INDEX TO PERIODICAL LITERATURE
ON CHRIST AND THE GOSPELS

NEW TESTAMENT TOOLS
AND STUDIES

EDITED BY

BRUCE M. METZGER, Ph.D., D.D., L.H.D., D. Theol., D. Litt.

Professor of New Testament Language and Literature, Emeritus
Princeton Theological Seminary
and
Corresponding Fellow of the British Academy

AND

BART D. EHRMAN, Ph.D.

Associate Professor, Department of Religious Studies
University of North Carolina at Chapel Hill

VOLUME XXVII

INDEX TO PERIODICAL LITERATURE ON CHRIST AND THE GOSPELS

EDITED BY

WATSON E. MILLS, Th.D., Ph.D.

BRILL
LEIDEN · BOSTON · KÖLN
1998

This book is printed on acid-free paper.

This work is an updating (to 1996) of the *Index to Periodical Literature on Christ and the Gospels* (E.J. Brill, 1966) by Prof. Bruce M. Metzger.

Library of Congress Cataloging-in-Publication Data

Mills, Watson E.
    Index to periodical literature on Christ and the Gospels / edited
by Watson E. Mills.
        p.   cm. — (New Testament tools and studies ; v. 27)
    ISBN 9004100989 (alk. paper)
    1. Jesus Christ—Periodicals—Indexes.   2. Bible. N.T.   Gospels–
–Periodicals—Indexes.   I. Title.   II. Series.
    Z7806.M55   1998
    [BT202]
    016.232'05—dc21
                                                                            98-39186
                                                                                CIP

Die Deutsche Bibliothek – CIP-Einheitsaufnahme

Mills, Watson, E.:
Index to periodical literature on Christ and the Gospels / ed. by
Watson E. Mills. - Leiden ; Boston ; Köln : Brill, 1998
    (New Testament tools and studies ; Vol. 27)
    ISBN 90–04–10098–9

ISSN 0077-8842
ISBN 90 04 10098 9

PRINTED IN THE NETHERLANDS

Dedication

In loving recognition and affirmation
of
Kim and Michael Mills
on their wedding day
September 12, 1998
καὶ ἔσονται οἱ δύο εἰς σάρκα μίαν

TABLE OF CONTENTS

PREFACE TO THE ORIGINAL EDITION

Work on the present index was begun during the academic year 1959-60, when several graduate students in New Testament at Princeton Theological Seminary made a survey of a score of periodicals, collecting the titles of articles on Christ and the Gospels. During the following three years other students continued the survey in additional periodicals. Now the combined labor of some thirty-five students and their supervisor is offered as a bibliographical tool to assist international New Testament scholarship.

The index includes articles in one hundred sixty periodicals, written in sixteen languages, namely Afrikaans, Danish, Dutch, English, French, German, Greek, Italian, Latin, Lithuanian, Norwegian, Portuguese, Russian, Serbian, Spanish, and Swedish. It was the aim of the project to index completely every periodical mentioned in the list below (pp. xxiii-xxix), from the year of its inception to the close of 1961 (or, if it ceased being issued prior to 1961, to the last year of its publication). It will be seen from the dates following the titles in the list that many periodicals span half a century, and several have had continuous publication for considerably more than a century.

All articles that bear on Christ and the Gospels, except a few of a purely homiletic nature, have been cited. In the section on Lexicography (pp. 287-303) the articles are arranged alphabetically in accord with the Greek or English words which are treated in the articles. In several sections which list critical and exegetical studies of individual passages[1] the articles are arranged in accord with the Scriptural sequence of the passages. Here the more extensive passages precede the more limited; that is, articles which deal with, for example, the Sermon on the Mount as a whole (Mt. 5-7) are cited before those that deal with single chapters, and articles that discuss, for example, Mt. 5: 1-12 stand before those that deal with Mt. 5:1. For the rest, the articles are listed in chronological order.

---

[1] There are four such sections, namely, "Individual Text-Critical Problems," pp. 172-174, "Critical and Exegetical studies of Individual Passages in the Gospels," pp. 311-606, "Pauline Christological Texts," pp. 646-652, and "Passages in the Old Testament Regarded as Prophetic and Typological," pp. 836-842.

Those who consult this index will doubtless wish to join the editor in expressing gratitude to the following persons who assisted in surveying the periodicals: Messrs. William P. Anderson, Norman A. Beck, Gerald L. Bell, Jr., James M. Boice, Bruce L. Blackie, Donald M. Borchert, Gerald L. Borchert, Plutarco Bonilla-Acosta, James A. Brooks, J. Daniel Brown, Laurence A. Brown, Jr., James S. A. Cunningham, Andries J. G. Dreyer, Jay H. Ellens, Thomas A. Erickson, Richard T. Foulkes, S. David Garber, John G. Gibbs, Arvin W. Glandon, Charles H. Immendorf, Werner H. Kelber, Kenei Kira, Andrew T. L. Kuo, David C. Lachmann, Chong Wan Lee, George D. McCall, John S. Metallides, Kenneth F. Morris, Arthur G. Patzia, Donald W. Shaner, J. Bartram Shields, Donald J. Sneen, Marshall P. Stanton, Allison A. Trites, and Morris A. Weigelt. Besides completing the assignments of several students who found it impossible to finish their work, the editor surveyed a number of periodicals, most of which were not available in the libraries at Princeton. In this connection he wishes to record his thanks for the courtesies extended to him at the following institutions: the Bodleian Library, the British Museum, the Catholic University of America, Dumbarton Oaks Research Center, Notre Dame University, the Library of Congress, Union Theological Seminary, and the University of Uppsala.[2]

Perhaps the greatest single task was the classification of the articles. Each student, following a list of subject-headings drawn up by the editor, entered a preliminary judgment on the slip which he made. The next stage was the production of a greatly expanded scheme of classification that grew out of the accumulated mass of materials. For valuable assistance in developing these subject headings the editor is indebted to two of his assistants, John G. Gibbs and S. David Garber. Whenever it was feasible titles were entered in the sections arranged in accordance with the Scriptural sequence of the Gospels (pp. 311-606). Finally, after the slips had been filed in accord with the enlarged classification, the editor went through them twice, rearranging and reclassifying many in what seemed to be more appropriate categories. For various reasons some of the slips required a second examination of the periodical. The editor is also responsible for the

---

[2]A trip to the last-mentioned library after the index was typed and ready for the printer enabled the editor to supplement previous surveys of periodicals. The additional titles are included in an appendix and are keyed by cross-references from the appropriate sections in the body of the index. In these cases the cross-reference numerals are printed in italics.

insertion of cross-references in certain cases where articles fall into two or more categories of the classification. It was taken for granted, however, that the user of the index, after consulting the table of contents for the appropriate topical classification, would turn, without being prompted by cross-references, to seek articles listed under the appropriate Scriptural passage(s). Thus, if one wishes to find articles on, for example, the Transfiguration of Christ, he should consult the titles listed under the appropriate passages in the Synoptic Gospels as well as those collected under the heading of Transfiguration.

The task of typing the ten thousand slips—written in all kinds of legible and illegible hands!—was executed with remarkable success by Mrs. Michel Pradervand. In the preparation of the index of the names of authors, the alphabetizing of the slips was undertaken by James B. Metzger and John M. Metzger, and the typing was done by Norman A. Beck. The editor is grateful to S. David Garber for assistance in the onerous task of proofreading.

It is most devoutly to be wished that works could issue from the press perfectly free from errors, but every author and editor must say with Alexander Pope,

"Whoever thinks a faultless piece to see, Thinks what ne'er was, nor is, nor e'er shall be."

It is particularly in a composite work involving a vast number of details that the possibility of error is multiplied. In the case of the present volume every effort was made in the collecting, the typing, and the proofreading to keep mistakes to a minimum.

Princeton Theological Seminary
Princeton, New Jersey

BRUCE M. METZGER

PREFACE TO THE NEW EDITION

The "New Testament Tools and Studies" series has served the field of biblical scholarship for more than thirty-five years. That this indispensble research resource is so frequently cited in the secondary literature attests to its enduring importance.

Of course the need arises over time to update these monumental works of the past. In this present update of Volume 6 of NTTS all of the original citations in Bruce M. Metzger's 1966 edition have been included as well as an additional 4,500 references from the years 1961 through 1996.

The categories remain as they were assigned by Professor Metzger and his assistants with the newer citations continuing the previous numbering scheme by using a "decimal extension" after the final number in each original category, e.g., **29.1** indicates the first new entry in the category ending in the 1966 edition with the number 29.

As with the 1966 edition all new entries are chronologically listed except for the section on individual passages in each of the gospels where they are listed by chapter and verse.

The original "canon" of some one hundred and sixty periodicals has been retained as well. Obviously some of these have ceased publication in the interim. And many new periodicals in the field of New Testament studies have been launched. Typical examples of the latter group are *Filología Neotestamentaria* and *The Journal for the Study of the New Testament*.

The tedium of this kind of work is well documented and widely recognized. I can only apologize for the errors that remain.

Watson E. Mills
Mercer University
Macon GA 31207 USA
July 1998

LIST OF PERIODICALS

A   ῎Αγγελος. Archiv für neutestamentliche Zeitgeschichte und Kulturkunde (Leipzig, 1925-34)

ABR   Australian Biblical Review (Melbourne, 1951 ff.)

AJP   American Journal of Philology (Baltimore, 1880 ff.)

AJT   American Journal of Theology (Chicago, 1897-1920)

ATR   Anglican Theological Review (New York; Evanston, Ill., 1918 ff.)

B   Biblica (Rome, 1920 ff,)

BA   Biblical Archaeologist (New Haven, 1938 ff.)

BBC   Bulletin of the Bezan Club (Leiden, [1926]-1937)

Bes   Bessarione, pubblicazione periodica di studi orientali (Rome, (1896-1923)

BETS   Bulletin of the Evangelical Theological Society (Wheaton, Ill, 1958 ff); named changed to Journal of the Evangelical Theological Society (JETS)

BibZ   Biblische Zeitschrift (Freiburg, 1903-1939; Paderborn, 1957 ff.)

BJRL   Bulletin of the John Rylands Library (Manchester, 1903 ff.)

BK   Bibel und Kirche (Stuttgart, 1946 ff.)

BLE   Bulletin de littérature ecclésiastique (Paris; Toulouse, 1899 ff.)

BO   Biblia et Oriente (Milan, 1959 ff.)

BR   Biblical Review (New York, 1916-1930)

Bres   Biblical Research; Papers of the Chicago Society of Biblical Research (Amsterdam; Chicago, 1956-57 ff.)

BS   Bibliotheca Sacra (New York; Andover; Oberlin; St. Louis; Dallas, 1844 ff.)

BT   Biblical Theology (Belfast, 1950 ff.)

BTr   Bible Translator (London, 1950 ff.)

BVC   Bible et vie chrétienne (Paris, 1953 ff.)

BW   Biblical World (Chicago, 1893-1920)

C   Catholica. Vierteljahresschrift für Kontroverstheologie

(Paderborn; Münster, 1932 ff.)

CB   Cultura bíblica (Segovia, 1943 ff.)

CBQ   Catholic Biblical Quarterly (Washington, 1939 ff.)

CJRT   Canadian Journal of Religious Thought (Toronto, 1924-1932)

CJT   Canadian Journal of Theology (Toronto, 1955 ff.)

CM   Classica et Mediaevalia (Copenhagen, 1939 ff.)

CQ   Crozer Quarterly (Chester, Pa., 1924-1952)

CS   Cahiers Sioniens (Paris, 1947-1955)

CT   Cuadernos teológicos (Buenos Aires, 1950 ff.)

CTM   Concordia Theological Monthly (St. Louis, Mo., 1930 ff.)

Div   Divinitas; pontificiae academiae theologicae Romanae commentarii (Rome, 1957 ff.)

DS   Dominican Studies (Oxford, 1948-54)

DTT   Dansk teologisk tidsskrift (Copenhagen, 1938 ff.)

EB   Estudios bíblicos (Madrid, 1929-36); segunda época (Madrid, 1941 ff.)

EE   Estudios eclesiásticos (Madrid, 1926 ff.)

EQ   Evangelical Quarterly (London, 1929 ff.)

ET   Expository Times (Edinburgh, 1889 ff.)

ETL   Ephemerides theologicae Lovanienses (Louvain et Bruges, 1924 ff.)

EvT   Evangelische Theologie (Munich, 1934 ff.)

Exp   The Expositor (London, 1880-1925)

FF   Faith and Freedom, A Journal of Progressive Religion (Leeds; Oxford, 1947 ff.)

FilN   Filologia Neotestamentaria (Córdoba, 1988 ff)

FZPT   Freiburger Zeitschrift für Philosophie und Theologie (Freiburg [Schweiz], 1954 ff.)

GOTR   Greek Orthodox Theological Review (Brookline, Ma., 1954ff)

GRBS   Greek, [Roman] and Byzantine Studies (Cambridge, Ma., 1958 ff.)

GTT   Gereformeerd theologisch tijdschrift (Heusden; Kampen, 1909 ff.)

Herm   Hermathena; a Series of Papers on Literature, Science, and Philosophy by Members of Trinity College, Dublin (Dublin, 1873 ff.)

HeyJ   Heythrop Journal (Oxford, 1960 f.)

HJ   Hibbert Journal (London, 1902 ff.)

HQ   The Hartford Quarterly (Hartford, Ct., 1960 f.)

HS   Hispania sacra. Revista de historia eclesiástica (Barcelona, 1948 ff.)

HTR   Harvard Theological Review (Cambridge, Ma., 1908 ff.)

Interp   Interpretation; a Journal of Bible and Theology (Richmond, Va., 1947 ff.)

ITQ   Irish Theological Quarterly (Dublin; Maynooth, 1906 ff.)

J   Judaica. Beiträge zum Verständnis der jüdischen Schicksals in Vergangenheit and Gegenwart (Zurich, 1945 ff.)

JBL   Journal of Biblical Literature (New Haven; Boston; Philadelphia, 1881 ff.)

JBR   Journal of Bible and Religion (Wolcott, N.Y.; Brattleboro, Vt, 1933 ff.)

JCP   Christian Philosophy Quarterly (from vol. 2 onwards, = The Journal of Christian Philosophy) (New York, 1881-84)

JCSP   Journal of Classical and Sacred Philology (Cambridge, England, 1854-59)

JEH   Journal of Ecclesiastical History (London, 1950 ff.)

JJS   Journal of Jewish Studies (London, 1948 ff.)

JNES   Journal of Near Eastern Studies (Chicago, 1942 ff.)

JQR   Jewish Quarterly Review (London, 1889-1908; New Series, Philadelphia, 1910 ff.)

JR   Journal of Religion (Chicago, 1921 ff.)

JSNT   Journal for the Study of the New Testament (Sheffield, 1978 ff.)

JTS   Journal of Theological Studies (Oxford, 1899 ff.; N.S., 1950 ff.)

K   Kyrios; Vierteljahresschrift für Kirchen- und Geistesgeschichte Osteuropas (Berlin, 1936-40; N.F., 1960 f.)

KD   Kerygma und Dogma; Zeitschrift für theologische Forschung und
        kirchliche Lehre (Göttingen, 1955 ff.)
KhV   Христіанскій Востокъ (St. Petersburg, 1912-22)
L   Lumen. Katolsk teologisk tidsskrift (Copenhagen, 1957 ff.)
LCQ   Lutheran Church Quarterly (Gettysburg, Pa., 1928-49)
LCR   Lutheran Church Review (Philadelphia, 1882-1927)
LQ   The Quarterly Review of the Evangelical Lutheran Church; from
        1878, The Lutheran Quarterly (Gettysburg, Pa., 1871-1927,
        reviewed in 1949 ff)
LumV   Lumière et vie (Lyons, 1951 ff.)
MTZ   Münchener theologische Zeitschrift (München, 1950 ff.)
Mu   Le Muséon (Louvain, 1882 ff.)
NedTT   Nederlands theologisch tijdschrift (Wageningen, 1946 ff.)
NGTT   Nederduitse gereformeerde teologiese tydskrif (Kaapstad, 1959ff.)
NJDT   Neue Jahrbücher für deutsche Theologie (Bonn, 1892-95)
NKZ   Neue kirchliche Zeitschrift; from 1934, Luthertum (Erlangen,
        1890-1939)
NTR   Nouvelle revue théologique (Paris, Leipzig, Tournai; Louvain,
        1869 ff.)
NT   Novum Testamentum; an International Quarterly for New
        Testament and Related Studies based on International Cooperation
        (Leiden, 1956 ff.)
NTS   Nieuwe theologische studiën (Groningen; Wageningen, 1918-42)
NTSt   New Testament Studies; an International Journal Published
        Quarterly under the Auspices of Studiorum Novi Testamenti
        Societas (Cambridge, England, 1954 ff.)
NTT   Norsk teologisk tidsskrift (Christiania; Oslo, 1900 ff.)
Num   Numen; International Review for the History of Religions (Leiden,
        1954 ff.)
Nunt   Nuntius sodalicii neotestamentici Upsaliensis (Uppsala, 1949-52)
O   Orpheus; rivista di umanità classica e cristiana (Catania, 1954ff.)
OC   Oriens christianus (Rome, 1901-40; Wiesbaden, 1953 ff.)

OCP   Orientalia christiana periodica (Rome, 1935 ff.)

OS   L'orient syrien (Paris, 1956 ff.)

OSt   Ostkirchliche Studien (Würzburg, 1952 ff.)

PCTSA Proceedings of the Catholic Theological Society of America (Yonkers, N.Y., 1946 ff.)

PSB   The Princeton Seminary Bulletin (Princeton, 1907 ff.)

PTR   Princeton Theological Review (Philadelphia; Princeton, 1903-29)

RB   Revue biblique (Paris, 1892 ff.)

Rbén   Revue Bénédictine (Maredsous, 1884 ff.)

RE   [Baptist] Review and Expositor (Louisville, Ky., 1904 ff.)

REB   Revista eclesiástica brasileira (Pétropolis, 1942 ff.)

RclB   Religion och Bibel, Nathan Söderblom-Sällskapets Årsbok Stockholm, 1942-51)

RET   Revista española de teología (Madrid, 1940 ff.)

RHE   Revue d'histoire ecclésiastique (Louvain, 1900 ff.)

RHLR   Revue d'histoire et de littérature religieuses (Paris, 1896 ff.)

RHPR   Revue d'histoire et de philosophie religieuses (Strasbourg, 1921 ff.)

RivB   Rivista biblica (Rome, 1953 ff.)

RL   Religion in Life (New York, 1932 ff.)

RMAL   Revue du moyen âge latin (Lyon; Strasbourg, 1945-52)

ROC   Revue de l'orient chrétien (Paris, 1896-1946)

RQ   Römische Quartalschrift für christliche Alterthumskunde und für Kirchengeschichte (Rome, 1887 ff.)

RQu   Revue de Qumran (Paris, 1959 ff.)

RR   Review of Religion (New York, 1936-58)

RSPT   Revue des sciences philosophiques et théologiques (Paris, 1907ff.)

RSR   Recherches de science religieuse (= Science religieuse, travaux et recherches, 1943-44), (Paris, 1910 ff.)

RSRel Revue des sciences religieuses (Strasbourg, 1921 ff.)

RT   Revue de théologie et de philosophie chrétienne (Paris, Geneva, Strasbourg, 1850-57); Nouvelle revue de théologie (1858-62);

Revue de théologie, troisième série (1863-69)

RTP   Revue de théologie et de philosophie (Geneva; Lausanne, 1868 ff.)

RTQR   Revue de théologie et des questions religieuses (Montaubon, 1891-
        1914)

RTR   The Reformed Theological Review (Melbourne, 1942 ff.)

Σ   Σωτήρ. Religijos mokslo laikraštis (Kaunas, 1924-35)

S   Synoptica: commentarii trimestres a Primo Vannutelli sacerdote
        editi (Rome, 1936-40)

Sal   Salmanticensis (Salamanca, 1954 ff.)

Scr   Scripture; The Quarterly of the Catholic Biblical Association
        (London, 1948 ff.)

SJT   Scottish Journal of Theology (Edinburgh, 1948 ff.)

SR   Science religieuse, travaux et recherches (cf. RSR) (Paris, 1943 f.)

ST   Studia theologica (Lund, 1948 ff.)

STK   Svensk teologisk kvartalskrift (Lund, 1925 ff.)

STZ   Theologische Zeitschrift aus der Schweiz: from 1900 =
        Schweizerische theologische Zeitschrift (Zürich, 1884-1920)

Θ   Θεολογία (Athens, 1923 ff.)

TB   Theologische Blätter (Leipzig, 1922-42)

Th   Theology; A Journal of Historic Christianity (London, 1920 ff.)

ThSt   Theological Studies (New York; Woodstock, Md., 1940 ff.)

TLZ   Theologische Literaturzeitung (Leipzig, 1876 ff.)

TQ   Theologische Quartalschrift (Tübingen; Ravensburg, 1819 ff.)

TR   Theologische Rundschau (Tübingen, 1897 ff.)

TRev   Theologische Revue (Münster, 1902 ff.)

TS   Theologische studiën (Utrecht, 1883 ff.)

TSK   Theologische Studien und Kritiken (Hamburg; Gotha, 1828-1938)

TT   Theologisch tijdschrift (Amsterdam; Leiden, 1867-1919)

TTDF   Teologisk tidsskrift for den Danske Folkekirke (Copenhagen,
        1884-1937)

TTK   Tidsskrift for theologi og kirke (Oslo, 1930 ff.)

TTod   Theology Today (Princeton, 1944 ff.)

TvT   Tijdschrift voor teologie (Nijmegen, 1961)

TZ   Theologische Zeitschrift (Basel, 1945 ff.)

USQR   Union Seminary Quarterly Review (New York, 1945 ff.)

USR   Union Seminary Magazine; since 1913, Union Seminary Review
        (Hampden-Sidney, Va.; Richmond, Va., 1890-1946)

Vcar   Verbum Caro (Neuchâtel, 1947 ff)

Vch   Vigiliac Christianae (Amsterdam, 1947 ff.)

VD   Verbum Domini (Rome, 1920 ff.)

VP   Vivre et Penser; recherches d'exégèse et d'histoire (= RB) (Paris,
        1941-44)

VT   Vox theologica; Interacademicaal theologisch tijdschrift (Assen,
        1930 ff.)

WJT   Westminster Theological Journal (Philadelphia, 1938 ff.)

Z   Zalmoxis. Revue des études religieuses (Paris, 1938)

ŽA   Živa Antika (Skoplje, 1951 ff.)

ZEE   Zeitschrift für evangelische Ethik (Gütersloh, 1957 ff.)

ZKT   Zeitschrift für katholische Theologie (Innsbruck, 1876 ff.)

ZMW   Zeitschrift für die neutestamentliche Wissenschaft und die Kunde
        des Urchristentums (. . . Kunde der älteren Kirche, 1921-)
        (Giessen; Berlin, 1900 ff.)

ZRGG   Zeitschrift für Religions- und Geistesgeschichte (Köln; Erlangen,
        1948 ff.)

ZST   Zeitschrift für systematische Theologie (Gütersloh, 1923-55)

ZTK   Zeitschrift für Theologie und Kirche (Freiburg i.Br., 1891 ff.)

ZWT   Zeitschrift für wissenschaftliche Theologie, ed. Adolf Hilgenfeld
        (Jena, Leipzig, 1858-1914)

ZWTh   Zeitschrift für wissenschaftliche Theologie, ed. G. B. Winer
        (Sultzbach, 1826-27)

BIBLIOGRAPHICAL ARTICLES ON CHRIST
AND THE GOSPELS

A. THE GOSPELS (IN GENERAL)

1. A. Hilgenfeld, "Die Evangelien-Forschung nach ihrem Verlaufe und gegenwärtigen Stande," *ZWT* 4 (1861): 1-71, 137-203.

2. A. Hilgenfeld, "Die Evangelienfrage und ihre neuesten Bearbeitungen," *ZWT* 5 (1862): 1-45.

3. A. Hilgenfeld, "Die neuesten Leistungen in der Evangelien-Forschung," *ZWT* 13 (1870): 151-88.

4. A. Hilgenfeld, "Die neueste Evangelienforschung. I. W. Beyschlag und das Johannesevangelium. II. B. Weiss und die synoptischen Evangelien," *ZWT* 20 (1877): 1-47.

5. A. Hilgenfeld, "Papias von Hierapolis und die neueste Evangelienforschung," *ZWT* 29 (1886): 257-91.

6. W. Bousset, "Der gegenwärtige Stand der neutestamentlichen Einleitungswissenschaft," *TR* 1 (1897-1898): 4-16.

7. A. Hilgenfeld, "Drei Evangelienforscher der Gegenwart (W. Beyschlag, A. Harnack, J. Weiss)," *ZWT* 41 (1898): 137-50.

8. Clyde W. Votaw and Charles F. Bradley, "Books Recommended for New Testament Study," *BW* 16 (1900): 42-80.

9. Clyde W. Votaw, "Books for New Testament Study: Popular and Professional," *BW* 26 (1905): 271-320.

10. J. Weiss, "Wellhausens Evangelienkommentar," *TR* 8 (1905): 1-9.

11. Arthur S. Peake, "Bibliographical Notes for Students of the Old and New Testament," *BJRL* 2 (1914-1915): 51-65.

12. Frederick C. Grant, "A New Testament Bibliography, 1914-1917," *ATR* 1 (1918-1919): 58-91.

13.   L. Fonck, "Commentarii in Evangelia et in vitam Christi," *VD* 1 (1921): 351-52, 378-79; 2 (1922): 64, 95-96.

14.   H. Windisch, "English-amerikanische Literatur zum Neuen Testament in den Jahren 1914-1920," *ZNW* 20 (1921): 69-90, 147-65.

15.   H. Windisch, "Literature on the New Testament in Germany, Austria, Switzerland, Holland, and the Scandinavian Countries, 1914-1920," *HTR* 15 (1922): 115-216.

16.   Frederick C. Grant, "A New Testament Bibliography for 1918 to 1922 inclusive," *ATR* 6 (1923-1924): 309-19; 7 (1924-1925): 40-54.

17.   Lyder Brun, "Nye veier i studiet av den evangeliske overlevering," *NTT* 25 (1924): 24-43.

18.   Hans Windisch, "Literature on the New Testament in Germany, Holland, and the Scandinavian Countries, 1921-1924," *HTR* 19 (1926): 1-114.

19.   Clarence T. Craig, "The New Testament in 1931," *RL* 1 (1932): 36-46.

20.   Walter Gutbrod, "Aus der neueren englischen Literatur zum Neuen Testament," *TR* 11 (1939): 263-77; 12 (1940): 1-23.

21.   K. H. Schelkle, "Zur neueren katholischen Exegese des Neuen Testaments," *TR* 14 (1942): 173-99.

22.   Cuthbert Lattey, "Bibliography of Christ and the Gospels," *Scr* 1 (1946): 38-41; 5 (1952-1953): 153-60.

23.   Kendrick Grobel, "Amerikanische Literatur zum Neuen Testament seit 1938," *TR* 17 (1948-1949): 142-56.

24.   C. H. Dodd, "Thirty Years of New Testament Study," *RL* 19 (1950): 323-33.

25.   G. Lindeskog, "Nordische Literatur zum Neuen Testament, 1939-1949," *TR* 18 (1950): 216-38; 288-317.

26.   W. F. Albright, "The Bible After Twenty Years of Archeology," *RL* 21 (1952): 537-50.

27.   John J. Collins, "Bulletin of the New Testament," *ThSt* 13 (1952): 205-19.

28.   C. K. Barrett, "New Testament Commentaries—Gospels and Acts," *ET* 65 (1953-1954): 143-46.

29.   John J. Collins, "Bulletin of the New Testament," *ThSt* 15 (1954): 389-15.

        See also numbers 2013, 3126, 3131.

29.1   André M. Dubarle, "Bulletin de théologie biblique," *RSPT* 44 (1960): 111-39; 45 (1961): 68-101; 46 (1962): 153-93; 47 (1963): 67-98; 48 (1964): 47-84.

29.2   F. G. Dreyfus, "Bulletin de théologie Biblique: Nouveau Testament," *RSPT* 48 (1964): 316-41; 50 (1966): 98-118; 53 (1969): 320-40.

29.3   X. Léon-Dufour, "Bulletin d'exégèse du Nouveau Testament," *RSR* 59 (1971): 583-618; 62 (1974): 261-97.

29.4   Yves M. J. Congar, "Pour une christologie pneumatologique: note bibliographique," *RSPT* 63 (1979): 435-42.

29.5   André Viard, "Ouvrages généraux d'études bibliques," *RSPT* 67 (1983): 186-200.

29.6   Sean P. Kealy, "Gospel Studies Since 1970," *ITQ* 56 (1990): 161-69; 57 (1991): 93-104.

29.7   Helmut Merkel, "Israel im lukanischen Werk," *NTSt* 40 (1994): 371-98.

B. THE SYNOPTIC GOSPELS

30.   H. B. Hackett, "Synoptical Studies of the Gospels, and Recent Literature Pertaining to it," *BS* 3 (1846): 1-21.

31.   A. Hilgenfeld, "Der gegenwärtige Stand der Evangelienforschung; I. Der gegenwärtige Stand der synoptischen Evangelienforschung; II. Der gegenwärtige Stand der johanneischen Evangelien forschung, *ZWT* 25 (1882): 189-226.

32.   A. Hilgenfeld, "Die neueste synoptische Evangelienforschung (C. Halcyon und C. Weizsacker)," *ZWT* 30 (1887): 1-42.

33.   A. Hilgenfeld, "Die synoptische Zweiquellen-Theorie in neuester Fassung," *ZWT* 36, pt. 1 (1893): 1-56.

34.   J. E. Belser, "Das Lukasevangelium nach den neuesten Forschungen," *TQ* 79 (1897): 298-345.

35.   Lyder Brun, "Nyere verker om Markusevangeliet," *NTT* 5 (1904): 182-201.

36.   E. Wendling, "Neuere Schriften zu den synoptischen Evangelien und zur Apostelgeschichte," *ZWT* 51 (1909): 135-68.

37.   Clyde W. Votaw, "Books on the Gospel of Matthew," *BW* 35 (1910): 62-65.

38.   E. Wendling, "Neuere französische Werke über die Synoptiker," *ZWT* 52 (1910): 231-38 [Alfred Loisy and M. Goguel].

39.   Lyder Brun, "Nye Lukas studier," *NTT* 13 (1912): 194-201.

40.   Rudolf Bultmann, "Kurze Anzeigen und Mitteilungen," *TR* 20 (1917): 102-103.

41.   W. K. Lowther Clarke, "Recent Literature on the Synoptic Gospels," *Th* 10 (1925): 278-88.

42.   Vincent Taylor, "The Synoptic Gospels, and Some Recent British Criticism," *JR* 8 (1928): 225-46.

43.   Julius Schniewind, "Zur Synoptiker-Exegese," *TR* N.F. 2 (1930): 129-89.

44.   C. S. C. Williams, "Commentaries and Books on St. Luke's Gospel," *Th* 62 (1959): 408-14.

45.   Owen E. Evans, "Synoptic Criticism since Streeter," *ET* 72 (1960-1961): 295-99.

46.   C. S. C. Williams, "Luke-Acts in Recent Study," *ET* 73: (1961-1962): 133-36.

46.1   X. Léon-Dufour, "Bulletin d'exégèse du Nouveau Testament: Evangiles synoptiques; histoire et interprétation," *RSR* 53 (1965): 600-446.

46.2   Ralph P. Martin, "St. Matthew's Gospel in Recent Study," *ET* 80 (1968-1969): 132-36.

46.3   R. S. Barbour, "Recent Study of the Gospel According to St. Mark," *ET* 79 (1968-1969): 324-29.

46.4   Howard C. Kee, "Mark as Redactor and Theologian: A Survey of Some Recent Markan Studies," *JBL* 90 (1971): 333-36.

46.5   X. Léon-Dufour, "Autour de la question synoptique," *RSR* 60 (1972): 491-518.

46.6   X. Léon-Dufour, "Synopses évangéliques," *RSR* 60 (1972): 615-346.

46.7   D. J. Harrington, "Matthean Studies since Joachim Rohde," *HeyJ* 16 (1975): 375-88.

46.8   Charles H. Talbert, "Shifting Sands: The Recent Study of the Gospel of Luke," *Interp* 30 (1976): 381-95.

46.9   Howard C. Kee, "Mark's Gospel in Recent Research," *Interp* 32 (1978): 353-68.

46.10   William L. Lane, "From Historian to Theologian: Milestones in Markan Scholarship," *RE* 75 (1978): 601-17.

46.11   X. Léon-Dufour, "Bulletin d'exégèse du Nouveau Testament: exégèse des évangiles synoptiques," *RSR* 66 (1978): 113-51.

46.12   Jacques Guillet, "Bulletin d'exégèse synoptique," *RSR* 68 (1980): 575-90; 69 (1981): 425-42; 71 (1983): 403-20; 74 (1986): 221-52; 77 (1989): 379-416; 81 (1993): 459-73; 84 (1996): 425-446.

46.13   J. A. Ziesler, "What is the Best Commentary? I. The Gospel According to St Matthew," *ET* 97/3 (1985): 67-71.

46.14   Bernard Sesboüé, "Bulletin de théologie dogmatique: christologie," *RSR* 77 (1989): 531-65.

46.15   I. Howard Marshall, "Commentaries on the Synoptic Gospels: Mark and Luke," *BTr* 45 (1994): 139-50.

46.16   Andreas Lindemann, "Literatur zu den Synoptischen Evangelien 1984-1991," *TR* 59 (1994): 41-100.

C. THE GOSPEL OF JOHN

47.   A. Hilgenfeld, "Das Johannes-Evangelium und seine gegenwärtigen Auffassungen," *ZWT* 2 (1859): 281-348, 377-448.

48. A. Hilgenfeld, "Das Johannes-Evangelium und die neuesten Schriften von Hofstede de Grot, Keim und Scholten," *ZWT* 11 (1868): 213-31.

49. A. Hilgenfeld, "Das Johannes-Evangelium und die Vertheidigung seiner Aechtheit durch F. Godet und C. E. Luthardt," *ZWT* 23 (1880): 1-31.

50. A. Hilgenfeld, "Das neueste Forscher-Paar über das Johannes Evangelium," *ZWT* 28 (1885): 393-425.

51. A. Meyer, "Die Behandlung der johanneischen Frage im letzten Jahrzehnt," *TR* 2 (1899): 255-63, 295-305, 333-45.

52. Arnold Meyer, "Johanneische Litteratur," *TR* 5 (1902): 316-33, 497-507; 7 (1904): 473-84, 519-31; 9 (1906): 302-11, 340-59, 381-97; 13 (1910): 15-26, 63-75, 94-100, 151-62; 15 (1912): 239-49, 278-93, 295-305.

53. A. Hilgenfeld, "Das Johannes-Evangelium und seine neuesten Kritiker," *ZWT* 47 (1904): 21-56.

54. F. C. Conybeare, "Recent French and English Criticism of the Fourth Gospel," *TT* 40 (1906): 39-62.

55. Catharina Gleise, "Beiträge zu der Frage nach der Entstehung und dem Zweck des Johannesevangeliums," *NKZ* 18 (1907): 470-98, 548-91, 632-72, 673-88.

56. J. E. Belser, "Das Johannesevangelium und seine neueste Beurteilung," *TQ* 93 (1911): 404-49, 569-614.

57. Walter Bauer, "Johannesevangelium und Johannesbriefe," *TR* 1 (1929): 135-60.

58. John H. Scammon, "Studies in the Fourth Gospel, 1931-1940," *ATR* 23 (1941): 103-17.

59. Johannes Behm, "Der gegenwärtige Stand der Erforschung des Johannesevangeliums," *TLZ* 73 (1948): 21-30.

60. Mary E. Andrews, "The Fourth Gospel since 1940," *JBR* 17 (1949): 168-74.

61. Walter G. Heyne, "John's Gospel in Current Literature," *CTM* 21 (1950): 819-33.

62. Angel Gonzáles, "Bibliography sobre San Juan," *CB* 12

(1955): 306-12.

63. Ernst Haenchen, "Aus der Literatur zum Johannes-Evangelium, 1929-1956," *TR* 23 (1955-1956): 295-335.

64. J. N. Sanders, "Commentaries on the Gospel According to St. John," *Th* 61 (1958): 327-31.

65. James M. Robinson, "Recent Research in the Fourth Gospel," *JBL* 78 (1959): 242-52.

See also numbers 31, 2864.

65.1 H. S. Songer, "The Gospel of John in Recent Research," *RE* 62/4 (1965): 417-28.

65.2 X. Léon-Dufour, "Bulletin d'exégèse du Nouveau Testament 1. Autour du quatrième évangile," *RSR* 55 (1967): 556-86.

65.3 J. Gnilka, "Neue katholische Literatur zum Johannesevangelium," *TRev* 63 (1967): 145-52.

65.4 S. Marcus Ward, "The Fourth Gospel in Recent Study," *ET* 81/3 (1969-1970): 68-72.

65.5 P.-M. Bogart, "Quelques ouvrages récents sur l'évangile selon saint Jean," *BVC* 102 (1971): 80-82.

65.6 A. Moda, "Quarto Vangelo: 1966-1972: Una selezione bibliografica," *RivB* 22 (1974): 53-86.

65.7 John Bogart, "Recent Johannine Studies," *ATR* 60 (1978): 80-87.

65.8 J. Becker, "Aus der Literatur zum Johannesevangelium (1978-1980)," *TR* 47 (1982): 279-301, 305-47.

65.9 X. Léon-Dufour, "Bulletin de littérature johannique," *RSR* 68 (1980): 271-316.

65.10 J. Becker, "Johanneische Literarkritik," *TR* 47 (1982): 294-301.

65.11 X. Léon-Dufour, "Bulletin d'exégèse du Nouveau Testament: L'évangile de Jean," *RSR* 73 (1985): 245-80; 75 (1987): 77-96; 82 (1994): 227-50.

65.12 M. Morgen, "Les bulletins johanniques de Xavier

Léon-Dufour," *RSR* 83 (1995): 187-91.

D. THE LIFE OF CHRIST

66.   Samuel J. Andrews, "Works on the Life of Christ," *BS* 22 (1865): 177-206.

67.   Charles M. Mead, "More Recent Works on the Life of Christ," *BS* 22 (1865): 207-22.

68.   E. F. Williams, "Recent Lives of Christ," *BS* 43 (1886): 221-38.

69.   E. Elmer Harding, "The Resurrection and Ascension of Jesus Christ; Literature and Hints for Study," *ET* 5 (1893-1994): 404-405.

70.   Shailer Mathews, "Helps to the Study of the Life of Christ," *BW* 6 (1895): 524-29.

71.   L. Fonck, "Leben und Lehre Jesu in der neuesten Literatur," *ZKT* 27 (1903): 293-322.

72.   H. L. Oort, "Een leven van Jezus," *TT* 40 (1906): 511-26.

73.   William H. Ryder, "The Recent Literature upon the Resurrection of Christ," *HTR* 2 (1909): 1-27.

74.   Shirley Jackson Case, "Jesus in the Light of Modern Scholarship," *BW* 38 (1911): 262-71, 331-40, 409-15; 39 (1912): 55-62.

75.   G. Esser, "Literatur zur Christusfrage," *TRev* 10 (1911): 1-6, 41-47.

76.   M. Meinertz, "Jesus-Literatur," *TRev* 13 (1914): 433-43.

77.   G. Baldensperger, "Un demi-siecle de recherches sur l'historicite de Jesus," *RTP* N.S. 12 (1924): 161-201.

78.   Shirley Jackson Case, "The Life of Jesus During the Last Quarter-Century," *JR* 5 (1925): 561-75.

79.   M. Goguel, "Quelques ouvrages recents sur Jesus," *RHPR* 1 (1929): 53-73.

80.   E. F. Scott, "Recent Lives of Jesus," *HTR* 27 (1934): 1-32.

81.   J. A. Robertson, "The Best Books on the Life of Christ," *ET* 48 (1936-1937): 65-68.

82.   J. Sickenberger, "Neuere Leben-Jesu-Literatur," *Trove* 35 (1936): 385-93, 433-39.

83.   Donald W. Riddle, "Jesus in Modern Research," *JR* 17 (1937): 170-82.

84.   U. Holzmeister, "Neueste Leben-Jesu-Werke," *B* 23 (1942): 209-17.

85.   A. M. Hunter, "The Life of Christ in the Twentieth Century," *ET* 61 (1949-1950): 131-35.

86.   John Wick Bowman, "From Schweitzer to Bultmann," *TTod* 11 (1954): 160-78.

87.   Alexander C. Purdy, "Recent Books on Jesus and his Ministry," *RL* 24 (1955): 436-42.

88.   M. de Jonge, "Nieuwe bijdragen tot de Leben-Jesu-Forschung in Duitsland," *VT* 29 (1958-1959): 129-44.

89.   Paul Winter, "Anlässlich eines neuen Jesus-Buches," *ZRGG* 11 (1959): 165-68.

        See also numbers 779, 790.

89.1   Marcus J. Borg, "Portraits of Jesus in Contemporary North American Scholarship," *HTR* 84 (1991): 1-22.

89.2   Dieter Georgi, "The Interest in Life of Jesus Theology as a Paradigm for the Social History of Biblical Criticism," *HTR* 85 (1992): 51-83.

89.3   R. Aguirre, "Estado actual de los estudios sobre el Jesús histórico después de Bultmann," *EB* 54 (1996): 433-63.

89.4   M. Eugene Boring, "The 'Third Quest' and the Apostolic Faith," *Interp* 50 (1996): 341-54.

E. THE THEOLOGY OF CHRIST AND THE GOSPELS

90   Lyman Abbott, et al., "The Kingdom of God: A Symposium," *BW* 12 (1898): 12-19.

91.   George S. Goodspeed, "Some Books on Messianic Prophecy," *BW* 12 (1898): 444-47.

92.   Lyder Brun, "Nytestamentlig teologi," *NTT* 13 (1912):

361-80.

93. J. K. Mozley, "Recent Works on the Atonement," *Th* 1 (1920): 222-32, 265-77.

94. Alexander C. Purdy, "Das Neue Testament in der amerikanischen Theologie," *TR* N.F. 3 (1931): 367-86.

95. A. Lemonnyer, "Bulletin de Théologie Biblique: Nouveau Testament," *RSPT* 3 (1909): 158-71; 4 (1910): 174-86; 5 (1911): 168-90.

96. C. Spicq, "Bulletin de Théologie Biblique: Nouveau Testament," *RSPT* 22 (1933): 123-34; 23 (1934): 120-28; 24 (1935): 167-75; 25 (1936): 191-203; 26 (1937): 120-40; 27 (1938): 123-35; 28 (1939): 126-45; 29 (1940): 334-44; 32 (1948): 84-105; 33 (1949): 76-94; 34 (1950): 30-57; 35 (1951): 34-60; 36 (1952): 150-83; 37 (1953), 139-83; 38 (1954): 137-63.

97. Hans Windisch, "Urchristentum," *TR* N.F. 5 (1933): 186-200, 239-58, 289-301, 319-34.

98. W. F. Howard, "The Best Books on the Kingdom of God," *ET* 48 (1936-1937): 393-96.

99. Werner Georg Kümmel, "Die Eschatologie der Evangelien. Ihre Geschichte und ihr Sinn," *TB* 5 (1936): 225-41.

100. Werner G. Kümmel, "Das Urchristentum," *TR* N.F. 14 (1942): 81-95, 155-73; 17 (1948-1949): 3-50, 103-42; 18 (1950): 1-53; 22 (1954): 138-70.

101. Rudolf Bultmann, "Zum Thema: Christentum und Antike," *TR* N.F. 16 (1944): 1-20; 21 (1953): 1-14; 23 (1955-1956): 207-29.

102. André Viard, "Bulletin de Theologie Biblique: Nouveau Testament," *RSPT* 39 (1955): 266-96; 40 (1956): 139-70; 41 (1957): 249-73; 42 (1958): 324-48; 43 (1959): 301-24; 44 (1960): 262-98; 45 (1961): 284-313.

See also numbers 7353, 7359.

102.1 X. Léon-Dufour, "Bulletin d'exégèse du Nouveau Testament: sur la résurrection de Jésus," *RSR* 57 (1969): 583-622.

102.2 D. Suter, "The Drama of Christian Theology in the Gospel of

John," *JR* 49 (1969): 275-80.

102.3   Eric F. Osborn, "Negative and Positive Theology in John," *ABR* 31 (1983): 72-80.

HISTORICAL STUDIES OF THE LIFE OF JESUS

A. GENERAL STUDIES

103.   A. M. Fairbairn, "Studies in the Life of Christ," *Exp* 1st ser., 3 (1876), 321-42; 4 (1876): 430-46; 7 (1878): 59-73, 161-76, 388-404; 8 (1878): 23-40, 98-116, 182-202, 288-304, 431-49; 9 (1879): 122-37, 178-201; 10 (1879): 253-74; 11 (1880): 44-65; 12 (1880): 47-70, 258-88, 356-80, 405-43.

104.   E. Barnaud, "Qui est Jésus?" *RTP* 25 (1892): 576-612.

105.   A. B. Bruce, "Jesus Mirrored in Matthew, Mark and Luke," *Exp* 5th ser., 3 (1896): 15-29, 95-111, 200-17, 295-312, 321-35, 418-33; 4 (1896): 27-42, 99-114, 212-27.

106.   Shailer Mathews, "An Outline of the Life of Jesus," *BW* 11 (1898): 328-40.

107.   Ernest DeW. Burton, "Sources of the Life of Jesus Outside the Gospels," *BW* 15 (1900): 26-35.

108.   Ernest DeW. Burton and Shailer Mathews, "Constructive Studies in the Life of Jesus Christ," *BW* 15 (1900): 36-69, 119-42, 193-210, 273-94, 360-75, 433-53; 16 (1900): 25-41, 118-36, 210-21, 283-94, 362-77, 451-62.

109.   John MacPherson, "The Gospels as a Source for the Life of Christ," *AJT* 5 (1901): 496-504.

110.   F. Warburton Lewis, "The Visits of Jesus to Nazareth," *ET* 16 (1904-1905): 381.

111.   Irving F. Wood, et al., "Expository and Practical Studies on the Life of Christ," *BW* 27 (1906): 63-72, 135-46, 304-15, 374-84, 458-67; 28 (1906): 59-67, 142-49, 205-12, 274-80, 334-41.

112.   H. U. Meyboom, "Ecce Deus," *TT* 46 (1912): 36-53.

113.   Llewellyn Phillips, "The Beginning of the Christian Movement," *BW* 42 (1913): 214-18.

114.   Philip Wendell Crannell, "The Five Portraits of Jesus," *RE* 18 (1921): 129-51 [Synoptics; Paul and Peter; Epistle to

Hebrews; Earth Gospel; Revelation].

115. Kirsopp Lake, "The Problem of Christian Origins," *HTR* 15 (1922): 97-114.

116. W. Emery Barnes, "A Reconstruction of Early Christian History," *JTS* 31 (1929-1930): 364-72.

117. J. Randel Harris, "On the Stature of Our Lord," *BJRL* 10 (1926): 112-26.

118. Samuel S. Cohon, "The Place of Jesus in the Religious Life of his Day," *JBL* 48 (1929): 82-108.

119. Morton S. Enslin, "An Additional Step Toward the Understanding of Jesus," *JR* 9 (1929): 419-35.

120. François Jansen, "Jésus a-t-il ri?" *NRT* 56 (1929): 352-72.

121. J. Hugh Michael, "The Close of the Galilean Ministry," *ET* 43 (1931-1932): 562-65.

122. J. O. F. Murray, "The Waiting Time at Nazareth," *Th* 32 (1936): 269-78.

123. Morton S. Enslin, "Changing Horizons in the Gospels," *CQ* 16 (1939): 3-15.

124. Ellis E. Jensen, "The First Century Controversy over Jesus as a Revolutionary Figure," *JBL* 60 (1941): 261-72.

125. Berkeley G. Collins, "The Hidden Years," *ET* 54 (1942-1943): 109-12.

126. Roderic Dunkerley, "The Context of the Gospel Story," *ET* 59 (1947-1948): 4-7.

127. Leslie Farmer, "Jesus' Mountain Tops," *ET* 65 (1953-1954): 250-51.

128. John F. Walvoord, "The Earthly Life of the Incarnate Christ," *BS* 117 (1960): 291-306.

129. John F. Walvoord, "The Ministry of Christ in his Life on Earth," *BS* 118 (1961): 3-7.

See also numbers 3130, 3169.

129.1 J. Blinzler, "Die Heimat Jesu," *BK* 25 (1970): 14-20.

129.2 David Hill, "Is the Search for the Historical Jesus Religiously Irrelevant?" *ET* 88 (1976): 82-85.

129.3   Étienne Trocmé, "Albert Schweitzer et la vie de Jésus," *RHPR*, 56 (1976): 28-36.

129.4   J. Jervell and T. Wyller, "Den historiske Jesus - 'andre' fase. Samtale med Jacob Jervell," *NTT* 96 (1995): 167-75.

B. THE LIFE OF JESUS ACCORDING TO MATTHEW

130.   A. Hilgenfeld, "Über Particularismus und Universalismus in dem Leben Jesu nach Matthäus, zur Vertheidigung gegen Hrn. D. Keim," *ZWT* 8 (1865): 43-61.

131.   John C. Granbery, "Jesus' Galilean Ministry: Period of Popularity; According to Matthew," *BW* 35 (1910): 197-203.

132.   T. W. Manson, "The Life of Jesus: A Survey of the Available Material: (4) The Gospel According to Matthew," *BJRL* 29 (1945-1946): 392-428.

          See also number 10057.

132.1   F. W. Beare, "Concerning Jesus of Nazareth," *JBL* 87 (1968): 125-35.

132.2   A. Ogawa, "L'histoire de Jesus chez Mathieu," *TLZ* 103 (1978): 81-96.

C. THE LIFE OF JESUS ACCORDING TO MARK

133.   A. Gemberg, "Über Jesu Wirksamkeit in Galiläa nach Markus," *TSK* 18 (1845): 62-112.

134.   W. H. Bennett, "The Life of Christ According to St. Mark," *Exp* 6th ser., 8 (1903): 106-15, 306-17, 397-400; 9 (1904): 76-80, 201-14, 301-309; 10 (1904): 18-29, 220-29, 302-12; 11 (1905): 133-39, 275-82; 12 (1905): 128-36, 262-68; 7th ser., 1 (1906): 346-52; 2 (1906): 56-64, 340-47, 545-52; 3 (1907): 153-58.

134.1   Jürgen Roloff, "Das Markusevangelium als Geschichtsdarstellung," *EvT* 29 (1969): 73-93.

D. LIFE OF JESUS ACCORDING TO LUKE

135.   Ernst von Dobschütz, "Jesu Wanderungen nach Lukas," *ZWT* 54 (1912): 366-80.

136.   G. W. H. Lampe, "The Lucan Portrait of Christ," *NTSt* 2 (1955-1956): 160-75.

136.1   M. Völkel, "Der Anfang Jesu in Galiläa. Bemerkungen zum Gebrauch und zur Funktion Galiläas in den lukanischen Schriften," *ZNW* 64 (1973): 222-32.

136.2   Merrill C. Tenney, "Historical Verities in the Gospel of Luke," *BS* 135 (1978): 126-38.

E. THE LIFE OF JESUS ACCORDING TO JOHN

137.   Bernhard Jacobi, "Ueber die Data zur Chronologie des Lebens Jesu in dem Evangelium des Johannes," *TSK* 11 (1838): 845-916.

138.   J. C. Jacoby, "The Length of our Savior's Public Ministry According to the Gospel of St. John," *LQ* 13 (1883): 49-56.

139.   A. Hilgenfeld, "Johannes und Jesus nach J. Wellhausen's Darstellung," *ZWT* 41 (1898): 481-501.

140.   Edward Day, "The Jesus of the Fourth Gospel," *BW* 34 (1909): 410-17.

141.   C. J. Cadoux, "The Johannine Account of the Early Ministry of Jesus," *JTS* 20 (1919): 311-20.

142.   J. H. Philp, "The Seeming Egotism of Jesus in the Fourth Gospel," *CJRT* 3 (1926): 462-66.

143.   Charles C. Torrey, "In the Fourth Gospel the Last Supper was the Paschal Meal," *JQR* 42 (1951-1952): 237-50.

144.   S. Zeitlin, "The Last Supper as an Ordinary Meal in the Fourth Gospel," *JQR* 42 (1951-1952): 251-60.

144.1   Ernst Haenchen, "History and Interpretation in the Johannine Passion Narrative," *Interp* 24 (1970): 198-219.

F. THE BIRTH OF JESUS, HIS GENEALOGY AND CHILDHOOD

145.   Jules Bovon, "La naissance du Sauveur," *RTP* 25 (1892): 557-75.

146.   Hr. Wandel, "Die Kindheitsgeschichte Jesu Christi nach Nösgen und Nebe," *NKZ* 5 (1894): 286-315, 449-65.

147.   David Brown, "The Life of Jesus prior to his Public

Ministry," *ET* 6 (1894-1895): 415-16.

148.   A. C. Zenos, "The Birth and Childhood of Jesus," *BW* 6 (1895): 433-43.

149.   Joseph Edkins, "The Star in the East," *ET* 8 (1896-1897): 565.

150.   George T. Purves, "The Story of the Birth," *BW* 8 (1896): 423-34.

151.   A. H. Sayce, "Discovery of Evidence for Enrollments in Syria," *ET* 10 (1898-1899): 231.

152.   W. Canton, "The Nativity: An Outline," *Exp* 5th ser., 9 (1899): 123-35.

153.   W. Canton, "The Star of the Magi," *Exp* 5th ser., 9 (1899): 465-72.

154.   R. B. Perry, "Jesus with the Doctors," *LQ* 30 (1900): 565-74.

155.   Edward Bosworth, "What the Nazareth Years did for Jesus," *BW* 18 (1901): 424-33.

156.   W. Montgomery, "Was Jesus Born in a Cave?" *ET* 14 (1902-1903): 384.

157.   H. Usener, "Geburt und Kindheit Christi," *ZNW* 4 (1903): 1-21.

158.   G. H. Box, "The Gospel Narratives of the Nativity and the alleged Influence of Heathen Ideas," *ZNW* 6 (1905): 80-101.

159.   J. Rendel Harris, "The Present State of the Controversy over the Place and Time of the Birth of Christ," *Exp* 7th ser., 5 (1908): 208-23.

160.   J. K. Fotheringham, "The Star of Bethlehem," *JTS* 10 (1908-1909): 116-19.

161.   Wm. Weber, "Der Census des Quirinius nach Josephus," *ZNW* 10 (1909): 307-19.

162.   W. Weber, "The Birth and Childhood of Jesus," *LQ* 39 (1909): 31-47.

163.   Gerald B. Smith, "Biblical Criticism and the Christmas Message," *BW* 36 (1910): 368-78.

164.   M.-J. Lagrange, "Où en est la question du récensement de

Quirinius?" *RB* 20 (1911): 60-84.

165.   F. Steinmetzer, "The Star of the Wise Men," *ITQ* 7 (1912): 51-63.

166.   W. van Koeverden, "La Grotte de la nativité sur un tableau de 1519," *RB* 22 (1913): 259-61.

167.   Louis H. Gray, "The Wise Men from the East," *ET* 25 (1913-1914): 256-57.

168.   E. Abbey Tindall, "The Star of Bethlehem," *ET* 25 (1913-1914): 45-46.

169.   F. Conrad Hamlyn, "The Visit of the Child Jesus to the Temple," *ET* 27 (1915-1916): 43-44.

170.   H. W. Magoun, "The Two Genealogies of Jesus," *BS* 72 (1915): 34-48.

171.   J. W. Ballantyne, "The Star in the East," *ET* 28 (1916-1917): 327.

172.   William Noty, "The Star of Bethlehem and the Magi," *BS* 73 (1916): 537-45.

173.   William H. Bates, "A Study in the Genealogy of Jesus," *BS* 74 (1917): 321-29.

174.   L. Melikset-Bekov, "Фрдгментъ грузинской версіи 'Дѣтстваа христа," *KhV* 6 (1922): 315-20.

175.   J. Sickenberger, "Zur Quiriniusfrage," *BibZ* 16 (1922-1924): 215-16.

176.   G. Kuhn, "Die Geschlechtsregister Jesu bei Lukas und Matthäus nach ihrer Herkunft untersucht," *ZNW* 22 (1923): 206-28.

177.   Norman W. DeWitt, "The Birth of the Child," *CJRT* 2 (1925): 137-41.

178.   Wm. M. Everts, "The Genealogies of Jesus Christ," *BS* 82 (1925): 203-209.

179.   J. Schaumberger, "Zusatzbemerkungen," *B* 7 (1926): 296-301 [the star at the birth of Jesus].

180.   Karl Schoch, "Der Stern des Messias," *B* 7 (1926): 295-96.

181.   David G. Stevens, "The Hearts that Cradled the Christ," *CQ*

3 (1926): 403-16.

182.   H. C. Carter, "The Education of Jesus," *ET* 39 (1927-1928): 562-66.

183.   P. Pons, "Genealogia Christi altera," *VD* 7 (1927): 267-71.

184.   L. Fonck, "De veritate historica narrationis sacrae de Infantia Christi," *VD* 7 (1927): 289-95.

185.   Ferdinand Prat, "La parenté de Jésus," *RSR* 17 (1927): 127-38.

186.   Morton S. Enslin, "The Christian Stories of the Nativity," *JBL* 59 (1940): 317-38.

187.   Joh. B. Schaumberger, "Stella Magorum et coniunctio Saturni cum Iove annis 7 a. Chr. et 1940-1," *VD* 20 (1940): 333-39.

188.   Joh. B. Schaumberger, "Ein neues Keilschriftfragment über den angeblichen Stem der Weisen," *B* 24 (1943): 162-69.

189.   Andrés Avelino Esteban, "En la casa de su Padre," *CB* 4 (1947): 1-7.

190.   P. Sträter, "De probabili origine historiae infantiae Christi," *VD* 25 (1947): 321-27.

191.   J. Fernández, "El encuentro del Niño Jesús en el Templo," *CB* 5 (1948): 3-8.

192.   A. Herranz, "Presentación de Jesús en el Templo," *CB* 6 (1949): 35-42.

193.   Leonhard Fendt, "Der heutige Stand der Forschung über das Geburtsfest Jesu am 25.X11. und über Epiphanias," *TLZ* 78 (1953): 1-10.

194.   Uuras Saarnivaara, "The Genealogies of Jesus in Matthew and Luke," *LQ* 6 (1954): 348-50.

195.   Jesús San-Pedro, "Valor apologético de la infancia de Jesu-cristo," *CB* 11 (1954): 39-41.

196.   Jose Alves Motta Filho, "Onde Cristo Nasceu," *REB* 16 (1956): 861-78.

197.   Emma Brunner-Traut, "Die Geburtsgeschichte der Evangelien im Lichte agyptologischer Forschungen," *ZRGG*

12 (1960): 97-111.

See also numbers 1083ff., 3312, 6873, 8148, 8304, 8414-8474, 9852, 9903

197.1 Jacques Dupont, "La genealogia di Gesu secondo Matteo 1,1-17," *BO* 4/1 (1962): 3-6.

197.2 J. Gnilka, "Der Hymnus des Zacharias [Lk. 1:67-79]," *BibZ* 6/2 (1962): 215-38.

197.3 A. R. C. Leaney, "The Birth Narratives in St. Luke and St. Matthew," *NTSt* 8 (1962): 158-66.

197.4 C. H. Cave, "St. Matthew's Infancy Narrative," *NTSt* 9 (1962-1963): 382-90.

197.5 H. H. Oliver, "The Lucan Birth Stories and the Purpose of Luke-Acts," *NTSt* 10 (1963-1964): 202-26.

197.6 J. G. Davies, "The Ascription of the Magnificat to Mary," *JTS* 15 (1964): 307-308.

197.7 E. Pascual, "La Genealogia de Jesus segun S. Mateo," *EB* 23/2 (1964): 109-49

197.8 C. Spicq, " 'Joseph, son mari, etant juste. . .' (Mt. 1, 19)," *RB* 70 (1964): 206-14.

197.9 A. Vögtle, "Die Genealogie Mt. 1, 2-16 und die matthaische Kindheitsgeschichte (I. Teil)," *BibZ* 8/1 (1964): 45-58; 9 (1965): 32-49

197.10 H. Schürmann, "Aufbau Eigenart und Geschichtswert von Lukas 1-2," *BK* 21 (1966): 106-11.

197.11 Stephen Benko, "The Magnificat: A History of the Controversy," *JBL* 86 (1967): 263-75.

197.12 H. Schöllig, "Die Zählung der Generationen im matthäischen Stammbaum," *ZNW* 59 (1968): 261-68.

197.13 Roy A. Harrisville, "Jesus and the Family," *Interp* 23/4 (1969): 425-38.

197.14 C. T. Ruddick, "Birth Narratives in Genesis and Luke," *NT* 12 (1970): 343-48.

197.15 T. Stramare, "Giuseppe 'uomo giusto' in Mt. 1,18-25," *RivB* 21 (1973): 287-300.

197.16   E. L. Abel, "The Genealogies of Jesus *o Khristos*," *NTS* 20 (1973-1974): 203-10.

197.17   F. Gryglewicz, "Die Herkunft der Hymnen des Kindheitsevangeliums des Lucas," *NTSt* 21 (1974-1975): 265-73.

197.18   P. Schmidt, "Maria und das Magnificat," *C* 29 (1975): 230-46.

197.19   Barclay M. Newman, "Matthew 1:1-18: Some Comments and a Suggested Restructuring," *BTr* 27 (1976): 209-12.

197.20   D. E. Nineham, "The Genealogy in St. Matthew's Gospel and Its Significance for the Study of the Gospels," *BJRL* 58 (1976): 421-44.

197.21   Herman C. Waetjen, "The Genealogy as the Key to the Gospel According to Matthew," *JBL* 95/2 (1976): 205-30.

197.22   Michelangelo Alessandri, "Partenogenesi e Miracolo," *Div* 21 (1977): 425-28.

197.23   Roger T. Beckwith, "St Luke, the Date of Christmas and the Priestly Courses at Qumran," *RQu* 9 (1977): 73-94.

197.24   C. H. Gordon, "Paternity at Two Levels" *JBL* 96 (1977): 101.

197.25   Ernst Hansack, "Luk 2,14: 'Friede den Menschen auf erden, die Guten Willens sind'? Ein Beitrag zur Übersetzungstechnik der Vulgata," *BibZ* 21 (1977): 117-18.

197.26   M. J. Down, "The Matthaean Birth Narratives: Matthew 1:18-2:23" *ET* 90 (1978): 51-52.

197.27   Reginald H. Fuller, "The Conception/Birth of Jesus as a Christological Moment," *JSNT* 1 (1978): 37-52.

197.28   A. T. Hanson, "Rahab the Harlot in Early Christian Tradition," *JSNT* (1978): 53-60.

197.29   R. T. France, "Herod and the Children of Bethelem," *NT* 21/2 (1979): 98-120.

197.30   M. Herranz Marco, "Substrato arameo en el relato de la Anunciación a José," *EB* 38 (1979-1980): 35-55, 237-68.

197.31   René Virgoulay, "Conçu du Saint Esprit, né' de la vierge

Marie: réflexions sur le rapport du fait et du sens dans le dogme chrétien," *RSR* 69 (1981): 509-28.

197.32 Laurence Cantwell, "The Parentage of Jesus: Mt. 1:18-21," *NT* 24/4 (1982): 304-15.

197.33 C. L'Eplattenier, "Une série pour l'Avent," *ETL* 57 (1982): 569-82.

197.34 A. R. C. McLellan, "Into Egypt," *ET* 95 (1983): 84-86.

197.35 Édouard Delebecque, "Sur la salutation de Gabriel à Marie (Lc 1,28)," *B* 65 (1984): 352-55.

197.36 T. Stramare, "La circoncisione di Gesù: Signifcato esegetico e teologico," *BO* 26 (1984): 193-203.

197.37 Alberto Valentini, "Magnifcat e lopera lucana," *RivB* 33 (1985): 395-423.

197.38 Raymond E. Brown, "Gospel Infancy Narrative Research from 1976 to 1986: Part I (Matthew)," *CBQ* 48 (1986): 468-83; 48/4 (1986): 660-80.

197.39 Pierre Grelot, "Le Cantique de Siméon," *RB* 93/4 (1986): 481-509.

197.40 T. P. Wiseman, "There Went Out a Decree from Caesar Augustus . . . ," *NTSt* 33 (1987): 497.

197.41 Michael Oberweis, "Beobachtungen zum AT-Gebrauch in der matthäische Kindheitsgeschichte," *NTSt* 35/1 (1989): 131-49.

197.42 T. Stramare, "L'Annunciazione a Giuseppe in Mt. 1:18-25: Analisi letteraria e significato teologico [pt 2]," *BO* 31 (1989): 199-217.

197.43 D. J. Harrington, "Jesus, the Son of David, the Son of Abraham," *ITQ* 57 (1991): 185-95.

197.44 John P. Heil, "The Narrative Roles of the Women in Matthew's Genealogy," *B* 72 (1991): 538-45.

197.45 Savas Agourides, "The Birth of Jesus and the Herodian Dynasty: An Understanding of Matthew, Chapter 2," *GOTR* 37 (1992): 135-46.

197.46 S. Willis, "Matthew's Birth Stories: Prophecy and the Magi,"

ET 105 (1993): 43-45.

197.47   N. de Chazal, "The Women in Jesus' Family Tree," *Th* 97 (1994): 413-19.

197.48   J. M. Jones, "Subverting the Textuality of Davidic Messianism: Matthew's Presentation of the Genealogy and the Davidic Title," *CBQ* 56 (1994): 256-72.

197.49   L. H. Silbermann, "A Model for the Lukan Infancy Narratives?" *JBL* 113 (1994): 491-93.

197.50   Charles H. Talbert, "Jesus' Birth in Luke and the Nature of Religious Language," *HeyJ* 35 (1994): 391-400.

197.51   Joseph A. Fitzmyer, "Another Query about the Lucan Infancy Narrative and Its Parallels," *JBL* 114 (1995): 295-96.

G. THE BAPTISM AND TEMPTATION OF JESUS

1 The Baptism of Jesus

198.   Leonhard Usteri, "Nachrichten über den Täufer Johannes. die Taufe und über Versuchung Christi," *TSK* 2 (1829): 439-68.

199.   Erich Haupt, "Jesu Eintritt in den messianischen Beruf. Zur Geschichte der Taufe und Versuchung Jesu," *TSK* 44 (1871): 205-49.

200.   A. B. Bruce, "The Baptism of Jesus," *Exp* 5th ser., 7 (1898): 187-201.

201.   Samuel Dickey, "The Significance of the Baptism of Jesus for his Conception of his Authority," *BW* 37 (1911): 359-68.

202.   Walter E. Bundy, "The Meaning of Jesus' Baptism," *JR* 7 (1927): 56-71.

203.   G. O. Williams, "The Baptism in Luke's Gospel," *JTS* 45 (1944): 31-38.

204.   F. E Lownds, "The Baptism of our Lord," *ET* 62 (1950-51): 274-75.

205.   Herbert Braun, "Entscheidende Motive in den Berichten über die Taufe Jesu von Markus bis Justin," *ZTK* N.F. 50 (1953): 39-43.

206.   P. Roulin et G. Carton, "Le baptême du Christ," *BVC* no. 25

(1959): 39-48.

See also numbers 1328-1376, 8498, 9898, 9902.

206.1 C. A. Poirier, "The Sacrament of Baptism and the Word," *JT* 9 (1963): 75-81.

206.2 A. Vögtle, "Die historische und theologische Tragweite de heutigen Evangelienforschung," *ZKT* 86 (1964): 385-471.

206.3 S. Lewis Johnson, "The Baptism of Christ," *BS* 123 (1966): 220-29.

206.4 P. G. Bretscher, "Exodus 4:22-23 and the Voice from Heaven," *JBL* 87 (1968): 301-11.

206.5 P. Colella, "De Mamona iniquitatis," *RivB* 19 (1971): 427-28.

206.6 B. Marconcini, "La predicazione del Battista in Marco e Luca confrontata con la redazione di Matteo," *RivB* 20 (1972): 451-66.

206.7 G. W. Trompf, "La section médiane de l'évangile de Luc: L'organisation des documents," *RHPR* 53 (1973): 141-54.

206.8 Stephen Gero, "The Spirit as a Dove at the Baptism of Jesus," *NT* 18 (1976): 17-35.

206.9 S. Légasse, "Le baptême administré par Jésus et l'origine du baptême chrétien," *BLE* 78 (1977): 3-30.

206.10 Michel Gourgues, "À propos du symbolisme christologique et baptismal de Marc 16:5," *NTSt* 27 (1980-1981): 672-78.

206.11 A. E. Harvey, " 'The Workman is Worthy of His Hire': Fortunes of a Proverb in the Early Church," *NT* 2 (1982): 209-21.

206.12 C. Grappe, "Baptême de Jésus et baptême des premiers chrétiens," *RHPR* 73 (1993): 377-93.

206.13 Joel Marcus, "Jesus' Baptismal Vision," *NTSt* 41 (1995): 512-21.

2. The Temptation of Jesus

207. Anonymous, "Ueber die Versuchungsgeschichte Jesu," *TQ* 8 (1827): 25-72, 195-234.

208.   C.A. Hasert, "Einige Bemerkungen über die Ansichten der Herren Prof. Dr. Ullmann und Usteri von der Versuchung Christi," *TSK* 3 (1830): 66-78.

209.   Leonhard Usteri, "Beitrag zur Erklärung der Versuchungs-geschichte," *TSK* 5 (1832): 768-91.

210.   F.W. Laufs, "Ueber die Versuchung Jesu, Matth. 4:1-11; Luk. 4:1-13," *TSK* 26 (1853): 355-86.

211.   William A. Stearns, "The Temptation in the Wilderness," *BS* 11 (1854): 155-66.

212.   Samuel S. Potwin, "The Temptation," *BS* 22 (1865): 127-38.

213.   Otto Pfleiderer, "Die evangelische Erzählung von der Versuchung Jesu in der Wüste, auf ihren historischen Kern untersucht," *ZWT* 13 (1870): 188-213.

214.   Friedrich Stawars, "Die Zeit der bekannten drei Versuchungen Jesu durch Satan," *TQ* 56 (1874): 632-57.

215.   A. M. Fairbairn, "The Temptation of Christ," *EXP* 1st ser., 3 (1876): 321-42.

216.   J. J. Murphy, "The Temptation of Christ," *Exp* 2nd ser., 4 (1882): 312-19.

217.   W. W. Peyton, "The Bread Problem of the World: Our Lord's First Temptation," *Exp* 3rd ser., 9 (1889): 369-91.

218.   W.W. Peyton, "The Hebrew Problem of the Period," *Exp* 4th ser., 2 (1890): 360-78, 439-54 [Our Lord's Second Temptation].

219.   W.W. Peyton, "The Human Splendours, Our Lord's Third Temptation," *Exp* 4th ser., 4 (1891): 223-36, 340-60.

220.   R. Macpherson, "Christ's Temptation and Ours," *ET* 3 (1891-92): 418-19.

221.   J. H. Bernard, "The Temptation of Christ," *ET* 9 (1897-1998): 503-506.

222.   William B. Hill, "The Temptation in the Wilderness," *BW* 11 (1898): 28-36.

223.   E. Wendling, "Synoptische Studien; I. Die Versuchungsgeschichte," *ZNW* 8 (1907): 256-73.

224.   Richard Roberts, "A Study and an Application of our Lord's Temptation," *BR* 1 (1916): 77-85.

225.   Harmon H. McQuilkin, "The Unifying Principle in the Threefold Temptation of Jesus," *BR* 3 (1918): 188-206.

226.   C. C. McCown, "The Temptation of Jesus Eschatologically and Socially Interpreted," *BW* 53 (1919): 402-407.

227.   William M. McPheeters, "The Testing of Jesus," *BR* 4 (1919): 517-36.

228.   Albert Weston Moore, "The Temptation in the Wilderness," *BS* 77 (1920): 249-71.

229.   Henry Offermann, "The Temptation of Jesus," *LCR* 42 (1923): 240-49.

230.   Daniel G. Stevens, "The Wilderness Crises of the Christ," *CQ* 1 (1924): 258-82.

231.   Friedrich Freese, "Die Versuchlichkeit Jesu," *TSK* 96-97 (1925): 312-18.

232.   H. J. Vogels, "Die Versuchungen Jesu," *BibZ* 17 (1925-1926): 238-55.

233.   Lindsay Dewar, "Our Lord's Temptations," *Th* 16 (1928): 79-88.

234.   Melvin B. Wright, "If Thou Art the Son of God," *CQ* 10 (1933): 216-34.

235.   R. H. Stewart, "Christ's Temptations are ours Today," *ET* 46 (1933-1934): 505-507.

236.   F. E. Lownds, "A Study in the Temptation of our Lord," *ET* 47 (1925-1926): 220-22.

237.   E. F. Synge, "Our Lord's Temptation," *Th* 33 (1936): 104-105.

238.   Ernst Lohmeyer, "Die Versuchung Jesu," *ZST* 14 (1937): 619-50.

239.   Theodore J. Jansma, "The Temptation of Jesus," *WTJ* 5 (1943): 166-81.

240.   John A. T. Robinson, "The Temptations," *Th* 50 (1947): 43-48.

241.   A. Victor Murray, "The Temptation of Jesus," *ET* 60 (1948-1949): 99-101.

242.   F. J. Glendenning, "The Devil and the Temptations of our Lord According to St. Luke," *Th* 52 (1949): 102-105.

243.   Rudolf Schnackenburg, "Der Sinn der Versuchung Jesu bei den Synoptikern," *TQ* 132 (1952): 297-326.

244.   E. González Vila, "Ayuno y tentaciones de Nuestro Señor en el desierto," *CB* 9 (1952): 68-72, 101-106.

245.   Célestin Charlier, "Les tentations de Jésus au désert," *BVC* no. 5 (1954): 85-92.

246.   Peter Doble, "The Temptations," *ET* 72 (1960-1961), 91-93.

247.   W. Powell, "The Temptation," *ET* 72 (1960-1961): 248.

           See also numbers 909, 2282, 3150, 8491.

247.1   H. A. Kelly, "The Devil in the Desert," *CBQ* 26 (1964): 190-220.

247.2   H. F. G. Swanston, "The Lukan Temptation Narrative," *JTS* 17 (1966): 71.

247.3   C. U. Wolf, "The Continuing Temptation of Christ in the Church. Searching and Preaching on Matthew 4:1-11," *Interp* 20 (1966): 288-301.

247.4   J. A. Kirk, "The Messianic Role of Jesus and the Temptation Narrative: A Contemporary Perspective," *EQ* 44 (1972): 11-29.

247.5   P. Pokorný, "The Temptation Stories and their Intention," *NTSt* 20 (1974): 115-27.

247.6   K. Grayston, "The Temptations," *ET* 88 (1977): 143-44.

247.7   J. A. Davidson, "The Testing of Jesus," *ET* 94 (1982-1983): 113-15.

247.8   C. H. Giblin, "Confrontations in John 18:1-27," *B* 65 (1984): 210-32.

247.9   William R. Stegner, "The Temptation Narrative: A Study in the Use of Scripture by Early Jewish Christians," *BRes* 35 (1990): 5-17.

H. THE PUBLIC MINISTRY OF JESUS

1. General Studies

248. W. H. Luckenbach, "The Comparatively Small Success of Christ's Personal Ministry," *LQ* 15 (1885): 371-86.

249. Arnold Stevens, "The Ministry of Christ," *BW* 6 (1895): 444-54.

250. W. H. Wynn, "Lacunae in the Life of Our Lord; Or the Gospel of Circumstance," *LQ* 25 (1895): 25-49.

251. M.L. Gordon, "Notes and Opinions: In Whose House did Jesus Eat with Publicans and Sinners?" *BW* 10 (1897): 78-79 [the house of Levi].

252. Walter Rauschenbusch, "Jesus as an Organizer of Men," *BW* 11 (1898): 102-11.

253. J. D. Bernard, "The Judaean Ministry of Jesus," *ET* 12 (1900-1901): 11-15, 210-15, 307-11.

254. Edward Bosworth, "The Period of Doubt among the Friends of Jesus; A Study in the Life of Jesus," *BS* 57 (1900): 445-64.

255. Dean A. Walker, "The Strategy of Jesus," *BW* 18 (1901): 101-104.

256. I. Herzog, "Jesus als Prediger," *ZTK* 14 (1904): 44-92.

257. Paul Heinisch, "Clemens von Alexandrien und die einjährige Lehrtätigkeit des Herrn," *BibZ* 4 (1906): 402-407.

258. Franz Schubert, "Das Zeugnis des Irenaeus über die öffentliche Tätigkeit Jesu," *BibZ* 4 (1906): 39-48.

259. C. West-Watson, "The Peraean Ministry," *JTS* 11 (1909-1910): 269-74.

260. F. C. Burkitt, "The Peraean Ministry: A Reply," *JTS* 11 (1909-1910): 412-15.

261. John William Bailey, "The Later Ministry—A Critical Period," *BW* 36 (1910): 55-64.

262. Warren P. Behan, "Jesus' Work in Galilee: The Beginnings of Opposition," *BW* 35 (1910): 273-81.

263. Olaf Moe, "Hvorfor valgte Jesus Galilaea til sin arbeids-

mark?" *TTDF* 3rd ser., 9 (1918): 81-93.

264. John E. Sampey, "The Prophetic Note in the Ministry of Jesus," *BR* 3 (1918): 278-89.

265. D. Plooij, "Jesus and the Temple," *ET* 42 (1930-1931): 36-39.

266. W. Fraser Munro, "The Close of the Galilean Ministry," *ET* 44 (1932-1933): 476-77.

267. Frederick C. Grant, "The Beginning of Jesus' Ministry," *JBL* 52 (1933): 189-202.

268. Edward Shillito, "What Jesus made of Men," *ET* 49 (1937-1938): 490-93.

269. J. L. Lilly, "Jesus and his Mother during the Public Life," *CBQ* 8 (1946): 52-57, 197-200.

270. H. G. Brueggemann, "The Public Ministry in the Apostolic Age," *CTM* 22 (1951): 81-109.

271. John R. Gray, "The Mind of Christ—Whom Jesus Loved," *ET* 62 (1950-1951): 291-94.

272. William R. Mewell, "With Jesus in Five Cities," *BS* 108 (1951): 286-99.

273. Harold G. Newsham, "Why Jesus Feared the Pharisees," *ET* 63 (1951-1952): 67-69.

274. George Johnston, "Soul Care in the Ministry of Jesus," *CJT* 5 (1959): 263-68; 6 (1960): 25-30.

See also numbers 131, 1119, 1198.

274.1 J. Julius Scott, "Gentiles and the Ministry of Jesus: Further Observations on Matthew 10:5-6; 15:21-28," *JETS* 33 (1990): 161-69.

274.2 Frans Neirynck, "apo tote erxato and the structure of Matthew," *ETL* 64 (1988): 21-59.

274.3 Maurice Carrez, "Que représente la vie de Jésus pour l'apôtre Paul," *RHPT* 68 (1988): 155-61.

274.4 Frank J. Matera, "The Prologue as the Interpretative Key to Mark's Gospel," *JSNT* 34 (1988): 3-20.

274.5 Herbert Giesbrecht, "The Evangelist John's Conception of the Church as Delineated in His Gospel," *EQ* 58 (1986): 101-19.

274.6　Jeffrey B. Gibson, "The Rebuke of the Disciples in Mark 8:14-21," *JSNT* 27 (1986): 31-47.

274.7　Fritz Neugebauer, "Die wunderbare Speisung und Jesu Identität," *KD* 32 (1986): 254-77.

274.8　Heinz Kruse, "Jesu Seefahrten und die Stellung von Joh 6," *NTSt* 30 (1984): 508-30.

274.9　F. G. Dreyfus, "Ministre de Jésus-Christ ou le sacerdoce de l'Evangile," *RB* 77 (1970): 292-93.

2. The Miracles of Jesus

275.　Ed. Scherer, "Des miracles de Jésus Christ," *RT* 4 (1852): 141-60.

276.　Ed. Ensfelder, "Études sur les miracles du Nouveau Testament," *RT* 6 (1860): 46-72.

277.　J. H. Scholten, "Les miracles de Jésus," *RTP* 2 (1869): 223-236.

278.　J. R. Lumby, "Christ feeding the Multitudes," *Exp* 1st. ser., 8 (1878): 148-55.

279.　A. Peloni, "Miracles—The Problem stated," *Exp* 2nd ser., 4 (1882): 241-64.

280.　G. A. Chadwick, "The Miracles of Christ," *Exp* 4th ser., 5 (1892): 39-50, 126-39, 270-80.

281.　G. A. Chadwick, "The First Miracle," *Exp* 4th ser., 5 (1892): 347-58.

282.　M.L. Young, "Evidential Value of the Miracles," *LQ* 22 (1892): 429-40.

283.　G .A. Chadwick, "Some Minor Miracles," *Exp* 4th ser., 8 (1893): 456-64 [Matt. 9:27; 9:32; 12:22].

284.　J. Jaeger, "Ist Jesus Christus ein Suggestionstherapeut gewesen?" *NKZ* 8 (1897): 454-81.

285.　J. H. Bernard, "The Evidential Value of Miracle," *Exp* 5th ser., 10 (1899): 331-39.

286. M. Dods, "Jesus as Healer," *BW* 15 (1900): 169-77.

287. Herbert Kelly, "The Relation of Miracles to Christian Doctrine," *JTS* 2 (1900-1901): 505-26.

288. W. Sanday, "Miracles and the Supernatural Character of the Gospels," *ET* 14 (1902-1903): 62-66.

289. H. B. Swete, "The Two Greatest Miracles of the Gospel History," *ET* 14 (1902-1903): 214-17.

290. Mich. Seisenberger, "Das grösste Wunder Jesu," *BibZ* 3 (1905): 40-42.

291. William Steinbicker, "The Miracles of Jesus," *LCR* 24 (1905): 82-87.

292. John Wilson, "The Miracles of the Gospels," *AJT* 9 (1905): 10-33.

293. A. Allen Brockington, "Miracles as Signs," *ET* 17 (1905-1906): 493-95.

294. Frank H. Foster, "The New Testament Miracles: An Investigation of their Function," *AJT* 12 (1908): 369-91.

295. William H. Johnson, "Miracles and History," *PTR* 8 (1910): 529-59.

296. James H. Ropes, "Some Aspects of the New Testament Miracles," *HTR* 3 (1910): 482-99.

297. Theodore G. Soares, "Jesus' Work in Galilee: His Healing Ministry," *BW* 35 (1910): 118-24.

298. Arthur Dakin, "The Belief in the Miraculous in New Testament Times," *ET* 23 (1911-1912): 37-39.

299. T. E. Schmauk, "The Miracles of Christ," *LCR* 30 (1911): 183-91.

300. S. Grébaut, "Aperçu sur les miracles de Notre Seigneur," *ROC* 16 (1911): 255-65, 356-67; 17 (1912): 427-31.

301. Paul Fiebig, "Die Wunder Jesu und die Wunder der Rabbinen," *ZWT* 54 (1912): 158-79.

302. George Henry Hubbard, "The Message of the Miracles to Modern Minds," *BW* 42 (1913): 204-13.

303. G.W. Wade, "Miracles and Christianity," *HJ* 12

(1913-1914): 162-73.

304. Léonce de Grandmaison, "Les signes divins et le miracle," *RSR* 5 (1914): 105-22.

305. Benjamin B. Warfield, "Kikuyu, Clerical Veracity and Miracles," *PTR* 12 (1914): 529-85.

306. C. W. Hodge, "What is a Miracle?" *PTR* 14 (1916): 202-64.

307. S Grébaut, "Aperçu sur les miracles de Jésus," *ROC* 21 (1918-1919): 94-112.

308. Albert Thomas Steele, "Jesus' Attitude toward his Miracles," *BW* 51 (1918): 195-203.

309. W. F. Adeney, "Miracle and Prophecy," *HJ* 19 (1920-1921): 133-42.

310. M. D. Jeffries, "Miraculous Healing, as Recorded in the Scriptures, and as Claimed since that Day," *RE* 19 (1922): 64-73.

311. W. W. Everts, "Jesus Christ, No Exorcist," *BS* 81 (1924): 355-62.

312. D. A. Frøvig, "Hvorfor Jesus gjorde undere," *NTT* 26 (1925): 65-87.

313. Robert Mackintosh, "Two Johannine Miracles," *ET* 37 (1925-1926): 43-44.

314. Campbell Bonner, "Traces of Thaumaturgic Technique in the Miracles," *HTR* 20 (1927): 171-81.

315. Vincenzo Anzalone, "Jesus et Maria ad nuptias in Cana Galilaeae," *VD* 9 (1929): 364-69.

316. Hermann Dieckmann, "De miraculorum Iesu Christi explicatione 'occultistica'," *VD* 9 (1929): 33-38.

317. Frederic C. Spurr, "The Miracles of Christ, and their Modern Denial," *RE* 27 (1930): 324-34.

318. C. H. Dodd, "Miracles in the Gospel," *ET* 44 (1932-1933): 504-509.

319. Leander S. Keyser, "The Rationale of Christ's Miracles," *EQ* 5 (1933): 357-64.

320. S. Rivière, "M. Guignebert et les miracles de l'Évangile,"

BLE 34 (1933): 145-72.

321.   G. J. Jordan, "The Classification of the Miracles," ET 46 (1934-1935): 310-16.

322.   Robert H. Miller, "An Appreciation of the Miracles," JBR 2 (1934): 68-71.

323.   J. Samain, "L'accusation de magie contre le Christ dans les Évangiles," ETL 15 (1938): 449-90.

324.   Gordon H. Clark, "Miracles, History, and Natural Law," EQ 12 (1940): 23-34.

325.   C.P. Coffin, "An Old Testament Prophecy and Some New Testament Miracle Stories," JBR 11 (1943): 162-66.

326.   Vergilius Ferm, "Miracles—Possible or Probable?" CQ 26 (1949): 215-18.

327.   J. Calvin Keene, "The Possibility of Miracles," CQ 26 (1949): 208-14.

328.   Frederic Niedner, "The Great Physician," CTM 24 (1953): 262-72.

329.   Georges Crespy, "La curación en los evangelios y en la iglesia apostólica," CT 13 (1955): 28-41.

330.   Gerhard Delling, "Das Verständnis des Wunders im Neuen Testament," ZST 24 (1955): 265-80.

331.   William Neil, "The Nature Miracles," ET 67 (1955-1956): 369-72.

332.   John R. Burne, "Jean-Jacques Rousseau and the Bible," EQ 28 (1956): 141-47.

333.   Robert H. Culpepper, "The Problem of Miracles," RE 53 (1956): 211-24.

334.   Augustin George, "Les miracles de Jésus dans les évangiles synoptiques," LumV No. 33 (1957): 7-24.

335.   S. Vernon McCasland, "Signs and Wonders," JBL 76 (1957): 149-52.

336.   Rudolf Bultmann, "The Problem of Miracle," RL 27 (1958): 63-75.

337.   T. A. Burkill, "The Notion of Miracle with Special Reference

to St. Mark's Gospel," *ZNW* 50 (1959): 33-73.

See also numbers 2891, 3127, 3215, 3303, 3317, 7118, 7166.

337.1   Paul J. Achtemeier, "Person and Deed: Jesus and the Storm-Tossed Sea," *Interp* 16 (1962): 169-76.

337.2   R. J. Dillon, "Wisdom Tradition and Sacramental Retrospect in the Cana Account," *CBQ* 24 (1962): 268-96.

337.3   J. D. M. Derrett, "Water into Wine: The Situation at Cana," *BibZ* 7 (1963): 80-97.

337.4   J. Wilkinson, "A Study of Healing in the Gospel according to John," *SJT* 20 (1967): 442-61.

337.5   John Craghan, "The Gerasene Demoniac," *CBQ* 30/4 (1968): 522-36.

337.6   E. Schuyler English, "A Neglected Miracle," *BS* 126 (1969): 300-305.

337.7   F. S. Parnham, "The Miracle at Cana," *EQ* 42 (1970): 105-109.

337.8   Paul J. Achtemeier, "Gospel Miracle Tradition and the Divine Man," *Interp* 26 (1972): 174-97.

337.9   Paul J. Achtemeier, "The Origin and Function of the Pre-Marcan Miracle Catenae," *JBL* 91 (1972): 198-221.

337.10   Paul J. Achtemeier, "The Lucan Perspective on the Miracles of Jesus: A Preliminary Sketch," *JBL* 94 (1975): 547-62.

337.11   A. B. Kolenkow, "Healing Controversy as a Tie between Miracle and Passion Material for a Proto-Gospel," *JBL* 95 (1976): 623-38.

337.12   Ernest Best, "Exorcism in the New Testament and Today," *BT* 27 (1977): 1-9.

337.13   Frans Neirynck, "Foi et miracle. Le fonctionnaire royal de Capharnaüm et 4:46-54," *ETL* 53 (1977): 451-78.

337.14   R. L. Sturch, "The Markan Miracles and the Other Synoptists," *ET* 89 (1977-1978): 375-76.

337.15   Jack D. Kingsbury, "Observations on the 'Miracle Chapters' of Matthew 8-9," *CBQ* 40/4 (1978): 559-73.

337.16   Ernest Best, "The Miracles in Mark," *RE* 75 (1978): 539-54.

337.17   John P. Heil, "Significant Aspects of the Healing Miracles in Matthew," *CBQ* 41/2 (1979) 274-87.

337.18   Dieter Zeller, "Wunder und Bekenntnis," *BiZ* 25 (1981): 204-22.

337.19   M.-É. Boismard, "Rapports entre foi et miracles dans l'évangile de Jean," *ETL* 58 (1982): 357-64.

337.20   Harold Remus, "Does Terminology Distinguish Early Christian from Pagan Miracles?" *JBL* 101 (1982): 531-51.

337.21   Sarrae Masuda, "The Good News of the Miracle of the Bread: The Tradition and Its Markan Redaction," *NTSt* 28 (1982): 191-219.

337.22   Stephen C. Barton, "The Miraculous Feedings in Mark," *ET* 97/4 (1985-1986): 112-13.

337.23   Howard M. Jackson, "The Death of Jesus in Mark and the Miracle from the Cross," *NTSt* 33/1 (1987): 16-37.

337.24   Ivor Bailey, "The Cripple's Story," *ET* 99 (1987-1988): 110-12.

337.25   Joel B. Green, "Jesus and a Daughter of Abraham (Luke 13:10-17): Test Case for a Lucan Perspective on Jesus' Miracles," *CBQ* 51 (1989): 643-54.

337.26   Frank J. Matera, " 'He Saved Others; He Cannot Save Himself': A Literary-Critical Perspective on the Markan Miracles," *Interp* 47 (1993): 15-26.

337.27   J. D. M. Derrett, "Miracles, Pools and Sight," *BO* 36 (1994): 71-85.

337.28   B. D. Ellenburg, "A Review of Selected Narrative-Critical Conventions in Mark's Use of Miracle Material," *JETS* 38 (1995): 171-80.

337.29   M. R. Saucy, "Miracles and Jesus' Proclamation of the Kingdom of God," *BS* 153 (1996): 281-307.

3. The Transfiguration of Jesus

338.   Hugh Macmillan, "Water-Marks in the Narratives of our Lord's Transfiguration," *ET* 7 (1895-1896): 25-27.

339.   Alexander B. Grosart, "Water-Marks in the Narratives of our
        Lord's Transfiguration," *ET* 7 (1895-1896): 95-96.

340.   Hugh Macmillan, "The Mount of Transfiguration," *ET* 7
        (1895-1896): 139-41.

341.   E. Petavel-Olliff, "La kénose après la transfiguration," *RTP*
        29 (1896): 138-62.

342.   B. W. Bacon, "The Transfiguration Story," *AJT* 6 (1902):
        236-65.

343.   A. E. Burn, "The Transfiguration," *ET* 14 (1902-1903):
        442-47.

344.   R. Holmes, "The Purpose of the Transfiguration," *JTS* 4
        (1902-1903): 543-47.

345.   H. A. A. Kennedy, "The Purpose of the Transfiguration,"*JTS*
        4 (1902-1903): 270-73.

346.   A. T. Fryer, "The Purpose of the Transfiguration," *JTS* 5
        (1903-1904): 214-17.

347.   G. Stringer Rowe, "The Transfiguration," *ET* 15
        (1903-1904): 336.

348.   W. C. Braithwaite, "The Teaching of the Transfiguration,"
        ET 17 (1905-1906): 372-75.

349.   J. Mathieson Forson, "The Transfiguration," *ET* 17 (1905-
        1906): 140-41.

350.   A. T. Fryer, "The Transfiguration," *ET* 17 (1905-1906): 431-
        32.

351.   Friedrich Spitta, "Die evangelische Geschichte von der Ver-
        klärung Jesu," *ZWT* 53 (1911): 97-167.

352.   F. J. Badcock, "The Transfiguration," *JTS* 22 (1921):
        321-26.

353.   Ernst Lohmeyer, "Die Verklärung Jesu nach dem
        Markus-Evangelium," *ZNW* 21 (1922): 185-215.

354.   Wm. L. Groves, "The Significance of the Transfiguration of
        our Lord," *Th* 11 (1925): 86-92.

355.   E.J. Martin, "The Transfiguration," *ET* 38 (1926-1927): 189.

356.   Joseph B. Bernardin, "The Transfiguration," *JBL* 52 (1933):

36   HISTORICAL STUDIES OF THE LIFE OF JESUS

181-89.

357.   W.P. Brodley, "The Transfiguration—Credential, or Answer?" *CQ* 12 (1935): 57-76.

358.   Everett F. Harrison, "The Transfiguration," *BS* 93 (1936): 315-30.

359.   G. H. Boobyer, "St. Mark and the Transfiguration," *JTS* 41 (1940): 119-40.

360.   U. Holzmeister, "Einzeluntersuchungen über das Geheimnis der Verklärung Christi," *B* 21 (1940): 200-10.

361.   J.A. Oñate, "Noches de Jesús," *CB* 9 (1952): 83-86 [the Transfiguration].

362.   André Feuillet, "Les perspectives propres à chaque évangeliste dans les récits de la transfiguration," *B* 39 (1958): 281-301.

363.   Hans-Peter Müller, "Die Verklärung Jesu," *ZNW* 51 (1960): 56-64.

364.   Charles E. Carleston, "Transfiguration and Resurrection," *JBL* 80 (1961): 233-40.

See also numbers 543, 1226.

364.1   S. Lewis Johnson, "The Transfiguration of Christ," *BS* 124 (1967): 133-43.

364.2   Margaret Thrall, "Elijah and Moses in Mark's Account of the Transfiguration," *NTSt* 16/4 (1969-1970): 305-11.

364.3   J. A. Ziesler, "The Transfiguration Story and the Markan Soteriology," *ET* 81 (1969-1970): 263-68.

364.4   F. C. Synge, "The Transfiguration Story," *ET* 82 (1970-1971): 82-83.

364.5   Walter Schmithals, "Der Markusschluss, die Verklärungs-geschichte und die Aussendung der Zwölf," *ZTK* 69 (1972): 379-411.

364.6   Robert H. Stein, "Is the Transfiguration a Misplaced Resurrection Account?" *JBL* 95/1 (1976): 79-96.

364.7   A. A. Trites, "The Transfiguration of Jesus: The Gospel in Microcosm," *EQ* 51 (1979): 67-79.

364.8   Jerome H. Neyrey, "The Apologetic Use of the Transfiguration in 2 Peter 1:16-21," *CBQ* 42 (1980): 504-19.

364.9   Morton Smith, "The Origin and History of the Transfiguration Story," *USQR* 36 (1980): 39-44.

364.10   Bruce D. Chilton, "The Transfiguration: Dominical Assurance and Apostolic Vision," *NTS* 27/1 (1980-1981): 115-24.

364.11   Margaret Pamment, "Moses and Elijah in the Study of the Transfiguration," *ET* 92 (1981): 338-39.

364.12   Geir Hellemo, "Transfigurasjonen og det kristologiske paradoks," *NTT* 86/2 (1985): 65-78.

364.13   Barbara Reid, "Voices and Angels: What Were They Talking About at the Transfiguration? A Redaction-Critical Study of Luke 9:28-36," *BRes* 34 (1989): 19-31.

364.14   C. Deutsch, "Wisdom in Matthew: Transformation of a Symbol," *NT* 32 (1990): 13-47.

364.15   A. del Agua, "La transfiguratión como preludio 'Exodo' de Jesús en Lc 9,28-36," *Sal* 40 (1993): 5-19.

4. The Entry into Jerusalem

365.   Dr. Aberle, "Die Letzte Reise Jesu nach Jerusalem," *TQ* 56 (1874): 127-64.

366.   George Cross, "Jesus' Last Journey to Jerusalem," *BW* 36 (1910): 126-33.

367.   Friedrich Spitta, "Der Volksruf beim Einzug Jesu in Jerusalem," *ZWT* 52 (1910): 307-20.

368.   J. Blenkinsopp, "The Hidden Messiah and his Entry into Jerusalem," *Scr* 13 (1961): 81-88.

369.   J. Blenkinsopp, "The Oracle of Judah and the Messianic Entry," *JBL* 80 (1961): 55-64.

370.   E. D. Freed, "The Entry into Jerusalem in the Gospel of John," *JBL* 80 (1961): 329-38.

See also number 1137.

370.1   B. A. Mastin, "The Date of the Triumphal Entry," *NTSt* 16 (1969-1970): 76-82.

370.2   J. D. M. Derrett, "Law in the New Testament: The Palm
           Sunday Colt," *NT* 13 (1971): 241-58.

370.3   Roman Bartnicki, "Das Zitat von Zach IX, 9-10 und die Tiere
           im Berichte von Matthaus über dem Einzug Jesu in
           Jerusalem," *NT* 18/3 (1976): 161-66.

370.4   Roman Bartnicki, "Il carattere messianico delle pericopi di
           Marco e Matteo sull'ingresso di Gesù in Gerusalemme (Mc.
           11,1-10; Mt. 21,1-9)," *RivB* 25 (1977): 5-27.

370.5   Robert Lunt, "The Chronology of John 12:12-19," *BTr* 38
           (1987): 445-46.

370.6   Paul B. Duff, "The March of the Divine Warrior and the
           Advent of the Greco-Roman King: Mark's Account of Jesus'
           Entry into Jerusalem," *JBL* 111 (1992): 55-71.

370.7   J. F. Coakley, "Jesus' Messianic Entry into Jerusalem," *JTS*
           46 (1995): 461-82.

I. THE TEACHING OF JESUS

1. General Studies

371.   Ed. Scherer, "Les prédications de Jésus-Christ," *RT* 5 (1852):
           365-377; 6 (1853): 47-56.

372.   Ed. Scherer, "De l'enseignement de Jésus-Christ," *RT* 7
           (1853): 37-49, 65-74.

373.   L. Vaucher, "Essai de restitution des discours de N.S.
           Jésus-Christ contenus dans les évangiles synoptiques," *RT* 9
           (1862): 1-12.

374.   F. Gardiner, "The Unity of our Lord's Discourses," *BS* 31
           (1874): 416-35.

375.   A.B. Bruce, "A Chapter of Gospel History: Or, Jesus Judging
           his Contemporaries and himself," *Exp* 1st ser., 5 (1877):
           11-26, 98-113, 197-214, 257-73, 387-400, 421-35; 6 (1877):
           61-80, 142-57 [Mt. 11].

376.   R.W. Hufford, "Answers of Jesus," *LQ* 21 (1891): 406-13.

377.   David Eaton, "Professor Wendt's 'Teaching of Jesus,'" *ET*
           4 (1892-1893): 10-14.

378.   A. Riddervold, "Das Momentane in Jesu Reden," *NKZ* 4

(1893): 1017-25.

379. J. Stalker, "The Difficult Words of Christ," *Exp* 4th ser., 7 (1893): 29-37 [Matt. 11:16-19], 224-31 [Matt. 11:12]; 8 (1893): 63-71.

380. John Watson, "The Premier Ideas of Jesus," *Exp* 4th ser., 9 (1894): 34-42, 127-37, 211-21, 302-14.

381. A. B. Bruce, "The Teaching of Christ iu the Gospels of Matthew, Mark, and Luke," *BW* 6 (1895): 455-66.

382. D. M. Ross, "The Mind of the Master," *Exp* 5th ser., 4 (1986): 228-40; 5 (1897): 1-16.

383. J. Stalker, "Wendt's Untranslated Volume: On the Teaching of Christ," *Exp* 5th ser., 3 (1896): 401-17.

384. J. G. Tasker, "The Words of the Lord Jesus," *ET* 8 (1896-1897): 361-62.

385. J. T. Marshall, "Dalman's 'Die Worte Jesu,'" *ET* 10 (1898-1899): 320-24.

386. C. Bruston, "Les prédications de Jésus," *RTP* 32 (1899): 389-426.

387. Oskar Pfister, "Modernes Antichristentum, antimodernes Christentum und das Evangelium Jesu," *STZ* 16 (1899): 97-116, 174-86, 193-202.

388. A. T. Robertson, "Jesus and Questions of his Time," *LCR* 20 (1901): 371-77.

389. Joseph Stump, "The Teaching of Jesus," *LCR* 21 (1902): 22-25.

390. C. W. Kambli, "Einige Gedanken über Christus und das Christentum," *STZ* 20 (1903): 143-81.

391. H. B. Swete, "The Teaching of Christ," *Exp* 6th ser., 7 (1903): 81-94, 259-73, 401-16; 8 (1903): 116-30, 267-82, 440-55.

392. Georg Hollmann, "Leben und Lehre Jesu," *TR* 7 (1904): 149-71, 197-212, 246-55.

393. James H. Moulton, "Synoptic Studies; II, The Epistle of James and the Sayings of Jesus," *Exp* 7th ser., 4 (1907):

45-55.

394.   Edward B. Pollard, "Aesthetic and Imaginative Elements in the Words of Jesus," *BW* 30 (1907): 339-45.

395.   Frank C. Porter, "The Sufficiency of the Religion of Jesus," *AJT* 11 (1907): 74-94.

396.   R. M. Lithgow, "The Development of Christ's Doctrine during his Earthly Ministry," *ET* 20 (1908-1909): 126-31.

397.   F. P. Mayser, "The Preaching of Jesus," *LCR* 27 (1908): 331-42.

398.   Lic. Schwen, "Zu den Kreuzesworten Jesu," *TSK* 82 (1909): 309-10.

399.   Shirley Jackson Case, "The Religion of Jesus," *AJT* 14 (1910): 234-52.

400.   Richard M. Vaughan, "The Teaching of Jesus in the Temple," *BW* 36 (1910): 193-202.

401.   Ludwig Ihmels, "The Gospel of Jesus Christ," *LQ* N.S. 42 (1912): 62-102.

402.   Lucius Hopkins Miller, "The Teaching of Jesus," *BW* 43 (1914): 238-50.

403.   Lester Reddin, "Christ's Estimate of the Human Personality," *BS* 71 (1914): 132-44.

404.   A. T. Robertson, "The Teaching of Jesus in Mark's Gospel," *BW* 52 (1918): 83-91.

405.   T. Stephenson, "Our Lord's Teaching in St. Mark's Gospel," *JTS* 22 (1921): 6-13.

406.   A. Ancel, "De oratoria progression in orationibus Christi Domini," *VD* 6 (1926): 273-80, 299-308.

407.   M. Goguel, "Une étude sur la pensée de Jésus," *RHPR* 7 (1927): 51-56.

408.   J. B. Green, "The Gospel which Jesus Preached," *USR* 41 (1929-1930): 151-61, 292-303.

409.   Carl S. Patton, "Some Late Elements in the Teachings of Jesus," *JR* 9 (1929): 389-97.

410.   Jules Lébreton, "La prédication de l'Évangile par le Christ

notre Seigneur," *RSR* 21 (1931): 6-37.

411. A. E. Morris, "What Did Jesus Say?" *HJ* 30 (1931-1932): 91-102.

412. Donald W. Riddle, "The Bearing of Recent Gospel Research upon the Study of the Teaching of Jesus," *JR* 14 (1934): 150-67.

413. W. Hersey Davis, "The Relation to the Jewish People Claimed by Jesus in his Sabbath Teaching," *RE* 32 (1935): 366-75.

414. R. Thibaut, "Le complément natural des paroles du Christ," *NRT* 62 (1935): 1009-23.

415. H. H. Horne, "The Philosophy held by Jesus," *USR* 47 (1935-1936): 175-80.

416. R. W. Stewart, "The Idea of 'Growth' in the Teaching of Jesus," *ET* 47 (1935-1936): 390-94.

417. F. Ménégoz, "L''illusion' dans l'espérance de Jésus," *RHPR* 7 (1937): 413-23.

418. R. Thibaut, "Les précieuses reliques des paroles du Christ," *NRT* 64 (1937): 113-38.

419. R. Thibaut, "Les trois degrés d'originalité des paroles du Christ," *NRT* 64 (1937): 929-43.

420. Elmer W. K. Mould, "The World-View of Jesus," *JBR* 6 (1938): 133-37.

421. Edward J. Byrne, "Father Lagrange on Jesus and his Message," *CBQ* 1 (1939): 239-42.

422. Graham Gilmer, "Our Lord's Outline of the New Testament," *BS* 96 (1939): 198-204.

423. Julian Price Love, "Current Attitudes Toward the Teachings of Jesus," *JBR* 7 (1939): 115-20, 160.

424. T. F. Glasson, "Jesus' Questions and Ours," *ET* 52 (1940-1941): 466-69.

425. Edgar M. McKown, "Methods and Materials in Teaching the Message of Jesus," *JBR* 10 (1942): 155-58.

426. F. W. A. Bosch, "The Freedom of the Spirit; I, The

Teachings of Jesus," *USR* 54 (1942-1943): 140-61.

427.   Laura H. Wild, "The Basic Teachings of Jesus," *JBR* 12 (1944): 26-32.

428.   David Daube, "Public Pronouncement and Private Explanation in the Gospels," *ET* 57 (1945-1946): 175-77.

429.   Olaf Moe, "Lov og evangelium i Jesu forkynnelse," *TTK* 17 (1946): 1-11.

430.   E. Paul Smith, "The Witness of Nature to the Message of Jesus," *CQ* 23 (1946): 363-68.

431.   James H. Ropes, "The Religious Radicalism of Jesus," *CQ* 24 (1947): 113-19.

432.   H. H. Cadman, "The Mind of Christ—The Rule of the Father," *ET* 62 (1950-1951): 323-26.

433.   J. Isaac, "Jesus and Israel," *RHPR* 31 (1951): 365.

434.   Matthew Black, "Ernst Percy's 'Message and Mission of Jesus' (Die Botschaft Jesu)," *ET* 66 (1954-1955): 68-71.

435.   J. A. E. van Dodewaard, "Jésus s'est-il servi lui-même du mot 'Évangile'?" *B* 35 (1954): 160-73.

436.   James M. Robinson, "Jesus' Understanding of History," *JBR* 23 (1955): 17-24.

437.   John Baker, "Christ's Challenge to Straight Thinking," *ET* 67 (1955-1956): 179-81.

438.   Paul E. Davies, "Trends Toward Individualism in the Teaching of Jesus," *JBR* 24 (1956): 10-17.

439.   Joaquín Salaverri, "Cristo, Maestro," *EE* 32 (1958): 5-19.

440.   Henry J. Cadbury, "Intimations of Immortality in the Thought of Jesus," *HTR* 53 (1960): 1-26.

440.1   A. W. Mosley, "Jesus' Audiences in the Gospels of St. Mark and St. Luke," *NTS* 10 (1963-1964): 139-49.

440.2   D. G. Calvert, "An Examination of the Criteria for Distinguishing the Authentic Words of Jesus," *NTS* 18 (1971-1972): 209-19.

440.3   Paul S. Minear, "Jesus' Audiences according to Luke," *NT* 16 (1974): 81-109.

440.4   Johannes Nissen, "Autoritet i forkyndelse og handling: om evangeliets formidling hos Jesus og Paulus," *DTT* 46/2 (1983): 107-43.

440.5   Douglas J. Moo, "Jesus and the Authority of the Mosaic Law," *JSNT* 20 (1984): 3-49.

440.6   Gerard Luttikhuizen, "The Evaluation of the Teaching of Jesus in Christian Gnostic Revelation Dialogues," *NT* 30 (1988): 158-68.

440.7   Ronald Youngblood, "Christ and the Kingdom in the Old and New Testaments," *JETS* 35 (1992): 3-49.

2. Jesus' Teaching Methods

441.   Richard Montague "The Dialectic Method of Jesus," *BS* 41 (1884): 549-72.

442.   George B. Stevens, "The Teaching of Jesus; II, The Methods of his Teaching," *BW* 5 (1895): 106-13.

443.   William C. Wilkinson, "Jesus as a Preacher," *BW* 6 (1895): 476-89.

444.   Ernest DeW. Burton, "Jesus as a Thinker," *BW* 10 (1897): 245-58.

445.   Charles F. Thwing, "Jesus as a Teacher," *BW* 10 (1897): 166-73.

446.   D. Macfadyen, "Did our Lord ever Speak in Irony?" *ET* 13 (1901-1902): 47.

447.   David Smith, "Our Lord's Use of Common Proverbs," *Exp* 6th ser., 6 (1902): 441-54.

448.   Samuel MacComb, "The Irony of Christ," *BW* 23 (1904): 104-109.

449.   H. Peters, "Jesus as a Teacher," *LCR* 23 (1904): 241-54.

450.   T. H. Bindley, "The Method of the Christ," *ET* 16 (1904-1905): 201-205.

451.   M. Cunningham Wilson, "Did Christ Preach from a Text?" *ET* 19 (1907-1908): 187-88.

452.   Lester Reddin, "Jesus the Rabbi," *BS* 69 (1912): 693-706.

453.   A. H. Tuttle, "Jesus the Teacher," *BR* 2 (1917): 275-88.

454.   J. Warschauer, "Jesus as a Teacher: Toward an Interpretation," *AJT* 23 (1919): 146-64.

455.   John Lendrum, "Our Lord's Use of 'We,'" *ET* 35 (1923-1924): 507-10.

456.   C. G. Montefiore, "The Originality of Jesus," *HJ* 28 (1929-1930): 98-111.

457.   H. Bluth, "Mehrdeutige Herrenworte. Ein Beitrag Zur Methodik der Verkündigung Jesu," *NKZ* 42 (1931): 38-56.

458.   J. M. C. Crum, "Jesus as a Poet Teacher," *ET* 46 (1934-1935): 197-200.

459.   Harold A. Guy, "The Element of Abruptness in the Teaching of Jesus," *ET* 52 (1940-1941): 238-39.

460.   D. H. C. Read, "His Way with Inquirers," *ET* 63 (1951-1952): 37-40.

461.   H. Clavier, "L'ironie dans l'enseignement de Jésus," *NT* 1 (1956): 3-20.

           See also numbers 394, 425, 2893ff., 2911, 2974.

461.1   C. L. Mitton, "Threefoldness in the Teaching of Jesus," *ET* 75 (1963-1964): 228-30.

461.2   Wilfred Tooley, "The Shepherd and Sheep Image in the Teaching of Jesus," *NT* 7 (1964-1965): 15-25.

461.3   Aloysius M. Ambrozic, "Mark's Concept of the Parable," *CBQ* 29 (1967): 220-27.

461.4   John D. Crossan, "Parable and Example in the Teaching of Jesus," *NTSt* 18 (1972): 285-307.

J. THE PASSION OF JESUS

  1. General Studies

462.   C. Pius Zingerle, "Ueber und aus Reden von zwei syrischen Kirchenvätern über das Leiden Jesu," *TQ* 52 (1870): 92-114; 53 (1871): 409-26.

463.   Arthur Carr, "Hostile and Alien Evidence for Christ at Passiontide," *Exp* 6th ser., 7 (1903): 417-25.

464. Samuel Whittlesey Howland, "The Reason and Nature of Christ's Sufferings," *BS* 62 (1905): 514-37.

465. J. M. Pfättisch, "Christus und Sokrates bei Justin," *TQ* 90 (1908): 503-23.

466. B. A. Greene, "Jesus' Last Interviews," *BW* 36 (1910): 274-81.

467. A. M. Haggard, "Problems of the Passion Week," *BS* 69 (1912): 664-92.

468. William F. Bostick, "Jesus and Socrates," *BW* 47 (1916): 248-52.

469. James Moffatt, "Jesus as Prisoner," *ET* 28 (1916-1917): 57-62.

470. N. M. Plum, "Lidelseshistoriens Harmonisering," *TTDF* 3rd ser., 7 (1916): 177-208.

471. E. S. Buchanan, "New Light on the Passion of our Lord Jesus Christ," *BS* 74 (1917): 610-13.

472. James Moffatt, "Jesus and the Four Men," *ET* 32 (1920-1921): 486-49.

473. Albert D. Belden, "The Spirit of Expiation," *RE* 22 (1925): 228-33.

474. Martin Dibelius, "Das historische Problem der Leidensgeschichte," *ZNW* 30 (1931): 193-201.

475. Eric F. F. Bishop, "With Jesus on the Road from Galilee to Calvary: Palestinian Glimpses into the Days Around the Passion," *CBQ* 11 (1949): 428-44.

476. Ernst Benz, "Christus und Sokrates in der alten Kirche," *ZNW* 43 (1950-1951): 195-224.

477. Constantin Hope, "The Story of the Passion and Resurrection in the English Primer," *JTS* N.S., 2 (1951): 68-82.

478. Erich Fascher, "Sokrates und Christus," *ZNW* 45 (1954): 1-41.

479. Juan Leal, "La nueva fecha de la Cena y el orden de los hechos de la Pasión de Nuestro Señor," *EE* 31 (1957): 173-88.

480.   X. Léon-Dufour, "Mt et Mc dans le récit de la Passion," *B* 40 (1959): 684-96.

480.1   J. Riaud, "La gloire et la royauté de Jésus dans la passion selon Saint Jean," *BVC* 56 (1964): 28-44.

480.2   Hans Conzelmann, "History and Theology in the Passion Narratives of the Synoptic Gospels," *Interp* 24 (1970): 178-97.

480.3   R. Desjardins, "Les Vestiges du Seigneur au Mont des Oliviers," *BLE* 73 (1972): 51-72.

480.4   Gerhard Schneider, "Das Problem Einer Vorkanonischen Passionserzahlung," *BibZ* 16/2 (1972): 222-44.

480.5   Robert Smith, "Darkness at Noon: Mark's Passion Narrative," *CTM* 44 (1973): 325-38.

480.6   Marcel Bassin, "L'annonce de la passion et les critères de l'historicíte," *RevSR* 50 (1976): 289-329; 51 (1977): 187-213.

480.7   H. Klein, "Die lukanisch-johanneische Passionstradition," *ZNW* 67 (1976): 155-86.

480.8   Leander E. Keck, "Mark and the Passion," *Interp* 31 (1977): 432-34.

480.9   William A. Smalley, "Translating Luke's Passion Story from the TEV," *BTr* 28 (1977): 231-35.

480.10   Julius Oswald, "Die Beziehungen zwischen Psalm 22 und dem vormarkinischen Passionsbericht," *ZKT* 101 (1979): 53-66.

480.11   George W. E. Nickelsburg, "The Genre and Function of the Markan Passion Narrative," *HTR* 73 (1980): 153-84.

480.12   Paul Beauchamp, "Narrativité biblique du récit de la passion," *RSR* 73 (1985): 39-59.

480.13   Edgar Haulotte, "Du récit quadriforme de la passion au concept de croix," *RSR* 73 (1985): 187-228.

480.14   Jean Delorme, "Sémiotique du récit et récit de la passion," *RSR* 73 (1985): 85-109.

480.15   Joseph Moingt, "Narrativité et théologie dans les récits de la passion," *RSR* 73 (1985): 6-160; 161-244.

480.16   Paul Ricoeur, "Le récit interprétatif: exégèse et théologie dans les récits de la passion," *RSR* 73 (1985): 17-38.

480.17   John M. Perry, "The Three Days in the Synoptic Passion Predictions," *CBQ* 48/4 (1986): 637-54.

480.18   Donald Senior, "Matthew's Special Material in the Passion Story: Implications for the Evangelist's Redactional Technique and Theological Perspective," *ETL* 63 (1987): 272-94.

480.19   Reinhard Feldmeier, "Die Krisis des Gottessohnes: die markinische Gethsemaneperikope als Markuspassion," *TLZ* 113 (1988): 234-36.

480.20   Daniel P. Jamros, "Satisfaction for Sin: Aquinas on the Passion of Christ," *ITQ* (1990): 307-28.

480.21   B. Kinman, "Jesus' 'Triumphal Entry' in the Light of Pilate's," *NTSt* 40 (1994): 442-48.

480.22   Donald Senior, "Revisiting Matthew's Special Material in the Passion Narrative: A Dialogue with Raymond Brown," *ETL* 70 (1994): 417-24.

480.23   Donald J. Verseput, "Jesus' Pilgrimage to Jerusalem and Encounter in the Temple: A Geographical Motif in Matthew's Gospel," *NT* 36 (1994): 105-21.

480.24   I. R. Kitzberger, "Mary of Bethany and Mary of Magdala—Two Female Characters in the Johannine Passion Narrative: A Feminist, Narrative-Critical Reader- Response," *NTSt* 41 (1995): 564-86.

480.25   B. Shellard, "The Relationship of Luke and John: A Fresh Look at an Old Problem," *JTS* 46 (1995):71-98.

2. The Last Supper

481.   Dr. Aberle, "Die Begebenheiten bei dem letzten Abendmahl," *TQ* 51 (1869): 69-126.

482.   Nathaniel Schmidt, "The Character of Christ's Last Meal," *JBL* 11 (1892): 1-21.

483.   E. P. Gray, "The Last Passover, and its Harmonies," *BS* 51 (1894): 339-46.

484.   James B. Johnston, "Professor Blass and St. Luke on the Lord's Supper," *ET* 9 (1897-1898): 520.

485.   Raphaël Proust, "Le comput Pascal," *RBén* 16 (1899): 25-35, 145-58.

486.   A. H. Sayce, "The Four Ways of Understanding the Words of Institution," *ET* 11 (1899-1900): 564-65.

487.   T. G. Selby, "The Passover and the Lord's Supper," *Exp* 9 (1899): 210-17.

488.   C. P. Coffin, "Two Sources for the Synoptic Account of the Last Supper," *AJT* 5 (1901): 102-16.

489.   Wilhelm Koch, "Die neutestamentlichen Abendmahlsberichte und die neueste Abendmahlsforschung," *TQ* 87 (1905): 230-57.

490.   P. Volz, "Ein heutiger Passahabend," *ZNW* 7 (1906): 247-51.

491.   G. Wohlenberg, "Die biblischen Abendmahlsberichte und ihre neuere Kritik," *NKZ* 17 (1906): 181-99, 247-71, 358-67.

492.   Willoughby C. Allen, "The Last Supper was a Passover Meal," *ET* 20 (1908-1909): 377.

493.   A. R. Eagar, "St. Luke's Account of the Last Supper: A Critical Note on the Second Sacrament," *Exp* 7th ser., 5 (1908): 252-62, 343-61.

494.   George Milligan, "The Last Supper not a Paschal Meal," *ET* 20 (1908-1909): 334.

495.   M. A. R. Tuker, "The Words of Institution at the Last Supper," *HJ* 9 (1910-1911): 134-45.

496.   William Fredrick, "Did Jesus Eat the Passover?" *BS* 68 (1911): 503-509.

497.   B. C. Bacon, "The Lukan Tradition of the Lord's Supper," *HTR* 5 (1912): 322-48.

498.   A. E. Suffrin, "The Last Supper and the Passover," *ET* 29 (1917-1918): 475-77.

499.   E. J. Kissane, "Date of the Last Supper," *ITQ* 15 (1920): 365-68.

500.   Paul Haupt, "The Last Supper," *JBL* 40 (1921): 178-80.

501. L. von Sybel, "Das letzte Mahl Jesu," *TSK* 95 (1923-1924): 116-24.

502. Robert Eisler, "Das letzte Abendmahl," *ZNW* 24 (1925): 161-92; 25 (1926): 5-37.

503. Gottfried Kittel, "Die Wirkungen des Christlichen Abendmahls nach dem Neuen Testament," *TSK* 96-97 (1925): 215-37.

504. George G. Monks, "The Lucan Account of the Last Supper," *JBL* 44 (1925): 228-60.

505. H. M. Christie, "Did Christ Eat the Passover with his Disciples? or, The Synoptics *versus* John's Gospel," *ET* 43 (1931-1932): 515-19.

506. Conrad H. Moehlman, "The Origin of the Lord's Supper," *RL* 2 (1933): 571-82.

507. A. E. Morris, "Jesus and the Eucharist," *Th* 26 (1933): 242-66.

508. Percy J. Heawood, "The Last Passover in the Gospels," *ET* 53 (1941-1942): 295-97.

509. A. Herranz, "La Última Cena," *CB* 4 (1947): 65-70.

510. Joachim Jeremias, "Zur Exegese der Abendmahlsworte Jesu," *EvT* 7 (1947-1948): 60-63.

511. Lambert Nolle, "Did our Lord Eat the Pasch of the Old Testament before his Passion?" *Scr* 3 (1948): 43-45.

512. David Daube, "Two Notes on the Passover 'Haggadah,' " *JTS* 50 (1949): 53-57.

513. Joachim Jeremias, "The Last Supper," *JTS* 50 (1949): 1-10.

514. Joachim Jeremias, "Zur Exegese der Abendmahlsworte Jesu," *Nunt* 1 (1949): 3-5.

515. K. G. Kuhn, "Die Abendmahlsworte," *TLZ* 75 (1950): 399-407.

516. Willi Marxsen, "Der Ursprung des Abendmahls," *EvT* 12 (1952-1953): 293ff.

517. T. A. Burkill, "The Last Supper," *Nun* 3 (1956): 161-77.

518. D. Frangipane, "Una nuova ipotesi sul giorno in cui Gesù

celebrò la Pasqua," *RivB* 4 (1956): 233-52.

519. Jean Deloune, "La cène et la pâque dans le Nouveau Testament," *LumV* No. 31 (1957): 9-48.

520. L. Johnston, "The Date of the Last Supper," *Scr* 9 (1957): 108-15.

521. John A. O. Flynn, "The Date of the Last Supper," *ITQ* 25 (1958): 58-63.

522. Jean-Baptist du Roy, "Le dernier repas de Jésus," *BVC* 26 (1959): 44-52.

523. Johannes Steinbeck, "Das Abendmahl Jesu unter Berücksichtigung moderner Forschung," *Num* 6 (1959): 51-60.

524. Sydney Temple, "The Two Traditions of the Last Supper, Betrayal, and Arrest," *NTSt* 7 (1960-1961): 77-85.

See also numbers 479, 1087, 1090 ff., 3195, 3201, 5183 ff.

524.1 G. H. C. MacGregor, "The Eucharist in the Fourth Gospel," *NTSt* 9 (1962-1963): 111-19.

524.2 Oscar S. Brooks, "The Johannine Eucharist: Another Interpretation," *JBL* 82 (1963): 293-300.

524.3 Frank Stagg, "The Lord's Supper in the New Testament," *RE* 66/1 (1969): 5-14.

524.4 G. J. Bahr, "The Seder of Passover and the Eucharistic Words," *NT* 12 (1970): 181-202.

524.5 Norman A. Beck, "The Last Supper as an Efficacious Symbolic Act," *JBL* 89 (1970): 192-98.

524.6 J. D. G. Dunn, "John VI. A Eucharistic Discourse?" *NTSt* 17 (1970-1971): 328-38.

524.7 Kenneth Hein, "Judas Iscariot: Key to the Last Supper Narratives?" *NTSt* 17/2 (1970-1971): 227-32.

524.8 Paul H. Ballard, "Reasons for Refusing the Great Supper," *JTS* 23/2 (1972): 341-50.

524.9 A. Shaw, "Breakfast by the Shore and the Mary Magdalene Encounter as Eucharistic Narratives," *JTS* 25 (1974): 12-26.

524.10 A. R. Winnett, "The Breaking of the Bread: Does it

Symbolize the Passion?" *ET* 88 (1976-1977): 181-82.

524.11   Michel Gourgues, "Section christologique et section eucharistique en Jean VI. Une proposition," *RB* 88 (1981): 515-31.

524.12   David E. Klemm, " 'This is my Body': Hermeneutics and Eucharistic Language," *ATR* 64/3 (1982): 293-310.

524.13   J. D. M. Derrett, "The Upper Room and the Dish," *HeyJ* 26 (1985): 373-82.

524.14   John D. Laurence, "The Eucharist as the Imitation of Christ," *ThSt* 47/2 (1986): 286-96.

524.15   Kenneth Durkin, "A Eucharistic Hymn in John 6?" *ET* 98 (1987): 168-70.

524.16   Peter Lampe, "The Eucharist: Identifying with Christ on the Cross," *Interp* 48 (1994): 36-49.

524.17   Barry D. Smith, "The Chronology of the Last Supper," *WTJ* 53 (1991): 29-45.

524.18   Norman Theiss, "The Passover Feast of the New Covenant," *Interp* 48 (1994): 17-35.

  3. Judas and the Betrayal

525.   G. A. Chadwick, "Judas Iscariot," *Exp* 3rd ser., 10 (1889): 161-74.

526.   F. R. Whittaker, "The Fate of the Traitor," *ET* 23 (1911-1912): 478.

527.   G. Schläger, "Die Ungeschichtlichkeit des Verräters Judas," *ZNW* 15 (1914): 50-59.

528.   Marg. Plath, "Warum hat die urchristliche Gemeinde auf die Überlieferung der Judaserzählungen Wert gelegt?" *ZNW* 17 (1916): 178-88.

529.   B. W. Bacon, "What Did Judas Betray?" *HJ* 19 (1920-1921): 476-93.

530.   Richard Delbrueck, "Antiquarisches zu den Verspottungen Jesu," *ZNW* 41 (1942): 124-45.

531.   Herbert Preisker, "Der Verrat des Judas und das

Abendmahl," *ZNW* 41 (1942): 151-55.

532.   Kurt Lüthi, "Das Problem des Judas Ischariot—neu untersucht," *EvT* 16 (1956): 98-114.

532.1   Alasdair B. Gordon, "The Fate of Judas according to Acts 1:18," *EQ* 43/2 (1971): 97-100.

532.2   T. F. Glasson, "Davidic Links with the Betrayal of Jesus," *ET* 85 (1973-1974): 118-19.

532.3   L. Paul Trudinger, "Davidic Links with the Betrayal of Jesus: Some Further Observations," *ET* 86 (1974-1975): 278-79.

532.4   Yoël Arbeitman, "The Suffix of Iscariot," *JBL* 99 (1980): 122-23.

4. Gethsemane

533.   J. Gilbert, "The Agony in the Garden," *Exp* 3rd ser., 5 (1887): 180-93.

534.   W. W. Keen, "Further Studies on the Bloody Sweat of our Lord," *BS* 54 (1897): 483-96.

535.   J. W. Schwartz, "Jesus in Gethsemane," *LQ* 22 (1892): 267-71.

536.   C. Malan, "La crainte que ressent le seigneur Jésus à l'approche de la mort," *RTP* 31 (1898): 439-52.

537.   A. Eugene Thomson, "The Gethsemane Agony," *BS* 67 (1910): 598-610.

538.   John Monro Gibson, "The Gethsemane of the Fourth Gospel," *ET* 30 (1918-1919): 76-79.

539.   Camden M. Cobern, "Gethsemane," *BW* 54 (1920): 139-41.

540.   A. L. Vail, "Gethsemane," *RE* 20 (1923): 188-200.

541.   L. Fonck, "Passio SS. Cordis in horto Gethsemani," *VD* 8 (1928): 161-70, 193-204.

542.   K. G. Kuhn, "Jesus in Gethsemane," *EvT* 12 (1952-1953): 260-85.

543.   Anthony Kenny, "The Transfiguration and the Agony in the Garden," *CBQ* 19 (1957): 444-52.

544.   A. Colunga, "La agonía de Jesús en Getsemaní," *CB* 16

(1959): 13-17.

See also numbers 4671 ff.

544.1   Thor Boman, "Der Gebetskampf Jesu," *NTSt* 10 (1963-1964): 261-73.

544.2   Mark Kiley, " 'Lord Save My Life' (Ps 116:4) as a Generative Text for Jesus' Gethsemane Prayer (Mark 14:36a)," *CBQ* 48/4 (1986): 655-59.

544.3   E. A. Obeng, "Abba, Father: The Prayer of the Sons of God," *ET* 99 (1987-1988): 363-66.

544.4   Barbara Saunderson, "Gethsemane: The Missing Witness," *B* 70/2 (1989): 224-33.

5. The Trials of Jesus

545.   C. M. Genelli, "Jesus Christus vor seinen Richtern," *TQ* 22 (1840): 3-64.

546.   Dr. Aberle, "Die Berichte der Evangelisten über Gefangennehmung und Verurteilung Jesu," *TQ* 53 (1871): 3-63.

547.   B. Tideman, "De Overoordeling van Jezus," *TT* 5 (1871): 57-66.

548.   Henry C. Vedder, "The Trial of Christ: A Diatessaron," *BS* 39 (1882): 648-73.

549.   S. Cox, "A Day in Pilate's Life," *Exp* 2nd ser., 8 (1884): 107-28.

550.   A. Taylor Innes, "The Trials of Jesus Christ," *ET* 10 (1898-1899): 522-23.

551.   F. J. Lamb, "The Trial of Jesus: Its Value in the Foundation of Faith," *BS* 56 (1899): 223-40.

552.   W. M. Macgregor, "Christ's Three Judges," *Exp* 6th ser., 2 (1900): 59-68, 119-29.

553.   Andreas Brüll, "Die Ergreifung und Überlieferung Jesu an Pilatus," *TQ* 83 (1901): 161-86, 396-411.

554.   Ernst von Dobschütz, "Der Process Jesu nach den Acta Pilati," *ZNW* 3 (1902): 89-114.

555.   Henry M. Cheever, "The Legal Aspects of the Trial of Christ," *BS* 60 (1903): 495-509.

556.   Orlo J. Price, "Jesus' Arrest and Trial," *BW* 36 (1910): 345-53.

557.   Karl Kastner, "Nochmals die Verspottung Christ," *BibZ* 9 (1911): 56.

558.   Martin Dibelius, "Herodes und Pilatus," *ZNW* 16 (1915): 113-26.

559.   Burton S. Easton, "The Trial of Jesus," *AJT* 19 (1915): 430-52.

560.   Herbert G. Wood, "A Mythical Incident in the Trial of Jesus," *ET* 28 (1916-1917): 459-60.

561.   Richard W. Husband, "The Pardoning of Prisoners by Pilate," *AJT* 21 (1917): 110-16.

562.   S. Langdon, "The Release of a Prisoner at the Passover," *ET* 29 (1917-1918): 328-30.

563.   H. Danby, "The Bearing of the Rabbinical Criminal Code on the Jewish Trial Narratives in the Gospels," *JTS* 21 (1920): 51-76.

564.   G. Baldensperger, "Il a rendu témoignage devant Ponce Pilate," *RHPR* 2 (1922): 1-25, 95-117.

565.   George A. Barton, "On the Trial of Jesus Before the Sanhedrin," *JBL* 41 (1922): 205-11.

566.   Parke P. Flourney, "What Frightened Pilate?" *BS* 82 (1925): 314-20.

567.   Gunnar Rudberg, "Die Verhöhnung Jesu vor dem Hohenpriester," *ZNW* 24 (1925): 307-309.

568.   Cuthbert Lattey, "The Praetorium of Pilate," *JTS* 31 (1929-1930): 180-82.

569.   M. Goguel, "À propos du procès de Jésus," *ZNW* 31 (1932): 289-301.

570.   Hans Lietzmann, "Bemerkungen zum Prozess Jesu," *ZNW* 30 (1931): 211-15; 31 (1932): 78-84.

571.   U. Holzmeister, "Christus Dominus spinis coronatur," *VD* 17

(1937): 65-69.

572.   Charles B. Chavel, "The Releasing of a Prisoner on the Eve of the Passover in Ancient Jerusalem," *JBL* 60 (1941): 273-78.

573.   Stephen Liberty, "The Importance of Pontius Pilate in Creed and Gospel," *JTS* 45 (1944): 38-56.

574.   Horace A. Rigg, "Barabbas," *JBL* 64 (1945): 417-56.

575.   Paul Gächter, "The Hatred of the House of Annas," *ThSt* 8 (1947): 3-34.

576.   M. Leroux, "Responsabilitiés dans le procès du Christ," *CS* 1 (1947): 102-21.

577.   Everett F. Harrison, "Jesus and Pilate," *BS* 105 (1948): 307-19.

578.   Joachim Jeremias, "Zur Geschichtlichkeit des Verhors Jesu vor dem Hohen Rat," *ZNW* 43 (1950-1951): 145-50.

579.   Jean Cantinat, "Jésus devant le Sanhédrin," *NRT* 75 (1953): 300-308.

580.   J. Blinzler, "Der Entschied des Pilatus—Exekutionsbefehl oder Todesurteil?" *MTZ* 5 (1954): 171-84.

581.   J. A. Drossaart Bentfort, "Enige beknopte beschouwingen met betrekking tot de processen van de Here Jezus Christus en van de Apostel Paulus," *GTT* 55 (1955): 33-68.

582.   V. E. Harlow, "The Destroyer of Jesus: The Story of Herod Antipas," *RHPR* 26 (1956): 85-86.

583.   Paul Winter, "Marginal Notes on the Trial of Jesus," *ZNW* 50 (1959): 14-33, 221-51.

584.   Joseph B. Tyson, "Jesus and Herod Antipas," *JBL* 79 (1960): 239-46.

        See also numbers 3200, 3234, 10055.

584.1   Paul Lamarche, "Le 'blasphème' de Jésus devant le Sanhédrin," *RSR* 50 (1962): 74-85.

584.2   Paul Winter, "The Marcan Account of Jesus' Trial by the Sanhedrin," *JTS* 14 (1963): 94-102.

584.3   A. Bajsíc, "Pilatus, Jesus und Barabbas," *B* 48 (1967): 7-28.

584.4   P. Valentin, "Les comparutions de Jésus devant le
            Sanhédrin," *RSR* 59 (1971): 230-36.

584.5   M. Herranz Marco, "El proceso ante el Sanhedrin y el
            Ministerio Público de Jesus," *EB* 34 (1974): 83-111; 35
            (1975): 49-78, 187-222; 36 (1976): 35-55.

6. The Crucifixion and Death of Jesus

a. *General Studies*

585.   J. E. W. Gericke, "Die Wirkungen des Todes Jesu in
            Beziehung auf seine eigene Person," *TSK* 16 (1843):
            261-314.

586.   D. W. Simon, "The Death of Christ in its Outward
            Appearance and its Historical Influence," *BS* 25 (1868):
            733-64.

587.   Thomas A. Hoyt, "The Physiological Features of the
            Crucifixion," *JCP* 3 (1883-1884): 481-90.

588.   Wm. O. Ayres, "The Death of Jesus Christ: Its Physiological
            Significance," *BS* 44 (1887): 293-305.

589.   Ernest Martin, "La mort de Jésus-Christ," *RTP* 22 (1889):
            51-62.

590.   John J. Young, "Religious Fanaticism and the Death of
            Christ," *LQJ* 25 (1895): 516-26.

591.   Edward M. Merrins, "Did Jesus die of a Broken Heart?" *BS*
            52 (1905): 38-53, 229-44.

592.   W S Fleck, "How Long was Christ in the State of the Dead?"
            ET 17 (1905-1906): 42-44.]

593.   Alfred E. Garvie, "The Desolation of the Cross," *Exp* 7th
            ser., 3 (1907): 507-27.

594.   Karl Kastner, "Christi Dornenkrönung und Verspottung
            durch die römische Soldateska," *BibZ* 6 (1908): 378-92.

595.   W. S. Rutherford, "The Seamless Coat," *ET* 22 (1910-1911):
            44-45.

596.   J. H. Farmer, "The Death of Christ in the Gospels," *RE* 15
            (1918): 394-410.

597.   Norvelle Wallace Sharpe, "A Study of the Definitive Cause of Death of the Lord Jesus Christ," *BS* 87 (1930): 423-52.

598.   Adhemar d'Alès, "La condition du corps du Christ dans la mort," *RSR* 21 (1931): 200-201.

599.   William Southerland, "The Cause of Christ's Death," *BS* 88 (1931): 476-85.

600.   G. L. Young, "The Cause of our Lord's Death," *BS* 88 (1931): 197-206.

601.   J. W. Hewitt, "The Use of Nails in the Crucifixion," *HTR* 25 (1932): 29-46.

602.   G. L. Young, "The Cause of Christ's Death," *BS* 89 (1932): 96-97.

603.   Carl Schneider, "Der Hauptmann am Kreuz," *ZNW* 33 (1934): 1-17.

604.   S. Zeitlin, "The Crucifixion of Jesus Re-examined," *JQR* 31 (1940-1941): 327-69; 32 (1941-1942): 175-89, 279-301.

605.   U. Holzmeister, "Die Finsternis beim Tode Jesu," *B* 22 (1941): 404-11.

606.   U. Holzmeister, "Crucifixio Christi et martyrium S. Bartholomaei," *VD* 22 (1942): 82-85.

607.   N. B. Stonehouse, "Who Crucified Jesus?" *WTJ* 5 (1943): 137-65.

608.   W. B. Primrose, "A Surgeon Looks at the Crucifixion," *IIJ* 47 (1948-1949): 382-88.

609.   Samuel Rosenblatt, "The Crucifixion of Jesus from the Standpoint of Pharisaic Law," *JBL* 75 (1956): 315-21.

            See also numbers 811, 1094 ff.

609.1   H.-W. Bartsch, "Die Bedeutung des Sterbens Jesu nach den Synoptikern," *TZ* 20 (1964): 87-102.

609.2   José R. Scheifler, "El Salmo 22 y la Crucifixión del Señor," *EB* 24 (1965): 5-83.

609.3   S. Lewis Johnson, "The Death of Christ," *BS* 125 (1968): 10-19.

609.4   Birger Gerhardsson, "Jésus livré et abandonne d'après la

Passion selon saint Matthieu," *RB* 76 (1969): 206-27.

609.5   R. S. Barbour, "Gethsemane in the Tradition of the Passion," *NTSt* 16 (1969-1970): 231-51.

609.6   J. M. Ford, " 'Crucify Him, Crucify Him' and the Temple Scroll," *ET* 87 (1975-1976): 275-78.

609.7   Paul Beauchamp, "Jésus Christ n'est pas seul: l'accomplissement des écritures dans la croix," *RSR* 65 (1977): 243-78.

609.8   Virgil Howard, "Did Jesus Speak About His Own Death?" *CBQ* 39/4 (1977): 515-27.

609.9   Miguel de Burgos Nuñez, "La communión de Dios con el crucificado. Cristología de Marcos 15,22-39," *EB* 37 (1978): 243-66.

609:10   Christopher L. Chase, "A Note on the Theological Origins of the Iconography of the Dead Christ," *GOTR* 24 (1979): 58-64.

609.11   Grant R. Osborne, "Redactional Trajectories in the Crucifixion Narrative," *EQ* 51 (1979): 80-96.

609.12   Dieter Zeller, "Die Handlungsstruktur der Markuspassion. Der Frtrag strukturalistischer Literaturwissenschaft für die Exegese," *TQ* 59 (1979): 213-27.

609.13   Lewis Sperry Chafer, "For Whom Did Christ Die?" *BS* 137 (1980): 310-26.

609.14   Haim H. Cohn, "Jesus' Cry on the Cross: An Alternative View," *ET* 93 (1981-1982): 215-17.

609.15   Frank J. Matera, "The Death of Jesus according to Luke: A Question of Sources," *CBQ* 47 (1985): 469-85.

609.16   Daniel J. Antwi, "Did Jesus Consider His Death to Be an Atoning Sacrifice?" *Interp* 45 (1991): 17-28.

609.17   Gerald O'Collins and D. Kendall, "Did Joseph of Arimathea Exist?" *B* 75 (1994): 235-41.

b. *The Seven Words from the Cross*

610.   Eb. Nestle, "The Seven Words from the Cross," *ET* 11 (1899-1900): 423-24.

611. W. Rüdel, "Die letzten Worte Jesu," *NKZ* 21 (1910): 199-227.

612. W. H. Griffith Thomas, "The Words from the Cross," *ET* 27 (1915-1916): 46.

613. William E. Wilson, "Our Lord's Cry on the Cross," *ET* 31 (1919-1920): 519-20.

614. R. Galdos, "De septum verbis Jesu morientis," *VD* 7 (1927): 71-79, 101-10.

615. T. E. Young, "A Fresh Exposition of the Cries upon the Cross," *ET* 39 (1927-1928): 93.

See also number 398.

615.1 J. Wilkinson, "The Seven Words from the Cross," *SJT* 17 (1964): 69-82.

615.2 S. J. Kistemaker, "The Seven Words from the Cross," *WTJ* 38 (1976): 182-91.

615.3 J.-N. Aletti, "Mort de Jésus et théorie de récit," *RSR* 73 (1985): 147-60.

c. *The Burial of Jesus*

616. L.-H. Vincent, "Garden Tomb: histoire d'un mythe," *RB* 34 (1925): 401-31.

617 Karl Bornhäuser, "Die Kreuzesabnahme und das Begräbnis Jesu," *NKZ* 42 (1931): 137 68.

618. Heinrich Holtzmann, "Das Begräbnis Jesu," *ZNW* 30 (1931): 311-13.

619. F.-M. Braun, "La sépultire de Jésus," *RB* 45 (1936): 34-52, 184-200, 346-63.

620. J. Mehlmann, "De sepulcro Domini quaestiones archaeologicae," *VD* 21 (1941): 74-81.

621. David Daube, "The Annointing at Bethany and Jesus' Burial," *ATK* 32 (1950): 186-99.

622. J. Spencer Kennard, Jr., "The Burial of Jesus," *JBL* 74 (1955): 227-38.

See also numbers 4723 ff.

622.1   K. P. G. Curtis, "Three Points of Contact between Matthew and John in the Burial and Resurrection Narratives," *JTS* 23 (1972): 440-44.

622.2   Helen F. Bergin, "The Death of Jesus and Its Impact on God —Jurgen Moltmann and Edward Schillebeeckx," *ITQ* 52 (1986): 193-211.

622.3   Raymond E. Brown, "The Burial of Jesus," *CBQ* 50 (1988): 233-45.

K. THE RESURRECTION OF JESUS AND HIS POST-RESURRECTION APPEARANCES

623.   Ludwig Paul, "Über die geschichtliche Beglaubigung einer realen Auferstehung Christi nach den neutestamentlichen Berichten," *ZWT* 6 (1863): 182-209, 297-311.

624.   A. Hilgenfeld, "Nachwort zu den neuesten Verhandlungen über die Auferstehung Christi," *ZWT* 7 (1864): 95-98.

625.   J. O. Dykes, "The Identity of the Lord Jesus after his Resurrection," *Exp* , 1st ser., 3 (1876): 161-74.

626.   Benjamin B. Warfield, "The Resurrection of Christ as an Historical Fact, Evinced by Eye-Witnesses," *JCP* 3 (1883-1984): 305-18.

627.   M. Schiffers, "La question d'Emmaus," *RB* 2 (1893): 26-40.

628.   Samuel Hutchings, "The Nature of the Resurrection Body of Christ," *BS* 52 (1895): 708-23.

629.   J.-Alfred Porret, "Jésus-Christ est-il ressuscité?" *RTP* 31 (1898): 481-532.

630.   Newport J. D. White, "The Appearances of the Risen Lord to Individuals," *Exp* 5th ser., 10 (1899): 66-74.

631.   C. J. Ellicott, "The Testimony of the Tomb," *ET* 14 (1902-1903): 508-11.

632.   E. Petavel-Olliff, "La résurrection de Jésus-Christ en face de la science contemporaine," *RTP* 38 (1905): 369-400.

633.   H. J. Holtzmann, "Das leere Grab und die gegenwärtigen Verhandlungen über die Auferstehung Jesu," *TR* 9 (1906): 79-86, 119-32.

634.   William P. Armstrong, "The Resurrection and the Origin of the Church in Jerusalem," *PTR* 5 (1907): 1-25.

635.   J. A. Cramer, "Het historisch getuigenis aangaande de opstanding van Jesus Christus," *TT* 43 (1909): 51-78.

636.   J. S. Banks, "The Disciples and Christ's Resurrection," *ET* 21 (1909-1910): 419-21.

637.   J. M. Shaw, "The Visibility of our Lord's Resurrection Body," *ET* 21 (1909-1910): 544-47.

638.   William P. Armstrong, "The Resurrection of Jesus and Historical Criticism," *PTR* 8 (1910): 247-70.

639.   J. A. Cramer, "De berichten aangaande de verschijningen van Jezus Christus," *TT* 44 (1910): 189-222.

640.   Margaret D. Gibson and Agnes Smith Lewis, "The Stone Rolled Away," *ET* 24 (1912-1913): 383-84.

641.   J. Armitage Robinson, "The Resurrection Appearances," *JTS* 14 (1912-1913): 196-206.

642.   William P. Armstrong, "The Resurrection of Jesus," *PTR* 12 (1914): 586-616.

643.   G. Wohlenberg, "Welshes war der Schauplatz der Wirksamkeit Jesu?" *NKZ* 26 (1915): 662-75.

644.   T. J. Agius, "Hallucination and the Resurrection," *ITQ* 11 (1916): 351-68.

645.   James H. Snowden, "The Historical Proofs of the Resurrection of Christ," *BR* 6 (1921): 352-79; 541-63.

646.   T. Haering, "Noch einmal das 'Wie' der 'Auferstehung' Jesu," *ZTK* N.F. 4 (1923): 27-46.

647.   W. H. Turton, "The First Easter Day," *BS* 80 (1923): 57-73.

648.   E. Bickermann, "Das leere Grab," *ZNW* 23 (1924): 281-92.

649.   Sophie Radford de Meissner, "The Journey to Emmaus," *BS* 84 (1927): 158-67.

650.   S. Vernon McCasland, "Peter's Vision of the Risen Christ," *JBL* 47 (1928): 41-59.

651.   S. Vernon McCasland, "The Scripture Basis of 'On the Third Day," *JBL* 48 (1929): 124-37.

652.   William J. Thompson, "Christ's Resurrection: Delusion, Illusion, or Hallucination?" *CQ* 6 (1929): 162-69.

653.   A. Vitti, "Quid de Christi resurrection in apocryphis inveniatur," *VD* 9 (1929): 103-11.

654.   B. W. Bacon, "The Resurrection in Judean and Galilean Tradition," *JR* 11 (1931): 506-16.

655.   George L. Hurst, "The Post-Resurrection Appearances of Jesus," *CJRT* 8 (1931): 302-305.

656.   S. Vernon McCasland, "The Basis of the Resurrection Faith," *JBL* 50 (1931): 211-26.

657.   W. J. Sparrow Simpson, "The Empty Tomb," *ET* 43 (1931-1932): 123-28.

658.   G. Baldensperger, "Le tombeau vide," *RPHR* 12 (1932): 413-43; 13 (1933): 105-44; 14 (1934): 97-125.

659.   U. Holzmeister, "Inscriptio urbis Nazareth nuper publici facta, novus testis resurrectionis Domini (?)," *VD* 17 (1937): 117-18.

660.   W. J. Sparrow Simpson, "The Evidence for our Lord's Resurrection," *Th* 34 (1937): 198-206.

661.   Everett F. Harrison, "The Ministry of our Lord During the Forty Days," *BS* 95 (1938): 45-68.

662.   W. Tom, "Waar was Jezus gedurende de veertig dagen tusschen zijn opstanding en hemelvaart?" *GTT* 39 (1938): 404-11.

663.   C. J. Goslinga, "Een herhaalde hemelvaart?" *GTT* 39 (1938): 557-60 [No; reply to W. Tom].

664.   W. Tom, "Nog eens: waar was Jezus gedurende de veertig dagen tusschen zijn upstanding en hemelvaart?" *GTT* 40 (1939): 303-306 [reply to Goslinga].

665.   C. J. Goslinga, " 'Tot op den dag, in welken hij opgenomen is'," *GTT* 40 (1939): 519-22 [second reply to W. Tom].

666.   W. H. McClellan, "Saint John's Evidence of the Resurrection," *CBQ* 1 (1939): 253-55.

667.   P. E. Kretzmann, "Die Erscheinungen des auferstandenen

Heilandes," *CTM* 11 (1940): 661-67.

668.   Cuthbert Lattey, "The Apparitions of Christ Risen," *CBQ* 2 (1940): 195-214.

669.   R. A. Edwards, "The Evidence for the Resurrection," *HJ* 40 (1941-1942): 252-59.

670.   U. Holzmeister, "Num Christus post resurrectionem benedictae Matri apparuerit," *VD* 22 (1942): 97-102.

671.   J. L. Lilly, "The Appearances of the Risen Christ," *CBQ* 4 (1942): 22-36.

672.   Eric F. F. Bishop, "With Saint Luke in Jerusalem from Easter Day till Pentecost," *ET* 56 (1944-1945): 192-94, 220-23.

673.   J. A. Oñate, "Noches de Jesús," *CB* 4 (1947): 255-62; 5 (1948): 114-19.

674.   Roland D. Sawyer, "Was Peter the Companion of Cleopas on Easter Afternoon?" *ET* 61 (1949-1950): 91-93.

675.   Charles Masson, "Le problème historique de la résurrection de Jésus-Christ," *RTP* N.S., 38 (1950): 178-86.

676.   Morton S. Enslin, " 'And that he heath been raised,' " *JQR* 43 (1952-1953): 27-56.

677.   Valdo Galland, "El problema histórico de la resurrectión de Jesu Cristo," *CT* No. 6 (1952): 12 ff.

678.   Eric F. F. Bishop, "The Risen Christ and the Five Hundred Brethren (1 Cor. 15.6)," *CDQ* 18 (1956): 341-44.

679.   Jacques Dupont, "Le repas d'Emmaus," *LumV* 31 (1957): 77-92.

680.   C. F. D. Moule, "Post-Resurrection Appearances in the Light of Festival Pilgrimages," *NTSt* 4 (1957-1958): 58-61.

681.   Rupert Annand, "He was seen of Peter," *SJT* 11 (1958): 180-87.

682.   L. A. Garrard, "What Happened on the First Easter?" *HJ* 57 (1958-1959): 213-22.

683.   León Villuendaz Polo, "La geografía de las apariciones de Cristo resucitado en la 'Vida de Jesucristo' del P. A. Fernáddez," *EE* 34 (1960): 929-34.

684.   J. W. D. Smith, "The Resurrection of Christ: Myth or History?" *ET* 72 (1960-1961): 370-75.

            See also numbers 69, 73, 477, 811, 1105, 2243, 3313, 3327, 8811-8912, 8920 f., 10037, 10045.

684.1   Félix Gils, "Pierre et la foi au Christ Ressuscité," *ETL* 38 (1962): 5-43.

684.2   M. Balagué, "La prueba de la resurrección," *EB* 25 (1966): 169-92.

684.3   L. H. Duparc, "Le premier signe de la Résurrection chez saint Jean. Jean 20:7," *BVC* 86 (1969): 70-77.

684.4   Bernd Steinseifer, "Der Ort der Erscheinungen des Auferstandenen," *ZNW* 62/3 (1971): 232-65.

684.5   J. K. Elliott, "Does Luke 2:41-52 Anticipate the Resurrection?" *ET* 83 (1971-1972): 87-89.

684.6   G. Ghiberti, " 'Resurrexit': Gli Atti di un simposio e la discussione successiva," *RivB* 23 (1975): 413-40.

684.7   G. Ghiberti, "Discussione sulla risurrezione di Gesù," *RivB* 24 (1976): 57-93.

684.8   Donald Senior, "The Death of Jesus and the Resurrection of the Holy Ones (Mt. 27:51-53)," *CBQ* 38 (1976): 312-29.

684.9   Albert Descamps, "À propos d'un Ouvrage important sur la Resurrection de Jesus," *B* 58 (1977): 84-105.

684.10   Joseph Doré, "Résurrection de Jésus a l'épreuve du discours théologique," *RSR* 65 (1977): 279-304.

684.11   D. Muñoz León, "El sustrato targúmico del Discurso del Pan de Vida. Nuevas aportaciones: La equivalencia 'venir' y 'aprender/creer' y la conexión 'vida eterna' y 'resurrección'," *EB* 36 (1977): 217-26.

684.12   R. Alan Culpepper, "The Passion and Resurrection in Mark," *RE* 75 (1978): 583-600.

684.13   Gerald O'Collins, "Peter as Easter Witness," *HeyJ* 22 (1981): 1-18.

684.14   Gerald O'Collins, "Luminous Appearances of the Risen Christ," *CBQ* 46 (1984): 247-54.

684.15 Rowan Williams, "The Resurrection Of Jesus: A New Survey of the Material," *ITQ* 51 (1985): 225-31.

684.16 Roland Kany, "Der Lukanische Bericht von Tod und Auferstehung Jesu aus der Sicht eines hellenistischen Romanlesers," *NT* 28/1 (1986): 75-90.

684.17 Gerald O'Collins, "Mary Magdalene as Major Witness to Jesus' Resurrection," *ThSt* 48 (1987): 631-46.

684.18 John P. Galvin, "The Origin of Faith in the Resurrection of Jesus: Two Recent Perspectives," *ThSt* 49 (1988): 25-44.

684.19 J. D. M. Derrett, "Miriam and the Resurrection," *BO* 33 (1991): 211-19.

684.20 Charles H. Talbert, "The Place of the Resurrection in the Theology of Luke," *Interp* 46 (1992): 19-30.

684.21 J. M. Winger, "When Did the Women Visit the Tomb? Sources for Some Temporal Clauses in the Synoptic Gospels," *NTSt* 40 (1994): 284-88.

L. "LIFE-OF-JESUS" RESEARCH AND ITS THEOLOGICAL IMPLICATIONS

685. Dr. Marck, "Bericht über die kritische Bearbeitung des Lebens Jesu von D. Strauss," *TQ* 19 (1837): 35-91, 259-325, 425-57, 633-86.

686. Alex. Schweizer, "Das Leben Jesu von Strauss im Verhältnisse zur Schleiermacher'schen Dignität des Religionsstifters," *TSK* 10 (1837): 459-510.

687. Jul. Müller, "Bemerkung zum dritten Hefte der Streitschriften über das Leben Jesu von Dr. D. Fr. Strauss," *TSK* 11 (1838): 370-82.

688. H. B. Hackett, "Critique on Strauss's Life of Jesus," *BS* 2 (1845): 48-79.

689. J. Colani, "Des quatre évangiles canoniques considérés comme documents historiques de la vie de Jésus-Christ," *RT* 1 (1850): 223-43, 294-316; 2 (1851): 22-56.

690. A. Hilgenfeld, "Die Evangelien und die geschichtliche Gestalt Jesu," *ZWT* 6 (1863): 311-41.

691. Carl Beck, "Kritische Anzeige von 'Strauss, das Leben Jesu,

für das deutsche Volk bearbeitet,' " *TSK* 38 (1865): 71-126.

692.   Dr. Weiss, "W. Schenkel's Charakterbild Jesu, besonders von Seiten der Quellenbenutzung und geschichtlichen Behandlungsweise beleuchtet," *TSK* 38 (1865): 277-318.

693.   Dr. Kähler, "Das Charakterbild Jesu von D. Schenkel unter dogmatischen Gesichtspunkten betrachtet," *TSK* 39 (1866): 53-86.

694.   M. A. N. Rovers, "Over de methode van Renan," *TT* 12 (1878): 59-84.

695.   H. Schmidt, "Über die Grenzen der Aufgabe eines Lebens Jesu mit besonderer Rücksicht auf den gottmenschlichen Charakter seiner Person," *TSK* 51 (1878): 393-457.

696.   A. Hilgenfeld, "Ein conservatives 'Leben Jesu,' " *ZWT* 26 (1883): 386-455.

697.   Erich Haupt, "Das Leben Jesu von B. Weiss," *TSK* 57 (1884): 7-79.

698.   Paul Ewald, "Der biblische Christus unseres Glaubens Grund," *NKZ* 3 (1892): 949-77.

699.   W. Herrmann, "Der geschichtliche Christus, der Grund unseres Glaubens," *ZTK* 2 (1892): 232-73.

700.   M. M. Oliver, "Renan's Life of Christ," *BS* 1 (1893): 309-30.

701.   Otto Ritschl, "Der geschichtliche Christus, der christliche Glaube und die theologische Wissenschaft," *ZTK* 3 (1893): 371-426.

702.   Ernest DeW. Burton, "The Sources of the Life of Christ," *BW* 6 (1895): 424-32.

703.   J. van Loon, "De vraag naar karakter en oorsprong der evangelische geschiedenis (W. Brandt, 'Die Evang. Geschichte und der Ursprung des Christenthums')," *TT* 29 (1895): 457-96.

704.   K. F. Nösgen, "Die apostolische Verkündigung und die Geschichte Jesu," *NJDT* 4 (1895): 46-94.

705.   H. A. Redpath, "Prof. Albert Réville's Jésus de Nazareth," *Exp* 5th ser., 6 (1897): 90-102.

706.   M. Reischle, "Der Streit über die Begründung des Glaubens auf den 'geschichtlichen' Jesus Christus," *ZTK* 7 (1897): 171-264.

707.   T. Häring, "Gäbe es Gewissheit des Christlichen Glaubens, wenn es geschichtliche Gewissheit von der Ungeschichtlichtkeit der Geschichte Jesu Christi gäbe?" *ZTK* 8 (1898): 468-93.

708.   C. J. H. Ropes, "The Christ of History and of Faith," *AJT* 2 (1898): 80-96.

709.   Eberhard Vischer, "Die geschichtliche Gewissheit und der Glaube an Jesus Christus," *ZTK* 8 (1898): 195-260.

710.   W. Baldensperger, "Leben Jesu," *TR* 2 (1899): 59-67.

711.   Pfarrer Hadorn, "Der geschichtliche Christus," *STZ* 16 (1899): 50-59, 85-97.

712.   H. Scholz, "Der gegenwärtige Stand der Forschung über den dogmatischen Christus und den historischen Jesus," *TR* 2 (1899): 169-81, 211-24.

713.   W. Baldensperger, "Leben Jesu," *TR* 3 (1900): 9-19, 342-56.

714.   P. Schwartzkopf, "Einige Bemerkungen zur wahrhaft geschichtlichen Methode in der Erforschung des Lebensbildes Christi," *TSK* 73 (1900): 284-303.

715.   H. Borg-Schüttmann, "Der geschichtliche Christus als Glaubensgrund," *NKZ* 12 (1901): 667-93.

716.   David Smith, "Recent New Testament Criticism; III, Second Century Rivals of the Evangelic Jesus," *Exp* 6th ser., 4 (1901): 139-52; "IV, The Testimony of Christian Experience to the Historicity of the Evangelic Jesus," 208-20; "V, The Supreme Evidence of the Historicity of the Evangelic Jesus," 280-94.

717.   H. Weinel, "Leben Jesu," *TR* 5 (1902): 231-45, 278-91.

718.   Henri Bois, "La personne de Jésus et l'évangile de Jésus d'après Harnack," *RTQR* 12 (1903): 389-419, 534-70; 13 (1904): 45-59.

719.   Paul Chapuis, "Quelques problèms de la vie de Jésus à propos de quelques publications récentes," *RTP* 36 (1903):

408-49.

720. D. A. Frøvig, "Historicisme og kristelig aabenbaringstro," *NTT* 4 (1903): 328-39.

721. M.-J. Lagrange, "Jésus et la critique des évangiles," *BLE* (1903): 3-26.

722. D. S. Margoliouth, "The Historical Character of Jesus of Nazareth," *Exp* , 6th ser., 10 (1904): 401-12.

723. Romanus, "The Historical Jesus and the Christ of Experience," *HJ* 3 (1904-1905): 574-84.

724. G. Hollmann, "Leben und Lehre Jesu," *TR* 9 (1906): 132-48, 253-75.

725. W. Sanday, "The Spiritual Meaning of the Life of Christ," *Exp* 7th ser., 1 (1906): 385-403.

726. John W. Buckham, "Did Theology Create Christ?" *ET* 19 (1907-1908): 476-77.

727. Albertina A. Forrest, "The Cry 'Back to Christ': Its Implication," *AJT* 11 (1907): 56-73.

728. G. Hollmann, "Leben und Lehre Jesu," *TR* 11 (1908): 243-57, 265-77.

729. Chr. Glarbo, "Om den historiske Erkendelse af Jesu Person," *TTDF* 3rd ser., 1 (1909-1910): 287-98.

730. Hans Windisch, "Leben und Lehre Jesu," *TR* 12 (1909): 145-62, 171-83.

731. André Arnal, "Jésus historique," *RTQR* 19 (1910): 261-75.

732. Howard N. Brown, "Jesus and his Modern Critics," *HTR* 3 (1910): 437-53.

733. Alfred E. Garvie, "The Living Christ and the Historical Jesus," *ET* 22 (1910-1911): 402-409.

734. Friedrich Schulz, "Hat sich Jesus über lebt?" *STZ* 28 (1911): 241-62.

735. H. Weinel, "Ist unsere Verkündigung von Jesus unhaltbar geworden?" *ZTK* 20 (1910): 1-38.

736. Hans Windisch, "Der geschichtliche Jesus," *TR* 13 (1910): 163-82, 199-220.

737. W. Bousset, "Noch einmal 'der vorchristliche Jesus'," *TR* 14 (1911): 373-85.

738. Shirley Jackson Case, "The Historicity of Jesus: An Estimate of the Negative Argument," *AJT* 15 (1911): 20-42.

739. Shirley Jackson Case, "Is Jesus a Historical Character? Evidence for an Affirmative Opinion," *AJT* 15 (1911): 205-27.

740. Shirley Jackson Case, "Jesus' Historicity: A Statement of the Problem," *AJT* 15 (1911): 265-68.

741. K. Dunkmann, "The Christ Myth," *BS* 63 (1911): 34-47.

742. K. W. Feyerabend, "Ist unsere Verkündigung von Jesus unhaltbar geworden? Ein Wort zu der von Professor Weinel gestellten und beantworteten Frage," *ZTK* 21 (1911): 123-40.

743. Douglas C. Mackintosh, "Is Belief in the Historicity of Jesus Indispensable to Christian Faith?" *AJT* 15 (1911): 362-72.

744. Shailer Mathews, "Is Belief in the Historicity of Jesus Indispensable to Christian Faith?" *AJT* 15 (1911): 614-17; 16 (1912): 106-10.

745. William B. Smith, "The Pre-Christian Jesus," *AJT* 15 (1911): 259-65.

746. Hermann Werner, "Der historische Jesus der liberalen Theologie—ein Geisteskranker," *NKZ* 22 (1911): 347-90.

747. Hans Windisch, "Leben und Lehre Jesu," *TR* 14 (1911): 114-37, 199-236; 15 (1912): 110-32, 145-64, 198-210; 16 (1913): 319-41, 386-400, 436-50; 17 (1914): 404-23, 425-46; 18 (1915): 331-49; 19 (1916): 1-21, 283-93, 353-69; 20 (1917): 18-58, 305-41.

748. Karl Beth, "Die Bindung des Glaubens an die Person Jesu," *TR* 15 (1912): 1-21.

749. Wilhelm Fresenius, "Die Bedeutung der Geschichtlichkeit Jesu für den Glauben," *ZTK* 22 (1912): 244-68.

750. J. C. Mattes, "The Reconstructed Christ and the Reconstructionists," *LCR* 31 (1912): 264-71, 456-65, 678-96.

751.   Jacob Müller, "Der 'historische Jesus' der protestantischen freisinnigen Leben-Jesu-Forschung," *ZKT* 36 (1912): 425-63, 665-714.

752.   Rush Rhees, "Did Jesus Ever Live?" *BW* 39 (1912): 80-87.

753.   Rush Rhees, "What Did Jesus Undertake to Do?" *BW* 39 (1912): 167-74.

754.   Rush Rhees, "What Did Jesus Accomplish?" *BW* 39 (1912): 243-48.

755.   A. Kielholz, "Psychiatrische Leben-Jesu-Forschung," *STZ* 30 (1913): 285-86.

756.   H. U. Meyboom, "De tegenwoordige stand van het 'Jesus'-probleem," *TT* 47 (1913): 391-432.

757.   Lucius Hopkins Miller, "The Source of our Information regarding the Life of Jesus," *BW* 42 (1913): 290-303.

758.   C. A. Scott, "The Church's Interpretation of the Historic Christ," *ET* 25 (1913-1914): 439-44.

759.   Friedrich Karl Feigel, "Geschichtlichkeit Jesu und christlicher Glaube," *ZTK* 24 (1914): 171-79.

760.   K. G. Goetz, "Genügt der geschichtliche Jesus für die praktische Theologie und Frömmigkeit oder niche?" *ZWT* 55 (1914): 193-230.

761.   Lucius Hopkins Miller, "The Life of Jesus in the Light of Modern Criticism," *BW* 43 (1914): 75-85.

762.   William Walker Rockwell, "The Jesus as portrayed by non-Catholic Historians," *HTR* 7 (1914): 358-77.

763.   Gerald B. Smith, "The Christ of Faith and the Jesus of History," *AJT* 18 (1914): 521-44.

764.   M.-J. Lagrange, "La vie de Jésus d'après Renan," *RB* 27 (1918): 432-506.

765.   F. Schnedermann, "Zum Erweise geschichtlicher Treue bei den Evangelisten," *NKZ* 29 (1918): 638-56.

766.   Ernest DeW. Burton, "Jesus of Nazareth," *BW* 53 (1919): 547-54, 655-69; 54 (1920): 104-12, 214-24, 316-36.

767.   J. E. Flow, "The Character of Jesus is Proof of his

Historicity," *USR* 31 (1919-1920): 319-35.

768. J. de Zwaan, "De oorsprong van het Christendom ontraadseld?" *NTSt* 2 (1919): 111-17.

769. W. Schmidt, "Das Verhältnis der Christologie zur historischen Leben-Jesu-Forschung," *ZTK* N.F. 1 (1920): 323-53.

770. W. Mundle, "Der Christus des Glaubens und der historische Jesus," *ZTK* N.F. 2 (1921): 247-73.

771. E. Weber, "Die Geschichte des Christus," *NKZ* 32 (1921): 451-81.

772. J. R. Arkroyd, "The Christ Myth Theory: Its Service to the Understanding of Christianity," *RE* 19 (1922): 182-87.

773. F. Ménégoz, "Trois problèmes de philosophie religieuse," *RHPR* 2 (1922): 46-68.

774. Rudolf Paulus, "Geschichtliche und über geschichtliche Grundlagen des Glaubens. Eine Studie zum Christusproblem in der heutigen Theologie," *ZTK* N.F. 3 (1922): 180-202, 226-94.

775. A. Fornerod, "Le Christ de l'histoire et le Christ des consciences," *RTP* N.S. 10 (1922): 81-102.

776. Anton Fridrichsen, "Eduard Meyers syn paa kristendommens urhistorie," *NTT* 24 (1923): 40-54.

777. George F. Moore, "A Jewish Life of Jesus," *HTR* 16 (1923): 93-103.

778. Shirley Jackson Case, "The Next 'Life of Jesus,' " *CJRT* 1 (1923): 371-79.

779. Ernst von Dobschütz, "Der heutige Stand der Leben-Jesu-Forschung," *ZTK* N.F. 5 (1924): 64-84.

780. M. Goguel, "Jésus de Nazareth, mythe ou histoire?" *RHPR* 4 (1924): 169-78.

781. Kirsopp Lake, "Jesus," *HJ* 23 (1924-1925): 5-19.

782. Gregory Papamichael, " 'Ο Renan καὶ ὁ 'βίος τοῦ 'Ινσοῦ'," *Θ* 2 (1924): 309-43.

783. Karl Staab, "Wege zur 'Christusmythe' von A. Drews," *B* 5

(1924): 26-38.

784.   Dr. Strathmann, "Ursprung und Anfänge des Christentums," *NKZ* 35 (1924): 557-76.

785.   M. Goguel, "La vie et la pensée de Jésus. Leur rôle dans le christianisme primitif," *RHPR* 5 (1925): 509-39.

786.   M. Goguel, "Recent French Discussion of the Historical Existence of Jesus Christ," *HTR* 19 (1926): 115-42.

787.   Lyder Brun, "Et nyt Jesusbillede (R. Bultmann: Jesus)," *NTT* 28 (1927): 97-109.

788.   Burton S. Easton, "Dr. Case's Biography of Jesus," *ATR* 10 (1927-1928): 250-57.

789.   Robert Jelke, "Der Glaube an Jesus Christus und die historische Erforschung seines Lebens," *NKZ* 38 (1927): 341-97.

790.   Friedrich Traub, "Leben-Jesu-Forschung und Glaube," *NKZ* 38 (1927): 819-34.

791.   Milton G. Evans, "Christian Faith and the Historicity of Jesus," *CQ* 5 (1928): 5-14.

792.   Erich Foerster, "Rudolf Bultmanns Jesusbuch," *ZTK* N.F. 9 (1928): 28-50.

793.   M. Goguel, "Critique et histoire. À propos de la vie de Jésus," *RHPR* 8 (1928): 113-48.

794.   A. Nairne, "Books that have influenced our Epoch; Renan's 'Life of Jesus'," *ET* 40 (1928-1929): 439-43.

795.   John Dow, "The Historic Jesus," *CJRT* 6 (1929): 298-308.

796.   M. Goguel, "Le Jésus de l'histoire et le Christ de la foi," *RHPR* 2 (1929): 115-39.

797.   J. A. Robertson, "Books that have influenced our Epoch; Glover's Jesus of History," *ET* 41 (1929-1930): 124-26.

798.   Hans Windisch, "Das Problem der Geschichtlichkeit Jesu; die ausserchristlichen Zeugnisse," *TR* 1 (1929): 266-88.

799.   M. Goguel, "The Problem of Jesus," *HTR* 23 (1930): 93-120.

800.   W. Staerk, "Jesus im Lichte der jüdischen theologischen Wissenschaft," *TB* 9 (1930): 25-38.

801. Hans Windisch, "Das Problem der Geschichtlichkeit Jesu: die Christusmythe," *TR* 2 (1930): 207-52.

802. Paul Feine, "Die Aufgabe der heutigen Jesusforschung," *TSK* 103 (1931): 161-78.

803. M. Goguel, "La vie de Jésus," *RHPR* 12 (1932): 67-73.

804. Oswald W. S. McCall, "The Modern Interest in Jesus," *RL* 1 (1932): 288-93.

805. W. C. Robinson, "The Quest of the Historical Jesus," *EQ* 4 (1932): 113-27.

806. M. Goguel, "Le 'Jésus' de M. Ch. Guignebert," *RHPR* 13 (1933): 409-47.

807. G. H. C. Macgregor, "Recent Gospel Criticism, and our Approach to the Life of Jesus," *ET* 45 (1933-1934): 198-203, 283-86.

808. E. Mersch, "La vie historique de Jésus et sa vie mystique," *NRT* 60 (1933): 5-20.

809. C. J. Cadoux, "The Historical Jesus: A Study of Schweitzer and After," *ET* 46 (1934-1935): 406-10.

810. R. A. Edwards, "The 'Peasant' Theory of Jesus," *HJ* 33 (1934-1935): 521-35.

811. G. Baldensperger, "L'historicité de Jésus. À propos des récits évangéliques de la passion et de la résurrection," *RHPR* 15 (1935): 193-209.

812. Heinrich Frick, "Wider die Skepsis in der Leben-Jesu-Forschung (R. Ottos Jesus-Buch)," *ZTK* N.F. 16 (1935): 1-20.

813. Alfred Loisy, "Was Jesus an Historical Person?" *HJ* 36 (1937-1938): 380-94, 509-29.

814. Paul-Louis Couchoud, "The Historicity of Jesus; A Reply to Alfred Loisy," *HJ* 37 (1938-1939): 193-214.

815. C. J. Callan, "A Recent Life of Christ," *CBQ* 1 (1939): 145-49.

816. Eugene S. Tanner, "Recent Jewish Interpretations of Jesus," *JBR* 8 (1939): 80-82.

817.   C. J. Cadoux, "Is it Possible to Write a Life of Christ?" *ET* 53 (1941-1942): 175-77.

818.   T. W. Manson, "Is it Possible to Write a Life of Christ?" *ET* 53 (1941-1942): 248-51.

819.   Donald W. Riddle, "The Central Problem of the Gospels," *JBL* 60 (1941): 97-111.

820.   J. Schelhaas, "Christus en de Historische Stoffen in de Prediking," *GTT* 42 (1941): 107-28.

821.   Vincent Taylor, "Is it Possible to Write a Life of Christ?" *ET* 53 (1941-1942): 60-65.

822.   T. W. Manson, "The Life of Jesus: A Survey of the Available Material," *BJRL* 27 (1942-1943): 323-37; 28 (1944): 119-36, 382-403; 29 (1945-1946): 392-428; 30 (1946-1947): 312-29.

823.   Chr. Ihlen, "Troens Kristus og historiens Jesu. Antitese eller syntese under spenning," *TTK* 14 (1943): 97-113.

824.   Roderic Dunkerley, "The Life of Jesus: A New Approach," *ET* 57 (1945-1946): 264-68.

825.   Joseph Bonsirven, "Un témoignage juif sur Jésus," *CS* 1 (1947): 50-62 [Shalom Asch, *The Nazarene*].

826.   J. Guitten, "Le problème de Jésus et les fondements du témoignage chrétien," *RHPR* 28 (1948): 164-67.

827.   Hans von Campenhausen, "Maurice Goguel: Jésus et les origines du christianisme: La naissance du christianisme," *Nunt* 3 (1949): 19-24.

828.   S. MacLean Gilmour, "Schweitzer's Jesus of History," *RL* 18 (1949): 427-33.

829.   Thomas S. Kepler, "The Problem of Modernizing Jesus," *JBR* 17 (1949): 163-67.

830.   J. T. Noonan, "Renan's Life of Jésus: A Re-examination," *CBQ* 11 (1949): 26-39.

831.   H. Clavier, "La figure historique de Jesus," *RHPR* 30 (1950): 41-50.

832.   Olof Linton, "Hebreerbrevet och 'den historiske Jesus'," *STK* 26 (1950): 335-45.

833. Donald T. Rowlingson, "On the Neglect of the Jesus of History," *RL* 20 (1951): 541-52.

834. Ernst Ludwig Dietrich, "Gedanken zu Heinrich Ackermann, Jesus. Seine Botschaft und deren Aufnahme im Abendland, 1952," *ZRGG* 5 (1953): 365-67.

835. Ernst Käsemann, "Zum Thema der Nichtobjektivierbarkeit," *EvT* 12 (1952-1953): 455-66.

836. Robert C. Johnson, "The Jesus of History and the Christian Faith," *TTod* 10 (1953): 170-84.

837. Renate Ludwig, "Zwischen Licht und Schatten. Randgestalten der Geschichte Jesu in der neueren Literatur," *EvT* 13 (1953-1954): 277-81.

838. C. L. Mitton, "Goguel's 'Life of Jesus'," *ET* 65 (1953-1954): 259-63.

839. Paul E. Davies, "The Tradition of Jesus at the Point of Origin," *JBR* 22 (1954): 94-98.

840. Hans Engelland, "Gewissheit um Jesus von Nazareth," *TLZ* 79 (1954): 65-74.

841. Ernst Käsemann, "Das Problem des historischen Jesus," *ZTK* N.F. 51 (1954): 125-53.

842. W. Norman Pettinger, "The Problem of the Historical Jesus," *ATR* 36 (1954): 89-93.

843. N. A. Dahl, "Der historische Jesus als geschichtswissenschaftliches und theologisches Problem," *KD* 1 (1955): 104-32.

844. Otto Michel, "Der 'historische Jesus' und das theologische Gewissheitsproblem," *EvT* 15 (1955): 349-63.

845. Ernst Fuchs, "Die Frage nach dem historischen Jesus," *ZTK* N.F. 53 (1956): 210-29.

846. Holt H. Graham, "The 'Lives' of Jesus," *ATR* 38 (1956): 285-90.

847. Ernst Heitsch, "Die Aporie des historischen Jesus als Problem theologischer Hermeneutik," *ZTK* 53 (1956): 192-210.

848.   Matthew J. Newley, "The Historic Life of Jesus," *CJT* 2 (1956): 126-28.

849.   Peter Biehl, "Zur Frage nach dem historischen Jesus," *TR* 24 (1957-1958): 54-76.

850.   Ernst Fuchs, "Glaube und Geschichte im Blick auf die Frage nacx dem historischen Jesus. Eine Auseinandersetzung mit G. Bornkamms Buch über 'Jesus von Nazareth," *ZTK* N.F. 54 (1957): 224-52.

851.   Franz Mussner, "Der historische Jesus und der Christus des Glaubens," *BibZ* 1 (1957): 224-52.

852.   Ralph W. Odom, "An Analytical Approach to the Study of Jesus," *JBR* 25 (1957): 199-202.

853.   James M. Robinson, "The Historical Jesus and the Church's Kerygma," *RL* 26 (1957): 40-49.

854.   Gerhard Ebeling, "Jesus und Glaube," *ZTK* N.F. 55 (1958): 64-110.

855.   Ernst Fuchs, "Jesus und der Glaube," *ZTK* N.F. 55 (1958): 170-85.

856.   Joachim Jeremias, "The Present Position in the Controversy Concerning the Problem of the Historical Jesus," *ET* 69 (1958): 333-39.

857.   Léonce de Grandmaison, "La personne de Jésus et ses témoins," *RHPR* 28 (1958): 289-90.

858.   M. Gutiérrez Marín, "El Cristo histórico," *CT* 27-28 (1958): 39-44.

859.   Friedrich Mildenberger, "Kerygmatische Historie?" *EvT* 18 (1958): 419-24.

860.   James T. Ross, "Source Analysis for Study of the Life of Christ," *JBR* 26 (1958): 314-17.

861.   B. Rigaux, "L'historicité de Jésus deviant l'exégèse récente," *RB* 65 (1958): 481-522.

862.   James M. Robinson, "The Quest of the Historical Jesus Today," *TTod* 15 (1958): 183-97.

863.   Hans-Joachim Schoeps, "Protestantische Neuerscheinungen

zur Erkenntnis Jesu Christi," *ZRGG* 10 (1958): 160-65.

864.   Hans Conzelmann, "Zur Methode der Leben-Jesu Forschung," *ZTK* N.F. 56 (1959 - Beiheft 1): 2-13.

865.   Gerhard Ebeling, "Die Frage nach dem historischen Jesus und das Problem der Christologie," *ZTK* N.F. 56 (1959-Beiheft 1): 14-30.

866.   Frederick C. Grant, "The Jesus of History," *USQR* 14, no. 4 (March, 1959): 1-16.

867.   Bent Noack, "Om Stauffers Jesubog," *DTT* 22 (1959): 16-35.

868.   L. Randellini, "Possiamo ricostruire una biography di Gesù?" *BO* 1 (1959): 82-88.

869.   Rudolf Schnackenburg, "Jesusforschung und Christusglaube," *C* 13 (1959): 1-17.

870.   William R. Farmer and Norman Perrin, "The Kerygmatic Theology and the Question of the Historical Jesus," *RL* 29 (1960): 86-97.

871.   Ernst Fuchs, "Die Theologie des Neuen Testaments und der historische Jesus," *ZTK* N.F. 57 (1960): 296-301.

872.   Rene Marle, "The Problem of the Historical Jesus," *HeyJ* 1 (1960): 229-32.

873.   Hejne Simonsen, "Den historiske Jesus og menighedens Kristuskerygma," *DTT* 23 (1960). 193-208.

874.   W. D. Davies, "A Quest to be Resumed in New Testament Studies," *USQR* 15 (1960): 83-98.

875.   Dwight Marion Beck, "The Never-Ending Quest for the Historical Jesus," *JBR* 29 (1961): 227-31.

876.   E. C. Blackman, "Jesus Christ Yesterday: The Historical Basis of the Christian Faith," *CJT* 7 (1961): 118-27.

877.   Oscar Cullmann, "Out of Season Remarks on the 'Historical Jesus' of the Bultmann School," *USQR* 16 (1961): 131-48.

878.   Patrick Fannon, "Can We Know Jesus?" *Scr* 13 (1961): 44-51.

879.   Ernst Fuchs, "Muss man an Jesus glauben, wenn man an

Gott glauben will?" *ZTK* N.F. 58 (1961): 45-67.

880.   Peter C. Hodgson, "The Son of Man and the Problem of Historical Knowledge," *JR* 41 (1961): 91-108.

881.   W. Matthias, "Der historische Jesus und der irdische Jesus," *TLZ* 86 (1961): 571-74.

882.   J. D. MacCaughey, "The Question of the Historical Jesus," *RTR* 20 (1961): 1-12.

883.   Donald T. Rowlingson, "Jesus in History and in Faith," *JBR* 29 (1961): 35-38.

884.   Van A. Harvey and Schubert M. Ogden, "Wie neu ist die 'Neue Frage nach demhistorischen Jesus'?" *ZTK* N.F. 59 (1962): 46-87.

884.1   Thomas J. J. Altizer, "Word and History," *TTod* 22 (1965): 380-93.

884.2   Erich Grässer, "Der historische Jesus im Hebräerbrief," *ZNW* 56 (1965): 63-91.

884.3   James M. Robinson, "Kerygma und Geschichte im Neuen Testament," *ZTK* 62 (1965): 294-337.

884.4   Donald T. Rowlingson, "Gospel-Perspective and the Quest of the Historical Jesus," *JBR* 33 (1965): 329-36.

884.5   John H. Elliott, "Historical Jesus, the Kerygmatic Christ, and the Eschatological Community," *CTM* 37 (1966): 470-91.

884.6   Jack D. Kingsbury, "Jesus of History and the Christ of Faith: In Relation to Matthew's View of Time—Reactions to a New Approach," *CTM* 37 (1966): 500-10.

884.7   George E. Ladd, "History and Theology in Biblical Exegesis," *Interp* 20 (1966): 54-64.

884.8   D. Moody Smith, "The Historical Jesus in Paul Tillich's Christology," *JR* 46 (1966): 131-47.

884.9   Peter R. Ackroyd, "What Kind of Belief about Jesus?" *ATR* 49 (1967): 281-95.

884.10   William E. Hull, "New Quest of the Historical Jesus," *RE* 64 (1967): 323-39.

884.11   A. Vögtle, "Die hermeneutische Relevanz des

geschichtlichen Charakters der Christusoffenbarung," *ETL* 43 (1967): 470-87.

884.12   Hermann Fischer, "Die geschichtliche Christologie und das Problem des historischen Jesus: Erwägungen zur Christologie Friedrich Gogartens," *ZTK* 65 no 3 (1968): 348-70.

884.13   David W. Lotz, "Two Levels of History," *CTM* 39 (1968): 28-35.

884.14   Harvey K. McArthur, "From the Historical Jesus to Christology," *Interp* 23 (1969): 190-206.

884.15   William O. Walker, "Quest for the Historical Jesus: A Discussion of Methodology," *ATR* 51 (1969): 38-56.

884.16   Paul Merkley, "New Quests for Old: One Historian's Observations on a Bad Bargain," *CJT* 16 (1970): 203-18.

884.17   Stewart R. Sutherland, "History and Belief," *Th* 73 (1970): 4-9.

884.18   Harvey K. McArthur, "Burden of Proof in Historical Jesus Research," *ET* 82 (1971): 116-19.

884.19   H.-W. Bartsch, "Theologie und Geschichte in der Uberlieferung vom Leben Jesu," *EvT* 32 (1972): 128-42.

884.20   A. M. Ramsey, "Christian Faith and the Historical Jesus," *Th* 75 (1972): 118-26.

884.21   Gerhard Delling, "Die Jesusgeschichte in der Verkundigung nach Acta," *NTSt* 19 (1973): 373-89.

884.22   Erich Grässer, "Christologie und historischer Jesus: kritische Anmerkungen zu Herbert Brauns Christologieverständnis," *ZTK* 70 (1973): 404-19.

884.23   Jürgen Roloff, "Auf der Suche nach einem neuen Jesusbild: Tendenzen und Aspekte der gegenwärtigen Diskussion," *TLZ* 98 (1973): 561-72.

884.24   Falk Wagner, "Systematisch-theologische Erwägungen zur neuen Frage nach dem historischen Jesus," *KD* 19 (1973): 287-304.

884.25   John G. Gager, "Gospels and Jesus: Some Doubts about Method," *JR* 54 (1974): 244-72.

884.26   Robert P. Scharlemann, "Argument from Faith to History,"
           RL 43 (1974): 137-49.

884.27   H.-W. Bartsch, "Der Ursprung des Osterglaubens," *TZ* 31
           (1975): 16-31.

884.28   Brian A. Gerrish, "Jesus, Myth, and History: Troeltsch's
           Stand in the Christ-Myth Debate," *JR* 55 (1975): 13-35.

884.29   David Cairns, "Motives and Scope of Historical Inquiry about
           Jesus," *SJT* 29 (1976): 335-55.

884.30   Traugott   Koch,   "Albert   Schweitzers   Kritik   des
           christologischen Denkens und die sachgemässe Form einer
           gegenwärtigen Beziehung auf den geschichtlichen Jesus,"
           ZTK 73 (1976): 208-40.

884.31   Willi Marxsen, "Die urchristlichen Kerygmata und das
           Ereignis Jesus von Nazareth," *ZTK* 73 (1976): 42-64.

884.32   Daniel L. Migliore, "How Historical Is the Resurrection: A
           Dialogue," *TTod* 33 (1976): 5-14.

884.33   Nikolaus Walter, "Historischer Jesus und Osterglaube: ein
           Diskussionsbeitrag zur Christologie," *TLZ* 101 (1976):
           321-38.

884.34   André M. Dubarle, "Témoignage de Josèphe sur Jésus
           d'après des publications récentes," *RB* 84 (1977): 38-58.

884.35   Per Bilde, "Den nyere evangelieforsknings metoder og
           sporgsmalet om den historiske Jesus," *DTT* 41 (1978):
           217-43.

884.36   Michael L. Cook, "Call to Faith of the Historical Jesus:
           Questions for the Christian Understanding of Faith," *ThSt* 39
           (1978): 679-700.

884.37   David L. Mealand, "Dissimilarity Test," *SJT* 31 (1978):
           41-50.

884.38   C. F. D. Moule, "Christ of Experience and the Christ of
           History," *Th* 81 (1978): 164-72.

884.39   Halvor Moxnes, "Jesus som utfordring: 'Problemet den
           historiske Jesus' i norsk debatt etter 1953," *NTT* 80 (1979):
           1-18.

884.40   Per Bilde, "Josefus' beretning om Jesus," *DTT* 44 (1981): 99-135.

884.41   Stewart C. Goetz and Craig L. Blomberg, "The Burden of Proof," *JSNT* 11 (1981): 39-63.

884.42   Robert A. Guelich, "The Gospels: Portraits of Jesus and His Ministry," *JETS* 24 (1981): 117-25.

884.43   Donald A. Hagner, "Interpreting the Gospels: The Landscape and the Quest," *JETS* 24 (1981): 23-37.

884.44   Heinrich Kraft, "Die Evangelien und die Geschichte Jesu," *TZ* 37 (1981): 321-41.

884.45   Mogens Müller, "Evangeliet og evangelierne: et stykke problemorienteret forskningshistorie," *DTT* 44 (1981): 1-16.

884.46   Albrecht Dihle, "Die Evangelien und die biographische Tradition der Antike," *ZTK* 80 (1983): 33-49.

884.47   D. Moody Smith, "Mark 15:46: The Shroud of Turin as a Problem of History and Faith," *BA* 46 (1983): 251-54.

884.48   Hugo Staudinger, "The Resurrection of Jesus Christ as Saving Event and as 'Object' of Historical Research," *SJT* 36 (1983): 309-26.

884.49   Erich Grässer, "Norman Perrin's Contribution to the Question of the Historical Jesus," *JR* 64 (1984): 484-500.

884.50   Gerard Loughlin, "On Telling the Story of Jesus," *Th* 87 (1984): 323-29.

884.51   J. Neville Birdsall, "The Continuing Enigma of Josephus's Testimony about Jesus," *BJRL* 67 (1985): 609-22.

884.52   Don A. Carson, "Historical Tradition in the Fourth Gospel," *JSNT* 23 (1985): 73-81.

884.53   Hans P. Göll, "Offenbarung in der Geschichte: Theologische Überlegungen zur sozialgeschichtlichen Exegese," *EvT* 45 (1985): 532-45.

884.54   John Strange, "Frelsehistorie og historie: et synspunkt pa bibelsk teologi," *DTT* 48 (1985): 225-37.

884.55   Nikolaus Walter, "Paulus und die urchristliche Jesustradition," *NTSt* 31 (1985): 498-522.

884.56   F. Gerald Downing, "Towards a Fully Systemic Scepticism: In the Service of Faith," *Th* 89 (1986): 355-61.

884.57   Ieuan Ellis, "Dean Farrar and the Quest for the Historical Jesus," *Th* 89 (1986): 108-15.

884.58   Hans F. Geisser, "Glück und Unglück eines Theologen mit seiner Kirche," *ZTK* 83 (1986): 85-110.

884.59   Paul Merkley, "The Gospels as Historical Testimony," *EQ* 58 (1986): 319-36.

884.60   Nicholas T. Wright, "Constraints and the Jesus of History," *SJT* 39 (1986): 189-210.

884.61   Sven Hermin, "Albert Schweitzers teologi och religion," *STK* 63 (1987): 145-53.

884.62   Marcus J. Borg, "A Renaissance in Jesus Studies," *TTod* 45 (1988): 280-92.

884.63   Stephen Fowl, "Reconstructing and Deconstructing the Quest of the Historical Jesus," *SJT* 42 (1989): 319-33.

884.64   William Madges, "D. F, Strauss in Retrospect: His Reception among Roman Catholics," *HeyJ* 30 (1989): 273-92.

884.65   Amos N. Wilder, "Norman Perrin and the Relation of Historical Knowledge to Faith," *HTR* 82 (1989): 201-11.

884.66   James H. Charlesworth, "Jesus Research: A Paradigm Shift for New Testament Scholars," *ABR* 38 (1990): 18-32.

884.67   John P. Meier, "The Historical Jesus: Rethinking Some Concepts," *ThSt* 51 (1990): 3-24.

884.68   John P. Meier, "Jesus in Josephus: A Modest Proposal," *CBQ* 52 (1990): 76-103.

884.69   Jerome Murphy-O'Connor, "John the Baptist and Jesus: History and Hypotheses," *NTSt* 36 (1990): 359-74.

884.70   Gerd Theissen, "Theologie und Exegese in den neutestamentlichen Arbeiten von Günther Bornkamm," *EvT* 51 (1991): 308-32.

884.71   Martin Karrer, "Der lehrende Jesus Neutestamentliche Erwägungen," *ZNW* 83 (1992): 1-20.

884.72   Keith F. Nickle, "More about Jesus Would I know," *TTod* 49

(1992): 398-407.

884.73 Étienne Trocmé, "Un Christianisme sans Jésus-Christ?" *NTSt* 38 (1992): 321-36.

884.74 Craig A. Evans, "Life-of-Jesus Research and the Eclipse of Mythology," *ThSt* 54 (1993): 3-36.

884.75 Bengt Holmberg, "En historisk vändning i forskningen om Jesus," *STK* 69 (1993): 69-76.

884.76 Jeffrey A. Trumbower, "The Historical Jesus and the Speech of Gamaliel," *NTSt* 39 (1993): 500-17.

884.77 Nicholas T. Wright, "Taking the Text with Her Pleasure: A Post-Post-Modernist Response to J. Dominic Crossan," *Th* 96 (1993): 303-10.

884.78 Hans Dieter Betz, "Jesus and the Cynics: Survey and Analysis of a Hypothesis," *JR* 74 (1994): 453-75.

884.79 John P. Galvin, "From the Humanity of Christ to the Jesus of History: A Paradigm Shift in Catholic Christology," *ThSt* 55 (1994): 252-73.

884.80 Frans Neirynck, "The Historical Jesus: Reflections on an Inventory," *ETL* 70 (1994): 221-34.

M. THE SELF-CONSCIOUSNESS AND SELF-DISCLOSURE OF JESUS

885. Dr. Kuhn, "Über den Bildungsgang Jesu, besonders über den Einfluss der jüdischen Erziehung auf die Entwicklung seines Messiasbewusstseins," *TQ* 20 (1838): 3-30.

886. P. Goy, "Du témoignage que Jésus-Christ se rend à lui-même," *RT* 1 (1850): 161-75.

887. J. Colani, "Des passages où Jésus parle de sa mort," *RT* 4 (1852): 365-79.

888. M. Schwalb, "Ce que Jésus a pensé de sa mort," *RT* 9 (1862): 342-59; 10 (1862): 106-18.

889. J. M. Usteri, "Die Selbstbezeichnung Jesu als des Menschen Sohn," *STZ* 3 (1886): 1-23.

890. W. H. Wynn, "God-Consciousness and the Christ," *LQ* 18 (1888): 538-56.

891.   Hermann Schmidt, "Bildung und Gehalt des messianischen Bewusstseins Jesu," *TSK* 62 (1889): 423-507.

892.   C. Bruston, "L'enseignement de Jésus sur son retour," *RTP* 23 (1890): 145-70, 344-74, 421-52.

893.   C. Holsten, "Biblische-theologische Studien. I. II. Die Bedeutung des Ausdrucks ὁ πατὴρ ὑμῶν (und ὁ πατήρ μου) ὁ ἐν τοῖς οὐπανοῖς (ὁ οὐράνιος) im Bewusstsein Jesu," *ZWT* 33 (1890): 129-180; "III. Die Bedeutung der Ausdrucksform ὁ υἱὸς τοῦ ἀνθρώπου im Bewusstsein Jesu," 34 (1891): 1-79; "IV. Zu Entstehung und Entwicklung des Messiasbewusstseins in Jesus," 385-449.

894.   Joh. Hausleiter, "Eine theologische Disputation über den Glauben Jesu," *NKZ* 3 (1892): 507-20.

895.   James Orr, "Wendt on the Self-Witness of Jesus," *ET* 5 (1893-1894): 23-28.

896.   T. H. Root, "The Self-Consciousness of Jesus," *BW* 2 (1893): 265-74, 353-62, 412-20.

897.   T. C. Hall, "The Faith of Jesus," *BW* 3 (1894): 247-51.

898.   G. A. Chadwick, "The Self-disclosure of Jesus when on Earth," *Exp* 5th ser., 2 (1895): 436-57.

899.   George B. Stevens, "The Teaching of Jesus; IV, His Teaching Concerning himself," *BW* 5 (1895): 266-72.

900.   C. Malan, "L'avènement, dans Jésus enfant, de la conscience religieuse," *RTQR* 5 (1896): 269-83.

901.   A. M. Fairbairn, "Christ's Attitude to his own Death," *Exp* 5th ser., 4 (1896): 277-90, 414-26; 5 (1897): 16-30, 105-19.

902.   W. M. Lisle, "Principal Fairbairn on 'Christ's Attitude to his own Death'," *BW* 10 (1897): 384-85.

903.   B. W. Bacon, "The Autobiography of Jesus," *AJT* 2 (1898): 527-60.

904.   A. B. Bruce, "Messiahship as Conceived by Jesus," *BW* 12 (1898): 369-79.

905.   W. F. Adeney, "The Transcendental Element in the Consciousness of Christ," *AJT* 3 (1899): 99-107.

906.   Ernest DeW. Burton, "The Personal Religion of Jesus," *BW* 14 (1899): 394-403.

907.   A. Klöpper, "Der Sohn des Menschen in den synoptischen Evangelien. Ein Beitrag zur Deutung dieser Selbstbezeichnung Jesu," *ZWT* 42 (1899): 161-86.

908.   J. de Visme, "Ce que Jésus a pensé de sa mort," *RTQR* 8 (1899): 353-406.

909.   B. W. Bacon, "The Temptation of Jesus: His Conception of the Messiahship," *BW* 15 (1900): 18-25.

910.   Oscar Holtzmann, "Der Messiasglaube Jesu," *ZNW* 2 (1901): 265-74.

911.   J. Felten, "Das messianische Bewusstsein Jesu," *TRev* 1 (1902): 233-37.

912.   Alfred E. Garvie, "Studies in the 'Inner Life' of Jesus. Introductory," *Exp* 6th ser., 5 (1902): 34-42; "II. The Virgin-Birth," 126-35; "III. The Growth in Wisdom and Grace," 260-70; "IV. The Vocation Accepted," 366-76; "V. The Temptation," 435-45; "VI. The Early Self-Disclosure," 6 (1902): 37-46; "VII. The Surrender of Home," 106-16; "VIII. The Judgment of Religious Rulers and Teachers," 196-208; "IX. The Scope of the Ministry," 296-308; "X. The Function of the Miracles," 353-66; "XI. The Companionship of the Twelve," 7 (1903): 337-52; "XII. The Limitation of Knowledge," 12 (1905): 241-54; "XIII. The Causes of Offence," 424-38; "XIV. The Perfection of Character," 7th ser., 1 (1906): 304-19; "XV. The Consciousness of the Son," 496-510; "XVI. The Foreshadowings of the Cross," 2 (1906): 410-26; "XVII. The Foregleams of the Glory," 518-30.

913.   George Jackson, "The Teaching of Jesus Concerning himself," *ET* 4 (1902-1903): 467-70.

914.   G. Milligan, "The Messianic Consciousness of Jesus," *Exp.*, 6th ser., 5 (1902): 72-80, 148-56.

915.   Emil Schürer, "Das messianische Selbstbewusstsein Jesu Christi," *ZTK* 13 (1903): 437-56,

916.   J. P. Sheraton, "Our Lord's Teaching Concerning himself,"
          PTR 1 (1903): 513-36.

917.   Robert Mackintosh, "The Dawn of the Messianic
          Consciousness," *ET* 16 (1904-1905): 157-58, 211-15,
          267-70.

918.   R. B. Perry, "Christ's Thought of the Cross," *LQ* 34 (1904):
          275-84.

919.   J. P. Sheraton, "Our Lord's Teaching Concerning himself,"
          PTR 2 (1904): 1-31.

920.   W. F. Adeney, "The Teaching of Jesus Christ concerning
          himself and his Work," *BW* 26 (1905): 447-54.

921.   B. W. Bacon, "Jesus' Voice from Heaven," *AJT* 9 (1905):
          451-73.

922.   Dwight Mallory Pratt, "The Consciousness of Christ the Key
          to Christianity," *BS* 62 (1905): 201-10.

923.   James M. Whiton, "The God-Consciousness of Jesus," *AJT*
          9 (1905): 263-74.

924.   H. A. A. Kennedy, "The Self-Consciousness of Jesus and the
          Servant of the Lord," *ET* 19 (1907-1908): 346-49, 394-97,
          442-46, 487-91.

925.   Dr. Rade, "Die Gewissheit des historischen Jesus," *ZTK* 18
          (1908): 478-81.

926.   T. E. Schmauk, "The Death of Christ and its Significance, as
          Forseen by himself," *LCR* 27 (1908): 53-61.

927.   Johannes Stier, "Zur Frage des Selbstbewusstseins Jesu,"
          NKZ 19 (1908): 911-34.

928.   Karl Thieme, "Die neusten Christologien im Verhältnis zum
          Selbstbewusstsein Jesu," *ZTK* 18 (1908): 401-72.

929.   Francis A. Christie, "The Personal Religion of Jesus," *BW* 34
          (1909): 224-31.

930.   Ph. Bachmann, "Vom Zeugnis des Gewissens hin zu Christi
          Kreuz," *NKZ* 21 (1910): 11-54.

931.   Adolf Harnack, " 'Ich bin gekommen.' Die ausdrücklichen
          Selbstzeugnisse Jesu über den Zweck seiner Sendung und

seines Kommens," *ZTK* 22 (1912): 1-30.

932. S. Greijdanus, "Eene bladzijde uit het zielelijden van onzen Heiland," *GTT* 14 (1913): 57-78, 107-20.

933. Albert G. Lawson, "The Personal Religion of Jesus," *BW* 44 (1914): 36-44.

934. J.-Alfred Porret, "Le Christ, d'après Jésus," *RTQR* 23 (1914): 266-85, 289-314.

935. Franz Diekamp, "Über das Wissen der Seele Christi," *TRev* 12 (1915): 97-108.

936. W. Morison, "Christ's Confidence in his Perpetual Presence," *ET* 27 (1915-1916): 557-59.

937. Benjamin B. Warfield, "Jesus' Mission, According to his own Testimony," *PTR* 13 (1915): 513-86.

938. Geerhardus Vos, "Modern Dislike of the Messianic Consciousness in Jesus," *BR* 1 (1916): 170-85.

939. William Morison, "Christ's Confidence in himself as a Teacher," *ET* 28 (1916-1917): 263-64.

940. David Foster Estes, "Contents of the Consciousness of Jesus," *BS* 74 (1917): 351-76.

941. Jesse H. Bond, "The Origin of Jesus' Consciousness of Divine Sonship," *BW* 52 (1918): 264-69.

942. Rudolf Bultmann, "Die Frage nach dem messianischen Bewusstsein Jesu und das Petrus-Bekenntnis," *ZNW* 19 (1919-1920): 165-74.

943. G. Pierce, "Our Lord's Experiential Knowledge," *ITQ* 15 (1920): 113-25.

944. Geerhardus Vos, "The Messiahship, Formal or Essential to the Mind of Jesus?" *BR* 5 (1920): 196-208.

945. W. Mundle, "Die Geschichtlichkeit des messianischen Bewusstseins Jesu," *ZNW* 21 (1922): 299-311.

946. H. H. Horne, "What did the Cross Mean to Christ?" *BR* 8 (1923): 565-77.

947. Olaf Moe, "Til spørsmaalet om Jesu messianitet," *NTT* 24 (1923): 64-68.

948. Hans Rust, "Das Gnadenbewusstsein Christi und der Kreuzesruf," *TB* 2 (1923): 49-51.

949. S. Greijdanus, "Eene nieuwe verklaring van's Heeren Messiasbewustzijn," *GTT* 26 (1925-1926): 130-42.

950. Walther Bleibtreu, "Jesu Selbstbenennung als der Menschensohn," *TSK* 98-99 (1926): 164-211.

951. W. K. Lowther Clarke, " 'A Prophet like unto Me'," *Th* 12 (1926): 163-68.

952. H. W. Magoun, "Christ's Estimate of himself," *BS* 83 (1926): 13-28.

953. Shirley Jackson Case, "The Alleged Messianic Consciousness of Jesus," *JBL* 46 (1927): 1-19.

954. Frederick B. Greul, "Jesus' Interest in his own Humanity," *CQ* 4 (1927): 191-202.

955. Robert C. Hallock, "The Innermost Thinking of Jesus, the Perfect Norm of Truth," *BS* 84 (1927): 307-16.

956. Oliver C. Quick, "A Note on the Kenosis in Relation to our Lord's Knowledge," *ATR* 10 (1927-1928): 223-29.

957. A. McCaig, "Christ's Teaching Concerning his own Death," *BR* 13 (1928): 196-215.

958. D. A. Frøvig, "Til spørsmålet Jesu eksistens og selvberissthet," *NTT* 30 (1929): 199-203.

959. H. J. Flowers, "Christ's View of his own Death," *RE* 27 (1930): 183-94.

960. Hugo Vondran, "Der Leidensgedanke im Spiegel des Selbstbewusstseins Jesu," *NKZ* 43 (1932): 257-75.

961. K. G. Goetz, "Hat sich Jesus selbst für den Messias gehalten und ausgegeben?" *TSK* 105 (1933): 117-37.

962. George Arthur Clarke, "The Attitudes of Jesus," *CQ* 11 (1934): 443-50.

963. Olaf Moe, "Hoad vilde Jesus? Korsets plass i Jesu kallsbevissthet," *TTK* 6 (1935): 197-210.

964. Norman Hook, "The Problem of our Lord's Knowledge," *ET* 48 (1936-1937): 540-42.

965. H. Pfotenhauer, "Christi Selbstzeugnis von seiner Person und seinem Amt," *CTM* 10 (1939): 175-79.

966. Alexander Ross, "Our Lord's Self-Witness," *EQ* 12 (1940): 215-22.

967. William H. Baker, "Did Jesus Foresee his Passion?" *ET* 55 (1943-1944): 249-50.

968. U. Holzmeister, "Christus passionem suam discipulis suis saepius praedicit," *VD* 23 (1943): 33-41.

969. Robert E. Speer, "The Consciousness of Christ," *USR* 55 (1943-1944): 93-119.

970. C. J. Cadoux, "Did Jesus foresee his Passion?" *ET* 56 (1944-1945): 83.

971. W. Manson, "The ἐγώ εἰμι of the Messianic Presence in the New Testament," *JTS* 48 (1947): 137-45.

972. C. Ryder Smith, "When did Jesus Foresee the Crucifixion?" *ET* 59 (1947-1948): 25.

973. D. Mollat, "Les déclarations de Jésus sur lui-même dans le IVᵉ évangile," *NRT* 70 (1948): 854-55.

974. A. W. Argyle, "The Evidence for the Belief that our Lord himself Claimed to be Divine," *ET* 61 (1949-1950): 228-32.

975. Alex. Durand, "La science du Christ," *NRT* 71 (1949): 497-503.

976. Cuthbert Lattey, "The Evidence for the Belief that our Lord himself Claimed to be Divine," *ET* 62 (1950-1951): 31.

977. Anton T. Boisen, "What did Jesus Think of himself?" *JBR* 20 (1952): 7-12.

978. R. W. Stewart, "Jesus' own Thoughts about his Death," *ET* 64 (1952-1953): 174-78.

979. William C. Berkemeyer, "How did Jesus regard himself?" *LQ* 5 (1953): 290-97.

980. 980.Leo Scheffczyk, "Der Wandel in der Auffassung vom menschlichen Wissen Christi bei Thomas von Aquin und seine bleibende Bedeutung für die Frage nach den Prinzipien der Problemlösung," *MTZ* 8 (1957): 278-88.

981.   Jean Galot, "Science et conscience de Jésus," *NRT* 82 (1960): 113-31.

982.   Paul W. Meyer, "The Problem of the Messianic Self-consciousness of Jesus," *NT* 4 (1960): 122-38.

983.   Joseph Ratzinger, "Bewusstsein und Wissen Christi," *MTZ* 12 (1961): 78-81.

984.   E. Schillebeeckx, "Het bewustzijnsleven van Christus," *TvT* 1 (1961): 227-51.

984.1   Charles Desanto, "Theological Key to the Gospel of John," *EQ* 34 (1962): 83-90.

984.2   K. H. Rengstorf, "Old and New Testament Traces of a Formula of the Judaean Royal Ritual," *NT* 5 (1962): 229-44.

984.3   W. C. van Unnik, "Jesus the Christ," *NTSt* 8 (1962): 101-16.

984.4   Otto Betz, "Die Frage nach dem messianischen Bewusstsein Jesu," *NT* 6 (1963): 20-48.

984.5   F. H. Borsch, "Son of Man," *ATR* 45 (1963): 174-90.

984.6   Ulrich Luz, "Das Geheimnismotiv und die markinische Christologie," *ZNW* 56 (1965): 9-30.

984.7   J. van Goudoever, "Place of Israel in Luke's Gospel," *NT* 8 (1966): 111-23.

984.8   John H. Hayes, "Resurrection as Enthronement and the Earliest Church Christology," *Interp* 22 (1968): 333-45.

984.9   Sherman E. Johnson, "Davidic-Royal Motif in the Gospels," *JBL* 87 (1968): 136-50.

984.10   C. J. Maurer, "Das Messiasgeheimnis des Markus-evangeliums," *NTSt* 14 (1968): 515-26.

984.11   S. H. Russell, "Calvin and the Messianic Interpretation of the Psalms," *SJT* 21 (1968): 37-47.

984.12   James R. Schaefer, "Relationship between Priestly and Servant Messianism in the Epistle to the Hebrews," *CBQ* 30 (1968): 359-85.

984.13   Alfred Suhl, "Der Davidssohn im Matthaus-Evangelium," *ZNW* 59 (1968): 57-81.

984.14   Paul Hoffmann, "Die Versuchungsgeschichte in der

Logienquelle: zur Auseinandersetzung der Judenchristen mit dem politischen Messianismus," *BibZ* NS 13 (1969): 207-23.

984.15   André Feuillet, "La personnalité de Jésus entrevue à partir de sa soumission au rite de repentance du précurseur," *RB* 77 (1970): 30-49.

984.16   Georg Fohrer, "Das Alte Testament und das Thema 'Christologie'," *EvT* 30 (1970): 281-98.

984.17   Birger Gerhardsson, "Gottes Sohn als Diener Gottes: Messias, Agape und Himmelsherrschaft nach dem Matthäusevangelium," *ST* 27 (1973): 73-106.

984.18   P. von der Osten-Sacken, "Zur Christologie des lukanischen Reiseberichts," *EvT* 33 (1973): 476-96.

984.19   Lloyd Gaston, "Messiah of Israel as Teacher of the Gentiles: The Setting of Matthew's Christology," *Interp* 29 (1975): 24-40.

984.20   Jack D. Kingsbury, "Title 'Son of David' in Matthew's Gospel," *JBL* 95 (1976): 591-602.

984.21   Harald Sahlin, "Zum Verständnis der christologischen Anschauung des Markusevangeliums," *ST* 31 (1977): 1-19.

984.22   Matthew Black, "Jesus and the Son of Man," *JSNT* 1 (1979): 4-18.

984.23   Joseph Coppens, "Où en est le problème de Jésus 'fils de l'homme' [bar nash]," *ETL* 56 (1980): 282-302.

984.24   Morris M. Faierstein, "Why do the Scribes Say that Elijah Must Come First," *JBL* 100 (1981): 75-86.

984.25   Hans Hübner, "Der 'Messias Israels' und der Christus des Neuen Testaments," *KD* 27 (1981): 217-40

984.26   W. R. G. Loader, "Son of David, Blindness, Possession, and Duality in Matthew," *CBQ* 44 (1981): 570-85.

984.27   Gerhard Sauter, "Jesus der Christus: Die Messianität Jesu als Frage an die gegenwärtige Christenheit," *EvT* 42 (1982): 324-49.

984.28   Wolfgang Schrage, "Ja und Nein: Bemerkungen eines Neutestamentlers zur Diskussion von Christen und Juden,"

EvT 42 (1982): 126-51.

984.29   A. N. Sherwin-White, "The Messianic Mission," *JSNT* 17 (1983): 4-9.

984.30   Richard Weber, "Christologie und 'Messiasgeheimnis': ihr Zusammenhang und Stellenwert in den Darstellungsintentionen des Markus," *EvT* 43 (1983): 108-25.

984.31   J. O. Tuñi, "Pablo y Jesus: la vida de Jesus y la vida de Pablo," *EB* 45 (1987): 285-308.

984.32   Donald J. Verseput, "The Role and Meaning of the 'Son of God' Title in Matthew's Gospel," *NTSt* 33 (1987): 532-56.

984.33   Donald L. Berry, "Revisioning Christology: The Logic of Messianic Ascription," *ATR* 70 (1988): 129-40.

984.34   Michael Goldberg, "God, Action, and Narrative: Which Narrative, Action, God?" *JR* 68 (1988): 39-56.

984.35   I. de La Potterie, "C'est lui qui a ouvert la voie: la finale du prologue johannique," *B* 69 (1988): 340-70.

984.36   E. J. Waschke, "Die Frage nach dem Messias im Alten Testament als Problem alttestamentlicher Theologie und biblischer Hermeneutik," *TLZ* 113 (1988): 321-32.

984.37   Bertold Klappert, "Christologie in messianischen Dimensionen," *EvT* 50 (1990): 574-86.

See also numbers 4270 ff., 10024, 10039, 10046.

N. THE PERSONALITY OF JESUS; HIS CHARACTER AND HABITS

985.   C. Ullmann, "Noch ein Wort über die Persönlichkeit Christi und das Wunderbare in der evangelischen Geschichte. Antwortschreiben an Herrn Dr. Strauss," *TSK* 11 (1838): 277-369.

986.   Oliver S. Taylor, "Psychology in the Life, Work, and Teachings of Jesus," *BS* 27 (1870): 209-44.

987.   Alexander B. Grosart, "The Humour of our Lord," *ET* 2 (1890-1991): 36-39, 107-109.

988.   Alfred Plummer, "The Advance of Christ in σωφία," *Exp* 4th ser., 4 (1891): 1-14.

989. R. Glaister, "The Sympathy of Christ," *ET* 5 (1893-1894): 156-59.

990. J.-Alfred Porret, "L'éloquence de Jésus-Christ," *RTQR* 4 (1895): 313-33.

991. A. Austin Bierbower, "Jesus as a Man of Affairs," *BW* 11 (1898): 17-27.

992. A. Kingsley Glover, "The Dress of the Master (Illustrated)," *BW* 15 (1900): 347-57.

993. John Tomlinson, "The Moral Character of Jesus," *LQ* 30 (1900): 254-61.

994. F. G. Peabody, "The Character of Jesus Christ," *HJ* 1 (1902-1903): 641-60.

995. J. M. Robertson, "The Poverty of Christ," *Exp* , 6th ser., 11 (1905): 321-39.

996. Alfred E. Garvie, "Personality in God, Christ, Man," *HJ* (1906-1907): 558-71.

997. J. G. Skemp, "Jesus as Humanist," *ET* 18 (1906-1907): 500-501.

998. Shepherd Knapp, "Traces of Humor in the Sayings of Jesus," *BW* 29 (1907): 201-207.

999. André Arnal, "Contre la 'folie' de Jésus," *RTQR* 18 (1909): 171-79.

1000. P. T. Forsyth, "The Faith of Jesus," *ET* 21 (1909-1910): 8-9.

1001. Henry Preserved Smith, "The Faith of Jesus," *ET* 21 (1909-1910): 281.

1002. Raoul Dardel, "Le pessimisme de Jésus," *RTP* 43 (1910): 271-330.

1003. Jacob Müller, "Jesus ein Proletarier?" *ZKT* 34 (1910): 401-404

1004. G. Vorbrodt, "Zur Religionspsychologie der Persönlichkeit Jesu," *TSK* 83 (1910): 1-63.

1005. C. G. Montefiore, "The Significance of Jesus for his own Age," *HJ* 10 (1911-1912): 766-79.

1006. David Cairns, "The Person of Jesus Christ," *ET* 24

(1912-1913): 104-109.

1007.   H. Peters, "The Human Education of our Lord," *LCR* (1912): 623-34.

1008.   W. L. Walker, "The Subconscious, the Superconscious, and the Person of Christ," *Exp* , 8th ser., 4 (1912): 120-37.

1009.   Frederick J. Rae, "The Heart of Jesus," *ET* 26 (1914-1915): 250-53.

1010.   John R. Brown, "The Character of Jesus," *AJT* 19 (1915): 529-49.

1011.   F. Kramer, "Het Gebedsleven van Immanuel," *GTT* 16 (1915): 107-16, 150-62.

1012.   Ray O. Miller, "The Permanent and Transient Elements in the Life of Jesus," *BW* 46 (1915): 145-51.

1013.   E. F. Sutcliffe, "The Divine Carpenter," *ITQ* 11 (1916): 147-63.

1014.   A. D. Martin, "The Patriotism of Jesus," *ET* 28 (1916-1917): 237.

1015.   Henry H. Bothamley, "Our Lord's Clothing," *ET* 29 (1917-1918): 42-43.

1016.   William A. Elliott, "The Cosmopolitanism of Jesus as Related to Kingdom Ideals," *BW* 49 (1917): 139-46.

1017.   George H. Gilbert, "The Greatness of Jesus," *BW* 49 (1917): 147-50.

1018.   M. C. Hazard, "Humor in the Bible," *BW* 53 (1919): 514-19.

1019.   R. E. Neighbor, "The Religious Experience of Jesus Christ," *RE* 17 (1920): 167-74.

1020.   M. Goguel, "Quelques traits de la vie de Jésus au point de vue psychologique et psychanalytique, par Berguer," *RHPR* 1 (1921): 269-76.

1021.   Colonel Repord, "Le Costume du Christ," *B* 3 (1922): 3-14.

1022.   H. A. Williamson, "Jeremiah and Jesus—in Comparison and Contrast," *ET* 34 (1922-1923): 535-38; 35 (1923-1924): 39-42.

1023.   Christian Schjelderup, "Mystiken som element i Jesu fromhetsliv," *NTT* 24 (1923): 139-56.

1024.   Joachim Jeremias, "Das Gebetsleben Jesu," *ZNW* 25 (1926): 123-40.

1025.   H. H. Horne, "Jesus as a Philosopher," *BR* 12 (1927): 361-71.

1026.   J. A. Faulkner, "And This Man—What?" *RE* 26 (1929): 304-16.

1027.   J. Alexander Findlay, "The Secret of Jesus," *RL* 5 (1936): 216-22 [Jesus' obedience].

1028.   Fred Gealy, "Jesus the Layman," *CQ* 15 (1938): 176-86.

1029.   Jules Lebreton, "Études sur la contemplation dans le Nouveau Testament; 1. La contemplation dans la vie de notre Seigneur," *RSR* 29 (1939): 568-93.

1030.   Carl H. Kraeling, "Was Jesus Accused of Necromancy?" *JBL* 59 (1940): 147-57.

1031.   R. Thibaut, "La signification des gestes du Christ," *NRT* 67 (1940-1945): 14-31.

1032.   Amos N. Wilder, "Jesus and the Charismatic Type," *JBR* 9 (1941): 151-54.

1033.   Charles F. Nesbitt, "An Inquiry into the Physical Health of Jesus," *JR* 24 (1942): 302-12.

1034.   Louis M. Sweet, "The Relationship of Jesus to Men," *USR* 54 (1942-1943): 195-213.

1035.   Theophilus M. Taylor, "Jesus: Physician Extraordinary," *USR* 55 (1943-1944): 120-39.

1036.   Donald T. Rowlingson, "An Appreciative Spirit in the Historical Jesus," *RL* 16 (1947): 344-51.

1037.   Emile Lombard, "Charpentier ou maçon? Note sur le métier de Jésus," *RTP* N.S., 36 (1948): 161-92.

1038.   03J. Wedderspoon, "The Mind of Christ-Jesus as a Religious Man," *ET* 62 (1950-1951): 365-68.

1039.   R. A., "Aspecto físico de N. S. Jesucristo," *CB* 8 (1951): 266-69.

1040.   Bernhard Stövesand, "El lenguaje mímico de Jesús," *CB* 8

(1951): 21.

1041.   B. Leeming, "The Human Knowledge of Christ: The Beatific Vision," *ITQ* 19 (1952): 135-47, 234-53.

1042.   Jane Darroch, "The Personality of Jesus in the Light of Psychology," *FF* 7 (1953-1954): 83-86.

1043.   Juan Mairena Valdayo, "El 'Yo' de Cristo," *Sal* 4 (1957): 602-26.

1044.   Jean Galot, "La psychologie du Christ," *NRT* 80 (1958): 337-58.

1045.   Ch. V. Héris, "À propos d'un article sur la psychologie du Christ," *RSPT* 43 (1959): 462-71.

           See also numbers 117, 2131, 5735, 7126, 7654, 8234.

1045.1   Paul E. Davies, "Impact and Response: The Centrality of Jesus for Thought and Life," *Interp* 18 (1964): 276-84.

1045.2   Richard L. Strauss, "Like Christ: An Exposition of Ephesians 4:13," *BS* 143 (1986): 260-65.

1045.3   John B. Webster, "Christology, Imitability and Ethics," *SJT* 39 (1986): 309-26.

1045.4   Morna D. Hooker, "Pistis Christou," *NTSt* 35 (1989): 321-42.

O. THE LANGUAGES AND CULTURE OF JESUS' WORLD

1046.   G. H. Gwilliam, "The Vernacular of Palestine in the Time of Our Lord, and the Remains of It in St. Mark," *ET* 2 (1890-1891): 133-34.

1047.   A. Roberts, "That Christ Spoke Greek," *Exp* 1st ser., 6 (1877): 81-96, 161-76, 285-99, 367-83.

1048.   W. Sanday, "The Language Spoken in Palestine at the Time of Our Lord," *Exp*, 1st ser., 7 (1878): 81-99.

1049.   A. Roberts, "That Christ Spoke Greek—A Reply," *Exp* , 1st ser., 7 (1878): 278-95.

1050.   W. Sanday, "Did Christ Speak Greek?—A Rejoinder," *Exp*, 1st ser., 7 (1878): 368-88.

1051.   George H. Schodde, "Christ and the Theology of his Day,"

LQ 15 (1885): 1-10.

1052. D. L. J., "La langue parlée par Jésus et par les apôtres," *RBén* 8 (1891): 105-11, 145-51, 225-33.

1053. Jeremiah Zimmerman, "The Roman World in the Time of Christ," *LQ* 26 (1896): 269-84.

1054. Ernest DeW. Burton, "Jewish Family Life (Illustrated)," *BW* 8 (1896): 445-57.

1055. D. R. Fotheringham, "The New Testament Coinage," *ET* 10 (1898-1899): 45-46.

1056. H. M. Scott, "The Times of Christ," *BW* 6 (1895): 413-23.

1057. Allan Hoben, "The Land of Jesus," *BW* 26 (1905): 408-17.

1058. Lyder Brun, "Jesu forhold til Moseloven," *NTT* 8 (1907): 334-62.

1059. John A. Rice, "The Farewell Breakfast at Nazareth," *BW* 34 (1909): 239-48.

1060. Ferdinand Prat, "Le cours des monnaies en Palestine au temps de Jésus-Christ," *RSR* 15 (1925): 441-48.

1061. Karl Bornhäuser, "Die Bedeutung der sprachlichen Verhältnisse Palästinas zur Zeit Jesu für das Verständnis der Evangelien," *NKZ* 37 (1926): 187-200.

1062. Wm. C. Graham, "The Jewish World in which Jesus lived," *JR* 8 (1928): 566-80.

1063. É. Ha-Reubéni, "Recherches sur les plantes de l'évangile," *RB* 42 (1933): 230-34.

1064. Joachim Jeremias, "Hilfsmittel zum Studium der Muttersprache Jesu," *TLZ* 65 (1940): 177-80.

1065. R. O. P. Taylor, "Did Jesus speak Aramaic?" *ET* 56 (1944-1945): 95-97.

1066. W. G. M. Abbott, "Did Jesus speak Aramaic?" *ET* 56 (1944-1945): 305.

1067. J. Gwyn Griffiths, "Did Jesus speak Aramaic?" *ET* 56 (1944-1945): 327-28.

1068. F. F. Bruce, "Did Jesus speak Aramaic?" *ET* 56 (1944-1945): 328.

1069.   Paul Kahle, "Das zur Zeit Jesu in Palästina gesprochene Aramäisch," *TR* 17 (1948-1949): 201-16.

1070.   Sverre Aalen, "Jesu morsmål," *TTK* 26 (1955): 46-61. [Probably Aramaic].

1071.   Philip Carrington, "The Ichthyology of the Gospels," *ATR* 37 (1955): 50-55.

1072.   A. W. Argyle, "Did Jesus speak Greek?" *ET* 67 (1955-1956): 92-93, 383.

1073.   D. K. Russell, "Did Jesus speak Greek?" *ET* 67 (1955-1956): 246.

1074.   H. Mudie Draper, "Did Jesus speak Greek?" *ET* 67 (1955-1956): 317.

1075.   Matthew Black, "The Recovery of the Language of Jesus," *NTSt* 3 (1956-1957): 305-13.

1076.   R. McL. Wilson, "Did Jesus speak Greek?" *ET* 68 (1956-1957): 121-22.

1077.   Matthew Black, "Die Erforschung der Muttersprache Jesu," *TLZ* 82 (1957): 653-68.

1078.   Paul Kahle, "Das palästinische Pentateuchtargum und das zur Zeit Jesu gesprochene Aramäisch," *ZNW* 49 (1958): 100-16.

1079.   Heinz Schürmann, "Die Sprache des Christus," *BibZ* 2 (1958): 54-84.

1080.   Robert G. Bratcher, "Weights, Money, Measures, and Time," *BT* 10 (1959): 165-74.

1081.   E. Y. Kutscher, "Das zur Zeit Jesu gesprochene Aramäisch," *ZNW* 51 (1960): 46-54.

1082.   Paul Kahle, "Das zur Zeit Jesu gesprochene Aramäisch: Erwiderung," *ZNW* 51 (1960): 55.

        See also numbers 413, 2813, 3027, 3417, 10056.

1082.1 J. A. Emerton, "Did Jesus Speak Hebrew?" *JTS* NS 12 (1961): 189-202.

1082.2 J. C. Hindley, "Our Lord's Aramaic—A Speculation," *ET* 72 (1961): 180-81.

1082.3 Jens G. Moller, "Jesu forkyndelse og dagligsprogets logik,"

DTT 29 (1966): 42-51.

1082.4 Heinrich Ott, "Um die Muttersprache Jesu Forschungen seit Gustaf Dalman," *NT* 9 (1967): 1-25.

1082.5 H. P. Rüger, "Zum Problem der Sprache Jesu," *ZNW* 59 (1968): 113-22.

1082.6 Joseph A. Fitzmyer, "Languages of Palestine in the First Century AD," *CBQ* 32 (1970): 501-31.

1082.7 Pinchas Lapide, "Insights from Qumran into the Languages of Jesus," *RQu* 8 (1975): 483-501.

1082.8 G. R. Selby, "The Language in which Jesus Taught," *Th* 86 (1983): 185-93.

1082.9 Matthew Black, "Aramaic Barnasha and the 'Son of Man'," *ET* 95 (1984): 200-206.

1082.10 Günther Schwarz, "Egeirai, kai sothese," *ZNW* 76 (1985): 129-30.

1082.11 L. D. Hurst, "The Neglected Role of Semantics in the Search for the Aramaic Words of Jesus," *JSNT* 28 (1986): 63-80.

1082.12 Eric M. Meyers, et al., "Sepphoris: 'Ornament of All Galilee'," *BA* 49 (1986): 4-19.

1082.13 J. Naegele, "Translation of Talanton 'Talent'," *BTr* 37 (1986): 441-43.

1082.14 P. Maurice Casey, "General, Generic and Indefinite: The Use of the Term 'Son of Man' in Aramaic Sources and in the Teaching of Jesus," *JSNT* 29 (1987): 21-56.

1082.15 James Barr, "Abba, Father and the Familiarity of Jesus' Speech," *Th* 91 (1988): 173-79.

1082.16 James Barr, " 'Abba Isn't 'Daddy'," *JTS* NS 39 (1988): 28-47.

P. THE CHRONOLOGY OF JESUS' LIFE

1083. George E. Day, "The True Date of Christ's Birthday," *BS* 3 (1846): 166-84, 653-73.

1084. A. Paschke, "Über die Differenz der Evangelisten in der Angabe der Zeit, zu welcher Christus sein lutists Passamahl feierte," *TQ* 33 (1851): 410-15.

1085. Henry Browne, "S. Clemens Alex. on New Testament Chronology," *JCSP* 1 (1854): 327-36.

1086. Joseph Packard, "Sacred Chronology," *BS* 15 (1858): 289-300.

1087. Dr. Aberle, "Über den Tag des letzten Abendmahls," *TQ* 45 (1863): 537-68.

1088. F. L. Fred. Chavannes, "Essai sur la détermination de quelques dates de l'histoire évangélique," *RT* 1 (1863): 209-48.

1089. Ludwig Paul, "Erwiederung auf des Herrn Prof. Hilgenfeld 'Nachwort zu den neuesten Verhandlungen über die Auferstehung Christi'," *ZWT* 7 (1864): 396-408.

1090. Ludwig Paul, "Über die Zeit des Abendmahls nach Johannes," *TSK* 39 (1866): 362-74; 40 (1867): 524-39.

1091. Friedrich Stawars, "Die Ordnung Abia in Beziehung auf die Bestimmung des wahren Geburtsdatums Jesu," *TQ* 48 (1866): 201-25.

1092. Friedrich Stawars, "Tradition und Rechnung über den Geburtstag Jesu," *TQ* 49 (1867): 206-31.

1093. Friedrich Stawars, "Die Weissagung Daniel's 9, 24-27 in Beziehung auf das Taufjahr Jesu," *TQ* 50 (1868): 416-37.

1094. J. K. Aldrich, "The Crucifixion on Thursday—Not Friday," *BS* 27 (1870): 401-29.

1095. Charles Ed. Caspari, "The Date of the Passion of our Lord," *BS* 27 (1870): 469-84.

1096. Theodore D. Woolsey, "The Year of Christ's Birth," *BS* 27 (1870): 290-336.

1097. Prof. Hehle, "Das Geburtsjahr Christi," *TQ* 58 (1876): 85-101.

1098. Anonymous, "Das Geburtsjahr Christi," *ZKT* 4 (1880): 588-89.

1099. Matthias Flunk, "Nochmal das Geburtsjahr Christi," *ZKT* 7 (1883): 581-86.

1100.   H. Kellner, "Die patristische Tradition inbetreff des Geburtsjahres Christi," *ZKT* 15 (1891): 518-33.

1101.   E. Bratke, "Die Lebenszeit Christi im Daniel-Commentar des Hippolytus," *ZWT* 35 (1892): 129-76.

1102.   A. Hilgenfeld, "Die Zeiten der Geburt, des Lebens und des Leidens Jesu nach Hippolytus," *ZWT* 35 (1892): 257-81.

1103.   A. Hilgenfeld, "Die Lebenszeit Jesu bei Hippolytus," *ZWT* 36, 1 (1893): 106-17.

1104.   Arthur Wright, "On the Date of the Crucifixion," *BW* 2 (1893): 7-14, 106-12, 167-77, 275-82.

1105.   R. G. Jones, "The Time of the Death and Resurrection of Jesus Christ," *BS* 51 (1894): 505-11.

1106.   Eb. Nestle, "Zur kirchlichen Chronologie des Lebens Jesu," *ZWT* 37 (1894): 244-45.

1107.   E. Bratke, "Zur Chronologie des Lebens Jesu," *ZWT* 38 (1895): 465-66.

1108.   Charles W. Heisler, "On the Day of the Crucifixion of our Lord," *LQ* 25 (1895): 209-30.

1109.   J. E. Belser, "Der Tag des letzten Abendmahls und des Todes Jesu," *TQ* 78 (1896): 529-76.

1110.   G. Semeria, "Le jour de la mort de Jésus selon les synoptiques et selon saint Jean," *RB* 5 (1896): 78-87.

1111.   W. C. van Manen, "Harnack's Chronologie," *TT* 32 (1898): 168-93.

1112.   E. W. G. Masterman, "Was our Lord Crucified on the 14th or or 15th of Nisan?" *ET* 10 (1898-1899): 315-17.

1113.   E. P. Boys Smith, "The Day of the Crucifixion," *ET* 10 (1898-1899): 383-84.

1114.   J. E. Belser, "Zur Chronologie der evangelischen Geschichte," *TQ* 82 (1900): 23-42.

1115.   Erwin Preuschen, "Todesjahr und Todestag Jesu," *ZNW* 5 (1904): 1-17.

1116.   Hubert Klug, "Die Dauer der öffentlichen Wirksamkeit Jesu nach Daniel und Lukas," *BibZ* 3 (1905): 263-68.

1117.   Franz Schubert, "Das Jahr der Taufe Jesu bei Tertullian,"
          BibZ 3 (1905): 177-79.

1118.   D. J. Veen, "In welk jaar en op welken dag en datum is
          Christus gestorven?" *TS* 23 (1905): 429-38.

1119.   Clyde W. Votaw, "The Chronology of Jesus' Public
          Ministry," *BW* 26 (1905): 425-30.

1120.   John Chapman, "On an Apostolic Tradition that Christ was
          Baptized in 46 and Crucified under Nero," *JTS* 8
          (1906-1907): 590-606.

1121.   Peter Dausch, "Bedenken gegen die Hypothese von der bloss
          einjährigen öffentlichen Wirksamkeit Jesu," *BibZ* 4 (1906):
          49-60.

1122.   E. Schwartz, "Osterbetrachtungen," *ZNW* 7 (1906): 1-33.

1123.   B. W. Bacon, "Lucan versus Johannine Chronology," *Exp* 7th
          ser., 3 (1907): 206-20.

1124.   John Chapman, "Papias on the Age of our Lord," *JTS* 9
          (1907-1908): 42-61.

1125.   G. E. French, "The Hour of the Crucifixion," *ET* 20 (1908-
          1909): 380.

1126.   Margaret D. Gibson, "The Hour of the Crucifixion," *ET* 20
          (1908-1909): 183-84.

1127.   Maurice Neeser, "La durée du ministère de Jésus: étude
          exégétique et chronologique," *RTP* 41 (1908): 327-66,
          482-93.

1128.   W. M. Ramsay, "The Morning Star and the Chronology of
          the Life of Christ," *Exp* 7th ser., 5 (1908): 1-21.

1129.   W. M. Ramsay, "The Time of the Transfiguration," *Exp* 7th
          ser., 6 (1908): 557-62.

1130.   David Smith, "The Day of the Crucifixion," *ET* 20 (1908-
          1909): 514-18.

1131.   B. W. Bacon, "Notes on Gospel Chronology," *JBL* 28
          (1909): 130-48.

1132.   W. Weber, "The Census of Quirinus," *LQ* 39 (1909):
          358-71.

1133.   Julius Boehmer, "Der chronologische und der geographische Rahmen des Lebensganges Jesu," *ZWT* 52 (1910): 121-47.

1134.   Dr. Dausch, "Ein neuer Kämpe für die Hypothese von der bloss einjährigen offentlichen Wirksamkeit Jesu," *BibZ* 8 (1910): 377-86.

1135.   J. K. Fotheringham, "Astronomical Evidence for the Date of the Crucifixion," *JTS* 12 (1910-1911): 120-27.

1136.   Margaret D. Gibson, "Which was the Night of the Passover?" *ET* 22 (1910-1911): 378.

1137.   Theophil Bromboszcz, "Der Einzug Jesu in Jerusalem bei Mondschein? Ein Beitrag zur Chronologie der Leidensgeschichte," *BibZ* 9 (1911): 164-70.

1138.   Hans Windisch, "Die Dauer der öffentlichen Wirksamkeit Jesu nach den vier Evangelisten," *ZNW* 12 (1911): 141-75.

1139.   Kirsopp Lake, "The Date of Herod's Marriage with Herodias and the Chronology of the Gospels," *Exp*, 8th ser., 4 (1912): 462-77.

1140.   F. Steinmetzer, "Ein neuer Weg zur Bestimmung des Geburtsdatums Christ?" *TQ* 94 (1912): 497-511.

1141.   J. B. Nisius, "Zur Kontroverse über die Dauer der öffentlichen Wirksamkeit Jesu," *ZKT* 37 (1913): 457-503.

1142.   J. E. Belser, "Zur Abfolge der evangelischen Geschichte," *TQ* 96 (1914): 1-49

1143.   Petrus Dausch, "Neue Studien über die Dauer der öffentlichen Wirksamkeit Jesu," *BibZ* 12 (1914): 158-67.

1144.   Josef Linder, "Zur Frage nach dem Monatstage des letzten Abendmahles und Todes Christi," *ZKT* 39 (1915): 600-602.

1145.   M. Meinertz, "Methodisches und Sachliches über die Dauer der öffentlichen Wirksamkeit Jesu," *BibZ* 14 (1916-1917): 119-39, 236-49.

1146.   M. Chaumes, "Recherches sur la chronology de la vie de notre Seigneur," *RB* 27 [N.S. 15] (1918): 215-43, 506-49.

1147.   Roland H. Bainton, "Basilidian Chronology and New Testament Interpretation," *JBL* 42 (1923): 81-134.

1148.   Conrad Cichorius, "Chronologisches zum Leben Jesu," *ZNW* 22 (1923): 16-20.

1149.   E. Hampden-Cook, "The Hours of the Day in the Fourth Gospel," *ET* 35 (1923-1924): 286-87.

1150.   A. M. Perry, "Jesus in Jerusalem: A Note on the Chronology," *JBL* 43 (1924): 15-21.

1151.   P. Joh. Schaumberger, "Der 14. Nisan als Kreuzigungstag und die Synoptiker," *B* 9 (1928): 57-77.

1152.   Karl Schoch, "Christi Kreuzigung am 14. Nisan," *B* 9 (1928): 48-56.

1153.   J. Th. Ubbink, "Het z.g. verschil tusschen Joh. en de synoptici I ten aanzien van den datum van Jesus' sterfdag," *NTS* 11 (1928): 225-34.

1154.   E. J. Cook, "Synoptic Indications of the Visits of Jesus to Jerusalem," *ET* 41 (1929-1930): 121-23.

1155.   Theodor Kluge, "Der Geburtstag Christi," *RQ* 37 (1929): 435-36.

1156.   Charles C. Torrey, "The Date of the Crucifixion according to the Fourth Gospel," *JBL* 50 (1931): 227-41.

1157.   W. Agricol, "Wann wurde Jesus geboren?" *NKZ* 43 (1932): 724-41.

1158.   U. Holzmeister, "Neuere Arbeiten über das Datum der Kreuzigung Christi," *B* 13 (1932): 93-103.

1159.   U. Holzmeister, "Wann war Pilatus Prokurator von Judaea?" *B* 13 (1932): 228-32.

1160.   John Stewart, "The Dates of the Nativity and the Crucifixion of Our Lord—A New Discovery," *EQ* 4 (1932): 290-315.

1161.   Anonymous, "Wann wurde unser Herr Jesus geboren?" *CTM* 3 (1932): 725-37.

1162.   S. Zeitlin, "The Date of the Crucifixion according to the Fourth Gospel," *JBL* 51 (1932): 263-71.

1163.   Jean Levie, "La date de la mort du Christ," *NRT* 60 (1933): 141-47.

1164.   Martin Dibelius and Walther Köhler, "Der Todestag Jesu,"

TB 13 (1934): 65-71.

1165.   J. K. Fotheringham, "The Evidence of Astronomy and Technical Chronology for the Date of the Crucifixion," *JTS* 35 (1934): 146-62.

1166.   C. J. Cadoux, "A Tentative Synthetic Chronology of the Apostolic Age," *JBL* 56 (1937): 177-91.

1167.   Olaf Moe, "Jesu dødesdag efter synoptikerne og Johannes," *TTK* 8 (1937): 129-37.

1168.   J. H. McCubbin, "The Date of the Last Supper in the Synoptists and the Fourth Gospel," *Th* 37 (1938): 178-80.

1169.   T. Nicklin, "The Chronology of the New Testament," *ET* 50 (1938-1939): 418-21.

1170.   Graham Gilmer, "A Week in the Life of Christ," *BS* 96 (1939): 42-50.

1171.   Cyril C. Richardson, "Early Patristic Evidences for the Synoptic Chronology of the Passion," *ATR* 22 (1940): 299-308.

1172.   Cyril C. Richardson, "The Quartodecimans and the Synoptic Chronology," *HTR* 33 (1940): 177-90.

1173.   A. D. Doyle, "Pilate's Career and the Date of the Crucifixion," *JTS* 42 (1941): 190-93.

1174.   Paul Gächter, "The Chronology from Mary's Betrothal to the Birth of Christ," *Thst* 2 (1941): 145-70, 347 68.

1175.   Carl H. Kraeling, "Olmstead's Chronology of the Life of Jesus," *ATR* 24 (1942): 334-54.

1176.   George Ogg, "Is A.D. 41 the Date of the Crucifixion?" *JTS* 43 (1942): 187-88.

1177.   A. T. Olmstead, "The Chronology of Jesus' Life," *ATR* 24 (1942): 1-26.

1178.   Paulo Jaeschke, "A data do nasciemento e da morte de Jesus Christo," *REB* 3 (1943): 95-103.

1179.   Grace Amadon, "The Crucifixion Calendar," *JBL* 63 (1944): 177-90.

1180.   Salvador Muñoz Iglesias "Una opinión de Fr. Luis de León sobre la cronología de la Pascua," *EB* 3 (1944): 79-96.

1181.   J. Lamar Jackson, "Christmas," *RE* 41 (1944): 388-96.

1182.   Salvador Munoz Iglesias, "El año de la muerte de Herodes y la fecha del nacimiento del Señor," *CB* 2 (1945): 313-15.

1183.   T. Corbishley, "The Date of our Lord's Birth," *Scr* 1 (1946): 77-80.

1184.   D. J. O'Herlihy, "The Year of the Crucifixion," *CBQ* 8 (1946): 298-305.

1185.   V. Larrañaga, "Ensayo de reconstrucción de la última cena," *EB* 5 (1946): 381-402.

1186.   W. Georgi, "Timelog of Jesus' Last Days," *CTM* 18 (1947): 263-77.

1187.   J. Fernández, "Fecha del Nacimiento de Cristo," *CB* 6 (1949): 356-58.

1188.   Julian Morgenstern, "The Reckoning of the Day in the Gospels and in Acts," *CQ* 26 (1949): 232-40.

1189.   Miguel Balagué, "Los años de la vida del Señor," *CB* 7 (1950): 223-25.

1190.   Robert G. Bratcher, "Reckoning of Time in the Fourth Gospel," *RE* 48 (1951): 161-68.

1191.   Percy J. Heawood, "The Time of the Last Supper," *JQR* 42 (1951-1952): 37-44.

1192.   H. Mulder, "De datum der kruisiging," *GTT* 51 (1951): 176-89, 193-212.

1193.   D. W. B. Robinson, "The Date and Significance of the Last Supper," *EQ* 23 (1951): 126-33.

1194.   S. Zeitlin, "The Time of the Passover Meal," *JQR* 42 (1951-1952): 45-50.

1195.   Uuras Saarnivaara, "The Date of the Crucifixion in the Synoptics and John," *LQ* 6 (1954): 157-60.

1196.   J. Blinzler, "Qumran-Kalender und Passionschronologie," *ZNW* 49 (1958): 238-51.

1197.   Paul Gächter, "Eine neue Chronologie der Leidenswoche?" *ZKT* 80 (1958): 555-61.

1198.   G. Ogg, "The Age of Jesus when he taught," *NTSt* 5 (1958-1959): 291-98.

1199.   J. C. Quirant, "La nueva fecha de la Ultima Cena," *EB* 17 (1958): 47-81.

1200.   P. W. Skehan, "The Date of the Last Supper," *CBQ* 20 (1958): 192-99.

1201.   James A. Walther, "The Chronology of Passion Week," *JBL* 77 (1958): 116-22.

1202.   Norman Walker, "Concerning the Jaubertian Chronology of the Passion," *NT* 3 (1959): 317-20.

1203.   A. Jaubert, "Jésus et le calendrier de Qumrân," *NTSt* 7 (1960-1961): 1-30.

1204.   H. W. Montefiore, "When did Jesus Die?" *ET* 72 (1960-1961): 53-54.

1205.   A. Strobel, "Der Termin des Todes Jesu: Überschau und Losungsvorschlag unter Einschluss der Qumrankalenders," *ZNW* 51 (1960): 69-101.

1206.   Norman Walker, "Jaubert's Solution of the Holy Week Problem," *ET* 72 (1960-1961): 93-94.

1207.   Norman Walker, "The Reckoning of Hours in the Fourth Gospel," *NT* 4 (1960): 69-73.

1208.   K. G. Kuhn, "Zum essenischen Kalendar," *ZNW* 52 (1961): 65-73.

1209.   Massey H. Shepherd, Jr., "Are Both the Synoptics and John Correct about the Date of Jesus' Death?" *JBL* 80 (1961): 123-32.

         See also numbers 137, 138, 143, 144, 479, 520, 521, 5506 ff., 8514, 9883, 10078.

1209.1   Norman Walker, "Pauses in the Passion Story and Their Significance for Chronology," *NT* 6 (1963): 16-19.

1209.2   Norman Walker, "Yet Another Look at the Passion Chronology," *NT* 6 (1963): 286-89.

1209.3   D. Howard Smith, "Concerning the Duration of the Ministry of Jesus," *ET* 76 (1965): 114-16.

1209.4   W. E. Filmer, "Chronology of the Reign of Herod the Great," *JTS* NS 17 (1966): 283-98.

1209.5   N. C. Masterman, "Date of the Triumphal Entry," *NTSt* 16 (1969): 76-82.

1209.6   Jean Carmignac, "Les apparitions de Jésus ressuscité et le calendrier biblico-qumranien," *RQu* 7 (1971): 483-504.

1209.7   Harold W. Hoehner, "Chronological Aspects of the Life of Christ," *BS* 132 (1975): 47-65.

1209.8   Edgar Mezger, "Le sabbat'second-premier' de Luc," *TZ* 22 (1976): 138-43.

1209.9   M. J. Edwards, " 'Not Yet Fifty Years Old': John 8:57," *NTSt* 40 (1994): 449-54.

Q. THE GEOGRAPHY OF PALESTINE

1210.   J. F. Thrupp, "On the Borders of the Inheritance of the Tribe of Nephtali; and on the Site of the Cities denounced by our Saviour in the Gospels," *JCSP* 2 (1855): 290-308.

1211.   Adversaria, "Lucian the Martyr on the Locality of Calvary and the Sepulchre of our Lord," *JCSP* 3 (1857): 122-23.

1212.   S. P. Tregelles, "On the Eastern Boundary of Nephtali, and the Sites of Bethsaida and Capharnaum," *JCSP* 3 (1857): 141-54.

1213.   George Williams, "The Emmaus of S. Luke," *JCSP* 4 (1859): 262-67.

1214.   Selah Merrill, "Galilee in the Time of Christ," *BS* 31 (1874): 29-73, 235-65.

1215.   A. Kohut, "Talmudic Miscellanies, IV: Lakes of the Holy Land," *JQR* 4 (1891-92): 690-96.

1216.   M.-J. Lagrange, "Topographie de Jérusalem," *RB* 1 (1892): 17-38.

1217.   P. Savi, "Emmaüs," *RB* 2 (1893): 223-37.

1218.   Hughes Vincent, "Les fouilles de Jérusalem d'après M. Bliss," *RB* 5 (1896): 241-47.

1219.   W. Wright, "The Homeland of Jesus," *Exp* 5th ser., 4 (1896):

461-69.

1220. John R. Thurston, "The Place of the Crucifixion," *JBL* 18 (1899): 203-207.

1221. J.-Alfred Porret, "De Gethsémané au jardin de Joseph," *RTQR* 9 (1900): 134-70.

1222. George Milligan, "Gethsemane," *ET* 12 (1900-1901): 345-49.

1223. Eb. Nestle, "Bethesda," *ET* 13 (1901-1902): 332-33.

1224. K. Furrer, "Das Geographische im Evangelium nach Johannes," *ZNW* 3 (1902): 257-65.

1225. J. Kreyenbühl, "Der Ort der Verurteilung Jesu," *ZNW* 3 (1902). 15-22.

1226. W. Ewing, "The Mount of Transfiguration," *ET* 18 (1906-1907): 333-34.

1227. William Knight, "The Site of Capernaum," *Exp* 7th ser., 2 (1906): 48-56.

1228. R. Savignac, "Création d'un sanctuaire et d'une tradition á Jérusalem," *RB* 16 (1907): 113-26.

1229. Julius Boehmer, "Emmaus," *ET* 20 (1908-1909): 186-87, 429.

1230. Julius Boehmer, "Studien Zur Geographie Palästinas bes. im Neuen Testament," *ZNW* 9 (1908): 216-29.

1231. Lucien Gautier, "Emmaus," *ET* 20 (1908-1909): 279.

1232. Gebhard Kresser "Das Haus der hl. Familie in Nazareth," *TQ* 91 (1909): 212-47.

1233. Gottlieb Linder, "Bethesda," *RTP* 43 (1910): 494-506.

1234. J. H. A. Hart "Possible References to the Foundation of Tiberius in the Teaching of our Lord," *Exp* 8th ser., (1911): 74-84.

1235. Eb. Nestle, "The Lake of Tiberius," *ET* 23 (1911-1912): 41.

1236. Denis Buzy, "Emmaüs et l'ancienne tradition locale," *RSR* 5 (1914): 395-415.

1237. Carl Sachsse, "Golgatha und das Prätorium des Pilatus," *ZNW* 19 (1919-1920): 29-38.

1238.   F. Warburton Lewis "A Certain Village—not Bethany," *ET* 32 (1920-1921): 330.

1239.   L.-H. Vincent, "La cité de David," *RB* 30 (1921): 410-33, 541-69.

1240.   Th. Zahn, "Die Geburtsstätte Jesu in Geschichte, Sage und bildender Kunst," *NKZ* 32 (1921): 669-91.

1241.   Dr. Wandel, "Zur Lage des neutestamentlichen Golgatha," *TSK* 94 (1922): 132-61.

1242.   T. Nicklin, "Bethsaida," *ET* 35 (1923-1924): 475-76.

1243.   F.-M. Abel, "La distance de Jérusalem á Emmaüs," *RB* 34 (1925): 347-67.

1244.   Joachim Jeremias, "Wo lag Golgatha und das Heilige Grab? Die Überlieferung im Lichte der Formgeschichte," A 1 (1925): 141-73, und A Beiheft 1 (1926): 1-96.

1245.   Shirley Jackson Case, "Jesus and Sepphoris," *JBL* 45 (1926): 14-22.

1246.   Joachim Jeremias, "Golgatha und der heilige Felson," A 2 (1926): 74-128.

1247.   C. Anne E. Moberly, "An Historical Place in Jerusalem," *ET* 41 (1929-1930): 381.

1248.   W. P. Porter, "The Geographic Background of the Bible," *USR* 42 (1930-1931): 401-11.

1249.   Denis Buzy, "Béthanie au delà du Jourdain," *RSR* 21 (1931): 444-62.

1250.   C. C. McCown, "The Geography of Jesus' Last Journey," *JBL* 51 (1932): 107-29.

1251.   J. McKee Adams, "Comparatively New Centers Named in the Gospels and the Acts," *RE* 31 (1934): 356-71.

1252.   J. McKee Adams, "Palestinian Place Names in the Gospels and the Acts," *RE* 31 (1934): 194-204.

1253.   Paul Joüon, "Les mots employés pour désigner le temple dans l'Ancien Testament, le Nouveau Testament et Josèphe," *RSR* 25 (1935): 329-43.

1254.   L. Pujol, " 'In loco qui dicitur *Lithostrotos*'," *VD* 15 (1935):

180-86, 204-207, 233-37.

1255. L.-H. Vincent, "Bethléem, le sanctuaire de la nativité," *RB* 45 (1936): 544-74; 46 (1937): 93-121.

1256. Denis Buzy, "La Bethaïde de Galilée," *RSR* 28 (1938): 570-79.

1257. John J. Collins, "The Archaeology of the Crucifixion," *CBQ* 1 (1939): 154-59.

1258. C. C. McCown, "Gospel Geography: Fiction, Fact, and Truth," *JBL* 60 (1941): 1-25.

1259. Eric F. F. Bishop, "Where was Emmaus? Why not Imwas?" *ET* 55 (1943-1944): 152-53.

1260. J. Spencer Kennard, "Was Capernaum the Home of Jesus?" *JBL* 65 (1946): 131-41.

1261. Clemens Kopp, "Christian Sites around the Sea of Galilee; 1. Capernaum," *DS* 2 (1949): 213-35; "2. Bethsaida and El-Mingeh," 3 (1950): 10-40; "3. Chorazin," 275-84; "4. Magdala," 344-50; "5. The Sermon on the Mount and the Feeding of the Multitudes," 4 (1951): 35-68; "6. The Sermon on the Mount and the Feeding of the Multitudes (*concluded*): The Appearance of the Risen Christ by the Lake," 5 (1952): 185-204.

1262. Eric F. F. Bishop, "Jesus and the Lake," *CBQ* 13 (1951): 398-414.

1263. James Kelso, "New Testament Jericho," *BA* 14 (1951): 34-43.

1264. G. H. Boobyer, "Galilee and the Galileans in St. Mark's Gospel," *BJRL* 35 (1952-1953): 334-48.

1265. H. St. J. Hart, "Judea and Rome—The Official Commentary," *JTS* N.S., 3 (1952): 172-98.

1266. Ralph E. Knudsen, "Palestine in the Light of Contemporary Events," *RE* 49 (1952): 167-74.

1267. Werner Schmauch, "Der Ölberg. Exegese zu einer Ortsangabe besonders bei Matthäus und Markus," *TLZ* 77 (1952): 391-96.

1268.   Eric F. F. Bishop, "Jesus and Capernaum," *CBQ* 15 (1953): 305-14.

1269.   F. Spadafora, "Emmaus: critic a testuale e archeologica," *RivB* 1 (1953): 255-68.

1270.   Augustín Arce, "El topónimo natal del Precursor," *EE* 34 (1960): 825-36.

1271.   P. Teodorico da Castel S. Pietro, "Golgota e Santo Sepolcro," *RivB* 8 (1960): 351-63.

1272.   Charles F. Nesbitt, "The Bethany Traditions in the Gospel Narratives," *JBR* 29 (1961): 119-24.

          See also numbers 627, 683, 5599.

1272.1   V. Corbo, "Capharnaüm," *RB* 76 (1969): 557-63; 78 (1971): 588-91.

1272.2   Joachim Wanke, "Wie sie ihn beim Brotbrechen erkannten: zur Auslegung der Emmauserzählung Lk 24:13-35," *BibZ* 18 (1974): 180-92.

1272.3   Robert G. North, "Discoveries at Capernaum," *B* 58 (1977): 424-31.

1272.4   A. del Agua Pérez, "El cumplimiento del Reino de Dios en la misión de Jesús: Programa del Evangelio de Lucas," *EB* 8 (1979-1980): 269-93.

1272.5   Elizabeth S. Malbon, "Galilee and Jerusalem: History and Literature in Marcan Interpretation," *CBQ* 44 (1982): 242-55.

1272.6   James F. Strange, "Diversity in Early Palestinian Christianity, Some Archaeological Evidences," *ATR* 65 (1983): 14-24.

1272.7   V. Tzaferis, "New Archaeological Evidence on Ancient Capernaum," *BA* 46 (1983): 198-204.

1272.8   Bernard P. Robinson, "The Place of the Emmaus Story in Luke-Acts," *NTSt* 30 (1984): 481-97.

1272.9   Lloyd R. Bailey, "Gehenna: The Topography of Hell," *BA* 49 (1986): 187-91.

1272.10   Louis Dussaut, "Le triptyque des apparitions en Luc 24 (analyse structurelle)," *RB* 94 (1987): 161-213.

1272.11 Seán Freyne, "Galilee-Jerusalem Relations according to Josephus' Life," *NTSt* 33 (1987): 600-609.

1272.12 T. R. W. Longstaff, "Nazareth and Sepphoris: Insights into Christian Origins," *ATR* suppl. 11 (1990): 8-15.

1272.13 Robert M. Grant, "Early Christian Geography," *VCh* 46 (1992): 105-11.

1272.14 Rami Arav and J. Rousseau, "Bethsaïde, ville perdue et retrouvée," *RB* 100 (1993): 415-28.

1272.15 Z. Kallai, "Palestine—Biblical to Byzantine Periods," *BA* 56 (1993): 149-50.

1272.16 Stuart A. Irvine, "The Southern Border of Syria Reconstructed," *CBQ* 56 (1994): 21-41.

1272.17 Timothy Wiarda, "Simon, Jesus of Nazareth, Son of Jonah, Son of John: Realistic Detail in the Gospels and Acts," *NTS* 40 (1994): 192-209.

R. PERSONS AND GROUPS RELATED TO JESUS

1. Mary, the Mother of Jesus, and Joseph

1273. A. Whyte, "Joseph and Mary," *Exp* 3rd ser., 1 (1885): 120-27.

1274. Gustav Rösch, "Astarte—Maria," *TSK* 61 (1888): 265-99, 557-58.

1275. M.-J. Lagrange, "La dormition de la sainte verge et la, maison de Jean-Marc," *RB* 8 (1899): 589-600.

1276. Anton Baumstark, "Die leibliche Hirmnel fahrt der allerseligsten Jungfrau und die Lokaltradition von Jerusalem," *OC* 1. Serie, 4 (1904): 371-92.

1277. Anton Baumstark, "Zwei syrische Dichtungen auf das Entschlafen der allerseligsten Jungfrau," *OC* 1. Serie, 5 (1905): 82-125.

1278. W. M. Ramsay, "The Worship of the Virgin Mary at Ephesus," *Exp* , 6th ser., 11 (1905): 401-415; 12 (1905): 81-98.

1279. Eb. Nestle, "The Relation of Mary and Elisabeth," *ET* 17 (1905-1906): 140.

1280.   O. Bardenhewer, "Ist Maria zu Jerusalem oder zu Ephesus gestorben?" *TRev* 5 (1906): 569-77.

1281.   G. E. Price, "Gleanings anent the Immaculate Conception," *ITQ* 13 (1918): 297-310.

1282.   P. J. Toner, "Definability of the Assumption of the Blessed Virgin," *ITQ* 16 (1921): 16-19.

1283.   Pierre Aubron, "La Mariologie de Saint Bernard," *RSR* (1934): 543-77.

1284.   W. Staerk, " 'Eva-Maria.' Ein Beitrag zur Denk- und Sprechweise der altkirchlichen Christologie," *ZNW* 33 (1934): 97-104.

1285.   A. W. Burridge, "L'immaculée conception dans la théologie de l'Angleterre médiévale," *RHE* 32 (1936): 570-97.

1286.   Pierre Aubron, "Le Discours de Théophane de Nicée sur la Très Sainte Mère de Dieu," *RSR* 27 (1937): 257-74.

1287.   C. Chevalier, "Mariologie de Romanos (490-550 environ), le Roi des Mélodes," *RSR* 28 (1938): 48-71.

1288.   H. Barré, "La Royauté de Marie pendant les neuf premiers siècles," *RSR* 29 (1939): 129-62, 303-34.

1289.   E. Mersch, "Sainte Marie, Mère de Dieu," *NRT* 67 (1940-1945): 129-52.

1290.   B. Poschmann, "Zur Mariologie," *TRev* 39 (1940): 1-5.

1291.   Eug. Druwé, "Vers la définition dogmatique de l'Assomption. À propos d'une publication récente," *RSR* 33 (1946): 462-83.

1292.   Romualdo Galdoz, "María en la Biblia," *CB* 3 (1946): 113-15.

1293.   M. Peinador, "La Virgen María en Nazareth," *CB* 3 (1946): 238-40.

1294.   L. G. da Fonseca, "L'Assunzione di Maria nella Sacra Scrittura," *B* 28 (1947): 321-62.

1295.   Gerhard Ebeling, "Zur Frage nach dem Sinn des mariologischen Dogmas," *ZTK* N.F. 47 (1950): 383-91.

1296.   Mateus Hoepers, "A Assunção de Nossa Senhora e o Novo

Testamento," *REB* 10 (1950): 44-61.

1297. André M. Dubarle, "Les fondements bibliques du titre marial de Nouvelle Ève," *RSR* 39 (1951-1952): 49-64.

1298. Giovanni Miegge, "La Asunción de María," *CT* 3 (1951): 5-23.

1299. F. Quiévr\eux, "La maternité spirituelle de la mère de Jésus dans l'évangile de saint Jean," *VCar* 6 (1952): 15-38.

1300. P. Michalon, "Le témoignage du Nouveau Testament sur la mère de Jésus," *LumV* no. 10 (1953): 109-26.

1301. M.-A. Berrouard, "La foi de sainte Marie," *LMmV* no. 16 (1954): 19-34.

1302. Gerald Mitchell, "The Definition of the Immaculate Conception," *ITQ* 21 (1954): 1-15.

1303. Karl Rahner, "Le principe fondamental de la théologie mariale," *RSR* 42 (1954): 481-522.

1304. M.-B. de Vaux Saint-Cyr, "Grandeur de Marie et idéal évangelique," *LumV* no. 16 (1954): 95-108.

1305. G. Philips, "L'Immaculée Conception dans le mystère du Christ Rédempteur," *ETL* 31 (1955): 100-11.

1306. Hermann Volk, "Christus und Maria; dogmatische Grundlagen der marianischen Frömmigkeit," *C* 10 (1955): 85-107.

1307. Ch. Baumgartner, "Du Concile du Vatican au développement du Dogme," *RSR* 44 (1956): 573-75.

1308. J. Galot, "La plus ancienne affirmation de la corédemption mariale: le témoignage de Jean le Géomètre," *RSR* 45 (1957): 187-208.

1309. Aloísio Lorscheider, "O mistério de Maria pregação," *REB* 18 (1958): 671-86.

1310. Donal Flanagan, "The Image of the Bride in the Earlier Marian Tradition," *ITQ* 27 (1960): 111-24.

1311. S. Cavalletti, "I sogni di San Giuseppe," *BO* 2 (1960): 149-51.

1312. Donal Flanagan, "Mary, Bride of Christ," *ITQ* 28 (1961): 233-37.

See also numbers 269, 670, 1174, 2000, 3731-3733, 7304.

1312.1   Eric F. F. Bishop, "Mary (of) Clopas and Her Father," *ET* 73 (1962): 339.

1312.2   Ben F. Meyer, "But Mary Kept All These Things," *CBQ* 26 (1964): 31-49.

1312.3   J. M. Ford, "Mary's Virginitas, Post-Partum and Jewish Law" *B* 54 (1973): 269-72.

1312.4   Willibald Grimm, "Der Dank fur die empfangene Offenbarung bei Jesus und Josephus," *BibZ* 17 (1973): 249-56.

1312.5   John W. Wenham, "The Relatives of Jesus," *EQ* 47 (1975): 6-15.

1312.6   A. Tosato, "Joseph, Being a Just Man (Matt. 1:19)," *CBQ* 41 (1979): 547-51.

1312.7   George D. Kilpatrick, "Jesus, His Family and His Disciples," *JSNT* 15 (1982): 3-19.

1312.8   Joseph A. Grassi, "The Role of Jesus' Mother in John's Gospel: A Reappraisal," *CBQ* 48/1 (1986): 67-80.

1312.9   A. M. Allchin, "Mary: An Anglican Approach," *ITQ* 54 (1988): 120-30.

2. The Brethren of Jesus

1313.   C. Wieseler, "Die Söhne Zebedäi Vettern des Herrn," *TSK* 13 (1840):648-94.

1314.   Lic. Wieseler, "Über die Brüder des Herrn in ihrem Unterschiede von den Söhnen Alphäi, und namentlich, dass zu Pauli Zeit Jakobus, der Apostel und Sohn Alphäi, die Säule der jerusalemischen Gemeinde gewesen sei," *TSK* 15 (1842): 71-125.

1315.   Ed. Scherer, "Jacques, fils d'Alphée, et Jacques, frère du Seigneur," *RT* 3 (1851): 31-40.

1316.   Philip Schaff, "The Brethren of Christ," *BS* 21 (1864): 855-69.

1317.   Calvin Cutler, "The Brethren of our Lord," *BS* 26 (1869): 745-58.

1318.   Agnes Smith Lewis, "Who was Judas Thomas?" *ET* 14 (1902-1903): 397-99 [Perhaps Jude the brother of Jesus and perhaps twin of James].

1319.   J. Chapman, "The Brethren of the Lord," *JTS* 7 (1905-1906): 412-33.

1320.   Alfred Durand, "Les frères du Seigneur," *RB* 17 (1908): 9-35.

1321.   J. B. Mayor, "The Brethren of the Lord," *Exp* 7th ser., 7 (1909): 18-30.

1322.   Samuel Dickey, "Jesus and his Brethren," *BW* 35 (1910): 33-38.

1323.   Antoine Malvy, "Saint Jacques de Jérusalem était-il un des douze?" *RSR* 8 (1918): 122-31

1324.   Hans Leisegang, "Der Bruder des Erlösers," *A* 1 (1925): 24-33.

1325.   A. Marmorstein, "Ein Wort über den Bruder des Erlösers in der Pistis Sophia," *A* 2 (1926): 155-56.

1326.   S. Lyonnet, "Témoignages de saint Jean Chrysostome et de saint Jérôme sur Jacques le frère du Seigneur," *RSR* 29 (1939): 335-50.

1327.   John J. Collins, "The Brethren of the Lord and Two recently Published Papyri," *ThSt* 5 (1944): 484-94.

1327.1   John D. Crossan, "Mark and the Relatives of Jesus," *NT* 15 (1973): 81-113.

1327.2   Richard J. Bauckham, "The Brothers and Sisters of Jesus: An Epiphanian Response to John P. Meter," *CBQ* 56 (1994): 686-700.

3. John the Baptist

1328.   S. Hoekstra, "Johannes de Dooper en het Christendom," *TT* 18 (1884): 336-411.

1329.   Benjamin B. Warfield, "The Scene of the Baptist's Work," *Exp* 3rd ser., 1 (1885): 267-82.

1330.   A. D. Loman, "Het bericht van Flavius Josephus aangaande de oorzaak en het datum der executie van Johannes den

Dooper, vergeleken met de verhalen der Synoptici," *TT* 25 (1891): 293-315.

1331.   B. Whiteford, "The Ideal Preacher," *Exp* 5th ser., 3 (1896): 357-66.

1332.   T. Barns, "The Baptism of John: Its Place in New Testament Criticism," *Exp* 5th ser., 6 (1897): 139-53.

1333.   S. Sollertinsky, "The Death of St. John the Baptist," *JTS* 1 (1899-1900): 507-28.

1334.   Shailer Mathews, "Jesus and John: A Suggestion to Reformers," *BW* 17 (1901): 17-21.

1335.   B. W. Bacon, "The 'Coming One' of John the Baptist," *Exp* 6th ser., 10 (1904): 1-18.

1336.   Eb. Nestle, "Why was the Father of John the Baptist called Zacharias?" *ET* 17 (1905-1906): 146.

1337.   F. R. M. Hitchcock, "The Baptist and the Fourth Gospel," *Exp* 7th ser., 4 (1907): 534-53.

1338.   E. F. Scott, "John the Baptist and his Message," *Exp* 7th ser., 6 (1908): 68-76.

1339.   James Denney, "Jesus' Estimate of John the Baptist," *Exp* 7th ser., 7 (1909): 60-75.

1340.   Jas. B. Russell, "Was the Baptist Loyal to Jesus?" *ET* 21 (1909-1910): 333.

1341.   J. C. Todd, "The Logia of the Baptist," *ET* 21 (1909-1910): 173-75.

1342.   E. Wendling, "Synoptische Studien; Die Anfrage des Täufers und das Zeugnis über den Täufer," *ZNW* 10 (1909): 46-58.

1343.   W. P. Bradley, "John the Baptist as Forerunner," *BW* 35 (1910): 327-38, 396-404.

1344.   Henry Burton Sharman, "The Ministry of John the Baptist and the Beginning of Jesus' Ministry," *BW* 35 (1910): 57-61.

1345.   W. Brandt, "Ein talmudisches Zeugnis von dem Täufer Johannes?" *ZNW* 12 (1911): 289-95.

1346.   C. Bruston, "De quelques texts relatifs à Jean-Baptiste et non à Jésus Christ," *RTQR* 20 (1911): 337-67.

1347.   Clayton R. Bowen, "John the Baptist in the New Testament,"
         AJT 16 (1912): 90-106.

1348.   E. C. J. Kraeling, "The Baptism of John," *LCR* 31 (1912):
         65-71, 288-94.

1349.   B. H. Streeter, "Was the Baptist's Preaching Apocalyptic?"
         JTS 14 (1912-1913): 549-52.

1350.   Dennis Buzy, "Saint Jean-Baptiste a-t-il été sanctifié dans le
         sein de sa mère?" *RSPT* 7 (1913): 680-99.

1351.   Clayton R. Bowen, "Was John the Baptist the Sign of
         Jonah?" *AJT* 20 (1916): 414-21.

1352.   H. M. Treen, "Jesus and John the Baptist," *ET* 35
         (1923-1924): 521-22.

1353.   J. Randel Harris, "A New Life of John the Baptist," *BJRL* 11
         (1927): 329-498.

1354.   B. W. Bacon, "New and Old in Jesus' Relation to John," *JBL*
         48 (1929): 40-81.

1355.   Joachim Jeremias, "Der Ursprung der Johannestaufe," *ZNW*
         28 (1929): 312-20.

1356.   B. Brinkmann, "De predication christologica S. Iohannis
         Baptistae," *VD* 10 (1930): 309-13.

1357.   Ernst Lohmeyer, "Zur evangelischen Überlieferung von
         Johannes dem Täufer," *JBL* 51 (1932): 300-19.

1358.   Joshua Starr, "The Unjewish Character of the Markan
         Account of John the Baptist," *JBL* 51 (1932): 227-37.

1359.   Hans Windisch, "Die Notiz über Tracht und Speise des
         Täufers Johannes und ihre Entsprechungen in der
         Jesusüberlieferung," *ZNW* 32 (1933): 65-87.

1360.   G. H. C. Macgregor, "John the Baptist and the Origins of
         Christianity," *ET* 46 (1934-1935): 355-62.

1361.   Andrés Fernández, "Le Costume d'Elie et celui de Jean
         Baptiste," *B* 16 (1935): 74-84.

1362.   M. Kiddle, "The Teaching of John the Baptist," *ET* 48 (1936-
         1937): 396-400.

1363.   C. C. McCown, "The Scene of John's Ministry and its

Relation to the Purpose and Outcome of his Mission," *JBL* 59 (1940): 113-31.

1364.   M. Leimer, "Die Taufe Johannis des Täufers in ihrem Verhältnis zu Christi Taufe," *CTM* 14 (1943): 197-206.

1365.   Everett F. Harrison, "The Son of God among the sons of men; 1. Jesus and John the Baptist," *BS* 102 (1945): 74-83.

1366.   Alberto Vidal, "Vida de S. Juan Bautista," *CB* 2, núm. 17 (1945): 282-84; núm. 18, 308-11; 3 (1946): 55-58.

1367.   John M. T. Barton, "The Voice of One Crying...," *Scr* 4 (1947): 6-11.

1368.   T. W. Manson, "John the Baptist," *BJRL* 36 (1953-1954): 395-412.

1369.   J. Mouson, "Jean-Baptiste dans les fragments d'Héracléon," *ETL* 30 (1954): 301-22.

1370.   T. F. Glasson, "John the Baptist in the Fourth Gospel," *ET* 67 (1955-1956): 245-46.

1371.   S. Lewis Johnson, "The Message of John the Baptist," *BS* 113 (1956): 30-36.

1372.   A. S. Geyser, "The Youth of John the Baptist. A Deduction from the Break in the Parallel Account of the Lucan Infancy Story," *NT* 1 (1956): 70-74.

1373.   Paul Evdokimov, "Jean Baptiste," *BVC* no. 16 (1956-1957): 7-18.

1374.   John A. T. Robinson, "Elijah, John and Jesus: an Essay in Detection," *NTSt* 4 (1957-1958): 263-81.

1375.   James L. Jones, "References to John the Baptist in the Gospel According to St. Matthew," *ATR* 41 (1959): 298-302.

1376.   Raymond E. Brown, "Three Quotations from John the Baptist in the Gospel of John," *CBQ* 22 (1960): 292-98.

See also numbers 1270, 2270, 2726, 3225, 3257, 4236 ff., 5503, 6145, 7107, 7114.

1376.1   E. Galbiati, "La testimonianza di Giovanni Battista (Giov. 1:9-28)," *BO* 4 (1962): 227-33.

1376.2   M.-É. Boismard, "Les traditions johanniques concernant le

Baptiste," *RB* 70 (1963): 5-42.

1376.3　A. G. Patzia, "Did John the Baptist Preach a Baptism of Fire and Holy Spirit?" *EQ* 40 (1968): 21-27.

1376.4　Morna D. Hooker, "John the Baptist and the Johannine Prologue," *NTSt* 16 (1969-1970): 354-58.

1376.5　Ernst Bammel, "The Baptist in Early Christian Tradition," *NTSt* 18 (1971-1972): 95-128.

1376.6　Lamar Cope, "The Death of John the Baptist in the Gospel of Matthew; or, the Case of the Confusing Conjunction," *CBQ* 38/4 (1976): 515-19.

1376.7　John P. Meier, "John the Baptist in Matthew's Gospel," *JBL* 99 (1980): 383-405.

1376.8　Helmut Merklein, "Dei Umkehrpredigt bei Johannes dem Täufer und Jesus von Nazaret," *BibZ* 25 (1981): 29-46.

1376.9　S. L. Davies, "John the Baptist and Essene Kashruth," *NTSt* 29 (1983): 569-71.

1376.10　John J. Kilgallen, "John the Baptist, the Sinful Woman and the Pharisee," *JBL* 104/4 (1985): 675-79.

1376.11　Carl Kazmierski, "The Stones of Abraham: John the Baptist and the End of Torah (Matt. 3,7-10 Par. Luke 3,7-9)," *B* 68/1 (1987): 22-40.

1376.12　Michael Cleary, "The Baptist of History and Kerygma," *ITQ* 54 (1988): 211-27.

1376.13　Jan Lambrecht, "John the Baptist and Jesus in Mark 1:1-15: Markan Redaction of Q?" *NTSt* 38 (1992): 357-84.

1376.14　B. Kinman, "Luke's Exoneration of John the Baptist," *JTS* 44 (1993): 595-98.

1376.15　P. Katz, "Jesus als Vorläufer des Christus. Mögliche Hinweise in den Evangelien auf Elia als den 'Typos' Jesu," *TZ* 52 (1996): 225-35.

1376.16　J. E. Taylor, "John the Baptist and the Essenes," *JJS* 47 (1996): 256-85.

4. The Disciples of Jesus

1377.   G. A. Chadwick, "The Group of the Apostles," *Exp* 3rd ser., 9 (1889): 100-14, [Peter] 187-99, [Minor Figures] 434-48.

1378.   W. Milligan, "The Apostle John," *Exp* 3rd ser., 10 (1889): 321-41.

1379.   Eb. Nestle, "Matthias—Bartholomew," *ET* 9 (1897-1998): 566-67.

1380.   Edward Bosworth, "How Jesus Gathered his First Disciples," *BW* 15 (1900): 112-18.

1381.   Pastor Scholz, "Christus in seinem Verhalten zu den Zwölfen, ein Vorbild in der Seelsorge," *NKZ* 15 (1904): 956-73.

1382.   J. H. A. Hart, "Cephas and Christ," *JTS* 9 (1907-1908): 14-41.

1383.   Errett Gates, "Growth of Discipleship in the Company of Jesus," *BW* 33 (1909): 314-25.

1384.   Robert Mackintosh, " 'Peter and John'," *ET* 23 (1911-1912): 93-94.

1385.   Nicholas Oliver, "The Fisherman as Expositor," *ET* 28 (1916-1917): 229-31.

1386.   Otis and Frank Cary, "How Old Were Christ's Disciples?" *BW* 50 (1917): 3-12.

1387.   Kirsopp Lake, "Simon Zelotes," *HTR* 10 (1917): 57-63.

1388.   George Farmer, "A Group of Four Apostles," *ET* 31 (1919-1920): 331.

1389.   Kirsopp Lake, "Simon, Cephas, Peter," *HTR* 14 (1921): 95-97.

1390.   S. Ponkin, "The Psychology of the Twelve," *ET* 33 (1921-1922): 562-64.

1391.   H. J. Flowers, "The Calling of Peter and the Restoration of Peter," *ATR* 5 (1922-1923): 235-42.

1392.   Samuel Krauss, "Die Instruction Jesu an die Apostel," *A* 1 (1925): 96-102.

1393.   J. Farquhar, "The Apostle Thomas in North India," *BJRL* 10 (1926): 80-111.

1394.   R. B. Y. Scott, "Who Was Nathanael?" *ET* 38 (1926-1927): 93-94.

1395.   D. Browne, "Who Was Nathanael?" *ET* 38 (1926-1927): 286.

1396.   J. Farquhar, "The Apostle Thomas in South India," *BJRL* 11 (1927): 20-50.

1397.   W. H. P. Hatch, "The Apostles in the New Testament and in the Ecclesiastical Tradition of Egypt," *HTR* 21 (1928): 147-59.

1398.   P. Edm. Power, "St. Peter in Gallicantu and the House of Caiphas," *OC* III. Serie, 6 (1931): 182-208.

1399.   Hans Lauerer, "Der Anspruch Jesu an seine Jünger," *NKZ* (*Luthertum*): 45 (1934): 229-39, 280-83.

1400.   Everett Gill, "Jesus' Salt Covenant with the Eleven," *RE* 36 (1939): 197-98 [Acts 1:4].

1401.   F. Sühling und B. Altones, "Zur Petrusfrage," *TRev* 38 (1939): 361-66.

1402.   U. Holzmeister, "Nathaniel fuitne idem ac S. Bartholomaeus Apostolus?" *B* 21 (1940): 28-39.

1403.   W. S. Reilly, "The Training of the Twelve according to St. Mark," *CBQ* 2 (1940): 9-14.

1404.   W. Maxfield Garrott, "How Jesus Trained Leaders," *RE* 38 (1941). 401-409.

1405.   W. T. Whitley, "The Apostolic Band," *RE* 38 (1941): 371-85.

1406.   Charles C. Torrey, "The Name 'Iscariot'," *HTR* 36 (1943): 51-62.

1407.   J. Rendel Harris, "St. Luke's Version of the Death of Judas," *AJT* 18 (1914): 127-31 [Acts 1:16-20].

1408.   Everett F. Harrison, "The Son of God among the Sons of Men. I. Jesus and John the Baptist," *BS* 102 (1945): 74-83; "II. Jesus and Andrew," 170-78; "III. Jesus and Simon Peter," 300-10; "IV. Jesus and Nathaniel," 442-47; "V. Jesus and Nicodemus," 103 (1946): 50-56; "VI. Jesus and the Women of Samaria," 176-86; "VII. Jesus and the Impotent

Man," 306-15; "VIII. Jesus and the Woman Taken in Adultery," 431-39; "IX. Jesus and the Man Born Blind," 104 (1947): 49-58; "X. Jesus and Lazarus," 182-93; "XI. Jesus and Martha," 298-306; "XII. Jesus and Mary of Bethany," 441-50; "XIII. Jesus and Judas," 105 (1948): 170-81; "XIV. Jesus and Pilate," 307-19; "XV. Jesus and Mary Magdalene," 433-42; "XVI. Jesus and Thomas," 106 (1949): 65-74; "XVII. Jesus and John the Apostle," 228-38.

1409.   Anonymous, "The Disciple whom Jesus Loved," *EQ* 18 (1946): 81-83.

1410.   G. T. Manley, "Simon, Whose Surname Is Peter," *EQ* 18 (1946): 46-51.

1411.   K. M. Bishop, "St. Matthew and the Gentiles," *ET* 59 (1947-1948): 249.

1412.   Fr. Placid, "The South Indian Apostolate of St. Thomas," *OCP* 18 (1952): 229-45.

1413.   Warren M. Smelts, "John Son of Zebedee," *ATR* 35 (1953): 8-17.

1414.   Eduard Schweizer, "The Disciples of Jesus and the Post-Resurrection Church," *USQR* 15 (1960): 281-94.

1415.   S. Legacy, "Scribes et disciples de Jésus," *RB* 68 (1961): 321-345, 481-506.

1416.   Cecil Roth, "Simon-Peter," *HTR* 54 (1961): 91-98.

See also numbers 636, 674, 2313, 3419, 3420, 3566, 4477, 5069, 5071, 10027, 10043.

1416.1   Oscar Cullmann, "Le douzième apôtre," *RHPR* 42 (1962): 133-40.

1416.2   Otto Betz, "The Dichotomized Servant and the End of Judas Iscariot," *RQu* 5/17 (1964): 43-58.

1416.3   L. Johnson, "The Beloved Disciple: A Reply," *ET* 77 (1965-1966): 380.

1416.4   L. Johnson, "Who Was He Beloved Disciple?" *ET* 77 (1965-1966): 157-58.

1416.5   I. R. Porter, "Who Was the Beloved Disciple?" *ET* 77

(1965-1966) 213-14.

1416.6   Thomas L. Budesheim, "Jesus and the Disciples in Conflict with Judaism," *ZNW* 62/3 (1971): 190-209.

1416.7   Ulrich Luz, "Die Jünger im Matthäusevangelium," *ZNW* 62 (1971): 141-71.

1416.8   David J. Hawkin, "The Incomprehension of the Disciples in the Marcan Redaction," *JBL* 91 (1972): 491-500.

1416.9   B. de Solages, "Jean, fils de Zébédée et l'énigme du 'disciple que Jésus aimait'," *BLE* 73 (1972): 41-50.

1416.10   B. A. E. Osborne, "Peter, Stumbling-Block and Satan," *NT* 15/3 (1973): 187-90.

1416.11   Paul S. Mincar, "The Disciples and the Crowds in the Gospel of Matthew," *ATR* Suppl. 3 (1974): 28-44

1416.12   Camille Focant, "L'incompréhension des disciples dans le deuxième évangile. Tradition et rédaction," *RB* 82 (1975): 161-85.

1416.13   Paul S. Minear, "The Beloved Disciple in the Gospel of John: Some Clues and Conjectures," *NT* 19 (1977): 105-23.

1416.14   Robert C. Tannehill, "The Disciples in Mark: The Function of a Narrative Role," *JR* 57 (1977): 386-405.

1416.15   Ernest Best, "Peter in the Gospel According to Mark," *CBQ* 40/4 (1978): 547-58.

1416.16   James Thompson, "The Odyssey of a Disciple," *EQ* 23 (1980): 77-81.

1416.17   John J. Gunther, "The Relation of the Beloved Disciple to the Twelve," *TZ* 37 (1981): 129-48.

1416.18   E. D. Freed, "The Disciples in Mark and the *maskilim* in Daniel: A Comparison," *JSNT* 16 (1982): 7-23.

1416.19   Robert F. O'Toole, "Parallels between Jesus and his Disciples in Luke-Acts: A Further Study," *BibZ* 27 (1983): 195-212.

1416.20   Elizabeth S. Malbon, "Disciples/Crowds/Whoever: Markan Characters and Readers," *NT* 28 (1986): 104-30.

1416.21   Ekkehard W. Stegemann, "Zur Rolle von Petrus, Jakobus und Johannes im Markusevangelium," *TZ* 42 (1986): 366-74.

1416.22   R. Aguirre, "Pedro en el Evangelio de Mateo," *EB* 47 (1989): 343-61.

1416.23   Frank J. Matera, "The Incomprehension of the Disciples and Peter's Confession (Mark 6,14-8,30)," *B* 70/2 (1989): 153-72.

1416.24   David R. Bauer, "The Major Characters of Matthew's Story: Their Function and Significance," *Interp* 46 (1992): 357-67.

1416.25   J. J. Bartolomé, "El discipulado de Jesús en Marcos. Motivo y metodología de un modelo evangélico de vida cristiana," *EB* 51 (1993): 511-30.

5. Religious Sects

a. *The Pharisees and the Sadducees*

1417.   Ed. Reuss, "Le Pharisaïsme et le Sadducéisme," *RT* 3 (1851): 193-211.

1418.   James Moffatt, "The Righteousness of the Scribes and Pharisees," *ET* 13 (1901-1902): 201-206.

1419.   Chr. A. Bugge, "De tre Religionsretninger i Israel paa Christi Tid of deres Stilling i Israels Historie," *NTT* 9 (1908): 297-320.

1420.   Eb. Nestle, "Did the Pharisees Wear White Garments?" *ET* 20 (1908-1909): 188-89.

1421.   G. Margoliouth, "The Traditions of the Elders," *ET* 22 (1910-1911): 261-63.

1422.   C. T. Dominate, "The Synoptic Evangelists and the Pharisees," *Exp* 8th ser., 1 (1911), 231-44.

1423.   B. D. Eerdmans, "Farizeën en Sadduceën," *TT* 48 (1914): 1-26, 223-30.

1424.   H. L. Oort, "Iets over Farizeën en Sadduceën," *TT* 48 (1914): 214-22.

1425.   Theodore H. Robinson, "Jesus and the Pharisees," *ET* 28 (1916-1917): 550-54.

1426.   J. Ridderbos, "Farizeesche Heilsverwachting," *GTT* 17

(1916-1917): 1-14, 49-61.

1427.   B. W. Bacon, "Pharisees and Herodians in Mark," *JBL* 39
          (1920): 102-12.

1428.   F. C. Burkitt, "Jesus and the Pharisees," *JTS* 28 (1926-1927):
          392-97.

1429.   Louis Finkelstein, "The Pharisees: Their Origin and their
          Philosophy," *HTR* 22 (1929): 185-261.

1430.   H. Branscomb, "Jesus and the Pharisees," *USR* 44
          (1932-1933): 24-40.

1431.   Werner Foerster, "Der Ursprung des Pharisäismus," *ZNW* 34
          (1935): 35-51.

1432.   W. S. Reilly, "Our Lord and the Pharisees," *CBQ* 1 (1939):
          64-68.

1433.   John Bowman, "The Pharisees," *EQ* 20 (1948): 125-46.

1434.   Elie Bikermann, "La chaine de la tradition pharisienne," *RB*
          59 (1952): 44-54.

1435.   A. F. J. Klijn, "Scribes, Pharisees, Highpriests, and Elders in
          the New Testament," *NT* 3 (1959): 259-67.

          See also numbers 273, 3218, 3248, 5118, 5121.

1435.1   Sebastián Bartina, "Jesús y los saduceos: 'El Dios de
          Abraham, de Isaac y de Jacob' es 'El que hace existir'," *EB*
          21 (1962): 151-60.

1435.2   J. A. Ziesler, "Luke and the Pharisees," *NTS* 25 (1979):
          146-57.

1435.3   F. Schnider, "Ausschliessen und Ausseschlossen Werden:
          Beobachtungen zur Struktur der Gleichnisses vom Pharisaer
          und Zollner (Lk 18,10-14a)," *BibZ* 24 (1980): 42-56.

1435.4   A. I. Baumgarten, "The Name of the Pharisees," *JBL* 102
          (1983): 411-28.

1435.5   Robert A. Wild, "The Encounter between Pharisaic and
          Christian Judaism: Some Early Gospel Evidence," *NT* 27/2
          (1985): 105-24.

1435.6   John J. Kilgallen, "The Sadducees and Resurrection From the
          Dead: Luke 20:27-40," *B* 67/4 (1986): 478-95.

1435.7   A. I. Baumgarten, "The Pharisaic Paradosis," *HTR* 80 (1987): 63-77.

1435.8   Felix Böhl, "Das Fasten an Montagen und Donnerstagen: Zur Geschichte einer Pharisdischen Praxis (Lk 18,12)," *BibZ* 31 (1987): 247-50.

1435.9   Donald E. Cook, "A Gospel Portrait of the Pharisees," *RE* 84 (1987): 221-33.

1435.10   Dieter Lührmann, "Die Pharisäer und die Schriftgelehrten im Markusevangelium," *ZNW* 78 (1987): 169-85.

1435.11   Robert L. Mowery, "Pharisees and Scribes, Galilee and Jerusalem," *ZNW* 80/3-4 (1989): 266-68.

1435.12   Howard C. Kee, "The Transformation of the Synagogue after 70 ce: Its Import for Early Christianity," *NTSt* 36 (1990): 1-24.

1435.13   Steve Mason, "Pharisaic Dominance before 70 CE and the Gospels' Hypocrisy Charge," *HTR* 83 (1990): 363-81.

1435.14   Urban C. von Wahlde, "The Relationships between Pharisees and Chief Priests: Some Observations on the Texts in Matthew, John and Josephus," *NTSt* 42 (1996): 506-22.

b. *The Essenes, the Zealots, and the Herodians*

1436.   A. Hilgenfeld, "Der Essäismus und Jesus," *ZWT* 10 (1867): 97-111.

1437.   A. Réville, "Jésus et l'Essénisme," *RT* 5 (1867): 221-45.

1438.   B. Pick, "Christ and the Essenes," *LQ* 18 (1888): 217-45.

1439.   H. Maldwyn Hughes, "Anti-Zealotism in the Gospels," *ET* 27 (1915-1916): 151-54.

1440.   L. Cerfaux, "Le baptême des Esséniens," *RSR* 19 (1929): 248-65.

1441.   E. Biker Mann, "Les Hérodiens," *RB* 47 (1938): 184-97.

1442.   Paul Joüon, "Les 'Hérodiens' de l'Evangile (Marc III, 6; XII 13 Matthieu XXII, 14)," *RSR* 28 (1938): 585-88.

1443.   H. Rowley, "The Herodians in the Gospels," *JTS* 41 (1940): 14-29.

See also numbers 1427, 2326, 3225, 4776, 5118.

1443.1   C. Daniel, "Les Esséniens et 'Ceux qui sont dans les maisons des rois'," *RQu* 6 (1967): 261-77.

1443.2   C. Daniel, "Les 'Herodiens' du Nouveau Testament sont-ils des Esseniens?" *RQu* 6 (1967): 31-53.

1443.3   C. Daniel, "Esseniens et Eunuques (Matthieu 19,10-12)," *RQu* 6 (1968): 353-90.

1443.4   C. Daniel, "Les Esséniens et l'arrière-fond historique de la parabole du Bon Samaritain," *NT* 11 (1969): 71-104.

1443.5   C. Daniel, " 'Faux Prophete': Surnom des Esseniens dans le Sermon sur la Montagne," *RQu* 7/25 (1969): 45-79.

1443.6   W. A. Λ. Wilson, "Who Married Herodias? (And Other Questions from the Gospel of Mark)," *BTr* 21/3 (1970): 138-40.

1443.7   S. G. F. Brandon, "Jesus and the Zealots: Aftermath," *BJRL* 54 (1971-1972): 47-66.

1443.8   Oscar Cullmann, "Courants multiples dans la communauté primitive: à propos du martyre de Jacques fils ae Zébédée," *RSR* 60 (1972): 55-69.

1443.9   P. W. Barnett, " 'Under Tiberius All Was Quiet'," *NTSt* 21 (1975): 564-71.

1443.10   W. J. Bennett, "The Herodians of Mark's Gospel," *NT* 17/1 (1975): 9-14.

1443.11   J. M. Ford, "Zealotism and the Lukan Infancy Narratives," *NT* 18 (1976): 280-92.

1443.12   T. Gorringe, "A Zealot Option Rejected? Luke 12:13-14," *ET* 98 (1986-1987): 267-70.

1443.13   Émile Puech, "Un Hymne Essenien en Partie Retrouve et les Beatitudes: 1QH V 12-VI 18 (= Col. XIII-XIV 7) et 4QBeat," *RQu* 13/1 (1988): 59-88.

1443.14   W. Braun, "Were the New Testament Herodians Essenes? A Critique of an Hypothesis," *RQu* 14 (1989): 75-88.

6. Other Persons and Groups

1444.   H. Burton, "Christ and the Samaritans," *Exp* 1st ser., 6 (1877): 186-96.

1445.   M.-J. Ollivier, "Ponce Pilate et les Pontii," *RB* 5 (1896): 247-54, 394-600.

1446.   J. H. A. Hart, "The Scribes of the Nazarenes," *Exp* 7th ser., 3 (1907): 259-71.

1447.   A. R. Simpson, "Mary of Bethany; Mary of Magdala; and Anonyma," *Exp* , 7th ser., 8 (1909): 307-18.

1448.   Theodor Kluge, "Die apokryphe Erzählung des Joseph von Arimathäa über den Bau der ersten christlichen Kirche in Lydda," *OC* 11 Serie, 4 (1915): 24-38.

1449.   A. R. S. Kennedy, "The Samaritans," *ET* 31 (1919-1920): 374-75.

1450.   H. L. Oort, "Lazarus," *TT* 53 (1919): 1-5.

1451.   George Steven, "Nicodemus," *ET* 31 (1919-1920): 505-508.

1452.   A. T. Burbridge, "A Further Note on Simon the Crucifer," *ET* 35 (1923-1924): 186.

1453.   John R. Mackay, "The Other Mary," *ET* 40 (1928-1929): 319-21.

1454.   F. C. Burkitt, "Mary Magadlene and Mary, Sister of Martha," *ET* 42 (1930-1931): 157-59.

1455.   Clyo Jackson, "Joseph of Arimathea," *JR* 16 (1936): 332-40.

1456.   G. Ernest Wright, "Herod's Nabataean Neighbor," *BA* 1 (1938): 3-4.

1457.   J. A. Oñate, "María Magdalena, María de Betania y la pecadora del Evangélio...," *CB* 1 (1944): 215-18.

1458.   A. A. T. Ehrhardt, "Pontius Pilatus in der frühchristlichen Mythologie," *EvT* 9 (1949-1950): 433-47.

1459.   J. A. Oñate, "Noches de Jesús," *CB* 8 (1951): 137-42 [Nicodemus].

1460.   A. M. Micoud, "Les équipes d'Evangile," *BVC* no. 2 (1953): 100-105.

1461.   Alfred Marshall, "The Case of Mary Magdalene," *EQ* 28

1462.   Siegfried Mendner, "Nikodemus," *JBL* 77 (1958): 293-323.
             See also numbers 254, 545-584, 674, 1408.

1462.1   R. C. White, "Vindication for Zacchaeus," *ET* 91
             (1979-1980): 21.

1462.2   A. J. Kerr, "Zacchaeus's Decision to Make Fourfold
             Restitution," *ET* 98/3 (1986-1987): 68-71.

1462.3   J. F. Williams, "Discipleship and Minor Characters in Mark's
             Gospel," *BS* 153 (1996): 332-43.

CRITICAL STUDIES OF THE GOSPELS

A. TEXTUAL CRITICISM OF THE GOSPELS

1. The Materials of Textual Criticism

a. *Papyri and Ostraca*

1463.   G. Volkmar, "Der Wiener Evangelien-Papyrus," *STZ* 3 (1886): 40-42.

1464.   A. Knopf, "Eine Tonscherbe mit dem Texte des Vaterunsers," *ZNW* 2 (1901): 228-33.

1465.   A. Bludau, "Papyrusfragmente des neutestamentlichen Textes," *BibZ* 4 (1906): 25-38.

1466.   A. Bludau, "Griechische Evangelienfragmente auf Ostraka," *BibZ* 4 (1906): 386-97.

1467.   Hermann Müller, "Zu den neutestamentlichen Papyrus-fragmenten," *BibZ* 6 (1908): 25-29.

1468.   Edgar J. Goodspeed, "New Textual Materials from Oxyrhynchus," *BW* 33 (1909): 344-46.

1469.   Victor Martin, "Les papyrus du Nouveau Testament et l'histoire du texte," *RTP* N.S. 7 (1919): 43-72.

1470.   Henry A. Sanders, "An Early Papyrus Fragment of the Gospel of Matthew in the Michigan Collection," *HTR* 19 (1926): 215-26.

1471.   M.-J. Lagrange, "Un nouveau papyrus évangélique," *RB* 38 (1929): 161-77.

1472.   F. C. Burkitt, "The Chester Beatty Papyri," *JTS* 34 (1933): 363-68.

1473.   M.-J. Lagrange, "Un nouveau papyrus evangelic," *RB* 42 (1933): 402-404.

1474.   C. A. Phillips, "The Chester Beatty Biblical Papyri," *ET* 45 (1933-1934): 55-60.

1475.   Carl Schmidt, "Die Evangelienhandschrift der Chester Beatty-Sammlung," *ZNW* 32 (1933): 225-32.

1476.   Paul-Louis Couchoud, "Notes sur le texte de St. Marc dans le Codex Chester Beatty," *JTS* 35 (1934): 3-22.

1477. M.-J. Lagrange, "Les papyrus Chester Beatty pour les évangiles," *RB* 43 (1934): 5-41.

1478. Alexius Mallon, "De antiquissimo Evangeliorum manuscripto, *VD* 14 (1934): 20-22.

1479. E. R. Smothers, "Les Papyrus Beatty de la Bible Groucho," *RSR* 24 (1934): 12-34.

1480. W. Derouaux, "Litérature chrétienne antique et papyrologie," *NRT* 62 (1935): 810-43.

1481. Hans Lietzmann, "Neue Evangelienpapyri," *ZNW* 34 (1935): 285-93.

1482. R. V. G. Tasker, "The Readings of the Chester Beatty Papyrus in the Gospel of St. John," *JTS* 36 (1935): 387-91.

1483. L. Cerfaux, "Les récentes découvertes de texts évangéliques," *RSPT* 25 (1936): 331-41.

1484. Joachim Jeremias, "Das neugefundene Fragment des Johannesevangeliums (Pap. Ryl. Gk. 457)," *TB* 15 (1936): 97-99.

1485. Kirsopp and Silva Lake, "Some Recent Discoveries," *RL* 5 (1936): 89-102.

1486. C. H. Roberts, "An Unpublished Fragment of the Fourth Gospel in the John Rylands Library," *BJRL* 20 (1936): 45-55.

1487. H. C. Hoskier, "Some Study of P⁴⁵ with Special Reference to the Bezan Text," *BBC* 12 (1937): 51-57.

1488. R. V. G. Tasker, "The Chester Beatty Papyrus and the Ceasarean Text of John," *HTR* 30 (1937): 157-64.

1489. Jean Merell, "Nouveaux fragments du papyrus 4," *RQ* 47 (1938): 5-22.

1490. C. C. Tarelli, "Some Linguistic Aspects of the Chester Beatty Papyrus of the Gospels," *JTS* 39 (1938): 254-59.

1491. C. C. Tarelli, "The Chester Beatty Papyrus and the Caesarean Text," *JTS* 40 (1939): 46-55.

1492. C. C. Tarelli, "Omissions, Additions, and Conflations in the Chester Beatty Papyrus," *JTS* 40 (1939): 382-87.

1493.   C. C. McCown, "The Earliest Christian Books," *BA* 6 (1947): 21-31.

1494.   Bruce M. Metzger, "Recently Published Greek Papyri of the New Testament," *BA* 10 (1947): 25-44.

1495.   Georg Maldfeld and Bruce M. Metzger, "Detailed List of the Greek Papyri of the New Testament," *JBL* 68 (1949): 359-70.

1496.   Floyd V. Filson, "Nessana," *BA* 15 (1952): 47-48 [P^{59} and P^{60}].

1497.   Colin Roberts, "An Early Papyrus of the First Gospel," *HTR* 46 (1953): 233-38 [P^{64}].

1498.   Kurt Aland, "Neue neutestamentliche Papyri," *NTSt* 3 (1956-1957): 261-86.

1499.   V. Martin, "Un nouveau codex de papyrus du IVe Evangile," *ETL* 32 (1956): 547-48.

1500.   C. K. Barrett, "Papyrus Bodmer II: A Preliminary Report," *ET* 68 (1956-1957): 174-77.

1501.   A. F. J. Klijn, "Papyrus Bodmer II (John I-XIV) and the Text of Egypt," *NTSt* 3 (1956-1957): 327-33.

1502.   M.-E. Boismard, "Le papyrus Bodmer II," *RB* 64 (1957): 363-98.

1503.   Floyd V. Filson, "A New Papyrus Manuscript of the Gospel of John," *BA* 20 (1957): 54-63.

1504.   J. Ramsey Michaels, "Some Notable Readings of Papyrus Bodmer II," *BTr* 8 (1957): 150-54.

1505.   Martin H. Scharlemann, "Papyrus Sixty-Six," *CTM* 28 (1957): 573-78.

1506.   Edgar R. Smothers, "Papyrus Bodmer II: An Early Codex of St. John," *ThSt* (1957): 434-41.

1507.   François Lasserre, "Un nouveau manuscript de l'évangele de Jean," *RTP* sér. 3, 7 (1957): 45-57 [Bodmer Pap. II].

1508.   Bernard Botte, "Le texte du quatrième évangile et le Papyrus Bodmer II," *BVC* no. 24 (1958): 96-107.

1509.   G. Danesi, "Il paù antico codice del Vangelo di Giovanni. Il papiro Bodmer II recentemente scoperto," *RivB* 6 (1958): 295-322.

1510.   E. Massaux, "Quelques variants importantes de P. Bodmer III et leur accointance avec la Gnose," *NTSt* 5 (1958-1959): 210-12.

1511.   Edgar R. Smothers, "Two Readings in Papyrus Bodmer II," *HTR* 5 (1958): 109-22.

1512.   J. Harold Greenlee, "A Misinterpreted Nomen Sacrum in P^9," *HTR* 5 (1958): 187.

1513.   H. Zimmermann, "Papyrus Bodmer II und seine Bedeutung für die Textgeschichte des Johannes- Evangeliums," *BibZ* 2 (1958): 214-43.

1514.   R. Schippers, "De rest van P^{66}," *GTT* 59 (1959): 81-85.

1515.   Serafin de Ausejo, "El papiro Bodmer II y la exégesis del IV Evangelio," *EE* 34 (1960): 907-28.

1516.   M. A. King and R. Patterson, "Textual Studies in the Bodmer Manuscript of John," *BS* 117 (1960): 164-71, 258-66.

1517.   Ernst Bammel, "Ein neuer Vater-Unser-Text," *ZNW* 52 (1961): 280-81 [a third century papyrus].

1518.   Ernst Bammel, "A New Text of the Lord's Prayer," *ET* 73 (1961-1962): 54.

1519.   Bruce M. Metzger, "The Bodmer Papyrus of Luke and John," *ET* 73 (1961-1962): 201-203.

See also numbers 1892, 6064, 6067, 6455, 10079.

1519.1   Calvin L. Porter, "PBodmer XV [P^{75}] and the Text of Codex Vaticanus," *JBL* 81 (1962): 363-76.

1519.2   Kurt Aland, "Neue Neutestamentliche Papyri," *NTSt* 9 (1962-1963): 303-16; 10 (1963-1964): 62-79; 11 (1964-1965): 1-21; 12 (1965-1966): 193-210.

1519.3   R. V. G. Tasker, "The Chester Beatty Papyrus and the Caesarean Text of John," *HTR* 30 (1967): 157-64.

1519.4   E. F. Rhodes, "The Corrections of Papyrus Bodmer II," *NTSt* 14 (1967-1968): 271-81.

1519.5   J. B. Bauer, "Zur Datierung des Papyrus Bodmer II (p^{66}),"

BibZ 12 (1968): 121-22.

1519.6   J. K. Elliott, "The Text and Language of the Endings to Mark's Gospel," *TZ* 27 (1971): 255-62.

1519.7   José O'Callaghan, "Posible identificación de P44 C *recto* b como Mc 4,22-24," *B* 52 (1971): 398-400.

1519.8   C. Schedl, "Zur Schreibung von Johannes i.10a in Papyrus Bodmer XV," *NT* 14 (1972): 238-40.

1519.9   Kurt Aland, "Neue neutestamentliche Papyri? Ein Nachwort zu den angeblichen Entdeckungen von Professor O'Callaghan," *BK* 28 (1973): 19-20.

1519.10   Ernst Bammel, "P^{64} (67) and the Last Supper," *JTS* 24/1 (1973): 189.

1519.11   Chan-Hie Kim, "The Papyrus Invitation," *JBL* 94/3 (1975): 391-402.

1519.12   S. A. Edward, "P 75 under the Magnifying Glass," *NT* 18 (1976): 190-212.

1519.13   E. L. Miller, "P66 and P75 on John 1:3-4," *TZ* 41 (1985): 440-43.

1519.14   Mikeal C. Parsons, "A Christological Tendency in P75," *JBL* 105/3 (1986): 463-79.

1519.15   G. Aranda Pérez, "La versiónn sahídica de San Mateo en Bodmer XIX y Morgan 569," *EB* 46 (1988): 217-30.

1519.16   John W. Pryor, "Papyrus Egerton 2 and the Fourth Gospel," *ABR* 37 (1989): 1-13.

1519.17   Peter M. Head, "Observations on Early Papyri of the Synoptic Gospels, especially on the 'Scribal Habits'," *B* 71/2 (1990): 240-47.

   b. *Uncials*

     (1). Uncials in General

1520.   Ph. Buttmann, "Kritische Beobachtungen über den Text des codex Vaticanus B. Nr. 1209. und seine Geltung bei Feststellung des neutestamentlichen Textes überhaupt," *TSK* 33 (1860): 341-82.

1521.   T. K. Abbott, "On an Uncial Palimpsest Evangelistarium,"

Herm 5 (1885): 146-50 (with a Plate) [Greg. 0133].

1522.   Caspar René Gregory, "Der Kodex N der Evangelien," *TLZ* 21 (1896): 393-94.

1523.   Kirsopp Lake, "On the text of Codex Ψ in St. Mark," *JTS* 1 (1899-1900): 290-92.

1524.   Eb. Nestle, "John viii. 57 in the Codex Vaticanus," *ET* 12 (1900-1901): 480.

1525.   Agnes Smith Lewis, "John viii. 57 in the Codex Vaticanus," *ET* 12 (1900-1901): 524-25.

1526.   V. Scheil, "Archéologie," *RB* 1 (1892): 113-17 [Greek uncial fragments of Lk. 5 and 1:74 ff.].

1527.   Eb. Nestle, "Zum Codex Purpureus Petropolitanus (N)," *ZWT* 42 (1899): 621-23.

1528.   W. C. Braithwaite, "A New Uncial of the Gospels," *ET* 12 (1900-1901): 114-17.

1529.   Erwin Preuschen, "Codex aureo-purpureus Parisinus," *ZNW* 1 (1900): 264-65.

1530.   Erwin Preuschen, "Die neue Pariser Evangelienhandschrift," *ZNW* 3 (1902): 253-56.

1531.   H. S. Cronin, "An Examination of Some Omissions of the Codex Sinaiticus in St. John's Gospel," *JTS* 13 (1911-1912): 563-71.

1532.   Kirsopp Lake and R. P. Blake, "The Text of the Gospels and the Koridethi Codex," *HTR*, 16 (1923): 267-86.

1533.   M.-J. Lagrange, "Le manuscrit sinaïtique," *RB* 35 (1926): 89-97.

1534.   A. H. Salonius, "Die griechischen Handschriftenfragmente des Neuen Testaments in den Staatlichen Museen zu Berlin," *ZNW* 26 (1927): 97-109.

1535.   W. H. P. Hatch, "An Uncial Fragment of the Gospels," *HTR* 23 (1930): 149-52.

1536.   A. Vaccari, "Codicis evangeliorum purpurei N folium iterum repertum," *B* 12 (1931): 483-84.

1537.   P. E. Kretzmann, "The Koridethi Manuscript and the Latest

Discoveries in Egypt," *CTM* 3 (1932): 574-78.

1538. C. A. Phillips, "The Codex Sinaiticus and the Codex Alexandrinus," *ET* 51 (1939-1940): 299-301.

1539. William Duff McHardy, "Matthew xxv.37-xxvi.3 in 074," *JTS* 46 (1945): 190-91.

1540. Stanley Rypins, "Two Inedited Leaves of Codex N," *JBL* 75 (1956): 27-39.

1541. R. W. Lyon, "A Re-examination of Codex Ephraemi Rescriptus," *NTSt* 5 (1958-1959): 260-72.

1542. Kurt Treu, "Zur vermeintlichen Kontraktion von ἱεροσόλυμα in O188, Berlin P. 13416," *ZNW* 52 (1961): 278-80.

See also numbers 1943, 1946.

1542.1 Gordon D. Fee, "Codex Sinaiticus in the Gospel of John: A Contribution to Methodology in Establishing Textual Relationships," *NTSt* 15 (1968-1969): 23-44.

1542.2 I. A. Sparks, "A New Uncial Fragment of St. Matthew," *JBL* 88 (1969): 201-202.

1542.3 J. M. Plumley and C. H. Roberts, "An Uncial Text of St. Mark in Greek from Nubia," *JTS* 27 (1976): 34-45.

1542.4 Michael McCormick, "Two Leaves from the Lost Uncial Codex 0167: Mark 4:24-29 and 4:37-41," *ZNW* 70/3-4 (1979): 238-42.

1542.5 George Howard, "A Note on Codex Sinaiticus and Shem-Tob's Hebrew Matthew," *NTSt* 38 (1992): 187-204.

(2). Codex Bezae (D)

1543. Eb. Nestle, "Some Observations on the Codex Bezae," *Exp* 5th ser., 2 (1895): 235-40.

1544. Eb. Nestle, "Another Peculiarity of Codex Bezae," *ET* 9 (1897-1898): 140 [Iscariot].

1545. F. H. Chase, "The Name Iscariot in Codex Bezae," *ET* 9 (1897-1898): 189.

1546. Ferdinand Graefe, "Der Codex Bezae und das Lukas-evangelium," *TSK* 21 (1898): 116-40.

1547.   Ed. König, "The Origin of Ζαφθανεί in Cod. D of Matt. xxvii.46 and Mark xv.34," *ET* 11 (1899-1900): 237-38.

1548.   Eb. Nestle, "On Mark xv.34 in Codex D," *ET* 11 (1899-1900): 334-36.

1549.   Eb. Nestle, "The Reading of Codex D and its Allies in Matt. xxvii.46 and Mark xv.34," *ET* 11 (1899-1900): 287-88.

1550.   Dom J. Chapman, "The Order of the Gospels in the Parent of Codex Bezae," *ZNW* 6 (1905): 339-46.

1551.   John Chapman, "The Original Contents of Codex Bezae," *Exp* 6th ser., 12 (1905): 46-53 [It contained the book of Revelation].

1552.   Henry Quentin, "Le Codex Bezae à Lyon au IXe siècle?" *RBén* 23 (1906): 1-25.

1553.   E. A. Lowe, "The Codex Bezae and Lyons," *JTS* 25 (1923-1924): 270-74.

1554.   Paul Gächter, "Codex D and Codex A," *JTS* 35 (1934): 248-66.

1555.   A. H. A. Bakker, "The Textual Relations of Codex Bezae in Matthew," *BBC* 12 (1937): 74-76.

1556.   A. J. Wensinck, "The Semitisms of Codex Bezae and their Relation to the non-Western Text of the Gospel of Luke," *BBC* 12 (1937): 11-48.

1557.   J. de Zwaan, "Codex D en Emmaus," *NedTT* 6 (1951-1952): 112.

1558.   Otto Stegmüller, "Zu den Bibelorakeln im Codez Bezae," *B* 34 (1953): 13-22.

1559.   Paul Glaue, "Einige Stellen, die die Bedeutung des Codex D charakterisieren," *NT* 2 (1958): 310-15.

1560.   James D. Yoder, "The Language of the Greek Variants of Codex Bezae," *NT* 3 (1959): 241-48.

1560.1   S. Brock, "Note on Luke 9:16 [Codex Bezae Cantabrigiensis]," *JTS* 14 (1963): 391-93.

1560.2   I. A. Moir, "The Reading of Codex Bezae (D-05) at Mark 9:1," *NTSt* 20 (1973-1974): 105.

1560.3   E. L. Miller, "Codex Bezae on John i.3-4: One Dot or Two?"
           TZ 32 (1976): 269-71.

1560.4   Heinrich Greeven, "Nochmals Mk IX. 1 in Codex Bezae,"
           NTSt 23 (1977): 305-308.

1560.5   Ernst Bammel, "The Cambridge Pericope: The Addition to
           Luke 6:4 in Codex Bezae," *NTSt* 32/3 (1986): 404-26.

           (3). The Freer Gospels (W)

1561.   Edgar J. Goodspeed, "Exploration and Discovery: The Freer
           Gospels and Shenute of Atripe," *BW* 33 (1909): 201-206.

1562.   Edgar J. Goodspeed, "Notes on the Freer Gospels," *AJT* 13
           (1909): 597-603.

1563.   Edgar J. Goodspeed, "The Washington Manuscript of the
           Gospels," *AJT* 17 (1913): 240-49.

1564.   Edgar J. Goodspeed, "The Freer Gospels," *AJT* 17 (1913):
           395-416, 599-613; 18 (1914): 131-46, 266-81 [Collation
           with W-H text].

1565.   E. Jacquier, "Le manuscrit Washington des évangiles," *RB*
           22 (1913): 547-55.

1566.   B. H. Streeter, "The Washington MS and the Caesarean Text
           of the Gospels," *JTS* 27 (1925-1926): 144-47.

1567.   B. H. Streeter, "The Washington Manuscript of the Gospels,"
           HTR 19 (1926): 165-73.

1568.   C. S. C. Williams, "Syriasms in the Washington Text of
           Mark," *JTS* 42 (1941): 177-78.

1568.1   Klaus Haacker, "Bemerkungen zum Freer-Logion," *ZNW* 63
           (1972): 125-29.

1568.2   Günther Schwarz, "Zum Freer-Logion: ein Nachtrag," *ZNW*
           70 (1979): 119.

           c. *Minuscules*

1569.   W. H. Simcox, "Collation of the British Museum MS Evan.
           604 (for St. Luke)," *AJP* 5 (1884): 454-65.

1570.   Edgar J. Goodspeed, "A Twelfth Century Gospels
           Manuscript," *BW* 10 (1897): 277-80.

1571.   Edgar J. Goodspeed, "The Newberry Gospels," *AJT* 3 (1899): 116-37.

1572.   Edgar J. Goodspeed, "The Critical Value of the Newberry Gospels," *AJT* 5 (1901): 752-55.

1573.   Edgar J. Goodspeed, "The Haskell Gospels," *JBL* 21 (1902): 100-107.

1574   H. Gebhardt, "Untersuchungen zu der Evangelienhand-schrift 238," *ZNW* 7 (1906): 120-22.

1575.   Edgar J. Goodspeed, "The Harvard Gospels," *AJT* 10 (1906): 687-700 [Gregory 666].

1576.   Edgar J. Goodspeed, "The Toronto Gospels," *AJT* 15 (1911): 268-71 [ms. 2321]

1577.   Edgar J. Goodspeed, "The Text of the Toronto Gospels," *AJT* 15 (1911): 445-59.

1578   Henry A. Sanders, "A New Collation of MS 22 of the Gospels," *JBL* 33 (1914): 91-117.

1579.   R. P. Casey, "The 'Lost' Codex 106 of the Gospels," *HTR* 16 (1923): 394-96.

1580.   Ernst von Dobschütz, "The Notices Prefixed to Codex 773 of the Gospels," *HTR* 18 (1925): 280-84.

1581.   A. T. Robertson, "A Newly Discovered Tetra-Evangelion," *USR* 39 (1927-1928): 180-81 [MS 2358].

1582.   Donald W. Riddle, "The Rockefeller-McCormick Manuscript," *JBL* 48 (1929): 248-57.

1583.   Harold R. Willoughby, "The Reconstruction of Lost Rockefeller McCormick Miniatures," *JBL* 51 (1932): 253-62.

1584.   F. C. Burkitt, "The Rockefeller McCormick New Testament," *JTS* 34 (1933): 165-68.

1585.   Merrill M. Parvis, "The Janina Gospels and the Isle of Patmos," *CQ* 21 (1944): 30-40 [ms. 2409]

1586.   Joseph Reuss, "Die Evangelienkatenen in Cod. Athon. gr. Laura B 113," *ZNW* 42 (1949): 217-28.

1587.   K. W. Kim, "Codices 1582, 1739, and Origen," *JBL* 69 (1950): 167-75.

1588.   Joseph Reuss, "Die Evangelienkatenen im Cod. Archivio di
             S. Pietro Gr. B 59," *B* 35 (1954): 207-16.

1589.   J. Neville Birdsall, "The Missing Leaves of Codex 213 of the
             New Testament," *JTS* N.S., 9 (1958): 78-81.

             See also number 1943.

1589.1   H. J. de Jonge, "Manuscriptus Evangeliorum Antiquissimus
             of Daniel Heinsius," *NTS* 21 (1975): 286-94.

1589.2   William Reader, "Entdeckung von Fragmenten aus zwei
             zerstörten neutestamentlichen Minuskeln (338 und 612)," *B*
             61 (1980): 407-11.

1589.3   Alan D. Crown, "Samaritan Minuscule Palaeography," *BJRL*
             3 (1981): 330-68.

1589.4   Thomas C. Geer, "Codex 1739 in Acts and Its Relationship
             to Manuscripts 945 and 1891," *B* 69 (1988): 27-46.

d. *Lectionaries*

1590.   T. K. Abbott, "On a Fragment of an Uncial Lectionary,"
             Herm 5 (1885): 151-53.

1591.   Germain Morin, "Les notes liturgiques de l'évangéliaire de
             Burchard," *RBén* 10 (1893): 113-26.

1592.   Germain Morin, "Un nouveau type liturgique d'après le livre
             des Evangiles, Clm. 6224," *RBén* 10 (1893): 246-56.

1593.   G. Morin, "Le lectionnaire de l'Église de Paris au VIIe
             siècle," *RBén* 10 (1893): 438-41.

1594.   A. Wilmart, "Note sur les évangiles datés de Troyes N. 960,"
             RB 33 (1924): 391-96 [lect. 960].

1595.   E. C. Colwell, "Is there a Lectionary Text of the Gospels?"
             HTR 25 (1932): 73-84.

1596.   Allen Wikgren, "The Lectionary Text of the Pericope John 8
             1-11," *JBL* 53 (1934): 188-98.

1597.   C. C. Tarelli, "The Byzantine Text and the Lectionaries," *JTS*
             43 (1942): 181-83.

1598.   G. Zuntz, "The Byzantine Text and the Lectionaries: A
             Comment on Mr. Tarelli's Note," *JTS* 43 (1942): 183-84.

1599. Bruce M. Metzger, "A Treasure in the Seminary Library [Greek Gospel Lectionary 303]," *PSB* 36, no. 4 (March, 1943): 14-19.

1600. Heinrich Greeven, "Die Textgestalt der Evangelien-lektionare," *TLZ* 76 (1951): 513-22.

1601. Klaus Gamber, "Fragmente eines griechischen Perikopen-buches des 5. Jh. aus Ägypten," *OC* IV ser., 8 (1960): 75-87 [lect- 1043].

1601.1 Frederick W. Danker, "The Shape of Luke's Gospel in Lectionaries," *Interp* 30 (1976): 339-52.

e. *Versions*

(1). Ancient Versions in General

1602. H. J. Vogels, "Übersetzungsfarbe als Hilfsmittel zur Erforschung der neutestamentlichen Textgeschichte," *RBén* 40 (1928): 123-29.

1603. Gustave Bardy, "Simples remarques sur les ouvrages et les manuscrits bilingues," *RB* 52 (1944): 242-67.

1604. Bruce M. Metzger, "A Survey of Recent Research on the Ancient Versions of the New Testament," *NTSt* 2 (1955-1956): 1-16.

1605. A. F. J. Klijn, "The Value of the Versions for the Textual Criticism of the New Testament," *BTr* 9 (1958): 127-30.

(2). The Old Latin Versions

1606 J. R. Harris, "The 'Sortes Sanctorum' in the St. Germain Codex," *AJP* 9 (1888): 58-63.

1607. H. A. A. Kennedy, "The Old Latin Versions and Westcott-Hort's Theory of the Traditional Text of the New Testament," *ET* 10 (1898-1899): 187-88.

1608. F. C. Burkitt, "On St. Mark xv 34 in Cod. k," *JTS* 1 (1899-1900): 278-79.

1609. C. H. Turner, "Notes on the Old Latin Version of the Bible," *JTS* 2 (1900-1901): 600-10.

1610. F. C. Burkitt, "Further Notes on Codex k," *JTS* 5

(1903-1904): 100-107.

1611. C. H. Turner, "A Re-Collation of Codex k of the Old Latin Gospels (Turin G VII 15)," *JTS* 5 (1903-1904): 88-100.

1612. F. C. Burkitt, " 'Chief Priests' in the Latin Gospels," *JTS* 9 (1907-1908): 290-97.

1613. Eb. Nestle, " 'He said' in the Latin Gospels," *JTS* 12 (1910-1911): 607-608.

1614. D. De Bruyne, "Notes sur le manuscrit 6224 de Munich (MS *q* des évangiles)," *RBén* 28 (1911): 75-80.

1615. E. S. Buchanan, "A Sixth-Century Fragment of St. Mark," *JTS* 13 (1911-1912): 369-71 [Mk. 16:15-20].

1616. Eb. Nestle, "Von den lateinischen Übersetzern der Evangelien," *ZNW* 13 (1912): 88-90.

1617. H. J. White, "On the Reading of the Old Latin *Codex Veronensis* (h) in Luke i.34-38," *JTS* 15 (1913-1914): 600-602.

1618. H. J. Vogels, "Zur 'afrikanischen' Evangelien-übersetzung," *BibZ* 12 (1914): 251-68.

1619. H. J. Vogels, "Versuch einer Methode zur Erforschung der Geschichte der lateinischen Evangelien-übersetzung," *BibZ* 13 (1915): 322-33.

1620. H. J. Vogels, "Mk. 9, 15 in der Vetus Latina," *BibZ* 14 (1916-1917): 34-40.

1621. Chr. Wordsworth, "Extracts from a Gospel Lectionary (Old Latin) of the Spanish Church," *JTS* 18 (1916-1917): 169-76.

1622. H. J. Vogels, "Der Auferstehungsbericht bei Mk. 15, 47-16, 8 in altlateinischer Übersetzung," *TQ* 101 (1920): 365-85.

1623. A. Souter, "A Lost Leaf of Codex Palatinus (e) of the Old-Latin Gospels Recovered," *JTS* 23 (1921-1922): 284-86.

1624. E. A. Lowe, "On the African Origin of Codex Palatinus of the Gospels (*e*)," *JTS* 23 (1921-1922): 401-404.

1625. Benedikt Kraft, "Zwei unbekannte lateinische Evangelienhandschriften," *BibZ* 16 (1922-1924): 214-15.

1626. D. De Bruyne, "Deux feuillets d'un texte préhieronymien des évangiles," *RBén* 35 (1923): 62-80.

1627. A. Souter, "The Anonymous Latin Translation of Origen on St. Matthew (xxii. 34 to the end), and Old Latin MS *q* of the Gospels," *JTS* 35 (1934): 63-66.

1628. Pierre Minard, "Témoins inédits de la vieille version latine des évangiles. Les Canons à *Initia* des évangéliaires de Sainte-Croix de Poitiers et de la trinité de Vendôme," *RBén* 56 (1945-1946): 58-92.

1629. A. W. Adams, "The Old-Latin Version," *BTr* 5 (1954): 101-106.

See also numbers 5306, 6568.

1629.1 M. W. Anderson, "Erasmus the Exegete," *CTM* 40 (1969): 722-33.

1629.2 W. J. Gochee, "Latin Liturgical Text: A Product of Old Latin and Vulgate Textual Interaction," *CBQ* 35 (1973): 206-11.

1629.3 R. G. Bailey, "A Study of the Lukan Text of Manuscript 2533 of the Gospels," *NTSt* 23 (1977): 212-29.

1629.4 E. Lerle, "Die Ahnenverzeichnisse Jesu: Versuch einer christologischen Interpretation [Lk 3:23-38]," *ZNW* 72 (1981): 112-17.

1629.5 Alexander Globe, "The Dialogue of Timothy and Aquila as Witness to a Pre-Caesarean Text of the Gospels," *NTSt* 29 (1983): 233-46.

1629.6 J. K. Elliott, "Old Latin Manuscripts in Printed Editions of the Greek New Testament," *NT* 26 (1984): 225-48.

1629.7 David C. Parker, "The Translation of oun in the Old Latin Gospels," *NTSt* 31 (1985): 252-76.

1629.8 Christian Gnilka, "Eine Spur altlateinischer Bibelversion bei Prudentius," *VCh* 42 (1988): 147-55.

1629.9 J. C. Haelewyck, "Le cantique de la vigne. Histoire du texte vieux latin d'Is 5:1-7," *ETL* 65 (1989): 257-79.

1629.10 Gert Haendler, "Zur Arbeit an altlateinischen Bibelübersetzungen [Vetus Latina]," *TLZ* 114 (1989): 1-12.

1629.11 G. Quispel, "A Diatessaron Reading in a Latin Manichean

Codex," *VCh* 47 (1993): 374-78.

1629.12   D. Steen and T. Steiger, "Vetus Latina: Wurzel der abendlämdischen Kultur: Der archäologische Beitrag," *BK* 48 (1993): 226-29.

1629.13   P. Burton, "Fragmentum Vindobonense 563: Another Latin-Gothic Bilingual?" *JTS* 47 (1996): 141-56.

(3). The Latin Vulgate

1630.   P. Savi, "Le lectionnaire de Silos (Contribution à l'étude de l'histoire de la Vulgate en Espagne)," *RB* 2 (1893): 305-28.

1631.   J. H. Bernard, "The Vulgate of St. Mark," *Herm* 8 (1893): 122-26.

1632.   J. H. Bernard, "The Vulgate of St. Luke," *Herm* 8 (1893): 385-89.

1633.   J. H. Bernard, "The Vulgate of St. John," *Herm* 9 (1896): 181-90.

1634.   J. H. Bernard, "The Greek MSS. used by St. Jerome," *Herm* 11 (1901): 335-42.

1635.   Eb. Nestle, "The Gospels in the Latin Vulgate," *AJT* 11 (1907): 501-502.

1636.   Eb. Nestle, "John Mill on the Latin Gospels," *AJT* 13 (1909): 603-604.

1637.   G. Mallows Youngman, "Manuscripts of the Vulgate in the British Museum," *AJT* 14 (1910): 608-26.

1638.   A. Souter, "The Type or Types of Gospel Text Used by St. Jerome as the Basis of his Revision, with Special Reference to St. Luke's Gospel and Codex Vercellensis (*a*)," *JTS* 12 (1910-1911): 583-92.

1639.   E. S. Buchanan, "The Golden Gospels in Latin in the Library of Mr. J. Pierpont Morgan," *BS* 68 (1911): 416-28.

1640.   E. Mangenot, "Saint Jérôme réviseur du Nouveau Testament," *RB* 27 (1918): 244-53.

1641.   F. C. Burkitt, " 'Mémoire sur l'établissement du texte de la Vulgate,' by Dom Henri Quentin," *JTS* 24 (1922-1923): 406-14.

1642. John Chapman, "St. Jerome and the Vulgate New Testament," *JTS* 24 (1922-1923): 33-51, 113-25, 282-99.

1643. A. Royet, "Un manuscrit palimpseste de la Vulgate hiéronymienne des évangiles," *RB* 31 (1922): 518-51; 32 (1923): 39-58, 213-37, 372-82.

1644. E. A. Lowe, "On the date of the *Codex Toletanus*," *RBén* 35 (1923): 267-71.

1645. John Chapman, "The Codex Amiatanus and Cassiodorus," *RBén* 38 (1926): 139-50; 39 (1927): 12-32.

1646. H. J. Vogels, "Die Vorlage des Vulgatatextes der Evangelien," *RBén* 38 (1926): 123-38.

1647. Arthur Allgeier, "Die Psalmenzitate in der Vulgate des Neuen Testamentes," *RQ* 36 (1928): 21-42.

1648. A. Wilmart, "Débris d'un manuscrit des évangiles à Avranches et Léningrad," *RB* 38 (1929): 396-404 [12th century Latin Vulgate ms.].

1649. Bernhard Bischoff, "Zur Rekonstruktion des Sangallensis (Σ) und der Vorlage seiner Marginalien," *B* 22 (1941): 147-58.

1650. Alban Dold, "Neue Teile der ältesten Vulgata-Evangelien-handschrift aus dem 5. Jahrhundert," *B* 22 (1941): 105-46.

1651. Michael Metlen, "The Vulgate Gospels as a Translation," *CBQ* 8 (1946): 83-88, 230-35; 9 (1947): 106-10, 220-25.

1652. Lincoln Ramos, "A Vulgata e o Texto Primitivo dos Evangelhos," *REB* 16 (1956): 356-79.

1653. E. Massaux, "Deux fragments d'un manuscript oncial de la Vulgate (Lc., VI,48-VII,5, 11-13; Jo., XII,39-49; XIII,6-15)," *ETL* 37 (1961): 112-17.

1653.1 B. Fischer, "Codex Amiatinus und Cassiodor," *BibZ* NS 6 (1962): 57-79.

1653.2 Erdmann Schott, "Lex paedagogus noster fuit in Christo Jesu (Vulgata): zu Luthers Auslegung von Gal 3:24," *TZL* 95 (1970): 561-70.

1653.3 T. Stramare, "La neo-Volgata: impresa scientifica e pastorale insieme," *EB* NS 38 (1979-1980): 115-38.

1653.4   Klaus W. Müller, "Apechei (Mk 14:41): absurda lectio," *ZNW* 77 (1986): 83-100.

1653.5   David C. Parker, "A Copy of the Codex Mediolanensis," *JTS* NS 41 (1990): 537-41.

1653.6   C. P. Thiede, "The Magdalen Papyrus: A Reply," *ET* 107 (1996): 240-41.

1653.7   C. B. Tkacze, "Labor Tam Utilis: The Creation of the Vulgate," *VCh* 50 (1996): 42-72.

(4). The Syriac Versions (exclusive of Tatian)

1654.   Margaret D. Gibson, "The Palestinian Syriac Lectionary of the Gospels," *ET* 11 (1899-1900): 95.

1655.   F. C. Burkitt, "On the Gospel PHMATA Found in Syriac MSS," *JTS* 2 (1900-1901): 429-32.

1656.   Albert Bonus, " 'Our Lord' in the Lewis Palimpsest," *ET* 13 (1901-1902): 236-38, 334-35.

1657.   J. Rendel Harris, " 'Our Lord' in the Lewis Palimpsest," *ET* 13 (1901-1902): 283-84.

1658.   Agnes Smith Lewis, "What have we Gained in the Sinaitic Palimpsest?" *ET* 12 (1900-1901): 56-62, 206-209, 268-71, 359-61, 417-20, 518-20, 550-51.

1659.   Agnes Smith Lewis, "A Leaf Stolen from the Sinai Palimpsest," *ET* 13 (1901-1902): 405-406.

1660.   Chr. A. Bugge, "Om 'den sinaitiske Syrer'," *NTT* 4 (1903): 51-75.

1661.   Agnes Smith Lewis, "On the Antiquity of the Syro-Antiochene or Sinai Palimpsest," *USR* 15 (1903-1904): 359-63.

1662.   Hugo Gressmann, "Das syrische Tetraevangelium," *TR* 7 (1904): 443-52.

1663.   Hugo Gressmann, "Studien zum syrischen Tetraevangelium," *ZNW* 5 (1904): 248-52; 6 (1905): 135-52.

1664.   Edgar J. Goodspeed, "A Part of the Gospel of Matthew from the Beirut Syriac Codex," *JBL* 25 (1906) 58-81.

1665. L. Delaporte, "L'évangéliaire hérculéen de Homs," *RB* 16 (1907): 254-58.

1666. Agnes Smith Lewis, "The Sinaitic Syriac Gospels," *ET* 22 (1919-1911): 477-78.

1667. H. J. Vogels, "Drei parallele Varianten im altsyrischen Evangelium," *BibZ* 9 (1911): 263-65.

1668. Walter Bauer, "Die Bedeutung der alten syrischen Evangelienübersetzung," *ZWT* 54 (1912): 329-66.

1669. Fr. Herklotz, "Zur altsyrischen Evangelienübersetzung," *BibZ* 10 (1912): 132.

1670. A. Mingana, "Lewisian and Curctonian Versions of the Gospels," *ET* 25 (1913-1914): 475-77, 524-25; 26 (1914-1915): 47-48, 93-94, 235-36.

1671. A. Mingana, "The Remaining Syriac Versions of the Gospels," *ET* 26 (1914-1915): 379-81.

1672. Felix Haase, "Zur ältesten syrischen Evangelienübersetzung," *TQ* 101 (1920): 262-72.

1673. M.-J. Lagrange, "L'ancienne version syriaque des évangiles," *RB* 29 (1920): 321-52; 30 (1921): 11-14.

1674. J. Mathew, "Divergences between the Peshitta and the Sinai Syriac Accounts of Jesus' Reception of the Children," *ET* 33 (1921-1922): 331-32.

1675. E. E. Baldwin, "Divergences between the Peshitta and the Sinai Syriac Accounts of Jesus' Reception of the Children," *ET* 34 (1922-1923): 281-82.

1676. M.-J. Lagrange, "L'origine de la version Syro-Palestinienne des évangiles," *RB*, 34 (1925): 481-504.

1677. Arthur Allgeier, "Cod. Phillipps 1388 in Berlin und seine Bedeutung für die Geschichte der Pešitta," *OC* III. Serie, 7 (1932): 1-15.

1678. A. Rücker, "Die Zitate aus dem Matthäusevangelium im syrischen 'Buche der Stufen'," *BibZ* 20 (1932): 342-54.

1679. Curt Peters, "Die Zitate aus dem Matthäus-Evangelium in

der syrischen Übersetzung der Theophanie des Eusebius,"
OC III. Serie, 11 (1936): 1-25.

1680.   W. H. P. Hatch, "The Subscription in the Chester Beatty
Manuscript of the Harclean Gospels," *HTR* 30 (1937): 141-
56.

1681.   N. Pigoulewski, "Manuscripts syriaques bibliques de
Léningrad," *RB* 46 (1937): 83-92, 392-400, 556-62; 47
(1938): 83-88, 214-26.

1682.   Hope B. Downs, "The Peshitto as a Revision: Its Background
in Syriac and Greek Texts of Mark," *JBL* 63 (1944): 141-59.

1683.   William Duff McHardy, "Disputed Readings in the Syriac
Sinaitic Palimpsest," *JTS* 45 (1944): 170-74.

1684.   W. H. P. Hatch, "To What Syriac Version or Versions of the
Gospels did Thomas of Harqel Refer in his Margin?" *JBL* 65
(1946): 371-76.

1685.   William Duff McHardy, "Sigla for the Syriac Versions of the
New Testament," *JTS*, 47 (1946): 177-79.

1686.   William Duff McHardy, "The Text of Matthew and Mark in
White's *Versio Syriaca Philoxeniana* and in the New College
MS. 333," *JTS* 49 (1948): 175-78.

1687.   G. Zuntz, "Études Harkléenes," *RB* 57 (1950): 550-82.

1688.   A. Vööbus, "Neuentdecktes Textmaterial zur Vetus Syra,"
TZ 7 (1951): 30-38.

1689.   J. de Zwaan, "Harklean Gleanings from Mingana's
Catalogue," *NT* 2 (1958): 174-84.

1690.   A. F. J. Klijn, "Die Wörter 'Stein' und 'Felsen' in der
syrischen Übersetzung des Neuen Testaments," *ZNW* 50
(1959): 99-105.

1691.   R. Köbert, "Lc I,28.42 in den syrischen Evangelien," *B* 42
(1961): 229-30.

         See also numbers 6079, 6082.

1691.1   R. Köbert, "Lc 1:28, 42 in den Syrischen Evangelien," *B* 42
(1961): 229-30.

1691.2   R. Köbert, "Sabrâ tabâ im syrischen Tatian Luc 2:14," *B* 42

(1961): 90-91.

1691.3 A. Baker, "Fasting to the World," *JBL* 84 (1965): 291-94.

1691.4 Joseph Molitor, "Sozo und soteria in syrisch-georgischer Evangelienübersetzung," *BibZ* NS 11 (1967): 258-65.

1691.5 Daniel Sperber, "Mark 12:42 and Its Metrological Background: A Study in Ancient Syriac Versions," *NT* 9 (1967): 178-90.

1691.6 E. M. Yamauchi, "Greek, Hebrew, Aramaic, or Syriac? A Critique of the Claims of G. M.Lansa for the Syriac Peshitta," *BS* 131 (1974): 320-31.

1691.7 R. Köbert, "Zur Hs Vat Syr 268," *B* 56 (1975): 247-50.

1691.8 Bruce D. Chilton, "Amen: An Approach through Syriac Gospels," *ZNW* 69 (1978): 203-11.

1691.9 James Lagrand, "How Was the Virgin Mary 'Like a Man': A Note on Matthew 1:18b and Related Syriac Christian Texts," *NT* 22 (1980): 97-107.

1691.10 Stephen Gero, "The Gates or the Bars of Hades: A Aote on Matthew 16:18," *NTSt* 27 (1981): 411-14.

1691.11 S. P. Brock, "Passover, Annunciation and Epiclesis: Some Remarks on the Term Aggen in the Syriac Versions of Luke 1:35," *NT* 24 (1982): 222-33.

1691.12 Randall Buth, "Hebrew Poetic Tenses and the Magnificat," *JSNT* 21 (1984): 67-83.

1691.13 Rykle Borger, "Das Comma Johanneum in der Peschitta," *NT* 29 (1987): 280-84.

1691.14 Daniel L. McConaughy, "A Recently Discovered Folio of the Old Syriac (Sy) Text of Luke 16:13-17:1," *B* 68 (1987): 85-88.

1691.15 G. C. van de Kamp, "Sporen van pneuma-christologie in de vroege Syrische traditie," *NTT* 42 (1988): 208-19.

1691.16 Jan Joosten, "The Text of Matthew 13:21a and Parallels in the Syriac Tradition," *NTSt* 37 (1991): 153-59.

1691.17 Jesús Luzárraga, "Las versiones siríacas del Magníficat," *EB* 50 (1992): 103-22.

1691.18   F. J. Martínez-Fernández, "Un canto arameo a la encarnación
           del Hijo de Dios: San Efrén el Sirio, himno De Nativitate III,"
           EB 50 (1992): 475-91.

           (5). Tatian's Diatessaron and its Influence

1692.   H. Wace, "Tatian's Diatessaron," *Exp* 2nd ser., 2 (1881):
           1-11 128-37, 193-205.

1693.   H. Wace, "Professor Zahn on Tatian's Diatessaron," *Exp* 2nd
           ser., 4 (1882): 161-71, 294-312.

1694.   Isaac H. Hall, "A Pair of Citations from the Diatessaron,"
           JBL 10 (1891, part 2): 153-55 [Mt. 3:5].

1695.   R. J. H. Gottheil, "Quotations from the Diatessaron," *JBL* 11
           (1892): 68-71.

1696.   B. W. Bacon, "Tatian's Rearrangement of the Fourth
           Gospel," *AJT* 4 (1900): 770-95.

1697.   George A. Barton and Hans H. Spoer, "Traces of the
           Diatessaron of Tatian in Harclean Syriac Lectionaries," *JBL*
           24 (1905): 179-95.

1698.   R. H. Connolly, "The Diatessaron in the Syriac Acts of John,"
           JTS 8 (1906-1907): 571-81.

1699.   F. C. Burkitt, "Tatian's Diatessaron and the Dutch
           Harmonies," *JTS* 25 (1923-1924): 113-30.

1700.   R. H. Connolly, "Jacob of Serug and the Diatessaron," *JTS* 8
           (1906-1907): 581-90.

1701.   F. C. Conybeare, "An Armenian Diatessaron?" *JTS* 25
           (1923-1924): 232-45.

1702.   F. C. Conybeare, "John XVii.23-24 [according to Marutha],"
           HTR 17 (1924): 188-89 [δέδωκα αὐτοῖς]

1703.   F. C. Burkitt, "St. Luke ix.54-56 and the Western
           'Diatessaron'," *JTS* 28 (1926-1927): 48-53.

1704.   H. J.. Vogels, "Lk. 8,8 im Diatessaron," *BibZ* 18 (1929):
           83-84.

1705.   A. Vaccari, "Propaggini del Diatessaron in Occidente," *B* 12
           (1931): 326-54.

1706.   Anton Baumstark, "Zur Geschichte des Tatiantextes vor Aphrem," *OC* III. Serie, 8 (1933): 1-12 [Mk. 14:25].

1707.   Anton Baumstark, "Das griechische 'Diatessaron'-Fragment von Dura-Europos," *OC* III. Serie, 10 (1935): 244-52.

1708.   A. Baumstark, "Die syrische Übersetzung des Titus von Bostra und das 'Diatessaron'," *B* 16 (1935): 257-99.

1709.   F. C. Burkitt, "The Dura Fragment of Tatian," *JTS* 36 (1935): 255-59.

1710.   W. Heffening und Curt Peters, "Spuren des Diatessaron in liturgischer Überlieferung," *OC* III. Serie, 10 (1935): 225-38 [Matt. 19:3-11].

1711.   M. J. Lagrange, "Deux nouveaux texts relatifs à l'évangile," *RB* 44 (1935): 321-43.

1712.   Anton Baumstark, "Die himmelgartener Bruchstücke eines niederdeutschen 'Diatessaron'-Textes des 13. Jahrhunderts," *OC* III. Serie, 11 (1936): 80-96.

1713.   L. Cerfaux, "Un fragment du Diatessaron grec," *ETL* 13 (1936): 98-100.

1714.   A. Merk, "Ein griechisches Bruchstuck des Diatessaron Tatians," *B* 17 (1936): 234-41.

1715.   Anton Baumstark, "Die Schönbach'schen Bruchstücke einer Evangelienharmonie in bayrisch-österreichischer Mundart des 14. Jahrhunderts," *OC* III. Serie, 12 (1937): 103-18.

1716.   Paul Joüon, "La nouvelle édition du *Diatessaron* arabe de Tatien," *RSR* 27 (1937): 91-97.

1717.   Anton Baumstark, "Der Cambridger Text des mittelniederländischen *Leven van Jesus*," *OC* III Serie, 13 (1938): 108-22.

1718.   S. Lyonnet, "Vestiges d'un Diatessaron arménian," *B* 19 (1938): 121-50.

1719.   A. Merk, "Tatian in italienischem Gewande," *B* 20 (1939): 294-305.

1720.   Curt Peters, "Ein neues Fragment des griechischen Diatessaron?" *B* 21 (1940): 51-55.

1721.   C. Peters, "Zum Problem der Stilistik in Tatians Diatessaron," *OCP* 6 (1940): 508-17.

1722.   G. Messina, "Un Diatessaron Persiano del secolo XIII tradotto dal Siriaco," *B* 23 (1942): 268-305; 24 (1943): 59-106.

1723.   Curt Peters, "Der Diatessarontext von Mt. 2,9 und die westsächsische Evangelienversion," *B* 23 (1942): 323-32.

1724.   Curt Peters, "Neue Funde und Forschungen zum Diatessaronproblem," *B* 23 (1942): 68-77.

1725.   C. S. C. Williams, "Tatian and the Text of Mark and Matthew," *JTS* 43 (1942): 37-42.

1726.   P. R. Weis, "The Arabic Version of Tatian's Diatessaron," *JTS* 45 (1944): 187-205.

1727.   G. Messina, "Louisiana apocrife nel Diatessaron Persiano," *B* 30 (1949): 10-27.

1728.   Bruce M. Metzger, "Tatian's Diatessaron and a Persian Harmony of the Gospels," *JBL* 69 (1950): 261-80.

1729.   Louis Mariès, "Le Diatessaron à l'origine de la version arménienne," *RSR* 38 (1951-1952): 247-56.

1730.   A. J. B. Higgins, "The Persian Gospel Harmony as a Witness to Tatian's Diatessaron," *JTS* N.S., 3 (1952): 83-87.

1731.   Louis Leloir, "Le Diatessaron de Tatien," *OS* 1 (1956): 208-31, 313-34.

1732.   Louis Mariès, "Pour l'étude du Diatessaron," *RSR* 44 (1956): 228-33.

1733.   Louis Leloir, "L'original syriaque du commentaire de S. Ephrem sur le Diatessaron," *B* 40 (1959): 959-70.

1734.   I. Ortiz de Urbina, "Trama e carattere del Diatessaron di Taziano," *OCP* 25 (1959): 326-57.

1735.   Willy Krogmann, "Heliand, Tatian und Thomasevangeliun," *ZNW* 51 (1960): 255-68.

         See also numbers 1801, 1878, 1900, 2121-2127, 4150, 4151, 5480, 6920.

1735.1   Tjitze Baarda, "Syriac Fragment of Mar Ephraem's

Commentary on the Diatessaron," *NTSt* 8 (1962): 287-300.

1735.2   Hans Quecke, "Lk 1:34 im Diatessaron," *B* 45 (1964): 85-88.

1735.3   Aelred Baker, "Gospel of Thomas and the Diatessaron," *JTS* NS 16 (1965): 449-54.

1735.4   G. M. Lee, "Diatessaron and Diapente," *VCh* 21 (1967): 87.

1735.5   G. Quispel, "Some Remarks Diatessaron Haarense," *VCh* 25 (1971): 131-39.

1735.6   Edward A. Johnson, "The First Harmony of the Gospels: Tatian's Diatessaron and Its Theology," *JETS* 15 (1972): 227-38.

1735.7   R. van den Broek, "Jacob van Maerlant en het Nederlandse Diatessaron," *NTT* 28 (1974): 141-64.

1735.8   R. van den Broek, "Latin Diatessaron in the Vita Beate Virginis Marie et Salvatoris Rhythmica," *NTSt* 21 (1974): 109-32.

1735.9   Tjitze Baarda, "Archaic Element in the Arabic Diatessaron: Ta 46:18: John 15:2," *NT* 17 (1975): 151-55.

1735.10   J. Neville Birdsall, "Sources of the Pepysian Harmony and Its Links with the Diatessaron," *NTSt* 22 (1976): 215-23.

1735.11   Louis Leloir, "La version arménienne des actes apocryphes d'André, et le diatessaron," *NTSt* 22 (1976): 115-39.

1735.12   Daniel A. Bertrand, "L'Evangile des Ebionites: Une harmonie evangelique anterieure au Diatessaron," *NTSt* 26 (1980): 548-63.

1735.13   George Howard, "Harmonistic Readings in the Old Syriac Gospels," *HTR* 73 (1980): 473-91.

1735.14   William L. Petersen, "Romanos and the Diatessaron: Readings and Method," *NTSt* 29 (1983): 484-507.

1735.15   A. J. B. Higgins, "Luke 1-2 in Tatian's Diatessaron," *JBL* 103 (1984): 193-222.

1735.16   Tjitze Baarda, "Anoixas - Anaptyxas: Over de Vaststelling van de Tekst van Lukas 4,17 in het Diatessaron," *NedTT* 40/3 (1986): 199-208.

1735.17   Tjitze Baarda, "The Flying Jesus: Luke 4:29-30 in the Syriac

Diatessaron," *VCh* 40/4 (1986): 313-41.

1735.18   Tjitze Baarda, "To the Roots of the Syriac Diatessaron Tradition (TuA25:1-3)," *NT* 28 No 1 (1986): 1-25.

1735.19   Hildegard Must, "A Diatessaric Rendering in Luke 2:7," *NTSt* 32 No 1 (1986): 136-43.

1735.20   J. K. Elliott, "The Arabic Diatessaron in the New Oxford Edition of the Gospel According to St Luke in Greek: Additional Note [Lk 8:22]," *JTS* ns 38 (1987): 135.

1735.21   Louis Leloir, "Le commentaire d'Ephrem sur le Diatessaron: quarante et un folios retrouvés," *RB* 94 (1987): 481-518.

1735.22   Tjitze Baarda, "Geven als vreemdeling: over de herkomst van een merkwaardige variant van ms 713 in Mattheus 17:26," *NTT* 42 (1988): 99-113.

1735.23   William L. Petersen, "Textual Evidence of Tatian's Dependence upon Justin's apomnemoneumata," *NTSt* 36 (1990): 512-34.

1735.24   Jan Joosten, "West Aramaic Elements in the Old Syriac and Peshitta Gospels," *JBL* 110 (1991): 271-89.

1735.25   Tjitze Baarda, "John 1:5 in the Oration and Diatessaron of Tatian: Concerning the Reading Katalambanei," *VCh* 47 (1993): 209-25.

1735.26   Leslie McFall, "Tatian's Diatessaron: Mischievous or Misleading?" *WTJ* 56 (1994): 87-114.

1735.27   Tjitze Baarda, "John 8:57B. The Contribution of the Diatessaron of Tatian," *NT* 38 (1996): 336-43.

(6). The Coptic Versions

1736.   H. Hyvernat, "Étude sur les versions coptes de la Bible," *RB* 5 (1896): 427-33, 540-69; 6 (1897): 48-74.

1737.   W. E. Crum and F. G. Kenyon, "Two Chapters of St. John in Greek and Middle Egyptian," *JTS* 1 (1899-1900): 415-33 [John 3:5-4:49 in British Museum MS. Or. 5707].

1738.   Marius Chaîne, "Fragments sahidiques inédits du Nouveau Testament," *Bes* 8 (1905): 276-80.

1739.   J. David, "Fragments de l'évangile selon saint Matthieu en dialecte Moyen-Egyptien," *RB* 19 (1910): 80-92.

1740. Joseph Michael Heer, "Neue griechisch-saïdische Evangelienfragmente," *OC* II. Serie, 2 (1912): 1-47 [Mk. 16:2-20 and Lk. 24:1-12, 36].

1741. Ad. Hebbelynck, "Les manuscrits coptes-sahidiques du 'monastère blanc.' Recherches sur les fragments complémentaires de la collection Borgia. II. Les fragments des évangiles," *Mu* 31 (1912): 275-362.

1742. Joseph Michael Heer, "Zu den Freiburger griechisch-saïdischen Evangelienfragmenten," *OC* II. Serie, 3 (1913): 141-42.

1743. P. Meyer, "Neue griechisch-saïdische Evangelienfragmente," *TLZ* 38 (1913): 766.

1744. A. Vaschalde, "Ce qui a été publié des versions coptes de la Bible," *RB* 28 (1919): 220-43, 513-31; 29 (1920): 91-106, 241-58; 30 (1921): 237-46; 31 (1922): 81-88, 234-58.

1745. W. H. P. Hatch, "Six Coptic Fragments of the New Testament from Nitria," *HTR* 26 (1933): 99-108.

1746. Anton Baumstark, "Ein 'Evangelium'-Zitat der manichäischen Kephalaia," *OC* III. Serie, 12 (1938): 169-91.

1747. Walter Till, "Klein-koptische Bibelfragmente," *B* 20 (1939): 241-63, 361-86.

1748. L. Th. Lefort, "Fragments de S. Luc en Akhmîmique," *Mu* 62 (1949): 199-205.

1749. Ramón Roca-Puig, "Un pergamino copto en Barcelona. P. Barc. Inv. Num. 8. Lc. 9,29-32, 36-39, 42-45, 48-50," *EE* 34 (1960): 837-50.

    See also number 6726.

1749.1 R. Kasser, "Les dialectes coptes et les versions coptes bibliques," *B* 46 (1965): 287-310.

1749.2 P. Weigandt, "Zur Geschichte der koptischen Bibel-übersetzungen," *B* 50 (1969): 80-95.

1749.3 R. Kasser, "Réflexions sur quelques méthodes d'étude des versions coptes néotestamentaires," *B* 55 (1974): 233-56.

1749.4   R. Kasser, "Petites rectifications à propos de l'histoire des versions coptes de la Bible," *B* 61/4 (1980): 557-60.

1749.5   Hans Quecke, "Eine neue koptische Bibelhandschrift III," *OCP* 53/4 (1984): 462-63.

1749.6   W. P. Funk, "Zur Faksimileausgabe der koptischen Manichaica in der Chester-Beatty-Sammlung," *OCP* 59/4 (1990): 524-41.

1749.7   S. P. Brock, "A Palimpsest Folio of Matthew 20:23-31 (Peshitta) in Sinai Ar 514 ("Codex Arabicus")," *OCP* 61/2 (1992): 102-105.

(7). The Gothic Version

1750.   Ernst Müller, "Die Bedeutung der gotischen Bibelübersetzung für das Verständnis des griechischen Textes," *NKZ* 37 (1926): 210-17.

1751.   A. Wilmart, "Les évangiles gothiques," *RB* 36 (1927): 46-61.

1752.   G. W. S. Friedrichsen, "The Silver Ink of the Codex Argenteus," *JTS* 31 (1929-1930): 189-92.

1753.   C. C. Tarelli, "The Gothic Version and the Greek Text," *JTS* 40 (1939): 387-89.

1754.   Walter Henss, "Gotisches jah und -uh zwischen Partizipium und Verbum finitum. Zur Herleitung der gotischen und altlateinischen Version des Neuen Testaments," *ZNW* 48 (1957): 133-41.

1754.1   G. W. S. Friedrichsen, "Notes on the Gothic Bible," *NTSt* 9 (1962): 39-55.

1754.2   G. W. S. Friedrichsen, "The Gothic Text of Luke in Its Relation to the Codex Brixianus and the Codex Palatinus," *NTSt* 11 (1965): 281-90.

1754.3   J. B. Bauer, "Et adicietur vobis credentibus: Mk 4:24f," *ZNW* 71 (1980): 248-51.

(8). The Armenian Version

1755.   Louis Mariès, "Le texte Arménian de l'évangile d'après Matthieu et Marc," *RSR* 10 (1920): 28-54.

1756. Robert P. Blake, "Macler's Armenian Gospels," *HTR* 15 (1922): 299-303.

1757. Louis Mariès, "Le meilleur exemplaire de la version arménienne des évangiles," *RSR* 12 (1922): 69-72.

1758. N. Adonz, "Note sur les synaxaires arménians," *ROC* 24 (1923-1924): 211-18.

1759. A Merk, "Die Einheitlichkeit der armenischen Evangelien-übersetzung," *B* 4 (1923): 356-74.

1760. A. Merk, "Die armenischen Evangelien und ihre Vorlage," *B* 7 (1926): 70-72.

1761. R. P. Casey, "An Armenian Manuscript of the Gospels," *JTS* 30 (1928-1929): 356-61.

1762. R. P. Casey, "An Armenian Manuscript at Union Seminary," *JTS* 35 (1934): 188-89.

1763. S. Lyonnet, "La version arménienne des évangiles et son modèle grec," *RB* 43 (1934): 69-87.

1764. R. P. Casey, "An Early Armenian Fragment of Luke xvi. 3-25," *JTS* 36 (1935): 70-73.

1765. Allen Wikgren, "Armenian Gospel New Testament Manuscripts in the Kurdian Collection," *JBL* 55 (1936): 155-58; 59 (1940): 51-53; 64 (1945): 531-33; 72 (1953): 115-26.

1766. E. C. Colwell, "Mark 16.9-20 in the Armenian Version," *JBL* 56 (1937): 369-86.

1767. E. C. Colwell, "Slandered or Ignored: The Armenian Gospels," *JR* 17 (1937): 48-61.

1768. S. Lyonnet, "La première version arménienne des évangiles," *RB* 47 (1938): 355-82.

1769. C. S. C. Williams, "Syriasms in the Armenian Text of the Gospels," *JTS* 43 (1942): 161-67.

1770. A. Vööbus, "La première traduction arménienne des évangiles," *RSR* 37 (1950): 581-86.

See also number 9944

1770.1 Allen Wikgren, "New Armenian Manuscripts of the New

Testament in the Kurdian Collection," *JBL* 79 (1960): 52-56.

1770.2 Claude Cox, "Biblical Studies and the Armenian Bible, 1955-1980," *RB* 89 (1982): 99-113.

1770.3 Henning Lehmann, "Bygger det armeniske ny Testamente pa syrisk eller graesk Et forskninghistorisk rids," *DTT* 48 (1985): 25-50; 153-71.

1770.4 J. A. C. Greppin, "The Survival of Ancient Anatolian and Mesopotamian Vocabulary until the Present," *JNES* 50 (1991): 203-207.

(9). The Georgian Version

1771. Aurelio Palmieri, "Le versioni georgiane della Biblia," *Bes* 6 (1904): 72-77, 189-94.

1772. Theodor Kluge, "Mitteilung über mehrere neue Evangelien-handschriften aus den Klöstern der Kirchenprovinz Chaldin (Vilajet Tirabzon)," *ZNW* 13 (1912): 266-68.

1773. Gregor Peradse, "Die Probleme der georgischen Evangelienübersetzung," *ZNW* 29 (1930): 304-309.

1774. Joseph Molitor, "Die georgische Bibelübersetzung," *OC* IV. Serie 1 (1953): 23-29.

1775. Theodor Kluge, "Über zwei altgeorgische neutestamentliche Handschriften," *NT* 1 (1956): 304-21.

1776. Joseph Molitor, "Das Adysh-Tetraevangelium," *OC* IV. Serie, 1 (1953): 30-55; 2 (1954): 11-40; 3 (1955): 1-32; 4 (1956): 1-15; 5 (1957): 1-21; 6 (1958): 1-18; 7 (1959): 1-16; 8 (1960): 1-16; 9 (1961): 1-19.

1777. Joseph Molitor, "Evangelienzitate in einem altgeorgischen Väterfragment," *OC* IV. Serie, 4 (1956): 16-21.

1778. Joseph Molitor, "Chanmetifragmente—Ein Beitrag zur Textgeschichte der altgeorgischen Bibelübersetzung," *OC* IV. Serie 5 (1957): 22-34; 7 (1959): 17-23; 8 (1960): 17-24; 9 (1961): 115-26.

1779. Joseph Molitor, "Zur Harmonistik des altgeorgischen Evangelientextes," *BibZ* 1 (1957): 289-96.

1780. Joseph Molitor, "Mt. 15,3 in einer altgeorgischen Fassung,"

BibZ 1 (1957): 129-31.

1780.1   Joseph Molitor, "Die Bedeutung der altgeorgischen Bibel für die neutestamentliche Textkritik," *BibZ* NS 4 (1960): 39-53.

1780.2   J. Neville Birdsall, "Two Notes of New Testament Palaeography," *JTS* 26 (1975): 393-95.

1780.3   M. van Esbroeck, "Une homélie géorgienne anonyme sur la transfiguration," *OCP* 46 (1980): 418-45.

1780.4   D. Vateishvili, "The First Georgian Printed Bible," *EB* NS 41 (1983): 205-40.

1780.5   J. Neville Birdsall, "Georgian Studies and the New Testament," *NTSt* 29 (1983): 306-20.

1780.6   M. V. Songulashvili, "The Translation of the Bible into Georgian," *BTr* 41 (1990): 131-34.

(10). The Old Slavonic Version

1781.   Andrej Snoj, "Veteroslavicae versionis evangeliorum pro critica et exegesi sacri textus momentum," *B* 3 (1922): 180-87.

1782.   Louis Gillet, "Note sur les *nomina sacra* en paléoslave-ecclésiastique," *RBen* 35 (1923): 105-107.

1783.   Julius Hadžega, "Einige Bemerkungen zu dem Texte des Markusevangeliums im Evangelium von Wraca," *BibZ* 19 (1930-1931): 42-43.

1784.   R. P. Casey and Silva Lake, "A New Edition of the Old Slavic Gospels," *JBL* 55 (1936): 195-209.

1785.   Joseph Schweigl, "De textu recepto slavico Evangelii liturgici," *B* 24 (1943): 289-303.

1786.   Guiliano Bonfante and Bruce M. Metzger, "The Old Slavic Version of the Gospel according to Luke," *JBL* 73 (1954): 217-36.

1786.1   Christian Hannick, "The Old-Slavonic Version of the New Testament," *BTr* 25 (1974): 143-46.

(11). Other Versions (Arabic, Vaudois, Portuguese, English, etc.)

1787.   W. Sanday, "The Revised Version of the New Testament: III.

The Text," *Exp* 2nd ser., 2 (1881): 241-78 [Matthew], 372-98 [Mark, Luke, John], 401-18.

1788. C. Short, "The New Revision of King James' Revision of the New Testament," *AJP* 2 (1881): 149-80; 3 (1882): 139-69; 4 (1883): 253-82; 5 (1884): 417-53; 7 (1886): 283-309.

1789. T. S. Evans, "Critical Remarks on the Translation of the Revised Version," *Exp* 2nd ser., 3 (1882): 1-13, 144-51, 161-77.

1790. B. F. Westcott, "Some Lessons of the Revised Version of the New Testament," *Exp* 3rd ser., 5 (1887): 81-97, 241-58, 453-68; 6 (1887): 81-89, 241-57, 401-14.

1791. C. J. Gloucester and Bristol, "The Principle of the Revised Version," *Exp* 4th ser., 6 (1892): 401-18.

1792. A. C. Bouquet, "On some Early Protestant Documents preserved at Cambridge," *JTS* 19 (1918): 231-50 [Waldensian MSS: N.T. in Vaudois, sermons...].

1793. Anton Baumstark, "Markus Kap. 2 in der arabischen Übersetzung des Isaak Velasquez," *OC* III. Serie, 9 (1934): 226-39.

1794. Curt Peters, "Proben eines bedeutsamen arabischen Evangelientextes," *OC* III. Serie 11 (1936): 188-211.

1795. Curt Peters, "Der Text der soghdischen Evangelien-bruchstücke und das Problem der Pešitta," *OC* III. Serie 11 (1936): 153-62.

1796. Anton Baumstark, "Erbe christlicher Antike im Bildschmuck eines arabischen Evangelienbuches des 14. Jahrhunderts," *OC* III. Serie, 13 (1938): 1-38.

1797. W.C. Taylor, "The First Catholic Version of the Greek New Testament in Portuguese," *RE* 35 (1938): 54-61.

1798. Harold H. Hutson and Harold R. Willoughby, "The Ignored Taverner Bible of 1539," *CQ* 16 (1939): 161-76.

1799. Alan S. C. Ross, "On the 'Text' of the Anglo-Saxon Gloss to the Lindisfarne Gospels," *JTS* N.S., 9 (1958): 38-52.

1799.1 Robert P. Gordon, "Citation of the Targums in Recent

English Bible Translations (RSV, JB, NEB)," *JJS* 26 (1975): 50-60.

1799.2   Bruce M. Metzger, "Story behind the Making of the Revised Standard Version of the Bible," *PSB* NS 1 (1978): 189-200.

1799.3   Frank Stagg, "The New International Version: New Testament," *RE* 76 (1979): 377-85.

1799.4   Jan P. Sterk, "Key Structure Analysis, or, the Base and Model Approach Revisited," *BTr* 35 (1984): 112-22.

1799.5   Roger L. Omanson, "What do Those Parentheses Mean?" *BTr* 41 (1990): 205-14.

1799.6   Lamar Williamson, "Translations and Interpretation: New Testament," *Interp* 32 (1978): 158-70.

1799.7   G. R. Dunstan, "The Jerusalem Bible, English Version," *Th* 69 (1966): 529-30.

1799.8   Robert G. Bratcher, "The Nature and Purpose of the New Testament in Today's English Version," *BTr* 22 (1971): 97-107.

f. *Patristic Quotations*

1800.   J. Sickenberger, "Über griechische Evangelien-kommentare," *BibZ* 1 (1903): 182-93.

1801.   H. J. Vogels, "Der vim hl. Augustinus in der Schrift *De consensu evangelistarum* verwandte Evangelientext," *BibZ* 4 (1906): 267-95.

1802.   G. Morin, "Le commentaire inédit de l'évêque latin Epiphanius sur les évangiles," *RBén* 24 (1907): 336-59.

1803.   H. J. Vogels, "Die Lukaszitate bei Lucifer von Calaris," *TQ* 103 (1922): 23-27, 183-200.

1804.   F. C. Burkitt, "Dr. Sanday's New Testament of Irenaeus, with a Note on Valentinian Terms in Irenaeus and Tertullian," *JTS* 25 (1923-1924): 56-64.

1805.   H. J. Vogels, "Der Evangelientext des hl. Irenaeus," *RBén* 36 (1924): 21-23.

1806.   E. F. Sutcliffe, "Quotations in the Ven. Bede's Commentary on S. Mark," *B* 7 (1926): 428-39.

1807.   Robert Devreesse, "Notes sur les chaînes grecques de saint Jean," *RB* 36 (1927): 192-215.

1808.   C. H. Turner, "Prolegomena to the *Testimonia* and *Ad Fortunatum* of St. Cyprian," *JTS* 29 (1927-1928): 113-36.

1809.   Jacob Geerlings and S. New, "Chrysostom's Text of the Gospel of Mark," *HTR* 24 (1931): 121-42.

1810.   D. De Bruyne, "Les citations bibliques dans le *De civitate dei*," *RB* 42 (1933): 550-60.

1811.   Marcel Richard, "Les citations de Théodoret conservées dans la chaîne de Nicétas sur l'évangile selon saint Luc," *RB* 43 (1934): 88-96.

1812.   R. V. G. Tasker, "The Quotations from the Synoptic Gospels in Origen's *Exhortation to Martyrdom*," *JTS* 36 (1935): 60-65.

1813.   R. V. G. Tasker, "The Text Used by Eusebius in *Demonstratio Evangelica* in quoting from Matthew and Luke," *HTR* 28 (1935): 61-67.

1814.   Bruno Griesser, "Die handschriftliche Überlieferung der *Expositio IV evangeliorum* des Ps. Hieronymus," *RBén* 49 (1937): 279-321.

1815.   R. V. G. Tasker, "The Text of St. Matthew used by Origen in his Commentary on St. Matthew," *JTS* 38 (1937): 60-64.

1816.   Marcel Richard, "Les fragments exégétiques de Théophile d'Alexandrie et de Théophile d'Antioche," *RB* 47 (1938): 387-97.

1817.   Eric Burrows, "Origenes-Fragmente in Matthaeuskatenen," *B* 20 (1939): 401-407.

1818.   Joseph Sickenberger, "Eine Athoshandschrift der Lukaskatene der Niketas," *ZNW* 39 (1940): 151-61.

1819.   Joseph Reuss, "Der Exeget Ammonius und die Fragmente seines Matthäus- und Johannes-Kommentars," *B* 22 (1941): 13-20.

1820.   A. Souter, "Notes on Incidental Gospel Quotations in Jerome's Commentary on St. Matthew's Gospel," *JTS* 42 (1941): 12-18.

1821. Joseph Reuss, "Cyrill von Alexandrien und sein Kommentar zum Johannes-Evangelium," *B* 25 (1944): 207-209.

1822. C. C. Tarelli, "Clement of Rome and the Fourth Gospel," *JTS* 48 (1947): 208-209.

1823. Claude D. Dicks, "The Matthean Text of Chrysostom in his Homilies on Matthew," *JBL* 67 (1948): 365-76.

1824. K. W. Kim, "The Matthean Text of Origen in his Commentary on Matthew," *JBL* 68 (1949): 125-39.

1825. M.-E. Boismard, "Critique textuelle et citations patristiques," *RB* 57 (1950): 388-408.

1826. K. W. Kim, "Origin's Text of John in his *On Prayer, Commentary on Matthew*, and *Against Celsus*," *JTS* N.S., 1 (1950): 74-84.

1827. M.-E. Boismard, "Lectio brevoir, potior," *RB* 58 (1951): 161-68.

1828. A. J. B. Higgins, "The Latin Text of Luke in Marcion and Tertullian," *VCh* 5 (1951): 1-42.

1829. A. Vööbus, "Die Evangelienzitate in der Einleitung der persischen Märtyrerakten," *B* 33 (1952): 222-34.

1830. Nigel J. Abercrombie, "Origen's Text of Matthew in his *Against Celsus*," *JTS* N.S. 4 (1953): 42-50.

1831. Richard Heard, "Papias' Quotations from the New Testament," *NTSt* 1 (1954-1955): 130-34.

1832. J. Neville Birdsall, "The Text of the Gospels in Photius," *JTS* N.S. 7 (1956): 43-55, 190-98.

1833. M. J. Suggs, "The Eusebian Text of Matthew," *NT* 1 (1956): 233-45.

1834. M. J. Suggs, "Eusebius' Text of John in the 'Writings against Marcellus'," *JBL* 75 (1956): 137-42.

1835. M. J. Suggs, "Eusebius and the Gospel Text," *HTR* 50 (1957): 307-10.

1836. J. Neville Birdsall, "Photius and the Text of the Fourth Gospel," *NTSt* 4 (1957-1958): 61-63.

1837. M. J. Suggs, "The Use of Patristic Evidence in the Search for a Primitive New Testament Text," *NTSt* 4 (1957-1958): 139-47.

1838. J. Duplacy, "Citations patristiques et critique textuelle du Nouveau Testament," *RSR* 47 (1959): 391-400.

1839. Tjitze Baarda, "The Gospel Text in the Biography of Rabbula," *VCh* 14 (1960): 102-27.

1840. Albert Heitlinger, "Der 'Codex Cusanus 18' die Vorlage-handschrift der 'Corderius-Katene' zum Johannes-evangelium," *B* 42 (1961): 443-54.

See also numbers 5998, 6726.

1840.1 J. Mehlmann, "John 8:48 in Some Patristic Quotations," *B* 44/2 (1963): 206-209.

1840.2 Gordon D. Fee, "The Text of John in Origen and Cyril of Alexandria: A Contribution to Methodology in the Recovery and Analysis of Patristic Citations," *B* 52 (1971): 357-94.

1840.3 Gordon D. Fee, "The Lemma of Origen's Commentary on John, Book X: An Independent Witness to the Egyptian Textual Tradition?" *NTSt* 20 (1973-1974): 78-81.

1840.4 Gordon D. Fee, "The Text of John and Mark in the Writings of Chrysostom," *NTSt* 26 (1979-1980): 525-47.

1840.5 Bart D. Ehrman, "Heracleon, Origen, and the Text of the Fourth Gospel," *NTSt* 34/1 (1988): 24-44. See also *VCh* 47 (1993): 105-18.

2. The History of Textual Criticism

1841. M. Stuart, "On the Manuscripts and Editions of the Greek New Testament," *BS* 1843, 254-82.

1842. Caspar Renè Gregory, "Tischendorf," *BS* 33 (1876): 153-93.

1843. D. R. J., "L'évolution de la critique protestante," *RBén* 14 (1899): 49-59.

1844. B. W. Bacon, "A Century of Change in New Testament Criticism," *HJ* 11 (1912-1913): 611-22.

1845. J. W. Bailey, "Erasmus and the Textus Receptus," *CQ* 17 (1940): 271-79.

1844.   B. W. Bacon, "A Century of Change in New Testament Criticism," *HJ* 11 (1912-1913): 611-22.

1845.   J. W. Bailey, "Erasmus and the Textus Receptus," *CQ* 17 (1940): 271-79.

1846.   C. C. Tarelli, "Erasmus's Manuscripts of the Gospels," *JTS* 44 (1943): 155-62; 48 (1947): 207-208.

1847.   A. Cordoliani, "Le texte de la Bible en Irlande du Vᵉ au IXᵉ siècle," *RB* 57 (1950): 5-39.

1848.   Lyle O. Bristol, "New Testament Textual Criticism in the Nineteenth Century," *RE* 49 (1952): 36-40.

1848.1   Eldon Jay Epp, "Twentieth Century Interlude in New Testament Textual Criticism," *JBL* 93 (1974): 386-414.

1848.2   Eldon Jay Epp, "Eclectic Method in New Testament Textual Criticism: Solution or Symptom?" *HTR* 69 (1975): 211-57.

1848.3   David C. Parker, "Development of Textual Criticism since B. H. Streeter," *NTSt* 24 (1977): 149-62.

1848.4   Eldon Jay Epp, "New Testament Textual Criticism in America: Requiem for a Discipline," *JBL* 98 (1979): 94-98.

1848.5   J. K. Elliott, "Keeping up with Recent Studies, 16: New Testament Textual Criticism," *ET* 99 (1987): 40-45.

1848.6   Eldon Jay Epp, "New Testament Textual Criticism Past, Present, and Future: Reflections on the Alands' Text of the New Testament," *HTR* 82 (1989): 213-29.

3. The Theory, Method, and Practice of Textual Criticism

a. *General Studies*

1849.   F. Gardiner, "Principles of Textual Criticism," *BS* 32 (1875): 209-65.

1850.   W. H. van de Sande Bakhuyzen, "De critiek van den tekst des Nieuwen Testaments," *TT* 17 (1883): 588-612.

1851.   Alfred Watts, "Textual Criticism Illustrated from the Printing-Office," *Exp* 2nd ser., 5 (1883): 54-75, 229-44, 382-96.

(1910): 457-71.

1855.   H. J. Vogels, "Methodisches zur Textkritik der Evangelien," *BibZ* 11 (1913): 367-96.

1856.   Albert C. Clark, "The Primitive Text of the Gospels and Acts, A Rejoinder," *JTS* 16 (1914-1915): 225-40.

1857.   A. T. Robertson, "Romance and Tragedy in the History of the New Testament Text," *ET* 36 (1924-1925): 19-24.

1858.   M.-J. Lagrange, "Projet de critique textuelle rationnelle du Nouveau Testament," *RB* 42 (1933): 481-98.

1859.   Edward B. Warren, "The Pastor and his Greek New Testament," *RE* 31 (1934): 461-65.

1860.   Norman Huffman, "Suggestions from the Gospel of Mark for a New Textual Theory," *JBL* 56 (1937): 347-59.

1861.   C. C. Tarelli, "Historical Greek Grammar and Textual Criticism," *JTS* 38 (1937): 238-42.

1862.   F. G. Kenyon, "The Text of the Greek New Testament," *ET* 50 (1938-1939): 68-71.

1863.   Kirsopp and Silva Lake, "De Westcott et Hort au Père Lagrange et au-delà," *RB* 48 (1939): 497-505.

1864.   Jean Levie, "L'encyclique sur les études bibliques," *NRT* 68 (1946): 648-70.

1865.   Teófilo Ayuso Marazuela, "¿Texto arrecensional, recensional o prerecensional? Contribución al estudio de la critica textual de los evangelios," *EB* 6 (1947): 35-90.

1866.   Frederick C. Grant, "The Greek Text of the New Testament," *BTr* 2 (1951): 117-21.

1867.   E. A. Nida, "Spiritual Values in Better Manuscript Readings of the New Testament," *BTr* 3 (1952): 81-86.

1868.   A. W. Argyle, "The Elements of New Testament Textual Criticism," *BTr* 4 (1953): 118-25.

1869.   E. Massaux, "État actuel de la critique textuelle du Nouveau Testament," *NRT* 75 (1953): 703-26.

1870.   A. A. T. Ehrhardt, "Zur Theologie der neutestamentlichen Textkritik," *EvT* 15 (1955): 553-63.

1871. Manfred Karnetzki, "Textgeschichte als Überlieferungs-geschichte," *ZNW* 47 (1956): 170-80.

1872. George D. Kilpatrick, "The Transmission of the New Testament and its Reliability," *BTr* 9 (1958): 127-36.

1873. Heinrich Greeven, "Erwägungen zur synoptischen Textkritik," *NTSt* 6 (1959-1960): 281-96.

1874. Juan Leal, "El autógrafo del IV Evangelio y la arqueología," *EE* 34 (1960): 895-906.

See also numbers 1990, 2249f., 3055, 5615.

1874.1 Kenneth W. Clark, "The Theological Relevance of Textual Variation in Current Criticism of the Greek New Testament," *JBL* 85 (1966): 1-16.

1874.2 George D. Kilpatrick, "Some Thoughts on Modern Textual Criticism and the Synoptic Gospels," *NT* 19 (1977): 275-92.

1874.3 Klaus Junack, "The Reliability of the New Testament Text from the Perspective of Textual Criticism," *BTr* 29 (1978): 128-40.

1874.4 Joseph Reuss, "Studien zur Lukaserklarung des Presbyters Hesychius von Jerusalem," *B* 59 (1978): 562-71.

1874.5 H.-W. Bartsch, "Ein neuer Textus Receptus für das griechische Neue Testament?" *NTS* 27 (1980-1981): 585-92.

b. *Text Families*

1875. A. S. Wilkins, "The Western Text of the Greek Testament," *Exp* 4th ser., 10 (1894): 386-400, 409-28.

1876. Kirsopp Lake, "The Text of the Gospels in Alexandria," *AJT* 6 (1902): 79-89.

1877. Caspar René Gregory, "The Greek Text in 1611," *BW* 37 (1911): 255-61.

1878. J. Chapman, "The Diatessaron and the Western Text of the Gospels," *RBén* 29 (1912): 233-52.

1879. F. C. Burkitt, "W and Θ: Studies in the Western Text of St. Mark," *JTS* 17 (1915-1916): 1-21 and 139-52.

1880. B. H. Streeter, "The Caesarean Text of the Gospels," *JTS* 26

(1924-1925): 373-78; and F. C. Burkitt, "Note on the Preceding Note," *ibid.* 378-80.

1881.   C. H. Turner, "Western Readings in the Second Half of St. Mark's Gospel," *JTS* 29 (1927-1928): 1-16.

1882.   F. C. Burkitt, "The Caesarean Text," *JTS* 30 (1928-1929): 347-56.

1883.   Kirsopp Lake, R. P. Blake, and S. New, "The Caesarean Text of the Gospel of Mark," *HTR* 21 (1928): 207-404.

1884.   M.-J. Lagrange, "Le groupe dit césaréen des manuscrits des évangiles," *RB* 38 (1929): 481-512.

1885.   Edgar J. Goodspeed, "The Letter of Jesus Christ and the Western Text," *ATR* 15 (1933): 105-14.

1886.   Frank Granger, "Julius Africanus and the Western Text," *JTS* 35 (1934): 361-68.

1887.   Silva New, "A Patmos Family of Gospel Manuscripts," *HTR* 25 (1932): 85-92.

1888.   Henry A. Sanders, "The Egyptian Text of the Four Gospels and Acts," *HTR* 26 (1933): 77-98.

1889.   Teófilo Ayuso, "Texto cesariense o precesariense, su realidad y su trascendencia en la critic a textual del Nuevo Testamento," *B* 16 (1935): 369-415.

1890.   E. C. Colwell, "The Complex Character of the Late Byzantine Text of the Gospels," *JBL* 54 (1935): 211-21.

1891.   B. H. Streeter, "The Caesarean Text of Matthew and Luke," *HTR* 28 (1935): 231-35.

1892.   R. V. G. Tasker, "The Chester Beatty Papyrus and the Ceasarean Text of Luke," *HTR* 29 (1936): 345-52.

1893.   B. H. Streeter, "The Early Ancestry of the Textus Receptus of the Gospels," *JTS* 38 (1937): 225-29.

1894.   L. Cerfaux, "Remarques sur le texte des évangiles à Alexandrie au IIᵉ siècle," *ETL* 15 (1938): 674-82.

1895.   .C. C. Tarelli, "The Chester Beatty Papyrus and the Western and Byzantine Texts," *JTS* 41 (1940): 253-60.

1896.   G. Zuntz, "The Byzantine Text in New Testament Criticism,"

JTS 43 (1942): 25-30.

1897. George D. Kilpatrick, "Western Text and Original Text in the Gospels and Acts," *JTS* 44 (1943): 24-36.

1898. Bruce M. Metzger, "The Caesarean Text of the Gospels," *JBL* 64 (1945): 457-89.

1899. E. C. Colwell, "Genealogical Method: Its Achievements and its Limitations," *JBL* 66 (1947): 109-33.

1900. Edward F. Hills, "Harmonizations in the Caesarean Text of Mark," *JBL* 66 (1947): 135-52.

1901. W. B. Sedgwick, "St. Luke and the δ-text," *ET* 59 (1947-1948): 222-23.

1902. Jacob Geerlings, "Is MS 826 the Archetype of Fam. 13a?" *JBL* 67 (1948). 357-63.

1903. B. Kingston Soper, "St. Luke and the 'Western' Text," *ET* 60 (1948-1949): 83.

1904. C. S. C. Williams, "St. Luke and the 'Western' Text," *ET* 60 (1948-1949): 25-26.

1905. Hollis W. Houston, "Mark 6 and II in P^{45} and in the Caesarean Text," *JBL* 74 (1955): 262-71.

1906. D. S. Wallace-Hadrill, "Eusebius and the Gospel Text of Caesarea," *HTR* 49 (1956): 105-14.

1907. E. C. Colwell, "The Significance of Grouping of New Testament Manuscripts," *NTSt* 4 (1957-1958). 73-92.

1908. Barnabas Lindars, "Matthew, Levi, Lebbaeus and the Value of the Western Text," *NTSt* 4 (1957-1958): 220-22.

1909 A. F. J. Klijn, "A Survey of the Researches into the Western Text of the Gospels and Acts," *NT* 3 (1959): 1-27, 161-73.

1910. G. Quispel, "L'évangile selon Thomas et le 'Texte Occidental' du Nouveau Testament," *VCh* 14 (1960): 204-15.

See also number 10079.

1910.1 Bart D. Ehrman, "Heracleon and the 'Western' Textual Tradition," *NTS* 40 (1994): 161-79.

1910.2 A. Aejmelaeus and B. Aland, "Methodenfragen der

172 CRITICAL STUDIES OF THE GOSPELS

biblischen Textkritik. A. Altes Testament. B. Neues Testament," *TR* 60 (1995): 316-29.

c. Individual Text-Critical Problems

1911. W. Milligan, "Some Recent Critical Readings in the New Testament," *Exp* 1st ser., 7 (1878): 123-37 [Matt. 6:12; 7:29; Mk. 6:22; 6:20], 194-215 [Jn. 5:3-4; 9:4].

1912. F. W. Farrar, "A Few Various Readings in the New Testament," *Exp* 1st ser., 9 (1879): 375-93.

1913. Henry Hayman, "On Some Textual Questions in the Gospel of John," *BS* 40 (1883): 139-52.

1914. J. R. Harris, "Conflate Readings of the New Testament," *AJP* 6 (1885): 24-40.

1915. Ferdinand Graefe, "Textkritische Bemerkungen zu den drei Schlusskapiteln des Lukasevangeliums," *TSK* 69 (1896): 245-81.

1916. A. N. Jannaris, "Misreadings and Misrenderings in the New Testament," *Exp* 5th ser., 8 (1898): 422-32; 9 (1899): 296-310.

1917. Ch. Rauch, "Bemerkungen zum Markustexte," *ZNW* 3 (1902): 300-14 [Mk. 1:40-45; 6:29-31; 14:12-17].

1918. F. C. Conybeare, "Three Early Doctrinal Modifications of the Text of the Gospels," *HJ* 1 (1902-1903): 96-113 [Mt. 1:16; 28:19; Mk. 10:18].

1919. Eb. Nestle, "Neue Lesarten zu den Evangelien," *ZNW* 4 (1903): 255-63.

1920. J. E. Belser, "Textkritische Untersuchung zum Johannesevangelium," *TQ* 94 (1912): 32-58 [1:15; 5:3-4; 7:53-8:11; 19:35].

1921. R. G. Bury, "Two Notes on the Fourth Gospel," *ET* 24 (1912-1913): 232-33.

1922. J. E. Belser, "Zur Textkritik der Schriften des Johannes," *TQ* 98 (1916): 145-84.

1923. C. H. Turner, "A Textual Commentary on Mark 1," *JTS* 28 (1926-1927): 145-58.

1924.   F. C. Burkitt, "Capernaum, Capharnaum," *JTS* 34 (1933): 385-89.

1925.   I. A. Heikel, "Konjekturen zu einigen Stellen des neutestamentlichen Textes," *TSK* 106 (1934-1935): 314-17 [Mt. 22:36; Mk. 3:6; Mk. 14:3; Lk. 12:15].

1926.   Frederick C. Grant, "Studies in the Text of St. Mark," *ATR* 20 (1938): 103-19.

1927.   José M. Bover, "Harmonizaciones e interpolaciones en el texto del Nuevo Testamento," *EB* 2 (1943): 121-22.

1928.   Ernest W. Saunders, "Studies in Doctrinal Influences on the Byzantine Text of the Gospels," *JBL* 71 (1952): 85-92.

1929.   M.-E. Boismard, "Problèmes de critique textuelle concernant le quatrième évangile," *RB* 60 (1953): 347-71.

1930.   J. Neville Birdsall, "The Text of the Fourth Gospel: Some Current Questions," *EQ* 29 (1957): 195-205.

1931.   J. Neville Birdsall, "John X.29," *JTS* N.S. 11 (1960): 342-44.

    See also numbers 4166, 4817-4819, 4859, 4965, 4966, 4973, 5005, 5013, 5043, 5182, 5213, 5226, 5274 ff-, 5381, 5395, 5405, 5406, 5408, 5409, 5446ff, 5476, 5657, 5685, 5709, 5940 ff., 6064, 6067, 6103ff, 6125, 6423 ff-, 7405.

1931.1   Kenneth W. Clark, "The Text of the Gospel of John in Third Century Egypt," *NT* 5 (1962): 17-24.

1931.2   T. F. Glasson, "Did Matthew and Luke Use a 'Western' Text of Mark?" *ET* 77 (1965-1966): 120-21.

1931.3   J. M. Ross, "The 'Harder Reading' in Textual Criticism," *BTr* 33 (1982): 138-39.

1931.4   J. M. Ross, "Some Unnoticed Points in the Text of the New Testament," *NT* 25 (1983): 59-72.

1931.5   David A Black, "The Text of Matthew 5:22a Revisited," *NT* 30/1 (1988): 1-8.

1931.6   David A. Black, "The Text of Mark 6:20," *NTS* 34/1 (1988): 141-45.

1931.7   David A. Black, "Conjectural Emendations in the Gospel of Matthew," *NT* 31/1 (1989): 1-15.

1931.8   F. H. Cryer, "Eben Bohan. Det laenge savnwe hebraeiske Matthaeusevangelium?" *DTT* 56 (1993): 209-215.

1931.9   Tjitze Baarda, "An Unexpected Reading in the West-Saxon Gospel Text of Mark 16.11," *NTS* 41 (1995): 458-65.

d. *Prologues, Divisions, and Other Aids for Readers*

1932.   Charles F. Schaeffer, "The Exegetical Punctuation of the New Testament," *BS* 25 (1868): 593-644.

1933.   J. T. Bergman, "De opschriften der Evangeliën," *TT* 7 (1873): 206-14.

1934.   John Chapman, "Priscillian, the Author of the Monarchian Prologues to the Vulgate Gospels," *RBén* 23 (1906): 335-49.

1935.   D. De Bruyne, "Prologues bibliques d'origine marcionite," *RBén* 24 (1907): 1-16.

1936.   Eb. Nestle, "Die Eusebianische Evangelien-Synopse," *NKZ* 19 (1908): 40-51, 93-114, 219-32.

1937.   H. Jeannotte, "Les 'capitula' du Commentarius in Matthaeum de saint Hilaire de Poitiers," *BibZ* 10 (1912): 36-45.

1938.   B. W. Bacon, "The Latin Prologues of John," *JBL* 32 (1913): 194-217.

1939.   S. Grébaut, "Les dix canons d'Eusèbe et d'Ammonius," *ROC* 18 (1913): 314-17 [in Ethiopic].

1940.   D. De Bruyne, "Les plus anciens prologues latins des évangiles," *RBén* 40 (1928): 193-214.

1941.   Ad. Hebbelynck, "Les κεφάλαια et les τίτλοι des évangiles," *Mu* 41 (1928): 81-120.

1942.   A. Souter, "Traces of an Unknown System of *Capitula* for St. Matthew's Gospel," *JTS* 33 (1931-1932): 188-89.

1943.   Paul Gächter, "Zur Textabteilung von Evangelien-handschriften," *B* 15 (1934): 301-20.

1944.   Franz Taeschner, "Die monarchianischen Prologe zu den vier Evangelien in der spanisch-arabischen Bibelübersetzung des Isaak Velasquez nach der Münchener Handschrift Cod. Arab.

238," *OC* Serie III, 10 (1935): 80-99.

1945. W. F. Howard, "The Anti-Marcionite Prologues to the Gospels," *ET* 47 (1935-1936): 534-38.

1946. L. G. da Fonseca, "De clausula IV Evangelii in codice Sinaitico," *VD* 18 (1938): 63-64.

1947. Robert M. Grant, "The Oldest Gospel Prologues," *ATR* 23 (1941): 231-45.

1948. R. G. Heard, "The Old Gospel Prologues," *JTS* N.S. 6 (1955): 1-16.

1948.1 O. J. F. Seitz, "Gospel Prologues: A Common Pattern?" *JBL* 83 (1964): 262-68.

1948.2 Samuel Hornsby, "Punctuation in the Authorized Version of the Bible," *BTr* 24 (1973): 139-41.

1948.3 Norman A. Mundhenk, "Punctuation," *BTr* 32 (1981): 234-40.

1948.4 K. Romaniuk, "Exégèse du Nouveau Testament et ponctuation," *NT* 23 (1981): 195-209.

e. *The Printed Greek Text and its Apparatus*

1949. E. C. S. Gibson, "Westcott and Hort's Greek Testament as a Commentary," *Exp* 2nd ser., 5 (1883): 330-40.

1950. Eb. Nestle, "Some more Minutiae concerning Westcott and Hort's 'Greek Testament'," *ET* 9 (1897-1898): 95-96, 333-34.

1951. Kirsopp Lake, "Dr. Weiss's Text of the Gospels: The Thoughts of a Textual Critic on the Text of an Exegete," *AJT* 7 (1903): 249-58.

1952. M.-J. Lagrange, "Une nouvelle édition du Nouveau Testament," *RB* 22 (1913): 481-524.

1953. F. W. Grosheide, "Het tekstkritisch systeem van H. von Soden," *GTT* 15 (1914): 186-200, 230-49, 299-322.

1954. George D. Kilpatrick, "The Oxford Greek New Testament," *JTS* 43 (1942): 30-34.

1955. George D. Kilpatrick, "Three Recent Editions of the Greek

New Testament," *JTS* 50 (1949): 10-23, 142-54 [Nestle, Souter, and Merk].

1956.   Merrill M. Parvis, "The International Project to Establish a New Critical Apparatus of the Greek New Testament," *CQ* 27 (1950): 301-308.

1957.   Anonymous, "A New Edition of the Greek New Testament," *BTr* 10 (1959): 29-35.

1957.1   J. Neville Birdsall, "A Report of the Textual Complexion of the Gospel of Mark in Ms 2533," *NT* 11 (1969): 233-39.

1957.2   J. K. Elliott, "The International Project to Establish a Critical Apparatus to Luke's Gospel," *NTS* 29 (1983): 531-38.

1957.3   S. O. Abogunrin, "The Three Variant Accounts of Peter's Call: A Critical and Theological Examination of the Texts," *NTS* 31 (1985): 587-602.

B. LITERARY CRITICISM OF THE GOSPELS

1. The Four Gospels

a. *General Studies*

1958.   C. E. Stowe, "The Four Gospels as we now have them in the New Testament, and the Hegelian Assaults upon them," *BS* 8 (1851): 508-29; 9 (1852): 77-110.

1959.   H. U. Meyboom, "De Methode der Evangeliën-Critiek," *TT* 2 (1868): 497-523.

1960.   A. Hilgenfeld, "Volkmar und die Evangelien," *ZWT* 13 (1870): 354-77.

1961.   L. S. P. Meyboom, "Getallensymboliek in de canonieke Evangeliën," *TT* 5 (1871): 512-20.

1962.   H. Burton, "The Human Element in the Gospels," *Exp* 1st ser., 1 (1875): 462-70; 2 (1875): 18-28.

1963.   E. H. Plumptre, "The Samaritan Element in the Gospels and Acts," *Exp* 1st ser., 7 (1878): 22-40.

1964.   W. Beyschlag, "Zu dem vorstehenden Aufsatz von B. Weiss: 'Zur Evangelienfrage'," *TSK* 56 (1883): 594-602.

1965.   Bernhard Weiss, "Zur Evangelienfrage. Mit besonderer

Beziehung auf den Aufsatz von W. Beyschlag: 'Die apostolische Spruchsammlung und unsere vier Evangelien,' (Theol. Stud. u. Krit. 1881, Heft 4, 565 ff.)," *TSK* 56 (1883): 571-94.

1966. August Jacobsen, "Zur Kritik der Evangelien," *ZWT* 33 (1890): 257-69.

1967. A. Hilgenfeld, "Paul Ewald's Lösung der Evangelienfrage," *ZWT* 34 (1891): 80-95.

1968. J. Massie, "Dr. Martineau and the Gospels," *Exp* 4th ser., 3 (1891): 391-98.

1969. W. Brandt, "Methodologische Studie," *TT* 30 (1896): 270-93.

1970. J. H. Bernard, "The Omissions of the Gospel," *Exp* 5th ser., 7 (1898): 356-64.

1971. W. Beyschlag, "D. Adolf Harnacks Untersuchungen zur Evangelienfrage," *TSK* 71 (1898): 71-115.

1972. Ada Bryson, "New Testament Criticism," *ET* 10 (1898-1899): 487-92.

1973. Arthur Wright, "Oral Teaching," *ET* 11 (1899-1900): 473-74.

1974. W. F. Lofthouse, "The Hexateuch and the Gospels: A Parallel," *ET* 13 (1901-1902): 565-67.

1975. C. A. Briggs, "Problems in the Gospels," *ET* 14 (1902-1903): 538-41; 15 (1903-1904): 14-16, 67-69.

1976. W. Sanday, "La critique actuelle et les évangiles," *BLE* 1903, 233-41.

1977. William P. Armstrong, "The Witness of the Gospels," *PTR* 2 (1904): 32-64.

1978. A. Hilgenfeld, "J. Wellhausen und die synoptischen Evangelien," *ZWT* 49 (1906): 193-238.

1979. F. Blass, "The Origin and Character of our Gospels," *ET* 18 (1906-1907): 345-47, 395-400, 458-59, 491-93, 558-59.

1980. W. Bousset, "Wellhausens Evangelienkritik," *TR*, 9 (1906): 1-14, 43-51.

1981.   W. Sanday, "Professor Burkitt on Gospel History," *ET* 18 (1906-1907): 249-55.

1982.   O. Bardenhewer, "Die Evangelien," *BibZ* 5 (1907): 27-34.

1983.   Hugh Pope, "The Need of Literary Criticism of the Gospel Narratives," *ITQ* 2 (1907): 438-57.

1984.   C. W. Emmet, "M. Loisy and the Gospel Story," *ET* 20 (1908-1909): 488-95.

1985.   Newport J. D. White, "Assumptions Underlying Gospel Criticism," *Exp* 8th ser., 1 (1911): 244-55.

1986.   J. E. Belser, "Zur Evangelienfrage," *TQ* 95 (1913): 323-76.

1987.   B. W. Bacon, "After Six Days: A New Clue for Gospel Critics," *HTR* 8 (1915): 94-121.

1988.   Burton S. Easton, "Interwoven Gospel Passages," *BW* 45 (1915): 146-52.

1989.   Clyde W. Votaw, "The Gospels and Contemporary Biographies," *AJT* 19 (1915): 45-73, 217-49.

1990.   E. S. Buchanan, "Ancient Testimony to the Early Corruption of the Gospels," *BS* 73 (1916): 177-91.

1991.   Hans Windisch, "Kleine Beiträge zur evangelischen Überlieferung," *ZNW* 18 (1917): 73-83.

1992.   D. M. McIntyre, "The Earliest Witness to the Gospel Story," *ET* 33 (1921-1922): 309-12.

1993.   C. J. Cadoux, "The Gospel Story and the Higher Criticism of Today," *HJ* 23 (1924-1925): 611-21.

1994.   Auguste Bill, "L'étude historique du Nouveau Testament," *RHPR* 13 (1933): 324-69; 7 (1927): 570-75.

1995.   L. Cerfaux, "La probité des souvenirs évangeliques," *ETL* 4 (1927): 13-28.

1996.   Thomas Yates, "The Romance and the Realism of the Gospel," *ET* 42 (1930-1931): 269-71.

1997.   B. W. Bacon, "Reading the Gospels Backward," *HJ* 30 (1931-1932): 76-90.

1998.   C. H. Dodd, "Present Tendencies in the Criticism of the Gospels," *ET* 43 (1931-1932): 246-51.

1999. D. A. Frøvig, "Fra den nyere evangelieforskning," *TTK* 3 (1932): 230-34.

2000. Benjamin Murmelstein, "Die Gestalt Josefs in der Agada und die Evangeliengeschichte," *A* 4 (1932): 51-55.

2001. T. W. Manson, "Some Outstanding New Testament Problems," *ET* 47 (1935-1936): 7-11.

2002. Paul Joüon, "La clé traditionnelle des évangiles," *RSR* 27 (1937): 213-15.

2003. D. A. Frøvig, "Fra den nyeste evangelieforskning," *TTK* 10 (1939): 22-28.

2004. D. A. Frøvig, "Hovedspørsmalene i den moderne evangeliekritikk. Et varsel om et omslag," *TTK* 12 (1941): 145-59.

2005. F. F. Bruce, "Some Aspects of Gospel Introduction," *EQ* 14 (1942): 174-97, 264-80; 15 (1943): 3-20.

2006. Mary E. Andrews, "Early Gospel Criticism," *ATR* 27 (1945): 170-78.

2007. C. J. Cadoux, "The Character of the Gospel Record," *BJRL* 29 (1945-1946): 269-85.

2008. R. H. Lightfoot, " 'The Witness of Matthew and Mark to Christ' by Ned Bernard Stonehouse," *JTS* 46 (1945): 217-24.

2009. S. G. F. Brandon, "The Logic of New Testament Criticism," *HJ* 47 (1948-1949): 144-52.

2010. J. T. Noonan, "Hegel and Strauss: The Dialectic and the Gospels," *CBQ* 12 (1950): 136-52.

2011. Morton S. Enslin, "Along Highways and Byways," *HTR* 44 (1951): 67-92.

2012. Gustav Kafka, "Bild und Wort in den Evangelien," *MTZ* 2 (1951): 263-87.

2013. C. K. Barrett, "Chronicle: New Testament," *JTS* N.S. 3 (1952): 312-20; 4 (1953): 311-20.

2014. H. Sylvester, "Le 'De concordia et exposition quatuor evangeliorum' inédit de Wazlin II, abbé de Saint-Laurent à Liège (ca 1150-ca 1157)," *RBén* 63 (1953): 310-25.

2015.   Paul Winter, "The Gospels and Modern Study," *FF* 8 (1955): 63-70.

2016.   Ernst Käsemann, "Neutestamentliche Fragen von heute," *ZTK* N.F. 54 (1957): 1-21.

2017.   Alexander Kerrigan, "The Four Gospels in 1957: The Oxford Congress," *ITQ* 25 (1958): 63-82.

2018.   David Daube, "The Earliest Structure of the Gospels," *NTSt* 5 (1958-1959): 174-87.

2019.   Vincent T. O'Keefe, "Towards Understanding the Gospels," *CBQ* 21 (1959): 171-89.

2020.   Vincent Taylor, "Methods of Gospel Criticism," *ET* 71 (1959-1960): 68-72.

2021.   B. de Solages, "Mathématiques et Evangiles. Réponse au R. P. Benoit," *BLE* 61 (1960): 297-311.

             See also numbers 721, 10030.

2021.1   H. Hogarth, "History and the Four Gospels," *ET* (1963-1964): 295-99.

2021.2   John Drury, "What Are the Gospels?" *ET* 87 (1976): 324-28.

b. *Studies concerning Date, Author, and Language*

2022.   Georg Eduard Steitz, "Des Papias von Hierapolis 'Auslegung der Reden des Herrn' nach ihren Quellen und ihrem muthmasslichen Charakter," *TSK* 41 (1868): 63-95.

2023.   A. Hilgenfeld, "Papias über Marcus und Matthäus," *ZWT* 22 (1879): 1-18.

2024.   J. E. Belser, "Zur Abfassungzeit der synoptischen Evangelien und der Apostelgeschichte," *TQ* 75 (1893): 355-407.

2025.   John Chapman, "Clément d'Alexandrie sur les évangiles, et encore le fragment de Muratori," *RBén* 21 (1904): 369-74.

2026.   John Chapman, "St. Irenaeus on the Dates of the Gospels," *JTS* 6 (1904-1905): 563-69.

2027.   Parke P. Flourney, "The Real Date of the Gospels," *BS* 65 (1908): 657-78.

2028.   W. Schonack, "Evangelistenviten aus Kosmas Indikopleustes in einer griechischen Handschrift," *ZWT* 54 (1912): 97-110.

2029. Warren J. Moulton, "The Dating of the Synoptic Gospels," *JBL* 37 (1918): 1-19.

2030. R. J. Drummond, "Who Wrote the Gospels?" *EQ* 13 (1941): 81-91.

2031. Robert M. Grant, "Papias and the Gospels," *ATR* 25 (1943): 218-22.

2032. George B. King, "The Original Language of the Gospels," *CQ* 13 (1936): 117-25; 14 (1937): 33-42.

2033. W. S. Reilly, "Witness of the Early Church to the Authorship of the Gospels," *CBQ* 1 (1939): 115-24.

2034. H. S. Shelton, "The Authorship and Date of the Gospels Reconsidered," *HJ* 41 (1942-1943): 167-71.

2035. J. T. Curran, "St. Irenaeus and the Dates of the Synoptics," *CBQ* 5 (1943): 33-46, 160-78, 301-309, 445-57.

2036. Richard Heard, "The ἀπομνημονεύματα in Papias, Justin, and Irenaeus," *NTSt* 1 (1954-1955): 112-29.

2037. Rupert Annand, "Papias and the Four Gospels," *SJT* 9 (1956): 46-62.

2038. G. J. Sirks, "Auctor-Compositor," *NedTT* 12 (1957-1958): 81-91.

2039. F. Schulthess, "Zur Sprache der Evangelien," *ZNW* 21 (1922): 217-36, 241-58.

2040. Samuel J. Feigin, "The Original Language of the Gospels," *JNES* 2 (1943): 187-97.

2041. Carmelo Ballester, "El lenguaje del Evangelio," *CB* 2, núm. 9 (1945): 50-54.

2041.1 L. W. Barnard, "St. Mark and Alexandria," *HTR* 57 (1964): 145-50.

c. *The Origins and Sources of the Gospels*

2042. Bernhard Weiss, "Zur Entstehungsgeschichte der drei synoptischen Evangelien," *TSK* 34 (1861): 29-100, 646-713.

2043. J. Isidore Mombert, "The Origin of the Gospels," *BS* 23

(1866): 353-83, 529-64.

2044.   Anonymous, "The Origin of the First Three Gospels," *BS* 26 (1869): 1-37, 209-43.

2045.   W. Beyschlag, "Die apostolische Spruchsammlung und unsere vier Evangelien," *TSK* 54 (1881): 565-636.

2046.   Lester Bradner, "The First Written Gospel; Results of Some of the Recent Investigations," *BW* 1 (1893): 432-44.

2047.   B. W. Bacon, "Gospel Types in Primitive Tradition," *HJ* 4 (1905-1906): 877-95.

2048.   Ernest W. Parsons, "The Origin of the Gospels," *BW* 48 (1916): 248-54, 312-18, 377-81; 49 (1917): 50-56.

2049.   F. C. Burkitt, " 'The Four Gospels, a Study of Origins', by B. H. Streeter," *JTS* 26 (1924-1925): 278-94.

2050.   H. W. Magoun, "Some Vital but Neglected Factors in all 'Quelle' Theories," *BS* 87 (1930): 26-37.

2051.   Joachim Jeremias, "Die vier Stimmen im vierten Evangelium," *NTSt* 17 (1934): 37-46.

2052.   J. O. F. Murray, "On the Origin of the Gospels," *Th* 31 (1935): 330-37.

2053.   W. Kolfhaus, "The Spiritual Background of our Gospels," *EQ* 10 (1938): 56-60.

2054.   T. C. Lawson, "Dates and Origins of the Gospels," *EQ* 10 (1938): 276-91.

2055.   G. Baldensperger, "Trois études sur le Christianisme primitif," *RHPR* 14 (1939): 195-222 [La préhistoire des évangiles; etc.].

2056.   Floyd V. Filson, "Five Factors in the Production of the Gospels," *JBR* 9 (1941): 98-103.

2057.   Emanuel Hirsch, "Fragestellung und Verfahren meiner Frühgeschichte des Evangeliums," *ZNW* 41 (1942): 106-24.

2058.   J. W. Bailey, "Light from Paul on Gospel Origins," *ATR* 28 (1946): 217-26.

2059.   Jacques Guillet, "La naissance des évangiles dans l'église," *LumV* no. 6 (1952): 43-64.

2060.   Paul Winter, "Vorsynoptische Evangelien," *ZRGG* 6 (1954): 355-59.

2061.   Marcelo Azevedo, "Um evangelho primitivo à base dos três sinóticos?" *REB* 15 (1955): 349-62.

2062.   Everett F. Harrison, "The Gospel and the Gospels," *BS* 116 (1959): 109-16.

2063.   Otto A. Piper, "The Origin of the Gospel Pattern," *JBL* 78 (1959): 115-24.

2064.   Otto A. Piper, "El Origen del patrón de los evangelios," *CT* 33 (1960): 13-24.

2065.   David M. Stanley, "Liturgical Influences on the Formation of the Four Gospels," *CBQ* 21 (1959): 24-38.

2066.   Alex. Jones, "The Gospel and the Gospels," *Scr* 12 (1960): 65-74.

             See also number 10038.

2066.1   H. P. Hamann, "*Sic et Non*: Are We So Sure of Matthean Dependence on Mark?" *CTM* 41 (1971): 462-69.

2066.2   George B. Caird, "The Study of the Gospels: 1. Source Criticism," *ET* 87/4 (1975-1976): 99-104.

2066.3   G. R. Beasley-Murray, "Second Thoughts on the Composition of Mark 13," *NTS* 29 (1983): 414-20.

d. *Semitic Backgrounds and the Gospels (Aramaic Origins)*

2067.   J. T. Marshall, "The Aramaic Gospel," *Exp* 4th ser., 3 (1891): 1-17, 109-24, 205-20, 275-91, 375-90, 452-67; 4 (1891): 208-23, 373-88, 435-48; 6 (1892): 81-97.

2068.   J. T. Marshall, "The Aramaic Gospel," *ET* 4 (1892-1893): 260-67.

2069.   Colin Campbell, "Professor Marshall's Theory of an Aramaic Gospel," *ET* 4 (1892-1893): 468-70.

2070.   J. T. Marshall, "The Aramaic Gospel," *ET* 4 (1892-1893): 515-16.

2071.   Arthur Wright, "The Origin of the Gospels," *ET* 4 (1892-1893): 275.

2072.   W. C. Allen, "The Aramaic Gospel," *Exp* 4th ser., 7 (1893): 386-400, 454-70.

2073.   S. R. Driver, "Professor Marshall's Aramaic Gospel," *Exp* 4th ser., 8 (1893): 388-400, 419-31.

2074.   J. T. Marshall, "The Aramaic Gospel: Reply to Dr. Driver and Mr. Allen," *Exp* 4th ser., 8 (1893): 176-92.

2075.   J. T. Marshall, "The Semitic and the Greek Gospels," *ET* 8 (1896-1897): 90-91.

2076.   Eb. Nestle, "The Semitic and the Greek Gospels," *ET* 8 (1896-1897): 42-43, 138-39.

2077.   W. C. Allen, "Difficulties in the Text of the Gospels Explained from the Aramaic," *JTS* 2 (1900-1901): 298-300 [Mk. 12:3, 4; 9:50; Lk. 24:32].

2078.   W. C. Allen, "The Aramaic Element in St. Mark," *ET* 13 (1901-1902): 328-30.

2079.   C. J. Ball, "Had the Fourth Gospel an Aramaic Archetype?" *ET* 21 (1909-1910): 91-93.

2080.   Cuthbert Lattey, "The Semitisms of the Fourth Gospel," *JTS* 20 (1919): 330-36.

2081.   J. F. Springer, "Aramaic and the Synoptic Problem," *ATR* 9 (1926-1927): 47-55.

2082.   Paul Joüon, "Quelques aramaïsmes sous-jacents au grec des évangiles," *RSR* 17 (1927): 210-29.

2083.   James A. Montgomery, "Some Aramaisms in the Gospels and Acts," *JBL* 46 (1927): 69-73.

2084.   Oswald T. Allis, "The Alleged Aramaic Origin of the Fourth Gospel," *PTR* 26 (1928): 531-72.

2085.   Millar Burrows, "The Original Language of the Gospel of John," *JBL* 49 (1930): 95-139.

2086.   A. Frøvig, "Das Matthäusevangelium und die aramäische Matthäusschrift des Papias," *NKZ* 42 (1931): 344-90.

2087.   D. A. Frøvig, "Det aramaiske Matteusskrift og vårt greske Matteus-evangelium," *TTK* 2 (1931): 1-30.

2088.   P. E. Kretzmann, "Aramaismen im Neuen Testament," *CTM*

2 (1931): 513-20.

2089.   U. Holzmeister, "De quibusdam generibus *Hebraismorum in textu* N.T. occurrentium," *VD* A (1932): 295-302.

2090.   Millar Burrows, "Principles for Testing the Translation Hypothesis in the Gospels," *JBL* 53 (1934): 13-30.

2091.   P. E. Kretzmann, "The Question of Aramaic Originals," *CTM* 5 (1934): 530-37.

2092.   Ralph Marcus, "Notes on Torrey's Translation of the Gospels," *HTR* 27 (1934): 211-40.

2093.   James A. Montgomery, "Torrey's Aramaic Gospels," *JBL* 53 (1934): 79-99.

2094.   George A. Barton, "Professor Torrey's Theory of the Aramaic Origin of the Gospels and the First Half of the Acts of the Apostles," *JTS* 36 (1935): 357-73.

2095.   Enno Littmann, "Torreys Buch über die vier Evangelien," *ZNW* 34 (1935): 20-34.

2096.   Donald W. Riddle, "The Aramaic Gospels and the Synoptic Problems," *JBL* 54 (1935): 127-38.

2097   Charles C. Torrey, "Professor Marcus on the Aramaic Gospels," *JBL* 54 (1935): 17-28.

2098.   W. C. van Unnik, "C. F. Burney's Hypothese aangaande de Aramaesche achtergrond van het Joh. Evangelie," *VT* 7 (1935): 123-31.

2099.   R. H. Connolly, "Syriacisms in St. Luke," *JTS* 37 (1936): 374-85.

2100.   W. R. Taylor, "Aramaic Gospel Sources and Form Criticism," *ET* 49 (1937-1938): 55-59.

2101.   Michael MarYosip, "The Aramaic Origin of our Gospels," *USR* 49 (1937-1938): 307-18.

2102.   J. de Zwaan, "John Wrote in Aramaic," *JBL* 57 (1938): 155-72.

2103.   C. C. McCown, "Luke's Translation of Semitic into Hellenistic Custom," *JBL* 58 (1939): 213-20.

2104.   James T. Hudson, "The Aramaic Basis of St. Mark," *ET* 53

(1941-1942): 264-70.

2105. Edgar J. Goodspeed, "The Possible Aramaic Gospel," *JNES* 1 (1942): 315-40.

2106. A. T. Olmstead, "Could an Aramaic Gospel be Possible?" *JNES* 1 (1942): 41-75.

2107. Charles C. Torrey, "The Aramaic of the Gospels," *JBL* 61 (1942): 71-85.

2108. C. C. McCown, "Aramaic and Greek Gospels," *ATR* 25 (1943): 281-94.

2109. H. F. D. Sparks, "The Semitisms of St. Luke's Gospel," *JTS* 44 (1943): 129-38.

2110. David Daube, "Concerning the Reconstruction of the Aramaic Gospels," *BJRL* 29 (1945-1946): 69-105.

2111. D. Broughton Knox, "The Aramaic Background of the Gospels," *RTR* 6 (1947): 24-29.

2112. Matthew Black, "Unsolved New Testament Problems; The Problem of the Aramaic Element in the Gospels," *ET* 59 (1947-1948): 171-76.

2113. Matthew Black, "Aramaic Studies and the New Testament: The Unpublished Work of the late A. J. Wensinck of Leyden," *JTS* 49 (1948): 157-65.

2114. Joseph Bonsirven, "Les aramaïsmes de S. Jean l'évangéliste?" *B* 30 (1949): 405-32.

2115. Nigel Turner, "Were the Gospels Written in Greek or in Aramaic?" *EQ* 21 (1949): 42-48.

2116. Millar Burrows, "The Semitic Background of the New Testament," *BTr* 2 (1951): 67-73.

2117. Heinz Schürmann, "Die Semitismen im Einsetzungsbericht bei Markus und bei Lukas," *ZKT* 73 (1951): 72-77 [Mk. 14:22-24; Lk. 22:19-20].

2118. David Gonzalo Maeso, "¿En qué lengua se escribió el Evangelio de San Juan?" *CB* 12 (1955): 296-305 [in Hebrew or Aramaic].

2119. Werner Eiss, "Zur gegenwärtigen aramaistischen

Forschung," *EvT* 16 (1956): 170-81.

2120. J. C. Hindley, "Our Lord's Aramaic—A Speculation," *ET* 72 (1960-1961): 180-81.

See also numbers 1556, 1568, 2284, 2426, 2524, 2685, 2686, 2689, 3369, 4890, 4904, 5006, 5199, 5204 f., 5248, 5324, 5329, 5530, 5710, 6053, 6122, 6456, 8016.

2120.1 Joseph A. Fitzmyer, "The Aramaic Language and the Study of the New Testament," *JBL* 99 (1980): 5-21.

2120.2 P. W. van der Horst, "Notes on the Aramaic Background of Luke 2:41-52," *JSNT* 7 (1980): 61-66.

2120.3 Luis Diez Merino, "Testimonios judios sobre la existencia de un evangelio arameo," *EB* 41/1 (1983): 157-63.

2120.4 Paul R. Berger, "Zum Aramäischen der Evangelien und der Apostelgeschichte," *TRev* 82 (1986): 1-17.

2120.5 Matthew Black, "The Aramaic Dimension in Q with Notes on Luke 17:22, Matthew 24:26," *JSNT* 40 (1990): 33-41.

2120.6 P. Maurice Casey, "The Original Aramaic Form of Jesus' Interpretation of the Cup," *JTS* 41 (1990): 1-12.

2120.7 J. M. Casciaro Ramírez, "The Original Aramaic Form of Jesus' Interpretation of the Cup," *JTS* 41 (1990): 1-12.

e. *Gospel Harmonization*

2121. W. H. Settlemyer, "Studies in Gospel Harmony," *LQ* 8 (1878): 538-50.

2122. Christian Pesch, "Über Evangelienharmonien," *ZKT* 10 (1886): 225-44, 454-80.

2123. Otto Schmid, "Zacharias Chrysopolitanus und seine Evangelienharmonie," *TQ* 68 (1886): 531-47; 69 (1887): 231-75.

2124. Charles Leaman, "Notes on Dr. Riddle's Edition of Robinson's Harmony of the Gospels: Being a Contribution to a Complete Harmony of the Gospels," *BS* 46 (1889): 73-94, 293-304, 445-65; 47 (1890): 216-36.

2125. Alfred Durand, "*Pro consensu Evangelistarum*," *RSR* 2 (1911): 295-301.

2126.   Emil Boismard, "L'évangile à quatre dimensions," *LumV* no.
               1 (1951): 94-114.

2127.   Angelo Penna, "Il 'De consensu evangelistarum' ed i 'canoni
               Eusebiani'," *B* 36 (1955): 1-19.

               See also numbers 548, 1692-1735.

2127.1   Georg Strecker, "Eine Evangelien-Harmonie bei Justin und
               Pseudoklemens?" *NTS* 24 (1978): 297-316.

f. *The Historical Reliability of the Gospel Tradition*

2128.   O. P. Lange, "Die Authentie der vier Evangelien, erwiesen
               aus dem anerkannten Charakter der vier Evangelisten," *TSK*
               12 (1839): 7-68.

2129.   Ed. Scherer, "Les errata du Nouveau Testament," *RT* 9
               (1854): 129-68.

2130.   H. Wace, "The Authenticity of the Four Gospels," *JCP* 3
               (1883-1884): 27-52.

2131.   N. S. Burton, "The Character of Jesus a Basis of Confidence
               in the Gospel Record," *BW* 8 (1896): 30-36.

2132.   Paul Ewald, "Über die Glaubwürdigkeit der Evangelien,"
               NKZ 7 (1896): 593-617.

2133.   Warren P. Behan, "The Trustworthiness of the Gospels - A
               Brief Catechism," *BW* 26 (1905): 364-77.

2134.   Paul Wilh. Schmiedel, "The Article 'Gospels' and the
               Preface to Neumann's 'Jesus'," *ET* 18 (1906-1907): 189-91.

2135.   S. McComb, "Can the Gospels be Trusted?" *BW* 30 (1907):
               346-51.

2136.   J. D. White, "The Human Element in the Gospels," *Herm* 14
               (1907): 285-95.

2137.   W. Sanday, "The Bearing of Criticism upon the Gospel
               History," *ET* 20 (1908-1909): 103-14, 152-62.

2138.   Henry Riegal, "The Vitality of Literary History," *BW* 33
               (1909): 399-407.

2139.   William P. Armstrong, "Gospel History and Criticism," *PTR*
               12 (1914): 427-53.

2140. Camden M. Cobern, "Some Results of Recent Archaeological Studies Bearing upon the New Testament and the Primitive Church," *BW* 51 (1918): 259-68.

2141. C. W. Wade, "Does Historical Criticism Imperil the Substance of Christian Faith?" *HJ* 18 (1919-1920): 321-44.

2142. Edward Beal, "The Face Value of the Gospels," *ET* 34 (1922-1923): 559-61.

2143. Walther Völker, "Die Kritik des Celsus am Leben Jesu und die Korrekturen der Synoptiker," *TB* 5 (1926): 35-39.

2144. Adolf Deissmann, "The Historical Value of the New Testament," *LCQ* 2 (1929): 257-70.

2145. R. O. Hall, "Accuracy in Gospel Records," *HJ* 34 (1935-1936): 278-87.

2146. R. Thibaut, "Jésus-Christ n'a pu être inventé," *NRT* 67 (1940-1945): 280-95.

2147. W. W. D. Gardiner, "Autobiographical Fragments in the Gospels," *ET* 55 (1943-1944): 275-77.

2148. Roderic Dunkerley, "The Principle of Coherence in the Gospel Story," *ET* 58 (1946-1947): 133-36, 161-64.

2149. F. C. Atkinson, "The Historicity and Accuracy of Scripture," *EQ* 19 (1947): 81-92.

2150. Fred L. Fisher, "The Truth of the Gospels," *RE* 54 (1957): 22-41.

2151. D. E. Nineham, "Eye-Witness Testimony and the Gospel Tradition," *JTS* N.S. 9 (1958): 13-25, 242-52.

2152. Jules L. Moreau, "The Historical Value of the Gospel Materials, Epitome and Prospect," *BRes* 5 (1960): 27-43.

2153. J. Neville Birdsall, "The Historical Foundations of Christian Faith," *EQ* 33 (1961): 16-25.

See also numbers 409, 412, 1977, 3103.

2153.1 Charles H. Talbert, "The Gospel and the Gospels," *Interp* 33 (1979): 351-62.

2. The Synoptic Problem

  a. *General Studies*

2154.   Ed. Scherer, "Quelques observations sur les rapports des trois premiers évangiles," *RT* 8 (1861): 292-307.

2155.   H. U. Meyboom, "Proeve eener geschiedenis der Logiahypotese," *TT* 6 (1872): 303-24, 361-402, 481-513.

2156.   A. D. Loman, "Bijdragen tot de critiek der synoptische Evangeliën. VII. De synoptische quaestie en de methode harer behandeling, naar aanleiding van Dr. A. Pierson's Geschrift over de Bergrede. VIII. Vervolg van VII," *TT* 13 (1879): 157-96, 365-405.

2157.   A. Hilgenfeld, "Neutestamentliche Forschungen. I. Die neueste Marcus-Hypothese. II. Der Christus des Philipperbriefes," *ZWT* 27 (1884): 484-505.

2158.   A. Wright, "On the Proper Names in S. Mark's Gospel: A Study in the Synoptic Problem," *Exp* 4th ser., 9 (1894): 173-88.

2159.   F. Godet, "The Composition of the Synoptical Gospels: A Reply," *Exp* 3rd ser., 10 (1889): 379-86.

2160.   C. Plummer, "A Mediaeval Illustration of the Documentary Theory of the Origin of the Synoptic Gospels," *Exp* 3rd ser., 10 (1889): 23-35.

2161.   Edward Y. Hincks, "The Probable Use of the First Gospel by Luke," *JBL* 10 (1891, part 2): 92-106.

2162.   W. Sanday, "A Survey of the Synoptic Question," *Exp* 4th ser., 3 (1891): 81-91, 179-94, 302-16, 345-59, 411-26.

2163.   G. Semeria, "La question synoptique," *RB* 1 (1892): 520-59.

2164.   J. Weiss, "Die Komposition der synoptischen Wiederkunftsrede," *TSK* 65 (1892): 246-70.

2165.   M. A. N. Rovers, "Een nieuwe poging tot oplossing van het synoptisch probleem (F. P. Badham, The Formation of the Gospels)," *TT* 27 (1893): 593-609.

2166.   V. H. Stanton, "Some Points in the Synoptic Problem," *Exp* 4th ser., 7 (1893): 81-97, 179-96, 256-66, 336-53.

2167.   David Brown, "The Synoptic Problem," *ET* 6 (1894-1895):

272-74.

2168. C. H. van Rhijn, "De Synoptische Evangeliën," *TS* 15 (1897): 365-81.

2169. V. Ermoni, "Le noyau primitif des évangiles synoptiques," *RB* 6 (1897): 83-93, 254-64.

2170. J. E. Belser, "Zur Evangelienfrage," *TQ* 80 (1898): 177-239.

2171. A. Hilgenfeld, "Die synoptische Zweiquellen-Theorie und Papias von Hierapolis," *ZWT* 44 (1901): 151-56.

2172. J. Weiss, "Die synoptischen Evangelien," *TR* 1 (1897-1898): 288-97; 2 (1899): 140-52; 4 (1901): 148-61; 6 (1903): 199-211; 11 (1908): 92-105, 122-33; 16 (1913): 183-96, 219-25.

2173. H. Zimmermann, "Die vier ersten Christlichen Schriften der Jerusalemischen Urgemeinde in den Synoptikern und der Apostelgeschichte," *TSK* 74 (1901): 415-58.

2174. F. C. Burkitt, "The Early Church and the Synoptic Gospels," *JTS* 5 (1903-1904): 330-49.

2175. John C. Hawkins, "St. Luke's Passion-Narrative considered with Reference to the Synoptic Problem," *ET* 15 (1903-1904): 122-26, 273-76.

2176. Jean Chapman, "Le témoignage de Jean le protytre au sujet de s. Marc et de s. Luc," *RBén* 22 (1905): 357-76.

2177. Frederick Torm, "Det synoptiske Problem," *TTDF* N.S. 8 (1906-1907): 392-415.

2178. B. W. Bacon, "A Turning Point in Synoptic Criticism," *HTR* 1 (1908): 48-69.

2179. Willoughby C. Allen, "Recent Criticism of the Synoptic Gospels," *ET* 20 (1908-1909): 445-49.

2180. Henry T. Hooper, "The Origin of the Term 'Synoptic'," *ET* 20 (1908-1909): 380.

2181. Frederick Torm, "Det synoptiske Problem," *TTDF* NS 10 (1908-1909): 369-98.

2182. A. T. W. Steinhauser, "The Synoptic Problem," *LCR* 28 (1909): 438-54, 588-95.

2183.   Arthur Wright, "Professor Stanton on the Synoptic Problem,"
          ET 21 (1909-1910): 211-16.

2184.   Arthur Carr, "Further Notes on the Synoptic Problem," *Exp*
          7th ser., 10 (1910): 543-53.

2185.   Arthur Wright, "Oxford Studies in the Synoptic Problem,"
          ET 22 (1910-1911): 358-62.

2186.   Robinson Smith, "Fresh Light on the Synoptic Problem," *HJ*
          10 (1911-1912): 615-25.

2187.   Ernest DeW. Burton, "Some Phases of the Synoptic
          Problem," *JBL* 31 (1912): 95-113.

2188.   Hugh Pope, "A Neglected Factor in the Study of the Synoptic
          Problem," *ITQ* 8 (1913): 247-70.

2189.   W. Robinson Smith, "Fresh Light on the Synoptic Problem,"
          AJT 17 (1913): 614-21.

2190.   Willoughby C. Allen, "A Study in the Synoptic Problem," *ET*
          26 (1914-1915): 264-65.

2191.   F. W. Grosheide, "Enkele opmerkingen over het synoptische
          vraagstuk," *GTl* 16 (1915): 174-93.

2192.   W. F. Adeney, "Synoptic Variations," *ET* 31 (1919- 1920):
          487-91.

2193.   Frederick C. Grant, "A Critique of *Matthew's Sayings of
          Jesus* by Castor," *ATR* 2 (1919-1920): 27-34.

2194.   Cuthbert Lattey, "The Place of Memory in the Composition
          of the Synoptic Gospels," *B* 1 (1920): 327-40.

2195.   F. C. Burkitt, " 'The Solution of the Synoptic Problem'," *JTS*
          23 (1921-1922): 191-96.

2196.   K. G. Goetz, "Zwei Beiträge zur synoptischen Quellen-
          forschung," *ZNW* 20 (1921): 165-70.

2197.   T. Stephenson, "Fresh Light on the Synoptic Problem," *JTS*
          23 (1921-1922): 250-55.

2198.   B. H. Streeter, "Fresh Light on the Synoptic Problem," *HJ* 20
          (1921-1922): 103-12.

2199.   M. Goguel, "Introduction au Nouveau Testament; 1. Les
          évangiles synoptiques," *RHPR* 3 (1923): 174-75.

2200. Henry Offermann, "The Present State of the Synoptic Problem," *LCR* 42 (1923): 1-23.

2201. J. F. Springer, "The Synoptic Problem," *BS* 80 (1923): 539-58; 81 (1924): 59-88, 201-39, 323-54, 493-514; 82 (1925): 89-113, 210-37, 321-53, 472-500; 83 (1926): 85-103, 213-28, 335-54; 84 (1927): 75-102, 342-57.

2202. J. F. Springer, "A Synoptic Matter," *LQ* 53 (1923): 465-75.

2203. Frank Zanzibar, "The Synoptic Problem from a Missionary's Point of View," *Th* 7 (1923): 252-58.

2204. Arthur G. Sellen, "The Interpretative Value of the Synoptic Source Analysis," *JBL* 44 (1925): 34-38.

2205. Primo Vannutelli, "Les évangiles synoptiques," *RB* 34 (1925): 32-53, 321-46, 505-23; 35 (1926): 27-39.

2206. U. Holzmeister, "De exordiis evangeliorum synopticorum," *VD* 8 (1928): 134-39.

2207. F. W. Grosheide, "The Synoptic Problem; A Neglected Factor in its Solution," *EQ* 3 (1931): 57-67.

2208. Alfred Wikenhauser, "Zur synoptischen Frage," *RQ* 39 (1931): 43-61.

2209. R. Pautrel, "Des abréviations subies par quelques sentences de Jésus dans la rédaction synoptique," *RSR* 24 (1934): 344-65.

2210. E. Rideau, "En marge de la question synoptique," *B* 15 (1934): 484-504.

2211. Primo Vannutelli, "Viam ostende, inveniam veritatem," *S* 1 (1936): pp. vii-x.

2212. Primo Vannutelli, "Disputationis ordo," *S* 1 (1936): pp. xii-cviii.

2213. Gaetano Angilella, "In tema di questione sinottica," *S* 2 (1937): pp. xxix-xxxi.

2214. Primo Vannutelli, "De argumentis internis," *S* 2 (1937): pp. iii-xxix; xxxvii-xlv, lxxiii-cxxxiv; 3 (1938): pp. iii-ixiv, lxix-c;4 (1939): pp.iii-xxi.

2215. Charles Callan, "The Synoptic Problem," *CBQ* 1 (1939):

55-63.

2216.   J. N. Geldenhuys, "The Synoptic Problem," *EQ* 11 (1939): 300-26.

2217.   José M. Bover, "Bernabé, clave de la solucion del problema sinoptico?" *EB* 3 (1944): 55-57.

2218.   Allen Wikgren, "Wellhausen on the Synoptic Gospels: A Centenary Appraisal," *JBR* 12 (1944): 174-80.

2219.   Iver K. Madsen, "Lidt om det synoptiske Problem og nutidens Typepsykologi," *DTT* 10 (1947): 96-107.

2220.   L. Vaganay, "La question synoptique," *ETL* 28 (1952): 238-56.

2221.   B. C. Butler, "Notes on the Synoptic Problem," *JTS* N.S. 4 (1953): 24-27.

2222.   Charles W. F. Smith, "Dr. Parker's Synoptic Theory," *ATR* 36 (1954): 210-13.

2223.   Jean Levie, "La complexité du problème synoptique," *ETL* 31 (1955): 619-36.

2224.   L. Vaganay, "Autour de la question synoptique," *ETL* 31 (1955): 343-56.

2225.   L. Vaganay, "Le problème synoptique," *RHPR* 25 (1955): 244-45.

2226.   P. Vielhauer, "Zum synoptischen Problem," *TLZ* 80 (1955): 647-52.

2227.   M. Zerwick, "Progressus in 'Quaestione synoptica' [P. Parker]," *VD* 33 (1955): 18-23.

2228.   Juan Leal, "Nota al Problema Sinóptico. Con motivo del libro del señor Vaganay," *EE* 30 (1956): 469-79.

2229.   Francis J. McCool, "Revival of Synoptic Source-Criticism," *ThSt* 17 (1956): 459-93.

2230.   John P. Brown, "On Early Revision of the Gospel of Mark," *JBL* 78 (1959): 215-27.

2231.   Eugene Maio, "The Synoptic Problem and the Vaganay Hypothesis," *ITQ* 26 (1959): 167-81.

2232.   L. Randellini, "Recenti tentativi per resolver la questione sinottica," *RivB* 7 (1959): 159-72, 242-57.

See also numbers 488, 1873, 1987, 3179, 3626, 3958, 6914, 6917, 6927, 6938, 6946, 6998, 7329.

2232.1   R. T. Simpson, "The Major Agreements of Matthew and Luke against Mark," *NTSt* 12 (1965-1966): 273-84.

2232.2   William R. Farmer, "The Two-Document Hypothesis as a Methodological Criterion in Synoptic Research," *ATR* 48 (1966): 380-96.

2232.3   James L. Bailey, "Comparing the Contributions of the Synoptic Writers," *BT* 18 (1968): 54-57.

2232.4   A. M. Honoré, "A Statistical Study of the Synoptic Problem," *NT* 10 (1968): 95-147.

2232.5   Paul Aubin, "Le fait synoptique," *RSR* 60 (1972): 491-632.

2232.6   E. P. Sanders, "Priorités et dépendances dans la tradition synoptique," *RSR* 60 (1972): 519-40.

2232.7   C. K. Barrett, "John and the Synoptic Gospels," *ET* 85 (1973-1974): 228-33.

2232.8   F. W. Beare, "On the Synoptic Problem: A New Documentary Theory," *ATR* Supp. #3 (1974): 15-28.

2232.9   J. C. O'Neill, "The Synoptic Problem," *NTSt* 21 (1975): 273-85.

2232.10   William R. Farmer, "Modern Developments of Griesbach's Hypothesis," *NTSt* 23 (1977): 275-95.

2232.11   Reginald H. Fuller, "Baur versus Hilgenfeld: A Forgotten Chapter in the Debate on the Synoptic Problem," *NTSt* 24 (1978): 355-70.

2232.12   J. B. Orchard, "Why Three Synoptic Gospels?: A Statement of the Two-Gospel Hypothesis," *ITQ* 46 (1979): 240-55.

2232.13   D. Moody Smith, "John and the Synoptics: Some Dimensions of the Problem," *NTSt* 26 (1979-1980): 425-44.

2232.14   David L. Dungan, "Theory of Synopsis Construction," *B* 61 (1980): 305-29.

2232.15   Gordon D. Fee, "A Text-Critical Look at the Synoptic Problem," *NT* 22/1 (1980): 12-28.

2232.16   Malcolm Lowe, "The Demise of Arguments from Order for Markan Priority," *NT* 24 (1982): 27-36.

2232.17   William R. Stegner, "The Priority of Luke: An Exposition of Robert Lindsey's Solution to the Synoptic Problem," *BRes* 27 (1982): 26-38.

2232.18   Malcolm Lowe and D. Flusser, "Evidence Corroborating a Modified Proto-Matthean Synoptic Theory," *NTSt* 29/1 (1983): 25-47.

2232.19   M. E. Glaswell, "The Relationship between John and Mark," *JSNT* 23 (1985): 99-115.

2232.20   J. D. M. Derrett, "Marcan Priority and Marcan Skill," *BO* 29 (1987): 135-40.

2232.21   F. Gerald Downing, "Compositional Conventions and the Synoptic Problem," *JBL* 107 (1988): 69-85.

2232.22   Philippe Rolland, "La question synoptique demande-t-elle une response compliquee?" *B* 70/2 (1989): 217-23.

2232.23   Ronald V. Huggins, "Matthean Posteriority: A Preliminary Proposal," *Interp* 34/1 (1992): 1-22.

2232.24   M. H. de Lang, "The Prehistory of the Griesbach Hypothesis," *ETL* 69 (1993): 134-39.

2232.25   J. Halverson, "Oral and Written Gospel: A Critique of Werner Kelber," *NTSt* 40 (1994): 180-95.

2232.26   K. E. Bailey, "Middle Eastern Oral Tradition and the Synoptic Gospels," *ET* 106 (1995): 363-67.

b. *Synoptic Agreements*

2233.   Ed. Reuss, "Études comparatives sur les trois premiers évangiles au point de vue de leurs rapports d'origine et de dépendence mutuelle," *RT* 10 (1855): 65-83; 11 (1855): 163-88; 15 (1857): 1-32; "Nouvelles études. . .," *NRT* 1 (1858): 15-72.

2234.   234, Karl Nippel, "Das Verhältnis der Evangelien des Marcus und Lucas," *TQ* 58 (1876): 551-79.

2235.   Dr. Schanz, "Matthäius und Lucas," *TQ* 64 (1882): 517-60.

2236.   I. N. Sepp, "Die Markus- und Matthäusfrage und gewisse

Missverständnisse bei den Synoptikern," *TSK* 63 (1890): 357-67.

2237. G. Schläger, "Die Abhängigkeit des Matthäusevangeliums vom Lukasevangelium," *TSK* 69 (1896): 83-93.

2238. Rush Rhees, "A 'Striking Monotony' in the Synoptic Gospels," *JBL* 17 (1898): 87-102.

2239. H. Chavannes, "Les resemblances des évangiles synoptiques," *RTP* 37 (1904): 138-60.

2240. E. Wendling, "Synoptische Studien; Der Hauptmann von Kapernaum," *ZNW* 9 (1908): 96-109; 10 (1909): 219-29.

2241. B. H. Alford, "Variations Between Matthew and Mark," *HJ* 7 (1908-1909): 649-61.

2242. W. W. Holdsworth, "The Markan Narrative in the Synoptic Gospels," *Exp* 8th ser., 1 (1911): 449-60.

2243. W. J. Cunningham Pike, "The Angels at the Empty Tomb: A Study in Synoptics," *Exp* 8th ser., 4 (1912): 269-75.

2244 T. Stephenson, "The Classification of Doublets in the Synoptic Gospels," *JTS* 20 (1919): 1-8.

2245. T. Stephenson, "The Overlapping of Sources in Matthew and Luke," *JTS* 21 (1920): 127-45.

2246. J. F. Springer, "The Order of Events in Matthew and Mark," *BS* 79 (1922): 131-52, 321-50; 80 (1923): 115-32, 272-83.

2247. M. Goguel, "Luke and Mark: With a Discussion of Streeter's Theory," *HTR* 26 (1933): 1-56.

2248. Julian Price Love, "The Nature of the Synoptic Message," *JBR* 10 (1942): 80-87.

2249. T. F. Glasson, "Did Matthew and Luke Use a 'Western' Text of Mark?" *ET* 55 (1943-1944): 180-84; 57 (1945-1946): 53-54.

2250. C. S. C. Williams, "Did Matthew and Luke use a 'Western'Text of Mark?" *ET* 56 (1944-1945): 44-45; 58 (1946-1947): 251.

2251. V. C. MacMunn, "From St. Matthew to St. Luke," *Th* 7 (1923): 37-42.

2252.   B. Willaert, "La connexion littéraire entre la première prédiction de la passion et la confession de Pierre chez les synoptiques," *ETL* 32 (1956): 24-25.

2253.   Harald Sahlin, "Zwei Fälle von harmonisierendem Einfluss des Matthäus-Evangeliums auf das Markus-Evangelium," *ST* 13 (1959): 166-79.

2254.   A. W. Argyle, "Agreements Between Matthew and Luke," *ET* 73 (1961-1962): 19-22.

2254.1   E. P. Sanders, "The Argument from Order and the Relationship Between Matthew and Luke," *NTSt* 15/2 (1969): 249-61.

2254.2   Jean F. Bouhours, "Une étude de l'ordonnance de la triple tradition," *RSR* 60 (1972): 595-614.

2254.3   T. R. W. Longstaff, "The Minor Agreements: An Examination of the Basic Argument," *CBQ* 37 (1975): 184-92.

2254.4   M.-É. Boismard, "The Two-Source Theory at an Impasse," *NTSt* 26 (1979-1980): 1-17.

2254.5   Charles H. Dyer, "Do the Synoptics Depend on Each Other?" *BS* 138 (1981): 230-45.

2254.6   Carlo Buzzetti, "Parallels in the Synoptic Gospels: A Case Study," *BTr* 34 (1984): 425-431.

2254.7   Christopher M. Tuckett, "On the Relationship Between Matthew and Luke," *NTSt* 30/1 (1984): 130-42.

2254.8   Timothy A. Friedrichsen, "The Minor Agreements of Matthew and Luke against Mark: Critical Observations on R. B. Vinson's Statistical Analysis," *ETL* 65 (1989): 395-408.

2254.9   F. Gerald Downing, "A Paradigm Perplex: Luke, Matthew and Mark," *NTSt* 38/1 (1992): 15-36.

c. *"Q"*

2255.   W. C. Allen, "Did St. Matthew and St. Luke use the Logia?" *ET* 11 (1899-1900): 424-26.

2256.   W. Sanday, "A Plea for the Logia," *ET* 11 (1899-1900): 471-73.

2257. John C. Hawkins, "Some Internal Evidence for the Use of the Logia in the First and Third Gospels," *ET* 12 (1900-1901): 72-76.

2258. C. W. Emmet, "Professor Harnack on the Second Source of the First and Third Gospels," *ET* 19 (1907-1908): 297-300, 358-63.

2259. Kirsopp Lake, "The Date of Q," *Exp* 7th ser., 7 (1909): 494-507.

2260. James H. Moulton, "Synoptic Studies; III. Some Criticisms on Professor Harnack's 'Sayings of Jesus'," *Exp* 7th ser., 7 (1909): 411-23.

2261. George H. Gilbert, "The Jesus of 'Q'—the Oldest Source in the Gospels," *HJ* 10 (1911-1912): 533-42.

2262. George D. Castor, "The Relation of Mark to the Source Q," *JBL* 31 (1912): 82-91.

2263. Carl S. Patton, "Did Mark Use Q? or Q Use Mark?" *AJT* 16 (1912): 634-42.

2264. Anton Fridrichsen, "De nyere rekonstruktioner av Logiakilden (Q)," *NTT* 14 (1913): 193-244.

2265. B. W. Bacon, "The Nature and Design of Q, the Second Synoptic Source," *HJ* 22 (1923-1924): 674-88.

2266. Henry T. Fowler, "Paul, Q, and the Jerusalem Church," *JBL* 43 (1924): 9-14.

2267. John Line, "The Second Synoptic Source," *CJRT* 1 (1924): 313-22.

2268. J. M. C. Crum, "The 'Q' Document," *HJ* 24 (1925-1926): 346-49, 537-62.

2269. E. W. Lummis, "A Case against 'Q'," *HJ* 24 (1925-1926): 755-65.

2270. B. W. Bacon, "The Q Section on John the Baptist and the Shemoneh Esreh," *JBL* 45 (1926): 23-56.

2271. J. M. C. Crum, "Mark and 'Q'," *Th* 12 (1926): 275-82, 350-58.

2272. Joachim Jeremias, "Zur Hopothese einer schriftlichen

Logienquelle Q," *ZNW* 29 (1930): 147-49.

2273.   Wilhelm Bussmann, "Hat es nie eine schriftliche Logienquelle gegeben?" *ZNW* 31 (1932): 23-32.

2274.   Vincent Taylor, "Some Outstanding New Testament Problems; The Elusive Q," *ET* 46 (1934-1935): 68-74.

2275.   W. F. Howard, "The Origin of the Symbol 'Q'," *ET* 50 (1938-1939): 379-80.

2276.   George D. Kilpatrick, "The Disappearance of Q," *JTS* 42 (1941): 182-84.

2277.   Frederick C. Grant, "Was There a Document 'Q'?" *RL* 11 (1942): 35-44.

2278.   C. K. Barrett, "Q: A Re-examination," *ET* 54 (1942-1943): 320-23.

2279.   T. E. Floyd Honey, "Did Mark Use Q?" *JBL* 62 (1943): 319-31.

2280.   A. W. Argyle, "Parallels Between the Pauline Epistles and Q," *ET* 60 (1948-1949): 318-20.

2281.   B. H. Throckmorton, "Did Mark Know Q?" *JBL* 67 (1948): 319-29.

2282.   A. W. Argyle, "The Accounts of the Temptations of Jesus in Relation to the Q Hypothesis," *ET* 64 (1952-1953): 382.

2283.   A. W. Argyle, "Scriptural Quotations in Q," *ET* 65 (1953-1954): 285-86.

2284.   Frederick Bussby, "Is Q an Aramaic Document?" *ET* 65 (1953-1954): 272-75.

2285.   Bruce M. Metzger, "Scriptural Quotations in Q Material," *ET* 65 (1953-1954): 125.

2286.   Vincent Taylor, "The Order of Q," *JTS* N.S. 4 (1953): 27-31.

2287.   C. F. D. Moule and A. M. G. Stephenson, "R. G. Heard on Q and Mark," *NTSt* 2 (1955-1956): 114-19.

2288.   E. L. Bradby, "In Defense of Q," *ET* 68 (1956-1957): 315-18.

2289.   Hollis W. Huston, "The 'Q' Parties at Oxford," *JBR* 25 (1957): 123-28.

2290.   C. S. Petrie, " 'Q' is only What You Make it," *NT* 3 (1959): 28-33.

2291.   Theodore R. Rosché, "The Words of Jesus and the Future of the 'Q' Hypothesis," *JBL* 79 (1960): 210-20.

2292.   John P. Brown, "Mark as Witness to an Edited Form of Q," *JBL* 80 (1961): 29-44.

2293.   William R. Farmer, "A 'Skeleton in the Closet' of Gospel Research," *BRes* 6 (1961): 18-42.

            See also numbers 2050, 2344, 2407.

2293.1   C. Michaelis, "Die π Alliteration der Subjektsworte der ersten 4 Seligpreisungen in Mt. V 3-6 und ihre Bedeutung für den Aufbau der Seligpreisungen bei Mt., Lk. und in Q," *NT* 10 (1968): 148-61.

2293.2   E. P. Sanders, "The Overlaps of Mark and Q and the Synoptic Problem," *NTSt* 19 (1972-1973): 453-65.

2293.3   Giuseppe Frizzi, "Carattere originale e rilevanza degli 'apostoli inviati' in Q," *RivB* 21 (1973): 401-12.

2293.5   Ronald D. Worden, "Redaction Criticism of Q: A Survey," *JBL* 94 (1975): 532-46.

2293.6   Michael D. Goulder, "On Putting Q to the Test," *NTSt* 24 (1977-1978): 218-34.

2293.7   Petros Vassiliadis, "The Nature and Extent of the Q Document," *NT* 20 (1978): 49-73.

2293.8   Arland D. Jacobson, "The Literary Unity of Q," *JBL* 101 (1982): 365-89.

2293.9   David R. Catchpole, "Q and 'The Friend at Midnight'," *JTS* 34 (1983): 407-24.

2293.10   Christopher M. Tuckett, "1 Corinthians and Q," *JBL* 102 (1983): 607-19.

2293.11   David R. Catchpole, "Jesus and the Community of Israel: The Inaugural Discourse in Q," *BJRL* 68 (1985-1986): 296-316.

2293.12   Wendy J. Cotter, "The Parable of the Children in the Market-Place, Q (Lk) 7:31-35," *NT* 29 (1987): 289-304.

2293.13   John S. Kloppenborg, "Symbolic Eschatology and the

Apocalypticism of Q," *HTR* 80 (1987): 287-306.

2293.14   Robert J. Miller, "The Rejection of the Prophet in Q," *JBL* 107 (1988): 225-40.

2293.15   Dieter Lührmann, "The Gospel of Mark and the Sayings Collection Q," *JBL* 108 (1989): 51-71.

2293.16   Christopher M. Tuckett, "Q, Prayer, and the Kingdom," *JTS* 40 (1989): 367-76.

2293.17   Mary R. D'Angelo, "Theology in Mark and Q: Abba and 'Father' in Context," *HTR* 85 (1992): 149-74.

2293.18   D. Kosch, "Q and Jesus," *BibZ* 36/1 (1992): 30-38.

2293.19   I. Dunderberg, "Q and the Beginning of Mark," *NTSt* 41 (1995): 501-11.

2293.20   M. C. Moreland and James M. Robinson, "The International Q Project," *JBL* 114 (1995) 475-85.

2293.21   James M. Robinson, "The Incipit of the Sayings Gospel Q," *RHPR* 75 (1995): 9-33.

2293.22   Michael D. Goulder, "Is Q a Juggernaut?" *JBL* 115 (1996): 667-81.

2293.23   John S. Kloppenborg, "The Sayings Gospel Q and the Quest of the Historical Jesus," *HTR* 89 (1996): 307-44.

3. Literary Criticism of Matthew

   a. *General Studies*

2294.   H. B. Smith, "The Structure of the Gospel According to Matthew," *BS* 1 (1844): 86-97.

2295.   A. Hilgenfeld, "Das Matthäus-Evangelium, auf's Neue untersucht," *ZWT* 10 (1867): 303-23, 366-447; 11 (1868): 22-76.

2296.   A. D. Loman, "Bijdragen tot de kritiek der synoptische Evangeliën. II. De vijf spreukengroepen in het Mattheus-Evangelie," *TT* 4 (1870): 28-48.

2297.   A. D. Loman, "De samenstelling van het Mattheus-Evangelie in verband beschouwd met het vraagstuk omtrent het ontstaan der kanonische Evangeliën in het algemeen," *TT* 4 (1870): 570-605.

2298. J. Wieser, "Über Plan und Zweck des Matthäus-Evangeliums," *ZKT* 1 (1877): 564-94; 2 (1878): 129-70.

2299. F. Gardiner, "A Study in the First Gospel," *JBL* 9 (1890, part 1): 1-16.

2300. G. M. Harmon, "The Judaism of the First Gospel," *JBL* 14 (1895): 114-24.

2301. Ernest DeW. Burton, "The Purpose and Plan of the Gospel of Matthew," *BW* 11 (1898): 37-44, 91-101.

2302. Thomas Milne, "St. Matthew's Parallel Narratives," *JTS* 5 (1903-1904): 602-608.

2303. Francis A. Christie, "The Composition of Matthew's Gospel," *BW* 34 (1909): 380-90.

2304. Commission Biblique, "Évangile de saint Matthieu," *NRT* 43 (1911): 570-72.

2305. Jos. Hermans, "L'évangile hébreu de saint Matthieu," *NRT* 43 (1911): 484-502.

2306. E. F. Morison, "The Enthusiasm of the Gospel According to St. Matthew," *Exp* 8th ser., 1 (1911): 408-16.

2307. Joseph Sickenberger, "Das neue Dekret der Bibelkommission über das Mt. Evangelium und die sog. Zweiquellentheorie," *BibZ* 9 (1911): 391-96.

2308. J. R. Mozley, "The Distinctive Excellence of the First Gospel," *HJ* 17 (1918-1919): 272-81.

2309. B. W. Bacon, "Jesus and the Law: A Study of the First 'Book' of Matthew (Mt. 3-7)," *JBL* 47 (1928): 203-31.

2310. Ernest W. Parsons, "Some Pragmatic Elements in the Gospel of Matthew," *CQ* 6 (1929): 397-408.

2311. Burton S. Easton, "Professor Bacon's 'Studies in Matthew'," *ATR* 13 (1931): 49-55.

2312. Morton S. Enslin, "The Five Books of Matthew: Bacon on the Gospel of Matthew," *HTR* 24 (1931): 67-98.

2313. M. Kiddle, "The Conflict between the Disciples, the Jews, and the Gentiles in St. Matthew's Gospel," *JTS* 36 (1935): 33-44.

2314.   David Daube, "Three Questions of Form in Matthew v," *JTS* 45 (1944): 21-31.

2315.   John Henry Bennetch, "Matthew: An Apologetic," *BS* 103 (1946): 238-46, 477-84.

2316.   C. H. Dodd, "Matthew and Paul," *ET* 58 (1946-1947): 293-98.

2317.   J. Spencer Kennard, "The Reconciliation Tendency in Matthew," *ATR* 38 (1946): 159-63.

2318.   Kenneth W. Clark, "The Gentile Bias in Matthew," *JBL* 66 (1947): 165-72.

2319.   Paul Demann, "Le premier évangile est-il anti-juif?" *CS* 5 (1951): 240-57.

2320.   Austin Farrer, " 'The Originality of St. Matthew,' by B. C. Butler," *JTS* N.S. 3 (1952): 102-106.

2321.   Irénée Fransen, "Cahier de Bible: L'évangile selon Matthieu. La charte du royaume des cieux," *BVC* no. 6 (1954): 82-88.

2322.   V. Iacono, "Caratteristiche dell'Evangelo di san Matteo," *RivB* 3 (1955): 32-48.

2323.   S. Lewis Johnson, "The Argument of Matthew," *BS* 112 (1955): 143-53.

2324.   Floyd V. Filson, "Broken Patterns in the Gospel of Matthew," *JBL* 75 (1956): 227-31.

2325.   Massey H. Shepherd, "The Epistle of James and the Gospel of Matthew," *JBL* 75 (1956): 40-51.

2326.   C. U. Wolf, "The Gospel to the Essenes," *BRes* 3 (1958): 28-43 [i.e. Matthew].

          See also numbers 2490, 3382, 3390, 3398, 3531, 3636, 10063.

2326.1   Edgar Krentz, "The Extent of Matthew's Prologue: Toward the Structure of the First Gospel," *JBL* 83 (1964): 409-14.

2326.2   Georg Strecker, "Das Geschichtsverständnis des Matthäus," *EvT* 26 (1966): 57-74.

2326.3   G. Danieli, "Analisi strutturale ed esegesi di Matteo a proposito del recente libro di J. Radermakers," *RivB* 21

(1973): 433-39.

2326.4   C. E. Carlston, "Interpreting the Gospel of Matthew," *Interp* 29 (1975): 3-12.

2326.5   Arland J. Hultgren, "Interpreting the Gospel of Luke," *Interp* 30 (1976): 353-65.

2326.6   John M. Court, "The Didache and St. Matthew's Gospel," *SJT* 34/2 (1981): 109-20.

2326.7   Graham N. Stanton, "The Gospel of Matthew and Judaism," *BJRL* 66/2 (1984): 264-84.

2326.8   James E. Davison, "Anomia and the Question of an Antinomian Polemic in Matthew," *JBL* 104/4 (1985): 617-35.

2326.9   B. R. Doyle, "Matthew's Intention as Discerned by His Structure," *RB* 95 (1988): 34-54.

2326.10   Klyne Snodgrass, "Matthew's Understanding of the Law," *Interp* 46 (1992): 368-78.

2326.11   R. Aguirre, "La comunidad de Mateo y el judaísmo," *EB* 51 (1993): 233-49.

2326.12   Robert L. Mowery, "The Matthean References to the Kingdom: Different Terms for Different Audiences," *ETL* 70 (1994): 398-405.

2326.13   C. C. Rowland, "Apocalyptic, the Poor, and the Gospel of Matthew," *JTS* 45 (1994): 504-18.

b. *Studies concerning Date, Author, Sources, and Authenticity*

2327.   A. Hilgenfeld, "Die Einführung des kanonischen Matthäus-Evangeliums in Rom," *ZWT* 38 (1895): 447-51.

2328.   J. H. Wilkinson, "Were Matthew and Zacchaeus the same Person?" *Exp* 5th ser., 8 (1898): 37-42.

2329.   Eb. Nestle, "Die Fünfteilung im Werk des Papias und im ersten Evangelium," *ZNW* 1 (1900): 252-54.

2330.   W. Soltau, "Zur Entstehung des I. Evangeliums," *ZNW* 1 (1900): 219-48.

2331.   A. S. Barnes, "Suggestions on the Origin of the Gospel according to St. Matthew," *JTS* 6 (1904-1905): 187-203.

2332. Arthur Carr, "The Authenticity and Originality of the First Gospel," *Exp* 7th ser., 4 (1907): 339-49.

2333. Shirley Jackson Case, "The Origin and Purpose of the Gospel of Matthew," *BW* 34 (1909): 391-403.

2334. Willoughby C. Allen, "The Alleged Catholicism of the First Gospel and its Date," *ET* 21 (1909-1910): 439-44.

2335. Willoughby C. Allen, "Harnack and Moffatt on the Date of the First Gospel," *ET* 22 (1910-1911): 349-52.

2336. S. Grébaut, "Notice sur Matthieu l'évangéliste," *ROC* 18 (1913): 312-14 [in an Ethiopic ms.].

2337. T. Stephenson, "The Old Testament Quotations Peculiar to Matthew," *JTS* 20 (1919): 227-29.

2338. J. F. Springer, "The Apostolic Authorship of the First Gospel," *LQ* 54 (1924): 49-88.

2339. J. F. Springer, "Why Lose the Apostle Matthew as a Witness?" *LQ* 54 (1924): 419-37.

2340. Ernst von Dobschütz, "Matthäus als Rabbi und Katechet," *ZNW* 27 (1928): 338-48.

2341. W. Caspari, "Hebräische Spruchquelle des Matthäus und hellenistisch-phönikischer Schauplatz Jesu," *ZNW* 31 (1932): 209-33.

2342. Joseph Sickenberger, "Drei angebliche Hinweise auf die Matthäuspriorität," *BibZ* 21 (1933): 1-8.

2343. Frederick C. Grant, "Further Thoughts on the M-Hypothesis," *ET* 46 (1933-1934): 438-45.

2344. Alexius Mallon, "Papias Hierapolitanus quandonom opus de *Logiis Dominicis* exaraverit?" *VD* 14 (1934): 93-94.

2345. H. Grimme, "Studien zum hebräischen Urmatthäus," *BibZ* 23 (1935-1936): 244-65, 347-57.

2346. W. S. Reilly, "The Origin of St. Matthew's Gospel," *CBQ* 2 (1940): 320-29.

2347. J. Spencer Kennard, "The Place and Origin of Matthew's Gospel," *ATR* 31 (1949): 243-46.

2348. Ant. J. van der Voort, "The Originality of St. Matthew," *Scr* 5 (1952): 72-76.

2349. Bertil Gärtner, "The Habakkuk Commentary (DSH) and the Gospel of Matthew," *ST* 7 (1953): 1-24.

2350. Günther Bornkamm, "Matthäus als Interpret der Herrenworte," *TLZ* 79 (1954): 342-46.

2351. Anton Baumstark, "Die Zitate des Mt. Evangeliums aus dem Zwölfprophetenbuch," *B* 37 (1956): 296-313.

2352. Edward P. Blair, "Recent Study of the Sources of Matthew," *JBR* 27 (1959): 206-10.

2353. Joachim Jeremias, "Die Muttersprache des Evangelisten Matthäus," *ZNW* 50 (1959): 270-74.

2354. Josef Kurzinger, "Das Papiaszeugnis und die Erstgestalt des Matthäusevangeliums," *BibZ* 4 (1960): 19-38.

2355. S. Vernon McCasland, "Matthew Twists the Scriptures," *JBL* 80 (1961): 143-48.

    See also number 10051.

2355.1 C. E. Carlston, "A Positive Criterion of Authenticity?" *BRes* 7 (1962): 33-44.

4. Literary Criticism of Mark

a. *General Studies*

2356. F. C. Baur, "Kritisch-exegetische Bemerkungen über einige Stellen der Evangelien, namentlich des Marcusevangeliums," *ZWT* 2 (1859): 364-76.

2357. A. Hilgenfeld, "Das Marcus-Evangelium und die Marcus-Hypothese," *ZWT* 7 (1864): 287-333.

2358. A. Hilgenfeld, "Marcus zwischen Matthäus und Lucas," *ZWT* 9 (1866): 82-113.

2359. H. U. Meyboom, "Een plan in het Marcus-Evangelie," *TT* 1 (1867): 651-90.

2360. A. D. Loman, "Het evangelische epos en de Markus-Hypothese van Volkmar," *TT* 4 (1870): 269-311.

2361. H. B. Swete, "St. Mark in the New Testament," *Exp* 5th ser.,

6 (1897): 81-89.

2362.　Ernest DeW. Burton, "The Purpose and Plan of the Gospel of Mark," *BW* 15 (1900): 250-55, 331-40.

2363.　A. Hilgenfeld, "Der Evangelist Marcus und Julius Wellhausen," *ZWT* 47 (1904): 180-228, 289-332, 462-524.

2364.　W. H. Ramsay, "The Oldest Written Gospel," *Exp* 7th ser., 3 (1907): 410-32.

2365.　B. W. Bacon, "The Purpose of Mark's Gospel," *JBL* 29 (1910): 41-60.

2366.　F. C.Burkitt, "The Historical Character of the Gospel of Mark," *AJT* 15 (1911): 169-93.

2367.　Ludwig Schade, "Markusevangelium und Astralmythus," *BibZ* 10 (1912): 370-95.

2368.　Carl S. Patton, "Two Studies of the Gospel of Mark," *HTR* 6 (1913): 229-39.

2369.　W. T. Whitley, "The Scope of Mark's Work," *ET* 29 (1917-1918): 331-32.

2370.　L. Dieu, "Marc source des Actes?" *RB* 29 (1920): 555-69.

2371.　W. Larfeld, "Darf man noch von einer Markushypothese reden?" *NKZ* 33 (1922): 201-21.

2372.　B. W. Bacon, "Notes on the Gospel of Mark," *JBL* 42 (1923): 137-49.

2373.　C. H. Turner, "Marcan Usage: Notes, Critical and Exegetical, on the Second Gospel," *JTS* 25 (1923-1924): 377-86; 26 (1924-1925): 12-20, 145-56, 225-40; 27 (1925-1926): 58-62; 28 (1926-1927): 9-30, 349-62; 29 (1927-1928): 275-89, 346-61.

2374.　F. C. Burkitt, "Was the Gospel of Mark Written in Latin?" *JTS* 29 (1927-1928): 375-81.

2375.　D. Strömholm, "A Literary Examination of Mark," *HJ* 26 (1927-1928): 252-65.

2376.　Paul-Louis Couchoud (tr. by Morton S. Enslin): "Was the Gospel of Mark Written in Latin?" *CQ* 5 (1928): 35-79.

2377.　M.-J. Lagrange, "L'évangile de saint Marc n'a pas été écrit en latin," *RB* 37 (1928): 106-16.

2378. Donald W. Riddle, "The Martyr Motif in the Gospel according to Mark," *JR* 4 (1924): 397-410.

2379. Ernest W. Burch, "Tragic Action in the Second Gospel: A Study in the Narrative of Mark," *JR* 11 (1931): 346-58.

2380. Martin Rist, "Is Mark a Complete Gospel?" *ATR* 14 (1932): 143-51.

2381. M. Kiddle, "The Death of Jesus and the Admission of the Gentiles in St. Mark," *JTS* 35 (1934): 45-50.

2382. W. Emery Barnes, "Points that may be Missed in Reading the Gospel According to St. Mark," *Th* 34 (1937): 207-14 [Mk. 1:14, 2:1; 2:17; 3:5; 5:19, 20; 6:45; 8:24; 9:30, 31a; 9:39, 41; 13:10].

2383. Iver K. Madsen, "Om Markusevangeliet," *TTDF* 5th ser., 8 (1937): 241-57.

2384. G. H. Stevenson, "The Significance of St. Mark," *Th* 36 (1938): 37-42.

2385. Hans von Soden, "Ein erdichtetes Markusevangelium," *TB* 18 (1939): 65-81, 280-82 [M. Erich Winkel, *Das ursprüngliche Evangelium*, 1937].

2386. Morton S. Enslin, "The Artistry of Mark," *JBL* 66 (1947): 385-99.

2387. J. J. Pedreira de Castro, "Instantâneos de Jesus no Evangelho de S. Marcos," *REB* 11 (1951): 257-88.

2388. L. Vaganay, "L'absence du sermon sur la montagne chez Marc," *RB* 58 (1951): 5-46.

2389. F. N. Davey, " 'A Study in Mark,' by Austin Farrer," *JTS* N.S. 3 (1952): 239-42.

2390. Cecil S. Emden, "The Gospel of Mark made more Vivid," *ET* 64 (1952-1953): 334-36.

2391. A. G. Hebert, "Dr. Austin Farrer on St. Mark's Gospel," *RTR* 12 (1953): 61-74.

2392. Sherman E. Johnson, "A New Theory of St. Mark," *ATR* 35 (1953): 41-44.

2393.   Willibald Michaux, "Cahier de Bible; L'évangile selon
          Marc," *BVC* no. 1 (1953): 78-97.

2394.   L. Vaganay, "Existe-t-il chez Marc quelques traces du
          sermon sur la montagne?" *NTSt* 1 (1954-1955): 192-210.

2395.   John Coutts, "The Authority of Jesus and of the Twelve in St.
          Mark s Gospel," *JTS* N.S. 8 (1957): 111-18.

2396.   Robert G. Bratcher, "Introduction to the Gospel of Mark,"
          RE 55 (1958): 351-66.

2397.   Edwin M. Good, "The Bridge between Mark and Acts," *JBL*
          77 (1958): 67-74.

2398.   Alfred Kuby, "Zur Konzeption des Markus-Evangeliums,"
          ZNW 49 (1958): 52-64.

2399.   T. A. Burkill, "Anti-Semitism in St. Mark's Gospel," *NT* 3
          (1959): 34-53.

          See also numbers 1358, 2230, 2480, 2541, 2898, 2920,
          3382, 3456, 3576, 3606, 3640, 5142.

2399.1   Samuel Sandmel, "Prolegomena to a Commentary on Mark,"
          JBL 31 (1963): 294-300.

2399.2   Jean Delorme, "Aspects doctrinaux du second Évangile,"
          ETL 43 (1967): 74-99.

2399.3   Robert H. Stein, "The Proper Methodology for Ascertaining
          a Markan Redaction History," *NT* 13 (1971): 181-98.

2399.4   H. Hogarth, "A New Look at Mark's Gospel," *ET* 84
          (1972-1973): 88-90.

2399.5   R. Alan Culpepper, "An Outline of the Gospel according to
          Mark," *RE* 75 (1978): 619-22.

2399.6   Heinrich Baarlink, "Zur Frage nach dem Antijudaismus im
          Markusevangelium," *ZNW* 70 (1979): 166-93.

2399.7   Joanna Dewey, "Oral Methods of Structuring Narrative in
          Mark," *Interp* 43 (1989): 32-44.

2399.8   Joanna Dewey, "Mark as Interwoven Tapestry: Forecasts and
          Echoes for a Listening Audience," *CBQ* 53 (1991): 221-36.

2399.9   M. Cahill, "The Identification of the First Markan
          Commentary," *RB* 101 (1994): 258-68.

2399.10   B. Escaffre, "La mort de Jésus et la venue du Royaume dans l'évangile de Marc," *EB* 52 (1994): 329-39.

2399.11   R. Kieffer, "En ny måde at strukturere fortaellingerme om Jesus: En semiotisk doktoafhandling om Markusevangeliet," *DTT* 57 (1994): 40-51.

b. *Studies concerning Date, Author, Sources, and Authenticity*

2400.   Adversaria, "On the Epithet 'Stump-Fingered' applied to St. Mark," *JCSP* 2 (1855): 87-88.

2401.   S. P. Tregelles, "Why was the Epithet 'Stump- Fingered' applied to St. Mark?" *JCSP* 2 (1855): 224-26.

2402   Ephorus Bäumlein, "Die Nachricht des Papias über das Marcusevangelium," *TSK* 36 (1863): 111-13.

2403.   A. Hilgenfeld, "Das Urevangelium," *ZWT* 32 (1889): 1-42.

2404.   J. A. M. Mensinga, "Eine Eigenthümlichkeit des Marcus-Evangeliums," *ZWT* 32 (1889): 385-92.

2405.   Hans Graeven, "Der heilige Markus in Rom und in der Pentapolis," *RQ* 13 (1899): 109-26.

2406.   Vernon Bartlet, "Mark the 'Curt-Fingered' Evangelist," *JTS* 6 (1904-1905): 121-24.

2407.   C. A. Briggs, "The Use of the Logia of Matthew in the Gospel of Mark," *JBL* 23 (1904): 191-210.

2408.   K. Lincke, "Simon Petrus and Johannes Markus," *ZNW* 5 (1904): 191-203.

2409.   M. Brückner, "Die Petruserzählungen im Markusevangelium," *ZNW* 8 (1907): 48-65.

2410.   Warren J. Moulton, "The Relation of the Gospel of Mark to Primitive Christian Tradition," *HTR* 3 (1910): 403-36.

2411.   F. H. Colson, "Τάξει in Papias (The Gospels and the Rhetorical Schools)," *JTS* 14 (1912-1913): 62-69.

2412.   Arthur Wright, "Τάξει in Papias," *JTS* 14 (1912-1913): 298-300.

2413.   Shirley Jackson Case, "John Mark," *ET* 26 (1914-1915): 372-76.

2414.   Richard Drescher, "Das Markusevangelium und seine

Entstehung," *ZNW* 17 (1916): 228-56.

2415.   Edmund D. Jones, "Was Mark the Gardener of Gethsemane?" *ET* 33 (1921-1922): 403-404.

2416.   A. T. W. Steinhauser, "Petrine Elements in Mark's Gospel," *LCR* 41 (1922): 247-52.

2417.   B. W. Bacon, "La date et l'origine de l'evangile selon Marc," *RHPR* 3 (1923): 268-85.

2418.   J. Rendel Harris, "An Unrecognized Latinism in St. Mark," *ET* 35 (1923-24): 403-405.

2419.   George A. Barton, "The Question of 'Ur-Marcus' Once More," *JBL* 48 (1929): 239-47.

2420.   Paul Gächter, "Zur Abfassungszeit des Markusevangeliums," *ZKT* 54 (1930): 425-35.

2421.   B. T. Holmes, "Luke's Description of John Mark," *JBL* 54 (1935): 63-72.

2422.   Joachim Jeremias, "Zum Problem des Ur-Markus," *ZNW* 35 (1936): 280-85.

2423.   M. Buchanan, "The Fisherman's Gospel," *Th* 35 (1937): 111-16.

2424.   W. S. Reilly, "St. Mark the Disciple of St. Peter and St. Paul," *CBQ* 1 (1939): 223-231.

2425.   Donald F. Robinson, "The Sources of Mark," *JBL* 66(1947): 153-64.

2426.   Jean Levie, "L'évangile araméen de s. Matthieu est-il la source de l'évangile de s. Marc?" *NRT* 76 (1954): 689-715, 812-43.

2427.   Ant. J. van der Voort, "The Origin of St. Mark's Gospel," *Scr* 6 (1954): 100-107.

2428.   Horace A. Rigg, "Papias on Mark," *NT* 1 (1956): 161-83.

2429.   H. E. W. Turner, "The Tradition of Mark's Dependence upon Peter," *ET* 71 (1959-1960): 260-63.

2430.   G. F. Brandon, "The Date of the Markan Gospel," *NTSt* 7 (1960-1961): 126-41.

2431.   Terence Y. Mullins, "Papias on Mark's Gospel," *VCh* 14

(1960): 216-24.

2431.1   N. J. McEleney, "Authenticating Criteria and Mark 7:1-23," *CBQ* 34/4 (1972): 431-60.

2431.2   Paul J. Achtemeier, "Mark as Interpreter of the Jesus Traditions," *Interp* 32 (1978): 339-52.

2431.3   Adrien Delclaux, "Deux témoignages de Papias sur la composition de Marc?" *NTSt* 27 (1980-1981): 401-11.

2431.4   C. Clifton Black, "The Quest of Mark the Redactor: Why Has It Been Pursued, and What Has It Taught Us?" *JSNT* 33 (1988): 19-39.

2431.5   Ernest Best, "Mark's Narrative Technique," *JSNT* 37 (1989): 43-58.

2431.6   Matthew Black, "The Use of Rhetorical Terminology in Papias on Mark and Matthew," *JSNT* 37 (1989): 31-41.

2431.7   C. C. Günter "Was Mark a Roman Gospel," *ET* 105 (1993): 36-40.

2431.8   P. J. Botha, "The Historical Setting of Mark's Gospel: Problems and Possibilities," *JSNT* 51 (1993): 27-55.

2431.9   C.-J. Thornton, "Justin und das Markusevangelium," *ZNW* 84 (1993): 93-110.

2431.10   Michael D. Goulder, "The Pre-Marcan Gospel," *SJT* 47 (1994): 453-71.

2431.11   John R. Donahue, "Windows and Mirrors: The Setting of Mark's Gospel," *CBQ* 57 (1995): 1-26.

c. *The "Messianic Secret"*

2432.   Martin Schulze, "Der Plan des Marcusevangeliums in seiner Bedeutung für das Verständnis der Christologie desselben," *ZWT* 37 (1894): 332-73.

2433.   W. Bousset, "Das Messiasgeheimnis in den Evangelien," *TR* 5 (1902): 307-16, 347-62.

2434.   A. Hilgenfeld, "Der mysteriöse Marcus und der reactionäre Jacobus," *ZWT* 46 (1903): 1-39.

2435.   W. Sanday, "The Injunctions of Silence in the Gospels," *JTS* 5 (1903-1904): 321-29.

2436.   A. Bolliger, "Das Messiahgeheimnis bei Markus," *STZ* 23 (1906): 98-132.

2437.   Chr. A. Bugge, "Über das Messiasgeheimnis," *ZNW* 7 (1906): 97-111.

2438.   E. Bickermann, "Das Messiasgeheimnis und Komposition des Markusevangeliums," *ZNW* 22 (1923): 122-40.

2439.   Rene Guisan, "Le secret messianique," *RTP* N.S. 22 (1934): 222-35.

2440.   Elie Bikerman, "Latens Deus: La reconnaissance du Christ dans les évangiles," *HTR* 39 (1946): 169-88.

2441.   Vincent Taylor, "Unsolved New Testament Problems—The Messianic Secret in Mark," *ET* 59 (1947-1948): 146-51.

2442.   Vincent Taylor, "W. Wrede's The Messianic Secret in the Gospels (Das Messiasgeheimnis in den Evangelien)," *ET* 65 (1953-1954): 246-50.

2443.   James W. Leitch, "The Injunctions of Silence in Mark's Gospel," *ET* 66 (1954-1955): 178-82.

2444.   T. A. Burkill, "The Injunctions to Silence in St. Mark's Gospel," *TZ* 12 (1956): 585-604.

2445.   T. A. Burkill, "Concerning St. Mark's Conception of Secrecy," *HJ* 55 (1956-1957): 150-58.

2446.   Vincent Taylor, "The Messianic Secret in Mark," *HJ* 55 (1956-1957): 241-48.

2447.   G. H. Boobyer, "The Secrecy Motif in St. Mark's Gospel," *NTSt* 6 (1959-1960): 225-35.

2448.   Joseph B. Tyson, "The Blindness of the Disciples in Mark," *JBL* 80 (1961): 261-68 [Messianic secret].

    See also number 368.

2448.1   Frederick W. Danker, "Mark 1:45 and the Secrecy Motif," *CTM* 37 (1966): 492-99.

2448.2   Frederick W. Danker, "Postscript to the Markan Secrecy Motif," *CTM* 38 (1967): 24-27.

2448.3   Brian G. Powley, "The Purpose of the Messianic Secret: A Brief Survey," *ET* 80 (1968-1969): 308-10.

2448.4   David E. Aune, "The Problem of the Messianic Secret," *NT* 11 (1969): 1-31.

2448.5   R. N. Longenecker, "The Messianic Secret in the Light of Recent Discoveries," *EQ* 41 (1969): 207-15.

2448.6   W. C. Robinson, "The Quest for Wrede's Secret Messiah," *Interp* 27 (1973): 10-30.

2448.7   Morna D. Hooker, "The Johannine Prologue and the Messianic Secret," *NTSt* 21 (1974-1975): 40-58.

2448.8   D. Moody Smith, "Clement of Alexandria and Secret Mark: The Score at the End of the First Decade," *HTR* 75 (1982): 449-61.

2448.9   Jack D. Kingsbury, "The Parable of the Wicked Husbandmen and the Secret of Jesus' Divine Sonship in Matthew: Some Literary-Critical Observations," *JBL* 105 (1986): 643-55.

5. Literary Criticism of Luke

a. *General Studies*

2449.   M. Schwalb, "Paroles de Jésus-Christ propres a l'évangile de Luc," *RT* 8 (1861): 321-52.

2450.   H. U. Meyboom, "De Lucas-quaestie (naar aanleiding van geschriften van W. Stewart en Dr. G. J. Vos)," *TT* 8 (1874): 521-38.

2451.   August Jacobsen, "Über die lukanischen Schriften," *ZWT* 31 (1888): 129-58.

2452.   452 Shailer Mathews, "Introduction to the Gospel of LukeThe Criticism of the Gospel," *BW* 5 (1895): 336-42; "II. The Historical Details of the Gospel," 448-55.

2453.   Eb. Nestle, "Some Corrections to Plummer on St. Luke," *ET* 17 (1905-1906): 478-79, 522.

2454.   B. W. Bacon, "Professor Harnack on the Lukan Narrative," *AJT* 13 (1909): 59-76.

2455.   C. H. Dodd, "Changes of Scenery in Luke," *ET* 33 (1921-1922): 40-41.

2456.   John A. Hutton, "The Differentia of the Gospel according to St. Luke," *ET* 34 (1922-1923): 306-308.

2457. Frederick Smith, "The Gospel of Luke Considered as a Psychological Document," *BS* 80 (1923): 491-94.

2458. Philip Wendell Crannell, "The Watering of Luke," *RE* 23 (1926): 154-69.

2459. Mary E. Andrews, "*Tendenz* versus Interpretation: F. C. Baur's Criticisms of Luke," *JBL* 58 (1939): 263-76.

2460. Hans Conzelmann, "Zur Lukasanalyse," *ZTK* N.F. 49 (1952): 16-33.

2461. M. Goguel, "Quelques observations sur l'oeuvre de Luc," *RHPR* 33 (1953): 37-51.

See also numbers 493, 504, 2745, 2818, 5330, 5332.

2461.1 B. E. Beck, "The Common Authorship of Luke and Acts," *NTSt* 23 (1977): 346-52.

2461.2 I. de la Potterie, "Les deux noms de Jérusalem dans l'évangile de Luc," *RSR* 69 (1981): 57-70.

2461.3 Terrance Callan, "The Preface of Luke-Acts and Historiography," *NTSt* 31 (1985): 576-81.

2461.4 Jack D. Kingsbury, "The Plot of Luke's Story," *Interp* 48 (1994): 369-78.

2461.5 D. Marguerat, "Juden und Christen im lukanischen Doppelwerk," *EvT* 54 (1994): 261-64.

2461.6 D. Marguerat, "Juifs et chrétiens selon Luc-Actes," *B* 75 (1994): 126-46.

2461.7 Mark A. Powell, "Toward a Narrative-Critical Understanding of Luke," *Interp* 48 (1994): 341-46.

2461.8 F. Sieg, "Communication de masse et rythmes de prose dans Luc/Acts," *RHPR* 74 (1994): 113-27.

b. *Studies concerning Date, Author, Sources, and Authenticity*

(1). The Evangelist Luke

2462. Dr. van Vloten, "Zur näheren Beleuchtung meiner Lukas- und Silas-Conjectur," *ZWT* 14 (1871): 431-34.

2463. F. Nau, "Le martyre de saint Luc évangéliste," *ROC* 3 (1898): 151-67.

2464. G. Mercati, "Lucas or Lucanus?" *JTS* 6 (1904-1905): 435.

2465. G. Balestri, "Il martirio di S. Luca evangelista (Testo copto e traduzione)," *Bes* 8 (1905): 128-40.

2466. Prof. Kellner, "Sterbeort und Translation des Evangelisten Lukas und des Apostels Bartholomäus," *TQ* 87 (1905): 596-608.

2467. Adolf Harnack, "Noch einmal Lukas als Verfasser des 3. Evangeliums und der Apostelgeschichte," *TLZ* 31 (1906): 466-68.

2468. Carl Clemen, "Harnack's 'Lukas der Arzt'," *TR* 10 (1907): 97-113.

2469. J. D. MacRoy, "The Authorship of the Third Gospel and the Acts," *ITQ* 2 (1907): 190-202.

2470. J. Rendel Harris, "The Discovery of St. Luke's Name," *ET* 25 (1913-1914): 44.

2471. R. C. Ford, "St. Luke and Lucius of Cyrene," *ET* 32 (1920-1921): 219-20.

2472. B. W. Bacon, "Le témoignage de Luc sur lui-même," *RHPR* 8 (1928): 209-26.

2473. S. H. Price, "The Authorship of Luke-Acts," *ET* 55 (1943-1944): 194.

2474. Alfred Vögeli, "Lukas und Euripides," *TZ* 9 (1953): 415-38.

2475. Henry J. Cadbury, " 'He' and 'I' passages in Luke-Acts," *NTSt* 3 (1956-1957): 128-32.

2476. John Baker, "Luke, the Critical Evangelist," *ET* 68 (1956-1957): 123-25.

2476.1 A. J. Mattill, "Jesus-Paul Parallels and the Purpose of Luke-Acts,"*NT* 17 (1975): 15-46.

2476.2 Jan H. Solbakk, "Lukas—legen: En kritisk underokelse av debatten i moderne historieforskning om den profesjonelle bakgrunn og identitet til forfatteren av Lukas-Acta," *NTT* 94 (1993): 219-33.

(2). Sources used by Luke

(a). *General Studies*

2477.   C. F. Nösgen, "Der Ursprung und die Entstehung des dritten Evangeliums," *TSK* 53 (1880): 49-137.

2478.   Karl Stockmeyer, "Über die Quellen des Lukas-Evangeliums," *STZ* 1 (1884): 117-49.

2479.   August Jacobsen, "Zur Frage nach den Quellen des Lucasevangeliums," *ZWT* 33 (1890): 180-85.

2480.   F. P. Badham, "St. Luke's St. Mark," *ET* 7 (1895-1896): 457-59.

2481.   M.-J. Lagrange, "Les sources du troisième évangile," *RB* 4 (1895): 5-22; 5 (1896): 5-38.

2482.   D. Völter, "Die Apokalypse des Zacharias im Evangelium des Lukas," *TT* 30 (1896): 244-69.

2483.   P. Berg, "Die Quellen des Lukasevangeliums," *NKZ* 20 (1909): 282-313, 337-52.

2484.   J.-Alfred Porret, "La genèse de l'évangile de Luc," *RTQR* 23 (1914): 97-122.

2485.   V. T. Kirby, "Did S. Luke know the Old Testament?" *ET* 33 (1921-1922): 227-29.

2486.   Hugo Bévenot, "Alte und neue Lukanische Quellen," *TQ* 110 (1929): 428-47.

2487.   D. M. McIntyre, "The Building of the Third Gospel," *EQ* 1 (1929): 130-46.

2488.   A. M. Perry, "Luke's Disputed Passion-Source," *ET* 46 (1934-1935): 256-60 [Lk. 22-23].

2489.   M. Kiddle, "The Passion Narrative in St. Luke's Gospel," *JTS* 36 (1935): 267-80 [Lk. 22-23].

2490.   Christopher Butler, "St. Luke's Debt to St. Matthew," *HTR* 32 (1939): 237-308.

2491.   Allan Barr, "The Use and Disposal of the Marcan Source in Luke's Passion Narrative," *ET* 55 (1943-1944): 227-31.

2492.   George D. Kilpatrick, "Scribes, Lawyers, and Lucan Origins," *JTS* N.S. 1 (1950): 56-60.

2493.   Paul Winter, "On Luke and Lucan Sources," *ZNW* 47 (1956):

217-42.

2494. Paul Winter, "Liken Sources," *ET* 68 (1956-1957): 285.

2495. Paul Winter, "Sources of the Lucan Passion Narrative," *ET* 68 (1956-1957): 95.

2496. Michael D. Goulder and M. L. Sanderson, "St. Luke's Genesis," *JTS* N.S. 8 (1957): 12-30.

2497. Abdon M. Salazar, "Questions about St. Luke's Sources," *NT* 2 (1958): 316-17.

2498. Sidney Jellicoe, "St. Luke and the Letter of Aristeas," *JBL* 80 (1961): 149-55.

See also numbers 2099, 2103, 2109, 3112, 5922, 7103.

2498.1 F. Gerald Downing, "Common Ground with Paganism in Luke and Josephus," *NTSt* 28 (1982): 546-59.

(b). *Proto-Luke and "L"*

2499. Burton S. Easton, "Linguistic Evidence for the Lucan Source L," *JBL* 29 (1910): 139-80.

2500. Franz Dibelius, "Die Herkunft der Sonderstücke des Lukasevangeliums," *ZNW* 12 (1911): 325-43.

2501. Burton S. Easton, "The Special Source of the Third Gospel," *JBL* 30 (1911): 78-103.

2502. B. W. Bacon, "The 'Order' of the Lukan 'Interpolations.' I. General Survey," *JBL* 34 (1915): 166-79; "II. The Smaller Interpolation, Lk. 6:20-8:3," 36 (1917): 112-39; "III. The Longer Interpolation, Lk. 9:51-18:14," 37 (1918): 20-53.

2503. Vincent Taylor, "Proto-Luke," *ET* 33 (1921-1922): 250-52.

2504. Vincent Taylor, "The Value of the Proto-Luke Hypothesis," *ET* 36 (1924-1925): 476-77.

2505. J. W. Hunkin, "The Composition of the Third Gospel, with Special Reference to Canon Streeter's Theory of Proto-Luke," *JTS* 28 (1926-1927): 250-62.

2506. Vincent Taylor, "Is the Proto-Luke Hypothesis Sound?" *JTS* 29 (1927-1928): 147-55.

2507. Vincent Taylor, "The Proto-Luke Hypothesis: A Reply to Dr. W. K. Lowther Clarke's Queries," *Th* 14 (1927): 72-76.

2508. Vincent Taylor, "The First Draft of Luke's Gospel," *Th* 14

(1927): 131-64.

2509.   A. M. Perry, " 'Proto-Luke' and the 'Chicago Theory' of the Synoptic Problem," *JBL* 47 (1928): 91-116.

2510.   A. M. Perry, "A Judaeo-Christian Source in Luke," *JBL* 49 (1930): 181-94.

2511.   B. H. Streeter, "Die Ur-Lukas-Hypothese," *TSK* 102 (1930): 332-40.

2512.   Eric F. F. Bishop, "Local Colour in Proto-Luke," *ET* 45 (1933-1934): 151-56.

2513.   J. M. Creed, "Some Outstanding New Testament Problems: 'L' and the Structure of the Lucan Gospel: A Study of the Proto-Luke Hypothesis," *ET* 46 (1934-1935): 101-107.

2514.   Vincent Taylor, "Professor J. M. Creed and the Proto-Luke Hypothesis," *ET* 46 (1934-1935): 236-38.

2515.   J. M. Creed, "The Supposed 'Proto-Lucan' Narrative of the Trial before Pilate: A Rejoinder," *ET* 46 (1934-1935): 378-79.

2516.   W. J. Fournier, "The Third Gospel: A Hidden Source," *ET* 46 (1933-1934): 428.

2517.   L. Cerfaux, "À propos des sources du troisième évangel: Proto-Luc ou Proto-Matthieu?" *ETL* 12 (1935): 5-27.

2518.   Pierson Parker, "A Proto-Lukan Basis for the Gospel according to the Hebrews," *JBL* 59 (1940): 471-78.

2519.   R. P. C. Hanson, "Does δίκαιος in Luke xxiii.47 explode the Proto-Luke Hypothesis?" *Herm* no. 60 (1942): 74-78.

2520.   C. S. Petrie, "The Proto-Luke Hypothesis," *ET* 54 (1942-1943): 172-77.

2521.   Vincent Taylor, "The Proto-Luke Hypothesis: A Rejoinder," *ET* 54 (1942-1943): 219-22.

2522.   C. S. Petrie, "The Proto-Luke Hypothesis: Observations on Dr. Vincent Taylor's Rejoinder," *ET* 55 (1943-1944): 52-53.

2523.   S. MacLean Gilmour, "A Critical Re-examination of Proto-Luke," *JBL* 67 (1948): 143-52.

2524.   Eduard Schweizer, "Eine hebraisierende Sonderquelle des

Lukas?" *TZ* 6 (1950): 161-85.

2525. Vincent Taylor, "Important Hypotheses Reconsidered—The Proto-Luke Hypothesis," *ET* 67 (1955-1956): 12-16.

2526. Joachim Jeremias, "Perikopen-Umstellungen bei Lukas?" *NTSt* 4 (1957-1958): 115-19.

2527. H. W. Montefiore, "Does 'L' hold Water?" *JTS* N.S. 12 (1961): 59-60.

2528. Heinz Schürmann, "Protolukanische Spracheigentumlich-keiten? Zu Fr. Rehkopf, Die lukanische Sonderquelle. Ihr Umfang und Sprachgebrauch," *BibZ* 5 (1961): 266-86.

2528.1 John W. Wenham, "Synoptic Independence and the Origin of Luke's Travel Narrative," *NTSt* 27 (1981): 507-15.

(c.) *Paul, Marcion, and Luke's Gospel*

2529. G. Fr. Franck, "Über das Evangelium Marcions und sein Verhältnis zum Lukas-Evangelium," *TSK* 28 (1855): 296-364.

2530. H. U. Meyboom, "Het Paulinisme van Lukas (naar aanleiding van W. H. van de Sande Bakhuyzen)," *TT* 8 (1874): 521-38.

2531. E. H. Plumptre, "St. Luke and St. Paul: An Inquiry into their Mutual Relations," *Exp* 1st ser., 4 (1876): 134-56.

2532. T. E. Bleiben, "The Gospel of Luke and the Gospel of Paul," *JTS* 45 (1944): 134-40.

2532.1 Tjitze Baarda, "De Korte Tekst Van Het Onze Vader in Lucas 11:2-4: Een Marcionitische Coruptie?" *NedTT* 44 (1990): 273-87.

(3). The Plan, Method, and Purpose of Luke

2533. C. Wittichen, "Die Composition des Lucasevangeliums," *ZWT* 16 (1873): 499-522.

2534. C. F. Nösgen, "Das historiographische Verfahren des dritten Evangelisten," *TSK* 50 (1877): 440-97.

2535. H. Holtzmann, "Die Disposition des dritten Evangeliums," *ZWT* 26 (1883): 257-67.

2536. H. Lesêtre, "La méthode historique de S. Luc," *RB* 1 (1892):

171-85.

2537.   Arnold Rüegg, "Die Lukasschriften und der Raumzwang des antiken Buchwesens," *TSK* 69 (1896): 94-101.

2538.   Ernest DeW. Burton, "The Purpose and Plan of the Gospel of Luke," *BW* 16 (1900): 248-58, 342-50.

2539.   B. W. Bacon, "The Treatment of Mk. 6: 14-8: 26 in Luke," *JBL* 26 (1907): 132-50 [Lk. 9:7-17, etc.].

2540.   E. G. Selwyn, "The Carefulness of Luke the Prophet," *Exp* 7th ser., 7 (1909): 547-58; 10 (1910): 449-63; 8th ser., 1 (1911): 273-84.

2541.   A. Wilfred Richmond, "Note on the Great Omission by St. Luke of St. Mark VI.45-VIII.3," *Exp* 8th ser., 2 (1911): 547-53.

2542.   Th. Zahn, "Das dritte Buch des Lukas," *NKZ* 29 (1917): 373-95.

2543.   A. T. Robertson, "Luke's Method of Research," *BR* 5 (1920): 171-95.

2544.   Donald W. Riddle, "The Occasion of Luke-Acts," *JR* 10 (1930): 545-62.

2545.   A. M. Ramsey, "The Cross in St. Luke's Gospel. A Study in his Editing of Mark," *Th* 25 (1932): 250-59.

2546.   Otto A. Piper, "The Purpose of Luke," *USR* 57 (1945-1946): 15-25.

2547.   Lambert Nolle, "The 'Orderly Account' of St. Luke," *Scr* 1 (1946): 53-54.

2548.   Juan Leal, "El plan literario del III Evangelio y la geografia," *EE* 29 (1955): 197-215.

2549.   H. C. Snape, "The Composition of the Lukan Writings: A Re-assessment," *HTR* 53 (1960): 27-46.

See also numbers 3436, 3557.

(4). The Date and the Authenticity of Luke

2550.   W. H. Simcox, "The Authentic Pictures of St. Luke," *Exp* 3rd ser., 8 (1888): 152-56.

2551.   A. W. H. Ramsay, "Professor Harnack on Luke," *Exp* 7th ser., 2 (1906): 481-507.

2552. J. MacRory, "Professor Harnack and St. Luke's Historical Authority," *ITQ* 2 (1907): 317-29.

2553. W. S. Reilly, "St. Luke," *CBQ* 1 (1939): 314-24.

2554. E. F. Sutcliffe, "A Note on the Date of St. Luke's Gospel," *Scr* 3 (1948): 45-46.

2555. Jean Burnier, "Art littéraire, témoignage et histoire chez saint Luc," *RTP* N.S. 38 (1950): 219-25.

2556. C. S. C. Williams, "The Date of Luke-Acts," *ET* 64 (1952-1953): 283-84.

2557. Henry G. Russel, "Which was written first, Luke or Acts?" *HTR* 48 (1955): 167-74.

2558. Salvador Muñoz Iglesias, "El Evangelio de la Infancia en San Lucas y las infancies de los héroes bíblicos," *EB* 16 (1957): 329-82.

6. Literary Criticism of John

a. *General Studies*

2559. Pfarrer Hauff, "Einige Bemerkungen über die Abhandlung von D. v. Baur über die Composition und den Charakter des johanneischen Evangeliums," *TSK* 19 (1846): 550-629.

2560. M. Schwalb, "Notes sur l'évangile de Jean," *RT* 1 (1863): 113-48, 249-78.

2561. J. H. Scholten, "Étude historique et critique sur le quatrième évangile," *RT* 2 (1864): 184-227; 3 (1865): 97-144, 301-39; 4 (1866): 49-117, 161-207.

2562. J. C. Matthes, "De conservatieven en het vierde Evangelie. Eene critiek van Nederlandse apologetiek," *TT* 1 (1867): 521-49.

2563. W. Beyschlag, "Zur johanneischen Frage," *TSK* 47 (1874): 607-723; 48 (1875): 235-87, 413-79.

2564. A. Hilgenfeld, "Ein französischer Apologet des Johannes-Evangeliums," *ZWT* 32 (1889): 129-47 [Gédéon Chastand, L'apôtre Jean et le IVᵉ évangile, étude de critique et d'historie, Paris, 1888].

2565.   J. S. Banks, "St. John in Modern Christian Thought," *ET* 3 (1891-1992): 61-63.

2566.   J. Iverach, "Dr. H. H. Wendt on the Fourth Gospel," *Exp* 4th ser., 4 (1891): 161-78.

2567.   W. C. van Manen, "Het misverstand in het vierde Evangelie," *TT* 25 (1891): 407-32.

2568.   W. Sanday, "The Present Position of the Johannean Question," *Exp* 4th ser., 4 (1891): 321-39, 401-20; 5 (1892): 12-29, 161-82, 281-99, 372-91.

2569.   A. Spaeth, "Studies in the Gospel of St. John," *LCR* 10 (1891): 173-205; 11 (1892): 205-37; 12 (1893): 289-318.

2570.   J. A. Cross, "The Fourth Gospel," *Exp* 4th ser., 6 (1892): 127-31.

2571.   A. Williams. Anthony, "The Fourth Gospel: An Outline for the Study of its Higher Criticism," *BW* 1 (1893): 190-93.

2572.   Fr. Düsterdieck, "Über das Evangelium des Johannes," *TSK* 66 (1893): 783-96.

2573.   Erich Haupt, "Wendts Stellung zur johanneischen Frage," *TSK* 66 (1893): 217-50.

2574.   W. L. Ferguson, "The Fourth Gospel after a Century of Criticism," *BS* 53 (1896): 1-27.

2575.   James Drummond, "The Fourth Gospel and the Quarto-decimans," *AJT* 1 (1897): 601-57.

2576.   M. Labourt, "La question johannine," *RB* 7 (1898): 59-73.

2577.   A. Camerlynck, "La question johannine," *RHE* 1 (1900): 201-11, 419-29, 633-44.

2578.   A. van Hoonacker, "L'hypothèse de M. Wendt sur la composition du quatrième évangile," *RHE* 2 (1901): 747-70.

2579.   W. Soltau, "Zum Problem des Johannesevangeliums," *ZNW* 2 (1901): 140-49.

2580.   B. W. Bacon, "Recent Aspects of the Johannine Problem—I. The External Evidence," *HJ* 1 (1902-1903): 510-31; 2 (1903-1904): 323-46; 3 (1904-1905): 353-75.

2581.   Vernon Bartlet, "Two Notes on the Fourth Gospel," *ET* 14

(1902-1903): 118-21.

2582. F. R. M. Hitchcock, "Wendt's Theory of the Fourth Gospel," *Herm* 12 (1903): 322-39.

2583. G. Wauchope Stewart, "Wendt on the Fourth Gospel," *Exp* 6th ser., 7 (1903): 65-80, 135-46.

2584. W. Lock, "Notes on the Gospel according to St. John," *JTS* 6 (1904-1905): 415-18.

2585. Robert Small, "Problems of the Fourth Gospel," *ET* 18 (1906-1907): 24-26, 67-68, 129-34.

2586. Pfarrer van Bebber and Dr. [J. E.] Belser, "Beiträge zur Erklärung des Johannesevangeliums," *TQ* 89 (1907): 1-58.

2587. Ernst von Dobschütz, "Johanneische Studien," *ZNW* 8 (1907): 1-8.

2588. James Moffatt, "Wellhausen on the Fourth Gospel," *Exp* 7th ser., 4 (1907): 56-69.

2589. F. Warburton Lewis, "The Fourth Gospel," *ET* 19 (1907-1908): 142-43.

2590. Roland Schütz, "Zum ersten Teil des Johannesevangeliums," *ZNW* 8 (1907): 243-55.

2591. Gottlieb Linder, "Vier Proben aus dem Johannesevangelium," *STZ* 26 (1909): 205-13 [Ch. 4; 13:1-15; 20:1ff.; 20:19-23].

2592. J. A., "Au sujet du quatrième évangile," *NRT* 42 (1910): 238-41.

2593. Parke P. Flourney, "The Fourth Gospel at Yale and Chicago," *BS* 67 (1910): 695-723.

2594. Th. Zahn, "Das Evangelium des Johannes unter den Händen seiner neuesten Kritiker," *NKZ* 22 (1911): 28-58, 83-115.

2595. J. Kreyenbühl, "Kritische Randglossen zu Wellhausens Evangelium Johannis," *STZ* 30 (1913): 129-45, 177-204, 241-63.

2596. James Moffatt, "Ninety Years After: A Survey of Bretscheneider's 'Probabilia' in the Light of Subsequent Johannine Criticism," *AJT* 17 (1913): 368-76.

2597.   W. Soltau, "Das Problem des Johannesevangeliums und der Weg zu seiner Lösung," *ZNW* 16 (1915): 24-53.

2598.   Edgar J. Goodspeed, "The Gospel of John," *BW* 48 (1916): 255-60, 319-25, 382-87; 49 (1917): 57-62, 127-34.

2599.   Hans C. Juell, "The Johannine Problems," *BS* 73 (1916): 376-95.

2600.   W. Mallinckrodt, "Een vraagpunt uit het Evangelie van Johannes," *NTS* 2 (1919): 136-44.

2601.   Pfarrer Rüdel, "Das Missverständnis im Johannesevangelium," *NKZ* 32 (1921): 351-61.

2602.   Clayton R. Bowen, "Notes on the Fourth Gospel," *JBL* 43 (1924): 22-27.

2603.   A. T. Robertson, "The Problem of the Fourth Gospel Again," *BR* 9 (1924): 65-75.

2604.   A. G. Voigt, "The Discourses in the Gospel of St.John," *LCR* 43 (1924): 214-27.

2605.   M. Goguel, "Une nouvelle méthode pour l'étude du problème johannique," *RHPR* 6 (1926): 366-95.

2606.   Vincent Taylor, "The Fourth Gospel and Some Recent Criticism," *HJ* 25 (1926-1927): 725-43.

2607.   E.-B. Allo, "Aspects nouveaux du problème johannique," *RB* 37 (1928): 37-62, 198-220.

2608.   John Chapman, "Names in the Fourth Gospel," *JTS* 30 (1928-1929): 16-23.

2609.   M. Meinertz, "Zum Problem des Johannesevangeliums," *TRev* 27 (1928): 161-70.

2610.   Clayton R. Bowen, "Comments on the Fourth Gospel," *ATR* 12 (1929-1930): 225-38.

2611.   Ernst von Dobschütz, "Zum Charakter des 4. Evangeliums," *ZNW* 28 (1929): 161-77.

2612.   C. F. Nolloth, "The Fourth Gospel and its Critics," *HJ* 28 (1929-1930): 124-36.

2613.   W. L. Newton, "Difficulties in Translating St. John's Gospel," *CBQ* 1 (1939): 160-62.

2614.   Hugo Odeberg, "Über das Johannesevangelium," ZST 16 (1939): 173-88.

2615.   Mary E. Andrews, "Pioneer Work on the Gospel of John," JBL 59 (1940): 181-92 [F. C. Baur].

2616.   Philippe-H. Menoud, "Le problème johannique," RTP N.S., 29 (1941): 236-56; 30 (1942): 155-75; 31 (1943): 80-100.

2617.   H. P. V. Nunn, "Considerations on Some Recent Criticism of the Fourth Gospel," EQ 15 (1943): 169-78.

2618.   R. P. Casey, "Professor Goodenough and the Fourth Gospel," JBL 64 (1945): 535-42.

2619.   Erwin R. Goodenough, "A Reply," JBL 64 (1945): 543-44 [See no. 2618].

2620.   Siegfried Mendner, "Johanneische Literaturkritik," TZ 8 (1952): 418-34.

2621.   Francisco Maria López Melús, "Caracteristicas del Evangelio de San Juan," CB 12 (1955): 288-95.

2622.   Evaristo Martin Nieto, "Introducción a la lectura del 4° Evangelio," CB, 12 (1955): 193-206.

2623.   F.-M. Braun, "Où en est l'étude du quatrième évangile?" ETL 32 (1956): 535-46.

2624.   Pierson Parker, "Two Editions of John," JBL 75 (1956): 303-14.

2625.   C. H. Dodd, "A l'arrière-plan d'un dialogue johannique," RHPR 27 (1957): 5-17.

2626.   Ernst Haenchen, "Johanneische Probleme," ZTK N.F. 56 (1959): 19-54.

2627.   A. M. Hunter, "Recent Trends in Johannine Studies," ET 71 (1959-1960): 164-67, 219-22.

2628.   Everett F. Harrison, "The Discourses of the Fourth Gospel," BS 117 (1960): 23-31.

2629.   L. Johnston, "The Making of the Fourth Gospel," Scr 12 (1960): 1-13.

2630.   George D. Kilpatrick, "Some Notes on Johannine Usage," BTr 11 (1960): 173-77.

2631.   Merrill C. Tenney, "The Footnotes of John's Gospel," *BS* 117 (1960): 350-64.

2632.   S. Virgulin, "Caratteristiche del quarto Evangelo," *BO* 2 (1960): 152-56.

2633.   Frank Madeley, "A New Approach to the Gospel of St. John," *EQ* 33 (1961): 140-45.

           See also numbers 1929, 3148, 10059.

2633.1   C. De Santo, "A Theological Key to the Gospel of John," *EQ* 34 (1962): 83-90.

2633.2   B. Brinkmann, "Prolog und Johannes-Evangelium. Theologische Grundlinien, innere Einheit," *BK* 20 (1965): 106-13.

2633.3   J. E. Burns, "The Use of Time in the Fourth Gospel," *NTSt* 13 (1966-1967): 285-90.

2633.4   C. Dekker, "Grundschrift und Redaktion im Johannesevangelium," *NTSt* 13 (1966-1967): 66-80.

2633.5   Günther Bornkamm, "Zur Interpretation des Johannesevangeliums," *EvT* 28/1 (1968): 8-25.

2633.6   Olivier de Dinechin, "Kathos la similitude dans l'évangile selon saint Jean," *RSR* 58 (1970): 195-236.

2633.7   Barclay M. Newman, "Some Observations Regarding the Argument, Structure and Literary Characteristics of the Gospel of John," *BTr* 26 (1975): 234-39.

2633.8   F.-M. Braun, "La réduction du pluriel au singulier dans l'évangile et la première lenre de Jean," *NTSt* 24 (1977-1978): 40-67.

2633.9   J. M. Bassler, "The Galileans: A Neglected Factor in Johannine Community Research," *CBQ* 43 (1981): 243-57.

2633.10   Jean Zumstein, "Chronique johannique," *RTP* 114 (1982): 65-77.

2633.11   Jean Zumstein, "L'évangile Johannique: une Stratégie du croire," *RSR* 77 (1989): 217-32.

2633.12   M. C. de Boer, "Narrative Criticism, Historical Criticism, and the Gospel of John," *JSNT* 47 (1992): 35-48.

2633.13   H. Saxby, "The Time-Scheme in the Gospel of John," *ET*

104 (1992): 9-13.

2633.14   Stephen C. Barton, "The Believer, the Historian and the Fourth Gospel," *Th* 96 (1993): 289-302.

2633.15   Andrew T. Lincoln, "Trials, Plots and the Narrative in the Fourth Gospel," *JSNT* 56 (1994): 3-30.

2633.16   T. Tatcher, "A New Look at Asides in the Fourth Gospel," *BS* 151 (1994): 428-39.

2633.17   N. G. Timmins, "Variation in Style in the Johannine Literature," *JSNT* 53 (1994): 47-64.

b. *Studies concerning Date, Author, Sources, Authenticity, etc.*

(1). Date, Place of Origin, and Author

2634.   Wilibald Grimm, "Über das Evangelium und den ersten Brief des Johannes als Werke eines und desselben Verfassers," *TSK* 20 (1847): 171-87.

2635.   K. L. Weitzel, "Das Selbstzeugnis des vierten Evangelisten über seine Person," *TSK* 22 (1849): 578-638.

2636.   A. Réville, "Jean le prophète et Jean l'évangéliste," *RT* 9 (1854): 329-63; 10 (1855): 1-24.

2637.   A. Kayser, "L'école de Tubingue et l'évangile selon saint Jean," *RT* 12 (1856): 217-77; 13 (1856): 65-85.

2638.   Georg Eduard Steitz, "Das angebliche Zeugnis des Melito von Sardes für das johanneische Evangelium," *TSK* 30 (1857): 584-96.

2639.   J. T. Tobler, "Über den Ursprung des vierten Evangeliums," *ZWT* 3 (1860): 169-203.

2640.   L. W. E. Rauwenhoff, "Aantekeningen over zekeren Theodotus, door Prof. Hofstede de Groot Aangevoerd als een getuige van het oudheid der vierde Evangelie uit het midden der tweede eeu," *TT* 1 (1867): 338-52.

2641.   H. B. Hackett, "Self-Commendatory Allusions in John's Gospel," *BS* 25 (1868). 779-83.

2642.   Otto Pfleiderer, "Beleuchtung der neuesten Johannes-Hypothese," *ZWT* 12 (1869): 394-421.

2643.   J. H. Scholten, "De Apostel Johannes in Klein-Azië. Critisch onderzoek," *TT* 5 (1871): 597-691.

2644. M. A. N. Rovers, "Een paar hoofdstukken uit de Johannes literature van den jongsten tijd," *TT* 7 (1873): 60-74.

2645. H. Holtzmann, "Das Verhältnis des Johannes zu Ignatius und Polykarp," *ZWT* 20 (1877): 187-214.

2646. S. Leathes, "The Writer of the Fourth Gospel and St. John," *Exp* 1st ser., 5 (1877): 56-71.

2647. Fréd. Rambert, "De l'auteur du IVᵉ évangile," *RTP* 10 (1877): 88-109, 161-87; 11 (1878): 36-57; 12 (1879): 577-602.

2648. F.-C.-J. van Goens, "L'apôtre Jean: est-il l'auteur du IVᵉ évangile?" *RTP* 9 (1876): 481-528; 11 (1878): 58-93, 267-89.

2649. H. Holtzmann, "Papias und Johannes," *ZWT* 23 (1880): 64-77.

2650. J. S. Banks, "The Supposed Presbyter John of Asia Minor," *ET* 8 (1896-1897): 416-18.

2651. Vincent Rose, "Question Johannine. Les aloges asiates et les aloges romains," *RB* 6 (1897): 516-34.

2652. A. van Hoonacker, "L'auteur du qustrième évangile," *RB* 9 (1900): 226-47.

2653. C. W. Rishell, "Baldensperger's Theory of the Origin of the Fourth Gospel," *JBL* 20 (1901): 38-49.

2654. P. Corssen, "Warum ist das vierte Evangelium für ein Werk des Apostels Johannes erklärt worden?" *ZNW* 2 (1901): 202-27.

2655. A. N. Jannaris, "Who Wrote the Fourth Gospel?" *ET* 14 (1902-1903): 459-63.

2656. Charles W. Rishell, "Hints Relative to the Date of the Fourth Gospel," *BS* 60 (1903): 244-60.

2657. W. Bousset, "Der Verfasser des Johannesevangeliums," *TR* 8 (1905): 225-44, 277-95.

2658. George S. Rollins, "The Hand of Apollos in the Fourth Gospel," *BS* 62 (1905): 484-99.

2659. C. Bruston, "Le témoignage du quatrième évangile sur son auteur," *RTP* 39 (1906): 501-508.

2660. B. W. Bacon, "The Disciple whom Jesus Loved," *Exp* 7th ser., 4 (1907): 324-39.

2661. M. Lepin, "À propos de l'origine du quatrième évangile," *RB* 17 (1908): 84-102.

2662. J. MacRory, "Recent Criticism and the Authorship of the Fourth Gospel," *ITQ* 3 (1908): 50-72.

2663. J. MacRory, "The Authorship of the Fourth Gospel: Internal Evidence," *ITQ* 3 (1908): 151-71.

2664. W. Soltau, "Die Entstehung des vierten Evangeliums," *TSK* 81 (1908): 177-202.

2665. R. H. Strachan, "The Personality of the Fourth Evangelist," *Exp* 7th ser., 5 (1908): 97-117.

2666. Eb. Nestle, "Death of St. John in the Seventh Year of Trajan," *ET* 22 (1910-1911): 91.

2667. Hermann Dechent, "Wer hat das vierte Evangelium verfasst?" *SK* 84 (1911): 446-61.

2668. H. J. Bardsley, "The Testimony of Ignatius and Polycarp to the Apostleship of St. John," *JTS* 14 (1912-1913): 489-500.

2669. J. Ritchie Smith, "The Authorship of the Fourth Gospel," *PTR* 10 (1912): 437-64; 11 (1931): 16-40.

2670. W. Heitmüller, "Zum Johannes-Tradition," *ZNW* 15 (1914): 189-209.

2671. Eduard Schwartz, "Johannes und Kerinthos," *ZNW* 15 (1914): 210-19.

2672. W. Soltau, "Kannte der 4. Evangelist den Lieblingsjunger Jesu?" *TSK* 88 (1915): 371-80 [No].

2673. H. B. Swete, "I. The Disciple whom Jesus Loved; II. John of Ephesus," *JTS* 17 (1915-1916): 371-78.

2674. Alfred E. Garvie, "The Disciple whom Jesus Loved," *ET* 28 (1916-1917): 232; 29 (1917-1918): 287.

2675. Edward Shillito, "The Beloved Disciple," *ET* 29 (1917-1918): 473-74.

2676. George C. Walker, "The Disciple whom Jesus Loved," *ET*

29 (1917-1918): 140.

2677.   Frederick Torm, "Overleveringen om Apostlen Johannes,"
         TTDF 3rd ser., 10 (1919): 97-122.

2678.   H. Mudie Draper, "The Disciple whom Jesus Loved," *ET* 32
         (1920-1921): 428-29.

2679.   B. Grey Griffith, "The Disciple whom Jesus Loved," *ET* 32
         (1920-1921): 379-81.

2680.   James Hendry, "Lazarus = John?" *ET* 32 (1920-1921):
         474-75.

2681.   F. Warburton Lewis, "The Disciple whom Jesus Loved," *ET*
         33 (1921-1922): 42.

2682.   H. Rigg, "Was Lazarus 'the Beloved Disciple'?" *ET* 33
         (1921-1922): 232-34.

2683.   F. Warburton Lewis, "Dr. Garvie's Book on the Fourth
         Gospel ('The Beloved Disciple')," *ET* 34 (1922-1923):
         378-79.

2684.   M. Goguel, "Une nouvelle théorie sur l'origin du quatrième
         évangile," *RHPR* 3 (1923): 373-82.

2685.   Charles C. Torrey, "The Aramaic Origin of the Gospel of
         John," *HTR* 16 (1923): 305-44.

2686.   W. F. Albright, "Some Observations favoring the Palestinian
         Origin of the Gospel of John," *HTR* 17 (1924): 189-94.

2687.   J. A. Faulkner, "John's Gospel in Church History," *BR* 11
         (1926): 331-44.

2688.   B. W. Bacon, "The Elder John in Jerusalem," *ZNW* 26
         (1927): 187-202.

2689.   W. K. Lowther Clarke, "The Fourth Gospel as a Document
         of the Early Palestinian Church," *Th* 14 (1927): 100-101.

2690.   E. G. Sihler, "St. John of Galilee—Bishop at Ephesus," *BR*
         12 (1927): 199-226.

2691.   G. L. Tremenheere, "The Bearing of Certain Texts on the
         Authorship of the Fourth Gospel," *Th* 16 (1928): 258-61.

2692.   J. A. Faulkner, "The World Significance of John," *BR* 14
         (1929): 171-90.

2693.   B. W. Bacon, "The Anti-Marcionite Prologue to John," *JBL* 49 (1930): 43-54.

2694.   A. Mingana, "The Authorship of the Fourth Gospel," *BJRL* 14 (1930): 333-39.

2695.   C. F. Nolloth, "The Witness of the Fourth Gospel to its Author," *Th* 20 (1930): 262-71.

2696.   B. W. Bacon, "John and the Pseudo-John," *ZNW* 31 (1932): 132-50.

2697.   D. M. McIntyre, "The Fourth Gospel," *EQ* 4 (1932): 24-38.

2698.   M. Goguel, "La formation de la tradition johannique d'après B. W. Bacon," *RHPR* 14 (1934): 415-39.

2699.   Friedrich Vogel, "Das Johannesproblem in bündiger Fassung," *TB* 14 (1935): 105-106.

2700.   P. E. Kretzmann, "Das Datum der Verabfassung des Johannesevangeliums," *CTM* 8 (1937): 499-503.

2701.   Hans Windisch, "Das vierte Evangelium und Johannes," *TB* 16 (1937): 144-52.

2702.   E. K. Simpson, "The Authorship and Authenticity of the Fourth Gospel," *EQ* 10 (1938): 113-34.

2703.   E. F. Sutcliffe, "Dr. Eisler and the Fourth Evangelist," *B* (1939): 38-50.

2704.   Walter J. Burghardt, "Did Saint Ignatius of Antioch Know the Fourth Gospel?" *ThSt* 1 (1940): 1-26, 130-56 [Possibly].

2705.   Alexander Faure, "Das 4. Evangelium im muratorischen Fragment," *ZST* 19 (1942): 143-49.

2706.   F. F. Bruce, "Some Notes on the Fourth Evangelist," *EQ* 16 (1944): 101-109.

2707.   H. P. V. Nunn, "The Fourth Gospel in the Early Church," *EQ* 16 (1944): 173-91, 294-99.

2708.   A. M. Perry, "Is John an Alexandrian Gospel?" *JBL* 63 (1944): 99-106.

2709.   Mary E. Andrews, "The Authorship and Significance of the Gospel of John," *JBL* 64 (1945): 183-92.

2710.   W. F. Howard, "The Common Authorship of the Johannine

Gospel and Epistles," *JTS* 48 (1947): 12-25.

2711. W. G. Wilson, "An Examination of the Linguistic Evidence adduced against the Unity of Authorship of the First Epistle of John and the Fourth Gospel," *JTS* 49 (1948): 147-56.

2712. Floyd V. Filson, "Who was the Beloved Disciple?" *JBL* 68 (1949): 83-88 [Lazarus].

2713. Robert M. Grant, "The Origin of the Fourth Gospel," *JBL* 69 (1950): 305-22.

2714. Eric L. Titus, "The Identity of the Beloved Disciple," *JBL* 69 (1950): 323-28.

2715. Hugo Odeberg, "The Authorship of St. John's Gospel," *CTM* 22 (1951): 225-51.

2716. R. C. Fuller, "The Authorship of the Fourth Gospel," *Scr* 5 (1952): 8-11.

2717. Cuthbert Lattey, "St. John the Evangelist's Home Circle," *CBQ* 15 (1953): 2-10.

2718. H. C. Snape, "The Fourth Gospel, Ephesus and Alexandria," *HTR* 47 (1954): 1-14.

2719. Arthur Valentin, "The Johannine Authorship of Apocalypse, Gospel and Epistles," *Scr* 6 (1954): 148-50.

2720. C. L. Mitton, "The Provenance of the Fourth Gospel," *ET* 71 (1959-1960): 337-40.

2721. T. E. Pollard, "The Fourth Gospel—Its Background and Early Interpretation," *ABR* 7 (1959): 41-53.

2722. Pierson Parker, "John and John Mark," *JBL* 79 (1960): 97-110.

See also numbers 2102, 2114, 3266, 10065.

2722.1 Raymond E. Brown, "The Problem of Historicity in John," *CBQ* 24 (1962): 1-14.

2722.2 Merrill C. Tenney, "Literary Keys to the Fourth Gospel: The Author's Testimony to Himself," *BS* 120 (1963): 214-23.

2722.3 F. L. Cribbs, "A Reassessment of the Date of Origin and the Destination of the Gospel of John," *JBL* 89 (1970): 38-55.

2722.4 F. F. Bruce, "St. John at Ephesus," *BJRL* 60 (1978): 339-61.

2722.5   L. L. Johns and D. B. Miller, "The Signs as Witness in the Fourth Gospel: Reexamining the Evidence," *CBQ* 56 (1994): 519-35.

(2). Sources and Influences

(a). *The Old Testament and Jewish Sources*

2723.   Albrecht Thoma, "Das Alte Testament im Johannes-Evangelium," *ZWT* 22 (1879): 18-66, 171-224, 273-312.

2724.   G. Chastand, "Le quatrième évangile et le Judaïsme et l'ancien testament," *RTP* 20 (1887): 588-99.

2725.   R. H. Strachan, "The Newly Discovered Odes of Solomon, and their Bearing on the Problem of the Fourth Gospel," *ET* 22 (1910-1911): 7-14.

2726.   M. Goguel, "Les sources des récits du quatrième évangile sur Jean-Baptiste," *RTQR* 20 (1911): 12-44.

2727.   E. C. Hoskyns, "Genesis I-III and St. John's Gospel," *JTS* 21 (1920): 210-18.

2728.   Alexander Faure, "Die alttestamentlichen Zitate im 4. Evangelium und die Quellenscheidungshypothese," *ZNW* 21 (1922): 99-121.

2729.   Paul Fiebig, "Die Mekhilta und das Johannes-Evangelium," *A* 1 (1925): 57-59.

2730.   Friedrich Smend, "Die Behandlung alttestamentlicher Zitate als Ausgangspunkt der Quellenscheidung im 4. Evangelium," *ZNW* 24 (1925): 147-50.

2731.   C. H. Dodd, "The Background of the Fourth Gospel," *BJRL* 19 (1935): 329-43.

2732.   R. Abramowski, "Der Christus der Salomooden," *ZNW* 35 (1936): 44-69.

2733.   Edwin C. Broome, "The Sources of the Fourth Gospel," *JBL* 63 (1944): 107-21.

2734.   C. K. Barrett, "The Old Testament in the Fourth Gospel," *JTS* 48 (1947): 155-69.

2735.   David R. Griffiths, "Deutero-Isaiah and the Fourth Gospel: Some Points of Comparison," *ET* 65 (1953-1954): 355-60.

2736.   Charles Goodwin, "How did Johan Treat his Sources?" *JBL* 73 (1954): 61-75.

2737.   F.-M. Braun, "L'arrière fond judaïque du quatrième évangile et la communauté de l'alliance," *RB* 62 (1955): 5-44.

2738.   Franklin W. Young, "A Study of the Relations of Isaiah to the Fourth Gospel," *ZNW* 46 (1955): 215-33.

2739.   Jacob J. Enz, "The Book of Exodus as a Literary Type for the Gospel of John," *JBL* 76 (1957): 208-15.

2740.   Richard Morgan, "Fulfillment in the Fourth Gospel; the Old Testament Foundations," *Interp* 11 (1957): 155-65.

2741.   Georg Ziener, "Weisheitsbuch und Johannesevangelium," *B* 38 (1957): 396-418; 39 (1958): 37-60.

2742.   H. M. Teeple, "Qumran and the Origin of the Fourth Gospel," *NT* 4 (1960): 6-25.

             See also numbers 3113, 3266.

2742.1   R. H. Smith, "Exodus Typology in the Fourth Gospel," *JBL* 81 (1962): 329-42.

2742.2   J. Burns, "Some Reflections on Coheleth and John," *CBQ* 25 (1963): 414-16.

2742.3   Merrill C. Tenney, "Literary Keys to the Fourth Gospel: The OT and the Fourth Gospel," *BS* 120 (1963): 300-308.

2742.4   Bruce Vawter, "Ezekiel and John," *CBQ* 26 (1964): 450-58.

2742.5   James H. Charlesworth and R. Alan Culpepper, "The Odes of Solomon and the Gospel of John," *CBQ* 35 (1973): 298-322.

2742.6   Bruce D. Chilton, "John xii 34 and Targum Isaiah lii 13," *NT* 22 (1980): 176-78.

2742.7   John V. Dahms, "Isaiah 55:11 and the Gospel of John," *EQ* 53 (1981): 78-88.

2742.8   G. Reim, "Targum und Johannesevangelium," *BibZ* 27 (1983): 1-13.

2742.9   R. Alan Culpepper, "The Gospel of John and the Jews," *RE* 84 (1987): 273-88.

(b). *Mark, Paul, and other Christian Sources*

2743.   H. J. Flowers, "Mark as a Source for the Fourth Gospel," *JBL* 46 (1927): 207-36.

2744.   B. W. Bacon, "Pauline Elements in the Fourth Gospel; II. Parables of the Shepherd," *ATR* 11 (1928-1929): 305-20.

2745.   Frederick C. Grant, "Was the Author of John Dependent upon the Gospel of Luke?" *JBL* 56 (1937): 285-307 [Not Lk. but Mk.].

2746.   P. Gardner-Smith, "St. John's Knowledge of Matthew," *JTS* N.S. 4 (1953): 31-35.

2747.   Georg Ziener, "Johannesevangelium und urchristhche Passafeier," *BibZ* 2 (1958): 263-74.

2748.   Wilhelm Wilkens, "Evangelist und Tradition im Johannes evangelium," *TZ* 16 (1960): 81-90.

        See also number 2759.

2748.1 Raymond E. Brown, "The Relation of 'The Secret Gospel of Mark' to the Fourth Gospel," *CBQ* 36 (1974): 466-85.

2748.2 Don A. Carson, "Current Source Criticism of the Fourth Gospel: Some Methodological Questions," *JBL* 97 (1978): 411-29.

(c). *Gnosticism, Mandaeanism, and Hellenistis Mysticism*

2749.   A. Hilgenfeld, "Das Johannes-Evangelium alexandrinisch oder gnostisch?" *ZWT* 25 (1882): 388-435.

2750.   Ezra P. Gould, "The Alexandrian Gospel," *JBL* 19 (1900): 5-11.

2751.   E.-B. Allo, "Premiers rapports historiques du Christianisme et du syncrétisme gréco-oriental," *Bes* 6 (1909): 11-29.

2752.   E. F. Scott, "The Hellenistic Mysticism of the Fourth Gospel," *AJT* 20 (1916): 345-59.

2753.   Gillis Pison Wetter, "Eine gnostische Formel im 4. Evangelium," *ZNW* 18 (1917): 49-63.

2754.   J. Rendel Harris, "Stoic Origin of the Fourth Gospel," *BJRL* 6 (1921-1922): 439-51.

2755.   Rudolf Bultmann, "Die Bedeutung der neuerschlossenen mandaischen und manichäischen Quellen für das Verständnis des Johannesevangeliums," *ZNW* 24 (1925): 100-46.

2756. Vincent Kraeling, "The Mandaeans and the Fourth Gospel," *HJ* 28 (1929-1930): 531-46.

2757. Carl H. Crawling, "The Fourth Gospel and Contemporary Religious Thought," *JBL* 49 (1930): 140-59.

2758. Elbert Russell, "Possible Influence of the Mysteries on the Form and Interrelation of the Johannine Writings," *JBL* 51 (1932): 336-51.

2759. Burton S. Easton, "Bultmann's *RQ* Source," *JBL* 65 (1946): 143-56 [Bultmann's commentary on John].

2760. H. A. Fischel, "Jewish Gnosticism in the Fourth Gospel," *JBL* 65 (1946): 157-74.

2761. A. W. Argyle, "Philo and the Fourth Gospel," *ET* 63 (1951-1952): 385-86.

2762. R. McL. Wilson, "Philo and the Fourth Gospel," *ET* 65 (1953-1954): 47-49.

2763. G. Quispel, "Het Johannesevangelie en de Gnosis," *NedTT* 11 (1956-1957): 173-203.

2764. R. McL. Wilson, "The Fourth Gospel and Hellenistic Thought," *NT* 1 (1956): 225-27.

See also numbers 3297, 3284-3311, 3322, 6975.

2764.1 Michel Tardieu, "Les trois stèles de Seth: um écrit gnostique retrouvé à Nag Hammadi," *RSPT* 57 (1973): 545-75.

2764.2 Georg Strecker, "Chiliasm and Docetism in the Johannine School," *ABR* 38 (1990): 45-61.

(3). Historical Reliability and Authenticity

2765. Karl Fromman, "Über die Echtheit und Integrität des Evangeliums Johannis, mit besonderer Rücksicht auf Weisse's evangelischc Geschichte," *TSK* 13 (1840): 853-930.

2766. Busken-Huet, "De l'authenticité des écrits johanniques d'après Antonie Niermeyer," *RT* 12 (1856): 305-38; 13 (1856): 35-63, 171-90.

2767. George P. Fisher, "The Genuineness of the Fourth Gospel,"

BS 21 (1864): 225-84.

2768. J. B. Lightfoot, "Internal Evidence for the Authenticity and Genuineness of St. John's Gospel," *Exp* 4th ser., 1 (1890): 1-21, 81-92, 176-88.

2769. H. K. Hugo Delff, "Noch einmal das vierte Evangelium und seine Authenticität," *TSK* 65 (1892): 72-104.

2770. G. Wetzel, "Die geschichtliche Glaubwürdigkeit der im Evangelium Johannes enthaltenen Reden Jesu," *NKZ* 14 (1903): 665-92, 809-26, 827-42.

2771. Frederick Torm, "Am Johannesevangeliets Ægthied," *TTDF* N.S. 7 (1905-1906): 257-306, 385-402.

2772. Fulcranus Vigouroux et Laurentius Janssens, "De auctore et veritate historica a quarti Evangelii," *RB* N.S. 4 (1907): 321-22.

2773. Th. Zahn, "Zur Heimatkunde des Evangelisten Johannes," *NKZ* 18 (1907): 265-94, 593-608; 19 (1908): 31-39, 207-18.

2774. J. H. A. Hart, "A Plea for the Recognition of the Fourth Gospel as an Historical Authority," *Exp* 7th ser., 5 (1908). 361-79; 6 (1908): 42-59.

2775. J. MacRory, "The Historical Character of the Fourth Gospel," *ITQ* 3 (1908): 451-65.

2776. E. H. Askwith, "The Historical Value of the Fourth Gospel," *Exp* 7th ser., 8 (1909): 71-81, 244-63, 365-75, 431-47, 530-42; 9 (1910): 86-96, 132-38, 228-41, 440-49, 538-47; 10 (1910): 38-52, 254-65.

2777. William P. Merrill, "The Real Jesus," *BW* 34 (1909): 104-10 [John's representation is faithful].

2778. W. K. Lowther Clarke, "The Allegorical Element in the Fourth Gospel," *ET* 22 (1910-1911): 116-18.

2779. J. J. Lias, "The Theology of the Fourth Gospel a Guarantee for its Genuineness," *BS* 68 (1911): 285-307.

2780. Hans C. Juell, "The Fourth Gospel, a Genuine Narrative," *BS* 72 (1915): 374-96.

2781. H. H. B. Ayles, "The Credibility of the Fourth Gospel," *ET* 29 (1917-1918): 507-11.

2782.   E. G. Selwyn, "The Mind of St. John," *Th* 2 (1921): 243-51.

2783.   Joseph Huby, "La valeur historique du quatrième évangile d'après un ouvrage récent," *NRT* 49 (1922): 229-243.

2784.   Luther A. Fox, "The Genuineness of St. John's Gospel," *LQ* 54 (1924): 323-33.

2785.   J. M. Hantz, "Authenticity of John's Gospel," *BS* 82 (1925): 63-76.

2786.   Frederick Torm, "Die Psychologie des vierten Evangeliums: Augenzeuge oder niche?" *ZNW* 30 (1931): 124-44.

2787.   W. F. Howard, "The Johannine Sayings of Jesus," *ET* 46 (1933-1934): 486-91.

2788.   J. O. F. Murray, "The Historical Value of 'The Discoveries' in St. John," *Th* 33 (1936): 70-81.

2789.   M.-J. Lagrange, "Le réalisme historique de l'évangile selon saint Jean," *RB* 46 (1937): 321-41.

2790.   L. V. Lester-Garland, "The Historical Value of the Fourth Gospel," *HJ* 36 (1937-1938): 265-77.

2791.   Philippe-H. Menoud, "L'originalité de la pensée johannique," *RTP* N.S. 28 (1940): 233-61.

2792.   Erwin R. Goodenough, "John a Primitive Gospel," *JBL* 64 (1945): 145-82.

2793.   R. C. Fuller, "The Fourth Gospel, an Objective Record?" *Scr* 5 (1952): 27-32.

2794.   X. Leon-Dufour, "Actualité du quatrième évangile," *NRT* 76 (1954): 449-68.

2795.   J. Blinzler, "Eine Bemerkung zum Geschichtsrahmen des Johannesevangeliums," *B* 36 (1955): 20-35.

2796.   Eva Krafft, "Die Personen des Johannesevangeliums," *EvT* 16 (1956): 18-32.

2797.   Eric L. Titus, "The Fourth Gospel and History," *JBR* 24 (1956): 161-66.

2798.   Frederick C. Grant, "The Historical Element in the Fourth Gospel," *RL* 28 (1959): 56-67.

2799.   Everett F. Harrison, "Historical Problems in the Fourth

Gospel," *BS* 116 (1959): 205-11.

2800. Juan Leal, "El simbolismo histórico del IV Evangelio," *EB* 19 (1960): 328-48.

2801. Léon Ramlot, "L'évangile selon saint Jean et la critique historique," *BVC* no. 38 (1961): 80-87.

2802. Hejne Simonsen, "Factum og tydning i Johannesevangeliet," *DTT* 24 (1961): 93-110.

See also numbers 305, 1224, 1874.

(4). The Purpose of John; Anti-Semitism

2803. Dr. Aberle, "Über den Zweck des Johannesevangeliums," *TQ* 43 (1861): 37-94.

2804. H. Holtzmann, "Über die Disposition des vierten Evangeliums," *ZWT* 24 (1881): 257-90.

2805. A. Hilgenfeld, "Der Antijudaïsmus des Johannes-Evangeliums," *ZWT* 36, 2 (1893): 507-17.

2806. J. Kunze, "Is the Gospel of John an Anti-Jewish Polemic?" *LCR* 23 (1904): 455-70.

2807. B. W. Bacon, "The 'Defense' of the Fourth Gospel," *HJ* 6 (1907-1908): 118-41.

2808. J. Bonnar Russell, "The Object of the Fourth Gospel," *ET* 27 (1915-1916): 169-71.

2809. E. C. Colwell, "The Fourth Gospel and the Struggle for Respectability," *JR* 14 (1934): 286-305.

2810. W. E. Henry, "The Appeal of John's Gospel," *RE* 32 (1935): 57-62.

2811. Walter W. Sikes, "The Anti-Semitism of the Fourth Gospel," *JR* 21 (1941): 23-30.

2812. G. J. Cuming, "The Jews in the Fourth Gospel," *ET* 60 (1948-1949): 290-92.

2813. K. J. Carroll, "The Fourth Gospel and the Exclusion of Christians from the Synagogues," *BJRL* 40 (1957-1958): 19-32.

2814. John A. T. Robinson, "The Destination and Purpose of St. John's Gospel," *NTSt* 6 (1959-1960): 117-31.

See also numbers 2399, 10059.

2814.1   John W. Bowker, "The Origin and Purpose of St. John's Gospel," *NTSt* 11 (1964-1965): 398-408.

2814.2   Erich Grässer, "Die antijüdische Polemik im Johannesevangelium," *NTSt* 11 (1964-1965): 74-90.

2814.3   A. Wind, "Destination and Purpose of the Gospel of John," *NT* 14 (1972): 26-69.

2814.4   Robert G. Bratcher, " 'The Jews' in the Gospel of John," *BTr* 26 (1975): 401-409.

2814.5   G. Reim, "Joh 8:44: Gotteskinder-Teufelskinder: wie antijudaistisch ist 'die wohl antijudaistischste Ausserung des NT'," *NTSt* 30/4 (1984): 619-24.

2814.6   Wolfgang Feneberg, "Das Neue Testament: Sprache der Lieben: Zum Problem des Antijudaismus," *ZKT* 107 (1985): 333-40.

2814.7   Don A. Carson "The Purpose of the Fourth Gospel: John 20:31 Reconsidered," *JBL* 106 (1987): 639-51.

(5). The Synoptics and John

2815.   E. Robinson, "The Alleged Discrepancy Between John and the Other Evangelists Respecting our Lord's Last Passover," *BS* 2 (1845): 405-36.

2816.   H. Holtzmann, "Das schriftstellerische Verhältnis des Johannes zu den Synoptikern," *ZWT* 12 (1869): 62-85, 155-78, 446-56.

2817.   J. A. M. Mensinga, "Das Johannes-Evangelium und die Synopsis," *ZWT* 35 (1892): 98-104.

2818.   J. J. Halcombe, "The Gospels and Modern Criticism," *ET* 4 (1892-1893): 77-79, 215-17 [Advocates the priority of John].

2819.   G. H. Gwilliam, "Mr. Halcombe on 'The Historic Relation of the Gospels'," *ET* 3 (1891-1892): 312-16 [Advocates the priority of Synoptics].

2820.   J. J. Halcombe, "The Origin and Relation of the Four Gospels," *ET* 4 (1892-1893): 268-69, 313-19.

2821.   F. W. Bussell, "Mr. Halcombe and the Four Gospels," *ET* 3 (1891-1892): 351-53.

2822. J. M. Ramsay, "The Gospels and Modern Criticism," *ET* 4 (1892-1893): 355-58 [Supports Halcombe's theory of the ‚priority of John].

2823. Arthur Wright, "The Gospels and Modern Criticism," *ET* 4 (1892-1893): 358-62, 467-68, 497-501; 5 (1893-1894): 126-29, 168-70, 278-81 [Against Halcombe's theory of the priority of John].

2824. J. J. Halcombe, "The Gospels and Modern Criticism," *ET* 4 (1892-1893): 404-408; 5 (1893-1894): 224-26 [Rebuttal of Wright's criticism].

2825. Hellmuth Zimmerrnann, "Lukas und die johanneische Tradition," *TSK* 76 (1903): 586-605.

2826. Anson P. Atterbury, "The Many-Sided Christ," *BW* 25 (1905): 450-56.

2827. H. Gaussen, "The Lucan and Johannine Writings," *JTS* 9 (1907-1908): 562-68.

2828. F. W. Worsley, "The Relation of the Fourth Gospel to the Synoptists," *ET* 20 (1908-1909): 62-65.

2829. Edward Day, "Sayings of Jesus in the Fourth Gospel which are Reminiscent of his Sayings Recorded in the Synoptic Gospels," *BW* 34 (1909): 259-70.

2830. W. Soltau, "Welche Bedeutung haben die synoptischen Berichte des IV. Evangeliums für die Zeitstellung seines Entstehens?" *ZWT* 52 (1910): 33-66.

2831. Albert Weston Moore, "Why the Raising of Lazarus is not Reported by the Synoptists," *BS* 73 (1916): 73-89.

2832. K. F. Proost, "Waaraan is het too te schrijven dat in de 4de evangelie geen sprake is van 'vergeving van zonden'?" *TT* 51 (1917): 197-227.

2833. George A. Barton, "The Origin of the Discrepancy between the Synoptists and the Fourth Gospel as to the Date and Character of Christ's Last Supper with his Disciples," *JBL* 43 (1924): 28-31.

2834. Olaf Moe, "Spor av Johannes-traditionen hos Lukas," *NTT* 25 (1924): 103-28.

2835.   F. Büchsel, "Johannes und die Synoptiker," *ZST* 4 (1926-1927): 240-65.

2836.   W. F. Howard, "The Position of the Temple Cleansing in the Fourth Gospel," *ET* 44 (1932-1933): 284-85.

2837.   Paul Doncoeur, "Des silences de l'évangile de saint Jean," *RSR* 24 (1934): 606-609.

2838.   R. P. C. Hanson, "Further Evidence for Indications of the Johannine Chronology of the Passion to be Found in the Synoptic Evangelists," *ET* 53 (1941-1942): 178-80.

2839.   Grace Amadon, "The Johannine-Synoptic Argument," *ATR* 26 (1944): 107-15.

2840.   Willard L. Sperry, " 'Jesus Said'," *RL* 23 (1954): 375-83.

2841.   Miguel Balagué, "San Juan y los Sinópticos," *CB* 12 (1955): 347-52.

2842.   C. H. Dodd, "Some Johannine 'Herrnworte' with Parallels in the Synoptic Gospels," *NTSt* 2 (1955-1956): 75-86.

2843.   E. Kenneth Lee, "St. Mark and the Fourth Gospel," *NTSt* 3 (1956- 1957): 50-58.

2844.   Ivor Buse, "St. John and the Marcan Passion Narrative," *NTSt* 4 (1957-1958): 215-19.

2845.   S. Mendner, "Zum Problem 'Johannes und die Synoptiker'," *NTSt* 4 (1957-1958): 282-307.

2846.   Peder Borgen, "John and the Synoptics in the Passion Narrative," *NTSt* 5 (1958-1959): 246-59.

2847.   Ivor Buse, "St. John and 'The First Synoptic Pericope'," *NT* 3 (1959): 57-61.

2848.   Ivor Buse, "St. John and the Passion Narratives of St. Matthew and St. Luke," *NTSt* 7 (1960-1961): 65-76.

2849.   Raymond E. Brown, "Incidents that are Units in the Synoptic Gospels but dispersed in St. John," *CBQ* 23 (1961): 143-60. See also numbers 505, 1153, 1168, 1195, 5107.

2849.1   F. E. Williams, "Fourth Gospel and Synoptic Tradition: Two Johannine Passages," *JBL* 86 (1967): 311-19.

(6). Method and Structure of John

2850.   A. Hilgenfeld, "Das Johannes-Evangelium niche interpolirt," *ZWT* 11 (1868): 434-55.

2851.   H. Spaeth, "Nathanael. Ein Beitrag zum Verständnis der Composition des Logos-Evangeliums," *ZWT* 11 (1868): 168-231, 309-43.

2852.   W. Honig, "Die Construction des vierten Evangeliums," *ZWT* 14 (1871): 535-66.

2853.   A. D. Loman, "De bouw van het vierde Evangelie," *TT* 11 (1877): 371-437.

2854.   Dr. Bertling, "Eine Transposition im Evangelium Johannis," *TSK* 53 (1880): 351-53 [7:19-24 to chapter 5].

2855.   W. Milligan, "The Structure of the Fourth Gospel and of the Apocalypse," *Exp* 2nd ser., 5 (1883): 102-20.

2856.   A. H. Franca, "Die Anlage des Johannes-Evangeliums," *TSK* 57 (1884): 80-154.

2857.   August Becker, "Über die Komposition des Johannes-evangeliums," *TSK* 62 (1889): 117-40.

2858.   Fr. Roos, "Der Eingang des Evangeliums Johannis und die Reden Jesu, insbesondere die johanneischen," *NKZ* 3 (1892): 554-71.

2859.   Ernest DeW. Burton, "The Purpose and Plan of the Gospel of John," *BW* 13 (1899): 16-41, 102-105.

2860.   H. Holtzmann, "Unordnungen und Umordnungen im vierten Evangelium," *ZNW* 3 (1902): 50-60.

2861.   Walter Lock, "A Partition Theory of St. John's Gospel," *JTS* 4 (1902-1903): 194-205.

2862.   Cuthbert Lattey, "The Structure of the Fourth Gospel," *Exp* 7th ser., 1 (1906): 424-34.

2863.   F. J. Paul, "On Two Dislocations in St. John's Gospel," *HJ* 7 (1908-1909): 662-68.

2864.   W. Bousset, "Ist das vierte Evangelium eine literarische Einheit?" *TR* 12 (1909): 1-12, 39-64.

2865.   W. Soltau, "Thesen über die Entwicklung einer johanneischen Literatur," *ZWT* 53 (1911): 167-70.

2866.   R. H. Strachan, "Is the Fourth Gospel a Literary Unity?" *ET*

27 (1915-1916): 22-26, 232-37, 280-82, 330-33.

2867. W. Soltau, "Die Reden des vierten Evangeliums," *ZNW* 17 (1916): 49-60.

2868. Willoughby C. Allen, "A Keynote of the Fourth Gospel," *ET* 28 (1916-1917): 43-45

2869. Walter Lock, "The Literary Method of the Fourth Gospel," *HJ* 15 (1916-1917): 40-55.

2870. H. J. Flowers, "Interpolations in the Fourth Gospel," *JBL* 40 (1921): 146-61.

2871. Vincent McNabb, "Some Main Divisions of St. John's Gospel," *Th* 3 (1921): 170-73.

2872. Hubert M. Foston, "Two Johannine Parentheses," *ET* 32 (1920-1921): 520-23.

2873. R. H. Strachan, "The Development of Thought within the Fourth Gospel," *ET* 34 (1922-1923): 228-32, 246-50.

2874. M.-J. Lagrange, "Où en est la dissection littéraire du quatrième évangile?" *RB* 33 (1924): 321-42.

2875. B. W. Bacon, "Sources and Methods of the Fourth Evangelist," *HJ* 25 (1926-1927): 115-30.

2876. Thos. Cottam, "Some Displacements in the Fourth Gospel," *ET* 38 (1926-1927): 91-92.

2877. Vincent Taylor, "The Psychology of the Johannine Christ-Testimonies," *HJ* 27 (1928-1929): 123-37.

2878. James Muilenburg, "Literary Form in the Fourth Gospel," *JBL* 51 (1932): 40-53.

2879. Greville P. Lewis, "Dislocations in the Fourth Gospel: The Temple Cleansing,and the Visit of Nicodemus," *ET* 44 (1932-1933): 228-30.

2880. F. Warburton Lewis, "Disarrangements in the Fourth Gospel," *ET* 44 (1932-1933): 382.

2881. H. E. Dana, "The Stratification of Tradition in the Fourth Gospel," *JR* 17 (1937): 62-75.

2882. Edward A. McDowell, "The Structural Integrity of the Fourth Gospel," *RE* 34 (1937): 397-416.

2883. 883 Peter Fraenkel, "Method of Work of the Author of the Fourth Gospel," *ET* 53 (1941-1942): 242.

2884. F. J. Brown, "Displacement in the Fourth Gospel," *ET* 57 (1945-1946): 217-20.

2885. T. F. Glasson, "Inaccurate Repetitions in the Fourth Gospel," *ET* 57 (1945-1946): 111-12.

2886. Alexander Ross, "Displacements in the Fourth Gospel," *ET* 58 (1946-1947): 250.

2887. Albert Power, "The Original Order of St. John's Gospel," *CBQ* 10 (1948): 399-405.

2888. W. G. Wilson, "The Original Text of the Fourth Gospel," *JTS* 50 (1949): 59-60 [contra theory of displacements].

2889. F. Quiévreux, "La structure symbolique de l'évangile de saint Jean," *RHPR* 33 (1953): 123-65.

2890. H. Clavier, "La structure du quatrième évangile," *RHPR* 135 (1955): 174-95.

2891. André Feuillet, "L'heure de Jésus et le signe de Cana—Contribution à l'étude de la structure du quatrième évangile," *ETL* 36 (1960): 5-22.

2892. Sydney Temple, "A Key to the Composition of the Fourth Gospel," *JBL* 80 (1961): 220-32.

See also numbers 3115, 3392, 3597, 3660ff.

2892.1 H. M. Teeple, "Methodology in Source Analysis of the Fourth Gospel," *JBL* 81 (1962): 279-86.

2892.2 Merrill C. Tenney, "Literary Keys to the Fourth Gospel: The Symphonic Structure of John," *BS* 120 (1963): 117-25.

2892.3 D. G. Deeks, "The Structure of the Fourth Gospel," *NTSt* 15 (1968-1969): 107-29.

7. Literary Criticism and Theology of the Parables

2893. Ed. Scherer, "Herméneutique des paraboles," *RT* 1 (1850): 273-94.

2894. G. Goguel, "De l'enseignement parabolique," *RT* 7 (1853): 49-53.

2895. J. M. Usteri, "Zur Erklärung der Gleichnisse Jesu," *STZ* 3

(1886): 238-48; 5 (1888): 38-52.

2896. J. H. de Ridder, "De gelijkenissen (naar aanleiding van Jülicher, Die Gleichnisreden Jesu, I)," *TT* 21 (1887): 534-53.

2897. J. J. Murphy, "Two Parables: The Prodigal Son (Luke XV.II-32); The Labourers in the Vineyard (Matt. 19:27; 20:16)," *Exp* 3rd ser., 9 (1889): 290-303.

2898. J. Weiss, "Die Parabelrede bei Markus," *TSK* 64 (1891): 289-321.

2899. J. Dräseke, "Zu den Gleichnissen Jesu," *NKZ* 3 (1892): 665-69.

2900. W. Milligan, "A Group of Parables," *Exp* 4th ser., 6 (1892): 114-26, 186-99.

2901. J. M. S. Baljon, "Het doel van Jezus' gelijkenissen," *TS* 15 (1897): 178-94, 421-57.

2902. David Eaton, "Professor Jülicher on the Parables of Jesus," *ET* 10 (1898-1899). 539-43.

2903. Shailer Mathews, "The Interpretation of Parables," *AJT* 2 (1898): 293-311.

2904. W. Sanday, "A New Work on the Parables," *JTS* 1 (1899-1900): 161-80.

2905. C. H. van Rhijn, "Naar aanleiding van de jongste verklaring van de gelijkenissen van Jezus," *TS* 19 (1901): 145-74.

2906. J. Weiss, "Jülichers 'Gleichnisreden Jesu'," *TR* 4 (1901): 1-11.

2907. L. Fonck, "Zur neuesten Parabelauslegung," *ZKT* 26 (1902): 280-98.

2908. Eb. Nestle, "A New Work on the Parables," *ET* 14 (1902-1903): 473-74.

2909. A. Sverdrup, "Parabel-literatur," *NTT* 3 (1902): 369-77.

2910. Julius A. Bewer, "The Psychological Study of the Words of Jesus, Especially of his Parables," *BS* 61 (1904): 102-40.

2911. Benjamin W. Robinson, "Some Elements of Forcefulness in Jesus' Comparisons," *JBL* 23 (1904): 106-79.

2912. R. M. Lithgow, "A Simple Scheme of the Parables," *ET* 16

(1904-1905): 470-72.

2913. R. M. Lithgow, "The Theology of the Parables," *ET* 18 (1906-1907): 538-42.

2914. R. M. Lithgow, "Man's Spiritual Development as Depicted in Christ's Parables," *ET* 19 (1907-1908): 543-47.

2915. H. Wellejus, "Forskellige Hovedopfattelser af Jesu Ligneker," *TTDF* N.S. 9 (1907-1908): 353-85, 474-500.

2916. R. M. Lithgow, "The Symbolism of the Parables," *ET* 20 (1908-1909): 217-20.

2917. R. M. Lithgow, "The Nomenclature of the Parables," *ET* 20 (1908-1909): 360-65.

2918. R. M. Lithgow, "The Lucan Parables," *ET* 20 (1908-1909): 558-61.

2919. M.-J. Lagrange, "La parabole en dehors de l'évangile," *RB* 18 (1909): 198-212, 342-67.

2920. M.-J. Lagrange, "Le but des paraboles d'après l'évangile selon saint Marc," *RB* 19 (1910): 5-35.

2921. James Denney, "Criticism and the Parables; I. The Transmission of the Parables," *Exp* 8th ser., 2 (1911): 117-13. "II. The Interpretation of the Parables," 219-36.

2922. Edward Rockliff, "Parables," *ITQ* 6 (1911): 328-44.

2923. Rayner Winterbotham, "The Story of the Lost and Found," *Exp* 8th ser., 1 (1911): 255-61.

2924. R. M. Lithgow, "The Minor Parables, the Metaphors and Similes of the Synoptic Gospels," *ET* 23 (1911-1912): 537-40.

2925. Paul Fiebig, "Jesu Gleichnisse im Lichte der rabbinischen Gleichnisse," *ZNW* 13 (1912): 192-211.

2926. T. E. Schmauk, "Parables and their Interpretation," *LCR* 31 (1912): 492-506.

2927. Jean Calès, "L'authenticité et le but des paraboles évangéliques, d'après une introduction récente," *NRT* 45 (1913): 69-75.

2928. J. W. Hunkin, "The Synoptic Parables," *JTS* 16 (1914-1915): 372-91.

2929. Denis Buzy, "Pour commenter les paraboles évangéliques," *RB* 25 (1916): 406-22.

2930. Jesse H. Bond, "Reinvention of the Parables of Jesus: A Subjective Interpretation," *BW* 51 (1918): 339-45.

2931. Arnold Brooks, "The Teaching in Parables," *ET* 32 (1920-1921): 170-72.

2932. J. E. S. Harrison, "The Teaching in Parables," *ET* 32 (1920-1921): 281.

2933. Jules Breitenstein, "Les paraboles de Jésus," *RTP* N.S 9. (1921): 97-113.

2934. B. W. Bacon, "Parable and its Adaptation in the Gospels," *HJ* 21 (1922-1923): 127-40.

2935. B. W. Bacon, "Two Parables of Lost Opportunity," *HJ* 21 (1922-1923): 337-52.

2936. J. E. Compton, "Two Parables: A Study," *ET* 35 (1923-1924): 380-81.

2937. L. Cerfaux, "Les paraboles de Jésus," *NRT* 55 (1928): 186-98.

2938. Anders Nygren, "Till förståelsen av Jesu liknelser," *STK* 4 (1928): 217-36.

2939. Anton Fridrichsen, "Den nyere tids parabelforskning," *STK* 5 (1929): 34-55.

2940. Iver K. Madsen, "Zur Erklärung der evangelischen Parabeln," *TSK* 10 (1929): 297-312 [Mt. 22:1-14; 13:3-8; Mk. 4:3-8; Lk. 8:5-8].

2941. Denis Buzy, "Les sentences finales des paraboles évangéliques," *RB* 40 (1931): 321-44.

2942. A. Škrinjar, "Le but des paraboles sur le règne et l'économie des lumières divines d'après l'Ecriture Sainte," *B* 11 (1930): 291-321, 426-49; 12 (1931): 27-40.

2943. Denis Buzy, "Y a-t-il fusion de paraboles évangéliques?" *RB* 41 (1932): 31-49.

2944. C. H. Dodd, "The Gospel Parables," *BJRL* 16 (1932): 396-412.

2945. Iver K. Madsen, "Om Jesu Lignelser," *TTDF* 5th ser., 3

(1932): 1-33; 4 (1933): 1-33.

2946.   G. J. Jordan, "The Classification of the Parables," *ET* 45 (1933-1934): 246-51.

2947.   U. Holzmeister, "Vim angeblichen Verstockungszweck der Parabeln des Herrn," *B* 15 (1934): 321-64.

2948.   James D. Smart, "A Redefinition of Jesus' Use of the Parables," *ET* 47 (1935-1936): 551-55.

2949.   Ernst Lohmeyer, "Vom Sinn der Gleichnisse Jesu," *ZST* 15 (1938): 319-46.

2950.   Paul Joüon, "La parabole des mines (Luc 19, 13-27): et la parabole des talents (Matthew 25,14-30)," *RSR* 29 (1939): 489-94.

2951.   Paul Joüon, "La parabole du portier qui doit veiller (Marc 13, 33-37): et la parabole des serviteurs qui doivent veiller (Luc 12,35-40)," *RSR* 30 (1940): 365-68.

2952.   Allan Barr, "The Interpretation of the Parables," *ET* 53 (1941-1942): 20-25.

2953.   Otto A. Piper, "The Understanding of the Synoptic Parables," *EQ* 14 (1942): 42-53.

2954.   Teófilo Antolín, "El problema de las conclusiones finales aparentes en las parábolas evangélicas," *EB* 2 (1943): 3-22.

2955.   José M. Bover, "Las paraboles del Evangelio," *EB* 3 (1944): 229-57.

2956.   L. Baudiment, "La leçon des paraboles," *RB* 53 (1946): 47-55.

2957.   Ashley Sampson, "The Parables as Literature," *Th* 50 (1947): 96-99.

2958.   Colman Barry, "The Literary and Artistic Beauty of Christ's Parables," *CBQ* 10 (1948): 376-83.

2959.   Frederick C. Grant, "A New Book on the Parables," *ATR* 30 (1948): 118-21.

2960.   R. S. Wallace, "The Parable and the Preacher," *SJT* 2 (1948): 13-28.

2961.   Pierre Bonnard, "Estado actual del problema de las parábolas del Evangelio—de Jülicher (1888) a Jeremías (1947)," *CT* 2

(1950): 24-35.

2962.   G. H. Boobyer, "The Interpretation of the Parables of Jesus," *ET* 62 (1950-1951): 131-34.

2963.   Robert Morgenthaler, "Formgeschichte und Gleichnis-auslegung," *TZ* 6 (1950): 1-16.

2964.   A. D. Harcus, "Why the Parabolic Method?" *ET* 63 (1951-1952): 5-7.

2965.   Norman Victor Hope, "Bases for Understanding; The Interpretation of Christ's Parables," *Interp* 6 (1952): 301-307.

2966.   C. F. D. Moule, "The Use of Parables and Sayings as Illustrative Material in Early Christian Catechesis," *JTS* N.S., 3 (1952): 75-79.

2967.   Chr. Svanholm, "Hovedproblemer i fortolkningen av Jesu lignelser i den nyere teologi fra Jülicher av," *TTK* 24 (1953): 164-76.

2968.   C. F. D. Moule, "J. Jeremias, 'The Parables of Jesus' and 'The Eucharistic Words of Jesus'," *ET* 66 (1954-1955): 46-50.

2969.   Jean Danten, "La révélation du Christ sur Dieu dans les paraboles," *NRT* 77 (1955): 450-77.

2970.   A. Herranz, "Las parábolas. Un problema y una solution," *CB* 12 (1955): 129-38.

2971.   Sherman E. Johnson, "King Parables in the Synoptic Gospels," *JBL* 74 (1955): 37-39.

2972.   Willi Marxsen, "Redaktionsgeschichtliche Erklärung der sogenannten Parabeltheorie des Markus," *ZTK* N.F. 52 (1955): 255-71.

2973.   James M. Bulman, "The Parables of Revelation and Judgment," *RE* 53 (1956): 314-25.

2974.   T. A. Burkill, "The Cryptology of Parables in St. Mark's Gospel," *NT* 1 (1956): 246-62.

2975.   Alberto Colunga, "Las parábolas evangélicas," *CB* 13 (1956): 89-91.

2976.   Oscar Cullmann, "Que signifie le sel dans la parabole de

Jésus," *RHPR* 37 (1957): 36-43.

2977.   A. M. Hunter, "The Interpretation of the Parables," *ET* 69 (1958): 100-104.

2978.   Eduard Lohse, "Die Gottesherrschaft in den Gleichnissen Jesu," *EvT* 18 (1958): 145-58.

2979.   M. F. Wiles, "Early Exegesis of the Parables," *SJT* 11 (1958): 287-301.

2980.   M. Miguens, "La predicazione di Gesù in parabole," *BO* 1 (1959): 35-40.

2981.   Augustin George, "Les paraboles de la semence," *BVC* no. 32 (1960): 37-41.

2982.   A. M. Hunter, "Interpreting the Parables," *Interp* 14 (1960): 70-84, 167-85, 315-32, 440-54.

2983.   Terence Y. Mullins, "Parables as Literary Forms in the New Testament," *LQ* 12 (1960): 235-41.

2984.   L. Randellini, "Aspetti formali delle parabole," *BO* 2 (1961): 1-5.

2985.   Marco Adinolfi, "L'interpretazione delle parabole," *RivB* 9 (1961): 97-111, 243-58.

2986.   Georg Eichholtz, "Das Gleichnis als Spiel," *EvT* 21 (1961): 309-26.

         See also numbers 3179, 3181, 6931, 6932, 7585, 9107, 9436, 10082, 10084.

2986.1   C. H. Cave, "The Parables and the Scriptures," *NTSt* 11 (1964-1965): 374-87.

2986.2   Dan O. Via, "Matthew on the Understandability of the Parables," *JBL* 84 (1965): 430-32.

2986.3   George B. Caird, "Expounding the Parables: The Defendant," *ET* 77 (1965-1966): 36-39.

2986.4   P. G. Jarvis, "Expounding the Parables: Tower-Builder and King Going to War," *ET* 77 (1965-1966): 196-98.

2986.5   C. L. Mitton, "Expounding the Parables: The Workers in the Vineyard," *ET* 77 (1965-1966): 307-11.

2986.6   William Neil, "Expounding the Parables: II. The Sower

(Mark 4:3-8)," *ET* 77 (1965-1966): 74-77.

2986.7 Barnabas Lindars, "Two Parables in John," *NTSt* 16 (1969-1970): 318-29.

2986.8 Norman Perrin, "Historical Criticism, Literary Criticism, and Hermeneutics: The Interpretation of the Parables of Jesus and the Gospel of Mark Today," *JR* 52 (1972): 361-75.

2986.9 John Drury, "The Sower, the Vineyard, and the Place of Allegory in the Interpretation of Mark's Parables," *JTS* 24/2 (1973): 367-79.

2986.10 John D. Crossan, "The Seed Parables of Jesus," *JBL* 92 (1973): 244-66.

2986.11 Christian Mellon, "La parabole: manière de parler, manière d'entendre," *RSR* 61 (1973): 49-63.

2986.12 Louis J. Bataillon, "Un sermon de S Thomas d'Aquin sur la parabole du festin," *RSPT* 58 (1974): 451-56.

2986.13 Klaus Berger, "Zur Frage des traditionsgeschichtlichen wertes apokrypher Gleichnisse," *NT* 17 (1975): 58-76.

2986.14 Richard J. Bauckham, "Synoptic Parousia Parables and the Apocalypse," *NTS* 23 (1976-1977): 162-76.

2986.15 Étienne Trocmé, "Why Parables? A Study of Mark IV," *BJRL* 59/2 (1976-1977): 458-71.

2986.16 J. R. Kirkland, "The Earliest Understanding of Jesus' Use of Parables: Mark 4:10-12 in Context," *NT* 19/1 (1977): 1-21.

2986.17 R. L. Sturch, "Jeremias and John: Parables in the Fourth Gospel," *ET* 89 (1977-1978): 235-38.

2986.18 John R. Donahue, "Jesus as the Parable of God in the Gospel of Mark," *Interp* 32 (1978): 369-86.

2986.19 Norman Huffman, "Atypical Features in the Parables of Jesus," *JBL* 97 (1978): 207-20.

2986.20 Peter R. Jones, "The Seed Parables of Mark," *RE* 75 (1978): 519-38.

2986.21 C. E. Carlston, "Parable and Allegory Revisited: An Interpretive Review," *CBQ* 43 (1981): 228-42.

2986.22 Gerlad Diamond, "Reflections upon Recent Developments in the Study of Parables in Luke," *ABR* 29 (1981): 1-9.

2986.23   Paul Ricoeur, "The 'Kingdom' in the Parables of Jesus," *ATR* 63/2 (1981): 165-69.

2986.24   Richard J. Bauckham, "Synoptic Parousia Parables Again," *NTSt* 29 (1983): 129-34.

2986.25   Charles W. Hedrick, "Kingdom Sayings and Parables of Jesus in the Apocryphon of James: Tradition and Redaction," *NTSt* 29 (1983): 1-24.

2986.26   Craig A. Evans, "On the Vineyard Parables of Isaiah 5 and Mark 12," *BibZ* 28 (1984): 82-86.

2986.27   J. C. O'Neill, "The Source of the Parables of the Bridegroom and the Wicked Husbandman," *JTS* 39 (1988): 485-89.

2986.28   Mary Ann Beavis, "Ancient Slavery as an Interpretive Context for the New Testament Servant Parables with Special Reference to the Unjust Steward," *JBL* 111 (1992): 37-54.

2986.29   John P. Heil, "Reader-Response and the Narrative Context of the Parables about Growing Seed in Mark 4:1-34," *CBQ* 54 (1992): 271-86.

2986.30   K. E. Pagenkemper, "Rejection Imagery in the Synoptic Parables," *BS* 153 (1996): 179-98; 308-31.

8. Literary Criticism of the Resurrection Narratives

2987.   E. Graf, "Zu den evangelischen Berichten von der Auferstehung Jesu. Die Weisung nach Galiläa," *TSK* 42 (1869): 532-42.

2988.   Dr. Aberle, "Die Berichte der Evangelien über die Auferstehung Jesu," *TQ* 52 (1870): 48-91.

2989.   J. G. Boekenoogen, "De opstandingsverhalen," *TT* 22 (1888): 58-92.

2990.   J. G. Tasker, "Loofs on the Relative Value of the Resurrection Narratives," *ET* 9 (1897-1898): 304-305.

2991.   W. Beyschlag, "Die neueste Zurechtlegung der Auferstehungsberichte," *TSK* 72 (1899): 507-39.

2992.   William C. Wilkinson, "Are the Resurrection Narratives Legendary?" *AJT* 10 (1906): 628-47.

2993.   J. Kreyenbühl, "Der älteste Auferstehungsbericht und seine Varianten," *ZNW* 9 (1908): 257-96.

2994.   W. H. Turton, "How the Resurrection Narratives Explain one Another," *Exp* 7th ser. 7 (1909): 442-49.

2995.   Martin Albertz, "Zur Formengeschichte der Auferstehungs-berichte," *ZNW* 21 (1922): 259-69.

2996.   A. T. Cadoux, "The Resurrection Appearances of Jesus," *ET* 39 (1927-1928): 504-507.

2997.   U. Holzmeister, "Numquid relations de Resurrectione Domini sibi contradicunt?" *VD* 7 (1927): 119-23.

2998.   James Smyth, "The Problem of the Resurrection Narratives," *CJRT* 4 (1927): 41-44.

2999.   W. J. Limmer Sheppard, "The Resurrection Morning," *ET* 40 (1928-1929): 182-87.

3000.   J. W. Hunkin, "Some Outstanding New Testament Problems; The Problem of the Resurrection Narratives," *ET* 46 (1934-1935): 150-54.

3001.   F. B. Westbrook, "The Resurrection Narratives," *ET* 51 (1939-1940): 277-82.

3002.   J. L. Lilly, "Alleged Discrepancies in the Gospel Accounts of the Resurrection," *CBQ* 2 (1940): 98-111.

3003.   A. E. Morris, "The Narratives of the Resurrection of Jesus Christ," *HJ* 39 (1940-1941): 309-24.

3004.   Charles Masson, "Le tombeau vide: Essai sur la formation d'une tradition," *RTP* N.S. 32 (1944): 161-74.

3005.   Norman Huffman, "Emmaus among the Resurrection Narratives," *JBL* 64 (1945): 205-26.

3006.   Lambert Nolle, "The Holy Women on Easter Morning," *Scr* 3 (1948): 112-14.

3007.   W. E. Brown, "The First Day of the Week," *Scr* 7 (1955): 43-49.

3008.   Ralph Russell, "The Beloved Disciple and the Resurrection," *Scr* 8 (1956): 57-62.

3009.   John L. Cheek, "The Historicity of the Markan Resurrection Narrative," *JBR* 27 (1959): 191-200.

3010. Albert Descamps, "La structure des récits évangéliques de la résurrection," *B* 40 (1959): 726-41.

3010.1 Gabriel Hebert, "The Resurrection Narrative in St. Mark's Gospel," *SJT* 15 (1962): 66-73.

C. FORM-CRITICISM OF THE GOSPELS

1. General Studies

3011. A. Peloni, "The Oral and the Written Gospel," *Exp* 2nd ser., 4 (1882): 1-19.

3012. Paul Wernle, "Altchristliche Apologetik im Neuen Testament," *ZNW* 1 (1900): 42-65.

3013. Olaf Moe, "Hvem har skapt evangelieformen?" *TTDF* 3rd ser. 5 (1914): 1-20.

3014. G. Baldensperger, "L'apologétique de la primitive église: son influence sur la tradition des origines et du ministère galiléen de Jésus," *RTP* N.S. 8 (1920): 5-43.

3015. M. van Rhijn, "Over den vorm van de warden van Jezus," *NTS* 3 (1920): 105-13.

3016. Georg Bertram, "Die Geschichte der synoptischen Tradition," *TB* 1 (1922): 9-13, 32-34.

3017. Henry J. Cadbury, "Between Jesus and the Gospels," *HTR* 16 (1923), 81-92.

3018. M Rauer, "Zur Geschichte der synoptischen Tradition," *TRev* 22 (1923): 353-60.

3019. Oscar Cullmann, "Les récentes études sur la formation de la tradition évangélique," *RHPR* 5 (1925): 459-77, 564-79.

3020. Rudolf Bultmann, "The New Approach to the Synoptic Problem," *JR* 6 (1926): 337-62.

3021. Edward Beal, "The Unwritten Counterpart of the Gospels," *ET* 38 (1926-1927): 475-77.

3022. E. F. Scott, "The New Criticism of the Gospels," *HTR* 19 (1926): 143-65.

3023. J. N. Bakhuizen van den Brink, "Eine Paradosis zu der Leidensgeschichte," *ZNW* 26 (1927): 213-19.

3024. C. Bouma, "Formgeschichte," *GTT* 28 (1927-1928): 573-82.

3025.   Martin Dibelius, "The Structure and Literary Character of the Gospels," *HTR* 20 (1927): 151-70.

3026.   Martin Dibelius, "Zur Formgeschichte der Evangelien," *TR* N.F. 1 (1929): 185-216.

3027.   C. Bouma, "De taal van Jezus en van de rabbijnen," *GTT* 29 (1928-1929): 3-13.

3028.   Burton S. Easton, "The First Evangelic Tradition," *JBL* 50 (1931): 148-55.

3029.   Ian F. Mackinnon, " 'Formgeschichte' and the Synoptic Problem: Past and Present," *CJRT* 9 (1932): 190-96.

3030.   D. E. Florit, "La 'Storia delle Forme' nei vangeli in rapporto alla dottrina cattolica," *B* 14 (1933): 212-48.

3031.   R. W. Stewart, "A New Phase of New Testament Study," *ET* 45 (1933-1934): 181-83.

3032.   Frederick C. Grant, "Form Criticism: A New Method of Research," *RL* 3 (1934): 351-66.

3033.   Donald W. Riddle, "Die Verfolgungslogien in formgeschichtlicher und soziologischer Beleuchtung," *ZNW* 33 (1934): 271-89.

3034.   L. J. Collins, "The Gospels and History," *HJ* 34 (1935-1936): 430-42.

3035.   George A. Barton, "Legitimate and Illegitimate Uses of Form Criticism," *JBR* 4 (1936): 67-73.

3036.   James E. Bear, "Form Criticism," *USR* 48 (1936-1937): 287-311.

3037.   Archibald Chisholm, "Form-Criticism and Christian Ethics," *ET* 48 (1936-1937): 165-68.

3038.   Edgar P. Dickie, "God in History," *RL* 5 (1936): 494-513.

3039.   Frederick C. Grant, "Further Thought on Form Criticism," *RL* 5 (1936): 532-43.

3040.   Donald W. Riddle, "The Structural Units of the Gospel Tradition," *JBL* 55 (1936): 45-58.

3041.   Allan Barr, "The Factor of Testimony in the Gospels," *ET* 49 (1937-1938): 401-408.

3042. Julius Richter, "The Form Historical Study of the New Testament," *USR* 49 (1937-1938): 46-51.

3043. H. Aarup, "Den formhistoriske Retning og Evangelie-forskningen," *DTT* 1 (1938): 169-99, 209-44.

3044. C. H. Dodd, "The Gospel as History: A Reconsideration," *BJRL* 22 (1938): 122-43.

3045. G. J. Inglis, "The Gospels and the Early Church," *Th* 36 (1938): 270-80.

3046. Paul Seidelin, "Formhistorie og Synoptikerexegese," *DTT* 1 (1938): 18-37.

3047. W. Staerk, "Christusglaube und Heilanderwartung. Zur Formgeschichte der biblischen Christologie," *ZTK* N.F. 19 (1938): 109-17.

3048. N. B. Stonehouse, "Jesus in the Hands of a Barthian—Rudolf Bultmann's Jesus in the Perspective of a Century of Criticism," *WTJ* 1 (1938): 1-42.

3049. Vincent Taylor, "The Gospel and the Gospels," *ET* 50 (1938-1939): 8-12.

3050. Mary E. Andrews, "More Form Criticism," *JBR* 7 (1939): 180-83.

3051. Austin Farrer, " 'Fact' and 'Significance' in the Gospels," *Th* 39 (1939): 371-72.

3052. Frederick C. Grant, "Form Criticism and the Christian Faith," *JBR* 7 (1939): 9-17.

3053. I. J. Peritz, "Form Criticism as I see it," *JBR* 7 (1939): 172-76.

3054. Frederick C. Grant, "A Note on Dr. Peritz's Article," *JBR* 7 (1939): 177-80 [see no. 3053].

3055. Frederick C. Grant, "Where Form Criticism and Textual Criticism Overlap," *JBL* 59 (1940): 11-21.

3056. F. J. Badcock, "Form Criticism," *ET* 53 (1941-1942): 16-20.

3057. John J. Collins, "Form Criticism and the Synoptic Gospels," *ThSt* 2 (1941): 388-400.

3058. Oscar Cullmann, "Les origines des premieres confessions de foi," *RHPR* 21 (1941): 77-110.

3059.   R. H. Lightfoot, "Form Criticism and Gospel Study," *ET* 53 (1941-1942): 51-54.

3060.   Lawrence J. McGinley, "Form Criticism of the Synoptic Healing Narratives," *ThSt* 2 (1941): 451-80; 3 (1942): 47-68, 203-30.

3061.   Paul S.Minear, "How Objective is Biblical Criticism?" *JBR* 9 (1941): 217-22.

3062.   I. J. Peritz, "Form Criticism as an Experiment," *RL* 10 (1941): 196-211.

3063.   Donald W. Riddle, "The Influence of Environment on the Growing Gospel Tradition," *JR* 21 (1941): 135-46.

3064.   Mary E. Andrews, "Peirasmos: A Study in Form Criticism," *ATR* 24 (1942): 229-44.

3065.   John Gillies, "Form Criticism and the Gospels," *RTR* 1 (1942): 4-13.

3066.   Ernst Haenchen, "Frühgeschichte des Evangeliums," *TLZ* 67 (1942): 129-36.

3067.   Paul S. Minear, "The Needle's Eye; A Study in Form Criticism," *JBL* 61 (1942): 157-69.

3068.   Vincent Taylor, "The Passion Sayings," *ET* 54 (1942-1943): 249-50.

3069.   Mary E. Andrews, "The Historical Gospel," *JBL* 62 (1943): 45-57.

3070.   H. S. Shelton, "The Origin of the Gospels," *HJ* 42 (1943-1944): 71-76.

3071.   R. O. P. Taylor, "Form-Criticism in the First Centuries," *ET* 55 (1943-1944): 218-20.

3072.   S. E. Donlon, "Form-Critics, the Gospels, and St. Paul," *CBQ* 6 (1944): 159-79, 306-25.

3073.   William Scott, "Gospels in a Developing Church," *JBR* 12 (1944): 19-25.

3074.   Pierre Benoit, "Réflexions sur la 'formgeschichtliche Methode'," *RB* 53 (1946): 481-512.

3075.   George B. King, "A Problem in Form Criticism," *CQ* 23 (1946): 157-63.

3076.   Paul S. Minear, "Form Criticism and Faith," *RL* 15 (1946): 46-56.

3077.   George B. King, "A Problem in Form Criticism Again," *CQ* 24 (1947): 344-47.

3078.   Félix Puzo, "El ritmo oral en la exégesis evangélica," *EB* 6 (1947): 133-86.

3079.   Oscar Cullmann, " 'Κύριος' as Designation for the Oral Tradition," *SJT* 3 (1950): 180-97.

3080.   Kingsley Joblin, "The Earliest and the Latest Gospels," *TTod* 7 (1950): 42-53.

3081.   Harold H. Hutson, "Form Criticism of the New Testament," *JBR* 19 (1951): 130-33.

3082.   C. H. Dodd, "The Dialogue Form in the Gospels," *BJRL* 37 (1954-1955): 54-67.

3083.   Salvador Muñoz Iglesias, "Géneros literarios en los Evangelios," *EB* 13 (1954): 289-318.

3084.   David M. Stanley, "*Didachē* as a Constitutive Element of the Gospel-Form," *CQ* 17 (1955): 336-48.

3085.   B. Rigaux, "La formation des évangiles: problème synoptique et Formgeschichte," *ETL* 31 (1955): 658-64.

3086.   Willi Marxsen, "Bemerkungen zur 'Form' der sogenannten synoptischen Evangelien," *TLZ* 81 (1956): 345-48.

3087.   Gerhard Iber, "Zur Formgeschichte der Evangelien," *TR* 24 (1957-1958): 283-338.

3088.   Juan Leal, "Forma, historicidad y exégesis de las sentencias evangélicas," *EE* 31 (1957): 267-325.

3089.   Gottfried Schille, "Bemerkungen zur Formgeschichte des Evangeliums; I. Rahmen und Aufbau des Markus-evangeliums," *NTSt* 4 (1957-1958): 1-24; "II. Das Evangelium des Matthäus als Katechismus," 101-68, "III. Das Evangelium als Missionsbuch," 5 (1958-1959): 1-11.

3090.   C. F. Evans, "The Beginning of the Gospel Tradition," *Th* 61 (1958): 355-62.

3091.   Erich Fascher, "Eine Neuordnung der neutestamentlichen Fachdisziplin," *TLZ* 83 (1958): 609-18.

3092.   D. E. Nineham, "Eye-witness Testimony and the Gospel Tradition," *JTS* N.S. 9 (1958): 13-25, 243-52; 11 (1960): 253-64.

3093.   Harald Riesenfeld, "Evangelie-traditionens ursprung," *STK* 34 (1958): 243-61.

3094.   Krister Stendahl, "Implications of Form-Criticism and Tradition-Criticism for Biblical Interpretation," *JBL* 77 (1958): 33-38.

3095.   Peter Lengsfeld, "Der Traditionsgedanke bei Rudolf Bultmann," *C* 13 (1959): 17-49.

3096.   W. S. Taylor, "Memory and the Gospel Tradition," *TTod* 15 (1959): 470-79.

3097.   José Angel Ubieta, "El kerygma apostólico y los Evangelios," *EB* 18 (1959): 21-61.

3098.   Roger Balducelli, "Professor Riesenfeld on Synoptic Tradition," *CBQ* 22 (1960): 416-21.

3099.   Patrick Fannon, "The Formation of the Gospels," *Scr* 12 (1960): 112-19.

3100.   Francis J. McCool, "The Preacher and the Historical Witness of the Gospels," *ThSt* 21 (1960): 517-43.

See also numbers 2963, 2995, 3020, 3366, 4659.

3100.1   George B. Caird, "The Study of the Gospels. II. Form Criticism," *ET* 87/4 (1976): 137-41.

2. Form-Criticism of the Individual Gospels

a. *Form-Criticism of Matthew*

3101.   Charles H. Lohr, "Oral Techniques in the Gospel of Matthew," *CBQ* 23 (1961): 403-35.

3101.1   Bernard P. Robinson, "Peter and His Successors: Tradition and Redaction in Matthew 16:17-19," *JSNT* 21 (1984): 85-104.

b. *Form-Criticism of Mark*

3102.   C. H. Dodd, "The Framework of the Gospel Narrative," *ET* 43 (1931-1932): 396-400.

3103.   F. B. Clogg, "The Trustworthiness of the Marcan Outline,"

ET 46 (1933-1934): 534-38.

3104.   Harold A. Guy, "A Sayings-Collection in Mark's Gospel," JTS 42 (1941): 173-76.

3105.   R. P. Casey, "St. Mark's Gospel," Th 55 (1952): 362-70.

3106.   Vincent Taylor, "The Origin of the Markan Passion-Sayings," NTSt (1954-1955): 159-67.

3107.   Philip Carrington, "Important Hypotheses Reconsidered—The Calendrical Hypothesis of the Origin of Mark," ET 67 (1955-1956): 100-103.

3108.   Chalmer E. Faw, "The Heart of the Gospel of Mark," JBR 24 (1956): 77-82.

3109.   Chalmer E. Faw, "The Outline of Mark," JBR 25 (1957): 19-23.

3110.   Manfred Karnetzki, "Die galiläische Redaktion im Markusevangelium," ZNW 52 (1961): 238-72.

        See also number 5116.

3110.1 C. J. Maunder, "A Sitz im Leben for Mark 14:9," ET 99 (1987): 78-80.

3110.2 S. H. Smith, "Mark 3:1-6: Form, Redaction and Community Function," B 75 (1994): 153-74.

   c. Form-Criticism of Luke

3111.   A. M. Perry, "An Evangelist's Tableau: Some Sections of Oral Tradition in Luke," JBL 48 (1929): 206-32.

3112.   Edgar P. Dickie, "The Third Gospel: A Hidden Source," ET 46 (1934-1936): 326-30.

3112.1 Robert F. O'Toole, "The Literary Form of Luke 19:1-10," JBL 110 (1991): 107-16.

   d. Form-Criticism of John

3113.   Karl Kundsin, "Eine wenig beachtete Überlieferungsgeschichte im vierten Evangelium," ZNW 22 (1923): 80-91.

3114.   Rudolf Bultmann, "Untersuchungen zum Johannesevangelium," ZNW 27 (1928): 113-63.

3115.   Ernst Lohmeyer, "Über Aufbau und Gliederung des vierten

Evangeliums," *ZNW* 27 (1928): 11-36.

3116.   Rudolf Bultmann, "Untersuchungen zum Johannes-evangelium," *ZNW* 29 (1930): 169-92.

3117.   Rudolf Bultmann, "Zur johanneischen Tradition," *TLZ* 80 (1955): 521-26.

3117.1. D. Moody Smith, "The Life Setting of the Gospel of John," *RE* 85 (1988): 433-44.

3117.2   John Painter, "Quest and Rejection Stories in John," *JSNT* 36 (1989): 17-46.

3117.3   John Painter, "Quest Stories in John 1-4," *JSNT* 41 (1991): 33-70.

D. RELIGIONSGESCHICHTE WITH REFERENCE TO CHRIST AND THE GOSPELS

1. General Studies

3118.   Joseph P. Thompson, "Christmas and the Saturnalia," *BS* 12 (1855): 144-56.

3119.   C. P. Thiele, "Christus en Krishna," *TT* 11 (1877): 63-82.

3120.   S. H. Kellogg, "The Legend of the Buddha and the Life of the Christ," *BS* 39 (1882): 458-97.

3121.   F. F. Kramer, "Jesus Christ and Gautama Buddha as Literary Critics," *BW* 3 (1894): 252-59.

3122.   J. Dräseke, "R. Seydel's Untersuchungen über das Verhältnis von Buddha-Legende und Leben Jesu," *ZWT* 41 (1898): 502-14.

3123.   L. Hackspill, "Études sur le milieu religieux et intellectuel contemporain du Nouveau Testament," *RB* 9 (1900): 564-77; 10 (1901): 200-15, 377-84; 11 (1902): 58-73.

3124.   Maud Joynt, "The Gospel of Krishna and of Christ," *NJ* 6 (1907-1908): 77-89.

3125.   H. H. Wendt, "Offenbarungsbedeutung Jesu und religions-geschichtliche Anschauung im Christlichen Lehrsystem," *ZTK* 17 (1907): 443-51.

3126.   W. Bousset, "Ein grundlegender Beitrag zur Religions-geschichte des neutestamentlichen Zeitalters," *TR* 11 (1908): 323-41.

3127. G. A. van den Bergh van Eysinga, "Wonderbaarlijkheden van ouderen en nieuweren tijd," *TT* 43 (1909): 401-12.

3128. W. Wooding, "The Pre-Christian Jesus," *HJ* 9 (1910-1911): 855-74.

3129. Peter Dahmen, "The Doctrine of Incarnation in Hinduism," *ITQ* 6 (1911): 59-73.

3130. Alfred Jeremias, "Hat Jesus Christus gelebt?" *NKZ* 22 (1911): 143-66, 167-88.

3131. W. Bousset, "Die Religionsgeschichte und das Neue Testament," *TR* 15 (1912): 251-78.

3132. James A. Montgomery, "Some Correspondence between the Elephantine Papyri and the Gospels," *ET* 24 (1912-1913): 428-29 [Gnomic saying of Ahikar and Mt. 6:19; 5:40,45; 15:5; Lk. 12:32f.].

3133. J. Rendel Harris, "On the Name 'Son of God' in Northern Syria," *ZNW* 15 (1914): 98-113.

3134. Karl Beth, "Gibt es buddhistische Einflüsse in den kanonischen Evangelien?" *TSK* 89 (1916): 169-227.

3135. Tor Andrae, "De synoptiska evangelierna och deras utombibliska paralleller," *NTT* 20 (1919): 193-216.

3136. Richard Reitzenstein, "Iranischer Erlösungsglaube," *ZNW* 20 (1921): 1-23.

3137. Wilhelm Michaelis, "Sadhu-Überlieferung und Jesus-Überlieferung," *TB* 1 (1922): 275-77.

3138. J. Rendel Harris, "Athena, Sophia, and the Logos," *BJRL* 7 (1922-1923): 56-72.

3139. G. Klameth, "Harpokrato motivai apokrifu pasakojimuose a pie Jezaus vaikyste [Quomodo Aegyptii mythi de divino infante Harpocrato influxerint in narrationes apocryphas de infantia Christi Domini]," *Σ* 4 (1927): 62-67.

3140. Angus S. Woodburne, "The Indian Appreciation of Jesus," *JR* 7 (1927): 43-55.

3141. Rudolf Bultmann, "Urkristendom och religionshistoria," *STK* 6 (1930): 299-324.

3142. Rudolf Bultmann, "Urchristentum und Religionsgeschichte,"

TR 4 (1932): 1-21.

3143. Gwymre Dalrymple, "The Rubaiyat and the Christ," *BS* 89 (1932): 172-79.

3144. G. Messina, "Una presunta profezia di Zoroastro sulla ventura del Messia," *B* 14 (1933): 170-98.

3145. M.-J. Lagrange, "Les légendes pythagoriennes et l'évangile," *RB* 45 (1936): 481-511; 46 (1937): 5-28.

3146. Adam Hohenberger, "Gottesoffenbarung im Hinduismus und im Christentum," *NKZ* (Luthertum): 48 (1937): 53-57, 73-81.

3147. Herbert J. Rose, "Hercules and the Gospels," *HTR* 31 (1938): 113-42.

3148. Sverre Aalen, "Johannesevangeliet og religionshistorien," *TTK* 11 (1940): 160-80; 12 (1941): 20-33.

3149. Donald W. Riddle, "Syncretism and New Testament Religion," *JBR* 9 (1941): 17-22.

3150. Herbert P. Houghton, "On the Temptations of Christ and Zarathushtra," *ATR* 26 (1944): 166-75.

3151. Egon Hessel, "Christus' Buddha und die Götter," *EvT* 9 (1949-1950): 43-48.

3152. Alejandro Díez Macho, "¿Cesará la 'Torá' en la edad mesiánica?" *EB* 12 (1953): 115-58; 13 (1954): 5-51.

3153. A. A. T. Ehrhardt, "Greek Proverbs in the Gospel," *HTR* 46 (1953): 59-78.

3154. Victor White, "Incarnations and the Incarnation," *DS* 7 (1954): 1-21.

3155. Jes Peter Asmussen, "Kristendommen i Iran og dens Forhold til Zoroastrismen," *DTT* 22 (1959): 209-27.

3156. Heinrich Vogel, "Die Mystik Radhakrishnans und das Evangelium von Jesus Christus," *EvT* 21 (1961): 387-407.

See also number 8432.

3156.1 Otto Böcher, "Wölfe in Schafspelzen. Zum religions- geschichtlichen Hintergrund von Matth. 7,15," *TZ* 24 (1968): 405-26.

3156.2   E. Linnemann, "Die Hochzeit zu Kana und Dionysos oder das Unzureichende der Kategorien Übertragung und Identifkation zur Erfassung der religionsgeschichtlichen Beziehungen," *NTSt* 20 (1973-1974): 408-18.

3156.3   Roland Bergmeier, "Entweltlichung. Verzicht auf religionsgeschichtliche Forschung?" *NT* 16 (1974): 58-80.

3156.4   J. Becker, "Religionsgeschichtliche Fragen," *TR* 51 (1986): 56-65.

2. Judaism (exclusive of Qumran) and the Gospel Tradition

3157.   Ed. Scherer, "Jésus-Christ et le Judaïsme," *RT* 1 (1850): 154-61.

3158.   Gustav Rosch, "Die Jesusmythen des Judentums," *TSK* 46 (1873): 77-115.

3159.   Franz Delitzsch, "Jesus and Hillel," *LQ* 11 (1881): 530-57.

3160.   George H. Schodde, "The Messianic Views of Christ's Contemporaries," *BS* 41 (1884): 261-84.

3161.   B. Pick, "The Talmud a Witness to Christ and Christianity," *LCR* 5 (1886): 122-41.

3162.   C. G. Montefiore, "On Some Misconceptions of Judaism and Christianity by Each Other," *JQR* 8 (1895-1896): 193-216.

3163.   George B. Stevens, "The Teachings of Jesus; The Religious Ideas of the Jews in the Time of Jesus," *BW* 5 (1895): 7-15.

3164.   H. Trabaud, "Le cadre juif de l'histoire évangélique," *RTP* 30 (1897): 22-39.

3165.   Shailer Mathews, "The Jewish Messianic Expectation in the Time of Jesus," *BW* 12 (1898): 437-43

3166.   E. K. Mitchell, "The Jewish Synagogue and the Relation of Jesus to it," *BW* 16 (1900): 10-17.

3167.   James S. Riggs, "Some Types of Judaism in the Times of Jesus," *BW* 15 (1900): 105-11.

3168.   S. Schechter, "Some Rabbinic Parallels to the New Testament," *JQR* 12 (1900-1901): 415-33.

3169.   Ludwig Couard, "Jüdische Sagen über das Leben Jesu," *NKZ* 12 (1901): 164-76.

3170.　George A. Barton, "On the Jewish-Christian Doctrine of the Pre-existence of the Messiah," *JBL* 21 (1902): 78-91.

3171.　G. Klein, "Zur Erläuterung der Evangelien aus Talmud und Midrash," *ZNW* 5 (1904): 144-53.

3172.　C. G. Montefiore, "Impressions of Christianity from the Points of View of the Non-Christian Religions; I. The Synoptic Gospels and the Jewish Consciousness," *HJ* 3 (1904-1905): 649-67.

3173.　M.-J. Lagrange, "Notes sur le messianisme au temps de Jésus," *RB* 14 (1905): 481-514.

3174.　Henry S. Nash, "Jesus and Current Judaism," *BW* 26 (1905): 431-37.

3175.　Clyde W. Votaw, "The Modern Jewish View of Jesus," *BW* 26 (1905): 101-19.

3176.　M.-J. Lagrange, "Le règne de Dieu dans le judaïsme," *RB* 17 (1908): 350-66.

3177.　Edward A. Wicher, "Ancient Jewish Views of the Messiah," *BW* 34 (1909): 317-25, 404-409.

3178.　O. Holtzmann, "Die täglichen Gebetsstunden im Judentum und Urchristentum," *ZNW* 12 (1911): 90-107.

3179.　H. Weinel, "Der Talmud, die Gleichnisse Jesu und die synoptische Frage," *ZNW* 13 (1912): 117-32.

3180.　N. Bentwich, "Judaism in Early Christianity," *JQR* 1 (1909): 131-38.

3181.　Paul Fiebig, "Jüdische Gleichnisse der neutestamentlichen Zeit," *ZNW* 10 (1909): 301-306.

3182.　W. O. E. Oesterley, "Grace and Free-will: The Teaching of the Gospel and of the Rabbis Contrasted," *Exp* 7th ser., 10 (1910): 464-76.

3183.　J.-B. Frey, "L'angélologie juive au temps de Jésus Christ," *RSPT* 5 (1911): 75-110.

3184.　J.-B. Frey, "L'état originel et la chute de l'homme d'après les conceptions juives au temps de Jésus Christ," *RSPT* 5 (1911): 507-45.

3185.　C. Piepenbring, "Le messianisme Juif," *RTP* N.S., 2 (1914):

366-85.

3186.   Alfred Bertholet, "The Pre-Christian Belief in the Resurrection of the Body," *AJT* 20 (1916): 1-30.

3187.   J.-B. Frey, "Dieu et le monde d'après les conceptions juives au temps de Jésus Christ," *RB* 25 (1916): 33-60.

3188.   J.-B. Frey, "La révélation d'après les conceptions juives au temps de Jésus Christ," *RB* 25 (1916): 472-510.

3189.   C. G. Montefiore, "The Religious Teaching of the Synoptic Gospels in its Relation to Judaism," *HJ* 20 (1921-1922): 435-46.

3190.   Herbert Preisker, "Sind die jüdischen Apokalypsen in den drei ersten kanonischen Evangelien literarisch verarbeitet?" *ZNW* 20 (1921): 199-205.

3191.   Paul Fiebig, "Fra den nyere nytestamentlige forskning," *NTT* 24 (1923): 55-63.

3192.   A. Guillaume, "The Midrash in the Gospels," *ET* 37 (1925-1926): 392-98.

3193.   C. J. Cadoux, "Judaism and Universalism in the Gospels," *ET* 38 (1926-1927): 55-60, 136-40.

3194.   Hans Lietzmann, "Jüdische Passahsitten und der ἀφικόμενος. Kritische Randnoten zu R. Eislers Aufsatz über 'Das letzte Abendmahl'," *ZNW* 25 (1926): 1-5.

3195.   A. Marmorstein, "Das letzte Abendmahl und der Sederabend," *ZNW* 25 (1926): 249-53.

3196.   M. Goguel, "Jésus et la tradition religieuse de son peuple," *RHPR* 7 (1927): 154-75, 219-44.

3197.   Joseph Coppens, "Un nouveau texte rabbinique sur le Christ," *ETL* 6 (1929): 469-70.

3198.   Frederick C. Grant, "Economic Messianism and the Teaching of Jesus," *ATR* 12 (1929-1930): 443-47.

3199.   A. Lukyn Williams, " 'My Father' in Jewish Thought of the First Century," *JTS* 31 (1929-1930): 42-47.

3200.   F. Büchsel, "Die Blutgerichtsbarkeit des Synedrions," *ZNW* 30 (1931): 202-10; 33 (1934): 84-87.

3201.   Joseph Coppens, "Les soi-disant analogies juives de l'Eucharistie," *ETL* 8 (1931): 238-48.

3202.   Ethelbert Stauffer, "Die Messiasfrage im Judentum und Christentum," *ZTK* N.F. 12 (1931): 165-91.

3203.   Amos N. Wilder, "The Nature of Jewish Eschatology," *JBL* 50 (1931): 201-206.

3204.   Jean Calès, "Le judaïsme avant Jésus Christ," *NRT* 59 (1932): 538-46.

3205.   Sigmund Mowinckel, "Die Vorstellungen des Spätjudentums vom heiligen Geist als Fürsprecher und der johanneische Paraklet," *ZNW* 32 (1933): 97-130.

3206.   Carl Stange, "Jesus und die Juden," *ZST* 11 (1933-1934): 63-74.

3207.   J. W. Bailey, "The Temporary Messianic Reign in the Literature of Early Judaism," *JBL* 53 (1934): 170-87.

3208.   Joseph Bonsirven, "Les espérances messianiques en Palestine au temps de Jésus Christ," *NRT* 61 (1934): 113-39, 250-76.

3209.   Werner Georg Kümmel, "Jesus und der jüdische Traditionsgedanke," *ZNW* 33 (1934): 105-30.

3210.   Samuel Belkin, "Dissolution of Vows and the Problem of Anti-social Oaths in the Gospels and Contemporary Jewish Literature," *JBL* 55 (1936): 227-34.

3211.   J. S. Conning, "The Changing Attitude of Jews to Jesus," *USR* 48 (1936-1937): 323-32.

3212.   Paul Seidelin, "Der 'Ebed Jahwe und die Messiasgestalt im Jesajatargum," *ZNW* 35 (1936): 194-231.

3213.   R. T. Herford, "Repentance and Forgiveness in the Talmud, with some reference to the Teaching of the Gospels," *HJ* 40 (1941-1942): 55-64.

3214.   David Daube, "Two Haggadic Principles and the Gospels," *JTS* 44 (1943): 149-55.

3215.   Lawrence J. McGinley, "The Synoptic Healing Narrative and Rabbinic Analogies," *ThSt* 4 (1943): 53-99.

3216.   Paul Seidelin, "Bodfaerdighed og eschatologisk Forventning paa Jesu Tid," *DTT* 6 (1943): 145-61.

3217.   Manuel Tarrés, "El silencio de Filón sobre Jesus de Nazaret,"

CB 3 (1946): 187-88.

3218.   W. D. Davies, "Unsolved New Testament Problems: The Jewish Background of the Teaching of Jesus: Apocalyptic and Pharisaism," *ET* 59 (1947-1948): 233-37.

3219.   Harold Garner, "Christ and Temple Sacrifices," *ET* 59 (1947-1948): 223.

3220.   Philip W. Grossman, "Jewish Anticipation of the Cross," *BS* 106 (1949): 239-49, 367-76.

3221.   Joachim Jeremias, "Der Gedanke des 'Heiligen Restes' im Spätjudentum und in der Verkündung Jesu," *ZNW* 42 (1949): 184-94.

3222.   Morton Smith, "What is Implied by the Variety of Messianic Figures?" *JBL* 78 (1959): 66-72.

3223.   J. L. Teicher, "The Damascus Fragments and the Origin of the Jewish Christian Sect," *JJS* 2 (1950): 115-43.

3224.   S. Ben-Chorin, "Das Jesusbild im modernen Judentum," *ZRGG* 5 (1953): 231-57.

3225.   S. Zeitlin, "The Essenes and Messianic Expectations," *JQR* 45 (1954-1955): 83-119.

3226.   Raymund Schaeffer, "Die Auseinandersetzung Martin Bubers mit Jesus Christus," *MTZ* 6 (1955): 154-66.

3227.   Erik Sjøberg, "Justin als Zeuge vom Glauben an den verborgenen und den leidenden Messias im Judentum," *NTT* 56 (1955): 173-83.

3228.   Morton Smith, "The Jewish Elements in the Gospels," *JBR* 24 (1956): 90-96.

3229.   Georg Strecker, "Christentum und Judentum in den beiden ersten Jahrhunderten," *EvT* 16 (1956): 458-77.

3230.   David Daube, "Evangelisten und Rabbinen," *ZNW* 48 (1957): 119-26.

3231.   S. L. Edgar, "New Testament and Rabbinic Messianic Interpretation," *NTSt* 5 (1958-1959): 47-54.

3232.   Louis Ligier, "Autour du sacrifice eucharistique (anaphores Orientales et anamnese juive de Kippur)," *NRT* 82 (1960): 40-55.

3233. J. de Savignac, "Le messianisme de Philon d'Aléxandrie," *NT* 4 (1960): 319-24.

3234. J. Blinzler, "Das Synedrium von Jerusalem und die Strafprozessordnung der Mischna," *ZNW* 52 (1961): 54-65.

See also numbers 118, 413, 563, 609, 1054, 1345, 2729, 2737, 3027, 3152, 3390, 4375, 6097, 6500, 6701, 6856, 7642, 8108, 8129, 9617, 9624, 9636, 10035, 10052, 10054, 10058.

3234.1 Peder Borgen, "Observations on the Midrashic Character of John 6," *ZNW* 54/3-4 (1963): 232-40.

3234.2 Jean Carmignac, "La portée d'une négation devant un verbe au causatif," *RB* 72 (1965): 218-26.

3234.3 Z. W. Falk, "On Talmudic Vows," *HTR* 59 (1966): 309-12.

3234.4 W. Ziffer, "Two Epithets for Jesus of Nazareth in Talmud and Midrash," *JBL* 85 (1966): 356-57.

3234.5 Johannes A. Huntjens, "Contrasting Notions of Covenant and Law in the Texts from Qumran," *RQu* 8 (1974): 361-80.

3234.6 J. D. M. Derrett, "Midrash in Matthew," *HeyJ* 16 (1975): 51-56.

3234.7 George W. Buchanan, "Office of Teacher of Righteousness," *RQu* 9 (1977): 241-43.

3234.8 Joseph A. Fitzmyer, "Crucifixion in Ancient Palestine, Qumran Literature, and the New Testament," *CBQ* 40 (1978): 493-513.

3234.9 Marc Bregman, "Another Reference to 'a Teacher of Righteousness' in Midrashic Literature," *RQu* 10 (1979): 97-100.

3234.10 J. D. M. Derrett, "Mt. 23,8-10: A Midrash on Is. 54,13 and Jer. 31,33-34," *B* 62/3 (1981): 372-86.

3234.11 Jacob Neusner, "Death-Scenes and Farewell Stories: An Aspect of the Master-Disciple Relationship in Mark and in Some Talmudic Tales," *HTR* 79 (1986): 187-97.

3234.12 Scott Cunningham and Darrell L. Bock, "Is Matthew Midrash?" *BS* 144 (1987): 157-180.

3234.13 F. García Martínez, "La reprehensión fraterna en Qumran y

Mt. 18,15-17," *FilN* 2/1 (1989): 23-40.

3234.14 Marie Sabin, "Reading Mark 4 as Midrash," *JSNT* 45 (1992): 3-26.

3234.15 R. A. J. Gagnon, "The Shape of Matthew's Q Text of the Centurion at Capernaum: Did It Mention Delegations?" *NTSt* 40 (1994): 133-42.

3. The Qumran Documents and the Gospel Tradition

3235. William H. Brownlee, "A Comparison of the Covenanters of the Dead Sea Scrolls with pre-Christian Jewish Sects," *BA* 13 (1950): 49-72.

3236 Floyd V. Filson, "Some Recent Study of the Dead Sea Scrolls," *BA* 13 (1950): 96-99.

3237. Floyd V. Filson, "New Fragments of the Dead Sea Scrolls," *BA* 13 (1950): 99-100.

3238. Joseph Ziegler, "Der Handschriftenfund in der Nähe des Toten Meeres," *MTZ* 1, Heft 4 (1950): 23-39.

3239. Bleddyn J. Roberts, "Some Observations on the Damascus Documents and the Dead Sea Scrolls," *BJRL* 34 (1951-1952): 366-87.

3240. J. L. Teicher, "Jesus in the Habakkuk Scroll," *JJS* 3 (1951): 53-55.

3241. J. L. Teicher, "Die Schriftrollen vom Toten Meer— Dokumente der jüdisch-christlichen Sekte der Ebioniten," *ZRGG* 3 (1951): 193-209.

3242. K. Schubert, "Die jüdischen und judenchristlichen Sekten im Lichte des Handschriftenfundes von 'En Fešcha," *ZKT* 74 (1952): 1-62.

3243. Jean-Paul Audet, "Affinités littéraires et doctrinales du Manuel de Discipline," *RB* 60 (1953): 41-82.

3244. J. R. Mantey, "Baptism in the Dead Sea Manual of Discipline," *RE* 51 (1954): 522-27.

3245. Lucetta Mowry, "The Dead Sea Scrolls and the Background for the Gospel of John," *BA* 17 (1954): 78-97.

3246. F. F. Bruce, "Qumrân and Early Christianity," *NTSt* 2

(1955-1956): 176-224.

3247. Joseph A. Fitzmyer, "The Qumrân Scrolls, the Ebionites and their Literature," *ThSt* 16 (1955): 335-72.

3248. Robert J. North, "The Qumrân 'Sadducees'," *CQ* 17 (1955): 164-88.

3249. Erik Sjøberg, "Neuschöpfung in den Toten-Meer-Rollen," *ST* 9 (1955): 131-36.

3250. Edward J. Young, "The Teacher of Righteousness and Jesus Christ; Some Reflections upon the Dead Sea Scrolls," *WTJ* 18 (1955): 121-45.

3251. J. M. Allegro, "Further Messianic References in Qumrân Literature," *JBL* 75 (1956): 174-87.

3252. William H. Brownlee, "Messianic Motifs of Qumrân and the New Testament," *NTSt* 3 (1956-1957): 12-30, 195-210.

3253. A. Rolla, "I manoscritti di Qumrân, e i vangeli," *RivB* 4 (1956): 72-80.

3254. David M. Stanley, "The Johannine Literature," *ThSt* 17 (1956): 516-31 [Qumran and Jn.].

3255. Morris Ashcraft, "The Dead Sea Scrolls and Early Christianity," *RE* 54 (1957): 7-22.

3256. W. D. Davies, "The Dead Sea Scrolls and Christian Origins," *RL* 26 (1957): 246-63.

3257. F. Nötscher, "Die Handschriften aus der Gegend am Toten Meer," *TRev* 53 (1957): 49-58.

3258. John A. T. Robinson, "The Baptism of John and the Qumran Community," *HTR* 50 (1957): 175-92.

3259. Kurt Schubert, "Die Messiaslehre in den Texten von Chirbet Qumran," *BibZ* 1 (1957): 177-97.

3260. Paul Winter, "Das Neue Testament und die Rollen vom Toten Meer. Der gegenwärtige Stand der Erforschung der in Palästina neu gefundenen hebräischen Handschriften," *TLZ* 82 (1957): 833-40.

3261. J. M. Allegro, "Fragments of a Qumran Scroll of Eschatological Midrāšîm," *JBL* 77 (1958): 350-54.

3262. Otto Betz, "Jesu heiliger Krieg," *NT* 2 (1958): 116-37.

3263. Kurt Schubert, "Die Schriftrollen vom Toten Meer," *MTZ* 9 (1958): 142-48.

3264. Kevin Smyth, "The Teacher of Righteousness," *ET* 69 (1958): 340-42.

3265. John V. Chamberlain, "Toward a Qumran Soteriology," *NT* 3 (1959): 305-13.

3266. F. Gryglewicz, "Der Evangelist Johannes und die Sekte von Qumran," *MTZ* 10 (1959): 226-28.

3267. B. Hjerl-Hansen, "Did Christ know the Qumrân Sect?" *RQu* 1 (1959): 495-508 [Mt. 24:26-28].

3268. J. Liver, "The Doctrine of the Two Messiahs in Sectarian Literature in the Time of the Second Commonwealth," *HTR* 52 (1959): 149-86.

3269. J. Gnilka, "Die Erwartung des messianischen Hohenpriesters in den Schriften von Qumran und im Neuen Testament," *RQu* 2 (1960): 395-426.

3270. Pierre Benoit, "Qumran et le Nouveau Testament," *NTSt* 7 (1960-1961): 276-96.

3271. Otto Betz, "Qumran und das Neue Testament: Auswahl aus der neueren Literatur," *NTSt* 7 (1960-1961): 361-63.

3272. Joseph A. Fitzmyer, "The Use of Explicit Old Testament Quotations in Qumran Literature and in the New Testament," *NTSt* 7 (1960-1961): 297-333.

See also numbers 2349, 2737, 2742, 3415, 6301, 10060.

3272.1 J. Gnilka, " 'Die Kirche des Matthäus und die Gemeinde von Qumran," *BibZ* 7 (1963): 43-63.

3272.2 E. Earle Ellis, "Jesus, the Sadducees and Qumran," *NTSt* 10 (1963-1964): 274-79.

3272.3 Frederick Bussby, "Note on Matthew 5:22 and Matthew 6:7 in the Light of Qumran," *ET* 76 (1964-1965): 26.

3272.4 F. Fensham, "Judas' Hand in the Bowl and Qumran," *RQu* 5 (1965): 259-61.

3272.5 M. de Jonge and A. S. Van Der Woude, "11 Q Melchizedek and the New Testament," *NTSt* 12 (1965-1966): 301-26.

3272.6 Raymond E. Brown, "Second Thoughts: 10. The Dead Sea

Scrolls and the New Testament," *ET* 78 (1966): 19-23.

3272.7   Maurice Baillet, "Les manuscrits de la Grotte 7 de Qumrân et le Nouveau Testament," *B* 53 (1972): 508-16.

3272.8   Pierre Benoit, "Note sur les fragments grecs de la grotte 7 de Qumrân," *RB* 79 (1972): 321-24.

3272.9   José O'Callaghan, "Notas sobre 7Q tomadas en el 'Rockefeller Museum' de Jerusalén," *B* 53 (1972): 517-33.

3272.10   José O'Callaghan, "New Testament Papyri in Qumran Cave 7?" *JBL* Supplement 91/2 (1972): 1-20.

3272.11   C. H. Roberts, "On Some Presumed Papyrus Fragments of the New Testament from Qumran," *JTS* 23 (1972): 446-47.

3272.12   Maurice Baillet, "Les manuscrits de la Grotte 7 de Qumrân et le Nouveau Testament," *B* 54 (1973): 340-50.

3272.13   Pierre Benoit, "Nouvelle Note sur les Fragments Grecs de la Grotte 7 de Qumrân," *RB* 80/1 (1973): 5-12.

3272.14   Kurt Aland, "Neue neutestamentliche Papyri III," *NTSt* 20 (1973-1974): 357-81.

3272.15   Colin J. Hemer, "A Note on 7Q5," *ZNW* 65 (1974): 155-57.

3272.16   W. Boyd Barrick, "The Rich Man from Arimathea (Matt 27:57-60) and 1QIsaa," *JBL* 96 (1977): 235-39.

3272.17   G. Brooke, "The Feast of New Wine (Qumran Temple Scroll 19,11-21) and the Question of Fasting," *ET* 95 (1983-1984): 175-76.

3272.18   Craig A. Evans, "1Q Isaiah and the Absence of Prophetic Critique at Qumran," *RQu* 11/4 (1984): 537-42.

3272.19   C. P. Thiede, "7Q-Eine Ruckkehr zu den Neutestamentlichen Papyrus-Fragmenten in der Siebten Hohle von Qumran," *B* 65/4 (1984): 538-59.

3272.20   Hans-Udo Rosenbaum, "Cave 7Q5! Gegen die erneute inanspruchnahme des Qumran-Fragments 7Q5 als bruchstueck der aeltesten Evangelien-Handschrift," *BibZ* 31/2 (1987): 189-205.

3272.21   Ferdinand Rohrhirsch, "Das Qumranfragment 7Q5," *NT* 30 (1988): 97-99.

3272.22   José O'Callaghan, "Sobre el papiro de Marcos en Qumrán,"

FilN 5 (1992): 191-97.

3272.23 C. P. Thiede, "7Q5–Facts or Fiction?" *WTJ* 57 (1995): 471-74.

4. The Mystery Religions and the Gospel Tradition

3273. Ernst von Lasaulx, "The Expiatory Sacrifices of the Greeks and Romans, and their Relation to the one Sacrifice upon Golgotha," *BS* 1 (1844): 368-408.

3274. J. van Loon, "Historische of mytologische behandeling van de 'Evangelische geschiedenis'," *TT* 33 (1899): 197-266.

3275. Karl Vold, "Myther om døende og igjen til liv kommende guddomme og dermed sammenhoengende ritualer," *NTT* 11 (1910): 139-53.

3276. H. J. Toxopeüs, "Het Christendom als mysterie-godsdienst," *TT* 46 (1912): 327-36.

3277. M.-J. Lagrange, "Les mystères d'Éleusis et le Christianisme," *RB* 28 (1919): 157-217.

3278. M.-J. Lagrange, "Attis et le Christianisme," *RB* 28 (1919): 419-80.

3279. S. Angus, "Christianity and the Mystery-Religions," *RE* 18 (1921): 3-11, 318-41, 387-401.

3280. Auguste Bill, "La littérature religieuse hellénistique et les religions des mystères d'après Reitzenstein," *RHPR* 3 (1923): 443-57.

3281. Léonce de Grandmaison, "Dieux morts et ressuscités," *RSR* 17 (1927): 97-126.

3282. M.-J. Lagrange, "La régénération et la filiation divine dans les mystères d'éleusis," *RB* 38 (1929): 63-81, 201-14.

3283. Bruce M. Metzger, "Considerations of Methodology in the Study of the Mystery Religions and Early Christianity," *HTR* 48 (1955): 1-20.

See also number 5512, 8432.

3283.1 Charles Masson, "La transfiguration de Jesus (Marc 9:2-13)," *RTP* 97 (1964): 1-14.

278 CRITICAL STUDIES OF THE GOSPELS

5. Gnosticism, Hermeticism, Neo-Platonism, the Mandaeans, the Koran, and the Gospel Tradition

3284. Gustav Rösch, "Die Jesusmythen des Islam," *TSK* 49 (1876): 409-54.

3285. G. Gabrieli, "Gesù Christo nel Qorano," *Bes* 9 (1901): 32-60.

3286. C. F. Andrews, "Current Muhammadan Teaching as to the Gospels," *JTS* 7 (1905-1906): 278-81.

3287. David M. McIntyre, "The Mystical Doctrine of Christ," *Exp* 7th ser., 2 (1906): 161-75.

3288. F. W. von Herbert, "The Moslem Tradition of Jesus' Visit on Earth," *HJ* 7 (1908-1909): 27-48.

3289. W. Bousset, "Platons Weltseele und das Kreuz Christi," *ZNW* 14 (1913): 273-85.

3290. Hermann Cladder, "Cerinth und unsere Evangelien," *BibZ* 14 (1916-1917): 317-32.

3291. S. Michelet, "Om senjededommens problemer," *NTT* 22 (1921): 197-98.

3292. Paul Fiebig, "Mandäische Religion und Urchristentum," *TB* 1 (1922): 273-75.

3293. Gunnar Rudberg, "Einige Platon-Paralleln zu neutestamentlichen Stellen," *TSK* 94 (1922): 179-84.

3294. M.-J. Lagrange, "L'Hermétisme," *RB* 33 (1924): 481-97; 34 (1925): 82-104, 368-96, 547-74; 35 (1926): 240-64.

3295. F. Büchsel, "Mandäer und Johannesjünger," *ZNW* 26 (1927): 219-30.

3296. M.-J. Lagrange, "La gnose mandéenne et la tradition évangélique," *RB* 36 (1927): 321-49, 481-515; 37 (1928): 5-36.

3297. A. Greiff-Marienburg, "Platons Weltseele und das Johannesevangelium," *ZKT* 52 (1928): 519-31.

3298. Herbert Preisker, "Urchristlicher und mandäischer Erlösungsglaube," *TB* 7 (1928): 143-51.

3299. Mary Ely Lyman, "Hermetic Religion and the Religion of the Fourth Gospel," *JBL* 49 (1930): 265-76.

3300.   Adelaide P. Bostick, "A Comparison of the Portrait of Jesus in the Gospels with the Portrait of Socrates in the Writings of Plato and Xenophon," *JBR* 3 (1935): 94-101.

3301.   R. P. Casey, "The Study of Gnosticism," *JTS* 36 (1935): 45-60.

3302.   Carolus B. Hughes, "De notitia Christi quae ad Mohammed pervenit," *VD* 15 (1935): 238-42.

3303.   Lawrence J. McGinley, "Hellenic Analogies and the Typical Healing Narrative," *ThSt* 4 (1943): 385-419.

3304.   John W. Drummond, "Jesus in the Quran," *ET* 55 (1943-1944): 260-62.

3305.   S. M. Zwemer, "The Allah of Islam and the God of Jesus Christ," *TTod* 3 (1946): 64-77.

3306.   Ernst Haenchen, "Gab es eine vorchristliche Gnosis?" *ZTK* N.F. 49 (1952): 316-49.

3307.   Georg Kretschmar, "Zur religionsgeschichtlichen Einordnung der Gnosis," *EvT* 13 (1953-1954): 354-61.

3308.   Alan Richardson, "Gnosis and Revelation in the Bible and in Contemporary Thought," *SJT* 8 (1955): 31-45.

3309.   J. Ries, "Introduction aux études manichéennes; quatre siècles de recherches," *ETL* 33 (1957): 453-82; 35 (1959): 362-409.

3310.   R. McL. Wilson, "Some Recent Studies in Gnosticism," *NTSt* 6 (1959-1960): 1-15.

3311.   F. W. Beare, "New Light on the Church of the Second Century: Gnosticism and the Coptic Papyri of Nag-Hammadi," *CJT* 6 (1960): 211-16.

            See also numbers 2749-2764, 5512, 6086, 6854, 6855, 6899 ff., 7134, 10083.

3311.1   Hildebrecht Hommel, "Herrenworte im Lichte sokratischer Überlieferung," *ZNW* 57 (1966): 1-23.

3311.2   L. Schottroff, "Heil als innerweltliche Entweltlichung. Der gnostische Hintergrund der johanneischen Vorstellung von Zeitpunkt der Erlösung," *NT* 11 (1969): 294-317.

3311.3   J. M. Lieu, "Gnosticism and the Gospel of John," *ET* 90

(1978-1979): 233-37.

3311.4   Craig A. Evans, "Jesus in Gnostic Literarure," *B* 62 (1981): 4O6-12.

3311.5   Pheme Perkins, "Gnostic Christologies and the New Testamnet," *CBQ* 43 (1981): 590-606.

E. DEMYTHOLOGIZING THE GOSPELS

3312.   W. Telfer, "Are the Gospel Nativity Stories Legendary?" *Th* 27 (1933): 66-72.

3313.   Erich Fascher, "Anastasis—Resurrectio—Auferstehung, eine programmatische Studie zum Thema 'Sprache und Offen-arung'," *ZNW* 40 (1941): 166-229.

3314.   Paul Althaus, "Neues Testament und Mythologie. Zu R. Bultmanns Versuch der Entmythologisierung des Neuen Testamentes," *TLZ* 67 (1942): 337-44.

3315.   E. Thestrup Pedersen, "Kristendommens Afmythologisering og Forkyndelsen," *DTT* 8 (1945): 193-222.

3316.   Regin Prenter, "Mythe et évangile," *RTP* N.S. 35 (1947): 49-67.

3317.   Philip E. Hughes, "Miracle and Myth," *EQ* 20 (1948): 184-95.

3318.   Josef R. Geiselmann, "Der Glaube an Jesus Christus—mythos oder Geschichte?" *TQ* 129 (1949): 257-77, 418-39.

3319.   Anonymous, "Hessen-Nassauische Synode zur Frage der Entmythologisierung," *EvT* 11 (1951-1952): 93-94.

3320.   W. Arndt, "Entmythologisierung," *CTM* 22 (1951): 186-92.

3321.   G. Casalis, "Le problème du mythe," *RHPR* 31 (1951): 330-42.

3322.   H. Clavier, "Le problème du rite et du mythe dans le quatrième évangile," *RHPR* 31 (1951): 275-92.

3323.   Ernst Fuchs, "Das entmythologisierte Glaubensärgernis," *EvT* 11 (1951-1952): 398-415.

3324.   William Hallock Johnson, "Myth and Miracle at Mid-Century," *TTod* 8 (1951): 313-26.

3325.   John Nome, "Avmytologiseringen av det bibelske kerygma,"
         TTK 22 (1951): 97-122.

3326.   Rudolf Schnackenburg, "Von der Formgeschichte zur
         Entmythologisierung des Neuen Testaments. Zur Theologie
         Rudolf Bultmanns," *MTZ* 2 (1951): 345-60.

3327.   Karl Adam, "Das Problem der Entmythologisierung und die
         Auferstehung des Christus," *TQ* 132 (1952): 385-410.

3328.   S. G. F. Brandon, "Myth and the Gospel," *HJ* 51 (1952-
         1953): 121-32.

3329.   David Lerch, "Zur Frage nach dem Verstehen der Schrift,"
         ZTK N.F. 49 (1952): 350-67.

3330.   G. O. Rosengirst, "Det nytestamentliga budskapets
         'avmytologisering' och forkunnselsen," *STK* 28 (1952):
         16-25.

3331.   W. Arndt, "The Faculty at Bethel on the demythologizing,
         Championed by Professor Dr. Bullmann," *CTM* 24 (1953):
         785-809.

3332.   Rudolf Bultmann, "The Christian Hope and the Problem of
         Demythologizing," *ET* 65 (1953-1954): 228-30, 276-78.

3333.   Jérôme Hamer, "Zur Entmythologisierung Bullmanns," *C* 9
         (1953): 138-46.

3334.   Ian Henderson, "An Issue in the Enthmythologisierung
         Controversy," *ET* 65 (1953-1954): 367-69

3335.   Ian Henderson, "Karl Jaspers and Demythologizing," *ET* 65
         (1953-1954): 291-93.

3336.   A. Kolping, "Sola fide. Aus der Diskussion um Bultmanns
         Forderung nach Entmythologisierung des Evangeliums,"
         TRev 49 (1953): 121-34.

3337.   Ronald Gregor Smith, "What is Demythologizing?" *TTod* 10
         (1953): 34-44.

3338.   Allan Barr, "Bultmann's Estimate of Jesus," *SJT* 7 (1954):
         337-54.

3339.   Rudolf Bultmann, "Zur Frage der Entmythologisierung," *TZ*
         10 (1954): 81-95.

3340.   Sherman E. Johnson, "Bultmann and the Mythology of the

New Testament," *ATR* 36 (1954): 29-47.

3341. Wolfhart Pannenberg, "Mythus und Wort. Theologische überlegungen zu Karl Jaspers' Mythusbegriff," *ZTK* N.F. 51 (1954): 167-85.

3342. E. G. Selwyn, "Image, Fact and Faith," *NTSt* 1 (1954-1955): 235-47.

3343. Pierre Bonnard, "Les mythes du Nouveau Testament," *RTP* ser. 3, 5 (1955): 32-40.

3344. Heinrich Fries, "Das Anliegen Bultmanns im Licht der katholischen Theologie," *C* 10 (1955): 1-13.

3345. H. P. V. Nunn, "The Use of Myth and Symbol in Religious Thought," *EQ* 27 (1955): 81-93.

3346. Hannelis Schulte, " 'Rettet den Mythosl!'," *EvT* 15 (1955): 523-33.

3347. Peter L. Berger, "Demythologization—Crisis in Continental Theology," *RR* 20 (1955-1956): 5-24.

3348. C. K. Barrett, "How far does Myth enter into the New Testament?" *ET* 68 (1956-1957): 359-62.

3349. Paul Jacobs, "Barth in den Sielen der existentialen Interpretation," *EvT* 16 (1956): 310-19.

3350. John A. O'Flynn, "New Testament and Mythology," *ITQ* 23 (1956): 49-59, 101-10.

3351. Roland Schütz, "Ernste Sorge um die Mythen der Bibel," *EvT* 16 (1956): 274-81.

3352. Markus Barth, "Introduction to Demythologizing," *JR* 37 (1957): 145-55.

3353. Myles M. Bourke, "Rudolf Bultmann's Demythologizing of the New Testament," *PCTSA* 12 (1957): 103-33.

3354. Allan D. Galloway, "Religious Symbols and Demythologizing," *SJT* 10 (1957): 361-69.

3355. John A. O'Flynn, "New Testament and Mythology," *ITQ* 24 (1957): 1-12, 109-21.

3356. Schubert M. Ogden, "Bultmann's Project of Demythologizing and the Problem of Theology and Philosophy," *JR* 37 (1957): 156-73.

3357. Maria F. Sulzbach, "The New Testament and Myth," *RL* 26 (1957): 560-71.

3358. John Thompson, "Demythologizing," *BT* 7 (1957): 27-35.

3359. J. H. Thomas, "The Relevance of Kierkegaard to the Demythologizing Controversy," *SJT* 10 (1957): 239-52.

3360. J. N. Walty, "Bulletin de théologie protestante: L'oeuvre de Rudolf Bultmann," *RSPT* 42 (1958): 349-70.

3361. Kendrick Grobel, "The Practice of Demythologizing," *JBR* 27 (1959): 28-31.

3362. Schubert M. Ogden, "The Debate on 'Demythologizing'," *JBR* 27 (1959): 17-27.

3363. Eric C. Rust, "The Possible Lines of Development of Demythologizing," *JBR* 27 (1959): 32-40.

3364. Thomas J. J. Altizer, "Demythologizing and Jesus," *RL* 29 (1960): 564-74.

3365. H.-W. Bartsch, "The Still Unsettled Debate on Demythologizing," *RL* 30 (1961): 167-78.

3366. J. McDonald, "The Primitive Community and Truth," *HeyJ* 2 (1961): 30-41.

3367. Charles W. F. Smith, "Levels of Interpretation in the Gospels," *RL* 30 (1961): 231-42.

See also numbers 741, 772, 783, 801.

3367.1 Rudolf Bultmann, "On the Problem of Demythologizing," *JR* 42 (1962): 96-102.

3367.2 Karl Prümm, "Zur Früh- und Spätform der religions-geschichtlichen Christusdeutung von H Windisch," *B* 42 (1961): 391-22; 43 (1962): 22-56.

3367.3 Eldon R. Hay, "Demythologizing and the Post-Supernatural Era," *CJT* 10 (1964): 248-57.

3367.4 Horst Seebass, "Kirchliche Verkündigung und die sogenannte Entmythologisierung," *KD* 11 (1965): 143-63.

3367.5 Colin Duncan, "The Bible and Objectifying Thinking—What Does Bultmann Mean by Demythologizing?" *ABR* 14 (1966): 24-32.

3367.6   Ulrich Luz, "Entmythologisierung als Aufgabe der Christologie," *EvT* 26 (1966): 349-68.

3367.7   James M. Robinson, "Pre-History of Demythologization," *Interp* 20 (1966): 65-77.

3367.8   Pierre Grelot, "Que penser de l'interprétation existentiale?" *ETL* 43 (1967): 420-43.

3367.9   C. F. Geyer, "Die Gegenwärtigkeit der Wahrheit: Gedanken zu einer Neuinterpretation der Eschatologie," *TZ* 32 (1976): 282-300.

3367.10   K. Zizelkow, "Theologisches Denken heute," *TZ* 33 (1977): 30-40.

3367.11   Peter Stuhlmacher, "In verrosteten angeln," *ZTK* 77 (1980): 222-38.

3367.12   John Painter, "The Origins of Demythologizing Revisited," *ABR* 33 (1985): 2-14.

3367.13   K. H. Schelkle, "Entmythologisierung in existentialer Interpretation," *TQ* 165 (1985): 257-66.

3367.14   Schuyler Brown, "Reader Response: Demythologizing the Text," *NTSt* 34 (1988): 232-37.

3367.15   Heinrich Ott, "Die hermeneutische Problematik und das Entmythologisierungsprogramm," *TZ* 44 (1988): 222-38.

3367.16   James F. Kay, "Myth or Narrative? Bultmann's 'New Testament and Mythology' Turns Fifty," *TTod* 48 (1991): 326-32.

3367.17   David S. Russell, "Interpreting Scripture: Myth and Remythologizing," *ET* 104 (1993): 356-59.

3367.18   Michael H. Barnes, "Demythologization in the Theology of Karl Rahner," *ThSt* 55 (1994): 24-45.

F. PHILOLOGICAL STUDIES OF THE GOSPELS

  1. Lexicographical Studies of the Gospels
    a. *General Studies*

3368.   Theodore D. Woolsey, "Greek Lexicography," *BS* 1 (1844): 613- 32.

3369.   Lemuel S. Potwin, "Words in New Testament Greek

Borrowed from the Hebrew and Aramaean," *BS* 33 (1876): 52-62.

3370. Lemuel S. Potwin, "The New Testament Vocabulary," *BS* 32 (1875): 703-14; 33 (1876): 52-62; 37 (1880): 503-27, 640-60.

3371. Rayner Winterbotham, "On the Use of Certain Slang Words in the New Testament," *Exp* 1st. ser., 4 (1876): 29-35.

3372. J. Massie, "A Word Study in the New Testament," *Exp* 1st. ser., 9 (1879): 345-60, 459-75; 10 (1879): 48-60.

3373. J. A. Selbie, "Nestle on the Original Gospels and Acts," *ET* 8 (1896-1897): 75 [Nestle's *Philologia Sacra*, 1896].

3374. James H. Moulton, "Notes from the Papyri," *Exp* 6th ser., 3 (1901): 271-82.

3375. P. Boylan, "The New Testament and the Newly Discovered Texts of the Graeco-Roman Period," *ITQ* 4 (1909): 327-44; 5 (1910): 212-26.

3376. D. De Bruyne, "Notes de philologie biblique," *RB* 30 (1921): 400-409.

3377. Paul Haupt, "Philological and Archeological Studies," *AJP* 45 (1924): 238-59 [Mk. 10:25, Mt. 5:13].

3378. Henry J. Cadbury, "Lexical Notes on Luke-Acts," *JBL* 44 (1925): 214-27; 45 (1926): 190-209, 305-22; 48 (1929): 412-25, 52 (1933): 55-65.

3379. Paul Joüon, "Notes de philologie évangélique (Mt. 25,9; Mc. 3,17: Βοανηργές; Lc. 1,54-55)," *RSR* 15 (1925): 438-41.

3380. Paul Joüon, "Notes philologiques sur les évangiles," *RSR* 17 (1927): 537-40; 18 (1928): 345-59, 499-502.

3381. Paul Joüon, "Mots grecs de l'araméen d'Onkelos ou de l'hébreu de la Mishna qui se trouvent dans les évangiles," *RSR* 22 (1932): 463-69.

3382. Paul-Louis Couchoud, "Notes de critique verbale sur St. Marc et St. Matthieu," *JTS* 34 (1933): 113-38.

3383. Edward B. Warren, "The Pastor and his Greek New Testament," *RE* 31 (1934): 208-10.

3384. A. Souter, "Greek and Hebrew Words in Jerome's

Commentary on St. Matthew's Gospel," *HTR* 28 (1935): 1-4.

3385.   Ch. Jaeger, "Remarques philoloigques sur quelques passages des synoptiques," *RHPR* 16 (1936): 246-49.

3386.   Adhémar d'Alès, "Les particules réduplicatives dans les verbes du Nouveau Testament," *RSR* 27 (1937): 217-31.

3387.   Joachim Jeremias, "Beobachtungen zu neutestamentlichen Stellen an Hand des neugefundenen griechischen Henoch-Textes," *ZNW* 38 (1939): 115-24.

3388.   John Knox, "On the Vocabulary of Marcion's Gospel," *JBL* 58 (1939): 193-201.

3389.   William Nickerson Bates, "Cadmus and the Greek Alphabet," *CQ* 19 (1952): 126-34.

3390.   G. George Fox, "The Matthean Misrepresentation of Tephillin," *JNES* 1 (1942): 373-77.

3391.   Edgar J. Goodspeed, "Greek Idiom in the Gospels," *JBL* 63 (1944): 87-91.

3392.   C. C. Tarelli, "Johannine Synonyms," *JTS* 47 (1946): 175-77.

3393.   N. A. Dahl, "Ny litteratur om Jesu ord," *NTT* 52 (1951): 58-66.

3394.   J. R. Mantey, "Inadequately Translated Words in the New Testament," *RE* 48 (1951): 169-75.

3395.   William John Samarin, "A Caution on Greek Connectives,"*BTr* 2 (1951): 131-32.

3396.   Richard M. L. Waugh, "The Preacher and his Greek New Testament," *RL* 20 (1951): 286-294.

3397.   Edgar J. Goodspeed, "Some Greek Notes," *JBL* 73 (1954): 84-92.

3398.   Eric May, "Translation of Monetary Terms in St. Matthew's Gospel," *CBQ* 18 (1956): 140-43.

See also numbers 385, 1046-1082, 2418, 3027, 5142, 7013, 10063.

3398.1 Nigel Turner, "Philology in New Testament Studies," *ET* 71 (1960): 104-107.

3398.2 Leslie C. Allen, "The Old Testament Background of

(Pro)Orizein in the New Testament," *NTSt* 17/1 (1970-1971): 104-108.

3398.3   G. H. R. Horsley, "Divergent Views on the Nature of the Greek of the Bible," *B* 65 (1984): 393-403.

3398.4   Johannes H. Friedrich, "Wortstatistik als Methode am Beispiel der Frage einer Sonderquelle im Matthäusevangelium," *ZNW* 76 (1985): 29-42.

3398.5   David A. Günter "New Testament Semitisms," *BTr* 39 (1988): 215-23.

3398.6   Stanley E. Porter, "Greek Language and Linguistics," *ET* 103 (1992): 202-208.

   b. *Greek Lexicography*

      (1). Greek Words

3399.   C. Spicq, "Le verbe ἀγαπάω et ses dérivés dans le grec classic," *RB* 60 (1953): 372-97.

3400.   Paul Fiebig, "ἀγγαρεύω," *ZNW* 18 (1917): 64-72.

3401.   Charles S. Macalpine, "The Sanctification of Christ," *ET* 19 (1907-1908): 58-60 [ἁγιάζω].

3402.   Anton Fridrichsen, " 'Helliget vorde dit Navn'!" *TTDF* 3rd ser., 8 (1917): 1-16 [ἁγιάζω].

3403.   L. Morris, "The Biblical Use of the Term 'Blood'," *JTS* N.S., 3 (1952): 216-27 [αἷμα].

3404.   C. Egli, "Zur Bedeutung des Hahnes im Evangelium," *ZWT* 22 (1879): 517-25 [ἀλέκτωρ].

3405.   Dr. Rüling, "Der Begriff ἀλήθεια in dem Evangelium und den Briefen des Johannes," *NKZ* 6 (1895): 625-48.

3406.   A. Andersen, " 'Sandheden' i Johannesevangeliet," *TTDF* N.S. 1 (1899-1900): 353-80 [ἀλήθεια].

3407.   G. F. Hamilton and G. G. Findlay, "'Αληθής and ἀληθινός in St. John," *ET* 16 (1904-1905): 42-43.

3408.   Geerhardus Vos, " 'True' and 'Truth' in the Johannine Writings," *BR* 12 (1927): 507-20.

3409.   José Trepat, "San Juan: ideas características—La Verdad," *CB* 4 (1947): 355-56.

3410.   H. W. Hogg, " 'Amen.' Notes on its Signiffcance and Use in Biblical and Post-Biblical Times/," *JQR* 9 (1896-1897): 1-23.

3411.   J. C. O'Neill, "The Six Amen Sayings in Luke," *JTS* N.S. 10 (1959): 1-9.

3412.   Paul Joüon, "Le verbe ἀναγγέλλω dans saint Jean," *RSR* 28 (1938): 234-35.

3413.   W. Bell Dawson, "The Meaning of 'Antichrist' in the Greek of the New Testament," *EQ* 16 (1944): 71-80.

3414.   J. A. Kleist, " 'Axios' in the Gospels," *CBQ* 6 (1944): 342-46.

3415.   Krister Stendahl, "ἄξιος im Lichte der Texte der Qumran-Höhle," *Nunt* 7 (1952): 53-55.

3416.   Erik Peterson, "Die Einholung des Kyrios," *ZST* 7 (1929-1930): 682-702 [ἀπάντησις].

3417.   N. H. Parker, "Jewish Apocalypse in the Time of Christ," *CQ* 17 (1940): 33-46 [ἀποκαλύπτω].

3418.   W. Z. Goedbloed, "Het begrip ἀπολύτρωσις in het Nieuwe Testament," *GTT* 15 (1914): 356-64.

3419.   Jacques Dupont, "Le nom d'apôtres a-t-il été donné aux douze par Jésus?" *OS* 1 (1956): 267-90, 425-44 [ἀπόστολος].

3420.   L. Cerfaux, "Pour l'histoire du titre *apostolos* dans le Nouveau Testament," *RSR* 48 (1960): 76-92.

3421.   J. W. Hunkin, " 'Pleonastic' ἄρχομαι in the New Testament," *JTS* 25 (1923-1924): 390-402.

3422.   Albert R. Bond, "Baptism Into or Unto," *RE* 15 (1918): 197-207 [βαπτίζειν εἰς].

3423.   A. Ben Oliver, "Is βαττίζω Used with ἐν and the Instrumental?" *RE* 35 (1938): 190-97.

3424.   F. W. C. Schulte, "Bar-Abbas een bijnaam," *NTS* 3 (1920): 114-18.

3425.   J. Courtenay James, "Boanerges," *ET* 26 (1914-1915): 45-46.

3426.   Ludwig Koehler, "Boanerges," *ET* 26 (1914-1915): 236-37.

3427. Paul Joüon, "Les verbes βούλομαι et θέλω dans le Nouveau Testament," *RSR* 30 (1940): 227-38.

3428. C. H. Bird, "Some γάρ Clauses in St. Mark's Gospel," *JTS* N.S. 4 (1953): 171-87.

3429. Ferdinand Prat, "Cette génération," *RSR* 17 (1927): 316-24 [ψενεά].

3430. F. R. M. Hitchcock, "The Use of γράφειν," *JTS* 31 (1929-1930): 271-75.

3431. T. Stephenson, "On the Use of γραφή in N.T.," *ET* 14 (1902-1903): 475-78.

3432. Benjamin B. Warfield, " 'Scripture,' 'The Scriptures,' in the New Testament," *PTR* 8 (1910): 560-612 [γραφή].

3433. H G. Meecham, "The Term Scripture(s): in the New Testament," *ET* 44 (1932-1933): 384.

3434. E. C. E. Owen, "Δαίμων and Cognate Words," *JTS* 32 (1930-1931): 133-53.

3435. Herbert G. Miller, "The Rendering of δέ in the New Testament," *ET* 15 (1903-1904): 551-55.

3436. Otto Glombitza, "Die Titel διδάσκαλος und ἐπιστάτης für Jesus bei Lukas," *ZNW* 49 (1958): 275-78.

3437. R. B. Lloyd, "The Word 'Glory' in the Fourth Gospel," *ET* 43 (1931-1932): 546-48 [δόξα].

3438. E. C. E. Owen, "Δόξα and Cognate Words," *JTS* 33 (1931-1932): 132-50, 265-79.

3439. Christoph Burchard, "Ei nach einem Ausdruck des Wissens oder Nichtwissens," *ZNW* 52 (1961): 73-82.

3440. J. Harold Greenlee, "The Preposition εἰς in the New Testament," *BTr* 3 (1952): 12-14.

3441. Georg Eduard Steitz, "Über den Gebrauch des Pronomen ἐκεῖνος im vierten Evangelium," *TSK* 32 (1859): 497-506.

3442. Alex. Buttmann, "Über den Gebrauch des Pronomen ἐκεῖνος im vierten Evangelium," *TSK* 33 (1860): 505-36.

3443. Georg Eduard Steitz, "Der classische und der johanneische Gebrauch von ἐκεῖνος," *TSK* 34 (1861): 267-310.

3444.   J. Ross, "Ἐκεῖνος," *ET* 17 (1905-1906): 287.

3445.   E. Benj. Andrews, "The Conception ἐκκλησία in the New Testament," *BS* 40 (1883): 35-58.

3446.   Everett Gill, "The Nordic Origin of 'Ekklesia'," *RE* 32 (1935): 264-68.

3447.   W. Grossouw, "L'espérance dans le nouveau testament," *RB* 61 (1954): 508-32 [ἐλπίς].

3448.   Harald Riesenfeld, "ἐντός," *Nunt* 2 (1949): 11-12.

3449.   W. R. Hutton, "Considerations for the Translation of Greek *en*," *BTr* 9 (1958): 163-70.

3450.   Nigel Turner, "The Preposition *en* in the New Testament," *BTr* 10 (1959): 113-20.

3451.   C. Spicq, "Bénignité, mansuétude, douceur, clémence," *RB* 54 (1947): 321-39 [ἐπιείκεια, etc].

3452.   C. Spicq, "ἐπιποθεῖν, désirer ou chérir?" *RB* 64 (1957): 184-95.

3453.   P. Gardner-Smith, "ἐπιφώσκειν," *JTS* 27 (1925-1926): 179-81.

3454.   J. A. Kleist, " 'Ergon' in the Gospels," *CBQ* 6 (1944): 61-68.

3455.   P. Zondervan, "Het woord 'Evangelium'," *TT* 48 (1914): 187-213.

3456.   J. Weiss, "εὐθύς bei Markus," *ZNW* 11 (1910): 124-33.

3457.   Primo Vannutelli, "La voce εὐθυς (εὐθέως) negli evangeli e negli scrittori greci," *S* 1 (1936): cxiv-cxxvi.

3458.   Jean-Paul Audet, "Esquisse historique du genre littéraire de la bénédiction, juive et de l' 'eucharistie' chrétienne," *RB* 65 (1958): 371-99 [εὐλογία—εὐχαριστία].

3459.   A. Festugière, "Notules d'exégèse. εὐφροσύνη, μυστήριον, κύριος," *RSPT* 23 (1934): 359-62.

3460.   J. Massie, "Two New Testament Words Denoting Life: ζωή and ψυχή," *Exp* 2nd ser., 4 (1882): 380-97.

3461.   Hugh H. Birley, "The Use of the Word ZOE in the Gospel and Epistles of St. John," *Th* 33 (1936): 105-107.

3462.   J.-B. Frey, "Le concept de 'vie' dans l'évangile de Saint

Jean," *B* 1 (1920): 37-58, 211-39 [ζωή].

3463. Rudolf Bultmann, "W. H. S. Jones' A Note on the Vague Use of θεός," *TR* 17 (1914): 164.

3464. George D. Kilpatrick, "The Meaning of *THUEIN* in the New Testament," *BTr* 12 (1961): 130-32.

3465. Primo Vannutelli, "De voce ἰδού ut in synopticis evangeliis usurpatur," *S* 2 (1937): pp. xlvi-liii.

3466. Vernon Bartlet, "The Twofold Use of 'Jerusalem' in the Lucan Writings," *ET* 13 (1901-1902): 157-58.

3467. Roland Schütz, "'Ιερουσαλήν und 'Ιεροσόλυμα im Neuen Testament," *ZNW* 11 (1910): 169-87.

3468. W. L. Dulière, "Inventaire de quarante-et-un porteurs du nom de Jésus dans l'histoire juive écrite en grec," *NT* 3 (1959): 180-217 ['Ιησοῦς].

3469. E. P. Groenewald, "Jesus-Jesúrun," *NGTT* 2 (1961): 197-204.

3470. Innes Logan, "The Strange Word 'Propitiation'," *ET* 46 (1933-1934): 525-27 [ἱλαστήριον].

3471. E. H. Blakeney, "The 'Ecbatic' Use of ἵνα in N.T.," *ET* 53 (1941-1942): 377-78.

3472. C. J. Cadoux, "The Imperatival Use of ἵνα in the New Testament," *JTS* 42 (1941): 165-73.

3473. H. G. Meecham, "The Imperatival Use of ἵνα in the New Testament," *JTS* 43 (1942): 179-80.

3474. A. R. George, "The Imperatival Use of ἵνα in the New Testament," *JTS* 45 (1944): 56-60.

3475. J. Harold Greenlee, "῞Ινα Clauses and Related Expressions," *BTr* 6 (1955): 12-16.

3476. A. P. Salom, "The Imperatival Use of Greek in the New Testament," *ABR* 6 (1958): 123-41.

3477. E. Levesque, "Le mot 'Judée' dans le Nouveau Testament," *VP* 3 (1944): 104-111 ['Ιουδαία].

3478. Pfarrer Hübner in Freienhagen, "Zur Versöhnungslehre," *NKZ* 23 (1912): 75-88 [καταλλάσσειν, καταλλαγή].

292 CRITICAL STUDIES OF THE GOSPELS

3479. André Pelletier, "Le vocabulaire du commandment dans le Pentateuque des LXX et dans le Nouveau Testament," *RSR* 41 (1953): 519-24 [κελεύω et al.].

3480. Dr. Groos, "Der Begriff der κρίσις bei Johannes, exegetisch entwickelt, ein Beitrag zur neutestamentlichen Lehre vom Gericht," *TSK* 41 (1868): 244-73.

3481. I. de la Potterie, "L'origine et le sens primitif du mot 'laïc'," *NRT* 80 (1958): 840-53 [λαός].

3482. Ed. König, "Woher stammt der Name 'Maria'?" *ZNW* 17 (1916): 257-63.

3483. Wilibald Grimm, "Über den Namen Matthäus," *TSK* 43 (1870): 723-29.

3484. Otto Michel, "Die Umkehr nach der Verkündigung Jesu," *EvT* 5 (1938): 403-13 [μετανοιεῖν].

3485. E. Böklen, "μονογενής," *TSK* 101 (1929): 55-90.

3486. Francis Marion Warden, "God's Only Son," *RE* 50 (1953): 216-23 [μονογενής].

3487. Rudolf Hermann, "Über den Sinn des μορφοῦσθαι Χριστὸν ἐν ὑμῖν in Gal. 4:19," *TLZ* 80 (1955): 713-26.

3488. A. Festugière, "Notule d'exégèse. μυστήριον," *RSPT* 23 (1934): 588-89.

3489. H. U. Meyboom and H. Oort, "Jezus de Nazoraeër," *TT* 39 (1905): 512-36.

3490. Eb. Nestle, "He Shall Be Called a Nazarene," *ET* 19 (1907-1908): 523-24.

3491. P. Schwen, "Nazareth und die Nazoräer," *ZWT* 54 (1912): 31-55.

3492. J. de Zwaan, "Jesus de Nazoraeër," *NTS* 4 (1921): 136-37.

3493. W. O. E. Oesterley, "Nazarene and Nazareth," *ET* 52 (1940-1941): 410-12.

3494. W. F. Albright, "The Names 'Nazareth' and 'Nazoraean'," *JBL* 65 (1946): 397-401.

3495. J. Spencer Kennard, "Nazorean and Nazareth," *JBL* 66 (1947): 79-81.

3496. Henry M. Shires, "The Meaning of the Term 'Nazarene'," *ATR* 29 (1947): 19-27.

3497. I. de la Potterie, "οἶδα et γινώσκω—les deux modes de la connaissance dans le quatrième évangile," *B* 40 (1959): 709-25.

3498. John H. Reumann, "*Oikonomia* = 'Covenant'; Terms for *Heilsgeschichte* in Early Christian Usage," *NT* 3 (1959): 282-92.

3499. Douglas Webster, "The Primary Stewardship," *ET* 72 (1960): 274-76 [οἰκονόμος].

3500. Steven T. Byington, "Jesus' Mountain Sides," *ET* 65 (1953-1954): 94 [ὄρος].

3501. Paul Winter, "῞Οτι 'recitativum' in Lc. 1.25,61 und 2.23," *ZNW* 46 (1955): 261-63.

3502. Alfred Marshall, "Οὐ and μή in Questions," *BTr* 4 (1953): 41-42.

3503. Paul Joüon, "῎Οχλος au sens de 'peuple, population' dans le grec du Nouveau Testament et dans la lettre d'Artistée," *RSR* 27 (1937): 618-19.

3504. D. W. B. Robinson, "The Use of *Parabole* in the Synoptic Gospels," *EQ* 21 (1949): 93-108.

3505. James Hastings, "Paraclete—A Bible Word Study," *ET* 10 (1898-1899): 169-71 [παράκλητος].

3506. G. G. Findlay, "Christ's Name for the Holy Spirit," *ET* 12 (1900-1901): 445-49 [παράκλητος].

3507. James Wells, "The Two Paracletes and the Under-Paracletes," *ET* 14 (1902-1903): 562-65.

3508. N. H. Snaith, "The Meaning of 'the Paraclete'," *ET* 57 (1945-1946): 47-50.

3509. J. D. Davies, "The Primary Meaning of παράκλητος," *JTS* N.S. 4 (1953): 35-38.

3510. Franz Mussner, "Die johanneischen Parakletsprüche und die apostolische Tradition," *BibZ* 5 (1961): 56-70. [παράκλητος].

3511. Paul Joüon, "Divers sens de παρρησία dans le Nouveau

Testament," *RSR* 30 (1940): 239-42.

3512. Frederick Bussby, "A Note on πάσχα in the Synoptic Gospels," *ET* 59 (1947-1948): 194-95.

3513. J. Oliver Buswell, "The Ethics of 'Believe' in the Fourth Gospel," *BS* 80 (1923): 28-37 [πιστεύειν].

3514. W. H. Griffith Thomas, " 'Faith' in the Synoptic Gospels," *ET* 24 (1912-1913): 477 [πίστις].

3515. William R. Schoemaker, "The Use of an רוח in the Old Testament and of πνεῦμα in the New Testament," *JBL* 23 (1904): 13-67.

3516. F. J. Badcock, " 'The Spirit' and Spirit in the New Testament," *ET* 45 (1933-1934): 218-21.

3517. K. L. Schmidt, "Neutestamentliche Wortforschung: Pneuma, Wind, Geist," *TZ* 4 (1948): 898.

3518. J. Massie, "A New Testament Antithesis," *Exp* 1st. ser., 12 (1880): 459-80 [πνευματικός, ψυχικός].

3519. Alfred Durand, "Le Christ 'premier-né'," *RSR* 1 (1910): 56-66 [πρωτότοκος].

3520. Wilhelm Michaelis, "Die biblische Vorstellung von Christus als dem Erstgeborenen," *ZST* 23 (1954): 137-57.

3521. Gottlieb Linder, "Principe qui a présidé a l'ordonnance de l'évangile selon saint Jean," *RTP* 31 (1898): 168-79; 32 (1899): 190-94 [προφήτης].

3522. Otto Michel, "Eine philologische Frage zur Einzugs-geschichte," *NTSt* 6 (1959-1960): 81-82 [πῶλος].

3523. J. B. Bauer, "πῶς in der griechischen Bibel," *NT* 2 (1958): 81-91.

3524. Frederick Bussby, "A Note on Σάββατα and Σάββατον in the Synoptics," *BJRL* 30 (1946-1947): 157-58.

3525. Jean-Pierre Charlier, "La notion de signe (σημεῖον) dans le IVᵉ evangel," *RSPT* 43 (1959): 434-48.

3526. K. Schilder, "Over het 'skandalon'," *GTT* 32 (1931-1932): 49-67, 97-130 [σκάνδαλον].

3527. Louis Escoula, "Le verbe sauveur et illuminateur chez saint Irénée," *NRT* 66 (1939): 385-400, 551-67 [σώζω].

3528. Paul Wendland, "Σωτήρ," *ZNW* 5 (1904): 335-53.

3529. Eb. Nestle, "τέλειος = οἰκτιρυῶν," *TSK* 69 (1896): 737-39.

3530. Olaf Moe, "Fullkommenhetstanken i Det nye testamente. Opposisjonsinnlegg ved Torbjørn Osnes," *TTK* 26 (1955): 25-35 [τέλειος].

3531. A. H. McNeile, "Τότε in St. Matthew," *JTS* 12 (1910- 1911): 127-28.

3532. J. Massie, "Two New Testament Synonyms: υἱός and τέκνον," *Exp* 1st. ser., 11 (1880): 137-55.

3533. Eric F. F. Bishop, "Why 'Son of David'?" *ET* 47 (1935-1936): 21-25 [υἱός].

3534. Frederick W. Danker, "The υἱός Phrases in the New Testament," *NTSt* (1960-1961): 94.

3535. D. R. Goodwin, "The Use of ὑπέρ in the New Testament," *JBL* 5 (1885): 86-87.

3536. Friedrich Spitta, "Das Verbot von Schuhen und Stöcken für die Sendboten Jesu," *ZWT* 55 (1941): 39-45, 166-67 [ὑποδήματα, ὑπενδύματα, etc.].

3537. Lawrence J. Jones, "On a Double Sense of ὑπόκρισις and ὑποκριτής in the New Testament," *ET* 4 (1892-1893): 276.

3538. Donald Matheson, " 'Actors': Christ's Word of Scorn," *ET* 41 (1929-1930): 333-34 [ὑποκριτής].

3539. A. Festugière, "ὑπομονή dans la tradition grecque," *RSR* 21 (1931): 477-86.

3540. Cuthbert Lattey, "Le verbe ὑψοῦν dans saint Jean," *RSR* 3 (1912): 597-98.

3541. J. Morrison, "Grace, Philologically Viewed," *Exp* 1st. scr., 12 (1880): 86-88 [χάρις].

3542. Edward P. Gardner, "Christ in the Four Gospels," *BS* 69 (1912): 222-41 [Χριστός].

3543. S. Vernon McCasland, "Christ Jesus," *JBL* 65 (1946): 377-83.

3544. J. Harold Greenlee, "Psuchê in the New Testament," *BTr* 2 (1951): 73-75 [ψυχή].

3545.   Eric F. F. Bishop, "Hosanna: The Word of the Joyful Jerusalem Crowds," *ET* 53 (1941-1942): 212-14.

3546.   F. D. Coggan, "Note on the Word ὡσαννά," *ET* 52 (1940-1941): 76-77.

3547.   Eric Werner, " 'Hosanna' in the Gospels," *JBL* 65 (1946): 97-122.

3548.   J. Spencer Kennard, " 'Hosanna' and the Purpose of Jesus," *JBL* 67 (1948): 171-76.

           See also numbers 4991, 5003, 5031, 5360, 5261, 5345, 5364, 5585, 5676, 5763, 5873 ff., 5928, 5965, 5966, 6077, 6090, 6109 f., 6128, 6161, 6258, 6294, 6693, 7240, 7307, 7321 f., 7719, 7992 ff., 8106 ff., 8171, 8737, 8756, 8983, 9633.

3548.1   I. de la Potterie, "L'emploi dynamique de εἰς dans Saint Jean et ses incidences théologiques," *B* 43 (1962): 366-87.

3548.2   J. A. Emerton, "τὸ αἱμά μου τῆς διαθήκης : The Evidence of the Syriac Versions," *JTS* 13 (1962): 111-17.

3548.3   Josef Blank, "Der johanneische Wahrheitsbegriff," *BibZ* 7 (1963): 163-73.

3548.4   D. Meyer, "*Polla pathein*," *ZNW* 55 (1964): 132.

3548.5   E. D. Freed, "John 4:51: παῖς or υἱός," *JTS* 16 (1965): 448-49.

3548.6   J. C. Hindley, "Witness in the Fourth Gospel," *SJT* 18 (1965): 319-37.

3548.7   J. J. O'Rourke, "A Note Concerning the Use of *eis* and *en* in Mark," *JBL* 85 (1966): 349-51.

3548.8   S. M. Reynolds, "πυγμῇ (Mark 7:3) as 'Cupped Hand'," *JBL* 85 (1966): 87-88.

3548.9   George D. Kilpatrick, "*Idou* and *ide* in the Gospels," *JTS* 18 (1967): 425-26.

3548.10   H. K. Moulton, "πάντας in John 2:15," *BTr* 18 (1967): 126-27.

3548.11   Howard C. Kee, "The Terminology of Mark's Exorcism Stories," *NTSt* 14 (1967-1968): 232-46.

3548.12   H. Clavier, "Notes sur un Motclef du Johannisme et de la

Soteriologie Biblique: Hilasmos," *NT* 10/4 (1968): 287-304.

3548.13 J. D. M. Derrett, "Κορβᾶν, ὅ ἐστιν, Δῶρον," *NTSt* 16/4 (1969-1970): 364-68.

3548.14 G. M. Lee, "New Testament Gleanings: Three Notes on ἵνα," *B* 51 (1970): 239-40.

3548.15 Georg Richter, "Ist ἐν ein strukturbildendes Element im Logoshymnus Joh 1:1ff?" *B* 51 (1970): 539-44.

3548.16 Charles Kannengiesser, "Une nouvelle interpretation de la christologie d'Apollinaire," *RSR* 59 (1971): 27-36.

3548.17 S. M. Reynolds, "A Note on Dr. Hengel's Interpretation of πυγμῇ in Mark 7:3," *ZNW* 62 (1971): 295-96.

3548.18 B. Hemmerdinger, "Un elément pythagoricien dans le Pater," *ZNW* 63 (1972): 121.

3548.19 D. R. Hall, "The Meaning of συγχράμαι in John 4:9," *ET* 83 (1972-1973): 56-57.

3548.20 Vernon K. Robbins, "*Dynameis* and *Sēmeia* in Mark," *BRes* 18 (1973): 5-20.

3548.21 W. A. Holden, " 'Ekklesia' or 'Synagoge'," *ET* 85 (1973-1974): 184.

3548.22 Manuek Benéitez, "Notas sobre verbos 'sinónimos' en Jn," *EE* 49 (1974): 109-16.

3548.23 Giuseppe Frizzi, "L'ἀπόστολος delle tradizioni sinottiche (Mc, Q, Mt, Lc. e Atti)," *RivB* 22 (1974): 3-37 [6:30].

3548.24 Jack D. Kingsbury, "The Title 'Kyrios' in Matthew's Gospel," *JBL* 94 (1975): 246-55.

3548.25 J. J. O'Rourke, "The Article as a Pronoun in the Synoptic Gospels," *CBQ* 37 (1975): 492-99.

3548.26 Malcolm Lowe, "Who Were the Ἰουδαῖοι?" *NT* 18 (1976): 101-30.

3548.27 Joseph A. Comber, "The Verb θεραπεύω in Matthew's Gospel," *JBL* 97 (1978): 431-34.

3548.28 Jack D. Kingsbury, "The Verb ἀκολουθεῖν as an Index of Matthew's View of His Community," *JBL* 97 (1978): 56-73.

3548.29 Daniel C. Arichea, "Translating 'Believe' in the Gospel of

John," *BT* 30 (1979): 205-209.

3548.30   E. D. Freed, "*Egō Eimi* in John 1:20 and 4:25," *CBQ* 41 (1979): 288-91.

3548.31   C. H. Gordon, " 'ἐν' of Predication or Equivalence," *JBL* 100 (1981): 612-13.

3548.32   J. R. Royse, "A Philonic Use of πανδοχεῖον," *NT* 23 (1981): 193-94.

3548.33   Günther Schwarz, "ἄφες τοὺς νεκροὺς θάψαι τοὺς ἑαυτῶν νεκρούς," *ZNW* 72 (1981): 272-76.

3548.34   E. D. Freed, "*Egō Eimi* in John viii.24 in the Light of Its Context and Jewish Messianic Belief," *JTS* 33 (1982): 163-67.

3548.35   J. S. Hill, "τὰ βαῖα τῶν φοινίκων (John 12:13): Pleonasm or Prolepsis?" *JBL* 101 (1982): 133-35.

3548.36   John V. Dahms, "The Johannine Use of Monogenes Reconsidered," *NTSt* 29 (1983): 222-32.

3548.37   K. Kipgen, "Translating *kataluma* in Luke 2:7," *BTr* 34 No 4 (1983): 442-43.

3548.38   Dennis D. Sylva, "*Ierousalem* and *Hierosoluma* in Luke-Acts," *ZNW* 74 (1983): 207-21.

3548.39   Norman H. Young, " 'Hilaskesthai' and Related Words in the New Testament," *EQ* 55 (1983): 169-76. Luke 18:13

3548.40   J. D. M. Derrett, "The Lucan Christ and Jerusalem: τελειοῦμαι," *ZNW* 75 (1984): 36-43.

3548.41   J. D. M. Derrett, "παλιγγενεσίᾳ, (Matthew 19.28)," *JSNT* 20 (1984): 51-58.

3548.42   V. S. Poythress, "Testing for Johannine Authorship by Examining the Use of Conjunctions," *WTJ* 46 (1984): 350-69.

3548.43   V. S. Poythress, "The Use of the Intersentence Conjunctions *De, Oun, kai,* and *Asyndeton* in the Gospel of John," *NT* 26 (1984): 312-40.

3548.44   Don A. Carson, "The Homoios Word-Group as Introduction to Some Matthean Parables," *NTSt* 31 (1985): 277-82.

3548.45   K. L. McKay, "The Use of *Hoi De* in Matthew 28.17," *JSNT*

24 (1985): 71-72.

3548.46 Margaret Pamment, "Path and Residence Metaphors in the Fourth Gospel," *Th* 88 (1985): 118-24.

3548.47 P. W. van der Horst, "Once More: The Translation of *Hoi De* in Matthew 28.17," *JSNT* 27 (1986): 27-30.

3548.48 James R. Edwards, "The Use of *Proserchesthai* in the Gospel of Matthew," *JBL* 106/1 (1987): 65-74.

3548.49 Robert Hill, "Synoptic 'basileia' and Pauline 'mysterion'," *EB* 45/3-4 (1987): 309-24.

3548.50 Frans Neirynck, "Words Characteristic of Mark: A New List," *ETL* 63/4 (1987): 367-74.

3548.51 Robert G. Bratcher, " 'Righteousness' in Matthew," *BTr* 40/2 (1989): 228-35.

3548.52 J. K. Elliott, "ἐρωτᾶν and ἐπερωτᾶν in the New Testament," *FilN* 2 (1989): 205-206.

3548.53 R. A. Edwards, "Narrative Implications of γάρ in Matthew," *CBQ* 52 (1990): 636-55.

3548.54 Deirdre Good, "The Verb ἀναχωρέω in Matthew's Gospel," *NT* 32 (1990): 1-12.

3548.55 T. Hirunuma, "ἄνευυ τοῦ πατρός: 'Without (of) the Father'," *FilN* 3 (1990): 53-62.

3548.56 Alberto Maggi, "Nota sull'uso τῷ σῷ ὀνόματι e ἀνομία in Mt. 7:21-23" *FilN* 3 (1990): 145-49.

3548.57 Robert Schlarb, "Die Suche nach dem Messias: ζητέω als Terminus technicus der markinischen Messianologie," *ZNW* 81 (1990): 155-70.

3548.58 J. D. M. Derrett, "τί ἐργάζῃ: An Unrecognized Allusion to Is 45,9," *ZNW* 84 (1993): 142-44.

3548.59 J. D. M. Derrett, "ἀντιλεγόμενον, ῥομφαία, διαλογισμοί: The Hidden Context," *FilN* 6 (1993): 207-18.

3548.60 R. E. Oster, "Supposed Anachronism in Luke-Acts's Use of συναγωγή: A Rejoinder to H.C. Kee," *NTSt* 39 (1993): 178-208.

3548.61 K. Romaniuk, "ἠπόρει or ἐποίει in Mc 6,20?" *ETL* 69 (1993): 140-41.

3548.62 David C. Sim, "The Meaning of παλιγγενεσία, in Matthew 19:28," *JSNT* 50 (1993): 3-12.

3548.63 James R. Edwards, "The Authority of Jesus in the Gospel of Mark," *JETS* 37 (1994): 217-33.

3548.64 Marco Adinolfi, "'Αρχή, εὐαγγέλιον, Χριστός: Note filologiche a Mc 1,1," *RivBib* 43 (1995): 211-24.

3548.65 J. D. M. Derrett, "ζώννυμι, φέρω, ἄλλος: The Fate of Peter," *FilN* 8 (1995): 79-84.

3548.66 G. Pendrick, "μονογενής," *NTSt* 41 (1995): 587-600.

(2). Greek Phrases

3549. Hans Gottlieb, "Τὸ αἷμά μου τῆς διαθήκης," *ST* 14 (1960): 115-18.

3550. Karl Zickendraht, "ἐγώ εἰμι," *TSK* 94 (1922): 162-68.

3551. James, Bishop of East Bengal, " 'I Am' in the Gospels," *Th* 62 (1959): 235-38.

3552. Heinrich Zimmerman, "Das absolute ἐγώ εἰμι als die neutestamentliche Offenbarungsformel," *BibZ* N.F. 4 (1960): 54-69, 266-76.

3553. Eric F. F. Bishop, "εἰ μὴ εἷς θεός—A Suggestion," *ET* 49 (1937-1938): 363-66.

3554. W. Brandt, "Nog eens εἰς ὄνομα," *TT* 36 (1902): 193-217.

3555. George Gifford, "ἐπὶ τῆς θαλάσσης," *ET* 40 (1928-1929): 236.

3556. W. Michaelis, "Das unbetonte καὶ αὐτός bei Lukas," *ST* 4 (1950): 86-93.

3557. J. Pernot, "La construction du καὶ ἐγένετο dans les évangiles," *RHPR* 4 (1924): 553-58.

3558. Joachim Jeremias, "'Εν ἐκείνη τῇ ὥρᾳ, (ἐν) αὐτῇ τῇ ὥρᾳ," *ZNW* 42 (1949): 214-17.

3559. W. Lockton, "Liturgical Notes," *JTS* 16 (1914-1915): 548-52 [κύριε ἐλέησον].

3560. L. von Sybel, "Ξύλον ζωῆς," *ZNW* 19 (1919-1920): 85-91.

3561. J. Henry Thayer, "Σὺ εἶπας, in the Answers of Jesus," *JBL* 13 (1894): 40-49.

3562. A. Marshall, "A Note on τε . . . καί," *BTr* 5 (1954): 182-83.

3563. Oscar Cullmann, "Neutestamentliche Wortforschung. ὑπὲρ (ἀντὶ) πολλῶν," *TZ* 4 (1948): 471-73.

3564. D. F. Hudson, "ὡς ἐξουσίαν ἔχων," *ET* 67 (1955-1956): 17. See also numbers 5873 ff., 5984, 5989, 6116, 6120, 6151, 7313 ff., 8034 ff., 8120.

3564.1 André Feuillet, "Les *ego eimi* christologiques du quatrième évangile," *RSR* 54 (1966): 5-22; 213-40.

3564.2 Günther Schwarz, " . . . '*anthropoi eudokias*'," *ZNW* 75 (1984): 136-37.

3564.3 A. H. Maynard, "Τί ἐμοὶ καὶ σοί," *NTSt* 31 (1985): 582-86.

3564.4 Dennis D. Sylva, "The Cryptic Clause ἐν τοῖς τοῦ πατρός μου δεῖ εἶναί με in Luke," *ZNW* 78 (1987): 132-40.

c. *Word Studies Keyed to the English Translation*

3565. Eb. Nestle, " 'Arise' and 'Rise'," *ET* 15 (1903-1904): 528.

3566. Eugene Stock, "Disciples and Apostles," *ET* 28 (1916-1917): 188-89.

3567. J. S. Banks, "The Good and the Beautiful," *ET* 23 (1911-1912): 281-82.

3568. J. Massie, "New Testament Words denoting Care," *Exp* 1st. ser., 12 (1880): 104-23.

3569. J. Davies Bryan, "Cross-Bearing," *ET* 38 (1926-1927): 378-79.

3570 Donald Matheson, "Cross-Bearing," *ET* 38 (1926-1927): 188, 524-25.

3571. A. G. Hebert and N. H. Snaith, "A Study of the Words 'Curse' and 'Righteousness'," *BTr* 3 (1952): 111-16.

3572. John Foster, "Denying Oneself," *ET* 54 (1942-1943): 331.

3573. W. H. Griffith Thomas, "Discipleship," *ET* 28 (1916-1917): 92.

3574. F. Rendall, "History of the Word 'Eternal'," *Exp* 3rd ser., 7 (1888): 266-78.

3575. James Henderson Brown, "The N.T. Terms 'Eternal,' 'For

Ever,' etc.," *ET* 46 (1934-1935): 333-34.

3576.   Willoughby C. Allen, " 'Fear' in St. Mark," *JTS* 48 (1947): 201-203.

3577.   Buchanan Blake, "For Christ's Sake," *ET* 34 (1922-1923): 282.

3578.   S. Vernon McCasland, "Some New Testament Metonyms for God," *JBL* 68 (1949): 99-113.

3579.   Millar Burrows, "The Origin of the Term 'Gospel'," *JBL* 44 (1925): 21-33.

3580.   T. Nicklin, " 'House' and 'Home' in New Testament Greek," *ET* 49 (1937-1938): 566-68.

3581.   Charles T. P. Grierson, "The Last Day," *ET* 19 (1907-1908): 162-67.

3582.   F. C. Burkitt, "On 'Lifting Up' and 'Exalting'," *JTS* 20 (1919): 336-38.

3583.   John M. Sykes, "The Lordship of Jesus," *RE* 49 (1952): 20-35.

3584.   Benjamin B. Warfield, "The Terminology of Love in the New Testament," *PTR* 16 (1918): 1-45, 153-203.

3585.   Clayton R. Bowen, "Love in the Fourth Gospel," *JR* 13 (1933): 39-49.

3586.   Bernhard Citron, "The Multitude in the Synoptic Gospels," *SJT* 7 (1954): 408-18.

3587.   Fred B. Pearson, "Sheol and Hades in Old and New Testament," *RE* 35 (1938): 304-14.

3588.   W. H. Raney, "Who were the 'Sinners'?" *JR* 10 (1930): 578-91.

3589.   Joachim Jeremias, "Zöllner und Sünder," *ZNW* 30 (1931): 293-300.

3590.   Lewis Sperry Chafer, "Biblical Terminology Related to Christ's Sufferings and Death," *BS* 104 (1947): 135-53.

3591.   Jesse W. Ball, "The Biblical Use of the Word Temptation," *LCR* 24 (1905): 551-56.

3592.   A. L. Burns, "Two Words for 'Time' in the New Testament,"

ABR 3 (1953): 7-22.

3593.   Robert W. Funk, "The Wilderness," *JBL* 78 (1959): 205-14.

3594.   George Evans, "The World in the Writings of the Apostle John," *RE* 31 (1934): 66-80.

3594.1   Henri Bourgoin, "Epiousios expliqué par la notion de préfixe vide," *B* 60/1 (1979): 91-96.

3594.2   G. A. Mikre-Sellassie, "Problems in Translating Pronouns from English Versions," *BTr* 39 (1988): 230-37.

3594.3   J. L. W. Schaper, "The Unicorn in the Messianic Imagery of the Greek Bible," *JTS* NS 45 (1994): 117-36.

2. The Grammar and Syntax of the Gospels

3595.   William G. Ballantine, "Predicative Participles with Verbs in the Aorist," *BS* 41 (1884): 787-99.

3596.   E. H. Blakeney, "Note on Tense-Translation in the New Testament," *ET* 8 (1896-1897): 381-82.

3597.   Morton S. Enslin, "The Perfect Tense in the Fourth Gospel," *JBL* 55 (1936): 121-31.

3598.   Paul Joüon, "Imparfaits de 'continuation' dans la Lettre d'Aristée et dans les Évangiles," *RSR* 28 (1938): 93-96.

3599.   George D. Kilpatrick, "The Possessive Pronouns in the New Testament," *JTS* 42 (1941): 184-86.

3600.   H. G. Meecham, "The Use of the Participle for the Imperative in the New Testament," *ET* 58 (1946-1947): 207-208.

3601.   J. Harold Greenlee, "The Genitive Case in the New Testament," *BTr* 1 (1950): 68-70.

3602.   Arnulf Kuschke, "Das Idiom der 'relativen Negation' im NT," *ZNW* 43 (1950-1951): 263.

3603.   J. Harold Greenlee, "Verbs in the New Testament," *BTr* 3 (1952): 71-75.

3604.   A. Marshall, "The Genitive of Quality in the New Testament," *BTr* 3 (1952): 14-16.

3605.   H. G. Meecham, "The Present Participle of Antecedent Action—Some New Testament Instances," *ET* 64 (1952-

1953): 285-86.

3606.   Cecil S. Emden, "St. Mark's Use of the Imperfect Tense,"
         ET 65 (1953-1954): 146-49.

3607.   Cecil S. Emden, "St. Mark's Use of the Imperfect Tense,"
         BTr 5 (1954): 121-25.

3608.   J. Harold Greenlee, "New Testament Participles," *BTr* 5
         (1954): 98-101.

3609.   A. W. Argyle, "The Causal Use of the Relative Pronouns in
         the Greek New Testament," *BTr* 6 (1955): 165-69.

         See also number 10063.

3609.1   George D. Kilpatrick, "The Order of Some Noun and
         Adjective Phrases in the New Testament," *NT* 5 (1962):
         111-14.

3609.2   Donald S. Deer, "The Implied Agent in Greek Passive Verb
         Forms in the Gospel of Matthew," *BTr* 18/4 (1967): 167.

3609.3   R. W. F. Wootton, "The Implied Agent in Greek Passive
         Verbs in Mark, Luke and John," *BTr* 19 (1968): 159-64.

3609.4   S. M. Reynolds, "The Zero Tense in Greek: A Critical Note,"
         WTJ 32 (1969): 68-72.

3609.5   M. J. Niedenthal, "The Irony and the Grammar of the
         Gospel," *PSB* 64 (1971): 22-29.

3609.6   William G. Morrice, "The Imperatival ἵνα," *BTr* 23 (1972):
         326-30.

3609.7   William G. Morrice, "Translating the Greek Imperative," *BTr*
         24 (1973): 129-34.

3609.8   Donald S. Deer, "The Interpretation and Translation of
         Constructions with a Passive Meaning in the Greek of the
         Synoptic Gospels," *BTr* 26 (1975): 338-46.

3609.9   G. J. Wenham, "The Syntax of Matthew 19.9," *JSNT* 28
         (1986): 17-23.

3609.10 John Thorley, "Aktionsart in New Testament Greek: Infinitive
         and Imperative," *NT* 31 (1989): 290-315.

3. The Literary Style of the Gospels

a. *General Studies*

3610. Carolus Lachmann, "De ordine narrationum in evangeliis synopticis," *TSK* 8 (1835): 570-90.

3611. Ferdinand Prat, "Les doublets et la critique des évangiles," *RB* 7 (1898): 541-53.

3612. Albert Thumb, "Die sprachgeschichtliche Stellung des biblischen Griechisch," *TR* 5 (1902): 85-99.

3613. S. Angus, "The Koiné, the Language of the New Testament," *PTR* 8 (1910): 44-92.

3614. Frederick C. Grant, "Editorial Style in the Synoptic Gospels," *ATR* 3 (1920-1921): 51-58.

3615. W. K. Lowther Clarke, "The Style of our Lord's Discourses," *Th* 12 (1926): 282-83.

3616. H. Pernot, "Greek and the Gospels," *ET* 38 (1926- 1927): 103-108.

3617. Paul Fiebig, "Der Erzählungsstil der Evangelien," *A* 2 (1926): 39-43.

3618. Paul Fiebig, trans. by G. B. King, "The Story-Telling Style of the Gospels," *CJRT* 4 (1927): 112-18.

3619. F. G. Vial, "The Language of the Gospels," *CJRT* 5 (1928): 105-10.

3620. Robert E. Keighton, "The Poetry of the Gospels," *CQ* 7 (1931): 78-91.

3621. N. W. Lund, "The Influence of Chiasmus upon the Structure of the Gospels," *ATR* 13 (1931): 27-48.

3622. J. Konopásek, "Les 'questions rhétoriques' dans le Nouveau Testament," *RHPR* 12 (1932): 47-66, 141-61.

3623. Michel Willam, "Das historische Präsens, ein wesentliches Merkmal des evangelischen Erzählungsstiles," *BibZ* 21 (1933): 309-19

3624. U. Holzmeister, "De forma chiastica in N.T. adhibita," *VD* 14 (1934): 337-41.

3625. T. P. Stafford, "The Language of the Bible," *RE* 35 (1938):

298-303.

3626.   Kendrick Grobel, "Idiosyncracies of the Synoptists in their Pericope-Introductions," *JBL* 59 (1940): 405-10.

3627.   W. S. van Leeuwen, "Een zin van den kruisdood in de Synoptische Evangelieën," *NTS* 24 (1941): 68-81.

3628.   David Daube, "A Rhetorical Principle in the Gospels," *ET* 54 (1942-1943): 305-306.

3629.   E. Ll. Lewis, "A Rhetorical Principle in the Gospels," *ET* 55 (1943-1944): 166-67.

3630.   Johannes Munck, "Deux notes sur la langue du Nouveau Testament," *CM* 5 (1943): 187-208; 6 (1944): 110-50.

3631.   Juan Leal, "Las paradojas de los Evangelios," *CB* 14 (1957): 14-17.

3632.   Donald C. Swanson, "Diminutives in the Greek New Testament," *JBL* 77 (1958): 134-51.

3632.1   Bernard J. Cooke, "Synoptic Presentation of the Eucharist as Covenant Sacrifice," *ThSt* 21 (1960): 1-44.

3632.2   R. H. Gundry, "Language Milieu of First-Century Palestine: Its Bearing on the Authenticity of the Gospel Tradition," *JBL* 83 (1964): 404-408.

3632.3   F. Rundgren, "Synoptic Gospels as Language," *B* 46 (1965): 465-69.

3632.4   George D. Kilpatrick, "Language and Text in the Gospels and Acts," *VCh* 24 (1970): 161-71.

3632.5   H. M. Teeple, "Greek Article with Personal Names in the Synoptic Gospels," *NTSt* 19 (1973): 302-17.

3632.6   Wolfgang Harnisch, "Die Sprachkraft der Analogie: zur These vom argumentativen Charakter der Gleichnisse Jesu," *ST* 28 (1974): 1-20.

3632.7   E. M. Sidebottom, "So-Called Divine Passive in the Gospel Tradition," *ET* 87 (1976): 200-204.

3632.8   Lars Lode, "Narrative Paragraphs in the Gospels and Acts," *BTr* 34 (1983): 322-35.

3632.9   Philippe Rolland, "L'arrière-fond sémitique des évangiles synoptiques," *ETL* 60 (1984): 358-62.

3632.10 Birger Gerhardsson, "The Narrative Meshalim in the Synoptic Gospels: A Comparison with the Narrative Meshalim in the Old Testament," *NTSt* 34 (1988): 339-63.

3632.11 Helmut Koester, "From the Kerygma-Gospel to Written Gospels," *NTSt* 35 (1989): 361-81.

3632.12 Ernst Jenni, "Kausativ und Funktionsverbgefüge: Sprachliche Bemerkungen zur Bitte: 'Führe uns nicht in Versuchung'," *TZ* 48 (1992): 77-88.

3632.13 F. Sieg, "Eigentliche Präpositionen als gebundene Morpheme der Substantive im Evangelium nach Johannes und in der Offenbarung des Johannes," *FilN* 5 (1992): 135-66.

3632.14 Peter Doble, "Luke 23.47—The Problem of Dikaios," *BTr* 44 (1993): 320-31.

3632.15 Folker Siegert, "Communication de masse et rythmes de prose dans Luc/Actes," *RHPR* 74 (1994): 113-27.

3632.16 P. R. Whale, "More Efficient Teaching of New Testament Greek," *NTSt* 40 (1994): 596-605.

3632.17 Adrian Schenker, "Interprétations récentes et dimensions spécifiques du sacrifice hattat," *B* 75 (1994): 59-70.

3632.18 William Whallon, "The Pascha in the Eucharist," *NTSt* 40 (1994): 126-32.

h *The Literary Style of Matthew*

3633. J. F. K. Gurlitt, "Kleine Beiträge zur Erklärung des Evangeliums Matthäi," *TSK* 34 (1861): 310-22.

3634. E. Levesque, "Quelques procédés littéraires de Saint Matthieu," *RB* 25 (1916): 5-22, 387-405.

3635. Frederick C. Grant, "Editorial Style in the Synoptic Gospels: St. Matthew," *ATR* 1 (1918-1919): 278-87.

3636. N. W. Lund, "The Influence of Chiasmus upon the Structure of the Gospel According to Matthew," *ATR* 13 (1931): 405-33.

3636.1 Jack D. Kingsbury, "The Rhetoric of Comprehension in the Gospel of Matthew," *NTSt* 41 (1995): 358-77.

c. The Literary Style of Mark

3637. J. R. Lumby, "Of the Graphic and Dramatic Character of the Gospel of St. Mark," *Exp* 1st ser., 2 (1875): 269-84.

3638. Theodore C. Pease, "Peculiarities of Form and Color in Mark's Gospel," *JBL* 16 (1897): 1-16.

3639. A.. van Veldhuizen, "Taal en stijl van Markus," *NTS* 1 (1918): 129-36.

3640. J. Rohr, "Der Aufbau des Markusevangeliums," *TQ* 101 (1920): 272-306.

3641. Ernst von Dobschütz, "Zur Erzählerkunst des Markus," *ZNW* 27 (1928): 193-98.

3642. Leo Wohleb, "Beobachtungen zum Erzählungsstil des Markus-Evangeliums," *RQ* 36 (1928): 185-96.

3643. Millar Burrows, "Mark's Transitions and the Translation Hypothesis," *JBL* 48 (1929): 117-23.

3644. J. van Dodewaard, "Die sprachliche Übereinstimmung zwischen Markus-Paullus und Markus-Petrus," *B* 30 (1949): 91-108, 218-38.

3645. George D. Kilpatrick, "Some Notes on Marcan Usage," *BTr* 7 (1956): 2-9, 51-56, 146.

See also number 2386.

3645.1 J. Miller, "The Literary Structure of Mark. An interpretation based on 1 Corinthians 2:1-8," *ET* 106 (1995): 296-99.

d. The Literary Style of Luke

3646. C. F. Nösgen, "Der schriftstellerische Plan des dritten Evangeliums," *TSK* 49 (1876): 265-92.

3647. R. J. Knowling, "The Medical Language of St. Luke," *BW* 20 (1902): 260-70.

3648. Edgar J. Goodspeed, "The Vocabulary of Luke and Acts," *JBL* 31 (1912): 92-94.

3649. Frederick C. Grant, "A Critique of *The Style and Literary Method of Luke*," *ATR* 2 (1919-1920): 318-23.

3650. G. Mackinlay, "Special Lucan Words," *BS* 77 (1920): 419-23.

3651. R. V. G. Tasker, "The Partiality of Luke for 'Three,' and its Bearing on the Original of Q," *JTS* 37 (1936): 141-55.

3652. C. A. Phillips, "Luke's Partiality for 'Three'," *BBC* 12 (1937): 49-50.

3653. Albert Wifstrand, "Lukas och Septuaginta," *STK* 16 (1940): 243-62.

3654. Heinz Schürmann, "Die Doubletten im Lukasevangelium," *ZKT* 7S (1953): 338-45.

3655. Heinz Schurmann, "Die Doublettenvermeidungen im Lukas-evangelium," *ZKT* 76 (1954): 83-93.

3656. H. F. D. Sparks, "St. Luke's Transpositions," *NTSt* 3 (1956-1957): 219-23.

3657. J. C. O'Neill, "The Six Amen Sayings in Luke," *JTS* N.S. 10 (1959): 1-9.

3658. H. Schürmann, "Sprachliche Reminiszenzen an abgeänderte oder ausgelassene Bestandteile der Spruchsammlung im Lukas- und Matthäusevangelium," *NTSt* 6 (1959-1960): 193-210.

See also numbers 2175, 5430.

3658.1 M. Augsten, "Lukanische Miszelle," *NTSt* 14 (1967-1968): 581-83.

3658.2 David L. Mealand, "Luke-Acts and the Verbs of Dionysis of Halicarnassus," *JSNT* 63 (1996): 63-86.

e. *The Literary Style of John*

3659. Dr. Aberle, "Exegetische Studien," *TQ* 50 (1868): 3-64 [on John].

3660. Gottlieb Linder, "Gesetz der Stoffteilung im Johannes-evangelium," *ZWT* 40 (1897): 444-54; 42 (1899): 32-35.

3661. C. H. Turner, "Transpositions of Text in St. John's Gospel: St. John xviii 13-25," *JTS* 2 (1900-1901): 141-42.

3662. Paul Moore Strayer, "Transpositions of Text in St. John's Gospel; St. John viii, ix, and x 1-22," *JTS* 2 (1900-1901): 137-40.

3663. F. R. M. Hitchcock, "The Dramatic Development of the

Fourth Gospel," *Exp* 7th ser., 4 (1907): 266-79.

3664.   E. Butler Pratt, "The Gospel of John from the Standpoint of Greek Tragedy," *BW* 30 (1907): 448-59.

3665.   F. R. M. Hitchcock, "Is the Fourth Gospel a Drama?" *Th* 7 (1923): 307-17.

3666.   Clayton R. Bowen, "The Fourth Gospel as Dramatic Material," *JBL* 49 (1930): 292-305.

3667.   Charles B. Hedrick, "Pageantry in the Fourth Gospel," *ATR* 15 (1933): 115-24.

3668.   Martin Blumenthal, "Die Eigenart des johanneischen Erzählungsstiles," *TSK* 106 (1934-1935): 204-12.

3669.   Paul Gächter, "Strophen im Johannesevangelium," *ZKT* 60 (1936): 99-120, 402-23.

3670.   R. J. Du Brau, "Some Observations on the Vocabulary of the Fourth Gospel," *CTM* 12 (1941): 114-18.

3671.   E. K. Simpson, "The Apostle John's Diction," *EQ* 14 (1942): 81-87.

3672.   C. Milo Connick, "The Dramatic Character of the Fourth Gospel," *JBL* 67 (1948): 159-69.

3673.   Oscar Cullmann, "Der johanneische Gebrauch doppel-deutiger Ausdrücke als Schlüssel zum Verständnis des 4. Evangeliums," *TZ* 4 (1948): 360-72.

3674.   E. Hirsch, "Stilkritik und Literanalyse im vierten Evangelium," *ZNW* 43 (1950-1951): 128-43.

3675.   E. Kenneth Lee, "The Drama of the Fourth Gospel," *ET* 65 (1953-1954): 173-76.

3676.   Francis Clark, "Tension and Tide in St. John's Gospel," *ITQ* 24 (1957): 154-94.

3677.   X. Léon-Dufour, "Trois chiasmes johanniques," *NTSt* 7 (1960-1961): 249-55.

3678.   Edith Lovejoy Pierce, "The Fourth Gospel as Drama," *RL* 29 (1960): 453-55.

3678.1   G. Ghiberti, " 'Vecchio' e 'nuovo' in Giovanni. Per una rilettura di Giovanni (Vangelo e Lettere)," *RivBib* 43 (1995): 225-51.

3678.2   Gerald L. Borchett, "The Fourth Gospel and Its Theological Impact," *RE* 78 (1981): 249-58.

3678.3   Jean Zumstein, "L'évangile Johannique: une Stratégie du croire," *RSR* 77 (1989): 217-32.

3678.4   T. Thatcher, "Jesus, Judas, and Peter: Character by Contrast in the Fourth Gospel," *BS* 153 (1996): 435-48.

G. CRITICAL AND EXEGETICAL STUDIES of INDIVIDUAL PASSAGES IN THE GOSPELS

1. Critical and Exegetical Studies of Passages in Several Gospels

3679.   H. C. M. Rettig, "Exegetische Analekten," *TSK* 3 (1830): 96-114; 7 (1834): 81-100; 11 (1838): 205-44, 467-87, 775-805, 965-89 [Jn. 1:39; 4:6; 19.14, Mt. 3:3 & par.; Lk. 1:41, 37; Mk. 1:2; Lk. 3:15; Mt. 2:1; Lk. 1.66, 2:37, 22, 23; Mt. 4:12ff.; Mk. 1:16; Lk. 3:2, etc.].

3680.   J. R. Linder, "Bemerkungen über einige Stellen der Evangelien," *TSK* 32 (1859): 511-19 [Mt. 11:5; 27:9; Mk. 9:49; Jn. 8:58].

3681.   Ed. Scherer, "Notes sur les évangiles synoptiques," *RT* 3 (1859): 306-21 [Mk. 1:1-15; Lk. 4:16-28], 371-83 [Lk. 5:1-11; Mt. 3:13-17; 5-8]; 4 (1859): 36-60 [Lk. 7:36-50; Mt. 13:10-17; Mk. 7 and Mt. 15; Mk. 6], 65-77 [Mt. 16:17-19; 18]; 5 (1860): 101-34 [Lk. 12:1-12; 12:13-59; 6:6-11; 13:10-17; 14:1-6; 14:1-24; 14:15-24; 15:1-7; 16:1-13, 14-31; Mt. 19; 19:12, 21; 20:1-16].

3682.   J. R. Linder, "Gedanken und Bemerkungen zu einigen Stellen des Neuen Testaments," *TSK* 35 (1862): 553-76 [Mt. 4:15; 12:18, 19:10; 28:1; Mk. 3:21; 7:31; 9·11 ff., 9:23; 14:72; Lk. 6:40; 12:2; 12:15; 13:32; 18:14; 21:19; 22:51].

3683.   G. A. Chadwick, "The Nobleman's Son and the Centurion's Servant," *Exp* 4th ser., 5 (1892): 443-56 [Jn. 4:46; Mt. 8:5; Lk. 7:1].

3684.   F. C. Conybeare, "New Testament Notes," *Exp* 4th ser., 9 (1894): 451-62 [Mt. 3:16; 26:49; Mk. 1:10; 14:45; Lk. 3:22; 22:47; Jn. 19:23].

3685.   J. E. Völter, "Zu und aus den Evangelien," *TT* 33 (1899):

119-51 [Mic. 5:1-2; 4:9-10; Mt. 11; Mk. 1:21-28].

3686.   Friedrich Spitta, "Beiträge zur Erklärung der Synoptiker," *ZNW* 5 (1904): 303-26 [Mt. 3:11, 16; Mk. 1:10-13; Lk. 3:16, 22].

3687.   Eb. Nestle, "Little Contributions to the Greek Testament," *ET* 16 (1904-1905): 524 [Punctuation in Mt. 26:64; Lk. 7:47].

3688.   L. Fonck, "Cena Bethanica," *VD* 8 (1928): 65-74, 97-105 [Lk. 10:38-42; Jn. 11].

3689.   A. T. Robertson, "Martha and Mary, or Temperament in Religion," *BR* 13 (1928): 63-73 [Lk. 10:38-42; Jn. 11].

3690.   Robert Dollinger, "Kreuz," *EvT* 10 (1950-1951): 433-50 [Lk. 14:27; Mt. 10:38; Mk. 10:21; et al.].

3691.   Jules Isaac, "De quelques abus dans la traduction et l'interprétation des texts," *RHPR* 33 (1953): 52-65 [Lk. 16:16-17; Mt. 11:12-14; etc.].

3691.1   Birger Gerhardsson, "Parable of the Sower and Its Interpretation," *NTSt* 14 (1968): 165-93 [Mt.13:1-52; Mk. 4:1-34; Lk 8:4-18].

3691.2   O. J. F. Seitz, "Love Your Enemies: The Historical Setting of Matthew 5:43f," *NTSt* 16 (1969): 39-54 [Mt. 5:43-44; Lk. 6:27-28].

3691.3   I. Howard Marshall, "Fear Him Who Can Destroy both Soul and Body in Hell," *ET* 81 (1970): 276-80 [Mt.10:28; Lk. 12:4-5].

3691.4   J. K. Elliott, "Anointing of Jesus," *ET* 85 (1974): 105-107 [Mt. 26:6-13; Mk. 14:3-9; Lk. 7:36-50; Jn. 12:3-8].

3691.5   Daniel R. Schwartz, "Viewing the Holy Untensils (P Ox V,840)," *NTSt* 32 (1986): 153-59 [Mt. 15:1-20; 23:25-28; Mk. 7:1-23].

3691.6   John F. Healey, "Models of Behavior," *JBL* 108 (1989): 497-98 [Mt. 6:26; Lk. 12:24; Prov. 6:6-8].

3691.7   K. J. H. Petzer, "Style and Text in the Lucan Narrative of the Institution of the Lord's Supper," *NTSt* 37 (1991): 113-29 [Mt. 26:26-29; Mk. 14:22-25; Lk. 22:19-20; 1 Cor. 11:23-26].

3691.8   Wilhelm Wilkens, "Die Täuferüberlieferung des Matthäus und ihre Verarbeitung durch Lukas," *NTSt* 40 (1994): 542-57 [Mt. 11:2-19; Lk. 7:18-35].

2. Critical and Exegetical Studies of Passages in Matthew

3692.   A. T. Robertson, "The New Testament Translated from the Greek Text of Westcott and Hort," *RE* 32 (1935): 21-37, 121-37 [Mt. 1:1-14:22].

3693.   W. C. Allen, "The Dependence of St. Matthew i-xiii upon St. Mark," *ET* 11 (1899-1900): 279-84.

3694.   G. Doekes, "Het Evangelie naar Mattheus," *GTT* 12 (1911): 22-29; "Jezus Christus de wettige stichter van het Koninkrijk der Hemelen," 105-13, 142-47, 201-207, 281-94, 336-40; "Jezus' doop," 469-72; "Jezus' verzocking in de woestijn," 13 (1913): 38-47 [Mt. 1:1-4:11].

3695.   Salvador Muñoz Iglesias, "El género literario del Evangelio de la Infancia en San Mateo," *EB* 17 (1958): 243-73 [Mt. 1:1-2:23].

3696.   Eb. Nestle, "Eine Verhandlung über Matthäi I und II im Jahr 119?" *ZWT* 36 (1893): 435-38.

3697.   Myles M. Bourke, "The Literary Genus of Matthew 1-2," *CBQ* 22 (1960): 160-75.

3698.   Peter Schleyer, "Über die von Matthäus und Lukas mitgetheilten Genealogieen Jesu Christi," *TQ* 18 (1836): 403-34, 539-66.

3699.   I. Riggenbach, "Exegetische Bruchstücke," *TSK* 28 (1855): 575-612 [Mt. 1:1-17; 2:23; Lk. 3:23-34].

3700.   Andrew D. Heffern, "The Four Women in St. Matthew's Genealogy of Christ," *JBL* 31 (1912): 69-81 [Mt. 1].

3701.   E. Riggenbach, "Bemerkungen zum Text von Matthäus 1," *STZ* 31 (1914): 241-49.

3702.   W. C. Allen, "The Genealogy in St. Matthew, and its Bearing on the Original Language of the Gospel," *ET* 11 (1899-1900): 135-37 [Mt. 1:1-18].

3703.   Eb. Nestle, "The Genealogy in St. Matthew and the Septuagint of Chronicles," *ET* 11 (1899-1900): 191 [Mt.

1:1-18].

3704. K. Weiseler, "Die Geschlechtstafeln Jesu bei den Evangelisten Matthäus und Lukas," *TSK* 18 (1845): 361-400 [Mt. 1:1-17; Lk. 3:23-38].

3705. George M. Clelland, "The Genealogy of Christ," *BS* 18 (1861): 410-41 [Mt. 1:1-17; Lk. 3:23-38].

3706. F. Gardiner, "Patristic Views of the Two Genealogies of our Lord," *BS* 29 (1872): 593-601 [Mt. 1:1-17; Lk. 3:23-38].

3707. L. L[indeboom], "De geslachtregisters van Jezus Christus, onzen Heere," *GTT* 11 (1910): 359-86 [Mt. 1:1-17; Lk. 3:23-38].

3708. Friedrich Spitta, "Die Frauen in der Genealogie Jesu bei Matthäus," *ZWT* 54 (1912): 1-8 [Mt. 1:1-17].

3709. Henry A. Sanders, "The Genealogies of Jesus," *JBL* 32 (1913): 184-93 [Mt. 1:1-17; Lk. 3:23-38].

3710. George F. Moore, "Fourteen Generations: 490 Years: An Explanation of the Genealogy of Jesus," *HTR* 14 (1921): 97-103 [Mt. 1:1-17].

3711. P. Pons, "Liber generationis Iesu Christi," *VD* 5 (1925): 41-48 [Mt. 1:1-17].

3712. Chaim Kaplan, "Some New Testament Problems in the Light of Rabbinics and the Pseudepigrapha. The Generation Schemes in Matthew 1:1-17, Luke 3:24ff.," *BS* 87 (1930): 465-71.

3713. Markos Siotos, "Αἱ γυναῖκες τῆς κατὰ Ματθαῖον γενεαλογίας," *Θ* 20 (1949): 157-63 [Mt. 1:1-17].

3714. Charles C. Starbuck, "Exegesis of Matthew 1. 1," *BS* 38 (1881): 508-23.

3715. J. L. Leuba, "Note exégétique sur Matthieu 1,1a," *RHPR* 22 (1942): 56-61.

3716. Eb. Nestle, "Matthew 1:4,5; Luke 3:23," *ET* 10 (1898-1899): 91.

3717. Paul Wilh. Schmiedel, "Jesu Geburt nach Matth. 1,16-25," *STZ* 31 (1914): 69-82; 32 (1915): 16-31.

3718. E. Riggenbach, "Zur Erwiderung auf Prof. Schmiedels

Artikel 'Jesu Geburt nach Matth. 1,16-25'," *STZ* 31 (1914): 117-18.

3719. Paul Wilh. Schmiedel, "Über Jesu Geburt und die vierte Bitte im Vaterunser, gegenüber Riggenbach, Mader und Kappeler," *STZ* 32 (1915): 122-33 [Mt. 1:16-25].

3720. A. T. Robertson, "The Text of Matthew 1:16," *BR* 11 (1926): 345-55.

3721. W. C. van Manen, "De oorspronkelijke lesing van Mt. 1,16," *TT* 29 (1895): 258-62.

3722. Frederick Torm, "Om den rette Laesemaade i Matth. I,16," *TTDF* N.S. 4 (1902-1903): 110-16, 451-52.

3723. Albrecht Jochmann, "Zur Beurteilung der Lesarten von Mt. 1,16," *BibZ* 11 (1913): 161-67.

3724. William P. Armstrong, "Critical Note," *PTR* 13 (1915): 461-68 [Von Soden's text of Mt. 1:16].

3725. G. Kuhn, "Untersuchungen über die richtige Textgestalt von Matthäus 1,16," *NKZ* 34 (1923): 362-85.

3726. H. Grimme, "Der Schlussvers des Stammbaumes Jesu Christi (Mt. 1,16)," *BibZ* 20 (1932): 355-65.

3727. Bruce M. Metzger, "On the Citation of Variant Readings of Matt 1:16," *JBL* 77 (1958): 361-63.

3728. F. W. Grosheide, "Mattheus 1,16b," *TT* 49 (1915): 100-105, 490-92.

3729. X. Léon-Dufour, "Le juste Joseph," *NRT* 81 (1959): 225-31 [Mt. 1:18-25].

3730. Robert B. Pocock, "The Origin of Matthew i.18-25," *ET* 25 (1913-1914): 287.

3731. Thomas Fahy, "The Marriage of Our Lady and St. Joseph (St. Luke 1:26 ff.; St. Matthew 1:18 ff.)," *ITQ* 24 (1957): 261-67.

3732. R. Bulbeck, "The Doubt of St. Joseph," *CBQ* 10 (1948): 296-309 [Mt. 1:18-19].

3733. L. Fonck, " 'Joseph autem vir eius cum esset iustus' (Mt. 1,19)," *VD* 4 (1924): 65-71.

3734. W. R. Mackintosh, "The Name of Jesus," *ET* 26

(1914-1915): 151-55 [Mt. 1:21].

3735. Frederic C. Spurr, "The Great Name," *RE* 24 (1927): 377-87 [Matt. 1:21; Phil. 2:9-10].

3736. G. Martin-Favenc, "Ésaïe VII,14 et Matthieu I,22 sq.," *RTQR* 11 (1902): 375-79.

3737. Theodore G. Soares, "The Virgin Birth of the Son Immanuel," *BW* 23 (1904): 417-21 [Mt. 1:23; Isa. 7:14].

3738. Eb. Nestle, " 'He called' or 'she called'?" *Exp* 4th ser., 9 (1894): 123-26 [Mt. 1:25].

3739. M. Peinador, " 'Et non cognoscebat eam, donec peperit filium suum primogenitum' (Mt. 1,25)," *EB* 8 (1949): 355-63.

3740. R. Thibaut, "Et non cognoscebat eam (Mt. 1,25)," *NRT* 59 (1932): 255-56.

3741. B. B. Edwards, "[H. A. W. Meyer's] Commentary on the Second and Third Chapters of the Gospel of Matthew," *BS* 8 (1851): 85-99.

3742. E. C. S. Gibson, "The Two Accounts of our Lord's Infancy," *Exp* 2nd ser., 3 (1882): 116-28 [Mt. 2; Lk. 2].

3743. Alexander Ross, "Old Testament Quotations in the New Testament—with Special Reference to the Second Chapter of Matthew," *EQ* 1 (1929): 241-51.

3744. F. Ball, "Der Stern der Weisen," *ZNW* 18 (1917): 40-48 [Mt. 2].

3745. W. K. Lowther Clarke, "The Rout [sic] of the Magi," *Th* 27 (1933): 72-80 [Mt. 2].

3746. William Edgar, "The Wise Men and their Gifts," *ET* 51 (1939-1940): 172-74 [Mt. 2].

3747. Albert-Marie Denis, "L'adoration des mages vue par s. Matthieu," *NRT* 82 (1960): 32-39.

3748. Salvador Muñoz Iglesias, "Herodes y los Magos," *CB* 3 (1946): 124-27 [Mt. 2:1-18].

3749. J. E. Bruns, "The Magi Episode in Matthew 2," *CBQ* 23 (1961): 51-54.

3750. H. J. Richards, "The Three Kings," *Scr* 8 (1956): 23-28 [Mt. 2:1-12].

3751. Theodore Appel, "The Star of the East," *BS* 35 (1878): 147-78 [Mt. 2:1-10].

3752. Eugene D. Owen, "The Christmas Star," *BS* 93 (1936): 473-78.

3753. Agnes Smith Lewis, "The Star of Bethlehem," *ET* 19 (1907-1908): 139-40 [Mt. 2:2].

3754. P. J. Maclagan, "The Star of Bethlehem," *ET* 19 (1907-1908): 329-30 [Mt. 2:2].

3755. Agnes Smith Lewis, "Matt. ii.2," *ET* 19 (1907-1908): 237.

3756. Nigel Turner, "The New-Born King (Matthew 2:2)," *ET* 68 (1956-1957): 122.

3757. G. Messina, "Ecce Magi ab Oriente venerunt (Mt. 2,2)," *VD* 14 (1934). 7-10.

3758. José González Raposo, "A Estrela de Jacob e a Estrela dos Magos," *REB* 9 (1949): 877-92 [Mt. 2:2].

3759. E. P. Groenewald, "'n Aantekening vor Matt. 2:2," *NGTT* 2 (1961): 204-205.

3760. Eb. Nestle, "The Text of Matthew ii.9," *ET* 8 (1896-1897): 521.

3761. F. C. Conybeare, "Two Notes on the Text of the Gospels from Old Sources," *ET* 8 (1896-1897): 428-30 [Mt. 2:9; Mk. 10:18].

3762. Pierre Charles, "Obtulerunt. Ils ont offert (Mt. 2:11)," *NRT* 61 (1934): 511-14.

3763. Rafael Fuster, "¿Fué español el oro que ofrecierón los magos al Niño Diós?" *CB* 2, núm. 9 (1945): 19-21 [Mt. 2:11].

3764. W. G. Elmslie, "The Descent into Egypt," *Exp* 1st. ser., 6 (1877): 401-11 [Mt. 2:13-15].

3765. W. W. Peyton, "Vicarious Heredity: A Reading of the Child Massacre in Bethlehem," *Exp* 5th ser., 4 (1896): 440-61.

3766. U. Holzmeister, "Quot pueros urbis Bethelem Herodes rex occiderit?" *VD* 15 (1935): 373-79 [Mt. 2:16].

3767. José Llamas Simón, "La expresión evangélica 'de dos años para abajo' y la cronología de Jesús," *EB* 1 (1941-1942): 41-52 [Mt. 2:16].

3768.   Caspar René Gregory (trans.), "Dr. Biesenthal on Matthew II.23," *BS* 32 (1875): 161-74.

3769.   Dr. Gieseler, "Über Matth. 2,23," *TSK* 4 (1831): 588-92.

3770.   U. Holzmeister, " 'Quoniam Nazaraeus vocabitur' (Mt.2, 23)," *VD* 17 (1937): 21-26.

3771.   W. Caspari, " Ναζωραῖος Mt. 2,23, nach alttestamenlichen Voraussetzungen," *ZNW* 21 (1922): 122-27.

3772.   N. Krieger, "Barfuss Busse tun," *NT* 1 (1956): 227-28 [Mt. 3:1].

3773.   Denis Buzy, "Pagne ou ceinture? À propos de saint Jean-Baptiste," *RSR* 23 (1933): 589-98 [Mt. 3:4; Mk. 1:6].

3774.   Ernst Pickelmann, "Zu Mt. 3,4 und Mk. 1,6," *BibZ* 23 (1935-1936): 190-91.

3775.   L. A. Pooler, "The Baptism of John (St. Matt. iii. 5,6)," *ET* 27 (1915-1916): 382-83.

3776.   Eb. Nestle, " 'Generation of Vipers'," *ET* 23 (1911-1912): 185 [Mt. 3:7, etc.; Lk. 3:7].

3777.   Ursula Treu, " 'Otterngezücht.' Ein patristischer Beitrag zur Quellenkunde des Physiologus," *ZNW* 50 (1959): 113-22 [γεννήματα ἐχιδνῶν Mt. 3:7; 12:34; 23:33; Lk. 2:7].

3778.   D. S. Wallace-Hadrill, "A Suggested Exegesis of Matthew iii.9,10 (= Luke iii. 8,9)," *ET* 62 (1950-1951): 349.

3779.   Augustus Poynder, "Matt. 3,11," *ET* 11 (1899-1900): 334.

3780.   John Reid, "The Baptism of Water and the Baptism of Fire," *ET* 25 (1913-1914): 306-307 [Mt. 3:11].

3781.   H. J. Flowers, "ἐν πνεύματι ἁγίῳ καὶ πυρί," *ET* 64 (1952-1953): 155-56 [Mt. 3:11].

3782.   Eduard Schweizer, " 'With tine Holy Ghost and Fire'," *ET* 65 (1953-1954): 29 [Mt. 3:11].

3783.   L. W. Barnard, "Matt. 3 Luke 3,16," *JTS* N.S. 8 (1957): 107.

3784.   Eb. Nestle, "Matthew iii.11," *ET* 11 (1899-1900): 233-34.

3785.   S. A. Tippel, "The Holy Ghost as Dove and Fire," *Exp* 1st. ser., 9 (1879): 81-90 [Mt. 3:11,16].

3786.   Lorenzo Turrado, "El Bautismo 'in Spiritu sancto et igni'," *EE*

34 (1960): 807-18 [Mt. 3:11; Lk. 3:16].

3787. G. H. P. Thompson, "Called—Proved—Obedient: A Study in the Baptism and Temptation Narratives of Matthew and Luke," *JTS* N.S. 11 (1960): 1-12 [Mt. 3:13-4:11; Lk. 3:21-4:13].

3788. Donald Ross, "The Baptism of Jesus," *EQ* 18 (1946): 241-44 [Mt. 3:13].

3789. N. Krieger, "Ein Mensch in weichen Kleidern," *NT* 1 (1956): 228-30 [Mt. 3:13-14; 24:27].

3790. Melanchthon W. Jacobus, "Die Taufe Jesu. Eine Untersuchung zu Matth. 3,14. 15," *NKZ* 40 (1929): 44-53.

3791. J. M. Ross, "St. Matthew iii. 15," *ET* 61 (1949-1950): 30-31.

3792. D. R. Griffiths, "St. Matthew iii. 15: Ἄφες ἄρτι οὕτω γὰρ πρέπον ἐστὶν ἡμῖν πληρῶσαι πᾶσαν δικαιοσύνην," *ET* 62 (1950-1951): 155-57.

3793. F. D. Coggan, "Note on St. Matthew iii. 15: Ἄφες ἄρτι οὕτω γάρ πρέπον ἐστὶν ἡμῖν πληρῶσαι πᾶσαν δικαιοσύνην," *ET* 60 (1948-1949): 258.

3794. George Christie, "A Note to Matthew iii. 15," *ET* 9 (1897-1998): 378.

3795. Anton Fredrichsen, "Accomplir toute justice," *RHPR* 7 (1927): 245-52 [Mt. 3:15].

3796. Dr. Mack, "Praktische Erklärung der evangelization Perikope auf den ersten Sonntag in der Fasten Matth. 4,1-11," *TQ* 21 (1839): 195-224 [Mt. 4:1-11].

3797. Pfarrer Held, "Versuchung und Verklärung Jesu," *ZWT* 9 (1866): 384-97 [Mt. 4:1-11; Mt. 16:16-19, 20-28; 17:1-8, 11-21].

3798. Alfred E. Garvie, "The Temptation of Christ," *ET* 10 (1898-1999): 301-302, 356-58, 419-21, 453-55, 509-10.

3799. A. Hilgenfeld, "Die Versuchung Jesu," *ZWT* 45 (1902): 289-302 [Mt. 4:1-11 and parallels].

3800. F. Walther Scoffer, "Zu Randbemerkungen zu neutestamentlichen Stellen," *ZWT* 46 (1903): 316-18 [Mt. 4:1-11; 1 Cor. 15:28].

3801.   J. Dick Fleming, "The Threefold Temptation of Christ: Matt. 4:1-11," *BW* 32 (1908): 130-37.

3802.   E. Boklen, "Zu der Versuchung Jesu," *ZNW* 18 (1917): 244-48 [Mt. 4:1-11; Lk. 4:1-13].

3803.   L. Fonck, "Christus tentatur in deserto (Mt. 4,1-11)," *VD* 1 (1921): 1-15.

3804.   Agnes Mason, "The Temptation in the Wilderness: A Possible Interpretation," *Th* 4 (1922): 127-36 [Mt. 4:1-11].

3805.   A. Georgette Bowden-Smith, "A Suggestion towards a Closer Study of the Significance of the Imagery of the Temptation," *ET* 47 (1935-1936): 408-12 [Mt. 4:1-11; Mk. 1:12,13].

3806.   G. S. Freeman "The Temptation," *ET* 48 (1936-1937): 45 [Mt. 4:1-11; Lk. 4:1-13].

3807.   A. Kadić, "Momentum Messianicum tentationum Christi (Mt. 4.1s. et par)," *VD* 18 (1938): 93-96, 126-28, 151-60.

3808.   J. J. Pelican, "The Temptation of the Church : A Study of Matt. 4:1-11," *CTM* 22 (1951): 252-59.

3809.   J. Estill Jones, "The Temptation Narrative," *RE* 53 (1956): 303-13 [Mt. 4:1-11; Mk. 1:12,13; Lk. 4:1-13].

3810.   A. Kadić, "Momentum Messianicum tentationum Christi (Mt. 4.2 s. et par)," *VD* 18 (1938): 93-96, 126-28, 151-60.

3811.   Matthew A. Power, "The Testing of Christ by the Devil," *ITQ* 9 (1914): 61-79 [Mt. 4:3].

3812.   George D. Kilpatrick, "Matthew iv. 4," *JTS* 45 (1944): 176.

3813.   A. B. Bruce, "The Light of Galilee," *Exp* 5th ser., 7 (1898): 423-39 [Mt. 4:16].

3814.   Sebastián Bartina, "La red esparavel del Evangelio (Mt. 4, 18; Mc. 1,16)," *EB* 19 (1960): 215-27.

3815.   L. Cerfaux, "La mission de Galilee dans la tradition synoptique," *ETL* 27 (1951): 369-89; 28 (1952): 629-47 [Mt. 4:23-10:42; Mk. 3:7-6: 34; Lk. 6:12-10:24].

3816.   Bernhard Weiss, "Die Gesetzauslegung Christi in der Bergpredigt," *TSK* 31 (1858): 50-94 [Mt. 5-7].

3817.   Carpus, "The Sermon on the Mount," *Exp* 1st. ser., 1 (1875):

71-88, 128-42, 196-211 [Mt. 5-7].

3818. M. Schwalb, "Le discours sur la montagne et les texts qui y sont rattachés," *RT* 8 (1861): 257-91 [Mt. 5-7].

3819. A. Frickart, "Die Composition der Bergpredigt," *STZ* 6 (1889): 193-210; 7 (1890): 43-52, 107-25 [Mt. 5-7].

3820. Alfred H. Hall, "The Gospel in the Sermon on the Mount," *BS* 48 (1891): 322-31 [Mt. 5-7].

3821. F. H. Woods, "The Moral Teaching of the Sermon on the Mount," *ET* 4 (1892-1893): 254-59 [Mt. 5-7].

3822. L'abbé Azibert, "Le sermon 'in monte' selon S. Matthew (v, vi, vii); in 'loco campestri' selon S. Luc (vi,20-49)," *RB* 3 (1894): 94-109.

3823. E. P. Burtt, "A Free Translation of the Sermon on the Mount," *BW* 3 (1894): 336-44 [Mt. 5-7].

3824. Nathan Söderblom, "Le sens des commandments de Jésus dans le discours sur la montagne," *RTP* 30 (1897): 247-63 [Mt. 5-7].

3825. G. Herbert Davis, "The Practice of the Sermon on the Mount," *ET* 11 (1899-1900): 382 [Mt. 5-7].

3826. L. Goumaz, "Le sermon sur la montagne constitue-t-il tout l'évangile?" *RTP* 36 (1903): 105-35 [Mt. 5-7].

3827. James Moffatt, "Literary Illustrations of the Sermon on the Mount," *ET* 15 (1903-1904): 508-11 [Mt. 5-7].

3828. James Moffatt, "Literary Illustrations of the Sermon on the Mount," *ET* 16 (1904-1905): 353-56 [Mt. 5-7].

3829. Clyde W. Votaw, "Jesus' Ideal of Life," *BW* 35 (1910): 46-56 [Mt. 5-7].

3830. Burton S. Easton, "The Sermon on the Mount," *JBL* 33 (1914): 228-43 [Mt. 5-7].

3831. H. Kuhn, "Das Problem der Bergpredigt," *NKZ* 25 (1914): 227-50, 251-67.

3832. H. R. Offerhaus, "Random de verheerlijking op den Berg," *TT* 49 (1915): 317-24, 384-95 [Mt. 5-7].

3833. Carl S. Patton, "The Deviations of Matthew and Luke in the 'Sermon on the Mount'," *BW* 48 (1916): 288-90 [Mt. 5-7;

Lk. 6].

3834. Edward Norman Harris, "Is the Sermon on the Mount Homiletically Defensible?" *BS* 75 (1918): 331-83 [Mt. 5-7].

3835. Charles R. Brown, "The Religion of a Laynuan. A Study of the Semnon on the Mount," *BW* 53 (1919): 586-93; 54 (1920): 50-57, 122-29, 268-75, 363-70 [Mt. 5-7].

3836. A. R. Abernathy, "A Study of the Sermon on the Mount," *RE* 18 (1921) [Mt. 5-7].

3837. V. C. MacMunn, "Who compiled the Sermon on the Mount?" *ET* 35 (1923-1924): 221-25 [Mt. 5-7].

3838. Carl Stingy, "Zur Ethik der Bergpredigt," *ZST* 2 (1924-1925): 37-74 [Mt. 5-7].

3839. A. Runestam, "Bergspredikans etiska problem," *STK* 2 (1926): 107-24 [Mt. 5-7].

3840. Paul Schneider, "Bergpredigt und Christenleben," *NKZ* 37 (1926): 591-610 [Mt. 5-7].

3841. A. Runestam, "Das ethische Problem der Bergpredigt," *ZST* 4 (1926-1927): 555-72 [Mt. 5-7].

3842. D. M. Baillie, "The Sermon on the Mount," *ET* 39 (1927-1928): 443-47 [Mt. 5-7].

3843. A. W. F. Blunt, "The Sermon on the Mount," *ET* 39 (1927-1928): 545-50 [Mt. 5-7].

3844. A. J. Gossip, "The Sermon on the Mount," *ET* 39 (1927-1928): 342-47 [Mt. 5-7].

3845. W. M. Macgregor, "The Sermon on the Mount," *ET* 39 (1927-1928): 293-97 [Mt. 5-7].

3846. F. W. Norwood, "The Sermon on the Mount," *ET* 39 (1927-1928): 408-11 [Mt. 5-7].

3847. James Reid, "The Serrnon on the Mount," *ET* 39 (1927-1928): 486-90 [Mt. 5-7].

3848. Friedrich Nägelsbach, "Die Einheit der Bergpredigt," *NKZ* 39 (1928): 47-76 [Mt. 5-7].

3849. R. C. Gillie, "The Sermon on the Mount," *ET* 40 (1928-1929): 21-25 [Mt. 5-7].

3850.   Andrew W. Blackwood, "The Sermon on the Mount for
         Today," *USR* 41 (1929-1930): 162-78 [Mt. 5-7].

3851.   Paul Fiebig, "Der Sinn der Bergpredigt," *ZST* 7 (1929-1930):
         497-515 [Rabbinical influence in Mt. 5-7].

3852.   U. Holzmeister, "De veritate sermonum in Scriptura
         relatorum," *VD* 10 (1930): 135-41.

3853.   A. M. Perry, "The Framework of the Sermon on the Mount,"
         JB L 54 (1935): 103-15. [Mt. 5-7].

3854.   Rafael Gyllenberg, "Religion und Ethik in der Bergpredigt,"
         ZS T 13 (1936): 682-705 [Mt. 5-7].

3855.   Friedrich Traub, "Das Problem der Bergpredigt," *ZTK* N.F.
         17 (1936): 193-218 [Mt. 5-7; Lk. 6].

3856.   Oskar Hammelsbeck, "Die Bergpredigt in Andacht und
         Unterricht," *EvT* 5 (1938): 212-21 [Mt. 5-7].

3857.   Erik Beijer, "Gudsrikets rättfärdighet," *STK* 18 (1942):
         89-111 [Mt. 5-7].

3858.   Frederick C. Grant, "The Sermon on the Mount," *ATR* 24
         (1942): 131-44 [Mt. 5-7].

3859.   G. T. Tolson, "Universals and Particulars in the Sermon on
         the Mount," *ET* 57 (1945-1946): 82 [Mt. 5-7].

3860.   Alexander C. Purdy, "Biblical Theology and the Sermon on
         the Mount," *RL* 15 (1946): 498-508 [Mt. 5-7].

3861.   G. Palomero, "El sermón de la montaña," *CB* 3 (1946):
         33-36, 129-32, 161-63 [Mt. 5-7].

3862.   S. MacLean Gilmour, "Interpreting the Sermon on the
         Mount," *CQ* 24 (1947): 47-56 [Mt. 5-7].

3863.   St. Gallo, "Structura sermonis montani," *VD* 27 (1949):
         257-69 [Mt. 5-7].

3864.   M. M. Gomes, "A Argumentação de Jesus no Sermão da
         Montanha," *REB* 10 (1950): 333-51 [Mt. 5-7].

3865.   Lewis Sperry Chafer, "The Sermon on the Mount," *BS* 108
         (1951): 389-413 [Mt. 5-7].

3866.   A. M. Hunter, "The Meaning of the Sermon on the Mount,"
         ET 63 (1951-1952): 176-79 [Mt. 5-7].

3867.   John Nome, "Bergprekenens betydning i den kristne etikk," *TTK* 22 (1951): 49-68 [Mt. 5-7].

3868.   É. Massaux, "Le texte du sermon sur la montagne de Matthieu utilisé par saint Justin," *ETL* 28 (1952): 411-48 [Mt. 5-7].

3869.   Pierre Boneyard, "Le sermon sur la montagne," *RTP* sér. III, 3 (1953): 233-46 [Mt. 5-7].

3870.   Pierre Boneyard, "El Sermón del Monte," *CT* 9-10 (1954): 40-54 [Mt. 5-7].

3871.   James F. Rand, "Problems in a Literal Interpretation of the Sermon on the Mount," *BS* 112 (1955): 28-38, 125-36 [Mt. 5-7].

3872.   Kurt Schubert, "Bergpredigt und Texte von En Fešha," *TQ* 135 (1955): 320-37 [Mt. 5-7].

3873.   Henlee Barnette, "The Ethic of the Sermon on the Mount," *RE* 53 (1956): 23-33 [Mt. 5-7].

3874.   William A. Mueller, "Self-Defense and Retaliation in the Sermon on the Mount," *RE* 53 (1956): 46-54 [Mt. 5-7].

3875.   Heber F. Peacock, "The Text of the Sermon on the Mount," *RE* 53 (1956): 9-23 [Mt. 5-7].

3876.   Jacob J. Rabinowitz, "The Sermon on the Mount and the School of Shammai," *HTR* 49 (1956): 79 [Mt. 5-7].

3877.   J. Dwight Pentecost, "The Purpose of the Sermon on the Mount," *BS* 115 (1958): 128-35, 212-28, 313-19 [Mt. 5-7].

3878.   Irwin W. Batdorf, "How Shall we Interpret the Sermon on the Mount?" *JBR* 27 (1959): 211-17 [Mt. 5-7].

3879.   Josef Kurzinger, "Zum Komposition der Bergpredigt nach Matthäus," *B* 40 (1959): 569-89 [Mt. 5-7].

3880.   O. S. Margoliouth, "Studies in the Sermon on the Mount," *Exp* 7th ser., 9 (1910): 42-50, 143-52, 210-17, 357-66 [Mt. 5-7].

3881.   Henry Offermann, "Studies in the Gospel of Matthew," *LCR* 45 (1926): 1-16, 109-116; 46 (1927): 129-44, 242-53, 348-60 [Mt. 5:1-6:15].

3882.   Ernst Fuchs, "Jesu Selbstzeugnis nach Matthäus 5," *ZTK* N.F. 51 (1954): 14-34.

3883.   W. F. Edna, "The Beatitudes," *Exp* 5th ser., 2 (1895): 365-76 [Mt. 5:1-12].

3884.   Marshall B. Lang, "The Beatitudes in the Twenty-third Psalm," *ET* 10 (1898-1999): 46-47 [Mt. 5:1-12].

3885.   Henry C. King, "The Fundamental Conditions of Happiness, as Revealed in Jesus' Beatitudes," *BW* 24 (1904): 180-87 [Mt. 5:1-12].

3886.   James H. Moulton, "Synoptic Studies; I. The Beatitudes," *Exp* 7th ser., 2 (1906): 97-110 [Mt. 5:1-12].

3887.   Robert Mackintosh, "The Beatitudes," *ET* 26 (1914-1915): 415-18 [Mt. 5:1-12].

3888.   R. H. Charles, "The Beatitudes," *ET* 28 (1916-17): 536-541 [Mt. 5:1-12].

3889.   Robert Mackintosh, "The Beatitudes," *ET* 32 (1920-1921): 519-20 [Mt. 5:1-12].

3890.   L. Fonck, " 'Beati . . . !' (Mt. 5:1-12)," *VD* 2 (1922): 321-27.

3891.   A. Lemonnyer, "Le Messianisme des 'Béatitudes'," *RSPT* 11 (1922): 373-89 [Mt. 5:1-12].

3892.   John Wick Bowman, "An Exposition of the Beatitudes," *JBR* 15 (1947): 162-70 [Mt. 5:1-12].

3893.   Jon E. Murray, " 'The Beatitudes'," *Interp* 1 (1947): 374-76.

3894.   William C. MacDonald, "The Singer of the Beatitudes," *TTod* 5 (1948): 13-14 [Mt. 5:1-12].

3895.   Matthew Günter "The Beatitudes," *ET* 64 (1952-1953): 125-26 [Mt. 5:1-12].

3896.   Friedrich Buchholz, "Predigt obeyer Matthäus 5, 1-12," *EvT* 14 (1954): 97-104.

3897.   John Wick Bowman, "Travelling the Christian Way—The Beatitudes," *RE* 54 (1957): 377-92 [Mt. 5:1-12; Lk. 6:20-26].

3898.   George van Santvoord, "The Teacher," *ATR* 30 (1948): 156-58 [Mt. 5:1-2].

3899.   Henry B. Carry, "Matthew 5:1 and Related Passages," *JBL* 42 (1923): 39-48.

3900.   G. Braumalun, "Zu traditionsgeschichtlichen Problem der Seligpreisungen Mt. v, 3-12," *NT* 4 (1960): 253-60.

3901.   Sebastián Bartina, "Los macarismos del Nuevo Testamento; estudio de la fonna," *EE* 34 (1960): 57-88 [Mt. 5:3-11].

3902.   Dr. Tholuck, "Uebereinstimmung unter den Auslegern des N. Test., nebst einer Beurteilung der Auslegungen von Mt. 5,3-5," *TSK* 5 (1832): 325-54.

3903.   A. Klöpper, "Über den Sinn und die ursprungliche Form der ersten Seligpreisung der Bergpredigt bei Matthäus," *ZWT* 37 (1894): 175-91 [Mt. 5:3].

3904.   T. H. Weir, "Matthew v. 3," *ET* 24 (1912-1913): 44.

3905.   A. Sloman, " 'Blessed Are the Poor in Spirit' Matt. v. 3; cf. Luke vi 20," *JTS* 18 (1916-1917): 34-35.

3906.   R. Ejarque, "Beati pauperes spiritu," *VD* 8 (1928): 129-33, 234-37, 334-41 [Mt. 5:3].

3907.   Vittorio Macchioro, "The Meaning of the First Beatitude," *JR* 12 (1932): 40-49 [Mt. 5:3].

3908.   M. H. Franzmann, "Beggars before God. The First Beatitude," *CTM* 18 (1947): 889-99 [Mt. 5:3].

3909.   J. Smit Sibinga, " 'Zalig de armen van geest'," *VT* 29 (1958): 5-15.

3910.   Ernest Best, "Matthew v. 3," *NTSt* 7 (1960-1961): 255-58.

3911.   Walter Tebbe, "Die zweite Seligpreisung (Matth. 5,4)," *EvT* 12 (1952-1953): 121-28.

3912.   W. E. P. Cotter, "The Meek," *ET* 33 (1921-1922): 280 [Mt. 5:5].

3913.   W. K. Lowther Clarke, "Studies in Texts," *Th* 47 (1944): 131-33 [Mt. 5:5].

3914.   Arthur Jones, " 'Blessed are the pure in (of) heart, for they shall see God' (Matt. v. 8)," *ET* 31 (1919-1920): 522-23.

3915.   Robert Koch, " 'Beati Mundo corde' (Mt. 5' 8)," *VD* 20 (1940): 9-18.

3916.   Augustin George, "Heureux les coeurs purs! Ils variant Dieu! (Matth. 5.8)," *BVC* 13 (1956): 74-79.

3917.   F. G. Peabody, "The Peace-Makers," *NTR* 12 (1919): 51-66 [Mt. 5:9].

3918.   Guy H. Ranson, "Persecuted for Righteousness' Sake," *RE* 53 (1956): 55-60 [Mt. 5:10-12].

3919.   Eb. Nestle, "The Salt of the Earth and the Light of the World," *ET* 20 (1908-1909): 565 [Mt. 5:13-16].

3920.   F. W. Eberhardt, "The Social Imperatives of the Kingdom of Heaven on Earth," *RE* 37 (1940): 163-72, 286-94, 397-407

[Mt. 5:13-16].

3921. Georg Aicher, "Mt. 5' 13: Ihr seid das Salz der Erde?" *BibZ* 5 (1907): 48-59.

3922. J. ten Hove, "Het zout der aarde," *TT* 46 (1912): 252-54 [Mt. 5:13; Mk. 9:50; Lk. 14:34-35].

3923. Arthur Carr, "Salt," *ET* 26 (1914-1915): 139-40 [Mt. 5:13].

3924. Harold C. Wilson, "The Salt of the Earth," *ET* 35 (1923-1924): 136-37 [Mt. 5:13; Mk. 9:50; Lk. 14:34-35].

3925. J. H. Morrison, " 'Ye are the salt of the earth'," *ET* 46 (1934-1935): 525 [Mt. 5:13].

3926. A. J. Mee, " 'Ye are the salt of the earth'," *ET* 46 (1933-1934): 476-77 [Mt. 5:13].

3927. J. B. Bauer, " 'Quod si sal infatuatum fuerit' (Mt. 5,13; Mc. 9,50; Lc. 14,34)," *VD* 29 (1951): 228-30.

3928. W. Hersey Davis, "Don't Hide Your Light?" *RE* 33 (1936): 400-401 [Mt. 5:14-16].

3929. W. Taylor Smith, "Matthew v. 14," *ET* 8 (1896-1897). 138.

3930. P. M. Bretscher, "Brief Studies: The Light of the World," *CTM* 30 (1959): 931-36 [Mt. 5:14].

3931. A. Klöpper, "Zum Stellung Jesu gegenuber dem mosaischen Gesetze (Matth. 5,17-48)," *ZWT* 39 (1896): 1-23.

3932. Henry E. Turlington, "Jesus and the Law," *RE* 53 (1956): 34-45 [Mt. 5:17-48].

3933. H. C. Touw, "De exegese van Mattheus 5:17-48," *VT* 9 (1937-1938): 169-74.

3934. H. N. Ridderbos, "De exegese van Mattheus 5:17-48," *VT* 9 (1937-1938): 162-69.

3935. E. B. A. Poortman, "De exegese van Mattheus 5:17-48," *VT* 9 (1937-1938). 181-87.

3936. T. Dokter, "De exegese van Mattheus 5:17-48," *VT* 9 (1937-1938): 175-80.

3937. Augustin George, "Soyez parfaits comme votre Pere céleste (Matth. 5,17-48)," *BVC* no. 19 (1957): 85-90.

3938. Eduard Schweizer, "Matth. 5.17-20—Anmerkungen zu Gesetzesverständnis des Matthäus," *TLZ* 77 (1952): 479-84.

3939. Dean A. Walker, "Idealism and Opportunism in Jesus, Teaching: A Study of Matt. 5:17-20," *BW* 17 (1901): 433-38.

3940. Pastor Wiessen, "Zu Matth. 5,17.20," *ZNW* 3 (1902):

336-52.

3941. J. H. Semmelink, "Theologisch-exegetische Opmerkingen," *NedTT* 1 (1946-1946): 340-46 [Mt. 5:17; 23:23].

3942. N. Warner, "Mattheus 5:17," *GTT* 48 (1948): 33-50.

3943. E. Wending, "Zu Matthäus 5,18.19," *ZNW* 5 (1904): 253-56.

3944. A. M. Honeyman, "Matthew v. 18 and the Validity of the Law," *NTSt* 1 (1954-1955): 141-42.

3945. J. Conner, "Matthew v. 18," *ET* 38 (1926-1927): 469.

3946. E. F. Sutcliffe, "One Jot or Tittle, Mt. 5. 18," *B* 9 (1928): 458-60.

3947. Franz Dibelius, "Zu Worte Jesu," *ZNW* 11 (1910): 188-92 [Mt. 5:19; 11:11].

3948. Heinz Schurmann, "Wer taker eines dieser geringsten Gebote auflost . . .", *BibZ* 4 (1960): 238-50 [Mt. 5:19].

3949. H. Liese, "De iustitia evangelic a (Mt. 5,20-24)," *VD* 12 (1932): 16-67.

3950. Olivo Olivieri, "Dico enim vibes' quia nisi abundaverit iustitia vestry plus quam scribarum et pharisaeorum non intrabitis in regnum caelorum," *B* 5 (1924): 201-205 [Mt. 5:20].

3951. T. H. Weir, "Matthew v. 20," *ET* 23 (1911-1912): 430-31.

3952. M. Weise, "Mt. 5,21 f.—ein Zeugnis sakraler Rechtsprechung in der Urgemeinde," *ZNW* 49 (1958): 116-23.

3953. George A. Barton, "The Meaning of the 'Royal Law,' Matt. 5:21-48," *JBL* 37 (1918): 54-65.

3954. V. Hasler, "Das Herzstück der Bergpredigt. Zum Verständnis der Antithesen in Matth. 5.21-48," *TZ* 15 (1959): 90-106.

3955. C. F. D. Moule, "Matthew v. 21, 22," *ET* 50 (1938-1939): 189-90.

3956. J. Th. Ensfelder, "Étude exégétique sur Matthieu v, 21 & 22," *RT* 2 (1851): 171-75.

3957. John P. Peters, "On Matthew v. 21-22," *JBL* 11 (1892): 131-32.

3958. W. O. E. Oesterley, "The Study of the Synoptic Gospels Exemplified by Matthew v. 21, 22," *Exp*, 6th ser., 12 (1905): 17-32.

3959.   P. J. Gloag, "Our Lord's View of the Sixth Commandment," *ET* 4 (1892-1893): 492-96 [Mt. 5:21-22].

3960.   Kemper Fullerton, "Raka," *ET* 15 (1903-1904): 429-31 [Mt. 5:22].

3961.   David Smith, "Raka!" *ET* 15 (1903-1904): 235-37 [Mt. 5:22].

3962.   P. Wernberg Møller, "A Semitic Idiom in Matt. v. 22," *NTSt* 3 (1956-1957): 71-73.

3963.   Walter A. Raikes, "Thou Fool," *ET* 4 (1892-1893): 514-15 [Mt. 5:22].

3964.   W. K. Lowther Clarke, "Studies in Texts," *Th* 5 (1922): 37-38 [Mt. 5:22].

3965.   Eb. Nestle, "Matt. v. 22," *ET* 11 (1899-1900): 381-82

3966.   Konrad Kohler, "Zu Mt. 5,22," *ZNW* 19 (1919-1920): 91-95.

3967.   Edw. S. Reaves, "What did Jesus Teach about Forgiving?" *RE* 18 (1921): 282-86 [Mt. 5:23; 18:15ff.].

3968.   Joachim Germs, " 'Lass oldie deine Gabe' (Mt. 5,23 f.)," *ZNW* 36 (1937): 150-54.

3969.   Jos. Vecchi, "In locum quendam Salviani observations," *VCh* 4 (1950): 190-92 [Mt. 5:28].

3970.   F.-M. Abel, "Coup d'ceil sur la Koine," *RB* 35 (1926): 5-26 [Mt. 5:29,38; 18:9].

3971.   H. Clavier, "Matthew 5.29 et la non-résistance," *RHPR* 27 (1957): 44-57.

3972.   Joseph Sickenberger, "Zwei neue Ausserungen zum Ehebruchklausel bei Mt.," *ZNW* 42 (1949): 202-209 [Mt. 5:31ff.; 19:7].

3973.   Heinrich Graven, "Zu den Aussagen des Neues Testaments über die Ehe," *ZEE* 1 (1957): 109-25 [Mt. 5:31,32; 19:3-9; Mk. 10:2-12; Lk. 16:18].

3974.   Bruce Vawter, "The Divorce Clauses in Mt. 5,32 and 19,9," *CBQ* 16 (1954): 155-67.

3975.   W. K. Lowther Clarke, "The Excepting Clause in St. Matthew," *Th* 15 (1927): 161-62 [Mt. 5:32; 19:9].

3976.   U. Holzmeister, "Die Streitfrage über die Ehescheidungstexte bei Matthäus 5,32 and 19,9," *B* 26 (1945): 133-46.

3977.   A. Vaccari, "La clausola del divorcee in Mt. 5,32; 19,9," *RivB* 3 (1955): 97-119.

3978.   E. P. Groenewald, "Grond vir egskeiding volgens Matthëus," *NGTT* 1, no. 4 (1960): 5-12 [Mt. 5:32].

3979.   W. Bäumlein, "Die exegetische Grundlage der Gesetzgebung über Ehescheidung," *TSK* 30 (1857): 329-30 [Mt. 5:32; 19:3ff.].

3980.   A. Tafi, " 'Except a fornicationis causa' (Mt. 5,32)," *VD* 26 (1948): 18-26.

3981.   Bernard Leeming and R. A. Dyson, "Except it be for Fornication?" *Scr* 8 (1956): 75-82 [Mt. 5:32].

3982.   Heinrich Baltensweiler, "Die Ehebruchsklauseln bei Matthäus," *TZ* 15 (1959): 340-56 [Mt. 5:32; 19:9].

3983.   Friedrich Nägelsbach, "Die hohen Forderungen der Bergpredigt (Mt. 5:33-42)," *NKZ* 30 (1919): 510-32.

3984.   J. Weener, "Mt. 5. 33-37," *NTS* 4 (1921): 74-79.

3985.   Olivo Olivieri, "Nolite iurare omnio," *B* 4 (1923): 385-90 [Mt. 5:34].

3986.   E. F. Sutcliffe, "Not to Swear at all," *Scr* 5 (1952): 68-69 [Mt. 5:34].

3987.   David Daube, "Matthew v. 38 f.," *JTS* 45 (1944): 177-87.

3988.   H. E. Bryant, "Matthew v.38, 39," *ET* 48 (1936-1937): 236-37.

3989.   W. Hope Davidson, "Note on Matthew v. 39," *ET* 22 (1910-1911): 231.

3990.   E. Wallace Archer, "Matthew v.39," *ET* 42 (1930-1931): 190-91.

3991.   U. Holzmeister, "Vom Schlagen auf die rechte Wange (Mt. 5:39)," *ZKT* 45 (1921): 334-36.

3992.   J. Skvireckas, "Nesipriešinkite piktans ['Non resistere malo' Mt. 5,39]," Σ 5 (1928): 15-21.

3993.   E. F. Sutcliffe, "Not to resist Evil," *Scr* 5 (1952): 33-35 [Mt. 5:39].

3994.   J. Honeymoon, "Nochmals Matth. 5, 42 ff.," *BibZ* 24 (1938-1939): 136-38.

3995.   Paul Jouon, "Matthew v,43," *RSR* 20 (1930): 545-46.

3996.   Morton Smith, "Mt. 5. 43: 'Hate thine Enemy'," *HTR* 45 1952): 71-73.

3997.   J. E. Yates, "Studies in Texts," *Th* 44 (1942): 48-51 [Mt. 5:44].

3998. E. M. Sidebottom, " 'Reward' in Matthew v. 46, etc.," *ET* 67 (1955-1956): 219-20.

3999. Anton Fridrichsen, "Fullkomlighetskravet i Jesu förkunnelse," *STK* 9 (1933): 124-33 [Mt. 5:48].

4000. Ronald Gregor Smith, "Studies in Texts," *Th* 45 (1942): 93-95 [Mt. 5:48].

4001. W. K. Lowther Clarke, "Studies in Texts," *Th* 20 (1930): 43-44 [Mt. 5:48].

4002. C. Sandegren, "Be ye Perfect!" *ET* 61 (1949-1950): 383 [Mt. 5:48].

4003. Augustin George, "La justice a faire dans le secret," *B* 40 (1959): 590-98 [Mt. 6:1-6 and 6:16-18].

4004. T. Biebericher, "Christus en het eudaimonisme, naar aanleiding van Matth. vi.1-5," *TS* 28 (1910): 24-31.

4005. A. Buchler, "St. Matthew vi. 1-6 and Other Allied Passages," *JTS* 10 (1908-1909): 266-70.

4006. Albert Bonus, "Righteousness and Almsgiving and St. Matthew vi.1," *ET* 11 (1899-1900): 379-81.

4007. Walter Nagel, "Gerechtigkeit—oder Almosen?" *VCh* 15 (1961): 141-45 [Mt. 6:1].

4008. Erich Klostermann, "Zum Verständnis von Mt. 6, 2," *ZNW* 47 (1956): 280-81.

4009. A. van der Flier, "Een fijn trekje in de kekening der Farizeen in de Bergrede (Mt. 6. 2, 5)," *NTS* 1 (1918): 111.

4010. Eb. Nestle, "Matt. vi. 3," *ET* 13 (1901 1902): 524-25.

4011. Dr. Reinäcker, "Über die Abweichungen im Gebete des Herrn nach dem Lutherischen und nach dem Heidelberger Katechismus," *TSK* 10 (1837): 328-50 [Mt. 6:9-13].

4012. T. E. Page, "Critical Notes on the Lord's Prayer," *Exp* 3rd ser., 7 (1888): 433-40 [Mt. 6:9-13].

4013. Pfarrer Kind, "Das Gebet des Herrn," *STZ* 6 (1889): 210-26 [Mt. 6:9-13].

4014. Albert S. Cook, "The Evolution of the Lord's Prayer in English," *AJP* 12 (1891): 59-66 [Mt. 6:9-13].

4015. F. W. Farrar, "Exegetic Studies on the Lord's Prayer," *Exp* 4th ser., 7 (1893): 38-49, 283-93 [Mt. 6:9-13].

4016. A. N. Jannaris, "The Lord's Prayer," *ET* 6 (1894-1995): 190-91 [Mt. 6:9-13].

4017.   Lyder Brun, "Herrens bøn," *NTT* 1 (1900): 254-86, 305-49; 2 (1901): 230-62, 289-336 [Mt. 6:9-13].

4018.   Eb. Nestle, "The Arrangement of the Lord's Prayer," *ET* 13 (1901-1902): 431-32 [Mt. 6:9-13].

4019.   A. Wabnitz, "Le vrai sens de la quatrième demande de la prière dominicale," *RTQR* 11 (1902): 380-85 [Mt. 6:9-13].

4020.   Dr. Schneider, "Zum Gebet des Herrn," *STZ* 20 (1903): 123-24 [Mt. 6:9-13].

4021.   A. T. W. Steinhauser, "The Lord's Prayer in Matthew and Luke," *LCR* 23 (1904): 546-49 [Mt. 6:9-13; Lk. 11:2-4].

4022.   Gustav Honnicke, "Neue Forschungen zum Vaterunser bei Matthäus und Lukas," *NKZ* 17 (1906): 57-67, 106-20, 169-80.

4023.   G. Klein, "Die ursprüngliche Gestalt des Vaterunsers," *ZNW* 7 (1906): 34-50 [Mt. 6:9-13].

4024.   Charles H. Richards, "The Pearl of Prayers," *BS* 63 (1906): 635-52 [Mt. 6:9-13].

4025.   Ernst von Dobschütz, "The Lord's Prayer," *HTR* 7 (1914): 293-321 [Mt. 6:9-13].

4026.   J.-B. Frey, "Le Pater est-il juif ou chrétien?" *RB* 24 (1915): 556-63 [Mt. 6:9-13].

4027.   Margaret D. Gibson, "The Lord's Prayer," *ET* 28 (1916-1917): 41 [Mt. 6:9-13].

4028.   Donald B. Maclane, "The Lord's Prayer in a Dozen Languages," *BS* 75 (1918): 527-42 [Mt. 6:9-13].

4029.   George Hebert Palmer, "The Lord's Prayer," *HTR* 13 (1920): 124-35 [Mt. 6:9-13].

4030.   John A. Hutton, "'When ye pray, say' Our Father!," *ET* 36 (1924-1925): 121-24.

4031.   Walter G. White, "The Lord's Prayer," *ET* 36 (1924-1925): 90-91 [Mt. 6:9-13].

4032.   Werner Petersmann, "The Gospel in the Lord's Prayer," *BS* 87 (1930): 284-97.

4033.   Anton Fridrichsen, "Fader vår," *STK* 10 (1934): 128-51.

4034.   T. M. Donn, "The Lord's Prayer. Directory or Formula?" *EQ* 9 (1937): 426-34.

4035.   Ernst Lohmeyer, "Das Vater-Unser als Ganzheit," *TB* 17 (1938): 217-27.

4036. C. G. Sheward, "The Lord's Prayer: A Study in Sources," *ET* 52 (1940-1941): 119-20.

4037. Albert Kleber, "The Lord's Prayer and the Decalog," *CBQ* 3 (1941): 302-20.

4038. G. H. Smukal, "The Lord's Prayer, the Pastor's Prayer," *CTM* 16 (1945): 145-53, 236-49, 301-306, 396-404, 466-73, 505-13, 583-91, 666-72, 757-65, 842-48.

4039. M. Meinertz, "Das Vaterunser," *Trove* 45 (1949): 1-6.

4040. B. Schultze, "Untersuchungen über das Jesus-Gebet," *OCP* 18 (1952): 319-43.

4041. T. W. Manson, "The Lord's Prayer," *BJRL* 38 (1955-1956): 99-113, 436-48.

4042. J. Alonso Díaz, "El problema literario del Padre Nuestro," *EB* 18 (1959): 63-75.

4043. Wilhelm Fresenius, "Beobachtungen und Gedanken zum Gebet des Herrn," *EvT* 20 (1960): 235-39.

4044. Joachim Jeremias, "The Lord's Prayer in Modern Research," *ET* 71 (1959-1960): 151-56.

4045. Raymond E. Brown, "The Pater Noster as an Eschatological Prayer," *Theist* 22 (1961): 175-208.

4046. R. F. Cyster, "The Lord's Prayer and the Exodus Tradition," *ZWT* 64 (1961): 377-81.

4047. A. G., "Explicación exegética de las petitions del Padre Nuestro," *CB* 10 (1953): 375-77 [Mt. 6:9,10].

4048. E. F. Morrison, " 'Hallowed be thy Name'," *ET* 28 (1916-1917): 298-300 [Mt. 6:9].

4049. Walter G. White, " 'Thy Kingdom come'," *ET* 33 (1921-1922): 523-24 [Mt. 6:10].

4050. R. Thibaut, "Que votre regne advienne (Math. vi,10; Luc. xi,2)," *NRT* 49 (1922): 555-58 [Mt. 6:10].

4051. Millar Burrows, "Thy Kingdom Come," *JBL* 74 (1955): 1-8 [Mt. 6:10].

4052. G. H. P. Thompson, "Thy Will be Done in Earth, as it is in Heaven (Matthew vi.10). A Suggested Re-interpretation," *ET* 70 (1958-1959): 379-81.

4053. M.-E. Jacquemin, "La portee de la truism demande du Pater," *ETL* 25 (1949): 61-76 [Mt. 6:10b].

4054. Fr. Zero, "Noch einmal Matth. 6:11: τὸν ἄρτον ἡμῶν τὸν ἐπιούσιον δὸς ἡμῖν σήμερον," *TSK* 45 (1872): 709-15.

4055. Hermann Rönsch, "Die griechische Fassung der vierten Bitte im Vaterunser," *ZWT* 27 (1884): 385-93 [Mt. 6:11].

4056. J. K. Edwards, "The Word ἐπιούσιος in the Fourth Petition of the Lord's Prayer," *ZWT* 29 (1886): 371-78 [Mt. 6:11].

4057. H. W. Horwill and R. M. Spence, "Our 'Daily' Bread," *ET* 2 (1890-1891): 254-56 [Mt. 6:11].

4058. J. B. McClellen, "On the Rendering 'Daily Bread' in the Lord's Prayer," *ET* 2 (1890-1891): 184-88 [Mt. 6:11].

4059. J. A. Clapperton, Alfred Gill, J. T. Marshall, and F. Tilney Bassett, "The Lord's Prayer," *ET* 3 (1891-1892): 24-31 [Mt. 6:11].

4060. L. S. Potwin, "The Old Syriac Version of the Lord's Prayer: The Rendering of ἐπιουσιος," *BS* 51 (1894): 165-68 [Mt. 6:11].

4061. Eb. Nestle, "Unser täglich Brot," *ZNW* 1 (1900): 250-52 [Mt. 6:11].

4062. Lemuel S. Potwin, "Ἐπιουσιος," *JBL* 12 (1893): 15-22 [Mt. 6:11].

4063. Eb. Nestle, "Ἐπιουσιος in Hebrew and Aramaic," *ET* 21 (1909-1910): 43 [Mt. 6:11].

4064. Adolf Bulgier, "Die vierte Bitte des Unservaters," *STZ* 30 (1913): 276-85 [Mt. 6:11].

4065. Paul Wilh. Schmiedel, " 'Unser tägliches Brot'," *STZ* 30 (1913): 204-20 [Mt. 6:11].

4066. A. Debrunner, "Nochmals 'Unser tägliches Brot'," *STZ* 31 (1914): 38-41 [Mt. 6:11].

4067. A. Kappeler, "Die 4. Bitte im Unservater," *STZ* 31 (1914): 147-56 [Mt. 6:11].

4068. G. Kuhn, "Zu Verständnis des Wortes epiousios im Unservater," *STZ* 31 (1914): 33-38 [Mt. 6:11].

4069. Paul Wilh. Schmiedel, "Nochmals 'Unser tägliches Brot'," *STZ* 31 (1914): 41-69, 192-93 [Mt. 6:11].

4070. A. Kappeler, "Zum vierten Bitte im Unservater," *STZ* 32 (1915): 118-22 [Mt. 6:11].

4071. William Clifford, Give us this day our daily bread'," *ET* 28 (1916-1917): 523-24 [Mt. 6:11].

4072. J. Waterink, " 'Dagelijksch' brood," *GTT* 17 (1916-1917):

163-68 tMt.6:11].

4073. F. G. Chalmondeley, Give us this day our daily bread," *ET* 29 (1917-1918): 139-40 [Mt. 6:11].

4074. G. Kuhn, "Unser tägliches Brot," *STZ* 36 (1919): 191-96 [Mt. 6:11].

4075. D. T. James, "'Επιουσιος, (Luke xi. 3, Matt. vi. 11)," *ET* 32 (1920-1921): 428 [Mt. 6:11].

4076. Franz Zorell, "'Επιουσιος," *B* 6 (1925): 321-22 [Mt. 6:11; Lk. 11:3].

4077. Thomas G. Shearman, "Our Daily Bread," *JBL* 53 (1934): 110-17 [Mt. 6:11].

4078. Sigmund Mowinckel, "Artos epiousios," *NTT* 40 (1939): 247-55 [Mt. 6:11].

4079. Matthew Günter "The Aramaic of τὸν ἄρτον ἡμῶν τὸν ἐπιούσιον (Matt. vi. 11 = Luke xi. 3)," *JTS* 42 (1941): 186-89.

4080. John Hennig, "Our Daily Bread," *Theist* 4 (1943): 445-54.

4081. William K. Prentice, "Our 'Daily' Bread," *RR* 11 (1946-1947): 126-31.

4082. T. M. Donn, "Our Daily Bread," *EQ* 21 (1949): 209-18.

4083. E. L. Wenger, "Our Bread for the Morrow," *ET* 62 (1950-1951): 285.

4084. Bruce M. Metzger, "Num bis relata sit, extra orationem Dominicam, vox epiousios?" *VD* 34 (1956): 349-51 [Mt. 6:11].

4085. Bruce M. Metzger, "How Many Times does 'epiousios' Occur Outside the Lord's Prayer?" *ET* 69 (1957): 52-54 [Mt. 6:11].

4086. D. Y. Hadidian, "The Meaning of ἐπιούσιον and the Codices Sergii," *NTSt* 5 (1958-1959): 75-81.

4087. D. M. Grant, " 'Debts' or trespasses'?" *ET* 36 (1924-1925): 526 [Mt. 6:12].

4088. F. C. Burkitt, "As We Have Forgiven," *JTS* 33 (1931-1932). 253-55 [Mt. 6:12].

4089. F. Fensham, "The Legal Background of Mt. vi, 12," *NT* 4 (1960): 1-2.

4090. Lemuel S. Potwin, "Does the Lord's Prayer Make Mention of the Devil?" *BS* 48 (1891): 332-39 [Mt. 6:13].

4091. L. S. Potwin, "Critical Note—Further on τοῦ πνηροῦ in the Lord's Prayer," *BS* 48 (1891): 686-97 [Mt. 6A].

4092. Johns Heller, "Die sechste Bitte des Vaterunser," *ZKT* 25 (1901): 85-93 [Mt. 6:13].

4093. William Muss-Arnolt, "Professor Harnack on Two Words of Jesus," *BW* 32 (1908): 262-66 [Mt. 6:13; Lk. 16:16].

4094. Frank Eakin, "Why the 'the'?" *ET* 30 (1918-1919): 524-25 [Mt. 6:13].

4095. Ch. Jaeger, "À propos de deux passages du sermon sur la montagne (Matthew 6,13; 5,21 et 33)," *RHPR* 18 (1938): 415-18.

4096. H. R. Wilson, " 'And lead us not into temptation'," *Th* 37 (1938): 302-304 [Mt. 6:13].

4097. J. N. Hoare, " 'Lead us not into temptation'," *ET* 50 (1938-1939): 333.

4098. R. H. Mode, "Lead us not into Temptation," *CQ* 17 (1940): 93-97.

4099. A. J. B. Higgins, " 'Lead us not into temptation': Some Latin Variants," *JTS* 46 (1945): 179-83.

4100. E. H. Blakeney, "Matthew 6:13—Luke 11:4; cf. Mark 14:38," *ET* 57 (1945-1946): 279.

4101. A. J. B. Higgins, "Lead us not into Temptation," *ET* 58 (1946-1947): 250.

4102. G. B. Venty, "Lead us not into Temptation but . . .," *ET* 58 (1946-1947): 221-22.

4103. W. Powell, " 'Lead us not into Temptation but ...'," *ET* 59 (1947-1948): 25.

4104. W. Powell, " 'Lead us not into temptation'," *ET* 67 (1955-1956): 177-78.

4105. J. B. Bauer, "Libera nos a malo (Mt. 6,13)," *VD* 34 (1956): 12-15.

4106. T. van Bavel, "Inferas—Inducas. À propos de Matth. 6,13, dans les ceuvres de saint Augustin," *RBén* 69 (1959): 348-51.

4107. Marjorie H. Sykes, "And do not Bring us to the Test," *ET* 73 (1961-1962): 189-90.

4108. Michael Walker, "Lead us not into Temptation," *ET* 73 (1961-1962): 287.

4109.   I. Hoh, "Christus human I civilisque cultus fautor (Mt. 6, 17)," *VD* 2 (1922): 204-206.

4110.   W. Pesch, "Zur Exegese von Mt. 6,19-21 und Lk. 12,33-34," *B* 41 (1960): 356-78.

4111.   A. T. Burchridge, "Singleness of Vision," *Exp* 6th ser., 2 (1900): 277-87 [Mt. 6:22-23; Lk. 11:33-36].

4112.   Paul Fiebig, "Das Wore Jesu vom Auge," *TSK* 89 (1916): 499-507 tMt. 6:22, 23; Lk. 11:34-36].

4113.   J. van Gilse, "Exegetische Studien," *TT* 10 (1876): 537-48 [Mt. 6:22-23; Jn. 19:11].

4114.   Friednch Schwencke, "Das Auge ist des Leibes Licht, " *ZWT* 55 (1914): 251-60 [Mt. 6:22 f.; Lk. 11:34-36].

4115.   W Brandt, "Der Spruch vom lumen internum, " *ZNW* 14 (1913): 97-116 [Mt. 6:22f.].

4116.   Erik Sjøberg, "Das Licht in dir. Zum Deutung von Matth. 6,22f. Par.," *ST* 5 (1951): 89-105 [especially Mt. 6:23].

4117.   Henry J. Cadbury, "The Single Eye," *HTR* 47 (1954): 69-74 [Mt. 6:22; Lk. 11:34].

4118.   C. Ryder Smith, "The Evil Eye, "*ET* 54 (1942-1943): 26 [Mt. 6:23, etc.].

4119   J. Duncan Percy, "An Evil Eye," *ET* 54 (1942-1943): 26-27 [Mt. 6:23, etc.].

4120.   A. Whyte, "Christ the Interpreter of Nature (Mt. vi,24-34)," *Exp* 3rd ser., 2 (1885): 224-32.

4121.   P. Emmanuel a S. Marco, "Quaerite ergo premium regnum Dei et iustitiam eius (Mt. 6,24-33)," *VD* 10 (1930): 281-86.

4122.   U. Holzmeister, " 'Nemo potest duobus dominis servire, (Mt. 6,24)," *VD* 3 (1923): 304-306.

4123.   Eb. Nestle, "Matt. vi. 24 = Luke xvi. 13," *ET* 19 (1907-1908): 284.

4124.   C. Sandegren, "A Mostly Misunderstood Section of the Sermon on the Mount," *EQ* 23 (1951): 134-38 [Mt. 6:25 ff.].

4125.   Paul Schruers, "La paternity divine dans Mt. v,45 et vi, 26-32," *ETL* 36 (1960): 593-624.

4126.   George B. King, " 'Consider the Lillies'," *CQ* 10 (1933): 28-35.

4127.   T. C. Skeat, "The Lilies of the Field," *ZNW* 37 (1938): 211-14 [Mt. 6:28].

4128.   M. et Mme. É. Ha-Reubeni, "Les lis des champs: recherches sur les plantes de l'évangile," *RB* 54 (1947): 362-64 [Mt. 6:28; Lk. 12:27].

4129.   W. H. P. Hatch, "A Note on Matthew 6:33," *HTR* 38 (1945): 270-72.

4130.   F. Nötscher, "Das Reich (Gottes) und seine Gerechtigkeit," *B* 31 (1950): 237-41 [Mt. 6:33].

4131.   Franciscus Zorell, " ' Ἀρκετός, Mt. 6,34: 'Sufficit diei malitia sua'," *B* 1 (1920): 95-96.

4132.   Kenneth J. Foreman, "A Possible Interpretation of Matthew 7," *Interp* 1 (1947): 66-67.

4133.   George B. King, "The Mote and the Beam," *HTR* 17 (1924): 393-404. [Mt. 7:3-5].

4134.   Charles A. Webster, "The Mote and the Beam (Luke vi. 41,42 = Matt. vii. 3-5)," *ET* 39 (1927-1928): 91-92.

4135.   P. L. Headily, " 'The Mote and the Beam' and 'The Gates of Hades'," *ET* 39 (1927-1928): 427-28 [Mt. 7:3-5; 16:18].

4136.   George B. King, "A Further Note on the Mote and the Beam (Matt. vii. 3-5; Luke vi. 41-42)," *HTR* 26 (1933): 73-76.

4137.   L. Delaporte, "Matthew vii, 4-27, d'après un papyrus de la Bibliothèque Nationale," *RB* 25 (1916): 560-64.

4138.   A. M. Perry, " 'Pearls before Swine'," *ET* 46 (1934- 1935): 381-82 [Mt. 7:6].

4139.   Donald McGillivray, "Matthew vii. 6," *ET* 27 (1915-1916): 46.

4140.   G. Castellini, "Struttura letteraria di Mt. 7,6," *RivB* 2 (1954): 310-17.

4141.   T. F. Glasson, "Chiasmus in St. Matthew vii. 6," *ET* 68 (1956-1957): 302.

4142.   C. G. Chavannes, "Matth. 7,7-11," *TT* 29 (1895): 72-76.

4143.   Günther Bornkamm, " 'Bittet, suchet, klopfet an'," *EvT* 13 (1953-1954): 1-5 [Mt. 7:7].

4144.   James Coffin Stout, "Matthew 7:9-11—A Translation," *BR* 3 (1918): 132-37.

4145.   W. J. Ferrar, "A Note on St. Matthew vii. 9," *ET* 17 (1905-1906): 478.

4146.   Borge Hjerl-Hansen, "Le rapprochement poison-serpent dans la prédication de Jésus (Mt. vii,10 et Luc xi,11)," *RB* 55

(1948): 195-98.

4147. E. W. Hirst, "The Implications of the Golden Rule," *ET* 26 (1914-1915): 555-58 [Mt. 7:12, Lk. 6:13].

4148. E. A. Sonnenschein, "The Golden Rule and its Application to Present Conditions," *HJ* 13 (1914-1915): 859-66 [Mt. 7:12; Lk. 6:31].

4149. W. H. P. Hatch, "A Syriac Parallel to the Golden Rule," *HTR* 14 (1921): 193-95.

4150. R. H. Connolly, "A Negative Form of the Golden Rule in the Diatessaron?" *JTS* 35 (1934): 351-57.

4151. Owen E. Evans, "The Negative Form of the Golden Rule in the Diatessaron," *ET* 63 (1951-1952): 31-32.

4152. Bruce M. Metzger, "The Designation 'The Golden Rule'," *ET* 69 (1958): 304 [Mt. 7:12].

4153. L. Fonck, "Attendite a falsis prophetis (Mt. 7,15-21)," *VD* 2 (1922): 198-204.

4154. Peter Orr, "The Will of My Father," *Scr* 4 (1950): 146-48 [Mt. 7:21].

4155. A. B. Bruce, "The Wise and the Foolish Hearer," *Exp* 1st ser., 9 (1879): 90-105 [Mt. 7:24-27; Lk. 6:47-49].

4156. Eb. Nestle, "Matt. vii. 25, 27," *ET* 19 (1907-1908): 237-38.

4157. James P. Wilson, "In Matthew vii. 25 is προσέπεσαν a Primitive Error Displacing προσέπεψαν?" *ET* 57 (1945-1946): 138.

4158. L. Fonck, "Surdus et mutus sanatur (Mt. 7, 31-37)," *VD* 4 (1924): 231-36.

4159. John C. Hawkins, "The Arrangement of Materials in St. Matthew viii-ix," *ET* 12 (1900-1901): 471-74; 13 (1901-1902): 20-25.

4160. Irénée Fransen, "Cahier de Bible: La charte de l'apôtre (Matthieu 8,1-11,1)," *BVC* no. 37 (1961): 34-45.

4161. L. Fonck, "Leprosus sanatur (Mt. 8,2-4)," *VD* 4 (1924): 8-14.

4162. G. A. Chadwick, "The First Leper Healed," *Exp* 4th ser., 6 (1892): 443-454 [Mt. 8:2; Mk. 1:40; Lk. 5:12].

4163. H. F. D. Sparks, "The Centurion's παῖς," *JTS* 42 (1941): 179-80 [Mt. 8:5-13].

4164. G. Zuntz, "The 'Centurion' of Capernaum and his Authority

(Matt. viii. 5-13)," *JTS* 46 (1945): 183-90.

4165. S. H. Hooke, "Jesus and the Centurion:Matthew viii. 5-10," *ET* 69 (1957): 79-80.

4166. Anton Fridrichsen, "Quatre conjectures sur le texte du Nouveau Testament," *RHPR* 3 (1923): 439-42 [Mt. 8:6; Rom. 2:1; Gal. 1:6-9; Phil. 2:5 ff.].

4167. A. Pollyanna, "Miracles—The Problem Solved," *Exp* 2nd ser., 6 (1883): 161-85 [Mt. 8:8-9].

4168. Alfred E. Garvie, "A Man under Authority," *ET* 20 (1908-1909): 377 [Mt. 8:9].

4169. Herbert H. Stainsby, " 'Under Authority'," *ET* 30 (1918-1919): 328-29 [Mt. 8:9].

4170. T. H. Weir, "St. Matthew viii. 9," *ET* 33 (1921-1922): 280.

4171. C. J. Cadoux and George Farmel, "St. Matthew viii. 9," *ET* 32 (1920-1921): 474.

4172. L. Vail, "What Made the Captain's Faith so Great?" *RE* 19 (1922): 310-18 [Mt. 8:9].

4173. Maurice Frost, " 'I also am a man under authority'," *ET* 45 (1933-1934): 477-78 [Mt. 8:9].

4174. R. O. P. Taylor, "The Outer Darkness," *Th* 33 (1936): 277-83 [Mt. 8:12; 22:13; 25:30].

4175. U. Holzmeister, " 'Et ego homo sum sub pot estate constitutes' (Mt. 8,9)," *VD* 17 (1937): 27-32.

4176. G. A. Chadwick, "Peter's Wife's Mother," *Exp* 4th ser., 6 (1892): 335-64 [Mt. 8:14; Mk. 1:29; Lk. 4:38].

4177. E. L. Wenger, "Let the Dead Bury Their Dead," *ET* 62 (1950-1951): 255 [Mt. 8:18-22].

4178. Alexander Stewart, "The Homelessness of Christ," *ET* 8 (1896-1897): 247-50 [Mt. 8:19-20].

4179. John Robson, "The Homelessness of Christ," *ET* 8 (1896-1897): 221-26 [Mt. 8:19-20].

4180. S. Luria, "Zur Quelle von Mt. 8,19," *ZNW* 25 (1926): 282-86.

4181. Augustus Paynder, "The Homelessness of Christ," *ET* 9 (1897-1898): 143 [Mt. 8:20].

4182. Hugh Schonfield, "Floor (Matt. viii. 20)," *ET* 39 (1927-1928): 332.

4183. Eb. Nestle, "A Parallel to Matt. viii. 20," *ET* 11 (1899-1900):

285.

4184. H. G. Howard, "Was his Father Lying Dead at Home?" *ET* 61 (1949-1950): 350-51 [Mt. 8:21-22; Lk. 9:59-60].

4185. W. J. Davies, "Was his Father Lying Dead at Home?" *ET* 62 (1950-1951): 92 [Mt. 8:21; Lk. 9:59-60].

4186. C. S. S. Ellison, "Was his Father Lying Dead at Home?" *ET* 62 (1950-1951): 92 [Mt. 8:21-22; Lk. 9:59-60].

4187. Matthew Günter "Let the Dead Bury their Dead," *ET* 61 (1949-1950): 219-20 [Mt. 8:22; Lk. 9:60].

4188. T. M. Donn, " 'Let the dead bury their dead' (Mt. viii. 22, Lk. ix. 60)," *ET* 61 (1949-1950): 384.

4189. L. Fonck, "Christus imperat ventis et mari (Mt. 8,23-27)," *VD* 3 (1923): 321-28.

4190. Th. Zahn, "Das Land der Gadarener, Gerasener oder Gergesener," *NKZ* 13 (1902): 923-45 [Γεργεσηνῶν, Mt. 8:28-34].

4191. Pfarrer Stocks, "Ein Fall von Kynanthropie im Neuen Testament (Matth. 8,28 ff. und Parallelen)," *NKZ* 18 (1907): 499-506.

4192. Jacques Dupont, "Le paralytique pardonné (Mt. 9,1-8)," *NRT* 82 (1960): 940-58.

4193. L. Fonck, "Paralyticus in Caparnaum sanatur (Mt. 9,1-8)," *VD* 1 (1921): 267-73.

4194. L. Fonck, "Paralyticus per tectum demissus," *B* (1921): 30-44 [Mt. 9:1-8 and parallels].

4195. G. A. Chadwick, "The Paralytic," *Exp* 4th ser., 8 (1893): 226-38 [Mt. 9:1; Mk. 2:1; Lk. 5:17].

4196. F. Warburton Lewis, "New Garments and Old Patches," *ET* 13 (1901-1902): 522 [Mt. 9:14-17; Lk. 5:33-39].

4197. C. W. Atkinson, "The New Patch on an Old Garment (Matthew ix. 16, Mark ii. 21, Luke v. 36)," *ET* 30 (1918-1919) 233-34.

4198. Walter Nagel, "Neuer Wein in alten Schlauchen (Mt. 9,17)," *VCh* 14 (1960): 1-8.

4199. G. A. Chadwick, "The Daughter of Jairus and the Woman with an Issue of Blood (Mt. ix. 18; Mk. v. 22; Lk. viii. 41)," *Exp* 4h ser., 8 (1893): 309-20.

4200. P. Emmanuel a S. Marco, "Mulier hemorroissa sanatur (Mt.

9, 20-22; Mc. 5, 25-34; Lc. 8, 43-48)," *VD* 11 (1931): 321-25.

4201.   Frederick C. Grant, "The Mission of the Disciples," Mt 9:35-11:1 and Parallels," *JBL* 35 (1916): 293-314.

4202.   K. L. Schmidt, "Andacht über Mtth. 9, 35-38," *TB* (1928): 275-76.

4203.   Otto Weber, "Predigt über Matth. 9, 35-38," *EvT* 8 (1948-1949): 117-23.

4204.   Dr. Schegg, "Über Matth. 9, 49-50," *TQ* 50 (1868): 301-16.

4205.   E. Schott, "Die Aussendungsrede Mt 10. Mc 6. Lc 9.10," *ZNW* 7 (1906): 140-50.

4206.   P. Deusch, "Die Jüngerinstruktion Mt. 10 quellenkritisch untersucht," *BibZ* 14 (1916-1917): 25-33.

4207.   Cuthbert Lattey, "The Apostolic Groups," *JTS* 10 (1908-1909)," 107-15 [Mt. 10:2-4; Mk. 3:16-19; Lk. 6:14-16; Ac. 1:13].

4208.   W. Weber, "Die neutestamentlichen Apostellisten," *ZWT* 54 (1912): 8-31 [Mt. 10:2-4]

4209.   A. H. McNeile, "Matthew x. 11-15," *JTS* 11 (1909-1910): 558-59.

4210.   T. H. Weir, "Matthew x. 11," *ET* 28 (1916-1917): 41.

4211.   T. H. Weir, "Matthew x. 16," *ET* 28 (1916-1917): 186.

4212.   R. Ejarque, "Prudentes sicut serpents (Mt. 10, 16)," *VD* 3 (1923): 102-108.

4213.   J. B. Bauer, "Variants de traduction sur l'hébreu?" *Mu* 74 (1961): 435-39 [Mt. 10:16].

4214.   Paul Joüon, "Matthew 10,22: ὑπομένειν 'endurer' et non 'perseverer'," *RSR* 28 (1938): 310-11.

4215.   J. Newport, "Verklaring van Matth. 10,23. Bijdrage tot kenschetsing van het onderling verb en der synoptische Evangeliën," *TT* 13 (1879): 577-97.

4216.   Heinz Schürmann, "Zum Traditions- und Redaktionsgeschichte von Mt. 10,23," *BibZ* 3 (1959): 82-88.

4217.   W. G. Essame, "Matthew x. 23," *ET* 72 (1960-1961): 248.

4218.   Jacques Dupont, " 'Vous n'aurez pas achevé les villes d'Israël avant que le fils de l'homme ne vienne' (Mat. x. 23)," *NT* 2 (1958): 228-44.

4219.   T. H. Weir, "Matthew x. 23," *ET* 37 (1925-1926): 237.

4220. André Feuillet, "Les origines et la signification de Mt. 10,20b," *CBQ* 23 (1961): 182-98.

4221. Niger, "The Disciple not above his Master," *Exp* 1st. ser., 11 (1880): 178-91.

4222. George Christie, "A Text Illustrated," *ET* 29 (1917-1918): 559-60 [Mt. 10:28-33].

4223. W. Warren, "St. Matthew x. 28 and St. Luke xii. 5," *ET* 8 (1896-1897): 430-31.

4224. R. J. Drummond, "The Destroyer of Soul and Body," *ET* 8 (1896-1897): 191-92 [Mt. 10:28 = Lk. 12:5].

4225. Albinos Stolz, "Christi de passeribus parabola (Mt. 10, 29-31)," *VD* 14 (1934): 56.

4226. G. G. Findlay, "The Worth of Sparrows," *Exp* 2nd ser., 7 (1884)· 103-16 [Mt. 10:29-31; Lk. 12:6-7].

4227. F. R. Tenant, "Christ's Conception of Manhood," *ET* 52 (1940-1941): 50-53 [Mt. 10:31].

4228. T. A. Roberts, "Some Comments on Matthew x. 34-36 and Luke xii. 51-53," *ET* 69 (1958): 304-306.

4229. Melancthon W. Jacobus, A. T. Robertson, James S. Riggs, Charles E. Jefferson, Charles R. Brown, "Did Jesus Favor Militarism? A Symposium on Matt. 10:34," *BW* 46 (1915): 300-303.

4230. Paul Doncoeur, "Gagner ou perdre sa ψυχή," *RSR* 35 (1948): 114-19 [Mt. 10:37-39; 16:24-26; Mk. 8:35-37; Lk. 9:23-25; 14:26; 17:33; Jn 12:26].

4231. Frank S. Hickman, "He that Loseth his Life," *RE* 37 (1940): 387-96 [Mt. 10:38-39].

4232. T. Arvedson, "Phil. 2,6 und Mt. 10,39," *ST* 5 (1951): 49-51.

4233. S. Cox, "Service and Reward," *Exp* 2nd ser., 4 (1882): 81-100 [Mt. 10:41].

4234. H. L. Oort, "Mattheus xi. en de Johannes-gemeenten," *TT* 42 (1908): 299-333.

4235. Irénée Fransen, "Cahier de Bible: Le discours en paraboles (Matthew 11,2-13,53)," *BVC* no. 18 (1957): 72-84.

4236. Friedrich Spitta, "Die Sendung des Täufers zu Jesus," *TSK* 83 (1910): 534-51 [Mt. 11 2-19; Lk. 7:16-35].

4237. Salami Hirsch, "Studien zu Matthäus 11,2-26. Zugleich ein Beitrag zur Geschichte Jesu und zur Frage seines

Selbstbewusstseins," *TZ* 6 (1950): 241-60.

4238. M. Brink, "De legatione Johannis Baptistae (Mt. 11,2-24)," *VD* 35 (1957): 193-203, 262-70, 321-31.

4239. L. Fonck, "Nuntii Iohannis (Mt. 11,2-10)," *VD* 3 (1923): 357-65.

4240. Jacques Dupont, "L'ambassade de Jean-Baptiste (Matthew 11,2-6; Luc 7,18-23)," *NRT* 83 (1961): 805-21, 943-59.

4241. John Macleod, "John the Baptist's Question," *EQ* 1 (1929): 166-80 [Mt. 11:2-5].

4242. A. Spaeth, "An Exegetical Study of Matthew 11:3," *LCR* 2 (1883): 289-98.

4243. James Moffatt, "Matthew xi. 5," *ET* 18 (1906-1907): 286-87.

4244. John A. Hutton, " 'The Lame Walk' (Matt. xi. 5)," *ET* 35 (1923-1924): 164-68.

4245. H. A. A. Kennedy, "The Functions of the Forerunner and the Storming of the Kingdom," *Exp* 7th ser., 6 (1908): 537-46 [Mt. 11:7-15].

4246. C. P. Shannon, " 'A Reed Shaken with the Wind' (Matt. xi. 7)," *ET* 21 (1909-1910): 379.

4247. Anton Fredrickson, "Neutestamentliche Wortforschung zu Matth. 11, 11-15," *TZ* 2 (1946): 470-71.

4248. H. J. Toxopeüs, "Mattheus xi.ii," *TT* 49 (1915): 483-89.

4249. E. F. Scott, "The Kingdom of Heaven Suffereth Violence: An Exposition of Matt. 11:12,13," *BW* 30 (1907): 460-63.

4250. S. Cox, "Spiritual Forces," *Exp* 1st. ser., 3 (1876): 252-64 [Mt. 11:12].

4251. Fr. Zero, "Neue Auslegung der Stelle Matth. 11:12: ἀπὸ δὲ τῶν ἡμνερῶν Ἰωάννου τοῦ βαπτιστοῦ ἕως ἄρτι ἡ βασιλεία τῶν οὐραῶν βιάζεται καὶ βιασται ἁρπάζουσιν αὐτήν," *TSK* 46 (1873): 663-704.

4252. M. J. Birks, "St. Matthew xi.12," *ET* 22 (1910-1911): 425-26.

4253. J. Hugh Michael, "A Conjecture on Matthew 11.12," *HTR* 14 (1921): 374-77.

4254. Benjamin Ralph, " 'The Kingdom Of Heaven Suffereth Violence' (Matt. xi.12)," *ET* 28 (1916-1917): 427.

4255. W. Cowper Robertson, "Matthew xi. 12," *ET* 28 (1916-1917): 236.

4256. Georg Braumann, " 'Dem Himmelreich vrird Gewalt angetan' (Matth. 11,12 par.)," *ZNW* 52 (1961): 104-109.

4257. W. F. Rinck, "Über Matth. 11,12; 21,31, eine exegetische und kritische Bemerkung gegen Prof. Schweizer in Zürich," *TSK* 13 (1840): 1020-24.

4258. Charles Stratton, "Pressure for the Kingdom: An Exposition," *Interp* 8 (1954): 414-21 [Mt. 11:12].

4259. Fr. Zero, "Erklärung von Matth. 11,12," *TSK* 33 (1860): 398-410.

4260. S. Band, "Reincarnation (Matthew xi. 14 and John ix.2)," *ET* 25 (1913-1914): 474.

4261. Carpus, "Capacity involves Responsibility," *Exp* 1st. ser., 2 (1875): 472-84 [Mt. 11:15].

4262. Robert M. Grant, "Like Children," *HTR* 39 (1946): 71-73 [Mt. 11:16-19].

4263. Franz Moistener, "Der niche erkannte Kairos," *B* 40 (1959): 599-612 [Mt. 11:16-19; Lk. 7:31-35].

4264. Cavendish Moxon, "The Meaning of Matthew xi. 16-19," *ET* 23 (1911-1912): 237.

4265. Joseph M. Beaver, "Iustificata est sapientia a filiis suis. Mt. 11.19—a filiis an ab operibus?" *B* 6 (1925): 323-25, 461-65.

4266. T. H. Weir, "Matthew xi. 19," *ET* 27 (1915-1916): 382.

4267. Dr. Warth, "Die Rechtfertigung der Weisheit Matth. 11,19," *TSK* 66 (1893): 591-95.

4268. Dr. Warth, "Noch einmal von der 'blasphemischen Theodicee' oder gotteslästerlichen Rechtfertigung der Weisheit, Matth. 11, 19," *TSK* 67 (1894): 617-21.

4269. Ragnar Leivestad, "An Interpretation of Matt. 11:19," *JBL* 71 (1952): 179-81.

4270. A. Klöpper, "Zwei wichtige Aussagen Jesu über sein religiöses und messianisches Bewusstsein in den synoptischen Evangelien," *ZWT* 39 (1896): 481-516 [Mt. 11:25-30; 22:41-46].

4271. Martin Rist, "Is Matt. 11:25-30 a Primitive Baptismal Hymn?" *JR* 15 (1935): 63-77.

4272. A. E. Morris, "St. Matthew xi.25-30—St. Luke x.21-22," *ET* 51 (1939-1940): 436-37.

4273. L. Cerfaux, "Les sources scriptures de Mt. xi,25-30," *ETL*

30 (1954): 740-46; 31 (1955): 331-42.

4274. K. G. Steck, "Über Matthäus 11,25-30," *EvT* 15 (1955): 343-49.

4275. Celestin Charlier, "L'action de grâces de Jésus (Luc 10,17-24 et Matth. 11,25-30)," *BVC* no. 17 (1957): 87-99.

4276. S. Legacy, "La révélation aux νήποι," *RB* 67 (1960): 321-48 [Mt. 11:25-30; Lk. 10:21-22].

4277. W. D. Davies, " 'Knowledge' in the Dead Sea Scrolls and Matthew 11:25-30," *HTR* 46 (1953): 133-40.

4278. E. F. Scott, "An Exegetical Study of Matt. 11:25-30," *BW* 35 (1910): 186-90.

4279. N. P. Williams, "Matthew xi. 25-27—Luke x. 21,22," *ET* 51 (1939-1940): 182-86, 215-20.

4280. F. J. Badcock, "Matthew xi. 25-27—Luke x. 21-22," *ET* 51 (1939-1940): 436.

4281. Harold A. Guy, "Matthew xi. 25-27—Luke x. 21-22," *ET* 49 (1937-1938): 236-37.

4282. William M. McPheeters, "Our Lord 'Confesses' his Father—Matthew 11:25-26; Luke 10:21-22," *BR* 7 (1922): 173-95.

4283. Paul Winter, "Matthew xi, 27 and Luke x, 22 from the First to the Fifth Century. Reflections on the Development of the Text," *NT* 1 (1956): 112-48.

4284. F. C. Burkitt, "On Matt. xi. 27, Luke x. 22," *JTS* 12 (1910-1911): 296-97.

4285. V. Hugger, "Des hl. Athanasius Traktat in Mt. 11, 27," *ZKT* 42 (1918): 437-41.

4286. Ernst Kuhl, "Das Selbstbewusstsein Jesu als Sohn Gottes nach Matth. 11, 27," *NKZ* 16 (1905): 179-207.

4287. G. Mathewson, "Christianity's first Invitation to the World," *Exp* 1st ser., 11 (1880): 101-19 [Mt. 11:28-30].

4288. F. Gryglewicz, "The Gospel of the Overworked Workers," *CBQ* 19 (1957): 190-98 [Mt. 11:28-30; 20:1-8].

4289. J. B. Bauer, "Das milde Joch und die Ruhe, Matth. 11, 28-30," *TZ* 17 (1961): 99-106.

4290. Godfrey N. Curnock, "A Neglected Parallel," *ET* 44 (1932-1933): 141 [Mt. 11:28 and Ex. 33:14].

4291. A. B. Bruce, "The Easy Yoke," *Exp* 5th ser., 8 (1898):

102-18 [Mt. 11:30].

4292. G. Lam Bert, " 'Mon joug est aisé et mon fardeau léger'," *NRT* 77 (1955): 963-69 [Mt. 11:39].

4293. B. W. Bacon, "The Redaction of Matthew 12," *JBL* 46 (1927): 20-49.

4294. A. Kappeler, "Die Porkpie von Äihrenraufen und Urmatthäus," *STZ* 2 (1885): 134-46 [Mt. 12:1-8; Mk. 2:23-28; Lk. 6:1-5].

4295. A. Klöpper, "Eine apologetische Rede Jesu für seine des Sabbatbruches beschuldigten Jünger. Matth. 12, 1-8; Marc. 2, 23-28; Luc. 6, 1-5," *ZWT* 28 (1885): 129-45.

4296. Benjamin Murmelstein, "Jesu Gang durch die Saatfelder," *A* 3 (1928): 111-20 [Mt. 12:1-8].

4297. Boaz Cohen, "The Rabbinic Law Presupposed by Matthew xii. i and Luke vi. i," *HTR* 23 (1930): 91-92.

4298. A. Buchler, "The Ears of Corn," *ET* 20 (1908-1909): 278 [Mt. 12:6].

4299. J. M. Pfättisch, "Der Herr des Sabbats," *BibZ* 6 (1908): 172-78 [Mt. 12:8; Mk. 2:28; Lk. 6:5].

4300. Ernest Tootle, "St. Matthew and the Gentiles," *ET* 60 (1948-1949): 26 [Mt. 12:9-21].

4301. U. Holzmeister, " 'Si licet sabbatis curare?' (Mt. 12, 10)," *VD* 8 (1928): 264-70.

4302. P. van Dijk, "Het gekrookte riet en de rookende vlaswiek (Matth. 12:18 v.v.)," *GTT* 23 (1922-1923): 155-72.

4303. Robert A. Faulkner, "Jesus as the Prophetic Servant of the Lord (Matt. 12:18-21)," *BW* 24 (1904): 22-25.

4304. W. C. Allen, "Matthew xii. 19—Isaiah xlii. 2," *ET* 20 (1908-1909): 140-41.

4305. Eb. Nestle, "Matthew xii. Isaiah xlii. 2," *ET* 20 (1908-1909): 92-93.

4306. Eb. Nestle, "Matthew xii. 19—Isaiah xlii. 2," *ET* 20 (1908-1909): 189.

4307. Burton S. Easton, "The Beezebul Sections," *JBL* 32 (1913): 57-73 [Mt. 12:25-32; Mk. 3:23-30; Lk. 11:17-23; 12:20].

4308. O. Rodriguez, " 'Qui sunt fratres mei' (Mt. 12, 28)," *VD* 5 (1925): 132-37.

4309. S. Cox, "The Sin against the Holy Ghost," *Exp* 2nd ser., 3

(1882): 321-38 [Mt. 12:32-32; Mk. 3:28-30].

4310. G. Hurst, "The Unpardonable Sin," *ET* 11 (1899-1900): 94 [Mt. 12:31].

4311. F. F. Walrond, "The Sign of the Prophet Jonas," *Exp* 5th ser., 6 (1897): 36-48 [Mt. 12:38-42].

4312. J. Knabenbaucr, "De peccato in Spiritum Sanctum quod non remittatur (Matth. 12, 31. 32. Marc. 3, 28. Luc. 12, 10.)," *RB* 1 (1892): 161-70.

4313. J. Hugh Mitchell, "The Sign of John," *JTS* 21 (1920): 146-59 [Mt. 12:38-42; 16:1-4; Mk. 8:11-12; Lk. 11:16 ff.].

4314. C. S. Rodd, "Spirit or Finger," *ET* 72 (1960-1961): 157-58 [Mt. 12:38; Lk. 11:20].

4315. A. H. Blom, "Het teeken van Jona. Matth. XII, 39; xiv, 4," *TT* 1 (1867): 637-50.

4316. Stuart L. Tyson, "The Sign of Jonah," *BW* 33 (1909): 96-101 [Mt. 12:39; 16:4; Lk. 11:29].

4317. F. A. Rayner, "The Story of Jonah. An Easter Story," *EQ* 22 (1950): 123-25 [Mt. 12:40-41].

4318. Georg Rumze, "Das Zeichen des Menschensohnes und der Doppelsinn des Jonazeichens," *ZWT* 41 (1898): 171-85 [Mt. 12:40; Lk. 11:30].

4319. A. Reville, "Remarquues sur Matth. xii, 40," *RT* 1 (1858): 331-38.

4320. Johannes Chr. Spann, "Zu Mt. 12, 40," *TQ* 93 (1911): 60-62.

4321. M. Dods, "The Last State Worse than the First," *Exp* 3rd ser., 7 (1888): 123-31 [Mt. 12:43-45].

4322. John Landrum, "The Unclean Spirit and Seven Others," *ET* 16 (1904-1905): 313-15 [Mt. 12:43-45; Lk. 11:24-26].

4323. John C. Granbery, "The Demoniac and the Returning Demon. An Exposition of Matt. 12:43-45; Luke 11:23-26," *BW* 37 (1911): 100-106.

4324. E. P. Gould, "Matt. xii, 43-45," *JBL* 3 (1883): 62.

4325. A. T. Burbridge, "The Seed Growing Secretly," *ET* 40 (1928-1929): 139-41 [Mt. 12:43-45].

4326. C. A. Phillips, "Matt. 12, 43: Luke 11, 24," *BBC* 5 (1928): 30.

4327. A. D. Loman, "Bijdrage tot de critiek der synoptische Evangeliën. VI. Het mysterie der gelijkenissen," *TT* 7 (1873):

175-205 [Mt. 13].

4328. Friedrich Spitta, "Die Parabelschnitte Matth. 13, Mark. 4, Luk. 8 als typisches Beispiel des Verhältnisses der Synoptiker zueinander," *TSK* 84 (1911): 538-69.

4329. B. W. Bacon, "The Matthean Discourse in Parables, Mt. 13:1-52," *JBL* 46 (1927): 237-65.

4330. N. A. Dahl, "The Parables of Growth," *ST* 5 (1951): 132-66 [Mt. 13:1-33; Mk. 4:1-32; Lk. 8:4-18; 13:18-20].

4331. A. M. Denis, "De parabels over het koninkrijk (Mt. 13)," *TvT* 1 (1961): 273-87 (French résumé, 287-88).

4332. U. Holzmeister, " 'Aliud (fecit fructum) centesimum' (Mt. 13, 8. cf. Mc. 4, 8; Lc. 8, 8)," *VD* 20 (1940): 219-23.

4333. Wilhelm Link, "Die Geheimnisse des Himmelreichs; eine Erklärung von Matth. 13, 10-23," *EvT* 2 (1935): 115-27.

4334. R. D. Clark, "Why Speakest thou in Parables?" *EQ* 12 (1940): 129-37 [Mt. 13:10].

4335. J. I. Prins, "Matth. xiii, 10b: 'Waarom spreekt gij tot hen in gelijkenissen?" *TT* 18 (1884): 25-38.

4336. L. Cerfaux, "La Kansans des secrets du Royaume d'après Matt. xiii. 11 et par.," *NTSt* 2 (1955-1956): 238-49.

4337. Émile Suys, "Le commentaire de la parabole du semeur dans les synoptiques (Mat. xiii, 18-23; Marc iv, 13-20; Luc viii, 11-15)," *RSR* 14 (1924): 247-54.

4338. L. Fonck, "Senfkörnlein, Tollkorn, und höhere Parabelkritik," *ZKT* 26 (1902): 13-32 [Mt. 13:24-43].

4339. L. Fonck, "Parabola zizaniorum agri (Mt. 13, 24-30)," *VD* 6 (1926): 327-34.

4340. A. D. Loman, "Bijdragen tot de critiek der synoptic Evangelien. I. De gelijkenis van het onkruid (Matth 13:24-30), naar nare oorspronklike redactie en betekenis," *TT* 3 (1869): 577-85.

4341. Hubert G. Houseman, "The Parable of the Tares," *Th* 3 (1921): 31-55 [Mt. 13:24-30].

4342. Leslie H. Bunn, "The Parable of the Tares," *ET* 38 (1926-1927): 561-64 [Mt. 13:24-30].

4343. L. Fonck, "Granum sinapis (Mt. 13, 31 s.)," *VD* 1 (1921): 322-27.

4344. Fr. Fehle, "Senfkorn und Saurteig in der Heiligen Schrift,"

NKZ 34 (1923): 713-19 [Mt. 13:31 ff.].

4345.   Albert J. Matthews, "The Mustard 'Tree'," *ET* 39 (1927-1928): 32-34 [Mt. 13:31-43; Mk. 4:30-32].

4346.   B. Schultze, "Die ekklesiologische Bedeutung des Gleichnisses vom Senfkorn (Matth. 13, 31-32; Mk. 4, 30-32; Lk. 13, 18-19)," *OCP* 27 (1961): 362-86.

4347.   H. Liese, "Fermentum (Mt. 13, 33; Lc. 13, 20s.)," *VD* 13 (1933): 341-46.

4348.   Oswald T. Allis, "The Parable of the Leaven," *EQ* 19 (1947): 254-73 [Mt. 13:33].

4349.   Michel de Goedt, "L'explication de la parabole de l'ivraie (Mt. xiii, 36-43)," *RB* 66 (1959): 32-54.

4350.   U. A. Homes-Gore, "The Parable of the Tares," *Th* 35 (1937): 117 [Mt. 13:37-43].

4351.   J. H. Burn, "The Pearl of Great Price," *Exp* 2nd ser. 8, (1884): 468-72 [Mt. 13:44-46].

4352.   W. M. Metcalfe, "The Twin Parables," *Exp* 2nd ser., 8 (1884): 54-67 [Mt. 13:44-46].

4353.   S. Tonkin, "The Parable of the Hidden Treasure, and of the Pearl Merchant (Matt. 13:44 ff.)," *ET* 33 (1921-1922): 330-31.

4354.   R. H. Charles, "Two Parables: A Study," *ET* 35 (1923-1924): 265-69 [Mt. 13:44-46].

4355.   W. P. Paterson, "The Parables of the Treasure and to Pearl," *ET* 38 (1926-1927): 261-64, 295-99 [Mt. 13:44-46].

4356.   T. H. Weir, "The Parable of the Hid Treasure," *ET* (1917-1918): 523 [Mt. 13:44].

4357.   Hyac. Faccis, "De thesauro abscondito (Mt. 13:44)," *VD* 28 (1950): 237-42.

4358.   Hans Kulp, "Der Schatz im Acker," *EvT* 13 (1953-1954): 145-49.

4359.   Piero Rossano, "La parabola del tesoro e il diritto orientale," *RivB* 8 (1960): 365-66 [Mt. 13:44].

4360.   Eric F. F. Bishop, "θησαυρῷ κεκρυμμέῳ ἐν τῷ ἀγρῷ (Mt. xiii. 44) σκάψω περὶ (συνῆν) (Lk. xiii. 8)," *ET* 65 (1953-1954): 287.

4361.   Otto Glombitza, "Der Perlenkaufmann," *NTSt* 7 (1960-1961): 153-61 [Mt. 13:45-46].

4362. Herbert S. Hayman, "The Parable of the Pearl Merchant: Matthew xiii. 45, 46," *ET* 49 (1937-1938): 142.

4363. Pfarrer Wächtler, "Versuch einer Erklärung von Matth. 13, 45. 46. Die Parabel von der köstlichen Perle," *TSK* 19 (1846): 939-46.

4364. Pfarrer Wächtler, "Noch ein Wort über die Parabel Matth. 13, 45. 46," *TSK* 22 (1849): 416-22.

4365. H. Stephenson, "Über Matth. 13, 45. 46. Mit Beziehung auf Wächtlers Erklärungsversuch in den Stud. u. Krit. 1846. H. 4. 939-946," *TSK* 20 (1847): 718-22.

4366. J. Renié, "Elegerunt bonos in visa (Mt. xiii, 48)," *RSR* 35 (1948): 271-72.

4367. Joseph Hoh, "Die christliche γραμματεύς (Mt. 13, 52)," *BibZ* 17 (1925-1926): 256-69.

4368. A. Hilgenfeld, "Die Verwerfung Jesu in Nazaret nach den kanonischen Evangelien und nach Marcion," *ZWT* 45 (1902): 127-44 [Mt. 13:54-58; Lk. 4:16-30; Mk. 6:1-6].

4369. M. Goguel, "Le Roget de Jésus à Nazareth," *ZNW* 12 (1911): 321-24 [Mt. 13:53-58; Mk. 6:1-6].

4370. W. Sherlock, "The Visit of Christ to Nazareth," *JTS* 11 (1909-1910): 552-57 [Mt. 13:54-58; Lk. 4:16-30; Mk. 6:16].

4371. H. Höpfl, "Nonne hic est fabri filius?" *B* 4 (1923): 41-55 [Mt. 13:55; Mk. 6:3].

4372. J. Nicklin, "Matthew xiv. 12," *ET* 55 (1943-1944): 110.

4373. J. F. Belser, "Zu der Perikope von der Speisung der Fünftausend," *BibZ* 2 (1904): 154-76 [Mt. 14:13-21; Mk. 6:30-44; Lk. 9:10-17; Jn. 6:1-15].

4374. J. Renié, "Une antilogie évangélique; Mc. 6, 51-52; Mt. 14, 32-33," *B* 36 (1955): 223-26.

4375. Joseph A. Fitzmyer, "The Aramaic Qoibā Inscription from Jebel Hallet et-Tûri and Mark 7:11/Matt. 15:5," *JBL* 78 (1959): 60-65.

4376. Eb. Nestle, "The Quotation in Matt. xv. 9; Mark vii. 7," *ET* 11 (1899-1900): 330-31.

4377. Johannes Cropp, "Die Perikope vom cananäischen Weibe," *TSK* 43 (1870): 125-34 [Mt. 15:21-28].

4378. R. W. Dale, "The Syro-Phoenician Woman," *Exp* 5th ser., 5 (1897): 365-72 [Mt. 15:21-28].

4379.   F. G. Cholmondeley, "Christ and the Woman of Canaan," *ET*
          13 (1901-1902): 138-39 [Mt. 15:21-28].

4380.   David Smith, "Our Lord's Hard Saying to the
          Syro-Phoenician Woman," *ET* 12 (1900-1901): 319-21 [Mt.
          15:21-28; Mk. 7:24-30].

4381.   F. Warburton Lewis, "The Children's Bread and the Dogs
          (Matt. xv. 21-28)," *ET* 23 (1911-1912): 430.

4382.   R. J. Morrice, "Note on Matt. xv, 21-28 Compared with
          Matt. viii, 5-13," *Th* 32 (1936): 361.

4383.   M. Meinertz, "Die angebliche Heidenfreundlichkeit Jesu in
          der Perikope von der Kanaanäerin (Mt. 15, 21 ff.) nach dem
          Syrus Sinaiticus," *TQ* 89 (1907): 536-47.

4384.   B. Horace Ward, "Our Lord's Hard Sayings to the Syro-
          Phoenician Woman," *ET* 13 (1901-1902): 48 [Mt. 15:26;
          Mk. 7:27].

4385.   G. E. Ford, "The Children's Bread and the Dogs (Mt. xv.
          21-28; Mk. vii. 24-30)," *ET* 23 (1911-1912): 329-30.

4386.   J. Ireland Hasler, "The Incident of the Syrophoenician
          Woman (Matt. xv. 21-28, Mark vii. 24-30)," *ET* 45 (1933-
          1934): 459-61.

4387.   James D. Smart, "Jesus, the Syro-Phoenician Woman—and
          the Disciples," *ET* 50 (1938-1939): 469-72 [Mt. 15:21-28].

4388.   Herbert M. Gale, "A Suggestion concerning Matthew 16,"
          JBL 60 (1941): 255-60.

4389.   C. F. D. Moule, "Some Reflections on the 'Stone' Testi-
          monia in relation to the Name Peter," *NTSt* 2 (1955-1956):
          56-58.

4390.   Jean van Camp, "La primauté de saint Pierre dans le contexte
          évangélique," *NRT* 73 (1951): 405-408 [Mt. 16, Lk. 22, Jn.
          21].

4391.   Henry Burton and Almoni Petoni, "The Stone and the Rock,"
          Exp 2nd ser., 6 (1883): 430-48 [Mt. 16:13-19].

4392.   J. A. Beet, "The Stone and the Rock," *Exp* 2nd ser., 7 (1885):
          311-20 [Mt. 16:13-19].

4393.   Elisaeus Vardapet, "The Revelation of the Lord to Peter,"
          ZNW 23 (1924): 8-17 [Mt. 16:13-23].

4394.   D. A. Frøvig, "Jesus ved Caesarea Filippi," *NTT* 12 (1911):
          18-32 132-64 [Mt. 16:13-20; Mk. 8:27-9:1; Lk. 9:18-27; Jn.
          6:67-71].

4395.   A. Vögtle, "Messiasbekenntnis und Petrusverheissung," *BibZ*
1 (1957): 252-72; 2 (1958): 85-103 [Mt. 16:13-23].

4396.   Dominique Nothomb, "La nature du pouvoir de juridiction du
confesseur," *NRT* 82 (1960): 470-82 [Mt. 16:16-19; Jn.
20:21-23].

4397.   H. Guenser, "La confession de Saint Pierre," *ETL* 4 (1927):
561-76 [Mt. 16:16; Mk. 8:29; Lk. 9:20].

4398.   T. de Kruijf, " 'Filius Dei viventis' (Mt. 16, 16)," *VD* 39
(1961): 39-43.

4399.   Burton S. Easton, "St. Matthew 16:17-19," *ATR* 5 (1922-
1923): 116-26.

4400.   O. J. F. Seitz, "Upon this Rock: A Critical Re- examination
of Matt. 16:17-19," *JBL* 69 (1950): 329-40.

4401.   Otto Betz, "Felsenmann und Felsengemeinde (Eine Parallele
zu Mt. 16:17-19 in den Qumranpsalmen)," *ZNW* 48 (1957):
49-77.

4402.   Dan O. Via, "Jesus and his Church in Matthew 16:17-19,"
RE 55 (1958): 22-39.

4403.   August Dell, "Matthäus 16, 17-19," *ZNW* 15 (1914): 1-49.

4404.   A. Dell, "Zur Erklärung von Matthäus 16:17-19," *ZNW* 17
(1916): 27-32.

4405.   Hermann Dieckmann, "Neuere Ansichten über die Echtheit
der Primatsstelle," *B* 4 (1923): 189-200 [Mt. 16:17ff.].

4406.   Burton S. Easton, "St. Matthew 16:17-19," *ATR* 4
(1921-1922): 156-66.

4407.   W. Soltau, "Wann ist Matth. 16, 17-19 eingeschoben?" *TSK*
89 (1916): 233-37.

4408.   Werner Georg Kümmel, "Jesus und die Anfänge der
Kirche," *ST* 7 (1953): 1-27 [Mt. 16:17-19].

4409.   Albrecht Oepke, "Der Herrnspruch über die Kirche Mt. 16,
17-19 in der neuesten Forschung," *ST* 2 (1948): 110-65.

4410.   J. Chapman, "St. Paul and the Revelation to St. Peter: Matt.
xvi, 17," *RBén* 29 (1912): 133-47.

4411   D. R. Griffiths, "The Disciples and the Zealots," *ET* (1957):
29 [Mt. 16:17].

4412.   Vacher Burch, "The 'Stone' and the 'Keys' (Mt. 16:18 ff.),"
JBL 52 (1933): 147-52.

4413.   A. Vögtle, "Der Petrus der Verheissung und der Erfüllung.

Zum Petrusbuch von Oscar Cullmann," *MTZ* 5 (1954): 1-47 [Mt. 16:18 ff.].

4414. C. Bruston, "La promesse de Jésus à l'apôtre Pierre," *RTQR* 11 (1902): 326-41 [Mt. 16:18,19].

4415. Gustav Krüger, "Matthäus 16:18, 19 und der Primat des Petrus," *TB* 6 (1927): 302-307.

4416. Theodor Hermann, "Zu Matthäus 16, 18. 19," *TB* 5 (1926): 203-207.

4417. Karl Bornhäuser, "Zum Verständnis von Matth. 16, 18 u. 19," *NKZ* 40 (1929): 221-37.

4418. F. G. Cholmondeley, "Note on Matthew xvi. 18," *Exp* 2nd ser., 8 (1884): 75-77.

4419. C. Bruston, "Les portes de l'enfer," *RTQR* 10 (1901): 358-60 [Mt. 16:18].

4420. Wallace N. Stearns, "Note on Matthew xvi. 18," *JBL* 21 (1902): 115.

4421. H. H. B. Ayles, "St. Matthew xvi. 18," *Exp* 8th ser. 2 (1911): 474-80.

4422. C. Bruston, "Contre quoi ne prévaudront pas les portes de l'enfer?" *RTQR* 22 (1913): 16-21 [Mt. 16:18].

4423. Otto Immisch, "Matthäus 16, 18. Laienbemerkungen zu der Untersuchung Dells," *ZNW* 17 (1916): 18-26.

4424. C. J. Tottenham, " 'The Gates of Hell," (Matt. xvi. 18)," *ET* 29 (1917-1918): 378-79.

4425. L. Fonck, "Tu es Petrus," *B* 1 (1920): 240-64 [Mt. 16:18].

4426. Prosper Schepens, "L'authenticité de saint Matthieu, xvi, 18," *RSR* 10 (1920): 269-302.

4427. J. Sickenberger, "Eine neue Deutung der Primatstelle (Mt 16, 18)," *TRev* 19 (1920): 1-7.

4428. Hermann Dieckmann, "Mt. 16, 18," *B* 2 (1921): 65-69.

4429. E. H[ocedez], "L'authenticité de Mt. xvi, 18," *NRT* 48 (1921): 322-24.

4430. Ferdinand Kattenbusch, "Der Spruch über Petrus und die Kirche bei Matthäus," *TSK* 94 (1922): 96-131 [Mt. 16:18].

4431. C. Clare Oke, " 'My Testimony'," *ET* 37 (1925-1926): 476-78 [Mt. 16:18].

4432. J. E. L. Oulton, "An Interpretation of Matthew xvi. 18," *ET* 48 (1936-1937): 525-26.

4433. Hans Rheinfelder, "Philologische Erwägungen zu Matth. 16, 18," *BibZ* 24 (1938-1939): 139-63.

4434. Donald W. Riddle, "The Cephas-Peter Problem, and a Possible Solution," *JBL* 59 (1940): 169-80 [Mt. 16:18].

4435. C. Cotter, "Tu es Petrus," *CBQ* 4 (1942): 304-10 [Mt. 16:18].

4436. Teófilo Auyso, "Tu es Petrus," *CB* 1 (1944): 14-18 [Mt. 16:18].

4437. J. Warren, "Was Simon Peter the Church's Rock?" *EQ* 19 (1947): 196-210 [Mt. 16:18].

4438. W. A. Wordsworth, "The Rock and the Stones," *EQ* 20 (1948): 9-15 [Mt. 16:18].

4439. Louis E. Sullivan, "The Gates of Hell (Matt. 16:18)," *ThSt* 10 (1949): 62-64.

4440. Ricardo Rábanos, "Tu es Petrus," *CB* 7 (1950): 327-33 [Mt. 16:18].

4441. Hans Lehmann, " 'Du bist Petrus ...'," *EvT* 13 (1953-1954): 44-67 [Mt. 16:18].

4442. E. L. Allen, "On this Rock," *JTS* N.S. 5 (1954): 59-62 [Mt. 16:18].

4443. Jorge M. Girardet, "Petro, el fundamento de la Iglesia—en la obra de Oscar Cullmann," *CT* 14 (1955): 50-62 [Mt. 16:18].

4444. Paul De Vooght, "L'argument patristique dans l'interprétation de Matth. xvi, 18 de Jean Huss," *RSR* 45 (1957): 558-66.

4445. R. Köbert, "Zwei Fassungen von Mt. 16, 18 bei den Syrern," *B* 40 (1959): 1018-20.

4446. G. A. F. Knight, " 'Thou art Peter'," *TTod* 17 (1960- 1961): 168-80 [Mt. 16:18].

4447. F. J. M. Potgieter, "Die Wese van die Kerk van Christus," *NGTT* 3 (1961-1962): 271-78 [Mt. 16:18].

4448. G. Gander, "Le sens des mots: Πέτρος — πέτρα / KIPNÂ — KIPNÂ/ כיפא — כיפא dans Matthieu xvi, 18a," *RTP* N.S. 29 (1941): 5-29.

4449. Francesco Vattioni, "Porta o portieri dell'inferno in Mt. 16, 18b?" *RivB* 8 (1960): 251-55.

4450. J. R. Slotemaker de Bruine, "De sleutelmacht," *TS* 22 (1904): 23-43 [Mt. 16:19; 18:18; Jn. 20:23].

4451. W. C. Allen, "Keys of the Kingdom of Heaven," *ET* 19 (1907-1908): 248-50 [Mt. 16:19].

4452. J. Jensen, "Het vraagstuk van de sleutelmacht," *GTT* 11 (1910): 308-22 [Mt. 16:19].

4453. Clyde W. Votaw, "Peter and the Keys of the Kingdom," *BW* 36 (1910): 8-25 [Mt. 16:19].

4454. H. Bruders, "Mt. 16, 19; 18, 18 und Jo. 20, 22, 23 in früchristlicher Auslegung. 1 Tertullian, 2. Africa bis 251, 3. Africa bis 258, 4. Africa bis 312, 5. Die Kirche der Donatisten," *ZKT* 34 (1910): 659-77; 35 (1911): 79-111, 292-346, 464-81, 690-713.

4455. J. R. Mantey, "The Mistranslation of the Perfect Tense in John 20:23, Mt. 16:19, and Mt. 18:18," *JBL* 58 (1939): 243-49.

4456. Henry J. Cadbury, "The Meaning of John 20:23, Matthew 16:19, and Matthew 18:18," *JBL* 58 (1939): 251-54.

4457. Gustave Lambert, "Lier—délier: l'expression de la totalité par l'opposition de deux contraires," *RB* 52 (1943-1944): 91-103 [Mt. 16:19; 18:18].

4458. Robert A. Baker, "The Forgiveness of Sin," *RE* 41 (1944): 224-35 [Mt. 16:19; 18:18, and Jn. 20:23].

4459. A. M. Coleman, "Matthew xvi. 24," *ET* 32 (1920-1921): 139.

4460. John MacNeill, "Christ's Challenge to Sacrifice," *CQ* 10 (1933): 410-18 [Mt. 16:24].

4461. M. C. Mackenzie, "Bearing the Cross," *ET* 25 (1913-1914): 139 [Mt. 16:25].

4462. G. M. Lee, "Matthew 16:26," *ET* 65 (1953-1954): 251.

4463. Augustinus Bea, "Lucrari mundum—perdere animam," *B* 14 (1933): 435-47 [Mt. 16:26].

4464. G. Zuntz, "A Note on Matthew xvi. 34 and xxvi. 75," *JTS* 50 (1949): 182-83.

4465. L. Fonck, "Christus in monte transfiguratur (Mt. 17, 1-9)," *VD* 2 (1922): 72-79.

4466. T. Torrance, "The Transfiguration of Jesus," *EQ* 14 (1942): 214-40 [Mt. 17:1-9; Mk. 9:2-10; Lk. 9:28-36].

4467. Edward Evans, "The Transfiguration of Jesus," *EQ* 26 (1954): 97-104 [Mt. 17:1-9].

4468. P. Dabeck, "Siehe, es erschienen Moses und Elias," *B* 23 (1942): 175-89 [Mt. 17:3].

4469. A. Büchler, "The Three Tabernacles," *ET* 20 (1908-1909): 278 [Mt. 17:4; Mk. 9:5; Lk. 9:33].

4470. Jacques Guillet, " 'Cette génération infidèle et dévoyée'," *RSR* 35 (1948): 275-81 [Mt. 17:17; Mk. 9:19; Lk. 9:41].

4471. A. Peloni, "Faith as a Grain of Mustard Seed," *Exp* 2nd ser., 8 (1884): 207-15 [Mt. 17:20].

4472. D. W. Simon, "Faith as a Grain of Mustard Seed," *Exp* 1st. ser., 9 (1879): 307-16 [Mt. 17:20; Lk. 17:6].

4473. E. Omar Pearson, "Matthew xvii. 20," *ET* 25 (1913-1914): 378.

4474. M. Dods, "The Stater in the Fish's Mouth," *Exp* 3rd ser., 7 (1888): 461-72 [Mt. 17:24-27].

4475. D. F. Strauss, "Die Geschichte von dem Stater im Maule des Fisches, Matth. 17, 24-27," *ZWT* 6 (1863): 293-96.

4476. J. B. Weatherspoon, "The Spirit of Forgiveness," *RE* 41 (1944): 361-71 [Mt. 18].

4477. Ernest R. Martinez, "The Interpretation of οἱ μαθηταί in Matthew 18," *CBQ* 23 (1961): 281-92.

4478. L. Vaganay, "Le schématisme du discours communautaire à la lumière de la critique des sources," *RB* 60 (1953): 203-44 [Mt. 18:1-35; Mk 9 33-50; Lk. 9:46-50].

4479. John J. Collins, "The Gospel for the Feast of the Guardian Angels," *CBQ* 6 (1944): 423-34 [Mt. 18:1-10].

4480. H. B. Kossen, "Quelques remarques sur l'ordre des paraboles dans Luc xv et sur la construction de Matthieu xviii, 8-14," *NT* 1 (1956): 75-80.

4481. J. G. Berry, "Matthew xviii. 10, οἱ ἄγγελοι αὐτῶν," *ET* 23 (1911-1912): 182.

4482. Denis Buzy, "La brebis perdue," *RB* 39 (1930): 47-61 [Mt. 18:12-14].

4483. Walter H. Bouman, "The Practical Application of Matthew 18:15-18," *CTM* 18 (1947): 178-205.

4484. José M. Bover, "Si peccaverit in te frater tuus ... Mt. 18, 15," *EB* 12 (1953): 195-198.

4485. J.-A. Janssen, "Le publicain ou le 'aššar dans la tradition arabe," *RB* 33 (1924): 82-85.

4486. Stephen Hobhouse, "Matthew xviii. 17," *ET* 29 (1917-1918): 521-22.

4487. Francis L. Palmer, " 'As a Heathen Man and a Publican' (Matt. xviii. 17)," *ET* 30 (1918-1919): 426-27.

4488. Stephen Hobhouse, " 'Let him be unto thee as the Gentile and the publican'," *ET* 49 (1937-1938): 43-44 [Mt. 18:17].

4489. A. Henderson, "Matthew xviii. 19, 20," *ET* 28 (1916-1917): 139-40.

4490. Eb. Nestle, "Matthew xviii. 20," *ET* 10 (1898-1899): 43.

4491. A. Spaeth, "Matthew 18:20 and the Doctrine of the Church," *LCR* 9 (1890): 106-16.

4492. L. Fonck, "Servus nequam (Mt. 18, 23-35)," *VD* 1 (1921): 310-15.

4493. T. Herbert Darlow, "Divorce and Childhood. A Reading of St. Matt. xix. 3-15," *Exp* 4th ser. 7 (1893): 294-99.

4494. Francis M. Downtown, "Note on St. Matthew xix, 3-12," *Th* 32 (1936): 107-108, 235, 175.

4495. R. O. P. Taylor, "The Matthean 'Exception'," *Th* 35 (1937): 296-98 [Mt. 19:3-12].

4496. Georg Aicher, "Mann und Weib—ein Fleisch (Mt. 19, 4 ff.)," *BibZ* 5 (1907): 159-65.

4497. Dr. Storz, "Erklärung der Stelle Matthäus 19, 9," *TQ* 62 (1880): 384-410.

4498. J. MacRory, "Christian Writers of the First Three Centuries and St. Matt. xix. 9," *ITQ* 6 (1911): 172-85.

4499. Anonymous, "The Excepting Clause in St. Matthew," *Th* 36 (1938): 27-36 [Mt. 19:9].

4500. Joseph Bonsirven, *"Nisi fornicationis causa.* Comment résoudre cette 'crux interpretum'?" *RSR* 35 (1948): 442-64 [Mt. 19:9].

4501. Thomas Fahy, "St. Matthew xix. 9—Divorce or Separation?" *ITQ* 24 (1957): 173-75.

4502. J. Blinzler, " 'Εἰσίν εὐνοῦχοι' zur Auslegung von Mt. 19, 12," *ZNW* 48 (1957): 254-70.

4503. Hugh K. Wagner, "Suffer Little Children, and Forbid them not to come unto me," *BS* 65 (1908): 214-48 [Mt. 19:13-15].

4504. K. Wimmer, "Über Matth. 19:16-22 als Beitrag zur Lehre von der Sündlosigkeit Jesu und zur Charakteristik biblischer

Personen," *TSK* 18 (1845): 115-53.

4505. E. Macmillan, "The Place of an Adjective," *ET* 37 (1925-1926): 45-46 [Mt. 19:19].

4506. Carpus, "The Rich Young Ruler," *Exp* 1st ser. 6 (1877): 229-40 [Mt. 19:21].

4507. Aug. Baur, "Zur Auslegung von Matth. 19, 23-26 (Marc. 10, 23-29)," *ZWT* 19 (1876): 300-304.

4508. Irving F. Wood, "Two Biblical Attitudes Toward Riches: James 5:1-16; Matt. 19:23-26," *BW* 33 (1909): 408-13.

4509. E. Martin Nieto, "¿Se pueden salvar los ricos?" *CB* 11 (1954): 25-29 [Mt. 19:23, 24].

4510. F. W. Farrar, "Brief Notes on Passages of the Gospels," *Exp* 1st. ser. 3 (1876): 369-80 [Mt. 19:24; Mk. 10:25; Lk. 18:25].

4511. Fr. Herklotz, "Zu Mt. 19, 24 und Parall.," *BibZ* 2 (1904): 176-77; 3 (1905): 39.

4512. Jos. Denk, "Suum cuique. Nachtrag zu Mt. 19, 24: camelus, das Schiffstau (BZ II 176 und III 39)," *BibZ* 3 (1905): 367.

4513. Cuthbert Lattey, "Camelus per foramen acus (Mt. 19, 24)," *VD* 31 (1953): 291-92.

4514. Pierre Batiffol, "Trois notes exégétiques sur Matth. XIX, 28 et Luc. XXII, 30," *RB* 21 (1912): 541-42.

4515. E. J. Kissane, "A Forgotton Interpretation of Matthew xix. 28," *ITQ* 16 (1921): 356-66.

4516. Frank C. Porter, "The Sayings of Jesus about the First and the Last," *JBL* 25 (1906): 97-110 [Mt. 19:30].

4517. Charles Connor, "The Hire of the Labourers in the Vineyard," *ET* 2 (1890-1891): 261-63 [Mt. 20:1-16].

4518. F. G. Cholmondeley, "The Parable of the Labourers in the Vineyard," *ET* 6 (1894-1895): 137-40 [Mt. 20:1-16].

4519. F. P. Mayser, "The Parable of the Laborers in the Vineyard," *LCR* 21 (1902): 388-97 [Mt. 20:1-16].

4520. W. O. E. Oesterley, "The Parable of the Labourers in the Vineyard," *Exp* 7th ser. 5 (1908): 333-43 [Mt. 20:1-16].

4521. John A. F. Gregg, "A Study of the Parable of the Labourers in the Vineyard," *ET* 30 (1918-1919): 422-24 [Mt. 20:1-16].

4522. W. A. Curtis, "The Parable of the Labourers, Matt. xx. 1-16," *ET* 38 (1926-1927): 6-10.

4523. Th. Vargha, "Operarii in vinea (Mt. 20, 1-16)," *VD* 8 (1928):

302-304.

4524. W. Sanday, "The Parable of the Labourers in the Vineyard," *Exp* 1st. ser. 3 (1876): 81-101 [Mt. 20:1-15].

4525. F. T. Hill, "The Parable of the Labourers in the Vineyard," *Exp* 1st. ser. 3 (1876): 427-32 [Mt. 20:1-16].

4526. L. Fonck, "Operarii in vinea (Mt. 20, 1-16)," *VD* 4 (1924): 33-40.

4527. André Feuillet, "Les ouvriers de la vigne et la théologie de l'alliance," *RSR* 34 (1947): 303-27 [Mt. 20:1-16].

4528. H. Heinemann, "The Conception of Reward in Mat. xx, 1-16," *JJS* 1 (1948-1949): 85-89.

4529. C. G. Wilke, "Über die Parabel von den Arbeitern im Weinberg, Matth. 20, 1-16," *ZWTh* 1 (1826): 71-109.

4530. W. J. Williams, "The Parable of the Labourers in the Vineyard (Matt. xx. 1-16)," *ET* 50 (1938-1939): 526.

4531. F. W. Aveling, "The Parable of the Labourers in the Vineyard," *ET* 5 (1893-1894): 549-51 [Mt. 20:1-16].

4532. Johann M. Rupprecht, "Die Parabel von den Arbeitern im Weinberge. Matth. 20,1-16," *TSK* 20 (1847): 396-416.

4533. U. Holzmeister, "Zum Gleichnis von den Arbeitern im Weinberg (Mt. 20, 1-16)," *ZKT* 52 (1928): 407-12.

4534. Jacques Dupont, "La parabole des ouvriers de la vigne (Matthew xx, 1-16)," *NRT* 79 (1957): 785-97.

4535. J. B. Bauer, "Gnadenlohn oder Tageslohn?" *B* 42 (1961): 224-28 [Mt. 20:8-16].

4536. W. H. P. Hatch, "A Note on Matthew 20:15," *ATR* 26 (1944): 250-53.

4537. A. Škrinjar, "Dicta Christi de martyris (Mt. 20, 23 etc.)," *VD* 18 (1938): 168-77.

4538. H. Ernst, "Is het woord λύτρον (Matth. 20, 28): in juridischen of ethischen zin te verstaan?" *TS* 12 (1894): 323-47.

4539. George Milligan, " 'A Ransom for Many'," *ET* 13 (1901-1902): 311-13 [Mt. 20:28; Mk. 10:45].

4540. M. H. Franzmann, "A Ransom for Many," *CTM* 25 (1954): 497-516 [Mt. 20:28].

4541. E. Schaubach, "Bemerkungen über die Lehre von der Erlösung, mit Beziehung auf Matth. 20,28," *TSK* 3 (1831): 823-28.

4542. Karl Pieper, "Zum Einzug Jesu in Jerusalem," *BibZ* 11 (1913): 397-402 [Mt. 21:1-9].

4543. Rayner Winterbotham, "The Ass and the Ass's Colt," *ET* 28 (1916-1917): 380-81 [Mt. 21:1-7].

4544. J. Llynfi Davies, "Was Jesus Compelled?" *ET* 42 (1930-1931): 526-27 [Mt. 21:1-9; Mk. 11:1-10; Lk. 19:28-38; Jn. 12:12-16].

4545. James Mcikle, "Was Jesus Compelled?" *ET* 43 (1931-1932): 288 [Mt. 21:1-9].

4546. R. Scott Frayn and J. W. Jack, "Was Jesus Compelled?" *ET* 43 (1931-1932): 381-83 [Mt. 21:1-9].

4547. Basilius Haeusler, "Zu Mt. 23, 3b und Parallelen," *BibZ* 14 (1916-1917): 153-58.

4548. C. H. Johnson, "The Song of Entry: Matt. 21:9; Mark 11:9; Luke 19:38; John 12:13," *BW* 34 (1909): 47.

4549. Fr. Herklotz, "Zu Mt. 21:9, 15," *BibZ* 18 (1929): 39.

4550. C. T. Wood, "The Word ὡσαννά in Matthew xxi. 9," *ET* 52 (1940-1941): 357.

4551. H. McKeating, "The Prophet Jesus," *ET* 73 (1961-1962): 4-7, 50-53 [Mt. 21:11].

4552. F.-M. Braun, "L'expulsion des vendeurs du temple (Mt. xxi, 12-17, 23-27; Mc. xi, 15-19, 27-33; Lc. xix, 45; xx, 8; Jo. ii, 13-22)," *RB* 38 (1929): 178-200.

4553. John Glasgow and Galloway, "Studies in Texts," *Th* 46 (1943). 83-84 [Mt. 21:14].

4554. Eb. Nestle, "Matthew xxi. 15, 16," *ET* 10 (1898-1899): 525.

4555. J. J. S. Perowne, "The Laws of the Kingdom and the Invitation of the King," *Exp* 1st. ser. 7 (1878): 215-23, 249-63, 348-58 [Mt. 21:25-30].

4556. John Reid, "Why Jesus did not Answer," *ET* 14 (1902-1903): 506-508 [Mt. 21:27].

4557. W. M. Macgregor, "The Parable of the Two Sons," *ET* 38 (1926-1927): 498-501 [Mt. 21:28-32].

4558. Alex. Schweizer, "Erklärung der Erzählung Matth xxi. 28-32 nach der von Lachmann aufgenommenen Lesart ὁ ὕστερος V. 31," *TSK* 12 (1839): 944-64.

4559. Harold A. Guy, "The Parable of the Two Sons," *ET* 51 (1939-1940): 204-205 [Mt. 21:28-31].

4560.   J. A. Kleist, "Greek or Semitic Idiom: A Note on Mt. 21:32,"
         CBQ 8 (1946): 192-96.

4561.   Arthur Gray, "The Parable of the Wicked Husbandmen," *HJ*
         19 (1920-1921): 42-52 [Mt. 21:33-41].

4562.   R. Swaeles, "L'arrière-fond scriptuaire de Matt. xxi. 43 et
         son lien avec Matt. XXI. 44," *NTSt* 6 (1959-1960): 310-13.

4563.   R. Swaeles, "L'orientation ecclésiastique de la parabole du
         festin nuptial en Mt. XXII.1-14," *ETL* 36 (1960): 655-84.

4564.   W. B. Selbie, "The Parable of the Marriage Feast (Matt. xxii.
         1-14)," *ET* 37 (1925-1926): 266-69.

4565.   A. Vaccari, "La parabole du festin des noces (Mt. XXII, 1-14).
         Notes d exégèse," *RSR* 39 (1951-1952): 138-45.

4566.   Giorgio R. Castellino, "L'abito di nozze nella parabola del
         convito e une lettera di Mari (Matteo 22, 1-14)," *EE* 34
         (1960): 819-24.

4567.   E. H. Merriman, "Matthew xxii. 1-14," *ET* 66 (1954-1955):
         61.

4568.   Wolfgang Trilling, "Zur Überlieferungsgeschichte des
         Gleichnisses vom Hochzeitsmahl, Mt. 22, 1-14," *BibZ* 4
         (1960): 251-65.

4569.   L. Fonck, "Nuptiae filii regis (Mt. 22, 1-14)," *VD* 2 (1922):
         294-300.

4570.   A. Hilgenfeld, "Das Gleichnis vom Hochzeitsmahl, Mt. 22,
         1-14," *ZWT* 36 (1893): 126-42.

4571.   A. D. Loman, "Bijdrage tot de kritiek der Synoptische
         Evangelien. De gelijkenis van het Gastmaal, bij Mattheus (22,
         2 vgg.) en Lucas (14, 16 vgg.)," *TT* 6 (1872): 178-200.

4572.   Agnes Smith Lewis, "Matthew xxii. 4," *ET* 24 (1912-1913):
         427.

4573.   H. Chavannes, "Quelques gloses des évangiles," *RTP* 42
         (1909): 288-310 [Mt. 22:11-14].

4574.   K. R. J. Cripps, "A Note on Matthew xxii. 12," *ET* 69
         (1957): 30.

4575.   F. Giesekke, "Πολλοί εἰσιν κλητοί, ὀλίγοι δὲ ἐκλεκτοί," *TSK*
         21 (1898): 344-48 [Mt. 22:14].

4576.   Herbert A. Musurillo, " 'Many are Called, but Few are
         Chosen' (Matthew 22:14)," *ThSt* 7 (1946): 583-89.

4577.   M. Brunec, " 'Multi vocati—pauci electi' (Mt. 22, 14)," *VD*

26 (1948): 88-97, 129-43, 277-90.

4578. Friedrich Müller, "Berufung und Erwählung. Eine exegetische Studie," *ZST* 24 (1955): 38-71 [Mt. 22:14].

4579. H. Liese, "Numisma census (Mt. 22, 15-21; Mc. 12, 13-17; Lc. 20, 20-26)," *VD* 12 (1932): 289-94.

4580. M. Süsskind, "Beitrag zur Erklärung der Stelle Matth. 22, 23-33 (Luc. 20, 27-39)," *TSK* 3 (1830): 664-69.

4581. E. H. Blakeney, "A Note on St. Matthew xxii. 29," *ET* 4 (1892-1893): 382.

4582. Aloys Berthoud, "La réponse de Jésus aux Sadducéens sur la résurrection," *RTQR* 13 (1904): 446-51 [Mt. 22:30].

4583. C. Bruston, "Du vrai sens de la réponse de Jésus aux Sadducéens," *RTQR* 13 (1904): 529-537 [Mt. 22:30].

4584. Pierre Vallin, "Une retouche au *Scriptum super quarto Sententiarum*aint Thomas," *RSR* 49 (1961): 561-63 [Mt. 22:31f.; Mk. 12:26f.; Lk. 20:36ff.].

4585. L. Fonck, "Quaestio de mandato magno (Mt. 22, 35-46)," *VD* 5 (1925): 261-71.

4586. Hugo Rosén, "Kärlekens Lag," *STK* 3 (1927): 50-61 [Mt. 22:35-46].

4587. Fr. Herklotz, "Zur Form des Liebesgebotes," *ZKT* 27 (1903): 574-77 [Mt. 22:37; Mk. 12:30, 33; Lk. 10:27].

4588. Paul Althaus, "Andacht über Matth. 22, 41-46," *TB* 7 (1928): 274-75.

4589. W. O. Carver, "The Christian Message is Christ," *RE* 40 (1943): 296-303 [Mt. 22:41-46, etc.].

4590. David Smith, "Our Lord's Reductio ad absurdum of the Rabbinical Interpretation of Psalm cx," *ET* 16 (1904- 1905): 256-58 [Mt. 22:44].

4591. Ernst Haenchen, "Matthäus 23," *ZTK* N.F. 48 (1951): 38-63.

4592. H. Grimme, "Ein Herrenwort bei Matthäus in neuer Beleuchtung," *BibZ* 23 (1935-1936): 171-79 [Mt. 23:2ff.].

4593. Eb. Nestle, They Enlarge the Borders of their Garments," *ET* 20 (1908-1909): 188-89 [Mt. 23:5].

4594. Ferdinand Prat, "Les places d'honneur chez les juifs contemporains du Christ," *RSR* 15 (1925): 512-22 [Mt. 23:6 et al.].

4595. W. S. Reilly, "Titles in Mt. 23:8-12," *CBQ* 1 (1939): 249-50.

4596.   E. F. Brown, "St. Matthew xxiii. 8-10," *Th* 30 (1935): 43-44.

4597.   John T. Townsend, "Matthew xxiii. 9," *JTS* N.S. 12 (1961): 56-59.

4598.   L. Saggin, "Magister vester unus est Christus (Mt. 23, 10)," *VD* 30 (1952): 205-12.

4599.   C. Spicq, "Une allusion au docteur de justice dans Matthieu XXIII, 10?" *RB* 66 (1959): 387-96.

4600.   H. J. Flowers, "Matthew xxiii. 15," *ET* 73 (1961-1962): 67-69.

4601.   John Hoad, "On Matthew xxiii. 15: A Rejoinder," *ET* 73 (1961-1962): 211-12.

4602.   Charles C. Torrey, "Strain out a Gnat and adorn a Camel," *HTR* 14 (1921): 195-96 [Mt. 23:24].

4603.   H. Windisch, "Der Untergang Jerusalems (Anno 70): im Urteil der Christen und Juden," *TT* 48 (1914): 519-50 [Mt. 23:26 ff., Lk. 19:42-44].

4604.   H. Pernot, "Matthieu XXIII, 29-36. Luc xi, 47-51," *RHPR* 13 (1933): 262-67.

4605.   J. R. Wilkinson, "A Play on Words in the Logia Hitherto Unnoticed. A Note on St. Matt. XXIII. 29-31 = St. Luke xi. 47-48," *Exp* 7th ser. 10 (1910): 188-92.

4606.   Joachim Jeremias, "Drei weitere spätjüdische Heiligengräbe," *ZNW* 52 (1961): 95-101.

4607.   D. F. Strauss, "Jesu Weheruf über Jerusalem und die σοφία τοῦ θεοῦ. Matth. 23, 34-39, Luc. 11, 49-51; 13, 34 f.," *ZWT* 6 (1863): 84-93.

4608.   John Chapman, "Zacharias, Slain Between the Temple and the Altar," *JTS* 13 (1911-1912): 398-410 [Mt. 23:35; Lk. 11:51].

4609.   Eb. Nestle, Between the Temple and the Altar," *ET* 13 (1901-1902): 562 [Mt. 23:35; Lk. 11:51].

4610.   G. Mercati, "La lettera di Severo Antiocheno su Matt. 23, 35," *OC* Serie 11/4 (1915): 59-63.

4611.   Christ. Wilh. Müller, "Zur Erklärung des Ζαχαρίου υἱοῦ βαραχίου Matth. 23, 35," *TSK* 14 (1841): 673-80.

4612.   John Macpherson, "A Study of Matthew 23:35," *BW* 9 (1897): 26-31.

4613.   Lewis Sperry Chafer, "The Olivet Discourse," *BS* 109

(1952): 4-36 [Mt. 23:37 [sic]—24:46].

4614. A. D. Loman, "De Apostrophe aan Jeruzalem, Matth. XXIII. 37 vlg. beschouwd in verband met de vraag, of Jezus toen voor het eerst in Jeruzalem is opgetreden," *TT* 1 (1867): 550-60.

4615. André Feuillet, "La synthèse eschatologique de saint Matthieu (XXIV-XXV)," *RB* 56 (1949): 340-64; 57 (1950): 62-91, 180-211.

4616. C. E. Stowe, "The Eschatology of Christ, With Special Reference to the Discourse in Matt. XXIV and XXV," *BS* 7 (1850): 452-78.

4617. James F. Rand, "A Survey of the Eschatology of the Olivet Discourse," *BS* 113 (1956): 162-73, 200-13 [Mt. 24-25].

4618. Friedrich Spitta, "Die grosse eschatologische Rede Jesu," *TSK* 82 (1909): 348-401 [Mt. 24:1-51; Mk. 13:1-37; Lk. 21:5-36].

4619. Édouard Cothenet, "La IIe Épître aux Thessaloniciens et l'apocalypse synoptique," *RSR* 42 (1954): 5-39 [Mt. 24:1-44, Mk. 13:1-37; Lk. 21:5-40].

4620. William Barclay, "Great Themes of the New Testament. Matthew xxiv," *ET* 70 (1958-1959): 326-30, 376-79.

4621. J. A. Oñate, "El 'Reino de Dios,' ¿tema central del discurso escatológico?" *EB* 3 (1944): 495-522; 4 (1945): 15-34, 163-96, 421-46; 5 (1946): 101-10.

4622. Francisco de P. Solá, "Apostillas a un libro sobre el 'Reino de Diós'," *EE* 23 (1949): 359-75. [Mt. 24].

4623. J. Blenkinsopp, "The Hidden Messiah and his Entry into Jerusalem," *Scr* 13 (1961): 51-56 [Mt. 24:5, 23-24].

4624. H. Liese, "Sermo de Parusia (Mt. 24, 15-35)," *VD* 12 (1932): 321-26.

4625. John Gwynn, "Hippolytus on St. Matthew xxiv. 15," *Herm* 7 (1890): 137-50.

4626. Dr. Auberlen, "Die eschatologische Rede Jesu Christi Matth. 24, 25," *TSK* 35 (1862): 213-47.

4627. I de Marchi, " 'Ubicumque fuerit corpus, ibi congregabuntur et aquilae' (Mt. 24, 28; Lc. 17, 37)," *VD* 18 (1938): 329-33.

4628. E. Robinson, "The Coming of Christ, as Announced in Matt. 24:29, 31," *BS* 1843, 531-57.

4629. F. C. Burkitt, "On *Immediately* in Matt. XXIV, 29," *JTS* 12 (1910-1911): 460-61.

4630. Paul Joüon, " 'Les forces des cieux seront ébranlées,' (Matthieu 24, 29; Marc 13, 25; Luc 21, 26)," *RSR* 29 (1939): 114-15.

4631. Moses Stuart, "Observations on Matthew 24:29-31, and the Parallel Passages in Mark and Luke, with Remarks on the Double Sense of Scripture," *BS* 9 (1852): 329-55, 449-65.

4632. U. Holzmeister, "Ab arbore fici discite parabolam (Mt. 24, 32)," *VD* 20 (1940): 299-306.

4633. R. Thibaut, "La parabole du voleur," *NRT* 54 (1927): 688-92. [Mt. 24:43].

4634. U. Holzmeister, "Das Gleichnis vom Diebe in den Evangelien und beim hl. Paulus (Mt. 24, 43f.; Lc. 12, 39f.; 1 Thess. 5, 24)," *ZKT* 40 (1916): 704-36.

4635. J. J. Murphy, "The Parables of Judgment," *Exp* 4th ser. 4 (1891): 52-62 [Mt. 24:45-25:46; Lk. 12:35-48].

4636. Samuel Dickey, "Three Warnings Concerning Jesus' Second Coming," *BW* 36 (1910): 268-73 [Mt. 25:1-46].

4637. W. D. Ridley, "The Parable of the Ten Virgins," *Exp* 5th ser., 2 (1895): 342-49 [Mt. 25:1-13].

4638. A. Hilgenfeld, "Das Gleichnis von den zehn Jungfrauen Matth. 25, 1-13," *ZWT* 44 (1901): 545-53.

4639. Pastor Wiesen, "Das Gleichnis von den zehn Jungfrauen," *TSK* 72 (1899): 37-62 [Mt. 25:1-12].

4640. A. Strobel, "Zum Verständnis von Mat. xxv, 1-13," *NT* 2 (1958): 199-227.

4641. James Reid, "The Parable of the Ten Virgins, Matt. xxv. 1-13," *ET* 37 (1925-1926): 447-51.

4642. R. Cölle, "Die Pointe des Gleichnisses von den zehn Jungfrauen," *NKZ* 12 (1901): 904-908 [Mt. 25:1-13].

4643. F. C. Burkitt, "The Parable of the Ten Virgins," *JTS* 30 (1928-1929): 267-70 [Mt. 25:1-13].

4644. H. L. Goudge, "The Parable of the Ten Virgins," *JTS* 30 (1928-1929): 399-401 [Mt. 25:1-13].

4645. R. Wintenbotham, "The Second Advent," *Exp* 1st ser. 9 (1879): 67-80 [Mt. 25:5].

4646. W. Schmidt, "Die Bedeutung der Talente in der Parabel

Matth. 25, 14-30," *TSK* 56 (1883): 782-99.

4647. G. Matheson, "Scripture Studies of the Heavenly State; The Nature of the Heavenly Blessedness (Matt. xxv. 21)," *Exp* 2nd ser. 6 (1883): 204-15.

4648. John Mutch, "The Man with One Talent," *ET* 42 (1930-1931): 332-34 [Mt. 25:24ff.].

4649. W. Lock, "The Sheep and the Goats," *Exp* 5th ser. 10 (1899): 401-12 [Mt. 25:31-33].

4650. C. F. Burney, "St. Matthew xxv. 31-46 as a Hebrew Poem," *JTS* 14 (1912-13): 414-24.

4651. A. T. Cadoux, "The Parable of the Sheep and the Goats (Mt xxv. 31-46)," *ET* 41 (1929-1930): 559-62.

4652. Karl Bornhäuser, "Zur Auslegung von Matthäus 25, 31-46," *NKZ* 46 (1935): 77-82.

4653. Paul S. Minear, "The Coming of the Son of Man," *TTod* 9 (1953): 489-93 [Mt. 25:31-46].

4654. John A. T. Robinson, "The 'Parable' of the Sheep and the Goats," *NTSt* 2 (1955-1956): 225-37 [Mt. 25:31-46].

4655. C. L. Mitton, "Present Justification and Final Judgment—A Discussion of the Parable of the Sheep and the Goats," *ET* 68 (1945-1947): 46-50 [Mt. 25:31-46].

4656. N. A. Dahl, "Die Passionsgeschichte bei Matthaeus," *NTSt* 2 (1955-1956): 17-32 [Mt. 26-27].

4657. John Willcock, "St. Matt. xxv. 36; 2 Tim. i. 16-18," *ET* 34 (1922-1923): 43.

4658. L. von Sybel, "Die Salbungen," *ZNW* 23 (1924): 184-93 [Mt. 26:6-13; Mk. 14:3-9; Lk. 7:36-50; Jn. 12:1-8].

4659. André Legault, "An Application of the Form-Critique Method to the Anointings in Galilee (Lk. 7, 36-50) and Bethany (Mt. 26, 6-13; Mk. 14, 3-9; Jn. 12, 1-8)," *CBQ* 16 (1954): 131-45.

4660. T. W. Bevan, "The Four Anointings," *ET* 39 (1927-1928): 137-39 [Mt. 26:6-13; Mk. 14:3-9; Lk. 7:36-50; Jn. 12:1-11].

4661. U. Holzmeister, "Num Iudas Christum pretio vulgari servorum vendiderit," *VD* 23 (1943): 65-70 [Mt. 26:15; 27:3, 9].

4662. R. Follet. "Constituerunt ei triginta argenteos (Mt. 26, 15)," *VD* 29 (1951): 98-100.

4663. Axel Andersen, "Zu Mt. 26, 17 ff. und Lc. 22, 15 ff.," *ZNW* 7 (1906): 87-90.

4664. D. A. Frøvig, "Jesu ord til yppperstepresten om sit komme paa himmelens skyer (Mt. 26, 24). Til belysning av de synoptiske utsagn om Menneskesønnens snarlige komme," *TTDF* 4th ser., 1 (1920): 257-79.

4665. A. Andersen, "Mt. 26, 26 flg. und Parallelstellen im Lichte der Abendmahlslehre Justins," *ZNW* 7 (1906): 172-75.

4666. F. E. Vokes, "Eucharistia," *Herm* no. 92 (1958): 31-44 [Mt. 26:26ff.].

4667. Joseph Bonsirven, "Hoc est corpus meum," *B* 29 (1948): 205-19 [Mt. 26:26].

4668. Miguel Torres, "Un problema de traducion—¿'Este es mi cuerpo' o 'esto es mi cuerpo'?" *CB* 15 (1958): 10-13 [Mt. 26:26].

4669. Salvador Muñoz Iglesias, "Hic est sanguis meus (Mt. 26, 28)," *VD* 22 (1942): 74-81.

4670. Karl Pieper, "Einige Bemerkungen zu Mt. 26, 31 und Mk. 14, 27," *BibZ* 21 (1933): 320-23.

4671. E. Petavel, "The House of Gethsemane," *Exp* 4th ser., 3 (1891): 220-32 [Mt. 26:36; Mk. 14:32].

4672. F. S. Stooke-Vaughan, "Sit Ye Here," *ET* 6 (1894-1895): 94-95 [Mt. 26:36].

4673. John Robson, "The Meaning of Christ's Prayer in Gethsemane," *ET* 6 (1894-1895): 522-23 [Mt. 26:39].

4674. W. M. Alexander, J. G. Cunningham, D. G. Watt, and George Milne, "The Meaning of Christ's Prayer in Gethsemane," *ET* 7 (1895-1896): 34-38 [Mt. 26:39].

4675. Thomas West, James Whyte, John Reith, J. A. Stokes Little, and Mrs. I. Grant, "The Meaning of Christ's Prayer in Gethsemane," *ET* 7 (1895-1896): 118-21 [Mt. 26:39].

4676. E. F. M'Michael, John Ross, and R. E. Wallis, "Our Lord's Prayer in Gethsemane," *ET* 7 (1895-1896): 502-505.

4677. A. Eugene Thomson, "Our Lord's Prayer in the Garden," *BS* 97 (1940): 110-16 [Mt. 26:39].

4678. W. Tom, "De bede van Christus in Gethsemané," *GTT* 57 (1957): 213-19 [Mt. 26:39, 54; Mk. 14:36; Lk. 22:43; Heb. 5:7].

4679. J. Aars, "Zu Matth. 26, 45 und Marc. 14, 41," *ZWT* 38 (1895): 378-83.

4680. W. J. M. Starkie, "Gospel according to St. Matthew xxvi. 45 and xxviii. 2," *Herm* 19 (1922): 141-43.

4681. T. Chase, "τὸ λοιπόν Matt. xxvi. 45," *JBL* 6 (1886, part 1): 131-35.

4682. J. M. Ballard, "The Fourth Cry from the Cross," *ET* 33 (1921-1922): 332-33 [Mt. 27:46].

4683. Thomas C. Gordon, "The Fourth Cry from the Cross," *ET* 34 (1922-1923): 380 [Mt. 27:46].

4684. Theodore D. Woolsey, "On a Passage in Matthew XXVI, 50," *BS* 31 (1874): 314-32 [ἐφ' ὃ πάρει].

4685. Adolf Deissmann, "Friend, wherefore art thou Come?" *ET* 33 (1921-1922): 431-93 [Mt 26:50].

4686. E. C. E. Owen, "St. Matthew xxvi. 50," *JTS* 29 (1927-1928): 384-86.

4687. James P. Wilson, "Matthew xxvi. 50: 'Friend' wherefore art thou come?" *ET* 41 (1929-1930): 334.

4688. Friedrich Rehkopf, "Mt. 26, 50: ἑταῖρε ἐφ' ὃ πάρει," *ZNW* 52 (1961): 109-15.

4689. Hans Kosmala, "Matthew XXVI, a Quotation from the Targum," *NT* 4 (1960): 3-5.

4690. Jacob Naadland, "Ordet um sverdet, Matt. 26, 52," *NTT* 55 (1954): 162-73.

4691. Johann Michl, "Der Tod Jesu. Ein Beitrag zur Frage nach Schuld und Verantwortung eines Volkes," *MTZ* 1 (1950): 5-15 [Mt. 26:57ff.; 27:15ff.].

4692. J. J. Young, "Christ Under Oath," *LQ* 31 (1901): 402-12 [Mt. 26:63].

4693. Samuel J. Andrews, "Matt. xxvi. 64," *JBL* 7 (1887, part 1): 90-93.

4694. P. V. Smith, "St. Peter's Threefold Denial of our Lord," *Th* 17 (1928): 341-48 [Mt. 26:69-75; Mk. 14:66-72; Lk. 22:56-62].

4695. Harold P. Cooke, "Christ Crucified—and by whom?" *HJ* 29 (1930-1931): 61-74 [Mt. 27; Mk. 15].

4696. F. Barth, "Der Tod des Judas Iscarioth," *STZ* 11 (1894): 108-24 [Mt. 27:3-10].

4697.   J. Iverach Munro, "The Death of Judas (Matt. xxvii. 3-8;
          Acts i. 18-19)," *ET* 24 (1912-1913): 235-36.

4698.   J. W. Primrose, "Exegetical Note: Matthew 27, 4. Judas,"
          USR 2 (1890): 29-31.

4699.   J. Rendel Harris, "Did Judas Really Commit Suicide?" *AJT*
          4 (1900): 490-513 [Mt. 27:5; cf. Ac. 1:18].

4700.   J. H. Bernard, "The Death of Judas," *Exp* 6th ser., 9 (1904):
          422-30 [Mt. 27:5; Ac. 1:18].

4701.   Hugh Ross Hatch, "The Old Testament Quotation in
          Matthew 27: 9, 10," *BW* 1 (1893): 345-54.

4702.   William Caldwell, "The Death and Resurrection of Jesus
          Christ," *BW* 36 (1910): 415-23 [Matt. 27:11-50; 28:1-20].

4703.   W. Hersey Davis, "Origen's Comment on Matthew 27:17,"
          RE 39 (1942): 65-67.

4704.   Heberle, "Über Matthäus 27, 24," *TSK* 29 (1856): 859-64.

4705.   U. Holzmeister, "Christus Dominus flagellis caeditur (Mt.
          27. 26 et par.)," *VD* 18 (1938): 104-108.

4706.   U. Holzmeister, "Christus Dominus spinis coronatur," *VD* 17
          (1937): 65-69 [Mt. 27:29].

4707.   John Willcock, " 'When he had tasted' (Matt. xxvii. 34)," *ET*
          32 (1920-1921): 426.

4708.   Ernest Elliott, " 'When he had tasted' (Matt. xxvii. 34)," *ET*
          33 (1921-1922): 41-42.

4709.   H. J. Vogels, "Der Lanzenstich vor dem Tode Jesu," *BibZ* 10
          (1912): 396-405 [Mt. 27:45 ff.].

4710.   Fred Smith, "The Strangest 'Word' of Jesus," *ET* 44
          (1932-1933): 259-61 [Mt. 27:46; Mk. 15:34].

4711.   W. F. Lofthouse, "The Cry of Dereliction," *ET* 53
          (1941-1942): 188-92 [Mk. 15:34; Mt. 27:46; Ps. 22:1].

4712.   C. M. Macleroy, "Notes on the Cry of Forsakenness on the
          Cross," *ET* 53 (1941-1942): 326 [Mt. 27:46; Mk. 15:34].

4713.   W. J. Kenneally, " 'Eli, Eli, Lamma Sabacthani?' (Mt.
          27:46)," *CBQ* 8 (1946): 124-34.

4714.   Frank Zimmermann, "The Last Words of Jesus," *JBL* 66
          (1947): 465-66 [Mt. 27:46].

4715.   Martin Rehm, "Eli, Eli, lamma sabacthani," *BibZ* 2 (1958):
          275-78 [Mt. 27:46].

4716.   H. C. Veale, " 'The Merciful Bystander'," *ET* 28

(1916-1917): 324-25 [Mt. 27:48].

4717. John Simpson, "Matthew xxvii. 51-53," *ET* 14 (1902-1903): 527-28 [Mt. 27:51-53].

4718. Martin Graebner, "The Resurrection of Saints at the Death of Christ," *CTM* 12 (1941): 182-88 [Mt. 27:52-53].

4719. G. Vittonatto, "La risurrezione dei morti in Mt. 27, 52-53," *RivB* 3 (1955): 193-219.

4720. Hermann Zeller, "Corpora sanctorum. Eine Studie zu Mt. 27:52-53," *ZKT* 71 (1949): 385-465.

4721. Cameron Mann, "The Centurion at the Cross," *ET* 20 (1908-1909): 563-64 [Mt. 27:54].

4722. P. van Stempvoort, " 'Gods Zoon' of 'Een Zoon Gods' in Mtt. 27, 54," *NedTT* 9 (1954-1955): 79-89.

4723. J. Blinzler, "Zur Auslegung der Evangelienberichte über Jesu Begräbnis," *MTZ* 3 (1952): 403-14 [Mt. 27: 57-61].

4724. Werner Bulst, "Untersuchungen zum Begräbnis Christi," *MTZ* 3 (1952): 244-55 [Mt. 27:57-61].

4725. Paul Joüon, "Matthew XXVII, 59: σινδὼν καθαρά," *RSR* 24 (1934): 93-95.

4726. Kevin Smyth, "The Guard on the Tomb," *HeyJ* 2 (1961): 157-59 [Mt. 27:65].

4727. D. S. Margoliouth, "The Visit to the Tomb," *ET* 38 (1926-1927): 278-80 [Mt. 28:1-10; Mk. 16:1-8].

4728. Charles A. Webster, "St.. Matthew xxviii. 1-3," *ET* 42 (1930-1931): 381-82.

4729. Juan Leal, "San Mateo y la aparición de Cristo a Magdalena (Mt. 28, 1. 5-10)," *EB* 7 (1948): 5-28.

4730. W. K. Lowther Clarke, "Studies in Texts," *Th* 43 (1941): 300-302 [Mt. 28:2-4].

4731. José M. Bover, "La aparición del Señor resucitado a las piadosas mujeres," *EB* 4 (1945): 5-13 [Mt. 28:9 ff.].

4732. F. F. Bruce, "The End of the First Gospel," *EQ* 12 (1940): 203-14 [Mt. 28:16-20].

4733. S. M. Zwemer, "The Authenticity and Genuineness of the Great Commission (Matthew 28:16-20)," *USR* 54 (1942-1943): 47-54.

4734. H. B. Swete, "St. Matthew XXVIII. 16-20," *Exp* 6th ser., 6 (1902): 241-59.

4735. Otto Michel, "Der Abschluss des Matthäusevangeliums," *EvT* 10 (1950-1951): 16-26 [Mt. 28:16-20].

4736. W. D. Morris, "Matthew xxviii. 17," *ET* 47 (1935-1936): 142.

4737. S. del Páramo, "Un problema de exégesis neotestamentaria: Quidam autem dubitaverunt (Mt. 28, 17)," *EB* 14 (1955): 281-96.

4738. B. Eager, "The Lord is with you," *Scr* 12 (1960): 48-54 [Mt. 28:18 ff.].

4739. John H. Strong, " 'The Great Commission': Does it Merit the Name?" *BW* 29 (1907): 352-56 [Mt. 28:18-20].

4740. L. E. Barton, "Imperative or Participle?" *RE* 33 (1936): 44-48 [Mt. 28:18-20].

4741. L. Fonck, "Inauguratio Ecclesiae (Mt. 28, 18-20)," *VD* 2 (1922): 161-65.

4742. Carl Stange, "Das letzte Wort des Auferstandenen," *ZST* 9 (1931-1932): 637-44 [Mt. 28:18-20].

4743. J. Armitage Robinson, " 'In the Name'," *JTS* 7 (1905-1906): 186-202 [Mt. 28:19, 20].

4744. Frederick L. Anderson, "The Great Commission," *CQ* 3 (1926): 58-79, 170-83 [Mt. 28:19-20].

4745. E. T. Thompson, "The Great Commission," *USR* 44 (1932-1933): 124-39 [Mt. 28:19-20].

4746. H. E. Bindseil, "Erklärung der Redensart: Βαπτίζειν τινὰ εἰς τὸ ὄνομα τοῦ πατρὸς καὶ τοῦ υἱοῦ καὶ τοῦ ἁγίου πνεύματος Matth. 28, 19," *TSK* 5 (1832): 410-17.

4747. H. E. Bindseil, "Interpretation of the Baptismal Formula —Matt. 28:19," (trans. by H. B. Smith) *BS* 1 (1844): 703-708.

4748. F. C. Conybeare, "The Eusebian Form of the Text Matth. 28, 19," *ZNW* 2 (1901): 275-88.

4749. F. H. Chase, "The Lord's Command to Baptize (St. Matthew XXVIII 19)," *JTS* 6 (1904-1905): 481-512.

4750. F. H. Chase, "The Lord's Command to Baptize (St. Matthew XXVIII, 19)," *JTS* 8 (1906-1907): 161-84.

4751. George H. Gilbert, "The Baptismal Formula of Matt. 28:19," *BW* 34 (1909): 374-79.

4752. F. W. Grosheide, "Matth. 28:19," *TS* 34 (1916): 217-27.

4753.   Anton Fridrichsen, "Den treleddede formel Mt. 28:19 og daaben til de tre navn," *NTT* 23 (1922): 65-81.

4754.   Jules Lebreton, "Les origines du symbole baptismal," *RSR* 20 (1930): 97-124 [Mt. 28:19].

4755.   Roger F. Markham, "In (Into) the Name," *Th* 36 (1938): 236-37 [Mt. 28:19].

4756.   Giovanni Ongaro, "L'authenticità e integrità del comma trinitario in Mt. 28, 19," *B* 19 (1938): 267-79.

4757.   Hans Raeder, "Matthaeus 28. 19," *DTT* 9 (1946): 193-96.

4758.   Harold M. Parker, "The Great Commission," *Interp* 2 (1948): 74-75 [Mt. 28:19].

4759.   D. H. Ogden, "The Reality and the Living Presence of Jesus Christ," *USR* 41 (1929-1930): 366-75 [Mt. 28:20]. On Mt. 1:16, see number 1918; 2:1, 3679; 2:9, 1723; chaps 3-7, 2309; 3:3, 3679; 3:11 and 16, 3686; 3:13-17, 3681; 3:16, 3684; 4:1-11, 4789; 4:12 ff., 3679; 4:15, 3682; chaps. 5-7, 2388; 5.17, *10047*; 6:11, 3719; 8:5, 3683; 10:38, 3690; chap. 11, 3685; 11:5, 3680; 11:12-1, 3691; 11:12, 16-19, 379; 12:18, 3682; 12:43 ff., *10080*; 13:10-17, 3681; chap. 15, 3681; 16:19, 9545; 18:12, *10072*; 18:18, 4455, 4456, 4458; chap. 19, 3681; 19:10, 3682; 20:1-16, 3681; 21:12-13, *10069*; 21:18-19, 10076; 22:1-14, *10068*; 22:34-28:20, 1627; 22:36, 1925; 24:1-51, *10025*; 25:9, 3379; 26:49, 3684; 26: 64, 3687; 27:9, 3680; 27:46, 4682f.; 28:1, 3682; 28:19, 1918, *10040, 10041*; 28:19-20, *10033*.

4759.1   J. O. Tuñi, "La Tipologia Israel-Jesús en Mt. 1-2," *EE* 47 (1972): 361-76 [1-2].

4759.2   E. Galbiati, "Genere letterario e storia in Matteo 1-2," *BO* 15 (1973): 3-16 [1-2].

4759.3   A. Vicent Cernuda, "La dialéctica *gennô-tiktô* en Mt. 1-2," *B* 55 (1974): 408-17 [1-2].

4759.4   B. T. Benedict, "The Genres of Matthew 1-2: Light from 1 Timothy 1:4," *RB* 97 (1990): 31-53 [1 2].

4759.5   H. Milton, "The Structure of the Prologue to St. Matthew's Gospel," *JBL* 81 (1962): 175-81 [1:1-17].

4759.6   Léon Ramlot, "Les genealogies bibliques. Un genre litteraire oriental," *BVC* 60 (1964): 53-70 [1:1-17].

4759.7   F. Schnider and W. Stenger, "Die Frauen im Stammbaum Jesu nach Matthaus. Strukturale Beobachtungen zu Mt. 1,

1-17" *BibZ* 23 (1979): 187-96 [1:1-17].

4759.8 Thomas H. Graves, "Matthew 1:1-17," *RE* 86 (1989): 595-600 [1:1-17].

4759.9 Richard J. Bauckham, "Tamar's Ancestry and Rahab's Marriage: Two Problems in the Matthean Genealogy," *NT* 37 (1995): 313-29 [1:3].

4759.10 Yair Zakovitch, "Rahab als Mutter des Boaz in der Jesus-Genealogie (Matth. 1,5)," *NT* 17/1 (1975): 1-5 [1:5].

4759.11 Jerome D. Quinn, "Is Ῥαχάβ in Mt. 1,5 Rahab of Jericho?" *B* 62/2 (1981): 225-28 [1:5].

4759.12 Raymond E. Brown, "Rachab in Mt. 1,5 Probably Is Rahab of Jericho," *B* 63/1 (1982): 79-80 [1:5].

4759.13 C. T. Davis, "Tradition and Redaction in Matthew 1:18-2:23," *JBL* 90/4 (1971): 404-21 [1:18-2:23].

4759.14 David R. Bauer, "The Kingship of Jesus in the Matthean Infancy Narrative: A Literary Analysis," *CBQ* 57 (1995): 306-23 [1:18-2:23].

4759.15 F. Dumermuth, "Bemerkung zu Jesu Menschwerdung," *TZ* 20 (1964): 52-53 [1:18-25].

4759.16 M. Krämer, "Die globale Analyse des Stiles in Mt. 1,18-25," *B* 45/2 (1964): 4-22 [1:18-25].

4759.17 K. Grayston, "Matthieu 1:18-25: Essai d'interprétation," *RTP* 23 (1973): 221-32 [1:18-25].

4759.18 F. Schnider and W. Stenger, " 'Mit der Abstammung Jesu Christi verhielt es sich so: . . .' Struckturale Beobachtungen zu Mt. 1,18-25," *BibZ* 25 (1981): 255-64 [1:18-25].

4759.19 Sheila Klassen-Wiebe, "Matthew 1:18-25," *Interp* 46 (1992): 392-95 [1:18-25].

4759.20 David Hill, "A Note on Matthew 1:19," *ET* 76/4 (1965): 133-34 [1:19].

4759.21 A. Vicent Cernuda, "El domicilio de José y la fama de María," *EB* 46 (1988): 5-25 [1:19].

4759.22 A. R. C. McLellan, "Choosing a Name for the Baby," *ET* 93 (1981): 80-82 [1:21].

4759.23 Klaus Junack, "Zu einem neuentdeckten Unzialfragment des Matthäus-Evangeliums," *NTSt* 16 (1969-1970): 284-88 [1:23-25].

4759.24 J. M. James, "The God Who Is with Us," *ET* 91 (1979):

78-79 [1:23].

4759.25 E. Galbiati, "Esegesi degli Evangeli festivi. L'Adorazione dei Magi (Matt. 2,1-12). (Festa dell'Epifania)," *BO* 4/1 (1962): 20-29 [2:1-12].

4759.26 Paul Gächter, "Die Magierperikope (Mt. 2,1-12)," *ZKT* 90/3 (1968): 257-95 [2:1-12].

4759.27 W. A. Schulze, "Zur Geschichte der Auslegung von Matth. 2,1-12," *TZ* 31/3 (1975): 150-60 [2:1-12].

4759.28 W. A. Schulze, "Nachtrag zu meinem Aufsatz: Zur Geschichte der Auslegung von Matth. 2:1-12," *TZ* 31 (1975): 150-60 [2:1-12].

4759.29 Antonio Charbel, "Mt. 2,1.7: I Magi erano Nabatei?" *RivB* 20 (1972): 571-83 [2:1-7].

4759.30 M. Küchler, "Wir haben seinen Stern gesehen . . . ," *BK* 44 (1989): 179-86 [2:2].

4759.31 John P. Heil, "Ezekiel 34 and the Narrative Strategy of the Shepherd and Sheep Metaphor in Matthew," *CBQ* 55 (1993): 698-708 [2:6].

4759.32 S. Barting, "Casa o caserio? Los magos en Belen," *EB* 25 (1966): 355-57 [2:11].

4759.33 D. H. C. Read, "Three Gaudy Kings," *ET* 91 (1979): 84-86 [2:11].

4759.34 Norman Walker, "The Alleged Matthaean Errata," *NTSt* 9 (1962-1963): 391-94 [2:13-15].

4759.35 Sebastián Dartina, "Y desde Egipto lo he proclamado hijo mio (Mt. 2,15)," *EB* 29/1 (1970): 157-60 [2:15].

4759.36 T. L. Howard, "The Use of Hosea 11:1 in Matthew 2:15. An Alternative Solution," *BS* 143 (1986): 314-28 [2:15].

4759.37 David L. Bartlett, "Jeremiah 31:15-20," *Interp* 32/1 (1978): 73-78 [2:18].

4759.38 J. A. Sanders, "*Nazoraios* in Matt. 2,23," *JBL* 84 (1965): 169-72 [2:23].

4759.39 Ernst Zuckschwerdt, "Ναζωραῖος in Matth. 2,23," *TZ* 31/2 (1975): 65-77 [2:23].

4759.40 W. Barnes Tatum, "Matthew 2:23: Wordplay and Misleading Translations," *BTr* 27/1 (1976): 135-38 [2:23].

4759.41 H. P. Rüger, "Nazareth/Nazara Nazarenos/Nazaraios," *ZNW* 72/3 (1981): 257-63 [2:23].

4759.42 T. Stramare, "Sarà chiamato Nazareno. Era stato detto dai Profeti," *BO* 36 (1994): 231-49 [2:23].

4759.43 Klaus Berger, "Jesus als Nasoräer/Nasiräaer," *NT* 38 (1996): 323-35 [2:23].

4759.44 B. Marconcini, "Tradizione e redazione in Mt. 3,1-12," *RivB* 19 (1971): 165-86 [3:1-12].

4759.45 Jean Doignon, "L'Argumentation d'Hilaire de Poitiers dans l'Exemplum de la Tentation de Jesus (In Matthaeum, 3,1-5)," *BTr* 29/1 (1978): 126-28 [3:1-5].

4759.46 John P. Brown, "The Ark of the Covenant and the Temple of Janus," *BibZ* 30/1 (1986): 20-35 [3:10].

4759.47 P. G. Bretscher, "Whose Sandals? (Matt. 3,11)," *JBL* 86 (1967): 81-87 [3:11].

4759.48 Otto Eissfeldt, "πληρῶσαι πᾶσαν δικαιοσύνην in Matthäus 3:15," *ZNW* 61/3 (1970): 209-15 [3:15].

4759.49 William R. Stegner, "Wilderness and Testing in the Scrolls and in Matthew 4:1-11," *BRes* 18 (1967): 18-27 [4:1-11].

4759.50 Balmer Kelly, "An Exposition of Matthew 4:1-11," *Interp* 29/1 (1975): 57-62 [4:1-11].

4759.51 Wilhelm Wilkens, "Die Versuchung Jesu Hach Matthaus," *NTSt* 28/4 (1982): 479-89 [4:1-11].

4759.52 Walter Wink, "Matthew 4:1-11," *Interp* 37/4 (1983): 392-97 [4:1-11].

4759.53 Lamar Williamson, "Matthew 4:1-11," *Interp* 38/1 (1984): 51- 55 [4:1-11].

4759.54 C. Grappe, "Essai sur l'arrière-plan Pascal des récits de la dernière nuit de Jésus," *RHPR* 65 (1985): 105-25 [4:1-11].

4759.55 William R. Stegner, "The Temptation Narrative: A Study in the Use of Scripture by Early Jewish Christians," *BRes* 35 (1990): 5-17 [4:1-11].

4759.56 Pierre Grelot, "Les tentations de Jesus," *NRT* 117 (1995): 501-16 [4:1-11].

4759.57 Robert L. Mowery, "Subtle Differences: The Matthean 'Son of God' References," *NT* 32 (1990): 193-200 [4:3].

4759.58 D. Flusser, "Die Versuchung Jesu und ihr jüdischer Hintergrund," *J* 45 (1989): 110-28 [4:9-10].

4759.59 G. G. Gamba, "Gesù si stabilisce a Cafarnao (Mt. 4,12-16)," *BO* 16 (1974): 109-32 [4:12-16].

4759.60 T. Harley Hall, "An Exposition of Matthew 4:12-23," *Interp* 29/1 (1975): 63-67 [4:12-23].

4759.61 H. Dixon Slingerland, "The Transjordanian Origin of St. Matthew's Gospel," *JSNT* 1/3 (1979): 18-28 [4:15].

4759.62 K. Romaniuk, "Repentez-vous, car le Royaume des Cieux est tout proche (Matt. iv.17 par.)," *NTSt* 12 (1965-1966): 259-69 [4:17].

4759.63 J. Héring, "Le Sermon sur la Montagne dans la nouvelle traduction anglaise de la Bible," *RHPR* 42 (1962): 122-12 [5-7].

4759.64 J. Schmid, "Ich aber sage euch: Der Anruf der Bergpredigt," *BK* 19 (1964): 75-79 [5-7].

4759.65 Michel Corbin, "Nature et signification de la loi évangélique," *RSR* 57 (1969): 5-48 [5-7].

4759.66 E. Lerle, "Realisierbare Forderungen der Bergpredigt?" *KD* 16 (1970): 32-40 [5-7].

4759.67 Karlmann Beyschlag, "Zur Geschichte der Bergpredigt in der Alten Kirche," *ZTK* 74/3 (1977): 291-322 [5-7].

4759.68 Günther Bornkamm, "Der Aufbau der Bergpredigt," *NTSt* 24 (1978): 419-32 [5-7].

4759.69 M. Bouttier, "Hesiode et le sermon sur la montagne," *NTSt* 25 (1978-1979): 129-30 [5-7].

4759.70 Hans Dieter Betz, "The Sermon on the Mount: Its Literary Genre and Function," *JR* 59 (1979): 285-97 [5-7].

4759.71 N. J. McEleney, "The Principles of the Sermon on the Mount," *CBQ* 41/4 (1979): 552-70 [5-7].

4759.72 W. Egger, "I titoli delle pericope bibliche come chiave di lettura," *RivB* 29 (1981): 33-43 [5-7].

4759.73 H. Frankemölle, "Neue Literatur zur Bergpredigt," *TR* 79 (1983): 177-98 [5-7].

4759.74 S. L. Cahill, "The Ethical Implications of the Sermon on the Mount," *Interp* 41 (1987): 144-56 [5-7].

4759.75 Robert A. Guelich, "Interpreting the Sermon on the Mount," *Interp* 41 (1987): 131-40 [5-7].

4759.76 Jack D. Kingsbury, "The Place, Structure and Meaning of the Sermon on the Mount within Matthew," *Interp* 41/2 (1987): 131-43 [5-7].

4759.77 Dale C. Allison, "A New Approach to the Sermon on the

Mount," *ETL* 64 (1988): 405-14 [5-7].

4759.78   Karin Bornkamm, "Umstrittener 'spiegel eines Christlichen lebens': Luthers Auslegung der Bergpredigt in seinen Wochenpredigten von 1530 bis 1532," *ZTK* 85 (1988): 409-54 [5-7].

4759.79   C. E. Carlston, "Betz on the Sermon on the Mount: A Critique," *CBQ* 50 (1988): 47-57 [5-7].

4759.80   Hans Dieter Betz, "The Sermon on the Mount: In Defense of a Hypothesis," *BRes* 36 (1991): 74-80 [5-7].

4759.81   Ernest W. Saunders, "A Response to H. D. Betz on the Sermon on the Mount," *BRes* 36 (1991): 81-87 [5-7].

4759.82   Klyne Snodgrass, "A Response to H. D. Betz on the Sermon on the Mount," *BRes* 36 (1991): 88-94 [5-7].

4759.83   Loyd Allen, "The Sermon on the Mount in the History of the Church," *RE* 89 (1992): 245-62 [5-7].

4759.84   H. S. Songer, "The Sermon on the Mount and Its Jewish Foreground," *RE* 89 (1992): 165-77 [5-7].

4759.85   Glen H. Stassen, "Grace and Deliverance in the Sermon on the Mount," *RE* 89 (1992): 229-44 [5-7].

4759.86   Randall Buth, "Singular and Plural Forms of Address in the Sermon on the Mount," *BTr* 44 (1993): 446-47 [5-7].

4759.87   J. Smit Sibinga, "Exploring the Compoisition of Matthew 5-7: The Sermon on the Mount and Some of Its 'Structures'," *FilN* 7 (1994): 175-95 [5-7].

4759.88   Roger D. Congdon, "Did Jesus Sustain the Law in Matthew 5?" *BS* 135 (1978): 117-25 [5].

4759.89   Christian Dietzfelbinger, "Die Antithesen der Bergpredigt im Verständnis des Matthaus," *ZNW* 70/1 (1979): 1-15 [5].

4759.90   W. J. Dumbrell, "The Logic of the Role of the Law in Matthew 5:1-20," *NT* 23 (1981): 1-21 [5:1-20].

4759.91   Dalmazio Mongillo, "Les Béatitudes et la béatitude: Le dynamisme de la Somme de théologie de Thomas d'Aquin: une lecture de la Ia-IIae," *RSPT* 78 (1994): 373-88 [5:1-10].

4759.92   Barclay M. Newman, "Some Translational Notes on the Beatitudes," *BTr* 26/1 (1975): 106-20 [5:1-8].

4759.93   Dale C. Allison, "Jesus and Moses (Mt. 5:1-2)," *ET* 98/7 (1987): 203-204 [5:1-2].

4759.94   Joseph Coppens, "Les Béatitudes," *ETL* 50 (1974): 256-60

[5:3-12].

4759.95 Hans Dieter Betz, "Die Makarismen der Bergpredigt (Matthaus 5:3-12)," *ZTK* 75/1 (1978): 3-19 [5:3-12].

4759.96 Mark A. Powell, "Matthew's Beatitudes: Reversals and Rewards of the Kingdom," *CBQ* 58 (1996): 460-79 [5:3-12].

4759.97 Christopher M. Tuckett, "The Beatitudes: A Source-Critical Study: With a Reply by Michael D. Goulder," *NT* 25/3 (1983): 193-216 [5:3-10].

4759.98 Felix Böhl, "Die Demut ('nwh) als Höchste der Tugenden, Bemeekungen zu Mt 5:3-5," *BibZ* 20 (1976): 217-23 [5:3-5].

4759.99 Günther Schwarz, " 'Ihenn gehört das Himmelreich' (Matthäus V.3)," *NTSt* 23/3 (1977): 341-43 [5:3].

4759.100 Klaus Jörms, " 'Armut, zu der der Geist hilft' (Mt. 5:3) als *nota ecclesiae*," *TZ* 43 (1987): 59-70 [5:3].

4759.101 Rudolf Schnackenburg, "Die Sellgpreisung der Friedensstifter (Mt. 5,9) im Mattäischen Kontext," *BibZ* 26/2 (1982): 161-78 [5:9].

4759.102 Michael W. Holmes, "The Text of Matthew 5:11," *NTSt* 32/2 (1986): 283-86 [5:11].

4759.103 J. B. Soucek, "Salz der Erde und Licht der Welt. Zur Exegese von Matth. 5:13-16," *TZ* 19 (1962): 169-79 [5:13-16].

4759.104 Günther Schwarz, "Matthaus v. 13a und 14a: Emendation und Rückübersetzung," *NTSt* 17 (1970-1971): 80-86 [5:13-14].

4759.105 K. M. Campbell, "The New Jerusalem in Matthew 5:14," *SJT* 31/4 (1978): 335-63 [5:14].

4759.106 J. D. M. Derrett, "The Light and the City: Mt. 5:14," *ET* 103 (1992): 174-75 [5:14].

4759.107 J. D. M. Derrett, "Light Under a Bushel: The Hanukkah Lamp?" *ET* 78 (1966-1967): 18 [5:15].

4759.108 André Feuillet, "Morale Ancienne et Morale Chrétienne d'après Mt. 5.17-20; Comparaison avec la Doctrine de l'Épitre aux Romains," *NTSt* 17 (1970-1971): 123-37 [5:17-20].

4759.109 Robert Banks, "Matthew's Understanding of the Law: Authenticity and Interpretation in Matthew 5:17-20," *JBL* 93/2 (1974): 226-42 [5:17-20].

4759.110 Ulrich Luz, "Die Erfüllung des Gesetzes bei Matthäus," *ZTK* (1978-1979): 398-435 [5:17-20].

4759.111 C. Heubüly, "Mt. 5:17-20: Ein Beitrag zur Theologie des Evangelisten Matthäus," *ZNW* 71 (1980): 143-49 [5:17-20].

4759.112 Christine Heutuot, "Mt. 5,17-20," *ZNW* 71/3 (1980): 143-49 [5:17-20].

4759.113 J.-C. Ingelaere, "Universalisme et puticularisme dans l'Évangile de Matthieu. Matthieu et le Judaïsme," *RHPR* 75 (1995): 45-59 [5:17-20].

4759.114 J. W. Deenick, "The Fourth Commandment and Its Fulfillment," *RTR* 28/2 (1969): 54-61 [5:17].

4759.115 D. H. C. Read, " 'Thou Shalt Not!': Says Who?" *ET* 88 (1977): 209-11 [5:17].

4759.116 S. Clive Thexton, "The Word of God in the Old Testament," *ET* 93 (1981): 50-51 [5:17].

4759.117 Robert G. Hamerton-Kelly, "Attitudes to the Law in Matthew's Gospel: A Discussion of Matthew 5:18," *BRes* 17 (1972): 19-32 [5:18].

4759.118 Günther Schwarz, "ἰῶτα ἓν ἢ μία κεραία (Matthäus 5:18)," *ZNW* 66 (1975): 268-69 [5:18].

4759.119 Ingo Broer, "Die Antithesen und der Evangelist Mattaus," *BibZ* 19 (1975): 50-63 [5:20-48].

4759.120 Ingo Broer, "Die Antithesen der Bergpredigt: Ihre Bedeutung und Funktion für die Gemeinde des Matthäus," *BK* 48 (1993): 128-33 [5:20-48].

4759.121 H. Günther, "Die Gerechtigkeit des Himmelreiches in der Bergpredigt," *KD* 17 (1971): 113-26 [5:20].

4759.122 Robert A. Guelich, "The Antitheses of Matthew V. 21-48: Traditional and/or Redactional?" *NTSt* 22/4 (1976): 444-57 [5:21-48].

4759.123 Georg Strecker, "Die Antithesen der Bergpredigt (Mt 5,21-48 par)," *ZNW* 69 (1978): 36-72 [5:21-48].

4759.124 John R. Levison, "Responsible Initiative in Matthew 5:21-48," *ET* 98/8 (1987): 231-34 [5:21-48].

4759.125 G. Röhser, "Jesus–der wahre 'Schriftgelehrte'. Ein Beitrag zum Problem der 'Toraverschärfung' in den Antithesen der Bergpredigt," *ZNW* 86 (1995): 20-33 [5:21-48].

4759.126 P. Wick, "Die erste Antithese (Mt 5,21 -26): Eine

Pilgerpredigt," *TZ* 52 (1996): 236-42 [5:21-26].

4759.127 C. F. D. Moule, "Uncomfortable Words. Part I. The Angry Word: Matthew 5:21f.," *ET* 81/1 (1969): 10-13 [5:21].

4759.128 C. F. D. Moule, "The Angry Word: Mt. 5:21f.," *ET* 81 (1969-1970): 10-13 [5:21].

4759.129 Robert A. Guelich, "Mt. 5,22: Its Meaning and Integrity," *ZNW* 64 (1973): 39-52 [5:22].

4759.130 Raymond Schwager, "La mort de Jésus: René Girard et la théologie," *RSR* 73 (1985): 481-502 [5:27-48].

4759.131 Will Deming, "Mark 9:42-10:12, Matthew 5:27-32, and b. Nid, 13b: A First Century Discussion of Male Sexuality," *NTSt* 36/1 (1990): 130-41 [5:27-32].

4759.132 Klaus Haacker, "Der Rechtssatz Jesu zum Thema Ehebruch," *BibZ* 21/1 (1977): 113-16 [5:28].

4759.133 Herbert W. Basser, "The Meaning of 'Shtuth', Gen. 4.11 in Reference to Matthew 5.29-30 and 18.8-9," *NTSt* 31/1 (1985): 148-51 [5:29-30].

4759.134 S. D. Currie, "Matthew 5:30a: Resistance or Protest?" *HTR* 57 (1964): 140-45 [5:30].

4759.135 G. J. Wenham, "Matthew and Divorce: An Old Crux Revisited," *JSNT* 22 (1984): 95-107 [5:31].

4759.136 J. J. O'Rourke, "A Note on an Exception: Mt. 5:32 (19:9) and 1 Cor 7:12 Compared," *HeyJ* 5 (1964): 299-302 [5:32].

4759.137 T. Stramare, "Matteo Divorzista?" *Div* 15/2 (1971): 213-35 [5:32].

4759.138 H. Crouzel, "Le Texte Patristique de Matthieu V.32 et XIX.9," *NTSt* 19/1 (1972): 98-119 [5:32].

4759.139 John J. Kilgallen, "To What Are the Matthean Exception-Texts (5:32 and 19:9) an Exception?" *B* 61 (1980): 102-105 [5:32].

4759.140 Ben Witherington, "Matthew 5.32 and 19.9: Exception or Exceptional Situation?" *NTSt* 31/4 (1985): 571-76 [5:32].

4759.141 Markus N. A. Bockmuehl, "Matthew 5.32; 19.9 in the Light of Pre-Rabbinic Halakhah," *NTSt* 35/2 (1989): 291-95 [5:32].

4759.142 John L. Nolland, "The Gospel Prohibition of Divorce: Tradition History and Meaning," *JSNT* 58 (1995): 19-35 [5:32].

4759.143 Gerhard Dautzenberg, "Ist das Schwurverbot Mt. 5,33-37;

Jak 5,12 ein Beispiel für die Torakritik Jesu?" *BibZ* 25/1 (1981): 47-66 [5:33-37].

4759.144 J.-A. A. Brant, "Infelicitous Oaths in the Gospel of Matthew," *JSNT* 63 (1996): 3-20 [5:33-37].

4759.145 B. Kollmann, "Des Schwurverbot Mt 5,33-37/Jak 5,12 im Spiegel antiker Eidkritik," *BibZ* 40 (1996): 179-93 [5:33-37].

4759.146 Dennis C. Duling, "Do Not Swear . . . by Jerusalem Because It Is the City of the Great King," *JBL* 110 (1991): 291-309 [5:35].

4759.147 Jerome Rausch, "The Principle of Nonresistance and Love of Enemy in Mt. 5,38-48," *CBQ* 28/1 (1966): 31-41 [5:38-48].

4759.148 Markus Rathey, "Talion im NT? Zu Mt. 5,38-42," *ZNW* 82 (1991): 264-66 [5:38-42].

4759.149 Ingo Broer, "Des Ius Talionis im Neuen Testament," *NTSt* 40 (1994): 1-21 [5:38-42].

4759.150 Marcus J. Borg, "A New Context for Romans XIII," *NTSt* 19/2 (1973): 205-18 [5:39].

4759.151 O. Bayer, "Sprachbewegung und Weltveränderung. Ein systematischer Versuch als Auslegung von Mt. 5,43-48," *EvT* 35 (1975): 309-21 [5:43-48].

4759.152 Bonnie B. Thurston, "Matthew 5:43-48," *Interp* 41/2 (1987): 170-73 [5:43-48].

4759.153 David C. Sim, "The Gospel of Matthew and the Gentiles," *JSNT* 57 (1995): 19-48 [5:46-47].

4759.154 H. Bruppacher, "Was sagte Jesus in Matthäus 5,48?" *ZNW* 58 (1967): 145 [5:48].

4759.155 L. Sabourin, "Why Is God Called 'Perfect' in Mt 5:48?" *BibZ* 24 (1980): 266-68 [5:48].

4759.156 Christian Dietzfelbinger, "Die Frommigkeitsregeln von Mt. 6,1-18 als Zeugnisse Fruchristlicher Geschichte," *ZNW* 75/3 (1985): 184-201 [6:1-18].

4759.157 Wiard Popkes, "Die Gerechtigkeitstradition im Matthäus-Evangelium," *ZNW* 80/1 (1989): 1-23 [6:1].

4759.158 N. J. McEleney, "Does the Trumpet Sound or Resound? An Interpretation of Matthew 6,2," *ZNW* 76/1 (1985): 43-46 [6:2].

4759.159 Paul Ellingworth, " 'In Secret' (Matthew 6.4, 6, 18)," *BTr* 40 (1989): 446-47 [6:4].

4759.160 Philip B. Harner, "Matthew 6:5-15," *Interp* 41/2 (1987): 173-78 [6:5-15].

4759.161 G. Casalis, "Das Vater Unser und die Weltlage," *EvT* 29 (1969): 357-71 [6:9-15].

4759.162 D. W. Shriver, "The Prayer That Spans the World. An Exposition: Social Ethics and the Lord's Prayer," *Interp* 21 (1967): 274-88 [6:9-13].

4759.163 Daniel C. Arichea, "Translating the Lord's Prayer (Matthew 6:9-13)," *BTr* 31 (1980): 219-23 [6:9-13].

4759.164 L. Gil, "Versiones del *Pater noster* al castellano en el Siglo de Oro," *FilN* 1 (1988): 175-91 [6:9-13].

4759.165 W. M. Buchan, "Research on the Lord's Prayer," *ET* 100 (1989): 336-39 [6:9-13].

4759.166 J. C. O'Neill, "The Lord's Prayer," *JSNT* 51 (1993): 3-25 [6:9-13].

4759.167 James Swetnam, "Hallowed Be Thy Name," *B* 52 (1971): 556-63 [6:9].

4759.168 David E. Garland, "The Lord's Prayer in the Gospel of Matthew," *RE* 89 (1992): 215-28 [6:10-13].

4759.169 J. Starcky, "La Quatrième Demande du Pater," *HTR* 64 (1971): 401-409 [6:11].

4759.170 R. ten Kate, "Geef ons Heden ons 'Dagelijks Brood'," *NedTT* 32/2 (1978): 125-39 [6:11].

4759.171 Delores Aleixandre, "En torno a la cuarta peticion del Padrenuestro [Matt 6:11, Lk. 11:3]]," *EB* 45 (1987): 325-36 [6:11].

4759.172 Arland J. Hultgren, "The Bread Petition of the Lord's Prayer," *ATR* 11 (1990): 41-54 [6:11].

4759.173 M.-É. Boismard, " 'Notre pain quotidian'," *RB* 102 (1995): 371-78 [6:11].

4759.174 J. M. Ford, "The Forgiveness Clause in the Matthean Form of the Our Father," *ZNW* 59 (1968): 127-31 [6:12].

4759.175 Samuel Tobias Lachs, "On Matthew 6.12," *NT* 17/1 (1975): 6-8 [6:12].

4759.176 G. Smith, "Matthaean 'Additions' to Lord's Prayer," *ET* 82 (1970-1971): 54-55 [6:13].

4759.177 C. F. D. Moule, "An Unsolved Problem in the Temptation Clause in the Lord's Prayer," *RTR* 33/3 (1974): 65-75 [6:13].

4759.178 Davis McCaughey, "Matthew 6.13a: The Sixth Petition in the Lord's Prayer," *ABR* 33 (1985): 31-40 [6:13].

4759.179 Wiard Popkes, "Die letzte Bitte des Vater-Unser. Formgeschichte Beobachtungen zum Gebet Jesu," *ZNW* 81 (1990): 1-20 [6:13].

4759.180 E. Moore, "Lead Us Not into Temptation," *ET* 102 (1991): 171-72 [6:13].

4759.181 K. Grayston, "The Decline of Temptation—and the Lord's Prayer," *SJT* 46 (1993): 279-95 [6:13].

4759.182 Dale C. Allison, "The Eye is the Lamp of the Body (Matthew 6.22-23 = Luke 11.34-36)," *NTSt* 33/1 (1987): 61-83 [6:22-23].

4759.183 C. E. Carlston, "Matthew 6:24-34," *Interp* 41/2 (1987): 179-83 [6:24-34].

4759.184 H. P. Rüger, "Μαμωνας," *ZNW* 64 (1973): 127-31 [6:24].

4759.185 Hans Dieter Betz, "Kosmogonie und Ethik in der Bergpredigt," *ZTK* 81/2 (1984): 139-71 [6:25-34].

4759.186 J. J. Bartolomé, "Los pájaros y los lirios: Una aproximación a la cuestión ecológica desde Mt. 6,25-34," *EB* 49 (1991): 165-90 [6:25-34].

4759.187 J. Enoch Powell, "Those 'Lilies of the Field' Again," *JTS* 33/2 (1982): 490-92 [6:28].

4759.188 Julian V. Hills, "The Three 'Matthean' Aphorisms in the Dialogue of the Savior 53," *HTR* 84 (1991): 43-58 [6:34].

4759.189 George S. Hendry, "Judge Not: A Critical Test of Faith," *TTod* 40/2 (1983): 113-29 [7:1].

4759.190 H. P. Rüger, " 'Mit welchem Mass ihr meßt, wird euch gemessen werden'," *ZNW* 6 (1969): 174-82 [7:2].

4759.191 Günther Schwarz, "Matthäus vii 6a. Emendation und Rückübersetzung," *NT* 14 (1972): 18-25 [7:6].

4759.192 Thomas J. Bennett, "Matthew 7:6: A New Interpretation," *WTJ* 49/2 (1987): 371-86 [7:6].

4759.193 Hermann von Lips, "Schweine futtert man, Hunde nicht ein Versuch, das Ratsel von Matthäus 7:6 zu losen," *ZNW* 79/3 (1988): 165-86 [7:6].

4759.194 Stephen Llewelyn, "Mt. 7:6a: Mistranslation or Interpretation," *NT* 31/2 (1989): 97-103 [7:6].

4759.195 Georg Strecker, "Complaince - Love of One's Enemy - the

Golden Rule," *ABR* 29 (1981): 38-46 [7:12].

4759.196 Paul Ricoeur, "The Golden Rule: Exegetical and Theological Perplexities," *NTSt* 36 (1990): 392-97 [7:12].

4759.197 C. Theobald, "La règle d'or chez Paul Ricoeur. Une interrogation théologique," *RSR* 83 (1995): 43-59 [7:12].

4759.198 J. D. M. Derrett, "The Merits of the Narrow Gate," *JSNT* 15 (1982): 20-29 [7:13-14].

4759.199 A. J. Mattill, " 'The Way of Tribulation'," *JBL* 98/4 (1979): 531-46 [7:14].

4759.200 David A. Günter "Remarks on the Translation of Matthew 7:14," *FilN* 2 (1989): 193-95 [7:14].

4759.201 G. H. R. Horsley, "τί at Matthew 7:14: 'Because' not 'How'," *FilN* 3 (1990): 141-43 [7:14].

4759.202 David Hill, "The False Prophets and Charismatics: Structure and Interpretation in Matthew 7:15-23," *B* 57 (1976): 327-48 [7:15-23].

4759.203 Hans Dieter Betz, "Eine Episode im Jüngsten Gericht," *ZTK* 78/1 (1981): 1-30 [7:21-23].

4759.204 William G. Thompson, "Reflections on the Composition of Mt. 8:1-9:34," *CBQ* 33 (1971): 365-88 [8-9].

4759.205 C. Burger, "Jesu Taten nach Matthäus 8 und 9," *ZTK* 70 (1973): 272-87 [8-9].

4759.206 Jeremy Moiser, "The Structure of Matthew 8-9: A Suggestion." *ZNW* 76/1 (1985): 117-18 [8-9].

4759.207 E. F. Siegman, "St. John's Use of the Synoptic Material," *CBQ* 30/2 (1968): 182-98 [8:5-13].

4759.208 Christoph Burchard, "Zu Matthäus 8:5-13," *ZNW* 84 (1993): 278-88 [8:5-13].

4759.209 B Schwank, "Dort wird Heulen und Zähneknirschen sein," *BibZ* 16 (1972): 121-22 [8:12].

4759.210 Jack D. Kingsbury, "On Following Jesus: The 'Eager' Scribe and the 'Reluctant' Disciple (Matthew 8:18-22)," *NTSt* 34/1 (1988): 45-59 [8:18-22].

4759.211 Jarmo Killunen, "Der Nachfolgewillige Schriftgelehrte: Matthäus 8:19-20 im verständnis des Evangelisten," *NTSt* 37 (1991): 268-79 [8:18-22].

4759.212 R. H. Gundry, "On True and False Disciples in Matthew 8:18-22," *NTSt* 40 (1994): 433-41 [8:18-22].

4759.213 Byron R. McCane, " 'Let the Dead Bury Their Own Dead': Secondary Burial and Matthew 8:21-22," *HTR* 83 (1990): 31-43 [8:21-22].

4759.214 H. G. Klemm, "Das Wort von der Selbstbestattung der Toten," *NTSt* 16 (1969-1970): 60-75 [8:22].

4759.215 J. Duplacy, "Et il y eut un grand calme . . . La tempête apaisée (Matthieu 8:23-27)," *BVC* 74 (1967): 15-28 [8:23-27].

4759.216 Wolfgang Schenk, "Den Menschen, Mt. 9:8," *ZNW* 54 (1963): 272-75 [9:8].

4759.217 Mark Kiley, "Why 'Matthew' in Matt. 9, 9-13?" *B* 65/3 (1984): 347-51 [9:9-13].

4759.218 R. Pesch, "Levi-Matthäus (Mc. 2,14/Mt. 9,9; 10,3): Ein Beitrag zur Lösung eines alten Problems," *ZNW* 59 (1968): 40-56 [9:9].

4759.219 A. Alves de Melo, "O discipulado hoje. 'Levantando-se, O seguiu'," *REB* 55 (1995): 619-27 [9:9].

4759.220 Michael Theobald, "Der Primat der Synchronie vor der Diachronie als Grundaxiom der Literaturkritik: Methodische Erwagungen an Hand von Mk. 2,13-17, Mt. 9,9-13," *BibZ* 22/2 (1978): 161-86 [9:9-13].

4759.221 José O'Callaghan, "Tres casos de armonización en Mt. 9," *EB* 47 (1989): 131-34 [9:13-14].

4759.222 A. E. Harvey, "New Wine in Old Skins: II. Priest," *ET* 84/7 (1973): 200-203 [9:17].

4759.223 Roger L. Omanson, "A Question of Harmonization: Matthew 9:18-25," *BTr* 42 (1991): 241 [9:18-25].

4759.224 José O'Callaghan, "La Variante eis/Elthon en Mt. 9,18," *B* 62/1 (1981): 104-106 [9:18].

4759.225 E. Galbiati, "Gesù guarisce l'emorroissa e risuscita la figlia di Giairo (Matt. 9,18-26)," *BO* 6 (1964): 225-30 [9:18-26].

4759.226 Manfred Hutter, "Ein Altorientalischer Bittegestus in Mt. 9,20-22," *ZNW* 75/1 (1984): 133-35 [9:20-22].

4759.227 Schuyler Brown, "The Mission to Israel in Matthew's Central Section (Mt. 9:35-11:1)," *ZNW* 69/1 (1978): 73-90 [9:35-11:1].

4759.228 Robert E. Morosco, "Matthew's Formation of a Commissioning-Type Scene Out of the Story of Jesus' Commissioning of the Twelve," *JBL* 104/4 (1984): 539-56

[9:35-11:1].

4759.229 B. Charette, "A Harvest for the People? An Interpretation of Matthew 9:37f.," *JSNT* 38 (1990): 29-35 [9:37].

4759.230 F. W. Beare, "The Mission of the Disciples and the Mission Charge: Matthew 10 and Parallels," *JBL* 89/1 (1970): 1-13 [10:1-16].

4759.231 Morna D. Hooker, "Prohibition of Foreign Missions in Mt. 10,5-6," *ET* 82 (1970-1971): 361-65 [10:5-6].

4759.232 Morna D. Hooker, "Uncomfortable Words: X. The Prohibition of Foreign Missions," *ET* 82/12 (1971): 361-65 [10:5-6].

4759.233 Roman Bartnicki, "Der Bereich der Tätigkeit der Jünger nach Mt. 10,5b-6," *BibZ* 31 (1987): 250-56 [10:5-6].

4759.234 J. A. Kirk, "Did 'Officials' in the New Testament Church Receive a Salary?" *ET* 84/4 (1973): 105 108 [10:10].

4759.235 José O'Callaghan, "Dos retoques antioquenos: Mt. 10,10; Mc. 2,20," *B* 68/4 (1987) 564-67 [10:10].

4759.236 Bruce A. Stevens, "Jesus as the Divine Warrior," *ET* 94/1 (1983): 326-29 [10:14].

4759.237 C. H. Giblin, "Theological Perspective and Matthew 10:23b," *ThSt* 29/4 (1968): 637-61 [10:23].

4759.238 Roman Bartnicki, "Das Trostwort an die Juenger in Matth. 10,23," *TZ* 43/4 (1987): 311-19 [10:23].

4759.239 Volker Hampel, " 'Ihr werdet mit den Stadten Israels nicht zu Ende kommen'," *TZ* 45/1 (1989): 1-31 [10:23].

4759.240 Harry S. Pappas, "The 'Exhortation to Fearlesss Confession Mt 10:26-33," *GOTR* 25 (1980): 239-48 [10:26-33].

4759.241 I. Howard Marshall, "Uncomfortable Words. VI. 'Fear Him Who Can Destroy both Soul and Body in Hell'," *ET* 81/9 (1970): 276-82 [10:28].

4759.242 Matthew Günter "The Violent Word," *ET* 81 (1969-1970): 115-18 [10:34].

4759.243 C. L. Mitton, "Stumbling Block Characteristics of Jesus," *ET* 82 (1970-1971): 168-72 [11:6].

4759.244 Stephen Llewelyn, "The *Traditionsgeschichte* of Matthew 11:12-13, par. Luke 16:16," *NT* 36 (1994): 330-49 [11:12-13].

4759.245 W. E. Moore, "Biazō, arpazō and Cognates in Josephus,"

NTSt 21 (1975): 519-43 [11:12].

4759.246   B. E. Thiering, "Are the 'Violent Men' False Teachers?" *NT* 21/4 (1979): 293-97 [11:12].

4759.247   W. E. Moore, "Violence to the Kingdom: Josephus and the Syrian Churches," *ET* 100/5 (1989): 174-77 [11:12].

4759.248   Paolo Papone, "Il regno dei cieli soffre violenza? (Mt. 11:12)," *RivB* 38 (1990): 375-76 [11:12].

4759.249   Olof Linton, "The Parable of the Children's Game," *NTSt* 22/2 (1976): 159-79 [11:16-19].

4759.250   José O'Callaghan, "La variante 'se gritan . . . diciendo', de Mt. 11,16-17," *EE* 61 (1986): 67-70 [11:16-17].

4759.251   Joseph A. Comber, "The Composition and Literary Characteristics of Matt. 11:20-24." *CBQ* 39/4 (1977): 497-504 [11:20-24].

4759.252   Kenneth O. Gangel, "Leadership: Coping with Cultural Corruption," *BS* 144 (1987): 450-60 [11:25-30].

4759.253   Dale C. Allison, "Two Notes on a Key Text: Matthew 11:25-30," *JTS* 39 (1988): 477-85 [11:25-30].

4759.254   Walter Grundmann, "Matth. xi. 27 und die Johanneischen 'Der Vater-Der Sohn'-Stellen," *NTSt* 12 (1965-1966): 42-49 [11:27].

4759.255   Hans Dieter Betz, "The Logion of the Easy Yoke and of Rest," *JBL* 86 (1967): 10-24 [11:28-30].

4759.256   B. Charette, " 'To Proclaim Liberty to the Captives': Matthew 11:28-30 in the Light of OT Prophetic Expectation," *NTSt* 38 (1992): 290-97 [11:28-30].

4759.257   M. Maher, " 'Take My Yoke upon You' (Matt. xi.29)," *NTSt* 22 (1975-1976): 97-103 [11:29].

4759.258   Joseph A. Grassi, "The Five Loaves of the High Priest," *NT* 7 (1964-1965): 119-22 [12:1-8].

4759.259   M. Herranz Marco, "Las espigas arrancadas en sabado (Mt 12,1-8 par.): Tradición y elaboración literaria," *EB* 28 (1969): 313-48 [12:1-8].

4759.260   Daniel M. Cohn-Sherbok, "An Analysis of Jesus' Arguments concerning the Plucking of Grain on the Sabbath," *JSNT* 2 (1979): 31-41 [12:1-8].

4759.261   C. Tassin, "Matthieu 'targumiste?' L'exemple de Mt. 12,18 (= Is 42,1)," *EB* 48 (1990): 199-214 [12:18].

4759.262   Arland J. Hultgren, "The Double Commandment of Love in
            Mt 22:34-40: Its Sources and Composition," *CBQ* 36 (1974):
            373-78 [12:28-34].

4759.263   Robert G. Hamerton-Kelly, "A Note on Matthew 12:28 Par.
            Luke 11:20," *NTSt* 11/2 (1965): 167-69 [12:28].

4759.264   J. G. Williams, "A Note on the 'Unforgivable Sin' Logion,"
            NTSt 12 (1965): 75-77 [12:30-31].

4759.265   M. Eugene Boring, "The Unforgivable Sin Logion Mark
            3:28-29/Matt. 12:31-32/Luke 12:10: Formal Analysis and
            History of the Tradition," *NT* 18/4 (1976): 258-79
            [12:31-32].

4759.266   John Howton, "The Sign of Jonah," *SJT* 15 (1962): 288-304
            [12:38-42].

4759.267   Harvey K. McArthur, " 'On the Third Day'," *NTSt* 18/1
            (1971): 81-86 [12:40].

4759.268   François Bovon, "Parabole d'Evangile, parabole du
            Royaume," *RTP* 122/1 (1990): 33-41 [12:46-13:23].

4759.269   David Wenham, "The Interpretation of the Parable of the
            Sower," *NTSt* 20 (1974): 299-319 [13:1-23].

4759.270   Mark Achtemeier, "Matthew 13:1-23," *Interp* 44 (1990):
            61-65 [13:1-23].

4759.271   Barclay M. Newman, "To Teach or Not to Teach (A
            Comment on Matthew 13.1-3)," *BTr* 34/1 (1983): 139-43
            [13:1-3].

4759.272   David S. New, "The Occurrence of Auton in Matthew 13:15
            and the Process of Text Assimilation," *NTSt* 37 (1991):
            478-80 [13:15].

4759.273   William G. Doty, "An Interpretation: Parable of the Weeds
            and Wheat," *Interp* 25 (1971): 185-93 [13:24-30].

4759.274   David R. Catchpole, "John the Baptist, Jesus and the Parable
            of the Tares," *SJT* 31/6 (1978): 557-71 [13:24-30].

4759.275   R. K. McIver, "The Parable of the Weeds among the Wheat
            and the Relationship between the Kingdom and the Church as
            Portrayed in the Gospel of Matthew," *JBL* 114 (1995):
            643-59 [13:24-30].

4759.276   M.-É. Boismard, "De Justin à l'harmonie de Pepys: la
            parabole de la semence," *RB* 103 (1996): 433-40 [13:3-9].

4759.277   Elizabeth Waller, "The Parable of the Leaven: A Sectarian
            Teaching and the Inclusion of Women," *USQR* 35 (1980):

99-109 [13:33].

4759.278 J. M. Bassler, "The Parable of the Loaves," *JR* 66 (1986): 157-72 [13:33].

4759.279 J. D. M. Derrett, "Law in the New Testament: The Treasure in the Field," *ZNW* 54 (1963): 31-42 [13:44].

4759.280 Paul W. Meyer, "Context as a Bearer of Meaning in Matthew," *USQR* 42/1 (1988): 69-72 [13:44-46].

4759.281 Delmar Jacobson, "An Exposition of Matthew 13:44-52," *Interp* 29/3 (1975): 277-82 [13:44-52].

4759.282 J. D. M. Derrett, "Esan gar Halieis (Mark 1:16). Jesus' Fisherman and the Parable of the Net," *NT* 22/2 (1980): 108-37 [13:47-49].

4759.283 J. Horman, "The Source of the Version of the Parable of the Sower in the Gospel of Thomas," *NT* 21/4 (1979): 326-43 [13:5-6].

4759.284 J. Becker, "Erwagungen zu Fragen der Neutestamentlichen Exegese," *BibZ* 13/1 (1969): 99-102 [13:52].

4759.285 Dieter Zeller, "Zu Einer Judischen Vorlage von Mt. 13, 52," *BibZ* 20/2 (1976): 223-26 [13:52].

4759.286 David W. Gooding, "Structure littéraire de Matthieu 13:53 à 18:35," *RB* 85 (1978): 227-52 [13:53-18:35].

4759.287 George W. Buchanan, "Jesus and the Upper Class," *NT* 7/3 (1965): 195-206 [13:55].

4759.288 José O'Callaghan, "La Variante 'Ahogaron' en Mt 13,7," *B* 68/3 (1987): 402-403 [13:7].

4759.289 J. Bernardi, "Cent, soixante et trente," *RB* 36 (1991): 398-402 [13:8].

4759.290 R. K. McIver, "One Hundred-Fold Yield - Miraculous or Mundane? Matthew 13:8,23; Mark 4,8.20; Luke 8.8," *NTSt* 40 (1994): 606-608 [13:8,23].

4759.291 Frans Neirynck, "The Matthew-Luke Agreements in Matt 14:13-14 and Lk 9:10-11 (par Mk 6:30-34): The Two-Source Theory behind the Impasse," *ETL* 60/1 (1984): 25-44 [14:13-14].

4759.292 Ivor Buse, "The Gospel Accounts of the Feeding of the Multitudes," *ET* 74 (1962-1963): 167-70 [14:15-21].

4759.293 Jerome Murphy-O'Connor, "The Structure of Matthew XIV-XVII." *RB* 82/3 (1975): 360-84 [14:16].

4759.294 Charles R. Carlisle, "Jesus' Walking on the Water: A Note on Matthew 14.22-33," *NTSt* 31/1 (1985): 151-55 [14:22-33].

4759.295 Ralph Stehley, "Boudhisme et Nouveau Testament: Apropos de la Marche de Pierre sur l'Eau," *RHPR* 57/4 (1977): 433-37 [14:28].

4759.296 E. Lövestam, "Wunder und Symbolhandlung: Eine Studie über Matthaus 14:28-31," *KD* 8 (1962): 124-35 [14:28-31].

4759.297 Roy A. Harrisville, "The Woman of Canaan. A Chapter in the History of Exegesis," *Interp* 20 (1966): 274-87 [15:21-28].

4759.298 P. E. Scherer, "A Gauntlet with a Gift in It. From Text to Sermon on Matthew 15:21-28 and Mark 7:24-30," *Interp* 20 (1966): 387-99 [15:21-28].

4759.299 T. Lovison, "La pericopa della Cananea Mt. 15,21-28," *RivB* 19 (1971): 273-305 [15:21-28].

4759.300 S. Légasse, "L'épisode de la Cananéenne d'après Mt. 15,21-28," *BLE* 73 (1972): 21-40 [15:21-28].

4759.301 Mark C. Thompson, "Matthew 15:21-28," *Interp* 35/3 (1981): 279-84 [15:21-28].

4759.302 Alice Dermience, "La pericope de la Cananeenne (Matt. 15:21-28): redaction et theologie," *ETL* 58/1 (1982): 25-49 [15:21-28].

4759.303 John P. Meier, "Matthew 15:21-28," *Interp* 40 (1986): 397-402 [15:21-28].

4759.304 J. M. C. Scott, "Matthew 15:21-28: A Test-Case for Jesus' Manners," *JSNT* 63 (1996): 21-44 [15:21-28].

4759.305 J. Knackstedt, "Die beiden Brotvermehrungen im Evangelium," *NTSt* 10 (1963-1964): 309-35 [15:32-39].

4759.306 José O'Callaghan, "Consideraciones críticas sobre Mt. 15,35-36a," *B* 67 (1986): 360-62 [15:35-36].

4759.307 José O'Callaghan, "La variante 'palabra' o 'precepto' en Mt. 15,6," *EE* 61 (1986) 421-23. [15:6].

4759.308 Kair A Syreeni, "Separation and Identity: Aspects of the Symbolic World of Matthew 6:1-18," *NTSt* 40 (1994): 522-41 [16:1-18].

4759.309 X. Quinzá Lleó, "La reflexión bíblica sobre los signos de los tiempos," *EB* 48 (1990): 317-34 [16:1-4].

4759.310 José O'Callaghan, "La variante neotestamentaria levadura de los panes," *B* 67 (1986): 98-100 [16:12].

4759.311 Paul S. Berge, "An Exposition of Matthew 16:13-20," *Interp* 29/3 (1975): 283-88 [16:13-20].

4759.312 M. J. Suggs, "Matthew 16:13-20," *Interp* 39/3 (1985): 291-95 [16:13-20].

4759.313 André Feuillet, "Chercher à prsuader Dieu," *NT* 12 (1970): 350-60 [16:13-23].

4759.314 Bruce T. Dahlberg, "The Topological Use of Jeremiah 1:4-19 in Matthew 16:13-23," *JBL* 94/1 (1975): 73-80 [16:13-23].

4759.315 Benjamin G. Wright, "A Previously Unnoticed Greek Variant of Matt. 16:14: 'Some Say John the Baptist . . .'," *JBL* 105 (1986): 694-97 [16:14].

4759.316 Jean Doignon, "Pierre Fondement de l'Eglise et Foi de la Confession de Pierre 'Base de l'Eglise' chez Hilaire de Poitiers," *RSPT* 66/3 (1982): 417-25 [16:16-17].

4759.317 R. H. Gundry, "The Narrative Framework of Matthew 16:17-19," *NT* 7/1 (1964): 1-9 [16:17-19].

4759.318 Max Wilcox, "Peter and the Rock: A Fresh Look at Matthew 16:17-19," *NTSt* 22/1 (1975): 73-88 [16:17-19].

4759.319 Christoph Kähler, "Zur From- und Traditionsgeschichte von Matth. 16:17-19," *NTSt* 23/1 (1976): 36-58 [16:17-19].

4759.320 Ulrich Luz, "Das Primatwort Matthaus 16:17-19 aus wirkungsgeschichtlicher Sicht," *NTSt* 37 (1991): 415-33 [16:17-19].

4759.321 C. Grappe, "Mt. 16,17-19 et le récit de la Passion," *RHPR* 72 (1992): 33-40 [16:17-19].

4759.322 Christoph Kähler, "Satanischer Schriftgebrauch: Zur Hermeneutrik von Mt 4,1-11/Lk4,1-13," *TLZ* 119 (1994): 857-68 [16:17-19].

4759.323 Bruce M. Metzger, "The New Testament View of the Church," *TTod* 19 (1962): 369-80 [16:18].

4759.324 D. Broughton Knox, "De-Mythologising the Church," *RTR* 32/2 (1973): 48-55 [16:18].

4759.325 Peter Lampe, "Das Spiel mit dem Petrusnamen-Matt. xvi.18," *NTSt* 25/2 (1979): 221-27 [16:18].

4759.326 Carlo Buzzetti, " 'You Are a Rock, Peter. . .' in Italy," *BTr* 34/3 (1983): 308-11 [16:18].

4759.327 Raimund Lülsdorff, "Vom Stein zum Felsen: Anmerkungen zur biblischen Begruendung des Petrusamtes nach Mt.

16:18," *C* 44/4 (1990): 274-83 [16:18].

4759.328 Ulrich Luz, "The Primacy Text (Mt. 16:18)," *PSB* 12/1 (1991): 41-55 [16:18].

4759.329 K. L. Carroll, "Thou Art Peter," *NT* 6 (1963-1964): 268-76 [16:18-19].

4759.330 J. R. Mantey, "Distorted Translations in John 20:23; Matthew 16:18-19 and 18:18," *RE* 78/3 (1981): 409-16 [16:18-19].

4759.331 Roland Minnerath, "L'exégèse de Mt 16:18-19 chez Tertullien," *RHPR* 72 (1992): 61-72 [16:18-19].

4759.332 J. A. Emerton, "Binding and Loosing: Forgiving and Retaining," *JTS* 15 (1962): 325-31 [16:19].

4759.333 Stanley E. Porter, "Vague Verbs, Periphrastics, and Matt. 16:19," *FilN* 1/2 (1988): 155-73 [16:19].

4759.334 Kair A. Syreeni, "Between Heaven and Earth: On the Structure of Matthew's Symbolic Universe," *JSNT* 38 (1990): 9-13 [16:19].

4759.335 Herbert W. Basser, "Marcus's 'Gates': A Response," *CBQ* 52 (1990): 307-308 [16:20].

4759.336 James M. Efird, "Matthew 16:21-27," *Interp* 35/3 (1981): 284-89 [16:21-27].

4759.337 A. C. Winn, "Worship as a Healing Experience: An Exposition of Matthew 17:1-9," *Interp* 29/1 (1975): 68-72 [17:1-9].

4759.338 Justin Taylor, "The Coming of Elijah, Mt 17,10-13 and Mk 9,11-13: The Development of the Texts," *RB* 98 (1991): 107-19 [17:10-13].

4759.339 J. Wilkinson, "The Case of the Epileptic Boy," *ET* 79/3 (1967-1968): 39-42 [17:15].

4759.340 R. Merkelbach and D. Hagedorn, "Ein Neues Fragment aus Porphyrios 'Gegen die Christen',"*VCh* 20/2 (1966): 86-90 [17:20].

4759.341 J. D. M. Derrett, "Peter's Penny: Fresh Light on Matthew 17:24-27," *NT* 6/1 (1963): 1-15 [17:24-27].

4759.342 H. W. Montefiore, "Jesus and the Temple Tax," *NTSt* 11/1 (1964): 60-71 [17:24-27].

4759.343 N. J. McEleney, "Mt. 17:24-27: Who Paid the Temple Tax?" *CBQ* 38/2 (1976): 178-92 [17:24-27].

4759.344 Richard J. Cassidy, "Matthew 17:24-27: A Word on Civil

Taxes," *CBQ* 41/4 (1979): 571-80 [17:24-27].

4759.345 José O'Callaghan, "Discusion Critica en Mt. 17:25," *FilN* 3 (1990): 151-53 [17:25].

4759.346 H. A. Homeau, "On Fishing for Staters: Matthew 17:27," *ET* 85/11 (1974): 340-42 [17:27].

4759.347 Günther Schwarz, "ἀνοίξας τὸ στόμα αὐτοῦ (Matthäus 17.27)," *NTSt* 38 (1992): 138-41 [17:27].

4759.348 José O'Callaghan, "Discusion Critica en Mt 17,4," *B* 65/1 (1984): 91-93 [17:4].

4759.349 José O'Callaghan, "Mt. 17,7: Revision Critica," *B* 66/3 (1985): 422-23 [17:7].

4759.350 Savas Agourides, " 'Little Ones' in Matthew," *BTr* 35/3 (1984): 329-34 [18:14].

4759.351 Gerhard Barth, "Auseinandersetzungen im die Kirchenzucht im Umkreis des Matthausevangeliums," *ZNW* 69/3 (1978): 158-77 [18:15].

4759.352 Victor C. Pfitzner, "Purified Community-Purified Sinner: Explusion from the Communion According to Matthew 18:15-18 and 1 Corinthians 5:1-5," *ABR* 30 (1982): 34-55 [18:15-18].

4759.353 J. D. M. Derrett, "Binding and Loosing (Matt. 16:19; Matt. 18:18; John 20:23)," *JBL* 102 (1983): 112-17 [18:18].

4759.354 Herbert W. Basser, "Derrett's 'Binding' Reopened," *JBL* 104 (1985): 297-300 [18:18].

4759.355 Richard H. Hiers, " 'Binding' and 'Loosing': The Matthean Authorizations," *JBL* 104/2 (1985): 233-50 [18:18].

4759.356 J. D. M. Derrett, "Where Two or Three Are Convened in My Name . . . .': A Sad Misunderstanding," *ET* 91/3 (1979): 83-86 [18:19-20].

4759.357 Pietro Bolognesi, "Matteo 18:20 e la dottrina della Chiesa," *BO* 29 (1987): 171-77 [18:20].

4759.358 B. Weber, "Vergeltung oder Vergebung!? Matthäus 18,21-35 auf dem Hinterground des 'Erlassjahres'," *TZ* 50 (1994): 124-51 [18:21-35].

4759.359 B. Weber, "Alltagswelt und Gottesreich: Überlegungen zum Verstehenshintergrund des Gleichnisses vom 'Schalksknecht'," *BibZ* 37 (1993): 161-82 [18:23-34].

4759.360 L. G. Kelly, "Cultural Consistency in Translation," *BTr* 21/4

(1970): 170-75 [18:23-35].

4759.361 Christian Dietzfelbinger, "Das Gleichnis von der erlassenen Schuld. Eine theologische Untersuchung von Matthaus 18,23-35," *EvT* 32 (1972): 437-51 [18:23-35].

4759.362 M. C. de Boer, "Ten Thousand Talents: Matthew's Interpretation and Redaction of the Parable of the Unforgiving Servant (Matt. 18:23-35)," *CBQ* 50 (1988): 214-32 [18:23-35].

4759.363 Roger Balducelli, "The Decision for Celibacy," *ThSt* 36/2 (1975): 219-42 [19:10-12].

4759.364 Christian Wolff, "Niedrigkeit und Verzicht in Wort und Weg Jesu und in der apostolischen Existenz des Paulus," *NTSt* 34/2 (1988): 183-96 [19:10-12].

4759.365 A. F. J. Klijn, "The Question of the Rich Young Man in a Jewish-Christian Gospel," *NT* 8 (1966): 149-15 [19:16-30].

4759.366 Eric F. Osborn, "Origen and Justification: The Good Is One," *ABR* 24/1 (1976): 18-29 [19:17].

4759.367 J. D. M. Derrett, "A Camel through the Eye of a Needle," *NTSt* 32/3 (1986): 465-70 [19:24].

4759.368 José O'Callaghan, "Examen critico de Mt. 19,24," *B* 69/3 (1988): 401-05 [19:24].

4759.369 Fred W. Burnett, "παλιγγενεσία, in Matt. 19:28: A Window on the Matthean Community?" *JSNT* 17 (1983): 60-72 [19:28].

4759.370 Francis J. Moloney, "Matthew 19,3-12 and Celibacy. A Redactional and Form Critical Study," *JSNT* 1/2 (1979): 42-60 [19:3-12].

4759.371 José O'Callaghan, "Nota crítica sobre Mt. 19,30," *EB* 48 (1990): 271-73 [19:30].

4759.372 Antonio Vargas-Machuca, "Los casos de 'divorcio' admitidos por San Mateo (5,32 y 19,9). Consecuencias para la teologia actual," *EE* 50 (1975): 5-54 [19:9].

4759.373 H. Crouzel, "Quelques remarques concernant le texte patristique de Mt. 19,9," *BLE* 82 (1981): 82-92 [19:9].

4759.374 C. Marucci, "Clausole matteane e critica testuale. In merito alla teoria di H. Crouzel sul testo originale di Mt. 19,9," *RivB* 38 (1990): 301-25 [19:9].

4759.375 C. L. Mitton, "Expounding the Parables: The Workers in the Vineyard," *ET* 77 (1965-1966): 307-11 [20:1-16].

4759.376 A. Orbe, "San Ireneo y la parábola de los obreros de la viñ: Mt. 20,1-16," *EE* 46 (1971): 35-62, 183-206 [20:1-16].

4759.377 D. A. Nelson, "An Exposition of Matthew 20:1-16," *Interp* 29/3 (1975): 288-92 [20:1-16].

4759.378 B. R. Doyle, "The Place of the Parable of the Labourers in the Vineyard in Matthew 20:1-16," *ABR* 42 (1994) 39-58 [20:1-16].

4759.379 José O'Callaghan, "Fluctuación textual en Mt 20,21.26,27," *B* 71/4 (1990): 553-58 [20:21-26:27].

4759.380 F. C. Glover, "Workers for the Vineyard, Mt. 20,4," *ET* 86 (1975): 310-11 [20:4].

4759.381 Ulrich Luz, "Der Antijudaismus im Matthäusevangelium als historisches und theologisches Problem: Eine Skizze," *EvT* 53 (1993): 310-27 [21-28].

4759.382 Paul W. Meyer, "Matthew 21:11," *Interp* 40 (1986): 180-85 [21:11].

4759.383 H.-W. Bartsch, "Die 'Verfluchung' des Feigenbaums," *ZNW* 53 (1962): 256-60 [21:18-19].

4759.384 A. Ogawa, "Paraboles de l'Israel Veritable? Reconsideration Critique de Mt. XXI.28-XXII.14," *NT* 21/2 (1979): 121-49 [21:28-22:14].

4759.385 Jean Doignon, "L'exegese latine de la parabole des deux fils (Matth. 21:28-31): Hilaire de Poitiers devant le probleme de l'obeisance a Dieu," *RHPR* 65/1 (1985): 53-59 [21:28-31].

4759.386 J. Ramsey Michaels, "The Parable of the Regretful Son," *HTR* 61 (1968): 15-26 [21:28-32].

4759.387 Helmut Merkel, "Das Gleichnis von den 'ungleichen Söhnen' (Matth. xxi.28-32)," *NTSt* 20 (1974): 254-61 [21:28-32].

4759.388 W. L. Richards, "Another Look at the Parable of the Two Sons," *BRes* 23 (1978): 5-14 [21:28-32].

4759.389 E. K. Broadhead, "An Example of Gender Bias in UBS3," *BTr* 40/3 (1989): 336-38 [21:38-42].

4759.390 K. H. Kuhn, "Kakie Kakos in the Sahidic Version of Matthew 21:41," *JTS* 36/2 (1985): 390-93 [21:41].

4759.391 A. Frenz, "Mt. XXI.5.7," *NT* 13 (1971): 259-60 [21:5-7].

4759.392 Peter Dschulnigg, "Positionen des Gleichnisverständnisses im 20. Jahrhundert," *TZ* 45/4 (1989): 335-51 [22:1-10].

4759.393 V. Hasler, "Die königliche Hochzeit, Matth. 22,1-14," *TZ* 18

(1962): 25-35 [22:1-14].

4759.394 Dan O. Via, "The Relationship of Form to Content in the Parable: The Wedding Feast," *Interp* 25 (1971): 171-84 [22:1-14].

4759.395 Richard J. Bauckham, "The Parable of the Royal Wedding Feast and the Parable of the Lame Man and the Blind Man (Apocryphon of Ezekiel)," *JBL* 115 (1996): 471-88 [22:1-14].

4759.396 David C. Sim, "The Man without the Wedding Garment (Matthew 22:11-13)," *HeyJ* 31 (1990): 165-78 [22:11-13].

4759.397 Ben F. Meyer, "Many (=All) Are Called, But Few (=Not All) Are Chosen," *NTSt* 36/1 (1990): 89-97 [22:14].

4759.398 E. Manns, "La technique du 'Al Tiqra' dans les évangiles," *RevSR* 64 (1990): 1-7 [22:32].

4759.399 B. T. Viviano, "Social World and Community Leadership: The Case of Matthew 23:1-12, 34," *JSNT* 39 (1990): 3-21 [23:1-12, 34].

4759.400 John Hoad, "On Matthew 23:15: A Rejoinder," *ET* 73 (1962): 211-12 [23:15].

4759.401 Paul S. Minear, "Yes or No: The Demand for Honesty in the Early Church," *NT* 13 (1971): 1-13 [23:15].

4759.402 Mark A. Powell, "Do and Keep What Moses Says," *JBL* 114 (1995): 419-35 [23:2-7].

4759.403 J. D. M. Derrett, "Receptacles and Tombs (Mt. 23,24-30)," *ZNW* 77 (1986): 255-66 [23:24-30].

4759.404 Samuel Tobias Lachs, "On Matthew 23:27-28," *HTR* 68/3 (1975): 385-88 [23:27-28].

4759.405 H. van der Kwaak, "Die Klage über Jerusalem (Matth. xxiii. 37-39)," *NT* 8 (1966): 156-70 [23:37-39].

4759.406 Eduard Lohse, "Hosianna," *NT* 6/2 (1963): 113-19 [23:39].

4759 407 Hyam Maccoby, "The Washing of Cups," *JSNT* 14 (1982): 3-15 [23:5-6].

4759.408 R. S. Barbour, "Uncomfortable Words. VIII: Status and Titles," *ET* 82/5 (1971): 137-42 [23:8-9].

4759.409 Morris A. Inch, "Matthew and the House-Churches," *EQ* 43/4 (1971): 196-202 [24-25].

4759.410 John F. Walvoord, "Christ's Olivet Discourse on the End of the Age," *BS* 128 (1971): 109-16 [24-25].

4759.411 John F. Walvoord, "Christ's Olivet Discourse on the Time of the End," *BS* 129 (1972): 20-32 [24-25].

4759.412 Schuyler Brown, "The Matthean Apocalypse," *JSNT* 4 (1979): 2-27 [24-25].

4759.413 Bruce A. Ware, "Is the Church in View in Matthew 24-25?" *BS* 138 (1981): 158-72 [24-25].

4759.414 John F. Walvoord, "Will Israel Build a Temple in Jerusalem?" *BS* 125 (1968): 99-106 [24:1-2:15].

4759.415 Thomas S. McCall, "How Soon the Tribulation Temple?" *BS* 128 (1971): 341-51 [24:15-16].

4759.416 Graham N. Stanton, " 'Pray That Your Flight May Not Be in Winter or on a Sabbath'," *JSNT* 37 (1989): 17-30 [24:20].

4759.417 E. K.-C. Wong, "The Matthean Understanding of the Sabbath: A Response to G. N. Stanton," *JSNT* 44 (1991): 3-18 [24:20].

4759.418 John F. Walvoord, "Christ's Coming to Reign," *BS* 123 (1966): 195-203 [24:27-30].

4759.419 George C. Fuller, "The Olivet Discourse: An Apocalyptic Time-Table," *WTJ* 28/2 (1966): 157-63 [24:29].

4759.420 John S. Kloppenborg, "Didache 16:6-8 and Special Matthaean Tradition," *ZNW* 70/1 (1979): 54-67 [24:29-31].

4759.421 John F. Walvoord, "Christ's Olivet Discourse on the Time of the End: Prophecies Fulfilled in the Present Age," *BS* 128 (1971): 206-14 [24:4-14].

4759.422 Justin Taylor, " 'The Love of Many Will Grow Cold': Matt. 24:9-13 and the Neronian Persecution," *RB* 96/3 (1989): 352-57 [24:9-13].

4759.423 J. M. Ford, "The Parable of the Foolish Scholars (Matt. 25:1-13)," *NT* 9 (1967): 107-23 [25:1-13].

4759.424 K. P. Donfried, "The Allegory of the Ten Virgins (Matt. 25:1-13) as a Summary of Matthean Theology," *JBL* 93 (1974): 415-28 [25:1-13].

4759.425 Wolfgang Schenk, "Auferweckung der Toten oder Gericht nach den Werken. Tradition und Redaktion in Mattäus XXV: 1-13," *NT* 20/4 (1978): 278-99 [25:1-13].

4759.426 Nancy J. Duff, "Wise and Foolish Maidens, Matthew 25:1-13," *USQR* 40/3 (1985): 55-58 [25:1-13].

4759.427 J. D. M. Derrett, "Law in the New Testament: The Parable of the Talents and Two Logia," *ZNW* 56 (1966): 184-95 [25:14-28].

4759.428   E. Kamlah, "Kritik und Interpretation der Parabel von den anvertrauten Geldern," *KD* 14 (1968): 28-38 [25:14-30].

4759.429   L. C. McGauchy, "The Fear of Yahweh and the Mission of Judaism: A Postexilic Maxim and Its Early Christian Expansion in the Parable of the Talents," *JBL* 94 (1975): 235-45 [25:14-30].

4759.430   David C. Steinmetz, "Matthew 25:14-30," *Interp* 34/2 (1980): 172-76 [25:14-30].

4759.431   H. K. Nielsen, "Er den 'dovne' tjener doven? Om oversaettelsen af ὀκνηρός, i Matth 25,26," *DTT* 53 (1990): 106-15 [25:26].

4759.432   A. Marcus Ward, "Uncomfortable Words: IV. Unprofitable Servants," *ET* 81/7 (1970): 200-203 [25:30].

4759.433   James H. Smylie, "Uncle Tom's Cabin Revisited: The Bible, the Romantic Imagination and the Sympathies of Christ," *Interp* 27/1 (1973): 67-85 [25:31].

4759.434   J. Ramsey Michaels, "Apostolic Hardships and Righteous Gentiles," *JBL* 84 (1965): 27-37 [25:31-46].

4759.435   H. E. W. Turner, "Expounding the Parables: The Parable of the Sheep and the Goats," *ET* 77 (1965-1966): 243-46 [25:31-46].

4759.436   Lamar Cope, "Matthew 25:31-46: 'The Sheep and the Goats' Reinterpreted," *NT* 11 (1969): 32-44 [25:31-46].

4759.437   J.-C. Ingelaere, "La 'parabole' du Jugement Dernier (Matthieu 25,31-46)," *RHPR* 50 (1970): 23-60 [25:31-46].

4759.438   M. A. Chevallier, "Note à propos de l'exégète de Mt. 25:31-46," *RevSR* 48 (1974): 398-400 [25:31-46].

4759.439   Rudolf Brändle, "Jean Chrysostome: l'importance de Matth 25,31-46 pour son Éthique," *VCh* 31/1 (1977): 47-52 [25:31-46].

4759.440   Rudolf Brändle, "Zur Interpretation von Mt. 25:31-46 im Matthäuskommentar des Origenes," *TZ* 36 (1980): 17-25 [25:31-46].

4759.441   Martin Tripole, "A Church for the Poor and the World: At Issue with Moltmann's Ecclesiology," *ThSt* 42/4 (1981): 645-59 [25:31-46].

4759.442   John M. Court, "Right and Left: The Implications for

Matthew 25.31-46," *NTSt* 31/2 (1985): 223-33 [25:31-46].

4759.443 Dan O. Via, "Ethical Responsibility and Human Wholeness in Matthew 25:31-46," *HTR* 80/1 (1987): 79-100 [25:31-46].

4759.444 Manfred Hutter, "Mt. 25:31-46 in der Deutung Manis," *NT* 33 (1991) 276-82 [25:31-46].

4759.445 K. Wengst, "Wie aus Böcken Ziegen wurden. Zur Entstehung und Verbreitung einer Forshungslegende oder: Wissenschaft als 'stille Post'," *EvT* 54 (1994): 491-500 [25:32].

4759.446 P. H. Bligh, "Eternal Fire, Eternal Punishment, Eternal Life (Mt. 25,41.46)," *ET* 83 (1971-72): 9-11 [25:41-46].

4759.447 Jean Calloud, "Entre les écritures et la violence: la passion du témoin," *RSR* 73 (1985): 111-28 [26-27].

4759.448 Robert Holst, "The One Anointing of Jesus: Another Application of the Form-Critical Method," *JBL* 95 (1976): 435-46 [26:11].

4759.449 Arthur G. Arnott, " 'The First Day of the Unleavened . . . ' Mt 26.17, Mk 14.12, Lk 22.7," *BTr* 35 (1984): 235-38 [26:17].

4759.450 Phillip Sigal, "Another Note to 1 Corinthians 10.16," *NTSt* 29/1 (1983): 134-39 [26:27].

4759.451 D. Muñoz León, " 'Iré delante de vosotros a Galilea' (Mt. 26,32 y par.). Sentido mesiánico y posible sustrato arameo del logion," *EB* 48 (1990): 215-41 [26:32].

4759.452 Herbert Dennett, "The Need for a Neutral Idiom," *BTr* 17 (1966): 39-41 [26:34].

4759.453 Dale C. Allison, "Anticipating the Passion: The Literary Reach of Matthew 26:47-27:56," *CBQ* 56 (1994): 701-14 [26:47-27:56].

4759.454 G. M. Lee, "Matthew 26:50," *ET* 81 (1969-1970): 55 [26:50].

4759.455 Birger Gerhardsson, "Confession and Denial before Men: Observation on Matt. 26:57-27:2," *JSNT* 13 (1981): 46-66 [26:57-27:2].

4759.456 Ronald F. Thiemann, "The Unnamed Woman at Bethany," *TTod* 44/2 (1987): 179-88 [26:6-13].

4759.457 J. F. Coakley, "The Anointing at Bethany and the Priority of John," *JBL* 107/2 (1988): 241-56 [26:6-13].

4759.458 David R. Catchpole, "The Answer of Jesus to Caiaphas (Matthew 26:64)," *NTSt* 17/2 (1971): 213-26 [26:64].

4759.459 Frank J. Matera, "Matthew 27:11-54," *Interp* 38 (1984): 55-59 [27:11-54].

4759.460 Roland Kany, "Die Frau des Pilatus und ihr Name. Ein Kapitel aus der Geschichte neutestarnentlicher Wissenschaft," *ZNW* 86 (1995): 104-10 [27:19].

4759.461 M. Philonenko, "Le sang du Juste (I Hénoch 47:1-4; Matthieu 27:24)," *RHPR* 73 (1993): 395-99 [27:24].

4759.462 T. B. Cargal, " 'His Blood Be Upon Us and Upon Our Children': A Matthean Double Entendre?" *NTSt* 37/1 (1991): 102-12 [27:24-25].

4759.463 Terence L. Donaldson, "The Mockers and the Son of God (Matthew 27:37-44): Two Characters in Matthew's Story of Jesus," *JSNT* 41 (1991): 3-18 [27:37-44].

4759.464 M. de Jonge, "Matthew 27:51 in Early Christian Exegesis," *IITR* 79 (1986): 67-79 [27:51].

4759.465 R. Aguirre, "El Reino de Dios y la muerte de Jesús en el evangelio de Mateo," *EE* 54 (1979): 363-82 [27:51-53].

4759.466 John W. Wenham, "When Were the Saints Raised?" *JTS* 32/1 (1981): 150-52 [27:51-53].

4759.467 W. G. Essame, "Matthew 27:51-54 and John 5:25-29," *ET* 76 (1964-1965): 103 [27:51-54].

4759.468 Frank J. Matera, "Matthew 27:51-54," *Interp* 38 (1984): 55-59 [27:51-54].

4759.469 David C. Sim, "The 'Confession' of the Soldiers Matthew 27:54," *HeyJ* 34 (1993): 401-24 [27:54].

4759.470 C. Turiot, "Sémiotique et lisibilité du texte évangélique," *RSR* 73 (1985): 161-75 [27:57-28:15].

4759.471 P. H. Lai, "Production du sens par la foi. Autorités religieuses contestées/fondées. Analyse structurale de Matthieu 27,57-28,20," *RSR* 61 (1973): 65-96 [27:57-28:20].

4759.472 C. H. Giblin, "Structural and Thematic Correlation in the Matthaean Burial-Resurrection Narrative (Matt. 27:57-28:20)," *NTSt* 21 (1974-1975): 406-20 [27:57-28:20].

4759.473 M. J. J. Menken, "The References of Jeremiah in the Gospel According to Matthew (Mt. 2,17; 16,14; 27,9)," *ETL* 60/1 (1984): 5-24 [27:9].

4759.474 Kevin Smyth, "Matthew 28: Resurrection as Theophany," *ITQ* 42/4 (1975): 259-71 [28].

4759.475 G. R. Driver, "Two Problems in the New Testament," *JTS* 16 (1965): 327-37 [28:1].

4759.476 Paul S. Minear, "Matthew 28:1-10," *Interp* 38/1 (1984): 59-63 [28:1-10].

4759.477 Cynthia A. Jarvis, "Matthew 28:1-10," *Interp* 42/1 (1988): 63-68 [28:1-10].

4759.478 Dorothy J. Weaver, "Matthew 28:1-10," *Interp* 46 (1992): 399-402 [28:1-10].

4759.479 Edgar V. McKnight and Charles H. Talbert, "Can the Griesbach Hypothesis Be Falsified?" *JBL* 91/3 (1972): 338-68 [28:1-18].

4759.480 Nikolaus Walter, "Eine Vormatthaische Schilderung derr Auferstehung Jesus," *NTSt* 19/4 (1973): 415-29 [28:11-15].

4759.481 Robert D. Culver, "What Is the Church's Commission? Some Exegetical Issues in Matthew 28:16-20," *BETS* 10/2 (1967): 115-26 [28:16-20].

4759.482 Ulrich Luz, "Herrenwort und Geschichte in Matth. 28,16-20," *EvT* 27 (1967): 494-508 [28:16-20].

4759.483 B. J. Malina, "The Literary Structure and Form of Matt. 28:16-20," *NTSt* 17 (1970-1971): 87-103 [28:16-20].

4759.484 Jean Zumstein, "Matthieu 28:16-20," *RTP* 22 (1972): 14-33 [28:16-20].

4759.485 Jack D. Kingsbury, "The Composition and Christology of Matthew 28:16-20," *JBL* 93/4 (1974): 573-84 [28:16-20].

4759.486 James Tanis, "Reformed Pietism and Protestant Missions," *HTR* 67/1 (1974): 65-73 [28:16-20].

4759.487 C. H. Giblin, "A Note on Doubt and Reassurance in Mt. 28:16-20," *CBQ* 37 (1975): 68-75 [28:16-20].

4759.488 John P. Meier, "Two Disputed Questions in Matt. 28:16-20," *JBL* 96/3 (1977): 407-24 [28:16-20].

4759.489 L. G. Parkhurst, "Matthew 28:16-20 Reconsidered," *ET* 90 (1979): 179-80 [28:16-20].

4759.490 Oscar S. Brooks, "Matthew 28:16-20 and the Design of the First Gospel," *JSNT* 10 (1981): 2-18 [28:16-20].

4759.491 Cynthia M. Campbell, "Matthew 28:16-20," *Interp* 46 (1992): 402-405 [28:16-20].

4759.492   W. D. Davies and Dale C. Allison, "Matt. 28:16-20: Texts Behind the Text," *RHPR* 72 (1992): 89-98 [28:16-20].

4759.493   J. Kwik, "Some Doubted," *ET* 77 (1965-1966): 181 [28:17].

4759.494   I. P. Ellis, "But Some Doubted," *NTSt* 14 (1967-1968): 574-80 [28:17].

4759.495   K. Grayston, "The Translation of Matthew 28:17," *JSNT* 21 (1984): 105-109 [28:17].

4759.496   P. T. O'Brien, "The Great Commission of Matthew 28:18-20," *RTR* 35/3 (1976): 66-78 [28:18-20].

4759.497   Schuyler Brown, "The Matthean Community and the Gentile Mission," *NT* 22/3 (1980): 193-221 [28:18-20].

4759.498   J.-C. Basset, "Dernières paroles du ressuscité et mission de l'Église aujourd'hui. (à propos de Mt 28:18-20 et parallèles)," *RTP* 114 (1982): 349-67 [28:18-20].

4759.499   Gerhard Friedrich, "Die Formale Struktur von Mt. 28,18-20," *ZTK* 80/2 (1983): 137-83 [28:18-20].

4759.500   D. R. A. Hare and D. J. Harrington, "Make Disciples of All the Gentiles (Matthew 28:19)," *CBQ* 37 (1975): 359-69 [28:19].

4759.501   John P. Meier, "Nations or Gentiles in Matthew 28:19," *CBQ* 39/1 (1977): 94-102 [28:19].

4759.502   Luise Abramowski, "Die Entstehung der Dreigliedrigen Taufformel-ein Versuch-mit einem exkurs: Jesus der Naziraer," *ZTK* 81/4 (1984): 417-46 [28:19].

4759.503   Robert D. Culver, "What Is the Church's Commission?" *BS* 125 (1968): 239-53 [28:19-20].

4759.504   George Howard, "A Note on the Shorter Ending of Matthew," *HTR* 81/1 (1988): 117-20 [28:19-20].

4759.505   Frans Neirynck, "Note on Mt 28,9-10," *ETL* 71 (1995): 161-65 [28:9-10].

3. Critical and Exegetical Studies of Passages in Mark

4760.   E. Iliff Robson, "Rhythm and Intonation in St. Mark i-x," *JTS* 17 (1915-1916): 270-80.

4761.   B. W. Bacon, "The Prologue of Mark: A Study of Sources and Structure," *JBL* 26 (1907): 84-106.

4762.   J. O. F. Murray, "The Witness of the Baptist to Jesus," *ET* 37 (1925-1926): 103-109 [Mk. 1:1-11].

4763.   F. C. Burkitt, "The Baptism of Jesus," *ET* 38 (1926- 1927):
          198-202 [Mk. 1:1-11].

4764.   Ivor Buse, "The Markan Account of the Baptism of Jesus and
          Isaiah 53," *JTS* N.S. 7 (1956): 74-75 [Mk. 1:1-11].

4765.   J. W. Cohoon, "Two Glosses on Goodspeed's *Problems of
          New Testament Translation*," *JBL* 65 (1946): 403-404 [Mk.
          1:1-4; Acts 1:18].

4766.   Edgar J. Godspeed, "A Reply," *JBL* 65 (1946): 405-406 [Mk
          1:1-4; Acts 1:18].

4767.   Eb. Nestle, "How does the Gospel of Mark begin?" *Exp* 4th
          ser. 10 (1894): 458-60 [Mk. 1:1 ff.].

4768.   Fr. Herklotz, "Weiteres zu Mk. 1, 1," *BibZ* 3 (1905): 408.

4769.   Eb. Nestle, "Mark i. 1 and the Revisers," *JTS* 9 (1907-
          1909): 101.

4770.   F. E. Daubanton, "Mk. 1, 1," *NTS* 2 (1919): 168-70.

4771.   R. L. T. Haselhurst, "The Opening of the Second Gospel,"
          Th 12 (1926): 283-84.

4772.   F. W. Grosheide, "Het begin van het evangelie," *GTT* 28
          (1927-1928): 455-61.

4773.   Allen Wikgren, "Ἀρχή τοῦ εὐαγγελίου," *JBL* 61 (1942):
          11-20 [Mk. 1:1].

4774.   A. van Veldhuizen, "De aanhef van Mk. en nog wat vooraf,"
          NTS 2 (1919): 171-75.

4775.   Joseph Palmer, "Mark i. 2," *ET* 11 (1899-1900): 474-75.

4776.   J. Gnilka, "Die essenischen Tauchbäder und die
          Johannestaufe," *RQu* 3 (1961): 185-207 [Mk. 1:4; Lk. 3:3].

4777.   G. L. Marriott, "Locusts and Wild Honey'," *ET* 30
          (1918-1919): 280-81.

4778.   W. R. Weeks, "Mark i. 7," *ET* 73 (1961-1962): 54.

4779.   Kendrick Grobel, "He that cometh after me," *JBL* 60 (1941):
          397-401 [Mk. 1:7].

4780.   James Moffatt, "Mark i. 8," *ET* 8 (1896-1897): 522-23.

4781.   F. J. Botha, "Ἐβάπτισα in Mark i. 8," *ET* 64 (1952- 1953):
          286.

4782.   J. E. Yates, "The Form of Mark 1. 8b," *NTSt* 4 (1957- 1958):
          334-38.

4783.   S. Greijdanus, "Onzes Heilands doop door Joahannes," *GTT*
          19 (1918-1919): 49-77 [Mk. 1:9-11].

4784. C. E. B. Cranfield, "The Baptism of our Lord—A Study of St. Mark i. 9-11," *SJT* 8 (1955): 53-63.

4785. André Fuillet, "Le baptême de Jésus d'après l'évangile selon Saint Marc (1, 9-11)," *CBQ* 21 (1959): 468-90.

4786. André Feuillet, "Le symbolisme de la colombe dans les récits évangéliques du baptême," *RSR* 46 (1958): 524-44 [Mk. 1:10].

4787. B. W. Bacon, "On the Aorist εὐδόκησα in Mark i. 11 and Parallels'," *JBL* 16 (1897): 136-39; 20 (1901): 28-30.

4788. C. H. Turner, "Ὁ υἱός μου ὁ ἀγαπητός," *JTS* 27 (1925-1926): 113-29 [Mk. 1:11; 9:7].

4789. S. Eitrem, "Die Versuchung Christi. Mit Nachwort von Anton Fridrichsen," *NTT* 25, *Reihefte* (1924): 3-37 [Mt. 4:1-11; Mk. 1:12-13; Lk 4:1-12].

4790. Jacques Dupont, "L'arrière-fond biblique du récit des tentations de Jésus," *NTS* 3 (1956-1957): 287-304 [Mk. 1:12-13].

4791. André Feuillet, "L'épisode de la tentation d'après l'évangile selon Saint Marc (1, 12-13)," *EB* 19 (1960): 49-73.

4792. Christian Duquoc, "La tentation du Christ," *LumV* 53 (1961): 21-41 [Mk. 1:12-13].

4793. Joseph Huby, "Sur un passage de saint Marc (Marc 1, 13)," *RSR* 1 (1910): 66-67.

4794. Wilhelm August Schulze, "Der Heilige und die wilden Tiere; zur Exegese von Mc. 1. 13b," *ZNW* 46 (1955): 280-83.

4795. J. M. Creed, " 'The Kingdom of God has come'," *ET* 48 (1936-1937): 184-85 [Mk. 1:15].

4796. C. H. Dodd, " 'The Kingdom of God has come'," *ET* 48 (1936-1937): 138-42 [Mk 1:15].

4797. J. Y. Campbell, " 'The Kingdom of God has come'," *ET* 48 (1936-1937): 91-94 [Mk. 1:15].

4798. Peter Staples, "The Kingdom of God has Come," *ET* 71 (1959-1960): 87-88 [Mk. 1:15].

4799. W. R. Hutton, "The Kingdom of God has Come," *ET* 64 (1952-1953): 89-91 [Mk. 1:15].

4800. Martin A. Simpson, "The Kingdom of God has Come," *ET* 64 (1952-1953): 188 [Mk. 1:15].

4801. Matthew Black, "The Kingdom of God has Come," *ET* 63

(1951-1952): 289-90 [Mk. 1:15].

4802. M. Buchanan, "Some Fishing Stories in the Gospels," *Th* 28 (1934): 35-52 [Mk. 1:16-20 etc.].

4803. J. Smith, "Fishers of Men," *ET* 9 (1897-1898): 426 [Mk. 1:17].

4804. J. Mánek, "Fishers of Men," *NT* 2 (1958): 138-41 [Mk. 1:17].

4805. Charles W. F. Smith, "Fishers of Men," *HTR* 52 (1959): 187-204 [Mk. 1:17].

4806. G. R. Wynne, "Mending their Nets," *Exp* 7th ser. 8 (1909): 282-85 [Mk. 1:19].

4807. E. P. Barrows, "Our Saviour's Discourse in the Synagogue at Capernaum," *BS* 11 (1854): 693-729 [Mk. 1:21-28].

4808. H. J. Flowers, "ὡς ἐδουσίαν ἔχων," *ET* 66 (1954-1955): 254 [Mk. 1:22].

4809. E. M. Sidebottom, "ὅτι ἐν ἐξουσίᾳ ἦν ὁ λόγος αὐτοῦ," *ET* 66 (1954-1955): 350 [Mk. 1:22].

4810. David Daube, "ἐξουσία in Mark i. 22 and 27," *JTS* 39 (1938): 45-59.

4811. Joshua Stan, "The Meaning of 'Authority' in Mark 1. 22," *HTR* 23 (1930): 302-305.

4812. Franz Mussner, "Ein Wortspiel in Mk. 1, 24?" *BibZ* 4 (1960): 285-86.

4813. Kr. Sandfeld Jensen, "Markus 1, 29," *TTDF* 3rd ser., 2 (1910-1911): 386-89.

4814. W. Parton Shinton, "For the Sake of the Sufferer," *ET* 34 (1922-1923): 426-28 [Mk. 1:40-45].

4815. Charles Masson, "La péricope du lépreux," *RTP* N.S. 26 (1938): 287-95 [Mk. 1:40-45].

4816. Charles C. Ryrie, "The Cleansing of the Leper," *BS* 113 (1956): 262-67 [Mk. 1:40-45].

4817. Kirsopp Lake, "ἐμβριμησάμενος and ὀργισθείς, Mark 1, 40-43," *HTR* 16 (1923): 197-98.

4818. Edwyn Bevan, "Note on Mark i. 41 and John xi. 33, 38," *JTS* 33 (1931-1932): 186-88.

4819. José M. Bover, "Critica textual de Mc. 1, 41," *EE* 23 (1949): 355-57.

4820. George D. Kilpatrick, "Mark i. 45," *JTS* 42 (1941): 67-68.

4821.   George D. Kilpatrick, "Mark i. 45 and the Meaning of λόγος," *JTS* 40 (1939): 389-90.

4822.   T. Nicklin, "St. Mark i. 45," *ET* 51 (1939-1940): 252.

4823.   Allen Cabaniss, "A Fresh Exegesis of Mark 2:1-12," *Interp* 11 (1957): 324-27.

4824.   Ernest Best, "Mark ii. 1-12," *BTr* 3 (1953): 41-46.

4825.   Richard T. Mead, "The Healing of the Paralytic— Unit?" *JBL* 80 (1961): 348-54 [Mk. 2:1-12].

4826.   W. Wrede, "Zur Heilung des Gelähmten (Mc. 2, 1 ff.)," *ZNW* 5 (1904): 354-58.

4827.   R. H. Strachan, " 'The Man borne of Four'," *ET* 33 (1921-1922): 470-73 [Mk. 2:3].

4828.   W. K. Lowther Clarke, "Studies in Texts," *Th* 11 (1925): 339 [Mk. 2:3, 4].

4829.   David Daube, "ὄχλος in Mark ii. 4 (Luke v. 19)," *ET* 50 (1938-1939): 138-39.

4830.   Hedwig Jahnow, "Das Abdecken des Daches Mc. 2, 4 [und] Lc. 5, 19," *ZNW* 24 (1925): 155-58.

4831.   W. D. Morris, "Mark ii. 4; Luke v. 19," *ET* 35 (1923-1924): 141-42.

4832.   L. Fonck, "Zum Abdecken des Daches," *B* 6 (1925): 450-54 [Mk. 2:4 and Lk. 5:19]

4833.   R. W. Wallace, "Mark ii. 4; Luke v. 19," *ET* 35 (1923-1924): 381.

4834.   H. Branscomb, "Mark 2:5, 'Son, thy sins are forgiven'," *JBL* 53 (1934): 53-60.

4835.   Fred Gealy, "Son, thy Sins are Forgiven," *JR* 18 (1938): 51-59 [Mk. 2:5].

4836.   André Feuillet, "L'ἐξουσία du fils de l'homme (d'après Mc. II, 10-28 et par.)," *RSR* 42 (1954): 161-92.

4837.   R. E. Wallis, "Man's Power to Forgive Sins," *Exp* 2nd ser. 3 (1882): 106-16 [Mk. 2:10].

4838.   Douglas S. Sharp, "Mark ii. 10," *ET* 38 (1926-1927): 428-29.

4839.   C. P. Ceroke, "Is Mark 2,10 a Saying of Jesus?" *CBQ* 22 (1960): 369-90.

4840.   G. H. Boobyer, "Mark ii, 10a and the Interpretation of the Healing of the Paralytic," *HTR* 47 (1954): 115-20.

4841.   F. C. Burkitt, "Levi Son of Alphaeus," *JTS* 28 (1926-1927):
273-74 [Mk. 2:14].

4842.   J. Alonso, "La parábola del médico en Mc. 2. 16, 17," *CB* 16
(1959): 10-12.

4843.   F. Warburton Lewis, "Who were the Sons of the Bride-
Chamber? (Mark ii. 18-22)," *ET* 24 (1912-1913): 285.

4844.   F. W. Dillistone, "St. Mark ii. 18-22: A Suggested
Reinterpretation," *ET* 48 (1936-1937): 253-54.

4845.   H. J. Ebeling, "Die Fastenfrage (Mk. 2. 18-22)," *TSK* 108
(1937-1938): 387-96.

4846.   Roderic Dunkerley, "The Bridegroom Passage," *ET* 64
(1952-1953): 303-304 [Mk. 2:20].

4847.   A. Klöpper, "Der ungewalkte Flicken und das alte Kleid. Der
neue Wein und die alten Schläuche," *TSK* 58 (1885): 505-34
[Mk. 2:21-22].

4848.   F. C. Synge, "Mark ii. 21—Matthew ix. 16—Luke v. 36: The
Parable of the Patch," *ET* 56 (1944-1945): 26-27.

4849.   R. R. Lewis, "ἐπίβλημα ῥάκους ἀγνάφου," *ET* 45
(1933-1934): 185 [Mk. 2:21].

4850.   H. Weitbrecht, "New Wine in New Wine Skins," *ET* 19
(1907-1908): 142 [Mk. 2:22].

4851.   Henry Troadée, "Le fils de l'homme est maître même du
sabbat (Marc 2, 23-3, 6)," *BVC* no. 21 (1958): 73-83.

4852.   F. W. Beare, "The Sabbath was made for Man?" *JBL* 79
(1960): 130-36 [Mk. 2:23-28].

4853.   S. Lyonnet, "Quoniam Nazaraeus vocabitur," *B* 25 (1944):
196-206 [Mk. 2:23].

4854.   John W. Wenham, "Mark ii. 26," *JTS* N.S. 1 (1950): 156.

4855.   Alan D. Rogers, "Mark ii. 26," *JTS* N.S. 2 (1951): 44.

4856.   T. R. English, "The Sabbath," *USR* 11 (1899-1900): 262-73
[Mk. 2:27-28].

4857.   R. Thibaut, "L'enthymème de Mc. II. 27 suiv.," *NRT* 59
(1932): 257.

4858.   L. Cerfaux, L'aveuglement d'esprit' dans l'évangile de Saint
Marc," *Mu* 59 (1946): 267-79 [Mk. 3:5].

4859.   Hermann Cladder, "Textkntisches zu Mk. 3, 7, 8," *BibZ* 10
(1912): 261-72.

4860.   W. Burgers, "De Instelling van de Twaalf in het Evangelie van Marcus," *ETL* 36 (1960): 625-54.

4861. T. T. Lynch, "The Glorious Company of Apostles," *Exp* 1st. ser. 1 (1875): 29-43 [Mk. 3:14].

4862. H. J. Vogels, "Der Apostelkatalog bei Markus in der altlateinischen Übersetzung," *BibZ* 16 (1922-1924): 66-67 [Mk. 3:16-19].

4863. J. Rendel Harris, "Sons of Lightning," *ET* 36 (1924-1925): 139 [Mk. 3:17].

4864. Gustave Bardy, "Boanergès," *RSR* 15 (1925): 167-77 [Mk. 3:17].

4865. G. Birdie, "Boanergès," *RSR* 18 (1928): 344 [Mk. 3:17].

4866. A. D. Martin, "A Sequel to the Wilderness Temptation," *ET* 34 (1922-1923): 259-62 [Mk 3:20-35].

4867. F. Spadafora, "Mc. 3, 20-21," *RivB* 4 (1956): 98-113, 193-217.

4868. S. Monteil, "À propos de Marc iii. 20-21," *RTQR* 19 (1910): 317-25.

4869. Franz Zorell, "Zu Mark 3, 20, 21," *ZKT* 37 (1913): 695-97.

4870. Gerhard Hartmann, "Mk. 3, 20 f.," *BibZ* 11 (1913): 249-79.

4871. J. E. Belser, "Zu Markus 3, 20-21," *TQ* 98 (1916): 401-18.

4872. A. Wimmer, "Apostolos quosdam exisse (Mc. 3, 20 s.)," *VD* 31 (1953): 131-43.

4873. James H. Moulton, "Mark iii. 21," *ET* 20 (1908-1909): 476.

4874. A. Wabnitz, "Note sur Marc iii. 21," *RTQR* 18 (1909): 221-25.

4875. André Urinal, "De nouveau Marc iii, 21," *RTQR* 19 (1910): 326-27.

4876. Andre Arnal, "La folie de Jésus et le témoignage de Marc," *RTQR* 17 (1908): 304-21 [Mk. 3:21].

4877. C. Bruston, "Un passage obscur de l'évangile de Marc," *RTQR* 18 (1909): 82-87 [Mk. 3:21].

4878. P. Tarel, "Encore Marc III. 21," *RTQR* 18 (1909): 88-93.

4879. W. Mallinckrodt, "Want zij zeiden: Hij is buiten zijne zinner (Marc 3. 21)," *NTS* 3 (1920): 314-22.

4880. Owen E. Evans, "The Unforgivable Sin," *ET* 68 (1956-1957): 240-44 [Mk. 3:28 f.].

4881. Anton Fridrichsen, "Le péché contre le Saint Esprit," *RHPR*

3 (1923): 367-72 [Mk. 3:28].

4882.   R. T. Herford, "The Unpardonable Sin—A Theological Fiction," *FF* 1 (1947-1948): 27-30 [Mk. 3:29].

4883.   Fred Gealy, "The Composition of Mark iv," *ET* 48 (1936-1937): 40-43.

4884.   Donald W. Riddle, "Mark 4:1-34; The Evolution of a Gospel Source," *JBL* 56 (1937): 77-90.

4885.   C. E. B. Cranfield, "St. Mark iv. 1-34," *SJT* 4 (1951): 398-414; 4 (1952): 49-66.

4886.   C. J. H. Ropes, "The Parable of the Field," *BW* 8 (1896): 20-22 [Mk. 4:1-20].

4887.   S. K. Finlayson, "The Parable of the Sower," *ET* 55 (1943-1944): 306-307 [Mk. 4:1-20].

4888.   Paul Doncoeur, "La parabole du semeur qui sème à tout terrain," *RSR* 24 (1934): 609-11 [Mk. 4:1-9].

4889.   K. Grayston, "The Sower," *ET* 55 (1943-1944): 138-39 [Mk. 4:1-9].

4890.   J. Rendel Harris, "An Unnoticed Aramaism in St. Mark," *ET* 26 (1914-1915): 248-50 [Mk. 4:1].

4891.   Eric F. F. Bishop, "ἀκουέτω Mark 4:9, 23," *BTr* 7 (1956): 38-40.

4892.   José M. Bover, "Problemas inherentes a la interpretación de la parábola del Sembrador," *EE* 26 (1952): 169-85 [Mk. 4:10-25].

4893.   K. Knoke, "Jesu Selbstaussage über seine parabolische Lehrweise, Mark. 4, 10-13," *NKZ* 16 (1905): 137-64.

4894.   E. F. Siegman, "Teaching in Parables (Mk. 4, 10-12, Lk. 8, 9-10; Mt. 13, 10-15)," *CBQ* 23 (1961): 161-81.

4895.   W. Manson, "The Purpose of the Parables: A Re-Examination of St. Mark iv. 10-12," *ET* 68 (1956-1957): 132-35.

4896.   J. Arthur Baird, "A Pragmatic Approach to Parable Exegesis: Some New Evidence on Mark 4:11, 33-34," *JBL* 76 (1957): 201-207.

4897.   W. H. Turton, "Studies in Texts," *Th* 20 (1930): 228-29 [Mk. 4:11, 12].

4898.   Bertil Wiberg, "Forhaerdelsestanken i evangelierne," *DTT* 21 (1958): 16-23 [Mk. 4:11-12].

4899. Nils Johansson, "τὸ μυστήριον τῆς βασιλείας τοῦ θεοῦ," *STK* 16 (1940): 3-38.

4900. T. M. Donn, "Discerning the Mysteries of the Kingdom of Heaven," *BT* 4 (1954): 57-62 [Mk. 4:11].

4901. Eb. Nestle, "Mark iv. 12," *ET* 13 (1901-1902): 524.

4902. Augustus Poynder, "Mark iv. 12," *ET* 15 (1903-1904): 141-42.

4903. Hans Windisch, "Die Verstockungsidee in Mc. 4, 12 und das kausale ἵνα der späteren Koine," *ZNW* 26 (1927): 203-209.

4904. T. A. Sinclair, "Note on an Apparent Mistranslation," *BT* 5 (1954): 18 [Mk. 4:12].

4905. C. E. B. Cranfield, "Message of Hope, Mark 4, 21-32," *Interp* 9 (1955): 150-64.

4906. Joseph Huby, "Sur un passage du second évangile (Marc IV 21-25)," *RSR* 1 (1910): 168-74.

4907. H. A. A. Kennedy, "The Composition of Mark iv. 21-25: A Study in the Synoptic Problem," *ET* 25 (1913-1914): 301-305.

4908. José M. Bover, "Nada hay encubierto que no se descubra," *EB* 13 (1954): 319-23 [Mk. 4:21-22].

4909. James Moffatt, "The Peril and the Comfort of Exposure," *Exp* 6th ser. 2 (1900): 381-94 [Mk. 4:22 = Lk. 8:17; Mt. 10:26; Lk. 12:2].

4910. P. J. Maclagan, "Mark iv. 23," *ET* 24 (1912-1913): 381-82.

4911. Wm. J. Loader, "Mark iv. 23," *ET* 25 (1913-1914): 429-30.

4912. Paul Tillich, "El enigma de la desigualdad," *CT* 29 (1959): 3-10 [Mk. 4:25].

4913. Hugh Pope, "The Seed Growing Secretly," *ITQ* 5 (1910): 279-88 [Mk. 4:26-29].

4914. Harald Sahlin, "Zum Verständnis von drei Stellen des Markus-Evangeliums," *B* 33 (1952): 53-66 [Mk. 4:26-29; 7:18f.; 15:34].

4915. Siegfried Goebel, "Das Gleichnis Mark. 4, 26-29," *TSK* 51 (1878): 565-82.

4916. D. F. Strauss, "Das Gleichnis vom fruchtbringenden Acker bei Marcus 4, 26-29," *ZWT* 6 (1863): 209-14.

4917. Joseph Freundorfer, "Eine neue Auslegung der Parabel von der 'selbstwachsenden Saat' Mk. 4, 26-29," *BibZ* 17

(1925-1926): 51-62.

4918.   K. Weiss, "Mk. 4:26 bis 29—dennoch die Parabel vom zuversichtlichen Sämann!" *BibZ* 18 (1929): 45-68.

4919.   T. W. Manson, "A Note on Mark iv. 28 f.," *JTS* 38 (1937): 399-400.

4920.   Alexander Brown, "The Ears of Corn," *ET* 20 (1908- 1909): 377-78 [Mk. 4:28].

4921.   George D. Kilpatrick, "Mark iv. 29," *JTS* 46 (1945): 191.

4922.   J. Hunter Smith, "The Parable of the Mustard Seed," *ET* 23 (1911-1912): 428-30 [Mk. 4:30-32].

4923.   H.-W. Bartsch, "Eine bisher übersehene Zitierung der LXX in Mark. 4, 30," *TZ* 15 (1959): 126-28.

4924.   Franz Mussner, "IQ Hodajoth und das Gleichnis vom Senfkorn (Mk. 4, 30-32 par.)," *BibZ* 4 (1960): 128-30.

4925.   S. Pollard, "The Mustard Seed," *ET* 24 (1912-1913): 187 [Mk. 4:31].

4926.   Charles B. Warring, "Mr. Huxley and the Healing of the Gadarenes, or the 'Swine Miracle'," *BS* 50 (1893): 172-74 [Mk. 5:1-20].

4927.   Theodore G. Soares, "The Worth of a Man: An Exposition of Mark 5:1-20," *BW* 33 (1909): 107-12.

4928.   A. D. Martin, "The Loss of the Gadarene Swine," *ET* 25 (1913-14): 380-381 [Mk. 5:1-20].

4929.   J. E. Somerville, "The Gadarene Demoniac," *ET* 25 (1913-1914): 548-51.

4930.   Mary M. Baird, "The Gadarene Demoniac," *ET* 31 (1919-1920): 189.

4931.   Agnes Mason, "The Healing of the Gadarene Demoniac," *Th* 31 (1935): 152-56 [Mk. 5:1-20].

4932.   W. J. Cratchley, "Demoniac of Gadara," *ET* 63 (1951-1952): 193-94.

4933.   T. Hawthorn, "The Gerasene Demoniac: A Diagnosis, Mark v. 1-20; Luke viii. 26-39 (Matthew viii. 28-34)," *ET* 66 (1954-1955): 79-80.

4934.   Ernest Best, "The Gadarene Demoniac," *BT* 7 (1956): 3-9 [Mk. 5:1-20].

4935.   Francis Terry, "Jesus as a Psychological Healer," *FF* 4 (1950-1951): 72-80 [Mk. 5:2-19; 9:14-29].

4936. T. A. Burkill, "Concerning Mk. 5, 7 and 5, 18-20," *ST* 11 (1957): 159-66.

4937. Robert Leaney, "Dominical Authority for the Ministry of Healing," *ET* 65 (1953-1954): 121-23 [Mk. 5:14-15].

4938. R. Lindenmann, "Die Erweckung der Tochter des Jairus und die Heilung des blutflüssigen Weibes, aufgefasst als symbolische Erzählungen," *STZ* 19 (1902): 1-9 [Mk. 5:21-24, 35-43].

4939. G. Wohlenberg, "Wer war das blutflussige Weib?" *NKZ* 27 (1916): 687-90 [Mk. 5:25-34].

4940. W. Powell, "Mark v. 39," *ET* 66 (1954-1955): 215.

4941. R. E. Ker, "St. Mark v. 39," *ET* 66 (1954-1955): 125.

4942. W. Powell, "St Mark v. 39," *ET* 66 (1954-1955): 61.

4943. R. E. Ker, "St. Mark v. 39," *ET* 65 (1953-1954): 315-16.

4944. Eric F. F. Bishop, "πρασιαί and πληρώματα," *ET* 60 (1948-1949): 192-93 [Mk. 6:1].

4945. J. K. Russell, " 'The Son of Mary' (Mark vi. 3)," *ET* 60 (1948-1949): 195.

4946. S. Zhebelev, "Христосъ плотникъ," *KhV* 6 (1922): 303-14 [Mk. 6:4].

4947. Paul H. Furfey, "Christ as Tekton," *CBQ* 17 (1955): 324-35 [Mk. 6:3].

4948. R. Thibaut, "Sans bâton ni chaussures?" *NRT* 58 (1931): 54-56 [Mk. 6:8].

4949. Herman Ljungvik, "Zum Markusevangelium 6, 14," *ZNW* 33 (1934): 90-92.

4950. Charles A. Webster, "St. Mark vi. 20," *ET* 49 (1937- 1938): 93-94.

4951. Campbell Bonner, "Note on Mark 6. 20," *NTR* 37 (1944): 41-44.

4952. James C. G. Greig, "εὔκαιρος," *ET* 65 (1954-1955): 158-59 [Mk. 6:21 ff.].

4953. Eb. Nestle, "A Little Mistake in the Revised Version," *ET* 15 (1903-1904): 95 [Mk. 6:25].

4954. G. H. Boobyer, "The Miracle of the Loaves and the Gentiles in St. Mark's Gospel," *SJT* 6 (1953): 77-87 [Mk. 6:30-8:21].

4955. A. Linder, "Die Speisungen der Tausende in den vier Evangelien," *STZ* 19 (1902): 89-93 [Mk. 6: 30-44].

4956. L. V. Lester-Garland, "The Feeding of the Five Thousand," *Th* 36 (1938): 87-92 [Mk. 6:30-44; 8:19].

4957. A. M. Farrer, "Loaves and Thousands," *JTS* N.S. 4 (1953): 1-14 [Mk. 6:30-44].

4958. Donald F. Robinson, "The Parable of the Loaves," *ATR* 39 (1957): 107-15.

4959. Georg Ziener, "Die Brotwunder im Markusevangelium," *BibZ* 4 (1960): 282-85 [Mk. 6:30-44; 8:1-9].

4960. U. Holzmeister, " 'Venite seorsum in desertum locum et requiescite pusillum' Mc. 6. 31," *VD* 22 (1942): 161-65.

4961. Ethelbert Stauffer, "Zum apokalyptischen Festmahl in Mc. 6, 34ff.," *ZNW* 46 (1955): 264-66.

4962. Alan Richardson, "The Feeding of the Five Thousand; Mark 6:34-44," *Interp* 9 (1955): 144-49.

4963. F. Cawley, "Feeding the Five Thousand," *ET* 36 (1924-1925): 225-28. [Mk. 6:38-42].

4964. G. A. F. Knight, "The Direction of the Wind when Jesus walked on the Sea of Galilee," *ET* 4 (1892-1893): 323-25 [Mk. 6:45-52].

4965. L. Vaganay, "Marc VI, 45. Essai de critique textuelle," *RB* 49 (1940): 5-32.

4966. Primo Vannutelli, "Textualis criticae experimentum," *S* 5 (1940): iii-viii [Mk. 6:45].

4967. Maisie Spens, "The Mystery of Jesus Walking on the Sea," *Th* 28 (1934): 272-76 [Mk. 6:47-56].

4968. H. G. Meecham, "Mark vi. 48," *ET* 47 (1935-1936): 284-85.

4969. Johannes Horst, "Die Worte Jesu über die kultische Reinheit und ihre Verarbeitung in den evangelischen Berichten," *TSK* 87 (1914): 429-54 [Mk. 7].

4970. Frank Grant Lewis, "Jesus' Attitude to the Old Testament: An Exposition of Mark 7:1-23," *BW* 31 (1908): 131-37.

4971. A. Blüchler, "The Law of Purification in Mark vii. 1-23," *ET* 21 (1909-1910): 34-40.

4972. Eric F. F. Bishop, "ἀπ' ἀγορᾶς: Mark vii. 4," *ET* 61 (1949-1950): 219.

4973. Edgar J. Goodspeed, "The Greek Text of Mark vii. 11," *ET* 20 (1908-1909): 471-72.

4974. J. Skvireckas, "Qorban (Mk. 7, 11; Mt. 15, 5)," *Σ* 1 (1924):

59-61.

4975. F. W. Farrar, "Brief Notes on Passages of the Gospels," *Exp* 1st. ser. 3 (1876): 308-20 [Mk. 7:19].

4976. C. Ryder Smith, " 'An Evil Eye'," *ET* 53 (1941-1942): 181-82 [Mk. 7:22].

4977. J. A. Selbie, "The Syro-Phoenician Woman," *ET* 9 (1897-1898): 408 [Mk. 7:24-30].

4978. R. V. Foster, "The Syro-Phoenician Woman," *ET* 12 (1900-1901): 430 [Mk. 7:24-30].

4979. R. Glaister and F. Warburton Lewis, "Christ and the Syro-Phoenician Woman," *ET* 13 (1901-1902): 188-90 [Mk. 7:24-30].

4980. T. H. Weir, "St. Mark vii. 28," *ET* 28 (1916-1917): 524.

4981. A. S. Weatherhead, "The Healing of one Deaf and Dumb (Mark vii. 31-37)," *ET* 23 (1911-1912): 381.

4982. B. Whiteford, "Aside from the Multitude. A Study in St. Mark VII. 33," *Exp* 5th ser. 4 (1896): 380-87.

4983. E. G. Parrinder, "The Feeding of the Four Thousand; Mark viii. 1-10," *ET* 51 (1939-1940): 397-98.

4984. G. H. Boobyer, "The Eucharistic Interpretation of the Miracles of the Loaves in St. Mark's Gospel," *JTS* N.S. 3 (1952): 161-71 [Mk. 8:1-10].

4985. H. Liese, Altera multiplicatio panum (Mc. 8, 1-8; cf. Mt. 15, 32-39)," *VD* 11 (1931): 193-96.

4986. Eb. Nestle, "A Little Contribution to the Greek Testament," *ET* 16 (1904-1905): 429-30 [Mk. 8:2; Mt. 15:32].

4987. Børge Hjerl-Hansen, "Dalmanutha (Marc VIII. 10). Enigme géographique et linguistique dans l'évangile de s. Marc," *RB* 53 (1946): 372-84.

4988. N. Herz, "Dalmanutha," *ET* 9 (1897-1898): 95 [Mk. 8:10].

4989. N. Herz, "Dalmanutha," *ET* 9 (1897-1898): 426 [Mk. 8:10].

4990. Ludwig Koehler, K. L. Schmidt, A. Debrunner, "Hebräisches jāsā, und Markus 8, 11," *TZ* 3 (1947): 471-73 [ἐξῆλθον].

4991. N. D. Coleman, "Some Noteworthy Uses of εἰ or εἶ in Hellenistic Greek, with a Note on St. Mark viii. 12," *JTS* 28 (1926-1927): 159-67.

4992. F. C. Burkitt, "Mark viii. 12 and εἰ in Hellenistic Greek," *JTS* 28 (1926-1927): 274-76.

4993.   Frazer Hood, "Seeing Men as Trees Walking," *USR* 35 (1923-1924): 25-37 [Mk. 8:14-26].

4994.   D. Howard Smith, "An Exposition of Mark viii. 14-21," *ET* 59 (1947-1948): 125-26.

4995.   A. Black, "The Leaven of Herod," *Exp* 5th ser. 9 (1899): 173-86 [Mk. 8:15].

4996.   P. B. Emmet, "St. Mark viii. 15," *ET* 48 (1936-1937): 332-33.

4997.   F. C. Synge, "Studies in Texts," *Th* 50 (1947): 263-64 [Mk. 8:19, 20].

4998.   Adolf Jacoby, "Zur Heilung des Blinden von Bethsaida," *ZNW* 10 (1909): 185-94 [Mk. 8:22-26].

4999.   A. Watson Taggart, "St. Mark viii. 24," *ET* 27 (1915- 1916): 284-85.

5000.   D. J. Saunders, "The Confession of Peter," *ThSt* 10 (1949): 522-40 [Mk. 8:27-30].

5001.   Manuel Fernández Jiménez, "¿Fué en Cesarea de Filipo donde Jesús prometió a Pedro el primado?" *CB* 14 (1957): 106-12 [Mk. 8:27-30].

5002.   Hermann Schultz, "Wer saget denn ihr, dass ich sei?" *ZTK* 14 (1904): 1-43 [Mk. 8:29].

5003.   George A. Barton, "The Use of ἐπιτιμᾶν in Mark 8.30 and 3. 12," *JBL* 41 (1922): 233-36.

5004.   Norman Walker, "After three days," *NT* 4 (1960): 261-62 [Mk. 8:31].

5005.   F. C. Burkitt, "St. Mark viii. 32: A Neglected Various Reading," *JTS* 2 (1900-1901): 111-13.

5006.   Frederick Bussby, "Mark viii. 33: A Mistranslation from the Aramaic?" *ET* 61 (1949-1950): 159.

5007.   J. Kahmann, "Het volgen van Christus door zelfverloochening en kruisdragen; een beschouwing van Mk. 8, 34-38 en parallelplaatsen," *TvT* 1 (1961): 205-25 (French summary, 225-26).

5008.   Joseph Palmer, "Cross-Bearing," *ET* 14 (1902-1903): 288 [Mk. 8:34].

5009.   George M. Reith, "Cross-Bearing," *ET* 15 (1903-1904): 238 [Mk. 8:34].

5010.   J. Davies Bryan, "To take up the Cross," *ET* 37 (1925-1926):

551-53 [Mk. 8:34].

5011. Ernst Fuchs, "Was heisst: 'Du sollst deinen Nächsten lieben wie dich selbst'?" *TB* 11 (1932): 129-40 [Mk. 8:34].

5012. J. M. Bover, "Transfiguratio 'regnum Dei veniens in virtute' (Mk. 8, 38-39)," *VD* 19 (1939): 33-38.

5013. C. A. Phillips, "Mark 8.38," *BBC* 5 (1928): 30-31.

5014. B. Zieliński, "De doxa Christi transfigurati," *VD* 26 (1948): 291-303 [Mk. 9:2-13].

5015. B. Zieliński, "De sensu transfigurationis," *VD* 26 (1948): 335-43 [Mk. 9:2-13].

5016. George B. Caird, "The Transfiguration," *ET* 67 (1955-1956): 291-94 [Mk. 9:2-13].

5017. Eduard Engelhardt, "Biblische Studie über Mark. 9, 9-13," *TSK* 37 (1864): 673-90.

5018. Percy J. Heawood, "Mark 9: 11-13," *ET* 64 (1952-1953): 239.

5019. C. Clare Oke, "The Rearrangement and Transmission of Mark ix. 11-13," *ET* 64 (1952-1953): 187-88.

5020. Fr. Durwell, " 'Elias cum venerit primo...' (Mc. 9. 11s.)," *VD* 19 (1939): 269-78.

5021. C. E. B. Cranfield, "St. Mark ix. 14-29," *SJT* 3 (1950): 57-67.

5022. Wilhelm Hüster, " 'Ich glaube, lieber Herr; hilf meinem Unglauben," *EvT* 19 (1959): 185-94.

5023. Matthew Black, "The Marcan Parable of the Child in the Midst," *ET* 59 (1947-1948): 14-16 [Mk. 9:33-37].

5024. T. F. Glasson and E. L. Wenger, "The Marcan Parable of the Child in the Midst," *ET* 59 (1947-1948): 166-67.

5025. Wilhelm Nestle, "Wer niche mit mir ist, der ist wider mich," *ZNW* 13 (1912): 84-87.

5026. I. Köstlin, "Die Worte Jesu 'Wer niche mit mir ist, ist wider mich' und 'Wer niche wider uns (euch) ist, ist für uns (euch)," *TSK* 55 (1882): 307-24 [Mk. 9:40].

5027. Anton Fridrichsen, "Wer niche mit mir ist, ist wider mich," *ZNW* 13 (1912): 273-80 [Mk. 9:40].

5028. Otto Michel, " 'Diese Kleinen'—eine Jüngerbezeichnung Jesu," *TSK* 108 (1937-1938): 401-15 [Mk. 9:42-50 and Par.].

5029. N. D. Coleman, " 'Salt' and 'Salted' in Mark 9:49-50," *ET* 48 (1936-1937): 360-62.

5030. Dr. Bähr, "Exegetische Erörterungen," *TSK* 22 (1849): 673-96 [Mk. 9:49, 50].

5031. N. D. Coleman, "Note on Mark ix. 49, 50: A New Meaning for ἅλας," *JTS* 24 (1922-1923): 387-96.

5032. C. W. Jacob, "The 'Salt' Problem in St. Mark," *ET* 48 (1936-1937): 476 [Mk. 9:49-50].

5033. W. R. Hutton, "The Salt Sections," *ET* 58 (1946-1947): 166-68 [Mk. 9:49-50, etc.].

5034. D. R. Griffiths, "The Salt Sections in the Gospels," *ET* 59 (1947-1948): 81-82 [Mk. 9:49-50; Lk. 14 34-35].

5035. J. de Zwaan, "Met vuur gezouten worden (Marcus 9, 49)," *NTS* 11 (1928): 179-82.

5036. Tjitze Baarda, "Mark IX. 49," *NTSt* 5 (1958-1959): 318-21.

5037. H. Zimmermann, " 'Mit Feuer gesalzen warden': Eine Studie zu Mk. 9, 49," *TQ* 139 (1957): 28-39 [Mk. 9:49].

5038. J. Rendel Harris, "A Further Note on the 'Salt' Section at the End of Mark ix," *ET* 48 (1936-1937): 185-86 [Mk. 9:50].

5039. J. de Zwaan, "Het smakelooze zout bij Marcus (Marcus 9, 50)," *NTS* 11 (1928): 176-78.

5040. A. van Veldhuizen, "Zout en vrede (Mk. 9, 50)," *NTS* 15 (1932): 71-73.

5041. Wolfgang Nauck, "Salt as a Metaphor in Instructions for Discipleship," *ST* 6 (1952): 165-78 [Mk. 9:50, etc.].

5042. Hans Joachim Schoeps, "*Restitutio Principii* as the Basis for the *Nova Lex Jesu*," *JBL* 66 (1947): 453-64 [Mk. 10:1-12; Mt. 19:1-9].

5043. F. Hitzig, "Zwei Stellen der Evangelien, exegetisch und textkritisch erörtert," *ZWT* 2 (1859): 147-59 [Mk. 10:9; Jn. 3:34].

5044. Gerhard Delling, "Das Logion Mark. x. 11 (und seine Abwandlungen) im Neuen Testament," *NT* 1 (1956): 263-74.

5045. Nigel Turner, "The Translation of μοιχᾶται ἐπ' αὐτήν in Mark x. 11," *BTr* 7 (1956): 151-52.

5046. J. Weiss, "Zum reichen Jüngling," *ZNW* 11 (1910): 79-83 [Mk. 10:13-27].

5047. W. K. Lowther Clarke, "Studies in Texts," *Th* 16 (1928):

5047. W. K. Lowther Clarke, "Studies in Texts," *Th* 16 (1928): 161-63 [Mk. 10:13-16].

5048. Joachim Jeremias, "Mc 10, 13-16 Par. und die Übung der Kindertaufe in der Urkirche," *ZNW* 40 (1941): 243-45.

5049. E. Hampden-Cook, "Whom did the Disciples Rebuke?" *ET* 17 (1905-1906): 192 [Mk. 10:13].

5050. Lester Bradner, "The Kingdom and the Child," *ATR* 3 (1920-1921): 59-65 [Mk. 10:14].

5051. R. Ejarque, "Sinite parvulos ad me venire," *VD* 4 (1924): 41-47 [Mk. 10:14].

5052. John W. Clayton, "Who Was the Rich Young Ruler?" *ET* 39 (1927-1928): 83-85 [Mk. 10:17-31].

5053. John W. Clayton, "The Rich Young Ruler," *ET* 39 (1927-1928): 283 [Mk. 10:17-31].

5054. James Williams, "The Rich Young Ruler and St. Paul," *ET* 41 (1929-1930): 139-40 [Mk. 10:17-31].

5055. C. E. B. Cranfield, "Riches and the Kingdom of God— Mark x. 17-31," *SJT* 4 (1951): 302-13.

5056. Otto Weber, "Predigt über Mark. 10, 17-27," *EvT* 8 (1948-1949): 433-39.

5057. Chr. Glarbo, "Markus 10, 17-18. En eksegetisk Studie," *TTDF* 3rd ser. 1 (1909-1910): 27-52.

5058. Buchanan Blake, Good Master, (Mk. x. 17)," *ET* 43 (1931-1932): 334.

5059. B. W. Bacon, "Why Callest thou me Good?" *BW* 6 (1895): 334-50 [Mk. 10:18].

5060. Wilhelm Wagner, "In welchem Sinne hat Jesus das Prädikat ἀγαθός von sich abgewiesen?" *ZNW* 8 (1907): 143-61 [Mk. 10:18].

5061. Friedrich Spitta, "Jesu Weigerung, sich als 'gut' bezeichnen zu lassen," *ZNW* 9 (1908): 12-20 [Mk. 10:18].

5062. A. S. Martin, "Why callest thou me good?" *ET* 21 (1909-1910): 137-38 [Mk. 10:18].

5063. Benjamin B. Warfield, "Jesus' Alleged Confession of Sin," *PTR* 12 (1914): 177-228 [Mk. 10:18].

5064. F. B. Westbrook, "Mark x. 18," *ET* 39 (1927-1928): 331.

5065. W. Crooke, "The Camel and the Eye of the Needle," *ET* 21 (1909-1910): 283 [Mk. 10:25].

5066.   Harald Riesenfeld, "παρὰ ἀνθρώποις—παρὰ θεῷ. Zu Mk. 10, 27," *Nunt* 7 (1952): 51-52.

5067.   J. Fernández, "Hacia el Calvario," *CB* 4 (1947): 33-38 [Mk. 10:32-34, 46-52].

5068.   Théo Preiss, "The Son of Man Came to Minister," *Interp* 4 (1950): 189-92 [Mk. 10:35-45].

5069.   Friedrich Spitta, "Die neutestamentliche Grundlage der Ansicht von E. Schwartz über den Tod der Söhne Zebedäi," *ZNW* 11 (1910): 39-58 [Mk. 10:35-45].

5070.   Olaf Moe, "Jesu lidelsesdåp," *TTK* 19 (1948): 206-208 [Mk. 10:35-45].

5071.   E. Schwartz, "Noch einmal der Tod der Söhne Zebedaei," *ZNW* 11 (1910): 89-104.

5072.   A. J. B. Higgins, "St. Mark x. 36," *ET* 52 (1940-1941): 317-18.

5073.   A. J. B. Higgins, "St. Mark x. 36," *ET* 52 (1940-1941): 437.

5074.   J. H. Bernard, "A Study of St. Mark x. 38, 39," *JTS* 28 (1926-1927): 262-70.

5075.   Gerhard Delling, "βάπτισμα βαπτισθῆναι," *NT* 2 (1958): 92-115 [Mk. 10:38 f.].

5076.   A. Škrinjar, "Dicta Christi de martyrio (Mc. 10. 39 et par. etc.)," *VD* 18 (1938): 168-77.

5077.   Blomfield Jackson, "Note on Matt. xx. 23 and Mark x. 40," *JTS* 6 (1904-1905): 237-40.

5078.   W. F. Howard, "Great Texts Reconsidered," *ET* 50 (1938-1939): 107-10 [Mk. 10:45].

5079.   Buchanan Blake, "Should the Word 'Ransom' be used for λύτρον in Mark x. 45, and Matthew xx. 28?" *ET* 45 (1933-1934): 142.

5080.   A. Médebielle, "La vie donnée en rançon," *B* 4 (1923): 3-40 [Mk. 10:45; Mt. 20:28].

5081.   E. P. Boys-Smith, "Studies in Texts," *Th* 10 (1925): 112-13 [Mk. 10:45].

5082.   A. Runze, "Erläuternde Bemerkungen zu Marc. 10, 45," *ZWT* 32 (1889): 148-229.

5083.   J. Benjamin Bedenbaugh, "The Ransom Saying of our Lord," *LQ* 7 (1955): 26-31 [Mk. 10:45].

5084.   H. W. Parrott, "Blind Bartimaeus Cries out Again," *EQ* 32

(1960): 25-29 [Mk. 10:46-52].

5085.   J. A. Kleist, "De Bartimaei ad Jericho urbem facta sanatione," *VD* 10 (1930): 231-38, 297-303 [Mk. 10:46].

5086.   H. G. Meecham, "St. Mark x. 51," *ET* 52 (1940-1941): 437.

5087.   Otto A. Piper, "God's Good News; the Passion Story! According to Mark," *Intrep* 9 (1955): 165-82 [Mk. 11:1-16:20].

5088.   T. A. Burkill, "Strain on the Secret: an Examination of Mark 11, 1-13, 37," *ZNW* 51 (1960): 31-46.

5089.   Heinz-Wolfgang Kuhn, "Das Reittier Jesu in der Einzugsgeschichte des Markusevangeliums," *ZNW* 50 (1959): 82-91 [Mk. 11:1-10].

5090.   Walter Bauer, "The 'Colt' of Palm Sunday (der Palmesel)," *JBL* 72 (1953): 220-29 [Mk. 11:2-7].

5091.   Robert G. Bratcher, "A Note on Mark xi. 3: ὁ κύριος αὐτοῦ χρείαν ἔχει," *ET* 64 (1952-1953): 93.

5092.   Robert G. Bratcher, "A Note on Mark XI. 3," *BTr* 4 (1953): 52.

5093.   J. Smit Sibinga, "Het ezeltje aan de weg in Marcus 11, 4," *VT* 27 (1956-1957): 5-12.

5094.   T. Arvedson, " 'Jesu efterföljd' i Nya Testamentet. En exegetisk studie," *STK* 7 (1931): 134-61 [Mk. 11:9, etc.]

5095.   Cyril C. Richardson, "Blessed is He that Cometh in the Name of the Lord," *ATR* 29 (1947): 96-98 [Mk. 11.9].

5096.   Lambert Nolle, "Bethany," *Scr* 4 (1951): 262-64 [Mk. 11:11].

5097.   Eduard Schwartz, "Der verfluchte Feigenbaum," *ZNW* 5 (1904): 80-84 [Mk. 11:12-25].

5098.   Julius Boehmer, "The Cursing of the Fig Tree," *ET* 21 (1909-1910): 328-29 [Mk. 11:12-25].

5099.   S. Tonkin, "The Withered Fig-Tree," *ET* 34 (1922-1923): 323-26 [Mk. 11:12-25].

5100.   J. Neville Birdsall, "The Withering of the Fig-Tree (Mark xi. 12-14, 20-22)," *ET* 73 (1961-1962): 191 [Mk. 11: 12-25].

5101.   Charles W. F. Smith, "No Time for Figs," *JBL* 79 (1960): 315-27 [Mk. 11:12-25].

5102.   Pierre Charles, "Non enim erat tempus ficorum (Marc. 11, 13)," *NRT* 61 (1934): 514-16.

5103.	A. Caldecott, "The Significance of the 'Cleansing of the Temple'," *JTS* 24 (1922-1923): 382-86 [Mk. 11:15-19].

5104.	F. C. Burkitt, "The Cleansing of the Temple," *JTS* 25 (1923-1924): 386-90 [Mk. 11:15-19; Jn. 2:13-25].

5105.	C. E. Blakeway, "The Cleansing of the Temple," *ET* 22 (1910-1911): 279-82 [Mk 11:15-19].

5106.	Siegfried Mendner, "Die Tempelreiniging," *ZNW* 47 (1956): 93-112 [Mk. 11:15-19].

5107.	Ivor Buse, "The Cleansing of the Temple in the Synoptics and in John," *ET* 70 (1958-1959): 22-24 [Mk. 11:15-19; Jn. 2:13-25].

5108.	Cecil Roth, "The Cleansing of the Temple and Zechariah XIV, 21," *NT* 4 (1960): 174-81 [Mk. 11:15-19; Jn. 2:13-22].

5109.	Eric F. F. Bishop, "Jesus Walking or Teaching in the Temple (Mk. xi. 27, Jn. x. 23)," *ET* 63 (1951-1952): 226-27.

5110.	John C. Mattes, "A Study in Exegesis: The Parable of the Vineyard," *LCR* 29 (1910): 578-87 [Mk. 12:12].

5111.	Anton Fridrichsen, "Til lignelsen om de onde vingartnere," *STK* 4 (1928): 355-61 [Mk. 12:1-12].

5112.	Ernst Lohmeyer, "Das Gleichnis von den bösen Weingärtnern (Mark 12, 1-12)," *ZST* 18 (1941): 243-59.

5113.	Austin Farrer, "An Examination of Mark xii. 10," *JTS* N.S. 7 (1956): 75-79.

5114.	David Daube, "Four Types of Questions," *JTS* N.S. 2 (1951): 45-48 [Mk. 12:13-37].

5115.	James Denney, "Caesar and God," *Exp* 5th ser., 3 (1896): 61-69 [Mk. 12:13-17].

5116.	Martin Rist, "Caesar or God (Mark 12:13-17)? A Study in Formgeschichte," *JR* 16 (1936): 317-31.

5117.	Ivar Benum, "Gud og keiseren," *NTT* 42 (1941): 65-96 [Mk. 12:13-17].

5118.	Stephen Liberty, "Pharisees, Herodians, and 'just men', as the Questioners about the Tribute," *ET* 28 (1916-1917): 522-23 [Mk. 12:14].

5119.	S. Cox, "An Ancient Solution of a Modern Problem," *Exp* 1st. ser. 3 (1876): 16-27 [Mk. 12:15-21].

5120.	T. G. White, "Render Unto Caesar," *HJ* 44 (1945-1946): 263-70 [Mk. 12:17].

5121. James Denney, "The Sadducees and Immortality," *Exp* 4th ser., 10 (1894): 401-409 [Mk. 12:18-27].

5122. G. Carton, "Comme des anges dans le ciel (Marc 12, 18-27)," *BVC* 28 (1959): 46-52.

5123. G. Sevenster, "De 'opstanding des vleses' en het Nieuwe Testament bij Tertullianus," *NedTT* 9 (1954-1955): 364-72 [Mk. 12:25 & par.; 1 Cor. 15:50, etc.].

5124. F. G. Dreyfus, "L'argument scripturaire de Jésus en faveur de la résurrection des morts (Marc, XII, 26-27)," *RB* 66 (1959): 213-24.

5125. W. O. Carver, "Two Most Important Questions of Jesus," *RE* 37 (1940): 77-79 [Mk. 12:28-37].

5126. James Denney, "The Great Commandment (Mark xii. 28-34)," *Exp* 5th ser. 3 (1896): 312-20.

5127. A. Leslie Reed, "St. Mark xii. 29b," *ET* 17 (1905-1906): 523.

5128. Harold A. Hunt, "The Great Commandment," *ET* 56 (1944-1945): 82-83 [Mk. 12:30-31].

5129. Rudolf Bultmann, " 'Aimer son prochain' commandment de Dieu," *RHPR* 10 (1930): 222-41 [Mk. 12:31, etc.].

5130. G. H. Boobyer, "Mark xii. 35-37 and the Pre-Existence of Jesus in Mark," *ET* 51 (1939-1940): 393-94.

5131. James Denney, "David's Son and David's Lord," *Exp* 5th ser., 3 (1896): 445-56 [Mk. 12:35-37].

5132. Robert Paul Gagg, "Jesus und die Davidssohnfrage (zur Exegese von Markus 12, 35-37)," *TZ* 7 (1951): 18-30.

5133. James Denney, "The Dissolution of Religion," *Exp* 5th ser. 4 (1896): 263-76 [Mk. 12:38-40].

5134. W. M. Ramsay, "On Mark xii. 42," *ET* 10 (1898-1899): 336.

5135. F. Blass, "On Mark xii. 42 and xv. 16," *ET* 10 (1898-1899): 185-87.

5136. F. Blass, "On Mark xii. 42," *ET* 10 (1898-1899): 286-87.

5137. W. M. Ramsay, "On Mark xii. 42," *ET* 10 (1898-1899): 232.

5138. Eb. Nestle, "The Widow's Mites," *ET* 13 (1901-1902): 562 [Mk. 12:42].

5139. Francis Dewar, "Chapter 13 and the Passion Narrative in St. Mark," *Th* 64 (1961): 99-107.

5140. M. Loisy, "L'apocalypse synoptique," *RB* 5 (1896): 173-98,

335-59 [Mk. 13; Mt. 24-25; Lk. 21:5-38].

5141. M.-J. Lagrange, "L'avenement du fils de l'homme," *RB* 15 (1906): 382-411, 561-74.

5142. J. Rohr, "Der Sprachgebrauch des Markusevangeliums und die 'Markusapokalypse'," *TQ* 89 (1907): 507-36.

5143. B. W. Bacon, "The Apocalyptic Chapter of the Synoptic Gospels," *JBL* 28 (1909): 1-25 [Mk. 13; Mt. 24; Lk. 21].

5144. Elijah A. Hanley, "The Destruction of Jerusalem: Mark, Chap. 13," *BW* 34 (1909): 45-46.

5145. Burton S. Easton, "The Little Apocalypse," *BW* 40 (1912): 130-38 [Mk. 13:7-8, 14-20, 24-27].

5146. G. S. Hitchcock, "Apocalyptic," *ITQ* 8 (1913): 160-77 [Mk. 13].

5147. T. J. Walshe, "Eschatological Apologetics," *ITQ* 8 (1913): 19-29 [Mk. 13].

5148. D. Völter, "Die eschatologische Rede Jesu und seine Weissagung von der Zerstörung Jerusalems," *STZ* 32 (1915): 180-202 [Mk. 13; Mt. 24; Lk. 21].

5149. David Foster Estes, "The Eschatological Discourse of Jesus," *RE* 15 (1918): 411-36.

5150. A. Piganiol, "Observations sur la date de l'apocalypse synoptique," *RHPR* 4 (1924): 245-49.

5151. Gustav Hölscher, "Der Ursprung der Apokalypse Mrk. 13," *TB* 12 (1933): 193-202.

5152. Lyle O. Bristol, "Mark's Little Apocalypse: A Hypothesis," *ET* 51 (1939-1940): 301-303.

5153. A. C. Cotter, "The Eschatological Discourse," *CBQ* 1 (1939): 125-32, 204-13.

5154. André Feuillet, "Le discours de Jésus sur la ruine du temple d'après Marc xiii et Luc xxi, 5-36," *RB* 55 (1948): 481-502; 56 (1949): 61-92.

5155. Vincent Taylor, "Unsolved New Testament Problems— The Apocalyptic Discourse of Mark 13," *ET* 60 (1948-1949): 94-98.

5156. A. Jones, "Did Christ Foretell the End of the World in Mark xiii?" *Scr* 4 (1951): 264-73.

5157. John A. O'Flynn, "The Eschatological Discourse," *ITQ* 18 (1951): 277-81 [Mk. 13 et par.].

5158. G. R. Beasley-Murray, "The Rise and Fall of the Little Apocalypse Theory," *ET* 64 (1952-1953): 346-49.

5159. C. E. B. Cranfield, "St. Mark 13," *SJT* 6 (1953): 189-96.

5160. T. F. Glasson, "Mark xiii and the Greek Old Testament," *ET* 69 (1958): 213-15.

5161. Hans Conzelmann, "Geschichte und Eschaton nach Mc. 13," *ZNW* 50 (1959): 210-21.

5162. Charles Perrot, "Essai sur le discours eschatologique (Mc. XIII, 1-37; Mt. XXIV, 1-36; Lc. XXI, 5-36)," *RSR* 47 (1959): 481-514.

5163. G. R. Beasley-Murray, "The Eschatological Discourse of Jesus," *RE* 57 (1960): 153-66.

5164. George D. Kilpatrick, "Mark xiii. 9-10," *JTS* N.S., 9 (1958): 81-86.

5165. Graham Cotter, "The Abomination of Desolation," *CJT* 3 (1957): 159-64 [Mk. 13:14].

5166. B. Rigaux, "βδέλυγμα τῆς ἐρημώσεως," *B* 40 (1959): 675-83 [Mk. 13:14; Mt. 24:15].

5167. Harold A. Guy, "Mark xiii. 14: ὁ ἀναγινώσκων νοείτω," *ET* 65 (1953-1954): 30.

5168. R. Thibaut, "La grande tribulation," *NRT* 55 (1928): 373-76 [Mk. 13:19].

5169. Rayner Winterbotham, "The Shortening of the Days," *Exp* 5th ser. 4 (1896): 65-72 [Mk. 13:20].

5170. Cyril H. Valentine, "The Son of Man Coming in the Clouds," *Th* 23 (1931): 14-21 [Mk. 13:26].

5171. W. C. Shearer, "The Limitations of our Lord's Knowledge," *ET* 4 (1892-1893): 554-55 [Mk. 13:31-32].

5172. Paul Joüon, "Marc 14, 31: ὁ δὲ ἐκπερισσῶς ἐλάλει," *RSR* 29 (1939): 240-41.

5173. Jules Lebreton, "L'ignorance du jour du judgment," *RSR* 8 (1918): 281-89 [Mk 13:32].

5174. E. Zeller, "Zum Marcus-Evangelium," *ZWT* 8 (1865): 308-28, 385-408 [Mk. 13:32; 15:37f.; 3:13; 6:7].

5175. S. Pezzella, "Marco 13, 32 e la scienza di Cristo," *RivB* 7 (1959): 147-52.

5176. E. R. Buckley, "The Sources of the Passion Narrative in St. Mark's Gospel," *JTS* 34 (1933): 138-44 [Mk. 14-15].

426   CRITICAL STUDIES OF THE GOSPELS

5177.   A. van der Flier, "Markus 14, 2," *TS* 29 (1911): 109-11.

5178.   W. G. Elmslie, "At the Sign of the Bible," *Exp* 3rd ser. 7 (1888): 395-97 [Mk. 14:3-9; Jn. 12:1-8].

5179.   J. A. Wood, "The Anointing at Bethany and its Significance," *ET* 39 (1927-1928): 475-76.

5180.   Joachim Jeremias, "Die Salbungsgeschichte Mc. 14, 3-9," *ZNW* 35 (1936): 75-82.

5181.   J. B. Bauer, "Ut quid perditio ista?—zu Mk. 14, 4 f. und Par.," *NT* 3 (1959): 54-56.

5182.   George D. Kilpatrick, "'Επάνω Mark xiv. 5," *JTS* 42 (1941): 181-82.

5183.   J. Harold Greenlee, "Εἰς μνημόσυνον αὐτῆς 'For her Memorial': Mt. xxvi. 13, Mk. xiv. 9," *ET* 71 (1959-1960): 245.

5184.   Joachim Jeremias, "Mc. 14, 9," *ZNW* 44 (1952-1953): 103-107.

5185.   A. Wright, "Was Judas Isacriot 'The First of the Twelve'?" *JTS* 18 (1916-1917): 32-34 [Mk. 14:10].

5186.   J. H. Burn, "St. Mark xiv. 10," *ET* 28 (1916-1917): 278-79.

5187.   George D. Kilpatrick, "The Last Supper," *ET* 64 (1952-1953): 4-8 [Mk. 14:12-25].

5188.   Joachim Jeremias, "The Last Supper," *ET* 64 (1952-1953): 91-92 [Mk. 14:12-25].

5189.   Alfred Plummer, "St. Mark xiv. 14, 15; St. Luke xxii. 11, 12," *ET* 2 (1890-1891): 81-82.

5190.   Margaret D. Gibson, "The House in which the Last Supper was Held," *JTS* 17 (1915-1916): 398 [Mk. 14:14].

5191.   G. H. Guyot, "Peter denies his Lord," *CBQ* 4 (1942): 111-18 [Mk. 14:66-72].

5192.   H. B. Hackett, "The Last Days of Christ; Exegetical Notes on the Basis of Mark XIV. 17-XVI. 20," *BS* 36 (1879): 342-66, 471-96, 665-74.

5193.   Lyder Brun, "Disciplenes trosgjennembrudd efter Jesu død," *NTT* 19 (1918): 201-20 [Mk. 14:17-72, etc.].

5194.   Gerhard Loeschcke, "Zur Frage nach der Einsetzung und Herkunft der Eucharistie," *ZWT* 54 (1912): 193-205 [Mk. 14:22-25].

5195.   F. Ruffenach, "Hoc est corpus meum, hic est sanguis meus,"

VD 4 (1924): 264-68, 296-98 [Mk. 14: 22-25].

5196.   Nigel Turner, "The Style of St. Mark's Eucharistic Words," *JTS* N.S., 8 (1957): 108-11 [Mk. 14:22-25].

5197.   Jacques Dupont, " 'Ceci est mon corps', 'ceci est mon sang'," *NRT* 80 (1958): 1025-41 [Mk. 14:22-25; 1 Cor. 11:23-25].

5198.   Joachim Jeremias, "Das Brotbrechen beim Passahmahl und Mc. 14. 22 par.," *ZNW* 33 (1934): 203-204.

5199.   J. A. Emerton, "The Aramaic Underlying τὸ αἷμά μου τῆς διαθήκης in Mk. xiv. 24," *JTS* N.S., 6 (1955): 238-40.

5200.   C. F. Evans, "I Will Go Before you into Galilee," *JTS* N.S., 5 (1954): 3-18 [Mk. 14:28].

5201.   Miguel Balagué, "Las negaciones de San Pedro," *CB* 8 (1951): 79-82 [Mk. 14:29-31].

5202.   C. H. Mayo, "St. Peter's Token of the Cock Crow," *JTS* 22 (1921): 367-70 [Mk. 14: 30, 72].

5203.   William F. Wilson, "Our Lord's Agony in the Garden," *ET* 32 (1920-1921): 549-51 [Mk. 14:32-42].

5204.   S. Vernon McCasland, "Abba, Father," *JBL* 72 (1953): 79-91 [Mk. 14:36].

5205.   W. Marchel, "Abba Pater! Oratio Christi et christianorum (Mc. 14. 36)," *VD* 39 (1961): 240-47.

5206.   C. E. B. Cranfield, "The Cup Metaphor in Mark xiv. 36 and Parallels," *ET* 59 (1947-1948): 137-38.

5207.   Matthew Black, "The Cup Metaphor in Mark xiv. 36," *ET* 59 (1947-1948): 195.

5208.   J. H. Bernard, "St. Mark xiv. 41, 42," *ET* 3 (1891-1892): 451-53.

5209.   Anonymous, "Erklärung einiger dunklen Stellen des Neuen Testaments," *TSK* 16 (1843): 103-40 [Mk. 14:41; Mt. 24:1 ff.; 28:17, Lk. 12:15; Mk. 11:13].

5210.   G. H. Boobyer, "ἀπέχει in Mark XIV. 41," *NTSt* 2 (1955-1956): 44-48.

5211.   E. A. Smisson, "Mark xiv. 41: ἀπέχει," *ET* 40 (1928-1929): 528.

5212.   H. Zeydner, "ἀπέχει, Mark XIV. 41," *TS* 23 (1905): 439-42.

5213.   J. de Zwaan, "The Text and Exegesis of Mark XIV. 41, and the Papyri," *Exp* 6th ser. 12 (1905): 459-72.

5214.   James G. Hudson, "Irony in Gethsemane?" *ET* 46 (1934-1935): 382 [Mk. 14:41].

5215.   M. Rostovtzeff, "Οὖς δεξιὸν ἀποτέμνειν," *ZNW* 33 (1934): 196-99 [Mk. 14:43, 46-47].

5216.   F. W. Belcher, "A Comment on Mark xiv. 45," *ET* 64 (1952-1953): 240.

5217.   P. B. Emmet, "St. Mark xiv. 45," *ET* 50 (1938-1939): 93.

5218.   John Lendrum, "The Impression from the Gospels that All was fixed Beforehand," *ET* 42 (1930-1931): 345-50 [Mk. 14:49; Lk. 22:22].

5219.   A. W. Argyle, "The Meaning of καθ᾿ ἡμέραν in Mark xiv. 49," *ET* 63 (1951-1952): 354.

5220.   S. Cox, "The Young Man in the Linen Cloth," *Exp* 1st. ser. 1 (1875): 436-46 [Mk. 14:51-52].

5221.   George W. Buchanan, "Mark xiv. 43," *ET* 68 (1956-1957): 27.

5222.   T. A. Burkill, "The Trial of Jesus," *VCh* 12 (1958): 1-18 [Mk. 14:55-65].

5223.   Walter G. White, "Mark xiv. 55, 56," *ET* 29 (1917-1918): 138-39.

5224.   J. A. Kleist, "The Two False Witnesses (Mark 14:55 ff.)," *CBQ* 9 (1947): 321-23.

5225.   Robert Bruce Boswell, "Destroying and Rebuilding the Temple," *ET* 26 (1914-1915): 140-41 [Mk. 14:58].

5226.   J. Rendel Harris, "A Lost Verse in the Gospel of Mark," *ET* 39 (1927-1928): 456-58 [after Mk. 14:59].

5227.   W. C. Robinson, "The Greater Confession," *EQ* 7 (1935): 364-77 [Mk. 14:61-63].

5228.   F. C. Burkitt, "On Romans IX. 5 and Mark XIV. 61," *JTS* 5 (1903-1904): 451-55.

5229.   Rayner Winterbotham, "Was, then, our Lord mistaken?" *ET* 29 (1917-1918): 7-11 [Mk. 14:62].

5230.   T. F. Glasson, "The Reply to Caiaphas (Mark XIV. 62)," *NTSt* 7 (1960-1961): 88-93.

5231.   Harvey K. McArthur, "Mark XIV. 62," *NTSt* 4 (1957-1958): 156-58.

5232.   John A. T. Robinson, "The Second Coming—Mark xiv. 62," *ET* 67 (1955-1956): 336-40.

5233.   A. W. Rudolph, "Wie lässt sich das dreymalige Verläugnen des Herrn mit dem sonstigen Charakter des Petrus vereinigen?" *ZWTh* 1 (1826): 109-36 [Mk. 14: 66-72].

5234.   J. M. Danson, "The Fall of St. Peter," *ET* 19 (1907-1908): 307-308 [Mk. 14:66-72].

5235.   J. Courtenay James, "The Dialect of Peter's Denial," *ET* 19 (1907-1908): 524 [Mk. 14:66-72].

5236.   W. D. Gardiner, "The Denial of St. Peter," *ET* 26 (1914-1915): 424-26 [Mk. 14:66-72].

5237.   W. M. Ramsay, "The Denials of Peter," *ET* 27 (1915-1916): 296-301, 360-63, 410-13, 471-72, 540-42 [Mk. 14:66-72].

5238.   W. M. Ramsay, "The Denials of Peter," *ET* 28 (1916-1917): 276-81 [Mk. 16:66-72].

5239   M. Goguel, "Did Peter deny his Lord? A Conjecture," *HTR* 25 (1932): 1-28 [Mk. 14:66-72].

5240.   J. Ramsay Thomson, "Saint Peter's Denials," *ET* 47 (1935-1936): 381-82 [Mk. 14:66-72].

5241.   U. Holzmeister, "Petrus Dominum ter negat," *VD* 16 (1936): 107-12 [Mk. 14:66-72].

5242.   Charles E. Garritt, "St. Peter's Denials," *ET* 48 (1936-1937): 43-44 [Mk. 14:66-72].

5243.   Günter Klein, "Die Verleugnung des Petrus," *ZTK* N.F. 58 (1961): 285-328 [Mk. 14:66-72].

5244.   W. J. P. Boyd, "Peter's Denial—Mark xiv. 68, Luke xx. 57," *ET* 67 (1955-1956): 341.

5245.   Franz Rothenaicher, "Zu Mk. 14, 70 und Mt. 26, 73," *BibZ* 23 (1935-1936): 192-93.

5246.   J. Neville Birdsall, "τὸ ῥῆμα ὡς εἶπεν αὐτῷ ὁ ᾿Ιησοῦς Mk. XIV, 72," *NT* 2 (1958): 272-75.

5247.   G. M. Lee, "St. Mark xiv. 72: ἐπιβαλὼν ἔκλαιεν," *ET* 61 (1949-1950): 160.

5248.   F. Busby, "St. Mark XIV, 72: An Aramaic Mistranslation," *BJRL* 21 (1937): 273-74.

5249.   Georg Braumann, "Markus 15, 2-5 und Markus 14, 55-64," *ZNW* 52 (1961): 273-78.

5250.   T. Nicklin, " 'Thou sayest," *ET* 51 (1939-1940): 155 [Mk. 15:2].

5251.   A. H. Wratislaw, "The Scapegoat—Barabbas," *ET* 3

(1891-1892): 400-403 [Mk. 15:6-15].

5252. J. J. Twomey, "Barabbas was a Robber," *Scr* 8 (1956): 115-19 [Mk. 15:6-15].

5253. R. A. Watson, "They Cried the More," *Exp* 4th ser. 8 (1893): 471-72 [Mk. 15:14].

5254. H. Vollmer, "Der König mit der Dornenkrone," *ZNW* 6 (1905): 194-98 [Mk. 15:16].

5255. A. B. Kinsey, "Simon the Crucifer and Symeon the Prophet," *ET* 35 (1923-1924): 84-88 [Mk. 15:21, Ac. 13:1].

5256. Eric F. F. Bishop, "Simon and Lucius: Where did they come from?" *ET* 51 (1939-1940): 148-53 [Mk. 15:21; Acts 13:12].

5257. J. G. Davies, "Studies in Texts: The Cup of Wrath and the Cup of Blessing," *Th* 51 (1948): 178-80 [Mk. 15:23].

5258. A. de Waal, "Das Mora-Spiel auf den Darstellungen der Verlosung des Kleides Christi," *RQ* 8 (1894): 145-46 [Mk. 15:24].

5259. Manuel Gómez-Pallete, "Cruz y crucifixión (Notas para una exégesis de Mc. 15, 25)," *EE* 21 (1947): 85-109.

5260. C. C. Cowling, "Mark's Use of ὥρα," *ABR* 5 (1956): 153-60 [Mk. 15:25].

5261. Eric F. F. Bishop, "οὐά. Mark xv. 29: A Suggestion," *ET* 57 (1945-1946): 112.

5262. John Bligh, "Christ's Death Cry," *HeyJ* 1 (1960): 142-46 [Mk. 15:33-41].

5263. Eb. Nestle, "Mark xv. 34," *ET* 9 (1897-1898): 521-22.

5264. William Blight, "The Cry of Dereliction," *ET* 68 (1956-1957): 285 [Mk. 15:34].

5265. D. H. C. Read, "The Cry of Dereliction," *ET* 68 (1956-1957): 260-62 [Mk. 15:34].

5266. Nelson B. Baker, "The Cry of Dereliction," *ET* 70 (1958-1959): 54-55 [Mk. 15:34].

5267. J. Gnilka, " 'Mein Gott, mein Gott, warum hast du mich verlassen?' (Mk. 15, 34 Par.)," *BibZ* 3 (1959): 294-97.

5268. D. Brown, "The Veil of the Temple rent in twain from the Top to the Bottom," *Exp* 5th ser. 2 (1895): 158-60 [Mk. 15:38].

5269. William Harrison Williams, "The Veil was Rent," *RE* 48 (1951): 275-85 [Mk. 15:38].

5270.   André Pelletier, "La tradition synoptique du 'voile déchiré, à la lumière des réalites archéologiques," *RSR* 46 (1958): 161-80 [Mk. 15:38].

5271.   Robert G. Bratcher, "A Note on υἱὸς θεοῦ (Mark xv. 39)," *ET* 68 (1956-1957): 27-28.

5272.   Charles Masson, "L'ensévelissement de Jésus: Marc xv, 42-47," *RTP* N.S. 31 (1943): 193-203.

5273.   Paul Gächter, "Zum Begräbnis Jesu," *ZKT* 75 (1953): 220-25 [Mk. 15:46; Lk. 23:53; Mt. 27:59].

5274.   Edgar J. Goodspeed, "The Original Conclusion of the Gospel of Mark," *AJT* 9 (1905): 484-90 [Mk. 16].

5275.   Lyder Brun, "Der Auferstehungsbericht des Markus-evangeliums," *TSK* 87 (1914): 346-88 [Mk. 16].

5276.   C. E. B. Cranfield, "St. Mark xvi. 1-8," *SJT* 5 (1952): 282-98, 398-412.

5277.   Gabriel Hebert, "The Resurrection Narrative in St. Mark's Gospel," *ABR* 7 (1959): 58-65 [Mk. 16:1-8].

5278.   L. Fonck, Surrexit' (Mc. 16, 1-7)," *VD* 2 (1922): 115-20.

5279.   Anonymous, "The Easter Message in St. Mark's Gospel," *Th* 36 (1938): 224-25.

5280.   R. R. Ottley, "ἐφοβοῦντο γάρ Mark xvi. 8," *JTS* 27 (1925-1926): 407-409.

5281.   T. Nicklin, "St. Mark xvi. 8," *ET* 38 (1926-1927): 429.

5282.   Henry J. Cadbury, "Mark 16. 8," *JBL* 46 (1927): 344-45.

5283.   Morton S. Enslin, "ἐφοβοῦντο γάρ, Mark 16. 8," *JBL* 46 (1927): 62-68.

5284.   George D. Kilpatrick, "St. Mark xvi. 8. 'They were afraid' Why?" *JTS* 47 (1946): 46-49.

5285.   L. J. D. Richardson, "St. Mark xvi. 8," *JTS* 49 (1948): 144-45.

5286.   T. C. Skeat, "St. Mark xvi. 8: A Modern Greek Parallel," *JTS* 50 (1949): 57-58.

5287.   C. F. D. Moule, "St. Mark XVI. 8 once more," *NTSt* 2 (1955-1956). 58-59.

5288.   F. C. Conybeare, "Aristion, the Author of the Last Twelve Verses of Mark," *Exp* 4h ser. 8 (1893): 241-54.

5289.   J. Rendel Harris, "An Alternative Ending of St. Mark's Gospel," *JBL* 12 (1893): 96-97.

5290.   W. C. Shearer, "The Last Twelve Verses of St. Mark's Gospel," *ET* 5 (1893-1894): 227-28.

5291.   C. Taylor, "Some Early Evidence for the Twelve Verses St. Mark XVI. 9-20," *Exp* 4th ser. 8 (1893): 71-80.

5292.   Th. Zahn and A. Resch, "The Authorship of the Last Verses of Mark," *Exp* 4h ser. 10 (1894): 219-32.

5293.   F. C. Conybeare, "On the Last Twelve Verses of St. Mark's Gospel," *Exp* 5th ser. 2 (1895): 401-21.

5294.   J.-P. van Kasteren, "L'épilogue canonique du second évangile (Mr. 16, 9-20)," *RB* 11 (1902): 240-55.

5295.   T. S. Rördam, "What was the Lost End of Mark's Gospel?" *HJ* 3 (1904-1905): 769-90 [Mk. 16:9-20].

5296.   B. W. Bacon, "Again the Authorship of the Last Verses of Mark," *Exp* 6th ser. 12 (1905): 401-12.

5297.   Joh. Mader, "Der Markusschluss," *BibZ* 3 (1905): 269-72.

5298.   Hans Schmidt, "Zur Frage des ursprünglichen Markus-schlusses," *TSK* 80 (1907): 487-513 [Mk. 16:9-20].

5299.   Adolf Harnack, "Neues zum unechten Marcusschluss," *TLZ* 33 (1908): 168-70 [Mk. 16:9-20].

5300.   Hugo Koch, "Der erweiterte Markusschluss und die kleinasiatischen Presbyter," *BibZ* 6 (1908): 266-78.

5301.   Lyder Brun, "Bemerkungen zum Markusschluss," *TSK* 84 (1911): 157-80.

5302.   Fr. Herklotz, "Zu Mk. 16, 9-20," *BibZ* 15 (1918-1921): 149-50.

5303.   Charilaos I. Papaïoannes, "τὸ τέλος τοῦ κατὰ Μᾶρκον Εὐαγγελίου," *Θ* 1 (1923): 167-79.

5304.   Robert O. Kevin, "The Lost Ending of the Gospel according to Mark; A Criticism and a Reconstruction," *JBL* 45 (1926): 81-103.

5305.   C. E. Scott Montcrieff, "The Lost Ending of Mark," *Th* 12 (1926): 218-20 [Mk. 16:9-20].

5306.   Albert C. Clark, "Did Codex Vercellensis (*a*) Contain the Last Twelve Verses of St. Mark?" *JTS* 29 (1927-1928): 16-28.

5307.   J. M. Creed, "The Conclusion of the Gospel according to Saint Mark," *JTS* 31 (1929-1930): 175-80.

5308.   Olof Linton, "Der vermisste Markusschluss," *TB* 8 (1929):

229-34 [Mk. 16:9-20].

5309.   W. K. Lowther Clarke, "The Ending of St. Mark," *Th* 29 (1934): 106-107.

5310.   C. H. Roberts, "The Ancient Book and the Ending of St. Mark," *JTS* 40 (1939): 253-57.

5311.   W. L. Knox, "The Ending of St. Mark's Gospel," *HTR* 35 (1942): 13-24.

5312.   José M. Bover, "El final de San Marcos (16, 9-20)," *EB* 3 (1944): 561-62.

5313.   F. F. Bruce, "The End of the Second Gospel," *EQ* 17 (1945): 169-81 [Mk. 16:9-20].

5314.   S. M. Zwemer, "The Last Twelve Verses of the Gospel of Mark," *EQ* 17 (1945): 13-23.

5315.   J. E. Bruns, "A Note to Mark 16:9-20," *CBQ* 9 (1947): 358-59.

5316.   P. E. Kahle, "The End of St. Mark's Gospel. The Witness of the Coptic Versions," *JTS* N.S. 2 (1951): 49-57.

5317.   H. N. Fegley, "An Exegetical Study on Mark xvi: 17-20," *LCR* 11 (1892): 241-50.

On Mark. 1:1-15, see also numbers 3681; 1:10-13, 3686; 1:10, 3684; 1:16, 3679; 1:21-28, 3685; 3:6, 1925; 3:17, 3379; 3:21, 3682; 3:29, *10070*; 6:22, *10066*; 7:26, *10064*; 7:31, 3682; 9:11 ff., 3682; 9:16, 1620; 9:49, 3680; 10:18, 1918, 3761; 10:21, 3690; 10:25, 4510; 10:45, *10053*; 11:1-10, 4544ff.; 11:12, *10076*; 12:3 and 4, 2077; 13:33-37, 2951; 14:3, 1925; 14:22-24, 2117; 14:25, 1706; 14:31, 5172; 14:45, 3684; 14:72, 3682; 16:9-20, 1766; 16:14-20, 8938.

5317.1   Robert Butterworth, "The Composition of Mark 1-12," *HeyJ* 13/1 (1972): 5-26 [1-12].

5317.2   André Paul, "Récit (Biblique) comme surface: éléments théoriques pour une sémantique narrative," *RSPT* 58 (1974): 584-98 [1-9].

5317.3   W. Barnes Tatum, "The Epoch of Israel: Luke i-ii and the Theological Plan of Luke-Acts," *NTSt* 13 (1966-1967): 184-95 [1-2].

5317.4   O. J. F. Seitz, "Praeparatio Evangelica in the Markan Prologue," *JBL* 82 (1963): 201-206 [1:1-15].

5317.5   Leander E. Keck, "The Introduction to Mark's Gospel," *NTSt* 12 (1965-1966): 352-70 [1:1-15].

5317.6   Gerhard Dautzenberg, "Die Zeit des Evangeliums. Mk 1,1-15 und die Konzeption des Markusevangeliums," *BibZ* 21 (1977): 219-34 [1:1-15].

5317.7   Gerhard Dautzenberg, "Die Zeit des Evangeliums. Mk 1,1-15 und die Konzeption des Markusevangeliums [Pt. 2]," *BibZ* 22/1 (1978): 76-91 [1:1-15].

5317.8   Robert A. Guelich, "The Beginning of the Gospel," *BRes* 27 (1982): 5-15 [1:1-15].

5317.9   P. I. Sankey, "Promise and Fulfilment: Reader-Response to Mark 1.1-15," *JSNT* 58 (1995): 3-18 [1:1-15].

5317.10   R. T. France, "The Beginning of Mark," *RTR* 49 (1990): 11-19 [1:1-13].

5317.11   Lamar Williamson, "Mark 1:1-8," *Interp* 32 (1978): 400-404 [1:1-8].

5317.12   Frans Neirynck, "Mark and His Commentators: Mk 1,1-8,26," *ETL* 65 (1989): 381-89 [1:1-8:26].

5317.13   Gerhard Arnold, "Mk 1:1 und Eröffnungswendungen in griechischen und lateinischen Schriften," *ZNW* 68 (1977): 123-27 [1:1].

5317.14   André Feuillet, "Le 'Commencement' de l'économie chrétienne d'après He ii.3-4; Mc i.1 et Ac i.1-2," *NTSt* 24 (1977-1978): 163-74 [1:1].

5317.15   Alexander Globe, "The Caesarean Omission of the Phrase 'Son of God' in Mark 1:1," *HTR* 75 (1982): 209-18 [1:1].

5317.16   Detlev Dormeyer, "Die Kompositionsmetapher 'Evangelium Jesu Christi, des Sohnes Gottes' Mk 1:1: ihre theologische und literarische Aufgabe in Markus," *NTSt* 33/3 (1987): 452-68 [1:1].

5317.17   Peter M. Head, "A Text-Critical Study of Mark 1:1: 'The Beginning of the Gospel of Jesus Christ'," *NTSt* 37 (1991): 621-29 [1:1].

5317.18   R. P. Merendino, "Testi anticotestamentari in Mc 1,2-8," *RivB* 35 (1987): 3-25 [1:2-8].

5317.19   M.-É. Boismard, "Évangile des Ébionites et problème synoptique (Mc. I,2-6 et par.)," *RB* 73 (1966): 321-52 [1:2-6].

5317.20   Klyne Snodgrass, "Streams of Tradition Emerging from Isaiah 40:1-5 and Their Adaptation in the New Testament," *JSNT* 8 (1980): 24-45 [1:2-3].

5317.21 C. T. Ruddick, "Behold, I Send My Messenger," *JBL* 88 (1969): 381-417 [1:2].

5317.22 Christian Wolff, "Zur Bedeutung Johannes des Täufers im Markusevangelium," *TLZ* 102 (1977): 857-65 [1:4-8].

5317.23 J. K. Elliott, "Ho baptizōn and Mark i.4," *TZ* 31 (1975): 14-15 [1:4-5].

5317.24 U. Mell, "Jesu Taupe durch Johannes (Markus 1,9-15)–zur narrativen Christologie vom neuen Adam," *BibZ* 40 (1996): 161-78 [1:9-15].

5317.25 Dieter Zeller, "Jesu Taufe: ein literarischer Zugang zu Markus 1,9-11," *BK* 23 (1968): 90-94 [1:9-11].

5317.26 Georg Richter, "Zu den Tauferzahlungen Mk 1:9-11 und Joh 1:32-34," *ZNW* 65 (1974): 43-56 [1:9-11].

5317.27 Paul Ellingworth, "Translating Parallel Passages in the Gospels," *BTr* 34 (1983): 401-407 [1:10].

5317.28 C. H. Dodd, "New Testament Translation Problems II," *BTr* 28 (1977): 101-16 [1:11].

5317.29 Jacques Dupont, "L'origine du récit des tentations de Jésus au désert," *RB* 73 (1966): 30-76 [1:12-15].

5317.30 J. González-Faus, "Las tentaciones de Jesus y la tentacion cristiana," *EE* 47 (1972): 155-88 [1:12-15].

5317.31 Antonio Vargas-Machuca, "La tentacion de Jesus segun Mc. 1,12-13, ¿Hecho real o relato de tipo haggadico?" *EE* 48 (1973): 163-90 [1:12-15].

5317.32 Jeffrey B. Gibson, "Jesus' Wilderness Temptation according to Mark," *JSNT* 53 (1994): 3-34 [1:12-13].

5317.33 John H. Reumann, "Mark 1:14-20," *Interp* 32 (1978): 405-10 [1:14-20].

5317.34 Vernon K. Robbins, "Mark 1:14-20: An Interpretation at the Intersection of Jewish and Graeco-Roman Traditions," *NTSt* 28 (1982): 220 36 [1:14-20].

5317.35 James L. Mays, "Jesus Came Preaching: A Study and Sermon on Mark 1:14-15," *Interp* 26 (1972): 30-41 [1:14-15].

5317.36 Karl-Georg Reploh, " 'Evangelium' bei Markus. Das Evangelium des Markus als Anruf an die Gemeinde zu Umkehr und Glaube (1,14-15)," *BK* 27 (1972): 110-14 [1:14-15].

5317.37 John E. Alsup, "Mark 1:14-15," *Interp* 33 (1979): 394-98

[1:14-15].

5317.38   Gustavo Gutiérrez, "Mark 1:14-15," *RE* 88 (1991): 427-31 [1:14-15].

5317.39   Rudolf Schnackenburg, "Zur formgeschichtlichen Methode in der Evangelienforschung," *ZKT* 85 (1963): 16-32 [1:16-20].

5317.40   J. D. M. Derrett, "ἦσαν γὰρ ἁλιεῖς (Mk. 1,16)," *NT* 22 (1980): 108-37 [1:16].

5317.41   H. Gollwitzer, "Zur Frage der 'Sündlosigkeit Jesu'," *EvT* 31 (1971): 496-506 [1:17-18].

5317.42   David L. Dungan, "Synopses of the Future," *B* 66/4 (1985): 457-92 [1:21-3:19].

5317.43   David E. Garland, " 'I Am the Lord Your Healer': Mark 1:21-2:12," *RE* 85/2 (1988): 327-43 [1:21-2:12].

5317.44   Robert H. Stein, "The 'Redaktions geschichtlich' Investigation of a Markan Seam (Mc 1:21f.)," *ZNW* 61 (1970): 70-94 [1:21].

5317.45   A. W. Argyle, "The Meaning of ἐξουσία in Mark 1:22, 27," *ET* 80 (1969-1970): 343 [1:22].

5317.46   R. J. Dillon, " 'As One Having Authority' (Mark 1:22): The Controversial Distinction of Jesus' Teaching," *CBQ* 57 (1995): 92-113 [1:22].

5317.47   Francis Watson, "The Social Function of Mark's Secrecy Theme," *JSNT* 24 (1985): 49-69 [1:24].

5317.48   M. L. Rigato, "Tradizione e redazione in Mc. 1,29-31 (e paralleli). La guarigione della suocera di Simon Pietro," *RivB* 17 (1969): 139-74 [1:29-31].

5317.49   T. W. Kowalski, "Les sources pré-synoptiques de Marc 1,32-34 et parallèles. Phénomenes d'amalgame et independance mutuelle immédiate des évangélistes synoptiques," *RSR* 60 (1972): 541-73 [1:32-34].

5317.50   D. H. C. Read, "Recognizing Jesus as King Today," *ET* 92 (1980-1981): 81-82 [1:33].

5317.51   E. K. Broadhead, "Christology as Polemic and Apologetic: The Priestly Portrait of Jesus in the Gospel of Mark," *JSNT* 47 (1992): 21-34 [1:39-45].

5317.52   Manfred Wichelhaus, "Am ersten Tage der Woche. Mk. i,35-39 und die didaktischen Absichten des Markus-Evangelisten," *NT* 11 (1969): 45-66 [1:35-39].

5317.53 M. Herranz Marco, "La curación de un leproso según San Marcos (Mc 1,40-45)," *EB* 31 (1972): 399-433 [1:40-45].

5317.54 C. H. Cave, "The Leper: Mark 1:40-45," *NTSt* 25 (1978-1979): 245-50 [1:40-45].

5317.55 Vittorio Fusco, "Il segreto messianico nell'episodio del lebbroso (Mc. 1,40-45)," *RivB* 29 (1981): 273-313 [1:40-45].

5317.56 George B. Telford, "Mark 1:40-45," *Interp* 36 (1982): 54-58 [1:40-45].

5317.57 Michal Wojciechowski, "The Touching of the Leper (Mark 1:40-45) as a Historical and Symbolic Act of Jesus," *BibZ* 33/1 (1989): 114-19 [1:40-45].

5317.58 Carl Kazmierski, "Evangelist and Leper: A Socio-Cultural Study of Mark 1:40-45," *NTSt* 38 (1992): 37-50 [1:40-45].

5317.59 E. Galbiati, "La Visitazione (Luke 1:41-50)," *BO* 4 (1962): 139-44 [1:41-50].

5317.60 Kenneth W. Clark, "The Theological Relevance of Textual Variation in Current Criticism of the Greek New Testament," *JBL* 85 (1966): 1-16 [1:41].

5317.61 J. K. Elliott, "The Conclusion of the Pericope of the Healing of the Leper and Mark i.45," *JTS* 22 (1971): 153-57 [1:45].

5317.62 J. K. Elliott, "Is ὁ ἐξελθὼν a Title for Jesus in Mark 1:45?" *JTS* 27 (1976): 402-405 [1:45].

5317.63 L. Schottroff, "Das Magnificat und die älteste Tradition über Jesus von Nazareth," *ET* 38 (1978): 298-313 [1:46-56].

5317.64 E. G. Rupp, "A Great and Mighty Wonder!" *ET* 89 (1977-1978): 81-82 [1:52].

5317.65 Warren Carter, "Zechariah and the Benedictus (Luke 1,68-79): Practicing What He Preaches," *B* 69 (1988): 239-47 [1:68-79].

5317.66 Joanna Dewey, "The Literary Structure of the Controversy Stories in Mark 2:1-3:6," *JBL* 92/3 (1973): 394-401 [2:1-3:6].

5317.67 M. A. Chevallier, "L'analyse littéraire des textes du Nouveau Testament," *RHPR* 57 (1977): 367-78 [2:1-20].

5317.68 Paul J. Achtemeier, "The Ministry of Jesus in the Synoptic Gospels," *Interp* 35 (1981): 157-69 [2:1-10].

5317.69 H.-J. Klauck, "Die Frage der Sündenvergebung in der Perikope von der Heilung des Gelähmten Mk 2,1-12 Parr," *BibZ* 25/2 (1981): 223-48 [2:1-2].

438   CRITICAL STUDIES OF THE GOSPELS

5317.70   John Vannorsdall, "Mark 2:1-2," *Interp* 36/1 (1982): 58-63 [2:1-2].

5317.71   Jonathan Bishop, "Parabole and Parrhesia in Mark," *Interp* 40/1 (1986): 39-52 [2:1-2].

5317.72   Emilio Rasco, " 'Cuatro' y 'la fe': ¿quiénes y de quién? (Mc 2,3b.5a)," *B* 50 (1969): 59-67 [2:3-5].

5317.73   David A. Black, "Some Dissenting Notes on R. Stein's *The Synoptic Problem* and Markan 'Errors'," *FilN* 1 (1988): 95-101 [2:4].

5317.74   Joseph Keller, "Jesus and the Critics: A Logico-Critical Analysis of the Marcan Confrontation," *Interp* 40/1 (1986): 29-38 [2:6-12].

5317.75   L. Paul Trudinger, "No Room in the Inn: A Note on Luke 2:7," *ET* 102 (1990-1991): 172-73 [2:7].

5317.76   Ronald Ross, "Was Jesus Saying Something or Doing Something? (Mark 2:8-9)," *BTr* 41 (1990): 441-42 [2:8-9].

5317.77   F. Hunter and G. Hunter, "Which Is Easier," *ET* 105 (1993): 12-13 [2:9].

5317.78   J. D. M. Derrett, "Why 'bed'? (Mark 2,9d; John 5,8b)," *BO* 38 (1996): 111-16 [2:9].

5317.79   B. Prete, " 'Oggi vi è nato . . . il Salvatore che è il Cristo Signore' (Lc 2,11)," *RivB* 34 (1986): 289-325 [2:11].

5317.80   M. Völkel, " 'Freund der Zöllner und Sünder'," *ZNW* 69 (1978): 1-10 [2:13-17].

5317.81   John R. Donahue, "Tax Collectors and Sinners: An Attempt at Identification," *CBQ* 33 (1971): 39-61 [2:14-17].

5317.82   Fritz Herrenbrück, "Zum Vorwurf der Kollaboration des Zöllners mit Rom," *ZNW* 78 (1987): 186-99 [2:14-16].

5317.83   C. H. Dodd, "New Testament Translation Problems," *BTr* 27/3 (1976): 301-305 [2:14].

5317.84   L. Alexander, "Luke's Preface in the Context of Greek Preface-Writing," *NT* 28/1 (1986): 48-74 [2:14].

5317.85   Beltran Villegas, "Peter, Philip and James of Alphaeus," *NTSt* 33 (1987): 292-94 [2:14].

5317.86   H.-W. Bartsch, "Zur Problematik eines Monopoltextes des Neuen Testaments. Das Beispiel Markus 2, Vers 15 und 16," *TLZ* 105 (1980): 91-96 [2:15-16].

5317.87   Elizabeth S. Malbon, "τῇ οἰκίᾳ αὐτου: Mark 2:15 in

Context," *NTSt* 31/2 (1985): 282-92 [2:15].

5317.88 Robert G. Bratcher, "Unusual Sinners," *BTr* 39 (1988): 335-37 [2:15].

5317.89 George D. Kilpatrick, "Two Studies of Style and Text in the Greek New Testament," *JTS* 41 (1990): 94-98 [2:16].

5317.90 G. M. Lee, " 'They that are Whole Need Not a Physician'," *ET* 76 (1964-1965): 254 [2:17].

5317.91 Gottfried Schille, "Was ist ein Logion?" *ZNW* 61 (1970): 172-82 [2:18-22].

5317.92 Robert Banks, "Jesus and Custom," *ET* 84 (1972-1973): 265-69 [2:18-22].

5317.93 J. A. Ziesler, "The Removal of the Bridegroom: A Note on Mark 2:18-22 and Parallels," *NTSt* 19 (1972-1973): 190-94 [2:18-22].

5317.94 Curtis C. Mitchell, "The Practice of Fasting in the New Testament," *BS* 147 (1990): 455-69 [2:18-22].

5317.95 Franz G. Cremer, " 'Die Söhne des Brautgemachs' (Mk 2,19 parr) in der griechischen und lateinischen Schrifterklärung," *BibZ* 11 (1967): 246-53 [2:19].

5317.96 Georg Braumann, " 'An Jenem Tag' Mk 2:20," *NT* 6 (1963): 264-67 [2:20].

5317.97 E. Galbiati, "La Circoncisione di Gesù (Luke 2:21)," *BO* 8 (1966): 37-45 [2:21].

5317.98 Ferdinand Hahn, "Die Bildworte vom neuen Flicken und vom jungen Wein (Mk 2,21f. parr)," *EvT* 31 (1971): 357-75 [2:21].

5317.99 Lucien Legrand, "On l'appela du nom de Jésus (Luke 2:21)," *RB* 89 (1982): 481-91 [2:21].

5317.100 E. Galbiati, "La Presentazione al tempio (Luke 2:22-40)," *BO* 6 (1964): 28-37 [2:22-40].

5317.101 T. Stramare, "La presentazione di Gesu al tempio (Luke 2:22-40)," *BO* 25 (1983): 63-71 [2:22-40].

5317.102 Arland J. Hultgren, "The Formation of the Sabbath Pericope in Mark 2:23-28," *JBL* 91/1 (1972): 38-43 [2:23-28].

5317.103 Christoph Hinz, "Jesus und der Sabbat," *KD* 19 (1973): 91-108 [2:23-28].

5317.104 Lars Lode, "The Presentation of New Information," *BTr* 35 (1984): 101-108 [2:23-28].

5317.105 P. Maurice Casey, "Culture and Historicity: The Plucking of the Grain in Mark 2:23-28," *NTSt* 34/1 (1988): 1-23 [2:23-28].

5317.106 C. S. Morgan, " 'When Abiathar Was High Priest,' (Mark 2:26)," *JBL* 98 (1979): 409-10 [2:26].

5317.107 J. H. van Halsema, "Het raadsel als literaire vorm in Marcus en Johannes," *GTT* 83/1 (1983): 1-17 [2:26].

5317.108 Craig A. Evans, "Patristic Interpretation of Mark 2:26: 'When Abiathar was High Priest'," *VCh* 40/2 (1986): 183-86 [2:26].

5317.109 Félix Gils, " 'Le sabbat a été fait pour l'homme et non l'homme pour le sabbat': Réflexions à propos de Mc II,27-28," *RB* 69 (1962): 506-23 [2:27].

5317.110 George D. Kilpatrick, "*Laoi* at Luke ii.31 and Acts iv.25, 27," *JTS* 16 (1965): 127 [2:31].

5317.111 Pierre Benoit, "Et Toi-Même, Un Glaive Te Transpercera L'âme! (Luc 2:35) [Ezek. 14:7]," *CBQ* 25 (1963): 251-61 [2:35].

5317.112 Ivor Bailey, "Parental Heart-Break," *ET* 89 (1977-1978): 85-86 [2:35].

5317.113 A. T. Varela, "Luke 2:36-37: Is Anna's Age What is Really in Focus?" *BTr* 27 (1976): 446 [2:36-37].

5317.114 H. J. de Jonge, "Sonship, Wisdom, Infancy: Luke 2:41-51a," *NTSt* 24 (1977-1978): 317-54 [2:41-51].

5317.115 E. Galbiati, "Esegesi degli Evangeli festivi. Preparate la via del Signore," *BO* 5 (1963): 213-15 [3:1-6].

5317.116 C. S. Rodd, "Are the Ethics of Jesus Situation Ethics?" *ET* 79 (1967-1968): 167-70 [3:1-6].

5317.117 Jürgen Sauer, "Traditionsgeschichtliche Überlegungen Zu Mk 3,1-6," *ZNW* 73/3-4 (1982): 183-203 [3:1-6].

5317.118 J. D. M. Derrett, "Christ and the Power of Choice: Mark 3:1-6," *B* 65/2 (1984): 168-88 [3:1-6].

5317.119 Leander E. Keck, "Mark 3:7-12 and Mark's Christology," *JBL* 84/4 (1965): 341-58 [3:7-12].

5317.120 T. A. Burkill, "Mark 3:7-12 and the Alleged Dualism in the Evangelist's Miracle Material," *JBL* 87/4 (1968): 409-17 [3:7-12].

5317.121 W. Egger, "Die Verborgenheit in Mk 3,7-12," *B* 50 (1969): 466-90 [3:7-12].

5317.122 Günther Schwarz, "ἵνα πλοιάριον προσκαρτερῇ: Markus 3.9," *NTSt* 33/1 (1987): 151-52 [3:9].

5317.123 Ernest Best, "Mark's Use of the Twelve," *ZNW* 69/1-2 (1978): 11-35 [3:14].

5317.124 Randall Buth, "Mark 3:17: Βοανηργές and Popular Etymology," *JSNT* 10 (1981): 29-33 [3:17].

5317.125 J.-A. Morin, "Les deux derniers des Douze: Simon le Zelote et Judas Iskariôth," *RB* 80 (1973): 332-58 [3:18-19].

5317.126 R. Garafalo, "The Family of Jesus in Mark's Gospel," *ITQ* 57 (1991): 265-76 [3:20-35].

5317.127 Henry Wansbrough, "Mark iii.21: Was Jesus Out of His Mind?" *NTSt* 18 (1971-1972): 233-35 [3:21].

5317.128 David Wenham, "The Meaning of Mark III. 21," *NTSt* 21 (1975): 295-300 [3:21].

5317.129 Ernest Best, "Mark 3:20, 21, 31-35," *NTSt* 22/3 (1975-1976): 309-19 [3:21].

5317.130 Roland Meynet, "Qui Donc Esr 'Le Plus Fort'? Analyse Rhetorique de Mc 3,22-30; Mt 12,22-37; Luc 11,14-26," *RB* 90/3 (1983): 334-50 [3:22-30].

5317.131 Philippe Rolland, "Jésus connaissait leurs pensées," *ETL* 62 (1986): 118-21 [3:22].

5317.132 G. M. Lee, "Luke iii,23," *ET* 79 (1967-1968): 310 [3:23].

5317.133 S. Légasse, " 'Homme Fort' de Luc XI,21-22," *NT* 5 (1962): 5-9 [3:27].

5317.134 Robert Hulst, "Re-examining Mark 3:28f. and its Parallels," *ZNW* 63 (1972): 122-24 [3:28].

5317.135 M. Eugene Boring, "How May We Identify Oracles of Christian Prophets in the Synoptic Tradition? Mark 3:28, 29 as a Test Case," *JBL* 91/4 (1972): 501-20 [3:29].

5317.136 J. C. O'Neill, "The Unforgivable Sin," *JSNT* 19 (1983): 37-42 [3:29].

5317.137 Baird Tipson, "A Dark Side of 17th Century English Protestantism: The Sin Against the Holy Spirit," *HTR* 77/3-4 (1984): 301-30 [3:29].

5317.138 Elizabeth S. Malbon, "Echoes and Foreshadowings in Mark 4-8: Reading and Rereading," *JBL* 112 (1993): 166-70 [4-8].

5317.139 Wilhelm Wilkens, "Die Redaktion des Gleichniskapitels Mark 4 durch Matth," *TZ* 20 (1964): 305-27 [4].

5317.140   Craig A. Evans, "A Note on the Function of Isaiah vi,9-10 in Mark iv," *RB* 88 (1981): 234-35 [4].

5317.141   C. C. Marcheselli, "Le parabole del vangelo di Marco," *RivB* 29 (1981): 405-15 [4:1-34].

5317.142   Christopher M. Tuckett, "Mark's Concerns in the Parables Chapter (Mark 4,1-34)," *B* 69/1 (1988): 1-26 [4:1-34].

5317.143   Greg Fay, "Introduction to Incomprehension: The Literary Structure of Mark 4:1-34," *CBQ* 51/1 (1989): 65-81 [4:1-34].

5317.144   Gerhard Dautzenberg, "Mk 4:1-34 als Belehrung über das Reich Gottes: Beobachtungen zum Gleichniskapitel," *BibZ* 34/1 (1990): 38-62 [4:1-34].

5317.145   Elizabeth A. Bogert, "The Parable and the Greenhouse: Mark 4:1-20," *HQ* 4 (1964): 61-64 [4:1-20].

5317.146   K. D. White, "The Parable of the Sower," *JTS* 15 (1964): 300-307 [4:1-20].

5317.147   John W. Bowker, "Mystery and Parable: Mark 4:1-20," *JTS* 25/2 (1974): 301-17 [4:1-20].

5317.148   James R. Edwards, "Markan Sandwiches: The Significance of Interpolations in Markan Narratives," *NT* 31 (1989): 193-216 [4:1-20].

5317.149   Joachim Jeremias, "Palästinakundliches zum Gleichnis vom Säemann (Mark. IV.3-8 Par.)," *NTSt* 13 (1966-1967): 48-53 [4:3-9].

5317.150   Peter Lampe, "Die markinische Deutung des Gleichnisses vom Samann Markus 4:10-12," *ZNW* 65 (1974): 140-50 [4:3-9].

5317.151   J. A. L. Lee, "Some Features of the Speech of Jesus in Mark's Gospel," *NT* 27 (1985): 1-26 [4:3-9].

5317.152   Gerhard Lohfink, "Das Gleichnis vom Sämann: Mk 4,3-9," *BibZ* 30/1 (1986): 36-69 [4:3-9].

5317.153   Terence J. Keegan, "The Parable of the Sower and Mark's Jewish Leaders," *CBQ* 56 (1994): 501-18 [4:3-8].

5317.154   José O'Callaghan, "Dos vartantes en la parábola del sembrador," *EB* 48 (1990): 267-70 [4:4-7].

5317.155   Harald Sahlin, "Emendationsvorschläge zum griechischen Text des Neuen Testaments I," *NT* 24 (1982): 160-79 [4:6].

5317.156   Joel Marcus, "Mark 4:10-12 and Markan Epistemology," *JBL* 103/4 (1984): 557-74 [4:10-12].

5317.157 Günter Haufe, "Erwägungen zum Ursprung der sogenannten Parabeltheorie Markus 4,11-12," *EvT* 32 (1972): 413-21 [4:11-12].

5317.158 Klaus Haacker, "Erwagungen zu Mc IV,11," *NT* 14/3 (1972): 219-25 [4:11].

5317.159 Schuyler Brown, "The Secret of the Kingdom of God," *JBL* 92/1 (1973): 60-74 [4:11].

5317.160 Juan Mateos, "Algunas notas sobre el Evangelio de Marcos (part 1)," *FilN* 3 (1989): 197-204 [4:13].

5317.161 Juan Mateos, "Algunas notas sobre el Evangelio de Marcos (part 2)," *FilN* 3 (1990): 159-66 [4:13].

5317.162 T. V. Walker, "Luke 4:16-30," *RE* 85 (1988): 321-24 [4:16-30].

5317.163 Gerhard Schneider, "Das Bildwort von der Lampe. Zur Traditionsgeschichte eines Jesus-Wortes," *ZNW* 61 (1970): 183-209 [4:21].

5317.164 John L. Nolland, "Impressed Unbelievers as Witnesses to Christ (Luke 4:22a)," *JBL* 98 (1979): 219-29 [4:22].

5317.165 John J. Kilgallen, "Provocation in Luke 4:23-24," *B* 70/4 (1989): 511-16 [4:23-24].

5317.166 John L. Nolland, "Classical and Rabbinic Parallel to 'Physician, heal yourself' (Luke 4:23)," *NT* 21 (1979): 193-209 [4:23].

5317.167 Howard A. Hatton, "Unraveling the Agents and Events," *BTr* 37/4 (1986): 417-20 [4:24-25].

5317.168 Jacques Dupont, " 'Le royaume des cieux est semblable à . . .'," *BO* 6 (1964): 247-53 [4:26-30].

5317.169 Jacques Dupont, "La parabole de la semence qui pousse toute seule," *RSR* 55 (1967): 367-92 [4:26-29].

5317.170 Rainer Stuhlmann, "Beobachtungen und Überlegungen zu Markus IV.26-29," *NTS* 19/2 (1972-1973): 153-62 [4:26-29].

5317.171 J. D. M. Derrett, "Ambivalence: Sowing and Reaping at Mk 4,26-29," *EB* 48 (1990): 489-510 [4:26-29].

5317.172 George Aichele, "Two Theories of Translation with Examples from the Gospel of Mark," *JSNT* 47 (1992): 95-116 [4:26-29].

5317.173 H. Weder, "Metapher und Gleichnis. Bemerkungen zur Reichweite des Bildes in religiöser Sprache," *ZTK* 90 (1993):

444 CRITICAL STUDIES OF THE GOSPELS

382-408 [4:26-29].

5317.174 Gerd Theissen, "Der Bauer und die von selbst Frucht bringende Erde: Naiver Synergismus in Mk 4,26-29?" *ZNW* 85 (1994): 167-82 [4:26-29].

5317.175 W. G. Essame, "Καὶ ἔλεγεν in Mark 4:21, 24, 26, 30," *ET* 77 (1965-1966): 121 [4:26].

5317.176 E. J. Vardaman, "The Earliest Fragments of the New Testament," *ET* 83 (1971-1972): 374-76 [4:28].

5317.177 Robert W. Funk, "The Looking-Glass Tree Is for the Birds. Ezekiel 17:22-24; Mark 4:30-32," *Interp* 27 (1973): 3-9 [4:30-32].

5317.178 Alberto Casalegno, "La parabola del granello di senape (Mc. 4,30-32)," *RivB* 26 (1978): 139-61 [4:30-32].

5317.179 Olof Linton, "Coordinated Sayings and Parables in the Synoptic Gospels: Analysis versus Theories," *NTSt* 26 (1979-1980): 139-63 [4:30-32].

5317.180 Richard J. Bauckham, "The Parable of the Vine: Rediscovering a Lost Parable of Jesus," *NTSt* 33/1 (1987): 84-101 [4:30-32].

5317.181 F. C. Synge, "Intruded Middles," *ET* 92 (1981): 329-33 [4:31-32].

5317.182 Paul J. Achtemeier, "Person and Deed: Jesus and the Storm-Tossed Sea," *Interp* 16 (1962): 169-76 [4:35-41].

5317.183 Gottfried Schille, "Die Seesturmerzählung Markus 4:45-41 als Beispiel neutestamentlicher Aktualisierung," *ZNW* 56 (1965): 30-40 [4:35-41].

5317.184 Rainer Riesner, "Das Boot vom See Gennesaret," *BK* 41 (1986): 135-38 [4:38].

5317.185 George D. Kilpatrick, "Three Problems of New Testament Text," *NT* 21 (1979): 289-92 [5:1].

5317.186 Tullio Aurelio, "Mistero del regno e unione con Gesù: Mc 5:1-21," *BO* 19 (1977): 59-68 [5:1-21].

5317.187 J. D. M. Derrett, "Contributions to the Study of the Gerasene Demoniac," *JSNT* 3 (1979): 2-17 [5:1-20].

5317.188 Ulrich B. Müller, "Zur Rezeption Gesetzes-Kritischer Jesusuberlieferung im Fruhen Christentum," *NTSt* 27/2 (1980-1981): 158-85 [5:1-20].

5317.189 Günter Klein, "Die Berufung des Petrus," *ZNW* 58 (1967): 1-44 [5:1-11].

5317.190 Juan Mateos, "Términos relacionados con 'Légion' en Mc 5:2-20," *FilN* 1 (1988): 211-16 [5:2-20].

5317.191 D. P. Davies, "Luke 5:8 (Simon Peter)," *ET* 79 (1967-1968): 382 [5:8].

5317.192 J. D. M. Derrett, "James and John as Co-rescuers from Peril (Luke 5:10)," *NT* 22 (1980): 299-303 [5:10].

5317.193 J. D. M. Derrett, "Mark's Technique: The Haemorrhaging Woman and Jairus' Daughter," *B* 63/4 (1982): 474-505 [5:21-43].

5317.194 Lone Fatum, "En kvindehistorie om tro og køn," *DTT* 53 (1990): 278-99 [5:21-43].

5317.195 Vernon K. Robbins, "The Woman Who Touched Jesus' Garment: Socio-rhetorical Analysis of the Synoptic Accounts," *NTSt* 33 (1987): 502-15 [5.24-34].

5317.196 S. M. Reynolds, "The Zero Tense in Greek: A Critical Note," *WTJ* 32 (1969): 68-72 [5:35-42].

5317.197 Enrique López-Dóriga, "Y cogiendo la mano de la niña le dice: Talitha koumi (Mc 5,41). Nota exegético-filológica," *EE* 39 (1964): 377-81 [5:41].

5317.198 Erich Grässer, "Jesus in Nazareth (Mark 6:1-6a): Notes on the Redaction and Theology of St. Mark," *NTSt* 16 (1969-1970): 1-23 [6:1-6].

5317.199 J. T. Buchanan, "The 'Second-First Sabbath' (Luke 6:1)," *JBL* 97 (1978): 259-62 [6:1].

5317.200 Richard A. Batey, "Is Not This the Carpenter?" *NTSt* 30 (1984): 249-58 [6:3].

5317.201 Tal Ilan, "Man Born of Woman . . . (Job 14:1): The Phenomenon of Men Bearing Metronymes at the Time of Jesus," *NT* 34 (1992): 23-45 [6:3].

5317.202 John Bradshaw, "Oral Transmission and Human Memory," *ET* 92 (1980-1981): 303-307 [6:6-13].

5317.203 J. D. M. Derrett, "Peace, Sandals and Shirts," *HeyJ* 24 (1983): 253-65 [6:6-13].

5317.204 J. A. L. Lee, "A Non-Aramaism in Luke 6:7," *NT* 33 (1991): 28-34 [6:7].

5317.205 G. M. Lee, "Two Notes on St. Mark," *NT* 18/1 (1976): 36 [6:10].

5317.206 George B. Caird, "Uncomfortable Words: II. Shake Off the Dust from Your Feet," *ET* 81/2 (1969-1970): 40-43 [6:11].

5317.207 Édouard Delebecque, "Secouez la Poussiere de vos Pieds . . . sur l'Hellenisme de Luc IX,5," *RB* 89/2 (1982): 177-84 [6:11].

5317.208 Gottfried Schille, "Prolegomena zur Jesusfrage," *TLZ* 93 (1968): 481-88 [6:14].

5317.209 Sasagu Arai, "Zum 'Tempelwort' Jesu in Apostelgeschichte 6:14," *NTSt* 34/3 (1988): 397-410 [6:14].

5317.210 E. W. Deibler, "Translating from Basic Structure," *BTr* 19 (1968): 14-16 [6:17-25].

5317.211 Jean Delorme, "L'intégration des petites unités littéraires dans l'Évangile de Marc du point de vue de la sémiotique structurale," *NTSt* 25 (1978-1979): 469-91 [6:30-56].

5317.212 Lamar Williamson, "An Exposition of Mark 6:30-44," *Interp* 30 (1976): 169-73 [6:30-44].

5317.213 Ulrich H. J. Körtner, "Das Fischmotiv im Speisungswunder," *ZNW* 75/1 (1984): 24-35 [6:30-44].

5317.214 Gerhard Friedrich, "Die beiden Erzählungen von der Speisung in Mark 6,31-44; 8,1-9," *TZ* 20 (1964): 10-22 [6:31-44].

5317.215 W. C. van Unnik, "Die Motivierung der Feindesliebe in Lukas vi,32-35," *NT* 8 (1966): 284-300 [6:32-35].

5317.216 J. D. M. Derrett, "Leek-Beds and Methodology," *BibZ* 19 (1975): 101-103 [6:39-40].

5317.217 Hermann Binder, "Von Markus zu den Grossevangelien," *TZ* 35 (1979): 283-89 [6:45-8:26].

5317.218 T. Snoy, "La rédaction marcienne de la marche sur les eaux," *ETL* 44 (1968): 205-41, 433-81 [6:45-52].

5317.219 Hubert Ritt, "Der 'Seewandel Jesu' (Mk 6,45-52 Par)," *BibZ* 23/1 (1979): 71-84 [6:45-52].

5317.220 Harry T. Fleddermann, " 'And He Wanted to Pass by Them' (Mark 6:48c)," *CBQ* 45/3 (1983): 389-95 [6:48].

5317.221 C. Mazzucco, "E voleva oltrepassarloi," *RivB* 42 (1994): 44-66 [6:48].

5317.222 David Hill, "The Walking on the Water: A Geographic or Linguistic Answer?" *ET* 99 (1987-1988): 267-69 [6:49].

5317.223 Gordon D. Fee, "Some Dissenting Notes on 7Q5 = Mark 6:52-53," *JBL* 92 (1973): 109-12 [6:52-53].

5317.224 Jozef Verheyden, "Mark 1:32-34 and 6:53-56: Tradition or

Redaction?" *ETL* 64/4 (1988): 415-28 [6:53-56].

5317.225 G. Rinaldi, "Traversata del lago e sbarco a Genezaret in 'Marco' 6,53," *BO* 17 (1975): 43-46 [6:53].

5317.226 John P. Brown, "Synoptic Parallels in the Epistles and Form-History," *NTSt* 10 (1963-1964): 27-48 [7:1-23].

5317.227 Hans Hübner, "Mark VII.1-23 und das 'Jüdisch-Hellenistische' Gesetzesverständnis," *NTSt* 22/3 (1975-1976): 319-45 [7:1-23].

5317.228 Jan Lambrecht, "Jesus and the Law. An Investigation of Mark 7:1-23," *ETL* 53 (1977): 24-82 [7:1-23].

5317.229 Michael FitzPatrick, "From Ritual Observance to Ethics: The Argument of Mark 7:1-23," *ABR* 35 (1987): 22-27 [7:1-23].

5317.230 Elian Cuviller, "Tradition et rédaction en Marc 7:1-23," *NT* 34/2 (1992): 169-92 [7:1-23].

5317.231 Richard C. Brand, "Clean and Unclean," *ET* 98/1 (1986-1987): 16-17 [7:1-8].

5317.232 W. Storch, "Zur Perikope von der Syrophonizierin. Mk 7,2 und Ri 1,7," *BibZ* 14/2 (1970): 256-57 [7:2].

5317.233 W. D. McHardy, "Mark 7:3: A Reference to the Old Testament?" *ET* 87 (1975-1976): 119 [7:3].

5317.234 J. M. Ross, " 'With the Fist'," *ET* 87 (1975-1976): 374-75 [7:3].

5317.235 T. C. Skeat, "A Note on πυγμῇ in Mark 7:3," *JTS* 41 (1990): 525-27 [7:3].

5317.236 E. Galbiati, "La risurrezione del giovane di Naim (Lc 7:11-16)," *BO* 4 (1962): 175-77 [7:11-16].

5317.237 Helmut Merkel, "Markus 7,15: das Jesuswort über die innere Verunreinigung," *ZRGG* 20 (1968): 340-63 [7:15].

5317.238 Heikki Räisänen, "Jesus and the Food Laws: Reflectings on Mark 7.15," *JSNT* 16 (1982): 79-100 [7:15].

5317.239 T. A. Burkill, "The Syrophoenician Woman: The Congruence of Mark 7:24-31," *ZNW* 57 (1966): 23-37 [7:24-31].

5317.240 T. A. Burkill, "The Historical Development of the Story of the Syrophoenician Woman," *NT* 9 (1967): 161-77 [7:24-31].

5317.241 Barnabas Flammer, "Die Syrophoenizerin. Mk 7,24-30," *TQ* 148 (1968): 463-78. (See the English translation, "The Syro-Phoenician Woman (Mk 7:24-30)," *TD* 18 (1970): 19-24 [7:24-30].

5317.242 Gerd Theissen, "Lokal- und Sozialkolorit in der Geschichte von der Syrophönischen Frau (Mk 7:24-30)," *ZNW* 75/3-4 (1984): 202-25 [7:24-30].

5317.243 P. Pokorný, "From a Puppy to the Child: Some Problems of Contemporary Biblical Exegesis Demonstrated from Mark 7.24-30/Matt 15.21-8," *NTSt* 41 (1995): 321-37 [7:24-30].

5317.244 W. R. G. Loader, "Challenged at the Boundaries: A Conservative Jesus in Mark's Tradition," *JSNT* 63 (1996): 45-61 [7:24-30].

5317.245 Francis Dufton, "The Syrophoenician Woman and Her Dogs," *ET* 100 (1988-1989): 417 [7:26-28].

5317.246 Günther Schwarz, "Συροφοινίκισσα-χαναναία (Markus 7:26; Matthäus 15:22)," *NTSt* 30/4 (1984): 626-28 [7:26].

5317.247 R. S. Sugirtharajah, "The Syrophoenician Woman," *ET* 98/1 (1986-1987): 13-15 [7:26].

5317.248 Ernst Haenchen, "Die Komposition von Mk VII,27-IX,1 und Par.," *NT* 6 (1963): 81-109 [7:27-9:1].

5317.249 Isaac Rabinowitz, " 'Be Opened' = ephphatha (Mark 7:34): Did Jesus Speak Hebrew?" *ZNW* 53 (1962): 229-38 [7:34].

5317.250 Fred L. Horton, "Nochmals Εφφαθα in Mark 7:34," *ZNW* 77/1 (1986): 101-108 [7:34].

5317.251 Tom Baird, "Translating Orthō's at Mark 7:35," *ET* 92 (1980-1981): 337-38 [7:35].

5317.252 B. M. F. van Iersel, "Die wunderbare Speisung und das Abendmal in der synoptischen Tradition (Mk 6:35-44, 8:1-20)," *NT* 7/3 (1964-1965): 167-94 [8:1-20].

5317.253 Frederick W. Danker, "Mark 8:3," *JBL* 82 (1963): 215-16 [8:3].

5317.254 Jeffrey B. Gibson, "Jesus' Refusal to Produce a 'Sign'," *JSNT* 38 (1990): 37-66 [8:11-13].

5317.255 Gustav Stählin, "Zum Gebrauch von Beteuerungsformeln im Neuen Testament," *NT* 5 (1962): 115-43 [8:12].

5317.256 George W. Buchanan, "Some Vow and Oath Formulas in the New Testament," *HTR* 58 (1965): 319-26 [8:12].

5317.257 John Ferguson, "Mary Magdalene," *ET* 97/9 (1985-1986): 275-76 [8:12].

5317.258 Jeffrey B. Gibson, "Mark 8:12a: Why Does Jesus 'Sigh Deeply'?" *BTr* 38/1 (1987): 122-25 [8:12].

5317.259 J. Mánek, "Mark viii,14-21," *NT* 7 (1964-1965): 10-14 [8:14-21].

5317.260 Eugene E. Lemcio, "External Evidence for the Structure and Function of Mark IV.1-20, VII.14-23, and VIII.14-21," *JTS* 29/2 (1978): 323-38 [8:14-21].

5317.261 Norman A. Beck, "Reclaiming a Biblical Text: The Mark 8:14-21 Discussion about Bread in the Boat," *CBQ* 43/1 (1981): 49-56 [8:14-21].

5317.262 L. W. Countryman, "How Many Baskets Full? Mark 8:14-21," *CBQ* 47/4 (1985): 643-55 [8:14-21].

5317.263 C. L. Mitton, "Leaven," *ET* 84 (1972-1973): 339-43 [8:15].

5317.264 Earl S. Johnson, "Mark 8:22-26: The Blind Man from Bethsaida," *NTSt* 25/3 (1978-1979): 370-83 [8:22-26].

5317.265 J. K. Howard, "Men as Trees, Walking. Mark 8.22-26," *SJT* 37 (1984). 163-70 [8.22-26].

5317.266 J.-F. Collange, "La déroute de L'aveugle (Mc 8,22-26): Écriture et pratique chrétienne," *RHPR* 66/1 (1986): 21-28 [8:22-26].

5317.267 Paolo Neri, "Per guarire il cieco di Betsaida," *BO* 30 (1988): 138 [8:22-26].

5317.268 John Ellington, "Mark 8:23," *BTr* 34 (1983): 443-44 [8:23].

5317.269 G. M. Lee, "Mark viii.24," *NT* 20/1 (1978): 74 [8:24].

5317.270 J. I. Miller, "Was Tischendorf Really Wrong? Mark 8:26b Revisited," *NT* 28/2 (1986): 97-103 [8:26].

5317.271 J. M. Ross. "Another Look at Mark 8:26," *NT* 29/2 (1987): 97-99 [8:26].

5317.272 H.-J. Venetz, "Widerspruch und Nachfolge. Zur Frage des Glaubens an Jesus nach Mk 8,27-10,52," *FZPT* 19 (1972): 111-19 [8:27-10:52].

5317.273 René Lafontaine and Pierre Mourlon Beernaert, "Essai sur la structure de Marc, 8,27-9,13," *RSR* 57 (1969): 543-61 [8:27-9:13].

5317.274 James L. Mays, "An Exposition of Mark 8:27-9:1," *Interp* 30/2 (1976): 174-78 [8:27-9:1].

5317.275 Josef Ernst, "Petrusbekenntnis-Leidensankündigung-Satanswort: Tradition und Redaktion," *C* 32 (1978): 46-73 [8:27-33].

5317.276 H. Klein, "Das Bekenntnis des Petrus und die Anfänge des

Christusglaubens im Urchristentum," *EvT* 47 (1987): 176-92 [8:27-33].

5317.277   Athol Gill, "Women Ministers in the Gospel of Mark," *ABR* 35 (1987): 14-21 [8:28].

5317.278   C. J. Reedy, "Mark 8:31-11:10 and the Gospel Ending," *CBQ* 34/2 (1972): 188-97 [8:31-11:10].

5317.279   Georg   Strecker,   "Die   Leidens-   und Auferstehungs-voraussagen im Markusevangelium (Mk 8,31; 9,31; 10,32-34)," *ZTK* 64 (1964): 16-39 [8:31].

5317.280   Elian Cuviller, "Il proclamait ouvertement la parole: notule sur la traduction de Marc 8:32a," *TR* 63/3 (1988): 427-28 [8:32].

5317.281   C. H. Cave, "The Obedience of Unclean Spirits," *NTSt* 11 (1964-1965): 93-97 [8:33].

5317.282   J. G. Griffiths, "The Disciple's Cross," *NTSt* 16 (1969-1970): 358-64 [8:34-35].

5317.283   Ernest Best, "An Early Sayings Collection," *NT* 18/1 (1976): 1-16 [8:34].

5317.284   Günther Schwarz, "Der Nachfolgespruch Markus 8:34b,c parr: Emendation und Rückübersetzung," *NTSt* 33/2 (1987): 255-65 [8:34].

5317.285   Walter Rebell, " 'Sein Leben verlieren' (Mark 8.35 parr.) als Strukturmoment vor- und nachosterlichen Glaubens," *NTSt* 35/2 (1989): 202-18 [8:35].

5317.286   José O'Callaghan, "Nota Critica a Mc 8,36," *B* 64/1 (1983): 116-17 [8:36].

5317.287   Michael D. Goulder, "Those Outside (Mark 4:10-12)," *NT* 33 (1991): 289-302 [9].

5317.288   Kent E. Brower, "Mark 9:1: Seeing the Kingdom in Power," *JSNT* 6 (1980): 17-41 [9:1].

5317.289   Enrique Nardoni, "A Redactional Interpretation of Mark 9:1," *CBQ* 43/3 (1981): 365-84 [9:1].

5317.290   John J. Kilgallen, "Mark 9:1: The Conclusion of a Pericope," *B* 63/1 (1982): 81-83 [9:1].

5317.291   David Wenham and A. D. Moses, " 'There Are Some Standing Here. . .': Did They Become the 'Reputed Pillars' of the Jerusalem Church? Some Reflections on Mark 1:9," *NT* 36 (1994): 146-63 [9:1].

5317.292   Robert H. Stein, "Is the Transfiguration a Misplaced

Resurrection Account?" *JBL* 95/1.(1976): 79-96 [9:2-8].

5317.293 James M. Robinson, "Jesus: From Easter to Valentinus (or the Apostles' Creed)," *JBL* 101 (1982): 5-37 [9:2-8].

5317.294 Walter Wink, "Mark 9:2-8," *Interp* 36/1 (1982): 63-67 [9:2-8].

5317.295 Wolfgang Gerber, "Die Metamorphose Jesu, Mark. 9,2f. par.," *TZ* 23 (1967): 385-95 [9:2].

5317.296 Foster R. McCurley, " 'And After Six Days' (Mark 9:2): A Semitic Literary Device," *JBL* 93/1 (1974): 67-81 [9:2].

5317.297 Jeremy Moiser, "Moses and Elijah," *ET* 96 (1984-1985): 216-17 [9:4].

5317.298 B. T. Viviano, "Rabbouni and Mark 9:5," *RB* 97 (1990): 207-18 [9:5].

5317.299 Joseph A. Fitzmyer, "More about Elijah Coming First," *JBL* 104 (1985): 295-96 [9:11-13].

5317.300 Joel Marcus, "Mark 9:11-13: 'As It Has Been Written'," *ZNW* 80/1 (1989): 42-63 [9:11-13].

5317.301 Dale C. Allison, "Elijah Must Come First," *JBL* 103 (1984): 256-58 [9:11].

5317.302 J. D. M. Derrett, "Herod's Oath and the Baptist's Head (With an Appendix on Mk IX.12-13, Mal III.24, Micah VII.6)," *BibZ* 9 (1965): 49-59, 233-46 [9:12-13].

5317.303 Wolfgang Schenk, "Tradition und Redaktion in der Epileptikerperikope, Mk 9:14-29," *ZNW* 63 (1972): 76-94 [9:14-29].

5317.304 Paul J. Achtemeier, "Miracles and the Historical Jesus: A Study of Mark 9:14-29," *CBQ* 37/4 (1975): 471-91 [9:14-29].

5317.305 J. González-Faus, "Jesus y los demonios: Intróducción cristológica a la lucha por la justicia," *EE* 52 (1977): 487-519 [9:14-29].

5317.306 Dominique Stein, "Une lecture psychanalytique de la Bible," *RSPT* 72 (1988): 95-108 [9:14-29].

5317.307 Frans Neirynck and Timothy A. Friedrichsen, "Note on Luke 9:22," *ETL* 65/4 (1989): 390-94 [9:22].

5317.308 Rolf J. Erler, "Eine kleine Beobachtung an Karl Barths Lebensweg mit den Menschen 'ganz unten': 'Ich glaube, lieber Herr, hilf meinem Unglauben'," *EvT* 47 (1987): 166-70 [9:24].

452 CRITICAL STUDIES OF THE GOSPELS

5317.309   Paul J. Achtemeier, "An Exposition of Mark 9:30-37," *Interp* 30/2 (1976): 178-83 [9:30-37].

5317.310   Susan R. Garrett, "Exodus from Bondage: Luke 9:31 and Acts. 12:1-24," *CBQ* 52 (1990): 656-80 [9:31].

5317.311   Christopher M. Tuckett, "Paul and the Synoptic Mission Discourse?" *ETL* 60 (1984): 376-81 [9:33-50].

5317.312   David Wenham, "A Note on Mark 9:33-42/Matt. 18:1-6/Luke 9:46-50," *JSNT* 14 (1982): 113-18 [9:33-42].

5317.313   Andrea Strus, "Mc. 9,33-37. Problema dell'autenticità e dell' interpretazione," *RivB* Supp. 20 (1972): 589-619 [9:33-37].

5317.314   A. Calmet, "Pour nous Contre nous? Marc 9,37-39," *BVC* 79 (1968): 52-53 [9:37-39].

5317.315   Jacques Schlosser, "L'exorciste étranger," *RevSR* 56 (1982): 229-39 [9:38-39].

5317.316   J. D. M. Derrett, "μύλος ὀνικὸς (Mk 9,42 Par)," *ZNW* 76/3 (1985): 284 [9:42].

5317.317   Helmut Koester, "Mark 9:43-47 and Quintilian 8.3.75," *HTR* 71 (1978): 151-53 [9:43-47].

5317.318   Michael Lattke, "Salz der Freundschaft in Mk 9,50c," *ZNW* 75/1 (1984): 44-59 [9:50].

5317.319   Thomas L. Brodie, "The Departure for Jerusalem (Luke 9:51-56) as a Rhetorical Imitation of Elijah's Departure for the Jordan (2 Kgs 1:1-2:6)," *B* 70/1 (1989): 96-109 [9:51-56].

5317.320   Hugh J. Blair, "Putting One's Hand to the Plough," *ET* 79 (1967-1968): 342-43 [9:62].

5317.321   Paul T. Eckel, "Mark 10:1-16," *Interp* 42/3 (1988): 285-91 [10:1-16].

5317.322   Rykle Borger, "NA26 und die neutestamentliche Textkritik," *TR* 52 (1987): 1-58 [10:1-7].

5317.323   Paul Ellingworth, "Text and Context in Mark 10:2, 10," *JSNT* 5 (1979): 63-66 [10:2].

5317.324   Klaus Berger, "Hartherzigkeit und Gottes Gesetz: Die Vorgeschichte des Antijudischen Vorwurfs in Mc 10:5," *ZNW* 61/1 (1970): 1-47 [10:5].

5317.325   T. A. Burkill, "Two into One: The Notion of Carnal Union in Mark 10:8; 1 Cor 6:16; Eph 5:31," *ZNW* 62 (1971): 115-20 [10:8].

5317.326 Bernadette J. Brooten, "Konnten Frauen im alten Judentum die Scheidung betreiben? Überlegungen zu Mk 10,11-12 und 1 Kor 7,10-11," *EvT* 42 (1982): 65-80 [10:11-12].

5317.327 Bernadette J. Brooten, "Zur Debatte über das Scheidungsrecht der jüdischen Frau," *EvT* 43 (1983): 466-78 [10:11-12].

5317.328 Ernst Bammel, "Markus 10:11f. und das Judische Eherecht," *ZNW* 61/1 (1970): 95-101 [10:11].

5317.329 Berndt Schaller, " 'Commits Adultery with Her', Not 'Against Her', Mark 10:11," *ET* 83 (1971-1972): 107-108 [10:11].

5317.330 Howard C. Kee, " 'Becoming a Child' in the Gospel of Thomas," *JBL* 82 (1963): 307-14 [10:13-16].

5317.331 Jürgen Sauer, "Der ursprünglichen 'Sitz im Leben' von Mk 10,13-16," *ZNW* 72/1 (1981): 27-50 [10:13-16].

5317.332 J. D. M. Derrett, "Why Jesus Blessed the Children," *NT* 25/1 (1983): 1-18 [10:13-16].

5317.333 Gerhard Ringshausen, "Die Kinder der Weisheit. Zur Auslegung von Mk 10:13-16 par," *ZNW* 77/1 (1986): 34-63 [10:13-16].

5317.334 L. L. Eubanks, "Mark 10:13-16," *RE* 91 (1994): 401-405 [10:13-16].

5317.335 Nikolaus Walter, "Zur Analyse von Mc 10:17-31," *ZNW* 53 (1962): 206-18 [10:17-31].

5317.336 William J. Carl, "Mark 10:17-27 (28-31)," *Interp* 33/3 (1979): 283-88 [10:17-27].

5317.337 Theodor Lorenzmeier, "Wider das Dogma von der Sündlosigkeit Jesu," *EvT* 31 (1971): 452-71 [10:17-18].

5317.338 Kenneth J. Thomas, "Liturgical Citations in the Synoptics," *NTSt* (1975-1976): 205-14 [10:19].

5317.339 S. Légasse, "Jesus a-t-il Announce le Conversion Finale d'Israel? (à propos de Marc x.23-7)," *NTSt* 10/4 (1963-1964): 480-87 [10:23-27].

5317.340 Ernest Best, "Uncomfortable Words: VII. The Camel and the Needle's Eye (Mark 10:25)," *ET* 82/3 (1970-1971): 83-89 [10:25].

5317.341 R. Köbert, "Kamel und Schiffstau: Zu Markus 10,25 (Par.) und Koran 7,40/38," *B* 53 (1972): 229-33 [10:25].

5317.342 Gerd Theissen, " 'Wir Haben Alles Verlassen' (Mc X,28).

Nachfolge und Soziale Entwurzelung in der Jüdisch-Palästinischen Gesellschaft des I. Jahr-Hunderts N. Ch.," *NT* 19/3 (1977): 161-96 [10:28].

5317.343 C. Daniel, "Les Esséniens et l'arrière-fond historique de la parabole du Bon Samaritain," *NT* 11 (1969): 71-104 [10:30-37].

5317.344 Ray McKinnis, "An Analysis of Mark 10:32-34," *NT* 18/2 (1976): 81-100 [10:32-34].

5317.345 James D. Smart, "Mark 10:35-45," *Interp* 33/3 (1979): 288-93 [10:35-45].

5317.346 André Feuillet, "La coupe et le baptême de la Passion (Mc x,35-40; cf. Mt xx,20-23; Lc xii,50)," *RB* 74 (1967): 356-91 [10:35-40].

5317.347 S. Légasse, "Approche de l'épisode préévangélique des fils de Zébédée," *NTSt* 20/2 (1973-1974): 161-77 [10:35-40].

5317.348 Georg Braumann, "Leidenskelch und Todestaufe (Mc 10:38f.)," *ZNW* 56 (1965): 178-83 [10:38].

5317.349 André Feuillet, "Le logion sur la rançon," *RSPT* 51 (1967): 365-402 [10:45].

5317.350 Paul E. Davies, "Did Jesus Die as a Martyr-Prophet?" *BRes* 19 (1974): 37-47 [10:45].

5317.351 W. J. Moulder, "The Old Testament Background and the Interpretation of Mark 10:45," *NTSt* 24/1 (1977-1978): 120-27 [10:45].

5317.352 Marco Adinolfi, "Il servo di JHWH nel logion del servizio e del riscatto (Mc. 10,45)," *BO* 21 (1979): 43-61 [10:45].

5317.353 Bernd Janowski, "Auslösung des vervirkten Lebens: Zur Geschichte und Struktur der biblischen Lösegeldvorstellung," *ZTK* 79 (1982): 25-59 [10:45].

5317.354 B. Prete, "Il logion di Gesù: 'Dare la propria vita' in riscatto per molti," *RivBib* 44 (1996): 309-35 [10:45].

5317.355 Vernon K. Robbins, "The Healing of Blind Bartimaeus (10:46-52) in the Marcan Theology," *JBL* 92 (1973): 224-43 [10:46-52].

5317.356 Ernest Lee Stoffel, "An Exposition of Mark 10:46-52," *Interp* 30/3 (1976): 288-92 [10:46-52].

5317.357 Earl S. Johnson, "Mark 10:46-52: Blind Bartimaeus," *CBQ* 40/2 (1978): 191-204 [10:46-52].

5317.358 Michael G. Steinhauser, "The Form of the Bartimaeus

Narrative (Mark 10.46-52)," *NTSt* 32/4 (1986): 583-95 [10:46-52].

5317.359 S. H. Smith, "The Function of the Son of David Tradition in Mark's Gospel," *NTSt* 42 (1996): 523-39 [10:47-48].

5317.360 R. Alan Culpepper, "Mark 10:50: Why Mention the Garment?" *JBL* 101 (1982): 131-32 [10:50].

5317.361 Michael G. Steinhauser, "Part of a 'Call Story'?" *ET* 94 (1982-1983): 204-206 [10:50].

5317.362 Georg Braumann, "Die Schuldner und die Sunderin Luk. VII.36-50," *NTSt* 10/4 (1963-1964): 487-93 [10:52].

5317.363 Marion Smith, "The Composition of Mark 11-16," *HeyJ* 22/4 (1981): 363-77 [11-16].

5317.364 Stephen Hre Kio, "A Prayer Framework in Mark 11," *BTr* 37/3 (1986): 323-28 [11].

5317.365 J. M. Ross, "Names of God: A Comment on Mark 11.3 and Parallels," *BTr* 35 (1984): 443 [11:3].

5317.366 José L. Sicre, "El uso del Salmo 118 en la Cristología Neotestamentaria," *EE* 52 (1977): 73-90 [11:9].

5317.367 Richard H. Hiers, " 'Not the Season for Figs'," *JBL* 87/4 (1968): 394-400 [11:11-14].

5317.368 Michal Wojciechowski, "Marc 11.14 et Targum Gen. 3.22: les fruits de la loi enlevés à Israël," *NTSt* 33/2 (1987): 287-89 [11:11-14].

5317.369 E. Weir, "Fruitless Fig Tree–Futile Worship," *ET* 106 (1995): 330 [11:12-21].

5317.370 Gerhard Mündelein, "Die 19 Verfluchung des Fegenbaumes (Mk. XI. 12-14)," *NTSt* 10 (1963): 88-104 [11:12-14].

5317.371 K. Romaniuk, " 'Car ce n'était pas la saison des figues . . .' (Mk 11:12-14 parr)," *ZNW* 66 (1975): 275-78 [11:12-14]

5317.372 Heinz Giesen, "Der Verdorrte Feigenbaum:Eine Symbolische Aussage? zu Mk 11,12-14.20f.," *BibZ* 20 (1976): 95-111 [11:12-14].

5317.373 Cornelis J. den Heyer, " 'Want Het was de tijd niet voor vijgen'," *GTT* 76/3 (1976): 129-40 [11:13].

5317.374 Wendy J. Cotter, "For It Was Not the Season for Figs," *CBQ* 48/1 (1986): 62-66 [11:13].

5317.375 Neill Q. Hamilton, "Temple Cleansing and Temple Bank," *JBL* 83 (1964): 365-72 [11:15-19].

5317.376   R. Alan Culpepper, "Mark 11:15-19," *Interp* 34/2 (1980): 176-81 [11:15-19].

5317.377   Victor P. Furnish, "War and Peace in the New Testament," *Interp* 38 (1984): 363-79 [11:15-19].

5317.378   Jacob Neusner, "Money-Changers in the Temple: The Mishnah's Explanation," *NTSt* 35/2 (1989): 287-90 [11:15-19].

5317.379   George W. Buchanan, "Symbolic Money-Changers in the Temple?" *NTSt* 37 (1991): 280-90 [11:15-19].

5317.380   J. D. M. Derrett, "No Stone upon Another: Leprosy and the Temple," *JSNT* 30 (1987): 3-20 [11:15-18].

5317.381   Victor Eppstein, "The Historicity of the Gospel Account of the Cleansing of the Temple (Mc 11, Mt 21, Lc 19)," *ZNW* 55 (1964): 42-58 [11:15-17].

5317.382   T. S. Dokka, "Bibelsk historie og teologisk mening: En presentasjon av Jostein Ådnas doktoravhandling," *DTT* 95 (1994): 213-20 [11:15-17].

5317.383   J. M. Ford, "Money 'Bags' in the Temple (Mark 11:16)," *B* 57 (1976): 249-53 [11:16].

5317.384   John D. Crossan, "Redaction and Citation in Mark 11:9-10 and 11:17," *BRes* 17 (1972): 33-50 [11:17].

5317.385   Craig A. Evans, "Jesus' Action in the Temple: Cleansing or Portent of Destruction?" *CBQ* 51 (1989): 237-70 [11:17].

5317.386   Barry D. Smith, "Objections to the Authenicity of Mark 11:17 Reconsidered," *WTJ* 54 (1992): 255-71 [11:17].

5317.387   J. G. Kahn, "La parabole du figuier stérile et les arbres récalcitrants de la Genèse," *NT* 13 (1971): 38-45 [11:20-24].

5317.388   Giancarlo Biguzzi, "Mc. 11,23-25 e il Pater," *RivB* 27 (1979): 57-68 [11:23-25].

5317.389   Young-Heon Lee, "Jesus und die Jüdische Autorität: eine exegetische Untersuchung zu Mk 11,27-12,12," *ZKT* 106/4 (1984): 505-506 [11:27-12:12].

5317.390   Martin Hengel, "Das Gleichnis von den Weingärtnern Mc 12:1-12 im Lichte der Zenonpapyri und der rabbinischen Gleichnisse," *ZNW* 59 (1968): 1-39 [12:1-12].

5317.391   John D. Crossan, "The Parable of the Wicked Husbandmen," *JBL* 90/4 (1971): 451-65 [12:1-12].

5317.392   Dino Merli, "La parabola dei vignaioliinfedeli (Mc. 12,1-12)," *BO* 15 (1973): 97-108 [12:1-12].

5317.393 William G. Morrice, "Murder Amongst the Vines," *ET* 97/5 (1985-1986): 145-47 [12:1-8].

5317.394 T. W. Kowalski, " 'Gleichnisse vom Wein des Königs' mit dem neutestamentlichen Winzergleichnis Mk 12, 1," *J* 50 (1994): 18-33 [12:1].

5317.395 Arthur Ogle, "What Is Left for Caesar," *TTod* 35/3 (1978): 254-64 [12:12-17].

5317.396 H. G. Klemm, "De Cencu Caesaris. Beobachtungen zu J. D. M. Derrett's Interpretation der Perikope Mk. 12:13-17 Par," *NT* 24/3 (1982): 234-54 [12:13-17].

5317.397 John D. Crossan, "Mark 12:13-17," *Interp* 37/4 (1983): 397-401 [12:13-17].

5317.398 C. H. Giblin, " 'The Things of God' in the Question Concerning Tribute to Caesar," *CBQ* 33/4 (1971): 510-27 [12:17].

5317.399 Antonio Ammassari, "Gesù ha veramente insegnato la risurrezione!" *BO* 15 (1973): 65-73 [12:18-27].

5317.400 E. Main, "Les Sadducéens et la résurrection des morts: comparaison entre Mc 12, 18-27 et Lc 20, 27-38," *RB* 103 (1996): 411-32 [12:18-27].

5317.401 J. Gerald Janzen, "Resurrection and Hermeneutics: On Exodus 3:6 in Mark 12:26," *JSNT* 23 (1985): 43-58 [12:26].

5317.402 Walter Diezinger, "Zum Liebesgebot Mk XII,28-34 und Parr," *NT* 20/2 (1978): 81-83 [12:28-34].

5317.403 George W. Hoyer, "Mark 12:28-34," *Interp* 33/3 (1979): 293-98 [12:28-34].

5317.404 N. Lohfink, "Il 'comandamento primo' nell'Antico Testamento," *BO* 7 (1965): 49-60 [12:28].

5317.405 H. W. Montefiore, "Thou Shalt Love Thy Neighbour as Thyself," *NT* 5 (1962): 157-70 [12:31].

5317.406 Gerhard Schneider, "Die Davidssohnfrage," *B* 53 (1972): 65-90 [12:35-37].

5317.407 Dennis C. Duling, "Solomon, Exorcism, and the Son of David," *HTR* 68 (1975): 235-52 [12:35-37].

5317.408 Bruce D. Chilton, "Jesus *ben David*: Reflections on the *Davidssohnfrage*," *JSNT* 14 (1982): 88-112 [12:35-37].

5317.409 W. R. G. Loader, "Christ at the Right Hand - Ps. cx. 1 in the New Testament," *NTSt* 24 (1977-1978): 199-217 [12:35-36].

5317.410　Harry T. Fleddermann, "A Warning About the Scribes (Mark 12:37b-40)," *CBQ* 44/1 (1982): 52-67 [12:37-40].

5317.411　J. D. M. Derrett, " 'Eating Up the Houses of Widows': Jesus' Comment on Lawyers?" *NT* 14/1 (1972): 1-9 [12:40].

5317.412　Elizabeth S. Malbon, "The Poor Widow in Mark and Her Poor Rich Readers," *CBQ* 53 (1991): 589-604 [12:41-44].

5317.413　R. S. Sugirtharajah, "The Widow's Mites Revalued," *ET* 103/2 (1992-1993): 42-43 [12:41-44].

5317.414　Felix Flückiger, "Die Redaktion der Zukunftsrede in Mark 13," *TZ* 26/6 (1970): 395-409 [13].

5317.415　O. Vena, "La expectavia escatológica en el Evangelio de Marcos: Análisis literario y estructural de Marcos 13," *RivB* 56 (1994): 85-101 [13].

5317.416　S. H. Smith, "The Literary Structure of Mark 11:1-12:40," *NT* 31/2 (1989): 104-24 [13:1-2].

5317.417　Jacques Dupont, "Il n'en sera pas laissé pierre sur pierre," *B* 52 (1971): 301-20 [13:2].

5317.418　Frederick W. Danker, "Double-Entendre in Mark 13:9," *NT* 10/2 (1968): 162-63 [13:9].

5317.419　Sidney G. Sowers, "The Circumstances and Recollection of the Pella Flight," *TZ* 26 (1970): 305-20 [13:14-20].

5317.420　John J. Gunther, "The Fate of the Jerusalem Church: The Flight to Pella," *TZ* 29 (1973): 81-94 [13:14-20].

5317.421　W. Sibley Towner, "An Exposition of Mark 13:24-32," *Interp* 30/3 (1976): 292-96 [13:24-32].

5317.422　M. Stowasser, "Mk 13,26f und die urchristliche Rezeption des Menschensohns: Eine Anfrage an Anton Vogtle," *BibZ* 39 (1995): 246-52 [13:26].

5317.423　Jacques Dupont, "La parabole du figuier qui bourgeonne," *RB* 75 (1968): 526-48 [13:28-29].

5317.424　John B. Trotti, "Mark 13:32-37," *Interp* 32 (1978): 410-15 [13:32-37].

5317.425　Jacques Winandy, "Le logion de l'ignorance (Mc, XIII,32; Mt., XXIV,36)," *RB* 75 (1968): 63-79 [13:32].

5317.426　H.-W. Bartsch, "Historische Erwägungen zur Leidensgeschichte," *EvT* 22 (1962): 449-59 [14-15].

5317.427　John P. Heil, "Mark 14:1-52: Narrative Structure and Reader Response," *B* 71/3 (1990): 305-32 [14:1-52].

5317.428 Frederick W. Danker, "The Literary Unity of Mark 14:1-25," *JBL* 85/4 (1966): 467-72 [14:1-25].

5317.429 Stephen C. Barton, "Mark as Narrative: The Story of the Anointing Woman (Mark 14:3-9)," *ET* 102 (1990-1991): 230-34 [14:3-9].

5317.430 Tjitze Baarda, "Markus 14:11: ἐπηγγείλαντο: 'Bron' or 'Redaktie'?" *GTT* 73 (1973): 65-75 [14:11].

5317.431 Stanislas Dockx, "Le récit du repas pascal. Marc 14,17-26," *B* 46 (1965): 445-53 [14:17-26].

5317.432 J.-M. van Cangh, "Le déroulement primitif de la Cène (Mc 14, 18-26 et par.)," *RB* 102 (1995): 193-225 [14:18-26].

5317.433 William J. Carl, "Mark 14:22-25," *Interp* 39/3 (1985): 296-301 [14:22-25].

5317.434 B. E. Thiering, " 'Breaking of Bread' and 'Harvest' in Mark's Gospel," *NT* 12 (1970): 1-12 [14:22].

5317.435 Joachim Jeremias, " 'This is My Body'," *ET* 83 (1971-1972): 196-203 [14:22].

5317.436 J. A. Emerton, "Mark 14:24 and the Targum to the Psalter," *JTS* 15 (1964): 58-59 [14:24].

5317.437 P. Maurice Casey, "No Cannibals at Passover," *Th* 96 (1993): 199-205 [14:24].

5317.438 Helmut Merklein, "Erwägungen zur überlieferungsgeschichte der Neutestamentlichen abendmalstraditionen," *BibZ* 21 (1977): 88-101; 235-44 [14:25].

5317.439 Max Wilcox, "The Denial Sequence in Mark xiv.26-31, 66-72," *NTSt* 17 (1970-1971): 426-36 [14:26-31].

5317.440 John Ellington, "The Translation of ὑμνέω, 'Sing a Hymn' in Mark 14:26 and Matthew 26:30," *BTr* 30 (1979): 445-46 [14:26].

5317.441 Thorwald Lorenzen, "Ist der Auferstandene in Galiläa erschienen? Bemerkungen zu einem Aufsatz von B. Steinseifer," *ZNW* 64 (1973): 209-21 [14:27-28].

5317.442 J.-M. van Cangh, "La Galilée dans l'évangile de Marc: un lieu théologique?" *RB* 79 (1972): 59-75 [14:28].

5317.443 Robert H. Stein, "A Short Note on Mark 14:28 and 16:7," *NTSt* 20 (1973-1974): 445-52 [14:28].

5317.444 David Brady, "The Alarm to Peter in Mark's Gospel," *JSNT* 4 (1979): 42-57 [14:30].

5317.445 M. Öhler, "Der zweimalige Hahnschrei der Markuspassion: Zur Textüberlieferung von Mk 14,30.68.72," *ZNW* 85 (1994): 145-50 [14:30].

5317.446 Werner H. Kelber, "Mark 14:32-42: Gethsemane. Passion Christology and Discipleship Failure," *ZNW* 63 (1972): 166-87 [14:32-42].

5317.447 Werner Mohn, "Gethsemane (Mk 14:32-42)," *ZNW* 64/3 (1973): 195-208 [14:32-42].

5317.448 Karen E. Smith, "Mark 14:32-42," *RE* 88 (1991): 433-37 [14:32-42].

5317.449 Gerhard Schneider, "Die Verhaftung Jesu: Traditionsgeschichte von Mk 14:43-52," *ZNW* 63/3 (1972): 188-209 [14:43-52].

5317.450 S. Légasse, "L'arrestation de Jésus d'après Maec 14,43-52," *ETL* 68 (1993): 241-47 [14:43-52].

5317.451 B. T. Viviano, "The High Priest's Servant's Ear: Mark 14:47," *RB* 96 (1989): 71-80 [14:47].

5317.452 Robin Scroggs and Kent I. Groff, "Baptism in Mark: Dying and Rising with Christ," *JBL* 92 (1973): 531-48 [14:51-52].

5317.453 Harry T. Fleddermann, "The Flight of a Naked Young Man (Mark 14:51-52)," *CBQ* 41/3 (1979): 412-18 [14:51-52].

5317.454 Albert Vanhoye, "La fuite du jeune homme nu (Mc 14,51-52)," *B* 52 (1971): 401-406 [14:51-52].

5317.455 Ernst L. Schnellbächer, "Das Rätsel des νεανίσκος bei Markus," *ZNW* 73/1 (1982): 127-35 [14:51].

5317.456 Mary Ann Beavis, "The Trial before the Sanhedrin (Mark 14:53-65): Reader Response and Greco-Roman Readers," *CBQ* 49 (1987): 581-96 [14:53-65].

5317.457 Paul Winter, "Markus 14:53b., 55-56: Ein Geblide des Evangelisten," *ZNW* 53 (1962): 260-63 [14:53].

5317.458 Josef Ernst, "Noch einmal: Die Verleugnung Jesu durch Petrus," *C* 30 (1976): 207-26 [14:54, 66-72].

5317.459 Gerhard Schneider, "Gab es Eine Vorsynoptische Szene 'Jesus vor dem Synedrium'?" *NT* 12/1 (1970): 22-39 [14:55-64].

5317.460 Dieter Lührmann, "Markus 14:55-64: Christologie und Zerstörung des Tempels im Markusevangelium," *NTSt* 27 (1980-1981): 457-74 [14:55-64].

5317.461 Giancarlo Biguzzi, "Mc. 14,58: un tempio ἀχειροποίητον

ἀχειροποίητον," *RivB* 26 (1978): 225-40 [14:58].

5317.462 B. Prete, "Formazione e storicità del detto di Gesù sul tempio secondo Mc. 14,58," *BO* 27 (1985): 3-16 [14:58].

5317.463 Klaus Berger, "Der 'brutale' Jesus. Gewaltsames in Wirken und Verküundigung Jesu," *BK* 51 (1996): 119-27 [14:58].

5317.464 J. C. O'Neill, "The Silence of Jesus," *NTSt* 15/2 (1968-1969): 153-69 [14:61].

5317.465 A. M. Goldberg, "Sitzend zur Rechten der Kraft. Zur Gottesbezeichnung Gebura in der frühen rabbinischen Literatur," *BibZ* 8 (1964): 284-93 [14:62].

5317.466 F. H. Borsch, "Mark 14:62 and I Enoch 62:5," *NTSt* 14 (1967-1968): 565-67 [14:62].

5317.467 Renatus Kempthorne, "The Marcan Text of Jesus' Answer to the High Priest (Mark 14:62)," *NT* 19/3 (1977): 197-208 [14:62].

5317.468 Antonio Vargas-Machuca, "¿Por qué condenaron a muerte a Jesús de Nazaret?" *EE* 54 (1979): 441-70 [14.62].

5317.469 J. D. M. Derrett, "The Reason for the Cock-Crowings," *NTSt* 29 (1983): 142-44 [14:68-72].

5317.470 G. M. Lee, "Mark 14,72: *epibalōn eklaien*," *B* 53 (1972): 411-12 [14:72].

5317.471 Robert L. Merritt, "Jesus Barabbas and the Paschal Pardon," *JBL* 104 (1985): 57-68 [15:7-15].

5317.472 G. M. Lee, "Mark xv.8," *NT* 20 (1978): 74 [15:8].

5317.473 Jack T. Sanders, "Tradition and Redaction in Luke xv.11-32," *NTSt* 15 (1968-1969): 433-38 [15:11-32].

5317.474 Pierre Grelot, "Le père et ses deux fils: Luke 15:11-32," *RB* 84 (1977): 321-48, 538-65 [15:11-32].

5317.475 R. G. Forrest, "I Believe in the Forgiveness of Sins," *ET* 92 (1980-1981): 18-19 [15:11-24].

5317.476 Klaus Berger, "Zum Problem der Messianität Jesu," *ZTK* 71 (1974): 1-30 [15:18].

5317.477 G. M. Lee, "Mark 15:21: 'The Father of Alexander and Rufus'," *NT* 17/4 (1975): 303 [15:21].

5317.478 Michal Wojciechowski, "Le Nazireat et la Passion (Mc 14,25a; 15,23)," *B* 65/1 (1984): 94-96 [15:23].

5317.479 Matthew Mahoney, "A New Look at 'The Third Hour' of Mark 15:25," *CBQ* 28 (1966): 292-99 [15:25].

5317.480 Jack D. Kingsbury, "The Significance of the Cross within Mark's Story," *Interp* 47 (1993): 370-79 [15:27-39].

5317.481 M. Josuttis, "Die permanente Passion. Predigt über Markus 15,33-39," *EvT* 38 (1978): 160-63 [15:33-39].

5317.482 B. Rinaldi, "Ora terza, sesta, nona, le ore della Passione di Cristo," *BO* 23 (1981): 86 [15:33-34].

5317.483 Christoph Burchard, "Markus 15,34," *ZNW* 74/1 (1983): 1-11 [15:34].

5317.484 David Atkinson, "A Cry of Faith," *ET* 96 (1984-1985): 146-47 [15:34].

5317.485 Kent E. Brower, "Elijah in the Markan Passion Narrative," *JSNT* 18 (1983): 85-101 [15:35-39].

5317.486 Harry L. Chronis, "The Torn Veil: Cultus and Christology in Mark 15:37-39," *JBL* 101/1 (1982): 97-114 [15:37-39].

5317.487 M. de Jonge, "De berichten over het scheuren van het voorhangsel bij Jezus' dood in de synoptische evangeliën," *NTT* 21 (1966-1967): 90-114 [15:38].

5317.488 S. Légasse, "Les voiles du Temple de Jérusalem," *RB* 87 (1980): 560-89 [15:38].

5317.489 S. Motyer, "The Rending of the Veil: A Markan Pentecost?" *NTSt* 33/1 (1987): 155-57 [15:38].

5317.490 David Ulansey, "The Heavenly Veil Torn: Mark's Cosmic Inclusio [linking 1:10 and 15:38]," *JBL* 110 (1991):123-25 [15:38].

5317.491 J. Ramsey Michaels, "The Centurion's Confession and the Spear Thrust," *CBQ* 29 (1967): 102-109 [15:39].

5317.492 P. H. Bligh, "A Note on υἱὸς θεοῦ in Mark 15:39," *ET* 80 (1968-1969): 51-53 [15:39].

5317.493 T. F. Glasson, "Mark 15:39: The Son of God," *ET* 80 (1968-1969): 286 [15:39].

5317.494 Harold A. Guy, "Son of God in Mark 15:39," *ET* 81 (1969-1970): 151 [15:39].

5317.495 Klemens Stock, "Das Bekenntnis des Centurio. Mk 15,39 im Rahmen des Markusevangeliums," *ZKT* 100 (1978): 289-301 [15:39].

5317.496 Earl S. Johnson, "Is Mark 15:39 the Key to Mark's Christology?" *JSNT* 31 (1987): 3-22 [15:39].

5317.497 Ernst L. Schnellbächer, "Sachgemässe Schriftauslegung," *NT* 30 (1988): 114-31 [15:39].

5317.498 L. Schottroff, "Maria Magdalena und die Frauen am Grabe Jesu," *EvT* 42 (1982): 3-25 [15:40-16:8].

5317.499 Corina Combet-Galland, "Qui roulera la peur? Finales d'évangile et figures de lecteur (a partir du chapitre 16 de l'Evangile de Marc)," *TR* 65/2 (1990): 171-89 [16].

5317.500 Josef A. Sint, "Die Auferstehung Jesu in der Verkündigung der Urgemeinde," *ZKT* 84 (1962): 129-51 [16:1-8].

5317.501 E. Galbiati, "È risorto, non è qui (Marco 16,1-8)," *BO* 5 (1963): 67-72 [16:1-8].

5317.502 Z. C. Hodges, "The Women and the Empty Tomb," *BS* 123 (1966): 301-309 [16:1-8].

5317.503 Robert Smith, "New and Old in Mark 16:1-8," *CTM* 43/8 (1972): 518-27 [16:1-8].

5317.504 Peter Stuhlmacher, " 'Kritischer müssten mir die Historisch-Kritischen sein!'," *TQ* 3 (1973): 244-51 [16:1-8].

5317.505 Antonio Ammassari, "Il racconto degli awenimenti della mattina di Pasqua secondo Marco 16,1-8," *BO* 16 (1974): 49-64 [16:1-8].

5317.506 Heinz-Wolfgang Kuhn, "Predigt über Markus 16,1-8," *EvT* 38 (1978): 155-60 [16:1-8].

5317.507 F.-J. Niemann, "Die Erzählung vom leeren Grab bei Markus," *ZKT* 101 (1979): 188-99 [16:1-8].

5317.508 Andreas Lindemann, "Die Osterbotschaf des Markus. Zur Theologischen Interpretation von Mark 16.1-8," *NTSt* 26/3 (1979-1980): 298-17 [16:1-8].

5317.509 Henning Paulsen, "Mark 16:1-8," *NT* 22/2 (1980): 138-75 [16:1-8].

5317.510 John S. Kloppenborg, "The Dishonoured Master (Luke 16:1-8a)," *B* 70/4 (1989): 474-95 [16:1-8].

5317.511 W. R. G. Loader, "Jesus and the Rogue in Luke 16:1-8a: The Parable of the Unjust Steward," *RB* 96 (1989): 518-32 [16:1-8].

5317.512 J. D. Hester, "Dramatic Inconclusion: Irony and the Narrative Rhetoric of the Ending of Mark," *JSNT* 57 (1995): 61-86 [16:1-8].

5317.513 D. W. Palmer, "The Origin, Form, and Purpose of Mark XVI.4 in Codex Bobbiensis," *JTS* 27/1 (1976): 113-22

[16:4].

5317.514 J. H. McIndoe, "The Young Man at the Tomb," *ET* 80 (1968-1969): 125 [16:5-7].

5317.515 Allan K. Jenkins, "Young Man or Angel?" *ET* 94/8 (1982-1983): 237-40 [16:5].

5317.516 Andrew T. Lincoln, "The Promise and the Failure: Mark 16:7-8," *JBL* 108/2 (1989): 283-300 [16:7-8].

5317.517 B. M. F. van Iersel, " 'To Galilee' or 'in Galilee' in Mark 14:28 and 16:7?" *ETL* 58 (1982): 365-70 [16:7].

5317.518 Jesús Luzarraga, "Retraducción semítica de φοβέομαι en Mc 16,8," *B* 50 (1969): 497-510 [16:8].

5317.519 Robert P. Meye, "Mark 16:8: The Ending of Mark's Gospel," *BRes* 15 (1969): 33-43 [16:8].

5317.520 P. W. van der Horst, "Can a Book End with γάρ? A Note On Mark 16:8," *JTS* 23 (1972): 121-24 [16:8].

5317.521 Thomas E. Boomershine, "Mark 16:8 and the Apostolic Commission," *JBL* 100/2 (1981): 225-39 [16:8].

5317.522 Thomas E. Boomershine and Gilbert L. Bartholomew, "The Narrative Technique of Mark 16:8," *JBL* 100/2 (1981): 213-23 [16:8].

5317.523 J. K. Elliott, "The Text and Language of the Endings to Mark's Gospel," *TZ* 27 (1971): 255-62 [16:9-20].

5317.524 G. W. Trompf, "The *Markusschluß* in Recent Research," *ABR* 21 (1973): 15-26 [16:9-20].

5317.525 Félix Asensio, "Trasfondo profético-evangélico πᾶσα ἐξουσία de la 'Gran Mision'," *EB* 27 (1968): 27-48 [16:14-20].

5317.526 Dale C. Allison, "Paul and the Missionary Discourse," *ETL* 61 (1985): 369-75 [16:14-18].

4. Critical and Exegetical Studies of Passages in Luke

5318.   F. C. Conybeare, "Ein Zeugnis Ephräms über das Fehlen von c. I und 2 im Texte des Lucas," *ZNW* 3 (1902): 192-97.

5319.   Ludwig Köhler, "Zu den kanonischen Geburts- und Jugendgeschichten Jesu," *STZ* 19 (1902): 215-27 [Lk. 1-2; Mt. 1-2].

5320.   H. Zimmermann, "Evangelium des Lukas Kap. 1 u. 2. Ein Versuch der Vermittlung zwischen Hilgenfeld und Harnack," *TSK* 76 (1903): 247-90.

5321. Friedrich Spitta, "Die chronologischen Notizen und die Hymnen in Lc 1. u. 2.," *ZNW* 7 (1906): 281-317.

5322. D. Völter, "Das angebliche Zeugnis Ephräms über das Fehlen von c. 1 und 2 im Texte des Lukas," *ZNW* 10 (1909): 177-80.

5323. Fr. Herklotz, "Zum Zeugnisse Ephräms über Lk. 1 und 2," *BibZ* 8 (1910): 387-88.

5324. R. A. Aytoun, "The Ten Lucan Hymns of the Nativity in their Original Language," *JTS* 18 (1916-1917): 274-88 [Lk. 1-2].

5325. J. Ridderbos, "Maria's Heilsverwachting," *GTT* 19 (1918-1919): 234-43 [Lk. 1-2].

5326. Emmanuele a S. Marco, "Bonorum Messianicorum conspectus," *VD* 18 (1938): 313-18, 343-49.

5327. Howard Tillman Kuist, "Sources of Power in the Nativity Hymns; An Exposition of Luke 1 and 2," *Interp* 2 (1948): 288-98.

5328. Paul Winter, "The Cultural Background of the Narrative in Luke i and ii," *JQR* 45 (1954-1955): 159-67, 230-42.

5329. Paul Winter, "Some Observations on the Language in the Birth and Infancy Stories of the Third Gospel," *NTSt* 1 (1954-1955): 111-58.

5330. Paul Winter, "Two Notes on Luke I, II With Regard to the Theory of 'Imitation Hebraisms'," *ST* 7 (1954): 158-65.

5331. N. Turner, "The Relation of Luke I and II to Hebraic Sources and to the Rest of Luke-Acts," *NTSt* 2 (1955- 1956): 100-50.

5332. R. Laurentin, "Traces d'allusions étymologiques en Luc 1-2," *B* 37 (1956): 435-56; 38 (1957): 1-23.

5333. Paul Winter, " 'Nazareth' and 'Jerusalem' in Luke chs. 1 and 2," *NTSt* 3 (1956-1957): 136-42.

5334. Salvador Muñoz Iglesias, "Estructura y teologia de Lucas i-ii," *EB* 17 (1958): 101-107.

5335. Paul Winter, "On the Margin of Luke I, II," *ST* 12 (1958): 103-107.

5336. Ae. De Roover, "De evangelii infantiae (Lc I-II) chronologia," *VD* 36 (1958): 65-82.

5337. J. Gresham Machen, "The Hymns of the First Chapter of Luke," *PTR* 10 (1912): 1-38, 212-77.

5338. Paul Winter, "The Proto-Source of Luke i," *NT* 1 (1956):

184-99.

5339.   Pierre Benoit, "L'enfance de Jean-Baptiste selon Luc I," *NTSt* 3 (1956-1957): 169-94.

5340.   Dr. Aberle, "Exegetische Studien," *TQ* 45 (1863): 84-134 [Lk. 1:1-4].

5341.   Lemuel S. Potwin, "Does the Preface to Luke's Gospel belong also to the Acts?" *BS* 38 (1881): 328-32.

5342.   A. Hilgenfeld, "Prolegomena zum Lucas-Evangelium," *ZWT* 40 (1897): 411-32 [Lk. 1:1-4].

5343.   A. Hilgenfeld, "Das Vorwort des dritten Evangelisten (Luc. 1, 1-4)," *ZWT* 44 (1901): 1-10.

5344.   A. T. Robertson, "The Implications in Luke's Preface," *ET* 35 (1923-1924): 319-21 [Lk. 1:1-4].

5345.   James H. Ropes, "St. Luke's Preface; ἀσφάλεια and παρακολουθεῖν," *JTS* 25 (1923-1924): 67-71.

5346.   F. H. Colson, "Notes on St. Luke's Preface, suggested by reading the second volume of Foakes-Jackson and Lake's *Beginnings of Christianity*," *JTS* 24 (1922-1923): 300- 309.

5347.   A. M. Pope, "The Key Word of the Lucan Narratives," *CJRT* 3 (1926): 44-52 [Lk. 1:1-4; πληροφορέω].

5348.   M. Devoldere, "Le prologue du troisième évangile," *NRT* 56 (1929): 714-19.

5349.   U. Holzmeister, "Officium exegetae iuxta prologum S. Lucae (1, 1-4)," *VD* 10 (1930): 6-9.

5350.   Vinzenz Hartl, "Zur synoptischen Frage. Schliesst Lukas durch 1, 1-3 die Benutzung des Matthäus aus?" *BibZ* 13 (1925): 334-37.

5351.   J. B. Bauer, "πολλοί, Luk. i, 1," *NT* 4 (1960): 263-66.

5352.   G. M. Lee, "Luke i. 1," *ET* 66 (1954-1955): 350.

5353.   W. A. Lambert, "Luke i: 2. An Exegetical Study," *LCR* 18 (1899): 712-25.

5354.   Edward White, "Questions on the Logos in St. Luke, Chap. i ver. 2," *ET* 4 (1892-1893): 129-30.

5355.   Eb. Nestle, "Luke i. 3," *ET* 13 (1901-1902): 139-40.

5356.   W. C. van Unnik, "Opmerking over het doel van Lucas' geschiedwerk (Luc. 1:4)," *NedTT* 9 (1954-1955): 323-31.

5357.   Friedrich Vogel, "Zu Luk. 1, 4," *NKZ* 44 (1933): 203-205.

5358.   A. Hilgenfeld, "Die Geburts- und Kindheitsgeschichte Jesu

Luc. 1, 5-2, 52," *ZWT* 44 (1901): 177-235.

5359.   H. L. MacNeill, "The *Sitz im Leben* of Luke 1. 5-2. 20," *JBL* 65 (1946): 123-30.

5360.   W. M. Ramsay, "Luke's Narrative of the Birth of Christ," *Exp* 8th ser. 4 (1912): 385-407, 481-507.

5361.   F. P. Badham, "The Integrity of Luke 1, 5-11," *ET* 8 (1896-1897): 116-19.

5362.   Aug. Thenn, "Locus Lucaneus 1, 6 ab Origine graece explanatus," *ZWT* 35 (1892): 105-108.

5363.   Aug. Thenn, "Locus Lucaneus 1, 22-23 ab Origine graece explanatus," *ZWT* 36² (1893): 274-80.

5364.   Paul Winter, "῞Οτι Recitativum in Luke 1, 25, 61; 11, 23," *HTR* 48 (1955): 213-16.

5365.   J. Gresham Machen, "The Integrity of the Lucan Narrative of the Annunciation," *PTR* 25 (1927): 529-86 [Lk. 1:26-38].

5366.   Jean-Paul Audet, "L'annonce à Marie," *RB* 63 (1956): 346-74 [Lk. 1:26-38].

5367.   Michel Allard, "L'annonce à Marie et les annonces de naissances miraculeuses de l'Ancien Testament," *NRT* 78 (1956): 730-33.

5368.   Simon Landersdorfer, "Bemerkungen zu Lk. 1, 26-38," *BibZ* 7 (1909): 30-48.

5369.   S. del Páramo, "La anunciación de la Virgen. Reparos exegéticos y doctrinales a una reciente interpretación," *EB* 16 (1957): 161-85.

5370.   Paul Joüon, "L'annonciation (Luc 1, 26-38)," *NRT* 66 (1939): 793-98.

5371.   C. Beckermann, "Et nomen virginis Maria (Lc. 1. 27)," *VD* 1 (1921): 130-36.

5372.   Anonymous, "Studies in Texts," *Th* 23 (1931): 42-43 [Lk. 1:27].

5373.   S. P. Canisius, "Historia evangelica Annuntiationis et Communio Paschalis," *VD* 9 (1929): 65-70 [Lk. 1:28-31].

5374.   Juan Leal, "El saludo del Angel a la Virgen," *CB* 11 (1954): 293-301 [Lk. 1:28].

5375.   W. Schwarz, "Examples of Luther's Biblical Translation," *JTS* N.S. 6 (1955): 199-209 [Lk. 1:28].

5376.   David Gonzálo Maeso, "Exégesis lingüística del Avemaría,"

CB 11 (1954): 302-19 [Lk. 1:28].

5377. Pedro Franguesa, "Sugerencias en torno a Luc. 1, 28," *CB* 11 (1954): 320-32.

5378. U. Holzmeister, " 'Dominus tecum' (Lc. 1, 28)," *VD* 23 (1943): 232-37, 257-62.

5379. Julio Fantini, "κεχαριτωμένη (Luc. 1, 28)," *S* 1 (1954): 760-63.

5380. A. Hilgenfeld, "Die Geburt Jesu aus der Jungfrau in dem Lucas-Evangelium," *ZWT* 44 (1901): 313-17 [Lk. 1:31 ff.; 3:23].

5381. H. J. Vogels, "Zur Textgeschichte von Lc 1. 34 ff.," *ZNW* 43 (1950-1951): 256-60.

5382. F. E. Gigot, "The Virgin Birth in St. Luke's Gospel," *ITQ* 8 (1913): 123-43, 412-34 [Lk. 1:34-35].

5383. B. Brinkmann, "Die Jungfrauengeburt und das Lukas-evangelium," *B* 34 (1953): 327-32 [Lk. 1:34, 35].

5384. J. M. Pfättisch, "Zu Lukas 1, 34-35," *BibZ* 6 (1908): 364-77.

5385. Adolf Harnack, "Zu Lc 1, 34-35," *ZNW* 2 (1901): 53-57.

5386. K. L. Schmidt, "Die jungfräuliche Geburt Jesu Christi," *TB* 14 (1935): 289-97 [Lk. 1:34-35].

5387. U. Holzmeister, " 'Quomodo fiet istud, quoniam virum non cognosco?' (Lc 1. 34)," *VD* 19 (1939): 70-75.

5388. Nicolás López Martínez, "Porque no conozco varón," *CB* 11 (1954): 333-35 [Lk. 1:34].

5389. C. P. Ceroke, "Luke 1, 34 and Mary's Virginity," *CBQ* 19 (1957): 329-42.

5390. Marciano Villanueva, "Nueva controversia en torno al voto de virginidad de Nuestra Señora," *EB* 16 (1957): 307-28 [Lk. 1:34].

5391. J. B. Bauer, "Monstra te esse matrem, Virgo singularis! Zur Diskussion um Lk. 1, 34," *MTZ* 9 (1958): 124-35.

5392. Mariano Deikhans, "Lc 1, 34 e a virginidade de Maria Ssma," *REB* 20 (1960): 29-35.

5393. Josef Gewiess, "Die Marienfrage Lk. 1, 34," *BibZ* 5 (1961): 221-54.

5394. M.-J. Lagrange, "La conception surnaturelle du Christ d'après Saint Luc," *RB* 23 (1914): 60-71, 188-208 [Lk.

1:35].

5395.	Ioseph M. Bover, "Quod nascetur (ex te) sanctum vocabitur filius Dei," *B* 1 (1920): 92-94 [Lk. 1:35].

5396.	C. J. Ellicott, "St. Luke and the Incarnation," *ET* 12 (1900-1901): 222-24 [Lk. 1:35].

5397.	Johannes Hehn and Arthur Allgeier, "Ἐπισκιάζειν Lk. 1, 35," *BibZ* 14 (1916-1917): 147-52, 338-43.

5398.	Charles C. Torrey, "Medina and πόλις, and Luke 1. 39," *HTR* 17 (1924): 83-91.

5399.	J. F. Springer, "No Mistranslation in Luke 1:39," *ATR* 10 (1927-1928): 37-46.

5400.	Benjamin B. Warfield, "Messianic Psalms of the New Testament (Lk i. 42-45; 45-55; 68-79; ii. 29-32)," *Exp* 3rd ser., 2 (1885): 301-309, 321-27.

5401.	Paul Haupt, "Magnificat and Benedictus," *AJP* 40 (1919): 64-75 [Lk. 1:46-55, 67-79].

5402.	John V. Grier Koontz, "Mary's Magnificat," *BS* 116 (1959): 336-49 [Lk. 1:46-58].

5403.	A. Durand, "L'origine du *Magnificat*," *RB* 7 (1898): 74-77 [Lk. 1:46-55].

5404.	J. H. Bernard, "The Magnificat," *Exp* 7th ser. 3 (1907): 193-206 [Lk. 1:46-55].

5405.	H. A. Köstlin, "Das Magnificat Lc 1, 46-55 Lobgesang der Maria oder der Elisabeth?" *ZNW* 3 (1902): 142-45.

5406.	F. C. Burkitt, "Who Spoke the *Magnificat*?" *JTS* 7 (1905-1906): 220-27 [Elizabeth].

5407.	Thomas Barns, "The *Magnificat* in Niceta of Remesiana and Cyril of Jerusalem," *JTS* 7 (1905-1906): 449-53.

5408.	C. W. Emmet, "Should the Magnificat be Ascribed to Elisabeth?" *Exp* 7th ser. 8 (1909): 521-29 [No].

5409.	J. Rendel Harris, "Mary or Elisabeth?" *ET* 41 (1929-1930): 266-67 [Lk 1:46-55].

5410.	J. Rendel Harris, "Again the Magnificat," *ET* 42 (1930-1931): 188-90.

5411.	Irving F. Wood, "τῆς δούλης in the Magnificat, Luke i. 48," *JBL* 21 (1902): 48-50.

5412.	J. F. Springer, "St. Luke 1:64 and 39," *ATR* 4 (1921-1922): 332-37.

5413.   J. M. Bover, " 'Mariae' nomen in cantico Zechariae," *VD* 4 (1924): 133-34 [Lk. 1:67-79].

5414.   P. Vielhauer, "Das Benedictus des Zacharias (Luk. 1, 68-79)," *ZTK* N.F. 49 (1952): 266-72.

5415.   Adolf Jacobi, "ἀνατολὴ ἐξ ὕψους," *ZNW* 20 (1921): 205-14 [Lk. 1:78].

5416.   M.-J. Lagrange, "Le récit de l'enfance dans saint Luc," *RB* 4 (1895): 160-85 [Lk. 2].

5417.   C. T. Diomont, "The Source of St. Luke's Gospel of the Infancy," *ET* 11 (1899-1900): 378-79 [Lk. 2].

5418.   W. M. Ramsay, "Professor Harnack on Luke 2," *Exp* 7th ser. 3 (1907): 97-124.

5419.   Vincent Taylor, "Is the Lukan Narrative of the Birth of Christ a Prophecy?" *ET* 30 (1918-1919): 377-78.

5420.   Paul Winter, "The Main Literary Problem of the Lucan Infancy Story," *VT* 28 (1957): 117-22 [Lk. 2].

5421.   Alfonso Rivera, "Glosas exegéticas al misterio de navidad," *CB* 4 (1947): 351-54 [Lk. 2:1 ff.].

5422.   J. W. Doeve, "Het 'teken' in Lucas 2," *VT* 25 (1954): 55-59.

5423.   Paul Winter, "The Main Literary Problem of the Lucan Infancy Story," *ATR* 40 (1958): 257-64 [Lk. 2].

5424.   R. Galdos, "Evangelica de Christi nativitate narratio (Lc. 2, 1-20)," *VD* 8 (1928): 11-16.

5425.   P. G. Kunst, "Kribbe of korfje," *GTT* 40 (1939): 509-18 [Lk. 2:1-20].

5426.   James H. Moulton, "St. Luke and the Census," *ET* 19 (1907-1908): 40-41 [Lk. 2:1-5].

5427.   A. G. Roos, "Volkstelling in Egypte en Lk. 2, 1-5," *NTS* 5 (1922): 1-7.

5428.   Anonymous, "Il censo di San Luca e l'iscrizione di Quirinio," *Bes* 1 (1896): 580-96 [Lk. 2:1-2].

5429.   R. D. C. Robbins, "A Vindication of Luke Chap. ii. 1, 2. When did the Taxing Spoken of in These Verses Take Place?" *BS* 1 (1844): 443-64.

5430.   Hermann Dieckmann, "Kaisernamen und Kaiser-bezeichnung bei Lukas," *ZKT* 43 (1919): 213-34 [Lk. 2:1; 3:1; 20:22-25; 23:2].

5431.   Theodore D. Woolsey, "On the Latin Equivalent of the Name in Luke ii. 2, Translated Cyrenius," *BS* 35 (1878): 499-513.

5432. A. T. Robertson, "The Romance of the Census in Luke's Gospel," *BR* 5 (1920): 491-506 [Lk. 2:2].

5433. W. Lodder, "Nieuw licht over 'n oude kwestic?" *NTS* 13 (1930): 82-86 [Lk. 2:2].

5434. Salvador Muñoz Iglesias, "Herodes y el censo de Quirino," *CB* 3 (1946): 25-30 [Lk. 2:2].

5435. W. J. de Wilde, "Het offer 'aangenaam om te verzoenen," *NTS* 22 (1939): 192-99 [Lk. 2:4].

5436. U. Holzmeister, "Cur S. Ioseph iter Bethlehemiticum susceperit et Maria eum comitata sit (Lc. 2, 4)," *VD* 22 (1942): 263-70.

5437. A. Wabnitz, "Observations sur Luc 2, 7; Jésus est-il né dans une étable?" *RTQR* 10 (1901): 262-67.

5438. Dionisio Yubero, "Una opinión original del 'Brocense' sobre Luc 2:7," *CB* 11 (1954): 3-6.

5439. J.-B. Frey, "La signification du terme πρωτότοκος d'après une inscription juive," *B* 11 (1930): 373-90 [Lk. 2:7].

5440. Karl Kastner, "Zu Lk. 2, 7," *TQ* 98 (1916): 184-87.

5441. M. Miguens, "In una mangiatoia, perchè non c'era posto," *BO* 2 (1960): 193-98 [Lk. 2:7].

5442. Eb. Nestle, "The Shepherds of Bethlehem," *ET* 17 (1905-1906): 430-31 [Lk. 2:8-20].

5443. Aug. Thenn, "Locus Lucaneus 2, 8-16 ab Origine graece explanatus," *ZWT* 34 (1891): 483-87.

5444. Paul Winter, "Lc 2, 11 χριστὸς κύριος oder χριστὸς κυρίου?" *ZNW* 49 (1958): 67-75.

5445. A. van Veldhuizen, "De kribbe van Bethlehem," *NTS* 13 (1930): 175-78.

5446. Georg Aicher, "Zu Gloria (Lk. 2, 14)," *BibZ* 5 (1907): 381-91.

5447. J. Sickenberger, "Zu Lk. 2, 14," *BibZ* 5 (1907): 402-403.

5448. G. Wohlenberg, "Zur Harnackschen Auffassung von Luk. 2, 14 (Hymnus angelicus)," *NKZ* 27 (1916): 812-26.

5449. James H. Ropes, "Good Will Toward Men (Luke 2:14)," *HTR* 10 (1917): 52-56.

5450. A. Merk, "Der Engelgesang Lukas 2,14 bei den Syrern," *ZKT* 49 (1925): 625-28.

5451. Thomas Shearer Duncan, "The Rendering of Luke 2, 14," *BS* 84 (1927): 340-41.

5452. Th. Vargha, " 'Gloria in altissimis Deo' (Lc. 2, 14)," *VD* 8 (1928): 370-73.

5453. Joachim Jeremias, "῎Ανθρωποι εὐδοκίας (Lc 2, 14)," *ZNW* 28 (1929): 13-20.

5454. Gerhard von Rad, "Noch einmal Lc 2, 14 ἄνθρωποι εὐδοκίας," *ZNW* 29 (1930): 111-15.

5455. Fr. Herklotz, "Zu Lk. 2, 14," *ZKT* 58 (1934): 113-14.

5456. Paul Joüon, "ἐν ἀνθρώποις εὐδοκίας," *RSR* 24 (1934): 86-95 [Lk. 2:14].

5457. Joseph Wobbe, "Das Gloria (Lk. 2, 14)," *BibZ* 22 (1934): 118-52, 224-45; 23 (1935-1936): 358-64.

5458. C. C. Tarelli, "An Interpretation of Luke 2, 14," *ET* 48 (1936-1937): 332.

5459. Robert A. Moody, " 'Men of Good-Will," *ET* 50 (1938-1939): 563 [Lk. 2:14].

5460. A. Lukyn Williams, " 'Glory to God in the highest' And on earth peace among men of good-will' (Luke 2, 14)," *ET* 50 (1938-1939): 283-84.

5461. J. A. van Nieuwenhuijzen, "Een exegese van de Engelenzang Lukas 2, 14," *VT* 15 (1943): 49-56.

5462. José M. Bover, " 'Pax hominibus bonae voluntatis' (Lc. 2, 14)," *EB* 7 (1948): 441-49.

5463. C.-H. Hunzinger, "Neues Licht auf Lc 2, 14 ἄνθρωπος εὐδοκίας," *ZNW* 44 (1952-1953): 85-90.

5464. S. del Páramo, "La paz de Cristo en el Nuevo Testamento," *EE* 27 (1953): 5-20 [Lk. 2:14].

5465. E. V., "Pax hominibus bonae voluntatis," *B* 34 (1953): 427-29 [Lk. 2:14].

5466. C.-H. Hunzinger, "Ein weiterer Beleg zu Lc 2, 14 ἄνθρωπος εὐδοκίας," *ZNW* 49 (1958): 129f.

5467. Joseph A. Fitzmyer, "'Peace upon Earth among Men of his Good Will' (Lk. 2:14)," *ThSt* 19 (1958): 225-27.

5468. F[rancesco] V[attioni], "Pax hominibus bonae voluntatis," *RivB* 7 (1959): 369-70 [Lk. 2:14].

5469. Reinhard Deichgräber, "Lc 2, 14: ἄνθρωπος εὐδοκίας," *ZNW* 51 (1960): 132.

5470. H. Liese, "Pastores ad praesepe (Lc. 2, 15-20)," *VD* 13 (1933): 353-58.

5471. H. Liese, "In circumcision Domini (Lc. 2, 21)," *VD* 12 (1932): 6-10.

5472. Fl. Ogara, " 'Et vocabitur nomen eius Emmanuel ... Deus fortis' (Is. 7, 14; 9, 6). vocatum est nomen eius Iesus' (Lc 2, 21)," *V* 17 (1937): 3-9.

5473. W. H. P. Hatch, "The Text of Luke 2, 22," *HTR* 14 (1921): 377-81.

5474. F. X. Porporato, "Obtulerunt pro eo par turturum aut duos pullos columbarum," *VD* 15 (1935): 35-40 [Lk. 2:24].

5475. J. Rendel Harris, " 'A Light to lighten the Gentiles'," *ET* 29 (1917-1918): 88-89 [Lk. 2:32].

5476. H. J. Vogels, "Die 'Eltern' Jesu (Textkritisches zu Lk. 2, 33 ff.)," *BibZ* 11 (1913): 33-43.

5477. P. Pons, "In signum cui contradicetur (Lc. 2, 34)," *VD* 2 (1922): 34-37.

5478. T. Gallus, "De sensu verborum Lu 2, 35 eorumque momento mariologico," *B* 29 (1948): 220-39.

5479. Jacob Mann, "Anna, 'a prophetess of the tribe of Asher' (Luke ii. 36)," *ET* 28 (1916-1917): 331-32.

5480. H. J. Vogels, "Lk. 2, 36 im Diatessaron," *BibZ* 11 (1913): 168-71.

5481. Eb. Nestle, "The Widow of Fourscore and Four Years," *ET* 24 (1912-1913): 43 [Lk. 2:37].

5482. L. Fonck, "Duodennis inter doctores (Lc. 2, 41-52)," *VD* 2 (1922): 18-25.

5483. B. M. F. van Iersel, "The Finding of Jesus in the Temple," *NT* 4 (1960): 161-73 [Lk. 2:41-51].

5484. John R. Gray, "Was our Lord an Only Child?—Luke ii. 43-46," *ET* 71 (1959-1960): 53.

5485. A. W. Hastings and E. Hastings, "Was Our Lord an Only Child—Luke ii. 43-46?" *ET* 71 (1959-1960): 187.

5486. R. E. Wallis, " 'About my Father's Business': A Plea for a Rejected Translation," *Exp* 2nd ser., 8 (1884): 17-28 [Lk. 2:49].

5487. G. Philip Robertson, "Note on Luke ii. 49," *ET* 39 (1927-1928): 235-36.

5488.   Edgar R. Smothers, "A Note on Luke ii. 49," *HTR* 45 (1952): 67-69.

5489.   Patrick J. Temple, " 'House' or 'Business' in Lk. 2:49?" *CBQ* 1 (1939): 342-52.

5490.   Charles Leaman, "Note on St. Luke ii. 49," *Th* 29 (1934): 365.

5491.   Patrick J. Temple, "Origen and the Ellipsis in Lk, ii. 49," *ITQ* 21 (1954): 367-75.

5492.   Paul Winter, "Lc 2, 49 and Targum Yerushalmi again," *ZNW* 45 (1954): 145-79.

5493.   Patrick J. Temple, "What Is to be Understood by ἐν τοῖς Luke 2, 49?" *ITQ* 17 (1922): 248-63.

5494.   Paul Winter, "Lc 2, 49 and Targum Yerushalmi," *ZNW* 46 (1955): 140-41.

5495.   Norvelle Wallace Sharpe, "A Message of Grace to be found in Luke ii. 49, 'My Father's Business'," *BS* 77 (1920): 229-33.

5496.   E. Gonzáles Vila, "Aún sobre el versículo 50 del capítulo 2° de S. Lucas," *CB* 8 (1951): 349-50; 9 (1952): 15-16.

5497.   Matthew A. Power, "Who Were They Who 'Understood Not'?" *ITQ* 7 (1912): 261-81, 444-59 [Lk. 2:50].

5498.   José M. Bover, "Una nueva interpretación de Lc. 2, 50," *EB* 10 (1951): 205-15.

5499.   A. W. Argyle, "A Parallel between Luke ii. 51 and Genesis xxxvii. 2," *ET* 65 (1953-1954): 29.

5500.   B. Whiteford, "Christ and Popularity," *Exp* 5th ser. 2 (1895): 69-76 [Lk. 2:52].

5501.   Patrick J. Temple, "Christ's Holy Youth According to Lk. 2:52," *CBQ* 3 (1941): 243-50.

5502.   Eb. Nestle, "The Genealogy of Luke iii. as Genealogy of Mary," *ET* 14 (1902-1903): 567.

5503.   Arthur Wright, "The Baptist's Advice to the Several Classes," *ET* 27 (1915-1916): 408-10.

5504.   Irénée Fransen, "Ce que Jésus a fait et enseigné (Luc 3, 1-9,50)," *BVC* 22 (1958): 58-72.

5505.   Robert M. Grant, "The Occasion of Luke iii. 1-2," *HTR* 33 (1940): 151-54.

5506.   Hermann Dieckmann, "Das fünfzehnte Jahr des Tiberius (Lk.

3, 1)," *BibZ* 16 (1922-1924): 54-65.

5507. Hermann Dieckmann, "Das fünfzehnte Jahr des Caesar Tiberius," *B* 6 (1925): 63-67 [Lk. 3:I].

5508. H. S. Cronin, "Abilene, the Jewish Herods and St. Luke," *JTS* 18 (1916-1917): 147-51 [Lk. 3:1].

5509. A. Hilgenfeld, "Zu Lucas 3, 2," *ZWT* 44 (1901): 466-68.

5510. H. Gollwitzer, "Predigt über Lukas 3, 3-14," *EvT* 11 (1951-1952): 145-51.

5511. U. Holzmeister, " 'Parate viam Domino, (Lc. 3, 4)," *VD* 1 (1921): 366-68.

5512. T. F. Glasson, "Water, Wind and Fire (Lk. iii. 16) and Orphic Initiation," *NTSt* 3 (1956-1957): 69-71.

5513. W. A. Watkins, "Note on Luke iii. 16 (ἀπεκρίνατο)," *ET* 31 (1919-1920): 41

5514. Shirley Jackson Case, "The Circumstances of Jesus' Baptism: An Exposition of Luke 3:21," *BW* 31 (1908): 300-302.

5515. Konrad Köhler, "Die Genealogie Jesu im Lukasevangelium," *TSK* 86 (1913): 281-85 [Lk. 3:23-38].

5516. U. Holzmeister, "Genealogia S. Lucae (3, 23-38)," *VD* 23 (1943): 9-18.

5517. U. Holzmeister, "Ein Erklärungsversuch der Lukas-Genealogie (3,23-38)," *ZKT* 47 (1923): 184-218.

5518. Lambert Nolle, "Old Testament Laws of Inheritance and St. Luke's Genealogy of Christ," *Scr* 2 (1947): 38-41 [Lk. 3:23-38].

5519. John Willcock, "Cainan (Luke iii. 36)," *ET* 30 (1918- 1919): 86-87.

5520. André Feuillet, "Le récit lucanien de la tentation," *B* 40 (1959): 613-31 [Lk. 4:1-13].

5521. Eb. Nestle, " 'The Pinnacle of the Temple'," *ET* 23 (1911-1912): 184-85 [Lk. 4:9]

5522. Bruno Violet, "Zum rechten Verständnis der Nazareth-Perikope Lc 4, 16-30," *ZNW* 37 (1938): 251-71.

5523. Patrick J. Temple, "The Rejection at Nazareth," *CQ* 17 (1955): 349-62 [Lk. 4:16-30].

5524. Erwin Preuschen, "Das Wort vom verachteten Propheten," *ZNW* 17 (1916): 33-48 [Lk. 4:16 ff.].

5525.   Eb. Nestle, "Luc 4, 18. 19," *ZNW* 2 (1901): 153-57.

5526.   U. Holzmeister, "Das 'angenehme Jahr des Herrn' (Is. 61, 2 = Lk. 4, 19) und die Einjahrtheorie," *ZKT* 53 (1929): 272-82.

5527.   Edward P. Rice, "Fulfilled in your Ears," *ET* 29 (1917-1918): 45-46 [Lk. 4:21].

5528.   J. E. Belser, "Zu Luk. 4, 23," *TQ* 89 (1907): 365-73.

5529.   U. Holzmeister, " 'Clausum est caelum annis tribus et mensibus sex' (Lc. 4, 25)," *VD* 19 (1939): 167-73.

5530.   Albert Bonus, "Widow or Gentile?" *ET* 14 (1902-1903): 430 [Lk. 4:26].

5531.   U. Holzmeister, " 'Mons saltus' iuxta urbem Nazareth et miraculum Lc. 4. 30 relatum," *VD* 17 (1937): 50-57.

5532.   Joseph Schuster, "Zwei neue medizingeschichtliche Quellen zum 'grossen Fieber' Lk. 4, 38," *BibZ* 13 (1915): 338-43.

5533.   D. R. Fotheringham, "St. Luke iv. 44," *ET* 45 (1933-1934): 237.

5534.   L. Fonck, "Prima piscatio miraculosa (Lc. 5, 1-11)," *VD* 6 (1926): 170-80.

5535.   Gaétan de Raucourt, "La vocation des apôtres (Luc 5, 1-11; Matthieu 4, 18-22; Marc 1, 16-20)," *RSR* 29 (1939): 610-15.

5536.   Robert Leaney, "Jesus and Peter: the Call and Post-resurrection Appearance (Luke v. 1-2 and xxiv. 34)," *ET* 65 (1953-1954): 381-82.

5537.   J. A. Chadwick, "The First Miraculous Draught of Fish," *Exp* 4th ser., 6 (1892): 18-26 [Lk. 5:2-11].

5538.   Albert J. Matthews, " 'Depart from me; for I am a sinful man, O Lord' (Luke v. 8)," *ET* 30 (1918-1919): 425.

5539.   J. H. Michell Dabb, "Luke v. 26," *ET* 45 (1933-1934): 45.

5540.   Arthur J. Rich, "Luke v. 26," *ET* 44 (1932-1933): 428.

5541.   F. H. Colson, "Two Examples of Literary and Rhetorical Criticism in the Fathers," *JTS* 25 (1923-1924): 364-77 [Lk. 6].

5542.   H.-W. Bartsch, "Feldrede und Bergpredigt. Redaktionsarbeit in Luk. 6," *TZ* 16 (1960): 5-18.

5543.   J. M. Robertson, " 'Deuteroproton'," *ET* 14 (1902-1903): 474-75 [Lk. 6:1].

5544.   H. Meulenbelt, "Lk. 6, 1 en Sabbatooi deuteroprootooi," *NTS* 5 (1922): 140-42.

5545.   E. Vogt, "Sabbatum 'Deuteróproton' in Lc. 6, 1 et antiquum kalendarium sacerdotale," *B* 40 (1959): 102- 105.

5546.   Albert Bonus, "St. Luke vi. 19," *ET* 18 (1906-1907): 287-88.

5547.   Eb. Nestle, "Luke vi. 19," *ET* 17 (1905-1906): 431.

5548.   Eric May, " '. . . For power went forth from him...' (Luke 6, 19)," *CBQ* 14 (1952): 93-103.

5549.   Hermann Diem, "Predigt über Lukas 6, 20-31," *EvT* 14 (1954): 241-46.

5550.   C. A. Phillips, "Luke 6, 24: ὅτι ἀπέχετε τὴν παράκλησιν ὑμῶν," *BBC* 6 (1929): 27-29.

5551.   G. Currie Martin, " 'Know no Despair'!" *ET* 8 (1896-1897): 141 [Lk. 6:35].

5552.   B. Whitefoord, "The Christian 'Nil Desperandum': A Study of St. Luke vi. 35," *Exp* 6th ser., 5 (1902): 218-24.

5553.   Wilhelm Brückner, "Über die ursprüngliche Stellung von Luk. 6, 39. 4a = Matth. 15, 14; 20, 24. Ein Beitrag zur Evangelienkritik," *TSK* 42 (1869): 616-57.

5554.   C. F. Hogg, "Luke vii. 2," *ET* 29 (1917-1918): 475.

5555.   R. H. Wray, "Luke vii. 6, 7," *ET* 25 (1913-1914): 380.

5556.   Donald K. Campbell, "The Prince of Life at Nain," *BS* 115 (1958): 341-47 [Lk. 7:11-17].

5557.   L. Fonck, " 'Adolescens, tibi dico, surge!' (Lc. 7, 14)," *VD* 2 (1922): 258-64.

5558.   C. A. Phillips, "Luke vii. 21. καὶ τυφλοῖς πολλοῖς ἐχαρίσατο βλέπειν," *BBC* 5 (1928): 27-29.

5559.   W. K. Lowther Clarke, " 'The dead are raised up': An Interpretation," *Th* 25 (1932): 35-36 [Lk. 7:22].

5560.   John Reid, "The Difference Christ has made," *ET* 12 (1900-1901): 312-13 [Lk. 7:28].

5561.   G. Gander, "Notule sur Luc 7. 29-30," *VCar* 5 (1951): 141-44.

5562.   Rayner Winterbotham, "Simon and the Sinner," *Exp* 1st ser. 6 (1877): 214-29 [Lk. 7:36-50].

5563.   J. M. S. Baljon, "Lukas 7, 36-50 en 16, 1-9," *TT* 25 (1891): 478-86.

5564.   W. C. van Manen, "Jezus gezalfd," *TT* 35 (1901): 1-20 [Lk. 7:36-50].

5565.   Cuthbert Lattey, "The Sinner of the City," *Exp* 7th ser. 8 (1909): 55-63 [Lk. 7:36-50].

5566.   M.-J. Lagrange, "Jésus a-t-il été oint plusieurs fois et par plusieurs femmes?" *RB* 21 (1912): 504-32 [Lk. 7:36-50; Mt. 26:6-13; Mk. 14:3-9; Jn. 12:1-8].

5567.   Edward Grubb, "The Anointing of Jesus," *ET* 26 (1914-1915): 461-63 [Lk. 7:36-50].

5568.   Alfred Plummer, "The Woman that was a Sinner," *ET* 27 (1915-1916): 42-43 [Lk. 7:36-50].

5569.   R. K. Orchard, "On the Composition of Luke vii. 36-50," *JTS* 38 (1937): 243-45.

5570.   Paul Joüon, "La pécheresse de Galilée et la parabole des deux débiteurs (Luc 7, 36-50)," *RSR* 29 (1939): 615-19.

5571.   A. H. Dammers, "Studies in Texts," *Th* 49 (1946): 78-80 [Lk. 7:36-50].

5572.   Eloíno Nácar, "La parábola de los dos deudores a quienes les fue condonada la deuda y la aplicación que de ella hace Cristo N.S.," *CB* 4 (1947): 89-90 [Lk. 7:36-50].

5573.   St. Gallo, "Peccatrix in civitate (Lc. 7, 36-50)," *VD* 27 (1949): 84-93.

5574.   Aem. Suys, " 'Simon, habeo tibi aliquid dicere' (Lc. 7, 40)," *VD* 12 (1932): 199-202.

5575.   W. M. Macgregor, "The Parable of the Money-Lender and his Debtors (Luke vii. 41-47)," *ET* 37 (1925-1926): 344-47.

5576.   K. Weiss, "Der westliche Text von Lc 7, 46 und sein Wert," *ZNW* 46 (1955): 241-45.

5577.   H. G. Meecham, "Luke vii. 47," *ET* 38 (1926-1927): 286.

5578.   Joachim Jeremias, "Lukas 7:45: εἰσῆλθον," *ZNW* 51 (1960): 131.

5579.   David J. M'Laren, "Luke vii. 47," *ET* 30 (1918-1919): 378.

5580.   John Dublin, "οὗ χάριν," *ET* 37 (1925-1926): 525-26 [Lk. 7:47].

5581.   U. Holzmeister, " 'Exiit qui seminat seminare semen suum' (Lc. 8, 4-15)," *VD* 22 (1942): 8-12.

5582.   L. Fonck, "Parabola seminantis (Lc. 8, 4-15)," *VD* 2 (1922): 43-48.

5583.   L. Cerfaux, "Fructifiez en supportant (l'épreuve)," *RB* 64 (1957): 481-91 [Lk. 8:15].

5584. J. Kreyenbühl, "Ursprung und Stammbaum eines biblischen Wunders," *ZNW* 10 (1909): 265-76 [Lk. 8:41-56].

5585. H. G. Wood, "The Use of ἀγαπάω in Luke viii. 42, 47," *ET* 66 (1954-1955): 319-20.

5586. Charles Neil, "The Throng and the Touch," *ET* 10 (1898-1899): 122-24 [Lk. 8:45].

5587. Carl Amerding, "The Daughter of Jairus," *BS* 105 (1948): 56-58 [Lk. 8:52].

5588. T. H. Bindley, "The Taste of Death," *Exp* 5th ser., 6 (1897): 372-76 [Lk. 9:27].

5589. Augustin George, "La transfiguration (Luc 9, 28-36)," *BVC* no. 33 (1960): 21-25.

5590. F. V. Pratt, "The Exodus of Jesus (Luke ix. 28-31)," *ET* 41 (1929-1930): 376-77.

5591. Robert Leaney, "Jesus and the Symbol of the Child (Luke ix. 46-48)," *ET* 66 (1954-1955): 91-92.

5592. August Jacobsen, "Der lukanische Reisebericht," *ZWT* 29 (1886): 152-79 [Lk. 9:51-18:14].

5593. John C. Hawkins, "The Disuse of the Marcan Source in St. Luke ix. 51-xviii. 14," *ET* 14 (1902-1903): 18-23, 90-93, 137-40.

5594. Rektor Schaarschmidt, "Der Reisebericht im Lukasevangelium," *TSK* 82 (1909): 12-28 [Lk. 9:51-18:14].

5595. J. E. Belser, "Der sog. Reisebericht im Lukasevangelium," *TQ* 97 (1915): 336-57 [Lk. 9:51-18:14].

5596. H. E. Guilleband, "The Travel Narrative in St. Luke," *BS* 80 (1923): 237-45 [Lk.9:51-18:14].

5597. Dr. Schaarschmidt, "Die Einschaltung im Lukas-evangelium (9, 51-18, 14) als Grundlage der biblischen Geschichte von Jesus," *TSK* 101 (1929): 357-80.

5598. W. Gasse, "Zum Reisebericht des Lukas," *ZNW* 34 (1935): 293-99 [Lk. 9:51-18:14].

5599. C. C. McCown, "The Geography of Luke's Central Section," *JBL* 57 (1938): 51-66 [Lk. 9:51-18:14].

5600. Eduard Lohse, "Missionarisches Handeln Jesu nach dem Evangelium des Lukas," *TZ* 10 (1954): 1-13 [Lk. 9:51-18:14].

5601. Irénée Fransen, "La montée vers Jérusalem (Luc 9, 51-18,

14)," *BVC* 11 (1955): 68-87.

5602.   Bo Reicke, "Instruktion och diskussion i reseberättelsen hos Lukas," *STK* 33 (1957): 224-33 [Lk. 9:51-18:14].

5603.   Walter Grundmann, "Fragen der Komposition des lukanischen 'Reiseberichts'," *ZNW* 50 (1959): 252-70.

5604.   W. C. Robinson, "The Theological Context for Interpreting Luke's Travel Narrative (9:51 ff.)," *JBL* 79 (1960): 20-31.

5605.   J. Starcky, "Sens et portée de Luc IX, 51," *RSR* 39 (1951-1952): 197-202.

5606.   José M. Bover, "Autenticidad de Lc 9, 54-56," *EE* 27 (1953): 347-49.

5607.   J. R. Crockford, "St. Luke ix. 57-62," *ET* 58 (1946-1947): 307.

5608.   M. Dods, "Candidates for Discipleship," *Exp* 4th ser., 4 (1891): 286-97 [Lk. 9:57-62].

5609.   A. Vaccari, " 'Mittens manum in aratrum et respiciens retro' (Lc. 9. 62)," *VD* 18 (1938): 308-12.

5610.   L. Cerfaux, "Variants de Lc. IX, 62," *ETL* 12 (1935): 326-28.

5611.   M. R. James, "An Ancient English List of the Seventy Disciples," *JTS* 11 (1909-1910): 459-62 [Lk. 10:1-24].

5612.   A. L. Vail, "The Significance of the Seventy," *RE* 22 (1925): 433-49; 23 (1926): 3-21.

5613.   Bruce M. Metzger, "Seventy or Seventy-two Disciples," *NTSt* 5 (1958-1959): 299-306 [Lk. 10:1, 17].

5614.   Sidney Jellicoe, "St. Luke and the Seventy-Two," *NTSt* 6 (1959-1960): 319-21.

5615.   W. Arndt, "The Chief Principles of New Testament Textual Criticism," *CTM* 5 (1934): 577-84 [Lk. 10:1].

5616.   M. Zerwick, " '... alios septuaginta duos' (Lc. 10. 1)," *VD* 26 (1948): 53-57.

5617.   D. van Swigchem, "De terugkeer van de 72 (Lucas 10, 17-24)," *GTT* 49 (1949): 193-202; 50 (1950): 152-62.

5618.   M. Zerwick, " 'Vidi Satanam sicut fulgur de caelo cadentem' (Lc 10. 17-20)," *VD* 26 (1948): 110-14.

5619.   Friedrich Spitta, "Der Satan als Blitz," *ZNW* 9 (1908): 160-63 [Lk. 10:18].

5620.   W. K. Lowther Clarke, "Studies in Texts," *Th* 7 (1923): 101-104 [Lk. 10:18].

5621. E. Hampden-Cook, "The Text for May—Luke x. 18," *ET* 18 (1906-1907): 334.

5622. P. Thomson, "Luke x. 18," *ET* 19 (1907-1908): 191.

5623. Charles A. Webster, "St. Luke x. 18 ἐθεώρουν τὸν Σατανᾶν ὡς ἀστραπὴν ἐκ τοῦ οὐρανοῦ πεσόντα," *ET* 57 (1945-1946): 52.

5624. F. Warburton Lewis, " 'I beheld Satan fall as lightning from heaven' (Luke x. 18)," *ET* 25 (1913-1914): 232-33.

5625. M. Zerwick, "Exsultatio Domini (Lc. 10, 21-24)," *VD* 26 (1948): 229-33.

5626. John Chapman, "Dr. Harnack on Luke x. 22: 'No man knoweth the Son'," *JTS* 10 (1908-1909): 552-66.

5627. D. van Swigchem, "Geschiedenis van de exegese van Luc. 10, 22 (Matth. 11, 27) in de laatste decennia," *GTT* 52 (1952): 97-108.

5628. C. E. B. Cranfield, "The Good Samaritan," *TTod* 11 (1954): 368-72 [Lk. 10:25-37].

5629. Inman R. Johnson, "Interpretation Through Reading," *RE* 34 (1937): 315-17 [Lk. 10:25-37].

5630. J. Mann, "Jesus and the Sadducean Priests: Luke 10:25-37," *JQR* 6 (1914): 415-22.

5631. A. L. Vail, "The Good Samaritan as a Text," *RE* 21 (1924): 309-21 [Lk. 10:25-37].

5632. C. A. van Liempd, "Parabola boni Samaritani (Lc. 10, 25-37)," *VD* 11 (1931): 262-63.

5633. James C. Gordon, "The Parable of the Good Samaritan (St. Luke x. 25-37)," *ET* 56 (1944-1945): 302-304.

5634. Bertram Maura, "Luke x. 25-37," *ET* 58 (1946-1947): 168.

5635. T. C. Smith, "The Parable of the Samaritan," *RE* 47 (1950): 434-41 [Lk. 10:25-37].

5636. Frank H. Wilkinson, "Oded: Proto-Type of the Good Samaritan," *ET* 69 (1957): 94 [Lk. 10:25-37].

5637. Dominique Sanchis, "*Samaritanus ille.* L'exégèse augustinienne de la parabole du bon samaritain," *RSR* 49 (1961): 406-25 [Lk. 10:25-37].

5638. M. Zerwick, "Diliges Deum tuum ex toto corde tuo, (Lc. 10, 25-28)," *VD* 26 (1948): 365-69.

5639. P. Thomson, Tempted him' (Luke x. 25)," *ET* 37

(1925-1926): 526.

5640. W. J. Masson, "The Parable of the Good Samaritan," *ET* 48 (1936-1937): 179-81 [Mk. 10:29-37].

5641. John Bowman, "The Parable of the Good Samaritan," *ET* 59 (1947-1948): 151-53, 248-49 [Lk. 10:29-37].

5642. Hermann Binder, "Das Gleichnis vom barmherzigen Samariter," *TZ* 15 (1959): 176-94 [Lk. 10:30-37].

5643. E. S. G. Wickham, "Studies in Texts: Luke x. 29," *Th* 60 (1957): 417-18.

5644. M. Zerwick, "Homo quidam descendebat ab Ierusalem in Iericho," *VD* 27 (1949): 55-59 [Lk. 10:30].

5645. L. Szcepánski, " 'Homo quidam descendebat ab Ierusalem in Iericho' (Lc. 10. 30)," *VD* 1 (1921): 315-17.

5646. Morley Stevenson, "Martha and Mary," *ET* 28 (1916-1917): 478 [Lk. 10:38-42].

5647. A. Vitti, " 'Maria optimam partem elegit' (Lc. 10, 38-42)," *VD* 10 (1930): 225-30.

5648. A. O'Rahilly, "The Two Sisters," *Scr* 4 (1949): 68-76 [Lk. 10:38-42].

5649. T. Gillieson, "A Plea for Proportion: St. Luke x. 38-42," *ET* 59 (1947-1948): 111-12.

5650. Erling Laland, "Marta-Maria-perikopen Lukas 10, 38-42; dens kerygmatiske plass i urkirken," *NTT* 53 (1952): 10-27 [Lk. 10:38-42].

5651. Th. C. van Stockum, "Catholice, calvinistice, mystice, Lucas 10, 38-42," *NedTT* 12 (1957-1958): 32-37.

5652. Erling Laland, "Die Martha-Maria-Perikope Lukas 10, 38-42. Ihre kerygmatische Aktualität für das Leben der Urkirche," *ST* 13 (1959): 70-85.

5653. Félix Puzo, "Marta y María. Nota exegética a Lc 10, 38-42 y 1 Cor 7, 29-35," *EE* 34 (1960): 851-58.

5654. Arthur Stevens Phelps, "The Martha Heresy," *RE* 27 (1930): 176-82 [Lk. 10:41-42].

5655. Friedr. Strähl, "Kritische und exegetische Beleuchtung von Luc. 10, 41-42," *STZ* 4 (1887): 116-23.

5656. M. Zerwick, "Oratio Dominica (Lc. 11, 1-4)," *VD* 28 (1950): 176-80.

5657. Robert Leaney, "The Lucan Text of the Lord's Prayer (Lk.

XI, 2-4)," *NT* 1 (1956): 103-11.

5658.   Hélène Pétré, "Les leçons du *panem nostrum quotidianum*," *RSR* 40 (1951-1952): 63-79 [Lk. 11:3; Mt. 6:11].

5659.   M. Zerwick, "Perseverante orare (Lc. 11, 5-13)," *VD* 28 (1950): 243-47.

5660.   A. D. Martin, "The Parable concerning Hospitality," *ET* 37 (1925-1926): 411-14 [Lk. 11:5-6].

5661.   C. T. Dimont, "Children or Servants," *ET* 9 (1897-1898): 382 [Lk. 11:7].

5662.   A. Souter, "Children or Servants," *ET* 9 (1897-1898): 382 [Lk. 11:7].

5663.   L. Fonck, " 'Petite et dabitur vobis' (Lc. 11, 9)," *VD* 2 (1922): 144-49.

5664.   Herbert Pegg, " 'A scorpion for an egg' (Luke xi. 12)," *ET* 38 (1926-1927): 468-69.

5665.   M. Zerwick, "In Beelzebub principe daemoniorum (Lc. 11, 14-28)," *VD* 29 (1951): 44-48.

5666.   J. Weiss, "Die Verteidigung Jesu gegen den Vorwurf des Bündnisses mit Beelzebub," *TSK* 63 (1890): 555-69 [Lk. 11:14-26].

5667.   L. Fonck, "Regnum Christi et regnum Satanae (Lc. 11, 15-28)," *VD* 3 (1923): 74-81.

5668.   H. E. Bryant, "Note on Luke xi. 17," *ET* 50 (1938-1939): 525-26.

5669.   U. Holzmeister, "Fortis armatus (Lc. 11, 20-26)," *VD* 6 (1926): 71-75.

5670.   Alfred Plummer, "The Parable of the Demon's Return," *ET* 3 (1891-1892): 349-51 [Lk. 11:26].

5671.   Eb. Nestle, "Luke xi. 27," *ET* 20 (1908-1909): 380.

5672.   R. Thibaut, "Le signe de Jonas," *NRT* 60 (1933): 532-36 [Lk. 11:30].

5673.   A. A. Burd, "The Outside and the Inside of the Cup," *Exp* 5th ser., 5 (1897): 373-76 [Lk. 11:39-41].

5674.   J. E. Yonge, "Note on St. Luke xi. 41," *Exp* 2nd ser., 5 (1883): 318-19.

5675.   G. Brans, "Christus' leer over de hoeveelheid der aalmoes," *ETL* 6 (1929): 463-69 [Lk. 11:41].

5676.   Eric F. F. Bishop, "Rue—πήγανον," *ET* 59 (1947-1948): 81

[Lk. 11:42].

5677. Hughes Vincent, "Le tombeau des prophètes," *RB* 10 (1901): 72-88 [Lk. 11:47].

5678. Vacher Burch, "The Petitioning Blood of the Prophets (Luke xi. 49-51)," *ET* 30 (1918-1919): 329-30.

5679. W. D. Niven, "Luke xii. 4," *ET* 26 (1914-1915): 44-45.

5680. James Denney, "Speaking against the Son of Man and Blaspheming the Spirit," *Exp* 7th ser., 4 (1907): 521-32 [Lk. 12:10].

5681. John Reid, "The Poor Rich Fool," *ET* 13 (1901-1902): 567-68 [Lk. 12:13-21].

5682. Paul Joüon, "La parabole du riche insensé (Luc 12, 13-21)," *RSR* 29 (1939): 486-89.

5683. Harris E. Kirk, "Christ and the Secular Temper," *USR* 22 (1910-1911): 104-18 [Lk. 12:13-14].

5684. C. C. Tarelli, "A Note on Luke xii. 15," *JTS* 41 (1940): 260-62.

5685. Konrad Köhler, "Textkritische Bemerkungen zu der Perikope vom Sorgen im Lukasevangelium," *TSK* 86 (1913): 452-61 [Lk. 12:22-31].

5686. E. G. Selwyn, "Studies in Texts," *Th* 16 (1928): 163-64 [Lk. 12:27, 28].

5687. S. Cox, "A New Parable," *Exp* 1st. ser. 1 (1875): 249-58 [Lk. 12:29].

5688. W. Pesch, "Zur Formgeschichte und Exegese von Lk. 12, 32," *B* 41 (1960): 25-40.

5689. S. E. C. T. "The Kind Master," *Exp* 1st. ser. 8 (1878): 420-31 [Lk. 12:35-38].

5690. A. K. Clarke and N. E. W. Collie, "A Comment on Luke xii. 41-58," *JTS* 17 (1915-1916): 299-301.

5691. G. Graystone, " 'I have come to cast fire on the earth'," *Scr* 4 (1950): 135-41.

5692. Ronald A. Ward, "St. Luke xii. 49: καὶ τί θέλω εἰ ἤδη ἀνήφθη," *ET* 63 (1951-1952): 92-93 [Lk. 12:49].

5693. F. K. Seper, "καὶ τί θέλω εἰ ἤδη ἀνήφθη (Lc. 12, 49b)," *VD* 36 (1958): 147-53.

5694. C. Bruston, "Une parole de Jésus mal comprise," *RHPR* 5 (1925): 70-71. [Lk. 12:50; Mt. 26:38; Jn. 12:27].

5695. H. G. Wood, "Interpreting this time," *NTSt* 2 (1955-1956): 262-66 [Lk. 12:56].

5696. Dr. Thieme, "Über die Autonomie im sittlichen Denken Jesu und Luk. 12, 57," *ZTK* 17 (1907): 64-66.

5697. James Denney, "Three Motives to Repentance," *Exp* 4th ser. 7 (1893): 232-37 [Lk. 13:1-9].

5698. J. Herderschee, "Lucas XIII. 1-5," *TT* 15 (1881): 465-71.

5699. Sherman E. Johnson, "A Note on Luke xiii 1-5," *ATR* 17 (1935): 91-95.

5700. J. Blinzler, "Die Niedermetzelung von Galiläern durch Pilatus," *NT* 2 (1958): 24-49 [Lk. 13:1].

5701. H. Faccio, "De ficu sterili (Lc 13, 6-9)," *VD* 29 (1951): 233-38.

5702. Rayner Winterbotham, " 'Are they few that be saved'?" *ET* 29 (1917-1918): 468-71 [Lk. 13:23].

5703. E. Brian Packett, "Luke 13:25," *ET* 67 (1955-1956): 178.

5704. Allen H. Gilbert, "Σήμερον καὶ αὔριον, καὶ τῇ τρίτῃ (Luke 13:32)," *JBL* 35 (1916): 315-18.

5705. Leslie H. Bunn, "Herod Antipas and 'that fox'," *ET* 43 (1931-1932): 380-81 [Lk. 13:32].

5706. F. A. Farley, "A Text (Luke xiii. 33)," *ET* 34 (1922-1923): 429-30.

5707. X. de Meeûs, "Composition de Lc. xiv, et genre symposiaque," *ETL* 37 (1961): 847-70.

5708. H. Liese, "Dominus ad cenam invitatus die Sabbati (Lc. 14, 1-12)," *VD* 11 (1931): 257-61.

5709. J. Rendel Harris, "A Speculation in Textual Criticism," *Exp* 7th ser., 3 (1907): 444-54 [Lk. 14:5].

5710. Matthew Black, "The Aramaic Spoken by Christ and Luke 14. 5," *JTS* N.S. 1 (1950): 60-62.

5711. Edward Shillito, "The Gospel according to St. Luke xiv. 7-33," *ET* 52 (1940-1941): 432-34.

5712. E. Linnemann, "Überlegungen zur Parabel vom grossen Abendmahl Lc 14, 15-24 und Mt 22, 1-14," *ZNW* 51 (1960): 246-55.

5713. H. Liese, "Cena magna (Lc. 14, 16-24)," *VD* 13 (1933): 161-66.

5714. J. Louw, "The Parables of the Tower-Builder and the King going to War," *ET* 48 (1936-1937): 478 [Lk. 14:25-35].

5715.   Stewart Mechie, "The Parables of the Tower Builder and the King going to War," *ET* 48 (1936-1937): 235-36 [Lk. 14:25-35].

5716.   J. Louw, "Lucas 14, 25-33," *NTS* 19 (1936): 144-45.

5717.   T. C. Finlayson, "Christ Demanding Hatred," *Exp* 1st. ser., 9 (1879): 420-30 [Lk. 14:26].

5718.   James Denney, "The Word 'Hate' in Luke xiv. 26," *ET* 21 (1909-1910): 41-42.

5719.   W. Soltau, "Die Anordnung der Logia in Lukas 15-18," *ZNW* 10 (1909): 230-38.

5720.   Ernst Fink, "Die Parabeln Christi über die Zöllner und Pharisäer, Luk. 15 und 16," *TSK* 7 (1834): 313-34.

5721.   Siegfried Goebel, "Die Gleichnisgruppe Luk. 15 und 16, methodisch ausgelegt," *TSK* 47 (1874): 506-38; 48 (1875): 656-707.

5722.   J. Russell Howden, "The Trilogy of Parables in Luke 15," *BR* 14 (1929): 331-44.

5723.   Hay Watson Smith, "The Fifteenth Chapter of Luke," *USR* 8 (1896-1897): 104-10.

5724.   Charles Brown, "The Great Parable of Grace," *RE* 16 (1919): 127-35 [Lk. 15].

5725.   J. Cantinat, "Les paraboles de la misericorde (Lc. xv, 1-32)," *NRT* 77 (1955): 246-64.

5726.   L. Fonck, "Ovis perdita et iuventa (Lc. 15, 1-10)," *VD* 1 (1921): 173-77.

5727.   M. Dods, "The Lost Sheep and Lost Piece of Money," *Exp* 3rd ser., 2 (1885): 16-28 [Lk. 15:1-10].

5728.   Jean Monnier, "Sur la grâce—à propos de la parabole de la brebis perdue," *RHPR* 16 (1936): 191-95 [Lk. 15:3-7].

5729.   H. Faccio, "De ove perdita (Lc. 15, 3-7)," *VD* 26 (1948): 221-28.

5730.   A. F. Walls, " 'In the presence of the angels' (Luke xv. 10)," *NT* 3 (1959): 314-16.

5731.   S.E.C.T., "The Prodigal and his Brother," *Exp* 1 st. ser. 9 (1879): 137-50 [Lk. 15:11-32].

5732.   H. Baumgartner, "Christologie, und Parabel vom verlornen Sohn," *STZ* 5 (1888): 178-99 [Lk. 15:11-32].

5733. J. Laidlaw, "The Parable of the Lost Son: A Study of Luke xv. 11-32," *Exp* 3rd ser. 8 (1888): 268-76, 388-99.

5734. W. H. Simcox, "The Prodigal and his Brother," *Exp* 3rd ser. 10 (1889): 122-36 [Lk. 15:11-32].

5735. M.-J. Ollivier, "Études sur la physionomie intellectuelle de N.S. Jésus Christ. La parabole de l'enfant prodigue (Luc xv, 11-31)," *RB* 3 (1894): 489-502.

5736. David Brown, "The Elder Brother of the Prodigal Son," *ET* 7 (1895-1896): 325-26 [Lk. 15:11-32].

5737. A. Hilgenfeld, "Das Gleichnis von dem verlorenen Sohne, Luc. 15, 11-32," *ZWT* 45 (1902): 449-64.

5738. Donald M. Henry, "The Atonement and the Parable of the Prodigal Son," *ET* 17 (1905-1906): 523 [Lk. 15:11-32].

5739. Geo. H. Knight, "The Atonement and the Parable of the Prodigal Son," *ET* 17 (1905-1906): 239 [Lk. 15:11-32].

5740. Arthur W. Witherspoon, "The Atonement and the Parable of the Prodigal Son," *ET* 17 (1905-1906): 335-36 [Lk. 15:11-32].

5741. K. Knoke, "Zum Verständnis des Gleichnisses vom verlornen Sohn," *NKZ* 17 (1906): 407-18 [Lk. 15:11-32].

5742. Arthur Dakin, "The Elder Brother," *ET* 19 (1907-1908): 141-42 [Lk. 15:11-32].

5743. A. D. Martin, "The Word of the Cross and the Parable of the Prodigal," *ET* 24 (1912-1913): 526-27 [Lk. 15:11-32].

5744. J. Bonnar Russell, "The Word of the Cross and the Parable of the Prodigal," *ET* 24 (1912-1913): 358-60 [Lk. 15:11-32].

5745. W. P. Robertson, " 'The Word of the Cross and the Parable of the Prodigal'," *ET* 25 (1913-1914): 181-82 [Lk. 15:11-32].

5746. W. Gray Williams, "The Parable of the Prodigal Son (Luke xv. 11-32)," *ET* 26 (1914-1915): 141-42.

5747. Alex. A. Duncan, "The Prodigal Son," *ET* 28 (1916-1917): 327 [Lk. 15:11-32].

5748. Arthur Dakin, "The Parable of the Prodigal Son as Literature," *ET* 35 (1923-1924): 330-31 [Lk. 15:11-32].

5749. John Lendrum, "Into a Far Country," *ET* 36 (1924-1925): 377-80 [Lk. 15:11-32].

5750. I. Mortari, "Parabola de filio prodigo (Lc. 15, 11-32)," *VD* 5

(1925): 289-94; 321-29.

5751.   Adolf Deissmann, "The Parable of the Prodigal Son," *RL* 1 (1932): 331-38 [Lk. 15:11-32].

5752.   J. E. Yates, "Studies in Texts: Sons or Servants? A Note on Luke xv, 11 - end," *Th* 49 (1946): 15-18.

5753.   Eduard Schweizer, "Zur Frage der Lukasquellen, Analyse von Luk. 15, 11-32," *TZ* 4 (1948): 469-71.

5754.   Joachim Jeremias, "Zum Gleichnis vom verlorenen Sohn, Luk. 15, 11-32," *TZ* 5 (1949): 228-31.

5755.   Eduard Schweizer, "Antwort an Joachim Jeremias, S. 228-231," *TZ* 5 (1949): 231-33 [Lk. 15:11-32].

5756.   Gerhard Rosenkranz, "Das Gleichnis vom verlorenen Sohn im Lotus-Sûtra und im Lukasevangelium," *TLZ* 79 (1954): 281-82.

5757.   H. Meulenbelt, "Lk. 15, 12," *NTS* 2 (1919): 267-68.

5758.   John Willcock, "Luke xv. 16," *ET* 29 (1917-1918): 43.

5759.   Eb. Nestle, "The Best Robe," *ET* 10 (1898-1899): 93-94 [Lk. 15:22].

5760.   Alexander Stewart, "The Elder Brother," *ET* 22 (1910-1911): 247-51 [Lk. 15:25-32].

5761.   J. E. Compton, "The Prodigal's Brother," *ET* 42 (1930-1931): 187 [Lk. 15:25-32].

5762.   H. E. Stickler, "The Prodigal's Brother," *ET* 42 (1930-1931): 45-46 [Lk. 15:25-32].

5763.   Phillips Barry, "On Luke xv. 25, συμφωνία: Bagpipe," *JBL* 23 (1904): 180-90.

5764.   Fred Senior, "Luke xv. 30," *ET* 31 (1919-1920): 282.

5765.   Albert Bonus, "Luke xv. 30," *ET* 31 (1919-1920): 476.

5766.   Fried. Zyro, "Neuer Versuch über das Gleichnis vom klugen Verwalter, Luc. 16," *TSK* 4 (1831): 776-804.

5767.   E. Rodenbusch, "Die Komposition von Lucas 16," *ZNW* 4 (1903): 243-54.

5768.   J. D. M. Derrett, "Fresh Light on St. Luke XVI," *NTSt* 7 (1960-1961): 198-220, 364-80.

5769.   Pastor Brauns, "Nun noch ein Auslegungsversuch von Luk. 16, 1-14," *TSK* 15 (1842): 1012-22.

5770.   K. Jensen, "Ueber das Gleichnis vom ungerechten Haushalter, Luc. 16, 1-13," *TSK* 2 (1829): 699-714.

5771.   James Hendry, "The Parable of the Unjust Steward," *ET* 4 (1892-93): 431-32 [Lk. 16:1-13].

5772.   W. B. Ripon, "The Parable of the Unjust Steward," *Exp* 4th ser., 7 (1893): 21-29 [Lk. 16:1-13].

5773.   A. R. Eagar, "The Parable of the Unjust Steward," *Exp* 5th ser., 2 (1895): 457-70 [Lk. 16:1-13].

5774.   A. N. Jannaris, "The Unrighteous Steward and Machiavellism," *ET* 13 (1901-1902): 128-30 [Lk. 16:1-13].

5775.   Margaret D. Gibson, "On the Parable of the Unjust Steward," *ET* 14 (1902-1903): 334 [Lk. 16:1-13].

5776.   W. O. E. Oesterley, "The Parable of the 'Unjust' Steward (St. Luke XVI)," *Exp* 6th ser., 7 (1903): 273-83.

5777.   Harold Frith and Henry T. Hooper, "The Unjust Steward," *ET* 15 (1903-1904): 426-27 [Lk. 16:1-13].

5778.   George Murray, "The Unjust Steward," *ET* 15 (1903-1904): 307-10 [Lk. 16:1-13].

5779.   Andrew N. Bogle, "The Unjust Steward," *ET* 15 (1903-1904): 475-76 [Lk. 16:1-13].

5780.   W. D. Miller, "The Unjust Steward," *ET* 15 (1903-1904): 332-34.

5781.   E. Hampden-Cook and F. G. Dutton, "The Unjust Steward," *ET* 16 (1904-1905): 44.

5782.   John Grant and F. W. S. O'Neill, "The Unjust Steward," *ET* 16 (1904-1905): 239-40.

5783.   R. L. Collins, "Is the Parable of the Unjust Steward pure Sarcasm?" *ET* 22 (1910-1911): 525-26 [Lk. 16:1-13].

5784.   William Arnott, "The Unjust Steward in a New Light," *ET* 24 (1912-1913): 508-11 [Lk. 16:1-13].

5785.   Frederick Beames, "The Unrighteous Steward," *ET* 24 (1912-1913): 150-55 [Lk. 16:1-13].

5786.   W. H. Griffith Thomas, "The Unjust Steward," *ET* 25 (1913-1914): 44.

5787.   H. F. B. Compston, "Friendship without Mammon," *ET* 31 (1919-1920): 282 [Lk. 16:1-13].

5788.   Frederick Eden Pargiter, "The Parable of the Unrighteous Steward," *ET* 32 (1920-1921): 136-37 [Lk. 16:1-13].

5789.   W. P. Paterson, "The Example of the Unjust Steward," *ET* 35 (1923-1924): 391-95 [Lk. 16:1-13].

5790.   J. F. McFadyen, "The Parable of the Unjust Steward," *ET* 37 (1925-1926): 535-39 [Lk. 16:1-13].

5791.   H. S. Marshall, "The Parable of the Untrustworthy Steward," *ET* 39 (1927-1928): 120-22 [Lk. 16:1-13].

5792.   J. Steele, "The Unjust Steward," *ET* 39 (1927-1928): 236-37 [Lk. 16:1-13].

5793.   R. B. Y. Scott, "The Parable of the Unjust Steward (Luke xvi. 1 ff.)," *ET* 49 (1937-1938): 234-35.

5794.   William F. Boyd, "The Parable of the Unjust Steward," *ET* 50 (1938-1939): 46 [Lk. 16:1-13].

5795.   Alexander King, "The Parable of the Unjust Steward," *ET* 50 (1938-1939): 474-76 [Lk. 16:1-13].

5796.   C. H. Pickar, "The Unjust Steward," *CBQ* 1 (1939): 250-52 [Lk. 16:1-13]

5797.   L. M. Friedel, "The Parable of the Unjust Steward," *CBQ* 3 (1941): 337-48 [Lk. 16:1-13].

5798.   André Feuillet, "Les riches intendants du Christ (Luc XVI, 1-13)," *RSR* 34 (1947): 30-54.

5799.   Paul Gächter, "The Parable of the Dishonest Steward After Oriental Conceptions," *CBQ* 12 (1950): 121-31 [Lk. 16:1-13].

5800.   J. Th. Ensfelder, "Interprétation de la parabole de l'économe infidèle," *RT* 4 (1852): 182-85.

5801.   K. W. Th. Pfeiffer, "Gleichnis 'vom ungerechten Haushalter'," *STZ* 8 (1891): 42-49 [Lk. 16:1-9].

5802.   Fritz Tillmann, "Zum Gleichnis vom ungerechten Verwalter, Lk. 16, 1-9," *BibZ* 9 (1911): 171-84.

5803.   J. A. de Klerk, "Een crux uit Lukas," *VT* 3 (1931-1932): 127-31 [Lk. 16:1-9].

5804.   H. Liese, "Villicus iniquitatis (Lc. 16, 1-9)," *VD* 12 (1932): 193-98.

5805.   Gerda Krüger, "Die geistesgeschichtlichen Grundlagen des Gleichnisses vom ungerechten Verwalter, Lk. 16, 1-9," *BibZ* 21 (1933): 170-81.

5806.   C. B. Firth, "The Parable of the Unrighteous Steward (Luke xvi. 1-9)," *ET* 63 (1951-1952): 93-95.

5807.   Paul G. Bretscher, "Brief Studies: The Parable of the Unjust Steward-A New Approach to Luke 16:1-9," *CTM* 22 (1951):

756-62.

5808. J. A. Davidson, "A 'Conjecture' about the Parable of the Unjust Steward (Luke xvi. 1-9)," *ET* 66 (1954-1955): 31.

5809. F. J. Williams, "The Parable of the Unjust Steward (Luke xvi. 1-9), Notes on the Interpretation Suggested by the Rev. R. G. Lunt," *ET* 66 (1954-1955): 371-72.

5810. J. Smit Sibinga, "De onrechtvaardige rentmeester naar het evangelie van Lucas," *VT* 26 (1955-1956): 112-21 [Lk. 16:1-9]

5811. B. A. Hooley and A. J. Mason, "Some Thoughts on the Parable of the Unjust Steward (Luke xvi. 1-9)," *ABR* 6 (1958): 47-59.

5812. A. H. Baverstock, "The Unjust Steward: An Interpretation," *Th* 35 (1937): 78-83 [Lk. 16:1-8a].

5813. John Coutts, "Studies in Texts: The Unjust Steward," *Th* 52 (1949): 54-60 [Lk. 16:1-8a].

5814. Herbert Preisker, "Lukas 16, 1-7," *TLZ* 74 (1949): 85-92.

5815. G. W. Stemler, "De rentmeester en zijn heer. Luk. 16, 1-9," *TS* 12 (1894): 414-21.

5816. Friedrich Köster, "Analekten zur Auslegung der Parabel vom ungerechten Haushalter," *TSK* 38 (1865): 725-34 [Lk. 16:1ff.].

5817. Dr. Hölbe, "Versuch einer Erklärung der Parabel vom ungerechten Haushalter, Luk. 16, 1ff.," *TSK* 31 (1858): 527-42.

5818. Simon Weber, "Revision gegen die Freisprechung des ungerechten Verwalters Luk. 16, 5-8," *TQ* 93 (1911): 339-63.

5819. G. Gander, "Le procédé de l'économe infidèle décrit Luc 16. 5-7 est-il répréhensible ou louable?" *VCar* 7 (1953): 128-41.

5820. M. Krämer, "Ad parabolam de villico iniquo (Lc. 16, 8. 9)," *VD* 38 (1960): 278-91.

5821. J. Skvireckas, "Neteisusis užvaizdas [villicus, iniquitatis Lk. 16, 8]," *Σ* 3 (1926): 43-49.

5822. C. T. Wood, "Luke xvi. 8," *ET* 63 (1951-1952): 126.

5823. Albert Descamps, "La composition littéraire de Luc XVI, 9-13," *NT* 1 (1956): 47-53.

5824. W. T. Whitley, "Luke xvi. 9-12," *ET* 25 (1913-1914):

332-33.

5825.   J. C. Wanset, "The Parable of the Unjust Steward: An Interpretation," *ET* 47 (1935-1936): 39-40 [Lk. 16:9].

5826.   R. Pautrel, " 'Aeterna Tabernacula' (Luc 16, 9)," *RSR* 30 (1940): 307-27.

5827.   Otto Hof, "Luthers Auslegung von Lukas 16, 9,"*EvT* 8 (1948-1949): 151-66.

5828.   R. D. Middleton, "St. Luke xvi. 9," *Th* 29 (1934): 41.

5829.   Nivard Schlögl, "Die Fabel vom 'ungerechten Reichtum' und die Aufforderung Jesu, sich damit Schätze für den Himmel zu sammeln," *BibZ* 14 (1916-1917): 41-43 [Lk. 16:9, 11].

5830.   K. W. Th. Pfeiffer, "Gleichnis vom 'reichen Mann und vom armen Lazarus' (Lukas 16, 10-30)," *STZ* 8 (1891): 163-70.

5831.   Konrad Köhler, "Zu Luk. 16, 10-12," *TSK* 94 (1922): 173-78.

5832.   Fred C. Anderson, "Luke xvi. 10," *ET* 59 (1947-1948): 278-79.

5833.   K. Knoke, "Textkritische Bemerkungen zu Luk. 16,11," *TSK* 67 (1894): 369-73.

5834.   R. P. C. Hanson, "A Note on Luke xvi. 14-31," *ET* 55(1943-1944): 221-22.

5835.   Ernst Bammel, "Is Luke 16, 16-18 of Baptist's Provenience?" *HTR* 51 (1958): 101-106.

5836.   Frederick W. Danker, "Luke 16. 16—An Opposition Logion," *JBL* 77 (1958): 231-43.

5837.   M. Dods, "Dives and Lazarus," *Exp* 3rd ser., 1 (1885): 45-59 [Lk. 16:19-31].

5838.   R. Cölle, "Zur Exegese und zur homiletischen Verwertung des Gleichnisses vom reichen Mann und armen Lazarus: Luk. 16, 19-31," *TSK* 75 (1902): 652-65.

5839.   L. W. Grensted, "The Use of Enoch in St. Luke xvi. 19-31," *ET* 26 (1914-1915): 333-34.

5840.   A. O. Standen, "The Parable of Dives and Lazarus, and Enoch 22," *ET* 33 (1921-1922): 523.

5841.   R. A. Hafer, "Dives and Poor Lazarus in the Light of Today," *LQ* 53 (1923): 476-81 [Lk. 16:19-31].

5842.   Karl Bornhäuser, "Zum Verständnis der Geschichte vom reichen Mann und armen Lazarus. Luk. 16, 19-31," *NKZ* 39

(1928): 833-43.

5843. Karl Barth, "Miserable Lazarus (Text: Luke 16:19-31)," *USR* 46 (1934-1935): 259-68

5844. W. Powell, "Parable of Dives and Lazarus (Luke xvi. 19-31)," *ET* 66 (1954-1955): 350-51.

5845. N. Rimmer, "Parable of Dives and Lazarus (Luke xvi. 19-31)," *ET* 66 (1954-1955): 215-16.

5846. Roderic Dunkerley, "Lazarus," *NTSt* 5 (1958-1959): 321-27 [Lk. 16:19-31; Jn. 11].

5847. L. Th. Lefort, "Le nom du mauvais riche (Lc 16. 19) et la tradition copte," *ZNW* 37 (1938): 65-72.

5848. H. A. Leenmans, "Lk. 16:21b," *NTS* 1 (1918): 104-105.

5849. Paul Haupt, "Abraham's Bosom," *AJP* 42 (1921): 162-67 [Lk. 16:22].

5850. Mircea Eliade, "Locum refrigerii. . .," *Z* 1 (1938): 203-208 [Lk. 16:24].

5851. F. Hugh Cadron, " 'Son' in the Parable of the Rich Man and Lazarus," *ET* 13 (1901-1902): 523 [Lk. 16:25].

5852. James Moffatt, "Jesus upon 'Stumbling-blocks'," *ET* 26 (1914-1915): 407-409 [Lk. 17:1-2].

5853. D. MacGillivray, "Luke xvii. 3," *ET* 25 (1913-1914): 333.

5854. Frederic Relton, "Christian Faith," *ET* 5 (1893-1894): 261-64 [Lk. 17:5]

5855. J. J. Murphy, "Unprofitable Servants," *Exp* 3rd ser., 10 (1889): 131-36 [Lk. 17.7-10].

5856. S. E. C. T., "The Dutiful Servant," *Exp* 1st ser., 8 (1878): 365-78 [Lk. 17:7-10].

5857. E. Riggenbach, "Ein Beitrag zum Verständnis der Parabel vom arbeitenden Knecht Luk. 17, 7-10," *NKZ* 34 (1923): 439-43.

5858. H. Liese, "Decem leprosi mundatur (Lc. 17, 11-19)," *VD* 12 (1932): 225-31.

5859. André Feuillet, "La venue du règne de Dieu et du fils de l'homme (d'après Luc XVII, 20 à XVIII, 8)," *RSR* 35 (1948): 544-65.

5860. James T. Hudson, "Q's Eschatology: A Study of Luke xvii. 20-37," *ET* 34 (1922-1923): 187-88.

5861. Edward A. McDowell, "The Kingdom of God and the Day of the Son of Man," *RE* 39 (1942): 54-65 [Lk. 17:20-37].

5862.   E. Schaubach, "Exegetische Bemerkungen zu Luk. 17, 20, 21," *TSK* 18 (1845): 169-72.

5863.   Richard Wegener, "Lukas Kap. 17 Vers. 20 und 21," *NKZ* 7 (1896): 278-304.

5864.   Burton S. Easton, "Luke 17:20-21. An Exegetical Study," *AJT* 16 (1912): 275-83.

5865.   C. Lindeboom, "Het koninkrijk Gods is binnen ulieden," *GTT* 20 (1919-1920): 334-39 [Lk. 17:20, 21].

5866.   Paul M. Bretscher, "Luke 17:20-21 in Recent Investigations," *CTM* 22 (1951): 895-908.

5867.   A. Strobel, "Die Passa-Erwartung als urchristliches Problem in Lc 17, 20 f.," *ZNW* 49 (1958): 157-96.

5868.   Alexander Rüstow, "ἐντὸς ὑμῶν ἐστίν. Zur Deutung von Lukas 17, 20-21," *ZNW* 51 (1960): 197-224.

5869.   A. Strobel, "A. Merx über Lc 17, 20 f.," *ZNW* 51 (1960): 133-34.

5870.   T. Nicklin, " 'With Observation'," *ET* 27 (1915-1916): 475 [Lk. 17:20].

5871.   P. N. Waggett, "Studies in Texts," *Th* 8 (1924): 163-66 [Lk 17:20].

5872.   A. Wabnitz, "Note sur Luc XVII, 21," *RTQR* 18 (1909): 234-38; "Note supplémentaire sur Luc XVII, 21," 289-94; "Seconde note supplémentaire . . .," 456-66.

5873.   K. F. Proost, "Lukas 17, 21, ἐντὸς ὑμῶν," *TT* 48 (1914): 246-53.

5874.   Frank Ballard, "Luke xvii. 21," *ET* 38 (1926-1927): 331.

5875.   F. Warburton Lewis, "Luke xvii. 21," *ET* 38 (1926-1927): 187-88.

5876.   Albert Geo. Smith, " 'The Kingdom of God is within you'," *ET* 43 (1931-1932): 378-79 [Lk. 17:21].

5877.   P. M. S. Allen, "Luke xvii. 21: ἰδοὺ γάρ, ἡ βασιλεία τοῦ θεοῦ ἐντὸς ὑμῶν ἐστιν," *ET* 49 (1937-1938): 476-77; 50 (1938-1939): 333-35.

5878.   Andrew Sledd, "The Interpretation of Luke xvii. 21," *ET* 50 (1938-1939): 235-37.

5879.   Paul M. Bretscher, "Luke 17:21," *CTM* 15 (1944): 730-36.

5880.   Allen Wikgren, "ἐντός," *Nunt* 4 (1950): 27-28 [Lk. 17:21].

5881. J. Gwyn Griffiths, "ἐντὸς ὑμῶν (Luke xvii. 21)," *ET* 63 (1951-1952): 30-31.

5882. W. Powell, "The Days of the Son of Man," *ET* 67 (1955-1956): 219 [Lk. 17:22-37].

5883. W. Winstanley, "Days of the Son of Man," *ET* 24 (1912-1913): 533-38 [Lk. 17:22].

5884. Robert Leaney, "The Days of the Son of Man," *ET* 67 (1955-1956): 28-29 [Lk. 17:22].

5885. E. Ashby, "The Days of the Son of Man," *ET* 67 (1955-1956): 124-25 [Lk. 17:22].

5886. A. W. Argyle, "Luke xvii. 31 f.," *ET* 64 (1952-1953): 222.

5887. A. Strobel, "In dieser Nacht (Luk. 17, 34)," *ZTK* N.F. 58 (1961): 16-29.

5888. R. Thibaut, "Erunt duo in lecto uno," *NRT* 58 (1931): 56-57 [Lk. 17 34].

5889. R. Thibaut, "Le proverbe des vautours et du cadavre," *NRT* 58 (1931): 57-58 [Lk. 17:37; Mt. 24:28].

5890. C. Spicq, "La parabole de la veuve obstinée et du juge inerte aux décisions impromptues (Lc. XVIII, 1-8)," *RB* 68 (1961): 68-90.

5891. Denis Buzy, "Le juge inique (Saint Luc, XVIII, 1-8)," *RB* 39 (1930): 378-91.

5892. Benjamin B. Warfield, "The Importunate Widow and the Alleged Failure of Faith," *ET* 25 (1913-1914): 69-72, 136-39 [Lk. 18:1-8].

5893. J. A. Robertson, "The Parable of the Unjust Judge (Luke xviii.1-8)," *ET* 38 (1926-1927): 389-92.

5894. H. G. Meecham, "The Parable of the Unjust Judge," *ET* 57 (1945-1946): 306-307 [Lk. 18:1-8].

5895. Philipp Tag, "Zur Exegese von Luk. 18,7 und Gal. 2,3-6," *TSK* 57 (1884): 167-72.

5896. G. Philip Robertson, "Luke xviii. 8," *ET* 40 (1928-1929): 525-26.

5897. L. Fonck, "Pharisaeus et publicanus (Lc. 18,9-14)," *VD* 1 (1921): 194-99.

5898. R. S. Franks, "The Parable of the Pharisee and the Publican," *ET* 38 (1926-1927): 373-76 [Lk. 18:9-14].

5899. C. Clare Oke, "The Parable of the Pharisee and the

Publican," *CJRT* 5 (1928): 122-26.

5900. F. F. Bruce, "Justification by Faith in the Non-Pauline Writings of the New Testament," *EQ* 24 (1952): 66-67 [Lk. 18:10-14, etc.].

5901. Robert G. Hoerber, " 'God be merciful to me a sinner'- A Note on Luke 18:13," *CTM* 33 (1962): 283-86.

5902. H. Meulenbelt, "Lk. 18, 13," *NTS* 2 (1919): 5.

5903. L. Fonck, "Caecus in Iericho sanatur (Lc. 18,31-43)," *VD* 3 (1923): 34-42.

5904. Arnold Brooks, "Salvation and Loss in the Story of Zacchaeus," *ET* 33 (1921-1922): 286-88 [Lk. 19:1-10].

5905. John Willcock, "St. Luke xix. 8," *ET* 28 (1916-1917): 236-37.

5906. Lucien Gautier, "St. Luke xix. 8," *ET* 28 (1916-1917): 284.

5907. Eugene Stock, "The Pounds and the Talents," *ET* 22 (1910-1911): 424-25 [Lk. 19:11-27].

5908. W. McCulloch, "The Pounds and the Talents," *ET* 23 (1911-1912): 382-83 [Lk. 19:11-27].

5909. Robert Candlish, "The Pounds and the Talents," *ET* 23 (1911-1912): 136-37.

5910. J. G. Simpson, "The Parable of the Pounds," *ET* 37 (1925-1926): 299-303 [Lk. 19:11-27].

5911. Henry Clarence Thiessen, "The Parable of the Nobleman and the Earthly Kingdom," *BS* 91 (1934): 180-90.

5912. M. Zerwick, "Die Parabel vom Thronanwärter," *B* 40 (1959): 654-74 [Lk. 19:11-27].

5913. P. Thomson, " 'Carry on!' (Luke xix. 13)," *ET* 30 (1918-1919): 277.

5914. F. E. Brightman, "Six Notes," *JTS* 29 (1927-1928): 158-65 [Lk 19:21].

5915. Rayner Winterbotham, "Christ, or Archelaus?" *Exp* 8th ser., 4 (1912): 338-47 [Lk. 19:21].

5916. Prebendary Whitefoord, "A Study of St. Luke xix. 40," *ET* 8 (1896-1897): 362-64.

5917. J. Rendel Harris, "The Lachrymatory of Jesus," *ET* 51 (1939-1940): 109 [Lk. 19:41, 42].

5918. H. L. Oort, "Lucas 20, 18b," *TT* 43 (1909): 138-40.

5919. T. H. Weir, "Luke xx. 20," *ET* 28 (1916-1917): 426.

5920. Maurice Wiles, "Studies in Texts: Luke xx. 34-36," *Th* 60 (1957): 500-502.

5921. W. J. Ferrar, "A Note on Luke xx. 39," *ET* 30 (1918-1919): 39.

5922. Paul Winter, "The Treatment of his Sources by the Third Evangelist in Luke XXI-XXIV," *ST* 8 (1954): 138-72.

5923. Lloyd Gaston, "Sondergut und Markusstoff in Luk. 21," *TZ* 16 (1960): 161-72.

5924. C. A. Phillips, "Luke 21, 1: Mc. 12, 41," *BBC* 6 (1929): 25-26.

5925. Vincent Taylor, "A Cry from the Siege: A Suggestion regarding a non-Markan Oracle Imbedded in Luke xvi. 20-36," *JTS* 26 (1924-1925): 136-44.

5926. P. Christophorus a Vico Gargano, "Secundus Christi Adventus (Lc. 21, 25-33)," *VD* 19 (1939): 338-46.

5927. U. Holzmeister, " 'Respicite et levate capita vestra, quoniam appropinquat redemptio vestra' (Lc. 21, 28)," *VD* 18 (1938): 353-61.

5928. James Coffin Stout, "ἀγρυπνεῖν—Luke 21: 36," *BR* 3 (1918): 621-23.

5929. Irénée Fransen, "Le baptême de sang (Luc 22, 1-23, 56)," *BVC* no. 25 (1959): 20-28.

5930. Émile Osty, "Les points de contact entre le récit de la Passion dans saint Luc et dans saint Jean," *RSR* 39 (1951-1952): 146-54 [Lk. 22:3-23; 56; Jn 13; 18:1-19:42].

5931. O. Linton, "The Trial of Jesus and the Interpretation of Psalm cx," *NTSt* 7 (1960-1961): 258-62.

5932. Paul Winter, "Luke 22, 7-18," *VT* 26 (1955-1956): 88-91.

5933. John Foster, " 'Go and make ready' (Luke xxii. 8, John xiv. 2)," *ET* 63 (1951-1952): 193.

5934. Hugh MacMillan, "The Man Bearing a Pitcher of Water," *ET* 3 (1891-1892): 58-60 [Lk. xxii. 10].

5935. G. A. van den Bergh van Eysinga, "De breking des broods," *TT* 39 (1905): 244-69 [Lk. 22: 14-26].

5936. W. F. Skene, "St. Luke's Account of the Institution of the Lord's Supper," *Exp* 2nd ser., 3 (1882): 478-80 [Lk. 22:14-23].

5937. Herbert E. D. Blakiston, "The Lucan Account of the

Institution of the Lord's Supper," *JTS* 4 (1902-1903): 548-55 [Lk. 22:14-23].

5938. Ivar P. Seierstad, "Lukas 22, 14-20," *TTK* 18 (1947): 83-107.

5939. Lucien Delporte, "Un texte de Saint Luc sur notre solidarité avec le Christ (Ev. 22, 15-37)," *ETL* 3 (1926): 475-92.

5940. H. N. Bate, "The 'Shorter Text' of St. Luke xxii. 15-20," *JTS* 28 (1926-1927): 362-68.

5941. Pierre Benoit, "Le récit de la cène dans Lc. XXII, 15-20 (étude de critique textuelle et littéraire)," *RB* 48 (1939): 357-93.

5942. Henry Chadwick, "The Shorter Text of Luke XXII. 15-20," *HTR* 50 (1957): 249-58.

5943. F. Blass, "Zu Luk. 22, 15 ff.," *TSK* 69 (1896): 733-37.

5944. Heinz Schürmann, "Die Gestalt der urchristlichen Eucharistiefeier," *MTZ* 6 (1955): 107-22 [Lk. 22: 15 ff.].

5945. G. H. Box, "St. Luke xxii. 15, 16," *JTS* 10 (1908-1909): 106-107.

5946. A. E. Brooke and F. C. Burkitt, "St. Luke xxii. 15, 16: What is the General Meaning?" *JTS* 9 (1907-1908): 569-72.

5947. C. K. Barrett, "Luke xxii. 15: To Eat the Passover," *JTS* N.S. 9 (1958): 305-307.

5948. Matthew Black, "The 'Fulfilment' in the Kingdom of God," *ET* 57 (1945-1946): 25-26 [Lk. 22: 16].

5949. Harold McA. Robinson, "The Text of Luke XXII. 17-25," *PTR* 8 (1910): 613-56.

5950. F. C. Burkitt, "On Luke xxii. 17-20," *JTS* 28 (1926-1927): 178-81.

5951. W. A. Gray, "The Three Cups," *ET* 12 (1900-1901): 295-99 [Lk. 22: 18].

5952. F. X. Porporato, "De Lucana pericopa 22, 19b-20," *VD* 13 (1933): 114-22.

5953. K. Goetz, "Das vorausweisende Demonstrativom in Lc 22, 19-20 und 1 Cor. 11, 24," *ZNW* 38 (1939): 188-90.

5954. George D. Kilpatrick, "Luke xxii. 19b-20," *JTS* 47 (1946): 49-56.

5955. Pierre Benoit, "Luc xxii. 19b-20," *JTS* 49 (1948): 145-47.

5956. B. H. Throckmorton, "The Longer Reading of Luke 22: 19b-20," *ATR* 30 (1948): 55-56.

5957. H. Schürmann, "Lu 22, 19b-20—als ursprüngliche Textüberlieferung," *B* 32 (1951): 364-92, 522-41.

5958. Karl Th. Schäfer, "Zur Textgeschichte von Lk. 22, 19b-20," *B* 33 (1952): 237-39.

5959. Alfred Plummer, "This do in Remembrance of Me," *Exp* 3rd ser., 7 (1888): 441-49 [Lk. 22:19; 1 Cor. 11:24].

5960. Eb. Nestle, " 'This do in Remembrance of Me'," *ET* 16 (1904-1905): 144 [Lk. 22:19].

5961. J. C. Todd, " 'Do This in Remembrance of Me'," *ET* 23 (1911-1912): 378-379 [Lk. 22:19].

5962. F. X. Porporato, " 'Hoc facite in meam commemorationem' (Lc. 22, 19; 1 Cor. 11, 24. 25)," *VD* 13 (1933): 264-70.

5963. Walter Lock, "Studies in Texts," *Th* 7 (1923): 284-85 [Lk. 22:19].

5964. Werner Foerster, "Lukas 22, 31 f.," *ZNW* 46 (1955): 129-33.

5965. F. J. Botha, "ὑμᾶς in Luke xxii. 31," *ET* 64 (1952-1953): 125.

5966. P. Thomson, "ἐπιστρέφω (Luke xxii. 32)," *ET* 38 (1926-1927): 468.

5967. R. E. Lee, "Luke xxii. 32," *ET* 38 (1926-1927): 233-34.

5968. C. H. Pickar, "The Prayer of Christ for Saint Peter," *CBQ* 4 (1942): 133-40 [Lk. 22:32].

5969. R. T. O'Callaghan, " 'Et tu aliquando conversus,' St. Luke 22, 32," *CBQ* 15 (1953): 305-14.

5970. T. M. Napier, " 'The Enigma of the Swords' (Luke xxii. 35-38)," *ET* 51 (1939-1940): 204.

5971. Arthur Wright, "Study of St. Luke xxii. 35-38," *ET* 4 (1892-1893): 153-57.

5972. W. Western, " 'The Enigma of the Swords'," *ET* 50 (1938-1939): 377 [Lk. 22:35-38].

5973. Stephen Hobhouse, " 'And he that hath no sword, let him . . . buy one' (Luke xxii. 35-38)," *ET* 30 (1918-1919): 278-79.

5974. S. K. Finlayson, " 'The Enigma of the Swords'," *ET* 50 (1938-1939): 563 [Lk. 22:35-38].

5975. Carpus, "Principles, not Rules," *Exp* 1st ser., 6 (1877): 312-20 [Lk. 22:35-36].

5976. R. F. Wright, "Studies in Texts," *Th* 44 (1942): 296-300 [Lk. 22: 36, 38].

5977. Edward A. McDowell, "Exegetical Notes," *RE* 38 (1941): 44-48 [Lk. 22:36, 38; Mt. 10:23].

5978. W. Western, "The Enigma of the Swords, St. Luke xxii. 38," *ET* 52 (1940-1941): 357.

5979. Eric F. F. Bishop, "A Stone's Throw," *ET* 53 (1941-1942): 270-71 [Lk. 22:41].

5980. Heinz Schürmann, "Lk. 22, 42a das älteste Zeugnis für Lk. 22, 20," *MTZ* 3 (1952): 185-88.

5981. Lyder Brun, "Engel und Blutschweiss, Lc 22, 43-44," *ZNW* 32 (1933): 265-76.

5982. Harold Smith, "Acts xx. 8 and Luke xxii. 43," *ET* 16 (1904-1905): 478.

5983. U. Holzmeister, "Exempla sudoris sanguinei (Lc. 22, 44)," *VD* 18 (1938): 73-81.

5984. Paul Joüon, "Luc XXII, 50-51: τὸ οὖς, τοῦ ὠτίου," *RSR* 24 (1934): 473-74.

5985. Joseph B. Tyson, "The Lukan Version of the Trial of Jesus," *NT* 3 (1959): 249-58 [Lk. 22:66-23:25].

5986. Paul Winter, "Luke 22, 66b-71," *ST* 9 (1955): 112-15.

5987. A. W. Verrall, "Christ Before Herod. Luke xxiii. 1-16," *JTS* 10 (1908-1909): 321-53.

5988. Karl Bornhäuser, "Die Beteiligung des Herodes am Prozesse Jesu," *NKZ* 40 (1929): 714-18 [Lk. 23:6 ff.].

5989. Paul Joüon, "Luc 23, 2: ἐσθῆτα λαμπράν *RSR* 26 (1936): 80-85.

5990. E. Graf, "Ueber die Echtheit und die Bedeutung der Worte in Luk. 23, 34: Vater, vergib ihnen," *TSK* 34 (1861): 749-64.

5991. Eb. Nestle, " 'Father, forgive them'," *ET* 14 (1902-1903): 285-86 [Lk. 23: 34].

5992. Donald M. Henry, " 'Father, forgive them; for they know not what they do' (Luke xxiii. 34)," *ET* 30 (1918-1919): 87.

5993. A. H. Dammers, "Studies in Texts," *Th* 52 (1949): 138-39 [Lk. 23:34a].

5994. J. Bouton Lawrence, "The Penitent Thief," *BS* 53 (1896): 574-78 [Lk. 23:39-43].

5995. Theodore B. Blathwayt, "The Penitent Thief," *ET* 18 (1906-1907): 288 [Lk. 23:39-43].

5996. Agnes Smith Lewis, "A New Reading of Luke xxiii. 39," *ET*

18 (1906-1907): 94-95.

5997. G. Currie Martin, "A New Reading of Luke xxiii. 39," *ET* 18 (1906-1907): 334-35.

5998. F. von Himpel, "Das Fragment der Apologie des Aristides und eine Abhandlung über Luk. 23, 42. 43. Aus dem Armenischen übersetzt und erläutert," *TQ* 62 (1880): 109-27.

5999. Friedrich West, "Betrachtungen über einige eschatologische Stellen der heiligen Schrift," *TSK* 31 (1858): 248-78 [Lk. 23:43].

6000. Eb. Nestle, "Luke xxiii. 43," *ET* 11 (1899-1900): 429.

6001. W. K. Lowther Clarke, "St. Luke and the Pseudepigrapha: Two Parallels," *JTS* 15 (1913-1914): 597-99 [Lk. 23: 44-48; Acts 16:23-25].

6002. George D. Kilpatrick, "A Theme of the Lucan Passion Story and Luke xxiii. 47," *JTS* 43 (1942): 34-36.

6003. J. Rendel Harris, "The Origin of a Famous Lucan Gloss," *ET* 35 (1923-1924): 7-10 [Lk. 23:48].

6004. H. S. Cronin, "They Rested the Sabbath Day according to the Commandment," *ET* 16 (1904-1905): 115-18 [Lk. 23:56].

6005. T. H. Weir, " 'The Stone Rolled Away' (Luke xxiv. 2)," *ET* 24 (1912-1913): 284.

6006. A. R. C. Leaney, "The Resurrection Narratives in Luke (xxiv. 12-53)," *NTSt* 2 (1955-1956): 110-14.

6007. Clayton R. Bowen, "The Emmaus Disciples and the Purposes of Luke," *BW* 35 (1910): 234-45 [Lk. 24:13-35].

6008. C. Evelyn Charlesworth, "The Unnamed Companion of Cleopas," *ET* 34 (1922-1923): 233-34 [Lk 24:13-35]

6009. A. E. Burn, "The Unnamed Companion of Cleopas," *ET* 34 (1922-1923): 428-29 [Lk. 24:13-35].

6010. Alexander B. Grosart, "Lost or Latent Powers of the Five Senses," *Exp* 4th ser., 4 (1891): 108-19 [Lk. 24.13-35].

6011. G. M. Perrella—A. Vaccari, "De vi critices textus et archaeologiae circa Lc. 24, 13-28," *VD* 17 (1937): 186-91.

6012. J. Esslemont Adams, "The Emmaus Story, Lk. xxiv. 13-25: A Suggestion," *ET* 17 (1905-1906): 333-35.

6013. R. T. Murphy, "The Gospel for Easter Monday," *CBQ* 6 (1944): 131-41 [Lk. 24:13-25].

6014. A. Souter, " 'Emmaus' Mistaken for a Person," *ET* 13

(1901-1902): 429-30 [Lk. 24:13].

6015. P. A. Arce, "Emmaús y algunos textos desconocidos," *EB* 13 (1954): 53-90.

6016. William Olney, "The Divine Expositor," *ET* 27 (1915-1916) 184 [Lk. 24:27].

6017. I. H. Hall, "Luke xxiv. 32 in Syriac," *JBL* 3 (1883): 153-54.

6018. A. H. van Zyl, "Die Emmausgangers as Leerlinge van Jezus," *NGTT* 2 (1961): 113-14 [Lk. 24:32].

6019. Eb. Nestle, "Luke xxiv. 34 f.," *ET* 20 (1908-1909): 380.

6020. Kirsopp Lake, "Luke xxiv. 34 f.," *ET* 17 (1905-1906): 191.

6021. J. Hugh Michael, The Text of Luke xxiv. 34," *ET* 60 (1948-1949): 292.

6022. James Reid, "Luke xxiv. 35," *ET* 49 (1937-1938): 186-89.

6023. Eb. Nestle, "The Honeycomb in Luke xxiv," *ET* 22 (1910-1911): 567-68. [Lk. 24:42].

6024. Augustin George, "L'intelligence des Écritures (Luc 24, 44-53)," *BVC* no. 18 (1957): 65-71.

6025. G. Currie Martin, "Luke xxiv. 51," *ET* 8 (1896-1897): 182-83.

6026. Theodore D. Woolsey, "The End of Luke's Gospel and the Beginning of the Acts. Two Studies," *BS* 39 (1882): 593-619.

6027. Ferdinand Graefe, "Der Schluss des Lukasevangeliums und der Anfang der Apostelgeschichte," *TSK* 61 (1888): 522-41.

On Lk. 1:25 and 61, see also number 3501; 1:37 and 41, 3679; 1:54-55, 3379; 2:2, *10074*; 2:23, 3501; 3:2, 3679; 3:15, 3679; 3:16 and 22, 3686; 3:22, 3684; 4:16-28, 3681; 5:1-11, 3681; 6:40, 3682; 7:1, 3683; 7:36-50, 3681; 7:47, 3687, *10071*; 8:8, 1704; 8:10, *10082*; 9:51-11:13, *10073*; 9:54-56, 1703; 10:25-37, *10080*; 10:38-42, 3688, 3680, 6526; 11:24ff., *10080*; 11:47-48, 4605; 11:49-51, 4607 ff.; 12:1-59, 3681; 12:2 and 15, 3682; 12:15, 1925; 12:35-40, 2951; 13:32, 3682; 13:34 f., 4607; 14:15-24, *10068*; 16:1-13, *10049*; 16:16-17, 3691; 18:1-18, *10077*; 18:25, 4510; 19:28-38, 4544 ff.; 21:19, 3682; 22:19-20, 2117; 22:47, 3684; 22:51, 3682; 23:47, 2519; 24:32, 2077.

6027.1 Kurt Aland, "Eine neue Ausgabe des griechischen Neuen Testaments: Zur Oxforder Ausgabe von Luk. 1-12," *TR* 80 (1984): 441-48 [1-12].

6027.2   D. J. Sneed, "An Exegesis of Luke 1:1-4 with Special Regard to Luke's Purpose as a Historian," *ET* 83 (1971-1972): 40-43 [1:1-4].

6027.3   G. Menestrina, "L'incipit dell'espitola 'Ad Diognetum,' Luca 1:1-4 et Atti 1:1-2," *BO* 19 (1977): 215-18 [1:1-4].

6027.4   Roger L. Omanson, "A Note on Luke 1.1-4," *BTr* 30 (1979): 446-47 [1:1-4].

6027.5   R. J. Dillon, "Previewing Luke's Project from his Prologue (Luke 1:1-4)," *CBQ* 43 (1981): 205-27 [1:1-4].

6027.6   R. Dillmann, "Das Lukasevangelium als Tendenzschrift: Leserlenkung und Leseintention in Lk 1,1-4," *BibZ* 38 (1994): 86-93 [1:1-4].

6027.7   Thomas L. Brodie, "A New Temple and a New Law," *JSNT* 5 (1979): 21-45 [1:1-4:22].

6027.8   M. Völkel, "Exegetische Erwagungen zum Verständnis des Begriffs καθεξῆς im Lukanischen Prolog," *NTSt* 20 (1973-1974): 289-99 [1-3].

6027.9   A. Smitmans, "Die Hymnen der Kindheitsgeschichte nach Lukas," *BK* 21 (1966): 115-18 [1-2].

6027.10   G. Voss, "Die Christusverkündigung der Kindheitgeschichte im Rahmen des Lukasevangeliums," *BK* 21 (1966): 112-15 [1-2].

6027.11   L. R. Helyer, "Luke and the Restoration of Israel," *JETS* 36 (1993): 317-29 [1-2].

6027.12   André Feuillet, "Témoins oculaires et serviteurs de la parole," *NT* 15 (1973): 241-59 [1:2].

6027.13   Brigitte Kahl, "Armenevangelium und Heidenevangelium: 'Sola Scriptura' und die ökumenische Traditions Problematik," *TLZ* 110 (1985): 779-81 [1:3].

6027.14   Roland Meynet, "Dieu Donne Son Nom à Jésus: Analyse Rhétorique de Lc. 1:26-56 et de 1 Sam. 2:1-10," *B* 66/1 (1985): 39-72 [1:26-56].

6027.15   B. Prete, "Il racconto dell'Annunziazione di Luca 1,26-38," *BO* 15 (1973): 75-88 [1:26-38].

6027.16   D. Moody Smith, "Luke 1:26-38," *Interp* 29 (1975): 411-17 [1:26-38].

6027.17   Klemens Stock, "Die Berufung Marias (Luke 1:26-38)," *B* 61 (1980): 457-91 [1:26-38].

6027.18   D. T. Landry, "Narrative Logic in the Annunciation to Mary,"

JBL 114 (1995): 65-79 [1:26-38].

6027.19 Charles H. Talbert, "Luke 1:26-31," *Interp* 39 (1985): 288-91 [1:26-31].

6027.20 Jean Carmignac, "The Meaning of παρθένον in Lk 1,27: A Reply to C. H. Dodd," *BTr* 28 (1977): 327-30 [1:27].

6027.21 A. Strobel, "Der Gruss an Maria (Lc 1:28): Eine Philologische Betrachtung Zu Seinem Sinngehalt," *ZNW* 53/1-2 (1962): 86-110 [1:28].

6027.22 G. M. Verd, " 'Gratia plena' (Lc 1,28). Sentido de una traduccion," *EE* 50 (1975): 357-89 [1:28].

6027.23 Carlo Buzzetti, "κεχαριτωμένη, 'Favoured' (Lk 1:28), and the Italian Common Language New Testament," *BTr* 33 (1982): 243 [1:28].

6027.24 I. de la Potterie, "κεχαριτωμένη, en Lc 1,28: Étude philologique," *B* 68 (1987): 357-82 [1:28].

6027.25 Gerhard Schneider, "Lk 1,34.35 als redaktionelle Einheit," *BibZ* 15 (1971): 255-59 [1:34-35].

6027.26 Hans Quecke, "Lk. 1:34 in Den Alten Ubersetzungen und im Protevangelium des Jakobus," *B* 44/4 (1963): 499-520 [1:34].

6027.27 J. B. Bauer, "Philologische Bemerkungen zu Lk. 1:34," *B* 45/4 (1964): 535-40 [1:34].

6027.28 M. Orsatti, "Verso la decodificazione di un insolita espressione (Luke 1:34)," *RivB* 29 (1981): 343-57 [1:34].

6027.29 Tjitze Baarda, "Dionysios Bar Salibi and the Text of Luke 1:35," VC 17 (1963): 225-29 [1:35].

6027.30 A. Vicent Cernuda, "La presunta sustantivacion de *gennōmenon* en Lc 1,35b," *EB* 33 (1974): 265-73 [1:35].

6027.31 Silverio Zedda, "Lc 1,35b, 'Colui che nascerà santo sarà chiamato Figlio di Dio': I. Breve storia dell'esegesi recente," *RivB* 33 (1985): 29-43 [1:35].

6027.32 James P. Martin, "Luke 1:39-47," *Interp* 36 (1982): 394-99 [1:39-47].

6027.33 J. M. Salgado, "La visitation de la Sainte Vierge Marie: exercice de sa Maternité Spirituelle," *Div* 16 (1972): 445-52 [1:39-45].

6027.34 H. B. Beverly, "Luke 1:39-45," *Interp* 30 (1976): 396-400 [1:39-45].

6027.35 D. Minguez, "Poética generativa del Magnificat," *B* 61 (1980): 55-77 [1:46-55].

6027.36 Bruce H. Grigsby, "Compositional Hypotheses for the Lucan 'Magnificat': Tensions for the Evangelical," *EQ* 56 (1984): 159-72 [1:46-55].

6027.37 P. L. Schoonheim, "Der alttestamentliche Boden der Vokabel *uperêphanos*, Lukas i,51," *NT* 8 (1966): 235-46 [1:51].

6027.38 H. Vermeyen, "Mariologie als Befreiung. Luke 1:26-45, 56 im Kontext," *ZKT* 105 (1983): 168-83 [1:56].

6027.39 Gerard Mussies, "Vernoemen in de antieke wereld: De historische achtergrond van Luk. 1,59-63," *NTT* 42 (1988): 114-25 [1:59-63].

6027.40 Albert Vanhoye, "Structure du 'Benedictus'," *NTSt* 12 (1965-1966): 382-89 [1:68-79].

6027.41 P. Auffret, "Note sur la structure littéraire de Luke 1:68-79," *NTSt* 24 (1977-1978): 248-58 [1:68-79].

6027.42 F. Rousseau, "Les Structures du Benedictus (Luc 1:68-79)," *NTSt* 32/2 (1986): 268-82 [1:68-79].

6027.43 Darrell L. Bock, "The Son of David and the Saints' Task: The Hermeneutics of Initial Fulfillment," *BS* 150 (1993): 440-57 [1:68-79].

6027.44 G. Ogg, "The Quirinius Question Today," *ET* 79 (1967-1968): 231-36 [2:1-7].

6027.45 J. D. M. Derrett, "Further Light on the Narratives of the Nativity," *NT* 17 (1975): 81-108 [2:1-7].

6027.46 P. W. Barnett, "ἀπογραφὴ and ἀπογράφεσθαι in Luke 2:1-5," *ET* 85 (1973-1974): 377-80 [2:1-5].

6027.47 Royce L. B. Morris, "Why Αὐγούστος? A Note to Luke 2:1," *NTSt* 38 (1992): 142-44 [2:1].

6027.48 George D. Kilpatrick, "Luke 2:4-5 and Leviticus 25:10," *ZNW* 80/3-4 (1989): 264-65 [2:4-5].

6027.49 Alwyn Pritchard, "Our True Selves," *ET* 94 (1982-1983): 81-82 [2:12].

6027.50 Eric F. F. Bishop, "Men of God's Good Pleasure," *ATR* 48 (1966): 63-69 [2:14].

6027.51 J. Riedl, " 'Ehre sei Gott in der Höhe'. Meditation über Lukas 2:14," *BK* 21 (1966): 119-22 [2:14].

6027.52 Paul R. Berger, "Luke 2:14: ἀνθρώποις εὐδοκίας. Die auf

Gottes Weisung mit Wohlgefallen beschenkten Menschen," *ZNW* 74 (1983): 129-44 [2:14].

6027.53 Paul R. Berger, "Menschen Ohne 'Gottes Wohlgefallen' Lk. 2:14," *ZNW* 76/1-2 (1985): 119-22 [2:14].

6027.54 A. Wolters, "Anthrōpoi eudokias (Luke 2:14) and 'śy rṣwn (4Q416)," *JBL* 113 (1994): 291-92 [2:14].

6027.55 Christoph Burchard, "Fußnoten zum neutestamentlichen Griechisch II," *ZNW* 69 (1978): 143-57 [2:15].

6027.56 Christoph Burchard, "A Note on ῥῆμα in JosAs 17:1f.; Luke 2:15, 17; Acts 10:37," *NT* 27 (1985): 281-95 [2:15].

6027.57 Paul Ellingworth, "Luke 2:17: Just Who Spoke to the Shepherds?" *BTr* 31 (1980): 447 [2:17].

6027.58 D. Ogston, "A Time for Pause," *ET* 89 (1977-1978): 50-52 [2:19].

6027.59 G. Bellia, " 'Confrontando nel suo cuore.' Custodia sapienziale di Maria in Luke 2:19b," *BO* 25 (1983): 215-28 [2:19].

6027.60 Marion L. Soards, "Luke 2:22-40," *Interp* 44 (1990): 400-405 [2:22-40].

6027.61 P. Figueras, "Syméon et Anne, ou le témoignage de la loi et des prophètes," *NT* 20 (1978): 84-99 [2:22-38].

6027.62 A. R. C. McLellan, "What the Law Required," *ET* 94 (1982-1983): 82-83 [2:22].

6027.63 T. Stramare, " 'Sanctum Domino vocabitur' (Luke 2:23): Il crocevia dei riti è la Santità," *BO* 25 (1983): 21-34 [2:23].

6027.64 Robert C. Tannehill, "Israel in Luke-Acts: A Tragic Story," *JBL* 104 (1985): 69-85 [2:29-32].

6027.65 A. Smitmans, " 'Ein Licht zur Erleuchtung der Völker' (Luke 2:32). Meditation über das *Nunc dimittis*," *BK* 24 (1969): 138-39 [2:32].

6027.66 John J. Kilgallen, "Jesus, Savior, the Glory of Your People," *B* 75 (1994): 305-28 [2:32].

6027.67 M. P. John, "Luke 2,36-37: How Old Was Anna?" *BTr* 26 (1975): 247 [2:36-37].

6027.68 J. K. Elliott, "Anna's Age," *NT* 30 (1988): 100-102 [2:36-37].

6027.69 Otto Glombitza, "Der Zwölfjährige Jesus, Luk 2:40-52: Ein Beitrag zur Exegese der Lukanischen Vorgeschichte," *NT* 5

(1962): 1-4 [2:40-52].

6027.70   J. F. Jansen, "Luke 2:41-52," *Interp* 30 (1976): 400-404 [2:41-52].

6027.71   E. Schüssler Fiorenza, "Luke 2:41-52," *Interp* 36 (1982): 399-403 [2:41-52].

6027.72   John J. Kilgallen, "Luke 2:41-50: Foreshadowing of Jesus, Teacher," *B* 66/4 (1985): 553-59 [2:41-50].

6027.73   J. Bishop, "The Compulsion of Love," *ET* 85 (1973-1974): 371-73 [2:49].

6027.74   Juan M. Lozano, "Jesucristo en la Espiritualidad de San Antonio María Claret," *EE* 60 (1985): 157-79 [2:49].

6027.75   S. M. Harris, "My Father's House," *ET* 94 (1982-1983): 84-85 [2:50].

6027.76   B. Couroyer, "À propos de Luke 2:52," *RB* 86 (1979): 92-101 [2:52].

6027.77   W. Brueggemann, "Luke 3:1-4," *Interp* 30 (1976): 404-409 [3:1-4].

6027.78   V. E. McEachern, "Dual Witness and Sabbath Motif in Luke," *CJT* 12 (1966): 267-80 [3:1-2].

6027.79   A. Strobel, "Plädoyer fur Lukas: Zur Stimmigkeit des chronistischen Rahmens van Lk 3.1," *NTSt* 41 (1995): 466-69 [3:1].

6027.80   Gerd Theissen, "Lokalkoloritforschung in den Evangelien: Plädoyer für die Erneuerung Einer Alten Fragestellung," *EvT* 45 (1985): 481-99 [3:2-3].

6027.81   B. L. Robertson, "Luke 3:10-18," *Interp* 36 (1982): 404-409 [3:10-18].

6027.82   N. Lohfink, "Vom Täufer Johannes und den Törichten Jungfrauen: Das Evangelium und seine sozialen Konsequenzen," *BK* 50 (1995): 26-31 [3:10-18].

6027.83   P. Proulx and L. Alonso Schokel, "Las Sandalias del Mesías Esposo," *B* 59 (1978): 1-37 [3:16].

6027.84   James S. Alexander, "A Note on the Interpretation of the Parable of the Threshing Floor at the Conference at Carthage of A.D. 411," *JTS* 24/2 (1973): 512-19 [3:17].

6027.85   J. Rius-Camps, "Constituye Lc 3,21-38 un solo periodo? Propuesta de un cambio de puntuación," *B* 65 (1984): 189-209 [3:21-38].

6027.86 K. H. Schelkle, "Die Frauen im Stammbaum Jesu," *BK* 18 (1963): 113-15 [3:23-38].

6027.87 E. Lerle, "Die Ahnenverzeichnisse Jesu. Versuch einer christologischen Interpretation," *ZNW* 72 (1981): 112-17 [3:23-38].

6027.88 Homer Heater, "A Textual Note on Luke 3:33," *JSNT* 28 (1986): 25-29 [3:33].

6027.89 D. C. Hester, "Luke 4:1-13," *Interp* 31 (1977): 53-59 [4:1-13].

6027.90 F. Gerald Downing, "Cynics and Christians," *NTSt* 30/4 (1984): 584-93 [4:1-13].

6027.91 Roy Yates, "Jesus and the Demonic in the Synoptic Gospels," *ITQ* 44 (1977): 39-57 [4:1-12].

6027.92 C. Escudero Freire, "Jesús profeta, libertador del hombre: Visión lucana de su ministerio terrestre," *EE* 51 (1976): 463-96 [4:14-44].

6027.93 A. del Agua Pérez, "El cumplimiento del Reino de Dios en la misión de Jesús: Programa del Evangelico de Lucas (Luke 4:14-44)," *EB* 38 (1979-1980): 269-93 [4:14-44].

6027.94 Hugh Anderson, "Broadening Horizons: The Rejection at Nazareth Pericope of Luke 4:16-30 in Light of Recent Critical Trends," *Interp* 18 (1964): 259-75 [4:16-30].

6027.95 A. Strobel, "Das apokalyptische Terminproblem in der sogenannten Antrittspredigt Jesu," *TLZ* 92 (1967): 251-54 [4:16-30].

6027.96 David Hill, "The Rejection of Jesus at Nazareth: Luke 4:16-30," *NT* 13/3 (1971): 161-80 [4:16-30].

6027.97 M. Rodgers, "Luke 4:16-30: A Call for a Jubilee Year?" *RTR* 40 (1981): 72-82 [4:16-30].

6027.98 Joseph B. Tyson, "The Jewish Public in Luke-Acts," *NTSt* 30/4 (1984): 574-83 [4:16-30].

6027.99 G. de Virgilio, "Essenza e diaconia dell'evangelizzazione nel terzo vangelo," *BO* 35 (1993): 3-13 [4:16-30].

6027.100 Patrick D. Miller, "Luke 4:16-21," *Interp* 29 (1975): 417-21 [4:16-21].

6027.101 K. H. Schelkle, "Jesus und Paulus lesen die Bibel," *BK* 36 (1981): 277-79 [4:16-21].

6027.102 Dirk Monshouwer, "The Reading of the Prophet in the Synagogue at Nazareth," *B* 72 (1991): 90-99 [4:16-21].

6027.103   J. Smit Sibinga, "The Function of Verbal Forms in Luke-Acts," *FilN* 6 (1993): 31-50 [4:16-20].

6027.104   Heinrich Baarlink, "Ein gnädiges Jahr des Hern und Tage der Vergeltung," *ZNW* 73 (1982): 204-20 [4:18-19].

6027.105   R. Koch, "Le Christ et l'Esprit du Seigneur selon Luc 4, 18-19," *NRT* 115 (1993): 877-85 [4:18-19].

6027.106   B. Rinaldi, "Proclamare ai prigionieri la liberazione (Luke 4:18)," BO 18 (1976): 241-45 [4:18].

6027.107   S. Dawson, "The Spirit's Gift of Sight," *ET* 90 (1978-1979): 241-42 [4:18].

6027.108   Gerhard Sauter, "Leiden und 'Handeln'," *EvT* 45 (1985): 435-58 [4:18].

6027.109   Donald G. Miller, "Luke 4:22-30," *Interp* 40/1 (1986): 53-58 [4:22-30].

6027.110   John L. Nolland, "Words of Grace (Luke 4,22)," *B* 65 (1984): 44-60 [4:22].

6027.111   Feargus O'Fearghail, "Rejection in Nazareth: Lk 4,22," *ZNW* 75 (1984): 60-72 [4:22].

6027.112   L. C. Crockett, "Luke 4:25-27 and Jewish-Gentile Relations in Luke-Acts," *JBL* 88 (1969): 177-83 [4:25-27].

6027.113   B. E. Thiering, "The Three and a Half Years of Elijah," *NT* 23 (1981): 41-55 [4:25].

6027.114   Gerald Bostock, "Jesus as the New Elisha," *ET* 92 (1980-1981): 39-41 [4:27].

6027.115   J. D. M. Dorrott, "Getting on Top of a Demon," *EQ* 65 (1993): 99-109 [4:39].

6027.116   Michael Theobald, "Die Anfänge der Kirche: Zur Struktur von Lk. 5:1-6:19," *NTSt* 30 (1984): 91-108 [5:1-6:19].

6027.117   K. Zillessen, "Das Schiff des Petrus und die Gefährten vom andern Schiff (Lc 5,1-11)," *ZNW* 57 (1966): 137-39 [5:1-11].

6027.118   Jean Delorme, "Luc v.1-11. Analyse Structurale et Histoire de la Rédaction," *NTSt* 18 (1971-1972): 331-50 [5:1-11].

6027.119   J. A. Fishbaugh, "New Life in the Depths of His Presence," *ET* 90 (1978-1979): 146-48 [5:4].

6027.120   Anthony Pope, "More on Luke 5:8," *BTr* 41 (1990): 442-43 [5:8].

6027.121   F. Deltombe, "Désormais tu rendras la vie à des hommes (Luke 5:10)," *RB* 89 (1982): 492-97 [5:10].

6027.122   J. K. Elliott, "The Healing of the Leper in the Synoptic Parallels," *TZ* 34 (1978): 175-76 [5:12-16].

6027.123   C. B. Cousar, "Luke 5:29-35," *Interp* 40 (1986): 58-63 [5:29-35].

6027.124   Bo Reicke, "Die Fastenfrage nach Luk. 5,33-39," *TZ* 30 (1974): 321-28 [5:33-39].

6027.125   R. S. Good, "Jesus, Protagonist of the Old, in Luke 5:33-39," *NT* 25/1 (1983): 19-36 [5:33-39].

6027.126   A. Kee, "The Old Coat and the New Wine," *NT* 12 (1970): 13-21 [5:36-39].

6027.127   Jacques Dupont, "Vin Vieux, Vin Nouveau (Luc 5:39)," *CBQ* 25 (1963): 286-304 [5:39].

6027.128   Dennis J. Ireland, "A History of Recent Interpretation of the Parable of the Unjust Steward," *WTJ* 51 (1989): 293-318 [6:1-13].

6027.129   W. Dietrich, " ' . . . den Armen das Evangelium zu verkünden': Vom befreienden Sinn biblischer Gesetze," *TZ* 41 (1985): 31-43 [6:1-5].

6027.130   E. Isaac, "Another Note on Luke 6:1," *JBL* 100 (1981): 96-97 [6:1].

6027.131   T. C. Skeat, "The 'Second-First' Sabbath (Luke 6:1): The Final Solution," *NT* 30 (1988): 103-106 [6:1].

6027.132   J. Bernardi, "Des chiffres et des lettres: Le texte de Luke 6,1," *RB* 101 (1994): 62-66 [6:1].

6027.133   J. D. M. Derrett, "Luke 6:5D Reexamined," *NT* 37 (1995): 232-48 [6:5].

6027.134   Johannes Beutler, "Lk 6:16: Punkt Oder Komma?" *BibZ* 35/2 (1991): 231-33 [6:16].

6027.135   Raymond E. Brown, "Le 'Beatitudini' secondo Luca," *BO* 7 (1965): 3-8 [6:17-49].

6027.136   David L. Tiede, "Luke 6:17-26," *Interp* 40 (1986): 63-68 [6:17-26].

6027.137   J. Mánek, "On the Mount, On the Plain (Mt. 5:1, Lk. 6:17)," *NT* 9 (1967): 124-31 [6:17].

6027.138   G. Menestrina, "Matteo 5-7 e Luca 6:20-49 nell'Evangelo di Tommaso," *BO* 18 (1976): 65-67 [6:20-49].

6027.139   Georg Strecker, "Die Makarismen der Bergpredigt," *NTSt* 17 (1970-1971): 255-75 [6:20-26].

6027.140 N. J. McEleney, "The Beatitudes of the Sermon on the Mount/Plain," *CBQ* 43 (1981): 1-13 [6:20-26].

6027.141 H. Frankemölle, "Die Makarismen (Mt 5,1-12; Lk 6,20-23)," *BibZ* 15 (1971): 52-75 [6:20-23].

6027.142 P. Klein, "Die lukanischen Weherufe Luke 6:24-26," *ZNW* 71 (1980): 150-59 [6:24-26].

6027.143 Dieter Lührmann, "Liebet eure Feinde (Lk 6,27-36; Mt 5,39-48)," *ZTK* 69 (1972): 412-38 [6:27-36].

6027.144 Jürgen Sauer, "Traditionsgeschichtliche Erwägungen zu den synoptischen und paulinischen Aussagen über Feindesliebe und Wiedervergeltungsverzicht," *ZNW* 76 (1985): 1-28 [6:27-36].

6027.145 Gerhard Lohfink, "Der ekklesiale Sitz im Leben der Aufforderung Jesu zum Gewaltverzicht (Matt. 5:39-42/Luke 6:29)," *TQ* 162 (1982): 236-53 [6:29].

6027.146 J. D. M. Derrett, "Christ and Reproof (Matthew 7:1-5/Luke 6:37-42)," *NTSt* 34/2 (1988): 271-81 [6:37-42].

6027.147 M. Krämer, "Hütet euch vor den falschen Propheten. Eine überlieferungsgeschichtliche Untersuchung zu Mt 7:15-23/Lk 6:43-46/Mt 12.33-37," *B* 57 (1976): 349-77 [6:43-46].

6027.148 J. D. M. Derrett, "Law in the New Testament: The Syro-Phoenician Woman and the Centurion of Capernaum," *NT* 15 (1973): 161-86 [7:1-10].

6027.149 J. A. G. Haslam, "The Centurion at Capernaum: Luke 7:1-10," *ET* 96 (1984-1985): 109-10 [7:1-10].

6027.150 R. A. J. Gagnon, "Luke's Motives for Redaction in the Account of the Double Delegation in Luke 7:1-10," *NT* 36 (1994): 122-45 [7:1-10].

6027.151 D. A. S. Ravens, "The Setting of Luke's Account of the Anointing: Luke 7.2-8.3," *NTSt* 34 (1988): 282-92 [7:2-8:3].

6027.152 F. A. J. Macdonald, "Pity or Compassion?" *ET* 92 (1980-1981): 344-46 [7:11-17].

6027.153 Thomas L. Brodie, "Towards Unravelling Luke's Use of the Old Testament: Luke 7:11-17 as an Imitation of 1 Kings 17:17-24," *NTSt* 32/2 (1986): 247-67 [7:11-17].

6027.154 I. Kerr, "The Signs of Jesus," *ET* 94 (1982-1983): 49-51 [7:18-23].

6027.155 Wolfgang Beinert, "Jesus Christus: das Ursakrament Gottes," *C* 38/4 (1984): 340-51 [7:22].

6027.156 Dieter Zeller, "Die Bildlogik des Gleichnisses Mt 11,16f. / Lk 7,31f," *ZNW* 68 (1977): 252-57 [7:31-32].

6027.157 Otto Böcher, "Ass Johannes der Täufer kein Brot (Luk. vii.33)?" *NTSt* 18 (1971-1972): 90-92 [7:33].

6027.158 Thomas L. Brodie, "Luke 7:36-50 as an Internalization of 2 Kings 4:1-37: A Study in Luke's Use of Rhetorical Imitation," *B* 64 (1983): 457-85 [7:36-50].

6027.159 Christian D. Kettler, "The Vicarious Repentance of Christ in the Theology of John McLeod Campbell and R. C. Moberly," *SJT* 38/4 (1985): 529-43 [7:36-50].

6027.160 Antony Hurst, "The Woman with the Ointment," *ET* 101 (1989-1990): 304 [7:36-50].

6027.161 John J. Kilgallen, "À proposal for Interpreting Luke 7:36-50," *B* 72/3 (1991): 305-30 [7:36-50].

6027.162 James L. Resseguie, "Luke 7:36-50," *Interp* 46 (1992): 285-90 [7:36-50].

6027.163 Ben Witherington, "On the Road with Mary Magdalene, Joanna, Susanna, and Other Disciples (Luke 8:1-3)," *ZNW* 70 (1979): 243-48 [8:1-3].

6027.164 J. Toy, "The Parable of the Sower and its Interpretation," *ET* 92 (1980-1981): 116-18 [8:4-15].

6027.165 Michael Walker, "Luke 8:4," *ET* 75 (1963-1964): 151 [8:4].

6027.166 J. Gervais, "Les épines étouffantes (Luc 8,14-15)," *ET* 84 (1972-1973): 5-40 [8:14-15].

6027.167 J. M. García Pérez, "El endemoniado de Gerasa (Lc 8,26-39)," *EB* 44 (1986): 117-46 [8:26-39].

6027.168 Michael D. Goulder, "From Ministry to Passion in John and Luke," *NTSt* 29 (1983): 561-68 [9-10].

6027.169 David P. Moessner, "Luke 9:1-50: Luke's Preview of the Journey of the Prophet Like Moses of Deuteronomy," *JBL* 102 (1983): 575-605 [9:1-50].

6027.170 Robert F. O'Toole, "Luke's Message in Luke 9,1-50," *CBQ* 49 (1987): 74-89 [9:1-50].

6027.171 William R. Stegner, "Lucan Priority in the Feeding of the Five Thousand," *BRes* 21 (1976): 19-28 [9:10-17].

6027.172 G. Ogg, "The Central Section of the Gospel according to St. Luke," *NTSt* 18 (1971-1972): 39-53 [9:15-19:27].

6027.173 M. J. Kingston, "Suffering," *ET* 94 (1982-1983): 144-45

[9:18-27].

6027.174 D. E. Miller, "Luke 9:18-24," *Interp* 37 (1983): 64-68 [9:18-24].

6027.175 D. H. C. Read, "At the Centre of the Self," *ET* 5 (1986): 142-44 [9:23-24].

6027.176 D. R. Fletcher, "Condemned to Die. The Logion on Cross-Bearing: What Does It Mean?" *Interp* 18 (1964): 156-64 [9:23].

6027.177 D. Gill, "Observations on the Lukan Travel Narrative and Some Related Passages," *HTR* 63 (1970): 199-221 [9:51-18:14].

6027.178 John W. Wenham, "Synoptic Independence and the Origin of Luke's Travel Narrative," *NTSt* 27 (1980-1981): 507-15 [9:51-18:14].

6027.179 Frank J. Matera, "Jesus' Journey to Jerusalem: A Conflict with Israel," *JSNT* 51 (1993): 57-77 [9:51-19:46].

6027.180 Brian G. Powley, "Time and Place," *ET* 94 (1983): 371-72 [9:51-56].

6027.181 Craig A. Evans, " 'He Set His Face': A Note on Luke 9:51," *B* 63 (1982): 545-48 [9:51].

6027.182 J. Rius-Camps, "El καὶ αὐτὸς en los encabezamientos lucanos, ¿una fórmula anadórica?" *FilN* 2 (1989): 187-92 [9:51].

6027.183 C. Kenneth Lysons, "The Seven Deadly Sins Today, Pt. 3: Anger," *ET* 97/10 (1985-1986): 302-304 [9:52-56].

6027.184 J. M. Ross, "The Rejected Words of Luke 9,54-56," *ET* 84 (1972-1973): 85-88 [9:54-56].

6027.185 Otto Glombitza, "Die christologische Aussage des Lukas in seiner Gestaltung der drei Nachfolgeworte Lukas IX,57-62," *NT* 13 (1971): 14-23 [9:57-62].

6027.186 Bernhard Lang, "Grussverbot oder Besuchsverbot?" *BibZ* 26 (1982): 75-79 [10:4].

6027.187 William Klassen, " 'A Child of Peace' in First Century Context," NTS 27 (1980-1981): 488-506 [10:6].

6027.188 H. Helbling, "Hören und Gehörtwerden. Eine biblische Meditation," *FZPT* 24 (1977): 3-6 [10:16].

6027.189 David Crump, "Jesus: The Victorious Scribal-Intercessor in Luke's Gospel," *NTSt* 38 (1992): 51-65 [10:17-20].

6027.190   Ulrich B. Müller, "Vision und Botschaft. Erwägungen zur prophetischen Struktur der Verkündigung Jesu," *ZTK* 74 (1977): 416-48 [10:18].

6027.191   Pierre Grelot, "Étude critique de Luc 10:19," *RSR* 69 (1981): 87-100 [10:19].

6027.192   L. Randellini, "L'inno di giubulo: Mt. 11,25-30; Lc. 10,20-24," *RivB* 22 (1974): 183-235 [10:20-24].

6027.193   Willibald Grimm, "Selige Augenzeugen, Luk. 10,23f. Alttestamentlicher Hintergrund und ursprünglicher Sinn," *TZ* 26 (1970): 172-83 [10:23-24].

6027.194   Robert W. Funk, " 'How Do You Read?' A Sermon on Luke 10:25-37," *Interp* 18 (1964): 56-61 [10:25-37].

6027.195   Dietfried Gewalt, "Der 'Barmherzige Samariter': Zu Lukas 10:25-37," *EvT* 38 (1978): 403-17 [10:25-37].

6027.196   R. Kieffer, "Analyse sémiotique et commentaire. Quelques réflexions à propos d'études de Luc 10:25-37," *NTSt* 25 (1979): 454-68 [10:25-37].

6027.197   Walter Wink, "The Parable of the Compassionate Samaritan: A Communal Exegesis Approach," *RE* 76 (1979): 199-217 [10:25-37].

6027.198   M. J. Kingston, "Love Cannot Be Contained By Rules," *ET* 91 (1979-1980): 339-40 [10:25-37].

6027.199   F. S. Spencer, "Chronicles 28:5-15 and the Parable of the Good Samaritan," *WTJ* 46 (1984): 317-49 [10:25-37].

6027.200   P. Y. Bourdil, "L'église, un Monde et sa Pensée," *RHPR* 65/3 (1985): 297-314 [10:25-37].

6027.201   M. Gnanavaram, " 'Dalit Theology' and the Parable of the Good Samaritan," *JSNT* 50 (1993): 59-83 [10:25-37].

6027.202   John J. Kilgallen, "The Plan of the νομικός," *NTSt* 42 (1996): 615-19 [10:25-37].

6027.203   R. H. Gundry, "A Rejoinder on Manhean Foreign Bodies in Luke 10,25-28," *ETL* 71 (1995): 139-50 [10:25-28].

6027.204   Frans Neirynck, "The Minor Agreements and Lk 10,25-28," *ETL* 71 (1995): 151-60 [10:25-28].

6027.205   J. D. M. Derrett, "Law in the New Testament: Fresh Light on the Parable of the Good Samaritan," *NTSt* 11 (1964-1965): 22-37 [10:29-38].

6027.206   L. Ramaroson, "Comme 'Le Bon Samaritain' ne chercher qu'à aimer (Lc 10,29-37)," *B* 56 (1975): 533-36 [10:29-37].

6027.207   L. Paul Trudinger, "Once Again, Now, 'Who Is My Neighbour'?" *EQ* 48 (1976): 160-63 [10:29].

6027.208   Norman H. Young, "Once Again, Now, 'Who Is My Neighbour?' A Comment," *EQ* 49 (1977): 178-79 [10:29].

6027.209   H. G. Klemm, "Schillers ethisch-ästhetische Variationen zum Thema Lk 10,30ff.," *KD* 17 (1971): 127-40 [10:30].

6027.210   J. A. Davidson, "Things to be Understood and Things to be Done," *ET* 94 (1982-1983): 306-307 [10:38-42].

6027.211   Robert W. Wall, "Martha and Mary (Luke 10:38-42) in the Context of a Christian Deuteronomy," *JSNT* 35 (1989): 19-35 [10:38-42].

6027.212   Roy A. Harrisville, "God's Mercy: Tested, Promised, Done! An Exposition of Genesis 18:20-32; Luke 11:1-13; Colossians 2:6-15," *Interp* 3 (1977): 165-78 [11:1-13].

6027.213   Michael D. Goulder, "The Composition of the Lord's Prayer," *JTS* 14 (1963): 32-45 [11:2-4].

6027.214   R. Freudenberger, "Zum Text der zweiten Vaterunserbitte," *NTSt* 15 (1968-1969): 419-32 [11:2-4].

6027.215   P. Edmonds, "The Lucan 'Our Father': A Summary of Luke's Teaching on Prayer?" *ET* 91 (1979-1980): 140-43 [11:2-4].

6027.216   Pierre Grelot, "L'Arrière-Plan Araméen du 'Pater'," *RB* 91/4 (1984): 531-56 [11:2-4].

6027.217   M. Philonenko, " 'Que Ton Esprit Saint vienne sur nous et qu'il nous purifie': l'arrière-plan qoumrânien d'une variante lucanienne du 'Notre Pare'," *RHPR* 75 (1995): 61-66 [11:2].

6027.218   Pierre Grelot, "La Quatrième Demande du 'Pater' et son Arrière-Plan Sémitique," *NTSt* 25 (1978-1979): 299-314 [11:3].

6027.219   R. G. Kratz, "Die Gnade de täglichen Brots: Späte Psalmen auf dem Weg zum Vaterunser," *ZTK* 89 (1992): 1-40 [11:3].

6027.220   C. B. Houk, "*Peirasmos*, The Lord's Prayer, and the Massah Tradition," *SJT* 19 (1966): 216-25 [11:4].

6027.221   Stanley E. Porter, "Mt 6:13 and Lk 11:4: 'Lead Us Not into Temptation'," *ET* 101 (1989-1990): 359-62 [11:4].

6027.222   R. R. Rickards, "The Translation of Luke 11,5-13," *BTr* 28 (1977): 239-43 [11:5-13].

6027.223   Dale Goldsmith, "Ask, and It Will Be Given . . . : Toward Writing the History of a Logion," *NTSt* 35/2 (1989): 254-65

[11:9-13].

6027.224 Édouard Delebecque, "Sur un hellénisme de Saint Luc," *RB* 87 (1980): 590-93 [11:13].

6027.225 Bruce D. Chilton, "A Comparative Study of Synoptic Development: The Dispute between Cain and Abel in the Palestinian Targums and the Beelzebul Controversy in the Gospel," *JBL* 101 (1982): 553-62 [11:15-23].

6027.226 W. C. B. MacLaurin, "Beelzeboul," *NT* 20/2 (1978): 156-60 [11:18].

6027.227 Robert Shirock, "Whose Exorcists Are They? The Referents of οἱ υἱοὶ ὑμῶν at Matthew 12:27/Luke 11:19," *JSNT* 46 (1992): 41-51 [11:19].

6027.228 Gerhard Lohfink, "Die Korrelation von Reich Gottes und Volk Gottes bei Jesus," *TQ* 165/3 (1985): 173-83 [11:20].

6027.229 Robert W. Wall, "The Finger of God: Deuteronomy 9:10 and Luke 11:20," *NTSt* 33 (1987): 144-50 [11:20].

6027.230 John J. Kilgallen, "The Return of the Unclean Spirit," *B* 74 (1993): 45-59 [11:24-26].

6027.231 R. C. Wahlberg, "Jesus and the Uterus Image (Lc 11,27-28)," *ITQ* 41 (1974): 235-50 [11:27-28].

6027.232 H. Zimmermann, " 'Selig die das Wort Gotres hören und es bewahren': Eine exegetische Studie zu Lk 11,27f.," *C* 29 (1975): 114-19 [11:27].

6027.233 Dino Merli, "Il Segno di Giona," *BO* 14 (1972): 61-77 [11:29-32].

6027.234 G. Schmitt, "Das Zeichen des Jona," *ZNW* 69 (1978): 123-29 [11:29-32].

6027.235 James Swetnam, "No Sign of Jonah," *B* 66/1 (1985): 126-30 [11:29].

6027.236 Susan R. Garrett, "Lest the Light in You Be Darkness: Luke 11:33-36 and the Question of Commitment," *JBL* 110 (1991): 93-105 [11:33-36].

6027.237 E. Springs Steele, "Luke 11:37-54: A Modifed Hellenistic Symposium?" *JBL* 103 (1984): 379-94 [11:37-54].

6027.238 E. Earle Ellis, "Luke 11:49-51: An Oracle of a Christian Prophet?" *ET* 74 (1962-1963): 157-58 [11:49-51].

6027.239 Dale C. Allison, "The Hairs on Your Head Are Numbered," *ET* 102 (1990-1991): 334-36 [12:7].

6027.240 G. W. H. Lampe, "St. Peter's Denial," *BJRL* 55/2 (1973): 346-68 [12:8-9].

6027.241 J. M. McDermott, "Luke 12:8-9: Stone of Scandal," *RB* 84 (1977): 523-37 [12:8-9].

6027.242 D. R. Copestake, "Luke 12:8 and 'Silent Witness'," *ET* 94 (1982-1983): 335 [12:8].

6027.243 H. Sawatzky, "What's Gotten Into Us?" *ET* 91 (1979-1980): 245-47 [12:13-21].

6027.244 George W. E. Nickelsburg, "Riches, the Rich, and God's Judgment in 1 Enoch 92-105 and the Gospel according to Luke," *NTSt* 25 (1978-1979): 324-44 [12:15-21].

6027.245 J. D. M. Derrett, "The Rich Fool: A Parable of Jesus Concerning Inheritance," *HeyJ* 18 (1977): 131-51 [12.16-21].

6027.246 Paul Ellingworth, "Luke 12:46: Is There an Anti-Climax Here?" *BTr* 31 (1980): 242-43 [12:46].

6027.247 J. D. M. Derrett, "Christ's Second Baptism (Lk. 12:50; Mk. 10:38-40)," *ET* 100 (1988-1989): 294-95 [12:50].

6027.248 J. N. Sevenster, "Geeft den Keizer, Wat des Keizers is, en Gode, Wat Gods is," *NedTT* 17 (1962): 21-31 [12:54-56].

6027.249 Günter Klein, "Die Prüfung der Zeit (Lukas 12:54-56)," *ZTK* 61/4 (1964): 373-90 [12:54-56].

6027.250 F. W. Young, "Luke 13:1-9," *Interp* 31 (1977): 59-63 [13:1-9].

6027.251 J. Wilkinson, "The Case of the Bent Woman in Luke 13:10-17," *EQ* 49 (1977): 195-205 [13:10-17].

6027.252 Dennis Hamm, "The Freeing of the Bent Woman and the Restoration of Israel: Luke 13:10-17 as Narrative Theology," *JSNT* 31 (1987): 23-44 [13:10-17].

6027.253 Robert F. O'Toole, "Some Exegetical Reflections on Luke 13:10-17," *B* 73 (1992): 84-107 [13:10-17].

6027.254 Robert W. Funk, "Beyond Criticism in Quest of Literacy: The Parable of the Leaven," *Interp* 25 (1971): 149-70 [13:20-21].

6027.255 P. Hoffmann, "Pántes ergátai adikías, Redaktion und Tradition in Lc 13,22-30," *ZNW* 58 (1967): 188-214 [13:22-30].

6027.256 M. Minor, "Luke 13:22-30: The Wrong Question, The Right Door," *RE* 91 (1994): 551-57 [13:22-30].

6027.257 Dieter Zeller, "Das Logion Mt 8,11f./Lk 13,28f. und das Motiv der 'Völkerwallfahrt'," *BibZ* 15 (1971): 222-37; 16 (1972): 84-93 [13:28].

6027.258 Willibald Grimm, "Zum Hintergrund von Mt 8,11f., Lk 13,28.f," *BibZ* 16 (1972): 255-56 [13:28].

6027.259 B. Prete, "Il testo di Luca 13:31. Unità letteraria ed insegnamento cristologico," *BO* 24 (1982): 59-79 [13:31].

6027.260 J. Bishop, "The Power of the Single Purpose," *ET* 93 (1982-1983): 115-16 [13:33].

6027.261 F. D. Weinert, "Luke, the Temple, and Jesus' Saying about Jerusalem's Abandoned House (Luke 13:34-35)," *CBQ* 44 (1982): 68-76 [13:34-35].

6027.262 Dale C. Allison, "Matt. 23:39 = Luke 13:35b as a Conditional Prophecy," *JSNT* 18 (1983): 75-84 [13:35].

6027.263 Christian Dietzfelbinger, "Vom Sinn der Sabbatheilungen Jesu," *EvT* 38 (1978): 281-97 [14:1-10].

6027.264 Otto Glombitza, "Das Grosse Abendmahl: Luk 14:12-24," *NT* 5 (1962): 10-16 [14:12-24].

6027.265 Daniel L. Migliore, "The Open Banquet," *PSB* 6/1 (1985): 8-13 [14:12-24].

6027.266 L. Schottroff, "Das Gleichnis vom grossen Gastmahl in der Logienquelle," *EvT* 47 (1987): 192-211 [14:15-24].

6027.267 Victor E. Vine, "Luke 14:15-24 and Anti-Semitism," *ET* 102 (1990-1991): 262-63 [14:15-24].

6027.268 E. Galbiati, "Gli invitati al convito (Luke 14:16-24)," *BO* 7 (1965): 129-35 [14:16-24].

6027.269 R. W. Resenhöft, "Jesu Gleichnis von den Talenten, ergänzt durch die Lukas-Fassung," *NTSt* 26 (1979-1980): 318-31 [14:16-24].

6027.270 Siegfried Kreuzer, "Der Zwang des Boten: Beobachtungen zu Lk. 14:23 und 1 Kor 9:16," *ZNW* 76/1-2 (1985): 123-28 [14:23].

6027.271 Ieuan Ellis, "Jesus and the Subversive Family," *SJT* 38/2 (1985): 173-88 [14:26].

6027.272 J. D. M. Derrett, "*Nisi dominus aedificaverit domum:* Towers and Wars," *NT* 19 (1977): 241-61 [14:28-32].

6027.273 Norman A. Mundhenk, "Problems Involving Illustrations in Luke," *BTr* 44 (1993): 247-48 [14:28-32].

6027.274 H. Sawatzky, "Problem at the Party," *ET* 91 (1979-1980): 270-72 [15:1-10].

6027.275 J. Toy, "The Lost Sheep and the Lost Coin," *ET* 92 (1980-1981): 276-77 [15:1-10].

6027.276 Wilhelm Schmidt, "Der Gute Hirte: Biblische Besinnung über Luke 15:1-7," *EvT* 24/4 (1964): 173-77 [15:1-7].

6027.277 J. D. M. Derrett, "Fresh Light on the Lost Sheep and the Lost Coin," *NTSt* 26 (1979-1980): 36-60 [15:3-10].

6027.278 Eric F. F. Bishop, "The Parable of the Lost or Wandering Sheep," *ATR* 44 (1962): 44-57 [15:3-7].

6027.279 Frederick Bussby, "Did a Shepherd Leave Sheep Upon the Mountains or in the Desert?" *ATR* 45 (1963): 93-94 [15:4].

6027.280 Daniel Sheerin, "The Theotokion: Its Background in Patristic Exegesis of Luke 15:8-10 and Western Parallels," *VCh* 43/2 (1989): 166-87 [15:8-10].

6027.281 J. D. M. Derrett, "Law in the New Testament: The Parable of the Prodigal Son," *NTSt* 14 (1967-1968): 56-74 [15:11-32].

6027.282 J. J. O'Rourke, "Some Notes on Luke xv.11-32," *NTSt* 18 (1971-1972): 431-33 [15:11-32].

6027.283 Ingo Broer, "Das Gleichnis vom verlorenen Sohn und die Theologie des Lukas," *NTSt* 20 (1973-1974): 453-62 [15:11-32].

6027.284 C. E. Carlston, "Reminiscence and Redaction in Luke 15:11-32," *JBL* 94 (1975): 368-90 [15:11-32].

6027.285 James L. Price, "Luke 15:11-32," *Interp* 31 (1977): 64-69 [15:11-32].

6027.286 Otfried Hofius, "Alttestamentliche Motive im Gleichnis vom verlorenen Sohn," *NTSt* 24 (1977-1978): 240-48 [15:11-32].

6027.287 R. R. Rickards, "Some Points to Consider in Translating the Parable of the Prodigal Son," *BTr* 31 (1980): 243-45 [15:11-32].

6027.288 G. S. Gibson, "The Sins of the Saints," *ET* 96 (1984-1985): 276-77 [15:11-32].

6027.289 Roger D. Aus, "Luke 15:11-32 and R. Eliezer Ben Hyrcanus's *Rise to Fame*," *JBL* 104 (1985): 443-69 [15:11-32].

6027.290 Michael R. Austin, "The Hypocritical Son," *EQ* 57 (1985): 307-15 [15:11-32].

6027.291 J. G. Lees, "The Parable of the Good Father," *ET* 97/8 (1985-1986): 246-47 [15:11-32].

6027.292 E. Borghi, "Lc 15,11-32: Linee esegetiche globali," *RivBib* 44 (1996): 279-308 [15:11-32].

6027.293 J. A. Harrill, "The Indentured Labor of the Prodigal Son," *JBL* 115 (1996): 714-17 [15:15].

6027.294 I. MacLeod, "Enough and to Spare," *ET* 88 (1976-1977): 114-15 [15:17].

6027.295 J. C. Kellogg, "Enough to Spare," *ET* 94 (1982-1983): 272-73 [15:17].

6027.296 Gerhard Lohfink, " 'Ich habe gesundigt gegen den Himmel und gegen dich': Eine Exegese von Lk 15,18.21," *TQ* 15 (1975): 51-52 [15:18-21].

6027.297 C. H. Cave, "Lazarus and the Lukan Deuteronomy," *NTSt* 15 (1968-1969): 319-25 [15:19-31].

6027.298 Tom Corlett, "This Brother of Yours," *ET* 100 (1989-1990): 216 [15:30].

6027.299 R. M. Grández, "Las tinieblas en la muerte de Jésus: Historia de la exégesis de Lc 23,44-45a," *EB* 47 (1989): 177-223 [15:33].

6027.300 M. Ball, "The Parables of the Unjust Steward and the Rich Man and Lazrus," *ET* 106 (1995): 329-30 [16].

6027.301 Ronald G. Lunt, "Expounding the Parables: Parable of the Unjust Steward," *ET* 77 (1965-1966): 132-36 [16:1-35].

6027.302 D. R. Fletcher, "The Riddle of the Unjust Steward," *JBL* 82 (1963): 15-30 [16:1-13].

6027.303 Joseph A. Fitzmyer, "The Story of the Dishonest Manager," *ThSt* 25 (1964): 23-42 [16:1-13].

6027.304 L. J. Topel, "On the Injustice of the Unjust Steward: Lk 16:1-13," *CBQ* 35 (1975): 216-27 [16:1-13].

6027.305 D. L. Mathewson, "The Parable of the Unjust Steward (Luke 16:1-13): A Reexamination of the Traditional View in Light of Recent Challenges," *JETS* 38 (1995): 29-39 [16:1-13].

6027.306 F. J. Moore, "The Parable of the Unjust Steward," *ATR* 47 (1965): 103-105 [16:1-9].

6027.307 F. E. Williams, "Is Almsgiving the Point of the 'Unjust Steward'?" *JBL* 83 (1964): 293-97 [16:1-8].

6027.308 Bernard B. Scott, "A Master's Praise: Luke 16:1-8," *B* 64

(1983): 173-88 [16:1-8].

6027.309 Douglas M. Parrott, "The Dishonest Steward and Luke's Special Parable Collection," *NTSt* 37 (1991): 499-515 [16:1-8].

6027.310 Hermann Binder, "Missdeutbar oder eindeutig?–Gedanken zu einem Gleichnis Jesu," *TZ* 51 (1995): 41-49 [16:1-8].

6027.311 T. Hoeren, "Des Cleichnis vom ungerechten Verwalter (Lukas 16.1-8a)—zugleich ein Beitrag our Geschichte der Restschuldbefreiung," *NTSt* 41 (1995): 620-29 [16:1-8].

6027.312 H. Drexler, "Zu Lukas 16,1-7," *ZNW* 58 (1967): 286-88 [16:1-7].

6027.313 J. D. M. Derrett, "Take Thy Bond . . . and Write Fifty (Luke xvi.6): The Nature of the Bond," *JTS* 23 (1972): 438-40 [16:6].

6027.314 Gregorio Ruiz, "El Clamor de las Piedras (Lk. 19:40; Hab 2:11): el Reino Choca con la Ciudad Injusta en la Fiesta de Ramos," *EE* 59/230 (1984): 297-312 [16:8-53].

6027.315 I. Howard Marshall, "Luke xvi.8: Who Commended the Unjust Steward?" *JTS* 19 (1968): 617-19 [16:8].

6027.316 Michael G. Steinhauser, "Noah in His Generation: An Allusion in Luke 16,8b 'εἰς τὴν γενεὰν τὴν ἑαυτῶν'," *ZNW* 79 (1988): 152-57 [16:8].

6027.317 C. S. Mann, "Unjust Steward or Prudent Manager?" *ET* 102 (1990-1991): 234-35 [16:8].

6027.318 P. Colella, "Zu Lk 16,9," *ZNW* 64 (1973): 124-26 [16:9].

6027.319 J. B. Cortés and F. M. Gatti, "On the Meaning of Luke 16:16," *JBL* 106 (1987): 247-59 [16:16].

6027.320 Henry J. Cadbury, "A Proper Name for Dives," *JBL* 81 (1962): 399-402 [16:19-31].

6027.321 Kendrick Grobel, "Whose Name Was Neves," *NTSt* 10 (1963-1964): 373-82 [16:19-31].

6027.322 Henry J. Cadbury, "The Name for Dives," *JBL* 84 (1965): 73 [16:19-31].

6027.323 W. P. Huie, "The Poverty of Abundance. From Text to Sermon on Luke 16:19-31," *Interp* 22 (1968): 403-20 [16:19-31].

6027.324 Otto Glombitza, "Der reiche Mann und der arme Lazarus," *NT* 12 (1970): 166-80 [16:19-31].

6027.325 Thorwald Lorenzen, "A Biblical Meditation on Luke 16,19-31," *ET* 87 (1975-1976): 39-45 [16:19-31].

6027.326 E. S. Wehrli, "Luke 16:19-31," *Interp* 31 (1977): 276-80 [16:19-31].

6027.327 F. Schnider and W. Stenger, "Die offene Tür und die unüberschreitbare Kluft. Strukturanalytische Überlegungen zum Gleichnis vom reichen Mann und armen Lazarus," *NTSt* 25 (1978-1979): 273-83 [16:19-31].

6027.328 J. Toy, "The Rich Man and Lazarus," *ET* 91 (1979-1980): 274-75 [16:19-31].

6027.329 Vincent Tanghe, "Abraham, Son Fils et Son Envoyé (Luc 16:19-31)," *RB* 91/4 (1984): 557-77 [16:19-31].

6027.330 R. F. Hock, "Lazarus and Micyllus: Greco-Roman Backgrounds to Luke 16:19-31," *JBL* 106 (1987): 447-63 [16:19-31].

6027.331 Roger L. Omanson, "Lazarus and Simon," *BTr* 40 (1989): 416-19 [16:19-31].

6027.332 Eckart Reinmuth, "Ps-Philo, Liber Antiquitatum Biblicarum 33,1-5 und Die Auslegung der Parabel Lk. 16:19-31," *NT* 31 (1989): 16-38 [16:19-31].

6027.333 Richard J. Bauckham, "The Rich Man and Lazarus: The Parable and the Parallels," *NTSt* 37 (1991): 225-46 [16:19-31].

6027.334 Eric F. F. Bishop, "A Yawning Chasm," *EQ* 45 (1973): 3-5 [16:26].

6027.335 R. M. Shelton, "Luke 17:1-10," *Interp* 31 (1977): 280-85 [17:1-10].

6027.336 Ferdinand Hahn, "Jesu Wort vom birgeversetzenden Glauben," *ZNW* 76 (1985): 149-69 [17:6].

6027.337 J. D. M. Derrett, "Moving Mountains and Uprooting Trees," *BO* 30 (1988): 231-44 [17:6].

6027.338 John J. Kilgallen, "What Kind of Servants Are We?" *B* 63 (1982): 549-51 [17:10].

6027.339 Otto Glombitza, "Der dankbare Samariter," *NT* 11 (1969): 241-46 [17:11-19].

6027.340 Hans Dieter Betz, "The Cleansing of the Ten Lepers (Luke 17:11-19)," *JBL* 90 (1971): 314-28 [17:11-19].

6027.341 M. J. Kingston, "Modern-day Leprosy," *ET* 92 (1980-1981): 371 [17:11-19].

6027.342 Dennis Hamm, "What the Samaritan Leper Sees: The Narrative Christology of Luke 17:11-19," *CBQ* 56 (1994): 273-87 [17:11-19].

6027.343 K. S. Proctor, "Luke 17,20.21," *BTr* 33 (1982): 245 [17:20-21].

6027.344 Harald Riesenfeld, "Le règne de Dieu, parmi vous ou en vouse?" *RB* 36 (1991): 190-98 [17:20-21].

6027.345 A. Strobel, "Zu Lk. 17:20f," *BibZ* 7 (1963): 111-13 [17:20].

6027.346 D. H. C. Read, "Christ Comes Unexpectedly," *ET* 98/1 (1986-1987): 21-22 [17:21].

6027.347 Jacques Schlosser, "Les jours de Noé et de Lot: À propos de Luc, xvii,26-30," *RB* 80 (1973): 13-36 [17:26-30].

6027.348 Dieter Lührmann, "Noah and Lot (Lk 17,26-29): - ein Nachtrag," *ZNW* 63 (1972): 130-32 [17:26-29].

6027.349 X. Léon-Dufour, "Luc 17:33," *RSR* 69 (1981): 101-12 [17:33].

6027.350 Gerhard Delling, "Das Gleichnis vom gottlosen Richter," *ZNW* 53 (1962): 1-25 [18:1-18].

6027.351 R. Deschryver, "La parabole du juge malveillant," *RHPR* 48 (1968): 355-66 [18:1-18].

6027.352 C. E. B. Cranfield, "The Parable of the Unjust Judge and the Eschatology of Luke-Acts," *SJT* 16 (1963): 297-301 [18:1-8].

6027.353 E. D. Freed, "The Parable of the Judge and the Widow," *NTSt* 33 (1987): 38-60 [18:1-8].

6027.354 J. D. M. Derrett, "Law in the New Testament: The Parable of the Unjust Judge," *NTSt* 18 (1971-1972): 178-91 [18:6].

6027.355 Herman Ljungvik, "Zur Erklärung Einer Lukas-Stelle," *NTSt* 10 (1963-1964): 289-94 [18:7].

6027.356 Albert Wifstrand, "Lukas 18:7," *NTSt* 11 (1964-1965): 72-74 [18:7].

6027.357 K. H. Tyson, "Faith on Earth," *ET* 88 (1977): 111-12 [18:8].

6027.358 D. Muñoz León, "Jesus y la apocaliptica pesimista (a proposito de Lc 18:8b y Mt 24:12)," *EB* 46/4 (1988): 457-95 [18:8].

6027.359 J. Kodell, "Luke and the Children: The Beginning and End of the Great Interpolation (Luke 9:46-56; 18:9-23)," *CBQ* 49 (1987): 415-30 [18:9-23].

6027.360 A. Biesinger, "Vorbild und Nachahmung Imitations-psychologische und bibeltheologische Anmerkungen zu Lk 18:9-14," *BK* 32 (1977): 42-45 [18:9-14].

6027.361 Helmut Merklein, " 'Dieser ging als Gerechter nach Hause . . . ' Das Gottesbild Jesu und die Haltung der Menschen nach Lk 18:9-14," *BK* 32 (1977): 34-42 [18:9-14].

6027.362 S. Schmitz, "Psychologische Hilfen zum Verstehen biblischer Texte?" *BK* 38 (1983): 112-18 [18:9-14].

6027.363 Ralph P. Martin, "Two Worshippers, One Way to God," *ET* 96 (1984-1985): 117-18 [18:9-14].

6027.364 F. C. Holmgren, "The Pharisee and the Tax Collector: Luke 18:9-14 and Deuteronomy 26:1-15," *Interp* 48 (1994): 252-60 [18:9-14].

6027.365 F. Mahr, "Der Antipharisäer. Ein Kapitel 'Bibel verfremdet' zu Lk 18:10-14," *BK* 32 (1977): 47 [18:10-14].

6027.366 J. B. Cortés, "The Greek Text of Luke 18:14a: A Contribution to the Method of Reasoned Eclecticism," *CBQ* 46 (1984): 255-73 [18:14].

6027.367 Claude Coulot, "La structuration de la péricope de l'homme riche et ses différentes lectures," *RevSR* 56 (1982): 240-52 [18:18-30].

6027.368 C. M. Swezey, "Luke 18:18-30," *Interp* 37 (1983): 68-73 [18:18-30].

6027.369 J.-P. Gérard, "Les riches dens la communauté lucanienne," *ETL* 71 (1995): 71-106 [18:18-30].

6027.370 John W. Wenham, " 'Why Do You Ask Me about the Good?' A Study of the Relation between Text and Source Criticism," *NTSt* 28 (1982): 116-25 [18:18-19].

6027.371 E. Galbiati, "Esegesi degli Evangeli festivi," *BO* 4 (1962): 57-63 [18:31-43].

6027.372 F. W. Hobbie, "Luke 19:1-10," *Interp* 31 (1977): 285-90 [19:1-10].

6027.373 J. O'Hanlon, "The Story of Zacchaeus and the Lukan Ethic," *JSNT* 12 (1981): 2-26 [19:1-10].

6027.374 Dennis Hamm, "Zacchaeus Revisited Once More: A Story of Vindication or Conversion?" *B* 72 (1991): 248-52 [19:1-10].

6027.375 D. A. S. Ravens, "Zacchaeus: The Final Part of a Lucan Triptych," *JSNT* 41 (1991): 19-32 [19:1-10].

6027.376 Nigel M. Watson, "Was Zacchaeus Really Reforming?" *ET*

77 (1965-1966): 282-85 [19:8].

6027.377 A. P. Salom, "Was Zacchaeus Really Reforming?" *ET* 78 (1966-1967): 87 [19:8].

6027.378 B. W. Grindlay, "Zacchaeus and David," *ET* 99 (1987-1988): 46-47 [19:8].

6027.379 Dennis Hamm, "Luke 19:8 Once Again: Does Zacchaeus Defend or Resolve?" *JBL* 107 (1988): 431-37 [19:8].

6027.380 D. Howell-Jones, "Lost and Found," *ET* 92 (1980-1981): 371-72 [19:10].

6027.381 John F. Walvoord, "The Parable of the Talents," *BS* 129 (1972): 206-10 [19:11-27].

6027.382 Luke T. Johnson, "The Lukan Kingship Parable," *NT* 24 (1982): 139-59 [19:11-27].

6027.383 Jack T. Sanders, "The Parable of the Pounds and Lucan Anti-Semitism," *ThSt* 42 (1981): 660-68 [19:11-17].

6027.384 F. D. Weinert, "The Parable of the Throne Claimant Reconsidered," *CBQ* 39 (1977): 505-14 [19:12-27].

6027.385 J. D. M. Derrett, "A Horrid Passage in Luke Explained," *ET* 97 (1985-1986): 136-38 [19:27].

6027.386 Randall Buth, "Luke 19:31-34, Mishnaic Hebrew, and Bible Translation: Is *Kyrioi Tou Polou* Singular?" *JBL* 104/4 (1985): 680-85 [19:31-34].

6027.387 N. Fernández Marcos, "La unción de Salomón y la entrada de Jesús en Jérusalén: 1 Re 1,33-40/Lc 19,35-40," *B* 68 (1987): 89-97 [19:35-40].

6027.388 Heinrich Baarlink, "Friede im Himmel: die Lukanische Redaktion von Lk 19,38 und Ihre Deutung," *ZNW* 76/3 (1985): 170-86 [19:38].

6027.389 B. Kinman, " 'The Stones Will Cry Out': Joy or Judgment?" *B* 75 (1994): 232-35 [19:40].

6027.390 John A. T. Robinson, "The Parable of the Wicked Husbandmen: A Test of Synoptic Relationships," *NTSt* 21 (1974-1975): 443-61 [20:9-19].

6027.391 A. Scattolon, "L'agapêtos sinottico nella luce della tradizione giudaica," *RivB* 26 (1978): 2-32 [20:13].

6027.392 Robert Doran, "Luke 20:18: A Warrior's Boast?" *CBQ* 45 (1983): 61-67 [20:18].

6027.393 B. Prete, "L'insegnamento di Gesù sulla risurrezione dei morti nella formulazione di Lc 20,27-40," *RivBib* 41 (1993): 429-51 [20:27-40].

6027.394   C. Monanti, "Lc 20,34-36 e la filiazione divina degli uomini," *BO* 13 (1971): 255-75 [20:34-36].

6027.395   A. G. Wright, "The Widow's Mites: Praise or Lament? A Matter of Context," *CBQ* 44 (1982): 256-65 [21:1-4].

6027.396   A. del Agua Pérez, "Derás Lucano de Mc 13 a la luz de su 'teologia del Reino' Lc 21,5-36," *EB* 39 (1981): 285-313 [21:5-36].

6027.397   Matthew Mahoney, "Luke 21:14-15: Editorial Rewriting or Authenticity?" *ITQ* 47/3 (1980): 220-38 [21:14-15].

6027.398   Felix Flückiger, "Luk. 21,20-24 und die Zerstorung Jerusalems," *TZ* 28 (1972): 385-90 [21:20-24].

6027.399   Craig R. Koester, "The Origin and Significance of the Flight to Pella Tradition," *CBQ* 51 (1989): 90-106 [21:20-22].

6027.400   X. Léon-Dufour, "Das letzte Mahl Jesu und die testamentarische Tradition nach Lk 22," *ZKT* 103 (1981): 33-55 [22:1-38].

6027.401   Joel B. Green, "Preparation for Passover: A Question of Redactional Technique," *NT* 29 (1987): 305-19 [22:7-13].

6027.402   William S. Kurz, "Luke 22:14-38 and Greco-Roman and Biblical Farewell Addresses," *JBL* 104 (1985): 251-68 [22:14-38].

6027.403   M. Rese, "Zur Problematik von Kurz- und Langtext in Luk. xxii.17ff.," *NTSt* 22 (1975-1976): 15-31 [22:17].

6027.404   A. Vööbus, "A New Approach to the Problem of the Shorter and Longer Text in Luke," *NTSt* 15 (1968-1969): 457-63 [22:21-39].

6027.405   I. Sloan, "The Greatest and the Youngest: Greco-Roman Reciprocity in the Farewell Address," *SR* 22 (1993): 63-73 [22:24-30].

6027.406   Peter K. Nelson, "The Unitary Character of Luke 22:24-30," *NTSt* 40 (1994): 609-19 [22:24-30].

6027.407   Larry Rasmussen, "Luke 22:24-27," *Interp* 37 (1983): 73-76 [22:24-27].

6027.408   Jacques Schlosser, "La genèse de Luc XXII,25-27," *RB* 89 (1982): 52-70 [22:25-27].

6027.409   R. R. Rickards, "Lk 22:25: They Are Called 'Friends of the People'," *BTr* 28 (1977): 445-46 [22:25].

6027.410 Jürgen Roloff, "Anfänge der Soteriologischen Deutung des Todes Jesu (Mk. x.45 und Lk. xxii.27)," *NTSt* 19 (1972-1973): 38-64 [22:27].

6027.411 Jacques Guillet, "Luc 22,29: Une Jormule johannique dans l'évangile de Luc," *RSR* 69 (1981): 113-22 [22:29].

6027.412 Jerome H. Neyrey, "The Absence of Jesus' Emotions - The Lucan Redaction of Luke 22:39-49," *B* 61 (1980): 153-71 [22:39-49].

6027.413 André Feuillet, "Le récit lucanien de l'agonie de Gethsémani (Lc 22:39-46)," *NTSt* 22 (1975-1976): 397-417 [22:39-46].

6027.414 S. Tostengard, "Luke 22:39-46," *Interp* 34 (1980): 283-88 [22:39-46].

6027.415 Joel B. Green, "Jesus on the Mount of Olives (Luke 22:39-46): Tradition and Theology," *JSNT* 26 (1986). 29-48 [22:39-46].

6027.416 Marion L. Soards, "On Understanding Luke 22:39," *BTr* 36/3 (1985): 336-37 [22:39].

6027.417 T. Lescow, "Jesus in Gethsemane bei Lukas und im Hebräerbrief," *ZNW* 58 (1967): 215-39 [22:40-46].

6027.418 T. Lescow, "Jesus in Gethsemane," *EvT* 26 (1968): 141-59 [22:40-46].

6027.419 Tjitze Baarda, "Luke 22:42-47a: The Emperor Julian as a Witness to the Text of Luke," *NT* 30 (1988): 289-96 [22:42-47].

6027.420 Gerhard Schneider, "Engel und Blutschweiss," *BibZ* 20 (1976): 112-16 [22:43-44].

6027.421 Bart D. Ehrman and M. A. Plunkett, "The Angel and the Agony: The Textual Problem of Luke 22:43-44," *CBQ* 45 (1983): 401-16 [22:43-44].

6027.422 Jean Delorme, "Le procès de Jésus ou la parole risquée (Lc 22:54-23:25)," *RSR* 69 (1981): 123-46 [22:54-23:25].

6027.423 N. J. McEleney, "Peter's Denials: How Many? To Whom?" *CBQ* 52 (1990): 467-72 [22:54-62].

6027.424 John P. Heil, "Reader-Response and the Irony of Jesus Before the Sanhedrin in Luke 22:66-71," *CBQ* 51 (1989): 271-84 [22:66-71].

6027.425 R. Russ, "Des Vermächtnis des gekreuzigten Herrn. Jesu letzte Worte im Evangelium nach Lukas," *BK* 50 (1995): 128-35 [23].

6027.426   Marion L. Soards, "Tradition, Composition, and Theology in Luke's Account of Jesus before Herod Antipas," *B* 66/3 (1985): 344-64 [23:6-12].

6027.427   Marion L. Soards, "Herod Antipas' Hearing in Luke 23:8," *BTr* 37/1 (1986): 146-47 [23:8].

6027.428   Marion L. Soards, "The Silence of Jesus Before Herod: An Interpretative Suggestion," *ABR* 33 (1985): 41-45 [23:9].

6027.429   G. Rau, "Das Volk in der lukanischen Passionsgeschichte, eine Konjektur zu Lc 23,13," *ZNW* 56 (1965): 41-51 [23:13].

6027.430   Jerome H. Neyrey, "Jesus' Address to the Women of Jerusalem: A Prophetic Judgment Oracle," *NTSt* 29 (1983): 74-86 [23:27-31].

6027.431   Walter Käser, "Exegetische und Theologische Erwägungen zur Seligpreisung der Kinderlosen, Lc 23:29b," *ZNW* 54/3-4 (1963): 240-54 [23:29].

6027.432   B. Rinaldi, "Beate le sterili (Lc. 23,29)," *BO* 15 (1973): 61-64 [23:29].

6027.433   Jacobus H. Petzer, "Anti-Judaism and the Textual Problem of Luke 23:24," *FilN* 5 (1992): 199-203 [23:34].

6027.434   P. M. Webb, "Saved," *ET* 85 (1973-1974): 175-76 [23:35].

6027.435   J. M. García Pérez, "El relato del Buen Ladron (Lc 23,39-43)," *EB* 44 (1986): 263-304 [23:39-43].

6027.436   Dennis D. Sylva, "The Temple Curtain and Jesus' Death in the Gospel of Luke," *JBL* 105/2 (1986): 239-50 [23:44-46].

6027.437   J. F. A. Sawyer, "Why is a Solar Eclipse Mentioned in the Passion Narrative (Luke xxiii.44-45)?" *JTS* 23 (1972): 124-28 [23:44-45].

6027.438   Joel B. Green, "The Demise of the Temple as 'Culture Center' in Luke-Acts: An Exposition of the Rending of the Temple Veil," *RB* 101 (1994): 489-515 [23:45].

6027.439   E. Bons, "Das Sterbewort Jesu nach Lk 23,46 und sein alttestamentlicher Hintergrund," *BibZ* 38 (1994): 93-101 [23:46].

6027.440   Robert J. Karris, "Luke 23:47 and the Lucan View of Jesus' Death," *JBL* 105/1 (1986): 65-74 [23:47].

6027.441   G. Ghiberti, "Sepolcro, sepoltura e panni sepolcrali di Gesù. Riconsiderando i dati biblici relativi alla Sindone di Torino," *RivB* 27 (1979): 123-58 [23:50-52].

6027.442   Luke T. Johnson, "Luke 24:1-11," *Interp* 46 (1992): 57-61

[24:1-11].

6027.443 John Muddiman, "A Note on Reading Luke XXIV.12," *ETL* 48 (1972): 542-48 [24:12].

6027.444 J. M. Ross, "The Genuineness of Luke 24:12," *ET* 98 (1986-1987): 107-108 [24:12].

6027.445 Anton Dauer, "Zur Authentizität von Lk 24,12," *ETL* 70 (1994): 294-318 [24:12].

6027.446 Frans Neirynck, "Once More Luke 24,12," *ETL* 70 (1994): 319-40 [24:12].

6027.447 A. A. T. Ehrhardt, "Disciples of Emmaus," *NTSt* 10 (1963-1964): 182-201 [24:13-35].

6027.448 P. J. Berry, "The Road to Emmaus," *ET* 91 (1980-1981): 204-206 [24:13-35].

6027.449 Antoine Delzant, "Les Disciples d'Emmaüs (Luc 24:13-35)," *RSR* 73/2 (1985): 177-86 [24:13-35].

6027.450 Robert J. Karris, "Luke 24:13-35," *Interp* 41 (1987): 57-61 [24:13-35].

6027.451 E. Hölscher and M. Klessmann, "Die Auferstehung einer Geschichte: Eine bibliodramatische Bearbeitung von Lk 24,13-35," *EvT* 54 (1994): 391-99 [24:13-35].

6027.452 J.-N. Aletti, "Luc 24,13-33: Signes, accomplissement et temps," *RSR* 75 (1987): 305-20 [24:13-33].

6027.453 Hans Dieter Betz, "The Origin and Nature of Christian Faith According to the Emmaus Legend (Luke 24:13-32)," *Interp* 23 (1969): 32-46 [24:13-32].

6027.454 R. Abba, "The Unrecognized Guest," *ET* 92 (1980-1981): 210-12 [24:30-31].

6027.455 J. R. Gray, "The Lord is Risen Indeed," *ET* 93 (1981-1982): 179-80 [24:34].

6027.456 M. A. Chevallier, " 'Pentecôtes' lucaniennes et 'Pentecôtes' johanniques," *RSR* 69 (1981): 301-13 [24:36-49].

6027.457 George D. Kilpatrick, "Luke 24:42-43," *NT* 28/4 (1986): 306-308 [24:42-43].

6027.458 Jack D. Kingsbury, "Luke 24:44-49," *Interp* 35 (1981): 170-74 [24:44-49].

6027.459 J. A. Jáuregui, " 'Israel' y la Iglesia en la Teologia de Lucas," *EE* 61/237 (1986): 129-49 [24:44].

6027.460 G. Odasso, "L'ascensione nell'evangelo di Luca," *BO* 13

(1971): 107-18 [24:51].

5. Critical and Exegetical Studies of Passages in John

6028. Dr. de Wette, "Bemerkungen zu Stellen des Evang. Johannis," *TSK* 7 (1834): 924-44.

6029. Prof. Bäumlein, "Beiträge zur Erklärung des Evangeliums Johannis," *TSK* 19 (1846): 389-99.

6030. Pfarrer Hauff, "Bemerkungen über einige Stellen des vierten Evangeliums," *TSK* 22 (1849): 106-30.

6031. B. W. Bacon, "Pauline Elements in the Fourth Gospel; 1. A Study of John i-iv," *ATR* 11 (1928-1929): 199-223.

6032. E. Basil Redlich, "S. John i-iii: A Study in Dislocations," *ET* 55 (1943-1944): 89-92.

6033. Adolf Harnack, "Ueber das Verhältnis des Prologs des vierten Evangeliums zum ganzen Werk," *ZTK* 2 (1892): 189-231.

6034. R. A. Falconer, "The Prologue to the Gospel of John," *Exp* 5th ser., 5 (1897): 222-34.

6035. Gottlieb Linder, "Das erste Kapitel des Johannes-evangeliums als Leseprobe nach neuer Methode," *STZ* 15 (1898): 161-68.

6036. George H. Gilbert, "Exegetical Notes: John, Chapter 1," *BW* 13 (1899): 42-46.

6037. Harald Sahlin, "Zwei Abschnitte aus Joh 1 rekonstruiert," *ZNW* 51 (1960): 64-69 [Jn. 1:6-9; 1:19-25].

6038. Edward B. Pollard, "Two Poems of Beginnings: Gen. 1:1-5; John 1:1-18," *BW* 17 (1901): 107-10.

6039. Moses Stuart, "Exegetical and Theological Examination of John 1:1-18," *BS* 7 (1850): 13-54, 281-327.

6040. F. Godet, "The Prologue of St. John's Gospel," *Exp* 1st ser., 2 (1875): 49-59, 103-15, 177-86, 285-95, 386-96.

6041. Adolf Harnack, "Julian's des Apostaten Beurtheilung des johanneischen Prologs," *ZTK* 5 (1895): 92-100.

6042. I. Kaftan, "Das Verhältnis des evangelischen Glaubens zur Logoslehre," *ZTK* 7 (1897): 1-27.

6043. Th. Calmes, "Étude sur le prologue du quatrième évangile," *RB* 9 (1900): 5-29, 378-99; 10 (1901): 512-21.

6044. A. van Hoonacker, "Le prologue du quatrième évangile,"

RHE 2 (1901): 5-14.

6045. J. E. Belser, "Der Prolog des Johannesevangeliums," *TQ* 85 (1903): 483-519.

6046. Nivard Schlögl, "Joh. 1, 1-18," *ZKT* 35 (1911): 753-59.

6047. P. Szczygiel, "Joh. 1, 1-18," *ZKT* 36 (1912): 191-96.

6048. Geerhardus Vos, "The Range of the Logos-Title in the Prologue to the Fourth Gospel," *PTR* 11 (1913): 365-419, 557-602.

6049. J. Hugh Michael, "Notes on the Johannine Prologue," *ET* 31 (1919-1920): 276-79.

6050. Paul Haupt, "The Beginning of the Fourth Gospel," *AJP* 41 (1920): 177-80.

6051. Cecil Cryer, "The Prologue to the Fourth Gospel," *ET* 32 (1920-1921): 440-43.

6052. Donald McGillivray, "The Prologue of the Fourth Gospel," *ET* 32 (1920-1921): 281-82.

6053. Millar Burrows, "The Johannine Prologue as Aramaic Verse," *JBL* 45 (1926): 57-69.

6054. Dudley Tyng, "Prologue of the Fourth Gospel: Is it Jewish, Greek, or What?" *RL* 1 (1932): 551-56.

6055. U. Holzmeister, "Prologi) Iohannei (1, 1-18) idea principalis et divisio," *VD* 11 (1931): 65-70.

6056. R. J. Drummond, "Genesis i and John i. 1-14," *ET* 49 (1937-1938): 568.

6057. J. F. Strombeck, "Grace and Truth. Studies in the Gospel According to St. John," *BS* 96 (1939): 88-116, 205-23 [Jn. 1-16].

6058. Charles Masson, "Le prologue du quatrième évangile," *RTP* N.S. 28 (1940): 297-311.

6059. Carl Stange, "Der Prolog des Johannes-Evangeliums," *ZST* 21 (1950-1952): 120-41.

6060. P. A. van Stampvoort, "Het woord als aspect van de heilsgeschiedenis in de proloog van het vierde Evangelie," *VT* 25 (1954): 35-48.

6061. Humphrey C. Green, "The Composition of St. John's Prologue," *ET* 66 (1954-1955): 291-94.

6062. Miguel Balagué, "Presencia histórica del Verbo-Prólogo de San Juan," *CB* 12 (1955): 207-17.

6063.   Serafín de Ausejo, "¿Es un himno a Cristo el prólogo de San
         Juan? Los himnos cristológicos de la Iglesia Primitiva y el
         prólogo del IV evangelio. Fil. 2, 6-11; Col. 1, 15-20; 1 Tim.
         3, 16; Hebr. 1, 2-4; Jn. 1, 1-18," *EB* 15 (1956): 223-77,
         381-427.

6064.   G. Maldfeld, "Papyrus Bodmer 11 = Joh. Kap. 1-14," *NT* 1
         (1956): 153-55.

6065.   M.-F. Lacan, "Le prologue de Saint Jean," *LumV* 33 (1957):
         91-110.

6066.   Rudolf Schnackenburg, "Logos-Hymnus und johanneischer
         Prolog," *BibZ* 1 (1957): 69-109.

6067.   W. A. Wordsworth, "The Bodmer Papyrus and the Prologue
         of St. John's Gospel," *NT* 2 (1958): 1-7.

6068.   William Barclay, "Great Themes of the New Testament; John
         i. 1-14," *ET* 70 (1958-1959): 78-82, 114-17.

6069.   Frank S. Hickman, "That which was from the Beginning,"
         RE 37 (1940): 266-81 [Jn. 1:1-5, 14].

6070.   Wilhelm Gregersen, "Johannes-prologens struktur," *DTT* 17
         (1954): 34-36.

6071.   Nigel Turner, "St. John's Eternal Word," *EQ* 22 (1950):
         243-48 [Jn. 1:1,2].

6072.   A. Médebielle, " 'In principio erat Verbum' (Ioh. 1, 1)," *VD*
         2 (1922): 3-9.

6073.   F. W. Grosheide, "In den beginne was het woord," *VT* 15
         (1943): 104-12 [Jn. 1:1].

6074.   Leon Nemoy, "A Tenth Century Criticism of the Doctrine of
         the Logos (John I, 1)," *JBL* 64 (1945): 515-29.

6075.   H. Faccio, "De 'Verbo' Dei (Jo. I. 1)," *VD* 26 (1948): 27-32.

6076.   Bruce M. Metzger, "On the Translation of John i. 1," *ET* 63
         (1951-1952): 125-26.

6077.   H. G. Meecham, "The Anarthrous θεός in John i. 1 and I
         Corinthians iii. 16," *ET* 63 (1951-1952): 126.

6078.   Oliver C. Quick, "Note on St. John i. 2-4," *Th* 34 (1937):
         115, 244

6079.   F. C. Burkitt, "The Syriac Interpretation of S. John i. 3, 4,"
         JTS 4 (1902-1903): 436-38.

6080.   George D. Kilpatrick, "John i. 3-4 and Jerome," *JTS* 46
         (1945): 191-92.

6081. J. de la Potterie, "De interpunctione et interpretatione versuum Io. 1, 3-4," *VD* 33 (1955): 193-208

6082. G. H. Gwilliam, "The Punctuation of St. John i. 3, 4 in the Peshitta," *JTS* 4 (1902-1903): 606-607.

6083. T. F. Glasson, "A Trace of Xenophon in John 1:3?" *NTSt* 4 (1957-1958): 208-209.

6084. J. Mehlmann, "A Note on John i. 3," *ET* 67 (1955-1956): 340-41.

6085. T. E. Pollard, "Cosmology and the Prologue of the Fourth Gospel," *VCh* 12 (1958): 147-53 [Jn. 1:3]

6086. Justo Collantes, "Un comentario gnóstico a Io 1, 3," *EE* 27 (1953): 65-83.

6087. J. Macpherson, "The New Testament View of Life," *Exp* 1st ser., 5 (1877): 72-80 [Jn 1:4].

6088. M.-F. Lacan, "L'oeuvre du verbe incarné le don de la vie (Jn. 1, 4)," *RSR* 45 (1957): 61-78.

6089. Piero Rossano, " 'Et tenebrae eum non comprehenderunt' (Giov. 1, 5)," *RivB* 9 (1961): 187.

6090. C. K. Barrett, "κατέλαβεν in John i. 5," *ET* 53 (1941-1942): 297.

6091. Walter Nagel, "Die Finsternis hat's nicht begriffen (Joh I, 5)," *ZNW* 50 (1959): 132-37.

6092. W. G. Allan, "John i. 6-8," *ET* 4 (1892-93): 179-80.

6093. D. Frangipane, " 'Et gratiam pro gratia' (John I. 6)," *VD* 26 (1948): 3-17.

6094. Dr. Bleek, "Bemerkungen zu einzelnen Stellen des Evangeliums des Johannes, meistens mit besonderer Rücksicht auf den Lücke'schen Commentar," *TSK* 6 (1833): 413-51

6095. P. Thomson, "Note on John i. 9, ἦν τὸ φῶς τὸ ἀληθινὸν ὃ φωτίζει πάντα ἄνθρωπον ἐρχόμενον εἰς τὸν κόσμον," *ET* 8 (1896-97): 527-28.

6096. Heinrich Schulte, "Die Übersetzung von Johannes 1, 9," *BibZ* 21 (1933): 182-83

6097. T. F. Glasson, "John I, 9 and a Rabbinic Tradition," *ZNW* 49 (1958): 288-90.

6098. A. Henderson, "John i. 11-13," *ET* 29 (1917-1918): 89-91.

6099. Jacob Jervell, " 'Han kom til sitt eget.' En bemerkning til Joh.

I, 11," *NTT* 54 (1953): 129-43.

6100. A. Médebielle, " 'In propria venit...' (Ioh. I, 11)," *VD* 2 (1922): 137-44.

6101. A. T. Robertson, "The Meaning of John 1:13," *BR* 10 (1925): 569-79.

6102. John Reid, "John i. 13," *ET* 4 (1892-1893): 227.

6103. A. Henderson, "Note on Variant in the Text of John i. 13," *ET* 23 (1911-1912): 525-28.

6104. G. Castellini, "De Io. I, 13 in quibusdam citationibus patristicis," *VD* 32 (1954): 155-57.

6105. Josef Schmid, "Joh. I, 13," *BibZ* 1 (1957): 118-25.

6106. T. H. Weir, " 'The Only-Begotten'," *ET* 31 (1919-1920): 521-22 [Jn. 1:14, 18; 3:16, 18].

6107. Olaf Moe, "Begrepene nåden og sannheten i Johannes-evangeliet," *TTK* 29 (1958): 69-77 [Jn. 1:14ff.].

6108. W. S. Curzon-Siggers, "Grace and Truth," *ET* 4 (1892-1893): *ET* 4 (1892-1893): 480 [Jn 1:14].

6109. C. H. Turner, "On πλήρης in St. John 1:14," *JTS* 1 (1899-1900): 120-25, 561-62.

6110. A. N. Jannaris, "On πλήρης and μονογενής in John i. 14," *ET* 12 (1900-1901): 333-34.

6111. A. Médebielle, " 'Et verbum caro factum est' (Ioh. 1, 14)," *VD* 2 (1922): 137-44.

6112. R. W. Stewart, "The Christmas Glory," *ET* 47 (1935- 1936): 109-10 [Jn. 1:14].

6113. A. M. Perry, "The Word and the Flesh," *CQ* 25 (1948): 241-47 [Jn. 1:14].

6114. Andrew R. Osborn, " 'The Word Became Flesh'," *Interp* 3 (1949): 42-49 [Jn. 1:14].

6115. P. Kačur, "De textu Io. I, 14c," *VD* 29 (1951): 20-27.

6116. Paul Winter, "Μονογενὴς παρὰ πατρός," *ZRGG* 5 (1953): 335-65 [Jn. 1: 14].

6117. C. Lindeboom, " 'Die na mij komt, is voor mij geworden'," *GTT* 16 (1915): 438-46 [Jn. 1:15, 27, 30].

6118. A. Orbe, "El primer testimonio del Bautista sobre el Salvador, según Heracleón y Orígenes," *EE* 30 (1956): 5-36 [Jn. 1: 15-18].

6119. Edward A. Cerny, "The Translation of Jn. 1:15," *CBQ* 1

(1939): 363-68.

6120. Adhémar d'Alès, "χάριν ἀντὶ χάριτος (Ioan. I, 16)," *RSR* 9 (1919): 384-86.

6121. Paul Joüon, "Jean 1, 16," *RSR* 22 (1932): 206.

6122. Matthew Black, "Does an Aramaic Tradition Underlie John i. 16?" *JTS* 42 (1941): 69-70.

6123. Ioseph M. Bover, "χάριν ἀντὶ χάριτος," *B* 6 (1925): 454-60 [Jn. 1:16].

6124. David Eaglesham, "Note on John i. 17," *ET* 16 (1904-1905): 428.

6125. Ezra Abbot, "On the Reading 'Only-Begotten God,' in John 1:18; With Particular Reference to the Statements of Dr. Tregelles," *BS* 18 (1861): 840-72.

6126. A. M. Fairbairn, "The Idea of the Fourth Gospel and the Theology of Nature. (John I. 18; XIV. 8, 9)," *Exp* 6th ser., 6 (1902): 260-77.

6127. A. M. Fairbairn, "The Governing Idea of the Fourth Gospel. (John I. 18; XIV. 8-9)," *Exp* 6th ser., 6 (1902): 161-76.

6128. J. Hugh Michael, "The Meaning of ἐξηγήσατο in St. John i. 18," *JTS* 22 (1921): 13-16.

6129. M.-E. Boismard, " 'Dans le sein du Père' (Jn. 1, 18)," *RB* 59 (1952): 23-39.

6130. P. G. Gennaro, "Il Dio 'invisibile' e il Figlio 'unigenito' (Io. 1, 18)," *RivB* 4 (1956): 154-78.

6131. Jefferson R. Taylor, "A Note on St. John i. 18," *ET* 18 (1906-1907): 47.

6132. L. Fonck, "Testimonium praecursoris de Christo (Ioh. i, 19-28 (1927-1928)," *VD* 1 (1921): 360-65.

6133. L. W. Grensted, "2 Cor. x. 9; John i. 22," *ET* 35 (1923-1924): 331.

6134. G. S. Richards, "Studies in Texts," *Th* 11 (1925): 42 [Jn. 1:23].

6135. U. Holzmeister, " 'Medius vestrum stetit, quem vos nescitis' (Jn. 1, 26)," *VD* 20 (1940): 329-32.

6136. Pierson Parker, "Bethany Beyond Jordan," *JBL* 74 (1955): 257-261 [Jn. 1:28].

6137. E. J. Gilchrist, " 'And I knew him not'," *ET* 19 (1907-1908): 379-80 [Jn. 1:29-34].

6138.   Jean Giblet, "Pour rendre témoignage à la lumière (Jean I, 29-34)," *BVC* no. 16 (1956-1957): 80-86.

6139.   H. L. Oort, "Iets over 'het Lam Gods'," *TT* 42 (1908): 1-10 [Jn. 1:29].

6140.   A. D. Mozley, "St. John i. 29," *ET* 26 (1914-1915): 46-47.

6141.   C. K. Barrett, "The Lamb of God," *NTSt* 1 (1954-1955): 210-18 [Jn. I: 29].

6142.   Paul Joüon, "L'agneau de Dieu (Jean 1, 29)," *NRT* 67 (1940-1945): 318-21.

6143.   Juan Leal, "El condero de Diós (Jn. 1:29, 36)," *CB* 7 (1950): 134-38.

6144.   Juan Leal, "El sentido soteriológico del cordero de Dios en la exégesis católica (Io. I, 29. 36)," *EE* 24 (1950): 147-82.

6145.   Ernest DeW. Burton, "The Biblical Doctrine of Atonement: V. Atonement in the Teaching of John the Baptist," *BW* 31 (1908): 348-56 [Jn. 1:29].

6146.   J. Hugh Michael, "Great Texts Reconsidered," *ET* 50 (1938-1939): 359-63 [Jn. 1:29].

6147.   E. Riggenbach, "Jesus trug die Sünde der Welt," NKZ, 18 (1907): 295-307 [Jn. 1:29].

6148.   Benjamin W. Robinson, "A Study of John 1:29-34," *BW* 37 (1911): 30-39.

6149.   J. Th. Ubbink, "Kai emeinen ep' auton, Jh. 1:32," *NTS* 5 (1922): 8-10.

6150.   C. E. Blakeway, " 'Behold the Lamb of God'," *ET* 31 (1919-1920): 364-65 [Jn. 1:29].

6151.   Joachim Jeremias, "Ἀμνὸς τοῦ θεοῦ—παῖς θεοῦ," *ZNW* 34 (1935): 117-23 [Jn. 1:29, 36].

6152.   A. Crawford Watt, "John's Difficulty in Knowing the Christ-'and I knew him not'," *ET* 19 (1907-1908): 93-94.

6153.   Amos B. Hulen, "The Call of the Four Disciples in John I," *JBL* 67 (1948): 153-57.

6154.   P. Federekiewiez, "Ecce Agnus Dei," *VD* 12 (1932): 41-47, 83-88, 117-20, 156-60, 168-71 [Jn. 1:36].

6155.   Agnes Smith Lewis, "St. John i. 41," *ET* 20 (1908-1909): 229-31.

6156.   A. Souter, "St. John i. 41," *ET* 20 (1908-1909): 333-34.

6157.   James H. Moulton, "St. John i. 41," *ET* 20 (1908- 1909):

428.

6158. Donald, Bishop of Bendigo, "John i. 41," *ET* 41 (1929-1930): 43-44.

6159. W. D. Ridley, "The Revelation of the Son of Man to Nathanael," *Exp* 5th ser., 8 (1898): 336-43. [Jn. 1:43-51].

6160. H. Spencer, "John i. 43," *ET* 45 (1933-1934): 336.

6161. Paul Joüon, "θέλειν au sens d'être sur le point de' dans Jean I, 43," *RSR* 29 (1939): 620-21.

6162. Joachim Jeremias, "Die Berufung des Nathanael (Jn. I. 45-51)," *A* 3 (1928): 2-5.

6163. Jesús Enciso Viana, "La vocación de Natanael y el Salmo 24," *EB* 19 (1960): 229-36 [Jn. 1:45-51].

6164. Rush Rhees, "The Confession of Nathanael, John i. 45-49," *JBL* 17 (1898): 21-30.

6165. Philippe-H. Menoud, " 'Le fils de Joseph': étude sur Jean I, 4, et vi, 42," *RTP* 18 (1930): 275-88.

6166. John L. McKenzie, "The Commentary of Theodore of Mopsuestia on John 1:46-51," *ThSt* 14 (1953): 73-84.

6167. George F. Genung, "A Glimpse of the Inner Life of Christ's Time," *BW* 16 (1900): 337-50 [Jn. 1:47].

6168. Eb. Nestle, "Nathanael under the Fig Tree," *ET* 13 (1901-1902): 432 [Jn. 1:48, 50].

6169. C. F. D. Moule, "A Note on 'Under the Fig Tree' in John i. 48, 50," *JTS* N.S. 5 (1954): 210-11.

6170. A. D. Mozley, " 'Thou art the Son of God'," *ET* Zs (1913-1914): 474-75 [Jn. 1:49].

6171. George C. Walker, "The Faith of Nathanael," *ET* 29 (1917-1918): 560 [Jn. 1:49].

6172. Hans Windisch, "Angelophanien um den Menschensohn auf Erden," *ZNW* 30 (1931): 215-33 [Jn. 1:51].

6173. Hans Windisch, "Joh I, 51 und die Auferstehung Jesu," *ZNW* 31 (1932): 199-204.

6174. C. Bouma, "Het Evangelie van de ladder Gods," *GTT* 42 (1941): 313-17 [Jn. 1:51].

6175. G. Quispel, "Nathanael und der Menschensohn (Joh I, 51)," *ZNW* 47 (1956): 281-83.

6176. J. Fritsch, " ' . . . videbitis. . . angelos Dei ascendentes et descendentes super Filium Hominis' (Jn. 1, 51)," *VD* 37

(1959): 3-11.

6177.   W. Michaelis, "Joh. 1, 51, Gen. 28, 12 und das Menschensohn-Problem," *TLZ* 85 (1960): 561-78.

6178.   Jean Giblet, "Tu verras le ciel ouvert (Jean 1, 51)," *BVC* no. 36 (1960): 26-30.

6179.   Rayner Winterbotham, "The Angels ascending and descending on the Son of Man," *Exp* 1st ser., 3 (1876): 134-41 [Jn. 1:52].

6180.   Gottlieb Linder, "Ev. Joh. Cap. II und III erklärt nach neuer Leseweise," *STZ* 17 (1900): 118-24.

6181.   H. W. Montefiore, "The Position of the Cana Miracle and the Cleansing of the Temple in St. John's Gospel," *JTS* 50 (1949): 183-87 [Jn. 2].

6182.   S. Leathes, "The Marriage in Cana of Galilee," *Exp* 1st ser. 5 (1877): 304-11 [Jn. 2:1-11].

6183.   M. Bourlier, "Les paroles de Jésus à Cana," *RB* 6 (1897): 405-22 [Jn. 2:1-11].

6184.   K. J. Rützou, "Brylluppet i Kana," *TTDF* N.S. 2 (1900-1901): 26-57 [Jn. 2:1-11].

6185.   W. Spicer Wood, "The Miracle of Cana," *JTS* 6 (1904-1905): 438 [Jn. 2:1-11].

6186.   David Baines-Griffiths, "The Gospel of Cana. The Christian Affirmation of Life," *BS* 64 (1907): 19-32 [Jn. 2:1-11].

6187.   Paul Gächter, "Maria in Kana (Jo. 2, 1-11)," *ZKT* 55 (1931): 351-402.

6188.   V. Iacono, "Probaturne B. V. Mariae universalis gratiarum mediatio ex Ioh. 2, 1-11?" *VD* 18 (1938): 202-207.

6189.   P. A. Illingworth, "The Miracle at Cana," *ET* 65 (1953-1954): 287 [Jn. 2:1-11].

6190.   F. Spadafora, "Maria alle nozze di Cana," *RivB* 2 (1954): 220-47 [Jn. 2:1-11].

6191.   A. M. G. Stephenson, "The Miracle at Cana," *ET* 66 (1954-1955): 177 [Jn. 2:1-11].

6192.   C. P. Ceroke, "Jesus and Mary at Cana: Separation or Association?" *ThSt* 17 (1956): 1-38 [Jn. 2:1-11].

6193.   Vincenzo Anzalone, "Gesù e Maria alle nozze di Cana," *RivB* 6 (1958): 135-46.

6194.   Carl Amerding, "The Marriage of Cana," *BS* 118 (1961):

320-26 [Jn. 2:1-11].

6195. Arthur M. Vincent, "Water into Wine: A Sign for the Modern Ministry," *CTM* 32 (1961): 28-38 [Jn. 2:1-11].

6196. G. Temple, "Conversation Piece at Cana," *DS* 7 (1954): 104-13 [Jn. 2:1-5].

6197. J. Rendel Harris, "A Western Gloss in John ii. 3," *ET* 41 (1929-1930): 107-109.

6198. W. F. Besser, "Über Joh. 2, 4," *TSK* 18 (1845): 416-25.

6199. Rayner Winterbotham, "Our Lord's Words to his Mother at Cana," *Exp*, 1st ser., 4 (1876): 179-90 [Jn. 2:4].

6200. Ernst Bröse, "Ein Vorschlag zu Joh. 2, 4," *NKZ* 8 (1897): 841-43.

6201. Eb. Nestle, "John 2, 4," *ET* 9 (1897-1898): 331-32, 562.

6202. Eb. Nestle, "John ii. 4," *ET* 22 (1910-1911): 526.

6203. F. C. Burkitt, " 'Woman, what have I to do with thee'?" *JTS* 13 (1911-1912): 594-95 [Jn 2:4].

6204. Alfred Durand, "La réponse de Jésus aux noces de Cana," *RSR* 3 (1912): 157-59 [Jn. 2:4].

6205. John Mockridge, "John ii. 4," *ET* 24 (1912-1913): 187.

6206. Augustus Poynder, " 'Mine hour is not yet come'," *ET* 26 (1914-1915): 478-79 [Jn. 2:4].

6207. Harold Smith, "John ii. 4," *ET* 32 (1920-1921): 45.

6208. E. Power, " 'Quid mihi et tibi, mulier? Nondum venit hora mea' (Ioh. 2. 4)," *VD* 2 (1922), 129-35.

6209. B. Brinkmann, " 'Quid mihi et tibi, mulier? Nondum venit hora mea' (Ioh. 2.4)," *VD* 14 (1934): 135-41.

6210. T. Gallus, " 'Quid mihi et tibi, mulier?' (Ioh. 2,4)," *VD* 22 (1942): 41-50.

6211. R. B. Woodworth, " 'The Marriage at Cana in Galilee'," *Interp* 1 (1947): 372-74 [Jn. 2:4].

6212. Edgar J. Goodspeed, " 'The Marriage at Cana in Galilee': A Reply," *Interp* 1 (1947): 486-89 [Jn. 2:4].

6213. Herbert Preisker, "John 2,4 und 19, 26," *ZNW* 42 (1949): 209-14.

6214. Juan Leal, "La hora de Jesús, la hora de su Madre (Io 2,4)," *EE* 26 (1952): 147-68.

6215. Alfons Kurfess, "Zu Joh 2, 4," *ZNW* 44 (1952-1953): 257.

6216.　　David Gonzalo Maeso, "Una lección de exégesis lingüística sobre el pasaje evangélico de las bodes de Caná," *CB* 11 (1954): 352-64 [Jn. 2:4].

6217.　　Johann Michl, "Bemerkungen zu Jo. 2, 4," *B* 36 (1955): 492-509.

6218.　　Harry M. Buck, "On the Translation of John 2:4," *BTr* 7 (1956): 149-50.

6219.　　C. P. Ceroke, "The Problem of Ambiguity in John 2, 4," *CBQ* 21 (1959): 316-40.

6220.　　P. Dacquino, "Aqua vinum facta (Jo. 2,9)," *VD* 39 (1961): 92-96.

6221.　　Hans Windisch, "Die johanneische Weinregel," *ZNW* 14 (1913): 248-57 [Jn. 2:10].

6222.　　F. J. Moore, "The Miracle of the Wine," *CJRT* 1 (1924): 56-60 [Jn. 2:11].

6223.　　Henry de Julliot, "Le zèle pour Tu maison (Jean 2, 12-25; 3,22-36)," *BVC* no. 30 (1959): 31-33.

6224.　　George Ogg, "The Jerusalem Visit of John ii. 13-iii. 21," *ET* 56 (1944-1945): 70-72.

6225.　　Aaron Martin Crane, "The Cleansing of the Temple," *BS* 59 (1902): 36-57 [Jn. 2:13-22].

6226.　　W. L. Walker, "The Cleansing of the Temple in John ii. 13-22," *ET* 14 (1902-1903): 286-87.

6227.　　E. J. Roberts, "The Position of the Temple Cleansing in the Fourth Gospel," *ET* 44 (1932-1933): 427 [Jn. 2:13-22].

6228.　　T. Torrance, "The Cleansing of the Temple," *EQ* 9 (1937): 180-91 [Jn. 2:13-22].

6229.　　R. H. Lightfoot, "Unsolved New Testament Problems— The Cleansing of the Temple in St. John's Gospel," *ET* 60 (1948-1949): 64-68 [Jn. 2:13-22].

6230.　　T. W. Manson, "The Cleansing of the Temple," *BJRL* 33 (1950-1951): 271-82.

6231.　　F. A. Cooke, "The Cleansing of the Temple," *ET* 63 {1951-1952): 321-22 [Jn. 2:13-22].

6232.　　X. Léon-Dufour, "Le signe du temple selon saint Jean," *RSR* 39 (1951-1952): 155-75 [Jn. 2:13-22].

6233.　　H. van den Bussche, "Le signe du Temple (Jean 2, 13-22)," *BVC* no. 20 (1957-1958): 92-100.

6234. D. S. Margoliouth, "Note on John ii. 19, λύσατε τὸν ναὸν τοῦτον," *ET* 4 (1892-1893): 128-29.

6235. Alfred E. Garvie, "Jesus and the Priesthood," *ET* 5 (1893-1894): 334-35 [Jn. 2: 19].

6236. Arthur Carr, "Christus aediffcator: A Comparison between St. John II. 19 and Zechariah VI. 13," *Exp* 7th ser., 7 (1909): 41-49.

6237. T. H. Weir, "John ii. 19," *ET* 21 (1909-1910): 191-92.

6238. C. J. Ball, "John ii. 19," *ET* 21 (1909-1910): 281-82.

6239. F. P. Cheetham, " 'Destroy this temple, and in three days I will raise it up' (St. John ii. 19)," *JTS* 24 (1922-1923): 315-17.

6240. André M. Dubarle, "Le signe du temple," *RB* 48 (1939): 21-44 [Jn. 2: 19].

6241. Claude Mondésert, "À propos du signe du temple. Un texte de Clément d'Alexandrie," *RSR* 36 (1949): 580-84 [Jn.2:19].

6242. E. Power, "Jo. 2. 20 and the Date of the Crucifixion," *B* 9 (1928): 257-88.

6243. F. J. Badcock, "A Note on St. John ii. 20," *ET* 47 (1935-1936): 40-41.

6244. Henry de Julliot, "L'eau et l'esprit (Jean 3 et 4)," *BVC* no. 27 (1959): 35-42.

6245. L. Krummel, "Das dritte Kapitel des Johannes-Evangeliums," *NKZ* 1 (1890): 50-69.

6246. J. Hugh Michael, "The Arrangement of the Text in the Third Chapter of John," *ET* 37 (1925-1926): 428-29.

6247. F. Warburton Lewis, "The Arrangement of the Texts in the Third Chapter of St. John," *ET* 38 (1926-1927): 92-93.

6248. J.-G. Gourbillon, "La parabole du serpent d'Airain et la 'lacune' du ch. III de l'évangile selon S. Jean," *RB* 51 (1942): 213-26.

6249. Rudolf Schnackenburg, "Die 'situationsgelösten' Redestücke in Joh 3," *ZNW* 49 (1958): 88-99.

6250. J. M. Usteri, "Exegetische und historisch-kritische Bemerkungen zum Gespräch Jesu mit Nikodemus, Joh. 3, 1-21," *TSK* 63 (1890): 504-51.

6251. F. Roustang, "L'entretien avec Nicodème," *NRT* 78 (1956): 337-58 [Jn. 3:1-15].

6252.   George R. Wells, "Some Aspects of the Discourse with Nicodemus," *BW* 51 (1918): 3-8 [Jn. 3:1-15].

6253.   Miguel Balagué, "Diálogo con Nicodemo," *CB* 16 (1959): 193-206 [Jn. 3:1-15].

6254.   F.-M. Braun, "La vie d'en haut (Jo. III, 1-15)," *RSPT* 40 (1956): 3-24.

6255.   Charles Watson, "Short Study of St. John iii. 2-5," *ET* 15 (1903-1904): 239-40.

6256.   U. Holzmeister, "Grundgedanke und Gedankengang im Gespräche des Herrn mit Nikodemus (Joh. 3, 3-21)," *ZKT* 45 (1921): 527-48.

6257.   John Reid, "John iii. 3," *ET* 3 (1891-1892): 271.

6258.   J. Louw, "De vraag naar de betekenis van ἄνωθεν, Johannes 3, 3," *NTS* 23 (1940): 53-56.

6259.   R. E. Neighbor, "The New Birth and the Conversation with Nicodemus," *RE* 20 (1923): 28-39 [Jn. 3:4ff.].

6260.   Henry Cowles, "Baptismal Regeneration; As Supposed to be Taught in the Words of Jesus: 'Born of Water and Spirit,' John III. 5," *BS* 33 (1876): 425-37.

6261.   John Reid and R. A. Mitchell, "Born of Water and Spirit," *ET* 3 (1891-1892): 318-19 [Jn. 3:5].

6262.   Margaret D. Gibson, Albert H. Walker, and A. S. Aglen, " 'Born of Water and Spirit'," *ET* 13 (1901-1902): 429 [Jn.3:5].

6263.   John Reid, "Born of Water and Spirit," *ET* 15 (1903- 1904): 413-15 [Jn. 3:5].

6264.   William H. Bates, "Born of Water," *BS* 85 (1928): 230-36.

6265.   J. S. Murray, "Water and Spirit (John iii. 5)," *ET* 59 (1947-1948): 138-39.

6266.   J. F. Genung, "John iii. 8," *JBL* 4 (1884): 145-46.

6267.   Alexander Brown, "Christ and Nicodemus," *ET* 4 (1892-1893): 287-88 [Jn. 3:8].

6268.   John Reid, "The Spirit and the Spirit-born," *ET* 4 (1892-1893): 161-64 [Jn. 3:8].

6269.   John Reid, "The Spirit Breathes," *ET* 4 (1892-1893): 369-71 [Jn. 3:8].

6270.   T. M. Donn, "The Voice of the Spirit (John iii. 8)," *ET* 66 (1954-1955): 32.

6271.   Eric F. F. Bishop, "The Authorized Teacher of the Israel of God (John 3:10)," *BTr* 7 (1956): 71-83.

6272.   H. van den Bussche, "L'élévation du fils de l'homme (Jean 3, 11-21)," *BVC* no. 35 (1960): 16-25.

6273.   Anonymous, "Ueber Joh. 3, 13-21," *TQ* (1819): 575-92.

6274.   W. H. Rigg, "Studies in Texts," *Th* 20 (1930): 98-99 [Jn.3: 13].

6275.   G. H. C. Macgregor, "A Suggested Rearrangement of the Johannine Text (John iii. 14-36 and xii. 30-36)," *ET* 35 (1923-1924): 476-77.

6276.   B. Jacobi, "Ueber die Erhöhung des Menschensohnes. Joh. 3, 14, 15," *TSK* 8 (1835): 7-70.

6277.   C. Lindeboom, " 'Verhoogd worden' in Johannes 3, 14," *GTT* 15 (1914): 491-98.

6278.   Eb. Nestle, "John iii. 16 and its Surroundings," *ET* 20 (1908-1909): 564.

6279.   Dale Moody, "God's Only Son: The Translation of John 3:16 in the Revised Standard Version," *JBL* 72 (1953): 213-19.

6280.   G. Gander, "Jean III, 22 à IV, 3 parle-t-il d'un baptême administré par Jésus?" *RTP* N.S. 36 (1948): 133-37.

6281.   Dale Moody, "God's Only Son: The Translation of John 3:16 in the Revised Standard Version," *BTr* 10 (1959): 145-47.

6282.   A. J. Walker, "St. John's Gospel iii. 22-26," *ET* 46 (1934-1935): 380-81.

6283.   Wm. Arnold, "Aenon near Salim," *JBL* 3 (1883): 128-41 [Jn. 3: 23].

6284.   David Knapp, "Did Christ Baptize?" *ET* 4 (1892-1893): 227-28 [Jn. 3:22].

6285.   A. C. Bouquet, "St. John iii. 25-A Suggestion," *JTS* 27 (1925-1926). 181-82.

6286.   W. N. Clarke, "John iii. 31-36," *JBL* 8 (1888): 163.

6287.   U. Holzmeister, "Colloquium Domini cum muliere Samaritana (Ioh. 4, 1-41)," *VD* 13 (1933): 17-20, 51-55.

6288.   Lothar Schmid, "Die Komposition der Samaria-Szene Joh 4, 1-42," *ZNW* 28 (1929): 148-58.

6289.   John C. Slemp, "The Authority of Christian Experience," *RE* 30 (1933): 261-71 [Jn. 4:1-42].

6290.   F. Roustang, "Les moments de l'acte de foi et ses conditions de possibilité. Essai d'interprétation du dialogue avec la Samaritaine," *RSR* 46 (1958): 344-78 [Jn. 4:1-42].

6291. A. Thom, "Christ's Necessities," *ET* 21 (1909-1910): 429-30 [Jn. 4:4].

6292. G. A. Smith, "The Question of Sychar," *Exp* 4th ser., 6 (1892): 464-72 [Jn. 4:5].

6293. W. R. Hutton, " 'Spring' and 'Well' in John iv. 6, 11, 12," *ET* 57 (1945-1946): 27.

6294. David Daube, "Jesus and the Samaritan Woman: The Meaning of συνγχράομαι," *JBL* 69 (1950): 137-47.

6295. Francisco Planas, "Jesús, judío y la Samaritana," *CB* 12 (1922): 225-28 [Jn. 4:9, etc.].

6296. J. Rendel Harris, "A Lost Verse of St. John's Gospel," *ET* 38 (1926-1927): 342-43 [Jn. 4:12-13].

6297. A. E. J. Rawlinson, "In Spirit and in Truth: An Exposition of St. John iv. 16-24," *ET* 44 (1932-1933): 12-14.

6298. H. Highfield, "Didache xi. 4, 5 and John iv. 19, 40," *ET* 22 (1910-1911): 565.

6299. J. E. Belser, "Zu Joh. 4, 20-24 und Hebr. 13, 10," *TQ* 96 (1914): 323-40.

6300. T. Torrance, "Salvation is of the Jews," *EQ* 22 (1950): 164-73 [Jn 4:22].

6301. Rudolf Schnackenburg, "Die 'Anbetung in Geist und Wahrheit' (Joh. 4, 23) im Lichte von Qumran-Texten," *BibZ* 3 (1959): 88-94

6302. John Henry Bennetch, "John 4:24a: A Greek Study," *BS* 107 (1950): 71-83.

6303. Walter G. White, "St. John iv. 27," *ET* 26 (1914-1915): 180.

6304. John Foster, " 'What seekest thou?' John iv. 27," *ET* 52 (1940-1941): 37-38.

6305. Leslie H. Bunn, "John iv. 34-42," *ET* 41 (1929-1930): 141-42.

6306. Ioseph M. Bover, "Adhuc quattuor menses sunt, et messis venit," *B* 3 (1922): 442-44 [Jn. 4:35].

6307. Justo Collantes, "La más antigua interpretación de Io. 4, 35," *EE* 27 (1953): 339-45.

6308. Lewis Johnson, "John iv. 44," *ET* 50 (1938-1939): 93-94.

6309. W. A. Wordsworth, "A Prophet in his own Country (Jn. iv.

44)," *ET* 49 (1937-1938): 92-93.

6310. Lewis Johnson, "John iv. 44," *ET* 49 (1937-1938): 236.

6311. W. A. Wordsworth, "John iv. 44," *ET* 49 (1937-1938): 429-30.

6312. Hubert Klug, "Ist die Heilung des Beamtensohnes Jo. 4:46 ff. das zweite Wunder Jesu in Galiläa?" *BibZ* 9 (1911): 369-71.

6313. Eduard Schweizer, "Die Heilung des Königlichen: Joh. 4, 46-54," *EvT* 11 (1951-1952): 64-71.

6314. André Feuillet, "La signification théologique du second miracle de Cana (Jn. IV, 46-54)," *RSR* 48 (1960): 62-75.

6315. H. Liese, "Filius reguli sanatur (Ioh 4, 46-53)," *VD* 11 (1931): 289-93.

6316. U. Holzmeister, " 'Nisi signa et prodigia videritis, non creditis' (Ioh. 4. 48)," *VD* 18 (1938): 294-98.

6317. F. G. Cholmondeley, "St. John iv. 52," *ET* 24 (1912- 1913): 283.

6318. Robert Mackintosh, "John v.-x.—where were the disciples?" *ET* 2 (1909-1910): 379-80.

6319. Friedrich Stawars, "Das Joh. 5, 1 erwähnte Fest," *TQ* 53 (1871): 610-25.

6320. M. J. Evans, "This Unnamed Feast-What was it?" *Exp* 1st ser., 8 (1878): 391-96 [Jn. 5:1]

6321. G. A. Chadwick, "Christ at the Pool of Bethesda," *Exp* 4th ser., 7 (1893): 136-46 [Jn. 5:1].

6322. J. Th. Ubbink, "Jh. 5, I, 'Een feest' of het (paasch)feest?" *NTS* 5 (1922): 131-36.

6323. José M. Bover, "La fiesta de los judíos en Io. 5, I," *EE* 26 (1952): 79-82.

6324. van Bebber, "Der Teich Bethesda und die Gottheit Jesu," *TQ* 84 (1902): 1-73, 498-573; 85 (1903): 161-95, 369-417 [Jn. 5:22ff.; 9:7ff.].

6325. J. Rendel Harris, "The Pool of Bethesda," *Exp* 7th ser., 2 (1906): 508-17 [Jn. 5:2].

6326. James H. Moulton, "John v. 2," *ET* 22 (1910-1911): 563.

6327. José M. Bover, "Autenticidad de Jn. 5, 3b-4," *EB* 11 (1952): 69-72.

6328. John G. Morton, "Christ's Diagnosis of Disease at Bethesda," *ET* 33 (1921-1922): 424-25 [Jn. 5:6].

6329. Caspar René Gregory, "John 5:7, 8," *AJT* 11 (1907): 131-38.

6330. Ivor Buse, "John v. 8 and Johannine-Marcan Relationships," *NTSt* 1 (1954-1955): 134-36.

6331. H. Clavier, "Autour de Jean v, 17. L'action, le travail et l'acte en Dieu," *RHPR* 24 (1944): 82-90.

6332. Alexander Stewart, "The Supreme Claim," *EQ* 8 (1936): 423-33 [Jn. 5:18].

6333. C. Bruston, "Encore l'interprétation de Jean v, 19-30," *RTQR* 2 (1893): 295-305.

6334. W. F. Howard, "The Father and the Son, An Exposition of John 5: 19-24," *Interp* 4 (1950): 3-11.

6335. Chazel, "Essai d'interpretation de Jean v, 26-30," *RTQR* 2 (1893): 199-210.

6336. G. A. Derry, "The Incarnation and Judgment," *Exp* 5th ser., 7 (1898): 108-13 [Jn. 5:27].

6337. Jean Giblet, "Le témoignage du Père (Jean 5, 31-47)," *BVC*, no. 12 (1955-1956): 49-59.

6338. Fritz Neugebauer, "Miszelle zu Joh 5, 35," *ZNW* 52 (1961): 130.

6339. Albert Vanhoye, "L'oeuvre du Christ, don du Père (Jn. v, 36 et XVII, 4)," *RSR* 48 (1960): 377-419.

6340. M.-E. Boismard, "À propos de Jean v, 39. Essai de critique textuelle," *RB* 55 (1948)' 5-34.

6341. Stephan Dillmann, "Jo. 5, 45-47 in der Pentateuchfrage," *BibZ* 15 (1918-1921): 139-48, 219-28.

6342. Ernest P. H. Pfatteicher, "John VI and the Lord's Supper," *LCR* 20 (1901): 103-13.

6343. Ernest P. H. Pfatteicher, "Does the Sixth Chapter of the Gospel According to St. John Pertain to the Lord's Supper?" *LCR* 20 (1901): 330-34.

6344. F. Cavallera, "L'interprétation du chapitre VI de saint Jean. Une controverse exégétique au Concile de Trente," *RHE* 10 (1909): 687-709.

6345. J. F. Springer, "The Sixth Chapter of John not in Danger," *ATR* 6 (1923-1924): 132-140.

6346. Delia Lyttelton, "St. John VI. and the Question of the Author," *Th* 36 (1938): 230-32.

6347. Miguel Balagué, "El Pedagogo Divino," *CB* 4 (1947):

193-200 [Jn. 6].

6348. Patrick J. Temple, "The Eucharist in St. John 6," *CBQ* 9 (1947): 442-52.

6349. D. Mollat, "Le chapitre VIᵉ de Saint Jean," *LumV* no. (1957): 107-109.

6350. X. Léon-Dufour, "Le mystère du pain de vie (Jean VI)," *RSR* 46 (1958): 481-523.

6351. Peder Borgen, "The Unity of the Discourse in John 6," *ZNW* 50 (1959): 277-78.

6352. Henry de Julliot, "Le pain de vie (Jean 6, 1-17)," *BVC* no. 26 (1959): 38-43.

6353. Edward J. Kilmartin, "Liturgical Influence on John 6," *CBQ* 22 (1960): 183-91.

6354. Edward J. Kilmartin, "The Formation of the Bread of Life Discourse (John 6)," *Scr* 12 (1960): 75-78.

6355. L. Fonck, "Christus primum panes multiplicat (Ioh. 6, 1-15)," *VD* 1 (1921): 47-51.

6356. Peter Dausch, "Kane das Osterfest Jo. 6, 4 mit dem Osterfest Jo. 2, 13 identifiziert werden?" *BibZ* 4 (1906): 398-401.

6357. Hubert Klug, "Das Osterfest Jo. 6, 4," *BibZ* 4 (1906): 152-63.

6358. J. A. Bruins, "Joh. VI, 5b-56, eene interpolatie," *TT* 45 (1911): 240-54.

6359. Charles A. Webster, "The Walking on the Sea (St. John vi. 16-21)," *ET* 51 (1939-1940): 434-35.

6360. Dr. Mack, "Ueber Joh. vi. 22-59, und das Verhältnis dieser Stelle zum heiligen Abendmahle," *TQ* 14 (1832): 52-87.

6361. J. M. Bover, "De sermonis unitate Ioh. 6, 25-59," *VD* 2 (1922): 48-50.

6362. Juan Fernández, "Jesus, pan de vida," *CB* 12 (1955): 218-24 [Jn. 6:26-59].

6363. André Feuillet, "Les thèmes bibliques majeurs du discours sur le pain de vie (Jn. 6)," *NRT* 82 (1960): 803-22, 918-39, 1040-62.

6364. R. E. Lee, "John vi. 29-31," *ET* 38 (1926-1927): 188.

6365. Walter G. White, "John vi. 29," *ET* 30 (1918-1919): 142.

6366. E. A. Erwin, "Studies in Texts," *Th* 22 (1931): 34-35 [Jn. 6:31].

6367.   Anonymous, "Ueber die Stellen Joh. 6, 35; Matth. 5, 4. 5; 1
         Thess. 5, 19. 20; Joh. 1, 13," *TQ* 1 (1819): 210-17.

6368.   Paul Gächter, "Die Form der eucharistischen Rede Jesu,"
         ZKT 59 (1935): 419-41 [Jn. 6:35 ff.].

6369.   Cinette Ferrière, "Je suis le pain," *BVC* no. 26 (1959): 71-77
         [Jn. 6:35ff.].

6370.   A. Henderson, "Note on John vi. 37," *ET* 31 (1919-1920):
         37-38.

6371.   E. Alty, "John vi. 37," *ET* 4 (1892-1893): 287.

6372.   John Theodore Mueller, "Notes on Luther's Interpretation of
         John 6: 47-58," *CTM* 20 (1949): 802-29.

6373.   Günther Bornkamm, "Die eucharistische Rede im
         Johannes-Evangelium," *ZNW* 47 (1956): 161-69 [Jn.
         6:51-58].

6374.   G. M. Behler, "Le pain de vie (Jean 6, 51-58)," *BVC* no. 32
         (1960): 15-26.

6375.   Joachim Jeremias, "Joh 6, 51c-58-redaktionell?" *ZNW* 44
         (1952-1953): 256-57.

6376.   Heinz Schürmann, "Joh. 6:51c-ein Schlüssel zur grossen
         johanneischen Brotrede," *BibZ* 2 (1958): 244-62.

6377.   Gerhard Kittel, "Andacht über Joh. 6, 60-69," *TB* 7 (1928):
         277.

6378.   H. L. Oort, "Joh. 6, 60-63," *TT* 43 (1909): 525-37.

6379.   J. Hugh Michael, "The Actual Saying behind St. John vi. 62,"
         ET 43 (1931-1932): 427-28.

6380.   Henry Lowther Clarke, "The Abiding Cause of the Desertion
         of Jesus Christ," *Th* 6 (1923): 123-28 [Jn. 6:63-7:1; Mt.
         13:54-57].

6381.   Leone Tondelli, "Caro non prodest quidquam," *B* 4 (1923):
         320-27 [Jn. 6:64].

6382.   W. Weiffenbach, "Der Weg zu Christo," *ZTK* 4 (1894):
         79-90 [Jn. 6:66-69; 7:16-17].

6383.   K. M. Bishop, "Two Friends," *ET* 61 (1949-1950): 31 [Jn.
         6:66-71].

6384.   James Hastings, "The Great Texts of St. John's Gospel," *ET*
         8 (1896-1897): 35-38 [Jn. 6:68].

6385.   C. Egli, "Zu Joh. 6, 71," *ZWT* 9 (1866): 333-36.

6386.   F. H. Chase, "The Name Judas Iscariot in the Fourth

Gospel," *ET* 9 (1897-98): 285-86 [Jn. 6:71, etc.].

6387.   Eb. Nestle, "The Name of Judas Iscariot in the Fourth Gospel," *ET* 9 (1897-1898): 240 [Jn. 6:71, etc.].

6388.   C. Clare Oke, "At the Feast of Booths; A Suggested Rearrangement of John vii.-ix.," *ET* 47 (1935-1936): 425-27.

6389.   G. H. C. Macgregor, "The Rearrangement of John vii. and viii.," *ET* 33 (1921-1922): 74-78.

6390.   J. E. Belser, "Zu Joh. 7, 1-5," *TQ* 97 (1915): 16-41.

6391.   Johannes Schneider, "Zur Komposition von Joh 7, 1," *ZNW* 45 (1954): 108-19.

6392.   J. O. Dykes, "Our Lord's First Appearance at the Feast of Tabernacles," *Exp* 4th ser., 1 (1890): 49-59 [Jn. 7:2ff.].

6393.   George Baldon, "St. John vii. 10," *ET* 18 (1906-1907): 143.

6394.   J. O. Dykes, "The Self-Witness of the Son of God (John vii. 12-20)," *Exp* 4th ser., 3 (1891): 54-63.

6395.   James Hastings, "The Great Texts of St. John's Gospel," *ET* 8 (1896-1897): 85-88 [Jn. 7:17].

6396.   R. H. Charles, "The Will to Know," *ET* 14 (1902-1903): 354-58 [Jn 7:17]

6397.   Eberhard Waitz, "Zur Erklärung von Joh. 7, 22-24," *TSK* 54 (1881): 145-60.

6398.   N. Messel, "Den angivelig jødiske laere om Messias' ukjendte herkomst (Joh. 7, 27)," *NTT* 21 (1920): 67-81.

6399.   J. O. Dykes, "Abortive Attempt to Arrest Jesus," *Exp* 4th ser., 1 (1890): 391-400 [Jn. 7:30-36, 40-52].

6400.   André M. Dubarle, "Des fleuves d'eau vive (S. Jean VII, 37-39)," *VP* 3 (1943-1944): 238-41.

6401.   Cuthbert Lattey, "A Note on John vii. 37-38," *Scr* 6 (1954): 151-53.

6402.   J. Blenkinsopp, "The Quenching of Thirst: Reflections on the Utterance in the Temple, John vii. 37-39," *Scr* 12 (1960): 39-48.

6403.   J. M. Bover, "Christus, aqua vitae (Ioh. 7, 37-39)," *VD* 1 (1921): 109-14.

6404.   Lyder Brun, " 'Floder av levende vand,' Joh. 7, 37-39," *NTT* 29 (1928): 71-79.

6405.   J. Blenkinsopp, "John VII, 37-39: Another Note on a Notorious Crux," *NTSt* 6 (1959-1960): 95-98.

6406. J. E. Somerville, "The Invitation to the Thirsty," *ET* 15 (1903-1904): 77-79 [Jn. 7:37-38].

6407. Hugo Rahner, "Flumina de ventre Christi-Die patristische Auslegung von Joh. 7, 37-38," *B* 22 (1941): 269-302, 367-403.

6408. Willoughby C. Allen, "St. John vii. 37, 38," *ET* 34 (1922-1923): 329-30.

6409. K. H. Kuhn, "St. John Vll. 37-38," *NTSt* 4 (1957-1958): 63-65.

6410. George D. Kilpatrick, "The Punctuation of John vii. 37-38," *JTS* N.S. 11 (1960): 340-42.

6411. J. C. Quirant, "Torrentes de ague viva. ¿Une nueva interpretación de Jn. 7, 37-38?" *EB* 16 (1957): 279-306.

6412. Eb. Nestle, "The Earliest Quotation of John vii. 38, 39," *ET* 23 (1911-1912): 331.

6413. J. Abrahams, "John vii. 38, 39," *ET* 23 (1911-1912): 180.

6414. A. S. Lewis, Margaret D. Gibson, and F. Relton, "John vii. 38, 39," *ET* 23 (1911-1912): 235-37.

6415. Pierre Grelot, "À propos de Jean VII, 38," *RB* 67 (1960): 224-25.

6416. Jean-Paul Audet, " 'De son ventre couleront des fleuves d'eau'," *RB* 66 (1959): 369-86. [Jn. 7:38].

6417. M.-E. Boismard, "De son ventre couleront des fleuves d'eau (Jn. VII, 38)," *RB* 65 (1958): 523-46.

6418. David Smith, "Recent New Testament Criticism; VI. 'Nunquam sic locutus est Homo'," *Exp* 6th ser., 4 (1901): 374-94 [Jn. 7:46 et al.].

6419. Arthur Carr. "A Note on St. John VII. 52. A Prophet or the Prophet," *Exp* 6th ser., 8 (1903): 219-26.

6420. C. F. Dieck, "Ueber die Geschichte von der Ehebrecherin im Evangelium Johannis vom juristischen Standpunkte," *TSK* 5 (1832): 791-822 [Jn. 7:53-8:11].

6421. F. W. Farrar, "The Gospel for Penitents; And Christ Writing on the Ground," *Exp* 1st ser., 9 (1879): 24-42 [Jn. 7:53-8:11].

6422. Caspar René Gregory, " 'And they went out one by one.' John 7:53-8:11," *BW* 12 (1898): 303-306.

6423. Eb. Nestle, "John vii. 53-viii. 11," *ET* 13 (1901-1902): 94-95.

6424.   Bernhard Weiss, "Die Perikope von der Ehebrecherin," *ZWT* 46 (1903): 141-58 [Jn. 7:53-8:11].

6425.   Hans von Soden, "Die Perikope von der Ehebrecherin," *ZNW* 8 (1907): 110-24.

6426.   J.-P. van Kasteren, "Verisimilia circa pericopen de muliere adultera (Ioan. VII, 53-VIII, 11)," *RB* 20 (1911): 96-102.

6427.   J. Linder, "Papias und die Perikope von der Ehebrecherin (Joh. 7, 53-8,11) bei Agapius von Mamlig," *ZKT* 40 (1916): 191-99.

6428.   Henry J. Cadbury, "A Possible Case of Lukan Authorship," *HTR* 10 (1917): 237-44 [Jn. 7:53-8:11].

6429.   T. W. Manson, "The Pericope de Adultera (Joh 7, 53-8, 11)," *ZNW* 44 (1952-1953): 255-56.

6430.   C. Taylor, "The Pericope of the Adulteress," *JTS* 4 (1902-1903): 129-30 [Jn. 8:1-11].

6431.   F. Nau, "La péricope de la femme adultère et la didascalie," *ROC* 16 (1911): 425-27 [Jn. 8:1-11].

6432.   F. Warburton Lewis, "The Pericope Adulterae," *ET* 29 (1917-1918): 138 [Jn. 8:1-11].

6433.   Robert Eisler, "Jesus und die ungetreue Braut," *ZNW* 22 (1923): 305-307 [Jn. 8:1-11].

6434.   Karl Bornhäuser, "Jesus und die Ehebrecherin," *NKZ* 37 (1926): 353-63 [Jn. 8:1-11].

6435.   Eric F. F. Bishop, "The Pericope Adulterae: A Suggestion," *JTS* 35 (1934): 40-45.

6436.   Everett F. Harrison, "Jesus and the Woman Taken in Adultery," *BS* 103 (1946): 431-39.

6437.   J. A. Oñate, "¿Quién era la pecadora del Evangelio?" *CB* 3 (1946): 81-86, 116-21 [Jn. 8:1-11].

6438.   Samuel Läuchli, "Eine alte Spur von Joh. 8:1-11?" *TZ* 6 (1950): 151 [in Origen, *Hom. in Jer.* XVI].

6439.   F. A. Schilling, "The Story of Jesus and the Adulteress," *ATR* 37 (1955): 91-106 [Jn. 8:1-11].

6440.   David O. Voss, "The Sins of Each One of Them," *ATR* 5 (1933): 321-23 [Jn. 8: 6].

6441.   R. Köbert, "Ein Satz aus Hariris 29. Makame zur Beleuchtung von Joh. 8, 6-9," *B* 29 (1948): 409-10.

6442.   E. Power, "Writing on the Ground," *B* 2 (1921): 54-57 [Jn.

8:6-8].

6443.   Paul Humbert, "Jesus Writing on the Ground (John viii. 6-8)," *ET* 30 (1918-1919): 475-76.

6444.   D. S. Margoliouth, "Jesus Writing on the Ground," *ET* 31 (1919-1920): 38 [Jn. 8:8].

6445.   Walter Kern, "Der symmetrische Gesamtaufbau von Jo. 8, 12-58," *ZKT* 78 (1956): 451-54.

6446.   J. O. Dykes, "The Light of the World," *Exp* 4th ser., 2 (1890): 216-23 [Jn. 8:12].

6447.   James Hastings, "The Great Texts of St. John's Gospel," *ET* 8 (1896-1897): 163-65 [Jn. 8:12].

6448.   Jean-Pierre Charlier, "L'exégèse johannique d'un précepte légal: Jean VIII 17," *RB* 67 (1960): 503-15.

6449.   Dr. Nirschl, "Ueber Johannes 8, 25," *TQ* 37 (1855): 592-605.

6450.   Albert Condamin, "La réponse de Jésus aux juifs, Jn. VIII, 25," *RB* 8 (1899): 409-12.

6451.   G. S. Robertson, "On the Interpretation of John viii. 25," *ET* 8 (1896-1897): 424-26.

6452.   R. G. Bury, "St. John viii. 25," *ET* 8 (1896-1897): 522.

6453.   G. S. Robertson, "St. John viii. 25," *ET* 8 (1896-1897): 567.

6454.   Robert G. Hoerber, "The Problems in John 8:25," *CTM* 26 (1955): 689-92.

6455.   Robert W. Funk, "Papyrus Bodmer 2 (p66) and John 8.25," *HTR* 51 (1958): 95-100.

6456.   Théo. Preiss, "Aramäisches in Joh. 8, 30-36," *TZ* 3 (1947): 78-80.

6457.   J. O. Dykes, "Of Spiritual Bondage and Freedom," *Exp* 4th ser., 3 (1891): 292-301 [Jn. 8:31-36].

6458.   K. G. Steck, "Über Johannes 8, 31-36," *EvT* 15 (1955): 439-45.

6459.   James Hastings, "The Great Texts of St. John's Gospel," *ET* 8 (1896-1897): 216-18 [Jn. 8:31-32].

6460.   D. Macfadyen, "Personality in Miracles," *ET* 8 (1896-1897): 332-33 [Jn. 8:31].

6461.   W. Winstanley, "Freedom by the Knowledge of the Truth," *ET* 19 (1907-1908): 397-400 [Jn. 8:32].

6462.   Paul F. Laubenstein, "The Most Abused Biblical Verse,"

Interp 2 (1948): 337-39 [Jn. 8:32].

6463.   J. O. Dykes, "True or False Children of Abraham," *Exp* 4th ser., 6 (1892): 455-63 [Jn. 8:37-42].

6464.   Eb. Nestle, "John vii. 41," *ET* 11 (1899-1900): 235.

6465.   J. O. Dykes, "The Diabolic Image," *Exp* 5th ser., 6 (1897): 440-49 [Jn. 8:43-47].

6466.   H. Liese, "Controversia Christum inter et Iudaeos (Ioh. 8, 46-59)," *VD* 14 (1934): 66-70.

6467.   J. O. Dykes, "How Jesus met Recrimination," *Exp* 5th ser., 8 (1898): 381-90 [Jn. 8:48-51].

6468.   J. R. Linder, "Exegetische Bemerkungen zu einigen Stellen des Neuen Testamentes," *TSK* 40 (1867): 507-24 [Jn. 8:56; 13:10; 16:8-11].

6469.   S. Cox, "Abraham's Gospel," *Exp* 2nd ser., 6 (1883): 98-108 [Jn. 8:56].

6470.   Th. Vargha, " 'Abraham exultavit ut videret diem meum' (Ioh. 8, 56)," *VD* 10 (1930): 43-46.

6471.   T. Torrance, "The Giving of Sight to the Man Born Blind," *EQ* 9 (1937): 74-82 [Jn. 9].

6472.   Karl Bornhäuser, "Meister, wer hat gesündigt, dieser oder seine Eltern, dass er ist blind geboren? Joh. 9, 2," *NKZ* 38 (1927): 433-37.

6473.   W. Herbert Spencer, "John ix. 3," *ET* 55 (1943-1944): 110.

6474.   James Hastings, "The Great Texts of St. John's Gospel," *ET* 8 (1896-1897): 260-62 [Jn. 9:4].

6475.   Oswald T. Allis, "The Comment on John ix. 38 in the American Revised Version," *PTR* 17 (1919): 221-311.

6476.   James T. Hudson, "A Disarrangement in John x.," *ET* 38 (1926-1927): 329.

6477.   Friedrich Spitta, "Die Hirtengleichnisse des vierten Evangeliums," *ZNW* 10 (1909): 59-80, 103-27 [Jn. 10:1-39].

6478.   H. Z. Westerink, " 'De allegoric van de schaapskooi.' Een proeve tot de exegese van Joh. 10, 1-21," *GTT* 43 (1942): 112-32.

6479.   John Quasten, "The Parable of the Good Shepherd: Jn. 10:1-21," *CBQ* 10 (1948): 1-12, 151-69.

6480.   Endres, "Eine altchristliche Darstellung des guten Hirten im städtischen Museum zu Augsburg," *RQ* 6 (1892): 114-18

554   CRITICAL STUDIES OF THE GOSPELS

[Jn. 10:1-18].

6481.   Lyder Brun, "Joh. 10, 1-18," *NTT* 10 (1909): 1-36.

6482.   José M. Bover, "El símil del Buen Pastor (Jn. 10, 1-18)," *EB* 14 (1955): 297-308.

6483.   Juan Leal, "La eucaristía y la parábola del Buen Pastor (Io 10, 1-18)," *EE* 27 (1953): 317-24.

6484.   Arthur Carr, "The Foreshadowing of the Church," *Exp* 6th ser., 11 (1905): 60-67 [Jn. 10:1-16].

6485.   A. D. Mozley, "St. John x. 1-10," *ET* 25 (1913-1914): 565.

6486.   Paul W. Meyer, "A Note on John 10, 1-18," *JBL* 75 (1956): 232-35.

6487.   John A. T. Robinson, "The Parable of John 10, 1-5," *ZNW* 46 (1955): 233-40.

6488.   O. Holtzmann, "Die Schafe werden sich in Wölfe verwandeln," *ZNW* 11 (1910): 224-31 [Jn. 10:3].

6489.   G. Faccio, "Christus ovium ostium et pastor (Io. 10, 7-16)," *VD* 28 (1950): 168-75.

6490.   Eric F. F. Bishop, " 'The Door of the Sheep' (ἐγώ εἰμι ἡ θύρα τῶν προβάτων)—John x. 7-9," *ET* 71 (1959-1960): 307-309.

6491.   J. Gibb, "The Door of the Sheep," *Exp* 1st ser., 8 (1878): 359-65 [Jn. 10:7].

6492.   L. MacLean Watt, "Symbols of Christ," *ET* 9 (1897- 1898): 427-28 [Jn 10:7].

6493.   J. M. Ballard, "Two Translations in St. John's Gospel," *ET* 36 (1924-1925): 45 [Jn. 10:9; 17:5].

6494.   John A. F. Gregg, " 'I am the Good Shepherd'; A Study," *ET* 31 (1919-1920): 491-93.

6495.   L. Fonck, "Pastor bonus (Ioh. 10, 11-16)," *VD* 1 (1921): 85-89.

6496.   F. Gryglewicz, "Breaking of the Contract of Work as Mentioned in the Gospels," *Scr* 7 (1955): 109-113 [Jn. 10:12-13]

6497.   H. N. Fegley, "What does Jesus Mean by the One Fold and One Shepherd?" *LCR* 30 (1911): 66-74 [Jn. 10:16].

6498.   Arthur M. Ross, "A Critical Note on John 10:16-Fold or Flock?" *BETS* 4 (1961): 99-100.

6499.   Donald M. Henry, "John x. 17," *ET* 4 (1892-1893): 566-67.

6500. H. Höpfl, "Das Chanokafest," *B* 3 (1922): 165-79 [Jn. 10:22].

6501. R. A. Aytoun, " 'No one shall snatch them out of my hand'," *ET* 31 (1919-1920): 475-76.

6502. J. Hugh Michael, "The Text and Context of St. John x. 29," *JTS* 24 (1922-1923): 51-54.

6503. R. G. Bury, "St. John x. 29," *JTS* 41 (1940): 262-63.

6504. T. E. Pollard, "The Exegesis of John x. 30 in the Early Trinitarian Controversies," *NTSt* 3 (1956-1957): 334-48.

6505. P. E. Kretzmann, "Die Schrift kann nicht gebrochen werden," *CTM* 6 (1935): 114-21 [Jn. 10:35].

6506. Donald G. Miller, " 'Where... at the First'," *Interp* 1 (1947): 240-42 [Jn. 10:40 A.R.V.].

6507. Anonymous, "Über Lazarus Erweckung," *TQ* 2 (1820): 3-27 [Jn. 11:1-46].

6508. Fr. Gumlich, "Die Räthsel der Erweckung Lazari," *TSK* 35 (1862): 65-110 [Jn. 11:1-46].

6509. E. A. Abbott, "On Some Phrases in the Raising of Lazarus," *Exp* 5th ser., 3 (1896): 217-24 [Jn. 11].

6510. Margaret D. Gibson, "The Story of Lazarus," *ET* 18 (1906-1907): 334 [Jn. 11].

6511. F. W. Worsley, "The Raising of Lazarus and the Synoptic Gospels," *ET* 19 (1907-1908): 43-44 [Jn. 11:1].

6512. J. E. Roberts, "The Raising of Lazarus," *ET* 23 (1911-1912): 461-64.

6513. Edward Grubb, "The Raising of Lazarus," *ET* 33 (1921-1922): 404-407.

6514. A. Henderson, "Notes on John II," *ET* 32 (1920-1921): 123-26.

6515. T. Francis Forth, "The Tomb of Lazarus and the Text of St. John," *Th* 9 (1922): 232-34.

6516. I. Leal, "De amore Iesu erga amicum Lazarum (Ioh. 11)," *VD* 21 (1941): 59-64.

6517. Everett F. Harrison, "Jesus and Lazarus," *BS* 104 (1947): 182-93 [Jn. 11].

6518. E. Kenneth Lee, "The Raising of Lazarus," *ET* 61 (1949-1950): 145-47.

6519. José M. Bover, "La resurrección de Lázaro," *EE* 28 (1954):

57-72 [Jn. 11].

6520. Wilhelm Wilkens, "Die Erweckung des Lazarus," *TZ* 15 (1959): 22-39.

6521. Karl Zickendraht, "Ist Lazarus der Lieblingsjünger im vierten Evangelium?" *STZ* 31 (1914): 49-54 [Jn. 11:5].

6522. R. Steck, "Lazarus der Jünger, den Jesus liebt?" *STZ* 33 (1916): 91-94 [Jn. 11:5].

6523. J. N. Sanders, "Those whom Jesus loved: St. John XI. 5," *NTSt* 1 (1954-1955): 29-76

6524. George Milligan, " 'Are there not Twelve Hours in the Day'?" *ET* 6 (1894-1895): 332-33 [Jn. 11:9].

6525. Fr. Trechsel, "Gedanken über die Auferweckung des Lazarus (Joh XI)," *STZ* 18 (1901): 49-58 [Jn. 11:17-44].

6526. N. Nicholson, "Martha and Mary," *ET* 29 (1917-1918): 184-88 [Jn. 11:20ff.; 12:2].

6527. Harald Riesenfeld, "καὶ νῦν. Zu Joh. 11, 22," *Nunt* 6 (1952): 41-44.

6528. James Hastings, "The Great Texts of St. John's Gospel," *ET* 8 (1896-1897): 349-50 [Jn. 11:25, 26].

6529. J. R. Harris, "Note on John xi. 25," *BBC* 5 (1928): 5-8.

6530. I. Hoh, " 'Omnis qui vivit et credit in me non morietur in aeternum' (Ioh. 11. 26)," *VD* 2 (1922): 333-35.

6531. J. B. Kingsland, "The Tears of Jesus," *ET* 1 (1889-1990): 228 [Jn. 11:35].

6532. Margaret D. Gibson, "John xi. 43," *ET* 21 (1909-1910): 328.

6533. A. D. Mosley, "John xi. 45," *ET* 26 (1914-1915): 91-92.

6534. Prosper Schepens, *"Pontifex anni illius* (Év. de saint Jean XI, 49, 51; XVIII, 14)," *RSR* 11 (1921): 372-74.

6535. A. Lemonnyer, "L'onction de Béthanie (Jean XII, 1-8)," *RSR* 18 (1928): 105-17.

6536. Rudolf Schnackenburg, "Der johanneische Bericht von der Salbung in Bethanien (Joh. 12, 1-8)," *MTZ* 1 (1950): 48-52.

6537. W. M. Rankin, "Love's Offering," *ET* 15 (1903-1904): 495-97 [Jn. 12:2].

6538. Arch Alexander, "The House was filled with the Odour of the Ointment (Jn. xii. 3)," *ET* 16 (1904-1905): 425-27.

6539. W. Rühme, "Eine kritische Studie zu Joh. 12, 7," *TSK* 98-99 (1926): 476-77.

6540. William R. Farmer, "The Palm Branches in John xii. 13," *JTS* N.S. 3 (1952): 62-66.

6541. J. R. Harris, C. A. Phillips, D. Plooij, D. C. Hesseling, "Symposium on the Pith of Palm Trees (John xii. 13)," *BBC* 3 (1926): 14-17; 4 (1927): 16-19.

6542. S. Cox, "The Gospel to the Greeks (John xii. 20-36)," *Exp* 2nd ser., 7 (1884): 117-30, 174-90.

6543. A. J. Gossip, "How Christ Won Through," *ET* 37 (1925-1926): 500-505 [Jn. 12:20-32].

6544. T. Torrance, "We Would See Jesus," *EQ* 23 (1951): 171-82 [Jn. 12:21].

6545. George B. Caird, "Judgment and Salvation: An Exposition of John xii. 31-32," *CJT* 2 (1956): 231-37.

6546. F. B. Blomfield and H. G. Blomfield, "Studies in Texts," *Th* 16 (1928): 101-107 [Jn. 12:31].

6547. S. A. Fries, "Was bedeutet der Fürst der Welt in Joh 12, 31; 14, 30; 16, 11?" *ZNW* 6 (1905): 159-79.

6548. H. Bulcock, "John vii. 32-36," *ET* 21 (1909-1910): 333.

6549. T. H. Weir, "John xii. 32," *ET* 25 (1913-1914): 43-44.

6550. Charles C. Torrey, "When I am Lifted up from the Earth, John 12: 32," *JBL* 51 (1932): 320-22.

6551. Martin A. Hopkins, "The Son of Man," *USR* 39 (1927-1928): 145-57 [Jn. 12:34].

6552. W. C. van Unnik, "The Quotation from the Old Testament in John 12:34," *NT* 3 (1959): 174-79.

6553. B. Brinkmann, "De priore quodam sermone valedictorio Domini (Ioh. 12, 44-50)," *VD* 19 (1939): 300-307.

6554. David Connor, "John vii. 47, 48," *ET* 27 (1915-1916): 237-38.

6555. Lewis Sperry Chafer, "The Upper Room Discourse," *BS* 109 (1952): 103-35 [Jn. 13-17].

6556. Paul Gächter, "Der formale Aufbau der Abschiedsrede Jesu," *ZKT* 58 (1934): 155-207 [Jn. 13:31-16:33].

6557. Anton Fridrichsen, "Bemerkungen zur Fusswaschung Joh 13," *ZNW* 38 (1939): 94-96

6558. W. L. Knox, "John 13. 1-30," *HTR* 43 (1950): 161-63.

6559. George H. Gilbert, "Washing the Disciples' Feet: John 13:1-20," *BW* 30 (1907): 51-55.

6560.   W. Smith, "The Washing of the Disciples' Feet," *Exp* 4th ser., 7 (1893): 300-11 [Jn. 13:1-17].

6561.   B. W. Bacon, "The Sacrament of the Footwashing," *ET* 43 (1931-1932): 218-21 [Jn. 13:1-17].

6562.   Ernst Lohmeyer, "Die Fusswaschung," *ZNW* 38 (1939): 74-94 [Jn. 13:1-17].

6563.   E. Graf, "Bemerkung über Joh. 13, 1-4," *TSK* 40 (1867): 741-48.

6564.   A Clergyman, "Before the Feast of the Passover," *Exp* 1st ser., 11 (1880): 475-80 [Jn. 13:1].

6565.   J. A. Beet, "Before the Feast of the Passover: A Reply," *Exp* 1st ser., 12 (1880): 82-85 [Jn. 13:1].

6566.   J. de Zwaan, "Johannes en de Synopse inzake Avondmaal en Paasmaal," *NedTT* 6 (1951-1952): 271 [Jn. 13:1].

6567.   Robert Eisler, "Zur Fusswaschung am Tage vor dem Passah," *ZNW* 14 (1913): 268-71 [Jn. 13:2-16]

6568.   A. Wilmart, "Un ancien texte latin de l'évangile selon saint Jean: XIII, 3-17," *RB* 31 (1922): 182-202.

6569.   Johann Michl, "Der Sinn der Fusswaschung," *B* 40 (1959): 697-708 [Jn. 13:4-15].

6570.   F.-M. Braun, "Le lavement des pieds et la réponse de Jésus à saint Pierre (Jean XIII, 4-10)," *RB* 44 (1935): 22-33.

6571.   David Smith, "Ne illotis pedibus," *ET* 11 (1899-1900): 536-37 [Jn. 13:5].

6572.   Hans von Campenhausen, "Zur Auslegung von Joh 13, 6-10," *ZNW* 33 (1934): 259-71.

6573.   A. Peloni, "The Daily Washing of the once Bathed," *Exp* 2nd ser., 4 (1882): 146-56 [Jn. 13:10].

6574.   T. H. Weir, " 'Ye are clean, but not all' (John xiii. 10)," *ET* 24 (1912-1913): 476.

6575.   Paul Fiebig, "Die Fusswaschung," *A* 3 (1930): 121-28 [Jn. 13:10].

6576.   N. M. Haring, "Historical Notes on the Interpretation of John 13:10," *CBQ* 13 (1951): 355-80.

6577.   H. F. D. Sparks, "St. John's Knowledge of Matthew: The Evidence of John 13, 16 and 15, 20," *JTS* N.S. 3 (1952): 58-61.

6578.   Eric F. F. Bishop, " 'He that eateth bread with me hath lifted up his heel against me.'—Jn. xiii. 18 (Ps. xl. 9)," *ET* 70 (1958-1959): 331-32.

6579. Hugh MacMillan, "A Mock Sacrament," *ET* 3 (1891- 1892): 107-10 [Jn. 13:26].

6580. Alfred Durand, "Le discours de la cène (Saint Jean XIII, 31—XVII, 26)," *RSR* 1 (1910): 97-131, 513-39; 2 (1911): 321-49, 521-45.

6581. Robert H. Miller, "By This shall All Men Know," *RE* 37 (1940): 295-98.

6582. George L. Hurst, "A Triple Tradition in John xiii 33—xvi," *ET* 16 (1904-1905): 381-82.

6583. L. Cerfaux, "La charité fraternelle et le retour du Christ (Jn. xiii, 33-38)," *ETL* 24 (1948): 321-32.

6584. St. Gallo, "Sermo Christi Sacrificalis," *VD* 26 (1948): 33-43 [Jn. 13:33-17:26].

6585. Alv Kragerud, "Kjaerlighetsbudet i Johannesevangeliet," *NTT* 57 (1956): 137-49 [Jn. 13:34ff.].

6586. G. Pidgeon, "The Root and Fruit of Christian Love," *TTod* 9 (1952): 186-87.

6587. Olaf Moe, "Om det nye bud Joh. 13, 34," *TTK* 28 (1957): 39-42.

6588. P. Corssen, "Die Abschiedsreden Jesu in dem vierten Evangelium," *ZNW* 8 (1907): 125-42 [Jn. 14ff.].

6589. M. Peinador, "Idea central del discurso de Jesús después de la Cena (Jn. XIV-XVII)," *EB* 12 (1953): 5-28.

6590. Friedrich Nägelsbach, "Die Voraussagungen Jesu nach Joh. 14-16 und ihre Folgerungen," *NKZ* 22 (1911): 663-96.

6591. T. Nicklin, "A Suggested Dislocation in the Text of St. John xiv-xvi," *ET* 44 (1932-1933): 382-83.

6592. B. W. Bacon, "The Displacement of John xiv," *JBL* 13 (1894): 64-76.

6593. Helmut Koester, "John xiv. 1-20: A Meditation," *ET* 73 (1961-1962): 88.

6594. A. Menzies, "Jesus' Parting Words of Comfort to his Disciples: John 14:1-13," *BW* 32 (1908): 329-35.

6595. O. Schaefer, "Der Sinn der Rede Jesu von den vielen Wohnungen in seines Vaters Hause und von dem Weg zu ihm (Joh 14, 1-7)," *ZNW* 32 (1933): 210-19.

6596.   W. K. Lowther Clarke, "Studies in Texts," *Th* 9 (1924): 41-43 [Jn. 14:1-4].

6597.   Dr. Beck, "Ueber Joh. 14, 1. 2," *TSK* 4 (1831): 130-34.

6598.   G. LaRoche, "Versuch einer Erklärung der Stelle Joh. 14, 1. 2," *TSK* 3 (1830): 114-18.

6599.   W. S. Walford and D. R. Fotheringham, "John xiv. 1," *ET* 21 (1909-1910): 138-39.

6600.   Carpus, "Heaven," *Exp* 1st ser., 3 (1876): 62-73 [Jn. 14:23; 17:24].

6601.   T. S. Berry, "Critical Note on St. John xiv. 2," *Exp* 2nd ser., 3 (1882): 397-400.

6602.   S. Cox, "Some Features of the Life Everlasting," *Exp* 2nd ser., 2 (1881): 278-87 [Jn. 14:2, 23].

6603.   J. L. Davies, "The Many Mansions and the Restitution of all Things," *Exp* 4th ser., 6 (1892): 209-13 [Jn. 14:2].

6604.   James Hastings, "The Great Texts of St. John's Gospel," *ETJ* 8 (1896-1897): 496-98 [Jn. 14:2].

6605.   W. A. Gray, "The Father's House," *ET* 12 (1900-1901): 29-34 [Jn. 14:2].

6606.   William Hamilton, "Many Mansions for God," *ET* 25 (1913-1914): 75 [Jn. 14:2].

6607.   R. Scott Frayn, " 'Many Mansions'," *ET* 25 (1913-1914): 233 [Jn. 14:2].

6608.   J. Courtenay James, "Mansiones Multae," *ET* 27 (1915-1916): 427-28 [Jn. 14:2].

6609.   B. W. Bacon, " 'In my Father's house are many mansions' (Jn. xiv. 2)," *ET* 43 (1931-1932): 477-78.

6610.   A. Lewis Humphries, "A Note on πρὸς ἐμαυτόν (John xiv. 3) and εἰς τά ἴδια (John i. 11)," *ET* 53 (1941-1942): 356.

6611.   Marie Comeau, "Le Christ, chemin et terme de l'ascension spirituelle, d'après saint Augustin," *RSR* 40 (1951-1952): 80-89 [Jn. 14:6].

6612.   Ricardo Rábanos, "Jesús es el camino, la verdad y la vida," *CB* 12 (1955): 338-46 [Jn. 14:6].

6613.   G. G. Findlay, "Christ on the Christian Evidences," *Exp* 2nd ser., 2 (1881): 301-16 [Jn. 14:8-21].

6614.   James Hastings, "The Great Texts of St. John's Gospel," *ET* 9 (1897-1898): 22-24 [Jn. 14:8-10].

6615. John Lendrum, " 'Greater things than these'," *ET* 38 (1926-1927): 471-73 [Jn. 14:12].

6616. Juan Leal, "Ego sum via, veritas, et vita (Ioh. 14, 14)," *VD* 33 (1955): 336-41.

6617. W. R. Hutton, "John xiv. 17," *ET* 57 (1945-1946): 194.

6618. Richard Kugelman, "The Gospel for Pentecost," *CBQ* 6 (1944): 259-75 [Jn. 14:23-31].

6619. Howard Osgood, "If One Love Me, He Will Keep My Word," *BS* 51 (1894): 674-95 [Jn. 14:23].

6620. U. Holzmeister, "Paraclitus autem Spiritus Sanctus (Ioh. 14, 26)," *VD* 12 (1932): 135-39.

6621. A. R. Gordon, "The Peace of Jesus," *ET* 30 (1918-1919): 504-506 [Jn. 14:27].

6622. Joh. Dräseke, "Evangelium Iohannis 14, 28, 'Der Vater ist grösser denn ich,' Byzantinisch-mittelalterliche Schrifterörterungen aus den Quellen mitgeteilt," *NKZ* 27 (1916): 881ff.

6623. C. Moss, "S. Amphilochius of Iconium on John 14, 28: *'The Father who sent me, is greater than I'*," *Mu* 43 (1930): 317-64.

6624. Augusto Segovia, "El texto 'Peter major me est' (S. Juan 14, 28) explicado por un polemista antimacedoniano," *RET* 1 (1940-1941): 603-609.

6625. Adversaria, "St. John xiv. 30, 31," *JCSP* 2 (1855): 231.

6626. Kozue Tomoi, "Is not John xiv. 45 a Dislocation?" *ET* 72 (1960-1961): 31.

6627. J. E. Roberts, "The Parable of the Vine," *ET* 32 (1920-1921): 73-75 [Jn. 15:1ff.].

6628. George Johnston, "The Allegory of the Vine: An Exposition of John 15: 1-17," *CJT* 3 (1957): 150-58.

6629. H. van den Bussche, "La vigne et ses fruits (Jean 15, 1 8)," *BVC* no. 26 (1959): 12-18.

6630. U. Holzmeister, " 'Ego sum vitis vera' (Ioh. 15, 1-7)," *VD* 5 (1925): 129-32.

6631. E. Power, " 'Ego sum vitis vera'," *VD* 1 (1921): 147-52.

6632. F. G. Engel, "The Ways of Vines," *ET* 60 (1948-1949): 111 [Jn. 15:1].

6633. Juan Leal, "La alegoria de la vid y la necesidad de la gracia,"

EE 26 (1952): 5-38 [Jn. 15:5].

6634. Lowell Russell Ditzen, "The Heart of the Gospel," *TTod* 7 (1950): 157-58 [Jn. 15:12].

6635. Walter Grundmann, "Das Wort von Jesu Freunden (Joh. xv, 13-16) und das Herrenmahl," *NT* 3 (1959): 52-69.

6636. James Strahan, "The Perfect Friendship," *ET* 23 (1911-1912): 70-73 [Jn. 15:14-15].

6637. John McNaugher, "The Witnessing Spirit and the Witnessed Christ," *BS* 88 (1931): 207-19 [Jn. 15:26].

6638. W. W. Holdsworth, "The Life of Faith," *ET* 21 (1909- 1910): 310-12 [Jn. 16:1-15].

6639. N. Messel, "Joh. 16, 5-15," *NTT* 13 (1912): 22-41.

6640. H. Liese, "Spiritus Sancti testimonium (Ioh. 16, 5-15)," *VD* 14 (1934): 101-107.

6641. J. T. Mueller, "Notes on John 16:5-16," *CTM* 23 (1952): 16-23.

6642. L. J. Lutkemeyer, "The Role of the Paraclete: Jn. 16:7-15," *CBQ* 8 (1946): 220-29.

6643. H. W. Tribble, "The Convicting Work of the Holy Spirit," *RE* 32 (1935): 269-80 [Jn. 16:7-11].

6644. B. van der Werff, "Overtuiging van zonde, van gerechtigheid en van ordeel," *GTT* 17 (1916-1917): 62-68 [Jn. 16:8-11].

6645. W. H. P. Hatch, "The Meaning of John XVI, 8-11," *HTR* 14 (1921): 103-105.

6646. M. F. Berrouard, "Le paraclète, défenseur du Christ devant la conscience du croyant (Jn. XVI, 8-11)," *RSPT* 33 (1949): 361-89.

6647. A. H. Stanton, "Convince or Convict (John xvi. 8)," *ET* 33 (1921-1922): 278-79.

6648. Arthur W. Wotherspoon, "Note on St. John xvi. 10," *ET* 33 (1921-1922): 521-22.

6649. Frederic Relton, "The Unfinished Teaching of Christ," *ET* 4 (1892-1893): 446-50 [Jn. 16:12].

6650. W. E. Bowen, "The Inspiration of the Church," *ET* 10 (1898-1899): 26-33 [Jn. 16:13].

6651. L. Fonck, "Duplex fructus Spiritus Sancti (Ioh. 16, 23-30)," *VD* 1 (1921): 115-20.

6652. E. Macmillan, "Note on St. John xvi. 23, 24," *ET* 34 (1922-1923): 379.

6653. Walther Bleibtreu, "Evang. Joh. 16, 23, 24," *NKZ* 22 (1911): 958-62.

6654. F. Warburton Lewis, "John xvi. 23," *ET* 15 (1903-1904): 381.

6655. Erich Fascher, "Johannes 16, 32," *ZNW* 39 (1940): 171-230.

6656. Hampton Adams, "Tribulation. . . Good Cheer," *RL* 12 (1943): 163-71 [Jn. 16:33].

6657. A. Wellington Tyler, "Our Lord's Sacerdotal Prayer-A New Critical Text Digest and Translation," *BS* 27 (1870): 323-32 [Jn. 17].

6658. George H. Gilbert, "An Important Unnoticed Argument in John, Chapter 17," *BW* 13 (1899): 308-11.

6659. W. W. Holdsworth, "The Life of Faith," *ET* 22 (1910-1911): 275-77 [Jn. 17]

6660. Joseph Bonsirven, "Pour une intelligence plus profonde de saint Jean," *RSR* 39 (1951-1952): 176-96 [Jn. 17].

6661. Augustin George, " 'L'heure' de Jean XVII," *RB* 61 (1954): 392-97.

6662. Adalbert Hamman, "La prière de Jésus," *BVC* no. 10 (1955): 7-21 [Jn 17].

6663. Jean Cadier, "The Unity of the Church; An Exposition of John 17," *Interp* 11 (1957): 166-76.

6664. W. W. English, "St. John xvii. 1-3," *ET* 13 (1901-1902): 47-48.

6665. Walter G. White, "St. John xvii. 1," *ET* 27 (1915-1916): 477.

6666. Fl. Ogava, " 'Et nunc clarifica me tu, Pater' (Ioh. 17, 5)," *VD* 18 (1938): 129-36.

6667. J. M. Ballard, "The Translation of John xvii. 5," *ET* 47 (1935-1936): 284.

6668. Evaristo Martín Nieto, "El nombre de Dios en S. Jn. 17, 11-12," *EB* 11 (1952): 5-30.

6669. G. G. Findlay, "Sanctification According to Christ," *Exp* 6th ser., 4 (1901): 1-15 [Jn 17:17-19].

6670. P. Pons, " 'Sanctifica eos in veritate' (Ioh. 17, 17)," *VD* 1 (1921): 247-50.

6671. John Reid, "The Sanctification of Christ and his Disciples,"

ET 24 (1912-1913): 459-60 [Jn. 17:19].

6672.   J. B. Weatherspoon, "The Consecration of Life," *RE* 23 (1926): 129-36 [Jn. 17:19].

6673.   T. E. Pollard, " 'That they all may be one' (John xvii. 21)-and the Unity of the Church," *ET* 70 (1958-1959): 149-50.

6674.   E. L. Wenger, " 'That they all may be one'," *ET* 70 (1958-1959): 333 [Jn. 17:21].

6675.   Salvador Gil Salafranca, " 'Agápe' en San Juan 17:26," *CB* 12 (1955): 272-81.

6676.   F.-M. Braun, "La passion de notre Seigneur Jésus Christ d'après saint Jean (XVIII-XIX)," *NRT* 60 (1933): 289-302, 385-400, 481-99.

6677.   W. Randolph Church, "The Dislocations in the Eighteenth Chapter of John," *JBL* 49 (1930): 375-83.

6678.   C. A. Phillips and J. Rendel Harris, "A Mediaeval Interpretation of John xiii. 1," *ET* 38 (1926-1927): 233.

6679.   Hans Reynen, "Συνάγεσθαι, Joh. 18, 2," *BibZ* N.F. 5 (1961): 86-90.

6680.   Sebastián Bartina, " 'Yo soy Yahweh.' Nota exegética a Io. 18, 4-8," *EE* 32 (1958): 403-26.

6681.   James H. Hingston, "John xviii. 5, 6," *ET* 32 (1920- 1921): 232.

6682.   P. Mein, "A Note on John xviii.6," *ET* 65 (1953-1954): 286-87.

6683.   Duff MacDonald, "Malchus' Ear," *ET* 10 (1898-1899): 188 [Jn. 18:10].

6684.   Norbert Krieger, "Der Knecht des Hohenpriesters," *NT* 2 (1958): 73-74 [Jn. 18:10].

6685.   Joseph Huby, "Un double problème de critique textuelle et d'interprétation: Saint Jean XVIII, 11-12," *RSR* 27 (1937): 408-21.

6686.   J. M. Farquhar, "The First Trial of Christ," *ET* 6 (1894-1895): 284-88, 429-31 [Jn. 18:12-28].

6687.   G. G. Findlay, "The Connexion of John xviii. 12-28," *ET* 6 (1894-1895): 335-36, 478-79.

6688.   Arthur Wright, "The First Trial of Jesus," *ET* 6 (1894- 1895): 523-24 [Jn. 18:12-28].

6689.   Johannes Schneider, "Zur Komposition von Joh 18, 12-27,"

ZNW 48 (1957): 111-19.

6690. P. B. Klövekorn, "Jesus vor der jüdischen Behörde," *BibZ* 9 (1911): 266-76 [Jn. 18:13ff.].

6691. Walter Drum, " 'The Disciple known to the High Priest'," *ET* 25 (1913-1914): 381-82 [Jn. 18:15].

6692. E. Abbey Tindall, "John xvii. 15," *ET* 28 (1916-1917): 283-84.

6693. F. Gardiner, "On the Aorist ἀπέστειλεν in Jn. xvii. 24," *JBL* 6 (1886, part I): 45-55.

6694. Ernst Haenchen, "Jesus vor Pilatus (Joh. 18, 28-19, 15)," *TLZ* 85 (1960): 93-102.

6695. D. Mollat, "Jésus devant Pilate (Jean 18, 28-38)," *BVC* no. 39 (1961): 23-31.

6696. Josef Blank, "Die Verhandlung vor Pilatus Joh. 18, 28-19, 16 im Lichte johanneischer Theologie," *BibZ* N.F. 3 (1959): 60-81.

6697. Dr. von Buchrucker, "Mein Reich ist nicht von dieser Welt," *NKZ* 4 (1893): 20-35 [Jn. 18:36].

6698. M. Chaning-Pearce, "The Ethics of a Kingdom not of this World," *HJ* 34 (1935-1936): 45-56 [Jn. 18:36].

6699. Newport J. D. White, "The Johannine View of the Crucifixion," *Exp* 6th ser., 7 (1903): 434-41 [Jn. 19].

6700. H. St. J. Hart, "The Crown of Thorns in John 19, 2-5," *JTS* N.S. 3 (1952): 66-75.

6701. Joseph Bonsirven, "Hora Talmudica," *B* 33 (1952): 511-15 [Jn. 19:4].

6702. John Porteous, "Note on John xix. 11: 'The Greater Sin'," *ET* 15 (1903-1904): 428-29.

6703. A. R. Eagar, "The Greater Sin. A Note on S. John xix. ii," *Exp* 6th ser., 12 (1905): 33-40.

6704. R. Thibaut, "La réponse de Notre Seigneur à Pilate (Jean XIX, ii)," *NRT* 54 (1927): 208-11.

6705. A. Roberts, "On the Proper Rendering of ἐκάθισεν in John xix. 13," *Exp* 4th ser., 8 (1893): 296-308.

6706. I. de la Potterie, "Jésus roi et juge d'après Jn. 19, 13," *B* 41 (1960): 217-47.

6707. I. de la Potterie, "Jesus King and Judge according to John XIX. 13," *Scr* 13 (1961): 97-111.

6708. John Aulay Steele, "The Pavement," *ET* 34 (1922-1923): 562-63 [Jn. 19:13].

6709. Sebastián Bartina, "Ignotum episèmon gabex (Ioh. 19, 14)," *VD* 36 (1958): 16-37.

6710. H. G. Grey, "A Suggestion on St. John xix. 14," *Exp* 7th ser., 2 (1906): 451-54.

6711. B. W. Bacon, "Exegetical Notes: John 19:17- 20:20," *BW* 13 (1899): 423-25.

6712. A. R. S. Kennedy, "The Soldiers' Portions (John xix. 23, 24)," *ET* 24 (1912-1913): 90-91.

6713. Dominic Unger, "A Note on John 19: 25-27," *CBQ* 9 (1947): 111-12.

6714. Eric F. F. Bishop, "Mary Clopas-John xix. 25," *ET* 65 (1953-1954): 382-83.

6715. George E. Evans, "The Sister of the Mother of Jesus," *RE* 44 (1947): 475-85 [Jn. 19:25].

6716. Eric F. F. Bishop, "Mary (of) Clopas and her Father," *ET* 73 (1961-1962): 339 [Jn. 19:25]

6717. Paul Gächter, "Die geistige Mutterschaft Marias. Ein Beitrag zur Erklärung von Jo. 19, 26 f.," *ZKT* 47 (1923): 391-429.

6718. C. A. Kneller, "Joh. 19, 26-27 bei den Kirchenvätern," *ZKT* 40 (1916): 597-612.

6719. José M. Bover, "La maternidad de María espresada por el redentor en la cruz," *EB* 1 (1941-1942): 627-46 [Jn. 19:26, 27].

6720. Iar. Tobola, "S. Ioannes Evangelista 'trium matrum filius'," *VD* 22 (1942): 271-72 [Jn. 19:26-27].

6721. Juan Leal, "Sentido literal mariológico de Jo. 19, 26. 27," *EB* 11 (1952): 303-19 [Jn. 19:26-27].

6722. J. M. Bover, " 'Mulier, ecce filius tuus'," *VD* 4 (1924): 225-31 [Jn. 19:26].

6723. T. Gallus, " 'Mulier, ecce filius tuus' (Joh. 19, 26)," *VD* 21 (1941): 289-97.

6724. W. Milligan, "St. John's View of Jesus on the Cross," *Exp* 1st ser., 6 (1877): 17-36, 129-42 [Jn. 19:28-37].

6725. A. R. Simpson, "The Broken Heart of Jesus," *Exp* 8th ser., 2 (1911): 310-21 [Jn. 19:34].

6726. Benedikt Kraft, "Das koptische Irenäus-Fragment de

Lagardes zu Jo. 19, 34," *BibZ* 13 (1915): 354-55 ["water and blood"].

6727. R. Galdos, "Apertumne est militis lancea emortui Iesu latus?" *VD* 5 (1925): 161-68 [Jn. 19:34].

6728. A. Vaccari, " 'Exivit sanguis et aqua' (Joh. 19, 34)," *VD* 17 (1937): 193-98.

6729. H. Dechent, "Zur Auslegung der Stelle Joh. 19, 35," *TSK* 72 (1899): 446-67.

6730. F. Blass, "Über Ev. Joh. 19, 35," *TSK* 75 (1902): 128-33.

6731. Basilius Haensler, "Zu Jo. 19, 35," *BibZ* 11 (1913): 44-48.

6732. F. H. Chase, "Two Notes on St. John's Gospel," *JTS* 26 (1924-1925): 381 [Jn. 19:35; 8:56].

6733. George A. Barton, "A Bone of him shall not be Broken, John 19, 36," *JBL* 49 (1930): 13-19.

6734. Eb. Nestle, "John xix. 37," *ET* 24 (1912-1913): 92.

6735. F.-M. Braun, "Le linceul de Turin et l'évangile de saint Jean," *NRT* 66 (1939): 900-35. 1025-46 [Jn 19:39-40; 20:5-7].

6736. Barnabas Lindars, "The Composition of John xx," *NTSt* 7 (1960-1961): 142-47.

6737. F. Spadafora, "Sulla risurrezione di Gesù, Jo. 20, 3-10," *RivB* 1 (1953): 99-115.

6738. Franz Michel Willam, "Johannes am Grabe des Auler-standenen," *ZKT* 71 (1949): 204-13 [Jn. 20:2-10].

6739. K. J. Kapteijn, "Maria Magdalena bij het graf van Jezus," *GTT* 13 (1913): 176-88, 215-32 [Jn. 20:11-18].

6740. Basilius Haensler, "Zu Jo. 20, 17," *BibZ* 11 (1913): 172-77.

6741. T. H. Farmer, " 'Touch me not'," *ET* 28 (1916-1917): 92-93 [Jn. 20:17].

6742. Basilius Haensler, "Zu Jo. 20, 9," *BibZ* 14 (1916-1917): 159-63.

6743. George Henslow, " 'Touch me not'," *ET* 28 (1916-1917): 189 [Jn. 20:17].

6744. Bruno Violet, "Ein Versuch zu Joh 20, 17," *ZNW* 24 (1925): 78-80.

6745. W. D. Morris, "John xx. 17," *ET* 40 (1928-1929): 527-28.

6746. W. E. P. Cotter, " 'Touch me not; for I am not yet ascended unto the Father' (St. John xx. 17)," *ET* 43 (1931-1932):

45-46.

6747. T. Nicklin, "Noli me tangere," *ET* 51 (1939-1940): 478 [Jn 20:17].

6748. W. Tom, "Het vraagteeken gehandhaafd," *GTT* 41 (1940): 129-31 [Jn. 20:17; Mt. 28:10].

6749. Alberto Vidal, " 'Noli me tangere'," *CB* 2 (1945): 78-81, 221-22 [Jn. 20:17].

6750. C. Spicq, "Noli me tangere," *RSPT* 32 (1948): 226-27 [Jn. 20:17].

6751. Joseph Crehan, "The Dialektos of Origen and John 20: 17," *ThSt* 11 (1950): 368-73.

6752. Walter Grundmann, "Zur Rede Jesu vom Vater im Johannes-Evangelium (eine redaktions- und bekennatnis- geschichtliche Untersuchung zu Joh 20, 17 und seiner Vorbereitung)," *ZNW* 52 (1961): 213-30.

6753. H. Liese, "Dominus apparet apostolic bis (Ioh. 20, 19-31. Cf. Mc. 16, 14; Lc. 24, 36-43)," *VD* 12 (1932): 97-102.

6754. F. W. Beare, "The Risen Jesus Bestows the Spirit: A Study of John 20: 19-23," *CJT* 2 (1958): 95-100.

6755. Pierre Etienne, " 'Comme le père m'a envoyé moi aussi je vous envoie,' (Saint Jean 20. 21)," *LumV* 15 (1961): 129-31.

6756. J. B. Umberg, "Die richterliche Bussgewalt nach Jo. 20, 23," *ZKT* 50 (1926): 337-70.

6757. T. Stephenson, "Doubting Thomas," *ET* 27 (1915-1916): 185 [Jn. 20:24-29].

6758. W. T. Thompson, "Thomas: A Character Study," *USR* 39 (1927-1928): 217-26 [Jn. 20:24-29].

6759. Wilfrid J. Moulton, "Note on John xx. 29," *ET* 12 (1900-1901): 382.

6760. Helmut Wenz, "Sehen und Glauben bei Johannes," *TZ* 17 (1961): 17-25 [Jn. 20:29b].

6761. Harold St. John, " 'Written that Ye Might Believe'," *EQ* 25 (1953): 195-201 [Jn. 20:31].

6762. S. Hoekstra, "Het laatste hooldstuk van het vierde Evangelie vergeleken met dit Evangelie self," *TT* 1 (1867): 407-24 [Jn. 21].

6763. A. Klöpper, "Das 21. Capitel des 4. Evangeliums," *ZWT* 42 (1899): 337-81.

6764. Thomas Barns, "A Study in St. John XXI," *Exp* 7th ser. 4 (1907): 533-42.

6765. R. H. Strachan, "Spitta on John XXI," *Exp* 8th ser., 4 (1912): 363-69, 554-61.

6766. Arthur Gray, "The Last Chapter of St. John's Gospel as interpreted by Early Christian Art," *HJ* 20 (1921-1922): 690-700.

6767. L. Vaganay, "La finale du quatrième évangile," *RB* 45 (1936): 512-28.

6768. M.-E. Boismard, "Le chapitre XXI de saint Jean: essai de critique littéraire," *RB* 54 (1947): 473-501.

6769. Bishop Cassian, "John XXI," *NTSt* 3 (1956-1957): 132-36.

6770. Eric F. F. Bishop, " 'A Fire of Coals with Fish laid thereon, and Bread'," *ET* 50 (1938-1939): 264-66 [Jn. 21:9].

6771. A. Hilgenfeld, "Die Rätselzahl Joh. 21, 11," *ZWT* 41 (1898): 480.

6772. Daniel T. Jenkins, "The Catch which is Perfect," *PSB* 42, no. 4 (1949): 7-9 [Jn. 21:11].

6773. J. A. Emerton, "The Hundred and Fifty-Three Fishes in John xxi. 11," *JTS* N.S. 9 (1958): 86-89.

6774. Peter R. Ackroyd, "The 153 Fishes in John xxi. 11-A Further Note," *JTS* N.S. 10 (1959): 94.

6775. William G. Ballantine, "Lovest Thou Me?" *BS* 46 (1889): 524-42 [Jn. 21:15ff.].

6776. B. W. Bacon, "The Motivation of John 21 15-25," *JBL* 50 (1931): 71-80.

6777. J. A. Seiss, "Christ's Questioning of Peter," *LCR* 17 (1898) 1-5 [Jn. 21:15-19].

6778. William G. Ballantine, " 'Loves thou me'?" *BS* 46 (1889) 524-42 [Jn. 21:15-17]

6779. J. A. Cross, "On St. John XXI. 15-17," *Exp* 4th ser., 7 (1893): 312-20.

6780. Julius A. Bewer, "The Original Words of Jesus in John 21: 15-17," *BW* 17 (1901): 32-34.

6781. W. K. Lowther Clarke, "Studies in Texts," *Th* 8 (1924): 281-82 [Jn. 21:15-17].

6782. G. F. Nicolassen, "A Discussion of John 21: 15-17," *USR* 37 (1925-1926): 55-58.

6783. Edward A. McDowell, "Lovest Thou Me?" *RE* 32 (1935): 422-41 [Jn. 21:15-17].

6784. J. B. Bauer, " 'Oves meae' quaenam sunt? (Jo. 21, 15ss et 10, 16)," *VD* 32 (1954): 321-24.

6785. Gabriel Pérez, "El primado de San Pedro en Jn. 21:15-17," *CB* 12 (1955): 229-37.

6786. E. G. Selwyn, "Studies in Texts: The Leadership of Love," *Th* 42 (1941): 173-75 [Jn. 21:16].

6787. Andrew Miller, "St. Peter's Despair," *ET* 11 (1899-1900] 432 [Jn. 21:17].

6788. J. E. Belser, "Zu Joh. 21, 18," *TQ* 95 (1913): 509-14.

6789. Jean Berthoud, "Remarques sur quelques passages de l'évangile de Jean et des Actes des Apôtres," *RTQR* 9 (1900): 422-60, 506-36 [Jn. 21:19, 23].

6790. G. M. Lee, "John xxi. 20-23," *JTS* N.S. 1 (1950): 62-63.

6791. P. N. Bushill, "A Note on John xxi. 21," *ET* 47 (1935-1936): 523-24.

6792. Willibald Grimm, "Ueber Evangelium Joh. 21, 22 f.," *ZWT* 18 (1875): 270-78.

6793. Lionel L. K. Ford, "Studies in Texts," *Th* 20 (1930): 229 [Jn. 21:23-25].

6794. C. Bouma, "De dood van den Apostel Johannes," *GTT* 24 (1923-1924): 145-55 [Jn. 21:23].

6795. John Chapman, "We Know that his Testimony is True," *JTS* 31 (1929-1930): 379-87 [Jn. 21:24].

6796. Charles Masson, "Le témoignage de Jean," *RTP* N.S. 3, (1950): 120-27 [Jn. 21:24].

6797. C. H. Dodd, "Note on John xxi. 24," *JTS* N.S. 4 (1953): 212-13.

6798. A. Peloni, "The Great Hyperbole," *Exp* 2nd ser., 3 (1882): 241-49 [Jn. 21:25].

6799. John Gwynn, "On the external Evidence alleged against the Genuineness of St. John xxi. 25," *Herm* 8 (1893): 368-84.

6800. James H. Moulton, " 'The Things which Jesus did'," *ET* 27 (1915-1916): 488-91 [Jn. 21:25].

On Jn. 1:15, see also number 1920; 1:39, 3679; 4:6, 3679; 4:46, 3683; 5:34, 1920; 7:53-8:11, 1596, 1920; 8:58, 3680; 10:22-39, *10073*; 10:29, 1931; 11:1ff., 3689; 12:12-16,

4544ff.; 16:8-11, *10026*; 17:1-26, *10032*; 19:14, 3679; 19:23, 3684; 19:35, 1920; 20: 17, *10042*; 20:23, 4455, 4456, 4458.

6800.1 E. A. Nida, "Rhetoric and the Translator: With Special Reference to John 1," *BTr* 33 (1982): 324-28 [1].

6800.2 H. Mowvley, "John 1 in the Light of Exodus 33-34," *ET* 95 (1983-1984): 135-37 [1].

6800.3 John Ashton, "The Transformation of Wisdom: A Study of the Prologue of John's Gospel," *NTSt* 32/2 (1986): 161-86 [1].

6800.4 Meynet Roland, "Analyse rhétorique du Prologue de Jean," *RB* 96 (1989): 481-510 [1].

6800.5 L. M. Dewailly, "La Parole parlait à Dieu? [Jean 1:1b-21]. Note d'exégèse biblique," *RTP* 1 (1967): 123-28 [1:1-21].

6800.6 John A. T. Robinson, "The Relation of the Prologue to the Gospel of St. John," *NTSt* 9 (1962-1963): 120-29 [1:1-18].

6800.7 P. M. Galopin, "Le Verbe, témoin du Père, Jean 1:1-18," *BVC* 53 (1963): 16-34 [1:1-18].

6800.8 Ernst Haenchen, "Probleme des johanneischen 'Prologs'," *ZTK* 60 (1963): 305-34 [1:1-18].

6800.9 P. Lemarche, "Le Prologue de Jean," *RSR* 52 (1964): 497-537 [1:1-18].

6800.10 W. Beilner, "Aufbau und Aussage des Johannesprologs," *BK* 20 (1965): 98-106 [1:1-18].

6800.11 Raymond B. Brown, "The Prologue of the Gospel of John," *RE* 62/4 (1965): 429-39 [1:1-18].

6800.12 H. Langkammer, "Zur Herkunf t des Logostitels im Johannesprolog," *BibZ* 9 (1965): 91-94 [1:1-18].

6800.13 T. Schitzler, "Der Prolog des Johannes-Evangeliums im Zusammenhang der dritten Weihnachtsmesse," *BK* 20 (1965): 116-19 [1:1-18].

6800.14 J. Boulet, "Dieu ineffable et Parole incarnée. Saint Jean de la Croix et le Prologue du 4;sse Évangile," *RHPR* 46 (1966): 227-40 [1:1-18].

6800.15 H. Ridderbos, "The Structure and Scope of the Prologue to the Gospel of John," *NT* 8 (1966): 180-201 [1:1-18].

6800.16 C. Demke, "Der sogenannte Logos-Hymnus im johanneischen Prolog," *ZNW* 58 (1967): 45-68 [1:1-18].

6800.17 Kurt Aland, "Eine Untersuchung zu Johannes 1:3-4: Über die Bedeutung eines Punktes," *ZNW* 59 (1968): 174-209 [1:1-18].

6800.18 Sebastián Bartina, "La vida como historia, en el prólogo al cuarto evangelio," *B* 49 (1968): 91-96 [1:1-18].

6800.19 J. C. O'Neill, "The Prologue of St. John's Gospel." *JTS* 20 (1969): 41-52 [1:1-18].

6800.20 P. Picard, "Le prologue de saint Jean," *BVC* 87 (1969): 84-87 [1:1-18].

6800.21 Peder Borgen, "Observations on the Targumic Character of the Prologue of John," *NT* 16 (1969-1970): 288-95 [1:1-18].

6800.22 Robert Kysar, "The Background of the Prologue of the Fourth Gospel: A Critique of Historical Methods," *CJT* 16 (1970): 250-55 [1:1-18].

6800.23 Robert Kysar, "Rudolf Bultmann's Interpretation of the Concept of Creation in John 1:3-4: A Study of Exegetical Method," *CBQ* 32 (1970): 77-85 [1:1-18].

6800.24 Peder Borgen, "Logos Was the True Light. Contributions to the Interpretation of the Prologue of John," *NT* 14 (1972): 115-30 [1:1-18].

6800.25 H. Thyen, "Aufweis der Forschungstrends an neueren Interpretationsversuchen des Johannesprologs," *TR* 39 (1974): 53-69, 222-52 [1:1-18].

6800.26 J. S. King, "The Prologue to the Fourth Gospel: Some Unsolved Problems," *ET* 86 (1974-1975): 372-75 [1:1-18].

6800.27 Mathias Rissi, "Die Logoslieder im Prolog des vierten Evangeliums," *TZ* 31 (1975): 321-36 [1:1-18].

6800.28 Barclay M. Newman, "Some Observations Regarding a Poetic Restructuring of John 1:1-18," *BTr* 29 (1976): 206-12 [1:1-18].

6800.29 Mathias Rissi, "John 1:1-18 (The Eternal Word)," *Interp* 31 (1977): 394-401 [1:1-18].

6800.30 E. D. Freed, "Theological Prelude to the Prologue of John's Gospel," *SJT* 32 (1979): 257-69 [1:1-18].

6800.31 P. Hofrichter, " 'Egeneto anthropos': Text und Zusätze im Johannesprolog," *ZNW* 70 (1979): 214-37 [1:1-18].

6800.32 E. L. Miller, "The New International Version on the Prologue of John," *HTR* 72 (1979): 307-11 [1:1-18].

6800.33 Walter Schmithals, "Der Prolog des Johannesevangeliums,"

ZNW 70 (1979): 16-43 [1:1-18].

6800.34 R. Alan Culpepper, "The Pivot of John's Prologue," *NTSt* 27 (1980-1981): 1-31 [1:1-18].

6800.35 Craig A. Evans, "On the Prologue of John and the Trimorphic Protennoia," *NTSt* 27 (1980-1981): 395-401 [1:1-18].

6800.36 C. H. Giblin, "Two Complementary Literary Structures in John 1:1-18," *JBL* 104 (1985): 87-103 [1:1-18].

6800.37 Elizabeth Johnson, "Jesus, the Wisdom of God: A Biblical Basis for Non-Androcentric Christology," *ETL* 61/4 (1985): 261-94 [1:1-18].

6800.38 Jeffrey L. Staley, "The Structure of John's Prologue: Its Implications for the Gospel's Narrative Structure," *CBQ* 48/2 (1986): 241-64 [1:1-18].

6800.39 John W. Pryor, "Covenant and Community in John's Gospel," *RTR* 47 (1988): 44-51 [1:1-18].

6800.40 Warren Carter, "The Prologue and John's Gospel: Function, Symbol and the Definitive Word," *JSNT* 39 (1990): 35-58 [1:1-18].

6800.41 Thomas H. Tobin, "The Prologue of John and Hellenistic Jewish Speculation," *CBQ* 52 (1990): 252-69 [1:1-18].

6800.42 G. Siegwalt, "Introduction à une théologie chrétienne de la récapitulation. Remarques sur le contenu dogmatique du prologue," *RTP* 113 (1991): 259-78 [1:1-18].

6800.43 W. Bindemann, "Der Johannesprolog: Ein Versuch, ihn zu verstehen," *NT* 37 (1995): 330-54 [1:1-18].

6800.44 S. R. Valentine, "The Johannine Prologue—a Microcosm of the Gospel," *EQ* 68 (1996): 291-304 [1:1-18].

6800.45 C. Clifton Black, "St. Thomas's Commentary on the Johannine Prologue: Some Reflections on Its Character and Implications," *CBQ* 48/4 (1986): 681-98 [1:1-14].

6800.46 H. van den Bussche, "De tout être la Parole était la vie," *BVC* 69 (1966): 57-65 [1:1-5].

6800.47 M. de Jonge, "An Analysis of 1 John 1:1-4," *BTr* 29 (1978): 322-30 [1:1-4].

6800.48 Charles Masson, "Pour une traduction nouvelle de Jean 1:1b et 2," *RTP* 98 (1965): 376-81 [1:1-2].

6800.49 Philip B. Harner, "Qualitative Anarthrous Predicate Nouns: Mark 15:39 and John 1:1," *JBL* 91 (1973): 75-87 [1:1].

6800.50 M. O'Rourke, "Sermo: Reopening the Conversation on Translating John 1:1," *VCh* 31 (1977): 161-68 [1:1].

6800.51 Bruce Vawter, "What Came to Be in Him was Life (John 1:3b-4a)," *CBQ* 25 (1963): 401-406 [1:3-4].

6800.52 H. Langkammer, "Die Zugehörigkeit des Satzteiles Ho gegonen in Johannes 1:3, 4 bei Hieronymus," *BibZ* 8 (1964): 295-98 [1:3-4].

6800.53 F. W. Schlatter, "The Problem of John 1:3b-4a," *CBQ* 34/1 (1972): 54-58 [1:3-4].

6800.54 P. van Minnen, "The Punctuation of John 1:3-4," *FilN* 7 (1994): 33-41 [1:3-4].

6800.55 Klaus Haacker, "Eine formgeschichtliche Beobachtung zu Johannes 1:3," *BibZ* 12 (1968): 119-21 [1:3].

6800.56 Georg Korting, "Johannes 1:3," *BibZ* 33/1 (1989): 97-104 [1:3].

6800.57 J. P. Louw, "Jon 1:5-'n vertaalprobleem," *NTT* 6 (1965): 47-52 [1:5].

6800.58 Earl Richard, "Expressions of Double Meaning and Their Function in the Gospel of John," *NTSt* 31 (1985): 96-112 [1:5].

6800.59 H. van den Bussche, "Il était dans le monde," *BVC* 81 (1968): 19-25 [1:9-11].

6800.60 A. Vicent Cernuda, "Engañan la oscuridad y el mundo; la luz era y manifiesta lo verdadero," *EB* 27 (1968): 153-75, 215-32 [1:9].

6800.61 B. Prete, "La concordanza del participio épxóuevov in Giov. 1:9," *BO* 17 (1975): 195-208 [1:9].

6800.62 W. E. Reiser, "Der Eindringling: Legende zu Johannes 1:11-12," *BK* 30 (1975): 123-25 [1:11-12].

6800.63 John W. Pryor, "Jesus and Israel in the Fourth Gospel," *NT* 32 (1990): 201-18 [1:11].

6800.64 Michael Mees, "Johannes 1:12, 13 nach frühchristlicher Überlieferung," *BibZ* 29/1 (1985): 107-15 [1:12-13].

6800.65 A. Vicent Cernuda, "La doble generación de Jesucristo según Jean 1:13-14," *EB* 40 (1982): 49-117, 313-44 [1:13-14].

6800.66 B. Schwank, "Eine textkritische Fehlentscheidung (Johannes 1:13) und ihre Auswirkungen im holländischen Katechismus," *BK* 24 (1969): 16-19 [1:13].

6800.67 A. Vicent Cernuda, "La huella cristológica de Jn 1:13 en el siglo 2 y la insólita audacia de esta fórmula joanea," *EB* 43/3-4 (1985): 275-320 [1:13].

6800.68 A. T. Hanson, "John i.14-18 and Exodus xxxiv," *NTSt* 23 (1976-1977): 90-101 [1:14-18].

6800.69 D. H. C. Read, "Inside John's Gospel: Introducing Jesus," *ET* 88 (1976-1977): 42-47 [1:14-18].

6800.70 J. Becker, "Schwerpunkte in der Auslegung einzelner Abschnitte," *TR* 47 (1982): 317-32 [1:14-18].

6800.71 L. J. Kuyper, "Grace and Truth: An OT Description of God, and Its Use in the Johannine Gospel," *Interp* 18 (1964): 3-19 [1:14].

6800.72 H. Leroy, " 'Und das Wort ist Fleisch geworden...': Eine theologische Meditation," *BK* 20 (1965): 114-16 [1:14].

6800.73 J. Riedl, "Strukturen christologischer Glaubensentfaltung im NT," *ZKT* 87 (1965): 443-52 [1:14].

6800.74 Frederick C. Grant, " 'Only-Begotten': A Footnote to the R.S.V.," *BTr* 17 (1966): 11-14 [1:14].

6800.75 J. C. Meagher, "John 1:14 and the New Temple," *JBL* 88 (1969): 57-68 [1:14].

6800.76 J. M. Rist, "St. John and Amelius," *JTS* 20 (1969): 230-31 [1:14].

6800.77 H. Schneider, " 'The Word Was Made Flesh': An Analysis of the Theology of Revelation in the Fourth Gospel," *CBQ* 31 (1969): 344-56 [1:14].

6800.78 Klaus Berger, "Zu 'Das Wort ward Fleisch' Johannes 1:14a," *NT* 16 (1974): 161-66 [1:14].

6800.79 R. G. Cole, "We Beheld His Glory," *ET* 90 (1978): 50-51 [1:14].

6800.80 L. D. Hynson, "The Flesh Became Word: An Advent Meditation," *PSB* 3 (1980): 54-55 [1:14].

6800.81 C. E. B. Cranfield, "John 1:14: 'Became'," *ET* 93 (1981-1982): 215 [1:14].

6800.82 Robert G. Bratcher, "What Does 'Glory' Mean in Relation to Jesus? Translating δόξα and δοξάζω in John," *BTr* 42 (1991): 401-408 [1:14].

6800.83 J. C. O'Neill, "The Word Did Not 'Become' Flesh," *ZNW* 82 (1991): 125-27 [1:14].

6800.84   Z. C. Hodges, "Grace and Grace," *BS* 135 (1978): 34-45 [1:16].

6800.85   Ruth B. Edwards, "χάριν ἀντὶ χάριτος (John 1:16): Grace and the Law in the Johannine Prologue," *JSNT* 32 (1988): 3-15 [1:16].

6800.86   Christian Amphoux, "À propos de Jacques 1:17," *RHPR* 50 (1970): 127-36 [1:17].

6800.87   C. T. R. Hayward, "The Holy Name of the God of Moses and the Prologue of St. John's Gospel," *NTSt* 25 (1978-1979): 16-32 [1:17].

6800.88   J. M. Ross, "Two More Titles of Jesus [John 1:18-34]," *ET* 85 (1973-1974): 281 [1:18-34].

6800.89   Francis J. Moloney, "John 1:18: 'In the Bosom of' or 'Turned towards' the Father?" *ABR* 31 (1983): 63-71 [1:18].

6800.90   David A. Fennema, "John 1.18: 'God the Only Son'," *NTSt* 31 (1985): 124-35 [1:18].

6800.91   Otfried Hofius, "Der in des Vaters Schoss ist: Johannes 1:18," *ZNW* 80/3-4 (1989): 163-71 [1:18].

6800.92   Charles H. Talbert, "Artistry and Theology. An Analysis of the Architecture of John 1:19-5:47," *CBQ* 32 (1970): 341-66 [1:19-5:47].

6800.93   Wolfgang Roth, "Scriptural Coding in the Fourth Gospel," *BRes* 32 (1987): 6-29 [1:19-4:54].

6800.94   L. Paul Trudinger, "The Seven Days of the New Creation in St John's Gospel: Some Further Reflections," *EQ* 44 (1972): 154-58 [1:19-51].

6800.95   R. Infante, "L'Agnello net Quarto Vangelo," *RivBib* 43 (1995): 331-61 [1:19-51].

6800.96   B. M. F. van Iersel, "Tradition und Redaktion in Johannes 1:19-36," *NT* 5 (1962): 245-67 [1:19-36].

6800.97   Georg Richter, " 'Bist du Elias?' (Johannes 1:21)," *BibZ* 6 (1962): 79-92, 238-56; 7 (1963): 63-80 [1:21].

6800.98   M. J. J. Menken, "The Quotation from Isa 40,3 in John 1,23," *B* 66 (1985): 190-205 [1:23].

6800.99   C. B. Cousar, "John 1:29-42," *Interp* 31 (1977): 401-406 [1:29-42].

6800.100   A. Rose, "Jésus Christ, Agneau de Dieu," *BVC* 62 (1965): 27-32 [1:29-34].

6800.101   J. E. Wood, "Isaac Typology in the New Testament," *NTSt* 14 (1967-1968): 583-89 [1:29-34].

6800.102   F. Gryglewicz, "Das Lamm Gottes," *NTSt* 13 (1966-1967): 133-46 [1:29].

6800.103   D. Greeves, "The Recognized Saviour," *ET* 93 (1981-1982): 84-86 [1:29].

6800.104   G. Tosatto, "Il battesimo di Gesù e alcuni passi trascurati dello Pseudo-Filone," *B* 56 (1975): 405-409 [1:32-34].

6800.105   B. Marconcini, "La predicazione del Battista: Interpretazione storica e applicazioni," *BO* 15 (1973): 49-60 [1:33].

6800.106   J. Williams, "Proposed Renderings for Some Johannine Passages," *BTr* 25 (1974): 351-53 [1:34-43].

6800.107   P. Cohee, "John 1.34," *NTSt* 41 (1995): 470-77 [1:34].

6800.108   Claude Coulot, "Les figures du maître et de ses disciples dans les premières communautés chrétiennes," *RSR* 59 (1985): 1-11 [1:35-51].

6800.109   D. H. C. Read, "From the Roots of Our Religion," *ET* 92 (1980): 21-22 [1:35-42].

6800.110   H.-J. Klauck, "Gemeinde ohne Amt: Erfahrungen mit der Kirche in den johanneischen Schriften," *BibZ* 29/2 (1985): 193-220 [1:35-42].

6800.111   John K. Thornecroft, "The Redactor and the 'Beloved' in John," *ET* 98 (1987): 135-39 [1:35].

6800.112   Robert Smith, "Seeking Jesus in the Gospel of John," *CTM* 15 (1988): 48-55 [1:38].

6800.113   A. H. Maynard, "The Role of Peter in the Fourth Gospel," *NTSt* 30/4 (1984): 531-48 [1:40-49].

6800.114   J. Ramsey Michaels, "Nathanael under the Fig Tree," *ET* 78 (1966-1967): 182-83 [1:43-51].

6800.115   J. D. M. Derrett, "Figtrees in the New Testament," *HeyJ* 14 (1973): 249-65 [1:43-51].

6800.116   E. Leidig, "Natanael, ein Sohn des Tholomäus," *TZ* 36 (1980): 374-75 [1:43-51].

6800.117   I. Willi-Plein, "Israel als Bezeichnung eines nachisraelitischen Gottesvolk, I. Nathanael. II. Jüdische 'Restgemeinden' als 'wahres Israel'?" *J* 37 (1981): 70-75, 148-53 [1:43-51].

6800.118   L. Paul Trudinger, "An Israelite in Whom There Is No Guile: An Interpretative Note on John 1:45-51," *EQ* 54 (1982):

117-20 [1:45-51].

6800.119   Peter J. Gomes, "John 1:45-51," *Interp* 43 (1989): 282-86 [1:45-51].

6800.120   Craig R. Koester, "Messianic Exegesis and the Call of Nathanael," *JSNT* 39 (1990): 23-34 [1:45-51].

6800.121   John Ashton, "The Identity and Function of the *Ioudaioi* in the Fourth Gospel," *NT* 27 (1985): 40-75 [1:49].

6800.122   Jerome H. Neyrey, "The Jacob Allusions in John 1:51," *CBQ* 44 (1982): 586-605 [1:51].

6800.123   C. C. Rowland, "John 1.51, Jewish Apocalyptic and Targumic Tradition," *NTSt* 30 (1984): 498-507 [1:51].

6800.124   M. Morgen, "La promesse de Jésus à Nathanaël éclairée par la hagaddah de Jacob-Israél," *RSRel* 67 (1993): 3-21 [1:51].

6800.125   T. C. Smith, "The Book of Signs, John 2-12," *RE* 62/4 (1965): 441-57 [2-12].

6800.126   B. Olsson, "Att omgås med texter," *STK* 52 (1976): 49-58 [2:1-12].

6800.127   R. F. Collins, "Cana (John 2:1-12) - The First of His Signs or the Key to His Signs?" *ITQ* 47 (1980): 79-95 [2:1-12].

6800.128   Allan Mayer, "Elijah and Elisha in John's Signs Source," *ET* 99 (1988): 171-73 [2:1-12].

6800.129   Rainer Riesner, "Fragen um 'Kana in Galiläa'," *BK* 43 (1988): 69-71 [2:1-12].

6800.130   Sydney Temple, "The Two Signs in the Fourth Gospel," *JBL* 81 (1962): 169-74 [2:1-11].

6800.131   Sebastián Bartina, " 'Cada uno a lo suyo': Una frase hecha en Os 14,19," *EB* 28 (1968): 247-49 [2:1-11].

6800.132   Joseph A. Grassi, "The Wedding at Cana: A Pentecostal Meditation?" *NT* 14 (1972): 131-36 [2:1-11].

6800.133   O. Bächli, " 'Was habe ich mit Dir zu schaffen?' Eine formelhafte Frage im A.T. und N.T.," *TZ* 33 (1977): 69-80 [2:1-11].

6800.134   S. D. Toussaint, "The Significance of the First Sign in John's Gospel," *BS* 134 (1977): 45-51 [2:1-11].

6800.135   K. T. Cooper, "The Best Wine: John 2:1-11," *WTJ* 1 (1978-1979): 364-80 [2:1-11].

6800.136   R. M. Mackowski, "Scholar's Qanah. A Re-Examination of the Evidence in Favor of Khirbet-Qanah," *BibZ* 23 (1979):

278-84 [2:1-11].

6800.137 M. Conti, " 'Non hanno più vino' (Gv 2,3)," *BO* 11 (1969): 76 [2:3].

6800.138 Albert Vanhoye, "Interrogation johannique et exégèse de Cana (Jean 2:4)," *B* 55 (1974): 157-67 [2:4].

6800.139 J. Villescas, "John 2: The Capacity of Six Jars," *BTr* 28 (1977): 447 [2:6].

6800.140 Paul W. Meyer, "John 2:10," *JBL* 86 (1967): 191-97 [2:10].

6800.141 J. B. Bauer, " 'Literarische' Namen und 'literarische' Bräuche (zu Johannes 2:10 and 18:39)," *BibZ* 26 (1982): 258-64 [2:10].

6800.142 John Hennig, "Was ist eigentlich geschehen?" *ZRGG* 15/3 (1963): 276-86 [2:11].

6800.143 C. J. Bjerkelund, "En tradisjons- og redaksjonshistorisk analyse an perikopeno om tempelrendelsen," *NTT* 69 (1968): 206-18 [2:13-22].

6800.144 Étienne Trocmé, "L'expulsion des marchands du Temple," *NTSt* 15 (1968-1969): 1-22 [2:13-22].

6800.145 Richard H. Hiers, "Purification of the Temple: Preparation for the Kingdom of God," *JBL* 90 (1971): 82-90 [2:13-22].

6800.146 Joachim Jeremias, "Zwei Miszellen. 2. Zur Geschichtlichkeit der Tempelreinigung," *NTSt* 23 (1976-1977): 179-80 [2:13-22].

6800.147 William P. Wood, "John 2:13-22," *Interp* 45 (1991): 59-63 [2:13-22].

6800.148 A. Orbe, "San Ireneo y la primera Pascua del Salvador," *EE* 44 (1969): 297-344 [2:13-3:21].

6800.149 P. Colella, "Cambiamonete (Jean 2:15)," *RivB* 19 (1971): 429-30 [2:15].

6800.150 Heinrich Vogel, "Die Tempelreinigung und Golgotha," *BibZ* 6/1 (1962): 102-107 [2:19-22].

6800.151 L. J. Topel, "A Note on the Methodology of Structural Analysis in John 2:23-3:21," *CBQ* 33 (1971): 211-20 [2:23-3:21].

6800.152 Z. C. Hodges, "Untrustworthy Believers," *BS* 135 (1978): 139-52 [2:23-25].

6800.153 William C. Grese, "Unless One Is Born Again: The Use of a Heavenly Journey in John 3," *JBL* 107 (1988): 677-93 [3].

6800.154 Roland Bergmeier, "Gottesherrschaft, Taufe und Geist. Zur Tauftradition in Joh 3," *ZNW* 86 (1995): 53-73 [3].

6800.155 John Bligh, "Four Studies in St. John. 2. Nicodemus," *HeyJ* 8 (1967): 40-51 [3:1-21].

6800.156 W. A. Wolfram and R. W. Fasold, "A Black English Translation of John 3:1-21 with Grammatical Annotations," *BTr* 20 (1969): 48-54 [3:1-21].

6800.157 G. T. Fish and W. A. Wolfram, "Correspondence [John 3:1-21 in Black English]," *BTr* 21 (1970): 44-46 [3:1-21].

6800.158 D. H. C. Read, "Nicodemus," *ET* 87 (1975-1976): 208-209 [3:1-21].

6800.159 Marc Michel, "Nicodème ou le non-lieu de la vérité," *RevSR* 55 (1981): 227-36 [3:1-21].

6800.160 Donald G. Miller, "John 3:1-21," *Interp* 35 (1981): 174-79 [3:1-21].

6800.161 Francis P. Cotterell, "The Nicodemus Conversation: A Fresh Appraisal," *ET* 96 (1984-1985): 237-42 [3:1-21].

6800.162 J. M. Bassler, "Mixed Signals: Nicodemus in the Fourth Gospel," *JBL* 108 (1989): 635-46 [3:1-21].

6800.163 Michael D. Goulder, "Nicodemus," *SJT* 44 (1991): 153-68 [3:1-21].

6800.164 Sandra M. Schneiders, "Born Anew," *TTod* 44 (1987): 189-96 [3:1-15].

6800.165 R. G. Forrest, "The Lord God Formed Man. . .," *ET* 91 (1979-1980): 15-17 [3:1-8].

6800.166 D. Howell-Jones, "The Second Birth," *ET* 92 (1981-1982): 85-86 [3:3].

6800.167 Barnabas Lindars, "John and the Synoptic Gospels: A Test Case," *NTSt* 27 (1980-1981): 287-94 [3:3-5].

6800.168 R. Fowler, "Born of Water and the Spirit (John 3:5)," *ET* 82 (1970-1971): 159 [3:5].

6800.169 G. Spriggs, "Meaning of 'Water' in John 3:5," *ET* 85 (1973-1974): 149-50 [3:5].

6800.170 Z. C. Hodges, "Water and Spirit," *BS* 135 (1978): 206-20 [3:5].

6800.171 Margaret Pamment, "John 3:5," *NT* 25 (1983): 189-90 [3:5].

6800.172 Ben Witherington, "The Waters of Birth: John 3:5 and 1 John 5:6-8," *NTSt* 35/1 (1989): 155-60 [3:5].

6800.173 C. H. Smith, "οὕτως ἐστὶν πᾶς ὁ γεγεννημένος ἐκ τοῦ πνεύματος," *ET* 81 (1969-1970): 181 [3:8].

6800.174 Jean Doignon, "L'esprit souffie où il veut dans la plus ancienne tradition patristique latine," *RSPT* 62 (1978): 345-59 [3:8].

6800.175 M. Morgen, "Le Fils de l'homme élevé en vue de la vie éternelle," *RevSR* 68 (1994): 5-17 [3:14-15].

6800.176 Roman Heiligenthal, "Das Heil entscheidet sich durch die Tat: Strukturverwandte Elemente der neutestament und der Bekehrungspredigt in den Gathas der Awesta," *ZRGG* 36/2 (1984): 131-40 [3:16-21].

6800.177 J. D. M. Derrett, "The Bronze Serpent," *EB* 49/3 (1991): 311-29 [3:16-21].

6800.178 H. K. Moulton, "John 3:16 - God so Loved the World" *BTr* 27 (1973): 242 [3:16].

6800.179 J. Williams, "John 3:16 [Croatian Version]," *BTr* 25 (1974): 248 [3:16].

6800.180 N. E. Block-Hoell, "Extra ecclesiam nulla salus?" *NTT* 80 (1979): 19-27 [3:16].

6800.181 Z. C. Hodges, "Coming to the Light," *BS* 135 (1978): 314-22 [3:20-21].

6800.182 J.-F. Collange, " 'Faire la vérité' considérations éthiques sur Jean 3,21," *RHPR* 62 (1982): 415-23 [3.21].

6800.183 H. van den Bussche, "Les paroles de Dieu," *BVC* 55 (1964): 23-28 [3:22-26].

6800.184 J. Wilson, "The Integrity of John 3:22-36," *JSNT* 10 (1981): 34-41 [3:22-36].

6800.185 Walter Klaiber, "Der irdische und der himmlische Zeuge: eine Auslegung von Johannes 3:22-36," *NTSt* 36 (1990): 205-33 [3:22-36].

6800.186 M.-É. Boismard, "Aenon, près de Salem," *RB* 80 (1973): 218-29 [3:23].

6800.187 Barnabas Lindars, "The Parable of the Best Man," *NTSt* 16 (1969-1970): 324-29 [3:29].

6800.188 John W. Pryor, "The Great Thanksgiving and the Fourth Gospel," *BibZ* 35/2 (1991): 157-79 [3:35].

6800.189 Gail R. O'Day, "Narrative Mode and Theological Claim: A Study in the Fourth Gospel," *JBL* 105/4 (1986): 657-68 [4].

6800.190   R. G. Maccini, "A Reassessment of the Woman at the Well in John 4 in Light of the Samaritan Context," *JSNT* 53 (1994): 35-46 [4].

6800.191   H. Rondet, "Au puits de Jacob. Saint Augustin et la conversion d'une âme," *BLE* 70 (1969): 100-109 [4:1-42].

6800.192   E. DeVries, "Johannes 4:1-42 in geest en hoofdzaak" *GTT* 78 (1978): 93-114 [4:1-42].

6800.193   C. M. Carmichael, "Marriage and the Samaritan Woman," *NTSt* 26 (1979-1980): 332-46 [4:1-42].

6800.194   J. D. M. Derrett, "The Samaritan Woman in India c. AD 200," *ZRGG* 39/4 (1987): 328-36 [4:1-42].

6800.195   N. Hyldahl, "Samtalen med den samaritanske kvinde," *DTT* 56 (1993): 153-65 [4:1-42].

6800.196   J. Neugebauer, "Die Textbezüge von Joh 4,1-42 und die Geschichte der johanneischen Gruppe," *ZNW* 84 (1993): 135-41 [4:1-42].

6800.197   J.-L. Ska, "Jésus et la Samaritaine (Jn 4). Utilité de l'Ancien Testament," *NRT* 118 (1996): 641-52 [4:1-42].

6800.198   D. A. Lee, "The Story of the Woman at the Well: A Symbolic Reading," *ABR* 41 (1993): 35-48 [4:1].

6800.199   J. D. M. Derrett, "The Samaritan Woman's Purity," *EQ* 60 (1988): 291-98 [4:4-52].

6800.200   C. Molina and J. Grandos, "Jesús y los Samaritanos: Análisis estructural de Juan 4:4-44," *CT* 6/3 (1983): 19-32 [4:4-44].

6800.201   Adrien Lenglet, "Jésus de passage parmi les Samaritans Jean 4:4-42," *B* 66/4 (1985): 493-503 [4:4-42].

6800.202   A. F. Wedel, "John 4:5-26 (5-42)," *Interp* 31 (1977): 406-12 [4:5-42].

6800.203   Laurence Cantwell, "Immortal Longings in Sermone Humili: A Study of John 4:5-26," *SJT* 36 (1983): 73-86 [4:5-26].

6800.204   L. Schottroff, "Johannes 4:5-15 und die Konsequenzen des johanneischen Dualismus," *ZNW* 60 (1969): 199-214 [4:5-15].

6800.205   Eric F. F. Bishop, "Constantly on the Road," *EQ* 41 (1969): 14-18 [4:6].

6800.206   George D. Kilpatrick, "John 4:9," *JBL* 87 (1968): 327-28 [4:9].

6800.207   T. E. Pollard, "Jesus and the Samaritan Woman," *ET* 92

(1980-1981): 147-48 [4:9].

6800.208 Jerome H. Neyrey, "Jacob Traditions and the Interpretation of John 4:10-26," *CBQ* 41 (1979): 419-37 [4:10-26].

6800.209 P. W. van der Horst, "A Wordplay in John 4:12?" *ZNW* 63 (1972): 280-82 [4:12].

6800.210 R. J. Bull, "An Archaeological Footnote to 'Our Fathers Worshipped on This Mountain'," *NTSt* 23 (1976-1977): 460-62 [4:20].

6800.211 I. de la Potterie, " 'Nous adorons, nous, ce que nous connaissons, car le salut vient des Juifs': Histoire de l'exégèse et interprétation de Jean 4:22," *B* 64 (1983): 74-115 [4:22].

6800.212 J. P. Cuthbert Lattey, "A Semiotic Approach to Discourse Analysis with Reference to Translation Theory," *BTr* 36/1 (1985): 101-107 [4:27].

6800.213 A. W. Argyle, "A Note on John 4:35," *ET* 82 (1970-1971): 247-48 [4:35].

6800.214 A. Niccacci, "Siracide 6:19 e Giovanni 4:36-38," *BO* 23 (1981): 149-53 [4:36-38].

6800.215 R. Walker, "Jüngerwort und Herrenwort: Zur Auslegung von Johannes 4:39-42," *ZNW* 57 (1966): 49-54 [4:39-42].

6800.216 George D. Kilpatrick, "John 4:41: πολλῷ πλείους," *NT* 18 (1976): 131-32 [4:41].

6800.217 Andrés Torres-Queiruga, "La teoría de la revelación en Wolfhart Pannenberg," *EE* 59/229 (1984): 139-78 [4:42].

6800.218 Craig R. Koester, "The Savior of the World," *JBL* 109 (1990): 665-80 [4:42].

6800.219 R. L. Sturch, "The πατρίς of Jesus," *JTS* 28 (1977): 94-96 [4:43-45].

6800.220 G. Reim, "John IV.44 - Crux or Clue? The Rejection of Jesus at Nazareth in Johannine Composition," *NTSt* 22 (1975-1976): 476-80 [4:44].

6800.221 John W. Pryor, "John 4:44 and the Patris of Jesus," *CBQ* 49 (1987): 254-63 [4:44].

6800.222 M.-É. Boismard, "Saint Luc et la réaction du quatrième évangile (Jean 4:46-54)," *RB* 69 (1962): 185-211 [4:46-54].

6800.223 Rudolf Schnackenburg, "Zur Traditionsgeschichte von Joh 4,46-54," *BibZ* 8 (1964): 58-88 [4:46-54].

6800.224 C. H. Giblin, "Suggestion, Negative Response, and Positive Action in St. John's Portrayal of Jesus," *NTSt* 26 (1979-1980): 197-211 [4:46-54].

6800.225 A. Hugh Mead, "The βασιλικός in John 4:46-53," *JSNT* 23 (1985): 69-72 [4:46-53].

6800.226 Frans Neirynck, "John 4:46-51: Signs Source and/or Synoptic Gospels," *ETL* 60/4 (1984): 367-75 [4:46-51].

6800.227 Günther Schwarz, " 'καὶ ἦν τις βασιλικὸς . . .'," *ZNW* 75 (1984): 138 [4:46].

6800.228 G. Van Belle, "Jean 4:48 et la foi du centurion," *ETL* 61 (1985): 167-69 [4:48].

6800.229 C. H. Dodd, "Une parabole cachée dans le quatrième Évangile," *RHPR* 42 (1962): 107-15 [5].

6800.230 John Bligh, "Jesus in Jerusalem," *HeyJ* 4 (1963): 115-34, 176 [5].

6800.231 John Painter, "Text and Context in John 5," *ABR* 35 (1987): 28-34 [5:1-47].

6800.232 H. van den Bussche, "Guérison d'un paralytique à Jérusalem le jour du Sabbat," *BVC* 61 (1965): 18-28 [5:1-18].

6800.233 H. Van Dyke Parunak, "Transitional Techniques in the Bible," *JBL* 102 (1983): 525-48 [5:1-18].

6800.234 L. T. Witkamp, "The Use of Traditions in John 5:1-18," *JSNT* 25 (1985): 19-47 [5:1-18].

6800.235 Michael Mees, "Die Heilung des Kranken vom Bethesdateich aus Johannes 5:1-18 in frühchristlicher Sicht," *NTSt* 32/4 (1986): 596-608 [5:1-18].

6800.236 John C. Thomas, "The Fourth Gospel and Rabbinic Judaism," *ZNW* 82 (1991): 159-182 [5:1-18].

6800.237 H. Weiss, "The Sabbath in the Fourth Gospel," *JBL* 110 (1991): 311-21 [5:1-16].

6800.238 Paul D. Duke, "John 5:1-5," *RE* 85 (1988): 539-42 [5:1-15].

6800.239 M. L. Rigato, "Era festa dei Giudei (Gv 5:1): quale?" *RivB* 39 (1991): 25-29 [5:1].

6800.240 D. J. Wieand, "John v.2 and the Pool of Bethesda," *NTSt* 12 (1965-1966): 392-404 [5:2].

6800.241 D. B. Wallace, "John 5:2 and the Date of the Fourth Gospel," *B* 71/2 (1990): 177-205 [5:2].

6800.242 Gordon D. Fee, "On the Inauthenticity of John 5:3b-4," *EQ*

54 (1982): 207-18 [5:3b-4].

6800.243 Z. C. Hodges, "The Angel at Bethesda," *BS* 136 (1979): 25-39 [5:4].

6800.244 D. B. Johnson, "A Neglected Variant in Gregory 33 (John 5,8)," *NTSt* 18 (1971-1972): 231-32 [5:8].

6800.245 H. J. de Jonge, "Een nieuwe tekstgetuige van het Griekse Nieuwe Testament in Nederland," *NTT* 32 (1978): 305-309 [5:17-28].

6800.246 G. Ferraro, "Il senso di 'heos arti' nel testo di Giovanni 5:17," *RivB* 20 (1972): 529-45 [5:17].

6800.247 Michael Mees, "Jesu Selbstzeugnis nach Johannes 5:19-30 in frühchristlicher Sicht," *ETL* 62/1 (1986): 102-17 [5:19-30].

6800.248 M. Eugene Boring, "John 5:19-24," *Interp* 45 (1991): 176-81 [5:19-24].

6800.249 H. J. de Jonge, "Een recente aanwinst onder de Nieuw Testamentische tekstgetuigen in Nederland," *NTT* 31 (1977): 2-7 [5:24-30].

6800.250 C. J. Pinto de Oliveira, "Le verbe didonai comme expression des rapports du Père et du fils dans le IVe Evangile," *RSPT* 49 (1965): 81-104 [5:26-27].

6800.251 Z. C. Hodges, "Those Who Have Done Good," *BS* 136 (1979): 158-66 [5:28-29].

6800.252 Urban C. von Wahlde, "The Witnesses to Jesus in John 5:31-40 and Belief in the Fourth Gospel," *CBQ* 43 (1981): 385-404 [5:31-40].

6800.253 Roland Mörchen, "Johanneisches 'Jubeln'," *BibZ* 301/2 (1986): 248-50 [5:35].

6800.254 Ernst Haenchen, " 'Der Vater, der mich gesandt hat'," *NTSt* 9 (1962-1963): 208-16 [5:36].

6800.255 F. J. Moore, "Eating the Flesh and Drinking the Blood. A Reconsideration," *ATR* 48 (1966): 70-75 [6].

6800.256 Michael Mees, "Sinn und Bedeutung westlicher Textvarianten in Johannes 6," *BibZ* 13 (1969): 244-51 [6].

6800.257 Marco M. Herranz, "El Jordán y el mar de Galilea en el marco geográfico de los Evangelios," *EB* 29 (1970): 327-52 [6].

6800.258 T. Snoy, "Le chapitre 6 de l'Évangile de Jean," *BVC* 94 (1970): 5-7 [6].

6800.259 M. Shorter, "The Position of Chapter VI in the Fourth Gospel," *ET* 84 (1972-1973): 181-83 [6].

6800.260 J.-N. Aletti, "Le discours sur le pain de la vie (Jean 6). Problèmes de composition et fonction des citations de l'Ancien Testament," *RSR* 62 (1974): 169-97 [6].

6800.261 J. S. Croatto, "Riletture dell'Esodo nel cap. 6 di San Giovanni," *BO* 17 (1975): 11-20 [6].

6800.262 D. Muñoz León, "Las fuentes y estadios de composición del Cap. 6. de San Juan segúin Boismard-Lamouille," *EB* 39 (1981): 315-38 [6].

6800.263 S. Légasse, "Le pain de la vie," *BLE* 83 (1982): 243-61 [6].

6800.264 H. Weder, "Die Menschwerdung Gottes: Uberlegungen zur Auslegungsproblematik des Johannesevangeliums am Beispiel von Johannes 6," *ZTK* 82/3 (1985): 325-60 [6].

6800.265 Raymond Bailey, "John 6," *RE* 85 (1988): 95-98 [6].

6800.266 L. T. Witkamp, "Some Specific Johannine Features in John 6:1-21," *JSNT* 40 (1990): 43-59 [6:1-21].

6800.267 P. E. Cousins, "The Feeding of the Five Thousand," *EQ* 39 (1967): 152-54 [6:1-15].

6800.268 F. Quiévreux, "Le récit de la multiplication des pains dans le quatrième évangile," *RevSR* 41 (1967): 97-108 [6:1-15].

6800.269 C. T. Ruddick, "Feeding and Sacrifice. The Old Testament Background of the Fourth Gospel," *ET* 79 (1967-1968): 340-41 [6:1-15].

6800.270 J.-M. Van Cangh, "Le thème des poissons dans les récits évangéliques de la multiplication des pains," *RB* 78 (1971): 71-83 [6:1-15].

6800.271 Bruce H. Grigsby, "The Reworking of the Lake-Walking Account in the Johannine Tradition," *ET* 100 (1989-1990): 295-97 [6:16-26].

6800.272 P. Zarrella, "Gesù cammina sulle acque: Significato teologico di Giovanni 6:16-21," *BO* 10 (1968): 181-87 [6:16-21].

6800.273 J. D. M. Derrett, "Why and How Jesus Walked on the Sea," *NT* 23 (1981): 330-48 [6:16-21].

6800.274 C. H. Giblin, "The Miraculous Crossing of the Sea," *NTSt* 29 (1983): 96-103 [6:16-21].

6800.275 L. Schenke, "Die Formale und Gedankliche Struktur von Joh 6:26-58," *BibZ* 24 (1980): 21-41 [6:26-58].

6800.276 L. Schenke, "Die literarische Vorgeschichte von Joh 6:26-58," *BibZ* 29/1 (1985): 68-89 [6:26-58].

6800.277 G. Gamibino, "Struttura, composizione e analisi letterario-teologica di Gv. 6:26-51b," *RivB* 24 (1976): 337-58 [6:26-51].

6800.278 F. Grob, " 'Vous me cherchez, non parce que vous avez vu des signes. . .' Essai d'explication cohérente de Jean 6/26," *RHPR* 60 (1980): 429-39 [6:26].

6800.279 Roland Bergmeier, "Glaube als Werk? Die 'Werke Gottes' in Damaskusschrift II,14-15 und Johannes 6:28-29," *RQu* 6 (1967): 253-60 [6:28-29].

6800.280 Urban C. von Wahlde, "Faith and Works in Jean 6:28-29. Exegesis or Eisegesis?" *NT* 22 (1980): 304-15 [6:28-29].

6800.281 Georg Richter, "Zur Formgeschichte und literarischen Einheit von Johannes 6.31-58," *ZNW* 60 (1969): 21-55 [6:31-58]

6800.282 Urban C. von Wahlde, "*Wiederaufnahme* as a Marker of Redaction in John 6:51-58," *B* 64 (1983): 542-49 [6:51-58].

6800.283 Rudolf Schnackenburg, "Zur Rede vom Brot aus dem Himmel: eine Beobachtung zu Joh 6,52," *BibZ* 12 (1968): 248-52 [6:52].

6800.284 E. Galbiati, "Il pane della vita (Giov. 6:55-58)," *BO* 5 (1963): 101-10 [6:55-58].

6800.285 G. Crocetti, "Le linee fondamentali del concetto di vita in Io. 6:57," *RivB* 19 (1971): 375-94 [6:57].

6800.286 R. Le Déaut, "Une aggadah targumique et les 'murmures' de Jean 6," *B* 51 (1970): 80-83 [6:58-61].

6800.287 G. Ferraro, "Giovanni 6,60-71. Osservazioni sulla struttura letteraria e il valore della pericope nel quarto vangelo," *RivB* 26 (1978): 33-69 [6:60-71].

6800.288 L. Schenke, "Das johanneische Schisma und die 'Zwölf' (Johannes 6:60-71)," *NTSt* 38 (1992): 105-21 [6:60-71].

6800.289 S. Ben-Chorin, "Deuteworte, Dornenkrone und Evangelien-struktur: drei exegetische Randbemerkungen," *ZRGG* 38/3 (1986): 270 [6:60].

6800.290 D. H. C. Read, "Your Bible - Dead or Alive?" *ET* 91 (1979-1980): 49-51 [6:63-64].

6800.291 G. Boccali, "Un 'mashal' evangelico e la sua applicazione (Gv 6:63)," *BO* 10 (1968): 53-58 [6:63].

6800.292 G. Krodel, "John 6:63," *Interp* 37 (1983): 283-88 [6:63].

6800.293 E. K. Broadhead, "Echoes of an Exorcism in the Fourth Gospel," *ZNW* 86 (1995): 111-19 [6:66-71].

6800.294 L. Schenke, "Joh 7-10: Eine dramatische Szene," *ZNW* 80/3-4 (1989): 172-92 [7-10].

6800.295 G. Rochais, "Jean 7: Une construction littétaire dramatique, à la manière d'un scénario," *NTSt* 39 (1993): 355-78 [7:1-52].

6800.296 H. W. Attridge, "Thematic Development and Source Elaboration in John 7:1-36," *CBQ* 42 (1980): 160-70 [7:1-36].

6800.297 Christoph Burchard, "Fußnoten zum neutestamentlichen Griechisch (Johannes 2:23, 7:11)," *ZNW* 61 (1970): 157-71 [7:11].

6800.298 B. Hedman, "No Middle Ground," *ET* 90 (1978-1979): 368-69 [7:12].

6800.299 J. D. M. Derrett, "Circumcision and Perfection: A Johannine Equation," *EQ* 63 (1991): 211-24 [7:22-23].

6800.300 Ernst Bammel, "Joh 7:35 in Manis Lebensbeschreibung," *NT* 15 (1973): 191-92 [7:35].

6800.301 M. Costa, "Simbolismo battesimale in Giov. 7:37-39; 19:31-37; 3:5," *RivB* 13 (1965): 347-83 [7:37-39].

6800.302 H. van den Bussche, "Jésus l'unique source d'eau vive," *BVC* 65 (1965): 17-23 [7:37-39].

6800.303 M. Miguéns, "El Agua y el Espítitu en Jean 7:37-39," *EB* 41 (1972): 369-93 [7:37-39].

6800.304 Gordon D. Fee, "Once More - John 7:37-39," *ET* 89 (1977-1978): 116-18 [7:37-39].

6800.305 Z. C. Hodges, "Water," *BS* 136 (1979): 239-48 [7:37-39].

6800.306 Bruce H. Grigsby, "If Any Man Thirsts: Observations on the Rabbinic Background of John 7:37-39," *B* 67/1 (1986): 101-108 [7:37-39].

6800.307 J. B. Cortés, "Yet Another Look at John 7:37-38," *CBQ* 29 (1967): 75-86 [7:37-38].

6800.308 G. Leanza, "Testimonianze della tradizione indiretta sul alcuni Testamento (Giov. 7:7-38 e altri passi)," *RivB* 15 (1967): 407-18 [7:37-38].

6800.309 Pierre Grelot, "Joh 7:38: Eau du rocher ou source du temple?" *RB* 70 (1963): 43-51 [7:38].

6800.310 M. Balagué, "Flumina de ventre credentis (Jean 7:38)," *EB* 26 (1967): 187-201 [7:38].

6800.311 L. F. Ladaria, "Juan 7:38 en Hilario de Poitiers. un análisis de Tr. Ps. 64,13-16," *EE* 52 (1977): 123-28 [7:38].

6800.312 S. H. Hooke, "The Spirit Was Not Yet [John 7:39]," *NTSt* 9 (1963): 372-80 [7:39].

6800.313 S. Pancaro, "The Metamorphosis of a Legal Principle in the Fourth Gospel: A Closer Look at John 7:51," *B* 53 (1972): 340-61 [7:40-52].

6800.314 A. A. Trites, "The Woman Taken in Adultery," *BS* 131 (1974): 137-46 [7:53-8:11].

6800.315 Hans von Campenhausen, "Zur Perikope von der Ehebrecherin," *ZNW* 68 (1977): 182-96 [7:53-8:11].

6800.316 F. Rousseau, "La femme adultère: Structure de Jean 7:53-8:11," *B* 59 (1978): 463-80 [7:53-8:11].

6800.317 Z. C. Hodges, "The Woman Taken in Adultery," *BS* 136 (1979): 318-32, 137 (1980): 41-53 [7:53-8:11].

6800.318 John Ferguson, "The Woman Taken in Adultery," *ET* 93 (1981-1982): 280-81 [7:53-8:11].

6800.319 Bart D. Ehrman, "Jesus and the Adulteress," *NTSt* 34/1 (1988): 24-44 [7:53-8:11].

6800.320 Philip Comfort, "The Pericope of the Adulteress," *BTr* 40 (1989): 145-47 [7:53-8:11].

6800.321 Reginald H. Fuller, "The Decalogue in the New Testament," *Interp* 43 (1989): 243-55 [7:53-8:11].

6800.322 John P. Heil, "The Story of Jesus and the Adulteress Reconsidered," *B* 72/2 (1991): 182-91 [7:53-8:11].

6800.323 J. Rius-Camps, "Origen lucano de la pericopa de la mujer adultera," *FilN* 6 (1993): 149-75 [7:53-8:11].

6800.324 D. B. Wallace, "Reconsidering 'The Story of Jesus and the Adulteress Recosidered," *NTSt* 39 (1993): 290-96 [7:53-8:11].

6800.325 J. I. H. McDonald, "The So-Called Pericope de adultera," *NTSt* 41 (1995): 415-27 [7:53-8:11].

6800.326 J. D. M. Derrett, "Exercitions on John 8," *EB* 52 (1994): 433-51 [8].

6800.327 J. D. M. Derrett, "Law in the NT: The Story of the Woman Taken in Adultery," *NTSt* 10 (1963-1964): 1-26 [8:1-11].

6800.328   G. Colombo, "La critica testuale di fronte alla pericope dell'adultera." *RivB* 42 (1994): 81-102 [8:1-11].

6800.329   Dieter Lührmann, "Die Geschichte von einer Sünderin und andere Apokryphe Jesusüberlieferungen bei Didymos von Alexandrien," *NT* 32 (1990): 289-316 [8:3-11].

6800.330   Henry Troadée, "Le témoignage de la lumière, Jean 8:12-59," *BVC* 49 (1963): 16-26 [8:12-59].

6800.331   Urban C. von Wahlde, "Literary Structure and Theological Argument in Three Discourses with the Jews in the Fourth Gospel," *JBL* 103 (1984): 575-84 [8:13-59].

6800.332   Jerome H. Neyrey, "Jesus the Judge: Forensic Process in John 8:21-59," *B* 68/4 (1987): 509-42 [8:21-59].

6800.333   F. J. Leenhardt, "Abraham et la conversion de Saul de Tarse, suivi d'une note sur 'Abraham' dans Jean VIII," *RHPR* 53 (1973): 331-51 [8:21-30].

6800.334   T. B. Dozeman, "Sperma Abraam in John 8 and Related Literature: Cosmology and Judgment," *CBQ* 42 (1980): 342-58 [8:21-30].

6800.335   H. W. Hollander, " 'Vrijheid' en 'slavernij' in Johannes 8:31-36," *NTT* 48 (1994): 265-74 [8:31-36].

6800.336   Giuseppe Segalla, "Un appello alla perseveranza nella fede in Gv 8:31-32?" *B* 62 (1981): 387-89 [8:31-32].

6800.337   James Swetnam, "The Meaning of Pepisteoukotas in John 8:31," *B* 61 (1980): 106-109 [8:31].

6800.338   N. A. Dahl, "Manndraperen og hans far (Joh 8:44)," *NTT* 64/3 (1963): 129-62 [8:44].

6800.339   S. Ben-Chorin, "Antijüdische Elemente im Neuen Testament," *EvT* 40 (1980): 203-14 [8:44].

6800.340   D. Muñoz León, "El principio trinitario inmanente y la interpretación del Nuevo Testamento (a propósito de la cristología epifánica restrictiva), pt 3," *EB* 41/3-4 (1983): 241-83 [8:44].

6800.341   Pierre Grelot, "Jean 8:56 et Jubilés 16:16-29," *RQu* 13 (1988): 621-28 [8:56].

6800.342   Édouard Delebecque, "Jésus contemporain d'Abraham selon Jean 8:57," *RB* 93/1 (1986): 85-92 [8:57].

6800.343   E. D. Freed, "Who or What Was before Abraham in John 8:58?" *JSNT* 17 (1983): 52-59 [8:58].

6800.344   J. M. Lieu, "Blindness in the Johannine Tradition," *NTSt* 34/1

(1988): 83-95 [9].

6800.345 J. W. Holleran, "Seeing the Light: A Narrative Reading of John 9," *ETL* 69 (1993): 354-82 [9].

6800.346 Thomas L. Brodie, "Jesus as the New Elisha: Cracking the Code (John 9:1-41)," *ET* 93 (1981-1982): 39-42 [9:1-41].

6800.347 John Bligh, "Four Studies in St John: 1. The Man Born Blind," *HeyJ* 7 (1966): 129-44 [9:1-12].

6800.348 F. A. Garcia Romero, "Breve comentario a Jn 9:1-3: objeciones al supuesto cristianismo de Trifiodoro," *FilN* 2 (1989): 93-97 [9:1-3].

6800.349 Karl Müller, "Joh 9,7 und das jüdische Verständnis des Siloh-Spruches," *BibZ* 13 (1969): 251-56 [9:7].

6800.350 G. Reim, "Joh 9: Tradition und zeitgenössische messianische Diskussion," *BibZ* 22 (1978): 245-53 [9:7].

6800.351 Bruce H. Grigsby, "Washing in the Pool of Siloam: A Thematic Anticipation of the Johannine Cross," *NT* 27 (1985): 227-35 [9:7].

6800.352 Ernst Bammel, "Johannes 9:17," *NTSt* 40 (1994): 455-56 [9:17].

6800.353 Calvin L. Porter, "John IX,38.39a: A Liturgical Addition to the Text," *NTSt* 13 (1966-1967): 387-94 [9:38-39].

6800.354 Ulrich Busse, "Offene Fragen zu Joh 10," *NTSt* 33/4 (1987): 516-31 [10].

6800.355 Augustin George, "Je suis la porte des brebis," *BVC* 51 (1963): 18-25 [10:1-10]

6800.356 James P. Martin, "John 10:1-10" *Interp* 32 (1978): 171-75 [10:1-10].

6800.357 F. Manns, "Traditions targumiques en Jean 10:1-30," *RevSR* 60/3-4 (1986): 135-57 [10:1-30].

6800.358 David J. Hawkin, "Orthodoxy and Hersey in John 10:1-21 and 15:1-17," *EQ* 47 (1975): 208-13 [10:1-21].

6800.359 Miguel Rodríguez Ruiz, "El discurso del Buen Pastor: coherencia theologico-literaria e interpretacion," *EB* 48/1 (1990): 5-45 [10:1-18].

6800.360 P. Weigandt, "Zum Text von Joh. x 7. Ein Beitrag zum Problem der koptischen Bibelübersetzung," *NT* 9 (1967): 43-51 [10:7].

6800.361 D. Mollat, "Le bon pasteur," *BVC* 52 (1963): 25-35

[10:11-18].

6800.362   Raymond E. Brown, " 'Other Sheep Not of This Fold': The Johannine Perspective on Christian Diversity in the Late First Century," *JBL* 97 (1978): 5-22 [10:16].

6800.363   Jean Giblet, "Et il y eut la dédicace, Jean 10:22-39," *BVC* 66 (1965): 17-25 [10:22-39].

6800.364   J. R. Lancaster and R. L. Overstreet, "Jesus' Celebration of Hanukkah in John 10," *BS* 152 (1995): 318-33 [10:22-39].

6800.365   Robert Kysar, "John 10:22-30," *Interp* 43 (1989): 66-70 [10:22-30].

6800.366   J. Whittaker, "A Hellenistic Context for John 10:29," *VCh* 24 (1970): 241-60 [10:29].

6800.367   A. T. Hanson, "John's Citation of Ps 82," *NTSt* 11 (1964-1965): 158-62 [10:33-36].

6800.368   Richard Jungkuntz, "Approach to the Exegesis of John 10:34-36," *CTM* 35 (1964): 556-65 [10:34-36].

6800.369   J. S. Ackerman, "The Rabbinic Interpretation of Psalm 82 and the Gospel of John: John 10:34 and the Prologue," *HTR* 59 (1966): 186-91 [10:34].

6800.370   A. T. Hanson, "John's Citation of Psalm LXXXII Reconsidered," *NTSt* 13 (1966-1967): 363-67 [10:36].

6800.371   Sandra M. Schneiders, "Death in the Community of Eternal Life: History, Theology, and Spirituality in John 11," *Interp* 41 (1987): 44-56 [11].

6800.372   Barnabas Lindars, "Rebuking the Spirit: A New Analysis of the Lazarus Story of John 11," *NTSt* 38 (1992): 89-104 [11].

6800.373   D. Burkett, "Two Accounts of Lazarus' Resurrection in John 11," *NT* 36 (1994): 209-32 [11].

6800.374   M. Aubineau, "Un Ps. Athanase, In Lazarum (e Vat. Ottob. gr. 14) restitué à Léonce de Constantinople," *JTS* 25 (1974): 442-47 [11:1-44].

6800.375   J. N. Suggit, "The Raising of Lazarus," *ET* 95 (1983-1984): 106-108 [11:1-44].

6800.376   Mark W. G. Stibbe, "A Tomb with a View: John 11:1-44 in Narrative Critical Perspective," *NTSt* 40 (1994): 38-54 [11:1-44].

6800.377   Iver Larsen, "Walking in the Light: A Comment on John 11:9-10," *BTr* 37/4 (1986): 432-36 [11:9-10].

6800.378 Édouard Delebecque, "Lazare est mort (note sur Jean 11:14-15)," *B* 67/1 (1986): 89-97 [11:14-15].

6800.379 Francis J. Moloney, "The Faith of Martha and Mary: A Narrative Approach to John 11:17-40," *B* 75 (1994): 471-93 [11:17-40].

6800.380 Max Wilcox, "The 'Prayer' of Jesus in John xi.41b-42," *NTSt* 24 (1977-1978): 128-32 [11:41-42].

6800.381 B. Osborne, "A Folded Napkin in an Empty Tomb: John 11:44 and 20:7 Again," *HeyJ* 14 (1973): 437-40 [11:44].

6800.382 W. E. Reiser, "The Case of the Tidy Tomb: The Place of the Napkins of John 11:44 and 20:7," *HeyJ* 14 (1973): 47-57 [11:44].

6800.383 J. D. M. Derrett, "Lazarus and his Grave-Clothes," *BO* 35 (1993): 129-37 [11:44].

6800.384 Johannes Beutler, "Two Ways of Gathering: The Plot to Kill Jesus in John 11:47-53," *NTSt* 40 (1994): 399-406 [11:47-53].

6800.385 J. Kennedy, "The Abuse of Power," *ET* 85 (1973-1974): 172-73 [11:50].

6800.386 Otfried Hofius, "Die Sammlung der Heiden zur Herde Israels (Joh 10,16; 11,51f.)," *ZNW* 58 (1967): 289-91 [11:51].

6800.387 J. Ramsey Michaels, "John 12:1-11," *Interp* 43 (1989): 287-91 [12:1-11].

6800.388 K. Tsuchido, "Tradition and Redaction in John 12:1-43," *NTSt* 30/4 (1984): 609-19 [12:1-43].

6800.389 J. E. Bruns, "A Note on John 12,3," *CBQ* 28 (1966): 219-22 [12:3].

6800.390 B. Prete, "Un'aporia giovannea: il testo di Giov. 12:3," *RivB* 25 (1977): 357-73 [12:3].

6800.391 G. M. Lee, "John xii 9 [ὁ] ὄχλος πολύς," *NT* 22 (1980): 95 [12:9].

6800.392 D. Moody Smith, "John 12:12ff. and the Question of John's Use of the Synoptics," *JBL* 82 (1963): 58-64 [12:12].

6800.393 R. L. Jeske, "John 12:20-36," *Interp* 43 (1989): 292-95 [12:20-36].

6800.394 J. L. Kovacs, " 'Now Shall the Ruler of This World Be Driven Out': Iesus' Death as Cosmic Battle in John 12:20-36," *JBL* 114 (1995): 227-47 [12:20-36].

6800.395   J. E. Lone, "Thunder or Angel? (John 12:20-32)," *ET* 66 (1984-1985): 145-46 [12:20-32].

6800.396   Augustin George, "Qui veut sauver sa vie, la perdra; qui perd sa vie, la sauvera," *BVC* 83 (1968): 11-24 [12:20-26].

6800.397   W. E. Moore, " 'Sir, We Wish to See Jesus': Was This an Occasion of Temptation?" *SJT* 20 (1967): 75-93 [12:21].

6800.398   A. W. Argyle, "Fruitfulness through Death (John 12:24)," *ET* 89 (1977-1978): 149 [12:24].

6800.399   Craig A. Evans, "The Voice from Heaven: A Note on John 12:28," *CBQ* 43 (1981): 405-408 [12:28].

6800.400   W. C. MacDonald, "The Outstretched Arms," *ET* 92 (1980-1981): 182-84 [12:32-33].

6800.401   W. Thüsing, " 'Wenn ich von der Erde erhöht bin. . . ': Die Erhohung Jesu nach dem Jo-Ev.," *BK* 20/2 (1965): 40-42 [12:32].

6800.402   B. McNeil, "The Quotation at John xii 34," *NT* 19 (1977): 22-23 [12:34].

6800.403   G. D. Bampfylde, "More Light on John XII 34," *JSNT* 17 (1983): 87-89 [12:34].

6800.404   Roland Mörchen, " 'Weggehen'. Beobachtungen zu Joh 12,36b," *BibZ* 28 (1984): 240-42 [12:36].

6800.405   B. Hollenbach, "Lest They Should Turn and Be Forgiven: Irony," *BTr* 34 (1983): 312-21 [12:40].

6800.406   Peder Borgen, "The Use of Tradition in John 12:44-50," *NTSt* 26 (1979-1980): 18-35 [12:44-50].

6800.407   Frank Stagg, "The Farewell Discourses," *RE* 62/4 (1965): 459-72 [13-17].

6800.408   H.-J. Klauck, "Der Weggang Jesu. Neue Arbeiten zu Joh 13-17," *BibZ* 40 (1996): 236-50 [13-17].

6800.409   F. Manns, "Le lavement des pieds: Essai sur la structure et la signification de Jean 13," *RSR* 55 (1981): 149-69 [13].

6800.410   D. Tripp, "Meanings of Foot-Washing: John 13 and Oxyrhynchus Papyrus 840," *ET* 103 (1992): 237-39 [13].

6800.411   Francis J. Moloney, "A Sacramental Reading of John 13:1-38," *CBQ* 53 (1991): 237-56 [13:1-38].

6800.412   J. D. G. Dunn, "The Washing of the Disciples' Feet in John 13:1-20," *ZNW* 61 (1970): 247-52 [13:1-20].

6800.413   H. Weiss, "Foot Washing in the Johannine Community," *NT*

21 (1979): 298-325 [13:1-20].

6800.414   Sandra M. Schneiders, "The Foot Washing (John 13:1-20): An Experiment in Hermeneutics," *CBQ* 43 (1981): 76-92 [13:1-20].

6800.415   M. Sabbe, "The Footwashing in John 13 and Its Relation to the Synoptic Gospels," *ETL* 58 (1982): 279-308 [13:1-20].

6800.416   Michal Wojciechowski, "La source de Jean 13:1-20," *NTSt* 34/1 (1988): 135-41 [13:1-20].

6800.417   M.-É. Boismard, "Le lavement des pieds," *RB* 71 (1964): 5-24 [13:1-17].

6800.418   W. Grossouw, "A Note on John xiii 1-3," *NT* 8 (1966): 124-31 [13:1-3].

6800.419   Karl T. Kleinknecht, "Johannes 13, die Synoptiker und die 'Methode' der johannischen Evangelienüberlieferung," *ZTK* 82/3 (1985): 361-88 [13:2-14:31].

6800.420   D. H. C. Read, "Happiness Is Doing What You Believe (John 13:7)," *ET* 85 (1973-1974): 240-41 [13:7].

6800.421   John C. Thomas, "A Note on the Text of John 13:10," *NT* 29 (1987): 46-52 [13:10].

6800.422   J. C. O'Neill, "John 13:10 Again," *RB* 101 (1994): 67-74 [13:10].

6800.423   J. D. M. Derrett, "Impurity and Idolatry: John 13:11; Ezekiel 36:25," *BO* 34 (1992): 87-92 [13:11].

6800.424   A. Weiser, "Joh 13:12-20: Zufügung eines späteren Herausgebers?" *BibZ* 12 (1968): 252-57 [13:12-20].

6800.425   G. F. Snyder, "John 13:16 and the Anti-Petrinism of the Johannine Tradition," *BRes* 16 (1971): 5-15 [13:16].

6800.426   David L. Bartlett, "John 13:21-30," *Interp* 43 (1989): 393-97 [13:21-30].

6800.427   G. Ferraro, " 'Pneuma' in Giov. 13,21," *RivB* 28 (1980): 185-211 [13:21].

6800.428   G. Granado, "El Espíritu Santo revelado como persana en el sermón de la Cena," *EB* 32 (1973): 157-73 [13:31-17:26].

6800.429   G. Reim, "Probleme der Abschiedsreden," *BibZ* 20 (1976): 117-22 [13:31-17:26].

6800.430   John Painter, "Glimpses of the Johannine Community in the Farewell Discourses," *ABR* 28 (1980): 21-38 [13:31-17:26].

6800.431   J. P. Kaefer, "Les discours d'adieu en Jean 13:31-17:26.

Rédaction et théologie," *NT* 26 (1984): 253-82 [13:31-17:26].

6800.432 J. Becker, "Die Abschiedsreden Jesu im Johannesevangelium," *ZNW* 61 (1970): 215-46 [13:31-16:33].

6800.433 A. Lacomara, "Deuteronomy and the Farewell Discourse (John 13:31-16:33)," *CBQ* 36 (1974): 65-84 [13:31-16:33].

6800.434 J. L. Boyle, "The Last Discourse (John 13:31-16:33) and Prayer (John 17): Some Observations on Their Unity and Development," *B* 56 (1975): 210-22 [13:31-16:33].

6800.435 M. Reese, "Literary Structure of John 13:31-14:31; 16:5-6; 16:16-33," *CBQ* 34 (1972): 321-31 [13:31-14:31].

6800.436 D. B. Woll, "The Departure of 'The Way': The First Farewell Discourse in the Gospel of John (John 13:31-14:31)," *JBL* 99 (1980): 225-39 [13:31-14:31].

6800.437 F. Porsch, "Der 'andere Paraklet': Das Wirken des Geistes nach den johanneischen Abschiedsreden," *BK* 37 (1982): 133-38 [14].

6800.438 Heribert Wahl, "Empathie und Text: das selbstpsychologische Modell interaktiver Texthermeneutik," *TQ* 169/3 (1989): 201-22 [14].

6800.439 J. Carmody, "The 'Death of God' and John 14-17," *BTr* 30 (1967): 2082-90 [14-17].

6800.440 R. H. Gundry, " 'In My Father's House Are Many Movaí' (John 14:2)," *ZNW* 58 (1967): 68-72 [14:2].

6800.441 G. Parrinder, "Only One Way? John 14:6," *ET* 107 (1995): 78-79 [14:6].

6800.442 Gordon D. Gordon, "John 14:8-17," *Interp* 43 (1989): 170-74 [14:8-17].

6800.443 Christian Dietzfelbinger, "Die Grösseren Werke (Joh 14:12f)," *NTSt* 35/1 (1989): 27-47 [14:12].

6800.444 G. M. Lee, "John xiv.16," *ET* 76 (1964-1965): 254 [14:16].

6800.445 J. E. Morgan-Wynne, "A Note on John 14:17b," *BibZ* 23 (1979): 93-96 [14:17].

6800.446 I. John Hesselink, "John 14:23-29," *Interp* 43 (1989): 174-77 [14:23-29].

6800.447 Josef Blank, "Bindung und Freiheit: Das Verhältnis der nachapostolischen Kirche zu Jesus von Nazaret," *BK* 33 (1978): 19-22 [14:25-26].

6800.448   R. L. Jeske, "John 14:27 and 16:33," *Interp* 38 (1984): 403-11 [14:27].

6800.449   Donald S. Deer, "More about the Imperatival ἵνα (John 14:31; 1 Cor 16:16; Col 2:41)," *BTr* 24 (1973): 328-29 [14:31].

6800.450   B. Sandvik, "Joh. 15 als Abendmahltext," *TZ* 23 (1967): 323-28.1 [15].

6800.451   G. Rinaldi, "Amore e odio (Giov. 15:1-16:4a)," *BO* 22 (1980): 97-106 [15:1-16:4].

6800.452   Francis J. Moloney, "The Structure and Message of John 15:1-16:3," *ABR* 35 (1987): 35-49 [15:1-16:3].

6800.453   M. Provera, "La cultura della vite nelle tradizione biblica ed orientale," *BO* 24 (1982): 97-106 [15:1-17].

6800.454   Fernando F. Segovia, "The Theology and Provenance of John 15:1-17," *JBL* 101 (1982): 115-28 [15:1-17].

6800.455   Peter Bolt, "What Fruit Does the Vine Bear? Some Pastoral Implications of John 15:1-8," *RTR* 51 (1992): 11-19 [15:1-8].

6800.456   J. G. van der Watt, " 'Metaphorik' in Johannes 15,1-8," *BibZ* 38 (1994): 67-80 [15:1-8].

6800.457   J. Carl Laney, "Abiding Is Believing: The Analogy of the Vine in John 15:1-6," *BS* 146 (1989): 55-66 [15:1-6].

6800.458   Joseph C. Dillow, "Abiding Is Remaining in Fellowship: Another Look at John 15:1-6," *BS* 147 (1990): 44-53 [15:1-6].

6800.459   G. W. Derickson, "Viticulture and John 15:1-6," *BS* 153 (1996): 34-52 [15:1-6].

6800.460   J. Foster, "A Note on St. Polycarp (John 15:5, 8)," *ET* 77 (1966): 319 [15:8].

6800.461   G. S. Gibson, "Joy (John 15:11)," *ET* 94 (1982-1983): 244-45 [15:11].

6800.462   G. M. Lee, "John xv 14 'Ye are My Friends'," *NT* 15 (1973): 260 [15:14].

6800.463   D. Heinz, "Brief Translation Note on John 15:19," *CTM* 39 (1968): 775 [15:19].

6800.464   S. Légasse, "Le retour du Christ d'après l'évangile de Jean, chapitre 14 et 16: une adaptation du motif de la Parousie," *BLE* 81 (1980): 161-74 [16].

6800.465   D. Moody Smith, "John 16:1-15," *Interp* 33 (1979): 58-62

[16:1-15].

6800.466   Don A. Carson, "The Function of the Paraclete in John 16:7-11," *JBL* 98 (1979): 547-66 [16:7-11].

6800.467   W. Stenger, "δικαιοσύνη in Jo. xvi 8:10," *NT* 21 (1979): 2-12 [16:8-10].

6800.468   D. Howell-Jones, "God's Pilgrim People," *ET* 90 (1978-1979): 45-46 [16:13-14].

6800.469   S. J. Stein, "Retrospection and Introspection. The Gospel according to Mary Baker Eddy," *HTR* 75 (1982): 97-116 [16:13].

6800.470   H. Hegstad, "Den Hellige Ånd som veileder til 'den fulle sannhet' - prinsippteologisk belyst," *TTK* 64 (1993): 95-109 [16:13].

6800.471   André Feuillet, "L'heure de la femme (Jean 16:21) et l'heure de la Mère de Jésus (Jean 19:5-27)," *B* 47 (1966): 169-84, 361-80, 551-73 [16:21].

6800.472   J. E. Bruns, "A Note on John 16:33 and 1 John 2:13-14," *JBL* 86 (1967): 451-53 [16:33].

6800.473   C. D. Morrison, "Mission and Ethic: An Interpretation of John 17," *Interp* 19 (1965): 259-73 [17].

6800.474   J. Becker, "Aufbau, Sichtung und theologiegeschichtliche Stellung des Gebetes in Johannes," *ZNW* 60 (1969): 56-83 [17].

6800.475   B. Rigaux, "Die Jünger Jesu in Johannes 17," *TQ* 150 (1970): 202-13 [17].

6800.476   Edward Malatesta, "The Literary Structure of John 17," *B* 52 (1971): 190-214 [17].

6800.477   Rudolf Schnackenburg, "Strukturanalyse von Joh 17," *BibZ* 17 (1973): 67-78, 196-202 [17].

6800.478   Jean Delorme, "Sacerdoce du Christ et ministère. (À propos de Jean 17). Sémantique et théologie biblique," *RSR* 62 (1974): 199-219 [17].

6800.479   D. Marzotto, "Giovanni 17 e il Targum di Esodo 19-20," *RivB* 25 (1977): 375-88 [17].

6800.480   Paul S. Minear, "Evangelism, Ecumenism, and John Seventeen," *TTod* 35 (1978): 5-13 [17].

6800.481   E. Gordon, "Our Lord's Priestly Prayer," *HTR* 92 (1992): 17-21 [17].

6800.482 Paul S. Minear, "John 17:1-11," *Interp* 32 (1978): 175-79 [17:1-11].

6800.483 André Laurentin, "Weattah - Kai nun: formule caractéristique des textes juridiques et liturgiques (à propos de Jean 17:5)," *B* 45/2 (1964): 168-97; 45/3 (1964): 413-32 [17:5].

6800.484 J. Riedl, "Die Funktion der Kirche nach Johannes. 'Vater, wie du mich in die Welt gesandt hast, so habe ich auch sie in die Welt gesandt' (Johannes 17:18)," *BK* 28 (1973): 12-14 [17:18].

6800.485 Royce G. Gruenler, "John 17:20-26," *Interp* 43 (1989): 178-83 [17:20-26].

6800.486 J. F. Randall, "The Theme of Unity in John 17:20-23," *ETL* 41 (1965): 373-94 [17:20-23].

6800.487 Margaret Pamment, "Short Note: John xvii 20-23," *NT* 24 (1982): 383-84 [17:20-23].

6800.488 J. C. Earwaker, "John 17:21," *ET* 75 (1963-1964): 316-17 [17:21].

6800.489 Martin Tetz, "Athanasius und die Einheit der Kirche: zur ökumenischen Bedeutung eines Kirchenvaters," *ZTK* 81/2 (1984): 196-219 [17:21].

6800.490 Albert Janssens de Varebeke, "La structure des scènes du récit de la Passion en Jean 18-19," *ETL* 38 (1962): 504-22 [18-19].

6800.491 M. Weise, "Passionswoche und Epiphaniewoche im Johannes-Evangelium. Ihre Bedeutung für Komposition und Konzeption des vierten Evangelium," *KD* 12 (1966): 48 62 [18-19].

6800.492 David E. Garland, "John 18-19: Life Through Jesus' Death," *RE* 85 (1988): 485-99 [18-19].

6800.493 J. D. M. Derrett, "Peter's Sword and Biblical Methodology," *BO* 32 (1990): 180-92 [18:8-11].

6800.494 Arthur J. Droge, "The Status of Peter in the Fourth Gospel: A Note on John 18:10-11," *JBL* 109 (1990): 307-11 [18:10-11].

6800.495 R. T. Fortna, "Jesus and Peter at the Hight Priest's House: A Test Case for the Question of the Relation between Mark's and John's Gospels," *NTSt* 24 (1977-1978): 371-83 [18:12-24].

6800.496 Craig A. Evans, " 'Peter Warming Himself': The Problem of an Editorial 'Seam'," *JBL* 101 (1982): 245-49 [18:25-27].

6800.497 A. Jaubert, "Une discussion patristique sur la chronologie de la passion," *RSR* 54 (1966): 407-10 [18:28-19:16].

6800.498 T. Horvath, "Why Was Jesus Brought to Pilate?" *NT* 11 (1969): 174-85 [18:28-19:16].

6800.499 H. Z. Maccoby, "Jesus and Barabbas," *NTSt* 16 (1969-1970): 55-60 [18:28-19:16].

6800.500 Ernst Haenchen, "History and Interpretation in the Johannine Passion Narrative," *Interp* 24 (1970): 198-219 [18:28-19:16].

6800.501 F. Chenderlin, "Distributed Observance of the Passover: A Hypothesis," *B* 56 (1975): 369-93 [18:28-19:16].

6800.502 D. Rensberger, "The Politics of John: The Trial of Jesus in the Fourth Gospel," *JBL* 103 (1984): 395-411 [18:28-19:16].

6800.503 F. Genuyt, "La comparution de Jésus devant Pilate: analyse sémiotique de Jean 18:28-19:16," *RSR* 73 (1985): 133-46 [18:28-19:16].

6800.504 C. H. Giblin, "John's Narration of the Hearing before Pilate," *B* 67/2 (1986): 221-39 [18:28-19:16].

6800.505 A. Vicent Cernuda, "La aporía entre Jean 18:31 y 19:6," *EB* 42/1-2 (1984): 71-88 [18:31].

6800.506 J. Ramsey Michaels, "John 18:31 and the 'Trial' of Jesus," *NTSt* 36 (1990): 474-79 [18:31].

6800.507 J. D. M. Derrett, "Christ, King and Witness (John 18:37)," *BO* 31 (1989): 189-98 [18:37].

6800.508 M. Herranz Marco, "Un problema de critica histórica en el relato de la Pasión: la liberación de Barrabás," *EB* 30 (1971): 137-60 [18:38].

6800.509 J. N. Suggit, "John 19:5: 'Behold the Man'," *ET* 94 (1982-1983): 333-34 [19:5].

6800.510 D. W. Head, "We Have a Law," *NT* 11 (1969): 185-89 [19:7].

6800.511 L. M. Dewailly, "D'où es-tu? (Jean 19:9)," *RB* 92 (1985): 481-96 [19:9].

6800.512 J. J. O'Rourke, "Two Notes on St. John's Gospel," *CBQ* 25 (1963): 124-28 [19:13].

6800.513 M. Balagué, "Y lo sentó en el tribunal: Reparas a la nueva traducción litúrgica," *EB* 33 (1974): 63-67 [19:13].

6800.514 Julio T. Barrera, "Posible substrato semitico del uso transitivo o intransitivo del verbo ἐκάθισεν en Jn 19:13," *FilN* 4 (1991): 51-54 [19:13].

6800.515 M. Sabbe, "The Johannine Account of the Death of Jesus and Its Synoptic Parallels," *ETL* 70 (1994): 34-64 [19:16-42].

6800.516 I. de la Potterie, "La tunique sans couture, symbole du Christ grand prêtre?" *B* 60 (1979): 255-69 [19:16-27].

6800.517 David A. Hubbard, "John 19:17-30," *Interp* 43 (1989): 397-40 [19:17-30].

6800.518 Max Wilcox, "The Text of the Titulus in John 19:19-20 as Found in Some Italian Renaissance Painting," *JSNT* 27 (1986): 113-16 [19:19-20].

6800.519 F.-M. Braun, "Quatre 'signes' johanniques de l'unité Chrétienne (Jean 6:12-13, 11:47-52, 19:23-4, 21:1-11)," *NTSt* 9 (1963): 147-55 [19:23-24].

6800.520 Anton Dauer, "Das Wort des Gekreuzigten an seine Mutter und den 'Jünger, den er liebte': Eine traditionsgeschichtliche und theologische Untersuchung zu Joh 19:25-27," *BibZ* 11 (1967): 222-39; 12 (1968) 80-93 [19:25-27].

6800.521 J. G. Patrick, "Motherhood: Its Tragedy and Its Triumph," *ET* 94 (1982-1983): 145-46 [19:25-26].

6800.522 L. T. Witkamp, "Jesus' Thirst in John 19:28-30: Literal or Figurative?" *JBL* 115 (1996): 489-510 [19:28-30].

6800.523 G. D. Bampfylde, "John xix,28: A Case for a Different Translation," *NT* 11 (1969): 247-60 [19:28].

6800.524 F. G. Beetham and P. A. Beetham, "A Note on John 19:29," *JTS* 44 (1993): 163-69 [19:29].

6800.525 A. Kirchgässner, "Erneigte das Haupt und gab den Geist auf. Meditation über Johannes 19:30," *BK* 25 (1970): 48-52 [19:30].

6800.526 Roland Borgmeier, "Tetelestai (Johannes 19:30)," *ZNW* 79/3-4 (1988): 282-90 [19:30].

6800.527 H.-J. Venetz, "Zeuge des Erhöhten: Ein exegetischer Beitrag zu Joh 19:31-37," *FZPT* 23 (1976): 81-111 [19:31-37].

6800.528 J. M. Ford, " 'Mingled Blood' from the Side of Christ (John xix,34)," *NTSt* 15 (1968-1969): 337-38 [19:34].

6800.529 J. Wilkinson, "The Incident of the Blood and Water in John 19:34," *SJT* 28 (1975): 149-72 [19:34].

6800.530 Dennis D. Sylva, "Nicodemus and His Spices," *NTSt* 34/1 (1988): 148-51 [19:39].

6800.531 B. Prete, "E lo legarono con bende (Giov. 19:40)," *BO* 10 (1968): 189-96 [19:40].

6800.532 Gert Hartmann, "Die Vorlage der Osterberichte in Joh 20," *ZNW* 55/3-4 (1964): 197-220 [20].

6800.533 Jacques Dupont, et al., "Recherche sur la structure de Jean 20," *B* 54 (1973): 482-98 [20].

6800.534 J. Kremer, "Entstehung und Inhalt des Osterglaubens: Zur neuesten Diskussion," *TR* 72 (1976): 1-14 [20].

6800.535 D. H. C. Read, "How to Hear the Easter Story," *ET* 79 (1977-1978): 178-79 [20].

6800.536 F. Manns, "En marge des récits de la résurrection dans l'évangile de Jean: le verbe voir," *RevSR* 57 (1983): 10-28 [20].

6800.537 I. de la Potterie, "Genèse de la foi pascale d'après Jean 20," *NTSt* 30 (1984): 26-49 [20].

6800.538 B. Byrne, "The Faith of the Beloved Disciple and the Community in John 20," *JSNT* 23 (1985): 83-97 [20].

6800.539 W. G. Kümmel, "Das Urchristentum II. Arbeiten zu Spelialproblemen," *TR* 50/2 (1985): 132-64 [20].

6800.540 D. A. Lee, "Partnership in Easter Faith: The Role of Mary Magdalene and Thomas in John 20," *JSNT* 58 (1995): 37-49 [20].

6800.541 Frank J. Matera, "John 20:1-18," *Interp* 43 (1989): 402-406 [20:1-18].

6800.542 C. Bernabé, "Trasfondo derásico de Jn 20," *EB* 49 (1991): 209-28 [20:1-18].

6800.543 A. Jasper, "Interpretative Approaches to John 20:1-18: Mary at the Tomb of Jesus," *ST* 47 (1993):107-18 [20:1-18].

6800.544 Paul S. Minear, " 'We Don't Know Where . . . ' John 20:2," *Interp* 30 (1976): 125-39 [20:2].

6800.545 K. P. G. Curtis, "Luke XXIV.12 and John XX.3-10," *JTS* 22 (1971): 512-15 [20:3-10].

6800.546 M. Shorter, "The Sign of the Linen Cloths: The Fourth Gospel and the Holy Shroud of Turin," *JSNT* 17 (1983): 90-96 [20:5-10].

6800.547 A. Webster, "My Master," *ET* 85 (1973-1974): 206-208 [20:11-18].

6800.548 T. Hearn, "Reach Hither, Touch Me Not," *RE* 59 (1962):

200-204 [20:17-27].

6800.549 D. C. Fowler, "The Meaning of 'Touch me not' in John 20:17," *EQ* 47 (1975): 16-25 [20:17].

6800.550 Antonio Charbel, "Giov. 20:17a: 'Nondum enim ascendi ad Patrem'?" *BO* 21 (1979): 79-83 [20:17].

6800.551 Michael McGehee, "A Less Theological Reading of John 20:17," *JBL* 105/2 (1986): 299-302 [20:17].

6800.552 Mary R. D'Angelo, "A Critical Note: John 20:17 and Apocalypse of Moses 31," *JTS* 41 (1990): 529-36 [20:17].

6800.553 Félix Asensio, "Los pasajes biblicos de la 'Gran Misión' y el Vaticano II," *EB* 29 (1970): 213-26 [20:19-23].

6800.554 M. G. DeDurand, "Pentecôte johannique et Pentecôte lucanienne chez certains Pères," *BLE* 79 (1978): 97-126 [20:19-23].

6800.555 Reginald H. Fuller, "John 20:19-23," *Interp* 32 (1978): 180-84 [20:19-23].

6800.556 Heino Falcke, "Kirchen im Friedensbund Gottes: ekklesiologische Aspekte des Friedensauftrags der Kirchen heute," *EvT* 45 (1985): 348-66 [20:19-21].

6800.557 James Swetnam, "Bestowal of the Spirit in the Fourth Gospel," *B* 74 (1993): 556-76 [20:22-23].

6800.558 G. M. Lee, "Presbyters and Apostles," *ZNW* 62 (1971): 122 [20:23].

6800.559 B. De Margerie, "La mission sacerdotale de retenir les péchés en liant les pécheurs. Intérêt actuel et justification d'une exégèse tridentine," *RevSR* 58 (1984): 300-17 [20:23].

6800.560 Paulino Bellet, "Analecta Coptica," *CBQ* 40 (1978): 37-52 [20:24-29].

6800.561 A. Hilhorst, "The Wounds of the Risen Jesus," *EB* 41/1-2 (1983): 165-67 [20:24-29].

6800.562 B. Prete, "Beati coloro che non vedono e credono (Giov. 20:29)," *BO* 9 (1967): 97-114 [20:29].

6800.563 Michael Lattke, "Joh 20:30f als Buchschluss," *ZNW* 78/3-4 (1987): 288-92 [20:30-31].

6800.564 B. de Solages and J.-M. Vacherot, "Le chapitre xxi de Jean est-il de la même plume que la reste de l'Évangile?" *BLE* 80 (1970): 96-101 [21].

6800.565 Stephen S. Smalley, "The Sign in John xxi," *NTSt* 20

(1973-1974): 275-88 [21].

6800.566 Paul S. Minear, "The Original Functions of John 21," *JBL* 102 (1983): 85-98 [21].

6800.567 Wolfgang Schenk, "Interne Strukturierungen im Schluss-Segment Johannes 21," *NTSt* 38 (1992): 507-30 [21].

6800.568 Édouard Delebecque, "La mission de Pierre et celle de Jean: note philologique sur Jean 21," *B* 67/3 (1986): 335-42 [21:1-25].

6800.569 Timothy Wiarda, "John 21:1-23: Narrative Unity and Its Implications," *JSNT* 46 (1992): 53-71 [21:1-23].

6800.570 D. H. C. Read, "Ongoing Easter: The Sign of the Fish," *ET* 85 (1973-1974): 208-209 [21:1-14].

6800.571 Mathias Rissi, "Voll grosser Fische, hundertdreiundfünfzig, Joh 21:1-14," *TZ* 35 (1979): 73-89 [21:1-14].

6800.572 Marion L. Soards, "τὸν ἐπενδύτην διεζώσατο, ἦν γὰρ γυμνός," *JBL* 102 (1983): 283-84 [21:1-14].

6800.573 Sandra M. Schneiders, "John 21:1-14," *Interp* 43 (1989): 70-75 [21:1-14].

6800.574 Bernd Steinseifer, "Der Ort der Erscheinungen des Auferstandenen," *ZNW* 63/3 (1971): 232-65 [21:1-11].

6800.575 D. H. Gee, "Why Did Peter Spring into the Sea?" *JTS* 40 (1989): 481-89 [21:7].

6800.576 N. J. McEleney, "153 Great Fishes (John 21:11)—Gematriacal Atbash," *B* 58 (1977): 411-17 [21:11].

6800.577 J. A. Romeo, "Gematria and John 21:11: The Children of God," *JBL* 97 (1978): 263-64 [21:11].

6800.578 Bruce H. Grigsby, "Gematria and John 21:11: Another Look at Ezekiel 47:10," *ET* 95 (1983-1984): 177-78 [21:11].

6800.579 Michael Oberweis, "Die Bedeutung der neutestamentlichen 'Rätselzahlen' 666 (Apk 13:18) und 153 (Joh 21:11)," *ZNW* 77/3-4 (1986): 226-41 [21:11].

6800.580 J. M. Ross, "One Hundred and Fifty-Three Fishes," *ET* 100 (1989): 357 [21:11].

6800.581 Kenneth Cardwell, "The Fish on the Fire: John 21:9," *ET* 102 (1990): 12-14 [21:11].

6800.582 L. Paul Trudinger, "The 153 Fishes: A Response and a Further Suggestion," *ET* 102 (1990): 11-12 [21:11].

6800.583 Otto Glombitza, "Petrus: der Freund Jesu. Uberlegungen zu Joh 21:15-17," *NT* 6 (1963): 277-85 [21:15-17].

6800.584 K. L. McKay, "Style and Significance in the Language of John 21:15-17," *NT* 27 (1985): 319-33 [21:15-17].

6800.585 Richard J. Bauckham, "The Beloved Disciple as Ideal Author," *JSNT* 49 (1993): 21-44 [21:20-25].

6800.586 Richard J. Bauckham, "Papias and Polycrates on the Origin of the Fourth Gospel," *JTS* 44 (1993): 24-69 [21:20-25].

6800.587 I. de la Potterie, "Le témoin qui demeure: le disciple que Jésus aimait," *B* 67/3 (1986): 343-59 [21:24-25].

6800.588 R. Kieffer, "Å gjenkjenne den ukjente," *NTT* 91/3 (1990): 129-39 [21:25].

6800.589 J. Neville Birdsall, "The Source of the Catena Comments on John 21:25," *NT* 36 (1994): 271-79 [21:25].

H. THE GOSPELS IN THE NEW TESTAMENT CANON

6801. A. Hilgenfeld, "Altchristliche Prolegomena zu den kano nischen Evangelien," *ZWT* 40 (1897): 432-44.

6802. Vincent Rose, "L'église primitive a-t-elle lu plus de quatre évangiles?" *RB* 7 (1898): 491-510.

6803. Julius A. Bewer, "The History of the New Testament Canon in the Syrian Church," *AJT* 4 (1900): 64-98, 345-63.

6804. F. H. Knubel, "Why There are Just Four Gospels," *LCR* 21 (1902): 339-46.

6805. Th. Zahn, "Outline of the History of the New Testament Canon," *LCR* 24 (1905): 296-306, 536-44.

6806. C. H. Turner, "Historical Introduction to the Textual Criticism of the New Testament; II. The Contents of the Canon of the New Testament: (A) The Four Gospels," *JTS* 10 (1908-1909): 161-82.

6807. Edgar J. Goodspeed, "The Making of the New Testament," *BW* 37 (1911): 379-90

6808. A. Kluikenberg, "De plaats der Evangelieën in bet Nieuwe Testament," *NTS* 9 (1926): 201-11.

6809. B. W. Bacon, "As to the Canonization of Matthew," *HTR* 22 (1929): 151-73.

6810. M.-J. Lagrange, "L'histoire ancienne du canon du Nouveau Testament," *RB* 44 (1935): 212-19.

6811.   L.-M. Dewailly, "Canon du Nouveau Testament et histoire des dogmes," *VP* 1 (1941): 78-93.

6812.   Oscar Cullmann, "Die Pluralität der Evangelien als theologisches Problem. Eine dogmengeschichtliche Studie," *TZ* 1 (1945): 23-42

6813.   Werner Georg Kümmel, "Notwendigkeit und Grenze des neutestamentlichen Kanons," *ZTK* N.F. 47 (1950): 278-313.

6814.   P. Saydon, "The Order of the Gospels," *Scr* 4 (1950): 190-96.

6815.   A. A. T. Ehrhardt, "The Gospels in the Muratorian Fragment," *OSt* 2 (1953): 121-38.

6816.   K. L. Carroll, "The Creation of the Four-Fold Gospel," *BJRL* 37 (1954-1955): 68-77.

6817.   K. L. Carroll, "The Earliest New Testament," *BJRL* 38 (1955-1956): 45-57

6818.   Olof Linton, "Nya Testamentets tanker om profeter och profetia," *STK* 12 (1936): 146-67.

         See also number 6981.

6818.1   A. C. Sundberg, "Canon Muratori: A Fourth-Century List," *HTR* 66 (1973): 1-41.

6818.2   Merrill C. Tenney, "The Canon of the Gospels," *BETS* 10 (1967): 36-43.

6818.3   F. F. Bruce, "Some Thoughts on the Beginning of the New Testament Canon," *BJRL* 65 (1983): 37-46.

6818.4   Helmut Merkel, "Clemens Alexandrinus über die Reihenfolge der Evangelien," *ETL* 60 (1984): 382-85.

SECTION IV

EARLY NON-CANONICAL LITERATURE RELATED
TO CHRIST AND THE GOSPELS

A. OLD TESTAMENT APOCRYPHA AND PSEUDEPIGRAPHA

6819.   George H. Schodde, "The New Greek Enoch Fragments,"
         BW 1 (1893): 359-62.

6820.   Léon Gry, "Le Roi-Messie dans Hénoch (parties anciennes),"
         Mu, 24 (1905): 129-39.

6821.   H. J. Lawlor, "The Book of Enoch in the Egyptian Church,"
         Herm 13 (1905): 178-83.

6822.   Léon Gry, "Le messie des Psaumes de Salomon," *Mu* 25
         (1906): 231-48.

6823.   Léon Gry, "Le messianisme des paraboles d'Henoch,"*Mu* 27
         (1908): 319-67.

6824.   Léon Gry, "Le messianisme des paraboles d'Hénoch et la
         théologie juive contemporaine,"*Mu* 28 (1909): 143-54.

6825.   N. Messel, "Messiasideen og den 17de Salomo-salme," *NTT*
         10 (1909): 105-29.

6826.   James Barrelet, "Un pont de l'Ancien au Nouveau Testa-
         ment: les Apocryphes et les Pseudépigraphes," *RTP* 43
         (1910): 5-38.

6827.   Pierre Batiffol, "Les Odes de Salomon," *RB* 20 (1911):
         161-97.

6828.   Ernest W. Parsons, "The Testaments of the Twelve
         Patriarchs," *BW* 37 (1911): 176-88.

6829.   Wilh. Schencke, "De nylig fundne saakaldte 'Salomos oder',"
         NTT 12 (1911): 116-31.

6830.   William R. Newbold, "The Descent of Christ in the Odes of
         Solomon," *JBL* 31 (1912): 168-209.

6831.   W. Weber, "Der Auferstehungsglaube im eschatologischen
         Buche der Weisheit Salomos," *ZWT* 54 (1912): 205-39.

6832.   Phillips Barry, "The Apocalypse of Ezra," *JBL* 32 (1913):
         261-72.

6833.   Gustav Hölscher, "Über die Entstehungszeit der
         'Himmelfahrt Moses'," *ZNW* 17 (1916): 108-27, 149-58.

6834.   Vacher Burch, "The Literary Unity of the *Ascensio Isaiae*,"

JTS 20 (1919): 17-23.

6835. W. Greitemann, "De messia eiusque regno in Testamentis duodecim Patriarcharum," *VD* 11 (1931): 156-60, 184-92.

6836. Xaverius Vallisoleto, "Christologia in Apocalypsi Baruch syriaca," *VD* 11 (1931): 212-21.

6837. Sigmund Mowinckel, "Henok og 'Menneskesønnen'," *NTT* 45 (1944): 67-69.

6838. A. R. Hastouris, "The Conception of the Messiah in the Apocryphal Literature," *Θ* 23 (1952): 109-21.

6839. Joshua Bloch, "Some Christological Interpretations in the Ezra-Apocalypse," *HTR* 51 (1958): 87-94.

6840. Allen Cabaniss, "Wisdom 18: 14f.: An Early Christmas Text," *VCh* 10 (1956): 97-102.

also number 6001, *10029, 10044.*

6840.1 P. W. Barnett, "Who Were the 'Biastai'?" *RTR* 36/3 (1977): 65-70.

6840.2 Morris M. Faierstein, "Why Do the Scribes Say That Elijah Must Come First?" *JBL* 100 (1981): 75-86.

6840.3 James H. Charlesworth, "Research on the Historical Jesus Today," *PSB* 6/2 (1985): 98-115.

B. NEW TESTAMENT APOCRYPHA

1. Non-canonical Gospels

a. *General Studies*

6841. M. W. Moggridge, "Lost Gospels," *Exp* 1st ser., 12 (1880): 325-45.

6842. Ludwig Couard, "Urchristliche Sagen über das Leben Jesu," *NKZ* 12 (1901): 234-60.

6843. William Muss-Arnolt, "The New Testament Apocrypha, with Special Reference to Recent German Contributions," *BW* 28 (1906): 50-58, 136-41.

6844. M. R. James, "Irish Apocrypha," *JTS* 20 (1919): 9-16.

6845. Alfred Plummer, "The Apocryphal Gospels," *ET* 34 (1922-1923): 373-76, 473-74.

6846. Hans Waitz, "Neue Untersuchungen über die sogen. judenchristlichen Evangelien," *ZNW* 36 (1937): 60-81.

6847. U. Holzmeister, "Relationes de miraculis Christi extra Evangelia canonica existentes," *VD* 21 (1941): 257-63.

6848.   J. de Ghellinck, "Récentes découvertes de littérature chrétienne antique," *NRT* 71 (1949): 83-86.

6849.   A. Vööbus, "Ta'āmera Iyasus. Zeuge eines älteren äthiopischen Evangelientypus," *OCP* 17 (1951): 462-67.

6850.   Paulino Bellet, "Testimonios coptos de la aparición de Cristo resucitado a la Virgen," *EB* 13 (1954): 199-205.

6851.   Lorenzo Turrado, "María en los Evangelios apócrifos," *CB* 11 (1954): 380-90.

6852.   Søren Giversen, "Johannes' apokryfon og Genesis," *DTT* 20 (1957): 65-80.

6853.   W. C. van Unnik, "The Origin of the Recently Discovered 'Apocryphon Jacobi'," *VCh* 10 (1956): 149-56.

6854.   Jes Peter Asmussen, "Manikaeiske Jesus-tekster fra kinesisk Turkestan," *DTT* 21 (1958): 129-45.

6855.   Andrew Helmbold, "The Coptic Gnostic Texts from Nag Hammadi," *BETS* 2, no. 2 (1959): 15-19.

6856.   A. Orbe, "Une théologie du judéo-christianisme," *RSR* 47 (1959): 544-59.

6857.   G. C. Stead, "New Gospel Discoveries," *Th* 62 (1959): 321-27.

6858.   A. D. Nock, "The Apocryphal Gospels," *JTS* N.S. 11 (1960): 63-70.

6859.   Félix M. Pareja, "Un relato morisco sobre la vida de Jesús y de María," *EE* 34 (1960): 859-72.

    see also numbers 653, 9899.

6859.1   Jean D. Kaestli, "Où en est l'étude de l'Evangile de Barthélemy?" *RB* 95 (1988): 5-33.

b. *The Gospel According to the Hebrews*

6860.   A. Hilgenfeld, "Das Evangelium der Hebräer," *ZWT* 6 (1863): 345-85.

6861.   J. R. Lumby, "Some Traces of a Hebrew Gospel," *Exp* 1st ser., 9 (1879): 316-25.

6862.   A. Hilgenfeld, "Das Hebräer-Evangelium und sein neuester Bearbeiter," *ZWT* 32 (1889): 280-302.

6863.   Eb. Nestle, "A Fragment of the Original Hebrew Gospel," *Exp* 5th ser., 2 (1895): 309-15.

6864.   A. S. Barnes, "The Gospel According to the Hebrews," *JTS*

6 (1904-1905): 356-71.

6865.   Vacher Burch, "The Gospel according to the Hebrews: Some
          New Matter Chiefly from Coptic Sources," *JTS* 21 (1920):
          310-15.

6866.   M.-J. Lagrange, "L'évangile selon des Hébreux," *RB* 31
          (1922): 161-81, 321-49.

6867.   Roderic Dunkerley, "The Gospel according to the Hebrews,"
          ET 39 (1927-1928): 437-42, 490-95.

6868.   J. Theodore Dodd, "The Appearance of Jesus to St. James,"
          Th 18 (1929): 189-97 [the Gospel according to the Hebrews].

6869.   Alfred Schmidtke, "Zum Hebräerevangelium," *ZNW* 35
          (1936): 24-44.

6870.   G. Quispel, "Das Hebräerevangelium im gnostischen
          Evangelium nach Maria," *VCh* 11 (1957): 139-44.

   c. *Protevangelium of James*

6871.   Primo Vannutelli, "Protevangelium Jacobi," *S* 5 (1940):
          1-151.

6872.   L. M. Peretto, "Testi sacri nel Protevangelo di Giacomo,"
          RivB 3 (1955): 174-78, 235-56.

6873.   Johann Michl, "Die Geburtsgrotte zu Bethlehem," *MTZ* 7
          (1956): 115-19 [according to the Protevangelium Jacobi
          18:1].

6874.   Gérard Garitte, "Le 'Protévangile de Jacques' en georgien,"
          Mu 70 (1957): 233-65.

6875.   Salvador Muñoz Iglesias, "Los Evangelios de la Infanc las
          infancias de los héroes," *EB* 16 (1957): 5-36.

6875.1   Malcolm Lowe, "Ioudaios of the Apocrypha: A fresh
          approach to the Gospels of James, Pseudo-Thomas, Peter and
          Nicodemus," *NT* 23 (1981): 56-90.

   d. *The Gospel of Peter*

6876.   James H. Moulton, "The 'Gospel of Peter' and the Four," *ET*
          4 (1892-1893): 299-300.

6877.   W. Emery Barnes, "The Newly-Found Gospel in its Relation
          to the Four," *ET* 5 (1893-1894): 61-64.

6878.   Lester Bradner, "An Important Discovery of MSS," *BW* 1
          (1893): 33-35 [Revelation of Peter, Gospel of Peter,
          fragments of Enoch].

6879.   A. Hilgenfeld, "Das Petrus-Evangelium über Leiden und Auferstehung Jesu," *ZWT* 36, pt. 1 (1893): 439-54.

6880.   A. Hilgenfeld, "Das Petrus-Evangelium," *ZWT* 36, pt. 2 (1893): 220-67.

6881.   A. Hilgenfeld, "Das κήρυγμα Πέτρου (καὶ Παύλου)," *ZWT* 36, pt. 2 (1893): 518-41.

6882.   Johannes Kurze, "Das Petrusevangelium," *NKDT* 2 (1893): 581-604; 3 (1894): 58-104.

6883.   John Macpherson, "The Gospel of Peter," *ET* 5 (1893-1894): 556-61.

6884.   W. C. van Manen, "Het Evangelie van Petrus," *TT* 27 (1893): 317-33, 379-432, 517-72.

6885.   J. O. F. Murray, "Evangelium secundum Petrum," *Exp* 4th ser., 7 (1893). 50-61.

6886.   Th. Zahn, "Das Evangelium des Petrus," *NKZ* 4 (1893): 143-218.

6887.   G. Semeria, "L'évangile de Pierre," *RB* 3 (1894): 522-60.

6888.   V. H. Stanton, "The 'Gospel of Peter': Its Early History and Character considered in Relation to the History of the Recognition in the Church of the Canonical Gospels," *JTS* 2 (1900-1901): 1-25.

6889.   H. Usener, "Eine Spur des Petrusevangeliums," *ZNW* 3 (1902): 353-58.

6890.   Pastor Stocks, "Zum Petrusevangelium," *NKZ* 13 (1902): 276-314; 14 (1903): 515-42.

6891.   Hans Waitz, "Eine Parallele zu den Seligpreisungen aus einem ausserkanonischen Evangelium," *ZNW* 4 (1903): 335-40 [Gosp. Pet.].

6892.   C. Bruston, "Un ancien recueil de paroles attribuées à Jésus," *RTQR* 14 (1905): 78-95 [The Gospel and Apocalypse of Peter].

6893.   D. Völter, "Petrusevangelium oder Ägypterevangelium," *ZNW* 6 (1905): 368-72.

6894.   C. H. Turner, "The Gospel of Peter," *JTS* 14 (1912-1913): 161-87.

6895.   Anton Baumstark, "Alte und neue Spuren eines ausserkanonischen Evangeliums (vielleicht des Ägypterevangeliums)," *ZNW* 14 (1913): 232-47.

6896.   P. Gardner-Smith, "The Gospel of Peter," *JTS* 27 (1925-1926): 255-71.

6897.   P. Gardner-Smith, "The Date of the Gospel of Peter," *JTS* 27 (1925-1926): 401-407.

6898.   A. F. J. Klijn, "Het evangelie van Petrus en de Westerse tekst," *NedTT* 15 (1960-1961): 264-69.

see also number *10062*.

6898.1   C. F. D. Moule, "The Angry Word: Mt. 5:21f.," *ET* 81 (1969-1970): 10-13.

6898.2   Raymond E. Brown, "The Gospel of Peter and Canonical Gospel Priority," *NTSt* 33 (1987): 321-43.

e. *The Gospel of Philip*

6899.   Hans-Martin Schenke, "Das Evangelium nach Philippus," *TLZ* 84 (1959): 1-26

6900.   Eric Segelberg, "The Coptic-Gnostic Gospel according to Philip and its Sacramental System," *Num* 7 (1960): 189-200.

6901.   Robert M. Grant, "The Mystery of Marriage in the Gospel of Philip," *VCh* 15 (1961): 129-40.

6901.1   J. J. Buckley, "A Cult-Mystery in the Gospel of Philip," *JBL* 99 (1980): 569-81.

6901.2   François Bovon, "The Synoptic Gospels and the Noncanonical Acts of the Apostles," *HTR* 81 (1988): 19-36.

f. *The Gospel of Thomas*

6902.   M. R. James, "The Gospel of Thomas," *JTS* 30 (1928-1929): 51-54.

6903.   L. Cerfaux et Gérard Garitte, "Les paraboles royaume dans l'évangile de Thomas,"*Mu* 70 (1957): 307-27.

6904.   Gérard Garitte, "Le premier volume de l'édition photographique des manuscrits gnostiques coptes et l'évangile de Thomas',"*Mu* 70 (1957): 59-73.

6905.   G. Quispel, "The Gospel of Thomas and the New Testament," *VCh* 11 (1957): 189-207.

6906.   B. Celada, "¿Se ha encontrado un quinto Evangelio?" *CB* 15 (1958): 366-75 [Gosp. Thos.].

6907.   J. Leipoldt, "Ein neues Evangelium? Das koptische Thomasevangelium übersetzt und besprochen," *TLZ* 83

(1958): 481-96.

6908. Olaf Moe, "Det nyfunne Thomas-evangelium," *TTK* 29 (1958): 217-18.

6909. G. Quispel, "L'évangile selon Thomas et les Clémentines," *VCh* 12 (1958): 181-96.

6910. G. Quispel, "Some Remarks on the Gospel of Thomas," *NTSt* 5 (1958-1959): 276-90.

6911. W. C. Till, "New Sayings of Jesus in the Recently Discovered Coptic 'Gospel of Thomas'," *BJRL* 41 (1958-1959): 446-58.

6912. R. McL. Wilson, "The Coptic 'Gospel of Thomas'," *NTSt* 5 (1958-1959): 273-76.

6913. R. McL. Wilson, "The Gospel of Thomas," *ET* 70 (1958-1959): 324-25.

6914. H.-W. Bartsch, "Das Thomas-Evangelium und di synoptischen Evangelien," *NTSt* 6 (1959-1960): 249-61.

6915. B. Celada, "Más acerca del supuesto quinto Evangelio," *CB* 16 (1959): 48-50 [Gosp. Thos.].

6916. Robert M. Grant, "Notes on the Gospel of Thomas," *VCh* 13 (1959): 170-80.

6917. Harvey K. McArthur, "The Dependence of the Gospel of Thomas on the Synoptics," *ET* 71 (1959-1960): 286-87.

6918. Otto A. Piper, "The Gospel of Thomas," *PSB* 53, no. 2 (1959): 18-24.

6919. P. Prigent, "L'évangile de Thomas. Etat de la question," *RHPR* 29 (1959): 39-45.

6920. G. Quispel, "L'évangile selon Thomas et le Diatessaron," *VCh* 13 (1959): 87-117.

6921. F. W. Beare, "The Gospel according to Thomas: A Gnostic Manual," *CJT* 6 (1960): 102-12.

6922. Ernest Best, "The Gospel of Thomas," *BT* 10 (1960): 1-10.

6923. Oscar Cullmann, "Das Thomasevangelium und die Frage nach dem Alter der in ihm enthaltenen Tradition," *TLZ* 85 (1960): 321-34.

6924. Frederick W. Danker, "The Gospel According to Thomas," *CTM* 31 (1960): 309-11.

6925. Robert M. Grant, "Two Gnostic Gospels," *JBL* 79 (1960): 1-11 [Thomas and Philip].

6926.   Otfried Hofius, "Das koptische Thomasevangelium und die Oxyrhynchus-Papyri Nr. I, 654 und 655," *EvT* 20 (1960): 21-42, 182-92.

6927.   C.-H. Hunzinger, "Aussersynoptisches Traditionsgut im Thomas-Evangelium," *TLZ* 85 (1960): 843-46.

6928.   Salvador Muñoz Iglesias, "El Evangelio de Tomás y algunos aspectos de la cuestión sinóptica," *EE* 34 (1960): 883-94.

6929.   K. H. Kuhn, "Some Observations on the Coptic Gospel according to Thomas," *Mu* 73 (1960): 317-23.

6930.   George W. MacRae, "The Gospel of Thomas-*Logia Iesou*?" *CBQ* 22 (1960): 56-71.

6931.   J. D. McCaughey, "Two Synoptic Parables in the Gospel of Thomas," *ABR* 8 (1960): 24-28.

6932.   H. W. Montefiore, "A Comparison of the Parables of the Gospel According to Thomas and of the Synoptic Gospels," *NTSt* 7 (1960-1961): 220-48.

6933.   Johannes Munck, "Bemerkungen zum koptischen Thomasevangelium," *ST* 14 (1960): 130-47.

6934.   John A. O'Flynn, "The Gospel According to Thomas," *ITQ* 27 (1960): 66-69.

6935.   William R. Schoedel, "Naassene Themes in the Coptic Gospel of Thomas," *VCh* 14 (1960): 225-34.

6936.   Kevin Smyth, "Gnosticism in *The Gospel according to Thomas*," *HeyJ* 1 (1960): 189-98.

6937.   A. F. Walls, "The References to Apostles in the Gospel of Thomas," *NTSt* 7 (1960-1961): 266-70.

6938.   R. McL. Wilson, "Thomas and the Synoptic Gospels," *ET* 72 (1960-1961): 36-39.

6939.   R. McL. Wilson, "The Gospel of Thomas," *BTr* 11 (1960): 132-35.

6940.   R. McL. Wilson, " 'Thomas' and the Growth of the Gospels," *HTR* 53 (1960): 231-50.

6941.   J. B. Bauer, "Arbeitsaufgaben am koptischen Thomasevangelium," *VCh* 15 (1961): 1-7.

6942.   E. M. J. M. Cornélis, "Quelques éléments pour une comparaison entre l'évangile de Thomas et la notice d'Hippolyte sur les Naassènes," *VCh* 15 (1961): 83-104.

6943.   Ernst Haenchen, "Literatur zum Thomasevangelium," *TR* 27

(1961): 147-78, 306-38.

6944. A. F. J. Klijn, "Das Thomasevangelium und das altsyrische Christentum," *VCh* 15 (1961): 146-59.

6945. R. Schippers, "Het evangelie van Thomas een onafhankelijke traditie?" *GTT* 61 (1961): 46-54.

6946. J. N. Sevenster, "Het evangeliec naar Thomas en de synoptische evangeliën," *VT* 32 (1961-1962): 9-17.

6947. Ernst Haenchen, "Spruch 68 des Thomasevangeliums,"*Mu* 75 (1962): 19-29.

See also numbers 1910, 7032f.

6947.1 J. Neville Birdsall, "Luke 12:16ff. and the Gospel of Thomas," *JTS* 13 (1962): 332-36.

6947.2 Raymond E. Brown, "The Gospel of Thomas and St. John's Gospel," *NTSt* 9 (1962-1963): 155-77.

6947.3 Howard C. Kee, " 'Becoming a Child' in the Gospel of Thomas," *JBL* 82 (1963): 307-14.

6947.4 Klyne Snodgrass, "The Parable of the Wicked Husbandmen: Is the Gospel of Thomas Version the Original?" *NTSt* 21 (1974-1975): 142-44.

6947.5 Benedict Englezakis, "Thomas, Logion 30," *NTSt* 25 (1979): 262-72.

6947.6 J. Horman, "The Source of the Version of the Parable of the Sower in the Gospel of Thomas," *NT* 21/4 (1979): 326-43.

6947.7 William L. Petersen, "The Parable of the Lost Sheep in the Gospel of Thomas and the Synoptics," *NT* 23 (1981): 128-47.

6947.8 William G. Morrice, "The Parable of the Dragnet and the Gospel of Thomas," *ET* 95/9 (1984): 269-73.

g. *The Gospel of Truth*

6948. J. Leipoldt, "Das 'Evangelium der Wahrheit'," *TLZ* 82 (1957): 825-34.

6949. C. K. Barrett, "The Gospel of Truth: The Editio Princeps of an Ancient Gnostic Text," *ET* 69 (1958): 167-70.

6950. H. I. Marrou, "L'Évangile de Vérité et la diffusion du comput digital dans l'antiquité," *VCh* 12 (1958): 98-103.

6951. J. D. McCaughey, "The Gnostic Gospel of Truth and the New Testament," *ABR* 6 (1958): 87-108.

6952.   Søren Giversen, "Evangelium Veritatis and the Epistle to the Hebrews," *ST* 13 (1959): 85-96.

6953.   W. Dunn, "What does 'Gospel of Truth' mean?" *VCh* 15 (1961): 160-64.

6954.   K. H. Schelkle, "Das Evangelium Veritatis als kanongeschichtliches Zeugnis," *BibZ* N.F. 5 (1961): 90-91.

        See also number 3311

6954.1 Alv Kragerud, "En gnostisk teodicé: om fall og frelse i Evangelium Veritatis," *NTT* 62 (1961): 144-71.

6954.2 Sasagu Arai, "Zur Lesung und Ubersetzung des Evangelium veritatis: ein Beitrag zum Verständnis seiner Christologie," *NT* 5 (1962): 214-18.

6954.3 Eric F. Osborn, "The Gospel of Truth," *ABR* 10 (1962): 32-41.

6954.4 Johannes Munck, "Evangelium Veritatis and Greek Usage as to Book Titles," *ST* 17 (1963): 133-38.

6954.5 Andrew C. Robison, "The Evangelium Veritatis: Its Doctrine, Character and Origin," *JR* 43 (1963): 234-43.

6954.6 R. McL. Wilson, "Note on the Gospel of Truth (33:8-9)," *NTSt* 9 (1963): 295-98.

6954.7 Helmer Ringgren, "Gospel of Truth and Valentinian Gnosticism," *ST* 18 (1964): 51-65.

6954.8 H. Ludin Jansen, "Tankesystemet i det nyfunne gnostiske skrift: evangelium Veritatis," *NTT* 66 (1965): 152-76.

6954.9 Alv Kragerud, "Evangelium Veritatis: en oversettelse," *NTT* 66 (1965): 177-93.

6954.10 J. E. Ménard, "La 'connaissance' dans l'Evangile de Vérité," *RSRel* 41 (1967): 1-28.

6954.11 J. E. Ménard, "La structure et la langue originale de l'Evangile de Vérité," *RSRel* 44 (1970): 128-37.

6954.12 J. E. Ménard, "L'Evangile de Vérité et le Dieu caché des littératures antiques," *RSRel* 45 (1971): 146-61.

6954.13 Jean D. Dubois, "Remarques sur le texte de l'evangile de verite (CG I, 2)," *VCh* 29 (1975): 138-40.

6954.14 Benoit Standaert, "Evangelium veritatis et veritatis evangelium: la question du titre et les témoins patristiques," *VCh* 30 (1976): 138-50.

6954.15 Benoit Standaert, "Evangile de vérité: critique et lecture,"

NTSt 22 (1976): 243-75.

6954.16   Christopher M. Tuckett, "Synoptic Tradition in the Gospel of Truth and the Testimony of Truth," *JTS* 35 (1984): 131-45.

6954.17   Anne McGuire, "Conversion and Gnosis in the Gospel of Truth," *NT* 28 (1986): 338-55.

h. *The Gospel of the Twelve Apostles*

6955.   Eugène Revillout, "L'évangile des douze apôtres," *Bes* 5 (1903): 14-21, 157-76, 309.

6956.   Eugène Revillout, "L'évangile des XII apôtres récemment découvert," *RB* 13 (1904): 167-87, 321-55.

6957.   Hans Waitz, "Das Evangelium der zwölf Apostel," *ZNW* 13 (1912): 338-48; 14 (1913): 38-64, 117-32.

6957.   Enzo Lucchesi, "D'un soi-disant Evangile (apocryphe) des douze Apôtres à l'Evangile (canonique) selon saint Jean," *OCP* 52 (1983): 267.

i. Other Gospels

6958.   Hans Windisch, "Das Evangelium des Basilides," *ZNW* 7 (1906): 236-46.

6959.   John W. Youngson, "The Discovery of the Gospel of Barnabas," *ET* 19 (1907-1908): 263-65.

6960.   Felix Haase, "Zur Rekonstruktion des Bartholomäus-evangeliums," *ZNW* 16 (1915): 93-112.

6961.   S. Grébaut, "La Pentecôte et la mission des apôtres," *ROC* 21 (1918-1919): 203-24; 22 (1920-1921): 57-64 [extract from *Les Miracles de Jésus*].

6962.   Emmanuel Cosquin, "Une épisode d'un évangile syriaque et les contes de l'Inde," *RB* 28 (1919): 136-57.

6963.   M.-J. Lagrange, "Un nouvel évangile de l'enfance, édité par M. R. James," *RB* 37 (1928): 544-57 [=Pseudo-Matthew].

6964.   J. Doresse, "Trois livres gnostiques inédits: *Évangile des Egyptiens.—Épître d'Eugnoste.—Sagesse de Jésus Christ*," *VCh* 2 (1948): 137-60.

6965.   Allen Cabaniss, "The Harrowing of Hell, Psalm 24, and Pliny the Younger: A Note," *VCh* 7 (1953): 65-74 [Gospel of Nicodemus].

6966.   L. Th. Lefort, "À propos de 'l'Histoire de Joseph le Charpentier," *Mu* 66 (1953): 201-23.

6967.   R. McL. Wilson, "The New Testament in the Gnostic Gospel of Mary," *NTSt* 3 (1956-1957): 236-42.

6968.   J. B. Bauer, "Hieronymus und das Nazaraerevangelium," *BibZ* N.F. 4 (1960): 122-28.

6969.   R. ten Kate, "Hrotsvits Maria und das Evangelium des Pseudo-Matthäus," *CM* 22 (1961): 195-204.

6969.1   John E. Fletcher, "Spanish Gospel of Barnabas," *NT* 18 (1976): 314-20.

6969.2   J. Gijsel, "Problème de la contamination," *NT* 18 (1976): 133-57.

6969.3   Christopher M. Tuckett, "Synoptic Tradition in Some Nag Hammadi and Related Texts," *VCh* 36 (1982): 173-90.

j. *Logia and Papyrus Fragments*

6970.   G. Bickell, "Ein Papyrusfragment eines nichtkanonischen Evangeliums," *ZKT* 9 (1885): 498-504.

6971.   G. T. S[toker], "The Fayûm Gospel Fragment," *Exp* 3rd ser., 2 (1885): 132-41.

6972.   A. Hilgenfeld, "Kein unentdecktes Evangelium," *ZWT* 29 (1886): 50-58.

6973.   G. T. Stokes, "The Latest Discoveries among the Fayûm Manuscripts," *Exp* 3rd ser., 7 (1888): 449-60.

6974.   P. Savi, "Le fragment évangélique du Fayoum," *RB* 1 (1892): 321-44.

6975.   J. A. Cross, "The Akhmim Fragment and the Fourth Gospel," *Exp* 4th ser., 10 (1894): 320 [Jn. 18:28; 19:14].

6976.   H. B. Swete, "The Oxyrhynchus Fragment," *ET* 8 (1896-1897): 544-50.

6977.   J. A. Cross, "The Sayings of Jesus," *Exp* 5th ser., 6 (1897): 257-67.

6978.   F. H. Fisher, "The New Logia of Jesus," *ET* 9 (1897-1898): 140-43.

6979.   J. A. Robinson, (translator): "The Recently Discovered Sayings of Jesus. By Professor Adolf Harnack, Berlin (Authorized Translation)," *Exp* 5th ser., 6 (1897): 321-40, 401-16, 417-21.

6980.   W. W. Moore, "The New Sayings of Jesus," *USR* 9 (1897-1898): 38-47.

6981.   H. A. Redpath, "The So-called Logia and their Relation to the

Canonical Scriptures," *Exp* 5th ser., 6 (1897): 224-30.

6982. C. H. van Rhijn, "Nienwe 'Woorden van Jezus'?" *TS* 15 (1897): 403-13.

6983. Emil Schürer, "Logia Christi," *TLZ* 22 (1897): 373-74.

6984. J. Weiss, "Neue Logia," *TR* 1 (1897-1898): 227-36.

6985. G. Frederick Wright, "The New 'Sayings of Jesus'," *BS* 54 (1897): 759-70.

6986. E. A. Abbott, "The Logia of Behnesa; or, the New 'Sayings of Jesus'," *AJT* 2 (1898): 1-27.

6987. A. B. Bruce, "Disciple-Logia," *Exp* 5th ser., 8 (1898): 1-16.

6988. G. Heinrici, "Notiz zu den Λόγια ᾿Ιησοῦ," *TLZ* 23 (1898): 229.

6989. H. Trabaud, "Les nouvelles paroles de Jésus," 31 (1898): 74-84.

6990. Th. Zahn, "Recently Discovered 'Logia of Jesus'," *LCR* 17 (1898): 168-83.

6991. James H. Ropes, "Resch's Logia," *AJT* 3 (1899): 695-98

6992. A. von Scholz, "Zu den Logia Jesu," *TQ* 82 (1900): 1-22.

6993. H. O. Lange, "Det sidste Papyrusfund: Et nyt Evangelien," *TTDF* N.S. 2 (1900-1901): 146-51.

6994. Pierre Batiffol, "Nouveaux fragments évangéliques de Behnesa," *RB* 13 (1904): 481-93.

6995. A. Hilgenfeld, "Neue Logia Jesu," *ZWT* 47 (1904): 414-18.

6996. A. Hilgenfeld, "Neue gnostische Logia Jesu," *ZWT* 47 (1904): 567-73.

6997. Clyde W. Votaw, "The Newly Discovered 'Sayings of Jesus' (Illustrated)," *BW* 24 (1904): 261-77.

6998. Kirsopp Lake, "The New Sayings of Jesus and the Synoptic Problem," *HJ* 3 (1904-1905): 332-41.

6999. A. Hilgenfeld, "Die neuesten Logia-Funde von Oxyrhynchus," *ZWT* 48 (1905): 343-53.

7000. J. Sickenberger, "Neuentdeckte Herrnworte," *BibZ* 3 (1905): 176.

7001. J. Sickenberger, "Fragment eines verlorenen Evangeliums," *BibZ* 3 (1905): 179.

7002. C. Taylor, "The Oxyrhynchus and other Agrapha," *JTS* 7 (1905-1906): 546-62.

7003.   Clyde W. Votaw, "The Oxyrhynchus Sayings of Jesus in Relation to the Gospel-making Movement of the First and Second Centuries," *JBL* 24 (1905): 79-90.

7004.   W. P. Workman, "Sayings of Jesus: A New Suggestion," *ET* 17 (1905-1906): 191.

7005.   W. H. van de Sande Bakhuyzen, "Het Evangeliefragment van Fayoem," *TT* 40 (1906): 155-57.

7006.   A. Hilgenfeld, "Noch einmal die neuesten Logia-Funde," *ZWT* 49 (1906): 270-73.

7007.   A. Büchler, "The New Fragment of an Uncanonical Gospel," *JQR* 20 (1907-1908): 330-46.

7008.   Ludwig Blau, "Das neue Evangelienfragment von Oxyrhynchos buch- und zaubergeschichtlich betrachtet, nebst sonstigen Bemerkungen," *ZNW* 9 (1908): 204-15.

7009.   J. Dräseke, "Zum neuen Evangelienbruchstück von Oxyrhynchos," *ZWT* 50 (1908): 485-89.

7010.   M.-J. Lagrange, "Nouveau fragment non-canonique relatif à l'évangile," *RB* 17 (1908): 538-53.

7011.   Erwin Preuschen, "Das neue Evangelien fragment von Oxyrhynchos," *ZNW* 9 (1908): 1-11.

7012.   Th. Zahn, "Neue Bruchstücke nichtkanonischer Evangelien," *NKZ* 19 (1908): 371-86.

7013.   George Milligan, "The Greek Papyri and the New Testament," *BW* 34 (1909): 151-58, 232-38.

7014.   Hugh G. Evelyn-White, "The Introduction to the Oxyrhynchus Sayings," *JTS* 13 (1911-1912): 74-76.

7015.   Hugh G. Evelyn-White, "The Fourth Oxyrhynchus Saying," *JTS* 14 (1912-1913): 400-403.

7016.   Hugh G. Evelyn-White, "The Second Oxyrhynchus Saying," *JTS* 16 (1914-1915): 246-50.

7017.   Edgar J. Goodspeed, "Recent Discoveries in Early Christian Literature," *BW* 46 (1915): 339-48.

7018.   James Moffatt, "Uncanonical Gospel-Fragments," *ET* 27 (1915-1916): 424.

7019.   M.-J. Lagrange, "Une des paroles attribuées à Jesus," *RB* 30 (1921): 233-37.

7020.   W. Schubart, "Das zweite Logion Oxyrhynchos Pap. IV 654," *ZNW* 20 (1921): 215-23.

7021. E. Riggenbach, "Das Wort Jesu im Gespräch mit dem pharisäischen Hohenpriester nach dem Oxyrhynchus Fragment V nr. 840," *ZNW* 25 (1926): 140-44.

7022. Roderic Dunkerley, "The Oxyrhynchus Gospel Fragments," *HTR* 23 (1930): 19-38.

7023. M.-J. Lagrange, "La seconde parole d'Oxyrhynque," *RB* 31 (1922): 427-33.

7024. L. Cerfaux, "Un nouvel évangile apocryphe," *ETL* 12 (1935): 579-81.

7025. B. A. van Groningen, "Fragmenten van een nienw evangelie," *NTS* 18 (1935) 210-14, 280.

7026. E. R. Smothers, "Un nouvel évangile du deuxième siècle," *RSR* 25 (1935): 358-62 [Pap. Egerton 2].

7027. H. Idris Bell, "Noch einmal: Ein bisher unbekanntes Evangelienfragment," *TB* 15 (1936): 72-74.

7028. L. Cerfaux, "Parallèles canoniques et extra-canoniques de 'l'évangile inconnu',"*Mu* 49 (1936): 55-77 [Pap. Egerton 2].

7029. C. H. Dodd, "A New Gospel," *BJRL* 20 (1936): 56-92.

7030. C. H. Roberts, "A Fragment of an Uncanonical Gospel," *JTS* 47 (1946): 56-57.

7031. Leon E. Wright, "The Oxyrhynchus Sayings of Jesus," *JBL* 65 (1946): 175-83.

7032. Joseph A. Fitzmyer, "The Oxyrhynchus *Logoi* of Jesus and the Coptic Gospel according to Thomas," *ThSt* 20 (1959): 505-60.

7033. Gérard Garitte, "Les 'Logoi' d'Oxyrhynque et l'apocryphe copte dit 'Évangile de Thomas',"*Mu* 73 (1960): 151-72.

7034. Gérard Garitte, "Les 'Logoi' d'Oxyrhynque sont traduits du copte,"*Mu* 73 (1960): 335-49.

7035. Antoine Guillaumont, "Les *Logia* d'Oxyrhynchos sont-ils traduits du copte?"*Mu* 73 (1960): 325-33.

7036. A. F. Walls, " 'Stone' and 'Wood' in Oxyrhynchus Papyrus 1," *VCh* 16 (1962): 71-76.

See also numbers 1885, *10036*.

7036.1 Andreas Schmidt, "Der mögliche Text von P. Oxy. III 405, Z 39-45," *NTSt* 37 (1991): 160.

2. Apocryphal Acts (with Gospel References)

7037.   H. Lietz, "Der gnostisch-christliche Charakter der apokryphen Apostel-Geschichten und -Legenden," *ZWT* 37 (1894): 34-57.

7038.   A. Hilgenfeld, "Das Johannes-Bild des Lykomedes," *ZWT* 42 (1899): 624-27 [Ac. Jn.].

7039.   A. Hilgenfeld, "Der gnostische und der kanonische Johannes über das Leben Jesu," *ZWT* 43 (1900): 1-61.

7040.   R. H. Connolly, "The Original Language of the Syriac Acts of John," *JTS* 8 (1906-1907): 249-61.

7041.   J. Flamion, "Les actes apocryphes de Pierre," *RHE* 9 (1908): 233-54, 465-80; 10 (1909): 5-29, [Doctrine] 245-77; [Histoire littéeraire] 11 (1910): 5-28, 223-56, 447-70, 675-92; 12 (1911): 209-30, 437-50.

7042.   Stephen Gaselee, "A Bohairic Fragment of the 'Martyrdom of St. Luke'," *JTS* 10 (1908-1909): 52-53.

7043.   J. S. MacArthur, "The Words of the 'Hymn of Jesus'," *ET* 36 (1924-1925): 136-38 [Acts of John, 94-96].

7044.   Primo Vannutelli, "Actorum Pilati textus synoptici," *S* 2 (1937): 1-180.

7045.   G. Quispel, "An Unknown Fragment of the Acts of Andrew," *VCh* 10 (1956): 129-48.

7046.   A. F. J. Klijn, "The So-Called Hymn of the Pearl (Acts of Thomas Ch. 108-113)," *VCh* 14 (1960): 154-64.

7046.1   Heinz-Wolfgang Kuhn, "Jesus als Gekreuzigter in der frühchristlichen Verkündigung bis zur Mitte des 2 Jahrhunderts," *ZTK* 72 (1975): 1-46.

7046.2   Heinz Kruse, "Das Brautlied der syrischen Thomas-Akten," *OCP* 50 (1984): 291-330.

7046.3   J. K. Elliott, "The Apocryphal Acts," *ET* 105 (1993): 71-77.

3. Apocryphal Epistles (Abgar; Epistle of the Apostles; etc.)

7047.   Ernst von Dobschütz, "Der Briefwechsel zwischen Abgar und Jesus," *ZWT* 43 (1900): 422-86.

7048.   J. P. Arendzen, "Syriac Text of the Apocalyptic Part of the 'Testament of the Lord'," *JTS* 2 (1900-1901): 401-16.

7049.   Anton Baumstark, "Ueberlieferung und Bezeugung der διαθήκη τοῦ κυρίου ἡμῶν 'Ιησοῦ χριστοῦ," *RQ* 14 (1900): 1-45.

7050.   Anton Baumstark, "Die arabischen Texte der διαθήκη τοῦ κυρίου," *RQ* 14 (1900): 291-300.

7051.   Pierre Batiffol, "Le soi-disant Testament de N.-S. Jésus. Christ," *BLE* [2] (1900): 51-57.

7052.   S. D. Dib, "Les versions arabes du 'Testamentum Domini, Nostri Jesu Christi," *ROC* 10 (1905): 418-23.

7053.   S. Dib, "Note sur deux ouvrages apocryphes arabes intitulés 'Testament de Notre Seigneur'," *ROC* 11 (1906): 427-30.

7054.   L. Guerrier, "Un 'Testament (éthiopien) de Notre Seigneur et Sauveur Jésus Christ' en Galilée," *ROC* 12 (1907): 1-8.

7055.   M. R. James, "The 'Epistola Apostolorum' in a New Text," *JTS* 12 (1910-1911): 55-56.

7056.   Anton Baumstark, "Hippolytos und die ausserkanonische Evangelienquelle des äthiopischen Galiläa-Testaments," *ZNW* 15 (1914): 332-35.

7057.   L. Melikset-Bekov, "Семипечатіе и еро толкованіе, ныія къ отвѣту Спасителя на посланіе Абгара Эдесскаро, въ редакціяхъ грузинской и армянской," *KhV* 3 (1915): 44-50.

7058.   Justin Boson, "La légende de Jésus Christ et du roi de Tyr," *ROC* 21 (1918-1919): 225-40.

7059.   S. Grébaut, "Les relations entre Abgar et Jésus, texte éthiopien," *ROC* 21 (1918-1919): 73-87, 190-203, 253-55.

7060.   J. Ziadé, "Un testament de N.-S. concernant les invasions des Mongols," *ROC* 21 (1918-1919): 261-73, 433-44.

7061.   Th. Schneider, "Das prophetische 'Agraphon' der Epistola apostolorum," *ZNW* 24 (1925): 151-54.

7062.   Gustav Klameth, "Über die Herkunft der Apocryphen Geschichte Josephs des Zimmermanns," *A* 3 (1928): 2-31.

7063.   L. Gry, "La date de la parousie l'après l'epistula apostolorum," *RB* 49 (1940): 86-97.

See also number 1885.

C. AGRAPHA

7064.   A. D. Loman, "De jongste uitgave der Agrapha (Alfred Resch, Aussercanonische Evangelienfragmente)," *TT* 23 (1889): 582-625.

7065.   D. S. Margoliouth, "Christ in Islam; Sayings Attributed to

Christ by Mohammedan Writers," *ET* 5 (1893-1894): 59-107, 177-78, 503-504, 561.

7066.   W. Lock, "Agrapha," *Exp* 4th ser., 9 (1894): 1-16, 97-109.

7067.   J.-P. van Kasteren, " 'Christum in cubile,' contribution à l'etude des Agrapha," *RB* 4 (1895): 65-66.

7068.   James H. Ropes, "The So-called Agrapha," *AJT* 1 (1897): 758-76.

7069.   Th. Zahn, "Neue Funde aus der alten Kirche," *NKZ* 16 (1905): 94-101, 165-78, 249-61, 415-27.

7070.   D. S. Margoliouth, "A Saying Attributed to Christ," *ET* 18 (1906-1907): 140 [Moslem *Bk. on Animals*, 3: 113; cf. Mt. 26:26-29].

7071.   Adolf Jacoby, "Agrapha," *ZNW* 13 (1912): 163-64.

7072.   E. Jacquier, "Les sentences du Seigneur extracanoniques (Les Agrapha)," *RB* 27 (1918): 93-135.

7073.   Roderic Dunkerley, "Jesus on Tabor," *ET* 36 (1924-1925): 523-25.

7074.   Sten Bugge, "Ord av Jesus fra kilder utenfor de kanoniske evangelier," *TTK* 4 (1933): 121-46.

7075.   Sten Bugge, " 'Verden er en bro.' Jesus-ord hos Al-Ghazali," *TTK* 4 (1933): 218-24.

7076.   Sherman E. Johnson, "Stray Pieces of Christian Writing," *JNES* 5 (1946): 40-54.

7077.   P. Andriessen, "À propos d'un agraphon cité par Hippolyte," *VCh* 2 (1948): 248-49.

7078.   Olaf Moe, "Ukjente ord av Jesus ('Agrapha')," *TTK* 22 (1951): 91-93.

7079.   Joachim Jeremias, "Unbekannte Jesusworte," *RHPR* 33 (1953): 77-79.

7080.   Joachim Jeremias, "The Saying of Jesus about the Bridge," *ET* 69 (1957): 7-9.

7081.   Helmut Köster, "Die ausserkanonischen Herrenworte," *ZNW* 48 (1957): 220-37.

7082.   R. McL. Wilson, "Further 'Unknown Sayings of Jesus'," *ET* 69 (1958): 182.

7083.   J. B. Bauer, "Das Jesuswort 'Wer mir nahe ist'," *TZ* 15 (1959): 446-50.

7083.1   William L. Lane, "Critique of Purportedly Authentic

Agrapha," *JETS* 18 (1975): 29-35.

D. THE EARLY CHURCH FATHERS

7084.   H. Holtzmann, "Barnabas und Johannes," *ZWT* 14 (1871): 336-51.

7085.   H. Holtzmann, "Hermes und Johannes," *ZWT* 18 (1875): 40-51.

7086.   P. Corssen, "Zur lateinischen Didascalia apostolorum," *ZNW* 1 (1900): 339-43 [reference to the Passion story of John].

7087.   Hugo Koch, "Zu Didache und Johannes-Evangelium," *BibZ* 4 (1906): 408.

7088.   C. Taylor, "Traces of a Saying of the Didache," *JTS* 8 (1906-1907): 115-17.

7089.   F. Nau, "Une didascalie de Notre Seigneur Jésus Christ (ou: Constitutions des Saints Apôtres)," *ROC* 12 (1907): 225-54.

7090.   Andreas ab Alpe, "Christologia in Psalmis Salomonis," *VD* 11 (1931): 56-59, 84-88, 110-20.

7091.   E. R. Buckley, "Justin Martyr's Quotations from the Synoptic Tradition," *JTS* 36 (1935): 173-76.

7092.   E. Massaux, "L'influence littéraire de l'évangile de saint Matthieu sur la Didachè," *ETL* 25 (1949): 5-41.

7093.   Louis Mariès, "Le Messie issu de Lévi chez Hippolyte de Rome," *RSR* 39 (1951-1952): 381-96.

7094.   F.-M. Braun, "La 'lettre de Barnabé et l'évangile de saint Jean," *NTSt* 4 (1957-1958): 119-24.

7095.   Richard Glover, "The *Didache*'s Quotations and the Synoptic Gospels," *NTSt* 5 (1958-1959): 12-29.

7095.1   C. P. Hammond, "Some Textual Points in Origen's Commentary on Matthew" *JTS* 24/2 (1973): 380-404.

7095.2   Eric F. Osborn, "Origen and Justification: The Good Is One," *ABR* 24/1 (1976): 18-29.

7095.3   B. De Margerie, " 'Hoc Facite in Meam Commemorationem': Les Exegeses des Peres Pre-Chalcedoniens (150-451)," *Div* 28 (1984): 137-49.

7095.4   Hermann Vogt, "Die Witwe als Bild der Seele in der Exegese des Origenes," *TQ* 165/2 (1985): 105-18.

7095.5   Ronald E. Heine, "Can the Catena Fragments of Origen's Commentary on John Be Trusted?" *VCh* 40/2 (1986): 118-34.

7095.6   H. B. Green, "Matthew, Clement and Luke: Their Sequence and Relationship," *JTS* 40/1 (1989): 1-25.

7095.7   Philippe Henne, "Pourquoi le Christ fut-il baptisé? La réponse de Justin," *RSPT* 77 (1993): 567-83.

E. JOSEPHUS AND THE GOSPEL TRADITION

7096.   H. Holtzmann, "Lucas und Josephus," *ZWT* 16 (1873): 85-93.

7097.   Max Krenkel, "Ein Nachtrag zu dem Aufsatze: Josephus und Lucas," *ZWT* 16 (1873): 441-44.

7098.   E. Schürer, "Lucas und Josephus," *ZWT* 19 (1876): 574-82.

7099.   H. Holtzmann, "Noch einmal Lucas und Josephus," *ZWT* 20 (1877): 535-49.

7100.   C. F. Nösgen, "Über 'Lukas und Josephus'," *TSK* 52 (1879): 521-40.

7101.   J. H. Scholten, "Flavius Josephus en Jezus," *TT* 16 (1882): 428-51.-

7102.   J. A. M. Mensinga, "Het getuigenis van Flavius Josephus over Jezus," *TT* 17 (1883): 145-52.

7103.   J. E. Belser, "Lukas und Josephus," *TQ* 77 (1895): 634-62; 78 (1896): 1-78.

7104.   H. W. Magoun, "The Testimony of Josephus Concerning Jesus," *BS* 69 (1912): 288-309.

7105.   F. C. Burkitt, "Josephus and Christ," *TT* 47 (1913): 135-44.

7106.   P. Corssen, "Die Zeugnisse des Tacitus und Pseudo-Josephus über Christus," *ZNW* 15 (1914): 114-40.

7107.   Bernhard Pick, "John the Baptist and Christ in the Slavic Translation of Josephus' *Jewish War*," *BW* 43 (1914): 172-77.

7108.   Hermann Dieckmann, "Die Zeugnisse über Christus in der altslavischen Übersetzung des Flavius Josephus," *ZKT* 50 (1926): 463-75.

7109.   Clyde Pharr, "The Testimony of Josephus to Christianity," *AJP* 48 (1927): 137-47.

7110.   P. Otzen, "Josefos' Bemaerkninger om Urkristendommen," *TTDF* 4th ser., 9 (1928): 273-317.

7111.   C. A. Kneller, "Zum Christuszeugnis bei Josephus," *ZKT* 52

(1928): 531-32.

7112. S. Zeitlin, "The Christ Passage in Josephus," *JQR* 18 (1928): 231-55.

7113. S. Zeitlin, "The Slavonic Josephus," *JQR* 19 (1929): 1-50.

7114. M.-J. Lagrange, "Jean-Baptiste et Jésus d'après le texte slave," *RB* 39 (1930): 29-46.

7115. Robert Eisler, "Flavius Josephus on Jesus called the Christ," *JQR* 21 (1930-1931): 1-60.

7116. F.-M. Braun, "La description de l'aspect physique de Jésus par Josephe," *RB* 40 (1931): 345-63, 519-43.

7117. S. Zeitlin, "Josephus on Jesus," *JQR* 21 (1931): 377-417.

7118. S. Vernon McCasland, "Portents in Josephus and in the Gospels," *JBL* 51 (1932): 323-35.

7119. P. E. Kretzmann, "The So-Called 'Christian Interpolations' in Josephus," *CTM* 4 (1933): 274-81.

7120. Franz Dornseiff, "Lukas der Schriftsteller, mit einem Anhang: Josephus und Tacitus," *ZNW* 35 (1936): 129-55.

7121. H. W. Kars, "Der älteste nichtchristliche Jesusbericht," *TSK* 108 (1937-1938): 40-64 [Josephus].

7122. Manuel Tarrés, "Flavio Josefo y su testimonio sobre Jesús de Nazaret," *CB* 3 (1946): 314-16.

7123. J. Spencer Kennard, "Gleanings from the Slavonic Josephus Controversy," *JQR* 39 (1948-1949): 161-70, 281.

7124. S. Zeitlin, "The Hoax of the 'Slavonic Josephus'," *JQR* 39 (1948-1949): 171-80.

7125. Franz Dornseiff, "Zum Testimonium Flavianum," *ZNW* 46 (1955): 245-50.

7126. B. Leeming, "Verbal Descriptions of Christ," *ITQ* 22 (1955): 293-312.

7127. José Múnera, "Eco insigne del Judaismo," *EE* 33 (1959): 441-46.

7128. H. W. Montefiore, "Josephus and the New Testament," *NT* 4 (1960): 139-60.

See also numbers 387, *10035*.

7128.1 Louis H. Feldman, "Origen's Contra Celsum and Josephus' Contra Apionem: The Issue of Jewish Origins," *VCh* 44 (1990): 105-35.

7128.2   Louis H. Feldman, "Pro-Jewish Intimations in Anti-Jewish Remarks Cited in Josephus' Against Apion," *JQR* 78 (1988): 187-251.

7128.3   William Horbury, "TheTtwelve and the Phylarchs," *NTSt* 32 (1986): 503-27.

7128.4   E. P. Sanders, "Judaism and the Grand 'Christian' Abstractions: Love, Mercy, and Grace," *Interp* 39 (1985): 357-72.

7128.5   Roger T. Beckwith, "The Daily and Weekly Worship of the Primitive Church in Relation to Its Jewish Antecedents," *EQ* 56 (1984): 65-80.

7128.6   Jaap Mansfeld, "Resurrection Added: The Interpretatio Christiana of a Stoic Doctrine," *VCh* 37 No 3 (1983): 218-33.

7128.7   F. Gerald Downing, "Ethical Pagan Theism and the Speeches in Acts," *NTSt* 27 (1981): 544-63.

7128.8   J. R. Busto-Saiz, "La carta de Judas a la luz de algunos escritos judíos," *EB* NS 39 (1981): 83-105.

F. VERGIL'S IV ECLOGUE; INSCRIPTIONS; ETC.

7129.   Jacques Zeiller, "L'inscription dite de Nazareth," *RSR* 21 (1931): 570-76.

7130.   David Atkinson, "The Sator-Formula and the Beginnings of Christianity," *BJRL* 22 (1938): 419-34.

7131.   Floyd V. Filson, "Were there Christians in Pompeii?" *BA* 2 (1939): 13-16 [Sator square].

7132.   Anton Fridrichsen, "Vergilius' fjärde eklog," *RelB* 3 (1944): 34-43.

7133.   Johannes Irmscher, "Zum Διάταγμα Καίσαρος von Nazareth," *ZNW* 42 (1949): 172-84.

7134.   R. P. Casey and R. W. Thomson, "A Dialogue between Christ and the Devil," *JTS* N.S. 6 (1955): 49-65.

7135.   Berndt Gustafsson, "The Oldest Graffiti in the History of the Church?" *NTSt* 3 (1956-1957): 65-69.

See also numbers 659, 5428.

7135.1   B. R. Voss, "Bemerkungen zu Euagrius von Antiochien Vergil und Sallust in der Vita Antonii," *VCh* 21 (1967): 93-102.

SECTION V

THEOLOGICAL STUDIES CONCERNING
JESUS CHRIST AND THE GOSPELS

A. STUDIES CLASSIFIED ACCORDING TO NEW TESTAMENT BOOKS
  1. Synoptic Gospels
    a. *General Studies*

7136. Anonymous, "La doctrine des synoptiques d'après Baur," *RT* 3rd ser., 3 (1865): 1-13.

7137. N. Gloubokovsky, "The Gospel and the Gospels," *ET* 13 (1900-1901): 101-104.

7138. Ernest DeW. Burton and Fred Merrifield, "The Origin and Teaching of the New Testament Books," *BW* 43 (1914): 65-72, 144-52, 209-16 [Synoptics].

7139. B. W. Bacon, "Immortality in the Synoptic Gospels," *RE* 19 (1922): 251-79.

7140. Hermann Dieckmann, "De testimoniis quibusdam disertis quae exhibent evangelia synoptica," *VD* 9 (1929): 15-22.

7141. Pfarrer Homann, "Der Begriff der Gnade in den synopti schen Evangelien," *ZST* 11 (1933-1934): 328-48.

7142. Alfred Loisy, "The Birth of the Christian Religion," *HJ* 45 (1946-1947): 289-303.

7143. Alphonse Humbert, "Essai d'une théologie du scandale dans les synoptiques," *B* 35 (1954): 1-28.

7144. Gérard Garitte, "Rufus, évêque de Šotep, et ses commentaires des évangiles," *Mu* 69 (1956): 11-33.

7145. S. MacLean Gilmour, "History and Theology in the Synoptic Gospels," *RL* 27 (1958): 567-76.

See also numbers 7538, 8674.

7145.1 A. W. H. Moule, "The Pattern of the Synoptists," *EQ* 43/3 (1971): 162-71.

7145.2 J.-N. Aletti, "Problème synoptique et théorie des permutations," *RSR* 60 (1972): 575-94.

7145.3 Dale C. Allison, "The Pauline Epistles and the Synoptic Gospels: The Pattern of the Parallels," *NTSt* 28/1 (1982): 1-32.

7145.4 J. Becker, "Johannes und die Synoptiker," *TR* 47 (1982):

289-94.

b. *Matthew*

7146. Dr. Aberle, "Ueber den Zweck des Matthäusevangeliums," *TQ* 41 (1859): 567-88; 42 (1860): 51-116, 654-81.

7147. Hermann Weiss, "Die Grundzüge der Heilslehre Jesu bei den Synoptikern, vorzüglich nach dem Evangelium Matthäi dargestellt," *TSK* 42 (1869): 59-103.

7148. Dr. Wetzel, "Praktische Auslegungen zum Matthäus-evangelium," *TLZ* 3 (1878): 425-27.

7149. Robert Kübel, "The Fundamental Thought and Purpose of the Gospel of Matthew," *BW* 1 (1893): 194-205, 263-69.

7150. C. H. Turner, "The Early Greek Commentators on the Gospel according to St. Matthew," *JTS* 12 (1910-1911): 99-112.

7151. Harold Smith, "Cramer's Catena on Matthew," *JTS* 16 (1914-15): 420.

7152. Harold Smith, "Some Catenae Fragments of Origen's Commentary on Matthew," *JTS* 17 (1915-1916): 101-103.

7153. Harold Smith, "Notes on Catenae on Matthew," *JTS* 18 (1916-1917): 317-19.

7154. M. L. W. Laistner, "A Ninth Century Commentator on the Gospel according to Matthew," *HTR* 20 (1927): 129-49.

7155. Georg Graf, "Der Matthäus-Kommentar des Moses bar Kepha in arabischer Übersetzung," *B* 21 (1940): 283-87.

7156. Germain Morin, "Les homélies latines sur s. Matthieu attribuées à Origène," *RBén* 54 (1942): 3-11.

7157. A. Herranz, "Santo Evangélio de Nuestro Señor Jesucristo según san Mateo," *CB* 1 (1944): 203-207; 2 (1945): 1-4, 65-69, 97-100, 171-73, 193-97, 225-29, 257-59, 321-23.

7158. Albert Descamps, "Le christianisme comme justice dans le premier évangile," *ETL* 22 (1946): 5-33.

7159. I. B. Pighi, "Incerti auctoris commentarius in evangelium secundum Matthaeum (P Bon 12)," *VCh* 2 (1948): 109-12.

7160. Dean G. McKee, "The Gospel according to Matthew," *Interp* 3 (1949): 194-205

7161. G. Rinaldi, "Il messianismo tra le genti in san Matteo," *RivB* 2 (1954): 318-24.

7161.1 A. W. Argyle, "M and the Pauline Epistles," *ET* 81 (1969): 340-42.

7161.2 E. L. Abel, "Who Wrote Matthew?" *NTSt* 17/2 (1971): 138-52.

7161.3 Dennis C. Duling, "The Therapeutic Son of David: An Element in Matthew's Christological Apologetic," *NTSt* 24 (1978): 392-410.

c. Mark

7162. James Hastings, "A New Commentary on St. Mark," *ET* 10 (1898-1899): 137-38 [by H. B. Swete].

7163. G. Wohlenberg, "Ein vergessener lateinischer Markuskommentar," *NKZ* 18 (1907): 427-69.

7164. Frédéric Bouvier, "Le *saint Marc* du P. Lagrange," *RSR* 2 (1911): 266-86.

7165. F. C. Caldwell, "The Power of Christ," *USR* 30 (1918-1919): 50-62 [Mk.].

7166. A. T. Robertson, "The Miraculous Element in Mark's Gospel," *BW* 51 (1918): 287-92.

7167. Harold Smith, "The Sources of Victor of Antioch's Commenary on Mark," *JTS* 19 (1918): 350-70.

7168. Herbert G. Wood, "Mark's Gospel and Paulinism," *ET* 51 (1939-1940): 327-33.

7169. Paul E. Davies, "Mark's Witness to Jesus," *JBL* 73 (1954): 197-202.

7170. Samuel A. Cartledge, "The Gospel of Mark," *Interp* 9 (1955): 186-99.

7171. Morton Smith, "Comment on Taylor's Commentary on Mark," *HTR* 48 (1955): 21-64.

7172. T. A. Burkill, "St. Mark's Philosophy of History," *NTSt* 3 (1956-1957): 142-48.

7173. James M. Robinson, "Mark's Understanding of History," *SJT* 9 (1956): 393-409.

7174. R. C. Briggs, "Exposition of the Gospel of Mark," *RE* 55 (1958): 367-92.

7175. Heber F. Peacock, "The Theology of the Gospel of Mark," *RE* 55 (1958): 393-99.

See also numbers 337, 8687.

7175.1 H. G. Leder, "Sündenfallerzählung und Versuchungsgeschichte: zur Interpretation von Mc 1:12f," *ZNW* 54 (1963): 188-216.

7175.2 John R. Donahue, "A Neglected Factor in the Theology of Mark," *JBL* 101 (1982): 563-94.

7175.3 Donald Senior, "The Struggle To Be Universal: Mission as Vantage Point for New Testament Investigation," *CBQ* 46 (1984): 63-81.

7175.4 Ole Davidsen, "Narrativitet og eksistens: et religionssemiotisk bidrag til bestemmelsen af den narrative Jesus i Markusevangeliet," *DTT* 49 (1986): 241-67.

7175.5 W. E. Moore, "Outside and 'Inside': A Markan Motif," *ET* 98 (1986): 39-43.

7175.6 Eugene E. Lemcio, "The Intention of the Evangelist, Mark," *NTSt* 32 (1986): 187-206.

7175.7 Dorothy A. Lee-Pollard, "Powerlessness as Power: A Key Emphasis in the Gospel of Mark," *SJT* 40 (1987): 173-88.

7175.8 Antonio Rodríguez-Carmona, "La iglesia en Marcos," *EE* 63 (1988): 129-63.

7175.9 Reinold Schmücker, "Zur Funktion der Wundergeschichten im Markusevangelium," *ZNW* 84 (1993): 1-26.

d. Luke

7176. J. Jungst, "Hat das Lukasevangelium paulinischen Charakter?" *TSK* 69 (1896): 215-44 [Yes].

7177. H. A. Redpath, "St. Luke in the International Critical Commentary," *ET* 8 (1896-1897): 218-21.

7178. Th. Zahn, "Die Predigten des Origenes über das Evangelium des Lukas," *NKZ* 22 (1911): 253-68.

7179. D. A. Frøvig, "Fra den nyere evangelieforskning. L. Bruns og Fr. Haucks kommentarer til Lukas-evangeliet," *TTK* 6 (1945): 163-68.

7180. James L. Price, "The Gospel according to Luke," *Interp* 7 (1953): 195-212.

7181. Eduard Lohse, "Lukas als Theologe der Heilsgeschichte," *EvT* 14 (1954): 256-75.

7182. J. Comblin, "La paix dans la théologie de saint Luc," *ETL* 32 (1956): 439-60.

7183. J. S. Javet, "L'évangile de la grâce," *RHPR* 18 (1958): 293-94 [Lk.].

7184. Robert Smith, "History and Eschatology in Luke-Acts," *CTM* 29 (1958): 881-901.

7185. Henri-Charles Puech et Pierre Hadot, "L'entretien d'Origène avec Héraclide et le commentaire de Saint Ambroise sur l'évangile de Saint Luc," *VCh* 13 (1959): 204-34.

7186. J. Mánek, "The Biblical Concept of Time and our Gospels," *NTSt* 6 (1959-1960): 45-51.

7187. Hans Conzelmann, "Geschichte, Geschichtsbild und Geschichtsdarstellung bei Lukas," *TLZ* 85 (1960): 241-50. See also numbers 3466, 8644.

7187.1 A. W. Argyle, "Evidence for the View that St. Luke Used St. Matthew's Gospel," *JBL* 83/4 (1964): 390-96.

2. The Johannine Literature

a. *The Fourth Gospel*

7188. Prof. Kling, "Bemerkungen über einzelne Stellen des Evang. Johannis, mit vorzüglicher Rücksicht auf den Commentar von Lücke 2. Ausg.," *TSK* 9 (1836): 125-60, 661-93.

7189. Wilibald Grimm, "Ueber den ersten Brief des Johannes und sein Verhältnis zum vierten Evangelium," *TSK* 22 (1849): 269-303.

7190. A. Hilgenfeld, "Die johanneische Theologie und ihre nueste Bearbeitung," *ZWT* 6 (1863): 96-116, 214-28.

7191. A. Hilgenfeld, "Hr. D. Riggenbach und das Johannes Evangelium," *ZWT* 10 (1867): 179-98.

7192. S. Hoekstra, "Oorsprong der verwantschap van den eersten brief van Johannes met het vierde Evangelie," *TT* 1 (1867): 137-88.

7193. Albrecht Thoma, "Justine literarisches Verhältnis zu Paulus und zum Johannes-Evangelium," *ZWT* 18 (1875): 383-412, 490-566.

7194. W. Milligan, "Double Pictures in the Fourth Gospel and the Apocalypse," *Exp* 2nd ser., 4 (1882): 264-78, 368-79, 430-47.

7195. W. Hönig, "Beiträge zur Aufklarung über das vierte Evangelium," *ZWT* 26 (1883): 216-34; 27 (1884): 85-125.

7196. J. B. Thompson, "The Theology of St. John," *JCP* 3 (1883-1884): 158-72.

7197. A. Hilgenfeld, "Neuer und alter Zweikampf wegen der Johannes-Schriften," *ZWT* 32 (1889): 330-48.

7198. H. Holtzmann, "Hugo Delff und das vierte Evangelium," *ZWT* 36 (1893): 503-507.

7199. C. G. Montefiore, "Fourth Gospel, Notes on its Religious Value," *JQR* 7 (1894-1895): 25-74.

7200. M. Dods, "The Teaching of Christ in the Gospel of John," *BW* 6 (1895): 467-75.

7201. A. B. Bruce, "Four Types of Christian Thought; IV. The Fourth Gospel," *BW* 7 (1896): 168-79.

7202. J. A. Cross, "The Theology of the Fourth Gospel," *Exp* 5th ser., 3 (1896): 151-52.

7203. J. Dräseke, "Das Johannesevangelium bei Celsus," *NKZ* 9 (1898): 139-55.

7204. J. Dräseke, "Johanneische Bedenken," *NKZ* 9 (1898): 579-604.

7205. James Moffatt, "The Autonomy of Jesus: A Study in the Fourth Gospel," *Exp* 6th ser., 3 (1901): 466-72; 4 (1901): 59-69, 122-39, 221-40.

7206. J. A. Cross, "The Argument of Wendt's 'Gospel according to St. John'," *ET* 14 (1902-1903): 331-33.

7207. G. G. Findlay, "The Theology of St. John," *ET* 15 (1903-1904): 501-508; 16 (1904-1905): 72-80, 324-32.

7208. Paul Dietze, "Die Briefe des Ignatus und das Johannesevangelium," *TSK* 78 (1905): 563-603.

7209. Parke P. Flourney, "A Unitarian on the Fourth Gospel," *BS* 62 (1905): 747-65.

7210. Paul Moore Strayer, "The Self-Revelation of Christ, with Special Reference to the Fourth Gospel," *BW* 27 (1906): 327-34.

7211. Carl Clemen, "Does the Fourth Gospel Depend upon Pagan Tradition?" *AJT* 12 (1908): 529-46 [No].

7212. Paul Ewald, "Die 'subjektive Form' der johanneischen Christusreden," *NKZ* 19 (1908): 824-53.

7213. W. Soltau, "Der eigenartige dogmatische Standpunkt der Johannesreden und seine Erklärung," *ZWT* 52 (1910): 341-58.

7214. Shailer Mathews, "The Struggle between the Natural and the Spiritual Order as Described in the Gospel of John," *BW* 42 (1913): 30-34, 76-79, 146-48, 368-79.

7215. Ernest DeW. Burton and Fred Merrifield, "The Origin and Teaching of the New Testament Books; x. Gospel and Epistles of John," *BW* 43 (1914): 419-26.

7216. Julius Graf, "Johannesevangelium und Geistesleben der Gegenwart," *TQ* 97 (1915): 42-70.

7217. W. Soltau, "Die Verwantschaft zwischen Evangelium Johannis und dem I. Johannesbrief," *TSK* 89 (1916): 228-33.

7218. Joseph Elkanah Walker, "The Ruling Ideas of the Fourth Gospel," *BS* 73 (1916): 581-92.

7219. H. A. A. Kennedy, "Irenaeus and the Fourth Gospel," *ET* 29 (1917-1918): 103-107, 168-72, 235-38, 312-14.

7220. Harry C. York, "A Note on the Interpretation of the Fourth Gospel," *JBL* 37 (1918): 100-104.

7221. Gustave Bardy, "Cérinthe," *RB* 30 (1921): 344-73.

7222. George H. Gilbert, "From John Mark to John the Theologian: The First Great Departure from Primitive Christianity," *HTR* 16 (1923): 235-58.

7223. James Jones, "Dr. Garvie's Book on the Fourth Gospel," *ET* 35 (1923-1924): 45.

7224. J.-M. Vosté, "Le commentaire de Théodore de Mopsueste sur saint Jean, d'après la version syriaque," *RB* 32 (1923): 522-48.

7225. Wilfrid Richmond, "The Gospel of Life: A Study of the Fourth Gospel," *Th* 8 (1924): 242-46, 307-16; 9 (1924): 62-66, 183-88, 302-305; 10 (1925): 68-71, 186-95.

7226. B. W. Bacon, "The New Testament Method of Differences," *HJ* 23 (1924-1925): 436-53.

7227. Jean Olivieri, "La conception qui domine le quatrième évangile," *RB* 35 (1926): 382-95.

7228. Xavier Ducros, "La traduction syriaque du commentaire de Théodore de Mopsueste sur l'évangile selon saint Jean," *BLE* 28 (1927): 145-59, 210-30.

7229. Hans Windisch, "Die Absolutheit des Johannes-evangeliums," *ZST* 5 (1927-1928): 3-54.

7230. Pierre Rousselot, "La grâce, d'après saint Jean et d'après saint Paul," *RSR* 18 (1928): 87-104.

7231. Ruth J. Dean, "An Early Fragment of a Manuscript of St. Augustine's Sermons on the Gospel according to St. John," *JTS* 36 (1935): 113-22.

7232. Herbert Preisker, "Das Evangelium des Johannes als erster Teil eines apokalyptischen Doppelwerkes," *TB* 15 (1936): 185-92.

7233. Walther von Loewenich, "Johanneisches Denken. Ein Beitrag zur Erkenntnis der johanneischen Eigenart," *TB* 15 (1936): 260-75.

7234. F. Büchsel, "Die Stelle des Johannesevangeliums in einer Theologie des Neuen Testaments," *TB* 16 (1937): 301-306.

7235. Rudolf Bultmann, "Hirschs Auslegung des Johannes-evangeliums," *EvT* 4 (1937): 115-42.

7236. C. H. Dodd, "The Epistle of John and the Fourth Gospel," *BJRL* 21 (1937): 129-56.

7237. Olaf Moe, "Johannes-evangeliet i lys av nyere forskning," *TTK* 8 (1937): 1-13.

7238. Jo. Cap. Bott, "De notione lucis in scriptis S. Iohannis," *VD* 19 (1939): 81-90, 117-22.

7239. L. J. Koch, "Professor Moes Johanneskommentar," *TTK* 10 (1939): 29-40.

7240. J. L. Koole, "Diorama Johanneum," *GTT* 42 (1941): [λόγος] 318-28, [σάρξ] 337-44, [ὁ υἱὸς τοῦ ἀνθρώπου] 410-19, [ὁ υἱὸς τοῦ θεοῦ] 458-69; 43 (1942): [πνεῦμα] 93-105, [ζωή] 276-84, [φῶς] 404-409; 46 (1946): [ἀγαπᾶν, κρίνειν, δοξάζειν. . .] 45-68.

7241. Martin Dibelius, "Ein neuer Kommentar zum Johannes-evangelium," *TLZ* 67 (1942): 257-64.

7242. Robert M. Grant, "The Fourth Gospel and the Church," *HTR* 35 (1942): 95-116

7243. Johannes Munck, "Bultmanns Kommentar til Johannes-evangeliet," *DTT* 5 (1942): 15-29.

7244. Philip Howard Wichern, "The Significance of the Fourth Gospel," *BS* 99 (1942): 231-34.

7245. Mary E. Andrews, "The Super-Historical Gospel: F. C. Baur's Criticism of the Gospel of John," *ATR* 26 (1944): 212-24.

7246. Benjamin Lotz, "The Gospel of St. John and the New Dogmatics," *LCQ* 17 (1944): 28-47.

7247. G. R. Beasley-Murray, "The Relation of the Fourth Gospel to the Apocalypse," *EQ* 18 (1946): 173-86.

7248. José Trepat, "San Juan: Idéas caracteristicas," *CB* 3 (1946):

145-48, 305-307; 4 (1947): 39-40, 263-64, 355-56.

7249. J. P. Weisengoff, "Light and its Relation to Life in St. John," *CBQ* 8 (1946): 448-51.

7250. Edwin Lewis, "Philosophy and the Fourth Gospel," *RE* 44 (1947): 271-84, 430-43; 45 (1948): 18-34.

7251. Geoffrey Styler, "The Place of the Passion in Johannine Theology," *ATR* 29 (1947): 232-37.

7252. M.-E. Boismard, "Clément de Rome et l'évangile de Jean," *RB* 55 (1948): 376-87.

7253. H. Ludin Jansen, "Typologien i Johannes-evangeliet," *NTT* 49 (1948): 144-90.

7254. R. J. Drummond, "The Johannine Writings: An Old Man's Speculations," *EQ* 21 (1949): 219-40.

7255. Charles B. Hedrick, "The Christianity of the Fourth Gospel," *ATR* 33 (1951): 209-19

7256. Paul F. Barackman, "The Gospel According to John," *Interp* 6 (1952): 63-78.

7257. A. Vergote, "L'exaltation du Christ en croix selon le quatrième évangile," *ETL* 28 (1952): 5-23.

7258. William Turner, "Believing and Everlasting Life-A Johannine Inquiry," *ET* 64 (1952-1953): 50-52.

7259. C. K. Barrett, "Zweck des 4. Evangeliums," *ZST* 22 (1953): 257-73.

7260. H. van den Bussche, "L'attente de la grande révélation dans le quatrième évangile," *NRT* 75 (1953). 1009-19.

7261. M. Meinertz, "Die 'Nacht' im Johannesevangelium," *TQ* 133 (1953): 400-407.

7262. D. E. Nineham, "Interpreting the Fourth Gospel," *Th* 56 (1953): 402-407.

7263. Taylor C. Smith, "The Secondary Purpose of the Fourth Gospel," *RE* 50 (1953): 67-86.

7264. Eduard Schweizer, "Orthodox Proclamation; The Reinterpretation of the Gospel by the Fourth Evangelist," *Interp* 8 (1954): 387-403.

7265. Godfrey Tietze, "Knowledge of God in the Fourth Gospel," *JBR* 22 (1954): 14-19.

7266. Paul Winter, "Zum Verständnis des Johannes- Evangeliums," *VT* 25 (1954): 149-59.

7267.   Rudolf Bultmann, "The Interpretation of the Fourth Gospel," *NTSt* 1 (1954-1955): 77-91.

7268.   E. L. Allen, "The Jewish Christian Church in the Fourth Gospel," *JBL* 74 (1955): 88-92.

7269.   J. Atkinson, "Einschätzung der theologischen Bedeutung des Johannesevangeliums durch Luther," *ZST* 24 (1955): 401-11.

7270.   Paul Winter, "Zum Verständnis des Johannes- Evangeliums," *TLZ* 80 (1955): 141-50.

7271.   Wilhelm Dehler, "Typen oder allegorische Figuren im Johannesevangelium?" *EvT* 16 (1956): 422-27.

7272.   Théo Preiss, "Die Rechtfertigung im johanneischen Denken," *EvT* 16 (1956): 289-310.

7273.   Helmut Köster, "Geschichte und Kultus im Johannesevangelium und bei Ignatius von Antiochien," *ZTK* N.F. 54 (1957): 56-69.

7274.   Alv Kragerud, "Jesu äpenbaring av de jordiske og de himmelske ting," *NTT* 58 (1957): 17-53.

7275.   Stephen S. Smalley, "Liturgy and Sacrament in the Fourth Gospel," *EQ* 29 (1957): 159-70.

7276.   Raymond T. Stamm, "The Preacher, the Scholar, and the Gospel of John; The Interpretation of the Gospel of John and the Pulpit," *Interp* 11 (1957): 131-54.

7277.   Paul W. Harkins, "The Text Tradition of St. Chrysostom's Commentary on John," *ThSt* 19 (1958): 404-12.

7278.   C. Spicq, "Notes d'exégèse johannique: la charité est amour manifeste," *RB* 65 (1958): 358-70.

7279.   Oscar Cullmann, "L'opposition contre le temple de Jérusalem, motif commun de la théologie johannique et du monde ambient," *NTSt* 5 (1958-1959): 157-73.

7280.   John S. Romanides, "Justin Martyr and the Fourth Gospel," *GOTR* 4 (1958-1959): 115-34.

7281.   Oscar Cullmann, "A New Approach to the Interpretation of the Fourth Gospel," *ET* 71 (1959-1960): 8-12, 39-43.

7282.   Yvonne Janssens, "Héracléon. Commentaire sur l'évangile selon saint Jean," *Mu* 72 (1959): 101-51, 277-99.

7283.   George B. Caird, "The Will of God in the Fourth Gospel," *ET* 72 (1960-1961): 115-17.

7284.   Eduard Ellwein, "Die Christusverkündigung in Luthers

Auslegung des Johannesevangeliums," *KD* 6 (1960): 31-68. See also numbers 142, 370, 666, 3408, 3409, 3437, 3441-3443, 3461, 3480, 3497, 3513, 3540, 3585, 3594, 8942, 8943, *10059, 10086.*

7284.1 Rudolf Schnackenburg, "Umschau und Kritik: Zur joh. Theologie," *BibZ* 6 (1962): 289-99; 7 (1963): 297-302.

7284.2 Erich Fascher, "Christologie und Gnosis im vierten Evangelium," *TLZ* 93 (1968): 721-30.

b. *Johannine Epistles and Apocalypse*

7285. Carl Clemen, "Beiträge zum geschichtlichen Verständnis der Johannesbriefe," *ZNW* 6 (1905): 271-81.

7286. Herbert Braun, "Literar-Analyse und theologische Schichtung im ersten Johannesbrief," *ZTK* N.F. 48 (1951): 262-92.

7287. Rudolf Schnackenburg, "Die Johannesbriefe," *RHPR* 25 (1955): 245-46.

7288. Lyle O. Bristol, "That which was from the Beginning," *RE* 48 (1951): 310-14 (1 Jn. 1:1ff.].

7289. J. Willemze, "1 Jh. 2:3-6," *NTS* 2 (1919): 1-2.

7290. J. Willemze, "1 Jh. 4:1-3," *NTS* 2 (1919): 3-4.

7291. Dale Moody, "God Is Love," *RE* 47 (1950): 427-33 [1 Jn. 4:7-21].

7292. James Denney, "He that Came by Water and Blood," *Exp* 7th ser., 5 (1908): 416-28 [1 John 5:6].

7293 H U Meyboom, "Jesus en Paulus in de Apokalypse," *TT* 17 (1883): 58-80.

7294. Jasper Seaton Hughes, "The Dramatic Interpretation of the New Testament Apocalypse," *BW* 42 (1913): 154-57.

7295. H. W. Tribble, "The Christ of the Apocalypse," *RE* 40 (1943): 167-76.

7296. Johannes Munck, "Peter and Paul in the Apocalypse of St. John," *Nunt* 4 (1950): 25-26.

7297. W. Milligan, "Inter-relation of the Seven Epistles of Christ," *Exp* 2nd ser., 4 (1882): 46-63 [Rev. 2-3].

7298. Sebastián Bartina, "En su mano derecha siete asteres," *EE* 26 (1952): 71-78 [Rev. 1:16].

7299. A. Škrinjar, " 'Ego sum α et ω," (Apoc. 22. 13)," *VD* 17 (1937): 10-20.

7300.   A. Škrinjar, " 'Fui mortuus et ecce sum vivens in saecula saeculorum' (Apoc. 1, 18)," *VD* 17 (1937): 97-106.

7301.   Augustin Fabre, "L'étoile du matin dans l'apocalypse," *RB* 17 (1908): 227-40 [Rev. 2:18-28; 22:12-16].

7302.   Dunlop Moore, "The Knocking Saviour," *ET* 7 (1895- 1896): 308-309 [Rev. 3:20]

7303.   E.-B. Allo, "Le donzième chapitre de l'apocalypse," *RB* N.S. 6 (1909): 529-54.

7304.   André Feuillet, "Le Messie et sa mère d'après le chapitre XII de l'Apocalypse," *RB* 66 (1959): 55-86.

7305.   Ray Summers, "Revelation 20: An Interpretation," *RE* 57 (1960): 176-83.

    See also numbers 3408, 3409, 3461.

7305.1   K. Karner, "Gegenwart und Endgeschichte in der Offenbarung des Johannes," *TTZ* 93 (1968): 641-52.

7305.2   Otto Böcher, "Johanneisches in der Apokalypse des Johannes," *NTSt* 27 (1981): 310-21.

7305.3   J. M. Lieu, "Authority to Become Children of God: A Study of 1 John," *NT* 23 (1981): 210-28.

7305.4   Christian Wolff, "Die Gemeinde des Christus in der Apokalypse des Johannes," *NTSt* 27 (1981): 186-97.

7305.5   J. W. Fuller, "I Will Not Erase His Name from the Book of Life," *JETS* 26 (1983): 297-306.

7305.6   Gregory K. Beale, "The Influence of Daniel upon the Structure and Theology of John's Apocalypse," *JETS* 27 (1984): 413-23.

7305.7   R. L. Jeske, "Spirit and Community in the Johannine Apocalypse," *NTSt* 31 (1985): 452-66.

7305.8   Eduard Lohse, "Wie christlich ist die Offenbarung des Johannes?" *NTSt* 34 (1988): 321-38.

7305.9   D. Edmond Hiebert, "An Expositional Study of 1 John," *BS* 146 (1989): 76-93; 198-216; 301-19; 420-36.

7305.10   David M. Scholer, "1 John 4:7-21," *RE* 7 (1990): 309-14.

7305.11   M. Eugene Boring, "Narrative Christology in the Apocalypse," *CBQ* 54 (1992): 702-23.

7305.12   Jens W. Taeger, " 'Gesiegt! O himmlische Musik des Wortes!': Zur Entfaltung des Siegesmotivs in den johanneischen Schriften," *ZNW* 85 (1994): 23-46.

3. Pauline Epistles (including the Pastorals)

a. *General Studies*

7306. Ed. Reuss, "Parallèle entre les apôtres Paul et Jean considérés comme théologiens," *RT* 1 (1850): 24-43.

7307. B. Spiegel, "Ueber εὐαγγέλιον und χριστός bei Paulus," *ZWT* 10 (1867): 330-32.

7308. A. Hilgenfeld, "Bemerkungen über den paulinischen Christus, *ZWT* 14 (1871): 182-98.

7309. F. Godet, "Paul's Gospel to the Romans," *Exp* 3rd ser., 3 (1886): 241-59.

7310. J. S. Banks, "St. Paul and the Gospels," *ET* 5 (1893-1894): 413-15.

7311. A. B. Bruce, "St. Paul's Conception of Christianity," *Exp* 4th ser., 7 (1893): 1-20, 118-36, 197-215, 267-82, 353-66, 416-30; 8 (1893): 21-37, 81-95, 192-207, 266-82, 348-61, 432-46; 9 (1894): 87-97, 189-203, 265-75, 342-55, 416-29; 10 (1894): 32-46, 112-26, 199-213, 300-13.

7312. W. C. van Manen, "Het Evangelie van Paulus verklaard?" *TT* 28 (1894): 358-73.

7313. J. S. Banks, "The New Testament Formula 'In Christ Jesus'," *ET* 9 (1897-1898): 18-20.

7314. C. A. Scott, "The Gospel According to St. Paul," *Exp* 6th ser., 2 (1900): 202-10.

7315. Arthur Carr, "Truth in Jesus: The Revelation of Christ and the Example of Christ," *Exp* 6th ser., 3 (1901): 118-27 [Eph.].

7316. A. G. S. Prior, "Paulus's Evangelium," *TTDF* N.S. 7 (1905-1906): 177-215.

7317. Gustave Roux, "Saint Paul et le quatrième évangile," *RTQR* 16 (1907): 405-18.

7318. G. J. A. Jonker, "De paulinische formule 'door Christus'," *TS* 27 (1909): 173-208

7319. John E. McFadyen, "Communion with God in the Bible," *BW* 34 (1909): 187-97 ["In Christ"].

7320. James H. Moulton, "The Gospel According to Paul," *Exp* 8th ser., 2 (1911): 16-28.

7321. Anton Fridrichsen, "τὸ εὐαγγέλιον hos Paulus," *NTT* 13 (1912): 153-70, 209-56.

7322.   C. Lindeboom, "Het geloof van Jezus Christus," *GTT* 14
        (1913): 340-52, 384-95, 414-22 [πίστις 'Ιησοῦ χριστοῦ].

7323.   Benjamin B. Warfield, "God our Father and the Lord Jesus
        Christ," *PTR* 15 (1917): 1-20 [Rom. 1:7, etc.].

7324.   Ioseph M. Bover, "De mystica unione 'In Christo Iesu'
        secundum B. Paulum," *B* 1 (1920): 309-26.

7325.   E. Weber, "Die Formel 'in Christo Jesu' und die paulinische
        Christusmystik," *NKZ* 31 (1920): 213-60.

7326.   Marius Hansen, "Omkring Paulus Formlen 'i Kristus',"
        TTDF 4th ser., 10 (1929): 135-59.

7327.   William E. Wilson, "The Development of Paul's Doctrine of
        Dying and Rising again with Christ," *ET* 42 (1930-1931):
        562-65.

7328.   Denis Buzy, "Saint Paul et saint Matthieu," *RSR* 28 (1938):
        473-78.

7329.   J. B. Orchard, "Thessalonians and the Synoptic Gospels," *B*
        19 (1938): 19-42.

7330.   Hunter B. Blakely, "The Gospel of Paul-A Study in the
        Prison Epistles," *TTod* 3 (1946): 345-57.

7331.   John W. Bailey, "Paul and Matthew and the Primitive
        Jewish-Christian Drama," *CQ* 24 (1947): 326-33.

7332.   Henry E. Turlington, "The Apostle Paul and the Gospel
        History," *RE* 48 (1951): 33-66.

7333.   John W. Bailey, "Gospel for Mankind; The Death of Christ
        in the Thinking of Paul," *Interp* 7 (1953): 163-74.

7334.   Otto Bauernfeind, "Zur Frage nach der Entscheidung
        zwischen Paulus und Lukas," *ZST* 23 (1954): 59-88.

7335.   Albert-Marie Denis, "L'apôtre Paul, prophète 'messianique'
        des Gentils," *ETL* 33 (1957): 245-318.

7336.   F. Neugebauer, "Das paulinische 'In Christo'," *NTSt* 4
        (1957-1958): 124-38.

7337.   Ragnar Bring, "Kristus såsom den nya lagen," *STK* 34
        (1958): 194-204;

7338.   J. A. Allan, "The 'In Christ' Formula in Ephesians," *NTSt* 5
        (1958-1959): 54-62.

7339.   Ragnar Bring, "Die Erfüllung des Gesetzes durch Christus,"
        KD 5 (1959): 1-22.

7340.   Chalmer E. Faw, "Death and Resurrection in Paul's Letters,"

JBR 27 (1959): 291-98.

7341. André Feuillet, "Mort du Christ et mort du chrétien d'après les épîtres pauliniennes," *RB* 66 (1959): 481-513.

7342. Ulrich Luck, "Kerygma, Tradition und Geschichte Jesu bei Lukas," *ZTK* N.F. 57 (1960): 51-66.

7343. J. K. S. Reid, "The Phrase 'in Christ'," *TTod* 17 (1960-1961): 353-65.

See also numbers 2058, 2530-2532, 7973, 7987, 8003, 8680, 8693.

7343.1 Michel Saillard, "C'est moi qui, par l'évangile, vous ai enfantés dans le Christ Jésus (1 Cor 4:15)," *RSR* 56 (1968): 5-40.

7343.2 John G. Strelan, "Burden-Bearing and the Law of Christ: A Re-Examination of Galatians 6:2," *JBL* 94 (1975): 266-76.

7343.3 Allen Cabaniss, "The Gospel according to Paul," *EQ* 48 (1976): 164-67.

7343.4 Richard A. Horsley, " 'How Can Some of You Say that There Is No Resurrection of the Dead?' Spiritual Elitism in Corinth," *NT* 20 (1978): 203-31.

7343.5 R. E. H. Uprichard, "The Person and Work of Christ in 1 Thessalonians," *EQ* 53 (1981): 108-14.

7343.6 Peter Lampe, "Theological Wisdom and the 'Word about the Cross': The Rhetorical Scheme in 1 Corinthians 1-4," *Interp* 44 (1990): 117-31.

7343.7 J. Frederick Holper, " 'As Often As You Eat This Bread and Drink this Cup'," *Interp* 48 (1994): 61-73.

b. *Jesus and Paul*

7344. J. H. McIlvaine, "Christ and Paul," *BS* 35 (1878): 425-60.

7345. G. Matheson, "The Historical Christ of St. Paul," *Exp* 2nd ser., 2 (1881): 27-47, 137-54, 287-301, 357-71.

7346. E. C. S. Gibson, "Sources of St. Paul's Teaching," *Exp* 2nd ser., 4 (1882): 33-45 [the Words of Jesus].

7347. A. Hilgenfeld, "Jesus und Paulus," *ZWT* 37 (1894): 481-541.

7348. Otto Schmoller, "Die geschichtliche Person Jesu nach den paulinischen Schriften," *TSK* 67 (1894): 656-705.

7349. H. H. Wendt, "Die Lehre des Paulus verglichen mit der Lehre Jesu," *ZTK* 4 (1894): 1-78.

7350. Paul Gloatz, "Zur Vergleichung der Lehre des Paulus mit der Jesu," *TSK* 68 (1895): 777-800.

7351. Arthur Hoyle, "Paul and Jesus," *ET* 8 (1896-1897): 487-92.

7352. Rhys Rhees Lloyd, "The Historic Christ in the Letters of Paul," *BS* 58 (1901): 270-93.

7353. Eberhard Vischer, "Jesus und Paulus," *TR* 8 (1905): 129-43, 173-88.

7354. M. Brückner, "Zum Thema Jesus und Paulus," *ZNW* 7 (1906): 112-19.

7355. L. Ihmels, "Jesus und Paulus," *NKZ* 17 (1906): 452-83, 485-516.

7356. William Hallock Johnson, "Was Paul the Founder of Christianity?" *PTR* 5 (1907): 398-422 [No].

7357. James Moffatt, "Paul and Jesus," *BW* 32 (1908): 168-73.

7358. W. Morgan, "The Jesus-Paul Controversy," *ET* 20 (1908-1909): 9-12, 55-58.

7359. Eberhard Vischer, "Jesus und Paulus," *TR* 11 (1908): 301-13.

7360. Arthur C. McGiffert, "Was Jesus or Paul the Founder of Christianity?" *AJT* 13 (1909): 1-20 [Both].

7361. P. Farel, "Jésus le Christ; Paul l'apôtre," *RTQR* 19 (1910): 242-60, 289-306.

7362. E. T. Horn, "Jesus and Paul," *LCR* 30 (1911): 628-35.

7363. W. Heitmüller, "Zum Problem Paulus und Jesus," *ZNW* 13 (1912): 320-37.

7364. G. Kittel, "Jesus bei Paulus," *TSK* 85 (1912): 366-402.

7365. John W. Buckham, "The Mysticism of Jesus and of Paul," *BW* 41 (1913): 309-13.

7366. J. G. James, "The Theology of Paul and the Teaching of Jesus Christ," *ET* 26 (1914-1915): 7-14.

7367. W. Heitmüller, "Jesus und Paulus. Freundschaftliche kritische Bemerkungen zu P. Wernles Artikel 'Jesus und Paulus'," *ZTK* 25 (1915): 156-79.

7368. Paul Wernle, "Jesus und Paulus. Antithesen zu Boussets Kyrios Christos," *ZTK* 25 (1915): 1-92.

7369. E. H. Wieringa, "Paulus en Jezus," *TS* 33 (1915): 257-82.

7370. H. Windisch, "Christuskult und Paulinismus," *TT* 50 (1916): 216-25.

7371. James H. Ropes, "Le radicalisme religieux de Jésus et la 'via media' de l'apôtre Paul," *RHPR* 1 (1921): 507-23.

7372. Paul Feine, "Jesus und Paulus," *NKZ* 36 (1925): 291-323.

7373. Fred G. Bratton, "Continuity and Divergence in the Jesus-Paul Problem," *JBL* 48 (1929): 149-61.

7374. Rudolf Bultmann, "Die Bedeutung des geschichtlichen Jesus für die Theologie des Paulus," *TB* 8 (1929): 137-51.

7375. Otto Michel, "Der Christus des Paulus," *ZNW* 32 (1933): 6-31.

7376. R. V. G. Tasker, "St. Paul and the Earthly Life of Jesus," *ET* 46 (1934-1935): 557-62.

7377. Hans Windisch, "Paulus und Jesus," *TSK* 106 (1934-1935): 432-68.

7378. W. C. Robinson, "The Theology of Jesus and the Theology of Paul," *EQ* 8 (1936): 373-97.

7379. G. J. Inglis, "St. Paul's Conception of Christ," *ET* 50 (1938-1939): 456-60.

7380. Alfred E. Garvie, "Jesus and Paul," *ET* 52 (1940-1941): 236-37.

7381. M. A. Guillebaud, "Paul's Gospel or Christ's?" *EQ* 14 (1942): 281-90.

7382. C. S. Petrie, "Paul and the Historical Jesus," *RTR* 2 (1943): 3-15.

7383. M. Goguel, "De Jésus à l'apôtre Paul," *RHPR* 28 (1948): 1-29.

7384. Ray Knight, "Jesus or Paul," *HJ* 47 (1948-1949): 41-49.

7385. G. S. Duncan, "From Paul to Jesus," *SJT* 2 (1949): 1-12.

7386. William A. Beardslee, "Was Jesus more Optimistic than Paul?" *JBR* 24 (1956): 264-68.

7387. Pierre Bonnard, "Mourir et vivre avec Jésus-Christ selon saint Paul," *RHPR* 36 (1956): 101-12.

7388. F. W. Beare, "Jesus and Paul," *CJT* 5 (1959): 79-86.

7389. J. Cambier, "Paul, apôtre du Christ et prédicateur de l'évangile," *NRT* 81 (1959): 1009-28.

7390. W. Joest, "Jesus, Paulus und wir," *TLZ* 86 (1961): 641-50.

7391. David M. Stanley, "Pauline Allusions to the Sayings of Jesus," *CBQ* 23 (1961): 26-39.

See also number 10050.

7391.1   Walter Schmithals, "Paulus und der historische Jesus," *ZNW* 53 (1962): 145-60.

7391.2   A. W. Argyle, "M and the Pauline Epistles," *ET* 81 (1970): 340-42.

7391.3   Joseph Coppens, "Fils de l'homme dans le dossier paulinien," *ETL* 52 (1976): 309-30.

7391.4   D. A. Koch, "Beobachtungen zum christologischen Schriftgebrauch in den vorpaulinischen Gemeinden," *ZNW* 71 (1980): 174-91.

7391.5   Hans C. C. Cavallin, "Parusi och uppstandelse: 1 Thess 4:13-18 som kombination av tva slags eskatologi," *STK* 59 (1983): 54-63.

7391.6   Gerald F. Hawthorne, "The Interpretation and Translation of Philippians 1:28b," *ET* 95 (1983): 80-81.

7391.7   Wolfgang Schenk, "Christus, das Geheimnis der Welt, als dogmatisches und ethisches Grundprinzip des Kolosserbriefes," *EvT* 43 (1983): 138-55 [Col 1:15-20].

7391.8   Rinaldo Fabris, "Gesù Cristo come fondatore del cristianesimo," *SM* 33 (1984): 277-304.

7391.9   Joseph Plevnik, "The Taking up of the Faithful and the Resurrection of the Dead in 1 Thessalonians 4:13-18," *CBQ* 46 (1984): 274-83.

7391.10   Ulrich Luck, "Die Bekehrung des Paulus und das paulinische Evangelium: zur Frage der Evidenz in Botschaft und Theologie des Apostels," *ZNW* 76 (1985): 187-208.

7391.11   M. A. Chevallier, "L'unité plurielle de l'église d'après le Nouveau Testament," *RHPR* 66 (1986): 3-20.

7391.12   L. D. Hurst, "Re-Enter the Pre-Existent Christ in Philippians 2:5-11," *NTSt* 32 (1986): 449-57.

7391.13   Otfried Hofius, "Das vierte Gottesknechtslied in den Briefen des Neuen Testamentes," *NTSt* 39 (1993): 414-37.

c. *Pauline Christological Texts (including the Pastorals)*

7392.   Ernst Bröse, "Zur Auslegung von Röm. 1, 3-4," *NKZ* 10 (1899): 562-73.

7393.   A. H. Blom, "Het belang van Jezus' opstanding, enz. naar Rom. 1, 4," *TT* 14 (1880): 388-94.

7394.   Alexander Brown, "Declared or Constituted Son of God," *ET* 5 (1893-1894): 308-309 [constituted].

7395. M.-E. Boismard, "Constitué Fils de Dieu (Rom. 1, 4)," *RB* 60 (1953): 5-17.

7396. F. W. Grosheide, "Rom. 1:6-7, 24 en 4:1," *TT* 46 (1912): 402-10.

7397. Charles R. Erdman, "The Power of the Gospel," *USR* 29 (1917-1918): 222-27 [Rom. 1:16-17]

7398. C. Bruston, "La justice de Dieu manifestée par le sacrifice de Jésus Christ," *RTP* 24 (1891): 231-332 [Rom. 2:25, 26].

7399. R. H. Miller, "An Exposition of Romans 3:21-31," *RE* 30 (1933): 424-31.

7400. Walther Bleibtreu, "Der Abschnitt Röm. 3:21-26, unter namentlicher Berücksichtigung des Ausdrucks ἱλαστήριον," *TSK* 56 (1883): 548-68.

7401. Rudolf Schnackenburg, "Todes- und Lebensgemeinschaft mit Christus. Neue Studien zu Röm. 6, 1-11," *MTZ* 6 (1955): 32-53.

7402. R. A. Mitchell, "Christ's Death to Sin," *ET* 5 (1893-1894): 265-67 [Rom. 6:10].

7403. T. Worden, "Christ Jesus who Died or Rather who has Been Raised up (Rom. viii. 34)," *Scr* 10 (1958): 33-43; 11 (1959): 51-59.

7404. Frederic C. Spurr, "Our Advocate and Mediator," *RE* 26 (1929): 163-70 [Rom. 8:34].

7405. E. Abbot, "Recent Discussions of Romans ix. 5," *JBL* 3 (1883): 90-112.

7406. Ernst Bröse, "Wird Christus Röm. 9, 5 θεός genannt?" *NKZ* 10 (1899): 645-57.

7407. Felix Flückiger, "Christus, des Gesetzes τέλος," *TZ* 11 (1955): 153-57 [Rom. 10:4]

7408. J. Havet, "Christ collectif ou Christ individuel en 1 Cor. XII, 12?" *ETL* 23 (1947): 499-520.

7409. J. W. Nott, "Ἐγήγερται in 1 Cor. xv," *JBL* 8 (1888): 41-42.

7410. Helga Rusche, "Die Leugner der Auferstehung von den Toten in der korinthischen Gemeinde. Stimmen zum Problem: Die 'Gegner' des Apostels Paulus von 1. Kor. 15," *MTZ* 10 (1959): 149-51.

7411. Paul Winter, "1 Corinthians XV 3b-7," *NT* 2 (1958): 142-50.

7412. Bruce M. Metzger, "A Suggestion Concerning the Meaning of 1 Cor. xv. 4b," *JTS* N.S. 8 (1957): 118-23.

7413.   Jean Boure, "Saint Paul et le Christ (dans la IIe épître aux Corinthiens)," *NRT* 65 (1938): 148-60.

7414.   W. A. Gray, "Christ's 'Yea'," *ET* 15 (1903-1904): 351-55 [2 Cor. 1:19].

7415.   Lic. Kittel, "Christus, der Sinn der Welt," *ZST* 6 (1998-1929): 96-100 [2 Cor. 1:20].

7416.   L. Krummel, "Exegetische und dogmatische Erörterung der Stelle 2 Cor. 3,17: der Herr ist der Geist," *TSK* 32 (1859): 39-100.

7417.   Samuel T. Lowrie, "Exegetical Note on 2 Cor. v. 16, 17," *PTR* 4 (1906): 236-41.

7418.   H. Francis Perry, "Knowing Christ after the Flesh. 2 Cor. 5: 16," *BW* 18 (1901): 284-86.

7419.   Frank C. Porter, "Does Paul Claim to Have Known the Historical Jesus? A Study of 2 Corinthians 5. 16," *JBL* 47 (1928): 257-75 [No].

7420.   J. B. Souček, "Wir kennen Christus nicht mehr nach dem Fleisch," *EvT* 19 (1959): 300-14 [2 Cor. 5:16].

7421.   Dr. Haussleiter, "Die Stelle 2 Kor. 5, 21 in den Predigten Novatians," *NKZ* 13 (1902): 270-75.

7422.   Alexander Ross, "The Grace of our Lord Jesus Christ," *EQ* 13 (1941): 219-40 [2 Cor. 8:9].

7423.   Prebendary Whitefoord, "The Captivity of the Mind to Christ," *ET* 6 (1894-1895): 488-90 [2 Cor. 10:5].

7424.   A. Hilgenfeld, "Die Stelle Gal. 3, 19. 20 und ihre neueste Auslegung," *ZWT* 8 (1865): 452-57.

7425.   Karl Bornhäuser, "Der 'Mittler.' Versuch einer Erklärung von Gal. 3, 19. 20," *NKZ* 39 (1928): 21-24.

7426.   Johannes Gründler, "Noch einmal: Der 'Mittler'," *NKZ* 39 (1928): 549-52 [Gal. 3:19-20].

7427.   Dr. Mack, "Ueber Gal. 3, 20," *TQ* 17 (1835): 453-92.

7428.   Wilhelm von Schütz, "Ueber Gal.3, 20," *TQ* 17 (1835): 623-45.

7429.   J. F. K. Gurlitt, "Noch ein Wort über Gal. 3, 20," *TSK* 10 (1837): 805-29.

7430.   Walther Bleibtreu, "Das Wort vom Mittler im Galaterbriefe," *NKZ* 6 (1895): 534-60 [Gal. 3:20].

7431. Wilh. Siebert, "Exegetisch-theologische Studie über Galater 3, 20 und 4, 4," *NKZ* 15 (1904): 699-733.

7432. Adolf Stegmann, "ὁ δὲ μεσίτης ἑνὸς οὐκ ἔστιν, Gal. 3, 20," *BibZ* 22 (1934): 30-42.

7433. Philipp Haeuser, "Der Gottessohn 'geworden unter dem Gesetze' (Gal. 4, 4)," *BibZ* 11 (1913): 178-84.

7434. H. J. Kouwenhoven, "Paulus' beroep op de lidteekenen van den Heere Jezus in zijn lichaam," *GTT* 13 (1913): 105-15 [Gal. 6:17].

7435. H. J. Flowers, "Election in Jesus Christ-A Study of Ephesians 1:3-4," *RE* 26 (1929): 55-67.

7436. André Feuillet, "L'église plérôme du Christ d'après Ephés. 1, 23," *NRT* 78 (1956): 449-72, 593-610.

7437. Harald Sahlin, "Omskärelsen i Kristus," *STK* 23 (1947): 11-24 [Eph. 2:11-22].

7438. L. Bostrup, "Kenodoxi," *TTDF* 3rd ser., 7 (1916): 26-48 [Phil. 2:1-11].

7439. O. P. Eaches, "The Self-Emptied Christ," *RE* 22 (1925): 216-27 [Phil. 2:1-6].

7440. André Feuillet, "L'Homme-Dieu considéré dans sa condition terrestre de serviteur et de rédempteur," *RB* 51 (1942): 58-79 [Phil 2:5ff.].

7441. C. N. Kähler, "Bemerkungen zu Philipper 2, 5-14, besonders in Betreff des οὐχ ἁρπαγμὸν ἡγήσατο τὸ εἶναι ἴσα θεῷ," *TSK* 30 (1857): 99-112.

7442. E. H. Gifford, "The Incarnation: A Study of Philippians II. 5-11," *Exp* 5th ser., 4 (1896): 161-77, 241-63.

7443. J. B. Nisius, "Zur Erklärung von Phil. 2, 5-11," *ZKT* 21 (1897): 276-306; 23 (1899): 75-113.

7444. Milton S. Terry, "The Great Kenotic Text (Phil. 2: 5-11)," *BW* 17 (1901): 292-96.

7445. K. F. Proost, "Adam-Christus-Satan," *TT* 50 (1916): 373-86 [Phil. 2:5-11].

7446. Jb. van Gilse, "Verklaring van Philippensen II vers 5-11," *TT* 51 (1917): 321-25.

7447. Nathan Söderblom, "Abschiedsandacht über Phil. 2, 5-11," *TB* 7 (1928): 280-82.

7448. Karl Bornhäuser, "Zum Verständnis von Philipper 2, 5-11,"

NKZ 44 (1933): 428-34, 453-62.

7449.   Paul Joüon, "Notes philologiques sur quelques versets de l'épître aux Philippiens (1, 21; 2, 5)," *RSR* 28 (1938): 89-93; "... Philippiens (11, 6-11)," 223-33.

7450.   A. A. T. Ehrhardt, "Jesus Christ and Alexander the Great," *JTS* 46 (1945): 45-51 [Plutarch and Phil. 2:5-11].

7451.   Josef Gewiess, "Zum altkirchlichen Verständnis der Kenosisstelle (Phil. 2, 5-11)," *TQ* 128 (1948): 463-87.

7452.   Ernst Käsemann, "Kritische Analyse von Phil. 2, 5-11," *ZTK* N.F. 47 (1950): 313-60.

7453.   Thor Boman, "Fil. 2, 5-11," *NTT* 53 (1952): 193-212.

7454.   Alva J. McClain, "The Doctrine of the Kenosis in Philippians 2: 5-8," *BR* 13 (1928): 506-27.

7455.   Fr. Ernesti, "Philipp. II, 6ff., aus einer Anspielung auf Genes. II. iii," *TSK* 21 (1848): 858-924.

7456.   Wilibald Grimm, "Ueber die Stelle Philipp. 2, 6-11," *ZWT* 16 (1873): 33-59.

7457.   Jacques Dupont, "Jésus Christ dans son abaissement et son exaltation, d'après Phil. 2, 6-11," *RSR* 37 (1950): 500-14.

7458.   Paul Galtier, "La *Forma Dei* et la *Forma servi* selon saint Hilaire de Poitiers," *RSR* 48 (1960): 101-18 [Phil. 2:6-7].

7459.   M. Stein, "Ueber Philipper 2, 6. Ein Versuch," *TSK* 10 (1837): 165-80.

7460.   Fr. Ernesti, "Noch ein Wort über Phil. 2, 6 gegen F. C. Baur's Bemerkungen in den Tübinger theologischen Jahrbüchern 1849, 502 ff.," *TSK* 24 (1851): 595-630.

7461.   E. Wetzel, "Über ἁρπαγμός in der Stelle Phil. 2, 6," *TSK* 60 (1887): 535-52.

7462.   Adhémar d'Alès, "Philip. II, 6. οὐχ ἁρπαγμὸν ἡγήσατο," *RSR* 1 (1910): 260-69.

7463.   L. Saint-Paul, "Note sur Philip. II, 6: οὐχ ἁρπαγμόν ἡγήσατο," *RB* 20 (1911): 550-53.

7464.   Martin Dibelius, "ἁρπαγμός," *TLZ* 40 (1915): 557-58 [Phil. 2:6].

7465.   Louis Bouyer, "ἁρπαγμός," *RSR* 39 (1951-1952): 281-88 [Phil. 2:6].

7466.   Victoriano Larrañaga, "El nombre sobre todo nombre dado a Jesús desde su Resurrección gloriosa (Phil. 2, 9-12)," *EB*

6 (1947): 287-305.

7467.   Sally Neill Roach, "The Power of his Resurrection," *RE* 24 (1927): 45-55, 297-304 [Phil. 3:10, etc.].

7468.   E. C. Caldwell, "The Fulness of Christ," *PTR* 16 (1918): 557-71 [Col.].

7469.   Ernst Bammel, "Versuch zu Col. 1, 15-20," *ZNW* 52 (1961): 88-95.

7470.   Chr. H. Weisse, "Christus, das Ebenbild des unsichtbaren Gottes (Coloss. 1, 15, 2 Korinth. 4, 4)," *TSK* 17 (1844): 913-66.

7471.   Johann Michl, "Die Versöhnung (Kol. 1, 20)," *TQ* 128 (1948): 442-62.

7472.   S. Lyonnet, "L'hymne christologique de l'épître aux Colossiens et la fête juive du Nouvel An (S. Paul, Col. 1, 20 et Philon, *De spec. leg.*, 192)," *RSR* 48 (1960): 93-100.

7473.   P. J. Gloag, "The Complement of Christ's Afflictions," *Exp* 1st ser., 7 (1878): 224-36 [Col. 1:24].

7474.   Sydnor L. Stealey, "Christ in You, the Hope of Glory," *RE* 40 (1943): 55-59 [Col 1:27, etc.].

7475.   Ferdinand Prat, "Le triomphe du Christ sur les principautés et les puissances," *RSR* 3 (1912): 201-29 [Col. 2:15].

7476.   Nolan P. Howington, "The Liberating Christ (Colossians 3:1-11)," *RE* 55 (1958): 196-202.

7477.   José M. Bover, "El 'gran misterio de la piedad'," *EE* 21 (1947): 225-33 [1 Tim. 3:16].

7478.   A. Klöpper, "Zur Christologie der Pastoralbriefe (1 Tim. 3, 16)," *ZWT* 45 (1902): 339-61.

See also number 2157.

7478.1   Georg Strecker, "Redaktion und Tradition im Christushymnus Phil 2:6-11," *ZNW* 55 (1964): 63-78.

7478.2   André Feuillet, "L'hymne christologique de l'Epître aux Philippiens 2:6-11," *RB* 72 (1965): 352-80; 481-507.

7478.3   John Harvey, "New Look at the Christ Hymn in Philippians 2:6-11," *ET* 76 (1965): 337-39.

7478.4   Joseph Coppens, "Les affinités littéraires de l'hymne christologique Phil 2, 6-11," *ETL* 42 (1966): 238-41.

7478.5   David H. Wallace, "Note on Morphe," *TZ* 22 (1966): 19-25.

7478.6   Joseph Coppens, "Une nouvelle structuration de l'hymne christologique de l'Epître aux Philippiens," *ETL* 43 (1967): 197-202.

7478.7   Charles H. Talbert, "Problem of Pre-Existence in Philippians 2:6-11," *JBL* 86 (1967): 141-53.

7478.8   Norman K. Bakken, "New Humanity: Christ and the Modern Age," *Interp* 22 (1968): 71-82 [Phil 2:6-11].

7478.9   Roy W. Hoover, "Harpagmos Enigma: A Philological Solution," *HTR* 64 (1971): 95-119 [Phil 2:6].

7478.10   Pierre Grelot, "Deux expressions difficiles de Philippiens 2:6-7," *B* 53 (1972): 495-507.

7478.11   Pierre Grelot, "Deux notes critiques sur Philippiens 2:6-11," *B* 54 (1973): 169-86.

7478.12   Pierre Grelot, "La valeur de ouk...alla... dans Philippiens 2 (1973): 6-7," *B* 54 (1973): 25-42.

7478.13   T. F. Glasson, "Two Notes on the Philippians Hymn 2:6-11," *NTSt* 21 (1974): 133-39.

7478.14   D. H. C. Read, "Gentle Jesus or Cosmic Christ," *ET* 96 (1985): 213-14 [Col 3:1].

7478.15   T. Y.-C. Wong, "The Problem of Pre-Existence in Philippians 2:6-11," *ETL* 62 (1986): 267-82.

7478.16   Hermann Binder, "Erwägungen zu Phil 2:6-7b," *ZNW* 78 (1987): 230-43.

7478.17   C. A. Wanamaker, "Philippians 2:6-11: Son of God or Adamic Christology?" *NTSt* 33 (1987): 179-93.

7478.18   Ulrich B. Müller, "Der Christushymnus Phil 2:6-11," *ZNW* 79 (1988): 17-44.

7478.19   J. C. O'Neill, "Hoover on Harpagmos Reviewed, with a Modest Proposal Concerning Philippians 2:6," *HTR* 81 (1988): 445-49.

7478.20   Roselyne Dupont-Roc, "De l'hymne christologique à une vie de koinonia: Etude sur la lettre aux Philippiens," *EB* 49 (1991): 451-72.

7478.21   Roland Bergmeier, "Weihnachten mit und ohne Glanz: Notizen zu Johannesprolog und Philipperhymnus," *ZNW* 85 (1994): 47-68.

4. The Rest of the New Testament (Acts, Hebrews, Catholic Epistles)

7479.   W. C. van Unnik, "The 'Book of Acts' the Confirmation of the Gospel," *NT* 4 (1960): 26-59.

7480. Immanuel Nitzsch, "Über παῖς θεοῦ, ob es Knecht oder Sohn Gottes bedeute. Zu Apostel-Geschichte 3, 13," *TSK* 1 (1828): 331-37.

7481. Charles Harris Nash, "Stephen, the Model Layman: The Unique Transcendent Image of Jesus in Life and Death 'Filled with all the Fulness of God.' Acts 6-7," *RE* 23 (1926): 452-75.

7482. Ulrich Wilckens, "Kerygma und Evangelium bei Lukas (zu Apg. 10, 34-43)," *ZNW* 49 (1958): 223-37.

7483. H. U. Meyboom, "Jesus en Paulus in den Hebraeërbrief," *TT* 18 (1884): 412-51.

7484. Geerhardus Vos, "Hebrews, the Epistle of the Diatheke," *PTR* 13 (1915): 587-632; 14 (1916): 1-61.

7485. F. Ogara, "Christi recens nati dignitas (Hebr. 1, 1-14)," *VD* 6 (1926): 33-42, 76-84.

7486. William M. Lewis, "Bringing the First-Begotten into the World," *BW* 12 (1898): 104-112 [Heb. 1:6].

7487. R. A. Mitchell, "Jesus Crowned with the Glory of Sonship: Hebrews II. 9," *ET* 3 (1891-1892): 455-57.

7488. Jean-Claude Dhôtel, "La 'sanctification' du Christ d'après Hébreux II, 11. Interprétations des Pères et des scolastiques médiévaux," *RSR* 47 (1959): 515-43; "Les commentaires de l'épître jusqu'à saint Thomas," 48 (1960): 420-52.

7489. A. B. Bruce, "The Epistle to the Hebrews: VII. Christ and Moses (Chap. III)," *Exp* 3rd ser., 9 (1889): 161-79.

7490. A. Strobel, "Die Psalmengrundlage der GethsemaneParallele Hbr. 5, 7 ff.," *ZNW* 45 (1954): 252-66.

7491. Reuben E. Omark, "The Saving of the Savior; Exegesis and Christology in Hebrews 5:7-10," *Interp* 12 (1958): 39-51.

7492. Georg Braumann, "Hebr. 5, 7-10," *ZNW* 51 (1960): 278-80.

7493. Mathias Rissi, "Die Menschlichkeit Jesu nach Hebr. 5, 7 und 8," *TZ* 11 (1955): 28-45.

7494. C. Spicq, "El sacerdocio de Cristo en la Epístola a los Hebreos," *CB* 13 (1956): 232-38 [Heb. 7ff.].

7495. Ricardo Rábanos, "Sacerdocio de Melquisedec, sacerdocio de Aarón y sacerdocio de Cristo," *CB* 13 (1956): 264-75 [Heb. 7ff.].

7496. Albert Vanhoye, "La structure centrale de l'épître aux Hébreux (Heb. 8, 1-9, 28)," *RSR* 47 (1959): 44-60.

7497.   F. Gardiner, "On Heb. x. 20," *JBL* 8 (1888): 142-46.

7498.   D. A. Hayes, "Jesus the Perfecter of Faith (Heb. 12:2)," *BW* 20 (1902): 278-87.

7499.   J. B. Nisius, "Zur Erklärung von Hebr. 12, 2," *BibZ* 14 (1916-1917): 44-61.

7500.   W. Childs Robinson, "Jesus Christ the Same Yesterday and To-day and Forever," *EQ* 16 (1944): 228-40 [Heb. 13:8].

7501.   R. L. T. Haslehurst, "The Fifth Gospel," *Th* 35 (1937): 96-103 [= Epistle of James].

7501.1 Ernest Best, "1 Peter and the Gospel Tradition," *NTSt* 16 (1969-1970): 95-113.

B. THEOLOGICAL STUDIES CLASSIFIED ACCORDING TO TOPIC

1. The Doctrine of the Word of God

a. *Inspiration*

7502.   Eml. V. Gerhart, "Relative Authority of the Gospels," *AJT* 3 (1899): 275-94.

7503.   M. Goguel, "Autorité di Christ et autorité de l'Ecriture," *RHPR* 18 (1938): 101-25.

7504.   Paulino Bellet, "El sentido de la analogía 'Verbum Dei Incarnatum = Verbum Dei Scriptum'," *EB* 14 (1955): 415-28.

7505.   J. H. Crehan, "The Analogy between 'Verbum Dei Incarnatum' and 'Verbum Dei Scriptum' in the Fathers," *JTS* N.S. 6 (1955): 87-90.

7506.   Wilhelm Dantine, "Christologische Grundlegung einer Lehre vom Worte Gottes," *TZ* 12 (1956): 471-81.

7507.   John A. Witmer, "The Incarnate and the Written Word of God," *BS* 113 (1956): 66-69.

7508.   Ch. Hauter, "Christologie et inspiration des Ecritures," *RHPR* 29 (1959): 83-96.

b. *The Kerygma*

7509.   Albert G. Lawson, "The Gospel Within the Gospel," *CQ* 4 (1927): 268-80.

7510.   Thomas S. Kepler, "The Gospel in the Gospels," *JBR* 5 (1937): 161-65.

7511.   Oliver C. Horsman, "What is the Gospel?" *CQ* 15 (1938): 241-50.

7512. Rittenhouse Meisser, "Reality and the Gospel," *CQ* 15 (1938): 167-75.

7513. W. H. P. Hatch, "The Primitive Christian Message," *JBL* 58 (1939): 1-13.

7514. Charles E. Schofield, "What is the Gospel?" *RL* 8 (1939): 388-98.

7515. R. Leijs, "Prédication des apôtres," *NRT* 69 (1947): 605-18.

7516. Bent Noack, "Johannesskrifternes kerygma," *DTT* 12 (1949): 65-80.

7517. C. H. Dodd, "Le kerygma apostolique dans le quatrième évangile," *RHPR* 31 (1951): 265-74.

7518. T. F. Glasson, "The Kerygma: Is Our Version Correct?" *HJ* 51 (1952-1953): 129-32.

7519. Krister Stendahl, "Kerygma und kerygmatisch. Von zweideutigen Ausdrücken der Predigt der Urkirche-und unserer," *TLZ* 77 (1952): 715-20.

7520. Martin Albertz, "Kerygma und Theologie im Neuen Testament," *TLZ* 81 (1956): 341-44.

7521. E. L. Allen, "The Lost Kerygma," *NTSt* 3 (1956-1957): 349-53.

7522. C. F. Evans, "The Kerygma," *JTS* N.S. 7 (1956): 25-41.

7523. William Baird, "What is the Kerygma? A Study of 1 Cor 15, 3-8 and Gal 1, 11-17," *JBL* 76 (1957): 181-91.

7524. John J. Vincent, "Didactic Kerygma in the Synoptic Gospels," *SJT* 10 (1957): 262-73.

7525. Paul Althaus, "Il considdetto kerygma e il Gesù della storia," *Div.* 6 (1962): 257-313.

See also numbers 873, 3325, 7342, 7482, 8825.

7525.1 Claude J. Geffré, "Kérygme et histoire chez Rudolf Bultmann," *RSPT* 49 (1965): 609-39.

7525.2 Paul Corset, "Le théologien face au conteur évangélique: à la recherche d'une théologie narrative," *RSR* 73 (1985): 61-84.

2. The Doctrine of God

a. *General Studies*

7526. George B. Stevens, "The Teaching of Jesus; III. His Teaching Concerning God," *BW* 5 (1895): 192-99.

7527. Charles M. Mead, "The Fatherhood of God," *AJT* 1 (1897):

577-600.

7528. R. W. Dale, "The Fatherhood of God," *Exp* 5th ser., 7 (1898): 56-69, 150-60.

7529. George B. Foster, "The Influence of the Life and Teaching of Jesus on the Doctrine of God," *BW* 11 (1898): 306-18.

7530. George W. Northrup, "The Fatherhood of God," *AJT* 5 (1901): 473-95.

7531. Robert D. Wilson, "The Names of God in the New Testament," *PTR* 19 (1921): 392-433.

7532. Edward Grubb, "The Wrath of God in the Teaching of Jesus," *ET* 34 (1922-1923): 214-17.

7533. Edward Grubb, "The God of Jesus Christ," *ET* 36 (1924-1925): 88-90.

7534. J. Gresham Machen, "The God of the Early Christians," *PTR* 22 (1924): 524-88.

7535. Gustaf Aulén, "Gudsbilden och Kristus," *STK* 3 (1927): 9-28.

7536. H. J. Flowers, "Christ's Doctrine of God," *RE* 24 (1927): 268-81, 435-54.

7537. Francis Pickens Miller, "The Significance of Jesus for our Conception of God," *RL* 4 (1935): 337-42.

7538. H. W. Montefiore, "God as Father in the Synoptic Gospels," *NTSt* 3 (1956-1957): 31-82.

7539. G. H. C. MacGregor, "The Concept of the Wrath of God in the New Testament," *NTSt* 7 (1960-1961): 101-109.

7540. C. L. Mitton, "The Will of God," *ET* 72 (1960-1961): 68-71. See also numbers 432, 7283, *10054*.

b. *The Doctrine of the Trinity*

7541. Edward Robie, "Doctrine of the Trinity," *BS* 27 (1870): 262-89.

7542. W. M. Thomson, "The Natural Basis of our Spiritual Language, Divine Names and Titles," *BS* 31 (1874): 136-58.

7543. R. E. Bartlett, "St. Paul on Trinity," *Exp* 2nd ser., 4 (1882): 321-31 [Eph. 2:18]

7544. E. R. Craven, "The Nicene Doctrine of the Homoousian," *BS* 41 (1884): 698-760

7545. Olaf Moe, "De trinitariske formler og forbindelser i de apostoliske breve, deres betydning og deres oprindelse," *NTT* 3 (1902): 53-75, 113-44.

7546. Benjamin B. Warfield, "Tertullian and the Beginnings of the Doctrine of the Trinity," *PTR* 3 (1905): 529-57; 4 (1906): 1-36, 145-67.

7547. F. R. M. Hitchcock, "The Apostolic Preaching of Irenaeus and its Light on his Doctrine of the Trinity," *Herm* 14 (1907): 307-37.

7548. Benjamin B. Warfield, "Calvin's Doctrine of the Trinity," *PTR* 7 (1909): 553-652.

7549. Arthur Carr, "The Indwelling Trinity," *Exp* 8th ser., 4 (1912): 263-68.

7550. Charles L. Dibble, "The Nicene Idea of God," *BW* 52 (1918): 240-47.

7551. Jules Lebreton, "Le dogme de la trinité dans l'ancienne église chrétienne: la foi du baptême," *RSR* 8 (1918): 1-35.

7552. Garrett Pierse, "Some Modern Sidelights on the Doctrine of the Trinity," *ITQ* 14 (1919): 201-12.

7553. Karl Thieme, "Zur Trinitätsfrage," *ZTK* N.F. 8 (1927): 251-68.

7554. Karl Thieme, "Zur Trinitätsfrage. 2. Ein Mittler-der Mensch Christus Jesus," *ZTK* [SC]N.F.[sc], 9 (1928): 99-129.

7555. Norman Bartlett, "The Realization of the Trinity," *RE* 27 (1930): 47-61.

7556. F. Cavallera, "Les premières formules trinitaires de saint Augustin," *BLE* 31 (1930): 97-123.

7557. T.-L. Penids, "La valeur de la théorie 'psychologique' de la trinité," *ETL* 8 (1931): 5-16.

7558. W. C. Robinson, "The Theocentric Theology Implicit in the Name of the Trinity," *EQ* 6 (1934): 225-54.

7559. Algernon Ward, "*Gloria Patri*: Text and Interpretation," *JTS* 36 (1935): 73-74.

7560. Raphaël Favre, "La communication des idiomes dans l'ancienne tradition latine," *BLE* 37 (1936): 130-45.

7561. Charles W. Lowry, "Origen as Trinitarian," *JTS* 37 (1936): 225-40.

7562. G. A. Wetter, "L. P. Karsarevins Ontologie der Dreieinheit. Die Struktur des kreatürlichen Seins als Abbild der göttlichen

Dreifaltigkeit," *OCP* 9 (1943): 366-405.

7563.   Jules Lebreton, "À propos de 'La doctrine trinitaire de saint Hilaire de Poitiers'," *RSR* 33 (1946): 484-89.

7564.   Paul Henry, "La mystique trinitaire du Bienheureux Jean Ruusbroec. La doctrine de Dieu," *RSR* 40 (1951-1952): 335-68; 41 (1953): 51-75.

7565.   Julian Stead, "Perichoresis in the Christological Chapters of the *De Trinitate* of Pseudo-Cyril of Alexandria," *DS* 6 (1953): 12-20.

7566.   Laurence Bright, "Saint Thomas on the Trinity: A Study of Philosophical Reasoning in Theology," *DS* 7 (1954): 48-58.

7567.   Leonard Hodgson, "The Doctrine of the Trinity: Some Further Thoughts," *JTS* N.S. 5 (1954): 49-55.

7568.   Ch. de Moré-Pontgibaud, "Sur l'analogie des noms divine. Au centre de l'analogie révélée," *RSR* 42 (1954): 321-60.

7569.   Francis Ruello, "Une source probable de la théologie trinitaire de saint Thomas," *RSR* 43 (1955): 104-28.

7570.   Jean Giblet, "La sainte trinité selon ltévangile de saint Jean," *LumV* no. 29 (1956): 95-126.

7571.   Jean Daniélou, "Trinité et angélologie dans la théologie judéo-chrétienne," *RSR* 45 (1957): 5-41.

7572.   Maurice Wiles, "Some Reflections on the Origins of the Doctrine of the Trinity," *JTS* N.S. 8 (1957): 92-106.

7573.   Herbert H. Farmer, "Monotheism and the Doctrine of the Trinity," *RL* 29 (1960): 32-41.

7574.   Jacob W. Heikkinen, "The Doctrine of the Trinity and the Bible," *RL* 29 (1960): 42-51.

7575.   Cyril C. Richardson, "The Ontological Trinity: Father and Son," *RL* 29 (1960): 7-15.

7576.   Claude Welch, "Mystery and Truth: A Preface to Trinitarian Theology," *RL* 29 (1960): 16-31.

7577.   Carl Andresen, "Zur Entstehung und Geschichte des trinitarischen Personbegriffes," *ZNW* 52 (1961): 1-39.

7578.   Paul M. Van Buren, "The Trinitarian Controversy Revisited,"

RL 30 (1961): 71-80.

See also number 9086.

3. The Doctrine of Christ

a. *Christology in General*

7579. J.-F. Astié, "Le problème christologique," *RTP* 7 (1874): 161-245.

7580. B. Spiegel, "Einiges über Christusdichtungen im Neuen Testament," *ZWT* 17 (1874): 519-30.

7581. Paul Chapuis, "Le problème christologique dans les limites du Nouveau Testament," *RTP* 10 (1877): 63-87.

7582. J. R. Lumby, "The Gospel in the Epistles," *Exp* 1st ser., 5 (1877): 1-11, 134-49, 289-304, 343-61, 451-73; 6 (1877): 96-113, 383-95, 429-44.

7583. N. Van Alstine, "The Fulness of Christ," *LQ* 8 (1878): 582-92.

7584. R. G. Balfour, "The First Principles of the Doctrine of Christ (Heb. vi. 1, 2)," *Exp* 3rd ser., 8 (1888): 438-47.

7585. Carl Pestalozzi, "Die Christologie der Gleichnisse," *STZ* 5 (1888): 87-104.

7586. E. H. Johnson, "The Idea of Law in Christology," *BS* 46 (1889): 599-625.

7587. J. W. Richard, "The Person, Work and States of Christ," *LQ* 19 (1889): 363-412.

7588. P. Lobstein, "Études christologiques," *RTP* 23 (1890): 205-49; 27 (1894): 105-53.

7589. J. G. Boekenoogen, "Het christologisch begrip," *TT* 26 (1892): 147-69.

7590. J. G. Boekenoogen, "Christologische beschouwingen; 2. De beteekenis van Jezus Christus voor het zedelijk leven," *TT* 26 (1892): 275-306.

7591. G. W. Stemler, "De roeping en optreding van Jezus als de Christus is, uit hetgeen de Evangeliën mededeelen, historisch te verklaren," *TS* 10 (1892): 308-28, 401-24; 11 (1893): 36-65.

7592. Frank H. Foster, "Studies in Christology," *BS* 52 (1895):

531-48.

7593. Louis Tomas, "Jésus-Christ, d'après la foi qu'il réclame: étude christologique," *RTP* 28 (1895): 46-68, 122-59.

7594. C. A. Briggs, "The Wisdom of Jesus the Messiah," *ET* 8 (1896-97): 393-98, 452-55, 492-96; 9 (1897-1898): 69-75.

7595. Frank H. Foster, "Studies in Christology," *BS* 53 (1896): 250-65, 444-65.

7596. Edwin Heyl, "The Christ of All Days," *LQ* 27 (1897): 118-31.

7597. G. Godet, "Messianisme ou évangile?" *RTQR* 10 (1901): 1-38.

7598. Wilfred Monod, "Évangile et messianisme," *RTQR* 10 (1901): 315-30.

7599. G. Godet, "Réplique de M. Godet à W. Monod (Évangile et messianisme)," *RTQR* 10 (1901): 331-41.

7600. Otto Jensen, "Hvorledes bør det kristologiske problem videnskabelig formuleres?" *NTT* 3 (1902): 209-24.

7601. L. H. A. Bähler, "Iets over de oud-christelijke belijdenissen in het N. Testament," *TS* 27 (1903): 119-38.

7602. George H. Gilbert, "The Supremacy of Jesus' Life and Teaching," *BW* 25 (1905): 215-23.

7603. T. Häring, "Einfachste Worte für eine grosse Sache, die Stellung Jesu im christlichen Glauben," *ZTK* 19 (1909): 177-203.

7604. James H. Moulton, " 'The Marks of Jesus'," *ET* 21 (1909-1910): 283-84.

7605. Rayner Winterbotham, "On the Omniscience of our Lord," *Exp* 7th ser., 8 (1909): 481-500.

7606. George Nye Boardman, "An Attested or a Self-developed Saviour-Which?" *BS* 67 (1910): 433-50.

7607. J. A. Bruins, "Het Jezus-Christus-geloof. Een antwoord aan Dr. H. T. de Graaf," *TT* 44 (1910): 17-40.

7608. Gabriel Campbell, "Christ and Philosophy," *BS* 67 (1910): 284-98.

7609. C. Caverno, "The Theistic Christ," *BS* 67 (1910): 472-85.89

7610. Jules Lebreton, "La foi au Seigneur Jésus dans l'église naissante," *RSR* 1 (1910): 2-26.

7611. George H. Gilbert, "A Critique on Professor Warfield's Article 'The Christology of the New Testament Writings' in the July Number of this Journal," *AJT* 15 (1911): 609-13. [cf. no 8319].

7612. Leander S. Keyser, "Christ's Personal Presence," *LQ* 41 (1911): 533-39.

7613. Julius Böhmer, "Absolutheit des Christentums und Absolutheit Jesu," *ZWT* 55 (1914): 153-66.

7614. M. Brückner, "Zur neutestamentlichen Christologie," *TR* 17 (1914): 169-87.

7615. James Moffatt, "The Christology of the Epistle to the Hebrews," *ET* 28 (1916-1917): 505-508, 563-66.

7616. Ernest W. Burch, "Christ in the Epistle to the Hebrews," *BS* 74 (1917): 613-20

7617. James Moffatt, "The Christology of the Epistle to the Hebrews," *ET* 29 (1917-1918): 26-30.

7618. Burton S. Easton, "The Development of Apostolic Christology," *ATR* 1 (1918-1919): 148-63, 371-82.

7619. Ed. Geismar, "Guds Vrede og Kristi Soning," *TTDF* 3rd ser., 9 (1918): 257-74.

7620. Frederic Palmer, "A Comparison of the Synoptic, Pauline, and Johannine Conceptions of Jesus," *AJT* 23 (1919): 300-18.

7621. Stewart Means, "The Mystery of Christ," *HJ* 18 (1919-1920): 734-52.

7622. S. J. Porter, "The Gospel Foci," *RE* 19 (1922): 127-42.

7623. S. G. Craig, "Genuine and Counterfeit Christianity," *PTR* 21 (1923): 1-41.

7624. A. Ancel, "Christus testis fidelis," *VD* 5 (1925): 137-46.

7625. A. Ancel, "Christus apologeta," *VD* 5 (1925): 247-50.

7626. A. Ancel, "Christus doctor ovium," *VD* 5 (1925): 271-79.

7627. A. Ancel, "Christus impugnatae veritatis defensor," *VD* 5 (1925): 353-60.

7628.   F. Cawley, "Christ in Paradox," *ET* 37 (1925-1926): 85-90.

7629.   Charles Harris Nash, "Jesus," *RE* 22 (1925): 311-32.

7630.   Charles B. Williams, "The Earliest Picture of Jesus the Christ," *CQ* 2 (1925): 265-76.

7631.   Daniel Evans, "The Theological Definition of the Authority of Jesus," *CQ* 5 (1928): 267-79.

7632.   Archibald G. Baker, "Jesus Christ as Interpreted by the Missionary Enterprise," *JR* 9 (1929): 1-11.

7633.   Albert D. Belden, "Vital Values of the Cross," *RE* 26 (1929): 329-35.

7634.   George Cross, "Christianity and Christology," *JR* 4 (1924): 600-10.

7635.   J. A. Faulkner, "The Strange Jesus," *RE* 26 (1929): 197-204.

7636.   W. H. Ellwanger, "The Christology of the Apocalypse," *CTM* 1 (1930): 512-28.

7637.   D. A. Frøvig, "Tilbedelsen av Kristus i det Nye Testament," *TTK* 1 (1930): 26-44

7638.   Harry F. Ward, "Is Jesus Superfluous?" *JR* 10 (1930): 471-86.

7639.   A. C. McGiffert, "The Significance of Jesus," *JR* 11 (1931): 47-62.

7640.   B. Botte, "La sagesse et les origines de la christologie," *RSPT* 21 (1932): 54-67.

7641.   Alfred E. Garvie, "Christological Notes," *ET* 44 (1932-1933): 20-25.

7642.   J.-B. Frey, "Le conflit entre le messianisme de Jésus et le messianisme des juifs de son temps," *B* 14 (1933): 133-49, 269-93.

7643.   Rafael Gyllenberg, "Die Christologie des Hebräerbriefes," *ZST* 11 (1933-1934): 662-90.

7644.   Jean Levie, "Per Iesum Christum, Filium tuum," *NRT* 60 (1933): 866-83.

7645.   Stewart G. Cole, "The Relevancy of Jesus," *JR* 35 (1935): 281-93.

7646.   Frederick C. Grant, "The Spiritual Christ," *JBL* 54 (1935):

1-15.

7647. William C. Bennett, "Scripture Unity Concerning Christ," *BS* 94 (1937): 239-46.

7648. Aage Bentzen, "Om kristologisk Exegese," *DTT* 1 (1938): 64-93.

7649. C Douglas Honeyford, "The Question of Christ," *BS* 95 (1938): 76-101.

7650. D. A. Frøvig, "Jesus som undergjører i den nyere teologi," *TTK* 11 (1940): 97-111.

7651. Walter Grundmann, "Das Problem der neutestamentlichen Christologie," *TLZ* 65 (1940): 65-73.

7652. Frederick C. Grant, "The Christ of the Four Gospels," *RL* 10 (1941): 430-42.

7653. Alfred E. Garvie, "The Prince of Peace," *ET* 54 (1942-1943): 68-69.

7654. Juan Bautista Manyá, "La psicología de la inteligencia en Cristo y sus derivaciones en la vida afectiva del Redentor," *RET* 3 (1943): 3-30.

7655. Jules Lebreton, "La foi en Jésus-Christ vie du chrétien; l'origine et le développement de cette foi dans l'église primitive," *RSR* 31 (1943): 17-69.

7656. Edmund D. Soper, "The Lord of Life," *RL* 12 (1943): 336-43.

7657. Robert E. Speer, "The Relationship of Jesus to the New Testament," *USR* 56 (1944-1945): 110-25.

7658. P. E. Kretzmann, "Kenotic Ignorance or Accommodation," *CTM* 17 (1946): 31-39.

7659. A. W. Argyle, "The Exaltation of our Lord Jesus Christ," *ET* 59 (1947-1948): 190-92.

7660. Humbert Bouëssé, "De la prise en charge de l'humanité par Jésus-Christ," *NRT* 69 (1947): 337-69.

7661. Paul E. Davies, "Jesus in Relation to Believing Man; Prolegomena to a Christology," *Interp* 1 (1947): 3-15.

7662. O. T. Owen, "Jesus Christ, Natural and Supernatural," *ET* 59 (1947-1948): 33-36.

7663. G. Pidgeon, "The Christological Basis of Historic Christianity," *RE* 44 (1947): 22-33.

7664. H. N. Ridderbos, "De Christologie van het Nieuwe Testament," *GTT* 47 (1947): 51-64.

7665. John Baker, "The Christological Problem," *ET* 60 (1948-1949): 176-79.

7666. A. J. Gossip, "The Mind of Christ-The Novelty of the Gospel," *ET* 62 (1950-1951): 195-200.

7667. Eva Krafft, "Christologie und Anthropologie im I. Petrusbrief," *EvT* 10 (1950-1951): 120-26.

7668. Jesús Solano, "Actualidades cristólogico-soteriológicas," *EE* 24 (1950):43-69.

7669. Martin Albertz, "Die 'Erstlinge' in der Botschaft des Neuen Testaments," *EvT* 12 (1952-1953): 151-55.

7670. Ch. Lemaître, "Pourquoi le Christ?" *NRT* 74 (1952): 688-705.

7671. E. L. Allen, "Representative-Christology in the New Testament," *HTR* 46 (1953): 161-70.

7672. J. Schmitt, "Les sources et les thèmes de la naissante foi apostolique au Christ Sauveur," *LumV* 15 (1954): 21-44.

7673. Josef Fink, "Die Anfänge der Christusdarstellung," *TRev* 51 (1955): 241-52.

7674. Eduard Schweizer, "Discipleship and Belief in Jesus as Lord from Jesus to the Hellenistic Church," *NTSt* 2 (1955- 1956): 87-99.

7675. Francisco de P. Solá, "Una nueva explicación del Yo de Jesucristo," *EE* 29 (1955): 443-78.

7676. Gabriel Pérez, "Humillación y exaltación de Cristo," *CB* 13 (1956): 4-10, 84-88.

7677. John Coutts, "Ephesians 1.3-14 and 1 Peter 1.3-12," *NTSt* 3 (1956-1957): 115-68.

7678. Klaus Dessecker, "Wie dünket euch um Christus?" *EvT* 16 (1956): 115-33.

7679. Reginald H. Fuller, "Some Problems of New Testament Christology," *ATR* 38 (1956): 146-52.

7680. L. A. Garrard, "The Diversity of New Testament Christology," *HJ* 5 (1956-1957): 213-22.

7681. John A. T. Robinson, "The Most Primitive Christology of All?" *JTS* N.S. 7 (1956): 177-89.

7682. Marcelo Azevedo, "As bases da Cristologia," *REB* 17 (1957): 582-605; 18 (1958): 373-84.

7683. Herbert Braun, "Der Sinn der neutestamentlichen Christologie," *ZTK* N.F. 54 (1957): 341-77.

7684. Eduard Schweizer, "Der Glaube an Jesus den 'Herrn' in seiner Entwicklung von den ersten Nachfolgern bis zur hellenistischen Gemeinde," *EvT* 17 (1957): 7ff.

7685. I. de la Potterie, "L'onction du Christ," *NRT* 80 (1958): 225-52.

7686. Felix Scheidweiler, "Paradoxie in der neutestamentlichen Christologie?" *ZNW* 49 (1958): 258-64.

7687. A. Gesché, "L'âme de Jésus dans la christologie du IVᵉ siècle," *RHE* 54 (1959): 385-425.

7688. C. F. D. Moule, "The Influence of Circumstances on the Use of Christological Terms," *JTS* N.S. 10 (1959): 247-63.

7689. Augustin George, "Gesù, la vite vera," *BO* 3 (1961): 121-206.

7690. Stephen S. Smalley, "The Christology of Acts," *ET* 73 (1961-1962): 358-62.

See also numbers 865, 1284, 1356, 3047, 6836 ff., 7090, 7295, 7299, 7478, 7506. 7508, 8766, 9621, *10005, 10075.*

(1) Synoptic Christology

7691. S. Hoekstra, "De Christologie van het canonieke Marcus-Evangelie, vergeleken met die van de beide andere synoptische Evangeliën," *TT* 5 (1871): 129-76, 313-33, 407-40.

7692. Karl Schmidt, "Gehört Jesus in das Evangelium, wie er selbst nach den Synoptikern verkündigt hat?" *NKZ* 13 (1902): 893-922.

7693. J. Kunze, "The Glory of Jesus Christ according to the First

Three Gospels," *LCR* 22 (1903): 695-724.

7694. W. T. Celestine Sheppard, "The 'Kenosis' according to St. Mark," *ITQ* 5 (1910): 265-78.

7695. L. von Sybel, "Vom Wachsen der Christologie im synoptischen Evangelium," *TSK* 100 (1927-1928): 362-401.

7696. Jean Giblet, "Jésus, messie et sauveur d'après les évangiles synoptiques," *LumV* no. 15 (1954): 45-82.

7697. Alv Kragerud, "Inntogshymne og engelsang. Til kristologien i Lukasevangeliet," *NTT* 57 (1956): 218-34.

7698. C. H. de Beus, "Een onderzoek naar formulecitaten bij Mattheus met het oog op het vroegste Christologisch denken volgens het Nieuwe Testament," *NedTT* 14 (1959-1960): 401-19.

7699. Johannes Schreiber, "Die Christologie des Markusevangeliums," *ZTK* N.F. 58 (1961): 154-83.

(2) Johannine Christology

7700. Otto Pfleiderer, "Zur johanneischen Christologie, mit Rücksicht auf W. Beyschlag's 'Chistologie des Neuen Testaments'," *ZWT* 9 (1866): 241-66.

7701. S. Hoekstra, "De Christologie der Apocalypse," *TT* 3 (1869): 363-402.

7702. Alex B. Orr, "Christ's Names in St. John's Gospel," *ET* 12 (1900-1901): 480.

7703. James Moffatt, "The Autonomy of Jesus: A Study in the Fourth Gospel," *Exp* 6th ser., 4 (1901): 122-39.

7704. E. A. Repass "Introduction to the Christology of St. John's Gospel," *LCR* 21 (1902): 568-73.

7705. Vincent M'Nabb, "The Christ of the Fourth Gospel," *ET* 18 (1906-1907): 171-74.

7706. F. Palmer, "The Christ of the Fourth Gospel," *HJ* 5 (1906-1907): 606-23.

7707. R. H. Strachan, "The Christ of the Fourth Gospel," *Exp* 7th ser., 8 (1909): 357-64, 501-507; 9 (1910): 139-43

7708. A. G. Voigt, "Christology from a Johannine Point of View,"

LCR 34 (1915): 68-74.

7709. Johannes Behm, "Die johanneische Christologie als Abschluss der Christologie des Neuen Testaments," *NKZ* 41 (1930): 577-601.

7710. Hans Erich Creutzig, "Zur johanneischen Christologie," *NKZ* (*Luthertum*): 49 (1938): 214-22.

7711. M.-E. Boismard, "Jésus, sauveur, d'après saint Jean," *LumV* no. 15 (1954): 103-22.

7712. J. H. Stelma, "De verkondiging der opstanding naar Johannes bij Rudolf Bultmann," *NedTT* 9 (1954-1955): 338-48.

7713. Bent Noack, "Johannesevangeliets messiasbillede og dets kristologi," *DTT* 19 (1956): 129-55.

7714. Everett F. Harrison, "The Christology of the Fourth Gospel in Relation to the Synoptics," *BS* 116 (1959): 303-309.

7715. Eugen Schmitt, "Die christologische Interpretation als das Grundlegende der Apokalypse," *TQ* 140 (1960): 257-90.

7715.1 Leander E. Keck, "Mark 3:7-12 and Mark's Christology," *JBL* 84/4 (1965): 341-58.

7715.2 J. Becker, "Wunder und Christologie: Zum literarkritischen und christologischen Problem der Wunder im Johannesevangelium," *NTSt* 16 (1969-1970): 130-48.

7715.3 Norman Perrin, "The Christology of Mark: A Study in Methodology," *JR* 51 (1971). 173-87.

7715.4 Werner H. Kelber, "Mark 14:32-42: Gethsemane. Passion Christology and Discipleship Failure," *ZNW* 63 (1972): 166-87.

7715.5 M. D. Johnson, "Reflections on a Wisdom Approach to Matthew's Christology," *CBQ* 36 (1974): 44-64.

7715.6 Jack D. Kingsbury, "The Composition and Christology of Matthew 28:16-20," *JBL* 93/4 (1974): 573-84.

7715.7 Dario Composta, "Cristologia e False Cristologie," *Div* 21 (1977): 408-12.

7715.8 Brunero Gherardini, "Lutero e le Cristologie Moderne: Rottura o Continuita?" *Div* 21 (1977): 5-22.

7715.9 Estella B. Horning, "Chiasmus, Creedal Structure, and

Christology in Hebrews 12:1-2," *BRes* 23 (1978): 37-48.

7715.10 Leander E. Keck, "Jesus in New Testament Christology," *ABR* 28 (1980): 1-20.

7715.11 Jack D. Kingsbury, "The 'Divine Man' as the Key to Mark's Christology: The End of an Era?" *Interp* 35 (1981): 243-57.

7715.12 Harry L. Chronis, "The Torn Veil: Cultus and Christology in Mark 15:37-39," *JBL* 101/1 (1982): 97-114.

7715.13 J. Becker, "Ich bin die Auferstehung und das Leben. Eine Skizze der johanneischen Christologie," *TZ* 39 (1983): 138-51.

7715.14 Elizabeth Johnson, "Jesus, the Wisdom of God: A Biblical Basis for Non-Androcentric Christology," *ETL* 61/4 (1985): 261-94.

7715.15 Earl S. Johnson, "Is Mark 15:39 the Key to Mark's Christology?" *JSNT* 31 (1987): 3-22.

7715.16 E. K. Broadhead, "Jesus the Nazarene: Narrative Strategy and Christological Imagery in the Gospel of Mark," *JSNT* 52 (1993): 3-18.

7715.17 E. K. Broadhead, "Linguistics and Christology: A Critical Note on Mark 6:31, 32-46," *ABR* 42 (1994): 69-70.

(3). Pauline Christology

7716. Otto Pfleiderer, "Die paulinische Christologie," *ZWT* 14 (1871): 502-35.

7717. J. Morison, "The Christology of St. Paul," *Exp* 1st ser., 9 (1879): 105-22.

7718. J. Morison, "The Christology of St. Paul," *Exp* 1st ser., 10 (1879): 149-62; 11 (1880): 309-20, 458-75.

7719. H. Holtzmann, "Die paulinische Christologie im Verhältnis zu dem Gegensatze von σάρξ und πνεῦμα," *ZWT* 31 (1888): 279-94.

7720. Emil Lingen, "Zur paulinischen Christologie," *ZKT* 20 (1896): 449-70.

7721. E. Medley, "The Conception of Christ Suggested to a Heathen Inquirer by Paul's Earliest Extant Writing," *Exp* 5th ser., 4 (1896): 359-70.

7722. Newport J. D. White, "A Point in the Christology of First Corinthians," *Exp* 6th ser., 2 (1900): 15-24.

7723. Vincent Rose, "Études sur la théologie de St. Paul," *RB* 11 (1902): 321-46; 12 (1903): 337-61.

7724. S. Odland, "Nogle hovedpunkter af den paulinske kristologi," *NTT* 4 (1903): 169-205.

7725. Alfred E. Garvie, "Studies in the Pauline Theology; III. The Doctrine of Christ," *Exp* 7th ser., 7 (1909): 126-38.

7726. J. Iverach, "The Epistle to the Colossians and its Christology," *ET* 25 (1913-1914): 150-53, 205-209.

7727. H. H. Lindemann, "Apostolic Christology: A Comparison of Paul with his Predecessors," *BW* 46 (1915): 14-25.

7728. Léonce de Grandmaison, "Le Christ de l'histoire dans l'oeuvre de saint Paul," *RSR* 13 (1923): 481-90.

7729. Ed. Rodhe, "Gottesglaube und Kyriosglaube bei Paulus," *ZNW* 22 (1923): 43-57.

7730. Emanuel Hirsch, "Zur paulinischen Christologie," *ZST* 7 (1929-1930): 605-30.

7731. Otto Michel, "Die Entstehung der paulinischen Christologie," *ZNW* 28 (1929): 324-33.

7732. Vincent McNabb, "Essai sur la christologie de saint Paul," *RB* 42 (1933): 320-27.

7733. Walter Dress, "Vom Problem paulinischer Christologie," *TB* 13 (1934): 43-58.

7734. Hans Windisch, "Zur Christologie der Pastoralbriefe," *ZNW* 34 (1935): 213-38.

7735. Ralph G. Turnbull, "The Christology of Paul," *USR* 57 (1945-1946): 121-37.

7736. D. J. O'Herlihy, "Witnesses to Christ; I. St. Paul," *Scr* 3 (1948): 103-106.

See also number 7308.

7736.1 Ronald Williamson, "Philo and New Testament Christology," *ET* 90 (1979): 361-65.

7736.2 C. N. Tsirpanlis, "Some Reflections on Philoxenos'

Christology," *GOTR* 25 (1980): 152-62.

7736.3   Issa A. Saliba, "The Bishop of Antioch and the Heretics: A Study of a Primitive Christology," *EQ* 54 (1982): 65-76.

(4). Patristic Christology

7737.   J. Dräseke, "Beron und Pseudo-Hippolytos. Ein Beitrag zur Geschichte der Christologie," *ZWT* 29 (1886): 291-318.

7738.   G. Voisin, "La doctrine christologique de saint Athanase," *RHE*, 1 (1900): 226-48.

7739.   Julius Boehmer, "Zum 2. Artikel des Apostolikums," *ZNW* 7 (1906): 176-81.

7740.   F. Nau, "Sur la christologie de Timothée Aelure," *ROC* 14 (1909): 99-103.

7741.   D. Plooij, "De Christologie van den Herder van Hermas," *TT* 43 (1909): 297-333.

7742.   Paul Galtier, "L'ὁμοούσιος de Paul de Samosate," *RSR* 12 (1922): 30-45.

7743.   R. P. Casey, "Clement and the Two Divine Logoi," *JTS* 25 (1923-1924): 43-56.

7744.   John Line, "The Beginnings of Christological Doctrine," *CJRT* 2 (1925): 211-21.

7745.   B. Capelle, "Le symbole romain au second siècle," *RBén* 39 (1927): 33-45.

7746.   F. J. Badcock, "Le crédo primitif d'Afrique," *RBén* 45 (1933): 3-9.

7747.   Gustave Bardy, "Sur la réitération du concile de Nicée," *RSR* 13 (1933): 430-50.

7748.   Paul Galtier, "Les anathematismes de saint Cyrille et le concile de Chalcédoine," *RSR* 23 (1933): 45-57.

7749.   G. Salet, "Le Christ, notre vie," *NRT* 62 (1935): 785-809.

7750.   Henri de Riedmatten, "Some Neglected Aspects of Apollinarist Christology," *DS* 1 (1948): 239-60.

7751.   Augusto Segovia, "Natus est-nascitur. La eterna generación del Hijo de Dios y su enunciación verbal en la literature patrística," *RET* 8 (1948): 385-407.

7752. Joseph Lécuyer, "Le sacerdoce céleste du Christ selon Chrysostome," *NRT* 72 (1950): 561-79.

7753. H. du Manoir, "Le quinzième centenaire du concile de Chalcédoine (451-1951)," *NRT* 73 (1951): 785-803.

7754. Wilhelm Schneemelcher, "Chalkedon 451-1951," *EvT* 11 (1951-1952): 241-59.

7755. Mauricio Gordillo, "El Concilio de Calcedonia en la historia del dogma católico a la luz de la Enciclica 'Sempiternus Rex Christus'," *EE* 26 (1952): 291-312.

7756. J. Schmitt, "Le Christ Jésus dans la foi et la vie de la naissante église apostolique," *LumV* no. 9 (1953): 23-42.

7757. Julian Stead, "Perichoresis in the Christological Chapters of the *De Trinitate* of Pseudo-Cyril of Alexandria," *DS* 6 (1953): 12-20.

7758. Jean Daniélou, "La charrou symbole de la croix (Irénée, *Adv. Haer.*, IV, 34,4)," *RSR* 42 (1954): 193-203.

7759. Werner Elert, "Christusbild und Christusdogma in der alten Kirche," *ZST* 23 (1954): 1-15.

7760. Jesús Solano, "Jesucristo bajo las denominaciones divinas en San Ignacio," *EE* 30 (1956): 325-42.

7761. G. Jouassard, " 'Impassibilité' du logos et 'impassibilité' de l'âme humaine chez saint Cyrille d'Alexandrie," *RSR* 45 (1957): 209-24.

7762. R. P. Casey, "The Earliest Christologies," *JTS* N.S. 9 (1958): 253-77.

7763. W. F. Macomber, "The Christology of the Synod of Seleucia-Ctesiphon A.D. 486," *OCP* 24 (1958): 142-54.

7764. Edmund Schlink, "La christologie de Chalcédoine dans le dialogue oecuménique," *VCar* 12 (1958): 23-30.

7765. M. Pellegrino, "Cristo e il martire nel pensiero di Origene," *Div* 3 (1959): 144-70.

7766. John S. Romanides, "Highlights in the Debate over Theodore of Mopsuestia's Christology and Some Suggestions for a Fresh Approach," *GOTR* 5 (1959-1960): 140-85.

7767. Suzanne Poque, "*Christus Mercator*. Notes augustiniennes,"

RSR 48 (1960): 564-77.

7768.   F. Refoulé, "La christologie d'Evagre et l'Origénisme," *OCP* 27 (1961): 221-66.

7769.   Martin Tetz, "Zum Streit zwischen Orthodoxie und Häresie an der Wende des 4. zum 5. Jahrhundert," *EvT* 21 (1961): 354-68.

See also numbers 1284, 7687, 7833, 8246, 9897, *10023*.

7769.1   C. N. Tsirpanlis, "Some Reflections on Philoxenos' Christology," *GOTR* 25 (1980): 152-62.

7769.2   Issa A. Saliba, "The Bishop of Antioch and the Heretics: A Study of a Primitive Christology," *EQ* 54 (1982): 65-76.

(5). Reformation and Modern Christology

7770.   M. Trottet, "De la vie et de l'oeuvre de Christ au point de vue de la théologie spéculative," *RT* 6 (1853): 193-223, 257-75.

7771.   W. H. Wynn, "Recent Studies in Christology," *LQ* 6 (1876): 161-86.

7772.   Dr. Doedes, "Ein Mandat Jesu Christ von Nikolaus Herman," *TSK* 51 (1878): 303-13.

7773.   Ph. H. Hugenholtz, "De Christologie en de huidige godsdienstwetenschap," *TT* 15 (1881): 30-52.

7774.   L. J. van Rhijn, "Gedachten over eene christelijke theologie voor de behoefte van onzen tijd," *TS* 4 (1886): 272-81.

7775.   J. G. Boekenoogen, "Christologische beschouwingen," *TT* 26 (1892): 147-69, 275-306, 514-43, 568-95.

7776.   Frank H. Foster, "Studies in Christology: With Criticisms upon the Theories of Professor Adolph Harnack," *BS* 49 (1892): 240-75.

7777.   William W. Kinsley, "Science and Christ," *BS* 50 (1893): 93-118, 291-308, 519-40, 656-67.

7778.   P. Kölbing, "Schleiermacher's Zeugnis vom Sohne Gottes nach seinen Festpredigten," *ZTK* 3 (1893): 277-310.

7779.   Prescott F. Jernegan, "Christological Implications of the Higher Criticism," *BW* 3 (1894): 420-28.

7780.   A. Verkouw, "Christus beteekenis voor de hedendaagsche

Godgeleerdheid," *TS* 12 (1894): 89-133, 181-230.

7781. Ludwig Kelber, "Das protestantische Christusdrama und die Kritik," *NKZ* 6 (1895): 137-55, 246-70.

7782. Milan C. Ayers, "The Christ of Today," *BS* 53 (1896): 739-44.

7783. Otto Jensen, "Hvorledes bør det kristologiske problem videnskabelig formuleres," *NTT* 3 (1902): 209-24.

7784. James Stalker, "The Article 'Jesus' in the Three Encyclopaedias," *BW* 19 (1902): 19-32.

7785. Charles G. Shaw, "Jesus Christ and Eternal Life," *BW* 22 (1903): 436-48.

7786. John W. Buckham, "The Christocentric Theology: Review and a Criticism," *BS* 62 (1905): 440-54.

7787. R. J. Drummond, "Forrest's 'Authority of Christ'," *ET* 17 (1905-1906): 547-50.

7788. Arnold Hein, "Die Christologie von D. Fr. Strauss," *ZTK* 16 (1906): 321-46.

7789. John Dickie, "Modern Positive Theology; III. Christology," *ET* 20 (1908-1909): 74-75.

7790. Ernst Günther, "Bemerkungen zur Christologie von David Friedrich Strauss," *ZTK* 18 (1908): 202-11.

7791. C. A. Drougge, "Albrecht Ritschls laere om Kristus," *NTT* 10 (1909): 70-96.

7792. C. A. Drougge, "Albrecht Ritschls kristologi i dens forhold til troen," *NTT* 10 (1909): 130-70.

7793. H. R. Mackintosh, "Christologies Ancient and Modern," *ET* 21 (1909-1910): 486-90, 553-58.

7794. Herman Bavinck, "Christological Movements in the Nineteenth Century," *BS* 68 (1911): 381-404.

7795. Henri Bois, "La christologie et le subconscient," *RTQR* 20 (1911): 289-324, 437-70.

7796. Shirley Jackson Case, "Modern Belief about Jesus," *BW* 37 (1911): 7-18.

7797. Frank H. Foster, "The Christology of a Modern Rationalist," *AJT* 15 (1911): 584-98.

7798. William A. Brown, "The Place of Christ in Modern Theology," *AJT* 16 (1912): 31-50.

7799. Ernst Günther, "Die christologische Aufgabe der Gegenwart," *ZTK* 22 (1912): 78-79.

7800. H. R. Mackintosh, "The Liberal Conception of Jesus in its Strength and Weakness," *AJT* 16 (1912): 410-25.

7801. Benjamin B. Warfield, "Christless Christianity," *HTR* 5 (1912): 423-73.

7802. D. C. Macintosh, "What is the Christian Religion?" *HTR* 7 (1914): 16-46.

7803. Ambrose W. Vernon, "A Modern Confession of Faith on Jesus Christ," *HJ* 14 (1915-1916): 760-68.

7804. E. S. Buchanan, "The Lost Christ," *BS* 73 (1916): 44-54.

7805. George Cross, "The Attitude of the Modern Theologian toward Jesus Christ," *BW* 47 (1916): 25-33.

7806. George E. Wolfe, "Troeltsch's Conception of the Significance of Jesus," *AJT* 20 (1916): 179-204.

7807. Jens Gleditsch, "Kristologienstorøtter," *NTT* 18 (1917): 1-18.

7808. J. H. Skrine, "Telepathy as Interpreting Christ," *HJ* 16 (1917-1918): 133-42.

7809. P. T. Forsyth, "The Christianity of Christ and Christ our Christianity," *RE* 15 (1918): 249-65.

7810. F. Büchsel, "Zum Jesusbilde Eduard Meyers," *NKZ* 33 (1922): 269-82.

7811. W. J. McConnell, "Christ and Christianity," *BS* 82 (1925): 139-45.

7812. Emanuel Hirsch, "Antwort an Rudolf Bultmann," *ZST* 4 (1926-1927): 631-61.

7813. J. Thijs, "De christologie bij de jong-modernen," *GTT* 28 (1927-1928): 389-405.

7814. J. M. Creed, "Christologie in der grossbritannischen Theologie der Gegenwart," *TB* 7 (1928): 242-43.

7815. Heinrich Frick, "Christologie im deutschen Protestantismus der Gegenwart," *TB* 7 (1928): 244-48.

7816. Heinrich Frick, "Rückblick auf die Aussprache," *TB* 7

(1928): 269-72.

7817. W. J. Sparrow Simpson, "Some German Thinkers on Christology," *ET* 40 (1928-1929): 406-11.

7818. Julius Kögel, "Das Christusproblem der Gegenwart," *NKZ* 40 (1929): 757-90, 801-10.

7819. Eugene W. Lyman, "The Place of Christ in Modern Theology," *JR* 9 (1929): 184-203.

7820. Martin Dibelius, "Jesus in Contemporary German Theology," *JR* 11 (1931): 179-211.

7821. Albert Salewski, "Die Sendung Jesu bei Bernhard von Clairvaux und in der Theologie der Gegenwart," *NKZ* 42 (1931): 519-39.

7822. W. Norman Pittenger, "An Essay in Christology," *ATR* 14 (1932): 34-41.

7823. Theodor Siegfried, "Zur Christologie Schleiermachers," *ZTK* N.F. 13 (1932): 223-35.

7824. A. Fornerod, "Théologie et métaphysique: le problème christologique," *RTP* N.S. 15 (1932): 20-45.

7825. T. Graebner, "The Modernistic Christ," *CTM* 4 (1933): 81-85.

7826. Emil Brunner, "The Absoluteness of Jesus," *USR* 46 (1934-1935): 269-82; 47 (1935-1936): 23-33.

7827. Albert E. Day, "The Significance of Jesus Christ for the Modern World," *RL* 3 (1934): 266-74.

7828. Ira A. Morton, "The Saviourhood of Jesus-A Psycho-Ethical View," *CQ* 11 (1934): 31-47.

7829. E. H. Blakeney, "The Liberal-Modernist View of Jesus," *HJ* 34 (1935-1936): 613-14

7830. C. J. Cadoux, "The Liberal-Modernist View of Jesus," *HJ* 34 (1935-1936): 614-17

7831. R. A. Edwards, "The Liberal-Modernist View of Jesus," *HJ* 34 (1935-1936): 443-49.

7832. E. Mersch, "L'objet de la théologie et le 'Christus Totus'," *RSR* 26 (1936): 129-57.

7833. A. L. Lilley, "A Christological Controversy of the Twelfth

Century," *JTS* 39 (1938): 225-38.

7834.   W. Norman Pittenger, "The Christology of the German Crisis-Theology," *ATR* 20 (1938): 1-15.

7835.   Ernst Strasser, "Die Bedeutung Jesu für Luther," *NKZ* (*Luthertum*): 49 (1938): 366-72.

7836.   Mary E. Andrews, "God's Continuing Revelation," *JBR* 7 (1939) 3-8.

7837.   Walter M. Horton, "Jesus our Contemporary," *RL* 9 (1940): 376-82.

7838.   E. L. Allen, "Suggestions for a Revised Christology," *HJ* 40 (1941-1942): 65-74.

7839.   Donald T. Rowlingson, "The Importance of Jesus for the Twentieth Century," *RL* 10 (1941): 121-29.

7840.   Anton Fridrichsen, "Söderbloms Jesustolkning, en forskningsuppgift," *RelB* 1 (1942): 58-63.

7841.   B. Schultze, "Problemi di teologia presso gli ortodossi; Christologia," *OCP* 9 (1943): 135-70.

7842.   Thomas S. Kepler, "The Dilemma Regarding Jesus," *JBR* 12 (1944): 12-16.

7843.   F. Ménégoz, "Études sur la personne et l'oeuvre de Jésus," *RHPR* 24 (1944): 61-81

7844.   Shirley Jackson Case, "The Lure of Christology," *JR* 25 (1945): 157-67.

7845.   Joseph L. Hromádka, "Jesus Christ and the Present Distress," *TTod* 2 (1945): 19-33.

7846.   John M. Shaw, "Our Lord and Saviour Jesus Christ," *TTod* 2 (1945): 316-28.

7847.   Ray Knight, "Gospels and Epistles," *HJ* 45 (1946-1947): 304-308.

7848.   Oscar Cullmann, "Christ et le temps," *RHPR* 28 (1948): 85-90.

7849.   Sherman E. Johnson, "A Fresh Approach to Christology," *ATR* 30 (1948): 170-72.

7850.   Thomas Coates, "Luther's Picture of Christ on the Basis of the Church Postil Sermons," *CTM* 20 (1949): 241-68.

7851. P. Maury, "Jésus-Christ, cet inconnu," *RHPR* 29 (1949): 343-45.

7852. G. T. Thomson, "The Presence of Christ," *EQ* 21 (1949): 133-60.

7853. John A. Mackay, "Jesus, Lord of Thought," *TTod* 7 (1950): 3-8.

7854. Rudolf Bultmann, "Das christologische Bekenntnis des ökumenischen Rates," *EvT* 11 (1951-1952): 1-13.

7855. T. H. Croxall, "Facets of Kierkegaard's Christology," *TTod* 1 (1951): 327-39

7856. A. Delhaye, "Jésus Christ raison de croire selon les apologistes catholiques du XIXᵉ siècle depuis l'epoque de Lacordaire," *ETL* 27 (1951): 5-29.

7857. Gerhard Gloege, "Gott im Widerspruch zur Christologie von Heinrich Vogel," *TLZ* 76 (1951): 79-90.

7858. Alden Drew Kelley, "A Functionalist Approach to Christology," *ATR* 33 (1951): 1-12.

7859. Guy Kendall, "Whither Christology?" *HJ* 50 (1951- 1952): 257-61.

7860. HeinrichVogel, "Fünfzig Thesen," *EvT* 11 (1951-1952): 513-17.

7861. D. M. Baillie, "The Christological Theory of William Sanday," *ET* 64 (1952-1953): 236-39

7862. Van A. Harvey, "On Interpreting Christ to America," *RL* 21 (1952): 527-36.

7863. John Marsh, "Christus Veritas," *ET* 64 (1952-1953): 14-18.

7864. D. E. Nineham, "The Christology of Leonard Hodgson's 'Doctrine of the Trinity'," *ET* 64 (1952-1953): 164-67.

7865. J. E. L. Oulton, "James Denney's 'Jesus and the Gospel'," *ET* 64 (1952-1953): 259-62

7866. A. R. Vine, "H. M. Relton's 'A Study in Christology'," *ET* 64 (1952-1953): 132-36

7867. J. Alonso, "Razón ontológica de la mediación pacificadora de Cristo," *RHT* 13 (1953): 549-56.

7868. Bruce M. Metzger, "The Jehovah's Witnesses and Jesus

Christ," *TTod* 10 (1953): 65-85.

7869.   Paul L. Holmer, "Philosophical Criticism and Christology," *JR* 34 (1954): 88-100.

7870.   William Hallock Johnson, "Science and Christ," *PSB* no. 47 (1954): 7-16.

7871.   Joseph Sittler, "A Christology of Function," *LQ* 6 (1954): 122-31.

7872.   Maria F. Sulzbach, "The Place of Christology in Contem porary Protestantism," *RL* 23 (1954): 206-15.

7873.   J. H. Thomas, "The Christology of Soren Kierkegaard and Karl Barth," *HJ* 53 (1954-1955): 280-88.

7874.   J. M. Delgado Varela, "El tema del 'YO de Cristo' en la teologia contemporánea española," *RET* 14 (1954): 567-81.

7875.   Heinrich Vogel, "Die Umdeutung der Christologie in der Religionsphilosophie Immanuel Kants," *EvT* 14 (1954): 399-413.

7876.   James Barr, "Christ in Gospel and Creed," *SJT* 8 (1955): 225-37.

7877.   Oscar Cullmann, "Zur Frage der Erforschung der neutestamentlichen Christologie," *KD* 1 (1955): 133-41.

7878.   Roger Hazelton, "Pascal and Jesus Christ: Reflections on the 'Mystère de Jésus'," *JR* 35 (1955): 65-73.

7879.   Alessandro Pellegrini, "La cristologia di Hölderlin, e la critica," *O* 2 (1955): 155-70.

7880.   Guy H. Ranson, "The Primary Emphasis in Christology," *RE* 52 (1955): 290-309.

7881.   A. R. Vine, "Important Hypotheses Reconsidered- Sanday's Christological Hypothesis," *ET* 67 (1955-1956): 49-52.

7882.   Siegfried Hansen, "Die Bedeutung des Leidens für das Christusbild Soren Kierkegaards," *KD* 2 (1956): 1-28.

7883.   W. Norman Pittenger, "Degree or Kind? A Christological Essay," *CJT* 2 (1956): 189-96.

7884.   John McIntire, "Christology and Revelation," *RTR* 15 (1956): 81-89; 16 (1957): 11-20, 44-52.

7885.   James M. Mallach, "Do we Need a Space Christology?" *ATR*

39 (1957): 169-74.

7886.   Heinrich Berchert, " 'Ohne Christus wäre ich Atheist'," *EvT* 18 (1958): 445-60.

7887.   Thorwald W. Bender, "Ferré's Christology: 'Christ in you, the hope of glory'," *BETS* 1, no. 2 (1958): 1-14.

7888.   Paul E. Davies, "Jesús en relación con los creyentes; prolegómenos a una cristología," *CT* 27-28 (1958): 25-38.

7889.   Helmut Dee, "Die Christologie in Paul Tillichs 'Systematischer Theologie'," *EvT* 18 (1958): 89-96.

7890.   Jerome Ficek, "The Christology of Paul Tillich: the New Being in Jesus as the Christ," *BETS* 1, no. 2 (1958): 15-23.

7891.   Charles R. Gresham, "The Christology of Current Religious Education," *BETS* 1, no. 2 (1958): 29-37

7892.   J. H. Hick, "The Christology of D. M. Baillie," *SJT* 11 (1958): 1-12.

7893.   Kenneth Kantzer, "The Christology of Karl Barth," *BETS* 1, no. 2 (1958): 25-28.

7894.   Johanna Konrad, "Friedrich Loofs Beitrag zur Christologie," *EvT* 18 (1958): 324-33.

7895.   J. M. Lochman, "The Problem of Realism in R. Niebuhr's Christology," *SJT* 11 (1958): 253-64.

7896.   Vincent Taylor, "Professor Oscar Cullmann's 'Die Christologie des Neuen Testaments'," *ET* 70 (1958-1959): 136-40.

7897.   David M. Stanley, "Cullmann's New Testament Christology: An Appraisal," *ThSt* 20 (1959): 409-21.

7898.   Paul M. Bretscher, "Luther's Christ," *CTM* 31 (1960): 212-14.

7899.   Oscar Cullmann, "Die Christologie des Neuen Testaments," *RHPR* 30 (1960): 185-87.

7900.   Grover Foley, "Ritschls Urteil über Zinzendorfs Christocentrismus," *EvT* 20 (1960): 314-26.

7901.   Woodbridge O. Johnson, "The Coming Copernican Christology," *HJ* 59 (1960): 10-20.

7902.   B. Leeming, "The 'Basis' of the World Council of

Churches," *HeyJ* 1 (1960): 234-37.

7903.   H. E. W. Turner, "Frank Weston's 'The One Christ'," *ET* 72 (1960-1961): 277-79.

7904.   Erich Beyreuther, "Christozentrismus und Trinität-sauffassung bei Zinzendorf," *EvT* 21 (1961): 28-47.

7905.   Jackson Lee Ice, "The Christ above the Christ," *FF* 14 (1961): 76-84.

7906.   Heinrich Steege, "Beneficia Christi," *EvT* 21 (1961): 264-84. See also numbers 8151 ff., 8539.

7906.1 John Macquarrie, "Recent Thinking on Christian Beliefs. I. Christology," *ET* 88 (1976): 36-39.

7906.2 Russell W. Palmer, "The Christology of Dietrich Bohnoeffer," *EQ* 49 (1977): 132-40.

7906.3 Michael F. Palmer, "Paul Tillich's Critique of Bultmann's Christology," *HeyJ* 20 (1979): 279-89.

7906.4 R. Krieg, "Cardinal Ratzinger, Max Scheler and Christology," *ITQ* 47 (1980): 205-19.

7906.5 Robert A. Krieg, "Is Jesus the Focus of Kung's Christology?" *HeyJ* 22 (1981): 243-60.

7906.6 Nigel M. Watson, "Willi Marxsen's Approach to Christology," *ET* 97 (1985-1986): 36-42.

b. *Christological Titles and Predicates*

(1). General Studies

7907.   F. H. Stead, "The Chief Pauline Names for Christ," *Exp* 3rd ser., 7 (1888): 386-95.

7908.   J. Watson, "The Name of Names," *Exp* 5th ser., 7 (1898): 81-92.

7909.   B. Whiteford, "The Name of Names: A Criticism," *Exp* 5th ser., 8 (1898): 234-40.

7910.   Benjamin B. Warfield, " 'Redeemer' and 'Redemption'," *PTR* 14 (1916): 177-201.

7911.   George Henderson, "The Names and Titles of Christ," *PTR* 20 (1922): 475-81.

7912.   K. L. Schmidt and E. C. Hoskyns, "'Ιησοῦς χριστός θεοῦ υἱός σωτήρ," *TB* 7 (1928): 254-57.

7913. Charles Edward Smith, "The Four Great Titles of our Lord which Cover his Entire Career," *BS* 86 (1929): 93-99.

7914. G. Hepperger, "De Ss. Nomine Iesu," *VD* 21 (1941): 345-46.

7915. D. Moule, "The Influence of Circumstances on the Use of Christological Terms," *JTS* N.S. 10 (1959): 247-63.

See also numbers 3436, 7480, 7542

7915.1 R. S. Wuest, "The Deity of Jesus in the Greek Texts of John and Paul," *BS* 119 (1962): 216-26.

7915.2 R. A. Rosenberg, "The a Star of the Messiah 'Reconsidered'," *B* 53 (1972): 105-109.

7915.3 Klaus Berger, "Die koniglichen Messiastraditionen des Neuen Testaments," *NTSt* 20 (1973-1974): 1-44.

7915.4 W. Barnes Tatum, " 'The Origin of Jesus Messiah' (Matt. 1:1, 18a): Matthew's Use of the Infancy Traditions," *JBL* 96 (1977): 523-35.

7915.5 Barnabas Lindars, "Jesus as Advocate: A Contribution to the Christology Debate," *BJRL* 62/2 (1980): 476-97.

7915.6 Jill Smith and Harold Fehderau, "Translating Christ and Messiah in the New Testament," *BTr* 32 (1981): 423-31.

7915.7 Joel Marcus, "Mark 14:61: 'Are You the Messiah-Son-of-God'?" *NT* 31 (1989): 125-41.

7915.8 B. W. Longenecker, "The Unbroken Messiah: A Johannine Feature and Its Social Functions," *NTSt* 41 (1995): 428-41.

(2). Messiah (Christ)

7916. A. Hilgenfeld, "Der Messias-Menschensohn," *ZWT* 35 (1892): 445-64.

7917. H. M. Scott, "The Teachings of Jesus and the Teachings of the Jews in the Time of Christ Respecting the Messiah and his Kingdom," *BW* 1 (1893): 408-19.

7918. Paul Chapuis, "Le messianisme de Jésus de Nazareth," *RTP* 37 (1904): 5-30

7919. George D. Castor, "Recent Discussions of the Messiahship of Jesus," *BW* 34 (1909): 111-19.

7920. H. T. de Graaf, "Jezus-Messias, volgens Dr. Bruins," *TT* 3 (1909): 413-34.

7921. Johs. Herrmann, "Der Messias aus Davids Geschlecht," *ZWT* 51 (1909): 260-68.

7922. Paul Humbert, "Le Messie dans le targum des prophétes," *RTP* 42 (1909): 420-47; 44 (1911): 5-46.

7923. Ferdinand Kattenbusch, "Das Messiastum Jesu," *ZNW* 12 (1911): 270-86.

7924. Geerhardus Vos, "The Ubiquity of the Messiahship in the Gospels," *BR* 1 (1916): 490-506.

7925. Shailer Mathews, "The Permanent Message of Messianism," *BW* 49 (1917): 267-74.

7926. D. A. Frøvig, "De nyere undersøkelser angaaende spørsmaalet om Jesu messianitet," *NTT* 20 (1919): 217-35.

7927. E. F. Scott, "What did the Idea of Messiah Mean to the Early Christians?" *JR* 1 (1921): 418-20.

7928. J. O. F. Murray, "The Messiahship of Jesus," *ET* 38 (1926-1927): 343-48, 401-405, 439-43.

7929. Hermann Dechent, "Der 'Gerechte'-eine Bezeichnung für den Messias," *TSK* 100 (1927-1928): 439-43.

7930. A. Guillaume, "The Messiah in Judaism and Christianity," *ET* 43 (1931-1932): 406-11.

7931. J. Héring, "Messie juif et Messie chrétien. (Questions et réponses)," *RHPR* 18 (1938): 419-31.

7932. D. F. Stamps, "Under Orders," *RE* 35 (1938): 71-79.

7933. Ralph Rogers Hawthorne, "The Significance of the Name of Christ," *BS* 103 (1946): 215-22, 348-62, 453-63.

7934. Charles C. Torrey, "The Messiah Son of Ephraim," *JBL* 66 (1947): 253-77.

7935. Knut Lundmark, "Till frågan om Messiasidéns och den nytestamentliga eskatologiens ursprung och utveckling," *STK* 26 (1950): 346-68.

7936. R. Lansing Hicks, "Messiah, Second Moses, Son of Man," *ATR* 33 (1951): 24-29.

7937. Millar Burrows, "The Messiahs of Aaron and Israel," *ATR* 34

(1952): 202-206.

7938.   N. Wieder, "The Doctrine of the Two Messiahs among the Karaites," *JJS* 6 (1955): 14-23.

See also numbers 904, 1335, 3144, 3198, 3202, 3207, 3208, 3542, 3543, 6838, 9657 ff.

7938.1   R. S. Wuest, "The Deity of Jesus in the Greek Texts of John and Paul," *BS* 119 (1962): 216-26.

7938.2   Otto Betz, "Die Frage nach dem messianischen Bewußtsein Jesu," *NT* 6 (1963): 20-48.

7938.3   R. A. Rosenberg, "The a Star of the Messiah 'Reconsidered'," *B* 53 (1972): 105-109.

7938.4   Klaus Berger, "Die koniglichen Messiastraditionen des Neuen Testaments," *NTSt* 20 (1973-1974): 1-44.

7938.5   Pennar Davies, "The Meaning of Messiahship," *ET* 87 (1975): 85-87.

7938.6   Lloyd Gaston, "The Messiah of Israel As Teacher of the Gentiles: The Setting of Matthew's Christology," *Interp* 29 (1975): 24-40.

7938.7   W. Barnes Tatum, " 'The Origin of Jesus Messiah' (Matt. 1:1, 18a): Matthew's Use of the Infancy Traditions," *JBL* 96 (1977): 523-35.

7938.8   Barnabas Lindars, "Jesus as Advocate: A Contribution to the Christology Debate," *BJRL* 62/2 (1980): 476-97.

7938.9   Jill Smith and Harold Fehderau, "Translating Christ and Messiah in the New Testament," *BTr* 32 (1981): 423-31.

7938.10   B. W. Longenecker, "The Unbroken Messiah: A Johannine Feature and Its Social Functions," *NTSt* 41 (1995): 428-41.

(3). Prophet

7939.   Canon R. H. Kennett, "Jesus the Prophet," *HJ* 5 (1906-1907): 136-55

7940.   Gerhard Kittel, C. H. Dodd, and Nathaniel Micklem, "'Ιησοῦς ὁ διδάσκαλος καὶ προφήτης," *TB* 7 (1928): 249-54.

7941.   Paul E. Davies, "Jesus and the Role of the Prophet," *JBL* 64

(1945): 241-54.

7942.   A. J. B. Higgins, "Jesus as Prophet," *ET* 57 (1945-1946): 292-94.

7943.   Franklin W. Young, "Jesus the Prophet: A Re-examination," *JBL* 68 (1949): 285-99.

See also number 264.

7943.1   Paul E. Davies, "Did Jesus Die as a Martyr-Prophet?" *BRes* 19 (1974): 37-47.

7943.2   M. W. Anderson, "P. T. Forsyth: Prophet of the Cross," *EQ* 47 (1975): 146-61. christology

7943.3   Johannes M. Nutzel, "Zum Schicksal der Eschatologischen Propheten," *BibZ* 20 (1976): 59-94.

7943.4   Gerd Theissen, "Die Tempelweissagung Jesu. Prophetie im Spannungsfeld von Stadt und Land," *TZ* 32 (1976): 144-58.

7943.5   J. D. G. Dunn, "Prophetic 'I'-Sayings and the Jesus Tradition: The Importance of Testing Prophetic Utterances within Early Christianity," *NTSt* 24 (1977-1978): 175-98.

7943.6   David B. Peabody, "A Pre-Markan Prophetic Sayings Tradition and the Synoptic Problem," *JBL* 97 (1978): 391-409.

7943.7   Yves M. J. Congar, "Sur la trilogie: prophète-roi-prêtre," *RSPT* 67 (1983): 97-115.

7943.8   Robert R. Hann, "*Christos Kyrios* in PsSol 17:32: 'The Lord's Anointed' Reconsidered," *NTSt* 31 (1985): 620-27.

7943.9   Richard A. Horsley, "Like One of the Prophets of Old: Two Types of Popular Prophets at the Time of Jesus," *CBQ* 47 (1985): 435-63.

7943.10   M. de Jonge, "The Earliest Christian Use of Christos: Some Suggestions," *NTSt* 32 (1986): 321-43.

7943.11   Charles P. Baylis, "The Woman Caught in Adultery: A Test of Jesus as the Greater Prophet," *BS* 146 (1989): 171-84.

7943.12   D. A. S. Ravens, "Luke 9:7-62 and the Prophetic Role of Jesus," *NTSt* 36 (1990): 119-29.

7943.13   Adela Y. Collins, "Jesus the Prophet," *BRes* 36 (1991):
           30-34.

7943.14   James M. Robinson, "Die Logienquelle: Weisheit oder
           Prophetie? Anfragen an Migaku Sato, Q und Prophetie," *ET*
           53 (1993): 367-89.

           (4). Servant of the Lord

7944.   George Milligan, "The Servant of the Lord in the Gospel
           according to St. Matthew," *Exp* 6th ser., 2 (1900): 463-72.

7945.   Clarence T. Craig, "The Identification of Jesus with the
           Suffering Servant," *JR* 24 (1944): 240-45.

7946.   John Wick Bowman, "Jesus and the Suffering Servant," *JR*
           25 (1945): 56-58.

7947.   Charles Masson, "Serviteur de Dieu et fils de David," *RTP*
           N.S. 34 (1946): 175-80.

7948.   Matthew Black, "Servant of the Lord and Son of Man," *SJT*
           6 (1953): 1-11.

7949.   C. J. Maurer, "Knecht Gottes und Sohn Gottes im
           Passionsbericht des Markusevangeliums," *ZTK* N.F. 50
           (1953): 1-38.

7950.   John A. Mackay, "The Form of a Servant," *TTod* 15 (1958):
           304-14.

7951.   George Johnston, "The Servant Image in the New
           Testament," *TTod* 15 (1958): 321-32.

7952.   James L. Price, "The Servant Motif in the Synoptic Gospels;
           A New Appraisal," *Interp* 12 (1958): 28-38.

7953.   Lewis S. Mudge, "The Servant Lord and his Servant People,"
           SJT 12 (1959): 113-28.

           See also numbers 9765 ff.

7953.1   I. Howard Marshall, "Son of God or Servant of Yahweh? A
           Reconsideration of Mark 1:11," *NTSt* 15 (1968-1969):
           326-36.

7953.2   David Hill, "Son and Servant: An Essay on Matthean
           Christology," *JSNT* 6 (1980); 2-16.

7953.3   David J. Lull, "The Servant-Benefactor as a Model of

Greatness," *NT* 28/4 (1986): 289-305.

(5). Priest

7954.   W. Milligan, "The Melchizedek or Heavenly Priesthood of our Lord," *Exp* 3rd ser., 8 (1888): 277-96, 337-59.

7955.   A. B. Bruce, "The Epistle to the Hebrews. IX. Christ not a Self-elected, but a God-appointed Priest (Chap. v. 1-10)," *Exp* 3rd ser., 9 (1889): 351-68.

7956.   David Knapp, "The Priesthood of Christ," *ET* 3 (1891-1892): 465.

7957.   Herm. Kutter, "Das Hohepriestertum Jesu Christi nach dem Hebräerbrief," *STZ* 14 (1897): 13-33, 114-28, 139-60, 197-211.

7958.   Geerhardus Vos, "The Priesthood of Christ in the Epistle to the Hebrews," *PTR* 5 (1907): 423-47, 579-604.

7959.   A. T. Robertson, "The Priesthood of Christ, a Book Study of Hebrews," *USR* 27 (1915-1916): 130-38.

7960.   J. Th. Ubbink, "De Hoogepriester en zijn offer in den brief aan de Hebreën," *NTS* 22 (1939): 172-84.

7961.   George Stoeckhardt, "The Sacerdotal Office of Christ According to the Epistle to the Hebrews," *CTM* 21 (1950): 561-75.

7962.   Gottfried Schille, "Erwägungen zur Hohenpriesterlehre des Hebräerbriefes," *ZNW* 46 (1955): 81-109.

7963.   P.-M. Galopias, "Le sacerdoce du Christ dans l'épître aux Hébreux," *BVC* no. 30 (1959): 34-44.

7964.   J. B. Rowell, "Our Great High Priest," *BS* 118 (1961): 148-53.

7964.1   A. E. Harvey, "New Wine in Old Skins: II. Priest," *ET* 84/7 (1973): 200-203.

7964.2   E. K. Broadhead, "Christology as Polemic and Apologetic: The Priestly Portrait of Jesus in the Gospel of Mark," *JSNT* 47 (1992): 21-34.

(6). Lamb of God

7965.   Alexander B. Grosart, "Christ the 'Little Lamb'," *ET* 3

(1891-1892): 57.

7966. J. M. Gibson, "In the Blood of the Lamb," *Exp* 5th ser., 6 (1897): 218-23 [Revelation 7:14].

7967. James R. Cameron, "The Lamb of God," *Exp* 7th ser., 10 (1910): 173-87.

7968. James R. Cameron, "The Lamb of God," *Exp* 7th ser., 10 (1910): 266-81.

7969. G. Florovsky, "The Lamb of God," *SJT* 4 (1951). 13-28.

7970. J. W. Doeve, "Agnus Dei," *NedTT* 14 (1959-1960): 57-65 (= 137-45).

7971. Stephen Virgulin, "Recent Discussion of the Title, Lamb of God," *Scr* 13 (1961): 74-80.

7971.1 E. W. Burrows, "Did John the Baptist Call Jesus 'The Lamb of God'?" *ET* 85 (1973-1974): 245-49.

7971.2 J. C. O'Neill, "The Lamb of God in the Testaments of the Twelve Patriarchs," *JSNT* 1 (1979): 2-30.

(7). The Last Adam

7972. C. Bruston, "La parallèle entre Adam et Jésus Christ," *RTP* 27 (1894): 33-62.

7973. James Denney, "Adam and Christ in St. Paul," *Exp* 6th ser., 9 (1904): 147-60.

7974. A. H. Tuttle, "The Last Adam," *BR* 1 (1916): 86-100.

7975. J. M. Bover, "Christus novus Adam (1 Cor 15, 20-23)," *VD* 4 (1924): 299-305.

7976. A. Vitti, "Christus-Adam: De Paulino hoc conceptu interpretando eiusque ab extraneis fontibus independentia vindicanda," *B* 7 (1926): 121-45, 270-85, 384-401.

7977. Xaverius Vallisoleto, " 'Christus-Adam'," *VD* 15 (1935): 87-93, 114-20.

7978. Matthew Black, "The Pauline Doctrine of the Second Adam," *SJT* 7 (1954): 170-79.

See also numbers 8003, 9636.

7978.1 Arthur C. Custance, "Theological Necessity of the Physical Immortality of the First and the Last Adam," *JETS* 21 (1978):

297-303.

(8). Lord

7979. G. Schläger, "Das Wort κύριος in seiner Beziehung auf Gott oder Jesus Christus," *TT* 32 (1898): 489-516; 33 (1899): 15-53.

7980. John Reid, " 'Lord' and 'the Lord' in the Gospels," *ET* 12 (1900-1901): 425-30, 479.

7981. Shirley Jackson Case, "κύριος as a Title for Christ," *JBL* 26 (1907): 151-61.

7982. B. W. Bacon, "Jesus as Lord," *HTR* 4 (1911): 204-28.

7983. Paul Althaus, " 'Unser Herr Jesus'," *NKZ* 26 (1915): 439-57, 513-45.

7984. Konrad Köhler, "Der κύριος Ἰησοῦς in den Evangelien und der Spruch vom Herr-Herr-sagen," *TSK* 88 (1915): 471-90.

7985. Geerhardus Vos, "The Continuity of the Kyrios-Title in the New Testament," *PTR* 13 (1915): 161-89.

7986. Geerhardus Vos, "The Kyrios-Christos Controversy," *PTR* 15 (1917): 21-89

7987. Henry Offermann, "The Lord of Glory in the Gospel of John," *LCR* 40 (1921): 299-317.

7988. L. Cerfaux, "Le titre 'Kyrios' et la dignité royale de Jésus," *RSPT* 11 (1922): 40-71; 12 (1923): 125-53.

7989. Geerhardus Vos, "The Name 'Lord' as Used of Jesus in the Gospels," *BR* 7 (1922): 515-36.

7990. A. Médebielle, "Christus Dominus," *VD* 4 (1924): 86-90, 117-19, 133-39.

7991. Erwin Wissmann, "Wilhelm Bousset oder Werner Foerster? Bemerkungen zu W. Foersters Schrift 'Herr ist Jesus.' Replik von W. Foerster," *TB* 4 (1926): 303-12.

7992. Hermann Sasse and A. E. J. Rawlinson, "ὁ κύριος," *RB* 7 (1928): 261-67.

7993. J. A. Smith, "The Meaning of κύριος," *JTS* 31 (1929-1930): 155-60.

7994. Ernst von Dobschütz, "κύριος Ἰησοῦς," *ZNW* 30 (1931):

97-123.

7995.   J. Héring, "Kyrios Anthropos," *RHPR* 16 (1936): 196-209.

7996.   L. Cerfaux, " 'Kyrios' dans les citations pauliniennes de l'Ancien Testament," *ETL* 20 (1943): 5-17.

7997.   Maximiano Andrés Blanco, "La Pedagogía y la Biblia—Jesús Maestro," *CB* 6 (1949): 78-80.

7998.   J. C. O'Neill, "The Use of κύριος in the Book of Acts," *SJT* 8 (1955): 155-74.

7999.   John A. Mackay, "The Lordship of Christ in the Soul," *TTod* 14 (1957): 309-14.

8000.   August Kimme, "Haupttypen der Christokratie," *KD* 5 (1959): 117-32.

        See also number 3583.

8000.1 A. J. B. Higgins, "The Sign of the Son of Man (Matt. 24:30)," *NTSt* 9 (1962-1963): 380-82.

8000.2 Eduard Schweizer, "The Son of Man again," *NTSt* 9 (1962-1963): 256-61.

8000.3 F. H. Borsch, "The Son of Man," *ATR* 45 (1963): 174-90.

8000.4 T. F. Glasson, "The Ensign of the Son of Man (Matt. 24:30)," *JTS* 15 (1964): 299-300.

8000.5 I. Howard Marshall, "The Synoptic Son of Man Sayings in Recent Discussion," *NTSt* 12 (1965-1966): 327-51.

8000.6 Ransom Marlow, "The Son of Man in Recent Journal Literature," *CBQ* 28 (1966): 20-30.

8000.7 Norman Perrin, "The Son of Man in the Synoptic Tradition," *BRes* 13 (1968): 3-25.

8000.8 Norman Perrin, "The Creative Use of the Son of Man Traditions by Mark," *USQR* 23 (1968): 357-65.

8000.9 William O. Walker, "The Kingdom of the Son of Man and the Kingdom of the Father in Matthew," *CBQ* 30/4 (1968): 573-79.

8000.10 Robert J. Maddox, "The Function of the Son of Man according to the Synoptic Gospels," *NTSt* 15 (1968-1969): 45-74.

8000.11 Matthew Black, "The 'Son of Man' Passion Sayings in the

Gospel Tradition," *ZNW* 60 (1969): 1-8.

8000.12 Matthew Black, "The Son of Man's Passion Sayings in the Gospel Tradition," *ZNW* 60 (1969): 58-65.

8000.13 J. Neville Birdsall, "Who is this Son of Man?" *EQ* 42/1 (1970): 7-17.

8000.14 L. S. Hay, "The Son of Man in Mark 2:10 and 2:28," *JBL* 89 (1970): 69-75.

8000.15 I. Howard Marshall, "The Son of Man in Contemporary Debate," *EQ* 42 (1970): 67-87.

8000.16 William O. Walker, "The Origin of the Son of Man Concept as Applied to Jesus," *JBL* 91/4 (1972): 482-90.

8000.17 W. J. Bennett, "The Son of Man," *NT* 17/2 (1975): 113-29.

8000.18 Pauline Giles, "The Son of Man in the Epistle to the Hebrews," *ET* 86 (1975): 328-32.

8000.19 Jack D. Kingsbury, "Title 'Son of Man' in Matthew's Gospel," *CBQ* 37 (1975): 193-202.

8000.20 Barnabas Lindars, "Re-Enter the Apocalyptic Son of Man," *NTSt* 22 (1975-1976): 52-72.

8000.21 Matthew Black, "The 'Parables' of Enoch (1 En 37-71) and the 'Son of Man'," *ET* 88 (1976): 5-8.

8000.22 P. Maurice Casey, "The Corporate Interpretation of 'One Like a Son of Man' (Dan. 7,13) at the Time of Jesus," *NT* 18 (1976): 167-80.

8000.23 P. Maurice Casey, "The Son of Man Problem," *ZNW* 67/3 (1976): 147-54.

8000.24 John W. Bowker, "The Son of Man," *JTS* 28 (1977): 19-48.

8000.25 John P. Brown, "The Son of Man: 'This Fellow'," *B* 58 (1977): 361-87.

8000.26 David R. Catchpole, "The Son of Man's Search for Faith (Luke 18:8)," *NT* 19 (1977): 81-104.

8000.27 David R. Catchpole, "The Poor on Earth and the Son of Man in Heaven: A Reappraisal of Matthew 25:31-46," *BJRL* 61/2 (1978-1979): 355-97.

8000.28 Joseph A. Fitzmyer, "Another View of the 'Son of Man' Debate," *JSNT* 4 (1979): 58-68.

8000.29   Paul Garnet, "The Baptism of Jesus and the Son of Man Idea," *JSNT* 9 (1980): 49-65.

8000.30   Barnabas Lindars, "The New Look on the Son of Man," *BJRL* 63 (1980-1981): 437-62.

8000.31   Francis J. Moloney, "The Re-interpretation of Psalm VIII and the Son of Man Debate," *NTSt* 27 (1980-1981): 656-72.

8000.32   David R. Catchpole, "The Angelic Son of Man in Luke 12:8," *NT* 2 (1982): 255-65.

8000.33   R. L. Sturch, "The Replacement of 'Son of Man' by a Pronoun (John 12:32)," *ET* 94 (1982-1983): 333.

8000.34   Darrell J. Doughty, "The Authority of the Son of Man," *ZNW* 74/3-4 (1983): 161-81.

8000.35   Mark S. Smith, "The 'Son of Man' in Ugaritic," *CBQ* 45 (1983): 59-60.

8000.36   William O. Walker, "The Son of Man: Some Recent Developments," *CBQ* 45 (1983): 584-607.

8000.37   P. Maurice Casey, "Aramaic Idiom and Son of Man Sayings," *ET* 96 (1984-1985): 233-36.

8000.38   P. Maurice Casey, "The Jackals and the Son of Man (Matt. 8.20//Luke 9.58)," *JSNT* 23 (1985): 3-22.

8000.39   David R. Jackson, "The Priority of the Son of Man Sayings," *WTJ* 47 (1985): 83-96.

8000.40   Chris L. Mearns, "The Son of Man Trajectory and Eschatological Development," *ET* 97/1 (1985-1986): 8-12.

8000.41   John R. Donahue, "Recent Studies on the Origin of 'Son of Man' in the Gospels," *CBQ* 48 (1986): 484-98.

8000.42   J. M. Casciaro Ramírez, "General, Generic and Indefinite: The Use of the Term 'Son of Man' in Aramaic Sources and in the Teaching of Jesus," *JSNT* 29 (1987): 21-56.

8000.43   Adela Y. Collins, "The Origin of the Designation of Jesus as 'Son of Man'," *HTR* 80 (1987): 391-407.

8000.44   Bruce A. Stevens, " 'Why Must the Son of Man Suffer?' The Divine Warrior in the Gospel of Mark," *BibZ* 31 (1987): 101-10.

8000.45   Robert L. Mowery, "God, Lord, and Father: The Theology of the Gospel of Matthew," *BRes* 33 (1988): 24-36.

8000.46 Mogens Müller, "Have You Faith in the Son of Man?" *NTSt* 37 (1991): 291-94.

8000.47 Joseph Plevnik, "Son of Man Seated at the Right Hand of God: Luke 22:69 in Lucan Christology," *B* 72/3 (1991): 331-47.

8000.48 William O. Walker, "John 1:43-51 and the 'Son of Man' in the Fourth Gospel," *JSNT* 56 (1994): 31-42.

(9). Son of Man

8001. H. J. Holtzmann, "Ueber den neustestamentlichen Ausdruck 'Menschensohn'," *ZWT* 8 (1865): 212-37.

8002. William S. Tyler, "The Son of Man," *BS* 22 (1865): 51-78.

8003. Dr. Krawutzcky, "Ueber die Bedeutung des neutestamentlichen Ausdrucks Menschensohn und sein Verhältnis zur paulinischen Bezeichnung Christi als des zweiten Menschen," *TQ* 51 (1869): 600-57.

8004. G. Frederick Wright, "The Term 'Son of Man' as used in the New Testament," *BS* 44 (1887): 575-601.

8005. W. Sanday, "On the Title 'Son of Man'," *Exp* 4th ser., 3 (1891): 18-32.

8006. Vernon Bartlet, "Christ's Use of the Term 'The Son of Man'," *Exp* 4th ser., 6 (1892): 427-43.

8007. R. H. Charles, "The Son of Man," *ET* 4 (1892-1893): 504-506.

8008. Vernon Bartlet, " 'The Son of Man': A Rejoinder," *ET* 5 (1893-1894): 41-42.

8009. B. D. Eerdmans, "De Oorsprong van de uitdrukking 'Zoon des Menschen' als Evangelische Messiastitel," *TT* 28 (1894): 153-76.

8010. B. D. Eerdmans, "De Oorsprong van de uitdrukking 'Zoon des Menschen' als Evangelische Messiastitel," *TT* 28 (1894): 177-92.

8011. W. C. van Manen, "Naschrift op Dr. Eerdmans' verhandeling over de uitdrukking 'Zoon des Menschen'," *TT* 28 (1894): 177-92.

8012. B. D. Eerdmans, "De witdrukking 'Zoon des Menschen' en het boek 'Henoch'," *TT* 29 (1895): 49-71.

8013. W. C. van Manen, " 'De Zoon des Menschen' bij Henoch," *TT* 29 (1895): 263-67.

8014. A. J. Th. Jonker, "De Zoon des Menschen," *TS* 13 (1895): 228-60.

8015. H. Burton, "The Son of Man," *Exp* 5th ser., 4 (1896): 388-400.

8016. Nathaniel Schmidt, "Was בר נשא a Messianic Title?" *JBL* 15 (1896): 36-53.

8017. A. Hilgenfeld, "Noch ein Wort über den Menschensohn," *ZWT* 42 (1899): 149-51.

8018. David Eaton, "Professor Dalman on 'The Son of Man'," *ET* 10 (1898-1899): 438-43.

8019. Fritz Hommel, "Apocalyptic Origin of the Expression 'Son of Man'," *ET* 11 (1899-1900): 341-45.

8020. L. A. Muirhead, "The Name 'Son of Man' and the Messianic Consciousness of Jesus," *ET* 11 (1899-1900): 62-65.

8021. W. Baldensperger, "Die neueste Forschung über den Menschensohn," *TR* 3 (1900): 201-10, 243-55.

8022. Milton G. Evans, "The Title 'The Son of Man'," *BS* 57 (1900): 680-95.

8023. Vincent Rose, "Études évangéliques.—III. Fils de l'homme et fils de Dieu," *RB* 9 (1900): 169-99.

8024. James Croskery, "Recent Discussions on the Meaning of the Title 'Son of Man'," *ET* 13 (1901-1902): 351-55.

8025. James Drummond, "The Use and Meaning of the Phrase 'The Son of Man' in the Synoptic Gospels," *JTS* 2 (1900-1901): 350-58, 539-71.

8026. Arthur Carr, "The Son of Man as the Light of the World," *Exp* 7th ser., 1 (1906): 115-23.

8027. David Smith, "The Nickname 'Son of Man'," *ET* 18 (1906-1907): 553-55.

8028. Vinzenz Hartl, "Anfang und Ende des Titels 'Menschensohn.' Ein Beitrag zur Lösung der johanneischen Frage,"

BibZ 7 (1909): 342-54.

8029.   B. W. Bacon, "Jesus as Son of Man," *HTR* 3 (1910): 325-40.

8030.   Henry Offermann, "The Son of Man and the Son of God," *LCR* 29 (1910): 710-20; 30 (1911): 120-26.

8031.   W. B. Kristensen, "De Term 'Zoon des Menschen'," *TT* 45 (1911): 1-38.

8032.   F. P. Badham, "The Title 'Son of Man'," *TT* 45 (1911): 395-448.

8033.   J. MacRory, "The Son of Man," *ITQ* 10 (1915): 50-63.

8034.   F. W. Grosheide, "υἱὸς τοῦ ἀνθρώπου in het Ev. naar Johannes," *TS* 35 (1917): 242-48.

8035.   E. Kuhnert, "ὁ υἱὸς τοῦ ἀνθρώπου," *ZNW* 18 (1917): 165-76.

8036.   R. Somervell, "The Son of Man," *ET* 29 (1917-1918): 522-23.

8037.   T. Stephenson, "The Title 'Son of Man'," *ET* 29 (1917-1918): 377-78.

8038.   Hermann Dieckmann, "ὁ υἱὸς τοῦ ἀνθρώπου," *B* 2 (1921): 69-71.

8039.   Paul Haupt, "Hidalgo and Filius Hominis," *JBL* 40 (1921): 167-70.

8040.   B. W. Bacon, "The 'Son of Man' in the Usage of Jesus," *JBL* 41 (1922): 143-82.

8041.   Carl S. Patton, "Did Jesus Call himself the Son of Man?" *JR* 2 (1922): 501-11.

8042.   A. M. Sanford, "Did Jesus Call himself the Son of Man? Another Point of View," *JR* 3 (1923): 308-13.

8043.   Arthur S. Peake, "The Messiah and the Son of Man," *BJRL* 8 (1924): 52-81.

8044.   J. Courtenay James, "The Son of Man: Origin and Uses of the Title," *ET* 36 (1924-1925): 309-14.

8045.   G. Baldensperger, " 'Le fils de l'homme'; essai historique et critique par Georges Dupont," *RHPR* 5 (1925): 262-73.

8046.   Christopher G. Hazard, "Why Jesus was called the Son of

God and the only begotten Son," *BS* 82 (1925): 169-76.

8047. Martin Wagner, "Der Menschensohn," *NKZ* 36 (1925): 245-78.

8048. Nathaniel Schmidt, "Recent Study of the Term 'Son of Man'," *JBL* 45 (1926): 326-49.

8049. A. McCaig, "The Title 'Son of Man' in its Lofty Associations," *BR* 12 (1927): 44-56.

8050. Hermann Dieckmann, "De Iesu Christi messianitate et divinitate quaestiones selectae; I, De nomine 'Filii hominis'," *VD* 8 (1928): 295-301.

8051. P. I. Bratsiotes, "'Ο Υἱὸς τοῦ 'Ανθρώπου, Συμβολή εἰς τὴν ἱστορίαν τοῦ ὅρου," *Θ* 7 (1929): 193-98.

8052. John McNaugher, "The Son of Man," *BS* 88 (1931): 90-104.

8053. Alexander Ross, "The Title 'Son of Man'," *EQ* 6 (1934): 36-49.

8054. Harold C. Phillips, "Jesus, Son of Man," *RL* 5 (1936): 207-15.

8055. Pierson Parker, "The Meaning of 'Son of Man'," *JBL* 60 (1941): 151-57.

8056. J. A. Burkill, "The Son of Man," *ET* 56 (1944-1945): 305-306.

8057. Sigmund Mowinckel, "Opharet til den senjødiske forestilling om Menneskesønnen," *NTT* 45 (1944): 189-244.

8058. Kenneth A. Fox, "The Son of Man.—A Criticism of Dr. Manson's Exposition in 'The Teaching of Jesus'," *ET* 57 (1945-1946): 328.

8059. T. W. Manson, "The Son of Man," *ET* 58 (1946-1947). 83.

8060. J. Y. Campbell, "The Origin and Meaning of the Term Son of Man," *JTS* 48 (1947): 145-55.

8061. John Bowman, "The Background of the Term 'Son of Man'," *ET* 59 (1947-1948): 283-88.

8062. Matthew Black, "Unsolved New Testament Problems. The 'Son of Man' in the Old Biblical Literature," *ET* 60 (1948-1949): 11-15.

8063. Matthew Black, "Unsolved New Testament Problems—The

'Son of Man' in the Teaching of Jesus," *ET* 60 (1948-1949): 32-36.

8064.   C. C. McCown, "Jesus, Son of Man. A Survey of Recent Discussion," *JR* 28 (1948): 1-12.

8065.   A. E. Guilding, "The Son of Man and the Ancient of Days," *EQ* 23 (1951): 210-12.

8066.   R. K. Harrison, "The Son of Man," *EQ* 23 (1951): 46-50.

8067.   W. Manson, "The Son of Man and History," *SJT* 5 (1952): 113-22.

8068.   André Feuillet, "Le fils de l'homme de Daniel et la tradition biblique," *RB* 60 (1953): 170-202, 321-46.

8069.   Th. Preiss, "Le fils de l'homme," *RHPR* 33 (1953): 71.

8070.   E. J. Tinsley, "The Way of the Son of Man," *Interp* 7 (1953): 418-25.

8071.   C. H. de Beus, "Achtergrond en inhoud van de uitdrukking 'de Zoon des Menschen' in de synoptische evangeliën," *NedTT* 9 (1954-1955): 272-95.

8072.   L. Johnston, "The Son of Man," *Scr* 6 (1954): 181-83.

8073.   E. J. Tinsley, "The Sign of the Son of Man," *SJT* 8 (1955): 297-306.

8074.   C. H. de Beus, "Het gebruik en de betekenis van de uitdrukking 'De Zoon des Menschen' in het Evangelie van Johannes," *NedTT* 10 (1955-1956): 237-51.

8075.   Jens Christensen, "Menneskesønnen gaar bort, som der staar skrevet om ham," *DTT* 19 (1956): 83-92.

8076.   Ethelbert Stauffer, "Messias oder Menschensohn?" *NT* 1 (1956): 81-102.

8077.   E. M. Sidebottom, "The Son of Man as Man in the Fourth Gospel," *ET* 68 (1956-1957): 231-35, 280-83.

8078.   E. M. Sidebottom, "The Ascent and Descent of the 'Son of Man' in the Gospel of St. John," *ATR* 39 (1957): 115-22.

8079.   J. A. Emerton, "The Origin of the Son of Man Imagery," *JTS* N.S. 9 (1958): 225-42.

8080.   Ian L. Sanders, "The Origin and Significance of the Title 'The Son of Man' as Used in the Gospels," *Scr* 10 (1958):

49-56.

8081. Walter Eichrodt, "Zum Problem des Menschensohnes," *EvT* 19 (1959): 1-3.

8082. Eduard Schweizer, "Der Menschensohn," *ZNW* 50 (1959): 185-209.

8083. Olaf Moe, "Der Menschensohn und der Urmensch," *ST* 14 (1960): 119-29.

8084. Eduard Schweizer, "The Son of Man," *JBL* 79 (1960): 119-29.

8085. E. Ashby, "The Coming of the Son of Man," *ET* 72 (1960-1961): 360-63.

8086. G. H. P. Thompson, "The Son of Man: The Evidence of the Dead Sea Scrolls," *ET* 72 (1960-1961): 125.

8087. T. A. Burkill, "The Hidden Son of Man in St. Mark's Gospel," *ZNW* 52 (1961): 189-213.

8088. Joseph Coppens, "Le fils d'homme daniélique et les relectures de Dan. VII, 13 dans les apocryphes et les écrits du Nouveau Testament," *ETL* 37 (1961): 5-51.

8089. Olaf Moe, "Menneskesønnen og urmennesket," *TTK* 32 (1961): 65-73.

See also numbers 880, 889, 950, 5068, 6551, 6837, 7848, 9419, 9568, 9595, 9796 ff.

8089.1 A. J. B. Higgins, "The Sign of the Son of Man (Matt. 24:30)," *NTSt* 9 (1962-1963): 380-82.

8089.2 Eduard Schweizer, "The Son of Man again," *NTSt* 9 (1962-1963): 256-61.

8089.3 F. H. Borsch, "The Son of Man," *ATR* 45 (1963): 174-90.

8089.4 T. F. Glasson, "The Ensign of the Son of Man (Matt. 24:30)," *JTS* 15 (1964): 299-300.

8089.5 I. Howard Marshall, "The Synoptic Son of Man Sayings in Recent Discussion," *NTSt* 12 (1965-1966): 327-51.

8089.6 Ransom Marlow, "The Son of Man in Recent Journal Literature," *CBQ* 28 (1966): 20-30.

8089.7 J. M. Ford, " 'The Son of Man': A Euphemism?" *JBL* 87 (1968): 257-66.

8089.8   Norman Perrin, "The Son of Man in the Synoptic Tradition,"
          BRes 13 (1968): 3-25.

8089.9   Norman Perrin, "The Creative Use of the Son of Man
          Traditions by Mark," *USQR* 23 (1968): 357-65.

8089.10   William O. Walker, "The Kingdom of the Son of Man and
          the Kingdom of the Father in Matthew," *CBQ* 30/4 (1968):
          573-79.

8089.11   Robert J. Maddox, "The Function of the Son of Man
          according to the Synoptic Gospels," *NTSt* 15 (1968-1969):
          45-74.

8089.12   Matthew Black, "The 'Son of Man' Passion Sayings in the
          Gospel Tradition," *ZNW* 60 (1969): 1-8.

8089.13   Matthew Black, "The Son of Man's Passion Sayings in the
          Gospel Tradition," *ZNW* 60 (1969): 58-65.

8089.14   J. Neville Birdsall, "Who is this Son of Man?" *EQ* 42/1
          (1970): 7-17.

8089.15   L. S. Hay, "The Son of Man in Mark 2:10 and 2:28," *JBL* 89
          (1970): 69-75.

8089.16   I. Howard Marshall, "The Son of Man in Contemporary
          Debate," *EQ* 42 (1970): 67-87.

8089.17   William O. Walker, "The Origin of the Son of Man Concept
          as Applied to Jesus," *JBL* 91/4 (1972): 482-90.

8089.18   W. J. Bennett, "The Son of Man," *NT* 17/2 (1975): 113-29.

8089.19   Pauline Giles, "The Son of Man in the Epistle to the
          Hebrews," *ET* 86 (1975): 328-32.

8089.20   Delmar Jacobson, "An Exposition of Matthew 13:44-52,"
          Interp 29/3 (1975): 277-82.

8089.21   Jack D. Kingsbury, "Title 'Son of Man' in Matthew's
          Gospel," *CBQ* 37 (1975): 193-202.

8089.22   Barnabas Lindars, "Re-Enter the Apocalyptic Son of Man,"
          NTSt 22 (1975-1976): 52-72.

8089.23   Matthew Black, "The 'Parables' of Enoch (1 En 37-71) and
          the 'Son of Man'," *ET* 88 (1976): 5-8.

8089.24   P. Maurice Casey, "The Corporate Interpretation of 'One
          Like a Son of Man' (Dan. 7,13) at the Time of Jesus," *NT* 18

(1976): 167-80.

8089.25 P. Maurice Casey, "The Son of Man Problem," *ZNW* 67/3 (1976): 147-54.

8089.26 John W. Bowker, "The Son of Man," *JTS* 28 (1977): 19-48.

8089.27 John P. Brown, "The Son of Man: 'This Fellow'," *B* 58 (1977): 361-87.

8089.28 David R. Catchpole, "The Son of Man's Search for Faith (Luke 18:8)," *NT* 19 (1977): 81-104.

8089.29 David R. Catchpole, "The Poor on Earth and the Son of Man in Heaven: A Reappraisal of Matthew 25:31-46," *BJRL* 61/2 (1978-1979): 355-97.

8089.30 Joseph A. Fitzmyer, "Another View of the 'Son of Man' Debate," *JSNT* 4 (1979): 58-68.

8089.31 Paul Garnet, "The Baptism of Jesus and the Son of Man Idea," *JSNT* 9 (1980): 49-65.

8089.32 Barnabas Lindars, "The New Look on the Son of Man," *BJRL* 63 (1980-1981): 437-62.

8089.33 Francis J. Moloney, "The Re-interpretation of Psalm VIII and the Son of Man Debate," *NTSt* 27 (1980-1981): 656-72.

8089.34 David R. Catchpole, "The Angelic Son of Man in Luke 12:8," *NT* 2 (1982): 255-65.

8089.35 Christopher M. Tuckett, "The Present Son of Man," *JSNT* 14 (1982): 58-81.

8089.36 R. L. Sturch, "The Replacement of 'Son of Man' by a Pronoun (John 12:32)," *ET* 94 (1982-1983): 333.

8089.37 Darrell J. Doughty, "The Authority of the Son of Man," *ZNW* 74/3-4 (1983): 161-81.

8089.38 Mark S. Smith, "The 'Son of Man' in Ugaritic," *CBQ* 45 (1983): 59-60.

8089.39 William O. Walker, "The Son of Man: Some Recent Developments," *CBQ* 45 (1983): 584-607.

8089.40 P. Maurice Casey, "Aramaic Idiom and Son of Man Sayings," *ET* 96 (1984-1985): 233-36.

8089.41 P. Maurice Casey, "The Jackals and the Son of Man (Matt. 8.20//Luke 9.58)," *JSNT* 23 (1985): 3-22.

8089.42   David R. Jackson, "The Priority of the Son of Man Sayings," *WTJ* 47 (1985): 83-96.

8089.43   Chris L. Mearns, "The Son of Man Trajectory and Eschatological Development," *ET* 97/1 (1985-1986): 8-12.

8089.44   John R. Donahue, "Recent Studies on the Origin of 'Son of Man' in the Gospels," *CBQ* 48 (1986): 484-98.

8089.45   J. M. Casciaro Ramírez, "General, Generic and Indefinite: The Use of the Term 'Son of Man' in Aramaic Sources and in the Teaching of Jesus," *JSNT* 29 (1987): 21-56.

8089.46   Adela Y. Collins, "The Origin of the Designation of Jesus as 'Son of Man'," *HTR* 80 (1987): 391-407.

8089.47   Adela Y. Collins, "The Origin of the Designation of Jesus as 'Son of Man'," *HTR* 80 (1987): 391-407.

8089.48   Bruce A. Stevens, " 'Why Must the Son of Man Suffer?' The Divine Warrior in the Gospel of Mark," *BibZ* 31 (1987): 101-10.

8089.49   Robert L. Mowery, "God, Lord, and Father: The Theology of the Gospel of Matthew," *BRes* 33 (1988): 24-36.

8089.50   Mogens Müller, "Have You Faith in the Son of Man?" *NTSt* 37 (1991): 291-94.

8089.51   Joseph Plevnik, "Son of Man Seated at the Right Hand of God: Luke 22:69 in Lucan Christology," *B* 72/3 (1991): 331-47.

8089.52   William O. Walker, "John 1:43-51 and the 'Son of Man' in the Fourth Gospel," *JSNT* 56 (1994): 31-42.

(10). Son of God

8090.   William S. Tyler, "The Son of God," *BS* 22 (1865): 620-42.

8091.   D. R. Goodwin, "θεοῦ υἱός, Matt. xxvii. 54, and Mark xv. 39," *JBL* 6 (1886, part 1): 129-31.

8092.   S. Schwarm, "Jesus the Son of God," *LQ* 20 (1890): 248-61.

8093.   M. Boy, "Der Sohn Gottes nach seinen Selbstzeugnissen im vierten Evangelium," *NJDT* 3 (1894): 337-49.

8094.   A. B. Taylor, "Was the Son of Man the Son of God?" *LQ* 29 (1899): 541-52.

8095. N. P. Rasmussen, "Bemaerkninger til Problemet: Jesus Kristus, Guds Søn," *TTDF* N.S. 4 (1902-1903): 1-33, 81-109, 449-50.

8096. C. Bruston, "De la notion du fils de Dieu dans l'épître aux Hébreux," *RTQR* 16 (1907): 39-66.

8097. B. W. Bacon, "Jesus the Son of God," *HTR* 2 (1909): 277-309.

8098. H. R. Offerhaus, "De Godszoon Jezus, volgens Mattheus," *TT* 49 (1915): 226-32.

8099. Hans Windisch, "Friedensbringer-Gottessöhne," *ZNW* 24 (1925): 240-60.

8100. W. F. Lofthouse, "Fatherhood and Sonship in the Fourth Gospel," *ET* 43 (1931-1932): 442-48.

8101. Ermenie Huntress, "Son of God in Jewish Writings prior to the Christian Era," *JBL* 54 (1935): 117-23.

8102. Manuel Gonzalez, "Jesucristo, 'El Hijo de Dios'," *CB* 3 (1946): 21-24, 151-54, 177-81.

8103. G. H. Donne Davis, "Jesus Christ, the Son of God," *EQ* 22 (1950): 45-55.

8104. Augustin George, "Le père et de fils dans les évangiles synoptiques," *LumV* no. 29 (1956): 27-40.

8105. Walter Grundmann, "Sohn Gottes," *ZNW* 47 (1956): 113-33. See also numbers 7949, *10061*.

8105.1 J. Howton, " 'Son of God' in the Fourth Gospel," *NTSt* 10 (1963-1964): 227-37.

8105.2 T. F. Glasson, "Mark 15:39: The Son of God," *ET* 80 (1968-1969): 286.

8105.3 Harold A. Guy, "Son of God in Mark 15:39," *ET* 81 (1969-1970): 151.

8105.4 Jan Slomp, "Are the Words 'Son of God' in Mark 1:1 Original?" *BTr* 28 (1977): 143-50.

8105.5 Matt Finlay, "Jesus, Son of God: A Translation Problem," *BTr* 30 (1979): 241-44.

8105.6 Alexander Globe, "The Caesarean Omission of the Phrase 'Son of God' in Mark 1:1," *HTR* 75 (1982): 209-18.

8105.7   Paul Ellingworth, " 'Like the Son of God': Form and Content in Hebrews 7:1-10," *B* 64 (1983): 255-62.

8105.8   Robert L. Mowery, "Subtle Differences: The Matthean 'Son of God' References," *NT* 32 (1990): 193-200.

8105.9   Terence L. Donaldson, "The Mockers and the Son of God (Matthew 27:37-44): Two Characters in Matthew's Story of Jesus," *JSNT* 41 (1991): 3-18.

(11). Word (Logos)

8106.   L. Lange, "Der λόγος des Johannes, grammatisch aufgefasst," *TSK* 3 (1830): 672-80.

8107.   C. Daub, "Ueber den Logos. Ein Beitrag zur Logik der göttlichen Namen," *TSK* 6 (1833): 355-410.

8108.   Dr. Röhricht, "Zur johanneischen Logoslehre," *TSK* 44 (1871): 503-509.

8109.   J. M. Danson, "The Doctrine of the Logos: Its Genesis and Corruptions," *Exp* 4th ser., 6 (1892): 65-79.

8110.   H. Holtzmann, "Der Logos und der eingeborene Gottessohn im 4. Evangelium," *ZWT* 36 (1893): 385-407.

8111.   C. Malan, "Le logos ou la parole éternelle," *RTQR* 6 (1897): 110-46.

8112.   A. N. Jannaris, "St. John's Gospel and the Logos," *ZNW* 2 (1901): 13-25.

8113.   E. P. Boys-Smith, "St. John's Gospel and the Logos," *ET* 13 (1901-1902): 140-44

8114.   E. W. Mayer, "Logos," *ZTK* 22 (1912): 315-20.

8115.   Herbert S. Turner, "Jesus Christ the Eternal Logos of the Father," *USR* 29 (1917-1918): 336-50.

8116.   W. F. Albright, "The Supposed Babylonian Derivation of the Logos," *JBL* 39 (1920): 143-51.

8117.   M.-J. Lagrange, "Le logos d'Héraclite," *RB* 32 (1923): 96-107.

8118.   M.-J. Lagrange, "Vers le logos de saint Jean," *RB* 32 (1923): 161-84, 321-71.

8119.   Archibald B. D. Alexander, "The Johannine Doctrine of the

Logos," *ET* 36 (1924-1925): 394-99, 467-72.

8120. Ethelbert Stauffer, "Vom λόγος τοῦ σταυροῦ und seiner Logik," *TSK* 103 (1931): 179-88.

8121. Jean-Joseph Maydieu, "La procession du logos d'après le commentaire d'Origène sur l'évangile de saint Jean," *BLE* 35 (1934): 3-16, 49-70.

8122. Irving E. Rouse, "The Logos in the Gospel of John," *RE* 32 (1935): 388-404.

8123. R. D. Middleton, "Logos and Shekinah in the Fourth Gospel," *JQR* 29 (1938-1939): 101-33.

8124. J. Thijs, "De Logos," *GTT* 39 (1938): 3-19.

8125. Kenneth Harper, "Christ, the Word," *ET* 60 (1948-1949): 200-202.

8126. Richard R. Caemmerer, "A Concordance Study of the Concept 'Word of God'," *CTM* 22 (1951): 170-86.

8127. T. F. Glasson, "Heraclitus' Alleged Logos Doctrine," *JTS* N.S. 3 (1952): 231-38.

8128. F. Buffière, "La notion du 'logos' dans l'exégèse d'Homère. Hermès, dieu de la parole et de la raison," *BLE* 54 (1953): 55-60.

8129. G. Quispel, "De joodse achtergrond van de Logos-christologie," *VT* 25 (1954): 48-55.

8130. Walter R. Roehrs, "The Word in the Word," *CTM* 25 (1954): 81-109.

See also numbers 3138, 8266, 8759, *10058*.

8130.1 D. Hill, "The Relevance of the Logos Christology," *ET* 78 (1966-1967): 136-39.

8130.2 N. Smart, "The Logos Doctrine and Eastern Beliefs," *ET* 78 (1966-1967): 168-71.

8130.3 M. McNamara, "Logos of the Fourth Gospel and Memra of the Palestinian Targum (Ex 12:42)," *ET* 79 (1967-1968): 115-17.

8130.4 Joachim Jeremias, "Zum Logos-Problem," *ZNW* 59 (1968): 82-85.

8130.5 G. H. Dix, "The Heavenly Wisdom and the Divine Logos in

Jewish Apocalyptic," *JTS* 26 (1975): 1-12.

8130.6   E. L. Miller, " 'The Logos Was God'," *EQ* 53 (1981): 65-77.

8130.7   E. L. Miller, "The Logos of Heraclitus: Updating the Report," *HTR* 74 (1981): 161-76.

8130.8   Pheme Perkins, "Logos Christologies in the Nag Hammadi Codices," *VCh* 35 (1981): 379-96.

8130.9   James Swetnam, "Jesus as Logos in Hebrews 4:12-13," *B* 62 (1981): 214-24.

8130.10   E. L. Miller, "The Logic of the Logos Hymn: A New View," *NTSt* 29 (1983): 552-61.

8130.11   Otfried Hofius, "Struktur und Gedankengang des Logos-Hymnus in Johannes 1:1-18," *ZNW* 78/1-2 (1987): 1-25.

8130.12   A. Jannière, " 'En arkhê ên o logos.' Notes sur des problèmes de traduction," *RSR* 83 (1995): 241-47.

(12). God

8131.   T. Dwight, "On Romans ix. 5," *JBL* 1 (1881): 22-55.

8132.   Ezra Abbot, "On the Construction of Romans ix. 5," *JBL* 1 (1881): 97-103.

8133.   Alfred Durand, "La divinité de Jésus Christ dans s. Paul, Rom. IX, 5," *RB* 12 (1903): 550-70.

8134.   A. W. Wainwright, "The Confession 'Jesus is God' in the New Testament," *SJT* 10 (1957): 274-99.

8135.   Vincent Taylor, "Does the New Testament Call Jesus God?" *ET* 73 (1961-1962): 116-18.

See also numbers 974, 976, 7406.

8135.1   P. Joseph Cahill, "The Johannine Logos as Center," *CBQ* 38 (1976): 54-72.

c. *The Person of Jesus Christ*

(1). General Studies

8136.   Henry B. Smith, "Dorner's History of the Doctrine of the Person of Christ," *BS* 6 (1849): 156-85.

8137.   Moses Stuart, "Doctrine Respecting the Person of Christ," *BS*

7 (1850): 696-732.

8138. T. Colani, "De la personne de Jésus Christ; étude critique des systèmes orthodoxes," *RT* 10 (1855): 349-70; 11 (1855): 93-122.

8139. Ern. Albaric, "De la personne de Jésus Christ," *RT* 9 (1862): 315-41.

8140. Dr. Schenkel, "La personne de Jésus," *RT* 2 (1864): 228-40.

8141. J. W. Richard, "Dr. Hodge on the Person of Christ," *LQ* 17 (1887): 410-27.

8142. P. M. Bikle, "The Superhuman Jesus," *LQ* 21 (1891): 431-46.

8143. H. Schmidt, "Zur Lehre von der Person Christi," *NKZ* 7 (1896): 972-1005.

8144. J. B. Strong, "The History of the Theological Term 'Substance'," *JTS* 2 (1900-1901): 224-35; 3 (1901-1902): 22-40; 4 (1902-1903): 28-45.

8145. R. Seeberg, "Die Person Christi der feste Punkt im fliessenden Strom der Gegenwart," *NKZ* 14 (1903): 437-57.

8146. William H. Walker, "The Development of the Doctrine of the Person of Christ in the New Testament," *AJT* 8 (1904): 452-69.

8147. J. O. Dykes, "The Person of our Lord," *ET* 17 (1905-1906): 7-10, 55-59, 103-107, 151-56.

8148. Leander S. Keyser, "Christ in the Temple Among the Doctors," *LCR* 24 (1905): 337-43.

8149. F. Nau, "Dans quelle mesure les Jacobites sont-ils monophysites?" *ROC* 10 (1905): 113-34.

8150. George H. Gilbert, "Justin Martyr on the Person of Christ," *AJT* 10 (1906): 663-74.

8151. Philip Wendell Crannell, "The Problem of Christ's Person in the Twentieth Century," *BS* 64 (1907): 331-52.

8152. R. Roberts, "Jesus or Christ? An Appeal for Consistency," *HJ* 7 (1908-1909): 352-69.

8153. G. K. Chesterton, "Jesus or Christ?—(A Reply to Mr. Roberts)," *HJ* 7 (1908-1909): 746-58.

8154.   James H. Moulton, "Jesus or Christ (A Reply to Mr. Roberts)," *HJ* 7 (1908-1909): 759-66.

8155.   Anonymous, "Translation of M. Loisy's Article on 'Jesus ou le Christ (Jesus or Christ)'," *HJ* 8 (1909-1910): 487-97.

8156.   R. Roberts, "Jesus or Christ: A Rejoinder," *HJ* 8 (1909-1910): 83-101.

8157.   V. G. A. Tressler, "The Most Recent Assaults of the Higher Critical Theology on the Person of Christ," *LQ* 41 (1911): 474-504.

8158.   John Oman, "Personality and Grace; VII. Jesus Christ," *Exp* 8th ser., 4 (1912): 57-60.

8159.   A. Williams Anthony, "The Person of Jesus Christ," *BW* 47 (1916): 363-70.

8160.   Herman Bavinck, "Christ and Christianity," *BR* 1 (1916): 214-36.

8161.   J. E. Todd, "How was Jesus Limited in Knowledge and Power?" *BS* 73 (1916): 481-84.

8162.   Edgar Whitaker Work, "The Message of the Epistle to the Colossians," *BR* 2 (1917): 100-29.

8163.   Leonard Hodgson, "The Metaphysic of Nestorius," *JTS* 19 (1918): 46-55.

8164.   A. Wilmart, "Un discours théologique d'Eusèbe d'Emèse: Le Fils image du Père," *ROC* 22 (1920-1921): 72-94.

8165.   W. J. Ferrar, "Modernism and the Person of Christ," *ET* 33 (1921-1922): 487-91.

8166.   James Harper, "The Mediatorial Person of Christ," *BS* 80 (1923): 317-27.

8167.   D. M. Edwards, "The Doctrine of the Person of Christ," *HJ* 23 (1924-1925): 454-67.

8168.   C. W. Hodge, "The Person of Christ in Recent Religious Philosophy," *PTR* 22 (1924): 529-43.

8169.   William S. Bishop, "The Chalcedonian Decree as an Interpretation of our Lord's Person," *ATR* 8 (1925-1926): 29-47.

8170.   Sydney Cave, "Recent Thought on the Doctrine of the Person of Christ," *ET* 37 (1925-1926): 247-53.

8171. Gustaf Aulén, Paul Althaus, "ὁ ἐσταυρωμένος," *TB* 7 (1928): 258-61.

8172. Carl Stange, "Die Person Jesu Christi in der Theologie Luthers," *ZST* 6 (1928-1929): 449-83.

8173. Oswald T. Allis, "Was Jesus a Modernist?" *PTR* 27 (1929): 83-119.

8174. George A. Barton, "The Person of Christ in the Modern Literature Concerning his Life," *ATR* 13 (1931): 56-71.

8175. Adolphine Bakker, "Christ an Angel?" *ZNW* 32 (1933): 255-65.

8176. R. Abba, "Jesus—Man or Mediator?" *ET* 55 (1943-1944): 61-65.

8177. John C. Bennett, "The Person of Christ," *RL* 12 (1943): 503-13.

8178. Paula von Mirtow, "The Glory of Christ in the Fourth Gospel," *Th* 49 (1946): 336-40, 359-65.

8179. J. H. L. Brown, "The Authority of the Person of Jesus," *RTR* 8 (1949): 12-15.

8180. A. Herranz, "Jesucristo—su mensaje, sus pruebas," *CB* 7 (1950): 44-47, 82-85, 122-26.

8181. H. S. Shelton, "Jesus: God or Man," *HJ* 49 (1950-1951): 271-76.

8182. E. G. Lee, "The Jesus of History—A Unitarian Reflection," *HJ* 49 (1950-1951): 154-58.

8183. E. F. Kevan, "The Person and Work of Christ," *EQ* 23 (1951): 213-40.

8184. Ch. Moeller, "Textes 'monophysites' de Léonce de Jérusalem," *ETL* 27 (1951): 467-82.

8185. H. F. Lovell Cocks, "P. T. Forsyth's 'The Person and Place of Jesus Christ'," *ET* 64 (1952-1953): 195-98.

8186. Austin Fulton, "Who is Jesus Christ?" *BT* 2 (1952): 35-47.

8187. Philip S. Watson, "The Kenosis Doctrine in H. R. Mackintosh's 'The Person of Jesus Christ'," *ET* 64 (1952-1953): 68-71.

8188.	Heinrich Buhr, "Der Fürst des Fests," *ZTK* N.F. 52 (1955): 360-79.

8189.	Andreas Theodoros, "Χριστολογικὴ ὁρολογία κσὶ διδασκαλία Λεοντίου τοῦ βυζαντίνου," Θ 26 (1955): 584-619.

8190.	G. Weyne, "Nietzsche's voorstellung van de echte Christusfigur," *ETL* 32 (1956): 331-54.

8191.	Bartolomé M. Xiberta, "Observaciones al margen de la controversia sobre la conciencia humana de Jesucristo," *RHT* 16 (1956): 215-34.

8192.	A. de Halleux, "La christologie de Martyrios-Sahdona dans l'evolution du nestorianisme," *OCP* 23 (1957): 5-32.

8193.	L. Ciappi, "La persona di Gesù Cristo nell' Enciclica 'Pascendi'," *Div.* 2 (1958): 69-84.

8194.	Anton Krempel, "Das hl. Thomas Natur- und Personbegriff im Zusammenhang mit dem Dreifaltigkeits- und Menschwerdungsverständnis," *MTZ* 10 (1959): 114-22.

8195.	John F. Walvoord, "The Person of the Incarnate Christ," *BS* 117 (1960): 99-107, 195-203.

8196.	Maria F. Sulzbach, "Who Was Jesus?" *RL* 30 (1961): 179-86.

	See also numbers 201, 748, 767, 920, 985-1045, 2131, 2826, 2877.

8196.1	S. Van Tilborg, "Neerdaling en incarnatie. De christologie van Johannes," *TTod* 13 (1973): 20-34.

8196.2	F. L. Battles, "God Was Accommodating Himself to Human Capacity," *Interp* 31 (1977): 19-38.

8196.3	Dermot Lane, "The Incarnation of God in Jesus Christ," *ITQ* 46 (1979): 158-69.

8196.4	Michael MacConaill, "The Incarnation Death and Resurrection of Christ," *ITQ* 47 (1980): 146-51.

8196.5	M. Bouttier, "L'humanité de Jésus selon saint Luc," *RSR* 69 (1981): 33-43.

8196.6	Graham Brown, "Identity Statements and the Incarnation," *HeyJ* 22 (1981): 261-77. John 15:15

8196.7 R. G. Crawford, "The Relation of the Divinity and the Humanity in Christ," *EQ* 53 (1981): 237-40.

8196.8 James B. Torrance, "The Incarnation and 'Limited Atonement'," *EQ* 55 (1983): 83-94.

(2). The Incarnation; the Humanity of Jesus Christ

8197. James Gardiner Vose, "Anselm's Doctrine of the Incarnation and Atonement," *BS* 11 (1854): 729-76; 12 (1855): 52-83.

8198. John A. Reubelt, "The Incarnation," *BS* 27 (1870): 1-32, 43-59.

8199. A. J. F. Behrends, "The Incarnation, and the Problem of Modern Thought," *JCP* 2 (1882-1883): 179-94.

8200. J. R. Illingworth, "The Incarnation of the Eternal Word," *Exp* 3rd ser., 3 (1886): 161-75.

8201. J. M. Gibson, "Wisdom Personified, and Love Incarnate," *Exp* 3rd ser., 8 (1888): 193-202.

8202. J. G. Boekenoogen, "Christologische beschouwingen; 3. Het Godmenschelijke," *TT* 26 (1892): 514-43.

8203. F. A. Stentrup, "Notwendigkeit der Erlösung und Menschwerdung nach St. Anselm," *ZKT* 16 (1892): 653-91.

8204. T. C. Edwards, "On the God-Man," *Exp* 5th ser., 2 (1895): 81-92, 161-91, 240-61.

8205. F. C. N. Wendel, "The Incarnation as a Proof of the Doctrine of the Kenosis," *BS* 54 (1897): 729-45.

8206. G. A. Derry, "The Incarnation and Dogma," *Exp* 5th ser., 7 (1898): 210-16.

8207. Th. Calmes, "Le prologue du quatrième évangile et la doctrine de l'incarnation," *RB* 8 (1899): 232-48.

8208. A. N. Jannaris, "The *Locus Classicus* for the Incarnation Overlooked," *ET* 13 (1901-1902): 477-80; 14 (1902- 1903): 188.

8209. Duff MacDonald, "The *Locus Classicus* for the Incarnation Overlooked," *ET* 14 (1902-1903): 48.

8210. T. A. Gurney, "Two Oxford Teachers on the Incarnation," *ET* 15 (1903-1904): 402-405.

8211. Eugen Sachsse, "Die Logoslehre bei Philo und bei Johannes," *NKZ* 15 (1904): 747-67.

8212. Alfred H. Kellogg, "The Incarnation and Other Worlds," *PTR* 3 (1905): 177-90

8213. G. Wohlenberg, "Zwei Krippentheologen. Eine Weihnachtsstudie zum Krippengespräch des Hieronymus," *NRZ* 16 (1905): 897-903.

8214. André Arnal, "L'humanité du Christ selon l'épître aux Hébreux," *RTQR* 15 (1906): 454-71.

8215. Lyder Brun, "Jesu menneskelighed i de synoptiske evangelier," *NTT* 7 (1906): 289-339.

8216. P. J. Toner, "The Modern Kenotic Theory," *ITQ* 1 (1906): 67-92, 183-207.

8217. Thorleif Homme, "Jesu fornedrelse eller hens forhold til det goddommelige i hans jordeliv," *NTT* 8 (1907): 165-87.

8218. A. Thune Jacobsen, "Videnskaben og Jesu liv," *TTDF* 3rd ser., 1 (1909-1910): 193-206.

8219. Willis J. Beecher, "Concerning the Incarnation and the Atonement," *PTR* 9 (1911): 438-57.

8220. Alfred E. Garvie, "The Doctrine of the Incarnation in the Creeds," *ET* 23 (1911-1912): 353-55.

8221. Alfred E. Garvie, "The Doctrine of the Incarnation in the Creeds," *ET* 23 (1911-1912): 414-16, 448-49, 505-509, 548-49.

8222. Charles W. Gilkey, "Our Spiritual Inheritance in the Doctrine of the Incarnation," *BW* 42 (1913): 345-50.

8223. Edward S. Drown, "The Growth of the Incarnation," *HTR* 7 (1914): 507-25.

8224. Mileham L. O'Harra, "The Incarnation," *BS* 72 (1915): 433-45.

8225. A. H. Lloyd, "Incarnation: An Essay in Three Parts," *AJT* 20 (1916): 45-80.

8226. F. Cuthbert, "The Incarnation and Modern Thought," *HJ* 16 (1917-1918): 63-73.

8227. John Douglas, "The Incarnation: Some Implications for the

Church," *ET* 30 (1918-1919): 327-28.

8228. Leander S. Keyser, "The Incarnation," *LCR* 37 (1918): 156-68.

8229. H. R. Mackintosh, "Christ and God," *ET* 31 (1919- 1920): 74-78.

8230. Gerald B. Smith, "The Religious Significance of the Humanity of Jesus," *AJT* 24 (1920): 191-208.

8231. I. Hoh, "De amabili humanitate Christi," *VD* 3 (1923): 143-46, 165-68.

8232. W. H. T. Dau, "The God-Man," *BR* 9 (1924): 48-84.

8233. Pl. de Meester, "Le mystère de l'incarnation ou christologie," *ETL* 1 (1924): 518-43; 2 (1925): 199-222.

8234. F. D. Jenkins, "The Incarnate Life of our Lord from the Point of View of his Moral Character," *PTR* 23 (1925): 397-421.

8235. William F. Pierce, "Christ and Miracle," *ATR* 8 (1925-1926): 209-17 [Miracle of Advent].

8236. E. Hocedez, "L'idée d'incarnation et les religions nonchrétiennes," *NRT* 53 (1926): 401-408.

8237. E. Hocedez, "Le mystère de l'incarnation est-il spécifiquement chrétien?" *NRT* 53 (1926): 481-99.

8238. Theodor Rüther, "Die Leiblichkeit Christi nach Clemens von Alexandrien," *TQ* 107 (1926): 231-54.

8239. L. S. Keyser, "The Incarnation of the Son of God," *BS* 85 (1928): 309-22.

8240. Sigfrid von Engeström, "Människan Jesu såsom utgångspunkt för Luthers teologiske tänkande," *STK* 5 (1929): 17-33.

8241. Norman Hook, "Incarnation versus Inspiration," *ET* 41 (1929-1930): 38-42.

8242. E. G. Selwyn, "The Incarnation," *Th* 19 (1929): 35-43, 74-84.

8243. Irénée Hausherr, "Un précurseur de la théorie scotiste sur la fin de l'incarnation," *RSR* 22 (1932): 316-20.

8244. Polykarp Radó, "Die Ps.-Chrysostomische Homilie εἰς τὴν χριστοῦ γέννησιν," *ZKT* 56 (1932): 82-83.

8245.   H. B. Alexander, "Why God Became Man," *HJ* 33 (1934-1935): 37-54.

8246.   Eug. Schiltz, "Aux sources de la théologie du mystère de l'incarnation: la christologie de saint Augustin," *NRT* 63 (1936): 689-713.

8247.   Willis W. Virtue, "The Mystery of God in Christ," *BS* 93 (1936): 336-47.

8248.   Lewis Sperry Chafer, "The Incarnation of Christ," *BS* 94 (1937): 8-14.

8249.   E. E. Flack, "Die Inkarnation und die christliche Einheit," *ZST* 14 (1937): 281-302.

8250.   J. P. Arendzen, "The Incarnation: Fact or Fantasy? A Catholic Comment," *HJ* 37 (1938-1939): 634-38.

8251.   L. J. Collins, "The Incarnation: Fact or Fantasy. (The Loisy-Couchoud Controversy)," *HJ* 37 (1938-1939): 396-404.

8252.   Jules Lebreton, "Les leçons de l'incarnation," *RSR* 28 (1938): 72-88.

8253.   Charles W. Lowry, "Did Origen Style the Son a κτίσμα?" *JTS* 39 (1938): 39-42.

8254.   Paul Tillich, "Nicholas Berdyaev," *RL* 7 (1938): 407-15 [the God-Man in Berdyaev].

8255.   André M. Dubarle, "L'ignorance du Christ chez saint Cyrille d'Alexandrie," *ETL* 16 (1939): 111-20.

8256.   Howard C. Zabriskie, "The Seven-fold Purpose of the Incarnation," *BS* 96 (1939): 71-87.

8257.   E. Closen, "De incarnatione imaginis Dei," *VD* 20 (1940): 105-15.

8258.   John Laird, "The Philosophy of Incarnation," *HTR* 33 (1940): 131-50.

8259.   André M. Dubarle, "La connaissance humaine du Christ d'après saint Augustin," *ETL* 18 (1941): 5-25.

8260.   Hermann Weller, "*Awatars* und Menschwerdung Christi," *TQ* 122 (1941): 14-26.

8261.   H. W. Schmidt, "Die Menschwerdung Gottes," *ZST* 19

(1942): 122-42.

8262. Nils Johansson, "De urkristna föreställningarna om Människosonen och vår Kristustro," *STK* 21 (1945): 1-13.

8263. Harris E. Kirk, "The Word Became Flesh," *TTod* 2 (1945): 158-59.

8264. Jean Rivière, "Contribution au dossier des 'Cur Deus homo' populaires, une homélie de saint Amphiloque d'Iconium," *BLE* 46 (1945): 129-38.

8265. Harry M. Taylor, "Why God the Son Became a Man," *RL* 14 (1945): 351-64.

8266. G. Rabeau, "L'incarnation du verbe dans la théologie de Karl Barth," *BLE* 47 (1946): 23-59.

8267. Alex. Durand, "Incarnation et Christocentrisme," *NRT* 69 (1947): 475-86.

8268. A. W. Argyle, "The New Testament Doctrine of the Incarnation," *ET* 60 (1948-1949): 135-38.

8269. John Baker, "The Incarnation," *EQ* 20 (1948): 2-8.

8270. John F. Walvoord, "The Incarnation of the Son of God," *BS* 105 (1948): 36-43, 145-53.

8271. R. Abramowski, "Der theologische Nachlass des Diodor von Tarsus," *ZNW* 42 (1949): 19-69.

8272. John Baker, "Limitations of Christ's Human Body," *ET* 61 (1949-50): 282-86.

8273. J. B. Soucek, "Man in the Light of the Humanity of Jesus," *SJT* 2 (1949): 74-82.

8274. T. H. Croxall, "Anglicanism and the Incarnation," *SJT* 3 (1950): 242-54.

8275. Guy M. Davis, "The Humanity of Jesus in John," *JBL* 70 (1951): 105-12.

8276. Francis G. Ensley, "Phillips Brooks and the Incarnation," *RL* 20 (1951): 350-61.

8277. Sherman E. Johnson, " 'God was in Christ'," *ATR* 33 (1951): 96-101.

8278. J. D. A. Macnicol, "Word and Deed in the New Testament," *ABR* 1 (1951): 44-56.

8279.   Apolinar Morán, "La santidad sustancial de la humanidad de Cristo en la teología de los ss. XVI y XVII," *EE* 25 (1951): 33-62.

8280.   Marcel Richard, "Le pape saint Léon le Grand et les *Scholia de Incarnatione Unigeniti* de saint Cyrille d'Alexandrie," *RSR* 40 (1951-1952): 116-28.

8281.   E. Delaruelle, "La doctrine de la personne humaine signe de contradiction entre christianisme et paganisme au IIIᴇ siècle," *BLE* 43 (1952): 161-72

8282.   Geraint Vaughan Jones, "L. S. Thornton's 'The Incarnate Lord'," *ET* 64 (1952-1953): 324-28.

8283.   Carlos H. Dodd, "La Venida de Cristo," *CT* 8 (1953): 3-21.

8284.   Norman Nagel, "The Incarnation and the Lord's Supper in Luther," *CTM* 24 (1953): 625-53.

8285.   I. Ortiz de Urbina, "L'anima umana di Cristo secondo s. Atanasio," *OCP* 20 (1954): 27-43.

8286.   Rudolf Haubst, "Das hoch- und spätmittelalterliche 'Cur Deus homo'?" *MTZ* 6 (1955): 302-13.

8287.   Roger Baron, "Philosophies chrétiennes, humanismes chrétiens et incarnation," *NRT* 78 (1956): 63-72.

8288.   James Barr, "The Word Became Flesh; The Incarnation in the New Testament," *Interp* 10 (1956): 16-23.

8289.   J. C. Campbell, "In a Son; The Doctrine of Incarnation in the Epistle to the Hebrews," *Interp* 10 (1956): 24-38.

8290.   H. M. Diepen, "Théodoret et le dogme d'Ephèse," *RSR* 44 (1956): 243-47.

8291.   G. Jouassard, "Saint Cyrille d'Alexandrie et le schéma de l'incarnation verbe-chair," *RSR* 44 (1956): 234-42.

8292.   Balmer Kelly, "Word of Promise; the Incarnation in the Old Testament," *Interp* 10 (1956): 3-15.

8293.   Charles Drelincourt, "Prière et méditation sur l'incarnation et la naissance de notre Seigneur et Sauveur Jésus Christ," *VCar* 11 (1957): 302-12.

8294.   Paul Galtier, "Théodore de Mopsueste: sa vraie pensée sur l'incarnation," *RSR* 45 (1957): 161-86, 338-60.

8295.   Panayotis Trempelas, "The Doctrine of the Incarnation of the Logos," *GOTR* 3 (1957): 61-69.

8296.   Serafin de Ausejo, "El concepto de 'carne' aplicado a Cristo en el IV Evangelio," *EB* 17 (1958): 411-27.

8297.   Robert E. Cushman, "Is the Incarnation a Symbol?" *TTod* 15 (1958): 167-82.

8298.   Eugene R. Fairweather, "A Milestone in Canadian Theology: Bishop Kingdon's *God Incarnate*," *CJT* 2 (1958). 101-10.

8299.   Ragnar Holte, "Logos Spermatikos. Christianity and Ancient Philosophy according to St. Justin's Apologies," *ST* 12 (1958): 109-68.

8300.   J. Jocz, "The Invisibility of God and the Incarnation," *CJT* 3 (1958): 179-86.

8301.   B. de San Pablo, "Porqué no hen repercutido entre los orientales las discusiones occidentales respecto al motivo determinante de la Encarnación del Verbo," *RET* 18 (1958): 187-218.

8302.   H. J. Richards, "The Word of God Incarnate," *Scr* 10 (1958): 44-48.

8303.   Ragnar Bring, "Det tidsbestämda och det evigt giltiga i Bibelns ord och bud," *STK* 35 (1959): 21-42.

8304.   M. Aubineau, "Une homélie de Théodote d'Ancyre sur la nativité du Seigneur," *OCP* 26 (1960): 221-50.

8305.   H. Crouzel, "Origène devant l'incarnation et devant l'histoire," *BLE* 61 (1960): 81-110.

8306.   John F. Walvoord, "The Incarnation of the Son of God," *BS* 117 (1960): 1-12.

8307.   Wilhelm F. Kasch, "Die Lehre von der Inkarnation in der Theologie," *ZTK* N.F. 58 (1961): 86-103.

         See also numbers 128, 207-247, 533-544, 701, 956, 5171, 5173ff., 7438ff., 8759, *10067, 10088* f.

8307.1   S. Van Tilborg, "Neerdaling en incarnatie. De christologie van Johannes," *TTod* 13 (1973): 20-34.

8307.2   F. L. Battles, "God Was Accommodating Himself to Human Capacity," *Interp* 31 (1977): 19-38.

8307.3   Dermot Lane, "The Incarnation of God in Jesus Christ," *ITQ* 46 (1979): 158-69.

8307.4   Michael MacConaill, "The Incarnation Death and Resurrection of Christ," *ITQ* 47 (1980): 146-51.

8307.5   M. Bouttier, "L'humanité de Jésus selon saint Luc," *RSR* 69 (1981): 33-43.

8307.6   Graham Brown, "Identity Statements and the Incarnation," *HeyJ* 22 (1981): 261-77. John 15:15

8307.7   R. G. Crawford, "The Relation of the Divinity and the Humanity in Christ," *EQ* 53 (1981): 237-40.

8307.8   James B. Torrance, "The Incarnation and 'Limited Atonement'," *EQ* 55 (1983): 83-94.

(3). The Two Natures in One Person

8308.   J. T. Tucker, "The Twofold Life of Jesus Christ," *BS* 17 (1860): 95-110.

8309.   Edward A. Lawrence, "The Divine and Human Natures in Christ," *BS* 24 (1867): 41-73

8310.   President Robins, "The Union of the Divine and Human in Jesus Christ," *BS* 31 (1874): 615-29.

8311.   E. de M., "La question des deux natures de Christ," *RTP* 16 (1883): 635-37.

8312.   W. H. Wynn, "The God-Man," *LQ* 19 (1889): 1-31.

8313.   F. A. Stentrup, "Zur Frage über die innere Vollkommenheit der Genugthunng Christi," *ZKT* 15 (1891): 667-89.

8314.   F. A. Stentrup, "Zwei Grundfragen in der Lehre von der Genugthuung Christi," *ZKT* 15 (1891): 267-300.

8315.   J. A. Clapperton, "Christ's Knowledge: Was it Limited or Unlimited?" *ET* 5 (1893-1894): 275-78.

8316.   A. M. Fairbairn, "The Natural and the Supernatural in Christ," *BW* 6 (1895): 168-88.

8317.   George Philip, "Union of the Divine and Human Natures in Christ," *ET* 10 (1898-1899): 92-93.

8318.   N. S. Burton, "The Twofold Nature of Christ," *BS* 62 (1905): 640-49.

8319. Benjamin B. Warfield, "The 'Two Natures' and Recent Christological Speculation. I. The Christology of the New Testament Writings," *AJT* 15 (1911): 337-61, 546-68. [cf. no. 7611].

8320. E. Albert Cook, "Is the 'Two-Nature' Theory of the Incarnation a Mystery or a Contradiction?" *AJT* 16 (1912): 268-75.

8321. J. Louw, "Het goddelijke en menschelijke in den Persoon van Jezus volgens den brief aan de Hebreën," *GTT* 20 (1919-1920): 242-48.

8322. W. J. Farley, "The 'Two Natures' of our Lord," *ET* 34 (1922-1923): 184-86.

8323. R. Boigelot, "Le mot 'personne' dans les écrits trinitaires de saint Augustin," *NRT* 57 (1930): 5-16.

8324. Paul Galtier, "L'union hypostatique et l'entre-deux de saint Thomas," *ETL* 7 (1930): 425-70.

8325. Melanchthon W. Jacobus, "Wer war Jesus?" *NKZ* 41 (1930): 825-33.

8326. H. Steen, "Hernieuwd Apollinarisme," *GTT* 34 (1933): 369-92.

8327. François Jansen, "Le concept de 'personne' chez les latins entre 1150 et 1250," *NRT* 61 (1934): 389-95.

8328. Walter Albrecht, "The Enhypostasia of Christ's Human Nature," *CTM* 6 (1935): 561-80.

8329. Charles Lee Feinberg, "The Hypostatic Union," *BS* 19 (1935): 261-91, 412-26.

8330. Th. Spáčil, "Nova opinio auctoris orthodoxi de Unione Hypostatica," *OCP* 1 (1935): 53-92.

8331. Eug. Schiltz, "Le problème de l'unité d'être dans le Christ," *NRT* 65 (1938): 1044-57.

8332. Paul Galtier, "Unité ontologique et unité psychologique dans le Christ," *BLE* 42 (1941): 216-32.

8333. H. G. England, "The Godhead and Manhood of Jesus," *HJ* 43 (1944-45): 55-62.

8334. E. Hocedez, "L'unité de conscience du Christ," *NRT* 68

718 THEOLOGICAL STUDIES

(1946): 391-401.

8335. Prosper Schepens, "ὁμοούσιος," *RSR* 35 (1948): 289-90.

8336. Ch. Hauter, "Les deux natures en Christ," *RHPR* 32 (1952): 201-11.

8337. Max Thurian, "Jésus Christ, vrai Dieu et vrai homme," *VCar* 6 (1952): 49-58, 107-16, 126-35.

8338. Francisco de P. Solá, "Observaciones sobre un interesante libro de Monseñor Parente: 'L'io di Christo'," *EE* 27 (1953): 203-29.

8339. Kevin McNamara, "Theodoret of Cyrus and the Unity of Person in Christ," *ITQ* 22 (1955): 313-28.

8340. Kevin McNamara, "The Psychological Unity of Christ: A Problem in Christology," *ITQ* 23 (1956): 60-69.

8341. Wolfgang Kratz, "Christus-Gott und Mensch. Einige Fragen an Calvin's Theologie," *EvT* 19 (1959): 209-19.

See also number 695.

8341.1 Heinrich Vogel, "Die Predigt als gehörte Rede," *ET* 39 (1979): 88-100.

8341.2 A. T. Hanson, "Two Consciousnesses: The Modern Version of Chalcedon," *SJT* 37 (1984): 471-83.

8341.3 Paul C. Bruns, "Jesus Christ and Christ Jesus Are One Person, Not Two," *BTr* 37 (1986): 234-35.

(4). The Divinity of Jesus Christ

8342. Dr. Schneckenburger, "Ueber die Gottheit Christi nach den synoptischen Evangelien," *TSK* 2 (1829): 356-60.

8343. David B. Ford, "Scriptural Evidence of the Deity of Christ," *BS* 17 (1860): 535-74.

8344. C. F. Schaeffer, "Athanasius and the Arian Controversy," *BS* 21 (1864): 1-38.

8345. E. Pétavel-Olliff, "Thèses synthétiques sur la divinité de Jésus Christ," *RTP* 28 (1895): 240-66.

8346. Edmond J. Wolf, "The Super-Angelic Rank of the Redeemer," *LQ* 25 (1895): 188-208.

8347. C. Malan, "La personnalité divine de Jésus Christ ressentie par ce qu'il y a de divin dàns la vie actuelle de l'homme déchu," *RTP* 32 (1899): 267-72.

8348. Henry S. Nash, "Θειότης—θεότης, Rom. i. 20; Col, ii. 9," *JBL* 18 (1899): 26-34.

8349. Vincent Rose, "Études évangéliques: la conception surnaturelle de Jésus," *RB* 8 (1899): 206-31.

8350. E. Dorsch, "Die Gottheit Jesu bei Clemens von Rom (1 Cor.)," *ZKT* 26 (1902): 466-91, 701-28.

8351. Frank C. Porter, "Inquiries Concerning the Divinity of Christ," *AJT* 8 (1904): 10-29.

8352. F. H. Offerman, "The Eternal Divinity of Christ," *LCR* 25 (1906): 249-58.

8353. F. W. Orde Ward, "The Stature of Christ," *Exp* 7th ser., 2 (1906): 441-51.

8354. Newport J. D. White, "The Unchangeableness of Jesus Christ in Relation to Christian Doctrine," *Exp* 7th ser., 2 (1906): 175-85

8355. H. W. Wright, "Can the Human Character of Jesus be called Divine?" *AJT* 11 (1907): 290-93.

8356. R. Morris, "Was Jesus a 'Divine Man' and Nothing More?" *HJ* 6 (1907-1908): 623-31.

8357. B. Jansen, "Die Gottheit Jesu Christi bei den Synoptikern," *ZKT* 33 (1909): 248-72.

8358. C. Meersdom, "La divinité de Jésus Christ," *NRT* 41 (1909): 641-56.

8359. Fritz Tillmann, "Methodisches und Sachliches zur Darstellung der Gottheit Christi nach den Synoptikern gegenüber der modernen Kritik," *BibZ* 8 (1910): 146-61, 252-62.

8360. J. MacRory, "The Synoptic Gospels and our Lord's Divinity," *IQ* 7 (1912): 22-39

8361. William A. Brown, "Modern Theology and the Preaching of the Gospel; V. The Deity of Christ in the Light of Modern Thought," *BW* 43 (1914): 382-95.

8362. C. Caverno, "The Full Divinity of Christ," *BS* 71 (1914):

145-49.

8363. Lucius Hopkins Miller, "The Divinity of Christ," *BW* 43 (1914): 295-304.

8364. Benjamin B. Warfield, "Misconceptions of Jesus, and Blasphemy of the Son of Man," *PTR* 12 (1914): 367-410.

8365. Paul Schmid, "Die göttliche Verehrung Jesu muss auf Gott übertragen werden," *STZ* 32 (1915): 99-107, 161-79.

8366. A. Souter, "A Theological Tractate on the Divinity of the Son, from Paris MS B.N. Lat. 653," *JTS* 17 (1915-1916): 129-36.

8367. Garrett Pierse, "The Human Character of Jesus: A Proof of his Divinity," *ITQ* 11 (1916): 184-200.

8368. Norman Bartlett, "The Unreasonableness of Denying the Deity of Christ," *BS* 80 (1923): 328-32.

8369. Albert D. Belden, "Religion and Modern Thought: The Divinity of our Lord," *RE* 20 (1923): 40-46.

8370. J. M. Hantz, "Our Lord's Divinity," *LQ* 54 (1924): 340-48.

8371. F. D. Jenkins, "Is Jesus God?" *PTR* 23 (1925): 544-68; 24 (1926): 67-95.

8372. J. M. Hantz, "Our Lord's Divinity," *BS* 85 (1928): 179-87.

8373. Norman Bartlett, "The Deity of Jesus Christ as Set Forth in the Epistles," *BS* 86 (1929): 70-84.

8374. Norman Bartlett, "The Deity of Jesus Christ; After his Resurrection," *BS* 86 (1929): 197-212.

8375. H. Guenser, "La filiation divine de Jésus d'après les évangiles," *STK* 6 (1929): 245-51.

8376. W. F. Lofthouse, "Vater und Sohn im Johannesevangelium," *TB* 11 (1932): 289-300.

8377. W. C. Robinson, "Jesus Christ is Jehovah," *USR* 44 (1932-1933): 278-92, 380-400.

8378. W. C. Robinson, "Jesus Christ is Jehovah," *EQ* 5 (1933): 144-55, 271-90.

8379. M.-J. Lagrange, "Les origines du dogme paulinien de la divinité du Christ," *RB* 45 (1936): 5-33.

8380. J. Morton Sterrett, "The Mystery of God, Even Christ," *BS* 95 (1938): 157-71.

8381.   I. Ortiz de Urbina, "L'homousios' preniceno," *OCP* 8 (1942): 194-209.

8382.   A. C. Cotter, "The Divinity of Christ in Apologetics," *ThSt* 4 (1943): 369-84.

8383.   J. Burnaby, "The Divine Sonship," *JTS* 45 (1944): 129- 34.

8384.   A. C. Cotter, "The Divinity of Jesus Christ in St. Paul," *CBQ* 7 (1945): 259-89.

8385.   D. J. Saunders, "The Devil and the Divinity of Christ," *ThSt* 9 (1948): 536-53.

8386.   Frederick C. Grant, "The Divinity of Christ," *RL* 18 (1949): 483-92.

8387.   B. Schultze, "Der Streit um die Göttlichkeit des Names Jesu in der russischen Theologie," *OCP* 17 (1951): 321-94.

8388.   Pierre Benoit, "La divinité de Jésus dans les évangiles synoptiques," *LumV* no. 9 (1953): 43-74.

8389.   M.-E. Boismard, "La divinité du Christ d'après saint Paul," *LumV* no. 9 (1953): 75-100.

8390.   Donatien Mollat, "La divinité du Christ d'après saint Jean," *LumV* no. 9 (1953): 101-34.

8391.   André Feuillet, "Jésus et la sagesse divine d'après les évangiles synoptiques," *RB* 62 (1955): 161-96.

8392.   J. Harold Greenlee, " 'My Father'," *BTr* 6 (1955): 119-21.

8393.   Luis M. Mendizábal, "El Homoousios preniceno extra-eclesiástico," *EE* 30 (1956): 147-96.

8394.   J. B. Rowell, "The Deity of the Lord Jesus Christ Vindicated," *BS* 114 (1957): 70-77.

8395.   Frank R. Hancock, "Bible Miracles and the Godhead of Jesus," *FF* 13 (1960): 111-14.

See also numbers 974, 976, 8131ff., 10005.

8395.1   Raymond E. Brown, "Does the New Testament Call Jesus God?" *ThSt* 26 (1965): 545-73.

8395.2   Augustin George, "Jesus Fils de Dieu dans l'Evangile selon saint Luc," *RB* 72 (1965): 185-209.

8395.3   Raymond E. Brown, "How Much Did Jesus Know? A Survey of the Biblical Evidence," *CBQ* 29 (1967): 315-45.

8395.4   I. Howard Marshall, "Divine Sonship of Jesus," *Interp* 21 (1967): 87-103.

8395.5   Helmut Koester, "One Jesus and Four Primitive Gospels," *HTR* 61 (1968): 203-47.

8395.6   John A. Witmer, "Did Jesus Claim to be God," *BS* 125 (1968): 147-56.

8395.7   Morton Smith, "Prolegomena to a Discussion of Aretalogies, Divine Men, the Gospels and Jesus," *JBL* 90 (1971): 174-99.

8395.8   Jean Carmignac, "L'importance de la place d'une negation, ouch arpagmon egesato Philippiens 2:6," *NTSt* 18 (1972): 131-66.

8395.9   Richard J. Bauckham, "Sonship of the Historical Jesus in Christology," *SJT* 31 (1978): 245-60.

8395.10   Otto Knoch, "Er war wie Gott: Anmerkungen zur Übersetzung von morphe in der Einheitsübersetzung," *TQ* 161 (1981): 285-87.

8395.11   Helmut Merklein, "Die Auferweckung Jesu und die Anfänge der Christologie," *ZNW* 72 (1981): 1-26.

8395.12   Ludger Oeing-Hanhoff, "Der in Gottesgestalt war: Erneute Kritik der Einheitsübersetzung," *TQ* 161 (1981): 288-304.

8395.13   W. R. G. Loader, "Apocalyptic Model of Sonship: Its Origin and Development in New Testament Tradition," *JBL* 97 (1978): 525-54.

8395.14   Birger Gerhardsson, "An ihren Früchten sollt ihr sie erkennen: die Legitimitätsfrage in der matthäischen Christologie," *EvT* 42 (1982): 113-26.

8395.15   G. Reim, "Jesus as God in the Fourth Gospel: The Old Testament Background," *NTSt* 30 (1984): 158-60.

8395.16   Michael R. Austin, "Salvation and the Divinity of Jesus," *ET* 96 (1985): 271-75.

8395.17   Helmut Koester, "The Divine Human Being," *HTR* 78 1985): 243-52.

8395.18   Maximos Aghiorgoussis, "The Word of God in Orthodox Christianity," *GOTR* 31 (1986): 79-103.

8395.19   Francis J. Beckwith, "Of Logic and Lordship: The Validity of a Categorical Syllogism Supporting Christ's Deity," *JETS* 29 (1986): 429-30.

8395.20 Paul A. Rainbow, "Jewish Monotheism as the Matrix for New Testament Christology," *NT* 33 (1991): 78-91.

8395.21 Don N. Howell, "God-Christ Interchange in Paul: Impressive Testimony to the Deity of Jesus," *JETS* 36 (1993): 467-79.

8395.22 Daniel Doriani, "The Deity of Christ in the Synoptic Gospels," *JETS* 37 (1994): 333-50.

(5). The Pre-Existence and Eternity of Jesus Christ; Melchisedek

8396. Wilh. Benecke, "Ueber die Frage, ob das N.T. die Präexistenz lehre," *TSK* 5 (1832): 616-25.

8397. Henry L. Kendall, "Dr. Watts's Theory of Christ's Pre-Existent Human Nature," *BS* 32 (1875): 421-52.

8398. C. Goodspeed, "The Angel of Jehovah," *BS* 36 (1879): 593-615.

8399. H. Holtzmann, "Zur paulinischen Präexistenzlehre," *ZWT* 27 (1884): 129-39.

8400. A. H. Franke, "Die neutestamentlichen Grundlagen der Lehre von der Präexistenz Christ," *TSK* 60 (1887): 323-52.

8401. H. Cordey, "La foi à la préexistence de Jésus Christ et son importance pour la piété chrétienne," *RTQR* 2 (1893): 257-79, 337-52, 451-73.

8402. Henri Bois, "De quelques objections métaphysiques et morales contre la préexistence de Jésus Christ," *RTQR* 3 (1894): 197-226.

8403. V. von Strauss und Torney, "Christi Gottheit und Präexistenz," *NKZ* 7 (1896): 755-93.

8404. E. Steudel, "Die Wahrheit von der Präexistenz Christi in ihrer Bedeutung für christlichen Glauben und Leben," *NKZ* 11 (1900): 919-40; 12 (1901): 13-34.

8405. F. P. Mayser, "Melchizedek the Most Perfect Type of Christ," *LCR* 30 (1911): 692-97; 31 (1912): 88-95.

8406. R. H. Strachan, "The Idea of Pre-Existence in the Fourth Gospel," *AJT* 18 (1914): 81-105.

8407. Jan K. Van Baalen, "The Ritschlians and the Pre-existence of Christ," *PTR* 18 (1920): 493-514, 611-37.

8408. Gustave Bardy, "Melchisédech dans la tradition patristique," *RB* 35 (1926): 496-509; 36 (1927): 25-45.

8409. F. Ogara, "Christus Rex 'Sacerdos secundum ordinem Melchisedech," *VD* 13 (1933): 138-46, 167-72, 209-14.

8410. A. Vaccari, " 'Melchisedec, rex Salem, proferens panem et vinum' (Gen. 14, 18)," *VD* 18 (1938): 208-14, 235-43.

8411. John F. Walvoord, "The Pre-incarnate Son of God," *BS* 104 (1947): 25-34, 282-89, 415-25.

8412. Helga Rusche, "Die Gestalt des Melchisedek," *MTZ* 6 (1955): 230-52.

8413. M. Gutiérrez Marín, "La eternidad de Jesucristo," *CT* 18-19 (1956): 58-65.

See also number 5130.

8413.1 Pierre Benoit, "Préexistence et incarnation," *RB* 77 (1970): 5-29.

8413.2 David E. Aune, "Note on Jesus' Messianic Consciousness and 11 HQ Melchizedek," *EQ* 45 (1973): 161-65.

8413.3 G. Schimanowski, "Präexistenz und Christologie: (Weisheit und Messias in der jüdischen Tradition)," *TLZ* 107 (1982): 318.

(6). The Virgin Birth of Jesus

8414. D. Brown, "The Miraculous Conception," *Exp* 3rd ser., 7 (1888): 293-308.

8415. A. Hering, "Die dogmatische Bedeutung und der religiöse Werth der übernatürlichen Geburt Christ," *ZKT* 5 (1895): 58-91.

8416. Jean Friedel, "La naissance surnaturelle du Christ et la biologie," *RTQR* 8 (1899): 558-68.

8417. T. Allan Hoben, "The Virgin Birth," *AJT* 6 (1902): 473-506, 709-52.

8418. W. Sanday, "The Virgin Birth," *ET* 14 (1902-1903): 296-303.

8419. C. E. Beeby, "Doctrinal Significance of a Miraculous Birth," *HJ* 2 (1903-1904): 125-40.

8420. Wentworth Webster, "The Phrase 'The Virgin Birth of our Lord'," *ET* 15 (1903-1904): 331-32.

8421. Newport J. D. White, "The Virgin-Birth," *Exp* 6th ser., 7 (1903): 198-207.

8422. G. A. Derry and Raphoe, "The Virgin Birth," *Exp* 6th ser., 11 (1905): 50-59.

8423. J. Gresham Machen, "The New Testament Account of the Birth of Jesus," *PTR* 3 (1905): 641-70; 4 (1906): 37-81.

8424. B. W. Bacon, A. C. Zenos, Rush Rhees, and Benjamin B. Warfield, "The Supernatural Birth of Jesus," *AJT* 10 (1906): 1-30.

8425. Arthur Carr, "The Virgin Birth in St. John's Gospel," *ET* 18 (1906-1907): 521-22

8426. J. Häcker, "Die Jungfrauen-Geburt und das Neue Testament," *ZWT* 49 (1906): 18-61.

8427. Vincent McNabb, "St. Mark's Witness to the Virgin Birth," *JTS* 8 (1906-1907): 448-50.

8428. Arthur Carr, "The Testimony of St. John to the Virgin Birth of our Lord," *Exp* 7th ser., 3 (1907): 311-16.

8429. W. L. Lingle, "The Virgin Birth of our Lord," *USR* 19 (1907-1908): 173-80.

8430. C. A. Briggs, "The Virgin Birth of our Lord," *AJT* 12 (1908): 189-210.

8431. J. S. Cooper, "The Virgin Birth," *ET* 20 (1908-1909): 372-73.

8432. Louis M. Sweet, "Heathen Wonder Births and the Birth of Christ," *PTR* 6 (1908): 83-117.

8433. C.-E. Babut, "Un essai inachevé au sujet de la naissance surnaturelle du Sauveur," *RTQR* 20 (1911): 481-524.

8434. B. W. Bacon, "Matthew and the Virgin Birth," *AJT* 15 (1911): 83-95.

8435. G. Buchanan Gray, "The Virgin Birth in Relation to the Interpretation of Isaiah vii. 14," *Exp* 8th ser., 1 (1911):

289-308.

8436. A. T. W. Steinhauser, "The Virgin Birth in the Fourth Gospel," *LCR* 30 (1911): 60-65.

8437. J. Gresham Machen, "The Virgin Birth in the Second Century," *PTR* 10 (1912): 529-80.

8438. A. T. Fryer, "The Virgin Birth," *ET* 28 (1916-1917): 324.

8439. Horace Marion Ramsey, "A Sketch of the Early History of the Dogma of the Virgin Birth," *BS* 73 (1916): 343-68.

8440. L. Patterson, "Origin of the Name Panthera," *JTS* 19 (1918): 79-80.

8441. G. G. Warren, "Thoughts on the Virgin Birth," *BR* 7 (1922): 48-60.

8442. Norvelle Wallace Sharpe, "A Study of the Traditional 'Virgin Mary' in the Light of the Word," *BS* 80 (1923): 74-96.

8443. J. A. Singmaster, "The Virgin Birth," *LQ* 54 (1924): 411-18.

8444. D. H. Ogden, "Was Jesus Christ Born of a Virgin?" *USR* 37 (1925-1926): 28-35.

8445. W. K. Lowther Clarke, "The Virgin Birth and Recent Discussion," *Th* 13 (1926): 78-92.

8446. W. H. Guiton, "The Virgin Birth of our Lord," *PTR* 25 (1927): 389-416.

8447. B. T. Stafford, "The Science of the Virgin Birth," *BS* 84 (1927): 167-76.

8448. R. D. Miller, "Why Did Jesus Not Call Mary Mother?" *BS* 85 (1928): 46-52.

8449. A. J. Macdonald, "Berengar and the Virgin Birth," *JTS* 30 (1928-1929): 291-94.

8450. H. W. Magoun, "What is the Solution?" *BR* 14 (1929): 541-59 [Virgin Birth and genealogies of Jesus].

8451. A. Rendle Short, "The Virgin Birth of our Lord and Saviour Jesus Christ," *EQ* 1 (1929): 147-55.

8452. Philip Wendell Crannell, "The Supernatural Birth of (the) Christ," *RE* 29 (1932): 347-62.

8453. Arthur C. Baldwin, "The Religious Values of the Virgin Birth," *CQ* 10 (1933): 419-28.

8454. H. W. Magoun, "Unrecognized Testimony Concerning the Virgin Birth," *BS* 91 (1934): 303-16.

8455. A. M. van de haar Krafft, "De maagdelijke geboort ontvangen van den Heiligen Geest, geboren uit de maagd Maria," *NTS* 20 (1937): 211-22.

8456. J. W. Parker, "The Virgin Birth," *Th* 36 (1938): 199-205.

8457. H. J. Carpenter, "The Birth from Holy Spirit and the Virgin in the Old Roman Creed," *JTS* 40 (1939): 31-36.

8458. Hjalmar Lindroth, "Conceptus de spiritu sancto," *STK* 17 (1941): 281-97.

8459. T. W. Manson, " 'The Virgin Birth in History and Faith,' by Douglas Edwards," *JTS* 44 (1943): 212-15.

8460 Karl Barth, "El Misterio y el Milagro de Navidad," *CT* 2 (1950): 5-10.

8461 G. A. Danell, "Did St. Paul know the Tradition about the Virgin Birth?" *ST* 4 (1950): 94-101.

8462. Dale Moody, "On the Virgin Birth of Jesus Christ," *RE* 50 (1953): 453-62.

8463. E. F. Sutcliffe, "Dr. Cadoux on the Virgin Birth," *Scr* 6 (1953): 42-45.

8464. James M. Bulman, "The Virgin Birth in Recent Discussion," *RE* 51 (1954): 470-94.

8465. Dale Moody, "The Miraculous Conception," *RE* 51 (1954): 495-507; 52 (1955): 44-54, 310-24.

8466. William A. Mueller, "Karl Barth's View of the Virgin Birth," *RE* 51 (1954): 508-21.

8467. Loren J. Shiley, "A New Theory of Christ's Birth," *CTM* 26 (1955): 458-60.

8468. Reginald H. Fuller, "The Virgin Birth, Historical Fact or Kerygmatic Truth?" *BRes* 1 (1956): 1-8.

8469. Harold A. Guy, "The Virgin Birth in St. Luke," *ET* 68 (1956-1957): 157-58.

8470. H. E. W. Turner, "The Virgin Birth," *ET* 68 (1956-1957): 12-17

8471. Thomas Boslooper, "Jesus' Virgin Birth and Non-Christian

'Parallels'," *RL* 26 (1957): 87-97.

8472. Y. Feenstra, "Geboren uit de Maagd," *GTT* 57 (1957): 88-96, 161-68, 193-99; 58 (1958): 10-18, 44-53, 65-73, 97-110, 129-36.

8473. J. Galot, "La virginité de Marie et la naissance de Jésus," *NRT* 82 (1960): 449-69.

8474. Martin Smith, "The Virgin Birth," *BT* 10 (1960): 59-61.

See also number 912.

8474.1 Otto A. Piper, "The Virgin Birth. The Meaning of the Gospel Accounts," *Interp* 18 (1964): 131-48.

8474.2 S. Lewis Johnson, "The Genesis of Jesus," *BS* 122 (1965): 331-42.

8474.3 W. C. Robinson, "A Re-study of the Virgin Birth of Christ. God's Son Was Born of a Woman: Mary's Son Prayed 'Abba Father'," *EQ* 37/4 (1965): 198-211.

8474.4 Joseph A. Fitzmyer, "The Virginal Conception of Jesus in the New Testament," *ThSt* 34 (1973): 541-75.

8474.5 John W. Pryor, "Of the Virgin Birth or the Birth of Christians: The Text of John 1:13 Once More," *NT* 27 (1985): 296-318.

8474.6 Gerald Bostock, "Virgin Birth or Human Conception?" *ET* 97/9 (1986-1987): 260-63.

8474.7 C. E. B. Cranfield, "Some Reflections on the Subject of the Virgin Birth," *SJT* 41 (1988): 177-89.

8474.8 Philip A. Mellor, "The Virgin Birth and the Theology of Beauty," *ITQ* 57 (1991): 196-208.

8474.9 P. W. Thomas, "The Virginal Conception," *ET* 107 (1995): 11-14.

(7). The Sinlessness of Jesus

8475. C. Ullmann, "Ueber die Unsündlichkeit Jesu," *TSK* 1 (1828): 3-83.

8476. C. Ullmann, "Polemisches in Betreff der Sündlosigkeit Jesu mit besonderer Beziehung auf D. Chr. Fr. Fritzsche und D. Strauss," *TSK* 15 (1842): 640-710.

8477. C. Ullmann, "Theologische Aphorismen. (Zugleich Selbstanzeige der Schrift: die Sündlosigkeit Jesu)," *TSK* 20 (1847): 155-70.

8478. F. Godet, "The Holiness of Jesus Christ," *Exp* 1st ser., 6 (1877): 1-17, 196-205.

8479. J. Hawkins, "The Temptation of Christ and his Impeccability," *LQ* 20 (1890): 33-45.

8480. R. Balgarnie, "Could Jesus Err?" *ET* 8 (1896-1897): 475.

8481. John A. Clark, "Could Jesus Err?" *ET* 8 (1896-1897): 524.

8482. James Hastings, "Could Jesus Err?" *ET* 8 (1896-1897): 568.

8483. Thomas Whitelaw, "Could Jesus Err," *ET* 8 (1896-1897): 299-303, 365-67, 411-13, 467-68.

8484. Paul Chapuis, "La sainteté de Jésus de Nazareth," *RTP* 30 (1897): 297-321, 409-27, 539-69.

8485. L. Gilard, "La sainteté de Jésus ou l'homme normal," *RTP* 31 (1898): 201-35, 349-73, 405-38.

8486. J. H. Srawley, "St. Gregory of Nyssa on the Sinlessness of Christ," *JTS* 7 (1905-1906): 434-41.

8487. Edwin A. Rumball, "The Sinlessness of Christ," *HJ* 5 (1906-1907): 600-605.

8488. Heinrich Scholz, "Schleiermachers Lehre von der Sündlosigkeit Jesu," *ZTK* 17 (1907): 391-422.

8489. J. A. Singmaster, "The Impeccability of Christ," *LQ* 38 (1908): 266-74.

8490. John L. Dawson, "The Sinlessness of Jesus," *BW* 38 (1911): 126-34.

8491. H. J. Wicks, "The Possibility of Temptation in the Life of our Lord," *ET* 30 (1918-1919): 459-61.

8492. John C. Mattes, "The Impeccability of Our Lord," *LCR* 41 (1922): 143-67.

8493. James Harper, "The Sinlessness of Jesus," *BS* 82 (1925): 267-73.

8494. Th. Engelder, "The Active Obedience of Christ," *CTM* 1 (1930): 810-17, 888-96.

8495. L. W. Grensted, "The Sinlessness of Christ," *Th* 24 (1932):

207-21.

8496. Anton Fridrichsen, "Fullkomlighetskravet i Jesu för-kunnelse," *STK* 9 (1933): 124-33.

8497. P. E. Kretzmann, "Die Sündlosigkeit Jesu," *CTM* 6 (1935): 413-19.

8498. John W. Voorhis, "The Baptism of Jesus and his Sinlessness," *EQ* 7 (1935): 39-53.

8499. A. Durand, "La liberté du Christ dans son rapport à l'impeccabilité," *NRT* 70 (1948): 811-22.

8500. Josef Eichinger, "Die Heiligkeit der menschlichen Seele Jesu," *TQ* 129 (1949): 101-11.

8501. J. K. S. Reid, "Tempted, Yet Without Sin," *EQ* 21 (1949): 161-67.

8502. B. Leeming, "The Holiness of Christ," *TQ* 18 (1951): 238-53.

8503. George F. Tittmann, "How Can We Say that Jesus is Perfect?" *ATR* 36 (1954): 201-204.

8504. John F. Walvoord, "The Impeccability of Christ," *BS* 118 (1961): 195-202.

See also numbers 207-47.

8504.1 Roy A. Stewart, "Sinless High-Priest," *NTSt* 14 (1967): 126-35.

8504.2 Ronald Williamson, "Hebrews 4:15 and the Sinlessness of Jesus," *ET* 86 (1974): 4-8.

8504.3 William R. Barnett, "Historical Understanding and Theo-logical Commitment: The Dilemma of Ritschl's Christology," *JR* 59 (1979): 195-212.

8504.4 Joseph G. Sahl, "The Impeccability of Jesus Christ," *BS* 140 (1983): 11-20.

8504.5 Thoms R. Schreiner, "Is Perfect Obedience to the Law Possible: A Re-examination of Galatians 3:10," *JETS* 27 (1984): 151-60.

d. *The Work of Jesus Christ*

(1). General Studies

8505. S. Cox, "The Veil and Web of Death destroyed by Christ," *Exp* 2nd ser., 4 (1882): 331-42.

8506. B. F. Westcott, "Christus consummator: Lessons from the Epistle to the Hebrews," *Exp* 3rd ser., 3 (1886): 1-9, 127-35, 193-201, 346-54.

8507. G. G. Findlay, "Jesus Crowned for Death," *Exp* 3rd ser., 9 (1889): 222-31 [Heb. 2: 5-9].

8508. J. R. Lumby, "Both Lord and Christ," *Exp* 4th ser., 10 (1894): 321-29.

8509. R. Glaister, "Christ's Sympathy in Life's Commonplace," *ET* 10 (1898-1899): 360-63 [Heb. 2: 16].

8510. James Barrelet, "Le serviteur de l'éternel d'après des travaux récents," *RTP* 34 (1901): 236-55.

8511. Dr. Rittelmeyer, "Das Werk Christi," *ZTK* 22 (1912): 31-40.

8512. Ph. Bachmann, "Über den Gedanken der Mittlerschaft in der christlichen Religion," *NKZ* 25 (1914): 595-634.

8513. John T. Ward, "The Work of Christ," *BS* 72 (1915): 464-74.

8514. S. Greijdanus, "Rationes (redenen) voor den duur van onzes Heilands ambtsbediening op aarde," *GTT* 20 (1919-1920): 81-89.

8515. J. M. Bover, "Christus pastor: Messias et Deus," *VD* 3 (1923): 51-58.

8516. W. T. McConnell, "The Finality of the Authority of Christ," *BS* 80 (1923): 333-44.

8517. A. Ancel, "Christus auctor fidei et petra scandai)," *VD* 5 (1925): 179-87.

8518. George Stibitz, "Sanctified by Obedience," *BR* 10 (1925): 527-43.

8519. V. C. MacMunn, "The Two Ministries of Christ," *Th* 16 (1928): 252-58, 314-28.

8520. E. K. Simpson, "The Pivot of Christianity," *BR* 15 (1930): 523-37.

8521. P. E. Kretzmann, "Christi stellvertretende Genugtuung als das wesentliche Moment in seinem Erlösungswerk," *CTM* 3 (1932): 113-20.

8522. Johannes Witte, "Warum ist Christus im Gegensatz zu allen Weltreligionen der Retter der Welt?" *TB* 11 (1932): 225-38.

8523. H. Th. van Munster. "De beteekenis van Christus' zoenoffer voor de gemeene gratie," *GTT* 35 (1934): 245- 58.

8524. Dr. Schultz, "Der Erlöser als Gestalt," *ZTK* N.F. 17 (1936): 218-41.

8525. G. Salet, "La croix du Christ, unité du monde," *NRT* 64 (1937): 225-60.

8526. Paul Althaus, "Das Kreuz und der Böse. Bemerkungen zu Karl Heims Lehre vom Werke Christi," *ZST* 15 (1938): 166-93.

8527. E. Scharl, "Der Rekapitulationsbegriff des hl. Irenäus," *OCP* 6 (1940): 376-416.

8528. Lewis Sperry Chafer, "Three Things Accomplished by Christ in his Sufferings," *BS* 103 (1946): 261-82.

8529. Lewis Sperry Chafer, "Seven Things Accomplished by Christ in his Sufferings and Death," *BS* 103 (1946): 391-410.

8530. Lewis Sperry Chafer, "Things Accomplished by Christ in his Death," *BS* 104 (1947): 3-24.

8531. F. Mitzka, "Das Wirken der Menschheit Christ zu unserem Heil nach dem hl. Thomas von Aquin," *ZKT* 69 (1947): 189-208.

8532. E. Rideau, "La grâce du Christ (méditation théologique)," *NRT* 69 (1947): 897-905.

8533. J. K. S. Reid, "The Office of Christ in Predestination," *SJT* 1 (1948): 1-19, 166-83.

8534. Gustaf Aulén, "Chaos and Cosmos; The Drama of the Atonement," *Interp* 4 (1950): 156-67.

8535. Carl Stange, "Das Heilswerk Christi nach Luther," *ZST* 21 (1950-1952): 181-211.

8536. Heinrich Willkomm, "Jesus the Judge of the World," *CTM* 25 (1954): 257-76.

8537. Gustaf Wingren, "Welt und Kirche unter Christus, dem

Herrn," *KD* 3 (1957): 53-60.

8538. John B. Cobb, "Some Thoughts on the Meaning of Christ's Death," *RL* 28 (1959): 212-22.

8539. Josef Finkenzeller, "Die christologische und ekklesiologische Sicht der gratia Christi in der Hochscholastik," *MTZ* 11 (1960): 169-80.

See also numbers 753, 754, 920, 8183.

8539.1 George L. Balentine, "Death of Jesus as a New Exodus," *RE* 59 (1962): 27-41.

8539.2 John Downing, "Jesus and Martyrdom," *JTS* NS 14 (1963): 279-93.

8539.3 M. Wolter, "Der Apostel und seine Gemeinden als Teilhaber am Leidensgeschick Jesu Christi: Beobachtungen zur paulinischen Leidenstheologie," *NTSt* 36 (1990): 535-57.

8539.4 A. Vicent Cernuda, "La condena inopinada de Jesús," *EB* 48 no 3 (1990): 375-422; 49 (1991): 49-96.

(2). The Work of Jesus Christ as Prophet and Teacher

8540. Oskar Holtzmann, "Die Offenbarung durch Christus und das Neue Testament," *ZTK* 1 (1891): 367-425.

8541. J. Watson, "Jesus our Supreme Teacher," *Exp* 5th ser., 3 (1896): 225-36.

8542. Sylvester Burnham, "Jesus as a Prophet," *BW* 10 (1897): 327-32.

8543. Wilhelm Engelhardt, "Jesus als Schriftgelehrter," *NKZ* 9 (1898): 427-46.

8544. Edward B. Pollard, "The Prophetic Activity of Jesus," *BW* 24 (1904): 94-99.

8545. Henry S. Nash, "The Saving Truth as it is in Jesus," *BW* 32 (1908): 242-51.

8546. M. Wagner, "Jesus, der Lehrer," *NKZ* 20 (1909): 492-99, 558-80, 581-92.

8547. R. Kennard Davis, "Christ as 'The Truth'," *HJ* 10 (1911-1912): 780-89

8548. H. R. Mackintosh, "The Revelation of God in Christ," *ET* 27

(1915-1916): 346-50.

8549.   B. W. Bacon, "The 'Son' as Organ of Revelation," *HTR* 9 (1916): 382-415.

8550.   Alfred E. Garvie, "God's Purpose as Revealed in Jesus Christ," *ET* 34 (1922-1923): 520-23.

8551.   A. Ancel, "Christus perversas audientium dispositiones corrigit," *VD* 6 (1926): 118-23.

8552.   A. Ancel, "Christus in polemico dicendi genere magister," *VD* 6 (1926): 195-201.

8553.   John W. Wenham, "The Authority of Christ as a Teacher: Does Incarnation Involve Fallibility?" *EQ* 17 (1945): 91-105.

8554.   H. Holstein, "La révélation du Dieu vivant," *NRT* 81 (1959): 157-68.

8555.   R. H. W. Shepherd, "The Revelation of God through Jesus Christ," *RL* 28 (1959): 262-72.

8556.   William L. Bradley, "The Authority of Jesus Christ," *HQ* 1, no. 3 (1961): 83-93.

8557.   Jean Levie, "Le message de Jésus dans la pensée des apôtres," *NRT* 83 (1961): 25-49.

         See also number 264.

8557.1   P. W. Barnett, "The Jewish Sign Prophets - AD 40-70: Their Intentions and Origins," *NTSt* 27 (1981): 679-97.

8557.2   Georg Sauer, "Das 'prophetische Amt Christi' und das 'amt' des Propheten," *EvT* 41 (1981): 284-89.

8557.3   David E. Aune, "The Odes of Solomon and Early Christian Prophecy," *NTSt* 28 (1982): 435-60.

8557.4   Adela Y. Collins, "From Noble Death to Crucified Messiah," *NTSt* 40 (1984): 481-503.

8557.5   David P. Moessner, "The Christ Must Suffer: New Light on the Jesus, Peter, Stephen, Paul Parallels in Luke-Acts," *NT* 28 (1986): 220-56.

8557.6   Adele Reinhartz, "Jesus as Prophet: Predictive Prolepses in the Fourth Gospel," *JSNT* 36 (1989): 3-16.

8557.7   Manuek Benéitez, "Un Extraño interrogatorio: Jn 18,29-32," *EE* 68 (1993): 459-9.

(3). The Work of Jesus Christ as Priest

(a). *General Studies; the Atonement*

8558. Enoch Pond, "Atonement," *BS* 13 (1856): 130-53.

8559. Edwards A. Park, "Dr. Griffin's Theory of the Atonement," *BS* 15 (1858): 132-78.

8560. Daniel T. Fisk, "The Necessity of the Atonement," *BS* 18 (1861): 284-324.

8561. Edward Hitchcock, "The Cross in Nature and Nature in the Cross," *BS* 18 (1861): 253-84.

8562. Enoch Pond, "The Atonement in its Relations to God and Man," *BS* 19 (1862): 685-706.

8563. Lemuel S. Potwin, "The Atonement in the Light of Conscience," *BS* 24 (1867): 141-50.

8564. Edwards A. Park, "John McLeod Campbell's Theory of the Atonement," *BS* 30 (1873): 334-60.

8565. Carpus, "The Atonement," *Exp* 1st ser., 2 (1875): 226-44.

8566. John Morgan, "Atonement," *BS* 34 (1877): 632-71.

8567. John Morgan, "Theories of Atonement," *BS* 35 (1878): 114-47

8568. S.E.C.T., "The Atonement-An Illustration," *Exp* 1st ser., 9 (1879): 221-33 [Philemon 18-19].

8569. J. A. Beet, "Christ crucified and risen," *Exp* 3rd ser., 6 (1887): 372-80.

8570. George F. Magoun, "Dr. Samuel D. Cochran on 'The Moral System and the Atonement'," *BS* 46 (1889): 475-98; 47 (1890): 21-53.

8571. Frank H. Foster, "The Benevolence Theory of the Atonement," *BS* 47 (1890): 567-88, 48 (1891): 104-27.

8572. Christoph Lotz, "Zur Lehre vom Verdienst Christi," *STZ* 7 (1890): 220-31.

8573. J. A. Beet, "The Doctrine of the Atonement in the New Testament," *Exp* 4th ser., 5 (1892): 2-11, 115-26, 183-89, 358-71, 432-43; 6 (1892): 27-34, 132-43, 297-305, 343-55, 419-26.

8574. J. P. Lilley, "The Invincible Love," *ET* 5 (1893-1894): 518-

21.

8575.   James S. Candlish, "Elements of the Doctrine of the Atonement in the Facts of our Lord's Sufferings," *BW* 9 (1897): 87-97.

8576.   R. C. Moberly, "The Fulham Conference on Communion with the Atonement," *JTS* 2 (1900-1901): 321-49.

8577.   George Mooar, "Reminiscences of Atonement Theory," *BS* 58 (1901): 294-313.

8578.   H. Rashdall, "Dr. Moberly's Theory of the Atonement," *JTS* 3 (1901-1902): 178-211.

8579.   Robert Mackintosh, "The Fact of the Atonement," *ET* 14 (1902-1903): 344-50.

8580.   W. T. A. Barber, "Atonement in Christ," *ET* 15 (1903-1904): 540-41.

8581.   James Denney, "The Atonement and the Modern Mind," *Exp* 6th ser., 8 (1903): 81-105, 161-82.

8582.   William McLane, "A Working Theory of the Atonement," *BW* 22 (1903): 284-89.

8583.   Benjamin B. Warfield, "Modern Theories of the Atonement," *PTR* 1 (1903): 81-92.

8584.   J. Hugh Beibitz, "Some Modern Views on the Atonement," *ET* 18 (1906-1907): 441-46.

8585.   Ernest DeW. Burton, "The Biblical Doctrine of Atonement," *BW* 31 (1908): 420-31; 32 (1908): 19-24, 124-29, 183-97, 252-61, 397-404; John M. P. Smith and Ernest DeW. Burton, 33 (1909): 23-31.

8586.   Stephen G. Barnes, "The Atonement and the Time- Spirit," *BS* 66 (1909): 458-66.

8587.   John L. Darby, "Is there no Atonement?" *ET* 21 (1909-1910): 224-25.

8588.   Samuel Zane Batten, "The Salvation of the Life," *BW* 48 (1916): 213-23.

8589.   Albert Bruckner, "Die religiöse Beurteilung des Leidens Jesu im Neuen Testament," *TSK* 89 (1916): 71-137.

8590.   James E. Gregg, "Penology and Atonement," *BW* 49 (1917):

203-208.

8591. Chr. Ihlen, "Aabenbaring og stedfortraedende soning," *NTT* 18 (1917) *Reformationshefte*, 193-229.

8592. H. McLachlan, "St. Luke's Doctrine of the Atonement," *HJ* 17 (1918-1919): 688-93.

8593. W. H. Griffith Thomas, "A Study in the Atonement," *BR* 3 (1918): 39-68.

8594. William H. Walker, "The Atonement in Christian Consciousness," *BS* 77 (1920): 165-85.

8595. Shailer Mathews, "The Functional Value of Doctrines of Atonement," *JT* 1 (1921): 146-59.

8596. Adhémar d'Alès et Maurice de la Taille, "Le sacrifice céleste et l'ange du sacrifice," *RSR* 13 (1923): 218-43.

8597. E. G. Selwyn, "The Atonement," *Th* 7 (1923): 216-22; 8 (1923): 20-31, 139-50.

8598. Robert Mackintosh, "Recent Thought on the Doctrine of the Atonement," *ET* 37 (1925-1926): 198-203.

8599. P. J. Beveridge, "The Doctrine of the Atonement," *ET* 38 (1926-1927): 516-18.

8600. W. E. Davidson, "On the Atonement," *RE* 24 (1927): 318-20.

8601. A. Gordon James, "Jesus our Advocate," *ET* 39 (1927-1928): 473-75.

8602. Fernand de Lanversin, "Esquisse d'une synthèse du sacrifice," *RSR* 17 (1927): 193-209.

8603. J. H. Leckie, "Books that have influenced our Epoch; John McLeod Campbell's 'The Nature of the Atonement'," *ET* 40 (1928-1929): 198-204.

8604. N. P. Williams, "Books that have influenced our Epoch; Moberly's 'Atonement and Personality'," *ET* 40 (1928-1929): 486-89.

8605. G. K. MacBean, "Our Relationship to God and its Mediation through Christ," *ET* 42 (1930-31): 508-12.

8606. Frederick A. M. Spencer, "The Atonement in Terms of Personality," *ET* 43 (1931-1932): 58-63.

8607.   Ed. C. Unmack, "The Philosophy of Atonement," *EQ* 3 (1931): 244-56.

8608.   Norman Bartlett, "The Root Principle of the Atonement," *BS* 90 (1933): 396-411.

8609.   Kenneth M. Monroe, "Time Element in the Atonement," *EQ* 5 (1933): 397-408

8610.   Thomas Houghton, "The Atonement," *EQ* 6 (1934): 137-46.

8611.   S. Antonius Patavinus, "Iesus Sacerdos in cruce et in altari mediator Dei et hominum," *VD* 15 (1935): 97-98.

8612.   J. G. Riddell, "Recent Thoughts on the Doctrine of the Atonement," *ET* 47 (1935-1936): 246-50, 327-32.

8613.   C. J. Wright, "The Atonement: Some Reflections," *ET* 47 (1935-1936): 155-60.

8614.   David M. McIntyre, "Cleansing in the Blood of Christ," *EQ* 8 (1936): 290-96.

8615.   Fl. Ogara, "Christus . . . assistens Pontifex futurorum bonorum," *VD* 16 (1936): 65-74.

8616.   G. W. Bromiley, "Redemption as History and Revelation," *EQ* 12 (1940): 97-111.

8617.   David S. Cairns, "Some Thoughts on the Atonement," *ET* 52 (1940-1941): 16-20, 60-64.

8618.   S. Barton Babbage, " 'Saviours' and the Saviour," *EQ* 15 (1943): 224-40.

8619.   Jean Rivière, "Théologie du sacrifice rédempteur. Un témoignage d'Origène," *BLE* 45 (1944): 3-12.

8620.   Morton S. Enslin, "The Atoning Work of Christ in the New Testament," *NTR* 38 (1945): 39-62.

8621.   W. T. Conner, "Three Types of Teaching in the New Testament on the Meaning of the Death of Christ," *RE* 43 (1946): 150-66.

8622.   W. T. Conner, "Three Theories of the Atonement," *RE* 43 (1946): 275-90.

8623.   Albert C. Knudson, "A Doctrine of Atonement for the Modern World," *CQ* 23 (1946): 51-64.

8624.   Lewis Sperry Chafer, "Theories False and True of the Value of Christ's Death," *BS* 104 (1947): 263-81.

8625. W. T. Conner, "Theories of Atonement," *RE* 44 (1947): 301-11.

8626. Nels F. S. Ferré, "The Savior Still," *RE* 44 (1947): 285-300.

8627. Royden K. Yerkes, "Atonement," *ATR* 29 (1947): 28-33.

8628. Hugh Thompson Kerr, "Love's Intention; the Motive of the Atonement," *Interp* 4 (1950): 131-42.

8629. L. Froidevaux, "Sur trois passages de la *Démonstration* de saint Irénée (§§89, 33, 31)," *RSR* 39 (1951-1952): 368-80 [priestly work of Christ].

8630. J. G. Riddell, "Emil Brunner's 'The Mediator'," *ET* 64 (1952-1953): 292-95.

8631. G. Graystone, "Modern Theories of the Atonement," *ITQ* 20 (1953): 225-52, 366-88.

8632. J. L. M. Haire, "The Atonement," *BT* 3 (1953): 66-72.

8633. Leon L. Morris, "The Day of Atonement and the Work of Christ," *RTR* 14 (1955): 9-19.

8634. W. D. Chamberlain, "The Need of Man; The Atonement in the Fourth Gospel," *Interp* 10 (1956): 157-66.

8635. B. Fraigneau-Julien, "Le sacrifice du Christ et le sacrifice de l'humanité selon Scheeben," *RSR* 45 (1957): 361-95.

8636. D. E. H. Whiteley, "St. Paul's Thought on the Atonement," *JTS* N.S. 8 (1957). 240-54.

8637. T. Torrance, "Uppfattningen om försoningen i urkyrkan. Kristi ämbete," *STK* 35 (1959): 73-100.

See also numbers 462-480, 8219 ff., 8697, 8699, 8708, 8719, 8722, 8726, 8743, 8745, 8749, 8770.

8637.1 C. William Swain, "For Our Sins: The Image of Sacrifice in the Thought of the Apostle Paul," *Interp* 17 (1963): 131-39.

8637.2 T. C. G. Thornton, "Propitiation or Expiation?" *ET* 80 (1968): 53-55.

8637.3 R. G. Crawford, "Is the Penal Theory of the Atonement Scriptural?" *SJT* 23 (1970): 257-72.

8637.4 Paul Garnet, "Atonement Constructions in the Old Testament and the Qumran Scrolls," *EQ* 46 (1974): 131-63.

8637.5 John W. Drane, "Simon the Samaritan and the Lucan Concept of Salvation," *EQ* 47 (1975): 131-37.

8637.6 Ralph P. Martin, "Salvation and Discipleship in Luke's Gospel," *Interp* 30 (1976): 366-80.

8637.7 Maximos Aghiorgoussis, "The Theology and Experience of Salvation," *GOTR* 22 (1977): 405-15.

8637.8 John P. Newport, "The Theology and Experience of Salvation," *GOTR* 22 (1977): 393-404.

8637.9 R. G. Crawford, "A Parable of the Atonement," *EQ* 50 (1978): 2-7.

8637.10 Bernd Janowski, "Sühne als Heilsgeschehen: Studien zur Sühnetheologie der Priesterschrift und zur Wurzel," *TL* 106 (1981): 779-80.

8637.11 R. Loewe, " 'Salvation' Is Not of the Jews," *JTS* 32 (1981): 341-68.

8637.12 Stephen S. Smalley, "Salvation Proclaimed: VIII. John 1," *ET* 93 (1981-1982): 324-29.

8637.13 Barnabas Lindars, "Christ and Salvation," *BJRL* 64 (1982): 481-500.

8637.14 Graham N. Stanton, "Salvation Proclaimed: X. Matthew 11:28-30: Comfortable Words?" *ET* 94/1 (1982): 3-9.

8637.15 Jan van Baal, "A Neglected Crux in the Interpretation of the Sacrifice of Christ," *NTT* 37 (1983): 242-46.

8637.16 Richard A. Riesen, "Criticism and Faith: William Robertson Smith on the Atonement," *SCT* 37 (1984): 171-87.

8637.17 Colin Gunton, "Christus Victor Revisited: A Study in Metaphor and the Transformation of Meaning," *JTS* ns 36 (1985): 129-45.

8637.18 D. A. S. Ravens, "St. Luke and Atonement," *ET* 97 (1985-1986): 291-94.

8637.19 Megory Anderson and Philip Culbertson, "The Inadequacy of the Christian Doctrine of Atonement in Light of the Levitical Sin Offering," *ATR* 68 (1986): 303-28.

8637.20 John B. Webster, "Atonement, History and Narrative," *TZ* 42 (1986): 115-31.

8637.21 Paul Ellingworth, "For Our Sake God Made Him Share Our Sin," *BTr* 38 (1987): 237-41.

8637.22 F. W. Young, "Allegory and Atonement," *ABR* 35 (1987): 107-14.

8637.23 A. F. Lascaris, "De verzoeningsleer en het offer-christendom," *NTT* 42 (1988): 220-42.

8637.24 C. Behan McCullagh, "Theology of Atonement," *Th* 91 (1988): 392-400.

8637.25 Michael Walker, "The Atonement and Justice," *Th* 91 (1988): 180-86.

8637.26 Jacob Neusner, "The Absoluteness of Christianity and the Uniqueness of Judaism: Why Salvation Is Not of the Jews," *Interp* 43 (1989): 18-31.

8637.27 J. Becker, "Die neutestamentliche Rede vom Suhnetod Jesu," *ZTK* 8 (1990): 29-49.

8637.28 Max Turner, "Atonement and the Death of Jesus in John—Some Questions to Bultmann and Forestell," *EQ* 62 (1990): 99-122.

8637.29 P. Jensen, "Forgiveness and Atonement," *SJT* 46 (1993): 141-59.

8637.30 D. A. Lee, "Women as 'Sinners': Three Narratives of Salvation in Luke and John," *ABR* 44 (1996): 1-15.

(b). *The Death on the Cross*

8638. Enoch Pond, "The Sufferings of Christ," *BS* 7 (1850): 205-26.

8639. J. Hawkins, "The Sufferings of Christ," *LQ* 2 (1872): 193-202.

8640. F.-C.-J. van Goens, "L'évangile de la croix," *RTP* 7 (1874): 558-82.

8641. Adolf Petersen, "Über das Werk der Erlösung als einer Erlösung durch das Blut Jesu Christi," *NJDT* 3 (1894): 121-45.

8642. G. Matheson, "The Place of the Cross in the World," *Exp* 5th ser., 5 (1897): 416-24 [Revelation 13:8].

8643. F. Niebergall, "Die Heilsnotwendigkeit des Kreuzestodes Jesu Christi," *ZTK* 7 (1897): 461-512.

8644. George Milligan, "On the Lukan Interpretation of Christ's Death," *Exp* 6th ser., 2 (1900): 69-75.

8645. W. R. Paton, "Die Kreuzigung Jesu," *ZNW* 2 (1901): 339-41.

8646. W. Morgan, "The Death of Christ," *ET* 14 (1902-1903): 166-72.

8647. F. J. Krop, "Nog eens: Welke beteekenis heeft de dood van Jezus Christus, volgens Zijn eigen verklaringen in de evangeliën voor mensch en menschheid?" *TS* 24 (1906): 153-75.

8648. W. L. Walker, "The Cross in Relation to Sin," *Exp* 7th ser., 1 (1906): 209-26.

8649. P. T. Forsyth, "What is Meant by the Blood of Christ?" *Exp* 7th ser., 6 (1908): 207-25.

8650. G. Vellenga, "De dood des Heeren. Exegetisch onderzoek," *TS* 27 (1909): 209-31; 28 (1910): 172-200, 268-99; 29 (1911): 311-38; 30 (1912): 168-211.

8651. G. A. J. Ross, "The Cross: The Report of a Misgiving," *HJ* 9 (1910-1911): 497-512.

8652. Karl Zickendraht, "Stellvertretung und Sündenvergebung im Leiden Jesu," *ZTK* 23 (1913): 390-98.

8653. Benjamin B. Warfield, "The Essence of Christianity and the Cross of Christ," *HTR* 7 (1914): 538-94.

8654. W. L. Walker, "The Cross as Viewed by Dr. Denney," *ET* 29 (1917-1918): 281-87

8655. Adolf Deissmann, "The Power of the Cross," *ET* 32 (1920-1921): 299-301.

8656. W. A. Jarrel, "Christians Filling Up that which is Lacking of the Sufferings of Christ," *RE* 18 (1921): 275-81 [Col. 1:24, etc.].

8657. L. Lindeboom, "Jezus Christus en die gekruisigd, het kenmerk der apostolische prediking," *GTT* 23 (1922- 1923): 260-75.

8658. Johannes Ording, "En forsoningslaere; Bernhard Steffen: *Das*

Dogma vom Kreuz," *NTT* 23 (1922): 165-74.

8659. Paul Althaus, "Das Kreuz Christi," *ZST* 1 (1923): 107-52.

8660. Albert D. Belden, "The Meaning of the Death of Jesus," *RE* 20 (1923): 293-303.

8661. A. G. Hogg, "The Cross of Christ and my Uttermost Farthing," *ET* 35 (1923-1924): 182-85

8662. L. Fonck, "Verbum Crucis in schola apostolorum," *VD* 4 (1924): 97-107.

8663. Edwin M. Poteat, "The Death of Jesus," *BR* 10 (1925): 11-45; 11 (1926): 188-212.

8664. Edwin M. Poteat, "The Scandal of the Cross," *BR* 12 (1927): 11-43.

8665. Albert D. Belden, "Vital Values of the Cross," *ET* 39 (1927-1928): 327-29.

8666. F. W. Buckler, "The Meaning of the Cross," *ATR* 12 (1929-1930): 411-22.

8667. Ed. Geismar, "Jesu Christi Tod als offenbarende und sühnende Tat," *ZST* 10 (1932-33): 463-89.

8668. Martin Dibelius, "La signification religieuse des récits évangéliques de la passion," *RHPR* 13 (1933): 30-45.

8669. C. J. Cadoux, "What does the Crucifixion Mean?" *IIJ* 32 (1933-1934): 70-80.

8670. Anton Anwander, "Das Kreuz Christi und andere Kreuze," *TQ* 115 (1934): 491-515.

8671. W. T. Whitley, "The Blood of Christ," *RE* 31 (1934): 211-15.

8672. J. M. Shaw, "The Problem of the Cross," *ET* 47 (1935-1936): 18-21.

8673. J. Hartog, "In den nacht in welken Hij verraden werd," *NTS* 20 (1937): 117-23

8674. T. E. Bleiben, "The Synoptists' Interpretation of the Death of Christ," *ET* 54 (1942-1943): 145-49

8675. John Baker, "Meditation on the Cross," *EQ* 17 (1945): 161-68; 18 (1946): 161-68; 20 (1948): 161-65.

8676. A. W. Argyle, "The New Testament Interpretation of the Death of our Lord," *ET* 60 (1948-1949): 253-56.

8677.   G. W. Bromiley, "The Significance of Death in Relation to the Atonement," *EQ* 21 (1949): 122-32.

8678.   Dale Moody, "The Crux of Christian Theology," *RE* 46 (1949): 164-80.

8679.   Albert D. Belden, "Vital Values of the Cross," *RE* 47 (1950): 158-64.

8680.   H. W. Schmidt, "Das Kreuz Christi bei Paulus," *ZST* 21 (1950-1952): 145-59.

8681.   J. Stadlhuber, "Das Laienstundengebet vom Leiden Christi in seinem mittelalterlichen Fortleben," *ZKT* 72 (1950): 282-325.

8682.   Carl Fr. Wisløff, "Kristi kamp og seier som motiv i forkynnelsen," *TTK* 21 (1950): 169-84.

8683.   F. E. Mayer, "Christ's Death the End of our Dying," *CTM* 22 (1951): 126-29.

8684.   Albert C. Outler, "For Us Men and Our Salvation," *RL* 20 (1951): 163-79.

8685.   Henri Rondet, "Notes d'exégèse augustinienne," *RSR* 39 (1951-1952): 472-77 [Cross as symbol; Christ as new Samson].

8686.   Marcel Viller, "La mystique de la passion chez saint Paul de la Croix," *RSR* 40 (1951-1952): 426-45.

8687.   John A. Allan, "The Gospel of the Son of God Crucified; Recent Study in the Gospel according to Mark," *Interp* 9 (1955): 131-43.

8688.   Carl Stange, "Kreuz und Auferstehung," *ZST* 24 (1955): 379-400.

8689.   Otto Kuss, "Der theologische Grundgedanke des Hebräerbriefs," *MTZ* 7 (1956): 233-71.

8690.   F. J. Leenhardt, "Réflexions sur la mort de Jésus," *RHPR* 27 (1957): 18-23.

8691.   A. F. Sava, "The Wound in the Side of Christ," *CBQ* 19 (1957): 343-46.

8692.   T. A. Burkill, "St. Mark's Philosophy of the Passion," *NT* 2 (1958): 245-71.

8693.   François Grandchamp, "La doctrine du sang du Christ dans les épîtres de saint Paul," *RTP* sér. 3, 2 (1961): 262-71.

8694. John F. Walvoord, "Christ in his Suffering and Death," *BS* 118 (1961): 291-303.

See also numbers 462-480, 585-622, 901, 902, 908, 926, 957, 959, 978, 3590, 7333, 7403, 9627, *10028*.

8694.1 Walter Kreck, "Zum Verständnis des Todes Jesu," *EvT* 28 (1968): 277-93.

8694.2 Richard Zehnle, "Salvific Character of Jesus' Death in Lucan Soteriology," *ThSt* 30 (1969): 420-44.

8694.3 Ernst Käsemann, "Pauline Theology of the Cross," *Interp* 24 (1970): 151-77.

8694.4 Jürgen Moltmann, "The 'Crucified God': A Trinitarian Theology of the Cross," *Interp* 26 (1972): 278-99.

8694.5 S. K. Williams, "Jesus' Death as Saving Event: The Background and Origin of a Concept," *HTR* 65 (1972): 605.

8694.6 Augustin George, "Le sens de la mort de Jésus pour Luc," *RB* 80 (1973): 186-217.

8694.7 W. S. Reid, "Death of Christ: Historical and Contemporaneous," *EQ* 45 (1973): 69-80.

8694.8 Earl J. Breech, "Crucifixion as Ordeal: Tradition and Interpretation in Matthew," *HTR* 69 (1976): 421.

8694.9 Johan B. Hygen, "Doden i dogmatisk belysning," *NTT* 78 (1977): 65-76.

8694.10 A. D. Smith, "God's Death," *Th* 80 (1977): 262-68.

8694.11 Max Wilcox, "Upon the Tree: Deut 21:22-23 in the New Testament," *JBL* 96 (1977): 85-99.

8694.12 John P. Galvin, "Jesus' approach to death: an examination of some recent studies," *ThSt* 41 (1980): 713-44.

8694.13 Philip Hefner, "The Cultural Significance of Jesus' Death as Sacrifice," *JR* 60 (1980): 411-39.

8694.14 Konrad Stock, "Gott der Richter: Der Gerichtsgedanke als Horizont der Rechtfertigungslehre," *EvT* 40 (1980): 240-56.

8694.15 Bruce H. Grigsby, "The Cross as an Expiatory Sacrifice in the Fourth Gospel," *JSNT* 15 (1982): 51-80.

8694.16 Peter Hünermann, "Erlöse uns von dem Bösen: theologische

Reflexion auf das Böse und die Erlösung vom Bösen," *TQ* 162 (1982): 317-29.

8694.17 Karl Lehmann, "Er wurde für uns gekreuzigt: eine Skizze zur Neubesinnung in der Soteriologie," *TQ* 162 (1982): 298-317.

8694.18 Gunther Wenz, "Die Lehre vom Opfer Christi im Herrenmahl als Problem ökumenischer Theologie," *KD* 28 (1982): 7-41.

8694.19 Daniel R. Schwartz, "Two Pauline Allusions to the Redemptive Mechanism of the Crucifixion," *JBL* 102 (1983): 259-68.

8694.20 M. Rese, "Die Aussagen über Jesu Tod und Auferstehung in der Apostelgeschichte: ältestes Kerygma oder lukanische Theologumena?" *NTSt* 30 (1984): 335-53.

8694.21 Richard E. Taylor, "Why Did Christ Die," *ET* 95 (1984): 183-84.

8694.22 Horst Beintker, "Gottverlassenheit und Transitus durch den Glauben," *EvT* 45 (1985): 108-23.

8694.23 Hubert Ritt, "Wer war schuld am Tod Jesu: Zeitgeschichte, Recht und theologische Deutung," *BibZ* NS 31 (1987): 165-75.

8694.24 M. C. de Boer, "The Death of Jesus Christ and His Coming in the Flesh," *NT* 33 (1991): 326-46.

8694.25 Bernd Jaspert, "Das Kreuz Jesu als symbolishe Realität: ein Beitrag zum christlich-jüdischen Dialog," *ZTK* 88 (1991): 364-87.

8694.26 Hans Hübner, "Kreuz und Auferstehung im Neuen Testament," *TR* 57 (1992): 58-82.

8694.27 David Seeley, "Jesus' Death in Q," *NTSt* 38 (1992): 222-34.

8694.28 Thomas Söding, "Das Geheimnis Gottes im Kreuz Jesu (1 Kor): Die paulinische Christologie im Spannungsfeld von Mythos und Kerygma," *BibZ* NS 38 (1994): 174-94.

(c). *The Penal Substitutionary Aspect of Christ's Sacrifice*

8695. A. F. D. Munchmeyer, "Hatte der Tod Jesu wirklich den Zweck, 'die auf seine menschliche Natur übergegangene erbliche Verdorbenheit vollends zu vernichten'?" *TSK* 18 (1845): 319-61.

8696. F. C. Baur, "Die Lehre des Apostels Paulus vom erlösenden Tode Christi, mit Rücksicht auf Dr. A. Schweizers Abhandlung in den Theol. Stud. und Krit. 1858, S. 425 f.," *ZWT* 2 (1859): 225-51.

8697. William G. T. Shedd, "The Atonement, a Satisfaction for the Ethical Nature of both God and Man," *BS* 16 (1859): 723-63.

8698. William H. Cobb, "The New Testament View of Christ as Bearing Sin," *BS* 32 (1875): 475-98.

8699. D. W. Simon, "Dale on the Atonement," *BS* 33 (1876): 755-66.

8700. Frank H. Foster, "A Defence of the Catholic Faith Concerning the Satisfaction of Christ Against Faustus Socinus of Sienna Written by Hugo Grotius," *BS* 36 (1879): 105-56, 271-319, 401-59, 616-47.

8701. Hugo Grotius (translated and annotated by Frank H. Foster): "A Defense of the Catholic Faith Concerning the Satisfaction of Christ against Faustus Socinus of Sienna Written by Hugo Grotius," *BS* 36 (1879): 105-56, 271-319, 401-59, 616-47.

8702. A. Grétillat, "Thèses sur la propitiation," *RTP* 23 (1890): 615-17.

8703. J. A. M. Mensinga, "Opfertod und Auferstehung Jesu," *ZWT* 34 (1891): 257-73.

8704. William Hayes Ward, "The New Testament Relation of Christ's Death to the Old Testament Sacrificial System," *BS* 51 (1894): 246-68.

8705. Wilfred Monod, "Y a-t-il eu substitution? Non et oui," *RTQR* 5 (1896): 488-507.

8706. J. Watson, "The Doctrine of Grace," *Exp* 5th ser., 10 (1899): 1-15, 210-20.

8707. Geerhardus Vos, "The Alleged Legalism in Paul's Doctrine of Justification," *PTR* 1 (1903): 161-79.

8708. E. P. Boys-Smith, "The Atonement considered as Forgiveness," *ET* 15 (1903-1904): 26-30.

8709. Jacob Cooper, "Vicarious Suffering the Order of Nature," *PTR* 1 (1903): 554-78.

8710.   W. D. Maclaren, "Can we still Defend a Vicariously Penal Element in the Atonement?" *ET* 15 (1903-1904): 392-97.

8711.   E. Ménégoz, "La mort de Jésus et le dogme de l'expiation," *RTQR* 14 (1905): 330-68.

8712.   C. Bruston, "L'expiation substitutive est-elle enseignée par saint Paul?" *RTQR* 16 (1907): 461-69.

8713.   A. Wabnitz, "La notion de l'expiation dans l'enseignement de Jésus et des apôtres," *RTQR* 16 (1907): 555-66.

8714.   Ernest DeW. Burton, "The Biblical Doctrine of Atonement; XI. The Teaching of the First Epistle of Peter and of the Epistle to the Hebrews," *BW* 32 (1908): 336-48.

8715.   Paul Fiebig, "Das kultische Opfer im Neuen Testament," *ZWT* 53 (1911): 253-75.

8716.   John Shaw, "Sin and the Atonement," *ET* 25 (1913-1914): 352-57.

8717.   Louis Emery, "La doctrine de l'expiation et l'évangile de Jésus Christ," *RTP* N.S. 2 (1914): 273-300, 386-407.

8718.   M.-J. Lagrange, "La justification d'après saint Paul," *RB* 23 (1914): 321-43, 481-503.

8719.   William B. Green, "The Reasonableness of Vicarious Atonement," *PTR* 15 (1917): 423-42.

8720.   Benjamin B. Warfield, "Christ our Sacrifice," *PTR* 15 (1917): 385-422.

8721.   Benjamin B. Warfield, "The New Testament Terminology of 'Redemption'," *PTR* 15 (1917): 201-49.

8722.   C. W. Hodge, "Dr. Denney and the Doctrine of the Atonement," *PTR* 16 (1918): 623-41.

8723.   M. G. Glazebrook, "Hebrew Conceptions of Atonement, and their Influence upon Early Christian Doctrine," *JTS* 20 (1919): 109-26.

8724.   Albert D. Belden, "Jesus—the Sin Bearer," *RE* 18 (1921): 12-19.

8725.   A. M. Pope, "The Forensic Interpretation of the Cross," *ET* 33 (1921-1922): 323-26.

8726.   P. L. Snowden, "Theory of the Atonement," *Th* 4 (1922):

30-41, 93-101.

8727. Jean Rivière, "De la 'satisfaction' du Christ chez saint Ambroise," *BLE* 28 (1927): 160-64.

8728. Douglas S. Sharp, "For our Justification," *ET* 39 (1927-1928): 87-90.

8729. Heinrich Lang, "Die Bedeutung Christi für die Rechtfertigung in Luthers Römerbriefvorlesung," *NKZ* 39 (1928): 509-48.

8730. Martin Wagner, "Das richterliche Walten Gottes und das Kreuz Jesu Christi," *NKZ* 39 (1928): 288-316.

8731. Jean Rivière, "Sur la satisfaction du Christ," *BLE* 35 (1934): 173-87.

8732. Joseph Bonsirven, "Le sacerdoce et le sacrifice de Jésus Christ d'après l'épître aux Hébreux," *NRT* 66 (1939): 641-60.

8733. Joh. Trinidad, "De Sacrificio Christi in Epistola ad Hebraeos," *VD* 19 (1939): 180-86, 207-12.

8734. Cuthbert Lattey, "Sacrament and Sacrifice; II. A Catholic View," *HJ* 40 (1941-1942): 185-88.

8735. Richard Herman Seume, "Divine Propitiation," *BS* 99 (1942): 193-213; 100 (1943): 289-300.

8736. W. T. Conner, "Is Paul's Doctrine of Justification Forensic?" *RE* 40 (1943): 48-54.

8737. T. W. Manson, "ἱλαστήριον," *JTS* 46 (1945): 1-10.

8738. J. L. Lilly, "The Idea of Redemption in the Gospels," *CBQ* 9 (1947): 255-61.

8739. F. W. Camfield, "The Idea of Substitution in the Doctrine of the Atonement," *SJT* 1 (1948): 282-93.

8740. Lewis Sperry Chafer, "For Whom Did Christ Die?" *BS* 105 (1948): 7-35.

8741. Alfred Marshall, "Did Christ Pay Our Debts?" *EQ* 23 (1951): 284-86.

8742. Paul S. Minear, "The Truth About Sin and Death; The Meaning of Atonement in the Epistle to the Romans," *Interp* 7 (1953): 142-55.

8743.   G. B. Mather, "The Atonement: Representative or Substitutionary?" *CJT* 4 (1958): 266-72.

8744.   John F. Walvoord, "The Humilation of the Son of God," *BS*
118 (1961): 99-106.

8744.1   B. G. Worrall, "Substitutionary Atonement in the Theology
of James Denney," *SJT* 28 (1975): 341-57.

8744.2   Günter Bader, "Jesu Tod als Opfer," *ZTK* 80 (1983): 411-31.

(d). *The Exemplary Aspect of Christ's Sacrifice*

8745.   H. Rashdall, "Abelard's Doctrine of the Atonement: A
University Sermon," *Exp* 4th ser., 8 (1893): 37-50 [Mt.
20:28].

8746.   Jesse L. Fonda, "The Lamb that hath been Slain from the
Foundation of the World," *BW* 4 (1894): 94-97.

8747.   R. W. McLaughlin, "The Example of Jesus," *BS* 58 (1901):
383-86.

8748.   George Henry Hubbard, "The Sacrificial Element in Christian
Ethics," *BW* 31 (1908): 382-90 [Christ's sacrifice
exemplary].

8749.   John Oman, "The Idea of Atonement in Christian Theology,
by Hastings Rashdall," *JTS* 21 (1920): 267-75.

8749.1   Barnabas Lindars, "Salvation Proclaimed, 7: Mark 10:45 - A
Ransom for Many," *ET* 93 (1982): 292-95.

8749.2   Albert Vanhoye, "Esprit éternel et feu du sacrifice en He
9:14," *B* 64 (1983): 263-74.

(4). The Work of Jesus Christ as King

8750.   A. Réville, "De l'autorité de Jésus-Christ," *RT* 3 (1859):
213-42.

8751.   E. Harmsen, "Versuch einer Beantwortung der Frage: Wird
Christus als Mittler der Weltschöpfung Röm. 11, 36 und 1
Kor. 8, 6 gedacht und dargestellt?" *ZWT* 19 (1876): 388-96.

8752.   G. Matheson, "The Lamb on the Throne," *Exp* 5th ser., 5
(1897): 265-73 [Revelation 5-6].

8753.   A. Wabnitz, "Le trône de Dieu et le trône du Christ," *RTQR*
17 (1908): 111-18.

8754. S. Greijdanus, "Het wereldbestuur van den Christus en deze wereldoorlog," *GTT* 18 (1917-1918): 251-62, 291-302, 327-41.

8755. J. M. Bover, "Christi Regnum in epistulis Pauli," *VD* 5 (1925): 225-29.

8756. C. F. Burney, "Christ as the ἀρχή of Creation," *JTS* 27 (1925-1926): 160-77.

8757. E. Ebrard Rees, "The Cosmic Christ," *ET* 41 (1929- 1930): 335-36.

8758. L. E. Barton, "The Cosmic Christ," *RE* 29 (1932): 459- 69.

8759. Jean-Joseph Maydieu, "La création du monde et l'incarnation du verbe dans la philosophic de Malebranche," *BLE* 36 (1935): 49-74.

8760. Erik Peterson, "Christus als Imperator," *C* 5 (1936): 64-72.

8761. Clarence T. Craig, "Deliverance through Christ," *RL* 8 (1939): 525-41.

8762. A. Vitti, " 'Quem constituit heredem universorum per quem fecit et saecula' (Hb. 1, 2)," *VD* 21 (1941): 40-48, 82-87.

8763. Teófilo Ayuso, "Cristo Rey," *CB* 3 (1946): 267-68.

8764. J.-D. Benoît, "W. A. Visser't Hooft, 'La royauté de Jésus Christ'," *RHPR* 28-29 (1948-1949): 66-68.

8765. B. N. Wambacq, " 'Per eum reconciliare . . . quae in caelis sunt' (Col. 1, 20)," *RB* 55 (1948): 35-42.

8766. W. S. Boycott, "Creation and Christology," *Th* 52 (1949): 443-48.

8767. Günther Bornkamm, "Christus und die Welt in der urchristlichen Botschaft," *ZTK* N.F. 47 (1950): 212-26.

8768. J. Leclercq, "L'idée de la royauté du Christ au XIV siècle," *RET* 10 (1950): 205-26.

8769. Gottfried Voigt, "The Speaking Christ in his Royal Office," *CTM* 23 (1952): 161-76.

8770. Roland Potter, "The Hallowing of Creatures: an Exegetical and Theological Inquiry," *DS* 6 (1953): 21-41.

8771. E. G. Selwyn, "The Authority of Christ in the New Testament," *NTSt* 3 (1956-1957): 83-92.

8772.   M. de Jonge, "De verkondiging van Christus als Heer; verlegenheid, aanrechting en antwoord," *VT* 29 (1958-1959): 108-23.

8773.   E. Th. van Montfoort, "Het Heer-zijn van Christus over de wereld en over de kerk," *VT* 29 (1958-1959): 38-43.

8774.   Gerhard Koch, "Jesus Christus-Schöpfer der Welt," *ZTK* N.F. 56 (1959): 83-109.

8775.   Gabriel de la Dolorosa, "El reinado temporal de Christo en los Santos Evangelios," *CB* 17 (1960): 278-97.

         See also numbers 2971, *10087*.

8775.1   W. L. Dulière, "Les textes évangéliques sur des visées temporelles de Jésus Alternances de concepts autoritaires et de concepts iréniques," *ST* 22 (1968): 107-48.

8775.2   Sherman E. Johnson, "Notes on the Prophet-King in John," *ATR* 51 (1969): 35-37.

8775.3   Eduard Schweizer, "Jesus, the Lord of his Church," *ABR* 19 (1971): 52-67.

8775.4   Morris A. Inch, "Jesus is Lord!" *JETS* 15 (1972): 173-80.

8775.5   M. de Jonge, "Jesus as Prophet and King in the Fourth Gospel," *ET:* 49 (1973): 160-77.

8775.6   Dennis C. Duling, "Promises to David and Their Entrance into Christianity: Nailing down a Likely Hypothesis," *NTSt* 20 (1973): 55-77.

8775.7   E. Lövestam, "Jésus Fils de David chez les Synoptiques," *T* 28 (1974): 97-109.

8775.8   K. Wengst, "Versöhnung und Befreiung: ein Aspekt des Themas 'Schuld und Vergebung' im Lichte des Kolosserbriefes," *EvT* 36 (1976): 14-26.

8775.9   A. García-Moreno, "La realeza y el señorío de Cristo en Tesalonicenses," *EB* NS 39 (1981): 63-82.

8775.10 George Johnston, "Christ as Archegos," *NTSt* 27 (1981): 381-85.

8775.11 Livingston Blauvelt, "Does the Bible Teach Lordship Salvation?" *BS* 143 (1986): 37-45.

8775.12 David L. Tiede, "The Exaltation of Jesus and the Restoration of Israel in Acts 1," *HTR* 79 (1986): 278-86.

8775.13   Martin Karrer, "Christus der Herr und die Welt als Stätte der Prüfung: zur Theologie des Jakobusbriefs," *KD* 35 (1989): 166-88.

8775.14   Brian M. Nolan, "Rooting the Davidic Son of God of Matthew 1-2 in the Experience of the Evangelist's Audience," *EB* 50 (1992): 149-56.

8775.15   Eugene H. Merrill, "Royal Priesthood: An Old Testament Messianic Motif," *BS* 150 (1993): 50-61.

     (5). Descensus ad inferos

8776.   John Brown, "The Preaching by Christ to the Spirits in Prison," *BS* 4 (1847): 708-44 [1 Pet. 3:19].

8777.   Bethe, "Kritisches zu I. Petr. 3, 19," *TSK* 31 (1858): 524-26.

8778.   Joseph Muenscher, "On the Descent of Christ into Hell," *BS* 16 (1859): 309-53.

8779.   Teipel, "Ueber die Höllenfahrt Christi," *TQ* 42 (1860): 577-653.

8780.   James B. Miles, "Christ Preaching to the Spirits in Prison," *BS* 19 (1862): 1-31.

8781.   Michel Nicolas, "De la descente de Jésus Christ aux enfers," *RT* 3 (1865): 253-78.

8782.   Henry Cowles, "Christ Preaching to the Spirits in Prison; 1 Pet. 3.18-20," *BS* 32 (1875): 401-20.

8783.   S. C. Bartlett, "The Preaching to the Spirits in Prison," *BS* 40 (1883): 333-73.

8784.   Delitzsch and von Hofmann, "The Descent of Christ into Hades," *Exp* 4th ser., 3 (1891): 241-63, 361-74.

8785.   L. S. Potwin, "Christ's Descent into Hades," *BS* 50 (1893): 541-43.

8786.   C. Bruston, "Notion biblique de la descente du Christ aux enfers," *RTP* 30 (1897): 57-78, 169-82

8787.   J. A. Selbie, "Bruston on 'Christ's Descent to Hell'," *ET* 9 (1897-1898): 20-22.

8788.   Ernst Bröse, "Der *descensus ad inferos* Eph. 4, 8-10," *NKZ*

9 (1898): 447-55.

8789. S. Odland, "Kristi praediken for 'aanderne i forvaring' (I Petr. 3, 19)," *NTT* 2 (1901): 116-44, 185-229.

8790. C. Bruston, "La descente aux enfers," *RTQR* 14 (1905): 236-49, 438-56.

8791. J. H. A. Hart, "Scribes of the Nazarenes; II. The Gospel According to St. Luke and the Descent into Hades," *Exp* 7th ser., 3 (1907): 53-71.

8792. S. C. Parker, "Christ's Preaching to the Spirits in Prison," *ET* 25 (1913-1914): 234.

8793. D. Plooij, "De descensus in 1 Petrus 3, 19 en 4, 6," *TT* 47 (1913): 145-62.

8794. W. Bousset, "Zur Hadesfahrt Christi," *ZNW* 19 (1919-1920): 50-66.

8795. Buchanan Blake, " 'He Descended into Hell'," *ET* 37 (1925-1926): 521-24.

8796. Jos Frings, "Zu 1. Petr. 3, 19 und 4, 6," *BibZ* 17 (1925-1926): 75-88.

8797. A. Vitti, "Descensus Christi ad inferos (ex 1 Petri 3, 19-20; 4, 6)," *VD* 7 (1927): 111-18.

8798. A. Vitti, "Descensus Christi ad inferos iuxta apocrypha," *VD* 7 (1927): 138-44, 171-81.

8799. Paul Koenig, "Christ's Descent into Hell," *CTM* 3 (1932): 862-37.

8800. Paul Althaus, "Niedergefahren zur Hölle," *ZST* 19 (1942): 365-84.

8801. A. Grillmeier, "Der Gottessohn im Totenreich," *ZKT* 71 (1949): 1-53, 184-203.

8802. Joachim Jeremias, "Zwischen, Karfreitag und Ostern," *ZNW* 42 (1949): 194-201.

8803. Olivier Rousseau, "La descente aux enfers, fondement sotériologique du baptême chrétien," *RSR* 40 (1951-1952): 273-97.

8804. J. Zandee, "De Descensus ad Inferos bij de Kopten," Ned *TT* 9 (1954-1955): 158-74.

8805.   Martin H. Scharlemann, " 'He Descended into Hell.' An Interpretation of 1 Peter 3:18-20," *CTM* 27 (1956): 81-95.

8806.   Eugen Biser, "Abgestiegen zu der Hölle," *MTZ* 9 (1958): 205-12, 283-93.

8807.   H. J. Schulz, "Die 'Höllenfahrt' als 'Anastasis.' Eine Untersuchung über Eigenart und dogmengeschichtliche Voraussetzungen byzantinischer Osterfrömmigkeit," *ZKT* 81 (1959): 1-66.

8808.   Sherman E. Johnson, "The Preaching to the Dead," *JBL* 79 (1960): 48-51.

8809.   Jean Galot, "La descente du Christ aux enfers," *NRT* 83 (1961): 471-91.

8810.   J. Teixidor, "Le thème de la descente aux enfers chez saint Ephrem," *OS* 6 (1961): 385-412.

See also numbers 592, 9976

8810.1   Jean Lebourlier, "À propos de l'état du Christ dans la mort," *RSPT* 46 (1952): 629-49; 47 (1963): 161-80.

8810.2   Thomas Manteufel, "He Descended into Hell: A Mystery Play about Victory over Death," *CTM* 43 (1972): 389-96.

8810.3   Mary Rakow, "Christ's Descent into Hell: Calvin's Interpretation," *RL* 43 (1974): 218-26.

8810.4   Milton M. Gatch, "The Harrowing of Hell: A Liberation Motif in Medieval Theology and Devotional Literature," *USQR* 36 (1981): 75-88.

8810.5   Joseph R. Hoffman, "Confluence in Early Christian and Gnostic Literature: The Descensus Christi ad Infernos," *JSNT* 10 (1981): 42-60.

8810.6   A. T. Hanson, "Salvation Proclaimed, pt 1: 1 Peter 3:18-22," *ET* 93 (1982): 100-105.

8810.7   John S. Feinberg, "1 Peter 3:18-20, Ancient Mythology, and the Intermediate State," *WTJ* 48 (1986): 303-36.

8810.8   Werner Brändle, "Hinabgestiegen in das Reich des Todes," *KD* 35 (1989): 54-68.

8810.9   Randall E. Otto, "Descendit in Inferna: A Reformed Review of a Creedal Conundrum," *WTJ* 52 (1990): 143-50.

8810.10   Wayne A. Grudem, "He Did Not Descend into Hell: A Plea for Following Scripture instead of the Apostles' Creed," *JETS* 34 (1991): 103-13.

8810.11   David P. Scaer, "He Did Descend to Hell: In Defense of the Apostles' Creed," *JETS* 35 (1992): 91-99.

8810.12   W. Hall Harris, "The Ascent and Descent of Christ in Ephesians 4:9-10," *BS* 151 (1994): 198-214.

e. The Resurrection of Jesus Christ (theologically considered)

(1). General Studies

8811.   J. H. B. Lübkert, "Welche Kraft haben wir nach der Schrift der Auferstehung Jesu beizulegen?" *TSK* 15 (1842): 935-78.

8812.   E. Robinson, "The Nature of our Lord's Resurrection Body," *BS* 2 (1845): 292-312.

8813.   George P. Fisher, "The Apostle Paul, a Witness for the Resurrection of Jesus," *BS* 17 (1860): 620-34.

8814.   E. Russell, "The Resurrection and its Concomitants," *BS* 17 (1860): 755-86.

8815.   S. P. Hickok, "Jesus and the Resurrection," *BS* 32 (1875): 593-623.

8816.   H. Burton, "The Christ of Resurrection," *Exp* 1st ser., 5 (1877): 311-20, 378-87.

8817.   F. Godet, "The Resurrection of Jesus Christ," *Exp* 1st ser., 5 (1877): 161-72, 241-57, 335-43.

8818.   J. Ker, "The Better Resurrection," *Exp* 3rd ser., 1 (1885): 161-76.

8819.   E. G. Steude, "Die Verteidigung der Auferstehung Jesu Christi," *TSK* 60 (1887): 203-95.

8820.   Lemuel S. Potwin, "The Resurrection of Christ a Part of Christianity," *BS* 47 (1890): 177-90.

8821.   P. Lobstein, "Der evangelische Heilsglaube an die Auferstehung Jesu Christi," *ZTK* 2 (1891): 343-68.

8822.   James S. Candlish, "The Relation of Christ's Resurrection to Our Justification," *Exp* 4th ser., 8 (1893): 465-70.

8823.   C. Malan, "Le ressuscité," *RTQR* 4 (1895): 1-27.

8824.   P. Lobstein, "La foi en la résurrection de Jésus Christ," *RTP* 28 (1895): 97-121

8825.   Prebendary Whitefoord, "The Resurrection as the Cardinal Feature of Apostolic Teaching," *ET* 7 (1895-1896): 492-96.

8826.   Alfred E. Garvie, "The Ritschlian Denial of the Resurrection," *ET* 8 (1896-1897): 333-35.

8827.   Karl Ziegler, "Der Glaube an die Auferstehung Jesu Christi," *ZTK* 6 (1896): 219-64.

8828.   Thomas Adamson, "Our Lord's Resurrection Body," *ET* 9 (1897-1898): 391-95.

8829.   T. Häring, "Gehört die Auferstehung Jesu zum Glaubensgrund? *Amica exegesis* zu Professor D. M. Reischles 'Der Streit über die Begründung des Glaubens auf den geschichtlichen Jesus Christus'," *ZTK* 7 (1897): 332-51.

8830.   G. Schönholzer, "Die Auferstehung," *STZ* 16 (1899): 24-33, 75-85.

8831.   Alvah Hovey, "Stapfer on the Resurrection of Jesus Christ," *AJT* 4 (1900): 536-54.

8832.   Henry G. Weston, "The Resurrection of the Lord Jesus the Central Fact in Christianity," *BS* 57 (1900): 696-708.

8833.   S. McComb, "Professor Harnack on our Lord's Resurrection," *Exp* 6th ser., 4 (1901): 350-63.

8834.   H. Henson, "The Resurrection of Jesus Christ," *HJ* 1 (1902-1903): 476-93.

8835.   David Smith, "The Resurrection of our Lord," *Exp* 6th ser., 8 (1903): 344-60.

8836.   C. F. Nolloth, "The Resurrection of our Lord and Recent Criticism," *HJ* 3 (1904-1905): 529-42.

8837.   James S. Riggs, "The Resurrection of Christ," *BW* 23 (1904): 249-55.

8838.   T. W. Rolleston, "The Resurrection: A Layman's Dialogue," *HJ* 4 (1905-1906): 624-41.

8839.   F. S. Turner, "Do I Believe in the Resurrection?" *HJ* 4 (1905-1906): 375-87.

8840.   Alfred E. Garvie, "The Risen Lord," *Exp* 7th ser., 4 (1907):

1-19.

8841.   Elliott Williams Boone, "The Belief in the Resurrection among the First Christians," *BW* 32 (1908): 269-76.

8842.   W. W. Fenn and W. Douglas Mackenzie, "The Relation between the Resurrection of Jesus and the Belief in Immortality," *AJT* 12 (1908): 565-87.

8843.   James Orr, "The Resurrection of Jesus," *Exp* 7th ser., 5 (1908): 35-51, 142-57, 233-49, 314-33, 428-49, 504-24; 6 (1908): 97-118, 235-54, 306-25, 420-37.

8844.   Shirley Jackson Case, "The Resurrection Faith of the First Disciples," *AJT* 13 (1909): 169-92.

8845.   J. MacRory, "Some Theories of our Lord's Resurrection," *ITQ* 4 (1909): 200-15.

8846.   F. P. Mayser, "The Resurrection of Christ the Keystone in the Arch of his Redeeming Work," *LCR* 28 (1909): 176-85.

8847.   W. J. Sparrow Simpson, "Christ's Resurrection and Modern Thought," *LCR* 28 (1909): 169-75.

8848.   Charles Marsh, "Paul on the Resurrection of Christ," *BS* 67 (1910): 391-414, 546-69.

8849.   Neville S. Talbot, "A Study of the Resurrection," *HJ* 9 (1910-1911): 571-83.

8850.   B. W. Bacon, "The Resurrection in the Primitive Tradition and Observance," *AJT* 15 (1911): 373-403.

8851.   L. Ihmels, "Wie entsteht die Gewissheit um die Auferstehung Jesu?" *NKZ* 25 (1914): 853-901.

8852.   S. Bretteville Jensen, "Paaskeevangelium og paaskepraeken," *NTT* 16 (1915): 58-78.

8853.   Alban G. Widgery, "The Idea of Resurrection," *HJ* 14 (1915-1916): 149-55.

8854.   Francis B. Palmer, "The Resurrection of Jesus," *BS* 73 (1916): 445-53.

8855.   K. Goetz, "Der Auferstehungsglaube des Neuen Testaments," *STZ* 36 (1919): 107-23.

8856.   W. E. Henry, "Our Lord's Resurrection and himself," *RE* 16 (1919): 423-25.

8857. Constance Maynard, "Is Christ alive Today? Two or Three Witnesses," *HJ* 18 (1919-1920): 361-77.

8858. Jacob Fry, "The Resurrection-Thought in Lutheran Theology," *LCR* 39 (1920): 117-28.

8859. W. E. Henry, "Christ's Resurrection and the Forgiveness of Sins," *RE* 17 (1920): 24-36.

8860. V. T. Kirby, "Christ's Resurrection as Evidence to Itself," *ET* 34 (1922-1923): 523-24.

8861. Carl Stange, "Die Auferstehung Jesu," *ZST* 1 (1923): 705-40.

8862. G. S. Duncan, "The Resurrection Faith," *ET* 37 (1925-1926): 330-33.

8863. Oliver C. Quick, "The Fact and Doctrine of the Resurrection," *ATR* 8 (1925-1926): 114-23.

8864. L. E. Barton, "The Gospel of the Resurrection," *RE* 24 (1927): 282-96.

8865. Erich Fascher, "Die Auferstehung Jesu und ihr Verhältnis zur urchristlichen Verkündigung," *ZNW* 26 (1927): 1-26.

8866. Henry Offermann, "The Resurrection of our Lord," *LCR* 46 (1927): 97-105.

8867. Lyder Brun, "Le contenu religieux de la croyance à la résurrection du Christ dans le Christianisme primitif," *RHPR* 8 (1928): 503-12.

8868. Hermann Dieckmann, "De variis sententiis quae resurrectionem Iesu Christi spectant," *VD* 9 (1929): 97-102.

8869. S. Vernon McCasland, "The Origin of the Lord's Day," *JBL* 49 (1930): 65-82.

8870. M. Goguel, "Le caractère de la foi à la résurrection dans le Christianisme primitif," *RPHR* 11 (1931): 329-85.

8871. C. F. Nolloth, "The Meaning of the Resurrection," *HJ* 30 (1931-1932): 450-58.

8872. M. Goguel, "La foi à la résurrection de Jésus dans le Christianisme primitif," *RHPR* 13 (1933): 76-79.

8873. J. K. Cameron, "The Resurrection of Christ," *EQ* 6 (1934): 147-68.

8874. Anton Fridrichsen, "Uppstandelseteologi," *STK* 10 (1934):

51-70.

8875.   F. Ménégoz, "Résurrection," *RHPR* 16 (1936): 347-84.

8876.   A. Škrinjar, " 'Fui mortuus et ecce sum vivens in saecula saeculorum' (Apoc. 1, 18)," *VD* 17 (1937): 97-106.

8877.   Martin Doerne, "Der begrabene und der lebendige Christus," *NKZ* (*Luthertum*): 49 (1938): 321-40.

8878.   G. H. C. Macgregor, "The Growth of the Resurrection Faith," *ET* 50 (1938-1939): 217-20, 280-83.

8879.   Th. Aaberg, "Stod op fra de døde tredje dag. En evangelieharmonie," *TTK* 10 (1939): 41-51.

8880.   Emanuel Hirsch, "Zum Problem des Osterglaubens," *TLZ* 65 (1940): 295-301.

8881.   Paul S. Minear, "The Resurrection of Jesus," *RL* 9 (1940): 174-81.

8882.   N. Harman, "Resurrection," *HJ* 40 (1941-1942): 350-54.

8883.   John Murray, "Who Raised up Jesus?" *WTJ* 3 (1941): 113-23.

8884.   Carl Stange, "Zur Kritik des Auferstehungsglaubens," *ZST* 18 (1941): 589-601.

8885.   H. R. Williamson, "The Necessity of Resurrection," *HJ* 40 (1941-1942): 245-51.

8886.   Paul E. Davies, "Resurrection and the Coming of the Spirit," *JBR* 10 (1942): 187-94.

8887.   Amos N. Wilder, "Variant Traditions of the Resurrection in Acts," *JBL* 62 (1943): 307-18.

8888.   G. C. Ring, "Christ's Resurrection and the Dying and Rising Gods," *CBQ* 6 (1944): 216-29.

8889.   John M. Shaw, "The Centrality of the Resurrection of Jesus to the Christian Faith," *RL* 14 (1945): 246-57.

8890.   J. Leslie Dunstan, "The Resurrection," *RL* 15 (1946): 236-49.

8891.   Floyd V. Filson, "The Focus of History; The Resurrection in Biblical Theology," *Interp* 2 (1948): 24-38.

8892.   A. W. Argyle, "The New Testament Doctrine of the Resurrection of our Lord Jesus Christ," *ET* 61 (1949- 1950):

187-88.

8893. Herbert Braun, "Zur Terminologie der Acta von der Auferstehung Jesu," *TLZ* 77 (1952): 533-36.

8894. L. Cerfaux, "La résurrection du Christ dans la vie et la doctrine de saint Paul," *LumV* no. 3 (1952): 61-82.

8895. J. Schmitt, "La résurrection de Jésus dans la prédication apostolique et la tradition évangélique," *LumV* no. 3 (1952): 35-60.

8896. G. M. Lee, "The Resurrection Appearances in Luke," *ET* 65 (1953-1954): 158.

8897. G. Gander, "La notion chrétienne primitive de la résurrection," *VCar* 8 (1954): 33-51.

8898. G. Jouassard, "Témoignages peu remarqués de saint Irénée en matière sacramentaire," *RSR* 42 (1954): 528-39.

8899. F. Nötscher, "Zur Auferstehung nach drei Tagen," *B* 35 (1954): 313-19.

8900. Ethelbert Stauffer, "Der Auferstehungsglaube und das leere Grab," *ZRGG* 6 (1954): 146-48.

8901. Wolfgang Nauck, "Die Bedeutung des leeren Grabes für den Glauben an den Auferstandenen," *ZNW* 47 (1956): 243-67.

8902. H. E. W. Turner, "The Resurrection," *ET* 68 (1956-1957): 369-71.

8903. W. C. Robinson, "The Bodily Resurrection of Christ," *TZ* 13 (1957): 81-101.

8904. Frank R. Hancock, "The Man of Galilee," *HJ* 57 (1958-1959): 223-28 [the Resurrection].

8905. Edwin G. Kaiser, "The Theology of the Resurrection of Christ," *PCTSA* 14 (1959): 28-53.

8906. J. Mánek, "The Apostle Paul and the Empty Tomb," *NT* 2 (1958): 276-80.

8907. Zdeněk Trtík, "Gedanken über Cullmanns Interpretation der Auferstehung," *TZ* 14 (1958): 350-62.

8908. Jacques Dupont, "Ressuscité 'le troisième jour'," *B* 40 (1959): 742-61.

8909. Reginald H. Fuller, "The Resurrection of Jesus Christ," *BRes*

762 THEOLOGICAL STUDIES

4 (1960): 8-24.

8910. Paul Nordhues, "Die Auferstehung Christi als Heilsmysterium nach der Theologie des Louis de Thomassin)," *C* 15 (1961): 24-42.

8911. E. G. Rüsch, "Die Auferstehung Jesu im Denken Carl Hiltys," *TZ* 17 (1961): 26-39.

8912. Eric C. Rust, "Interpreting the Resurrection," *JBR* 29 (1961): 25-34.

See also numbers 623-684, 7712, 9670, *10037, 10045.*

8912.1 Thomas Corbett, "Origen's Doctrine on the Resurrection," *ITQ* 46 (1979): 276-90.

8912.2 A. Rodríguez Carmona, "El vocabulario neotestamentario de resurrección a la luz del Targum y literatura intertestamentaria," *EB* NS 38 (1979-1980): 97-113.

8912.3 H.-W. Bartsch, "Inhalt und Funktion des urchristlichen Osterglaubens," *NTSt* 26 (1980): 180-96.

8912.4 W. Royce Clark, "Jesus, Lazarus, and Others: Resuscitation or Resurrection?" *RL* 49 (1980): 230-41.

8912.5 Joseph Plevnik, "The Origin of Easter Faith according to Luke," *B* 61 (1980): 492-508.

8912.6 S. O. Abogunrin, "The Language and Nature of the Resurrection of Jesus Christ in the New Testament," *JETS* 24 (1981): 55-65.

8912.7 Daniel M. Cohn-Sherbok, "Jesus' Defense of the Resurrection of the Dead," *JSNT* 11 (1981): 64-73.

8912.8 Eduard Schweizer, "Auferstehung: Wirklichkeit oder Illusion?" *EvT* 41 (1981): 2-19.

8912.9 John Gillman, "Transformation in 1 Corinthians 15:50-53," *ETL* 58 (1982): 309-33.

8912.10 Michael S. Moore, "Resurrection and Immortality: Two Motifs Navigating Confluent Theological Streams in the Old Testament," *TLZ* 39 (1983): 17-34.

8912.11 R. Pesch, "Zur Entstehung des Glaubens an die Auferstehung Jesu: ein neuer Versuch," *FZPT* 30 (1983): 73-98.

8912.12 William L. Craig, "The Historicity of the Empty Tomb of

Jesus," *NTSt* 31 (1985): 39-67.

8912.13 David A. S. Fergusson, "Interpreting the Resurrection," *SJT* 38 (1985): 287-305.

8912.14 Dieter Müller, "Geisterfahrung und Totenauferweckung: Totenauferweckung bei Paulus und in den ihm vorgegebenen Uberlieferungen," *TLZ* 110 (1985): 73-75.

8912.15 W. G. Kümmel, "Eine jüdisch Stimme zur Auferstehung Jesu," *TR* 51 (1986): 92-97.

8912.16 Glenn D. Weaver, "Senile Dementia and a Resurrection Theology," *TTod* 42 (1986): 444-56.

8912.17 Joseph Plevnik, "The Eyewitnesses of the Risen Jesus in Luke 24," *CBQ* 49 (1987): 90-103.

8912.18 Rudolf Reinhardt, "David Friedrich Strauss und die Auferstehung der Toten: zu seiner Preisschrift aus dem Jahre 1828," *TQ* 168 (1988): 150-53.

8912.19 William L. Craig, "Pannenbergs Beweis für die Auferstehung Jesu," *KD* 34 (1988): 78-104.

8912.20 N. P. Harvey, "Frames of Reference for the Resurrection," *SJT* 42 (1989): 335-39.

8912.21 Norman L. Geisler, "The Significance of Christ's Physical Resurrection," *BS* 146 (1989): 148-70.

8912.22 Roberto Vignolo, "Una finale reticente: interpretazione narrativa di Mc 16: 8," *RivB* 38 (1990): 129-89.

8912.23 David A. Walker, "Resurrection, Empty Tomb and Easter Faith," *ET* 101 (1990): 172-75.

8912.24 Gabriel Fackre, "I Believe in the Resurrection of the Body," *Interp* 46 (1992): 42-52.

(2). The Apologetic Significance of the Resurrection of Jesus Christ

8913. E. Coquerel, "De la signification religieuse de la résurrection de Jésus Christ," *RTP* 18 (1885): 462-72

8914. Irving F. Wood, "The Religious Value of the Resurrection of Jesus in the Early Church," *BW* 36 (1910): 379-86.

8915. Henry B. Dickert, "The Apologetic Value of the Resurrection of Jesus," *LCR* 32 (1913): 63-88.

8916. Henry B. Dickert, "The Resurrection and its Apologetic Value Against the Unbeliever," *LCR* 32 (1913): 227-43.

8917. W. E. Henry, "Christ's Resurrection Makes Faith Easy," *RE* 17 (1920): 175-85.

8918. Lyder Brun, "Det religiøse indhold i troen paa Kristi opstandelse i urkristendommen," *NTT* 29 (1928): 137-46.

8919. F. Holtz, "La valeur sotériologique de la résurrection du Christ selon saint Thomas," *ETL* 29 (1953): 609-45.

See also numbers 3281, 9032.

8919.1 Z. C. Hodges, "Form Criticism and the Resurrection Accounts," *BS* 124 (1967): 339-48.

8919.2 John Bligh, "The Gerasene Demoniac and the Resurrection of Christ," *CBQ* 31 (1969): 383-90.

8919.3 F. Gerald Downing, "The Resurrection of the Dead: Jesus and Philo," *JSNT* 15 (1982): 42-50.

8919.4 Barnabas Lindars, "Jesus Risen: Bodily Resurrection but No Empty Tomb," *Th* 89 (1986): 90-96.

8919.5 B. de Margerie, "Le troisième jour, selon les Ecritures, il est ressuscité: importance théologique d'une recherche exégétique," *RSRel* 60 (1986): 158-88.

8919.6 Ben F. Meyer, "Did Paul's View of the Resurrection of the Dead Undergo Development?" *ThSt* 47 (1986): 363-87.

8919.7 Bernard Pouderon, "L'authenticité du traité sur la résurrection attribué à l'apologiste Athénagore," *VCh* 40 (1986): 226-44.

8919.8 Alwyn Pritchard, "Two Sides to the Resurrection Narratives," *ET* 98 (1987): 207-208.

8919.9 Francis Watson, "Historical Evidence and the Resurrection of Jesus," *Th* 90 (1987): 365-72.

8919.10 Gerald L. Borchert, "The Resurrection Perspective in John: An Evangelical Summons," *RE* 85 (1988): 501-13.

8919.11 C. E. B. Cranfield, "The Resurrection of Jesus Christ," *ET* 101 (1990): 167-72.

8919.12 G. T. Eddy, "The Resurrection of Jesus Christ: A

Consideration of Professor Cranfield's Argument," *ET* 101 (1990): 327-29.

8919.13   Raymond Winling, "Mort et résurrection du Christ dans les traités Contre Eunome de Grégoire de Nysse [2 pts]," *RSRel* 64 (1990): 127-40; 251-69.

8919.14   Norman L. Geisler, "In Defense of the Resurrection: A Reply to Criticisms," *JETS* 34 (1991): 243-61.

8919.15   Claudia Setzer, "You Invent a Christ!: Christological Claims as Points of Jewish-Christian Dispute," *USQR* 44 (1991): 315-28.

    f. *The Ascension, Exaltation, and Heavenly Intercession of Jesus Christ*

8920.   Gottfried Kinkel, "Historisch-kritische Untersuchung über Christi Himmelfahrt," *TSK* 14 (1841): 597-634.

8921.   Gottfried Kinkel, "Historical and Critical Inquiry Respecting the Ascension of Christ," *BS* 1 (1844): 152-78.

8922.   E. Robinson, "The Resurrection and Ascension of our Lord," *BS* 2 (1845): 162-89.

8923.   John Brubaker, "The Ascension of Christ," *LQ* 24 (1894); 155-63.

8924.   Wilhelm Vollert, "Die Bedeuting der Himmelfahrt für Christum," *NKZ* 7 (1896): 389-427.

8925.   Wilhelm Vollert, "Die Bedeutung der Himmelfahrt Christi für die Kirche und für den einzelnen Gläubigen," *NKZ* 7 (1896): 937-63.

8926.   E. R. Bernard, "The Value of the Ascension," *ET* 12 (1900-1901): 152-55.

8927.   B. W. Bacon, "The Ascension in Luke and Acts," *Exp* 7th ser., 7 (1909): 254-61.

8928.   Th. Zahn, "Die Himmelfahrt Jesu an einem Sabbath," *NKZ* 33 (1922): 535-41.

8929.   S. Joh. Crysostom, "In Christi Domini ascensionem," *VD* 3 (1923): 129-31.

8930.   Wilhelm Michaelis, "Zur Überlieferung der Himmelfahrtsgeschichte," *TB* 4 (1925): 101-109.

8931. E. G. Selwyn, "Our Lord's Ascension," *Th* 12 (1926): 241-44.

8932. Anton Fridrichsen, "Omkring himmelfartsberetningen," *NTT* 28 (1927): 32-47.

8933. Anton Fridrichsen, "Die Himmelfahrt bei Lukas," *TB* 6 (1927): 337-41.

8934. J. Ivor Wensley, "The Heavenly Intercession of Christ," *ET* 40 (1928-1929): 559-63.

8935. Morton S. Enslin, "The Ascension Story," *JBL* 47 (1928): 60-73.

8936. H. E. Dana, "Historical Evidence of the Ascension," *BR* 14 (1929): 191-209.

8937. U. Holzmeister, "Der Tag der Himmelfahrt des Herrn," *ZKT* 55 (1931): 44-82.

8938. H. Liese, "In Ascensione Domini (Mc. 16, 14-20)," *VD* 12 (1932): 129-34.

8939. C. E. Wager, "Eduard Meyer on our Lord's Ascension," *ET* 44 (1932-1933): 491-95.

8940. V. A. Holmes-Gore, "The Ascension and Apocalyptic Hope," *Th* 32 (1936): 356-58.

8941. V. Larrañaga, "De Ascensione Domini in Act. 1, 3-13," *VD* 17 (1937): 129-39.

8942. J. S. Billings, "The Ascension in the Fourth Gospel," *ET* 50 (1938-1939): 285.

8943. F. F. Bruce, "The Ascension in the Fourth Gospel," *ET* 50 (1938-1939): 478.

8944. George Evans, "Jesus Christ Exalted," *RE* 35 (1938): 315-27.

8945. Albrecht Oepke, "Unser Glaube an die Hirnmelfahrt Christi," *NKZ* (*Luthertum*): 49 (1938): 161-86.

8946. George Evans, "Jesus Christ Exalted,"*RE* 36 (1939): 158-71.

8947. Ralph G. Turnbull, "The Ascension in Paul's Christology," *USR* 57 (1945-1946): 303-19.

8948.   S. M. Zwemer, "The Ascension," *EQ* 19 (1947): 247-54.

8949.   Pierre Benoit, "L'Ascension," *RB* 56 (1949): 161-203.

8950.   A. W. Argyle, "The Heavenly Session of Christ," *Th* 55 (1952): 286-89.

8951.   John Mauchline, "Jesus Christ als Intercessor," *ET* 64 (1952-1953): 355-60.

8952.   Carl Stange, "Die Himmelfahrt Jesu," *ZST* 22 (1953): 218-22.

8953.   J. G. Davies, "The Peregrinatio Egeriae and the Ascension," *VCh* 8 (1954): 93-100.

8954.   A. W. Argyle, "The Ascension," *ET* 66 (1954-1955): 240-42.

8955.   J. G. Davies, "The Prefigurement of the Ascension in the Third Gospel," *JTS* N.S. 6 (1955): 229-33.

8956.   Joseph Haroutunian, "The Doctrine of the Ascension; A Study of the New Testament Teaching," *Interp* 10 (1956): 270-81.

8957.   Joseph Haroutunian, "La doctrine de la Ascensión—Un estudio de la enseñanza del Nuevo Testamento," *CT* 21 (1957): 54-65.

8958.   P. van Stempvoort, "The Interpretation of the Ascension in Luke and Acts," *NTSt* 5 (1958-1959): 30-90.

8959.   Augustin Dupré la Tour, "La *Doxa* du Christ dans les oeuvres exégétiques de saint Cyrille d'Alexandrie," *RSR* 48 (1960): 521-43; 49 (1961): 68-94.

8959.1 Gottfried Schille, "Die Himmelfahrt," *ZNW* 57 (1966): 183-99.

8959.2 W. J. P. Boyd, "Ascension according to St John: Chapters 14-17 Not Pre-Passion but Post-Resurrection," *Th* 70 (1967): 207-11.

8959.3 S. G. Wilson, "Ascension. A Critique and an Interpretation," *ZNW* 59 (1968): 269-81.

8959.4 L. Paul Trudinger, "*Arpagmós* and the Christological Significance of the Ascension," *ET* 79 (1968): 279.

8959.5 Eric Franklin, "Ascension and the Eschatology of Luke-Acts," *SJT* 23 (1970): 191-200.

8959.6   Michael Mees, "Erhöhung und Verherrlichung Jesu im Johannesevangelium nach dem Zeugnis neutestamentlicher Papyri," *BibZ* ns 18 (1974): 32-44.

8959.7   Charles H. Talbert, "Myth of a Descending-Ascending Redeemer in Mediterranean Antiquity," *NTSt* 22 (1976): 418-40.

8959.8   Brian K. Donne, "The Significance of the Ascension of Jesus Christ in the New Testament," *SJT* 30 (1977): 555-68.

8959.9   Veselin Kesich, "Resurrection, Ascension, and the Giving of the Spirit," *GOTR* 25 (1980): 249-60.

8959.10   Peter Toon, "Historical Perspectives on the Doctrine of Christ's Ascension. Part 1: Resurrected and Ascended: The Exalted Christ," *BS* 140 (1983): 195-205.

8959.11   Peter Toon, "Historical Perspectives on the Doctrine of Christ's Ascension. Part 2: The Meaning of the Ascension for Christ," *BS* 140 (1983): 291-301.

8959.12   Joseph A. Fitzmyer, "The Ascension of Christ and Pentecost," *ThSt* 45 (1984): 409-40.

8959.13   Peter Toon, "Historical Perspectives on the Doctrine of Christ's Ascension. Part 3: The Significance of the Ascension for Believers," *BS* 141 (1984):16-27.

8959.14   George C. Fuller, "The Life of Jesus, after the Ascension," *WTJ* 56 (1994): 391-98.

4. The Doctrine of the Holy Spirit

8960.   John Robson, "The Work of the Holy Spirit in Christ, the Norm of his Work in Man," *ET* 6 (1894-1895): 18-22.

8961.   T. W. Hodge, "The Paraclete and the World," *ET* 13 (1901-1902): 10-12.

8962.   Lyder Brun, "Guds aand," *NTT* 10 (1909): 305-29.

8963.   George Jackson, "What do we Mean by the Holy Spirit?" *HJ* 20 (1921-1922): 622-31.

8964.   Harmon H. McQuilkin, "The Evangelical Faith and the Holy Spirit," *PTR* 23 (1925): 422-31.

8965.   A. L. Vail, "Is the Holy Spirit Really God?" *RE* 27 (1930):

290-303, 380-86.

8966. R. E. Lee, "The Spirit of Jesus," *ET* 24 (1912-1913): 380.

8967. Z. T. Cody, "The Work of the Paraclete," *RE* 16 (1919): 164-80.

8968. John A. Hutton, "The Holy Spirit and Christ," *ET* 31 (1919-1920): 454-55.

8969. Arthur W. Wotherspoon, "Concerning the Name 'Paraclete'," *ET* 34 (1922-1923): 43-44.

8970. W. Bartlett, "The Coming of the Holy Ghost according to the Fourth Gospel," *ET* 37 (1925-1926): 72-75.

8971. Hermann Sasse, "Der Paraklet im Johannesevangelium," *ZNW* 24 (1925): 260-77.

8972. D. Torsten, "Christusglaube und Heiliger Geist," *ZTK* N.F. 12 (1931): 298-311.

8973. H. G. England, "The Christ and the Holy Spirit," *HJ* 39 (1940-1941): 325-32.

8974. W. F. Lofthouse, "The Holy Spirit in the Acts and the Fourth Gospel," *ET* 52 (1940-1941): 334-36.

8975. John F. Walvoord, "The Holy Spirit in Relation to the Person and Work of Christ," *BS* 98 (1941): 29-55.

8976. W. R. Hutton, "The Johannine Doctrine of the Holy Spirit," *CQ* 24 (1947): 334-44.

8977. C. K. Barrett, "The Holy Spirit in the Fourth Gospel," *JTS* N.S. 1 (1950): 1-15.

8978. Günther Bornkamm, "C. K. Barrett, The Holy Spirit and the Gospel Tradition," *Nunt* 6 (1952): 43-48.

8979. Yves M. J. Congar, "Le Saint-Esprit et le corps apostolique, réalisateurs de l'oeuvre du Christ," *RSPT* 36 (1952): 613-25; 37 (1953): 25-48.

8980. F. Terry, "Jesus and the Era of the Spirit," *HJ* 51 (1952-1953): 10-15.

8981. A. Solignac, "Le Saint-Esprit et la présence du Christ auprès de ses fidèles," *NRT* 77 (1955): 478-90.

8982. C. K. Barrett, "Important Hypotheses Reconsidered-The Holy Spirit and the Gospel Tradition," *ET* 67 (1955- 1956):

142-45.

8983. José Goitia, "La noción dinámica del πνεῦμα en los libros sagrados. Segunda parse: El πνεῦμα y Christo," *EB* 15 (1956): 341-80.

8984. Herbert J. A. Bouman, "The Baptism of Christ with Special Reference to the Gift of the Spirit," *CTM* 28 (1957): 1-15.

8985. Joseph Bourke, "The Wonderful Counsellor," *CBQ* 22 (1960): 123-43.

8986. Robert Hoeferkamp, "The Holy Spirit in the Fourth Gospel from the Viewpoint of Christ's Glorification," *CTM* 33 (1962): 517-29.

See also numbers 3205, 3505-3510, 6620 ff.

8986.1 Werner Foerster, "Der Heilige Geist im Spätjudentum," *NTSt* 8 (1962): 117-34.

8986.2 Fritz Lieb, "Der Heilige Geist als Geist Jesu Christi," *EvT* 23 (1963): 281-98.

8986.3 Robin Scroggs, "Exaltation of the Spirit by Some Early Christians," *JBL* 84 (1965): 359-73.

8986.4 G. R. Beasley-Murray, "Holy Spirit, Baptism, and the Body of Christ," *RE* 63 (1966): 177-85.

8986.5 Frank Stagg, "Holy Spirit in the New Testament," *RE* 63 (1966): 135-47.

8986.6 Raymond E. Brown, "Paraclete in the Fourth Gospel," *NTSt* 13 (1967): 113-32.

8986.7 R. G. Crawford, "The Holy Spirit," *EQ* 40 (1968): 165-72.

8986.8 R. P. C. Hanson, "Basil's Doctrine of Tradition in Relation to the Holy Spirit," *VCh* 22 (1968): 241-55.

8986.9 Abraham J. Malherbe, "Holy Spirit in Athenagoras," *JTS* NS 20 (1969): 538-42.

8986.10 J. K. Parratt, "Witness of the Holy Spirit: Calvin, the Puritans and St Paul," *EQ* 41 (1969): 161-68.

8986.11 C. K. Barrett, "The Holy Spirit," *ABR* 18 (1970): 1-9.

8986.12 J. D. G. Dunn, "Spirit and Kingdom," *ET* 82 (1970): 36-40.

8986.13 Leander E. Keck, "Spirit and the Dove," *NTSt* 17 (1970): 41-67.

8986.14   J. G. Patrick, "Promise of the Paraclete," *BS* 127 (1970): 333-45.

8986.15   J. K. Parratt, "Holy Spirit and Baptism: Pt 1: The Gospels and the Acts of the Apostles," *ET* 82 (1971): 231-35.

8986.16   J. D. G. Dunn, "Rediscovering the Spirit," *ET* 84 (1972): 7-12; 40-44.

8986.17   Edward Malatesta, "Spirit/Paraclete in the Fourth Gospel," *B* 54 (1973): 539-50.

8986.18   John F. Walvoord, "Contemporary Issues in the Doctrine of the Holy Spirit," *BS* 130 (1973): 315-28.

8986.19   Ulrich B. Müller, "Die Parakletenvorstellung im Johannesevangelium," *ZTK* 71 (1974): 31-77.

8986.20   Wesley Carr, "Towards a Contemporary Theology of the Holy Spirit," *SJT* 28 (1975): 501-16.

8986.21   Günter Haufe, "Taufe und Heiliger Geist im Urchristentum," *TLZ* 101 (1976): 561-66.

8986.22   Einar Molland, "Den hellige and i oldkirkens erfaring, tro og laere," *NTT* 77 (1976): 33-43.

8986.23   Aaron Milavec, "The Bible, the Holy Spirit, and Human Powers," *SJT* 29 (1976): 215-35.

8986.24   Edmond Robillard, "Aux sources de la priere: l'Esprit-Saint dans l'homme nouveau," *RSRel* 50 (1976): 157-68.

8986.25   M. Eugene Boring, "Influence of Christian Prophecy on the Johannine Portrayal of the Paraclete and Jesus," *NTSt* 25 (1978): 113-23.

8986.26   J. D. G. Dunn, "Birth of a Metaphor: Baptized in the Spirit," *ET* 89 (1978): 134-38;173-75.

8986.27   Augustin George, "L'Esprit Saint dans l'oeuvre de Luc," *RB* 85 (1978): 500-42.

8986.28   James McPolin, "Holy Spirit in Luke and John," *ITQ* 45 (1978): 117-31.

8986.29   D. G. Dawe, "Divinity of the Holy Spirit," *Interp* 33 (1979): 19-31.

8986.30   A. C. Winn, "Holy Spirit and the Christian life," *Interp* 33 (1979): 47-57.

8986.31 Richard J. Bauckham, "The Role of the Spirit in the Apocalypse," *EQ* 52 (1980): 66-83.

8986.32 Eduard Buess, "Geist und Gericht in der Gemeinde," *EvT* 41 (1981): 243-58.

8986.33 Rudolf Landau, "Komm, Heiliger Geist, du Tröster wert: Gestaltungen des Heiligen Geistes," *EvT* 41 (1981): 187-211.

8986.34 John Moorhead, "The Spirit and the World," *GOTR* 26 (1981): 113-17.

8986.35 Gerhard Sauter, "Geist und Freiheit: Geistvorstellungen und die Erwartung des Geistes," *EvT* 41 (1981): 212-23.

8986.36 M. A. Chevallier, "Luc et l'Esprit Saint: a la mémoire du P Augustin George (1915-1977)," *RSRel* 56 (1982): 1-16.

8986.37 J. D. G. Dunn, "Rediscovering the Spirit (2)," *ET* 94 (1982): 9-18.

8986.38 Curtis C. Mitchell, "The Holy Spirit's Intercessory Ministry," *BS* 139 (1982): 230-42.

8986.39 Edna McDonagh, "The Holy Spirit and Human Identity," *ITQ* 49 (1982): 37-49.

8986.40 Kilian McDonnell, "The Determinative Doctrine of the Holy Spirit," *TTod* 39 (1982): 142-61.

8986.41 M. A. Chevallier, "L'Evangile de Jean et le 'Filioque'," *RSRel* 57 (1983): 93-111.

8986.42 Nigel M. Watson, "Risen Christ and Spirit/Paraclete in the Fourth Gospel," *ABR* 31 (1983): 81-85.

8986.43 François Bovon, "Schön hat der heilige Geist durch den Propheten Jesaja zu euren Vätern gesprochen (Acts 28:25)," *ZNW* 75 (1984): 226-32.

8986.44 Jürgen Moltmann, "The Fellowship of the Holy Spirit: Trinitarian," *SJT* 37 (1984) 287-300.

8986.45 J. E. Morgan-Wynne, "The Holy Spirit and Christian Experience in Justin Martyr," *VCh* 38 (1984): 172-77.

8986.46 Roy B. Zuck, "The Role of the Holy Spirit in Hermeneutics," *BS* 141 (1984): 120-30.

8986.47 D. M. Belonick, "Revelation and Metaphors: The Significance of the Trinitarian Names, Father, Son, and Holy

Spirit," *USQR* 40 (1985): 31-42.

8986.48   Christian Dietzfelbinger, "Paraklet und theologischer Anspruch im Johannesevangelium," *ZTK* 82 (1985): 389-408.

8986.49   D. P. Francis, "The Holy Spirit: A Statistical Inquiry," *ET* 96 (1985): 136-37.

8986.50   Hans O. Kvist, "Der Heilige Geist in den Bekenntnisschriften der evangelisch-lutherischen Kirche," *KD* 31 (1985): 201-11.

8986.51   Michael Beintker, "Creator Spiritus: zu einem unerledigten Problem der Pneumatologie," *EvT* 46 (1986): 12-26.

8986.52   David M. Coffey, "A Proper Mission of the Holy Spirit," *ThSt* 47 (1986): 227-50.

8986.53   Silvia Schroer, "Der Geist, die Weisheit und die Taube: feministisch-kritische Exegese eines neutestamentlichen Symbols," *FZPT* 33 (1986): 197-225.

8986.54   John F. Walvoord, "The Holy Spirit and Spiritual Gifts," *BS* 143 (1986): 109-22.

8986.55   M. A. Chevallier, "Sur un silence du Nouveau Testament: l'Esprit de Dieu a l'oeuvre dans le cosmos et l'humanite," *NTSt* 33 (1987): 344-69.

8986.56   Michal Wojciechowski, "Le don de l'Esprit Saint dans Jean 20:22 selon Targum Gen 2:7," *NTSt* 33 (1987): 289-92.

8986.57   Anthony Byatt, "The Holy Spirit—A Further Examination," *ET* 100 (1989): 215-16.

8986.58   David M. Coffey, "The Holy Spirit as the Mutual Love of the Father and the Son," *ThSt* 51 (1990): 193-229.

8986.59   Hans Hübner, "Der Heilige Geist in der Heiligen Schrift," *KD* 36 (1990): 181-208.

8986.60   Walter Kasper, "Das Verhältnis von Schrift und Tradition: eine pneumatologische Perspektive," *TQ* 170 (1990): 161-90.

8986.61   Ernst Koch, "Die 'Himlische Philosophia des heiligen Geistes': zur Bedeutung alttestamentlicher Spruchweisheit im Luthertum des 16 und 17 Jahrhunderts," *TLZ* 115 (1990): 705-20.

8986.62   Michael Theobald, "Geist- und Inkarnationschristologie: zur

Pragmatik des Johannesprologs," *ZKT* 112 (1990): 129-49.

8986.63   Hermann Vogt, "Die Lehre des Origenes von der Inspiration der Heiligen Schrift: Ein Vergleich zwischen der Grundlagenschrift und der Antwort auf Kelsos," *TQ* 170 (1990): 97-103.

8986.64   Max Turner, "The Spirit and the Power of Jesus' Miracles in the Lucan Conception," *NT* 33 (1991): 124-52.

8986.65   A. de la Fuente, "Isabel, 'Llena de Espíritu Santo' Lc 1,41 a la luz de la tradición rabínica," *EB* 50 (1992): 73-83.

8986.66   Martin Camroux, "What's All This about the Holy Spirit?" *ET* 104 (1993): 239-40.

8986.67   Stephen H. Levinsohn, "Anarthrous References to the Holy Spirit: Another Factor," *BTr* 44 (1993): 138-44.

8986.68   Enrique Nardoni, "The Concept of Charism in Paul," *CBQ* 55 (1993): 68-80.

8986.69   Clark H. Pinnock, "The Role of the Spirit in Interpretation," *JETS* 36 (1993): 491-97.

8986.70   Robert A. Pyne, "The Role of the Holy Spirit in Conversion," *BS* 150 (1993): 203-18.

8986.71   J. Rius-Camps, "El seguimiento de Jesús, 'el Señor' y de su Espíritu en los prolegómenos de la misión," *EB* 51 (1993): 73-116.

8986.72   Stephen M. Swartz, "The Holy Spirit: Person and Power—the Greek Article and Pneuma," *BTr* 44 (1993): 124-38.

8986.73   John R. Levison, "The Debut of the Divine Spirit in Josephus's Antiquities," *HTR* 87 (1994): 123-38.

5. Satan and Demonology

8987.   G. A. Chadwick, "Some Cases of Possession," Ext. 4th ser., 6 (1892): 272-81 [1. The Demoniac in the Synagogue (Mk. 1:23-27; Lk. 4:33-36); 2. The Woman with a Spirit of Infirmity (Lk. 13:1-17); 3. The Man with a Deaf and Dumb Spirit (Mt. 9:32-34)].

8988.   J. van der Veen, "De daemonologie van Jezus, volgens de Synoptici," *TS* 10 (1892): 30-48.

8989.   P. Schwartzkopf, "Der Teufels- und Dämonenglaube Jesu," *ZTK* 7 (1897): 289-332.

8990.   Th. Braun, "Die Dämonischen des Neuen Testaments," *ZTK* 8 (1898): 494-533.

8991.   W. Wrede, "Zur Messiaserkenntnis der Dämonen bei Markus," *ZNW* 5 (1904): 169-77.

8992.   B. W. Bacon, "The Markan Theory of Demonic Recognition of the Christ," *ZNW* 6 (1905): 153-58.

8993.   Paul Galtier, "La rédemption et les droits du démon dans saint Irénée," *RSR* 2 (1911): 1-24.

8994.   Paul Galtier, "Les droits du démon et l'obéissance du Christ," *RSR* 3 (1912): 345-55.

8995.   William Caldwell, "The Doctrine of Satan; III. In the New Testament," *BW* 41 (1913): 167-71.

8996.   Jean Rivière et Paul Galtier, "La mort du Christ et la justice envers le démon; le démon dans la théologie rédemptrice de saint Irénée," *RSR* 4 (1913): 57-73, 263-70.

8997.   A. Wakefield Slaten, "Did Jesus Believe in Demons?" *BW* 54 (1920): 371-77.

8998.   Carl J. Schindler, "Demonic Possession in the Synoptic Gospels," *LCQ* 1 (1928): 385-414.

8999.   Anton Fridrichsen, "Jesu kamp mot de urene ånder," *STK* 5 (1929): 299-314.

9000.   Anton Fridrichsen, "The Conflict of Jesus with Unclean Spirits," *Th* 22 (1931): 122-35.

9001.   E. L. Lewis, "Christ and Unclean Spirits," *Th* 23 (1931): 87-88.

9002.   T. Graebner, "Demoniacal Possession," *CTM* 4 (1933): 589-603.

9003.   S. Vernon McCasland, "The Demonic 'Confessions' of Jesus," *JR* 24 (1944): 33-36.

9004.   Willard M. Aldrich, "Satan's Attempt to keep Christ from the Cross," *BS* 102 (1945): 468-73.

9005.   Victor White, "Satan," *DS* 2 (1949): 193-98.

9006.   Anders Nygren, "Kristus och fördärvsmakterna," *STK* 27

(1951): 1-11.

9007. Anders Nygren, "Christ and the Forces of Destruction," *SJT* 4 (1951): 363-75.

9008. Trevor Ling, "Christ's Conquest of Satan, in its Relation to the Individual," *Th* 56 (1953): 327-32.

9009. Otto Skrzypczak, "A Demonologia no Novo Testamento," *REB* 17 (1957): 26-41.

See also numbers 7214, 8385, *10081.*

9009.1 G. J. M. Bartelink, "Les démons comme brigands," *VCh* 21 (1967): 12-24.

9009.2 Frederick W. Danker, "Demonic Secret in Mark: A Reexamination of the Cry of Dereliction," *ZNW* 61 (1970): 48-69.

9009.3 Willem Berends, "Biblical Criteria for Demon-Possession," *WTJ* 37 (1975): 342-65.

9009.4 E. G. Rüsch, "Dämonenaustreibung in der Gallus-Vita und bei Blumhardt dem Alteren," *TZ* 34 (1978): 86-94.

9009.5 Roy Yates, "The Powers of Evil in the New Testament," *EQ* 52 (1980): 97-111.

9009.6 G. J. M. Bartelink, "Baskanos désignation de Satan et des démons chez les auteurs chrétiens," *OCP* 49 (1983): 390-406.

9009.7 J. K. Howard, "New Testament Exorcism and Its Significance Today," *ET* 96/4 (1984-1985): 105-109.

9009.8 Peter Pimentel, "The 'Unclean Spirits' of St Mark's Gospel," *ET* 99 (1988): 173-75.

9009.9 B. Kollmann, "Jesu Schweigegebote an die Dämonen," *ZNW* 82 (1991): 267-73.

9009.10 Richard H. Hiers, "Satan, Demons, and the Kingdom of God," *SJT* 27 (1974): 35-47.

9009.11 Heinz Kruse, "Das Reich Satans," *B* 58 (1977): 29-61.

9009.12 Nicole Zeegers-Vander Vorst, "Satan, Eve et le serpent chez Théophile d'Antioche," *VCh* 35 No 2 (1981): 152-69.

9009.13 Kees F. De Blois, "How to Deal with Satan?" *BTr* 37 (1986): 301-309.

9009.14 Samuel Vollenweider, "Ich Sah Den Satan wie Einen Blitz vom Himmel Fallen (Lk. 10:18)," *ZNW* 79/3-4 (1988): 187-203.

9009.15 Michael Perry, "Taking Satan Seriously," *ET* 101 (1990): 105-12.

9009.16 Elaine H. Pagels, "The Social History of Satan, the 'Intimate Enemy': A Preliminary Sketch," *HTR* 84 (1991): 105-28.

9009.17 Julian V. Hills, "Luke 10:18: Who Saw Satan Fall?" *JSNT* 46 (1992): 25-40.

9009.18 Charles J. Scalise, "Perspectives on Evil and Satan," *RE* 89 (1992): 461-526.

6. The Doctrine of Man and Sin

9010. William Dewar, "Jesus' Conception of Nature," *BW* 15 (1900): 414-23.

9011. André Arnal, "La personne humaine dans les évangiles," *RTQR* 19 (1910): 516-74; 20 (1911): 45-73, 97-129.

9012. Hans Windisch, "Das Erlebnis des Sünders in den Evangelien," *ZTK* 27 (1917): 292-313.

9013. Arthur C. Hill, "Christ and the Will," *ET* 31 (1919-1920): 174-76.

9014. Lester Reddin, "The Significance of Man as Viewed by the Son of Man," *RE* 20 (1923): 209-21.

9015. D. Russell Scott, "The Teaching of Jesus on Sin," *ET* 36 (1924-1925): 223-25.

9016. H. J. Flowers, "Christ's Doctrine of Man and Sin," *BS* 85 (1928): 64-81, 160-78.

9017. R. Thibaut, "L'univers rival de l'homme-Dieu," *NRT* 70 (1948): 245-56.

9018. André M. Dubarle, "Le péché originel dans les suggestions de l'évangile," *RSPT* 39 (1955): 603-14.

See also numbers 403, 416, 2414, 8648, 8716, 9008.

9018.1 William K. Harrison, "Origin of Sin," *BS* 130 (1973): 58-61.

9018.2 Marc Michel, "Le péche originel, question herméneutique," *RSRel* 48 (1974): 113-35.

9018.3   Samuel L. Hoyt, "The Judgment Seat of Christ in Theological Perspective. Part 1: The Judgment Seat of Christ and Unconfessed Sins," *BS* 137 (1980): 32-40.

9018.4   Samuel L. Hoyt, "The Judgment Seat of Christ in Theological Perspective. Part 2: The Negative Aspects of the Christian's Judgment," *BS* 137 (1980): 125-32.

9018.5   E. P. Sanders, "Jesus and the Sinners," *JSNT* 19 (1983): 5-36.

9018.6   Norman H. Young, "Jesus and the Sinners: Some Queries," *JSNT* 24 (1985): 73-75.

9018.7   Schuyler Brown, "Sin and Atonement: Biblical Imagery and the Experience of Evil," *USQR* 44 (1990): 151-56.

9018.8   Alfred Vanneste, "Le péché originel: un débat sans issue?" *ETL* 70 (1994): 359-83.

9018.9   Robert B. Strimple, "Bernard Ramm and the Theology of Sin," *WTJ* 49 (1987): 143-52.

7. The Doctrine of Reconciliation

a. *General Studies*

9019.   F. Niebergall, "Das Heil im Kreuze Jesu Christi," *ZTK* 7 (1897): 97-139.

9020.   Vincent Rose, "Etudes évangéliques; IV. La rédemption messianique," *RB* 9 (1900): 489-517

9021.   I. Gottschick, "Augustines Anschauung von den Erlöserwirkungen Christi," *ZTK* 11 (1901): 97-213.

9022.   Friedrich Lundgreen, "Die Heilsbedeutung des Todes Jesu," *NKZ* 12 (1901): 261-85.

9023.   A. Klöpper, "Zur Soteriologie der Pastoralbriefe," *ZWT* 47 (1904): 57-88 [Tit. 3:4-7; 2 Tim. 1:9-11; Tit. 2:11-14].

9024.   Pastor Westermann, "Was ist uns Jesus? Ein Wort der Versöhnung und zur Versöhnung in den augenblicklichen Kämpfen," *ZTK* 15 (1905): 516-42.

9025.   James Orr, "The Christian Doctrine of Salvation," *ET* 17 (1905-1906): 176-81.

9026.   P. J. Toner, "The Soteriological Teaching of Christ," *ITQ* 2

(1907): 88-109.

9027. Paul Althaus, "Unser Bekenntnis zu der Heilsbedeutung des Todes Jesu," *NKZ* 26 (1915): 22-51.

9028. John A. F. Gregg, "Christ our Redemption," *ET* 34 (1922-1923): 355-58.

9029. Charles Harris Nash, "The Salvation of the Triune God, Father-Son-Holy Spirit, as it is Interpreted by Jesus," *RE* 21 (1924): 408-18.

9030. H. J. Flowers, "Salvation from Sin in the Teachings of Jesus," *RE* 23 (1926): 421-32.

9031. Charles Harris Nash, "The Thrice-Born of the Spiritual Kingdom of God," *RE* 26 (1929): 27-51.

9032. Al. Janssens, "De valore soteriologico resurrectionis Christi," *ETL* 9 (1932): 225-33

9033. A. De Bondt, "In Christus geheiligd," *GTT* 46 (1945): 79-87.

9034. H. Framer Smith, "Is Jesus the Believer's Mercy Seat?" *BS* 102 (1945): 292-99.

9035. S. Paul Schilling, "How does Jesus Save?" *RL* 18 (1949): 163-74.

9036. Heinrich Treblin, "Soteriologie oder Doxologie? (Die Umkehr als theologisches Prinzip)," *EvT* 9 (1949-1950): 558-71.

9037. Walter Bartling, "The New Creation in Christ," *CTM* 21 (1950): 401-19.

9038. André Feuillet, "Le plan salvifique de Dieu d'après l'epître aux Romains," *RB* 57 (1950): 336-87, 489-529.

9039. S. Verkhowsky, "Der neue Mensch in Christus," *EvT* 11 (1951-1952): 332-43.

9040. André Marc, "L'idée de religion chrétienne; III. Le testament du rédempteur," *NRT* 76 (1954): 337-50.

9041. N. Burnett Magruder, "The Redemptive Sovereignty of Jesus Christ," *RE* 53 (1956): 332-40.

9042. David M. Stanley, "The Conception of Salvation in the Synoptic Gospels," *CBQ* 18 (1956): 345-63.

9043. T. Torrance, "Reconciliation in Christ and in his Church," *BT* 11 (1961): 26-35.

See also number 7141.

9043.1 Gottfried Fitzer, "Der Ort der Versöhnung nach Paulus: zu der Frage des Sühnopfers Jesu," *TZ* 22 (1966): 161-83.

9043.2 Klaus Koch, "Sühne und Sündenvergebung um die Wende von der exilischen zur nachexilischen Zeit," *EvT* 26 (1966): 217-39.

9043.3 Hermann Binder, "Versohnung als die grosse Wende," *TZ* 29 (1973): 305-12.

9043.4 Ferdinand Hahn, "Siehe, jetzt ist der Tag des Heils: Neuschöpfung und Versöhnung nach 2 Korinther 5:14-6:2," *EvT* 33 (1973): 244-53.

9043.5 Gerhard Sauter, "Versöhnung und Vergebung: die Frage der Schuld im Horizont der Christologie," *EvT* 36 (1976): 34-52.

9043.6 Hans G. Geyer, "Anfänge zum Begriff der Versöhnung," *EvT* 38 (1978): 235-51.

9043.7 Otfried Hofius, "Erwägungen zur Gestalt und Herkunft des paulinischen Versöhnungsgedankens," *ZTK* 77 (1980): 186-99.

9043.8 Ralph P. Martin, "New Testament Theology. A Proposal: The Theme of Reconciliation," *ET* 91 (1980): 364-68.

9043.9 Carl E. Braaten, "The Christian Doctrine of Salvation," *Interp* 35 (1981): 117-31.

9043.10 Hans Hübner, "Sühne und Versöhnung: Anmerkungen zu einem umstrittenen Kapitel Biblischer Theologie," *KD* 29 (1983): 284-305.

9043.11 Reimund Bieringer, "2 Kor 5:19a und die Versöhnung der Welt," *ETL* 63 (1987): 295-326.

9043.12 Brian Kelly, "Towards a Theology of Redemption," *ITQ* 57 (1991): 173-84.

b. *Faith*

9044. Anton Oehler, "Der Glaube und die Geburt aus Gott in ihrer Einheit dargestellt nach dem johanneischen Lehrbegriffe," *TQ* 20 (1838): 599-622.

9045. F.-C.-J. van Goens, "La foi d'après les synoptiques," *RTP* 19

(1886): 5-39.

9046. V. Barlet, "Fides divina et fides humana; Or Faith According to Christ," *Exp* 4th ser., 5 (1892): 401-17.

9047. H. Scholz, "Das persönliche Verhältnis zu Christus und die religiöse Unterweisung," *ZTK* 3 (1893): 342-70.

9048. Fr. Neelsen, "Hat der Herr Jesus Christus geglaubet?" *NKZ* 5 (1894): 668-76.

9049. J. Watson, "Faith the Sixth Sense," *Exp* 4th ser., 9 (1894): 381-94.

9050. Paul Chapuis, "Der Glaube an Christus," *ZTK* 5 (1895): 273-343.

9051. C. Lucassen, "Der Glaube Jesu Christi," *NKZ* 6 (1895): 337-47.

9052. Prescott F. Jernegan, "The Faith of Jesus Christ," *BW* 8 (1896): 198-202.

9053. Aug. Meyer, "Der Glaube Jesu und der Glaube an Jesum," *NKZ* 11 (1900): 621-44.

9054. F. Niebergall, "Christus und der Glaube," *ZTK* 11 (1901): 269-300.

9055. Johannes Ording, "Den kirkelige bekjendelse, dens karakter og dens betydning for den kristelige troslaere," *NTT* 5 (1904): 213-40.

9056. K. Feilberg, "Om tro og overtro," *NTT* 7 (1906): 340-54.

9057. James M. Campbell, "Jesus an Example of Faith," *BW* 30 (1907): 208-12.

9058. W. W. Holdsworth, "Faith in the Fourth Gospel," *Exp* 7th ser., 4 (1907): 182-92.

9059. Henri Bois, "La valeur de la personne de Jésus pour la foi," *RTQR* 22 (1913): 1-15.

9060. Alfred E. Garvie, "The Pioneer of Faith and of Salvation," *ET* 26 (1914-1915): 502-504, 546-50.

9061. R. Martin Pope, "Faith and Knowledge in Pauline and Johannine Thought," *ET* 41 (1929-1930): 421-27.

9062. Joseph Huby, "De la connaissance de foi dans saint Jean," *RSR* 21 (1931): 385-421.

782 THEOLOGICAL STUDIES

9063. Chr. Ihlen, "Der Glaube an Christus als Mittelpunkt der Theologie," *ZST* 12 (1934-1935): 665-704.

9064. Eugene W. Lyman, "Faith in Christ," *RL* 7 (1938): 323- 34.

9065. J. Lessel, "De natura et momento fidei quid eruatur ex evangelio S. Iohannis," *VD* 20 (1940): 19-28, 85-93, 241-55.

9066. Carl Stange, "Der Glaube an Gott im Sinne des Evangeliums," *ZST* 21 (1950-1952): 315-38.

9067. Ernst Fuchs, "Warum fordert der Glaube an Jesus Christus von uns ein Selbstverständnis?" *ZTK* N.F. 48 (1951): 342-59.

9068. Pierre Benoit, "La foi dans les évangiles synoptiques," *LumV* no. 22 (1955): 45-64

9069. D. Mollat, "La foi dans le quatrième évangile," *LumV* no. 22 (1955): 91-107.

9070. G. Salet, "La part de l'homme dans l'accomplissement du plan divin," *NRT* 78 (1956): 227-42.

9071. Eberhard Buder, "Fides iustificans und fides historica," *EvT* 13 (1953-1954): 67-83.

9072. Thomas Barrosse, "The Relationship of Love to Faith in St. John," *ThSt* 18 (1957): 538-59.

9073. George Gordh, "The Concept of Corporate Faith," *RE* 54 (1957): 67-78.

9074. Thomas Shearer, "The Concept of 'Faith' in the Synoptic Gospels," *ET* 69 (1957): 3-6.

9075. A. Decourtray, "La conception johannique de la foi," *NRT* 81 (1959): 561-76.

9076. Gerald F. Hawthorne, "The Concept of Faith in the Fourth Gospel," *BS* 116 (1959): 117-26.

9077. Walter Grundmann, "Verständnis und Bewegung des Glaubens im Johannes Evangelium," *KD* 6 (1960): 131-54.

See also numbers 3513 f.

9077.1 Günther Bornkamm, "Geschichte und Glaube im Neuen Testament: ein Beitrag zur Frage der 'historischen' Begründung theologischer Aussagen," *EvT* 22 (1962): 1-15.

9077.2 L. Hejdanek and P. Pokorný, "Jesus, Glaube, Christologie," *TZ* 18 (1962): 268-82.

9077.3   Eberhard Jüngel, "Theologische Wissenschaft und Glaube im Blick auf die Armut Jesu," *EvT* 24 (1964): 419-43.

9077.4   Heinrich Baltensweiler, "Wunder und Glaube im Neuen Testament," *TZ* 23 (1967): 241-56.

9077.5   Eric F. F. Bishop, " 'Faith Has Still Its Olivet and Love Its Galilee'," *EQ* 44/1 (1972): 3-10.

9077.6   Gerhard Dautzenberg, "Der Glaube im Hebraerbrief," *BibZ* NS 17 (1973): 161-77.

9077.7   Gerhard Barth, "Glaube und Zweifel in den Synoptischen Evangelien," *ZTK* 72 (1975): 269-92.

9077.8   Otto Merk, "Glaube und Tat in den pastoralbriefen," *ZNW* 66 (1975): 91-102.

9077.9   Eduard Lohse, "Emuna und pistis - jüdisches und urchristliches Verständnis des Glaubens," *ZNW* 68 (1977): 147-63.

9077.10   Daniel C. Arichea, " 'Faith' in the Gospels of Matthew, Mark and Luke," *BTr* 29 (1978): 420-24.

9077.11   T. McCaughey, "Paradigms of Faith in the Gospel of St. Luke," *ITQ* 45 (1978): 177-84.

9077.12   Eduard Schweizer, "The Portrayal of the Life of Faith in the Gospel of Mark," *Interp* 32 (1978): 387-99.

9077.13   G. C. Stead, "Foundation Documents of the Faith: I. The Aapostles Creed," *ET* 91 (1979): 4-8.

9077.14   Y. Watanabe, "Selbstwertanalyse und christlicher Glaube," *EvT* 40 (1980): 58-75.

9077.15   Luke T. Johnson, "Romans 3:21-26 and the Faith of Jesus," *CBQ* 44 (1982): 77-90.

9077.16   H. E. Lona, "Glaube und Sprache des Glaubens im Johannesevangelium," *BibZ* NS 28 (1984): 168-84.

9077.17   Johannes Fischer, "Uber die Beziehung von Glaube und Mythos: Gedanken im Anschluss an Kurt Hübners Die Wahrheit des Mythos," *ZTK* 85 (1988): 303-28.

9077.18   Michael Theobald, "Glaube und Vernunft: zur Argumentation des Paulus Römerbrief," *TQ* 169 (1989): 287-301.

9077.19   Eberhard Jüngel, "Die Heilsbedeutung des Kreuzes für

Glaube und Hoffnung des Christen," *ZTK* 8 (1990): 1-93.

9077.20   A. del Agua, "The Narrative of the Transfiguration as a Derashic Scenification of a Faith Confession," *NTSt* 39 (1993): 340-52.

9077.21   Wolfgang Weiss, "Glaube—Liebe—Hoffnung: Zu der Trias bei Paulus," *ZNW* 84 (1993): 196-217.

9077.22   Roy A. Harrisville, "Pistis Christou: Witness of the Fathers," *NT* 36 (1994): 233-41.

9077.23   Otfried Hofius, "Glaube und Taufe nach dem Zeugnis des Neuen Testaments," *ZTK* 91 (1994): 134-56.

9077.24   Eric F. Osborn, "Arguments for Faith in Clement of Alexandria," *VCh* 48 (1994): 1-24.

c. *Prayer*

9078.   Carpus, "The Biblical Conception of Prayer," *Exp* 1st ser., 5 (1877): 321-35; 6 (1877): 113-29.

9079.   D. W. Simon, "The Atonement and Prayer," *Exp* 1st ser., 6 (1877): 321-34

9080.   G. A. Chadwick, "Asking in Christ's Name," *Exp* 3rd ser., 6 (1887): 191-98.

9081.   J. S. Banks, "Professor Deissmann on Jesus at Prayer," *ET* 11 (1899-1900): 270-73.

9082.   D. W. Forrest, "Did Jesus Pray with his Disciples?" *ET* 11 (1899-1900): 352-57.

9083.   A. Stewart, "Did Jesus Pray with his Disciples?" *ET* 11 (1899-1900): 477-78.

9084.   J. M. Shaw, "Jesus' Thought of Prayer," *ET* 34 (1922-1923): 506-508.

9085.   John F. Walvoord, "Praying in the Name of the Lord Jesus Christ," *BS* 91 (1934): 463-72.

9086.   Charles Lee Feinberg, "Prayer in its Relation to the Three Persons of the Godhead," *BS* 96 (1939): 285-306.

9087.   Alfred de Quervain, "La prière du Christ et la prière du chrétien," *RTP* sér. 3, 2 (1952): 97-106.

See also numbers 1518, 4011ff.

9087.1   L. A. Snijders, "Het gebed naar de tempel toe: over gebedsrichting in het Oude Testament," *NTT* 19 (1964): 1-14.

9087.2   R. S. Barbour, "Gethsemane in the Tradition of the Passion," *NTSt* 16 (1970): 231-51.

9087.3   Jerome D. Quinn, "Apostolic Ministry and Apostolic Prayer," *CBQ* 33 (1971): 479-91.

9087.4   Stephen S. Smalley, "Spirit, Kingdom and Prayer in Luke-Acts," *NT* 15 (1973): 59-71.

9087.5   Jacques Dupont, "La prière et son efficacité sans l'évangile de luc," *RSRel* 69 (1981): 45-55.

9087.6   Curtis C. Mitchell, "The Case for Persistence in Prayer," *JET* 27 (1984): 161-68.

9087.7   Ralph Sauer, "Das Vaterunser als Modell für unser Sprechen von Gott und Mensch in der Glaubensvermittlung," *TQ* 164 (1984): 294-305.

9087.8   Roger L. Omanson, "The Certainty of Judgment and the Power of Prayer," *RE* 83 (1986): 427-38.

9087.9   Thomas Söding, "Gebet 1und Gebetsmahnung Jesu in Getsemani: eine redaktionskritische Auslegung von Mk 14:32-42," *BibZ* NS 31 (1987): 76-100.

9087.10   Volker Stolle, "Das Gebet der Gemeinde Jesu Christi nach dem Neuen Testament," *KD* 37 (1991): 307-31.

    d. *Evangelism (Mission to the Gentiles)*

9088.   Lyder Brun, "Jesus og hedningerne," *NTT* 4 (1903): 297-327; 5 (1904): 293-344.

9089   H. Gebhardt, "Die an die Heiden gerichtete Missionsrede der Apostel und das Johannesevangelium," *ZNW* 6 (1905): 236-49.

9090.   H. Weitbrecht, "Jesus Christ and Missions to the World according to the Gospels," *ET* 19 (1907-1908): 24-28, 69-72.

9091.   Joseph B. Mayor, "Did Christ Contemplate the Admission of the Gentiles into the Kingdom of Heaven?" *Exp* 7th ser., 8 (1909): 385-99.

9092.   George Jackson, "The Missionary Idea in the Gospels," *ET* 23

786   THEOLOGICAL STUDIES

(1911-1912) 54-62.

9093.   Arthur W. Hummel, "The Primitive Christian Mission," *BW* 44 (1914): 260-70.

9094.   A. van Veldhuizen, "Heeft Jezus de Heidenzending gewild?" *NTS* 1 (1918): 33-40 [Yes].

9095.   M. Goguel, "Jésus et les origines de l'universalisme chrétien," *RHPR* 12 (1932): 193-211.

9096.   M. Kiddle, "The Admission of the Gentiles in St. Luke's Gospel and Acts," *JTS* 36 (1935): 160-73.

9097.   Bengt Sundkler, "Jésus et les païens," *RHPR* 16 (1936): 462-99.

9098.   Morton S. Enslin, "Luke and the Samaritans," *HTR* 36 (1943): 277-98.

9099.   Bo Reicke, "Den primära Israelsmissionen och hednamissionen enligt synoptikerna," *STK* 26 (1950): 77-100.

9100.   J. W. Doeve, "L'évangile de Luc; un moyen de prédication de la mission chrétienne primitive," *NedTT* 9 (1954-1955): 332-37.

9101.   John J. Vincent, "The Evangelism of Jesus," *JBR* 23 (1955): 266-71.

9101.1 G. Baumbach, "Die Mission im Matthäus-Evangelium," *TLZ* 92 (1967): 889-93.

9101.2 A. Simón-Muñoz, "Cristo, luz de los gentiles: puntualizaciones sobre Lc 2: 32," *EB* 46 (1968): 27-44.

9101.3 Robert J. Karris, "Missionary Communities: A New Paradigm for the Study of Luke-Acts," *CBQ* 41 (1979): 80-97.

9101.4 Richar J. Coggins, "The Samaritans and Acts," *NTSt* 28 (1982): 423-34.

9101.5 Raymond E. Brown, "Not Jewish Christianity and Gentile Christianity but Types of Jewish/Gentile Christianity," *CBQ* 45 (1983): 74-79.

9101.6 Ernest Best, "The Revelation to Evangelize the Gentiles," *JTS* NS 35 (1984): 1-30.

9101.7 S. J. D. Cohen, "Crossing the Boundary and Becoming a Jew [ca 150 BC-400 AD]," *HTR* 82 (1989): 13-33.

9101.8 R. S. Sugirtharajah, "Luke's Second Volume and the Gentiles," *ET* 100 (1989): 178-81.

9101.9 Johannes Beutler, "Greeks Come to See Jesus (John 12:20f)," *B* 71 (1990): 333-47.

9101.10 Stephen Ire Kio, "Understanding and Translating 'Nations' in Mt 28:19," *BTr* 41 (1990): 230-38.

9101.11 Hendrikus Boers, "We Who Are by Inheritance Jews; Not from the Gentiles, Sinners," *JBL* 111 (1992): 273-81.

9101.12 Jeffrey S. Siker, "First to the Gentiles: A Literary Analysis of Luke 4:16-30," *JBL* 111 (1992): 73-90.

9101.13 S. G. Wilson, "Gentile Judaizers [70-200 CE]," *NTSt* 38 (1992): 605-16.

9101.14 Terence L. Donaldson, " 'Riches for the Gentiles' (Rom 11:12): Israel's Rejection and Paul's Gentile Mission," *JBL* 112 (1993): 81-98.

8. The Church

a. *General Studies*

9102. Pierre Batiffol, "Jésus et l'église," *BLE* 5 (1903): 27-61.

9103. Newport J. D. White, "The Presence of Christ in his Church," *Exp* 6th ser., 11 (1905): 446-54

9104. Ambrose W. Vernon, "The Founding of the Church," *HTR* 10 (1917): 64-83.

9105. M. Goguel, "Jésus et l'église," *RHPR* 13 (1933): 197-241.

9106. E. C. Blackman, "The Church and the Kingdom of God: Need for Discrimination," *ET* 47 (1935-1936): 369-73.

9107. P. van Stempvoort, "Kerk en Koninkrijk Gods in de gelijkenis van den vierderlei grond," *NedTT* 1 (1946- 1947): 347-69.

9108. H. J. Westerink, "Kerk en Koninkrijk Gods," *GTT* 48 (1948). 163-81; 49 (1949): 203-18; 50 (1950): 183-93.

9109. C. P. Plooy, " 'Kerk en Koninkrijk Gods' (critiek op Dr. H. J. Westerink in *GTT* 26 jg., p. 163 e.v.)," *GTT* 48 (1948): 210-18.

9110. T. W. Manson, "The New Testament Basis of the Doctrine of the Church," *JEH* 1 (1950): 1-11.

9111.   John H. Watson, "The Church and the Kingdom," *EQ* 22 (1950): 95-106.

9112.   R. Lansing Hicks, "Jesus and his Church," *ATR* 34 (1952): 85-94.

9113.   S. J. Park, "Jesus and the Church," BT, 3 (1953): 56-63.

9114.   Erich Fascher, "Jesus der Lehrer. Ein Betrag zur Frage nach dem 'Quellort der Kirchenidee'," *TLZ* 79 (1954): 325-42.

9115.   S. Cipriani, "La dottrina della Chiesa in S. Matteo," *RivB·* 3 (1955): 1-31.

9116.   Otto Kuss, "Bemerkungen zu dem Fragenkreis: Jesus und die Kirche im Neuen Testament," *TQ* 135 (1955): 28-55, 150-83.

9117.   Roberto L. Calhoun, "Christo y la Iglesia," *CT* 23-24 (1957): 68-95.

9118.   U. Lattanzi, "El primato di Pietro nella interpretazione di Oscar Cullmann," *Div.* 1 (1957): 54-70.

9119.   Johannes Betz, "Die Gründung der Kirche durch den historischen Jesus," *TQ* 138 (1958): 152-83.

9120.   Carl Fr. Wisløff, "The Unity of the Church and the Message of Christ," *CTM* 31 (1960): 30-37.

See also numbers 9555, 9565, 9569, 9572 f.

9120.1   D. J. Harrington, "Ernst Käsemann on the Church in the New Testament," *HeyJ* 12 (1971): 246-57, 365-76.

9120.2   Klaus Haacker, "Jesus und die Kirche nach Johannes," *TZ* 29 (1973): 179-201.

9120.3   Raymond E. Brown, "Johannine Ecclesiology: The Community's Origins," *Interp* 31 (1977): 379-93.

9210.4   Werner Bieder, "Das Volk Gottes in Erwartung von Licht und Lobpreis," *TZ* 40/2 (1984): 137-48.

b. *The Sacraments*

(1). General Studies

9121.   Wilh. Böhmer, "Das Fusswaschen Christi, nach seiner sacramentlichen Würde dargestellt," *TSK* 23 (1850): 829-42.

9122. V. von Strauss & Torney, "Taufe und Abendmahl im Johannesevangelium," *NKZ* 3 (1892): 459-70.

9123. P. T. Forsyth, "Sacramentalism the True Remedy for Sacerdotalism," *Exp* 5th ser., 8 (1898): 221-33, 262-75.

9124. H. J. C. Knight, "On the Relation of the Discourses of our Lord recorded in S. John III and VI to the Institution of the two Sacraments," *Exp* 5th ser., 10 (1899): 54-66.

9125. Robert Rainy, "The Sacraments in the New Testament," *ET* 14 (1902-1903): 504-506.

9126. John Line, "The Johannine Doctrine of the Sacrament," *CJRT* 4 (1927): 323-33.

9127. J. B. Bord, "De l'institution des sacraments par le Christ," *NRT* 56 (1929): 667-70.

9128. Clarence T. Craig, "Sacramental Interest in the Fourth Gospel," JBL:58 (1939): 31-41.

9129. F. W. Patterson, "The Ordinances of the Gospel," *CQ* 17 (1940): 105-11.

9130. J. P. Haran, "Christus secundum quod homo instituit sacramenta," *ThSt* 7 (1946): 189-212.

9131. E. Luther Copeland, "Baptism and the Lord's Supper," *RE* 47 (1950): 325-32.

9132. Roger Mehl, "Zur Bedeutung von Kultus und Sakrament im vierten Evangelium," *EvT* 15 (1955): 65-74.

9133. Bruce Vawter, "The Johannine Sacramentary," *ThSt* 17 (1956): 151-66.

9134. David W. Hay, "Baptism, Passover and Eucharist," *CJT* 1 (1958): 46-52.

9135. Eduard Lohse, "Wort und Sakrament im Johannes-evangelium," *NTSt* 7 (1960-1961): 110-25.

9136. B. J. Cooke, "The Sacraments as the Continuing Acts of Christ," *PCTSA* 16 (1961): 43-68.

9136.1 Francis J. Moloney, "When Is John Talking about Sacraments?" *ABR* 30 (1982): 10-33.

9136.2 M. Quesnel, "Le sacramentel dans le Nouveau Testament: Ambiguïté et diversité," *RSR* 75 (1987): 203-10.

9136.3 A. García-Moreno, "Teología sacramentaria en el IV evangelic," *Sal* 42 (1995): 5-27.

(2). Baptism

9137. S. Odland, "Daaben i det nye testamente," *NTT* 1 (1900): 1-59.

9138. John Robson, "Notes on the Institution of the Sacrament of Baptism," *ET* 16 (1904-1905): 554-55.

9139. Berkeley G. Collins, "The Sacrament of Baptism in the New Testament," *ET* 27 (1915-1916): 36-39, 70-73, 120-23.

9140. Percy J. Heawood, "Some Aspects of Baptism in the New Testament," *ET* 29 (1917-1918): 405-10.

9141. M. de Jonge, "Le baptême au nom de Jésus d'après les Actes des Apôtres," *ETL* 10 (1933): 647-53.

9142. Oscar Cullmann, "Les traces d'une vieille formule baptismale dans le Nouveau Testament," *RHPR* 17 (1937): 424-34.

9143. Cuthbert Lattey, "De baptismo activo Christi," *VD* 29 (1951): 28-30.

9144. Eduard Stommel, " 'Begraben mit Christus' (Röm. 6, 4) und der Taufritus," *RQ* 49 (1954): 1-20.

9145. Eduard Stommel, "Das 'Abbild seines Todes' (Röm. 6, 5) und der Taufritus," *RQ* 50 (1955): 1-21.

9146. David M. Stanley, "Baptism in the New Testament," *Scr* 8 (1956): 44-57.

9147. David Michael Stanley, "The New Testament Doctrine of Baptism: An Essay in Biblical Theology," *ThSt* 18 (1957): 169-215.

9148. Roger Mercurio, "A Baptismal Motif in the Gospel Narratives of the Burial," *CBQ* 21 (1959): 39-54.

9149. Wolfgang Trilling, "Die Täufertradition bei Matthäus," *BibZ* 3 (1959): 271-89.

9150. John H. Elliott, "Rudolf Bultmann and the Sacrament of Holy Baptism," *CTM* 32 (1961): 348-55.

9150.1 W. E. Moore, "One Baptism," *NTSt* 10 (1963-1964): 504-16.

9150.2 D. W. B. Robinson, "Born of Water and Spirit: Does John

3:5 Refer to Baptism?" *RTR* 25 (1966): 15-23.

9150.3 J. D. G. Dunn, "Spirit and Fire Baptism," *NT* 14/2 (1972): 81-92.

9150.4 Robin Scroggs and Kent I. Groff, "Baptism in Mark: Dying and Rising with Christ," *JBL* 92 (1973): 531-48.

9150.5 Robert W. Jenson, "The Mandate and Promise of Baptism," *Interp* 30 (1976): 271-87.

9150.6 S. Légasse, "Baptême juif des prosélytes et baptême Chrétin," *BLE* 77 (1976): 3-40.

9150.7 Schuyler Brown, " 'Water Baptism' and 'Spirit Baptism' in Luke-Acts," *ATR* 59 (1977): 135-51.

9150.8 Roy A. Stewart, "Engrafting: A Study in New Testament Symbolism and Baptismal Application," *EQ* 50 (1978): 8-22.

9150.9 Richard P. Carlson, "The Role of Baptism in Paul's Thought," *Interp* 47 (1993): 255-66.

(3). The Lord's Supper

9151. William Nast, "The Sacrament of the Lord's Supper," *BS* 19 (1862): 384-99.

9152. Alex. Brandt, "Die Einsetzungsworte des Abendmahls," *ZWT* 31 (1888): 30-36.

9153. P. Lobstein, "La doctrine de la sainte cène," *RTP* 21 (1888): 337-57, 449-511; 22 (1889): 5-50, 148-76, 225-69.

9154. E. Grafe, "Die neuesten Forschungen über die urchristliche Abendmahlsfeier," *ZTK* 5 (1895): 101-38.

9155. J. A. W. Haas, "New Theory of the Gospels and Lord's Supper," *LCR* 15 (1896): 336-37.

9156. E. P. Boys-Smith, "The Lord's Supper under a New or an Old Aspect," *ET* 9 (1897-1898): 551-54.

9157. Norman Macleod Caie, "The Lord's Supper," *ET* 10 (1898-1899): 90-91.

9158. R. M. Spence, "The Lord's Supper," *ET* 10 (1898-1899): 235.

9159. G. W. Stewart, "Harnack, Jülicher, and Spitta on the Lord's Supper," *Exp* 5th ser., 8 (1898): 43-61, 86-102.

9160.   A. Menzies, "The Lord's Supper: St. Mark or St. Paul," *Exp* 5th ser., 10 (1899): 241-62.

9161.   J. Henry Thayer, "Recent Discussions respecting the Lord's Supper," *JBL* 18 (1899): 110-31.

9162.   J. A. W. Haas, "The Lord's Supper in the Last Decade," *LCR* 19 (1900): 356-62.

9163.   G. H. Box, "The Jewish Antecedents of the Eucharist," *JTS* 3 (1901-1902): 357-69.

9164.   S. Odland, "Svar paa to spørgsmaal vedrørende nadveren i det nye testamente," *NTT* 2 (1901): 53-64.

9165.   Axel Andersen, "Das Abendmahl in den zwei ersten Jahrhunderten nach Chr.," *ZNW* 3 (1902): 115-41, 206-21.

9166.   John C. Lambert, "The Passover and the Lord's Supper," *JTS* 4 (1902-1903): 184-93.

9167.   Pierre Batiffol, "L'euchristie dans le nouveau testament d'après des critiques récentes," *RB* 12 (1903): 497-528.

9168.   P. Lechler, "Über die Bedeutung der Abendmahlsworte," *ZWT* 46 (1903): 481-86.

9169.   H. R. Mackintosh, "The Objective Aspect of the Lord's Supper," *Exp* 6th ser., 7 (1903): 180-98.

9170.   O. Holtzmann, "Das Abendmahl im Urchristentum," *ZNW* 5 (1904): 89-120.

9171.   Johannes Merkel, "Die Begnadigung am Passahfeste," *ZNW* 6 (1905): 293-316.

9172.   James Denney, "The Cup of the Lord and the Cup of Demons," *Exp* 7th ser., 5 (1908): 289-304.

9173.   W. M. Ramsay, "The Authorities for the Institution of the Eucharist," *ET* 21 (1909-1910): 246-52, 295-98, 343-47, 473-77. 515-19.

9174.   C. H. Dodd, "Eucharistic Symbolism in the Fourth Gospel," *Exp* 8th ser., 2 (1911): 530-46.

9175.   Thorleif Homme, "Den heilage nattverden," *NTT* 13 (1912): 81-89.

9176.   G. Schläger, "Der Abendmahls-, der Auferstehungsbericht und die Herrnworte im I. Brief an die Korinther," *TT* 46

(1912): 136-57.

9177. F. C. Burkitt, "The Last Supper and the Paschal Meal," *JTS* 17 (1915-1916): 291-97.

9178. Maurice de la Taille, "La royauté pacifique de Notre Seigneur Jésus Christ par l'Eucharistie," *NRT* 49 (1922): 285-94.

9179. G. Margoliouth, "The Institution of the Eucharist," *ET* 35 (1923-1924): 412-16.

9180. Innes Logan, "The Lord's Supper," *ET* 36 (1924-1925): 333-34.

9181. W. K. Lowther Clarke, "Eisler on the Last Supper," *Th* 12 (1926): 104-106.

9182. K. G. Goetz, "Zur Lösung der Abendmahlsfrage," *TSK* 108 (1937-1938): 81-123.

9183. Ernst Lohmeyer, "Das Abendmahl in der Urgemeinde," *JBL* 56 (1937): 217-52.

9184. Ernst Lohmeyer, "Vom urchristlichen Abendmahl," *TR* 9 (1937): 168-94, 195-227, 273-312; 10 (1938): 81-99.

9185. Hans Ording, "Versöhnung und Abendmahl," *ZST* 14 (1937): 263-80.

9186. Ernst Lohmeyer, "Om nattvarden i Nya testament," *STK* 14 (1938): 333-45.

9187. Clarence T. Craig, "From the Last Super to the Lord's Supper," *RL* 9 (1940): 163-73.

9188. H. Rowley, "Sacrament and Sacrifice; I. A Protestant View of the Lord's Supper," *HJ* 40 (1941-1942): 181-85.

9189. A. B. Johnston, "This is my Body," *ET* 54 (1942-1943): 250-51.

9190. G. V. Jourdan, " 'Agape' or 'Lord's Supper'," *Herm* 64 (1944): 32-43.

9191. George W. Forell, "The Lord's Supper and Christology," *LCQ* 18 (1945): 91-94.

9192. Eduard Schweizer, "Das Abendmahl eine Vergegenwärtigung des Todes Jesu oder ein eschatologisches Freudenmahl?" *TZ* 2 (1946): 81-101.

9193. Théo Preiss, "Le dernier repas de Jésus fut-il un repas pascal?" *TZ* 4 (1948): 81-101.

9194. Ralph Russell, "On the Holy Eucharist in the New Testament," *Scr* 4 (1949): 79-89.

9195. Eduard Schweizer, "Das johanneische Zeugnis vom Herrenmahl," *EvT* 12 (1952-1953): 341-63.

9196. Miguel Balagué, "La Cena Eucarística," *CB* 10 (1953): 100-105.

9197. A. J. B. Higgins, "H. Lietzmann's 'Mass and Lord's Supper' (Messe und Herrenmahl)," *ET* 65 (1953-1954): 333-36.

9198. A. J. B. Higgins, "The Origins of the Eucharist," *NTSt* 1 (1954-1955): 200-209.

9199. Eduard Schweizer, "Das Herrenmahl im Neuen Testament," *TLZ* 79 (1954): 577-92.

9200. Edwin M. Poteat, "The Body of Christ as Metaphor or Fact," *RL* 25 (1956): 378-85.

9201. Pierre Benoit, "Les récits de l'institution et leur portée," *LumV* no. 31 (1957): 49-76.

9202. Victoriano Larrañaga, "Las fuentes bíblicas de la Eucaristía en el N.T. Problemas de crítica histórica y literaria suscitados dentro del protestantismo y racionalismo moderno," *EE* 32 (1958): 71-92.

9203. Johannes Steinbeck, "Das Abendmahl Jesu unter Berücksichti gung moderner Forschung," *NT* 3 (1959): 70-79.

9204. Marjorie H. Sykes, "The Eucharist as 'Anamnesis'," *ET* 71 (1959-1960): 115-18.

9205. Bernard Cooke, "Synoptic Presentation of the Eucharist as Covenant Sacrifice," *ThSt* 21 (1960): 1-44.

9206. Cyril Vollert, "The Eucharist: Quests for Insights from Scripture," *ThSt* 21 (1960): 404-43.

See also numbers 8673, 9952.

9206.1 Joseph de Sainte-Marie, "L'Eucharistie, Sacrament et Sacrifice du Christ et del'Eglise," *Div* 18 (1974): 234-86; 396-436.

9206.2   John H. McKenna, "The Eucharist, the Resurrection and the Future," *ATR* 60/2 (1978): 144-65.

9206.3   Theodore G. Stylianopoulos, "Holy Eucharist and Priesthood in the New Testament," *GOTR* 23 (1978): 113-30.

9206.4   L. M. Dewailly, "Donne-nous notre pain: quel pain: notes sur la quatrième demande du Pater," *RSPT* 64 (1980): 561-88.

9206.5   Raymond Moloney, "The Early Eucharist: The Jewish Background," *ITQ* 47 (1980): 34-42.

9206.6   Robert Shepard, "The Eucharistic Presence and Reconciliation of Opposing Realities," *HeyJ* 22 (1981): 123-34.

9206.7   Patrick McGoldrick, "The Holy Spirit and the Eucharist," *ITQ* 50 (1983): 48-66.

9206.8   S. W. Sykes, "Story and Eucharist," *Interp* 37 (1983): 365-76.

9206.9   R. M. Ball, "Saint John and the Institution of the Eucharist (John 13:1)," *JSNT* 23 (1985): 59-68.

9206.10   Andre Feuillet, "L'Eucharistie, le Sacrifice du Calvaire et le Sacerdocedu Christ d'après quelques donnees du Quatrième Evangile Comparaison avec les Synoptiques et L'epître aux Hebreux," *Div* 29 (1985): 103-49.

9206.11   Kenneth Stevenson, "A Theological Reflection on the Experience of Inclusion/Exclusion at the Eucharist," *ATR* 68/3 (1986): 212-21.

9206.12   Christoph Burchard, "The Importance of Joseph and Aseneth for the Study of the New Testament: A General Survey and a Fresh Look at the Lord's Supper," *NTSt* 33/1 (1987): 102-34.

9206.13   D. B. Carmichael, "David Daube on the Eucharist and the Passover Seder," *JSNT* 42 (1991): 45-67.

9206.14   Barbara J. Fleischer, "The Eucharist as Parable," *ITQ* 57 (1991): 26-40.

9206.15   Ralph F. Smith, "Eucharistic Faith and Practice," *Interp* 48 (1994): 5-16.

9. Ethics.

a. General Studies

9207. J.-Alfred Porret, "La philosophie morale du temps présent et l'évangile de Jésus Christ," *RTQR* 6 (1897): 390-414.

9208. J. A. W. Hass, "The Ethic of the Gospel of John," *LCR* 20 (1901): 207-17.

9209. Eberhard Vischer, "Das Leben nach dem Evangelium," *ZTK* 15 (1905): 377-414.

9210. Johannes Ording, "Gammel og moderne kristendom-sopfatning," *NTT* 7 (1906): 97-119.

9211. Dr. Stange, "Die sittliche Bedeutung des Glaubens an die Person Jesu Christi," *NKZ* 17 (1906): 657-95.

9212. George D. Castor, "The Moral Paradox of Jesus," *BW* 40 (1912): 9-16

9213. Jacob Mann, "Oaths and Vows in the Synoptic Gospels," *AJT* 21 (1917): 260-74.

9214. W. Bornhausen, "Der Sinn des Lebens und der Glaube an Jesus Christus. Ein Kriegsbekenntnis zu W. Hermanns Religion," *ZTK* N.F. 1 (1920): 1-13.

9215. Hans Ording, "Estetikk og kristendom," *NTT* 25 (1924): 82-102.

9216. Morton S. Enslin, "The Essential Principles of Christian Morality as Gathered from the New Testament," *CQ* 6 (1928): 280-97.

9217. E. Mersch, "La morale et le Christ total," *NRT* 68 (1946): 633-47.

9218. Mary E. Clarkson, "The Ethics of the Fourth Gospel," *ATR* 31 (1949): 112-15.

9219. W. Manson, "The Norm of the Christian Life in the Synoptic Gospels," *SJT* 3 (1950): 33-42.

9220. Robert Koch, "Die Wertung des Besitzes im Lukas-evangelium," *B* 38 (1957): 151-69.

9221. Everett Tilson, "The Gospels and Christian Ethics," *JBR* 28 (1960): 423-31.

See also number 419, 3513, 9457.

9221.1   Klaus Berger, "Zu den sogenannten Sätzen heiligen Rechts," *NTSt* 17 (1970-1971): 10-40.

9221.2   G. Stecker, "Ziele und Ergebnisse einer Neutestamentlichen Ethik," *NTSt* 25 (1978): 1-15.

9221.3   H.-W. Bartsch, "Traditionsgeschichtliches zur 'goldenen Regel' und zum Aposteldekret," *ZNW* 75 (1984): 128-32.

9221.4   Mary Ann Beavis, " 'Expecting Nothing in Return': Luke's Picture of the Marginalized," *Interp* 48 (1994): 357-68.

b. *The Ethical Teaching of Jesus*

9222.   F. F. Emerson, "The Teaching of Christ Concerning the Use of Money," *Exp* 3rd ser., 8 (1888): 100-12.

9223.   Jul. Döderlein, "Das Lernen des Jesusknaben," *NJDT* 1 (1892): 606-19

9224.   Ernest DeW. Burton, "The Ethical Teachings of Jesus in Relation to the Ethics of the Pharisees and of the Old Testament," *BW* 10 (1897): 198-208.

9225.   J. Henry Thayer, "The Ethical Method of Jesus," *JBL* 19 (1900): 146-65.

9226.   Lyman Abbott, "Are the Ethics of Jesus Practicable?" *BW* 17 (1901): 256-64.

9227.   Lyman Abbott, "Christ's Attitude toward Malicious Accusations," *BW* 17 (1901): 446.

9228.   R. Schoeller, "Jesu Religion eine Religion der Liebe, der Tat und der Wahrhaftigkeit, nicht des Glaubens," *STZ* 18 (1901): 107-27, 185-91.

9229.   Karl Bornhuäsen, "Die Ethik und der historische Jesus," *ZTK* 17 (1907): 215-21.

9230.   S. G. Dunn, "The Romantic Element in the Ethics of Christ," *HJ* 6 (1907-1908): 826-35.

9231.   A. Williams Anthony, "The Ethical Principles of Jesus," *BW* 34 (1909): 26-32.

9232.   William H. Ryder, "Jesus' Attitude Toward Church and State," *BW* 33 (1909): 296-304.

9233.   G. Wauchope Stewart, "The Place of Rewards in the

798   THEOLOGICAL STUDIES

Teaching of Christ," *Exp* 7th ser., 10 (1910): 97-111, 224-41.

9234.   J. W. Diggle, "The Duty of Self-love," *Exp* 8th ser., 2 (1911):
         553-62.

9235.   C. W. Emmet, "Is the Teaching of Jesus an Interimsethik?"
         Exp 8th ser., 4 (1912): 423-34 [No!].

9236.   Seminarlehrer Winkler in Oels, "Die sittlichen Ideale der
         Gegenwart und die Ethik Jesu," *NKZ* 23 (1912): 108-34.

9237.   Rush Thees, "The Religion that Jesus Lived," *BW* 39 (1912):
         368-74.

9238.   C. C. Arbuthnot, "Did Jesus Teach Christian Socialism?" *BW*
         41 (1913): 147-60.

9239.   Shailer Mathews, "The Message of Jesus to our Modern
         Life," *BW* 44 (1914): 225-28, 297-300, 367-72, 431-40; 45
         (1915): 56-64, 120-28, 185-92, 250-56, 316-24, 382-88.

9240.   J. M. Wilson, "Christ's Sanction as well as Condemnation of
         War," *HJ* 13 (1914-1915): 839-58.

9241.   Henry C. King, "The Problem of Suffering and Sin; III, Light
         from Christ," *BW* 45 (1915): 152-60.

9242.   Clyde W. Votaw, "The Ethical Teaching of Jesus," *BW* 46
         (1915): 249-57, 319-25, 389-97; 47 (1916): 54-62.

9243.   D. Plooij, "Jezus en de oorlog," *TS* 34 (1916): 113-29.

9244.   Samuel Dickey, "The Revolutionary Attitude of Jesus," *BW*
         50 (1917): 276-82.

9245.   Paul Fiebig, "Jesu Worte über die Feindesliebe, im
         Zusammenhang mit den wichtigsten rabbinischen Parallelen
         erläutert," *TSK* 91 (1918): 30-64.

9246.   Lester Reddin, "Is War Compatible with the Ethics of
         Jesus?" *CQ* 9 (1932): 172-84.

9247.   H. H. Horne, "Christ in Man-Making," *RE* 21 (1924): 41-47,
         146-60, 296-308.

9248.   Emil E. Fischer, "The Apocalyptic Background of Jesus'
         Ethical Teaching," *LCR* 44 (1925): 1-13.

9249.   H. Mick, "The Ethical Message of Jesus and the World of
         To-day," *CJRT* 3 (1926): 217-28.

9250.   J. Ellwood Welsh, "Christ and our Social Disorders," *RE* 24

(1927): 416-23.

9251. A. B. D. Alexander, "The Kingdom of God and the Ethic of Jesus," *ET* 40 (1928-1929): 73-77.

9252. E. F. Scott, "The Originality of Jesus' Ethical Teaching," *JBL* 48 (1929): 109-15.

9253. Otto Michel, "Der Lohngedanke in der Verkündigung Jesu," *ZST* 9 (1931-1932): 47-54.

9254. Burton S. Easton, "The Ethic of Jesus in the New Testament," *ATR* 14 (1932): 1-12.

9255. Ronald Symond, "Justice in the Teaching of Jesus," *HJ* 31 (1932-1933): 498-509.

9256. Martin Wagner, "Der Lohngedanke im Evangelium," *NKZ* 43 (1932): 106-12, 129-39.

9257. Shirley Jackson Case, "The Ethics of Jesus from Strauss to Barth," *JR* 15 (1935): 389-99.

9258. W. H. P. Hatch, "Jesus' Summary of the Law and the Achievement of the Moral Ideal According to St. Paul," *ATR* 18 (1936): 129-40.

9259. Hans Lauerer, "Jesu Stellung zu den menschlichen Gemeinschaften," *NKZ* (*Luthertum*): 48 (1937): 238-48.

9260. John W. Buckham, "The Ethical Supremacy of Jesus," *RL* 7 (1938): 368-73.

9261. Walter Gutbrod, "Jesus and the Law-Some Considerations," *Th* 39 (1939): 123-27.

9262. Horace T. Houf, "Jesus' Way in our Time," *RL* 8 (1939): 32-43.

9263. Gordon Poteat, "Can We Teach the Ethics of Jesus?" *CQ* 16 (1939): 81-96.

9264. Thomas Saunders, "The Ethic of Jesus and the Gospel of the Church," *CQ* 17 (1940): 262-70.

9265. S. MacLean Gilmour, "How Relevant is the Ethic of Jesus?" *JR* 21 (1941): 253-64.

9266. Frederick C. Grant, "Ethics and Eschatology in the Teaching of Jesus," *JR* 22 (1942): 359-70.

9267. Hillyer H. Straton, "Jesus, Exegesis, and War," *ATR* 26

(1944): 42-48.

9268.   Amos N. Wilder, "Equivalents of Natural Law in the Teaching of Jesus," *JR* 26 (1946): 125-35.

9269.   Johannes Herz, "Die sozial-ethische Gedankenwelt in Jesu Verkündigung," *TLZ* 73 (1948): 747-52.

9270.   Alfred M. Rehwinkel, "The Ethics of Jesus," *CTM* 19 (1948): 172-89.

9271.   Guy Martin Davis, "An Opinion Concerning the Pacifism of Jesus," *JBR* 17 (1949): 181-86.

9272.   Olof Linton, "I vad mån är Jesu etik eskatologiskt betingad?" *STK* 25 (1949): 1-11.

9273.   Lucetta Mowry, "Jesus and the Ethical Problem of Man," *JBR* 18 (1950): 160-65.

9274.   A. C. Fox, "The 'Ethic' of Jesus and his 'Theology'," *HJ* 51 (1952-1953): 378-84.

9275.   G. H. Boobyer, "Christian Pacifism and the Way of Jesus," *HJ* 55 (1956-1957): 350-62.

9276.   Claude Tresmontant, "Jésus et la morale des prophètes," *BVC* no. 21 (1958): 26-34.

9277.   Jean Mouroux, "La conscience du Christ et le temps," *RSR* 47 (1959): 321-44.

See also number 3967.

9277.1 Wallace M. Alston, "Christ and the Military Mind," *Interp* 30/1 (1976): 26-35.

9277.2 Victor P. Furnish, "War and Peace in the New Testament," *Interp* 38 (1984): 363-79.

9277.3 John R. Donahue, "The 'Parable' of the Sheep and the Goats: A Challenge to Christian Ethics," *ThSt* 47 (1986): 3-31.

9277.4 Walter Wink, "Beyond Just War and Pacificism: Jesus' Nonviolent Way," *RE* 89 (1992): 197-214.

c. *The Imitation of Christ; Discipleship*

9278.   C. Allmann, "Wirklich ein neues Stück der 'Imitatio Christi' des Thomas von Kempen?" *TSK* 16 (1843): 63-89.

9279.   Walter L. Hervey [et al.], "The Modern Imitation of Christ.

A Symposium," *BW* 24 (1904): 248-60.

9280. Shailer Mathews, "The Imitation of Jesus," *BW* 26 (1905): 455-58.

9281. Dr. Hunzinger, "Das Frömmigkeitsideal der Imitatio Christi," *NKZ* 17 (1906): 534-50.

9282. Carl Stuckert, *"Propter Christum,"* *ZTK* 16 (1906): 143-74.

9283. Edgar T. Selby, "The Imitation of Christ," *ET* 19 (1907-1908): 499-501.

9284. P. Lobstein, "Propter Christum (pour l'amour de Jesus Christ)," *RHPR* 2 (1922): 141-50.

9285. A. Ancel, "Christus ad propositum certamen trahens voluntates," *VD* 6 (1926): 6-15.

9286. A. Ancel, "Christus fortiter suaviterque attrahens corda," *VD* 6 (1926): 163-69.

9287. A. Runestam, "Die Nachfolge Jesu," *ZST* 6 (1928- 1929): 747-75.

9288. A. Lemaître, "L'imitation de Jésus Christ et notre devoir présent," *RHPR* 13 (1933): 488-507.

9289. Orville A. Petty, "Following a Pioneer," *CQ* 11 (1934): 80-86.

9290. A. T. Robertson, "Christ's Call for Preachers," *RE* 33 (1936): 251-59.

9291. Jules Lebreton, "La doctrine du renoncement dans le Nouveau Testament," *NRT* 65 (1938): 385-412.

9292. John C. Slemp, "The Essence of Christianity," *RE* 37 (1940): 37-44.

9293. N. A. Dahl, " 'Guds folk' som uttrykk for urkristendommens kirkebevissthet," *NTT* 42 (1941): 193-237.

9294. Andreas ab Alpe, "De imitatione Christi in Novo Testamento," *VD* 22 (1942): 57-63.

9295. Amos N. Wilder, "Christian Ethics and the Way of the Cross," *CQ* 19 (1942): 135-40

9296. Joseph Huby, "Les origines de l'imitation de Jésus-Christ,' nouveaux aperçus," *RSR* 31 (1943): 102-39; "Les origines de l'imitation de Jésus-Christ': de Gérard Groote à Thomas a

Kempis," 32 (1944): 211-44.

9297.	Nils Johansson, "Lärljungaskap och efterföjelse i Nya testamentet och i vår förkunnelse," *STK* 23 (1947): 205-26.

9298.	Fritz und Liselotte Kern, "Die Thomas-a-Kempis-Frage," *TZ* 5 (1949): 169-86.

9299.	Nemesio González Caminero, " 'Ejemplaridad' de la vida de Cristo en la vida cristiana," *EE* 24 (1950): 267-394.

9300.	John Purves, "My Disciple," *EQ* 22 (1950): 227-40.

9301.	Gustaf Wingren, "Was bedeutet die Nachfolge Christi in evangelischer Ethik?" *TLZ* 75 (1950): 386-92.

9302.	W. F. Lofthouse, "Imitatio Christi," *ET* 65 (1953-1954): 338-42.

9303.	V. Lindström, "La théologie de l'imitation de Jésus Christ chez Sören Kierkegaard," *RHPR* 25 (1955): 379-92.

9304.	John J. Vincent, "Discipleship and Synoptic Studies," *TZ* 16 (1960): 456-69.

9305.	Reinhard Deichgräber, "Gehorsam und Gehorchen in der Verkündigung Jesu," *ZNW* 52 (1961): 119-22.

9306.	Martin E. Lehmann, "Movement toward the Mind of Christ," *LQ* 13 (1961): 165-72.

	See also number 3573.

9306.1	Theo Aerts, "Suivre Jésus. Évolution d'un thème biblique dans les Évangiles synoptiques," *ETL* 42 (1966): 476-512.

9306.2	Ernest Best, "Discipleship in Mark: Mark 8:22-10:52," *SJT* 23/3 (1970): 323-37.

9306.3	David Daube, "Responsibilities of Master and Disciples in the Gospels," *NTSt* 19 (1972-1973): 1-15.

9306.4	Ernest Best, "The Role of the Disciples in Mark," *NTSt* 23 (1976-1977): 377-401.

9306.5	Heber F. Peacock, "Discipleship in the Gospel of Mark," *RE* 75 (1978): 555-64.

9306.6	Harry T. Fleddermann, "The Discipleship Discourse (Mark 9:33-50)," *CBQ* 43/1 (1981): 57-75.

9306.7	Ernst Kasemann, "The Gospel and the Pious," *ABR* 30 (1982): 1-9.

9306.8 Dennis M. Sweetland, "Discipleship and Persecution: A Study of Luke 12,1-12," *B* 65 (1984): 61-80.

9306.9 Demetrios Trakatellis, "*Akolouthei moi*: Follow Me (Mk 2:14): Discipleship and Priesthood," *GOTR* 30 (1985): 271-85.

9306.10 Urban C. von Wahlde, "Mark 9:33-50: Discipleship: The Authority That Serves," *BibZ* 29/1 (1985): 49-67.

9306.11 Robert J. Karris, "Women and Discipleship in Luke," *CBQ* 56 (1994): 1-20.

d. *The Law and the Gospel*

9307. F. W. Farrar, "The Antagonism between Christ and the Oral Law," *Exp* 1st ser., 5 (1877): 214-34.

9308. F. W. Farrar, "The Antagonism of Christ against Externalism," *Exp* 1st ser., 5 (1877): 436-51.

9309. H. Wace, "The Gospel as a Law of Liberty," *Exp* 2nd ser., 2 (1881): 346-56 [James 2:12].

9310. Lester Reddin, "Did Jesus Teach the Religion of Legalism?" *CQ* 1 (1924): 307-17.

9311. Fernaard Ménégoz, Maurice Goguel, Auguste Lecerf, André Jundt, A. Wautier d'Aygalliers, and Charles Hauter, "L'évangile et la loi," *RHPR* 17 (1937): 1-57.

9312. Pierre Benoit, "La loi et la croix d'après saint Paul," *RB* 47 (1938): 481-509.

9313. Karl Mittring, "Gesetz und Evangelium im Neuen Testament," *EvT* 5 (1938): 428-42.

9314. Robert M. Grant, "The Decalogue in Early Christianity," *HTR* 40 (1947): 1-18.

9315. George B. Caird, "The Mind of Christ-Christ's Attitude to Institutions," *ET* 62 (1950-1951): 259-62.

9316. Hans-Joachim Schoeps, "Jésus et la loi juive," *RHPR* 33 (1953): 1-20.

9317. C. L. Mitton, "The Law and the Gospel," *ET* 68 (1956-1957): 312-15.

9318. L. W. Spitz, "The Freedom we have in Christ," *CTM* 29

804 THEOLOGICAL STUDIES

(1958): 801-11.

9318.1 Gustaf Wingren, "Law and Gospel and Their Implications for Christian Life and Worship," *ST* 17 (1963): 77-89.

9318.2 Charles C. Ryrie, "End of the Law," *BS* 124 (1967): 239-47.

9318.3 C. E. Carlston, "The Things that Defile (Mark 7:14) and the Law in Matthew and Mark," *NTSt* 15/1 (1968-1969): 75-96.

9318.4 George Howard, "Christ the End of the Law: The Meaning of Romans 10:4ff," *JBL* 88 (1969): 331-37.

9318.5 Eduard Schweizer, "Observance of the Law and Charismatic Activity in Matthew," *NTSt* 16 (1970): 213-30.

9318.6 Edward H. Schroeder, "Law-Gospel Reductionism in the History of the Lutheran Church—Missouri Synod," *CTM* 43 (1972): 232-47.

9318.7 Kenneth J. Thomas, "Torah Citations in the Synoptics," *NTSt* 24 (1977): 85-96.

9318.8 Wilhelm H. Wuellner, "Toposforschung und Torahinterpretation bei Paulus und Jesus," *NTSt* 24 (1978): 463-83.

9318.9 Peter Stuhlmacher, "Jesu vollkommenes Gesetz der Freiheit: Zum Verständnis der Bergpredigt," *ZTK* 79 (1982): 283-322.

9318.10 Gerhard O. Forde, "Law and Gospel in Luther's Hermeneutic," *Interp* 37 (1983): 240-52.

9318.11 Otfried Hofius, "Das Gesetz des Mose und das Gesetz Christi," *ZTK* 80 (1983): 262-86.

9318.12 Brice L. Martin, "Matthew on Christ and the Law," *ThSt* 44 (1983): 53-70.

9318.13 J. D. G. Dunn, "Mark 2:1-3:6: A Bridge Between Jesus and Paul on the Question of the Law," *NTSt* 30/3 (1984): 395-415.

9318.14 W. J. Dumbrell, "Law and Grace: The Nature of the Contrast in John 1:17," *EQ* 58/1 (1986): 25-37.

9318.15 Mark A. Seifrid, "Jesus and the Law in Acts," *JSNT* 30 (1987): 39-57.

9318.16 Wayne G. Strickland, "Preunderstanding and Daniel Fuller's Law-Gospel Continuum," *BS* 144 (1987): 181-93.

9318.17   Ruth B. Edwards, "Charin anti Charitos (John 1:16): Grace and the Law in the Johannine Prologue," *JSNT* 32 (1988): 3-15.

9318.18   M. J. Molldrem, "A Hermeneutic of Pastoral Care and the Law/Gospel Paradigm Applied to the Divorce Texts of Scripture," *Interp* 45 (1991): 43-54.

9318.19   Mogens Müller, "The Gospel of St Matthew and the Mosaic Law—A Chapter of a Biblical Theology," *ST* 46 (1992): 109-20.

e. *Social Implications*

9319.   Adam Stump, "Christ and the Labor Movement," *LQ* 20 (1890): 435-45.

9320.   John S. Sewall, "The Social Ethics of Jesus," *BS* 52 (1895): 271-96.

9321.   Loren Foster Berry, "The Social Teachings of Jesus," *BS* 55 (1898): 717-29.

9322.   C. R. Henderson, "The Influence of Jesus on Social Institutions," *BW* 11 (1898): 167-76.

9323.   Harry P. Judson, "The Political Effects of the Teaching of Jesus," *BW* 11 (1898): 229-38.

9324.   Newell Dwight Hillis, "The Influence of Jesus Christ in Civilization," *BS* 56 (1899): 327-40.

9325.   James Stalker, "The Social Teaching of Jesus," *Exp* 6th ser., 3 (1901): 141-56.

9326.   D. Macfadyen, "Social Theories and the Teaching of Jesus," *ET* 19 (1907-1908): 112-13, 160-61, 220-25, 282-83, 328-29.

9327.   William Knight, "The Social Outlook in Matthew and Luke," *BS* 66 (1909): 193-216.

9328.   Paul Moore Strayer, "Jesus and Modern Civic Life," *BW* 36 (1910): 387-94.

9329.   Daniel Evans, "The Ethics of Jesus and the Modern Mind," *HTR* 4 (1911): 418-38.

9330.   T. E. Schmauk, "Tolstoi and the Teachings of Jesus," *LCR*

30 (1911): 25-44.

9331.   David Finley Bonner, "Christ and the Industrial Problem," *BS* 69 (1912): 492-512.

9332.   Clayton R. Bowen, "Jesus and the Social Revolution," *BW* 42 (1913): 26-29.

9333.   James A. Chamberlin, "The Social Atonement," *BW* 42 (1913): 67-75.

9334.   J. Leipoldt, "Jesus und die Armen," *NKZ* 28 (1917): 784-810.

9335.   Henry J. Cadbury, "The Social Translation of the Gospel," *HTR* 15 (1922): 1-14.

9336.   Samuel Zane Batten, "The Power of the Cross in Social Redemption," *RE* 19 (1922): 5-18.

9337.   Kristen Skjeseth, "De kristnes stilling i nutidens sociale kamp," *NTT* 23 (1922): 212-25.

9338.   J. R. Ackroyd, "The Person of Jesus in Relation to Social Problems; A Way of Approach," *RE* 20 (1923): 304-10.

9339.   W. W. Everts, "Modern Scientific Sociology and the Christ," *BS* 82 (1925): 274-75.

9340.   A. Klinkenberg, "De beteekenis van Lucas voor de Sociale Kwestie," *NTS* 8 (1925): 25-34.

9341.   W. T. McConnell, "The Social Teachings of our Lord," *BS* 84 (1927): 40-49.

9342.   John Baillie, "The Mind of Christ on Moral Problems of Today," *ET* 41 (1929-1930): 261-65.

9343.   E. A. Burroughs, "The Mind of Christ on Moral Problems of Today," *ET* 41 (1929-1930): 438-46.

9344.   George Hibbert Driver, "Does Jesus Meet the Social Need of Man?" *BS* 86 (1929): 213-17.

9345.   A. Herbert Gray, "The Mind of Christ on Moral Problems of Today," *ET* 41 (1929-1930): 391-96.

9346.   Peter Green, "The Mind of Christ on Moral Problems of Today," *ET* 41 (1929-1930): 213-17.

9347.   J. L. Paton, "The Mind of Christ on Moral Problems of Today," *ET* 41 (1929-1930): 491-94.

9348. F. J. Rae, "The Mind of Christ on Moral Problems of Today," *ET* 41 (1929-1930): 355-58.

9349. Herbert G. Wood, "The Mind of Christ on Moral Problems of Today," *ET* 41 (1929-1930): 186-89.

9350. Reinhold Niebuhr, "The Ethic of Jesus and the Social Problem," *RL* 1 (1932): 198-208.

9351. James D. Rankin, "The Social Program of Jesus," *BS* 89 (1932): 284-94.

9352. Rolvix Harlan, "Economics and the Mind of Christ," *CQ* 11 (1934): 408-17.

9353. Stanley S. Stuber, "The Sword of Christ," *CQ* 11 (1934): 341-50.

9354. E. J. Trueblood, "Social Elements in the Christian Religion," *RE* 31 (1934): 427-39.

9355. John C. Bennett, "The Relevance of the Ethic of Jesus for Modern Society," *RL* 4 (1935): 74-83.

9356. Louis M. Sweet, "The Relationship of Jesus to Civilization," *USR* 53 (1941-1942): 179-96.

9357. Frederick C. Grant, "The Gospels and Civilization," *RL* 12 (1943): 231-37.

9358. Holmes Rolston, "Ministry to Need; The Teachings of Jesus Concerning Stewardship of Possessions," *Interp* 8 (1954): 142-54

9359. Wolf-Dieter Marsch, "Christologische Begründung des Rechts?" *EvT* 17 (1957): 145-70, 193-218.

9360. Franz Lau, "Die Königsherrschaft Jesu Christi und die lutherische Zweireichelehre," *KD* 6 (1960): 306-26.

See also numbers 3920, 9249, 9267, 9271, 9275.

9360.1 Halvor Moxnes, "New Testament Ethics—Universal or Particular?: Reflections on the Use of Social Anthropology in New Testament Studies," *ST* 47 (1993): 153-68.

9360.2 Halvor Moxnes, "The Social Context of Luke's Community," *Interp* 48 (1994): 379-89.

f. *Marriage and Divorce*

9361.   F. C. Burkitt, "St. Mark and Divorce," *JTS* 5 (1903-1904): 628-30.

9362.   E. Lyttelton, "The Teaching of Christ about Divorce," *JTS* 5 (1903-1904): 621-28.

9363.   Eb. Nestle, "Christ's Teaching about Divorce," *ET* 15 (1903-1904): 45-46.

9364.   Charles F. Thwing, "The Teachings of Christ, and the Modern Family," *BS* 61 (1904): 1-46.

9365.   Ernest DeW. Burton, "The Biblical Teaching concerning Divorce: II. New Testament Teaching," *BW* 29 (1907): 191-200.

9366.   Willoughby C. Allen, "Christ's Teachine on Divorce," *ET* 22 (1910-1911): 507-509.

9367.   Randolph H. M'Kim, "Our Lord's Teaching on Marriage and Divorce," *BS* 67 (1910): 143-55.

9368.   J. MacRoy, "The Teaching of the New Testament on Divorce," *ITQ* 5 (1910): 80-95; 6 (1911): 74-91.

9369.   W. P. Paterson, "Divorce and the Law of Christ," *Exp* 7th ser., 10 (1910): 289-305.

9370.   Robert Law, "Christ's Teaching regarding Divorce," *ET* 23 (1911-1912): 83-86.

9371.   Shirley Jackson Case, "Divorce and Remarriage in the Teaching of Jesus," *BW* 45 (1915): 18-22.

9372.   J. P. Arendzen, "Ante-Nicene Interpretations of the Sayings on Divorce," *JTS* 20 (1919): 230-41.

9373.   D. S. Margoliouth, "Christ's Answer to the Question about Divorce," *ET* 39 (1927-1928): 273-75.

9374.   E. G. Selwyn, "Christ's Teaching on Marriage and Divorce: A Reply to Dr. Charles," *Th* 15 (1927): 88-101.

9375.   Karl Staab, "Zur Frage der Ehescheidungstexte im Matthäusevangelium," *ZKT* 67 (1943): 36-44.

9376.   John Murray, "Divorce," *WTJ* 9 (1946-1947): 31-46, 181-97; 10 (1947-1948): 1-22, 168-91; 11 (1948-1949): 105-22; 12 (1949-1950): 30-51.

9377. M. Brunec, "Tertio de clausulis divortii Mt. 5, 32 et 19, 9," *VD* 27 (1949): 3-16.

9378. Bo Reicke, "Neuzeitliche und neutestamentliche Auffassung von Liebe und Ehe," *NT* 1 (1956): 21-34.

9379. H. J. Richards, "Christ on Divorce," *Scr* 11 (1959): 22-32. See also numbers 3972 ff., 4493 ff.

9379.1 Joseph Moingt, "Le divorce 'pour motif d'impudicité'," *RSR* 56 (1968): 337-84.

9379.2 Richard N. Soulen, "Marriage and Divorce: A Problem in New Testament Interpretation," *Interp* 23/4 (1969): 439-50.

9379.3 Wilfrid J. Harrington, "Jesus' Attitude towards Divorce," *ITQ* 37 (1970): 199-209.

9379.4 D. O'Callaghan, "How Far Is Christian Marriage Indissoluble?" *ITQ* 40/2 (1973): 162-73.

9379.5 Pierre Nautin, "Divorce et remariage dans la tradition de l'église latine," *RSR* 62 (1974): 7-54.

9379.6 Joseph A. Fitzmyer, "The Matthean Divorce Texts and Some New Palestine Evidence," *ThSt* 37/2 (1976): 197-226.

9379.7 Bruce Vawter, "Divorce and the New Testament," *CBQ* 39 (1977): 528-42.

9379.8 James R. Mueller, "The Temple Scroll and the Gospel Divorce Texts," *RQu* 10 (1980): 247-56.

9379.9 Antonio Vargas-Machuca, "Divorcio e indisolubilidad del matrimonio en la Sagrada Escritura," *EB* 39 (1981): 19-61.

9379.10 M. J. Down, "The Sayings of Jesus about Marriage and Divorce," *ET* 95/11 (1983-1984): 332-34.

9379.11 Barbara Green, "Jesus' Teaching on Divorce in the Gospel of Mark," *JSNT* 38 (1990): 67-75.

9379.12 Michael W. Holmes, "The Text of the Matthean Divorce Passages: A Comment on the Appeal to Harmonization in Textual Decisions," *JBL* 109 (1991): 651-54.

9379.13 Dale C. Allison, "Divorce, Celibacy and Joseph," *JSNT* 49 (1993): 3-10.

9379.14 A. E. Harvey, "Marriage, Sex and the Bible," *Th* 96 (1993): 364-72.

9379.15   David C. Parker, "The Early Traditions of Jesus' Sayings on Divorce," *Th* 96 (1993): 372-83.

9379.16   T. Stramare, "Supplement au Dictionnaire de la Bible: e le clausole di Maneo sul divorzio," *Div* 39 (1995): 269-73.

10. Eschatology
a. *General Studies*

9380.   L. Thomas, "Le jour du Seigneur," *RTP* 20 (1887): 136-67, 245-63, 403-56, 523-38; 22 (1889): 370-98, 529-76; 23 (1890): 250-75, 375-93, 581-614; 24 (1891): 575-616; 25 (1892): 169-96, 279-91, 360-82, 454-79, 528-56; 26 (1893): 24-61, 135-72.

9381.   Smith B. Goodenow, "Theories of the Parousia, Resurrection, and Judgment," *BS* 48 (1891): 342-46.

9382.   T. W. Chambers, "ὁ κύριος ἐγγύς, Philip. iv. 5," *JBL* 6 (1886, part 2): 108-10.

9383.   R. A. Falconer, "The Future of the Kingdom," *Exp* 5th ser., 10 (1899): 339-50.

9384.   S. A. Fries, "Jesu Vorstellungen von der Auferstehung der Toten," *ZNW* 1 (1900): 291-307.

9385.   J. Hugh Beibitz, "The End of the Age," *ET* 13 (1901-1902): 443-50.

9386.   George B. Stevens, "Is there a Self-Consistent New Testament Eschatology?" *AJT* 6 (1902): 666-84.

9387.   F. G. Peabody, "New Testament Eschatology and Ethics," *HTR* 2 (1909): 50-57.

9388.   E. F. Scott, "The New Testament Idea of the Future Life: I. The Formative Influences," *BW* 38 (1911): 18-27.

9389.   Herbert Alden Youtz, "The Christian Doctrine of the Future Life," *BW* 40 (1912): 254-74.

9390.   Rudolf Bultmann, "Die Bedeutung der Eschatologie für die Religion des Neuen Testaments," *ZTK* 27 (1917): 76-87.

9391.   Frederick C. Grant, "The Permanent Value of the Primitive Christian Eschatology," *BW* 49 (1917): 157-68.

9392.   Anton Fridrichsen, "Urkristelig apokalyptik og nutidskristendom," *NTT* 19 (1918): 73-88.

9393. W. Caspari, "Messianisch und endheilszeitlich," *ZST* 1 (1923): 700-704.

9394. F. Traub, "Die christliche Lehre von den letzten Dingen," *ZTK* N.F. 6 (1925): 29-49, 91-120.

9395. Louis Berkhof, "Christ in the Light of Eschatology," *PTR* 25 (1927): 83-102.

9396. Robert Winkler, "Eschatologie und Mystik. Zur Auseinandersetzung mit Albert Schweitzer und Hans Emil Weber," *ZTK* N.F. 12 (1931): 147-63.

9397. Johannes Schneider, "Eschatologie und Mystik im Neuen Testament," *ZTK* N.F. 13 (1932): 111-29.

9398. Lyder Brun, "Apokalyptikk i urkristendommen," *NTT* 33 (1932): 47-78.

9399. Joh. Lindblom, "Gudsrikets drama. En bibelteologisk skiss," *STK* 9 (1933): 17-25.

9400. Pierre Charles, "Spes Christi (Exposé d'une doctrine)," *NRT* 61 (1934): 1009-21; 64 (1937): 1057-75.

9401. Folke Holmström, "Tre utkast till en eskatologisk totalsyn," *STK* 11 (1935): 142-66.

9402. Otto Michel, "Zur Lehre vom Todesschlaf," *ZNW* 35 (1936): 285-90.

9403. Harald Diem, "Das eschatologische Problem in der gegenwärtigen Theologie," *TR* N.F. 11 (1939): 228-47.

9404. F.-M. Braun, "Où en est l'eschatologie du Nouveau Testament?" *RB* 49 (1940): 33-54.

9405. H. V. Martin, "The Messianic Age," *ET* 52 (1940-1941): 270-75.

9406. G. R. Beasley-Murray, "The New Testament Doctrine of the End," *EQ* 16 (1944): 202-18

9407. Theron M. Chastain, "Eschatology and Ethics," *RE* 41 (1944): 236-49.

9408. W. A. Visser 't Hooft, "Jesus is Lord; The Kingship of Christ in the Bible," *TTod* 4 (1947): 177-89.

9409. Ernst Fuchs, "Christus das Ende der Geschichte," *EvT* 8

(1948-1949): 447-61.

9410.   Miguel Balaguer [sic], "La paz mesiánica prometida," *CB* 9 (1952): 262-66.

9411.   Georg Osnes, "Kristus midt på den frelseshistoriske linje (Melding av Oscar Cullmann: Christus und die Zeit, 1946)," *TTK* 23 (1952): 105-17.

9412.   C. K. Barrett, "New Testament Eschatology," *SJT* 6 (1953): 225-43, 287-303.

9413.   M. H. Franzmann, "Christ, the Hope of Glory," *CTM* 24 (1953): 881-901.

9414.   Paul S. Minear, "The Time of Hope in the New Testament," *SJT* 6 (1953): 337-61.

9415.   T. Torrance, "The Modern Eschatological Debate," *EQ* 25 (1953): 45-54, 94-106, 167-78, 224-32.

9416.   Otto A. Piper, "Christian Hope and History," *EQ* 26 (1954): 82-89, 154-66.

9417.   Edmund Schlink, "Christus-die Hoffnung für die Welt," *TLZ* 79 (1954): 705-14.

9418.   Rudolf Bultmann, "History and Eschatology in the New Testament," *NTSt* 1 (1954-1955): 5-16.

9419.   Michael Zalampis, "The Relation of Eschatology to the Son of Man and the Kingdom of God," *RE* 53 (1956): 326-31.

9420.   George E. Ladd, "Eschatology and the Unity of New Testament Theology," *ET* 68 (1956-1957): 268-73.

9421.   Donald Joseph Selby, "Changing Ideas in New Testament Eschatology," *HTR* 50 (1957): 21-36.

9422.   W. F. Albright, "Bultmann's History and Eschatology," *JBL* 77 (1958): 244-48.

9423.   George E. Ladd, "The Place of Apocalyptic in Biblical Religion," *EQ* 30 (1958): 75-85.

9424.   C. C. Goen, "The Modern Discussion of Eschatology," *RE* 57 (1960): 107-25.

See also number 2164.

9424.1   James P. Martin, "History and Eschatology in the Lazarus Narrative," *SJT* 17 (1964): 332-43.

9424.2   D. M. Roark, "The Great Eschatological Discourse," *NT* 7 (1964-1965): 123-27.

9424.3   Hugo Lattanzi, "Eschatologici Sermonis Domini Logica Interpretatio," *Div* 11/1 (1967): 71-92.

9424.4   H. G. Coiner, "Those 'Divorce and Remarriage' Passages," *CTM* 39/6 (1968): 367-84.

9424.5   Brian M. Nolan, "Some Observations on the Parousia and New Testament Eschatology," *ITQ* 36 (1969): 283-314.

9424.6   Willibald Grimm, "Eschatologischer Saul wider eschatologischen David," *NT* 15 (1973): 114-33.

9424.7   David R. Catchpole, "The Synoptic Divorce Material as a Traditio-Historical Problem," *BJRL* 57/1 (1974): 92-127.

9424.8   Sigfred Pedersen, "Die Proklamation Jesu als des eschatologischen Offenbarungstragers," *NT* 17 (1975): 241-64.

9424.9   Theodore G. Stylianopoulos, "Historical and Eschatological Aspects of the Life of the Church according to the New Testament," *GOTR* 22 (1977): 181-213.

9424.10   R. P. C. Hanson, "The Significance of the Doctrine of the Last Things for Christian Belief," *BJRL* 62 (1979): 115-31.

9424.11   Chris L. Mearns, "Parables, Secrecy and Eschatology in Mark's Gospel," *SJT* 44 (1991): 423-42.

9424.12   T. R. Hatina, "John 20.22 in Its Eschatological Context: Promise or Fulfillment?" *B* 74 (1993): 196-219.

9424.13   John J. Kilgallen, "The Purpose of Luke's Divorce Text," *B* 76 (1995): 229-38.

b. *Jesus' Eschatological Teachings*

9425.   Henry Cowles, "On the Teachings of Christ in Regard to his then Future Comings, and the Phraseology of the Apostles on this Subject," *BS* 28 (1871): 485-522.

9426.   Cephas Kent, "Christ's Words on the Duration of Future Punishment," *BS* 35 (1878): 290-308.

9427.   B. Pünjer, "Die Wiederkunftsreden Jesu," *ZWT* 21 (1878): 153-208.

9428.   D. C. Marquis, "Eschatology as Taught by our Lord," *LQ* 17 (1887): 88-102.

9429.   W. C. van Manen, "Het onderzoek naar Jezus' verwachting van de toekomst (E. Haupt, Die eschatologischen Aussagen Jesu)," *TT* 29 (1895): 250-57.

9430.   Henry Kingman, "The Apocalyptic Teaching of our Lord," *BW* 9 (1897): 167-78.

9431.   Rayner Winterbotham, "Our Lord's Vision of the End," *Exp* 6th ser., 2 (1900): 401-13.

9432.   E. Ménégoz, "À propos de l'eschatologie de Jésus; réponse à M. le doyen Bruston," *RTQR* 12 (1903): 344- 61.

9433.   Ludwig Köhler, "Sind die aus den drei ersten Evangelien zu erhebenden religiös-sittlichen Ideen Jesu durch den Glauben an die Nähe des Weltendes beeinflusst?" *STZ* 23 (1906): 77-93, 161-88, 257-93; 24 (1907): 71-82, 97-104, 162-69, 205-17, 262-84.

9434.   B. W. Bacon, "Jewish Eschatology and the Teaching of Jesus," *BW* 34 (1909): 15-25.

9435.   J. G. Tasker, "Dr. Paul Feine on the Apocalyptic Teaching of Jesus," *ET* 21 (1909-1910): 454-56.

9436.   R. M. Lithgow, "The Eschatology of the Parables," *ET* 22 (1910-1911): 469-74.

9437.   Ernst von Dobschütz, "The Eschatology of the Gospels," *Exp* 7th ser., 9 (1910): 97-113, 193-209, 333-47, 398-417.

9438.   Alfred Plummer, "The Witness of the Four Gospels to the Doctrine of a Future State," *ET* 22 (1910-1911): 54-61.

9439.   C. Bruston, "De l'eschatologie de Jésus Christ," *RTP* 44 (1911): 91-117.

9440.   Ernst von Dobschütz, "Zur Eschatologie der Evangelien," *TSK* 84 (1911): 1-20

9441.   Arthur Dakin, "The Idea underlying the Eschatological Discourses of our Lord," *ET* 23 (1911-1912): 86-88.

9442.   G. Margoliouth, "Christ and Eschatology," *Exp* 8th ser., 1 (1911): 399-407.

9443.   E. F. Scott, "The New Testament Idea of the Future Life; II.

The Future Life in the Teaching of Jesus," *BW* 38 (1911): 103-12.

9444. W. Sanday, "The Apocalyptic Element in the Gospels," *HJ* 10 (1911-1912): 83-109.

9445. H. Erskine Hill, "The Apocalyptic Element in our Lord's Teaching," *Exp* 8th ser., 4 (1912): 193-211.

9446. E. F. Scott, "The Significance of Jesus for Modern Religion in View of his Eschatological Teaching," *AJT* 18 (1914): 225-40.

9447. H. J. Toxopeüs, "Jezus in het licht der eschatologie," *TT* 48 (1914): 38-80.

9448. C. H. Parez, "The Eschatology of Christ," *ET* 27 (1915-1916): 238-39.

9449. J. Ridderbos, "Jezus' houding tegenover de nationale zijde van Israëls heilsverwachting," *GTT* 17 (1916-1917): 381-95, 423-47.

9450. Charles H. Dickinson, "The Significance of Jesus' Hope," *JR* 1 (1921): 47-65.

9451. E. F. Scott, "The Place of Apocalyptical Conceptions in the Mind of Jesus," *JBL* 41 (1922): 137-42.

9452. Douglas Edwards, "The Eschatology of Christ," *Th* 24 (1932): 70-87.

9453. Olga Levertoff, "Eschatological Teaching in the Gospels," *Th* 32 (1936): 339-42.

9454. C. C. McCown, "The Eschatology of Jesus Reconsidered," *JR* 16 (1936): 30-46.

9455. Amos N. Wilder, "Historical and Transcendental Elements in Jesus' View of the Future," *JBR* 5 (1937): 117-19.

9456. Marion J. Bradshaw, "Jesus and the Coming Kingdom," *JR* 18 (1938): 422-36.

9457. Asmund Stubdal, "Forholdet mellem eskatologi og etikk i Jesu forkynnelse," *NTT* 40 (1939): 30-58, 93-111, 182-204.

9458. Rudolf Bultmann, "Zur eschatologischen Verkündigung Jesu," *TLZ* 72 (1947): 271-74.

9459. J. N. Geldenhuys, "Our Lord's Teaching Concerning the

End," *EQ* 19 (1947): 161-77.

9460. Amos N. Wilder, "The Eschatology of Jesus in Recent Criticism and Interpretation," *JR* 32 (1948): 177-85.

See also numbers 892, 4616ff., 4647, 9235, 9248, 9266, 9272, *10025, 10046, 10084.*

9460.1 John Bligh, "Eschatology and Social Doctrine," *HeyJ* 3 (1962): 262-67.

9460.2 G. R. Beasley-Murray, "New Testament Apocalyptic: A Christological Eschatology," *RE* 72 (1975): 317-30.

9460.3 C. E. B. Cranfield, "Thoughts on New Testament Eschatology," *SJT* 35 (1982): 497-512.

9460.4 Barry S. Crawford, "Near Expectation in the Sayings of Jesus," *JBL* 101/2 (1982): 225-44.

9460.5 Paul J. Achtemeier, "An Apocalyptic Shift in Early Christian Tradition: Reflections on Some Canonical Evidence," *CBQ* 45 (1983): 231-48.

9460.6 Gerhard Lohfink, "Die Not der Exegese mit der Reich-Gottes-Verkündigung Jesu," *TQ* 168 (1988): 1-15.

c. *Synoptic Eschatology*

9461. Willard Learoyd Sperry, "The Eschatology of the Synoptic Gospels: Its Fidelity to Religious Experience," *HTR* 5 (1912): 385-95.

9462. G. Weller, "Die Eschatologie ein unentbehrliches Stück des Evangeliums," *NKZ* 34 (1923): 15-49.

9463. T. Nicklin, "Eschatology in the Synoptists," *ET* 40 (1928-1929): 475-76.

9464. Paul Schubert, "The Synoptic Gospels and Eschatology," *JBR* 14 (1946): 151-57.

9465. A. Jones, "The Eschatology of the Synoptic Gospels," *Scr* 4 (1950): 222-30.

9466. Gerhard Friedrich, "Beobachtungen zur messianischen Hohepriestererwartung in den Synoptikern," *ZTK* N.F. 53 (1956): 265-311.

9467. Hans Conzelmann, "Gegenwart und Zukunft in der synoptischen Tradition," *ZTK* N.F. 54 (1957): 277-96.

9468.   Donald T. Rowlingson, "Prophetic and Apocalyptic Eschatology in the Synoptic Gospels," *RL* 30 (1961): 105-11. See also numbers 3190, 5140ff., 7139, 7184.

9468.1 Basil S. Brown, "The Great Apostasy in the Teaching of Jesus," *ABR* 10 (1962): 14-20.

9468.2 G. R. Beasley-Murray, "The Parousia in Mark," *RE* 75 (1978): 565-81.

9468.3 Meredith G. Kline, "Primal Parousia," *WTJ* 40 (1978): 245-80.

9468.4 Morna D. Hooker, "Trial and Tribulation in Mark 13," *BJRL* 65 (1982): 78-99.

9468.5 Richard J. Bauckham, "Synoptic Parousia Parables Again," *NTSt* 29 (1983): 129-34.

9468.6 B. Kinman, "Lucan Eschatology and the Missing Fig Tree," *JBL* 113 (1994): 669-78.

d. *Johannine Eschatology*

9469.   E. F. Scott, "The New Testament Idea of the Future Life: IV. The Future Life in the Johannine Teaching," *BW* 38 (1911): 321-30.

9470.   Edward Grubb, "The Eschatology of the Fourth Gospel," *ET* 28 (1916 1917): 308-11.

9471.   Gustav Stählin, "Zum Problem der johanneischen Eschatologie," *ZNW* 33 (1934): 225-59.

9472.   H. Ludin Jansen, "Til spørsmålet om Johanneisk eschatologi," *NTT* 41 (1940): 65 79.

9473.   G. R. Beasley-Murray, "The Eschatology of the Fourth Gospel," *EQ* 18 (1946): 97-108.

9474.   C. K. Barrett, "Unsolved New Testament Problems—The Place of Eschatology in the Fourth Gospel," *ET* 59 (1947-1948): 302-305.

9475.   M.-E. Boismard, "L'évolution du thème eschatologique dans les traditions johanniques," *RB* 68 (1961): 507-24.

See also number 3190.

9475.1 Robert A. Guelich, "The Matthean Beatitudes: 'Entrance-Requirements' or Eschatological Blessings," *JBL* 95 (1976): 415-34.

9475.2 David L. Mealand, "Christology of the Fourth Gospel," *SJT* 31 (1978): 449-67.

9475.3 Margaret Pamment, "Eschatology and the Fourth Gospel," *JSNT* 15 (1982): 81-85.

9475.4 Chaim Milikowsky, "Which Gehenna: Retribution and Eschatology in the Synoptic Gospels and in Early Jewish Texts," *NTSt* 34/2 (1988): 238-49.

e. *The Parousia*

9476. C. A. Kober, "La parousie dans les synoptiques," *RT* 5 (1867): 25-42.

9477. J. A. Beet, "New Testament Teaching on the Second Coming of Christ," *Exp* 4th ser., 9 (1894): 190-99, 287-99.

9478. Edgar M. Wilson, "The Second Coming in the Discourse of the Last Things," *PTR* 26 (1928): 65-79.

9479. Karl Kundsin, "Die Wiederkunft Jesu in den Abschiedsreden des Johannesevangeliums," *ZNW* 33 (1934): 210-15.

9480. U. Holzmeister, "Num Parusiam docente S. Petro (Act. 3, 19s. 2 Petr. 3, 12) accelerare possimus," *VD* 18 (1938): 299-307.

9481. S. Barton Babbage, "The Parousia as Revealed in the Gospels," *EQ* 12 (1940): 60-75.

9482. W. Powell, "Comments on 'The Second Advent' by Dr. T. F. Glasson," *ET* 58 (1946-1947): 109-10.

9483. Vincent Taylor, "The 'Son of Man' Sayings Relating to the Parousia," *ET* 58 (1946-1947): 12-15.

9484. André Feuillet, "Le triomphe eschatologique de Jésus d'après quelques textes isolés des évangiles," *NRT* 71 (1949): 701-22, 806-28.

9485. W. D. Chamberlain, "Till the Son of Man be Come," *Interp.* 7 (1953): 3-13.

9486. H.-W. Bartsch, "Zum Problem der Parusieverzögerung bei den Synoptikern," *EvT* 19 (1959): 116-31.

9487. J. Gnilka, "Parusieverzögerung und Naherwartung in den synoptischen Evangelien und in der Apostelgeschichte," *C* 13 (1959): 277-90.

9488. H. P. Owen, "The Parousia of Christ in the Synoptic Gospels," *SJT* 12 (1959): 171-92.

See also numbers 7063, *10048*.

9488.1 J. G. Davies, "Genesis of Belief in an Imminent Parousia," *JTS* NS 14 (1963): 104-107.

9488.2 Heinrich Greeven, "Kirche und Parusie Christi," *KD* 10 (1964): 113-35.

9488.3 Stephen S. Smalley, "Delay of the Parousia," *JBL* 83 (1964): 41-54.

9488.4 Stephen S. Smalley, "Theatre of Parousia," *SJT* 17 (1964): 407-13.

9488.5 J. K. Howard, "Our Lord's Teaching Concerning His Parousia: A Study in the Gospel of Mark," *EQ* 38 (1966): 52-58, 68-75, 150-57.

9488.6 Richard H. Hiers, "Problem of the Delay of the Parousia in Luke-Acts," *NTSt* 20 (1974): 145-55.

9488.7 Christian Dietzfelbinger, "Die eschatologische Freude der Gemeinde in der Angst der Welt, Joh 16,16-33," *EvT* 40 (1980): 420-36.

9488.8 David G. Dunbar, "The Delay of the Parousia in Hippolytus," *VCh* 37 (1983): 313-27.

9488.9 H. F. G. Swanston, "Liturgy as Paradise and as Parousia," *SJT* 36 (1983): 505-19.

9488.10 T. F. Glasson, "Theophany and Parousia," *NTSt* 34 (1988): 259-70.

9488.11 John Painter, "Theology, Eschatology and the Prologue of John," *SJT* 46 (1993): 27-42.

f. *Realized Eschatology*

9489. Clarence T. Craig, "Realized Eschatology," *JBL* 56 (1937) 17-26.

9490.   Kenneth W. Clark, "Realized Eschatology," *JBL* 59 (1940): 367-83.

9491.   J. A. McEvoy, "Realized Eschatology and the Kingdom Parables," *CBQ* 9 (1947): 329-57.

9492.   Rudolf Bultmann, "Weisung und Erfüllung," *ZTK* N.F. 47 (1950): 360-83.

9493.   A. W. Argyle, "Does 'Realized Eschatology' Make Sense?" *HJ* 51 (1952-1953): 385-87.

9494.   Miguel Balagué, "La paz mesiánica realizada," *CB* 9 (1952): 300-304.

9495.   Walther Zimmerli, "Verheissung und Erfüllung," *EvT* 12 (1952-1953): 34-59.

9496.   Herbert G. Wood, "Important and Influential Books- Albert Schweitzer and Eschatology," *ET* 65 (1953-1954): 206-209.

9497.   Hermann Schuster, "Die konsequente Eschatologie in der Interpretation des Neuen Testaments, kritisch betrachtet," *ZNW* 47 (1956): 1-25.

9498.   W. G. Kümmel, "Futurische und präsentische Eschatologie im ältesten Urchristentum," *NTSt* 5 (1958-1959): 113-56.

9499.   Julius Richter, "Die 'konsequente Eschatologie' im Feuer der Kritik," *ZRGG* 12 (1960): 147-66.

         See also numbers 436, 440.

9499.1   Eugene E. Wolfzorn, "Realized Eschatology: An Exposition of Charles H. Dodd's Thesis," *ETL* 38 (1962): 44-70.

9499.2   Robert F. Berkey, "Ellixein, Phthanein and Realized Eschatology," JBL 82 (1963): 177-87.

9499.3   W. G. Kümmel, "Futuristic and Realized Eschatology in the Earliest Stages of Christianity," *JR* 43 (1963): 303-14.

9499.4   William L. Lane, "1 Timothy 4:1-3: An Early Instance of Over-Realized Eschatology?" *NTSt* 11 (1965): 164-67.

9499.5   John F. Walvoord, "Realized Eschatology," *BS* 127 (1970): 313-23.

9499.6   Robert F. Berkey, "Realized Eschatology and the Post-Bultmannians," *ET* 84 (1972): 72-77.

9499.7   Anthony C. Thiselton, "Realized Eschatology at Corinth,"

NTSt 24 (1978): 510-26.

9499.8   Georg Strecker, "Charles Harold Dodd: Person und Werk," *KD* 26 (1980): 50-58.

g. *The Kingdom of God*

9500.   M. Valentine, "The Nature and Relations of Christ's Kingdom," *LQ* 19 (1889): 69-83.

9501.   F.-C.-J. van Goens, "La doctrine du royaume de Dieu dans le Nouveau Testament," *RTP* 25 (1892): 340-59, 434-53.

9502.   J. H. Bernard, James Orr, Caleb Scott, and Alexander Stewart, "The Kingdom of God," *ET* 4 (1892-1893): 464-67.

9503.   Erich Haupt, "The Kingdom of God," *ET* 4 (1892-1893): 248-51.

9504.   A. Kurrikoff, "Die Lehre des Neuen Testamentes vom Reiche Gottes," *NKZ* 4 (1893): 419-40, 487-509.

9505.   H. H. Wendt, "The Kingdom of God in the Teaching of Christ," *ET* 5 (1893-1894): 20-23, 69-72, 111-15, 217-20, 470-73.

9506.   M. Dods, "The Righteousness of Christ's Kingdom," Exp 4th ser., 9 (1894): 70-79, 161-73, 321-30; 10 (1894): 20-32.

9507.   Thomas J. Ramsdell, "The Kingdom of Heaven in the Gospel of Matthew," *BW* 4 (1894): 124-33.

9508.   A. C. Zenos, "Jesus' Idea of the Kingdom of God," *BW* 3 (1894): 35-44.

9509.   George B. Stevens, "The Teaching of Jesus; VI. The Kingdom of God," *BW* 5 (1895): 431-37.

9510.   J. Watson, "The Kingdom of God," *Exp* 5th ser., 2 (1895): 41-53.

9511.   Edward Mortimer Chapman, "The Idea of the Kingdom of God: Its Influence upon the History of the English- Speaking Peoples in the Present Century," *BS* 54 (1897): 525-41.

9512.   A. Klöpper, "Das gegenwärtige und zukünftige Gottesreich in der Lehre Jesu bei den Synoptikern," *ZWT* 40 (1897): 355-410.

9513.   A. Hering, "Die Idee Jesu vom Reiche Gottes und ihre

Bedeutung für die Gegenwart," *ZTK* 9 (1899): 472-513.

9514.   W. L. Walker, "The Gospel of the Kingdom of God," *ET* 12 (1900-1901): 85-86.

9515.   [W.] Bousset, "Das Reich Gottes in der Predigt Jesu," *TR* 5 (1902): 397-407, 437-49.

9516.   J.-E. Neel, "Les conceptions actuelles du royaume de Dieu," *RTQR* 11 (1903): 141-72, 229-63.

9517.   F. Traub, "Die Gegenwart des Gottesreichs in den Parabeln vom Senfkorn und Sauerteig, von der selbstwachsenden Saat, dem Unkraut und dem Fischnetz," *ZTK* 15 (1905): 58-75.

9518.   Thorleif Homme, "Jesu fornedrelse eller hans forhold til det guddommelige i hans jordliv," *NTT* 88 (1907): 165-87.

9519.   W. L. Walker, "Christ's Preaching of the Kingdom," *Exp* 7th ser., 3 (1907): 21-37.

9520.   Percy Gardner, "The Present and the Future Kingdom in the Gospels," *ET* 21 (1909-1910): 535-38.

9521.   Shailer Mathews, "The Kingdom of God," *BW* 35 (1910): 420-27.

9522.   A. G. Hogg, "Christ's Message of the Kingdom," *ET* 23 (1911-1912): 466.

9523.   Eugene Stock, "Professor Hogg on the Kingdom of God," *ET* 23 (1911-1912): 394-99.

9524.   J. Warschauer, "The Mystery of the Kingdom," *ET* 27 (1915-1916): 364-68.

9525.   William H. Bates, "Kingdom-Church: A Biblical Study," *BS* 73 (1916): 593-608.

9526.   Frederick C. Grant, "The Gospel of the Kingdom," *BW* 50 (1917): 129-91

9527.   David Foster Estes, "Christ's First Proclamation of the Kingdom," *RE* 16 (1919): 33-52.

9528.   F. J. Foakes-Jackson, "The Kingdom of God in Acts, and the 'City of God'," *HTR* 12 (1919): 193-200.

9529.   Fordyce H. Argo, "The Second Coming and the Kingdom," *BW* 54 (1920): 156-68.

9530. K. Goetz, "Der Reichgottesgedanke Jesu und sein Unterschied von anderen Sozial- und Staatsidealen," *STZ* 37 (1920): 67-74, 123-28.

9531. Arthur W. Wotherspoon, "A Note on the Kingdom of God," *ET* 32 (1920-1921): 469-73.

9532. E. Albert Cook, "The Kingdom of God as a Democratic Ideal," *JR* 1 (1921): 626-40.

9533. John McNicol, "The Kingdom of Heaven in the Mind of Jesus," *BR* 11 (1926): 169-87.

9534. C. H. Dodd, "Das innerweltliche Reich Gottes in der Verkündigung Jesu," *TB* 6 (1927): 120-22.

9535 K. L. Schmidt, "Das überweltliche Reich Gottes in der Verkündigung Jesu," *TB* 6 (1927): 118-20.

9536. W. J. Sparrow Simpson, "Our Lord's Teaching on the Kingdom of Heaven," *ET* 39 (1927-1928): 214-16.

9537. Hans Windisch, "Die Sprüche vom Eingehen in das Reich Gottes," *ZNW* 27 (1928): 163-92.

9538. L. von Sybel, "Die βασιλεία τοῦ θεοῦ im synoptischen Evangelium," *TSK* 103 (1931): 85-94

9539. D. A. Frøvig, "Jesu ord i synoptikerne om rikdommen," *TTK* 3 (1932): 113-29.

9540. Ralph E. Knudsen, "The Kingdom of God," *RE* 29 (1932): 443-58.

9541. R. Newton Flew, "Jesus and the Kingdom of God," *ET* 46 (1934-1935): 214-18.

9542. J. Grange Radford, "The Kingdom of God," *ET* 46 (1934-1935): 427-28.

9543. Lyder Brun, "Guds rike og Menneskesønnen," *NTT* 38 (1937): 105-25.

9544. Rudolf Bultmann, "Reich Gottes und Menschensohn," *TR* 9 (1937): 1-35.

9545. Rudolf Hermann, "Das christliche 'Selbstverständnis' und der Glaube an Gott in Christo-unter besonderer Berucksichtigung der 'Schlüssel des Himmelreiches'," *ZST* 14 (1937): 681-708.

9546.   J. Héring, "Le royaume de Dieu et sa venue; étude sur l'expérience de Jésus et de saint Paul," *RHPR* 17 (1937): 399-400.

9547.   Herbert Haslam, "Jesus and Reality," *CQ* 14 (1937): 200-206.

9548.   Floyd V. Filson, "The Kingdom: Present and Future," *JBR* 7 (1939): 59-63

9549.   Joh. Lindblom, "The Idea of the Kingdom of God," *ET* 51 (1939-1940): 91-96.

9550.   Patrick Cummins, "The Kingdom of Heaven in the Gospel of St. Matthew," *CBQ* 3 (1941): 43-49.

9551.   F. F. Bruse, "The Kingdom of God: A Biblical Survey," *EQ* 15 (1943) 263-68.

9552.   H. N. Ridderbos, "Verbond en koninkrijk Gods," *GTT* 44 (1943): 97-121.

9553.   Charles E. Schofield, "The Significance of the 'Kingdom of God' for Current Christianity," *RL* 12 (1943): 256-65.

9554.   J. A. Oñate, "El 'Reino de Dios' en la Sagrada Escritura," *EB* 3 (1944): 343-82.

9555.   Ernst Percy, "Guds Rike och Kyrkan i Nya testamentet," *STK* 21 (1944): 1-18.

9556.   William S. Hill, "Jesus' Teaching Concerning the Kingdom," *RL* 16 (1947): 373-80.

9557.   Otto A. Piper, "The Mystery of the Kingdom of God; Critical Scholarship and Christian Doctrine," *Interp* 1 (1947): 183-200.

9558.   Ivor Buse, "Spatial Imagery in New Testament Teaching about the Kingdom of God," *ET* 60 (1948-1949): 82.

9559.   H. Clavier, "The Kingdom of God: Its Coming and Man's Entry in it," *ET* 60 (1948-1949): 241-44.

9560.   Robert M. Grant, "The Coming of the Kingdom," *JBL* 67 (1948): 297-303.

9561.   Santiago Luque, "El Reino de Dios en las Parábolas," *CB* 5 (1948): 44-46, 200-202; 6 (1949): 20-23, 51-55.

9562.   Edward A. McDowell, "The Problem of the Kingdom," *RE*

45 (1948): 3-17.

9563. W. Powell, "Spatial Imagery in New Testament Teaching about the Kingdom of God," *ET* 60 (1948-1949): 194.

9564. W. O. Carver, "Jesus' Problem with the Kingdom of God," *RE* 46 (1949): 299-306.

9565. E. Quinn, "The Kingdom of God and the Church in the Synoptic Gospels," *Scr* 4 (1950): 237-44.

9566. Gilbert Cope, "The Kingdom When and Where?" *CQ* 28 (1951): 232-39.

9567. Juan Prado, "La Paz del Reino Mesiánico," *CB* 8 (1951): 17-20.

9568. C. F. Evans, "Otto's 'The Kingdom of God and the Son of Man'," *ET* 65 (1953 1954): 303-306.

9569. S. MacLean Gilmour, "The Kingdom and the Church," *Interp* 7 (1953): 26-33.

9570. W. Arndt, "The Kingdom of God and John," *CTM* 25 (1954): 144-46.

9571. P. van Stempvoort, "De betekenis van λέγων τὰ περὶ τῆς βασιλείας τοῦ θεοῦ Hand. 1, 3," *NedTT* 9 (1954-1955): 349-55.

9572. David M. Stanley, "Kingdom to Church," *ThSt* 16 (1955): 1-29.

9573. T. Torrance, "Kingdom and Church in the Thought of Martin Butzer," *JEH* 6 (1955): 48-59.

9574. Peter H. Igarashi, "The Mystery of the Kingdom," *JBR* 24 (1956): 83-89.

9575. H. Roux, "L'évangile du royaume," *RHPR* 27 (1957): 116 [Matt.].

9576. Sverre Aalen, "Innbydelsen til Guds rike, belyst at fra lingnelsen om kongessønnens bryllup," *TTK* 29 (1958): 119-26.

9577. Wilhelm Dantine, "Regnum Christi-Gubernatio Dei. Dogmatische Überlegungen zum Begriff der 'Herrschaft'," *TZ* 15 (1959): 195-208.

9578. M.-F. Lacan, "Conversion et royaume dans les évangiles synoptiques," *LumV* no. 47 (1960): 25-47.

9579.   Edward A. McDowell, "Jesus' Concept of the Kingdom of God," *RE* 57 (1960): 138-52.

9580.   John K. S. Reid, "A. S. Hogg's 'Christ's Message of the Kingdom'," *ET* 72 (1960-1961): 300-302.

See also numbers 1016, 4975ff., 9108 f., 9111, 9251, 9419, 9456, 9881.

9580.1   Robert F. Berkey, "ἐγγίζειν, φθάνειν, and Realized Eschatology," *JBL* 82 (1963): 177-87.

9580.2   Richard H. Hiers, "Satan, Demons, and the Kingdom of God," *SJT* 27 (1974): 35-47.

9580.3   Warren W. Glover, " 'The Kingdom of God' in Luke," *BTr* 29 (1978): 231-37.

9580.4   William S. Johnson, "The Reign of God in Theological Perspective," *Interp* 47 (1993): 127-39.

9580.5   R. D. Witherup, "Conversion in Mark's Gospel," *BTr* 31 (1993): 166-70.

9580.6   M. R. Saucy, "The Kingdom-of-God Sayings in Matthew," *BS* 151 (1994): 175-97.

9580.7   M. Wolter, " 'Reich Gottes' bei Lukas," *NTSt* 41 (1995): 541-63.

11. The Use of the Old Testament in the Gospels

a. *General Studies*

9581.   Charles A. Aiken, "The Citations of the Old Testament in the New," *BS* 11 (1854): 568-616.

9582.   W. Milligan, "Idea of Old Testament Priesthood fulfilled in the New Testament," *Exp* 3rd ser., 8 (1888): 161-80.

9583.   H. W. Horwill, "Christ and the Old Testament," *ET* 11 (1899-1900): 477.

9584.   W. C. Allen, "The Old Testament Quotations in St. Matthew and St. Mark," *ET* 12 (1900-1901): 187-89, 281- 85.

9585.   Rayner Winterbotham, "Nazareth and Bethlehem in Prophecy," *Exp* 6th ser., 3 (1901): 14-26.

9586.   Henry T. Sell, "Christ in the Old Testament; or, The

Development of the Messianic Ideas," *BS* 60 (1903): 737-49.

9587. John J. Young, "Christ and the Old Testament," *LQ* 33 (1903): 554-65.

9588. S. Michelet, "Om Det gamle testaments betydning for os," *NTT* 7 (1906): 185-240.

9589. Milton S. Terry, "The Old Testament and the Christ," *AJT* 10 (1906): 233-50.

9590. Lyder Brun, "Jesu forhold til Moseloven," *NTT* 8 (1907): 334-62.

9591. Shirley Jackson Case, "The New Testament Writers' Interpretation of the Old Testament," *BW* 38 (1911): 92-102.

9592. Ed. König, "The Consummation of the Old Testament in Jesus Christ," *Exp* 8th ser., 4 (1912): 1-19, 97-119.

9593. T. Haering, "Das Alte Testament im Neuen," *ZNW* 17 (1916): 213-27.

9594. E. St.G. Baldwin, "Gethsemane: The Fulfillment of Prophecy," *BS* 77 (1920): 429-36.

9595. H. O. Cavalier, "The Gospel of the Son of Man," *Th* 60 (123): 218-21.

9596. Charles C. Torrey, "The Influence of Second Isaiah in the Gospels and Acts," *JBL* 48 (1929): 24-36.

9597. Otto Proksch, "Christus im Alten Testament," *NKZ* 44 (1933): 57-83.

9598. Gerhard von Rad, "Das Christuszeugnis des Alten Testaments. Eine Auseinandersetzung mit Wilhelm Vischers gleichnamigem Buch," *TB* 14 (1935): 249-54.

9599. Fritz Feldges, "Die Frage des alttestamentlichen Christuszeugnisses," *TB* 15 (1936): 25-30.

9600. Hermann Strathmann, "Zum Ringen um das christliche Verständnis des Alten Testaments," *TB* 15 (1936): 257-60.

9601. Karl Elliger, "Das Christuszeugnis des Alten Testaments," *ZST* 14 (1937): 377-92.

9602. Lionel E. H. Stephens-Hodge, "Christ and the Old Testament," *EQ* 10 (1938): 367-73.

9603. Daniel G. Finestone, "The Vicarious Death of Christ in the

Light of the Old Testament," *BS* 97 (1940): 34-62.

9604.   Louis M. Sweet, "The Relationship of Jesus to the Old Testament," *USR* 53 (1941-1942): 109-24.

9605.   N. Warner, "De openbaring van den Christus onder het Oude Verbond volgens den Brief aan de Hebreën," *GTT* 42 (1941): 93-87; "II. Volgens de brieven van Paulus," 43 (1942): 3-24.

9606.   Sherman E. Johnson, "The Biblical Quotations in Matthew," *HTR* 36 (1943): 135-54.

9607.   John Macleod, "The Witness of Moses to Christ," *EQ* 17 (1945): 5-12.

9608.   John F. Walvoord, "Christological Typology," *BS* 105 (1948): 286-96, 404-17; 106 (1949): 27-33.

9609.   Martin Schmidt, "Kleine Nachlese zu Isaaks Opferung," *TZ* 8 (1952): 465-71.

9610.   Ludwig Koehler, "Christus im Alten und im Neuen Testament," *TZ* 9 (1953): 241-59.

9611.   Markus Barth, "The Christ in Israel's History," *TTod* 11 (1954): 342-53.

9612.   Albert Descamps, "Moïse dans les évangiles et dans la tradition apostolique," *CS* 8 (1954): 171-87 (= 289-305).

9613.   Hermann Diem, "Jesus, der Christus des Alten Testamentes," *EvT* 14 (1954): 437-48.

9614.   E. L. Allen, "Jesus and Moses in the New Testament," *ET* 67 (1955-1956): 104-106.

9615.   J. G. S. S. Thomson, "Christ and the Old Testament," *ET* 67 (1955-1956): 18-20.

9616.   Joseph A. Fitzmyer, " '42 Testimonia' and the New Testament," *ThSt* 18 (1957): 513-37.

9617.   Claudio Gancho Hernández, "Las citaciones del A.T. en los Sinópticos y en los Rabinos," *S* 4 (1957): 289-359.

9618.   J. Mánek, "The New Exodus in the Books of Luke," *NT* 2 (1958): 8-23.

9619.   Heinrich Gross, "Zum Problem Verheissung und Erfüllung," *BibZ* N.F. 3 (1959): 3-17.

9620.   Albert C. Sundberg, "On Testimonies," *NT* 3 (1959): 268-81.

9621.   A. J. B. Higgins, "The Old Testament and Some Aspects of New Testament Christology," *CJT* 6 (1960): 200-10.

9622.   Siegfried Schulz, "Markus und das Alte Testament," *ZTK* N.F. 58 (1961): 184-97.

9623.   Herbert Braun, "Das Alte Testament im Neuen Testament," *ZTK* N.F. 59 (1962): 16-31.

           See also numbers 2485, 2723, 2724, 2727, 2728, 2730, 2734, 2735, 2738-2740, 3743, 4701, 4923, 5636.

9623.1   M. C. De Boer, "Het bloed en het water van Jezus Christus in de eerste Johannesbrief," *GTT* 89 (1989): 131-39.

9623.2   Franz Mussner, "Wann Kommt das Reich Gottes? Die Antwort Jesu Nach Lk. 17:20b-21," *BibZ* 6/1 (1962): 107-11.

9623.3   Richard Sneed, "The Kingdom of God is Within You (Lk. 17:21)," *CBQ* 24 (1962): 363-82.

9623.4   F. A. Schilling, "What Means the Saying about Receiving the Kingdom of God as a Little Child? Mark 10:15; Luke 18:17," *ET* 77 (1965-1966): 56-58.

9623.5   Hartmut Gese, "Psalm 22 und das Neue Testament," *ZTK* 65/1 (1968): 1-22.

9623.6   Q. Quesnell, " 'Made Themselves Eunuchs for the Kingdom of Heaven'," *CBQ* 30/3 (1968): 335-58.

9623.7   William A. Beardslee, "Uses of the Proverb in the Synoptic Gospels," *Interp* 24 (1970): 61-73.

9623.8   Matthew Black, "The Christo-Logical Use of the Old Testament in the New Testament," *NTSt* 18/1 (1971-1972): 1-14.

9623.9   J. D. M. Derrett, "Allegory and the Wicked Vinedressers," *JTS* 25 (1974): 426-32.

9623.10   Paul Beauchamp, "Signifiance de l'Ancien Testament pour la foi chrétienne," *RSR* 63 (1975): 297-406.

9623.11   Maurice Carrez, "Présence et fonctionnement de l'Ancien Testament dans l'annonce de l'Evangile," *RSR* 63 (1975): 325-41.

9623.12   Barclay M. Newman, "The Kingdom of God/ Heaven in the

Gospel of Matthew," *BTr* 27/4 (1976): 427-34.

9623.13   David Hill, "On the Use and Meaning of Hosea 6:6 in Matthew's Gospel," *NTSt* 24 (1977): 107-19.

9623.14   Johannes Beutler, "Psalm 42/43 im Johannesevangelium," *NTSt* 25 (1978-1979): 33-57.

9623.15   E. D. Freed, "Psalm 42/43 John's Gospel," *NTSt* 29 (1983): 62-73.

9623.16   G. R. Beasley-Murray, "John 3:3, 5: Baptism, Spirit and the Kingdom," *ET* 97 (1985-1986): 167-70.

9623.17   Matthew Black, "The Theological Appropriation of the Old Testament by the New Testament," *SJT* 39/1 (1986): 1-17.

9623.18   Hervé Barreau, "Une dogmatique évangélique pour notre temps," *RSPT* 71 (1987): 549-59.

9623.19   Paul Beauchamp, "L'evangile de Matthieu et l'heritage d'Israel," *RSR* 76 (1988): 5-38.

9623.20   Joel Marcus, "The Gates of Hades and the Keys of the Kingdom," *CBQ* 50/3 (1988): 443-55.

9623.21   David Peel, "Missing the Signs of the Kingdom," *ET* 99 (1988): 114-15.

9623.22   S. L. Cook, "The Metamorphosis of a Shepherd: The Tradition Hisory of Zechariah 11:17 + 13:7-9," *CBQ* 55 (1993): 453-66.

9623.23   B. C. Frein, "Narrative Predictions, Old Testament Prophecies and Luke's Sense of Fulfilment," *NTSt* 40 (1994): 22-37.

b. *Messianic Prophecies*

(1). General Studies

9624.   Dr. Mack, "Die messianischen Erwartungen und Ansichten der Zeilgenossen Jesu," *TQ* 18 (1836): 193-226.

9625.   E. P. Barrows, "The Relation of David's Family to the Messiah," *BS* 11 (1854): 306-28.

9626.   David Green, "The Knowledge and Faith of the Old Testament Saints Respecting the Promised Messiah," *BS* 14 (1857): 166-99.

9627. Anonymous, "Jewish Sacrifices, with Particular Reference to the Sacrifice of Christ," *BS* 16 (1859): 1-56.

9628. S. C. Bartlett, "Theories of Messianic Prophecy," *BS* 18 (1861): 724-800.

9629. Ed. Riehm, "Zur Charakteristik der messianischen Weissagung und ihres Verhältnisses zu der Erfüllung," *TSK* 38 (1865): 3-71, 425-89; 42 (1869): 209-84.

9630. A. B. Davidson, "The Various Kinds of Messianic Prophecy," *Exp* 1st ser., 8 (1878): 241-57, 379-90.

9631. J. R. Lumby, "On the Coming of the Messiah," *Exp* 1st ser., 9 (1879): 393-97.

9632. S. D. F. Salmond, "Dr. Martineau's 'Messianic Mythology'," *ET* 2 (1890-1891): 125-29.

9633. Alexander B. Grosart, "Χριστός and ὁ χριστός in the Septuagint," *ET* 1 (1889-1890): 275-76.

9634. R. H. Charles, "Messianic Doctrine of the Book of Enoch, and its Influence on the New Testament," *ET* 4 (1892- 1893): 301-303.

9635. William R. Harper, "The Foreshadowing of the Christ in the Old Testament," *BW* 6 (1895): 401-11.

9636. George F. Moore, " 'The Last Adam': Alleged Jewish Parallels," *JBL* 16 (1897): 158-61.

9637. George S. Goodspeed, "Aids to Bible Readers: The Foreshadowings of the Christ," *BW* 8 (1896): 376-89, 485-491; 9 (1897): 34-44, 194-203, 285-90, 354-62, 457-67.

9638. George S. Goodspeed, "Israel's Messianic Hopes," *BW* 12 (1898): 400-36.

9639. Anonymous, "Jehovah-Jesus-Messiah," *BS* 59 (1902): 267-81.

9640. R. H. Charles, "The Messiah of Old Testament Prophecy and Apocalyptic and the Christ of the New Testament," *Exp* 6th ser., 5 (1902): 241-59.

9641. W. Emery Barnes, "A Messianic Prophecy," *Exp* 6th ser., 10 (1904): 376-88.

9642. G. H. Gwilliam, "The Prophet like unto Moses," *ET* 17

(1905-1906): 65-71.

9643.   H. A. Redpath, "Christ the Fulfilment of Prophecy," *Exp* 7th ser., 3 (1907): 1-20.

9644.   F. W. Woods, "The Messianic Interpretation of Prophecy," *ET* 24 (1912-1913): 320-24.

9645.   J. Ridderbos, "Het Jodendom en de verwachting van een lijdenden Messias," *GTT* 14 (1913): 3-14.

9646.   F.-M. Abel, "Saint Jérôme et les prophéties messianiques," *RB* 25 (1916): 423-40; 26 (1917): 247-69.

9647.   Benjamin B. Warfield, "The Divine Messiah in the Old Testament," *PTR* 14 (1916): 369-416.

9648.   I. G. Matthews, "How to Interpret Old Testament Prophecy," *BW* 53 (1919): 328-36.

9649.   W. R. Aytoun, "The Rise and Fall of the 'Messianic' Hope in the Sixth Century," *JBL* 39 (1920): 34-43.

9650.   W. Caspari, "Die Anfänge der alttestamentlichen messianischen Weissagung," *NKZ* 31 (1920): 455-81.

9651.   Sigmund Mowinckel, "Der Knecht Jahwäs," *NTT* 22 (1921): 1-69.

9652.   S. Michelet, "Det gamle testamentes praktiske anvendelse saerlig i forkyndelsen," *NTT* 23 (1922): 193-211.

9653.   Ed. König, "Are there any Messianic Predictions?" *Th* 9 (1924): 6-13. [Not outside of Israel].

9654.   George R. Berry, "Messianic Predictions," *JBL* 45 (1926): 232-37.

9655.   R. D. Wilson, "Jesus and the Old Testament," *PTR* 24 (1926): 632-61.

9656.   G. L. Young, "Messianic Prophecy and its Fulfilment," *BS* 86 (1929): 218-39.

9657.   A. Vaccari, "De Messia *Filio Dei* in Vet. Testamento," *VD* 15 (1935): 48-55, 77-86.

9658.   W. M. Mackay, "Messiah in the Psalms," *EQ* 10 (1938): 153-64.

9659.   J. Ridderbos, "The Messiah-King," *EQ* 11 (1939): 289-99.

9660.   Roderic Dunkerley, "Prophecy and the Gospels," *ET* 59

(1947-1948): 218-22.

9661. J. Alonso, "Descripción de los tiempos mesiánicos en la literature profética como una vuelta al Paraíso," *EE* 24 (1950): 459-77.

9662. Clyde T. Francisco, "Things New and Old," *RE* 47 (1950): 311-23.

9663. Aage Bentzen, "Han, som kommer," *DTT* 14 (1951): 112-24.

9664. P. Saydon, "Old Testament Prophecy and Messias Prophecies," *Scr* 4 (1951): 335-39.

9665. León Villvendas, "Profecías mesiánicas," *CB* 8 (1951): 198-200, 255-56, 307-308, 371-72; 9 (1952): 55-56, 190-91.

9666. Dionisio Yubero, "La Pasión de Cristo según. . . los Profetas," *CB* 8 (1951): 118-20; 9 (1952): 49-54, 77-82; 10 (1953): 73-76; 11 (1954): 90-95

9667. Rudolf Meyer, "Der Erlöserkönig des Alten Testaments," *MTZ* 3 (1952): 221-43, 367-84.

9668. Alberto Colunga, "Los vaticinios proféticos de la Pasión," *CB* 11 (1954): 67-74

9669. L. Froidevaux, "Sur trois textes cités par saint Irénée (*Adv. Haer.*, IV, 29, 3 et 55, 4; *Démonstration*, 79 et 88)," *RSR* 44 (1956): 408-21 [O.T. prophecy of the cross].

9670. Gabriel Hebert, "Hope Looking Forward; The Old Testament Passages Used by the New Testament Writers as Prophetic of the Resurrection of Jesus Christ," *Interp* 10 (1956): 259-69.

9671. B. Schultze, "Profetismo e messianismo nusso religioso. Essenza, origini e rappresentanti principali," *OCP* 22 (1956): 172-97.

9672 Johann Jakob Stamm, "Jesus Christus und das Alte Testament," *EvT* 16 (1956): 387-95.

9673. A. Colunga, "Los vaticinios proféticos de la Pasión y los sentidos de la S. Escritura," *Sal* 4 (1957): 634-41.

See also 3144, 3170, 3272, 8292, *10085*.

9673.1 Hugh J. Blair, "Kingship in Israel and Its Implications for the

Lordship of Christ Today," *EQ* 47 (1975): 70-77.

(2). Texts of the Old Testament Regarded as Prophetic and Typological

9674.   Prof. Himpel, "Die messianischen Weissagungen im Pentateuch," *TQ* 41 (1859): 105-256.

9675.   W. Engelkemper, "Das Protoevangelium," *BibZ* 8 (1910): 351-71 [Gen. 3:15].

9676.   U. Holzmeister, "De Christi crucifixione quid e Deut. 21, 22s. et Gal. 3, 13 consequatur," *B* 27 (1946): 18-29.

9677.   E. L. Curtis, "Messianic Prophecy in the Book of Job," *BW* 1 (1893): 119-21.

9678.   John H. Raven, "Job's Messianic Hope," *BR* 8 (1923): 35-60 [Jb. 19:25-27].

9679.   Fr. Stettler, "Über Hiob 19:25-27," *STZ* 18 (1901): 230-45.

9680.   H. N. Ridderbos, "Christus in de Psalmen," *GTT* 44 (1943): 129-49.

9681.   Augustin Rojo, "Jesucristo en los Salmos," *CB* 2, núm. 16 (1945): 229-32.

9682.   Hermann Schultz, "Über doppelten Schriftsinn. Eine Abhandlung zur Geschichte der Psalmen," *TSK* 39 (1866): 7-52.

9683.   André Feuillet, "Les psaumes eschatologiques du règne de Jahweh; III. Les psaumes du règne et le Nouveau Testament," *NRT* 73 (1951): 359-63.

9684.   George Dahl, "The Messianic Epectation in the Psalter," *JBL* 57 (1938): 1-12.

9685.   P. Saydon, "The Divine Sonship of Christ in Psalm 11," *Scr* 3 (1948): 32-35.

9686.   A. Robert, "Considerations sur le messianisme du psaume 11," *RSR* 39 (1951-1952): 88-98.

9687.   Jacques Dupont, "*Filius meus es Tu*. L'interprétation de Ps.11, 7 dans le Nouveau Testament," *RSR* 35 (1948): 522-43.

9688.   E. C. Bissell, "The 'Protevangelium' and the Eighth Psalm," *JBL* 6 (1886, part 2): 64-68.

9689. F. W. C. Umbreit, "Kritische Bemerkung zum 8. Psalm," *TSK* 9 (1836): 1007-18.

9690. F. W. C. Umbreit, "Über die typische Auslegung des achten Psalms," *TSK* 11 (1838): 599-618.

9691. M. Kies, "Bemerkung zum 8. Psalm in Beziehung auf F. W. C. Umbreits kritische Bemerkung zum 8. Psalm in den Theol. Stud. und Kritiken Jahrg. 1836, 4. Heft," *TSK* 11 (1838): 488-96.

9692. J. Th. Ubbink, "De messiaansche uitlegging van Psalm 8:5-7 LXX in Hebreën 2, 9," *NTS* 24 (1941): 181-85.

9693. F. W. C. Umbreit, "Ist Jesus Christus in dem 22. Psalm?" *TSK* 13 (1840): 697-708.

9694. Alvah Hovey, "The Twenty-second Psalm," *BW* 22 (1903): 107-15.

9695. A. Vaccari, "Psalmus Christi patientis (Ps. 21 [22])," *VD* 20 (1940): 72-80, 97-104.

9696. T. Worden, "My God, My God, Why hast thou Forsaken me?" *Scr* 6 (1953): 9-16 [Ps. 22:1].

9697. W. J. Beecher, " 'Thy throne, O God, is forever and ever,' Ps. xlv.7," *JBL* 8 (1888): 139-40.

9698. P. Ballegui, "La última profecía sobre Jesús vivo," *CB* 8 (1951): 83-89 [Ps.68].

9699. Andreas ab Alpe, "Regnum Messiae in Ps. 71," *VD* 13 (1933): 271-76, 302-10.

9700. Santiago Luque, "El reino messiánico descrito en el Salmo 71 es fundamentalmente social," *CB* 5 (1948): 167-70.

9701. Albert Condamin, "Notes d'exégèse de l'Ancien Testament; un psaume messianique massacré par la critique rationaliste," *RSR* 7 (1917): 94-98 [Ps.72].

9702. Joseph Coppens, "La portée messianique du psaume cx," *ETL* 32 (1956): 5-23.

9703. Eloino Nácar, "Rey y sacerdote; Salmo 110," *EB* 5 (1946): 281-302.

9704. T. H. Rich, "Psalm 110," *JBL* 7 (1887, part 2): 43-45.

9705. Van Sante, "Le psaume 110 (Vulg. 109) 'Dixit Dominus',"

836 THEOLOGICAL STUDIES

BibZ 12 (1914): 22-28.

9706. R. Tournay, "Le Psaume cx," *RB* 67 (1960): 5-41.

9707. Friedrich Wilhelm Maier, "Ps. 110, 1 (LXX 109, 1) im Zusammenhang von 1 Kor. 15, 24-26," *BibZ* 20 (1932): 139-56.

9708. Ryge Jensen, "Salme 110, 4b," *TTDF* 5th ser., 6 (1935): 274-79.

9709. William R. Harper, "The Child Prophecies of Isaiah," *BW* 8 (1896): 417-22.

9710. A. Merk, "De Regno Christi apud Isaiam prophetam," *VD* 5 (1925): 257-61, 301-308, 333-38.

9711. G. G. Findlay, "The Messianic Teaching of Isaiah," *ET* 17 (1905-1906): 200-205.

9712. R. P. Stebbins, "A Criticism of Some Passages in Isaiah which are interpreted by the Late J. B. Alexander, D.D., as predicting the Messiah," *JBL* 5 (1885): 79-82.

9713. Louise P. Smith, "The Messianic Ideal of Isaiah," *JBL* 36 (1917): 158-212.

9714. Volkmar Herntrich, "Gottes Knecht und Gottes Reich nach Jesaja 40-55," *ZST* 16 (1939): 132-70.

9715. André Feuillet, "Le messianisme du livre d'Isaïe. Les rapports avec l'histoire et les traditions d'Israël," *RSR* 36 (1949): 182-228.

9716. O. Loretz, "Der Glaube des Propheten Isaias an das Gottesreich," *ZKT* 82 (1960): 40-73, 159-81.

9717. G. Ch. Aalders, "Iets over exegese van profetische voorzeggingen," *GTT* 27 (1926-1927): 3-9 [Isa. 2:2-4; Mic. 4:1-4 et al.].

9718. A. van Veldhuizen, "Jesaja 6:9-10 in de Evangelieën," *NTS* 9 (1925): 129-36.

9719. Jean Calès, "Les trois discours prophétiques sur l'Emmanuel (Isaïe VII; VIII, 1-10; VIII, II-IX, 6)," *RSR* 12 (1922): 169-77.

9720. Karl Budde, "Das Immanuelzeichen und die Ahazbegegnung Jesaja 7," *JBL* 52 (1933): 22-54.

9721. A. Vaccari, "De signo Emmanuelis (Is. 7)," *VD* 17 (1937):

45-49, 75-81.

9722. Sigmund Mowinckel, "Immanuelprofetien Jes. 7. Streiflys fra Ugarit 1," *NTT* 42 (1941): 129-57.

9723. George W. Davis, "The Child Prophecies of Isaiah. Isaiah 7:1-9:7," *BW* 4 (1894): 259-65.

9724. André Feuillet, "Le signe proposé à Achaz et l'Emmanuel (Isaïe 7, 10-25)," *RSR* 30 (1940): 129-51.

9725. F. W. C. Umbreit, "Ueber die Geburt des Immanuel durch eine Jungfrau (Jes. 7, 11-16)," *TSK* 3 (1830): 538-48.

9726. F. W. C. Umbreit, "Jes. 7, 14. Immanuel doch der Messias," *TSK* 28 (1855): 573-75.

9727. Dr. Schultz, "Ueber Immanuel Jes. 7, 14 ff.," *TSK* 34 (1861): 713-46.

9728. 0. Schott, "Immanuel," *NKZ* 5 (1894): 1021-30 [Isa. 7:14].

9729. Frank C. Porter, "A Suggestion regarding Isaiah's Immanuel," *JBL* 14 (1895): 19-36 [Isa. 7:14].

9730. Dr. Giesebrecht, "Die Immanuelweissagung," *TSK* 61 (1888): 217-64.

9731. Jean Calès, "Le sens de *'Almah* en hébreu, d'après les données sémitiques et bibliques," *RSR* 1 (1910): 161-68 [Isa. 7:14].

9732. F. Cavallera, "Saint Augustin et la prophétie de la viergemère (Isaïe VII, 14)," *RSR* 1 (1910): 380-84.

9733. P. Boylan, "The Sign in Isaias vii. 14," *ITQ* 7 (1912): 203-15.

9734. A. M. Haggard, "A Difficult Messianic Prophecy," *BS* 72 (1915): 154-58 [Isa. 7:14-16].

9735. John H. Raven, "The Sign Immanuel," *BR* 2 (1917): 213-40 [Isa. 7:14].

9736. Jean Calès, "L'avénement d'Emmanuel est-il affirmé prochain dans Isaïe VII, 14 sqq.?" *RSR* 17 (1927): 314-16.

9737. Emil G. Kraeling, "The Immanuel Prophecy," *JBL* 50 (1931): 277-97 [Isa. 7:14].

9738. Annie E. Skemp, " 'Immanuel' and 'The Suffering Servant of Jahweh'," *ET* 44 (1932-1933): 94-95.

9739. E. Lund, "Immanuel—Sangene, en symmetrisk formet

Digtning," *TTDF* 5th ser., 7 (1936): 1-13.

9740.   J. Coleran, " 'Propter hoc debit Dominus ipse vobis signum' (Is. 7, 14)," *VD* 17 (1937): 303-12.

9741.   C. B. Hansen, "Immanuel," *DTT* 3 (1940): 31-47.

9742.   Johann Jakob Stamm, "La prophétie d'Emmanuel," *RTP* N.S. 32 (1944): 97-123 [Isa. 7:14].

9743.   E. Hammershaimb, "The Immanuel Sign," *ST* 3 (1949): 124-42.

9744.   Edward J. Young, "The Immanuel Prophecy, Isaiah 7:14-16," *WTJ* 15 (1952-1953): 97-124; 16 (1953-1954): 23-50.

9745.   Carl Gaenssle, "Another Look at 'Almah, Is. 7:14," *CTM* 24 (1953): 443-45.

9746.   William A. Irwin, "That Troublesome 'Almah and Other Matters," *RE* 50 (1953): 337-60.

9747.   Dale Moody, "Isaiah 7:14 in the Revised Standard Version," *RE* 50 (1953): 61-68.

9748.   John Joseph Owens, "The Meaning of 'Almah in the Old Testament," *RE* 50 (1953): 56-60.

9749.   Alfred von Rohr Sauer, "The Almah Translation in Isaiah 7:14," *CTM* 24 (1953): 551-60.

9750.   L. G. Rignell, "Das Immanuelszeichen," *ST* 11 (1957): 99-119.

9751.   Walter Mueller, "A Virgin Shall Conceive," *EQ* 32 (1960): 203-207.

9752.   Stefan Porúbčan, "The Word *'ôt* in Isaia 7, 14," *CBQ* 22 (1960): 144-59.

9753.   Johann Jakob Stamm, "Die Immanuel-Weissagung und die Eschatologie des Jesaja," *TZ* 16 (1960): 439-55.

9754.   F. W. C. Umbreit, "Jesus Christus in der Weissagung des Propheten Jesaja nach der Auslegung von Kap. 9, 1-6 und 11, 1-10 mit besonderer Berücksichtigung der Herrn D. Gesenius, D. Hengstenberg und D. Hitzig," *TSK* 8 (1835): 551-69, 869-81.

9755.   T. W. Chambers, "The Everlasting Father," *JBL* 1 (1881):

169-71 [Isa. 9:6].

9756.   J. van Katwijk, "Exegetica. Jes. 9, 5b," *GTT* 14 (1913): 328-39.

9757.   Hans Wildberger, "Die Thronnamen des Messias, Jes. 9, 5b," *TZ* 16 (1960): 314-32.

9758.   E. Power, " 'Parvulus natus est nobis' (Is. 9, 6)," *VD* 2 (1922): 360-63.

9759.   Hans-Peter Müller, "Uns ist ein Kind geboren...," *EvT* 21 (1961): 408-19 [Isa. 9:6].

9760.   Joseph Zingerle, "Die Weissagung des Propheten Isaias (11, 6-8) vom messianischen Friedensreich," *ZKT* 4 (1880): 651-61.

9761.   F. W. C. Umbreit, "Ueber den Knecht Gottes," *TSK* 1 (1828): 295-330.

9762.   Dr. de Wette, "Kritischer Versuch über den Knecht Gottes (Jes. 40-66) mit Berücksichtigung der neuesten darüber aufgestellten Meinungen," *TSK* 9 (1836): 982-1004.

9763.   Dr. Bahr, "Über den Knecht Gottes. Auszug aus einem Schreiben von Dr. Bähr an Dr. Umbreit," *TSK* 15 (1842): 129-33.

9764.   R. P. Stebbins, "Servant of Jehovah," *JBL* 4 (1884): 65-79.

9765.   William H. Cobb, "The Servant of Jahveh," *JBL* 14 (1895): 95-113.

9766.   J. Nikel, "Die neuere Literatur über Jes. 40-66, insbesondere über die Weissagungen vom Gottesknechte," *TRev* 1 (1902): 73-77, 105-11.

9767.   A. van Hoonacker, "L'ébed Iahvé et la composition littéraire des chapitres XI ss. d'Isaïe," *RB* 18 (1909): 497-528.

9768.   C. Bruston, "La prophétie du serviteur de l'Eternel dans le second Esaïe et l'idée de la rédemption," *RTQR* 22 (1913): 494-529.

9769.   Henry A. Sanders, "The New Testament Quotation of a Twice Repeated Prophecy," *BS* 71 (1914): 275-82 [Isa. 40:3-8; Mal 1:3].

9770.   André Feuillet, "Richesses du Christ 'Serviteur de

l'Eternel'," *RSR* 35 (1948): 412-41 [Isa. 42:1-7 et al.].

9771. R. Tournay, "Les chants du serviteur dans la seconde partie d'Isaïe," *RB* 59 (1952): 355-84, 481-572.

9772. Henri Cazelles, "Les poèmes du serviteur. Leur place, leur structure, leur théologie," *RSR* 43 (1955): 5-55 [Isa. 52f.].

9773. Joseph Scharbert, "Stellvertretendes Sühneleiden in den Ebed-Jahwe-Liedern und in altorientalischen Ritualtexten," *BibZ* 2 (1958): 190-213.

9774. Samuel I. Curtiss, "Is the Modern Critical Theory of the Servant in Isaiah 52:13-53 Subversive of its New Testament Application to Christ?" *BW* 8 (1896): 354-63.

9775. P. Kleinert, "Über das Subjekt der Weissagung Jes. 52, 13-53, 12," *TSK* 35 (1862): 699-752.

9776. Stanley A. Cook, "The Servant of the Lord," *ET* 34 (1922-1923): 440-42.

9777. John R. Mackay, "Isaiah lii. 13-liii. 12: an Analysis," *EQ* 3 (1931): 307-11.

9778. Christopher R. North, "Who was the Servant of the Lord in Isaiah 53?" *ET* 52 (1940-1941): 181-84, 218-21.

9779. Martin Noth, "Von der Knechtsgestalt des Alten Testaments," *EvT* 6 (1946-1947): 302-10.

9780. Taylor Lewis, "The Purifying Messiah-Interpretation of Isaiah 52: 15," *BS* 30 (1873): 166-77.

9781. Wilhelm Bötticher, "Der alttestamentliche Sühneopfer Gedanke im Neuen Testament," *ZWT* 55 (1914): 230-51 [Isa. 53].

9782. L. Waterman, "The Martyred Servant Motif of Is. 53," *JBL* 56 (1937): 27-34.

9783. Frederick A. Aston, "The Servant of the Lord in Isaiah LIII," *EQ* 11 (1939): 193-206.

9784. Christopher R. North, "The Suffering Servant: Current Scandinavian Discussions," *SJT* 3 (1950): 363-79.

9785. Edward J. Young, "Of whom speaketh the Prophet this?" *WTJ* 11 (1948): 133-55 [Isa. 53:7-8; Ac. 8:34].

9786. Edward J. Young, "The Origin of the Suffering Servant

Idea," *WTJ* 13 (1950): 19-33.

9787. V. de Leeuw, "De koninklijke verklaring van de Ebed Jahweh-zongen," *ETL* 28 (1952): 449-71.

9788. George Pidoux, "Le serviteur souffrant d'Esaïe 53," *RTP* sér. 3, 6 (1956): 36-46.

9789. Robert Lennox, "The Servant of Yahweh," *TTod* 15 (1958): 315-20.

9790. José M. González Ruiz, "Une profecía de Isaías sobre la sepultura de Cristo (Is. 53, 9)," *EB* 6 (1947): 225-32.

9791. H. Grimme, "Eine messianische Stelle in berichtigter Form," *BibZ* 8 (1910): 24-25 [Sam. 4:20].

9792. Jean Daniélou, "Christos Kyrios. Une citation des *Lamentations* de Jérémie dans les *Testimonia*," *RSR* 39 (1951-1952): 338-52 [Lam. 4:20].

9793. Ed. Ensfelder, "Les prophéties messianiques d'Ezéchiel," *RT* 2 (1864): 59-76.

9794. K. Begrich, "Das Messiasbild des Ezechiel," *ZWT* 47 (1904): 433-61.

9795. Nathaniel Schmidt, "The 'Son of Man' in the Book of Daniel," *JBL* 19 (1900): 22-28.

9796. Ed. König, "Der Menschensohn im Danielbuche," *NKZ* 16 (1905): 904-28.

9797. Fritz Tillmann, "Hat die Selbstbezeichnung Jesu 'der Menschensohn' ihre Wurzel in Dn. 7, 13?" *BibZ* 5 (1907): 35-47 [No].

9798. James Muilenburg, "The Son of Man in Daniel and the Ethiopic Apocalypse of Enoch," *JBL* 79 (1960): 197-209.

9799. Julian Morgenstern, "The 'Son of Man' of Daniel 7. 13 f. A New Interpretation," *JBL* 80 (1961): 65-77.

9800. J. van Katwijk, "Exegetica," *GTT* 16 (1915): 343-52 [Micah 5:1].

9801. Edward B. Pollard, "Some Traditional Misinterpretations," *CQ* 4 (1927): 92-94 [Hag. 2:7; Gen. 49:10].

9802. A. Škrinjar, "Veniet desideratus cunctis gentibus," *VD* 15 (1935): 355-62 [Hag. 2:7].

9803.   F. F. Bruce, "The Book of Zechariah and the Passion Narrative," *BJRL* 43 (1960-1961): 336-53.

9804.   Joseph Lécuyer, "Jésus, fils de Josédec, et le sacerdoce du Christ," *RSR* 43 (1955): 82-103 [Zach. 3:1-9].

9805.   Albert Condamin, "Le sens messianique de Zacharie XII, 10," *RSR* 1 (1910): 52-56.

9806.   Charles R. Brown, "The Interpretation of Malachi 3:1-3; 4:1-6," *BW* 14 (1899): 417-20.

         See also numbers 367, 2351, 4764.

9806.1   John M. Gibbs, "Purpose and Pattern in Matthew's Use of the Title 'Son of David'," *NTSt* 10 (1963-1964): 446-64.

c. *The Old Testament in the Teachings of Jesus*

9807.   Gotthard Victor Lechler, "Das alte Testament in den Reden Jesu," *TSK* 27 (1854): 787-851.

9808.   J. J. Murphy, "Christ's Use of Scripture," *Exp* 2nd ser., 4 (1882): 101-10.

9809.   George H. Schodde, "Christ's Testimony of Moses," *LQ* 13 (1883): 337-46.

9810.   R. F. Horton, "Christ's Use of the Book of Proverbs," *Exp* 3rd ser., 7 (1888): 105-23.

9811.   R. T. Smith, "The Old Testament and our Lord's Authority," *Exp* 4th ser., 2 (1890): 81-101.

9812.   Buchanan Blake, "Christ and the Old Testament," *ET* 3 (1891-1892): 518-19.

9813.   C. J. Ellicott, "The Teaching of our Lord as to the Authority of the Old Testament," *ET* 3 (1891-1892): 157-63, 256-59, 359-62, 457-63, 538-45.

9814.   C. J. Ellicott, "The Teaching of our Lord as to the Authority of the Old Testament," *ET* 4 (1892-1893): 169-72, 218-22, 362-69, 450-58.

9815.   Carl Stuckert, "Das alte Testament in den Reden Jesu," *STZ* 10 (1893): 176-90.

9816.   W. R. Harper, "What is Christ's Attitude toward the Old Testament?" *BW* 3 (1894): 241-46.

9817. John P. Peters, "Christ's Treatment of the Old Testament," *JBL* 15 (1896): 87-105.

9818. G. Currie Martin, "Our Lord's Use of the Book of Hosea," *ET* 10 (1898-1899): 281.

9819. Leander S. Keyser, "Christ's Witness to the Old Testament," *LQ* 44 (1914): 40-65.

9820. Alexander Mackenzie Lamb, "The Pentateuch in the Hands of Christ," *BR* 3 (1918): 395-408.

9821. J. Rendel Harris, "Did Jesus use Testimonies?" *ET* 36 (1924-1925): 410-13.

9822. Henry J. Cadbury, "Jesus and the Prophets," *JR* 5 (1925): 607-22.

9823. W. W. Keen, "The Attitude of Jesus Toward the Mosaic Law, and the Eating of Blood," *CQ* 3 (1926): 203-207.

9824. Henry J. Allen, "Our Lord's Conception of his Messiahship in relation to Old Testament Prophecy," *ET* 40 (1928-1929): 563-67.

9825. H. Branscomb, "Jesus' Attitude to the Law of Moses," *JBL* 47 (1928): 32-40.

9826. H. E. Dana, "Jesus' Use of the Old Testament," *BR* 16 (1931): 389-99.

9827. J. Hofbauer, "Quid Christus Dominus senserit de Vetere Testamento," *VD* 22 (1942): 136-40.

9828. Robert E. Speer, "Jesus and his Bible," *USR* 57 (1945-1946): 111-20.

9829. John MacLeod, "The Mind of Christ—What he Found in Scripture," *ET* 62 (1950-1951): 175-77.

9830. Claude Chavasse, "Jesus: Christ and Moses," *Th* 54 (1951): 244-50, 289-96.

9831. T. W. Manson, "The Old Testament in the Teaching of Jesus," *BJRL* 34 (1951-1952): 312-32.

9832. Elwyn E. Tilden, "The Study of Jesus' Interpretive Methods," *Interp* 7 (1953): 45-61.

9832.1 Jay B. Stern, "Jesus' Citation of Dt 6,5 and Lv 19,18 in the Light of Jewish Tradition," *CBQ* 28 (1966): 312-16.

9832.2   D. R. Jones, "The Background and Character of the Lukan Psalms," *JTS* 19 (1968): 19-50.

9832.3   John H. Reumann, "Psalm 22 at the Cross: Lament and Thanksgiving for Jesus Christ," *Interp* 28/1 (1974): 39-58.

9832.4   James A. Sanders, "Torah and Christ," *Interp* 29 (1975): 372-90.

9832.5   James A. Sanders, "Isaiah in Luke," *Interp* 36 (1982): 144-55.

9832.6   G. Geiger, "Aufruf an Rückkehrende. Zum Sinn des Zitats von Psalm 78:24b in Johannes 6:31," *B* 65 (1984): 449-64.

9832.7   Craig A. Evans, "On the Isaianic Background of the Parable of the Sower," *CBQ* 47/3 (1985): 464-68.

9832.8   Helmer Ringgren, "Luke's Use of the Old Testament," *HTR* 79 (1986): 227-35.

9832.9   M. J. J. Menken, "The Old Testament Quotation in John 6:45: Source and Redaction," *ETL* 64/1 (1988): 164-72.

9832.10   M. Quesnel, "Les citations de Jérémie dans l'évangile selon saint Matthieu," *EB* 47 (1989): 513-27.

9832.11   J. N. Jones, " 'Think of the Lilies' and Proverbs 6:6-11," *HTR* 88 (1995): 175-77.

d. *Heilsgeschichte*

9833.   Paul S. Minear, "The Conception of History in the Prophets and Jesus," *JBR* 11 (1943): 156-61.

9834.   E. F. Scott, "The Conception of God's Law in the Prophets and in Jesus," *JBR* 11 (1943): 152-55.

9835.   A. E. J. Rawlinson, "The Unity of the New Testament," *ET* 58 (1946-1947): 200-203.

9836.   Vincent Taylor, "The Unity of the New Testament," *ET* 58 (1946-1947): 256-59.

9837.   Max Warren, "In Christ the New has Come," *TTod* 3 (1947): 473-85.

9838.   J. Stanley Glen, "Jesus Christ and the Unity of the Bible," *Interp* 5 (1951): 259-67.

9839.   David Michael Stanley, "The Conception of our Gospels as

Salvation-History," *ThSt* 20 (1959): 561-89.

9840. Herbert Braun, "Die Heilstatsachen im Neuen Testament," *ZTK* N.F. 57 (1960): 41-50.

See also numbers 436, 774, 870, 7145, 7147, 7181, 7187, 8939 f.

9840.1 Jack D. Kingsbury, "The Structure of Matthew's Gospel and His Concept of Salvation-History," *CBQ* 35 (1973): 451-74.

9840.2 John P. Meier, "Salvation-History in Matthew: In Search of a Starting Point," *CBQ* 37/2 (1975): 203-15.

9840.3 J. A. Jáuregui, "En el centro del tiempo: La teología de Lucas," *EE* 68 (1993): 3-24.

THE INFLUENCE AND INTERPRETATION OF JESUS CHRIST AND THE GOSPELS IN WORSHIP, THE FINE ARTS, AND CULTURE

A. GENERAL STUDIES

9841.   A. Grotz, "Christ et l'âme humaine," *RT* 13 (1856): 86- 111.

9842.   Amory H. Bradford, "Christ and our Century," *JCP* 2 (1882-1883): 47-58.

9843.   W. H. Wynn, "The Religion of Evolution as Against the Religion of Jesus," *LQ* N.S. 12 (1882): 1-28.

9844.   T. K. Cheyne, "The Jews and the Gospel," *Exp* 3rd ser., 1 (1885): 401-18.

9845.   A. Mair, "Testimony of Napoleon I. with regard to Christ," *Exp* 4th ser., 1 (1890): 366-81.

9846.   William W. Kinsley, "Science and Christ," *BS* 50 (1893): 93-118, 291-308, 519-40, 656-67.

9847.   Wm. H. Dunbar, "Christ in Theology," *LQ* N.S. 25 (1895): 490-506.

9848.   A. M. Fairbairn, "Christ in History," *BW* 6 (1895): 518-23.

9849.   Charles R. Henderson, "Christianity and Children," *BW* 8 (1896): 473-84.

9850.   G. A. Derry, "The Incarnation and Culture," *Exp* 5th ser., 7 (1898): 288-95.

9851.   F. Niebergall, "Die Wahrheit des Christentums," *ZTK* 8 (1898): 435-67.

9852.   F. C. Conybeare, "The History of Christmas," *AJT* 3 (1899): 1-21.

9853.   John W. Buckham, "Savonarola and Jesus," *BS* 57 (1900): 748-59.

9854.   K. Feilberg, "Kristendommen som kulturprodukt," *NTT* 3 (1902): 1-24.

9855.   G. Grützmacher, "The Secret of the Triumph of Christianity over the Ancient World," *ET* 15 (1903-1904): 8-13.

9856.   F. W. Schiefer, "Der Christus in der jüdischen Dichtung,"

NKZ 14 (1903): 843-84.

9857. G. A. J. Ross, "The Indispensableness of Jesus," *Exp* 7th ser., 9 (1910): 187-92.

9858. G. Heinzelmann, "Das Wesen der Religion im Lichte des Kreuzes Christi," *NKZ* 22 (1911): 797-824.

9859. Alfred E. Garvie, "The Christ of God and the Soul of Man," *ET* 25 (1913-1914): 409-14.

9860. Cavendish Moxon, "Jesus' Teaching and Modern Thought," *ET* 26 (1914-1915): 537-40.

9861. George Cross, "Rival Interpretations of Christianity," *BW* 49 (1917): 12-24, 88-102, 151-56, 209-18, 281-89, 341-47; 50 (1917): 18-25, 101-107, 334-41; 51 (1918): 8-19.

9862. Richard Roberts, "The Offense of the Cross," *BW* 50 (1917): 342-47.

9863. H. T. Andrews, "The Legacy of Jesus to the Church," *AJT* 23 (1919): 458-70.

9864. Walter M. Horton, "Shall We Discard the Living Christ?" *BW* 53 (1919): 276-82.

9865. Shailer Mathews, "Why I Believe in Jesus Christ," *BW* 54 (1920): 351-53.

9866. A. T. Robertson, "The Cry for Christ Today," *BW* 54 (1920): 3-8.

9867. D. J. Evans, "The Master Among the Masters," *RE* 18 (1921): 443-61.

9868. William Louis Poteat, "The Supremacy of Christ in Human Culture," *CQ* 1 (1924): 251-57.

9869. W. H. Smith, "Christ and Creed," *CJRT* 4 (1927): 380-87.

9870. Carl Stange, "Jesu Verhältnis zu den andern Religionstiftern," *ZST* 7 (1929-1930): 259-83.

9871. S. Greijdanus, " 'Christianity Today'," *GTT* 31 (1930-1931): 209-20.

9872. J. C. Robertson, "Christ and Greek Thought," *CJRT* 7 (1930): 122-29.

9873. W. O. Carver, "Jesus Christ the Answer to Modern Need," *RE* 29 (1932): 470-88.

9874.   P. Prins, "Een nieuw 'dogma'," *GTT* 34 (1933): 305-38 [Hitler's National Socialism and Christ].

9875.   J. K. Mozley, "The Risen Christ and the Historical Order," *Th* 29 (1934): 135-46.

9876.   Gaines S. Dobbins, "Capturing Psychology for Christ," *RE* 33 (1936): 427-36.

9877.   Herbert Haslam, "The Permanent Relevancy of Jesus," *CQ* 13 (1936): 93-99.

9878.   Ray Knight, "Silence as to the Ministry of Jesus in Early Christian Belief," *HJ* 37 (1938-1939): 54-67.

9879.   Harry M. Taylor, "The Complete Faith," *RL* 8 (1939): 399-410.

9880.   Claude C. Douglas, "Have we a Modern Christ?" *CQ* 17 (1940): 245-52.

9881.   Everett Gill, "Europe and the Coming of the Kingdom," *RE* 37 (1940): 243-52.

9882.   H. R. Minn, "Christ and the Race Factor," *EQ* 12 (1940): 76-96.

9883.   J.-M. Vosté, "L'ére de l'Ascension de Notre Seigneur dans les manuscrits nestoriens," *OCP* 7 (1941): 233-50.

9884.   Robert Devreesse, "Le christianisme dans la province d'Arabie," *RB* 50-52 (1941-1944): 110-46.

9885.   John W. Shepard, "The Supremacy of Christianity," *RE* 38 (1941): 20-38.

9886.   Joseph R. Sizoo, "The most Revered Image," *RL* 11 (1942): 163-71.

9887.   Carl Stange, "Christus und die Gegenwart," *ZST* 19 (1942): 257-80.

9888.   W. H. Rigg, "Christ and Public Opinion," *ET* 55 (1943-1944): 317-20.

9889.   H. W. Schmidt, "Christentum ohne Christus," *ZST* 20 (1943): 34-67.

9890.   Clinton M. Cherry, "The New Testament and a Changing Liberalism," *RL* 14 (1945): 14-23.

9891.   Wayne Oates, "The Gospel and Modern Psychology," *RE* 46

(1949): 181-98.

9892. Robert A. Pfeiffer, "Is the Gospel Obsolete?" *CQ* 27 (1950): 289-96.

9893. Ethelbert Stauffer, "Antike Jesustradition und Jesuspolemik im mittelalterlichen Orient," *ZNW* 46 (1955) 1-30.

9894. Harold G. Barr, "Did Jesus Speak to our Society?" *JBR* 24 (1956): 255-63.

9895. J. C. Coetzee, "The Claim of Jesus Christ on Modern Education," *EQ* 28 (1956): 70-86.

9896. Joseph Crehan, "The Seven Orders of Christ," *ThSt* 19 (1958): 81-93.

9897. Barnabas M Ahern, "The Concept of Union with Christ after Death in Early Christian Thought," *PCTSA* 16 (1961): 3-22.

9897.1 Norman B. Orr, "Rehabilitation of the Gospel," *SJT* 24 (1971): 435-48.

9897.2 John G. Bishop, "Psychological Insights in Saint Paul's Mysticism," *Th* 78 (1975): 318-24.

9897.3 Hugh Jackson, "Resurrection Belief of the Earliest Church: A Response to the Failure of Prophecy?" *JR* 55 (1975): 415-25.

9897.4 Donald G. Bloesch, "Biblical Piety vs Religiosity," *RL* 46 (1977): 488-96.

9897.5 Lesslie Newbigin, "Christ and the Cultures," *SJT* 31 (1978) 1-22.

9897.6 Ernst Feil, "Verstehen und Verständigung: zur Problematisierung neuzeitlichen Wissenschafts-verständnisses," *FZPT* 28 (1981): 206-52.

9897.7 Johannes Dantine, "Sakrament als Gabe und Feier," *TZ* 38 (1982): 3-27.

9897.8 J.-C. Basset, "Théologie de la croix et culture indienne: l'interprétation de V Chakkarai à la lumière de Philippiens 2:6-11," *RHPR* 63 (1983): 417-33.

9897.9 Halvor Moxnes, "Paulus og den norske vaeremåten: 'skam' og 'aere' i Romerbrevet," *NTT* 86 (1985): 129-40.

See also numbers 804, *10087*.

B. CHRIST AND THE GOSPELS IN ART

9898.   J. P. Kirsch, "Ein altes Bleisiegel mit der Darstellung der Taufe Christi," *RQ* 1 (1887): 113-25.

9899.   A. de Waal, "Die apokryphen Evangelien in der altchristlichen Kunst," *RQ* 1 (1887): 173-96.

9900.   A. de Waal, "Ein Christusbild aus der Zeit Leos III," *RQ* 3 (1889): 386-93.

9901.   Rush Rhees, "Christ in Art," *BW* 6 (1895): 490-502.

9902.   A. de Waal, "Die Taufc Christi auf vorconstantinischen Gemälden der Katakomben," *RQ* 10 (1896): 335-49.

9903.   William C. Wilkinson, "The Child Jesus in Painting (Illustrated)," *BW* 8 (1896): 458-72 [Raphael, da Vinci, etc.].

9904.   John Powell Lenox, "The Supreme Face of the Christian Centuries (Illustrated)," *BW* 12 (1898): 380-99.

9905.   Clifton Harby Levy, "The Life of Jesus as Illustrated by J. James Tissot (Illustrated)," *BW* 13 (1899): 69-87.

9906.   J. Wilpert, "Maria als Fürsprecherin und mit dem Jesus-knaben auf einem Fresko der ostrianischen Katakomben," *RQ* 14 (1900): 309-15.

9907.   E. Wüscher-Becchi, "Der Crucifixus in der Tunica manicata," *RQ* 15 (1901): 201-15.

9908.   H. Achelis, "Altchristliche Kunst," *TR* 5 (1902): 112-19.

9909.   A. de Waal, "Zur Ikonographie der Transfiguration in der älteren Kunst," *RQ* 16 (1902): 25-40.

9910.   E. Wüscher-Becchi, "Die griechischen Wandmalereien in S. Saba," *RQ* 17 (1903): 54-69.

9911.   A. de Waal, "Tierbilder in Verbindung mit heiligen Zeichen auf altchristlichen Monumenten," *RQ* 18 (1904): 260-64.

9912.   A. de Waal, "Altchristliche Thonschüsseln," *RQ* 18 (1904): 308-21.

9913.   A. de Waal, "Die biblischen Totenerweckungen an den altchristlichen Grabstätten," *RQ* 20 (1906): 27-48.

9914.   Fr. J. Dölger, "ΙΧΘΥΣ, das altchristliche Fischsymbol in religionsgeschichtlicher Beleuchtung," *RQ* 23 (1909): 3-112, 145-82; 24 (1910): 51-89.

9915.   Anton Baumstark, "Der Crucifixus mit dem königlichen
         Diadem auf einem modernen mesopotamischen Silber-
         deckel," *RQ* 24 (1910): 30-50.

9916.   C. R. Morey, "The Origin of the Fish Symbol," *PTR* 8
         (1910): 93-106, 231-45, 401-32; 9 (1911): 268-89; 10
         (1912): 278-98.

9917.   Fr. J. Dölger, "Zur Chronologie des Fischsymbols auf
         altchristlichen Grabinschriften," *RQ* 27 (1913): 93-102.

9918.   Paul Styger, "Neue Untersuchungen über die altchristlichen
         Petrusdarstellungen," *RQ* 27 (1913): 16-74.

9919.   H. Achelis, "Altchristliche Kunst," *ZNW* 16 (1915): 1-23
         [Peter's denial, Baptism of Christ].

9920.   P. Corssen, "Der Schauplatz der Passion des romischen
         Bischofs Sixtus II," *ZNW* 16 (1915): 147-66.

9921.   Paul Styger, "Die Christusstatue im römischen Thermen-
         museum (mit 2 Tafeln)," *RQ* 29 (1915): 26-28.

9922.   A. de Waal, "Der gute Hirt auf Gemme inmitten anderer
         Symbole," *RQ* 29 (1915): 111-20.

9923.   H. Achelis, "Altchristliche Kunst," *ZNW* 17 (1916): 81-107
         [the Last Supper].

9924.   Joseph Hoh, "Zur Herkunft der vier Evangeliensymbole,"
         BibZ 15 (1918-1921): 229-34.

9925.   G. de Jerphanion, "Le développement iconographique de l'art
         chrétien," *Bes* 35 (1919): 42-66.

9926.   Guillaume de Jerphanion, "Quels sont les douze apôtres dans
         l'iconographie chrétienne?" *RSR* 10 (1920): 358-67.

9927.   Oluf Kolsrud, "Kristendom og kunst under gothiken," *NTT*
         21 (1920): 82-114.

9928.   Dr. Preuss, "Thorwaldsens Christusstatue. Eine Säkular-
         betrachtung," *NKZ* 34 (1923): 237-48.

9929.   Georg Stuhlfauth, "Zwei Streitfragen der altchristlichen
         Ikonographie; 2. Die Martha-Szene oder die Sünderin?" *ZNW*
         23 (1924): 54-64

9930.   J. Rendel Harris, "Jesus Christ and the Four Penitents," *ET*
         37 (1925-1926): 366-69 [Rubens].

9931.   Victor Schultze, "Die Christusstatue in Paneas," *ZNW* 24 (1925): 51-56.

9932.   Gustavus A. Eisen, "The Great Chalice of Antioch," *BR* 11 (1926): 40-75.

9933.   Arthur Allgeier, "Vidi aquam. Exegetisches zur Begriffsgeschichte der altchristlichen ἰχθύς - Symbolik," *RQ* 39 (1931): 23-41.

9934.   P. Thomas Michels, "Christus mit der Buchrolle-Ein Beitrag zur Ikonographie der Himmelfahrt Christi," *OC* III. Serie, 7 (1932): 138-46

9935.   U. Holzmeister, "Crux Domini eiusque crucifixio ex archaeologia Romana illustrantur," *VD* 14 (1934): 149-55, 216-20, 241-49, 257-63.

9936.   Adolf Knücke, "Der Engel am Grabe Christi," *ZNW* 33 (1934): 313-17.

9937.   E. C. Colwell, "The Fourth Gospel and Early Christian Art," *JR* 15 (1935): 191-206.

9938.   Leslie Webber Jones, "The Text of the Bible and the Script and Art of Tours," *HTR* 28 (1935): 135-79.

9939.   Gitta Wodtka, "Malereien der Synagoge in Dura und ihre Parallelen in der christlichen Kunst," *ZNW* 34 (1935): 51-62.

9940.   Johannes Kollwitz, "Christus als Lehrer und die Gesetzes übergabe an Petrus in der konstantinischen Kunst Roms," *RQ* 44 (1936): 45-66.

9941.   Ernst Schäfer, "Die Heiligen mit dem Kreuz in der altchristlichen Kunst," *RQ* 44 (1936): 67-104.

9942.   R. Will, "Le symbolisme de l'image du Christ. Essai d'iconographie chrétienne," *RHPR* 16 (1936): 400-28.

9943.   G. de Jerphanion, "L'image de Jésus Christ dans l'art chrétien," *NRT* 65 (1938): 257-83.

9944.   Anton Baumstark, "Der Bilderschmuck eines armenischen Evangelienbuches vom Jahre 1305," *OC* III. Serie, 13 (1939): 214-24.

9945.   J. Leclercq, "Pour l'iconographie des apôtres," *RBén* 56 (1945-1946): 216-17.

9946. E. A. Wuenschel, "The Shroud of Turin and the Burial of Christ," *CBQ* 7 (1945): 405-37.

9947. P. Morris, "The Symbols of the Four Evangelists," *Scr* 1 (1946): 14-15.

9948. E. A. Wuenschel, "The Shroud of Turin and the Burial of Christ," *CBQ* 8 (1946): 135-78

9949. Claude Dalbonne, "Bas-relief représentant l'ange de l'annonciation," *OCP* 13 (1947): 86-92.

9950. Erich Dinkler, "Zur Geschichte des Kreuzsymbols," *ZTK* N.F. 48 (1951): 148-72.

9951. Marcel Aubert, "L'adoration des mages dans l'art du haut moyen âge," *BVC* no. 4 (1953-1954): 34-39.

9952. Gervase Mathew, "The Origins of Eucharistic Symbolism," *DS* 6 (1953): 1-11.

9953. A. M. Ammann, "Eine neue Variante der Darstellung des bekleideten Christus am Kreuz," *OCP* 21 (1955): 21-35.

9954. J. Doresse, "Les premiers monuments chrétiens de l'Éthiopie et l'église archaïque de Yéha," *NT* 1 (1956): 209-24.

9955. Hugo Rahner, "Antenna crucis: Der Schiffbruch und die Planke des Heils," *ZKT* 79 (1957): 129-69.

9956. Kart Marti, "Christus, die Befreiung der bildenden Künste zur Profanität," *EvT* 18 (1958): 371-75.

9956.1 André Feuillet, "Le premier cavalier de l'Apocalypse," *ZNW* 57 (1966): 229-59.

9956.2 Ronald Williamson, "Expressionist Art and the Parables of Jesus," *Th* 78 (1975): 474-81.

9956.3 S. A. Bay, "Die Hahnszene der Sarkophage," *ST* 35 (1981): 107-35.

9956.4 Boniface Ramsey, "A Note on the Disappearance of the Good Shepherd from Early Christian Art," *HTR* 76 (1983): 375-78.

9956.5 Werner Bulst, "Turiner Grabtuch und Exegese heute, 2: Neues zur Geschichte des Tuches," *BibZ* 30 (1986): 70-91.

9956.6 Fausto Sardini, "Gesù Cristo: la figura che più ha affascinato gli scrittori," *BO* 28 (1986): 156-63.

9956.7   Barbara Saunderson, "Biblical and Non-Biblical Elements in Italian Renaissance Representations of the Crucifixion," *JSNT* 27 (1986): 89-112.

9956.8   Peter Plank, "Die Wiederaufrichtung des Adam und ihre Propheten: eine neue Deutung der Anastasis-Ikone," *OS* 41 (1992): 34-49.

         See also numbers 1240, 1796, 6766.

C. CHRIST AND THE GOSPELS IN MUSIC

9957.   Dorothy W. Lyon, " 'Christe qui lux es et dies' and its German, Dutch and English Translations," *AJP* 19 (1898): 70-85, 152-92.

9958.   S.Grébaut, "Hymne à Jésus Christ," *ROC* 18 (1913): 310-12.

9959.   A. Rücker, "Zwei nestorianische Hymnen über die Magier," *OC* II. Serie, 10-11 (1920-1921): 33-55.

9960.   Sophronios Eustratiades, "Ὁ Χριστὸς ἐν τῇ ὑμνογραφίᾳ ὑπὸ τοῦ πρῴην Λεοντοπόλεως," Θ 9 (1931): 80-87, 171-80, 260-67, 350-55; 10 (1932): 75-80, 173-79; 11 (1933): 69-74.

9961.   Samuel Läuchli, "Negro Spirituals als christliche Verkündigung," *TZ* 12 (1956): 445-70.

9961.1   Christoph Trautmann, "J. S. Bach: New Light on His Faith," *CTM* 42 (1971): 88-99.

9961.2   Paul S. Minear, "Matthew, Evangelist, and Johann, Composer," *TTod* 30 (1973): 243-55.

9961.3   Charles B. Naylor, "Bach's Interpretation of the Cross," *Th* 78 (1975): 397-404.

9961.4   Daniel Lys, "Evénement, parole, tradition, écriture: une illustration de la réflexion biblique par l'histoire d'un martyr du Désert," *ETR* 54 (1979): 99-110.

9961.5   K. M. Campbell, "The Role of Music in Worship," *EQ* 52 (1980): 43-46.

9961.6   Ron Grove, "A Note on the Byzantine Apolytikion," *OS* 30 (1981): 21.

9961.7   Elke Axmacher, "Untersuchungen z Wandel d Passions-erständnisses im frühen 18ten Jahrhundert," *TLZ* 107 (1982):

153-55.

9961.8   A. Vicent Cernuda, "La doble generación de Jesucristo según Jn 1:13-14," *EB* 40 (1982): 49-117; 313-44.

9961.9   Thomas H. Schattauer, "The Koinonicon of the Byzantine Liturgy: An Historical Study," *OCP* 49 (1983): 91-129.

9961.10   Lothar Steiger and Renate Steiger, "Es ist dir gesagt, Mensch, was gut ist: J. S. Bachs Kantate BWV 45: ihre Theologie und Musik," *KD* 32 (1986): 3-34.

9961.11   Paul A. Richardson, "Worship Materials for Use with Acts," *RE* 87 (1990): 465-71.

D. CHRIST AND THE GOSPELS IN LITERATURE

9962.   Mary A. Woods, "Studies in 'Paradise Lost': II. Milton's Christ," *ET* 3 (1891-1892): 391-94.

9963.   Frank W. Gunsaulus, "Christ in Poetry," *BW* 6 (1895): 504-16.

9964.   Myra Reynolds, "Material from English Literature Illustrative of the International Sunday-School Lessons: I. The Triumphal Entry. II. The Day of Judgment. III. The Last Super. Judas," *BW* 11 (1898): 344-47.

9965.   Myra Reynolds, "Material from English Literature Illustrative of the International Sunday-School Lessons. I. The Crucifixion. II. The Resurrection," *BW* 11 (1898): 448-50.

9966.   H. L. Oort, "Christus en Faust," *TT* 37 (1903): 36-54.

9967.   George H. Gilbert, "A Study of Christmas Poetry," *BW* 38 (1911): 366-72.

9968.   Stopford A. Brooke, "Shelley's Interpretation of Christ and his Teaching," *HJ* 16 (1917-1918): 366-76.

9969.   J. R. Mozley, "A New Text of the Story of the Cross," *JTS* 31 (1929-1930): 113-27 [A medieval legend of the Cross].

9970.   P. Laurence K. Mudie, "A Comment on the Nativity and 'The Winter's Tale'," *ET* 52 (1940-1941): 100-102.

9971.   R. G. Philip, "A Ninth Century Life of Christ: The Old Saxon Hêliand," *ET* 58 (1946-1947): 246-48.

9972.   Carl E. Purinton, "The Christ Image in the Novels of

Dostoevsky," *RL* 16 (1947): 42-54.

9973.   William R. Locke, "Novels on the Life of Jesus," *JBR* 18 (1950): 226-29.

9974.   Georg Wehrung, "Ödipus und Christus," *ZST* 22 (1953): 362-92.

9975.   John M. Steadman, "The 'Suffering Servant' and Milton's Heroic Norm," *HTR* 54 (1961): 29-44.

See also numbers 804, *10087*.

9975.1   G. Quispel, "Der Heliand und das Thomasevangelium," *VCh* 16 (1962): 121-51.

9975.2   Jason P. Rosenblatt, "Celestial Entertainment in Eden: Book V of Paradise Lost," *HTR* 62 (1969): 411-27.

9975.3   John D. Crossan, "Parable as Religious and Poetic Experience," *JR* 53 (1973): 330-58.

9975.4   Michael Lieb, "Holy Name: A Reading of Paradise Lost," *HTR* 67 (1974): 321-39.

9975.5   Miriam K. Starkman, "The 'Grace of the Absurd': Form and Concept in W. H. Auden's *For the Time Being*," *HTR* 67 (1974): 275-88.

9975.6   Ilona Opelt, "Die Szenerie bei Iuvencus: ein Kapitel historischer Geographie," *VCh* 29 (1975): 191-207.

9975.7   Eva C. Topping, "St. Romanos the Melodos and His First Nativity Kontakion," *GOTR* 21 (1976): 231-50.

9975.8   Anthony C. Yu, "Life in the Garden: Freedom and the Image of God in Paradise Lost," *JR* 60 (1980): 247-71.

9975.9   R. Ferwerda, "Two Souls: Origen's and Augustine's Attitude toward the Two Souls Doctrine," VC 37 (1983): 360-78.

9975.10   M. Aubineau and Nicolas Séd, "Une citation retrouvée de Jean Chrysostome, Catachesis de iuramento, chez Sévère d'Antioche, Contra additiones Juliani," *VCh* (1985): 340-52.

9975.11   Steven M. Baugh, "The Poetic form of Colossians 1:15-20," *WTJ* 47 (1985): 227-44.

9975.12   Richard Hillier, "Joseph the Hymnographer and Mary the Gate," *JTS* 36 (1985): 311-20.

9975.13   Michael Lieb, "Milton's 'Chariot of Paternal Deitie' as a

Reformation Conceit," *JR* 65 (1985): 359-77.

9975.14 Reinhard M. Hübner, "Ps-Athanasius Contra Sabellianos: eine Schrift des Basilius oder des Apolinarius," *VCh* 41 (1987): 386-95.

9975.15 Jonathan A. Draper, "Lactantius and the Jesus tradition in the Didache," *JTS* 40 (1989): 112-16.

9975.16 C. E. Hill, "Hades of Hippolytus or Tartarus of Tertullian? The Authorship of the Fragment of *De Universo*," *VCh* 43 2 (1989): 105-26.

9975.17 J. Van Amersfoort, "Tatianus en de Nederlanden: de invloed van het Diatessaron op enige Middelnederlandse levens van Jezus," *NTT* 45 (1991): 34-45.

9975.18 Ian Henderson, "Gnomic Quatrains in the Synoptics: An Experiment in Genre Definition," *NTSt* 37 (1991): 481-98.

9975.19 Traugott Koch, "Drei Passionslieder Paul Gerhardts--und das lutherische Verständnis der passion Christi," *KD* 37 (1991): 2-23.

9975.20 Wolfgang Harnisch, "Language of the Possible: The Parables of Jesus in the Conflict between Rhetoric and Poetry," *ST* 46 (1992): 41-54.

9975.21 Adela Y. Collins, "The Genre of the Passion Narrative," *ST* 47 (1993): 3-28.

9975.22 Jean D. Kaestli, "Mémoire et pseudépigraphie dans le christianisme de l'âge post post-apostolique," *RTP* 125 (1993): 41-63.

9975.23 Enrico Norelli, "Avant le canonique et l'apocryphe: aux origines des récits de naissance de Jésus," *RTP* 126 (1994): 305-24.

9975.24 Werner Thiede, "Ein süsses und doch schwerverdauliches Büchlein: Zur Auslegung der Johannes-Offenbarung in christlichen Sondergemeinschaften," *KD* 41 (1994): 213-42.

9975.25 Peter Bolt, "Mark 13(1995): An Apocalyptic Precursor to the Passion Narrative," *RTR* 54 (1995): 10-32.

9975.26 Stephen J. Patterson, "The End of Apocalypse: Rethinking the Eschatological Jesus," *TTod* 52 (1995): 29-48.

9975.27   Eckart Reinmuth, "Narratio und argumentatio—zur Auslegung der Jesus-Christus-Geschichte im Ersten Korintherbrief: Ein Beitrag zur mimetischen Kompetenz des Paulus," *ZTK* 92 1 (1995): 13-27.

E. Christ and the Gospels in Preaching

9976.   J. Reymond, "La prédication aux morts," *RTP* 12 (1879): 142-60.

9977.   Willard Brown Thorp, "The Significance of Christ for the Minister's Preaching," *BW* 28 (1906): 306-12.

9978.   Meade C. Williams, "Preaching Christ," *PTR* 4 (1906): 191-205.

9979.   Alfred E. Garvie, "The Restatement of the Gospel for Today," *Exp* 7th ser., 4 (1907): 385-406.

9980.   W. F. Lofthouse, "The Atonement and the Modern Pulpit," *HTR* 8 (1915): 182-204.

9981.   Friedrich Delakat, "Menschliche Erziehung und die Botschaft von Jesus Christus, ihre grundsätzliche Verschiedenheit und ihre tatsächlichen Beziehungen," *EvT* 4 (1937): 326-34, 335-56.

9982.   Peter Marstrander, "Unsere Predigt als Christusbotschaft," *ZST* 16 (1939): 290-310.

9983.   William P. Merrill, "Preaching Christ in War Time," *CQ* 18 (1941): 189-97.

9984.   Carl Stange, "Kristus och vår tic," *STK* 18 (1942): 320-37.

9985.   Frederick C. Grant, "Preaching the Easter Message," *ATR* 28 (1946): 53-59.

9986.   Sydney Cane, "The Teaching of Jesus and Christian Preaching," *TTod* 3 (1946): 50-63.

9987.   W. C. Mavis, "Jesus' Influence on the Pastoral Ministry," *TTod* 4 (1947): 357-67.

9988.   Johannes Schneider, "Revelation, the Word of God and our Proclamation," *RE* 49 (1952): 281-90, 425-34.

9989.   E. Schillebeeckx, "De kyriale waardigheid van Christus en de verkondiging," *VT* 29 (1958-1959): 34-38.

9990. Wayne E. Ward, "Preaching and the Word of God in the New Testament," *RE* 56 (1959): 20-30.

9991. Giles Hibbert, "Christ and Philosophy," *ITQ* 27 (1960): 228-35.

9992. Gerhard Koch, "Dominus praedicans Christum-id est Jesum praedicatum," *ZTK* N.F. 57 (1960): 238-73.

9992.1 Elizabeth Kinniburgh, "Preaching the Historical Jesus," *Th* 70 (1967): 201-207.

9992.2 James A. Sanders, "Outside the Camp," *USQR* 24 (1969): 239-46.

9992.3 Alfred Blenker, "Tilgivelse i Jesu forkyndelse," *DTT* 34 (1971): 105-109.

9992.4 Maurice Robinson, "Spermologos: Did Paul Preach from Jesus's Parables?" *B* 56 (1975) :231-40.

9992.5 Mogens Müller, "Historikerens Jesus, den historiske Jesus og kirkens Kristus-forkyndelse," *DTT* 38 (1975): 81-104.

9992.6 David G. Buttrick, "Preaching on the resurrection," *RL* 45 (1976): 278-95.

9992.7 Ulrich Hedinger, "Jesus und die Volksmenge: Kritik der Qualifizierung der Ochloi in der Evangelienauslegung," *TZ* 32 (1976): 201-206.

9992.8 E. G. Rüsch, "Eine Weihnachtsansprache Zwinglis," *TZ* 32 (1976): 360-72.

9992.9 André Dumas, "Prédication de Jésus Christ," *RSR* 65 (1977): 227-38.

9992.10 Heinrich Braunschweiger, "Auf dem Weg zu einer poetischen Homiletik: einige Aspekte der Hermeneutik Ricoeurs als Impuls für die Homiletik," *EvT* 39 (1979): 127-43.

9992.11 Jacques Schlosser, "Le règne de Dieu dans les dits de Jésus," *RSR* 53 (1979): 164-76.

9992.12 Thorwald Lorenzen, "Responsible Preaching," *SJT* 33 (1980): 453-69.

9992.13 Kjell Aartun, "Forkynnelsen over gammeltestamentlige tekster: hvordan den har vaert og hvordan den boer vaere," *NTT* 82 (1981): 141-52.

9992.14 Jean Galloud, "Paul devant l'Aréopage d'Athènes [Acts 17:16-34]," *RSR* 69 (1981): 209-48.

9992.15 Ferdinand Hahn, "Die christologische Begründung urchristlicher Paränese," *ZNW* 72 (1981): 88-99.

9992.16 Morna D. Hooker, "Beyond the Things that Are Written: St Paul's Use of Scripture," *NTSt* 27 (1981): 295-309.

9992.17 Robert F. O'Toole, "Activity of the Risen Jesus in Luke-Acts," *B* 62 (1981): 471-98.

9992.18 Vernon K. Robbins, "Summons and Outline in Mark: The Three-Step Progression," *NT* 23 (1981): 97-114.

9992.19 Stephen C. Barton, "Paul and the Cross: a sociological approach," *Th* 85 (1982): 13-19.

9992.20 John F. Havlik, "Kenosis According to Saint Paul," *GOTR* 27 (1982): 58-66.

9992.21 Stanley B. Marrow, "Parrhesia and the New Testament," *CBQ* 44 (1982): 431-46.

9992.22 Jerome H. Neyrey, "The Thematic Use of Isaiah 42:1-4 in Matthew 12," *B* 63 (1982): 457-73.

9992.23 Lorenz Oberlinner, "Verkündigung des Auferweckung Jesu im geöffneten und leeren Grab: Zu einem vernachlässigten Aspekt in der Diskussion um das Grab Jesu," *ZNW* 73 (1982): 159-82.

9992.24 Rainer Albertz, "Die 'Antrittspredigt' Jesu im Lukas-evangelium auf ihrem alttestamentlichen Hintergrund," *ZNW* 74 (1983): 182-206.

9992.25 Gerhard Lohfink, "Wem gilt die Bergpredigt: eine redaktionskritische Untersuchung von Matt 4:23-5:2 und 7:28f," *TQ* 163 (1983): 264-84.

9992.26 Holsten Fagerberg, "Har exegetiken någon betydelse för homiletiken," *STK* 60 (1984): 97-106.

9992.27 Rudolf Hoppe, "Gleichnis und Situation: zu den Gleichnissen vom guten Vater (Lk 15:11-32) und gütigen Hausherrn (Matt 20:1-15)," *BibZ* 28 (1984): 1-21.

9992.28   Hermann Vogt, "Origenes," *TQ* 165 (1985): 81-142.

9992.29   J. M. Prieur, "Que prêcher à Noël," *ETR* 62 (1987): 545-49.

9992.30   Sigfred Pedersen, "Helbredelse og forkyndelse," *DTT* 52 (1989): 41-54.

9992.31   Brian Horne, "Beyond Tragedy: Preaching the Ascension," *Th* 94 (1991): 168-73.

9992.32   Leslie Houlden, "Beyond Belief: Preaching the Ascension," *Th* 94 (1991): 173-80.

9992.33   John Fotopoulos, "John Chrysostom: On Holy Pascha," *GOTR* 37 (1992): 123-34.

See also numbers 804, 820, 3100.

F. CHRIST AND THE GOSPELS IN WORSHIP AND LITURGY

9993.   Th. Zahn, "The Adoration of Jesus in the Apostolic Age," *BS* 51 (1894): 314-30, 386-406.

9994.   Paul Chapuis, "L'adoration du Christ," *RTP* 28 (1895): 560-86; 29 (1896): 27-53.

9995.   Paul Chapuis, "Die Anbetung Christi. Historisch-dogmatische Erwägungen," *ZTK* 7 (1897): 28-79.

9996.   James Moffatt, "The Adoration of Jesus," *Exp* 6th ser., 5 (1902): 302-17.

9997.   James Moffatt, "The Bright and Morning Star," *Exp* 6th ser., 6 (1902): 424-41.

9998.   N. Paulus, "Zur Geschichte der Kreuzwegandacht," *ZKT* 33 (1909): 143-48.

9999.   E. D. J. de Jongh, "Het teeken des Kruises," *GTT* 14 (1913): 423-46, 473-92.

10000.   J.-V. Bainvel, "Notes sur quelques textes anciens souvent cités comme relatifs au Coeur de Jésus," *RSR* 6 (1916): 479-93.

10001.   Hugo Gressmann, "Das Gebet des Kyriakos," *ZNW* 20 (1921): 23-35.

10002.   Ernst von Dobschütz, "Kultusens betydning for urkristendommens fromhet og troslaere," *NTT* 23 (1922): 8-35.

10003.   J. A. Faulkner, "Were the Early Christians Mystics?" *RE* 19

(1922): 418-33.

10004.   Paul Galtier, "L'enseignement des Pères sur la vision béatifique dans le Christ," *RSR* 15 (1925): 54-68.

10005.   A. T. Robertson, "The Worship of Jesus in the New Testament," *RE* 28 (1931): 438-46.

10006.   Placidius Rupprecht, "Mysterium Crucis," *TQ* 128 (1948): 343-60.

10007.   Richard Paquier, "Le fondement christologique de la liturgie," *VCar* 4 (1950): 15-33.

10008.   L. H. Grondijs, "La mort du Christ et le Rit du Zéon," *NedTT* 8 (1953-1954): 213-33.

10009.   L. H. Grondijs, "Quelques remarques sur la liturgie céleste," *NedTT* 10 (1955-1956): 302-13.

10009.1   Jean Paul Montminy, "L'offrande sacrificielle dans l'anamnèse des liturgies anciennes," *RSPT* 50 (1966): 385-406.

10009.2   B. A. Mastin, "Jesus Said Grace," *SJT* 24 (1971): 449-56.

10009.3   Paul J. Achtemeier, "Origin and Function of the Pre-Marcan Miracle Catenae," *JBL* 91 (1972): 198-221.

10009.4   Gerd Theissen, "Soziale Integration und sakramentales Handeln: eine Analyse von I Cor 11:17-34," *NT* 16 (1974): 179-206.

10009.5   Edmund W. Fisher, "Let Us Look upon the Blood-of- Christ (1 Clement 7:4)," *VCh* 34 (1980): 218-36.

10009.6   Daniel M. Cohn-Sherbok, "A Jewish note on *to poterion tes eulogias*," *NTSt* 27 (1981): 704-709.

10009.7   G. A. M. Rouwhorst, "Das manichaeische Bemafest und das Passafest der syrischen Christen," *VCh* 35 (1981): 397-411.

10009.8   Gunther Wenz, "Die Lehre vom Opfer Christi im Herrenmahl als Problem ökumenischer Theologie," *KD* 28 (1982): 7-41.

10009.9   Ralph P. Martin, "New Testament Hymns: Background and Development," *ET* 94 (1983): 132-36.

10009.10   Maurice Sachot, "Réemploi de l'homélie 56 de Jean Chrysostome (BHGua 1984) dans 2 homélies byzantines sur transfiguration (BHG 1980k, 1985a)," *RSR* 57 (1983): 123-46.

10009.11   H. F. G. Swanston, "Liturgy as Paradise and as Parousia," *SJT* 36 (1983): 505-19.

10009.12   Werner Führer, "Herr ist Jesus: die Rezeption der urchristlichen Kyrios-Akklamation durch Paulus - Römer 10:9," *KD* 33 (1987): 137-49.

10009.13   Regin Prenter, "Grundtvig og Påsken," *DTT* 51 (1988): 139-48.

G. METHODS OF STUDYING AND TEACHING THE GOSPELS

10010.   George B. Foster [*et al.*], "Suggestions for the Questions of a Sunday-School Catechism; V. Jesus Christ," *BW* 17 (1901): 203-205.

10011.   George M. Forbes, William Byron Forbush, Josephine L. Baldwin, "How Shall We Teach the Life of Christ to Sunday School Classes?" *BW* 26 (1905): 469-78.

10012.   William P. Merrill, "How Shall We Teach the Infancy Stories to Our Children?" *BW* 26 (1905): 438-46.

10013.   O. Moppert, "Jesus im Religionsunterricht," *STZ* 24 (1907): 193-205.

10014.   James T. Cleland, "Ethical Emphases in Teaching New Testament," *JBR* 2 (1934): 24-26.

10015.   Mary Ely Lyman, "Teaching the Fourth Gospel," *JBR* 2 (1934): 19-22.

10016.   Mary Ely Lyman, "Teaching the Fourth Gospel," *JBR* 12 (1944): 36-41.

10017.   Elmer W. K. Mould, "Teaching the Life of Jesus," *JBR* 12 (1944): 17-18.

10018.   J. J. Dougherty and Richard J. Dobell, "A Symposium on the Gospels in the Classroom," *CBQ* 8 (1946): 281-89.

10019.   Laura H. Wild, "Teaching the Fourth Gospel," *JBR* 15 (1947): 26-33.

10020.   Margaret Avery, "Teaching the Gospels," *ET* 65 (1953-1954): 336-37.

10021.   Margaret Avery, "Various Ways of Studying a Gospel," *ET* 65 (1953-1954): 380-81.

10022.   Lindsey P. Pherigo, "Trends in 'Life and Teachings' of Jesus Courses," *JBR* 25 (1957): 196-98.

10022.1   E. C. Blackman, "New Methods of Parable Interpretation," *CJT* 15 (1969): 3-13.

10022.2   Jack D. Kingsbury, "Major Trends in Parable Interpretation," *CTM* 42 (1971): 579-96.

10022.3   Morton S. Enslin, "Some Help and Hindrances to Understanding the New Testament," *RL* 46 (1977): 400-14.

10022.4   P. Maurice Casey, "Method in Our Madness, and Madness in Their Methods: Some Approaches to the Son of Man Problem in Recent Scholarship," *JSNT* 42 (1981): 17-43.

10022.5   Andreas Lindemann, "Literaturbericht zu den synoptischen Evangelien 1978-1983," *TR* 49 (1984): 223-76.

10022.6   Sigfred Pedersen, "Die Gotteserfahrung bei Jesus," *ST* 41 (1987): 127-56.

10022.7   Anthony F. Buzzard, "The Kingdom of God in the Twentieth-Century Discussion and the Light of Scripture," *EQ* 64 (1992): 99-115.

See also numbers 425, 7997, 9263.

APPENDIX[1]

10023. Camillus Hay, "The Christology of Theodore of Mopsuestia," *ABR* 9 (1961): 43-45.

10024. Fr. Helveg, "Frelserens rette Naevnelse og de Kristnes rette Selvbetegnelse," *TTDF* 1 (1884): 249-65, 516-21.

10025. A. S. Poulsen, "Forreligger Herrens eschatologiske Tale Matth. 24, i sin oprindelige Skikkelse?" *TTDF* 1 (1884): 505-15.

10026. A. Lunddahl, "Ev. Joh. 16, 8-11. Exegetisk Studie," *TTDK* 2 (1885): 251-55.

10027. H. Lützhøft, "Var Matthias Apostel?" *TTDF* 4 (1887): 276-85.

10028. Fr. Helveg, "Efter-apostolske synsmader for det frelsende i Jesu død," *TTDF* 5 (1888): 367-429.

10029. Alfred Levinsen, "Bidrag til en Karakteristik af Apokryfevangelierne," *TTDF* 5 (1888): 207-36.

10030. Alfred Levinsen, "Et Bevis for, at der er dyb Plan i vore Evangelier," *TTDF* 5 (1888): 332-47.

10031. Fr. Helveg, "De apokryfe evangelier. En historisk undersøgelse," *TTDF* 7 (1890): 229-75.

10032. H. Ostenfeld, "Joh. 17," *TTDF* 7 (1890): 402-30.

10033. V. Dahlerup, "Daabsformularen og Ev. Matth. 28, 19-20," *TTDF* 9 (1893): 396-411, 604-18.

10034. V. Sthyr, "om den rette Forstaaelse af Ev. Matth. 28, 18-20)," *TDF* 9 (1893): 412-20, 619-23.

10035. Fr Helveg, "Fortielsen hos Josef og omtalen i Talmud af J'sju hannozri," *TTDF* 9 (1893): 62-90.

10036. Fr. Helveg, "Evangeliefragment fra et (fransk) fund i Øvre-Ægypten," *TTDF* 9 (1893): 542-55.

10037. J. E. Christensen, "Sandsynlighedsbeviset for Christi Opstandelse," *TTDF* 10 (1894): 129-52.

---

[1]The Titles included in the Appendix are keyed by cross-references from the appropriate sections in the body of the index.

10038.   Alf. Levensen, "Lids mere om Papias," *TTDF* 11 (1895): 109-37, 496.

10039.   Frederick Torm, "Hvad mente Jesus om sig selv?" *TTDF* 11 (1895): 557-605; 12 (1896): 1-47.

10040.   A. K. Damgaard, "om den kirkelige oversaettelse af μαθητεύσατε, Matth. 28, 19," *TTDF* 12 (1896): 344-61.

10041.   V. Sthyr, "Efterskrift om Matth. 28, 19," *TTDF* 12 (1896): 362-72.

10042.   N. Teisen, " 'Rør ikke ved mig!" *TTDF* 13 (1898): 624-29 [Jn. 20:17]

10043.   A. D. Damgaard, "Jesu og hans Disciples ydre Vilkaar," *TTDF* 13 (1898): 455-80.

10044.   N. A. Buchwaldt, "Et graesk Fragment af Enochs Bog," *TTDF* 14 (1899): 48-85.

10045.   M. J. Gjessing, "om Jesu Christi opstandelse," *TTDF* 14 (1899): 465-555.

10046.   C. Leunbach, "Ventede Jesus selv sin Genkomst som naer forestaaende?" *TTDF* 13 (1898): 481-88; 14 (1899): 19- 22.

10047.   F. R. Nielsen, "om oversaetttelsen af Matth. 5, 17," *TTDF* 14 (1899): 1-18.

10048.   K. J. Rützou, "Jesu og hans Disciples Udsagn om Parusiens Naerhed," *TTDF* 14 (1899): 23-47.

10049.   K. J. Rüstou, "Lignelsen om den utro Husfoged," *TTDF* 14 (1899): 176-217 [Lk. 16:1-13].

10050.   W. G. Kümmel, "Jesus und Paulus zu Joseph Klausners Darstellung des Urchristentums," *J* 4 (1948): 1-35.

10051.   Karl Thieme, "Matthäus, der schriftgelehrte Evangelist," *J* 5 (1949): 130-52, 161-82.

10052.   G. Lindeskog, "Jesus als religionsgeschichtliches und religiöses Problem in der moderne jüdischen Theologie," *J* 6 (1950): 190-229, 241-68.

10053.   Joachim Jeremias, "Der Lösegeld für Viele (Mk. 10, 45)," *J* 3 (1948): 249-64.

10054.   W. G. Kümmel, "Die Gottesverkündigung Jesu und der

Gottesgedenken des Spätjudentums," *J* 1 (1945): 40-68.

10055. K. L. Schmidt, "Der Todesprozess des Messias Jesus," *J* 1 (1945): 1-40.

10056. Rudolf Meyer, "Der Am ha-Ares, Ein Beitrag der Religionssoziologie Palestinas im ersten und zweiten nachchristlichen Jahrhundert," *J* 3 (1947): 169-99.

10057. E. K. Winter, "Der historische Christus secundum Proto-Matthacum," *J* 10 (1954): 193-230.

10058. Kurt Schubert, "Einige Beobachtungen zum Verständnis des Logosbegriffs im frührabbinischen Schrifttum," *J* 9 (1953): 65-80.

10059. J. Jocz, "Die Juden im Johannesevangelim," *J* 9 (1953): 129-42.

10060. Kurt Schubert, "Zwei Messiasse aus dem Regelbuch von Chirbet Qumran," *J* 2 (1955): 216-35.

10061. J. Jocz, "The Son of God," *J* 13 (1957): 129-42.

10062. Isaac H. Hall, "The Newly Discovered Apocryphal Gospel of Peter," *BW* 1 (1893): 88-98.

10063. J. E. B. Mayor, "Classical Illustrations of St. Matthew's Gospel," *JCSP* 1 (1854): 93-95.

10064. P. Douglas Hamilton, "The Syro-Phenician Woman: Another Suggestion," *ET* 46 (1933-1934): 477-78 [Mk. 7:26].

10065. G. Volkmar, "Berichtigung zur äussern Bezeugung des Johannes-Evangeliums," *ZWT* 3 (1860): 293-300.

10066. William Lillie, "Salome or Herodias?" *ET* 65 (1953- 1954): 251 [Mk. 6:22].

10067. Andreas Rask, "Ämbete och Incarnation," *L* 5 (1961): 67-75.

10068. José M. Bover, "Las dos parábolas de las bodes reales y de la gram cena (Mt. 22, 1-14; Lc., 14, 15-24)," *EB* 1 (1929-1930): 8-27.

10069. Andrés Herranz Arriba, "Expulsión de los profanadores del Templo," *EB* 1 (1929-1930): 39-59, 122-42 [Mt. 21:12-13; Jn. 2:13-22].

10070. Tomás Castrillo y Aguado, " 'Spiritus blasphemiae non remittetur'," *EB* 1 (1929-1930): 60-67 [Mk. 3:29].

10071. Tomás Castrillo y Aguado, "Remittuntur ei peccata multa, quoniam dilexit multum (Luc., 7, 47)," *EB* 1 (1929-1930): 354-76.

10072. Pablo Caballero Sanchez, "La oveja perdida," *EB* 2 (1930-1931): 270-93 [Mt. 18:12].

10073. José M. Bover, "El viaje a Jerusalém, narrado por Lc. 9, 51-11, 13, fué a la fiesta de las Encenias, narrada por Ioh. 10, 22-39," *EB* 3 (1931-1932): 3-10.

10074. Miguel Muniesa Allaza, "Ἐγένετο en II-2 del tercer Evangelio," *EB* 3 (1931-1932): 58-74.

10075. Juan Vilar, "La Christología de S. Pedro," *EB* 3 (1931-1932): 27-42, 119-31.

10076. Gabriel Palomero Dias, "La higuera maldita," *EB* 5 (1933): 114-25 [Mk. 11:12-14; Mt. 21:18-19].

10077. P.C., "El jurez inicuo," *EB* 5(1933): 95-105 [Lk. 18:1-18].

10078. P. C. S., "Cronología de la vida pública de Jesucritso," *EB* 6 (1934): 161-83.

10079. Teófilo Ayuso, "El Texto Cesariense del Papiro de Chester Beatty en el Evangelio de S. Marcos," *EB* 6 (1934): 268-81.

10080. Teófilo Ayuso, "Un pasaje diffcil de Evangelio, 'cum immudas spiritus exierit de homine' (Mt. xii. 43 ss., y Lc. xi. 24 ss.)," *EB* 6 (1934): 434-53.

10081. Teófilo Ayuso, "Un estudio sobre la expression ἀκάθαρτον πνεῦμα y su significado en el Nuevo Testamento," *EB* 6 (1934): 377-84.

10082. G. Canal de la Rosa, "Fin de las parábolas del Salvador (ut videntes non videant; Luc., viii, 10)," *EB* 6 (1934): 393-97.

10083. Justo Pérez Hernán, "Los vestigios bíblicos de Corán," *EB* 6 (1934): 214-20. [λόγος, Jn. 1:1; etc.].

10084. P. C. S., "¿Seis nuevas parábolas? El futuro Reino mesiánico," *EB* 6 (1934): 329-76, 478-84; 7 (1935): 51-74, 107-109.

10085. P. Arconada, "La citas textuales de los Salmos en labios del Señor," *EB* 6 (1934): 221-43, 454-77; 7 (1935): 81-96, 264-86.

10086. C. H. Marin, "Esbozo de una teología del IV Evangelio," *EB* 7 (1935): 22-50.

10087. P. Lenicque, "Kristus Pantokrator enligt Teilhard de Chardin," *L* 5 (1961): 48-66.

10088. Joh. Jong, "Kristus og embedet," *L* 5 (1961): 30-47.

10089. L. M. Dewailly, "Ämbete och Inkarnation," *L* 5 (1961): 76-87.

10090. Syster Marie-Nicole, "Liknelsen om den barmhärtige Samariten, Lukas 10:25-37," *L* 3 (1959-1960): 48-63.

AUTHOR INDEX

NEW TESTAMENT
TOOLS AND STUDIES

edited by

Bruce M. Metzger, Ph.D., D.D., L.H.D., D. Theol., D. Litt.

and

Bart D. Ehrman, Ph.D.

VOL. XX *The New Testament in Greek, IV. The Gospel According to St. John*, edited by the American and British Committees of the International Greek New Testament Project. Volume One: *The Papyri*, edited by W. J. Elliott and D. C. Parker. 1995. ISBN 90 04 09940 9

VOL. XXI *Comparative Edition of the Syriac Gospels: Aligning the Sinaiticus, Curetonianus, Peshîṭtâ and Ḥarklean Versions*, by George A. Kiraz; 4 volumes. Vol. 1: Matthew; Vol. 2: Mark; Vol. 3: Luke; Vol. 4: John. 1996. ISBN 90 04 10419 4 (set)

VOL. XXII *Codex Bezae*. Studies from the Lunel Colloquium, June 1994, edited by D. C. Parker and C.-B. Amphoux. 1996.
ISBN 90 04 10393 7

VOL. XXIII *Bibliography of Literature on First Peter*, by Anthony Casurella. 1996. ISBN 90 04 10488 7

VOL. XXIV *Life of Jesus Research: An Annotated Bibliography*, by Craig A. Evans. Revised edition. 1996. ISBN 90 04 10282 5

VOL. XXV *Handbook to Exegesis of the New Testament*, edited by Stanley E. Porter. 1997. ISBN 90 04 09921 2

VOL. XXVI *An Annotated Bibliography of 1 and 2 Thessalonians*, by Jeffrey A.D. Weima and Stanley E. Porter. 1998. ISBN 90 04 10740 1

VOL. XXVII *Index to Periodical Literature on Christ and the Gospels*, by Watson E. Mills. 1998. ISBN 90 04 10098 9